The Untried Life

JAMES T. FRITSCH

The Untried Life

THE TWENTY-NINTH OHIO VOLUNTEER INFANTRY IN THE CIVIL WAR

Swallow Press / Ohio University Press • Athens

Swallow Press / Ohio University Press, Athens, Ohio 45701
www.ohioswallow.com

© 2012 by James T. Fritsch
All rights reserved

To obtain permission to quote, reprint, or otherwise reproduce or distribute material from Swallow Press / Ohio University Press publications, please contact our rights and permissions department at (740) 593-1154 or (740) 593-4536 (fax).

Printed in the United States of America
Swallow Press / Ohio University Press books are printed on acid-free paper ∞ ™

20 19 18 17 16 15 14 13 12   5 4 3 2 1

Library of Congress Cataloging-in-Publication Data

Fritsch, James T. (James Thomas), 1959–
 The untried life : the Twenty-Ninth Ohio Volunteer Infantry in the Civil War / James T. Fritsch.
   p. cm.
 Includes bibliographical references and index.
 ISBN 978-0-8040-1139-6 (pbk. : acid-free paper) — ISBN 978-0-8040-4047-1 (electronic)
 1. United States. Army. Ohio Infantry Regiment, 29th (1861–1865) 2. Ohio—History—Civil War, 1861–1865—Regimental histories. 3. United States—History—Civil War, 1861–1865—Regimental histories. 4. Soldiers—Ohio—Biography. 5. Ohio—History—Civil War, 1861–1865—Personal narratives. 6. United States—History—Civil War, 1861–1865—Personal narratives. 7. United States. Army—Military life—History—19th century. I. Title.
 E525.529th .F74 2012
 973.7'471—dc23

2012008952

*For my mother and grandmothers,
who taught me to consider those
who passed this way before*

Contents

Preface ix

Acknowledgments xiii

Prologue: The Wonder of the Age 1

PART ONE. "MADLY FROM THEIR SPHERES": THE LONG ROAD INTO BATTLE

1. "We Are All War": April–July 1861 — 11
2. Founders' Club: July–September 1861 — 23
3. Camp Giddings: Early Promise, Fall 1861 — 29
4. Recruiting Wars: Fall 1861 — 39
5. Camp Giddings: Season of Complaint, Late Fall 1861 — 52
6. "The Emblem of Universal Freedom": Late Fall 1861 — 61
7. "At the Threshold of an Untried Life": Camp Chase, Columbus, December 1861–January 1862 — 70

PART TWO. WITH THE EASTERN ARMIES

8. A Good "Breaking-In": Winter on the Upper Potomac, 1862 — 83
9. The Ball Opens: The Battle of Kernstown, March 23, 1862 — 102
10. Chasing Jackson: March–June 1862 — 117
11. "Up the River and Back of the Mountains": The Battle of Port Republic, June 9, 1862 — 129
12. "Rest Now, Rest": Alexandria, Virginia, June–July 1862 — 142
13. "South of Anywhere": The Battle of Cedar Mountain, Virginia, August 9, 1862 — 156
14. "In the Hands of Devils": Prison Stories, 1862 — 166
15. Narrow Escapes: The Second Bull Run Campaign, August 1862 — 175
16. Restoration: Frederick, Maryland, Fall 1862 — 185

17. Our Valley Forge: Dumfries, Virginia, Winter 1863	201
18. Saving the Life of the Army: The Battle of Chancellorsville, May 1–3, 1863	216
19. Aquia Creek Interlude: May–June 1863	236
20. Saving the Life of the Nation: The Gettysburg Campaign, June–July 1863	248
21. Journeying Forth: Summer–Fall 1863	265

PART THREE: WITH THE WESTERN ARMIES

22. The Battles around Chattanooga: Fall 1863	279
23. Home and Back Again: Bridgeport, Alabama, Winter 1864	292
24. "They Called It a Demonstration": The Fight for Dug Gap, May 8, 1864	304
25. Continuous Battle: The Approach to Atlanta, May–August 1864	318
26. Closing on the Prize: The Fall and Occupation of Atlanta, July–November 1864	339
27. Tearing It Up: The March to the Sea, the Fall of Savannah, and the Carolinas Campaign, November 1864–April 1865	353
28. The Long Way Home: May–July 1865	368

Notes	381
Bibliography	467
Twenty-Ninth Ohio Volunteer Infantry Regiment Index	477
General Index	487

Illustrations following page 276

Preface

The state of Ohio organized nearly 230 infantry regiments for service in the Union army during the Civil War. This is the story of one of them, the Twenty-Ninth Ohio Volunteer Infantry Regiment, told by the soldiers and officers who marched under its flags. Years ago, I was driving through northeast Ohio filling in bare spots in my family tree. Interest in an uncle who had served in an Ohio regiment brought me to the door of a teacher of history in the Akron public schools. He handed me the original of a letter he owned, yellow and brittle, written in a fine, old-fashioned cursive hand. The letter was written in the 1880s by an old man of Cambridge, Massachusetts, named Thomas Clark, who had been colonel of the regiment. He was writing to one of his former sergeants, a soldier for whom he had particular affection, named Rollin L. Jones of Ashtabula County, Ohio.

> I will "fire away" . . . until I get tired and ready to go off into dreamland or until I think the one who thus receives my attentions is satisfied and generally not stopping to think whether he will give me a return fire or not. . . . Do the misty memories of '61 to '65 ever come welling up from the great storehouse of past experience as you halt in the onward march for a little midday, or at other times rest?

Of memory, he said,

> A soldier cannot forget while memory holds sway—and one of the worst things that can happen to a soldier is the loss of memory. Stirring incidents of the past are burned into it and become a part of his life. . . . You must remember it all.[1]

After I finished reading, the collector told me about an incident that befell Rollin Jones at a place called Pine Knob, Georgia, in the summer of 1864, and also what became of him after the war as a result of what had happened to him that night. In the ten years that followed, I traveled to every place the Twenty-Ninth Ohio Infantry had marched, camped, and fought. I had gathered documents by the boxful, and in the boxes were many voices, which, heard together, told the story of this regiment. Those of the regiment who survived the war hoped above all else that what they had done would be remembered by future generations. I felt the weight of obligation to let them speak to this modern age. More than anything, this book was written to allow them that chance.

The regiment was known by its admirers as the Giddings Regiment, after the nationally famous antislavery politician who was its mythic founder. To others, it was known as the Abolition Regiment, which was a salute to the equally well known radical political beliefs that dominated the distinctive counties in northeastern Ohio known as the Western Reserve, in which the regiment was raised. To the soldiers who served in it they were the Giddings Boys, or more commonly, the Boys.

The Twenty-Ninth Ohio fought on many of the storied fields of the Civil War and at two of its most prominent: Chancellorsville, where they played a heroic part during the fight's closing hours; and Gettysburg, where they stood the test of repeated rebel assaults against the Union defenses atop Culp's Hill. The regiment's hardest days in the war came at lesser-known places: Port Republic, Virginia, in June 1862; and Cedar Mountain, Virginia, August 9, 1862. Both these battles pushed the regiment to the edge of extinction. Their worst day in the war came at a place called Dug Gap, Georgia, in early May 1864.

They had the distinction of fighting in both of the war's major theaters. They marched under the banner of the Army of the Potomac until late summer 1863. Then they moved to the relief of Chattanooga, participating after that in the constant fighting that culminated in the taking of Atlanta. They marched across Georgia under Sherman, through the Carolinas, recrossed their old Virginia battlefields, and on to Washington for the Grand Review. Few regiments made a circuit as long as theirs.

The soldiers of this regiment, as of every other regiment in the Civil War, were prodigious letter writers. As they frequently reported, it was not uncommon in their camp, in the hour after mail from home arrived, to find every officer and soldier leaned against a tree, using drum tops and crate tops as tables, quietly writing letters home.

Research for this project discovered over three hundred letters written by the regiment's soldiers and officers for publication in their hometown newspapers. An additional 150 letters of a much more personal nature written by soldiers at the front were found in the records of the Pension Bureau at the National Archives. Most of these, which began with the same words, "Dear Parents, I seat myself to write," have not been examined since they were opened and read by families to whom they were addressed, and later sent to Washington to support dependents' claims well over a century ago. These letters express the writer's concern for topics of universal interest to the soldiers: visits from the paymaster, food, shelter, their health, weather, places visited, and scenes of battle, camp, and life in rebel prisons. Even the most humble of these reveal the soldier's deeper feelings, most often expressions of his war weariness and loneliness for familiar scenes, family members, and a favorite colt. Fortunately for the student of the Civil War, substantial collections of the letters of two particular soldiers, John G. Marsh and Wallace B. Hoyt, have survived. Both young men were keen observers of life in the regiment.

Letters written by the regiment's founders and its first staff officers pertaining to its organization and early days in camp and field were found in the Ohio adjutant general's office archives at the Library of the Ohio Historical Society, as was the copious correspondence of the regiment's figurehead and founder, Congressman Joshua R. Giddings. In the postwar years, the soldiers of the Twenty-Ninth Ohio wrote extensively of their experiences in the war. Many of these reminiscences were published in the *National Tribune,* the weekly newspaper of the Union veterans' largest organization, the Grand Army of the Republic. John White Geary, Pennsylvania politician and Western explorer, commanded the division in which the Twenty-Ninth Ohio served from August 1862 to the end of the war. He wrote to his wife, Mary, almost every day of the war and reported on every topic under the sun. His letters provide an erudite, richly detailed view of the war from the perspective of the general who made the day-to-day decisions that decided the fate of the Twenty-Ninth's soldiers.

The soldiers knew they were witnessing history, and making it. Most soldiers began a diary to record what they saw and did, not only as a document to fortify the flagging memories that must come with advancing age but as an important testament to be added to the family history and that of the nation. Only a handful of these survived, and two are remarkable. Nathan Parmater was a teacher in the rural neighborhoods of Ashtabula County, Ohio, when he enlisted in the regiment as a private. From 1861 to the end of the war, he remained true to his promise to write in his diary every day. To its pages he confided his boredom and terror, wonder and disgust, faith and doubt. He was a keen observer of the always changing terrain, both physical and emotional, over which he and his regiment passed. The regiment's second chaplain, Lyman D. Ames, came to the regiment when it had already been in the field one year. He was a man of reserved temperament, who found it difficult to make intimate connections with the regiment's officers and soldiers. He left a diary that reflects a man who came to the war fully mature, sober-minded and confirmed in his opinions about the nature of men and their weaknesses and strengths. With the regiment through most of its career, he traveled a course directly parallel to it, never really piercing its interior. His diary is valuable because of this separateness, which lends his myriad observations an impartiality and wider field of view than its soldiers knew.

There can be no truly comprehensive study of a Civil War regiment without a concurrent examination of the cities and villages that produced them. Every regiment, North and South, bore the particular imprint of the locale in which it was raised. The Twenty-Ninth Ohio was recruited and sustained throughout four long years of the war principally by two counties, Ashtabula and Summit. Both lie within the distinctive region known as the Western Reserve. Settled almost exclusively by New Englanders, the Reserve is a wedge-shaped tract, remote to the rest of Ohio, butting against Lake Erie to the north, Pennsylvania to the east, and the expanse of Ohio spread out below it to the south and west.

By 1861, Ashtabula and Summit Counties were rural places with roughly equal populations of about thirty thousand. Akron, the seat of Summit County, was still too small to be classified a city, but in it were the stirrings of great industry. In Jefferson, the capital of Ashtabula County, the principal business had always been the practice of law. Both places had high hopes of becoming cities of the first order, although only one succeeded, and that was largely because of the war. The responsibility for the raising troops for service in the Union army resided not with the federal government but with the loyal states. The president issued several calls for troops as the war continued and assigned each state its quota. The state in turn delegated the weight of that task to the counties, towns, and villages, so that in practice the enlisting of men to fill a regiment was a homegrown enterprise. Once the project of building the Twenty-Ninth Ohio Regiment was launched, the Jefferson group moved quickly to turn that vision into the reality of one thousand uniformed, trained, and armed young men marching out of the village and into the war with battle flags and a band to lead the way. Given the difficulties, all this was done in a remarkably brief time.

The locally raised volunteer infantry regiment was the basic building block upon which the gigantic structure of the Union armies rested. Consisting on paper of one thousand men, a regiment was made of ten companies of one hundred men each. During the regiment's first summer in the field in 1862, the Union armies were reorganized on the *corps d'armée* system, a plan Napoleon had found efficient. The regiment would serve with several others in a brigade, and three to four brigades would be combined to make up a division, which theoretically included from ten to fifteen thousand soldiers and their officers. Several divisions, most usually three, made up a corps, and several corps made one of many Union armies named usually after the major river that passed through its area of operations. After a few months of service, attrition by disease and battle casualties severely reduced the strength of these organizations from top to bottom. After the Battle of Cedar Mountain, Virginia, in August 1862, the Twenty-Ninth Ohio's brigade numbered hardly more than a regiment, and the Twenty-Ninth mustered no more men than had filled a company when it left Ohio for the front little more than half a year earlier.

Ohio supplied 320,000 of its sons to the various arms of the Union service. Three of every five men between the ages of eighteen and forty-five served, most in infantry outfits. Men from Ashtabula and Summit Counties, along with the contributions of neighboring counties, filled the Giddings Regiment to the required manpower level at the time of its formation, in 1861, and then over the next four years of the war kept it alive by supplying it with hundreds of replacements. This accomplishment is especially extraordinary considering that both counties sustained not only the Twenty-Ninth Regiment, but other regiments too, as the war deepened and federal troop levies fell with increasing weight on a steadily decreasing manpower pool.

To carry off this prodigious feat in thinly populated rural areas of the North demanded mobilization of every portion of society. Modern historians tend to regard the North, with its larger population and superior financial and industrial capacity, as having vanquished the Confederacy with one arm tied behind its back. That may be true in the broader national picture, but is less so when viewed at the level of the rural county and village, from which most of the Twenty-Ninth's boys came. To keep things running back home in the Reserve's shops and farms with husbands, sons, and brothers away at war required the contributions of children, the aged, and most particularly its women. To those left behind fell the burdens of caring for the wounded and sick soldiers who began sifting back home almost from the start, filling the never-ending demands of the several soldier's relief organizations, maintaining their institutions both familial and public, and carrying on from day to day despite the personal tragedies that were ultimately visited upon nearly every family.

Early on, I was asked why I intended to write a history of this regiment when one of its own soldiers already had. In the early 1880s, when nearly every regiment was rushing to memorialize what it had done in the war, a committee of Twenty-Ninth veterans organized for that purpose, and they chose one of their own to take on the daunting job of writing it. J. Hampton SeCheverell, or Little Hamp as he was known in the regiment, had enlisted as a drummer boy in 1861. The regimental bands were ordered broken up less than six months into their field service, and SeCheverell was mustered out and went home along with the other musicians.

The result of Little Hamp's labors was *Journal History of the Twenty-Ninth Ohio Veteran Volunteers, 1861–1865: Its Victories and Its Reverses.* The book was intended as merely a sketch, and in its 130 pages of narrative, SeCheverell did not pretend to present the regiment's full face, public or private. SeCheverell's work highlights the glorious charge into the face of the enemy's guns on the one hand, and the enormity of their endurance in the face of miserable conditions on the other. His is a portrait of their war in two colors: black and white.

To see the story of the Twenty-Ninth Regiment's real service requires myriad shadings, including a forthright reporting of its human frailties. The Giddings Regiment suffered desertions, and failures in morale, and large-scale discharges of its private soldiers on suspect medical grounds. There were feuds over leadership offices and on matters of morality, and there were accusations of cowardice against one of its commanders.

The Civil War left in its wake hundreds of thousands of pages of records, official and personal, which frequently reveal confusing and conflicting accounts of the same event. The individual soldier was necessarily concerned most with what happened in the few square yards of battlefield that enclosed him. Of affairs up the line a few more yards, or of tactical or strategic significance of a campaign or battle, he was ignorant. The present work attempts to provide the broader context for the Twenty-Ninth Ohio's war.

History shows that most Union soldiers were indifferent toward emancipation of the slaves. However, the men who enlisted in the Twenty-Ninth Regiment were, according to its lore, handpicked to ensure each was as pure in his antislavery beliefs as was Joshua Giddings. The regiment was so publicly associated with his radical brand of abolitionism that its soldiers feared they would be summarily hanged if captured. Whether its soldiers would fight harder and endure more than other soldiers, and whether the Reserve's residents would remain zealously devoted to their ideals, and to the regiment they had organized to represent them, were questions that could only be tested by the experiment of war.

For any mistakes of fact or misguided interpretation of events, I offer the words given by "Little Hamp" SeCheverell as apology for shortcomings in his book: "He has conscientiously endeavored to make the volume free from errors. If he has succeeded it will be the first of its kind."

Acknowledgments

Without John Gurnish of Mogadore, Ohio, this book would not have been written. He invited me into his home on a rainy October evening fifteen years ago, and the story he told me provided the spark for this project. The book would be far poorer were it not for John's lifelong pursuit of the history of the Twenty-Ninth Ohio Volunteer Infantry Regiment and of the Akron scene during the Civil War.

Friends and family accompanied me during many of my travels along the regiment's path. My mother, Margaret B. Fritsch, served tirelessly as my assistant during research trips to Washington, D.C., Virginia, Maryland, and Pennsylvania. She discovered several soldier-written letters during our visits to the National Archives. Bradley Jahnke of St. Paul, Minnesota, was my enthusiastic companion on tramps over battlefields in Pennsylvania and Virginia and was with me on the tracing of the Chattanooga-Atlanta-Savannah leg of the regiment's campaigning.

Betty Auten of Waterloo, New York, was instrumental in bringing to light the formative years in frontier upper New York of the Twenty-Ninth's revered first commander, Lewis P. Buckley. Susan Conklin and Irene Hogg Gates of Batavia, New York, provided provocative clues on Buckley's origins and boyhood. John G. Wilson of Warsaw, New York, opened his own research files for me on the history of Middlebury Academy, in Wyoming, New York, where Buckley took his first formal education. Judith A. Sibley, Alicia Mauldin, and Suzanne Christoff of the United States Military Academy at West Point provided material on Buckley's background and his cadet career, as well as a wealth of information on cadet life in the 1820s. Dozens of librarians in as many states provided help. Among them were Marion Davies, Summit County, Ohio; Carol W. Bell, Warren, Ohio; Evan Kelley, Dakota County, Minnesota; and Jenifer Zies, Scottsdale, Arizona.

Gary Arnold and Jeff Thomas of the Ohio Historical Society and Library, Columbus, gave freely of their time on every occasion it was requested. Mr. Arnold unearthed correspondence important to an understanding of the regiment's organization at Jefferson, Ohio, in the autumn of 1861. Elizabeth Reeb, formerly of the society, made valuable suggestions on the course of my research in the early going. The staff of the Military Records and Rare Documents sections at the National Archives, Washington, D.C., assisted me in every way and made the research room my second home during my many visits there. The Library of Congress staff retrieved records for the Grand Army of the Republic, Department of Ohio, illuminating the declining years of that great veterans' organization in Summit County. Duke University located and gave permission to use the letter by Col. Charles Candy recalling his brigade's harrowing day at the battle of Cedar Mountain, Virginia.

Mae Colling of Ashtabula, Ohio, spent dozens of hours locating for me important information that I otherwise might have overlooked. Marisa Simmons Back of Pinehurst, North Carolina, mined the information on which I recreated the life of one of the regiment's authentic heroes, Maj. Myron T. Wright. During moments of frustration, Marisa buoyed me with her constancy. She also led a campaign to restore the cemetery in which Wright is buried.

Dr. Lewis Leigh of Fairfax, Virginia, gave permission for my use of the poignant letters of soldier Alonzo Sterrett. James C. Roach and Scott Hartwig of Gettysburg National Military Park, Gettysburg, Pennsylvania, answered my endless questions regarding the Twenty-Ninth's experiences there. Bill Burnett of the Friends of Andersonville Prison, Andersonville, Georgia, provided records on the regiment's soldiers whose unhappy fate it was to find their way into that place. Steve Zerbe of Cherry Hill, New

Jersey, applied his knowledge of the collections of the Library of the Military Order of the Loyal Legion of the United States, Philadelphia, Pennsylvania, to this effort, and suggested profitable avenues for further research into the postwar activities of the Twenty-Ninth's officers.

Marvin Sauder and Polly Boggess of Dalton, Georgia, personified the hospitality for which the South is rightfully famous. Each provided valuable material on the battle of Dug Gap. Dan and Betty Shackelford of Rapidan, Virginia, live near Cedar Mountain battlefield in a house that sits in the woods where Stonewall Jackson rallied his troops. They know the battlefield's secret places and shared them with me during several visits to their home. At the time of my preliminary visits to Cedar Mountain, Bernard Inskeep owned the land on which the battle was fought. He very kindly allowed a Yankee stranger to wander his grain fields and pastures and also shared his encyclopedic knowledge of the battle.

With the hope that no further burden of work will befall her from this mention, I thank in particular Louise Arnold-Friend of the U.S. Army Military History Institute, in Carlisle Barracks, Pennsylvania. She never failed in supplying a prompt and informative response to my many inquiries.

Dr. Robert Krick, chief historian, Fredericksburg-Spotsylvania Military Park and author of *Stonewall Jackson at Cedar Mountain,* answered my questions about the battle, and helped plot the Twenty-Ninth Ohio's movements during that battle. Mr. Krick also searched his own research files and provided me with the only surviving copy of Capt. James B. Storer's postwar affidavit containing accusations of cowardice against Capt. Wilbur F. Stevens, the regiment's acting commander at the battles of Cedar Mountain (Virginia) and Gettysburg.

The late Robert Scaife of Atlanta, Georgia, provided invaluable aid in placing the Twenty-Ninth Ohio against the physical backdrop of geography and geology on which the Atlanta campaign was marched and fought. The finely detailed maps in Mr. Scaife's book were essential to my understanding of the Twenty-Ninth Ohio's role in the confusing combats that marked that campaign. His maps accompanied me on every field trip and sat always within reach at home.

Roberta Hurley Hagood of Hannibal, Missouri, supplied most of the information on the postwar life of Capt. Wilbur F. Chamberlain in her hometown. It was material she provided that enabled me to draw a picture of Chamberlain's long residence there in the nineteenth century. Mrs. Hagood located and gave me a rare, privately published collection of Chamberlain's essays on his postwar travels in the Old West. This small book revealed the man, and without her perseverance, Chamberlain's troubled thoughts on the modern American society soldiers like he had helped create would not have come to light.

The late Russell C. Shaw of Toledo, Iowa, was the grandson of Pvt. John C. Shaw, the regiment's only soldier to survive imprisonment at Andersonville, Georgia. Mr. Shaw reached out to me from across the miles and, during a weekend visit to my home, shared his memories of his grandfather's struggles as an Andersonville survivor and homesteader. Dr. Richard Waters of Jefferson, Ohio, invited me into his home and shared his rich storehouse of knowledge of the regiment's hometown during the years of the war and after. Nearly everyone I encountered in this journey suggested paths for further exploration, and many have become friends; to all of them I am grateful.

I owe thanks to all of the members of the Ohio University Press staff, and several individuals in particular. Gillian Berchowitz, Editorial Director; Kevin Haworth, Executive Editor; Nancy Basmajian, Managing Editor; and Beth Pratt, Production Manager, all contributed to the process of transforming my manuscript into a book. For those of the Press staff whom I have not named, but who contributed generously of their time and talent, I offer thanks.

To family and friends I offer my thanks for their patience through the years of research and their tolerance for my many absences. My wife, Gayl Howell, nudged me through periods of discouragement. Her faith in the project always exceeded my own. To the descendants and students of the Twenty-Ninth Ohio Volunteers who provided vital material and words of support, I offer thanks.

Prologue

THE WONDER OF THE AGE

Its soldiers came from many places in northeastern Ohio, but Jefferson, seat of Ashtabula County, was the hometown of the Twenty-Ninth Ohio Volunteer Infantry. The men who came up with the idea of founding the regiment lived in Jefferson, as did J. R. Giddings, the famous politician who led them in their quest to have a regiment whose membership reflected their fervent antislavery beliefs. The camp where the regiment organized, and where young men took their first clumsy soldier steps, sat on the edge of the village, and its first company, Capt. William Fitch's Company A, was of this place.

A few decades earlier Jefferson, Ohio, had been a muddy stopover in the middle of a lightless primeval forest. By 1860, the year before the war, Jefferson had become a fair facsimile of a New England village. It had an avenue of pretty churches, a fine courthouse, and shaded streets of white clapboard houses set back on neat lawns. Jefferson's population of 658 was only half that of the largest place in the county, the city of Ashtabula, and smaller by a third than the village of Conneaut, both of which, unlike Jefferson, enjoyed the advantages of fine natural harbors on Lake Erie and a place on the railroad.[1] The only real business of the village revolved around the battalion of lawyers who worked from a row of squatty cottages lining an alley next door to the courthouse. In the only surviving photograph taken before the Civil War, Jefferson looks about the same as any other village of the time: a dusty main street, a plank walk running along the front of a common-walled row of businesses, and a few men in linen dusters and stovepipe hats leaning against hitching rails and lounging in doorways.

The Howells family moved to Jefferson from southern Ohio in the 1850s, knowing it to be a place more in step with their own antislavery beliefs. The elder Howells, William Cooper Howells, took over the editorial responsibilities at Joshua R. Giddings's pulpit-newspaper, the *Ashtabula Sentinel*. His son William Dean Howells spent most of his adolescence there. Had he stayed in Jefferson he might have enlisted in the Twenty-Ninth Ohio and written the great American novel about it and the Civil War. But Howells grew bored with village life and left for better and larger opportunities in Columbus. Howells would become the best-known man of American letters of his day. As an old man, he looked back at the Jefferson of his boyhood and concluded that it had been "simply the high-water mark of American civilization, a place so charming and warm that only fiction could portray it faithfully."[2] It was worthy of a book, and Howells wrote one, which he titled *Years of My Youth*.

He remembered the people of Jefferson as affable but blunt in disposition, hard working, and hard thinking, and he described everyone in the village as amazingly literary. The people were universally poor, but their entertainments cost them nothing. There were organized excursions into the country to pick blackberries or gather chestnuts in their seasons, barn-raisings, and riotous Fourths of July. Young people slipped along the village streets, stopping to serenade at the homes of friends. The annual county-wide rendezvous that was the Ashtabula County Fair marked the summer's end. Christmas celebrations were something out of Charles Dickens. Antislavery zealots came to lecture, which in Jefferson was like preaching to the choir. From what can be seen in the photograph of the main street—and imagined through the recollections of Howells—Jefferson, Ohio, appears too fixed in its homely, charming customs for anything revolutionary to have occurred here, but thinking that would be a mistake.

There was another side to Jefferson beyond the field of view of the photograph, and apparently forgotten by Howells. Jefferson as it turns out is noteworthy for more than its sponsorship of the Twenty-Ninth Ohio Volunteer Infantry Regiment, and its notoriety explains in a very direct way why the regiment came into existence. Jefferson could rightly be considered one of the birthplaces of the Civil War. It was this particular neighborhood's harsh, insistent voice, and its defiant actions on the issue of slavery, that led in no small way to the calamity of civil war. The people that Howells remembered as open minded were also the troubling opposite.

The several counties making up the Western Reserve of northeastern Ohio were famously antislavery, but Ashtabula County was by national reputation the most notoriously abolitionist among them, and Jefferson, its county seat, was the epicenter. Two nationally famous politicians lived in the village; both were reviled in the South: U.S. senator Ben Wade, and U.S. congressman Joshua Reed Giddings. Howells remembered that by the late 1850s the churches stood empty. The people were no longer much interested in religion, and the young openly mocked it. They had replaced the old-fashioned orthodoxy of their New England grandfathers, first with a devotion to temperance, and then to the antislavery cause. It had begun in the 1830s with scholarly meetings in schoolhouses, and progressed to an open flaunting of the Fugitive Slave Law, until finally the believers threatened violent insurrection if the federal government dared to interfere. This region of small farms and tranquil, well-ordered villages was also the home, arsenal, and refuge of John Brown, the martyr of Harpers Ferry. Shock waves originating here rolled out across the nation and helped break otherwise peacefully disposed Americans loose from their reason. Over time, the people here came to believe that war was inevitable, and some, like J. R. Giddings, clamored for it.

For years, the Jefferson newspaper, like most others in this part of Ohio, was filled with relentless antislavery agitation: graphic, firsthand accounts of Southern cruelty; the full texts of Giddings's provocative floor speeches in Congress, and of those made by angry, frock-coated men from the courthouse steps. All these produced a hatred not just of slavery, but of all things Southern. If some in the county had had it their way, the Civil War would have been fought years earlier than it was. "That sooner than submit to such odious laws we will see the Union dissolved; sooner than see slavery perpetual we would see war; and sooner than be slaves we will fight!"[3] This resolution had been overwhelmingly approved in a sleepy village not far from Jefferson. The year: 1850.

Some Reserve residents feared what the hate mongering might produce and wanted no part of it. As early as the 1830s, with the antislavery movement already galloping through the Reserve, a group of citizens in Painesville, a picturesque place on Lake Erie, above Jefferson, met to consider the consequences of having the Reserve's name so intimately associated with so divisive an issue and concluded the one-sided discourse had in it the seeds of civil war.[4] Over the years, the voices of those who counseled restraint became more difficult to hear, until the Reserve was known at last as the most abolition-obsessed region in the entire nation.[5] As the Reserve's association with antislavery deepened, its people began to regard themselves as besieged by barbarians, leaders of a lonely crusade in a nation sunk down by the sin of slavery and cut loose from the sacred intentions of the Founding Fathers. They alone knew the course to redemption, and they had been led in that cause by their congressman of two decades, the Honorable Joshua Giddings.

Giddings's rise paralleled that of another midwestern politician, Abraham Lincoln. Both grew up in log cabins, both were self-educated to an extraordinary extent on borrowed books, both were champion wrestlers and rail splitters, and both took up the study of law. Giddings and Ben Wade opened a law office and were soon the wealthiest two men in Jefferson. Fussing over legal papers dragged Giddings down into episodes of depression. He turned to land speculation, which provided the excitement he craved, but his timing was bad and he lost his shirt in the Panic of 1837. His despair caused a psychic change, after which he pledged to devote himself to uplifting mankind. The antislavery movement drew him like a lodestone. When he went to Congress, in 1839, his was one of the first voices to rail against the slave interests, and his supporters thought him their Daniel in the lions' den. A pariah in Washington because of his outspoken views, he was welcomed in every kitchen and played baseball in his shirtsleeves when home in Jefferson.

In the South he was the personification of everything that was wrong with the North: a cold-blooded advocate of slave revolt, a demon who grinned happily at the prospect of Southerners awash in their own blood.[6] The most scurrilous of these epithets were invariably reprinted in the *Sentinel*. Giddings clipped them from the newspapers and pasted them into his scrapbook, suggesting that he took satisfaction in the animosity he had stirred up. He had powerful enemies in his own state, and even within the Reserve. The editors of the *Cleveland Herald* referred to him as the Old Reprobate and believed his radical ideas were "putrid excrescence."[7] In their own state, feelings toward the people of the Western Reserve were hardly more charitable. Some Ohioans regarded the Reserve as "one vast Coon Pen," for the number of runaway slaves that were given refuge there, and wished that the Reserve would dry up and blow away.[8]

The people's crusade against slavery had been one of words mostly, until the Fugitive Slave Law became the law of the land. After that, the faithful in the Reserve set themselves on a course of open subversion of the law. Those who favored violent action had their own champion. John Brown had been raised not far from Akron and his face was familiar to everyone. He led a Reserve band into the Kansas-Missouri border dispute. The authorities saw in Brown's bloody work not the hand of an avenging God but simple murder. He ended up in Jefferson, where he was concealed from the authorities by local sympathizers, including Joshua Giddings's son Grotius.[9] Brown received money, arms, and manpower from supporters in Ashtabula County for his assault on the federal arsenal at Harpers Ferry, Virginia. He had hoped to inspire a slave revolt, but the slaves did not rise up, and the raid was a failure. Brown himself had been captured, but a few of his band escaped, and at least four of them fled straight back to Ashtabula County.

Brown was sentenced to death for treason, and rumors began to circulate that men were plotting to break Brown out of the Richmond jail. The source of the plotting was Ashtabula County.[10] Brown was hanged, and across the Reserve he was immediately elevated to sainthood. Preachers climbed into their pulpits and interpreted his legacy: he had proved that the stain on the national soul could never be blotted out without the effusion of blood.[11] Some in Washington feared that beneath Brown's insurrection lay a broader, far more troubling conspiracy, and various committees were established to investigate.[12] Virginia senator James Mason and the Honorable Clement Vallandigham of Ohio began to investigate. It didn't take a bloodhound to see that the road to Harpers Ferry ran straight back in the direction of Ashtabula County, and some saw it leading right into Giddings's parlor.[13] Giddings admitted that he had entertained Brown over tea in his home, and that he had corresponded with Brown during the Kansas difficulties, but of his plan to raid Harpers Ferry, Giddings said he knew nothing until he read about it in the newspapers afterward.[14] Those interested in seeing Giddings brought to justice gave up after he threatened to sue them for libel, but they got in the last word on the John Brown affair: the ceaseless agitation of Giddings and men like him was responsible for the insurrectionary environment in which John Brown flourished.[15]

A Richmond newspaper posted a bounty of $5,000 for Giddings's head, and $5,000 more to the man who could bring him to Richmond alive.[16] Threats did not deter Giddings in the least; he continued to denounce the Fugitive Slave Law as piratical and told his listeners that if violence were necessary to resist it, then so be it. His followers in Jefferson followed his lead.

Wanted fugitives from the raid stood on the courthouse steps the day after Brown was hanged in Charleston, in 1859, and vowed vengeance. One thousand armed Ashtabula County men, known as the Black Strings for the dark hank of thread they looped through their buttonhole, swore oaths to protect the Harpers Ferry fugitives. The Black Strings manned outposts at every approach to the village and had the final say on who could pass by. A plaque mounted on the courthouse wall memorializing the resisters claims with defiant pride, "The Federal Government made little effort to arrest any person in Ashtabula County as a conspirator or witness for fear of invoking Civil War."

By 1859, J. R. Giddings's lifelong crusade against slavery had brought the nation to the edge of civil war, and his years of struggle were about to produce fruit. When the local nominating convention of the Republican Party he had helped found met in Jefferson that autumn, he was passed over in favor of a younger and less radical man. Giddings found himself involuntarily removed from the public spotlight.[17] The John Brown raid had dangerously breeched the dam holding back sectional hatred, and it would take only one more push to bring it down entirely, with the election of Abraham Lincoln as president of the United States. The Reserve geared up early in the campaign of 1860 to make sure voters lined up foursquare behind the Illinois Rail-Splitter. The campaign was a gigantic pageant, big on torchlight parades and spectacles of all sorts and short on serious consideration of the issues: union or disunion, war or peace. In every Reserve town, young men enlisted in a pro-Lincoln organization called the Wide Awakes. Their uniforms eerily resembled the costume later adopted by the U.S. Army for what was to come: kepi-style caps, dark-blue trousers and blouses, and oilcloth capes, worn to deflect the sparks their lamps threw off.

The newspapers pitched in for all they were worth and stepped up their longtime practice of encouraging revulsion toward the South. Scattered among legitimate news pieces were stories of outrages committed upon innocent Northern visitors: a young woman traveling through Virginia victimized by brutes who assailed her with foul language and spat tobacco juice on her white crinoline skirts when her accent gave her away as a Yankee; a young Illinois man who was bullwhipped to death by Texans when he let slip that he was against slavery.[18] Keeping the readers' emotions as inflamed as a case of poison ivy proved unnecessary. Lincoln took every free state except New Jersey. He did not get a single electoral vote in any Southern state. Votes for him in the Reserve amounted to a stampede, and local Republicans claimed that without their support, he might not have won in Ohio, where the contest had been less lopsided.[19]

The people had waited for this moment for decades, and with their man elected, they pulled out all the stops in a regular jubilee that made past celebrations seem puny and halfhearted in comparison. One train after another pulled into Akron, each car jammed to the roof with the joyful of the surrounding villages.[20] Torchlight parades snaked through the streets, skyrockets were fired from rooftops, every public place was illuminated by huge bonfires, and lurid forty-foot-tall images of Washington and Lincoln were projected by lanterns onto the sides of buildings. The jubilant were heedless of the animosity Lincoln's election had touched off in the South. Six weeks after the election South Carolina seceded from the Union, joined soon after by six other Southern states. For years, Reserve politicians had ridiculed the threats of Southern states to leave the Union; these had been bluffs, calculated by Southern fire-eaters to win concessions for their "darling institution" of slavery. At first, South Carolina's secession from the Union was not taken seriously in the Reserve.

Lincoln's inauguration train pulled into Columbus, where he addressed the state legislature. The listeners found Lincoln's speech oddly vague and introspective. In these dangerous times, he was sounding like a man with his head in the sand. "I have not maintained silence from any want of real anxiety. It is a good thing that there is no more than anxiety, for there is nothing going wrong. . . . We entertain different views upon political questions, but nobody is suffering anything."[21]

The train moved deeper into the Reserve, where the Christmas season just past had held little goodwill toward men. At John Brown's hometown of Hudson, in Summit County, five thousand people showed up to greet Lincoln. He appeared for a second on the platform, gave the spectators a look at a real live president, and disappeared back into his car.[22] At Ravenna, west of Akron, he said that he realized that not everyone in the Reserve had voted for him.

> But let me tell to those who did not vote for me, an anecdote of a certain Irish friend that I met yesterday. He said that he did not vote for me, but went for Douglas. "Now," I said to him, "I will tell you what you ought to do in that case. If we will all turn in and keep

the ship from sinking this voyage, there may be a chance for Douglas on the next; but if we let it go down now, neither he nor anybody else will have an opportunity of sailing in it again." Now, was that not good advice?

The crowd replied in one voice, "Yes, yes, that's the talk."[23] The town's local artillery fired a round, shattering the window through which Mrs. Lincoln was peering out nervously at the rambunctious crowd. At Cleveland, the Lincoln party rode two miles through the muddy snow to the Weddell House. The people of the Western Reserve were used to their politicians talking in language as hard as New England granite. But again, Lincoln's speech stuck them as soft and vague. "Why all this excitement? Why all these complaints? As I said before, this crisis is all artificial. It has no foundation in fact. It can't be argued up, and it can't be argued down. Let it alone and it will go down itself."[24]

The inaugural train pushed east, out along Ohio's north shore, stopping at every Reserve station along the line. At Ashtabula, a crowd of three thousand people had gathered around the city's depot. Lincoln appeared on the platform of the rearmost car. The band struck up and the crowd cheered. He said in a voice so hoarse only those nearest him could hear, "I can only say how do you do, and farewell, as my voice, you perceive will warrant nothing more."[25] The residents of Conneaut awoke to the sound of ringing bells and the booming of the town's cannon. They rushed into town and crowded dangerously close to the railroad track. Lincoln explained that he had lost his voice and could not speak. As the train began to move forward, parting the crowd, a spectator hollered above the din of music and screeching iron wheels, "Don't give up the ship," and Lincoln replied, "With your aid I will never, so long as life lasts."[26]

No where in the Reserve had Lincoln echoed the warlike sentiment of its people. Lincoln's words were meant to relax the grip on the trigger, but in the Reserve, they fell on the ears of a people whose hearing had been deafened by years of war talk. Nevertheless, there still might be a pulling back from the brink. A peace conference in Washington was presenting resolutions hoped to stave off war. When it got right down to it, most people, North and South, still had enough composure to see that the nation was sliding down into an abyss, and they wanted a peaceful solution. Faced now with the real possibility of taking up arms against their own countrymen, most Ohioans decided compromise was preferable to civil war. Perhaps the South deserved consideration of its grievances, especially over the Fugitive Slave Law.[27] At the statehouse, in Columbus, a movement toward compromise gained momentum. Up in the Western Reserve, the people dug in their heels and prepared to resist. With South Carolina gone out and other Southern states threatening to join her, Joshua Giddings addressed an anticompromise meeting in Jefferson. He raised his arms and declared, "Sir, whether those States remain in the Union, or shoot madly from their spheres . . . I have no fear of dissolution. . . . Our entire redemption from the slave power *must come,* whether it come in peace, or in blood, I know not, but whether in peace or in blood, let it come."[28]

In Akron the same intransigent attitude was broadcast: there would be no further compromise of principle with slavery, whatever the result.[29] Even if secession advanced further, Reserve citizens were confident that the strength of a Southern confederacy was puny compared to the might of the North; Fort Sumter, the vulnerable federal bastion out in Charleston harbor, was a perfect floating castle and, like the North, impregnable to anything the South might throw at them. In these fragile days, citizens of the Reserve continued to pass runaway slaves through to the safety of Canada. With Lincoln elected, it was predicted that the steady flow of refugees of years past would become a stampede.[30]

Lincoln was inaugurated on March 4, 1861, and he was immediately beset by office seekers. At the head of the line was J. R. Giddings. He had fastened on the remunerative and comfortable consulate post at Montreal.[31] He called in old favors from influential men like Salmon P. Chase and Charles Sumner and got the job and the remarkable $4,000 annual salary that went with it.[32] But Giddings was a man who craved the limelight, and the Montreal post would take him out of the country just when the issue he had championed was about to be tested.

With the national crisis deepening, the people of Ashtabula County became suddenly fascinated with the prospect of riches. Oil had been found oozing from the banks of a creek in the county near the time Texas had seceded from the Union, and a well drilled nearby produced an explosion of oil. Fever took hold that would outrun the excitement touched off by the discovery of gold in California a decade earlier. In a very short time, Ashtabula County seemed poised to outgrow its reputation as an antislavery headquarters and the state's foremost producer of cheese and to become famous as the new El Dorado. Farmers stood all day in their fields haggling with speculators, while unmilked cows bawled at their elbows. An oil company had formed near Kingsville and hoped to find enough oil there to "slide herself out of the Union," a jibe that showed the people here still were not taking Southern secession seriously.[33]

Running beside news of the wildfire spread of the oil fever were situation reports on the developing crisis in Charleston harbor, drawings of the new Southern flag, and scholarly analysis of the skill of the gunners lobbing shells into and out of Fort Sumter.[34] The residents of Warren, in Trumbull County, anticipated the day there *might* be a call for troops, and enrolled one hundred men in its new military company, every one of whom could "bite a cartridge and carry a knapsack 25 miles a day."[35] It was becoming clear that the national predicament was not going away. Reverend Olds climbed into the pulpit at Jefferson's Brick Church and reminded any in his congregation who needed reminding, "The blind can see it, and almost the dead can know it. Great events are soon to transpire, that are to make an impression on human destiny. . . . Surely we are living in an eventful time, and it is well to be impressed with such a fact, for our own example and influence will help to make the impression, whatever it may be, that is to stamp the coming ages."[36]

Life in the Western Reserve seemed to go on just as it always had. Yankee Robinson's circus still came to town featuring lions, tigers, Florida alligators, Pygmies direct from the African jungle, Chinese acrobats, beautiful female equestrians, wire walkers, and trick-shot artists. At the evening show, the crowds were treated to a full staging of the battle of Buena Vista. Gypsies continued to set up camp on the edge of the village as they always had, making their livings by examining the palms of the villagers and disclosing their destinies. Merchants continued their feverish pitching of new-fangled implements for the home and hay field, like Roger's Improved Washing Machine, and Howard's Reaper and Self-Raker. People suffering from diseases for which there was as yet no earthly cure shuffled into the local drugstore to buy patent medicines with lurid labels and claims to match, like Madame Bovin's Celebrated Silver-Coated Female Pills and Mexican Mustang Ointment. There were ads aplenty for the latest New York fashions so any man or woman could promenade down the muddy main streets of Akron or Jefferson and feel up to date. The big lake boats continued to call at Ashtabula and Conneaut, with reports of where they had been and where they were bound.

There were notices of Sunday school picnics in the grove out on the edge of the village, and announcements for meetings of literary and dramatic societies, and of the village glee club. There were reports of regular, bloody wrecks on the local railroads, and the news that a ship that had called recently in Conneaut had gone down with all hands in a squall out on the Great Lakes, and accounts of the first days of the Pony Express. Neighbors paused on the boardwalk in Jefferson and debated the efficacy of the sage advice published in every edition of the village newspaper: how best to break a colt or raise a boy, how to prune a fruit tree, or how to make a better cheese or homemade barn paint. There were the announcements of life's ceaseless beginnings and endings—births, marriages, and deaths. Farm women used to lives of staggering hardness pondered the advice a learned professor offered in the local newspaper on the important topic of "premature aging of American female beauty." His prescription: young women should engage in a more vigorous outdoor life, including sleigh riding and playing in the snow, and avoid pretty shoes, and bonnets, except for when out under the hot midwestern sun.

The steam trains whistled down brakes in Akron, Ashtabula city, and other places lucky enough to be on the railroad, and halted just long enough to unload passengers and the bounty of the outside world: buffalo robes, French corsets, fancy wallpapers, and kid gloves. Loaded aboard for the outbound trip was the output of the Reserve's farms and shops: casks of the Reserve's famous cheese, pig iron, crockery, bales of wool, boat oars, and, in their season, barrels of fresh passenger pigeon harvested by the hundreds of thousands from islands in the great Pymatuning Swamp, out on Ashtabula's eastern border.

Families climbed the steps to the rooms above Steinbachar's Drug to have the image of how they looked this spring of 1861 recorded for posterity by G. W. Manley, Akron's most successful photographer. He was ready to place their picture on a carte de visite, which was all the rage and which, he assured them, was "the ne plus ultra of Card Pictures." Spring advanced by fits and starts but the snow finally went away. Sleighs were dragged into the shed and covered with an old sheet; buggy and wagon axles were greased. T. S. Winship, Ashtabula County's most exuberant merchant, stepped into the show window of his mercantile and replaced the sealskin caps and beaver mufflers with the finery of summer. Out on the stump-covered clearings in the big woods where most of the boys who would join the Twenty-Ninth Ohio lived, farmers studied the planting tips in the *Almanac* and squeezed a handful of soil to see if it was dry enough to scour from the plow. Amateur poets of the neighborhood sent their impressions of the condition of nature in this springtime of 1861 to the local newspapers: the land was quiet except for the hopeful sound of melted snow running in every watercourse and the bickering of the waterfowl that floated in every marsh. At twilight a mist heavy with the fragrance of rot and new life hung close the ground, and the lights from the stars overhead flickered and wavered and could be seen only dimly. The war, predicted by some to be the most terrible of modern times, had been a long time in coming but its arrival now was merely a question of time.[37]

Something awful, perhaps beyond imagining, lay just out of sight past the bend in the road, so powerful that it began to send shockwaves backward into the present, troubling people in their sleep. Just north of Atlanta, Georgia, sat a drowsing, no-account railroad stop named Big Shanty, and not far from the tracks stood a small, worn-out house. One night the woman who lived in it awoke from a troubling dream. In it, blackbirds had filled the air around her so thickly she thought she would suffocate. There would come a time a few years into the future when she awoke to find dark-coated men marching into her yard, digging rifle pits in her garden, and setting up their tents outside her kitchen window. The road leading past would be trod by an endless procession of armed men. On an evening in July 1864, she pulled up a chair and confided her dream to a church pastor from Conneaut, Ohio, who was doing duty just then as chaplain for the Twenty-Ninth Ohio Infantry. The troubles seen in her dream had come to pass, and she would see that her dream had been a prophecy.[38]

People of that day looked for signs of things to come: in their dreams, in the sky, and in the blurry shapes left in the bottoms of teacups. War was coming, that much seemed likely, but not everyone saw it as Armageddon—Joshua Reed Giddings, for instance. When the war was but a few weeks old, and the depths of the thicket into which the nation had stumbled were not yet plumbed, he wrote to his son, "We are opening up a new page in the history of governments and nations, and those who now save their country will be remembered, and be cherished in coming time." To the old man, the war might be nothing less than the wonder of the coming age.[39]

PART I

"Madly from Their Spheres"
THE LONG ROAD INTO BATTLE

I

"We Are All War"

APRIL–JULY 1861

"Let the Dogs of War Be Loosed"

On a warm autumn morning in 1861, a group of nine young men hiked south the few miles from the hamlet of Kingsville, Ashtabula County, Ohio, to the village of Jefferson. They passed through the village and out the few blocks to the fairgrounds. The Kingsville squad had come to be soldiers in a new regiment, the Twenty-Ninth Ohio Volunteer Infantry, that was camped within the oval of the racetrack. Present in this happy group was Nathan Parmater, age twenty-five. Most recently, he had been a teacher in the country schools of the neighborhood and had used his earnings to pay for his tuition at the Kingsville Academy. He had been close to finishing his studies when he heard a regiment was taking shape just down the road, and he and a few others—including his best friend, Alonzo Sterrett, whom Parmater called Chum—decided to put their schoolbooks aside and go to be Union soldiers.

Settled in his tent that first night, Parmater folded back the stiff, red-morocco cover of a new diary book and on its first page wrote:

> September 23— Started from Kingsville with eight others to join Co. E. 29th Regt. at Jefferson. The weather being fine we all enjoyed the trip well. Co. E is from K. and surrounding towns and is commanded by Capt. Luce. We arrived at camp about two o'clock p.m. with a good appetite to relish the bread and beef which the boys had prepared for us. After dinner we pitched a tent and prepared to camp for the night.[1]

He promised to write in it every day as long as the war lasted, but after a few days, he gave it up and would not write in it again until the day the regiment was packing to leave this place. To explain the lapse he wrote, "I quit writing in this Diary until now for the want of a change in country, and now the Regt. has got orders to march tomorrow I will go on again."[2] After that, he would write in it faithfully every day, even on those days he had to be propped up in a hospital bed to do it. There seemed more than enough blank diary pages for him to record the full details of the brief war they all expected, with pages left over. Unknown to him, the war would require that he fill this volume and several more like it. The places he would visit, and the things he would do or would see others do, no one could foresee. One of the boys in this camp would survive what they would pass through, and as an old man he would look back to this innocent time and conclude that the new soldier's most valuable asset had been his inability to see into the future.

Another boy had come into this camp with an Akron company of soldiers a few days before Parmater. Before he became a private in Company D, Benjamin Franklin Pontius had been a wagonmaker, talented in the fashioning of wood and iron. His widowed mother did not want him to go off to war. He was her only son, and keeping their poor farm afloat was plenty hard enough even with his help. But he wore down her objections, and she finally gave her permission. One day he dug out a paper and pencil and walked to the top of a low rise. He wanted to show his mother the importance of what he had come here to be part of, which was something he could not likely put into words. He could see in his mind's eye what Camp Giddings looked like to a bird flying over it, and he made a drawing of the camp, complete down to the shakes on the cook room roof.[3] He got the perfect outline made by the track that enclosed the lines of the company streets just so, and along the lines of the company streets he drew evenly spaced dark triangles to show the tents in which the soldiers lived.

Camp Giddings was little more than a few weeks old when these two young men first saw it. But in its perfect arrangement, already fixed military rituals, and a population double that of the village, Camp Giddings must have seemed to have been here forever. The nation had been at war for going on half a year already when Parmater, Pontius, and hundreds of others were already in this camp, but little blood had yet been spilled, and only a little war pain felt. Boys coming into camp and those already there longed for a look at this war, and Camp Giddings was the nearest portal by which they might approach it and see the great thing with their own eyes.

Every soldier knew that old J. R. Giddings had founded this regiment, and if they had not known why he started it, he explained it to them on the chill day when he came out to this camp to present them with their flags. What they did not know was that the roots of this particular grand military establishment ran back into their common, peculiar Western Reserve history. The more direct explanation as to why the Giddings Regiment was begun, by whom, and to what purpose, lay as near to hand as the events of a few months before, on the day the war began.

∽

The most important news in the history of Jefferson, seat of Ashtabula County, Ohio, came to it over the telegraph wire on April 12, 1861. The rebels had fired on Fort Sumter in Charleston harbor. As the people were fond of expressing it, the "ball" had opened. The excitement could not have been greater had the rebels lobbed shells into the village's main street. The people were exhorted to awaken and show their faith in the Union by their actions, and their actions were instant and electric. Within a day following the news of Fort Sumter, companies of men were practicing marching drills in the streets of every town in the Reserve. The residents filled the plank walks and spilled over into the streets and broke spontaneously into "Yankee Doodle." Flags floated from every home and shop, lifted high on the hot breath of war fever. Military bands practiced martial tunes at all hours in the village square. *Supernatural* was the only word that came close to describing the intensity of feeling felt by everyone in the springtime of 1861.[4] If a modern sociopsychologist were transported back to that first week after the bombardment of Fort Sumter, he might well diagnose the people's behavior as a form of mass hysteria; it had all of the characteristics of that malady.

Groups of men hurried along previously quiet village streets from morning to night, scooping up the latest telegrams and guessing at their meaning. No one could, or wanted to, talk of anything but war. Rumors blew up and down the village streets like dust devils; everything might be true, or all of it false, but nothing could be discounted entirely. The critical instinct of the newspaper editors was swept away in the tidal wave of high feeling; they printed everything that came to hand. Close to home, it was reported that John Brown Jr. had gathered an armed force of four hundred Negroes in the Pennsylvania woods just across the Ashtabula County line and was expecting fifteen hundred more to return from refuge in Canada and join him within a few days.[5]

Northerners who fled home from the Southern states brought with them rumors being circulated there: New York City had taken up arms and joined the secession; Washington city had been destroyed and Lincoln and his cabinet taken prisoner. Lincoln was reported to have been drunk since the inauguration and locked up in the White House taking a cure of opium and brandy, going out only under disguise.[6] Reliable men just returned from the South reported that whiskey-fueled mobs produced the United States flag at public demonstrations, tore it into strips, and spit and trampled on it. Southerners believed their cause was making gigantic headway, even in the North.[7] The Akron editors put some stock in that claim and warned Summit County's would-be traitors to "bridle their tongues or emigrate to the Sunny South."[8] Harsher chastisements of those of suspect loyalty were in the offing. To fill President Lincoln's first call for troops, the phenomenon of the war meeting burst immediately into existence.

Committees of leading citizens were formed to enlist men and raise money for their equipment. Residents were summoned to crossroads schoolhouses, churches, and mechanics' halls, or in the middle of the street to hear fevered speeches interrupted by the spontaneous eruption of band music, singing and cheering, and the firing of the village artillery piece. Those places too small to afford artillery touched off a thick charge of black gunpowder sandwiched between a pair of anvils borrowed from the local blacksmith, producing an explosion equal that of any cannon, and sending the topmost anvil wailing through the air. When the excitement reached its peak, men were exhorted to step to the front and sign the enlistment roll. War meetings would become a fixture on the Reserve scene for the next four years. After just a year of active war, the people would grow sick to death of them, and the newspaper editors bored with reporting them.[9] Just now, with the crisis still novel, the announcements of meetings taking place everywhere proved that the people were impassioned, and united.

At the hitherto sleepy crossroads village of Johnsons Corners, a few miles north of Akron, three cannon shots brought the residents quick-stepping into the village for an impromptu war meeting. They were treated to soul-stirring fife and drum music played by one C. L. Fergusson and his musical sons. Every man spoke who was inclined, including fourteen-year-old Albert Wright. He mounted the farm wagon being used as a speaker's platform and brought some men to tears by his sudden maturity and the eloquence of his words. Everyone joined in singing "Yankee Doodle" and "Hail Columbia" accompanied by the village band, and the meeting concluded with a fourteen-volley salute fired by their very own Union Gun Squad.[10]

The Akron newspaper happily ticked off the list of communities surrounding it that had fallen in and saluted them for their speedy, efficient reaction to the challenge. The formerly serene villages of Boston and Northfield were "up to the time," and Richfield was "wheeling into line." Copley was "in earnest," and Cuyahoga Falls was "all in a blaze." Akron itself was "fully aroused," and Summit County as a whole, "completely astir."[11] At tiny Greensburg, in Summit County, a gallows was hammered together on the village common. A rope was thrown over the top timber and from it hung the warning "Death to Traitors."[12] In Richfield on a Saturday evening, the Stars and Stripes were run up to the top of a seventy-foot-tall Lincoln pole left over from the last election, and the crowd cheered until all were hoarse. Akron had reached the flood stage of its own war fever. The relentless enthusiasm of the war's first week, the number of flags now flying, banners stretched across the town's streets, the mustering ceremonies and company drills, the singing and cheering had all been exciting and gratifying beyond description.[13]

Everywhere, plans were made to raise at least one company of hometown soldiers. At every war meeting, at least a few brave-hearted patriots would step forward to sign up, and they were rewarded by the crowd with three cheers and a tiger for the Union, and three groans for the Southern Confederacy. Afterward, the committeemen who had put on the show hurried out to canvass every home in the neighborhood for recruits, and if the household had no son or husband to contribute, cash donations were requested for the support of the soldiers' dependents. The newspapers kept a careful count of the men enlisted in each town in their neighborhood, heaped praise on the successful, and admonished others to do more. Competing villages exchanged delegations of freshly recruited soldiers. Visiting military bands with names like the Brimfield Rub-a-Dubs serenaded.[14]

A single campaign would wipe out the rebellion, and restore peace and prosperity to the land, and the people had good reason to believe such a thing could be true.[15] There was the evidence of their own eyes: the rush of men to enlist, the constant drillings to and fro of newly formed companies in the village streets, and the exuberance of the war meetings. One Reserve newspaper ran a prophetic piece called "Where the War Strength Lies," which compared the population of Northern cities to those of the South and came to the confident conclusion: "Thus at a glance will be seen where the advantage is, and what chances even a consolidated South are against a consolidated North."[16] An observer watched the demonstrations of men eager to come to the nation's rescue in the streets of Ashtabula city and concluded that the president could have as many men as he wished. "There is no want of the sinews of war—men and money are both abundant—equal to any emergency that is likely to arise."[17]

Everyone was of the same mind: the deck was stacked against rebel success. The Confederacy had no navy and little capacity to provision itself with the implements of war. Most important, the South was bankrupt. Loans to it made by Northern bankers, including some in Ohio, far exceeded the real value of the South's assets, which were hardly worth counting.[18] There was no anxiety as to whether the South could be whipped. The only real fear was that some unlucky town would be left behind in putting its boys into the fight.

Editorial rhetoric had been bitterly anti-Southern through decades preceding the war, but in this splendid state of alarm, the gloves came off completely. The current rapture equaled that which talented preachers had conjured up in the tents of the great religious revivals that had roared through here thirty years earlier, but unlike those, an element of bloodlust rose to the top. The editors of Akron's *Beacon* cried, "The rebels have begun the War, and now let them have war to their savage and bloody heart's content. . . . Let the dogs of war be loosed, and let them never be called in . . . let them drink their fill!!! Let the traitors be annihilated."[19]

To carry out the sanguinary work, a Massachusetts regiment was reportedly furnished special axes capable of splitting a man from his head to his belt buckle.[20] At the Union Hall in Akron the largest crowd ever gathered at a meeting of any kind showed unanimous support of one speaker's resolve: "We will do all in our power to exterminate or conquer them . . . no sacrifice is too great."[21]

That slavery would be obliterated as a natural byproduct of the North's triumph may have seemed too obvious to mention, and it was not mentioned, except in private by men like Giddings. To his friend Senator Charles Sumner of Massachusetts, he expressed what to him seemed self-evident: "The first gun fired at Fort Sumter rang out the death-knell of slavery."[22] For everyone else caught up in this mystical state, everything being done now was for the Union, plain and simple. Party lines had been spontaneously obliterated, political bickering forgotten, and all real patriots regardless of stripe were coming to the rescue of their country. On speakers' platforms, former political enemies sat shoulder to shoulder, good Democrats and Republicans alike waiting for their chance to stir the crowd.[23] The people were reminded that they were the lineal descendants of the heroes of the Revolution, which most all were here in the Reserve, and that the foul spirit of the Southern traitors had viciously assaulted the sacred legacy of '76.[24]

The pages of the local papers suddenly gave way to a fascination with all things military. Fresh recruits wrote excited, detailed letters home from training camps no more than an easy walk from the town as if they were writing from the other side of the planet. Old soldiers offered their wisdom to new ones: avoid strong coffee and oily meat, grow beards as protection for the throat and neck, wear hats with high crowns to allow air to cool the brain, and sleep on an India rubber blanket to ward off rheumatism. Above all, the soldier must practice vigilant hygiene and guard against fevers brought on by sudden, sweaty exertions in cold night air. One veteran of the War of 1812 concluded factually, "More men die from sickness than by the bullet."[25]

Everyone got into the act, including the Reserve's Yankee storekeepers. The proprietor of Talcott's Hardware, across the street from the courthouse in Jefferson, bombarded the readership of the local newspaper with ads astutely tied to the grand excitement sweeping the countryside. He headlined his ad "Fight! Fight! Fight!" and urged his townsmen to give the rebels their due without sparing the grapeshot, while bearing in mind at all times that Talcott's Hardware was prepared now more than ever to furnish hemp rope, oil lamp wicks, fishing line, and bed cording at fair prices every time.[26]

Reserve ministers had long since given up preaching Christian forbearance as a solution to the simmering sectional conflict, nor had most made any attempt to keep politics out of the church house.

In the present crisis, divine services were concluded now with "Our Country, 'Tis of Thee" and other patriotic anthems. Reverend Adams of Akron reminded a company of local soldiers bound for the battlefield that secession had not been merely treason but religious sacrilege. "This conflict therefore, to which you offer yourselves, is for this reason, of a sacred character. It is a holy war. . . . You will therefore fight not only for your country but for your God—and God therefore will be with you."[27] To prove that the divine was on their side, it was reported that the God of lightning had thrown a bolt onto a Confederate gunpowder factory, blasting it to smithereens, just as he had earlier sent lightning down to destroy the campaign signs and even headquarters buildings of their political opponents during the Lincoln campaign.

The hoopla immediately produced a huge surplus of soldiers. Ohio's quota under Lincoln's call was thirteen thousand men. Columbus had been a town of twenty thousand souls, but overnight its population pushed past fifty thousand by some accounts, and it grew larger with every train that came into the depot with another cargo of excited recruits.[28] A correspondent for Jefferson's leading newspaper had gone to Columbus to report on the chaotic scene. Thousands of fresh volunteers marched round the clock through the city streets, excited boys trying to get some sleep on the floor of the senate chamber while their friends drilled in the hallways, boxed, and wrestled. Some fellows played leapfrog, and there was one big chap down on all fours with a general riding on his back shouting orders.[29] Outside, recruits burned off their energy running barefoot races on the statehouse lawn. In Jefferson, the editor of the *Ashtabula Sentinel*, William Cooper Howells, regarded the war preparations seen in the village streets and concluded, "Of local matters, it may be said, in round terms, we are all war."[30]

Headquarters, Jefferson, Ohio

In Jefferson, the *Sentinel* put on its war face and took on the role of command post, dispensing bulletins and encouraging volunteers to step forward immediately, as if the war might last only a few days: "Headquarters, Jefferson, Ohio, To Arms . . . Men of Ashtabula! Men Are Wanted Now!" and following that, the announcement of a mass meeting to consider the urgent matter of the village's response to the call for troops.[31] The timing of the village response would prove critical if it were to avoid being left behind in the stampede to get a company into the war. The ball had opened, but the dance floor was yet small, and it was immediately crammed to capacity. Every single printer employed at the *Painesville Press* had thrown down his apron and hurried out to enlist, leaving the abandoned editor to wonder how he was going to get out his paper.[32] Within two weeks of the war's start, as many as eighty thousand men had rushed forward to fill Ohio's quota, six times the number of recruits Lincoln had requested of the state, and several thousand more men than he had asked of the entire North.[33]

Jefferson lawyer and brigadier general in the state militia Darius Cadwell had rushed to Columbus to see about getting Jefferson's company into the war.[34] Neither Cadwell's rank nor his close connection to the influential J. R. Giddings got him special treatment. He had to stand in the line of men filling the adjutant general's office, all of them wanting to tender their own companies, and when he finally got inside, he was told that from the obvious looks of things Ohio had met its quota of recruits. Cadwell was given assurance that some companies *might* be accepted into regiments already organizing. Encouraged thus, he went back to Jefferson to begin organizing, but five days had already wound off the clock by the time the village held its first big war meeting at the courthouse, on April 20, the first such event of the Civil War held in Ashtabula County.[35] Sixty men stepped up to the table manned by the meeting's secretary, Jefferson attorney J. D. Ensign, and signed the rolls. First in line was U.S. senator Ben Wade. Wade was too old for field service, and had important work to do in Washington, but his demonstration of community spirit and patriotism was appreciated. The Jefferson Guards were organized on the spot.[36]

The fiery exhortations of speakers at other county villages produced enlistees for their pet companies. At tiny West Andover, ninety-four men enlisted in the Andover Union Guards. Rollin L. Jones, a young printer of the village of Wayne, signed up and was elected second lieutenant.[37] The villages of Kingsville and Pierpont combined efforts and organized a company. They chose a rotund Pierpont merchant and schoolteacher named Wilbur F. Stevens as their first lieutenant.[38] He could be seen leading them in practice on the village green most every afternoon. In Ashtabula city, a veteran of the Mexican-American War was raising men for his company of Rough and Ready Guards, and at Hartsgrove, Capt. Leverett Grover had his company of Red Coats ready to go.[39] While the Jefferson Guards were still getting organized, the Morgan Riflemen, from nearby Rock Creek, marched into Jefferson to show off their homemade uniforms and advanced state of preparedness.[40]

During his visit to Columbus, Cadwell had been given the disappointing news that the state of Ohio already had more men than it could use. Then, while the company-raising hullabaloo was still reaching its zenith, unhappy news came that Conneaut's offer to the state of the company it had raised, which included a thin-faced doctor of medicine named Amos Fifield, had been refused and its dejected men ordered to disband.

The soldiers of Jefferson's company were organized and ready to march when they received official notice that they would not be accepted. They had already elected officers, and each man had been presented with a Bible and two red-flannel shirts sewn by the ladies who had turned the county courthouse into a sewing room.[41] The Jefferson Boys drilled every day in the village streets while they waited for orders, but when an order did arrive from Columbus, it was for them to disband. One company of Jefferson men would be going to war, but that was a reflection more of a single man than of the village. Giddings's son Grotius had resigned his comfortable post as his father's assistant in Montreal and gone home to Jefferson to raise two companies of expert riflemen. That he could easily raise two companies in and around Jefferson, and that the addition of them would complete the county's own regiment, was guaranteed.[42] Grotius Giddings succeeded in raising only one company of men, and with his father's influence he got his gaily outfitted Zouaves accepted into the three years of service under the flag of the Twenty-Third Ohio Infantry, officered in part by future president Rutherford B. Hayes. The Twenty-Third Regiment was not a purely local organization, and Ashtabula County residents did not place their hopes in it. For now, the people of the village would have to be content with the maneuvers of an excited group of juvenile boys who had formed the Jefferson Light Artillery. The youngsters had resurrected the village's rusty cannon and entertained themselves by firing it off from time to time and strutting about the village in their showy uniforms.[43]

Within two weeks of the war's start, editor W. C. Howells had stated confidently, "Will those papers who have been so free in their remarks concerning this County, please inform their readers that this County will have *one Regiment* in the field by May 6."[44] The hoped-for regiment did not materialize. Eventually, four Ashtabula County companies would be allowed to join the war's first call to arms, and Howells tried to put a bright face on this accomplishment.[45]

The Reverend Crane, regarded as a "true Christian and a good shot," would be taking his Rock Creek Company, known also as the Morgan Riflemen, into the war.[46] He had found a slot for his men in Company D of the ninety-day-term Nineteenth Ohio Volunteer Infantry being recruited from several Reserve counties. Ashtabula city's company, the Ashtabula Guards, would be allowed into the Nineteenth as Company I, under the leadership of a local preacher who had as his motto, "Look to the Lord and keep your powder dry."[47] Jefferson and Andover, two towns that had been in the national spotlight as abettors of the John Brown insurrection, would have to sit it out. The disappointment felt in Jefferson was acute.

The principal interest of Akron, two hours to the west, had always been commerce, but since Fort Sumter, business was the last thing on anyone's mind. The busiest intersection in the town, at Howard and Market Streets, was filled with mobs of excited men. Competing recruiters delivered patriotic speeches from wagon beds decorated with flags, while their deputies circulated through the crowd with enlistment rolls. Enough Akron men came forward in just two days to fill three companies. There would be room in the young war for only two of the three. One of these, the Akron Union Light Infantry, led by local businessman and militia officer Lewis P. Buckley, got a place in the Nineteenth Ohio. The town's third company, the Akron Buckeye Light Infantry, could not get in and was ordered disbanded.

Two of its members, George Dice, son of a Pennsylvania widow, and Myron Wright, a miller's boy from Johnsons Corners, found places with Buckley.

Two weeks after Lincoln's call for volunteers, Akron's soldiers marched up the main street bound for Cleveland, and the war. Buckley's company formed up to receive its send-off. One soldier after another was called forward to receive the presentation of a Colt's pistol, a Bowie knife, or both, from friends, fathers, brothers, and fellow workers.[48] James B. Storer had been a clerk in his father Webster's prosperous iron store. His brother Daniel presented him with a six-shooter, and James responded with feeling-filled words: "My brother, I accept this revolver, and I pledge to you that while I have life, I shall stand by the flag of my country, and that the giver of this shall never have occasion to say that he has ever been disgraced by me."[49] The citizens of Copley brought packets of cash for its soldiers.[50] Bibles were the most popular parting gifts, now and throughout, given with the blessing that the Ruler of Battles would keep them safe.[51] Most soldiers were still in the clothes they had worn to tend the family's dairy herd, but the luckier few wore the outlandish uniforms of their local militia. The few that were armed carried old-fashioned smoothbore muskets retrieved from long storage at the local militia armory. With a giant crowd accompanying them, Captain Buckley led his men down to the rail depot through a crashing thunderstorm behind the celebrated Professor Marble's Band and set off for Cleveland.[52]

Summit County's third company, Hard's Light Infantry, got itself to Camp Taylor in Cleveland but found no room. Captain Hard was handed an order to disband and go home. Pulaski Hard had been named after a Polish hero of the Revolution, was a graduate of a New York law school, and was an officer with three years' service in a local militia outfit. Given his credentials, and the efforts he had invested in his company, he thought they should not be so easily dismissed, but there was really nothing he could do about it.[53] Hard and his dispirited men marched to the depot but the railroad refused to honor their transportation vouchers, and the men had no money for tickets. They started out for Akron on foot. To make matters worse, boat passengers tossed insults at the ragged men as they trudged the path along the Ohio and Erie Canal home, hollering out that they were marching away from the war, not toward it.[54]

Over at the tiny village of Rock Creek, in Ashtabula County, the exit of the Morgan Riflemen brought out over a thousand people, everyone of them cheering wildly as their boys marched down the steep main street, across the creek, and out onto the main road.[55] In Jefferson, there was no cheering. They had not succeeded in getting their company into the war. Countywide, the people would have to be content in the knowledge that they had succeeded in getting at least some of their boys into a war that everyone expected would be won by the end of the summer, or earlier.

The Origins of the Giddings Regiment: The Summertime War, 1861

The Nineteenth Ohio Volunteer Infantry crossed the Ohio River into western Virginia. Before their brief campaign under George B. McClellan ended, they would find battle at a place called Rich Mountain, and the victory they won there would be regarded as glorious, even monumental. They itched for a fight, and the rebels were up ahead in the hills ready to accommodate them. The rebel general, Robert S. Garnett, had his small force dug in at a pass over Rich Mountain, which sat above the town of Beverly, and was set to dispute McClellan's passage. McClellan's second in command, Brig. Gen. of Volunteers William Starke Rosecrans, got his skirmish line up the mountain and right into the rebels and a sharp little fight sputtered to life in the rain. The Nineteenth Regiment, the Reserve's pride, got their chance when the rebel line began to totter.[56] They fired two volleys and the rebels broke.[57] The Union boys rushed into the deserted enemy camp and ransacked it for trophies just in case this had been the war's first and last battle. Soldiers of an Akron company dove into abandoned trunks, costumed themselves in Confederate dress uniforms, and amused their fellows by strutting about issuing mock orders in what they believed to be Southern accents.[58]

The Nineteenth Regiment's soldiers were convinced they had fought one of history's capital battles, even though only three men had been slightly wounded and none were killed, an economy of bloodletting that was attributed to the rebels' poor marksmanship.[59] Two days after Rich Mountain the rebel general, Garnett, took a ball in the back while directing his rear guard and was killed. The curious citizens of Wheeling waylaid Garnett's remains on the way back to his Virginia home, and opened the sealed metal coffin to gape at him. They marveled at the remarkable damage done by the newfangled bullet that had killed him. Tearing the body like a cannonball, the lead, cone-shaped minié ball had pierced his coats, his vest, and his underwear, before exiting his chest through a hole the size of a dinner plate.[60]

Back home on the Reserve, the newspaper editors were crowing. Their boys had fought like hurricanes, as good as U.S. Regulars or better. Rosecrans singled out Lewis P. Buckley for his competence in managing his boys under fire.[61] It had been a fine summer's outing for the Nineteenth Regiment, but the campaign had not been entirely a lark, and despite the glory and good fun, some of the boys were carrying grievances home with them. First and foremost, they had not been paid. The soldiers had left their farms with crops half planted or lost several months' wages from jobs in shops and mills. Until they were paid, the soldiers would curse the government for failing to hold up its end of the bargain. They had other complaints of a far more serious nature, and the revelation of them would lead directly to the founding of the Twenty-Ninth Ohio Volunteer Infantry.

It would be a while longer before their soldiers returned and their grievances became public. In the meantime the people of the Reserve celebrated the sort of old-fashioned Fourth of July their grandfathers had enjoyed. There was a war on, but it seemed far away. In the years just around the corner, the Fourth of July would still be observed; it was far too important a milepost in the year's passage to ignore. Future celebrations would be carefully orchestrated to encourage enlistments and donations to keep the produce of the ladies' aid societies flowing toward the army hospitals. At dawn, July 4, 1861, the firing of Conneaut's big gun rattled window glass, and people jumped from their beds and went out to see what was in store. Down on the village green, they found an evergreen bower filled with young women in white robes, each wearing a banner representing all of the states, including those fallen away from the Union, seeming to suggest that there were at least some folks in Conneaut who still believed that the tear in the fabric of the Union could be mended. There were brass band competitions, picnic baskets, and plenty of speeches. For the youngsters, a forty-five-foot-high swing was erected between two giant trees.[62] Sunday school superintendents took their charges down to the cool shade of the nearest grove for games and ice cream. After the Fourth, it was back to the measured pace of a Reserve summer.

The weather had turned unrelievedly hot as July deepened, and although dark clouds ganged up over Lake Erie late every afternoon, the rain would not come. Farmers worried over grain crops that lay slumped in the fields. Men of commerce wrung their hands over the state of the Reserve's business, which after only three months of war had gone as flat and stale as the July weather.[63] The village folk were preparing homecomings for the soldiers from the Nineteenth Ohio. Their three-month period of enlistment would expire soon, and the boys would be returning home and sliding back into quiet country life. The news of their sons' successful exploits in western Virginia started to come in before the Independence Day decorations had been packed away, and the people were now convinced more than ever that the Johnnies would be whipped wherever encountered and that after a few more rebukes like Rich Mountain, they would quit entirely.[64]

"Dark Peril"

The sun was going down red and belligerent on a Sunday that had been as unremarkable as any other July Sabbath in Jefferson. Then, the first news hit that the federal army had engaged the enemy at Bull Run, Virginia. The first major battle of the war had been fought, the result as yet unknown. A group of citizens gathered in the street outside the post office, which also served as the village's telegraph station, to await the details.

Telegrams piled up, reporting victory in one, calamity in the next. Men became gloomy and women lowered their eyes and sighed deeply into cupped hands, thinking of the sad prospects in store for the country, and maybe for their own families. The people of the village finally turned out the lamps and tried to get some rest, but most could not sleep. They got up and hurried back to the post office, drawn by the ellipse of light thrown onto the dirt by the telegrapher's lantern. They stood and held nervous discussion with their neighbors, with the latest news from Washington still clacking in over the telegraph wire.

As the night progressed, the news kept getting worse, the carnage and the scale of the defeat far greater than first reported. Once the gasconade was separated from fact, there was no longer any doubt: the Union army had been trounced and was presently making its way back to Washington like the survivors of a colossal shipwreck. That such a thing had happened was beyond anyone's belief.[65]

Alvin Coe Voris and Sam Lane, both stars of Summit County's stump speaker's bureau during the past fall's presidential election, addressed a meeting convened in Akron the Monday after the battle, and resolutions were passed. Akronites were more ready than ever "to pour out our blood like water in defense of country and home against rebellious despotism." Another resolution suggested that this might be the right time for Lincoln to emancipate the slaves.[66] Howells of the *Sentinel* in Jefferson took a more restrained view for once and did not try to explain away the reverse as some had by saying the defeat had been purely accidental.[67] Howells wrote, "It will be seen that we have experienced a reverse, such as must cast a gloom over the whole North and such as will be a grave lesson to us for the future."[68] The lesson of Bull Run was that the people of the North must prepare for the longer war now in the cards.[69] Bull Run had been a necessary wake-up call, not a signal defeat. For the people of Ashtabula County, the dark cloud of Bull Run was silver lined. From this point forward, the war would be prosecuted with just the sort of iron hand they had been calling for from the start. At Bull Run the rebels had revealed themselves to be barbarians and deserving of harsher treatment.

Reliable sources provided dozens of reports that proved just how evil an enemy they were up against. Wounded Union soldiers had been bayoneted while they lay hurt and helpless. Boys gone missing were found pinioned to tree trunks and sliced in ways improper to mention, and a Union officer was discovered drawn and quartered.[70] Louisiana Zouaves had severed the heads of dead Union boys and amused themselves by kicking them around the battlefield.[71] Souvenir hunters had picked up poisoned musket balls, reported to be the rebel's secret weapon, and beheld what they sincerely believed to be history's largest wreckage of men and materiel.[72] The rebels had committed these and a thousand other outrages, forcing the editor of the *Ohio State Journal* to ask, "Are they civilized?"[73]

The faces on the street the morning after the news of Bull Run seemed to show a people too broken to carry on with a war, or anything else. Within a few days, the public heart recovered sufficiently for the editor in Conneaut to observe, "That an awful battle has been fought there is no doubt, and that our loss has been considerable is also certain, but that we are disheartened or discouraged in the least we do not think. On the contrary, we believe that the defeat will fire up the hearts and nerve the multitudes to rush to the conflict."[74] But there would be no rush into this new phase of the war. The patriotic hysteria visible on every street corner in the opening days of the war had fallen back to earth like a spent skyrocket and just at a time when the nation was entering its "dark hour of peril."[75] Despite the steely backbones and upbeat words of men like Voris and Lane in Akron about the people having been aroused to new levels of patriotism, nothing was seen on the streets this time around that resembled the rapture that had greeted the opening of hostilities three months earlier. Wiser men counseled that sober determination must now replace pure exuberance if the rebellion were to be put down.

A vast organization, as precise in its parts and predictable in its output as a steam engine, began to be set in place, one in which every man and woman, young and old, and even children, would be required to take a hand. Men signing on now would be away not for just a summer but for nearly three years, and as Bull Run had shown, it would not likely be a pleasant, bloodless summer's outing like the Rich Mountain campaign. Most important for the disappointed in Jefferson, every last man who could march and shoulder a musket would now have a place.

The Twenty-Ninth Ohio Infantry would be founded in these chastened times, but the timing of its birth was only coincidental to the debacle at Bull Run. The motivations for its organization lay back in the treatment of Reserve Boys in the recently concluded Rich Mountain campaign and deeper yet in

Ashtabula County's decades-long devotion to the antislavery movement. The soldiers had not been paid, which was cause for complaint, but they had also been mistreated by their own commanders in ways that stung the pride of the people. The details of these humiliations were finding their way back to the Reserve just ahead of the returning soldiers. Ashtabula County's reaction to these injuries to their soldiers, and to their common political beliefs, would lead to the birth of the Twenty-Ninth Ohio Volunteers.

Disappointment's Child

The lore of the Twenty-Ninth Ohio Volunteer Infantry gives the time of the regiment's birth as the evening of the day of the battle of Bull Run and its place as the street in front of the Jefferson post office. Joshua Reed Giddings came up the street, stepped onto the boardwalk, and made his overwrought neighbors a speech: "We must raise a regiment in this County, and I am ready to do anything and all in my power to promote it. . . . This reverse is necessary to excite us to action, and now is the time for us to move."[76]

These were memorable words, and Giddings might well have spoken them. The best known of the county's published histories memorialized Giddings's words, and over time they became the gospel of the how and when of the regiment's origin. The story, however, turns out to be more legend than fact. Giddings had taken the first step in building a new regiment before the armies had collided at Bull Run, and his motivation for taking that step came from a series of embarrassments suffered by the county's boys in the Nineteenth Ohio. The first incident had been humiliating enough, but the second struck directly against the war's higher purpose as the people of Jefferson and their neighbors envisioned it.

While the Nineteenth Ohio was camped in western Virginia, on its way to Rich Mountain, Lt. Joel Stratton of Company C, which had in it a squad of soldiers from Trumbull County, just below Ashtabula, took a detail out into the surrounding countryside to procure provisions. They discovered a house along the way and while they were rummaging through it, the owner surprised them and accused them of stealing his gold watch and his money stash.[77] Rosecrans had the men arrested and ordered them thrown out of the regiment and sent back to Ohio under an armed guard.[78] What's more, the entire company, not just the accused men, was paraded in front of the assembled regiment, ceremonially disarmed, and ordered to prepare for the humbling march home.[79] Some of the regiment's officers threatened to resign in protest over the injustice.[80] Rosecrans reconsidered and decided the balance of the company could have their muskets back and stay on, but the accused had to go.[81]

The indignant in Warren, Stratton's hometown, and Jefferson railed against the army commanders who had blighted the flower of Trumbull County's young manhood, attacked Governor William Dennison for failing to step between McClellan and Ohio's citizen-soldiers, and accused McClellan of mollycoddling traitors. The citizens demanded a fair and public trial for their boys, as if it was a case for the court of common pleas rather than a court martial.

At the same camp, at about the same time, a far more serious incident occurred. Their boys' high officers had tried to turn them into the lowest thing any Reserve man could become: slave catchers.[82] A company having in it dozens of Ashtabula County men had come close to mutiny, and for a time it looked as though the first casualties of the campaign might very well be their own commanders.

McClellan had given the inhabitants of western Virginia his personal guarantee that their houses and property, including their slaves, would not be disturbed as long as they kept their noses clean. A gentleman rode up to McClellan's headquarters to file a complaint that one of his slaves had come up missing. His man had disappeared about the time Rosecrans's brigade had come to town, which to him seemed a mighty compelling coincidence.[83] Judge Thomas Key, McClellan's advocate general, was sent to help the man locate his missing property.[84] While searching the Nineteenth's camp, the gentleman spied his slave tending a cook pot. The runaway was being escorted from the camp when members of two companies, with large representations of Ashtabula and Geauga County men in them, blocked their path. The soldiers were mad as hornets and threatened to kill Judge Key and his assistants. Some soldiers went so far as to swear they would avenge the execution of John Brown right there in the company streets. One of the companies involved had men in it from Rock Creek, in Ashtabula County. They expressed their outrage by painting a legend in large letters on the side of a U.S. government tent, "REMEMBER JOHN BROWN, BENIGHTED ASHTABULA THE HOME OF GIDDINGS AND WADE."[85] An armed escort arrived and covered the retreat of the slave, his owner, and the headquarters staff.

The good citizens in Jefferson and their neighbors at Rock Creek were livid. The front page of the *Sentinel* bristled with a headline that answered its own provocative question as to why the county had sent its finest young manhood off to western Virginia: "BLOOD-HOUNDS?—NO!" A public meeting was announced for July 20 at the academy in Rock Creek to consider what might be done to redress the degradation.[86] There had been other slights done the Reserve's boys by their own high officers, and for that the people pinned the responsibility on the man at the very top.

George B. McClellan was well liked in most places in Ohio. He was a native son after all and was currently basking in the praise of the Northern press for his victory at Rich Mountain. The editors of newspapers in the Reserve began to assail McClellan from every quarter. In their opinion, he had shrunk before the slave owner's lash like a whipped spaniel.[87] General Rosecrans, also a native son, fell in for most of the abuse, which was justified in the eyes of the Akron newspaper: "The troops from the Western Reserve have been made to understand that it was enough to know that they hailed from this section to ensure them any amount of annoyances and indignities from some quarters . . . these men have been made the victims of a prejudice that rankles in the bosom of Gen. Rosecrans towards the Western Reserve troops."[88]

Rosecrans had reportedly mouthed a comment that there was too much of the high-minded gentleman in Reserve troops for them to make good fighters.[89] In another story, he had ordered the keeper of a tavern to refuse food to hungry Reserve soldiers. The general feeling was that the Reserve's people were going to be persecuted in the military, just as they had been at home, all because of their antislavery beliefs.

"What Does Ashtabula Do?"

The people's champion, J. R. Giddings, was supposed to be in Montreal tending to his consulate post, but he was in Ohio as much as Canada these days, which put him in line for some of the heat coming Ashtabula County's way. His critics accused him of continuing his shameful beating of the antislavery drum even after war had begun, and he was being paid for it out of the public coffers. A Cleveland newspaper put its fingers on a spot that had recently become very sore to the people who had steadfastly supported the antislavery movement: "The people have enough of difficulty and trouble now on their hands arising out of the agitation of such demagogues as Giddings."[90] Giddings was feeling the sting of such accusations when in the first days of hostilities he wrote to persuade Governor Dennison to admit his son Grotius's company into the war: "You are well aware the people of that County [Ashtabula] have long been taunted with the charge of leading in the great antislavery struggle which now attracts the attention of the civilized world; and I submit to you the request of permitting them a corresponding opportunity to maintain their principles on the field."[91] Since the war's first days, editors of neighboring newspapers had needled each other regularly over whose village, town, or county had the higher population of patriots. As the ninety-day war wound down and a longer war loomed, the *Sentinel* began to regard accusations printed in other newspapers that Ashtabula County was not doing its part as downright "malignant." The county's neighbors were charging them with "backwardness" when it came to volunteering for the fight.[92]

Ashtabula County had fitted two infantry companies into the war, and, given the vast numbers of soldiers throughout Ohio competing for a place, they had done fairly well. The Nineteenth Regiment was being reformed for the three years' service, but having the county's men continue their service in that regiment after what had happened down in Buckhannon was out of the question. Ashtabula County was represented in other outfits: Grotius Giddings's company of soldiers in the Twenty-Third Ohio, Capt. John Carlin's battery from Conneaut, and the Geneva Artillery from up on the lakeshore. The Geneva boys had won the distinction of firing the war's first land-based artillery piece during the battle of Philippi, in western Virginia. However, there was no infantry regiment on the drawing board, or in the field, that fully embodied the fiery spirit of Ashtabula's moral crusaders.

A few days after the news of Fort Sumter, a headline in the Jefferson newspaper had posed the question, "What Does Ashtabula Do?"[93] This was more than a rhetorical lament to stir enlistment. It was a genuine expression of worry that the county would be left behind, to be remembered in history for having touched off the war and then done nothing of consequence while others spilled their blood.

A full week before Bull Run, Giddings had gone to Washington on a special mission.[94] He likely knew something of the grave injuries to the county's pride before he set off for the capital. His goal was to get authority from the secretary of war to organize an infantry regiment to be recruited within the boundaries of his old congressional district. Before Bull Run, many men were lobbying to have their own regiments shoehorned into service, but getting one in required a letter of special permission signed by the secretary of war, and that took some doing. The ocean of men who had crowded forward to enlist in the springtime just past were far more than the federal government thought necessary to tame secession.[95] Thus assured, Secretary Cameron ordered the national recruiting machine essentially closed down. A few three-year regiments ordered in the president's call following Fort Sumter were being accepted, but for the most part the War Department had taken the Help Wanted sign out of the window.[96]

Giddings shouldered aside knots of army officers, politicians, and contractors clogging the secretary of war's outer office, settled his bulk into an armchair at the desk of Simon Cameron, and commenced string-pulling. He returned to Jefferson on July 13 with the happy news that his lobbying effort with Cameron had been a success. Cameron had given his word that a regiment raised within Ashtabula and adjoining counties would be accepted into the federal service.[97] Giddings published "a card" in the Jefferson newspaper confirming that his mission had succeeded. He invited interested gentlemen to meet at his home on Chestnut Street on the afternoon of Thursday, July 25, to discuss the project, but four days before the meeting was held, news of the Federal calamity at Bull Run hit, and it changed everything.[98]

Bringing the South back into the fold would require far more than had been previously done, and the throttle on the idling recruiting machine was thrown wide open. Lincoln issued a new call for troops the day after Bull Run. Of the half a million fresh volunteers needed to get the job done, Ohio's quota was just over 67,300. For every man who had fought in the ninety-day service, six more would now be needed.[99] Bull Run had come at a propitious time for vindication of Ashtabula County's honor, and leading citizens in Jefferson set to work immediately to capitalize on it.

2

Founders' Club

JULY–SEPTEMBER 1861

Acting in Concert

On a raw day in late November 1861, Giddings made the short buggy ride out to the Ashtabula County fairgrounds to present his regiment with the flags it would carry in the war. He told the soldiers drawn up before him that a "few gentlemen," residents of Ashtabula County, had determined on raising the regiment.[1] He did not name names. The published history of the regiment, written two decades after the war by its one-time drummer boy J. Hampton SeCheverell, named J. R. Giddings as the founder, and two men who served as his principal assistants: U.S. senator Ben Wade and Jefferson resident Edward B. Woodbury. "Little Hamp" stated that other "well-known associates" of Giddings also contributed, but he did not identify them.[2] Of the two men SeCheverell named, only Woodbury actually helped. Ben Wade had little or nothing to do with the birth of the Twenty-Ninth Ohio.

Pairing the two men, Giddings and Wade, was natural enough since the two came from the same tiny Ohio place, and they marched under the banner of the same political party. As younger men, they had built a thriving law practice together, but by the time of the war, they had been bitter enemies for over twenty years. Wade had made a mean joke at Giddings's expense during a trial at the courthouse in Jefferson, and the enmity it generated far outlasted the sting of the jury's laughter.[3] Wade had tried to wrest Giddings's congressional seat from him in 1840, and failing in that he supported Giddings's enemies in his future battles for office. In the Giddings home, Ben Wade, the man who lived just a few doors up the street, was held up to the children as the type of person they should avoid becoming. In Giddings's mind, Wade was a man who was perfectly willing to sacrifice principle in his selfish drive for political power.[4] Most important, Wade was presently raising a regiment of his own, the Second Ohio Cavalry. The competition over which man would be the first to put a regiment in the field would be the last skirmish in a feud that Giddings and Wade had fought for almost a quarter century.

Less than a week following Bull Run the Jefferson newspaper reported that a three-man central committee had been formed and charged with the task of spreading the word through Giddings's old congressional district that a new three-year regiment would be accepting companies of good men at their camp in Jefferson. The members of the committee were listed as Abner Kellogg, C. S. Simonds, and J. D. Ensign. It would be these three men who would attend to the myriad details of launching this complex project: making the first casts of the recruiting net, filling the top command slots, selecting a site for the camp, and arranging for all its equipment, right down to kettles and uniforms. All these efforts would have to be coordinated with the governor and the adjutant general of the state. Three of the Giddings clique—Kellogg, Ensign, and Woodbury—were already serving as members of the county's military committee, and in a few weeks Woodbury would take over its leadership.[5] That committee was obligated to advance the interest of *every* military outfit being formed in part or wholly within their county, including that of Ben Wade's Second Ohio Cavalry. That this dual service might produce discord was not yet foreseen.

The founding fathers of the Twenty-Ninth Ohio were as alike as peas in a pod. All were descendants of Revolutionary War soldiers. Each had made the Lincoln-like ascent from frontier poverty to small-town gentility. All were practicing lawyers. They had all taken a hand in building up the village of Jefferson and the county, following one another through a succession of elected offices, from school board member to county clerk to state congressman. Above everything else, they were unified by their hatred of slavery and had been pillars of Giddings's local power base, and he had been their point man on the national political stage.

Abner Kellogg was accounted to be one of the pioneers of the county's antislavery movement.[6] He had been expressing his conviction for years that slavery could only be eradicated by war. Along with Giddings's son Joseph Addison, Kellogg had organized a "sympathy meeting" at the courthouse on a March evening in 1860 attended by the fugitives in residence at Harpers Ferry. Charles Stetson Simonds and J. D. Ensign had been strong antislavery men most of their lives. At the age of twenty-one, Simonds set off to seek his fortune in the wilds of New Mexico. He got only as far as St. Louis when he heard that a Negro had been burned at the stake further down the river for shooting a white man. He decided against going further south and returned to Ashtabula County an antislavery zealot.[7] Recently, he had served as secretary of the Jefferson committee that had tried in vain to put the village company into the ninety-day service.[8]

Woodbury had grown up near Kelloggsville, not far from the Lake Erie shore, in the same neighborhood as Kellogg, and like Kellogg, he moved into Jefferson to practice law and occupy local political offices. Woodbury would do more of the needed legwork than any of the other identified founders. He also contributed his namesake son to the Twenty-Ninth Ohio. None of the founders served in the regiment, although some were still young enough for service, and although most of them had sons of service age, none of them enlisted in the Twenty-Ninth Ohio except for Woodbury's son. What contribution Giddings could make toward building the regiment was questionable.

Giddings's health was reported to be in decline, again, and technically he was supposed to be at his post in Montreal. What he had already done was significant. He had given his name to the regiment and it would be known throughout Ohio ever afterward as the Giddings Regiment.[9] If the regiment made a reputation for itself, the credit would go to him, and if it faltered, his name would be associated with its failure. His name alone would serve as a powerful magnet to men wanting to enlist. It remained to be seen whether the younger generation from which the recruits must come was as devoted to Giddings as their parents and grandparents. Giddings, as everyone knew, had connections in Washington, and if the regiment ran into trouble of any kind, Giddings could pull the strings to lift them out of it.

Giddings went to Columbus the day after Bull Run to see to the arrangements for receiving his regiment, but at that point there was no regiment to be received. However, the founders were confident that once the word was out, volunteers would hurry into Jefferson to join up. Two other prominent Jefferson lawyers, Decius S. Wade and Darius Cadwell, were immediately dispatched by the Central Committee to ride out Paul Revere–like into the surrounding villages to organize war meetings and galvanize support behind the new regiment.[10] The Giddings group started out immediately to turn an abstraction into an organized, uniformed, properly officered army of a thousand men. Their hope was that in a few weeks the Giddings Regiment would march down the main street and into the war. Dozens of steps must be taken in the meantime, and the first was to pick a man to command the new regiment.

"Come Boys, Follow Me"

The Reserve's soldiers in the Nineteenth Ohio were filtering back to their homes to await mustering out and their pay. They were veterans now, trained in the basics of march and maneuver and tested under fire. The Giddings Regiment founders believed they would jump at the chance to enlist in a regiment founded on principles loftier than those enforced by the army despots they had served under in western Virginia. In the minds of the founders, enlistment of the new regiment's core from the ranks of the Nineteenth Ohio veterans would be automatic. Just as critical to the success of their project was the selection of the man who would lead it. A private's opinion counted for a great deal, and if his preference for a particular commander was ignored, he could hike over to the next county and enlist in an outfit led by a man more to his liking. The veterans of the Nineteenth Ohio showing an interest in joining the new regiment wanted Lewis P. Buckley, recently retired major of the Nineteenth, to lead them.[11]

There was much else to recommend Buckley to the Giddings circle. He had proven himself a capable leader of troops in the Rich Mountain campaign. Professionally trained officers were scarce as hen's teeth just now, and Buckley had been to West Point. He had organized and led his own company for the ninety-day war, and that company would naturally follow him to his new post. More than likely, soldiers from Akron's second company in the Nineteenth Ohio would come along too. Moreover, Summit County's population was only slightly less than Ashtabula's, and with Buckley at the helm, the new regiment would be assured a direct conduit into the prime recruiting ground of Summit County. Buckley had returned to Akron from the ninety days' service to a welcome fit for a Caesar.[12] Two men close to him, Jonas Schoonover and John Clemmer, turned out their companies to escort him the last miles back into Akron in high military style.[13] He had not finishing putting his things away when Woodbury came knocking at his door to offer him the command.[14]

Woodbury stepped down into a town of three thousand souls. Akron was several times larger than Jefferson but had little of Jefferson's New England stateliness. Akron had been blessed by its situation on the great Ohio Canal, and more recently by the railroad. The town was lagging behind its more progressive neighbors, cities such as Cleveland and even Ashtabula, up on the lake, and it had less of the charm of its nearer, smaller neighbors like Copley or Hudson. From high above, the town resembled a large park, filled with well-tended homes, businesses, and churches, all tucked cozily into the folds of the Cuyahoga River.[15] Down at ground level, many of Akron's neighborhoods looked like they had been targets of a prolonged artillery bombardment. Dirt piles cluttered the landscape, and garbage floated on the surface of the canal, which leaked water into malarial pools on the main street.[16] Unpainted boxy warehouses and small businesses careened down to the banks of the canal. Thrown among them were shanties occupied by the Irish "muckers" who had come to dig the canal and stayed. The Irish were handy targets for jokes published regularly in the local newspapers, written in exaggerated dialect, in which they were invariably pictured as drunkards, imbeciles, or both. Akron's more prosperous citizens lived in modest houses along the streets that climbed free of the downtown and onto the bluff overlooking the Little Cuyahoga River gorge.

The town's business center lay at Howard and Market Streets. Scattered at regular intervals along the blocks of two- and three-story businesses in the downtown were sooty vacant lots where buildings had burned and the owners not gotten around to rebuilding. The streets were ankle deep with dust in the summer, flowed with a heady mixture of mud and manure in the rainy season, and at all times were overrun by the town's most notorious nuisance—rutting, half-wild hogs. Commercial activity dominated the streets during business hours and gave the place enough hustle and bustle to suggest that the town might someday become something very much bigger than it was currently. Despite its scruffy, uneven appearance, the seeds of real industry were already sprouting. There were boat works here, flouring and woolen mills, and potteries and foundries with close access to shipping by either water or rail. Primarily Yankee in makeup, the town contained a sizable population of German immigrants with their own singing societies and orchestras. The town's boosters were justifiably proud of its singing clubs, literary and debating societies, philosophic groups, and progressive schools.

While Woodbury made his pitch to Buckley, Giddings and his associates waited at the telegraph office in Jefferson, expecting a wire from Woodbury confirming that Buckley had accepted their offer.[17] Buckley, however, turned them down. He had not declined because of any dislike of Giddings or the politics he represented. His reason was personal: the campaigning in western Virginia had thoroughly wrecked his health.[18] Buckley realized that a commanding officer needed physical strength just as much as military experience.[19] Camping, marching, and fighting ruined the health of men half his age, and he was fifty-six. He disliked starting anything he might not be able to finish. By 1861 a long, useful life lay stretched out behind Lewis P. Buckley. He had come out to Akron when it was a rough-and-tumble place, made a go of his various business enterprises, and helped to build up the town in whatever way he could. He had served honorably in the ninety-day service.

If his health held, he might go far in this war. He had all the qualities that promised military greatness. In battle he sat his horse as coolly as a man eating his lunch. In dangerous situations he told wry jokes, which broke the tension and saved the day. He gave his orders in a stentorian voice that could be heard a half mile away. His perfect military bearing did not invite second-guessing. The common soldiers who served under him remembered Buckley for his stern sense of discipline, but they also remembered the personal conversations they had with him, or the times when he poked his head into a tent of sleeping privates to announce that he had started their cooking fire and set their coffee boiling. In the hearts of the men whom he commanded, no man of any rank ever stood higher. Long after Buckley's death, an old man who had been a boy in the Twenty-Ninth Ohio remembered him as the type of man who never said "Go," but always "Come boys, follow me."[20] Years from now, the Union veterans of the Akron area would donate money to have a fine Gothic-style chapel erected in an Akron cemetery as a memorial to their fallen comrades. The costly stained-glass windows would come all the way from Italy, and far and away the largest of them was a life-sized image of Lewis P. Buckley. It would be placed above the altar from which their most sacred ceremonies were conducted.

He was of medium height but stood so perfectly erect that he looked taller. He had a high forehead and large wide-set eyes above a nose that was long and straight. His chin made a broad square. Around the time of the war, he wore his dark hair close cut and curling slightly over large ears. Buckley was a man with the set of facial characteristics that in his day spoke of high moral strength and personal conviction.[21]

He was born in the frontier village of East Cayuga, in western New York, in August 1804, when Thomas Jefferson was president of the United States.[22] The village was situated at the eastern end of a mile-long plank bridge that spanned a swampy lake. On the other side lay the wild frontier.[23] Buckley's father, Hugh, kept a tavern, collected tolls, operated a log jail, and opened the neighborhood's first school.[24] The grandest cavalcade of immigration in the nation's history passed by the boy's front door on its way west.[25] During the War of 1812, heavy columns of American troops passed through the village on their way to war.[26]

Everything was looking up for Hugh and his family, but quickly things began to sour. Lewis's mother died when the boy was not yet six. Hugh found another wife and mother for his children, and for a while they were a family again.[27] Another epidemic swept through, and this time it took Hugh, leaving behind him a wife and six children, eight-year-old Lewis among them.[28] The stepmother died a year later, and Lewis and his brothers and sisters were now orphans.[29] Salvation arrived in the person of Justus Ingersoll, a veteran of the War of 1812. He married Lewis's sister and took in all her brothers and sisters.[30]

Lewis showed promise and Ingersoll had the financial means to provide him an education. After two years of boarding out and absorbing the classics as taught at Middlebury Academy, Lewis Buckley was ready to move on. In considering his protégé's future, Ingersoll concluded that his own military service had been the shaping experience of his life.[31] A professional military officer was a man of considerable stature. Ingersoll began a campaign to get Lewis an appointment to the U.S. Military Academy at West Point.

Letters of recommendation were sent highlighting young Buckley's capacity, solemnity, and classical attainments.[32] His tutor at Middlebury, Rev. Joshua Bradley, wrote that Buckley was a natural orator and that he had many abilities of value to the new republic. After months of waiting, a letter arrived bearing the mark of the secretary of war's office, in Washington. Buckley had been accepted. He passed the rigorous oral examinations, and was admitted as a fourth classman in the West Point class of 1826.

A biographical sketch of him published in a history of Summit County years after the war reported that Lewis Buckley had resigned from the academy before graduating because he could not tolerate the insolence of the proslavery faculty.[33] In truth, the termination of his West Point cadet career had nothing to do with the political views of the academy's instructors. Buckley had flunked out. He had survived the first year's culling out, but his performance had been less than impressive. He was ranked sixtieth among the sixty-nine cadets who had made it that far.[34] By the end of his second year, he had slipped further. The academic board concluded he was too indifferent toward his studies to proceed, and he was peremptorily discharged from the academy, and the army, having satisfactorily completed a single year of study.[35]

There is no record of his life in the ten years that followed his dismissal from West Point, except that three years after it, he married a young woman in Ogden, New York, named Sarah Jackemay.[36] Then, he disappears from view again until 1834, when he landed in Akron.[37] One of Justus Ingersoll's brothers liked the look of the Summit County country, bought land, and moved there.[38] However he came to Akron, Lewis Buckley hit the ground with his feet moving and eyes open. He opened a grocery store on the bank of the newly built Ohio Canal and set up housekeeping in its basement.[39] His timing was perfect. Akron, founded just two years earlier and hitherto a village of 250 mostly Irish laborers, was about to awake to its possibilities. In a very short time it began to resemble a boomtown: raucous and noisy. The parade of commerce floated right by Buckley's establishment and he prospered.

His election as Portage Township treasurer proved that his neighbors trusted him with their money. Buckley established a foundry and plow works and followed that with a tin and stove shop. He won appointment to the lucrative office of collector of tolls on the canal.[40] After one of Buckley's employees was robbed of several thousand dollars in toll receipts, Buckley was on the hook to the state of Ohio for the missing money. The majority of his fellow citizens never doubted his integrity, but a few gossips hinted behind his back that Buckley might have staged the robbery.[41] He sold all his property to pay what he could and his bondsman made up the difference.

In 1849 the news of gold discoveries in California came roaring through. Buckley organized fifteen other hopeful gentlemen and formed the Akron Mining Company.[42] They rolled out of Akron in a caravan of wagons bound for the Pacific Slope via the Great American Desert.[43] Buckley spent three years at Sacramento, not far from the mill where Captain Sutter's discovery had started it all, returning to Akron no richer than when he had left.[44] He brought back with him a troubling cough and recurrent fever. Through the 1850s he pursued his business interests, steering clear of the rancorous political disputes that were bringing the war steadily closer. To cap it all, he had responded to his country's call for help and dodged bullets leading the local boys in their victory at Rich Mountain. He was on the threshold of a contented retirement, and he had earned it.

While Buckley stayed home and tried to recover his health, Sgt. Myron T. Wright, recently retired from Buckley's Company G in the Nineteenth, and Sgt. James Grinnell, formerly of Akron's Company K, were both sticking recruiting posters to lampposts and placing them in store windows throughout Summit County. Each was intent on raising his own company for the new regiment, already known in Akron as the Giddings Regiment. The Akron newspaper endorsed both men, saying they had been "tried and not found wanting."[45] Jonas Schoonover and John Clemmer were also expressing an interest in forming companies for the new regiment. Buckley had led them through the campaign in western Virginia, and judging from the sort of man he was, he would have disliked sending them and the other local boys back into the war alone. Their enthusiasm for the Giddings project may have helped overcome Buckley's hesitancy. After just two weeks at home, his health had rebounded and he began to think that he might be able to do more. He wrestled with Woodbury's proposition again and finally made up his mind. He decided to accept the command of the Twenty-Ninth Ohio Volunteer Infantry and would report for duty in the first week of September.[46] In a letter to the adjutant general, Buckley confided, "I feel the responsibility, and I face too, my physical inabilities. . . . God willing and my life is spared and health permitting, I design to see the end of this War."[47]

The Giddings group had successfully laid the cornerstone of the project. They were now waiting on the officer they had picked to come and take charge until Buckley arrived.[48]

Cast in a Brilliant Light

Ground-shaking events, national and local, were coming all at once in the Jefferson of late summer 1861, compressed tightly together one atop another. The Giddings "card" proposing a meeting to discuss organizing the regiment ran in the newspaper followed by notice of a meeting in Rock Creek to protest the insult suffered by the local boys at Buckhannon, and next to that a bulletin that the long-awaited march on Bull Run had begun.[49] The people looked for omens in the strange workings of nature. A comet was seen driving through the stars above Ohio while events unfolded in Jefferson, and its appearance just then struck the people who marveled at it as more than coincidental.

It had been cloudy for several days, and when the dark curtain parted, a comet could be seen riding through the heavens brighter than Venus, as luminous as the full autumn moon and trailing a fiery cape that spread over half the northern sky. It was so bright that the outline of it could be seen even when the sun was up. At night, it lit the tops of clouds floating along below it. In the first few days of its visit, it appeared in the evening and slid out of sight within a few hours. After a while it never set, making circles round the North Star. The simpleminded were frightened, and everyone was spellbound. The people puzzled over its mysterious origins and theorized on its destination. Astronomers proposed that this was the same comet that had last been seen in 1558, coincidental to the abdication of Charles V, and way back in the Dark Ages, when it had come to announce the death of a pope. Its passage through the heavens had always marked the occurrence of cataclysmic events down below.[50]

3

Camp Giddings

EARLY PROMISE, FALL 1861

First Steps

Although every outfit stepping forward now was sure of a chance to fight, fresh memories of being left behind in the ninety-day war nagged the founders in Jefferson, and to increase their anxiety, recruiters for other regiments were already beginning to appear in their neighborhood. The project was too important to wait on any man, even Buckley. The Giddings men would do what they could to get the regiment building off to a quick start, but they were politicians and attorneys and someone was needed immediately to take charge of the military end of things, experienced in turning farm boys and mill hands into proper soldiers.

Fortunately, there was a man available who had had experience in turning recruits into proper soldiers, and he could come at once. The founders appointed thirty-nine-year-old Thomas Clark of Cleveland as major and acting commander of the Giddings Regiment.[1] Like Buckley, he came with the highest of recommendations.[2] Clark's most important qualification for high office in the regiment was the same enjoyed by Buckley—the recently returned veterans of the Nineteenth Regiment wanted him to lead them.[3]

He was a big man, taller than most by a head, with thick dark hair and bushy eyebrows. He had been born out in the mountain country of New Hampshire.[4] He had attended the region's military academy, Norwich University, but dropped out short of graduation and turned to school teaching and running a village mercantile.[5] His first child, Ellen Louisa, lived barely two years. After that, Clark and his wife packed up and headed west for a fresh start. He landed in Cleveland, where he was working as a commission merchant when the war broke.

Clark volunteered his services to the governor and was appointed state drillmaster for the several regiments doing their hurry-up training at Camp Taylor.[6] It was at Cleveland that he first met Lewis P. Buckley, and he was deeply impressed by Buckley's military aplomb. Clark had been offered the adjutancy of the Nineteenth Regiment but he declined the post because he found its commander too indolent and intemperate for his liking. He had his eye on appointment as commandant of Camp Taylor. He had seen firsthand the gross inefficiency of the troop training practiced by incompetent men and was confident he could institute a better system, founded on discipline and proper military instruction. The Camp Taylor job did not materialize.[7] When the Nineteenth Ohio was ordered forward to western Virginia, he volunteered to accompany them in an ex officio capacity.[8]

Volunteers were notoriously resistant to discipline, but even they admitted that Clark was a capable instructor of green troops. The ability to stand and face enemy fire was not something that could be taught, but Clark knew the mechanics of the thing. Other regiments were forming for the three years' service in Cleveland just then, and Clark's service would have been prized by any of them.[9]

Upon leaving Cleveland for the war, Clark had been presented with a fancy sword by his fellow members in the Sons of Temperance. He had taken the pledge to avoid strong drink, but he was not humorless, nor was he a crusader.[10] He was forceful enough to give orders, and have them obeyed by independent-minded volunteers, but he was also approachable and forgiving. In their first winter in the war, many boys in the regiment felt marooned and forgotten, and every soldier was impoverished. Clark used his own money to buy tobacco for the men, distributing it personally to them, and shared his own small supply of "waterproof biscuit" with the enlisted men.[11] The soldiers referred to him as a "good-natured old son," which was high praise from the ranks.[12]

The regiment's historian reported that Clark's first task upon setting down in Jefferson was to scout locations for their camp.[13] Actually, the question as to where the camp should be placed had been made by the regiment's promoters in the week following the news of Bull Run.[14] It had not been a difficult decision. Of course, it had to be in or near Jefferson, because that was where the founders made their homes. Even the dullest of businessmen could see that a town might be enriched by its proximity to the camp of an army regiment. Warren, in Trumbull County, was expected to reap a fortune of $100,000 by the rumored location there of a cavalry camp.[15]

The fairgrounds of the Ashtabula County Agricultural Society were located just a few blocks from the village center, and they stood vacant the whole year except for the annual fair, which was coming right up. The fair board was willing to loan the use of their grounds. With a little planning, the fair could be carried off as usual, while the regiment continued its drill and recruiting, and both might benefit.

Most of the Ashtabula County boys coming into the regiment had known these fairgrounds in more peaceful days. They had laid aside the chores for one day of the entire year and rode into Jefferson from remote county corners with jars of pickled cucumbers and fine quilts tucked safely into the corners of the spring wagon. They made their way past the courthouse and the grand houses and churches lining Jefferson Street and out the few blocks to the edge of town, where the land opened up into a dish-shaped expanse of green. Before them lay the fairgrounds, built on the largest piece of cleared ground anyplace in the county. The Ashtabula County fairgrounds were made to order for a military camp. The packed-dirt racetrack was judged to be as dry as a macadam highway, even in wet weather—perfect for drilling soldiers. The wood-framed, whitewashed buildings already standing could be easily converted to soldier use. The ticket office inside the main entrance would do duty as the Twenty-Ninth's hospital.[16] Here, the regiment's surgeon would treat the ill and injured and examine the fitness of new recruits. The exhibition hall and horse sheds would be used as kitchen, pantry, and mess. Even such primitive structures as cattle sheds could be turned to military purposes once swept clear of straw and manure. The camp must have a name, and this one would naturally honor its sponsor and be called Camp Giddings. When full, Camp Giddings would be the most populous place a good number of these boys had ever visited.

Clark sent his first official communiqué, postmarked Camp Giddings, to the state adjutant general, C. P. Buckingham, on August 20.[17] He requested Buckingham send along the basic accounting books needed by the regiment, such as an adjutant's orderly book, a roster, and morning report books. He also asked for copies of the army regulations. Apparently, there was not a single copy in camp. As for the other how-to books of soldiering, many recruits brought along at least one, such as *Hardee's Rifle and Infantry Tactics*, Gilham's *Manual for Volunteers and Militia*, Scott's *Infantry Tactics*, or McClellan's *Bayonet Exercises*. The government did not provide any of these, but they could be mail-ordered for about a dollar each from suppliers in Cleveland or Columbus.[18] For doctors planning on entering the service, curious about how patching up soldiers on battlefields might be different than treating civilians in their office above the local mercantile, there were weighty tomes for sale, such as Trepler and Blackman's *Military Surgery*.

Clark concluded his first official report by asking if the state had any arms handy that they might furnish the regiment. Columbus wired back that the state arsenal was so strapped that for the time being only field officers could be provided weapons.[19] In comparison to the exuberant tally of soldiers already in camp made by the regiment's boosters, Clark reported that the number present, although they looked to be of outstanding material, were the seed stock merely. By the time Clark arrived to take the reins, the regiment-building project was already booming along.[20]

One company was already organized, informally mustered in, and moving its recruiting headquarters out to camp.[21] Another company from Pierpont village, just to the west, was ready to come on as soon as camp could be prepared for their reception, and a third was taking shape not far to the southeast, just over the county line in Trumbull County.[22] The morning after the Bull Run news, Giddings bustled into Columbus, a city still reeling from the shock of yesterday's news. Although not a single man had yet been enlisted in his regiment, the *Ohio State Journal,* swept along by Giddings's enthusiasm, reported that the Giddings Regiment was already nearly full and would be filled to capacity within the week.[23] The Columbus newspaper admitted that this time around, Old Ashtabula had been first.[24] At the same time, representatives of the central committee spread out from Jefferson intent on visiting every town and village in Ashtabula County.[25] Notices appeared in the county newspapers that men wanting to join should come in just as fast as they could, by themselves if necessary, although it was "desirable for efficiency's sake" that they report in companies. And to avoid the unhappy confusion suffered by the Nineteenth's men as to when a soldier was on the clock for his wages, it was pointed out that soldiers volunteering for service in the Giddings Regiment would draw pay from the time they passed through the camp gate.[26]

To stimulate enlistment, the project's principals addressed hastily called meetings on successive nights in Geneva, in Sheffield at Blodgett's Store, at Center Church in Williamsfield, and in Gustavus, just over the Trumbull County line.[27] The star of the enterprise, J. R. Giddings, spoke to a gathering at nearby Hartsgrove.[28] At every stopping place they made their pitch for the Giddings Regiment. Every evening in the two weeks after Bull Run the lamps were lighted in the normally dark village church or mercantile in one town after another. The residents were drawn by the yellow glow in the sky in the direction of the town center and drove in to listen to Kellogg and Cadwell extol the benefits of enlisting in the regiment. Some of them signed the enlistment roll on the spot and with the loud congratulations of their neighbors ringing in their ears took an oath in front of a justice of the peace.

Some of these men woke up the next morning to the realization that they had been carried away by the fine rhetoric of the speaker and the goading of their friends. Upon serious consideration of the weight of the commitment they were facing, some men changed their minds. This first step in enlistment taken at the village church in a paroxysm of patriotism was still reversible, so it was believed, and the bargain would not be completely sealed until a man was officially sworn in by a mustering officer. There was a good deal of this backsliding going on in the vicinity of Akron. The newspapers warned that a man was beholden to his enlistment from the time he signed the roll, and if he did not show up, he would be treated as a deserter; but aside from threats, there was little to be done about it.[29] That a few men might not honor their commitment did not seem important just now. The organizers had been so successful in whipping up interest in their first week that the Jefferson newspaper could report that the enterprise was progressing finely and that the people were "all alive to the subject and numbers."[30] Near the end of August, the Jefferson newspaper was able to proclaim that all questions about filling up the regiment were at an end.[31]

As a reflection of the booming hopes of the founders in these early days, the Twenty-Ninth Ohio Volunteer Infantry was not going to be an ordinary regiment. It was planned to be the grandest fighting force Ohio had yet placed in the field. The founders envisioned the Giddings Regiment as a small army in its own right, composed of a full regiment of infantry, two companies of sharpshooters, two companies of cavalry, and a battery of artillery.[32] This blueprint would soon be discarded, but the rumor that the Twenty-Ninth Infantry Regiment was looking to add a battery of six guns persisted for several weeks more.[33]

Post of Honor

In Jefferson and close by, some men did not require the exhortations of the war meeting speaker but signed up immediately. These men were the nucleus of the regiment's very first company, known locally as the Jefferson Company, or the National Guards, as they liked to call themselves. They had been organized by Jefferson lawyer William T. Fitch.[34] The thirty-seven-year-old Fitch wore a drooping dark mustache on his broad upper lip and tended toward baldness, which he covered by parting his hair low on the side of his head and combing his forelock up into a modest pompadour. With his large head and square jaw, he was the picture of self-confidence.[35] It was reported that Fitch had done service in Company D of the ninety-day Nineteenth Ohio.[36] It had been the men of Company D, known locally as the Rock Creek Company, who had painted the rebellious motto on the side of a tent during the slave-catching incident in western Virginia.

Fitch and his men had been lodging in the homes of the villagers, and enough men had been collected for them to elect their officers two days before Thomas Clark arrived.[37] They elected William Fitch as their captain and Comfort T. Chaffee as first lieutenant.[38] The twenty-three-year-old Chaffee was one of the regiment's two dozen Jefferson natives. Standing just a little over five feet tall with his boots on, his size made him the butt of good-natured kidding. Though small, he was absolutely fearless, as he would prove in the near future. William S. Crowell, a nineteen-year-old teacher in the Rock Creek neighborhood, was elected second lieutenant of Fitch's company, and another schoolteacher, twenty-two-year-old Everson J. Hurlburt, was appointed orderly sergeant.[39] To top the good fortune in winning his post, Everson married Isabel Chaffee the very next day.[40] The day after his wedding it was back to regimental business. Hurlburt posted a notice in the Jefferson newspaper of August 19, ordering all men who had signed the roll of Fitch's company to report to Camp Giddings immediately.

With Clark's arrival, camp was officially open, and the real business of putting the regiment together could proceed. Fitch's company had marched through the gates of their new camp several days before Clark had even arrived. As the first company to report to camp, they had won for themselves the post of honor in the regiment and would be designated hereafter as Company A. They had won this important distinction by a hair. The same morning that Fitch's men were packing to move the few blocks out to camp, a company was preparing to march in from Pierpont village, a dozen miles to the east.

Capt. Henry Hathaway had raised a company of Pierpont men for the ninety-day service, but they could not be squeezed into the war. Now, with room for all, Hathaway's company would have its chance. After Bull Run, Pierpont had sprung to the nation's call with a will. Captain Hathaway was nowhere to be seen when the Pierpont company marched into camp right on the heels of Fitch's hometown company. Leading the company was Hathaway's second in command, 1st Lt. Wilbur F. Stevens. At twenty-one, he was the regiment's youngest company commander, and ultimately he would prove to be its most controversial figure.

Stevens had been born in Pierpont of parents who were already middle-aged when he came along.[41] The young Wilbur seemed better suited by temperament to academics than to plowing or mending boots, which were the trades his father followed. He had been a student at nearby Kingsville Academy and a schoolteacher in the neighborhood.[42] Men of the village who knew Stevens before the war recalled him to have been a temperate young man.[43] He carried over 170 pounds on his five-foot eight-inch frame and tended toward heaviness.[44] Stevens had "gone west" as a sixteen-year-old and what he had done while there later became the source of unpleasantness.[45] When he returned to Pierpont, some said he claimed that he had fought in the Utah war against the Mormons, in 1857 and 1858. Decades into the future, some of his men would accuse Stevens of having lied to them about his military service, that they had been hoodwinked into electing him captain.[46]

Military experience or no, Stevens had signed up nearly every one of the men in his company.[47] The existence of the Pierpont company owed largely to his efforts, and election as the captain of a company that one had taken a chief role in raising was the customary reward, regardless of one's credentials. Reverend Hosier of Pierpont had steered most of the company's men in the direction of Stevens's recruiting net.[48] Even after Company B was in camp, the reverend kept on with his labors, bringing new recruits into camp in his buggy every day or two, and pausing there to see if his boys needed anything. The Jefferson newspaper encouraged other men of the cloth to take hold of the cause with the same zeal. When

Hathaway bowed out, Stevens found himself in command of the company in which he had been merely a recruiting lieutenant. Fifty men of Stevens's company marched into camp only to find Fitch's company had arrived earlier that same day and were busy staking out their camp.

The regiment's third company was being gotten up by a handsome young farmer named Edward Hayes, who was living at his ancestral home, near Gustavus, in Trumbull County. The Hayes men had jumped whenever their country called. Edward's great-grandfather Titus Hayes had been with Washington at Valley Forge, and his grandfather Richard was famous all over the Reserve for his valiant service in the War of 1812. When the other young men of the neighborhood rushed off to enlist at the war's start, Edward had stayed at the family place on Burgh Hill and kept to his plowing. To those who asked why he had not enlisted, he explained that he felt his higher duty was to his young family, and to his aged parents. Now, Hayes could no longer stand aside. As a teenager, Giddings had served under Hayes's grandfather, and he recalled that the old colonel could be in more places, and think of more things to do once he got there, than any man he had ever known. Edward now got busy getting up his own company with an energy that put the old folks in mind of his famous grandfather.

It took one hundred men to fill up a company, but to muster as a recognized company, which ensured that boys enlisted in the same neighborhood could stay together, half that number was acceptable. The understanding was that they would recruit up to full strength within one week of their arrival.[49] By August 21, Edward Hayes already had fifty men on his enlistment roll, and to take up the slack he ran an advertisement in the Warren newspaper titled "20 Riflemen Wanted!" the particulars of which read:

> Wanted immediately, 20 good marksmen to fill up a company to go into the Twenty-Ninth Reg't and go into camp at Jefferson, Ashtabula County, Ohio. Apply at Burgh Hill, Trumbull County, to Edward Hayes. Recruiting Officer.[50]

Companies A and B supported themselves during their first three days in camp by supping in the village or enjoying picnics brought out to camp by the residents. In the last week of August, the first shipment of camp equipage arrived from Columbus, and it included tents. The racetrack infield at the county fairgrounds blossomed with canvas as farm boys sorted through tangles of rope, pegs, and yards of canvas, while their comrades stood around offering sage advice. From their musty odor, the Boys suspected the tents had last seen service in the Mexican-American War. Despite their condition, the soldiers were reported to be delighted with them.

Groups of novice soldiers could be seen at all hours practicing military steps on the track, or crouched around smudgy fires making their first tries at cooking while folk from the village stood around enjoying the novelty of it. A Mr. Ray, a local man who happened to sit on the board of the county agricultural society, which governed the use of the grounds, had bid on, and won, a contract with the federal government to supply rations to Camp Giddings. Soon after, a regular flow of government-provided foods began to arrive in camp.[51] Each soldier was to receive a precisely measured daily ration consisting of fresh beef or salted pork, white beans, fresh bread, potatoes, sugar, vinegar, coffee, candles, soap, and salt. For a time, the soldiers believed that Ray's commissariat provided everything that could possibly be asked for.[52]

The future of the regiment looked exceedingly bright. The rapid formation of three companies had inflated the promoters' optimism. Patriotic men were being held on their farms by the summer's last cutting of hay, and when this final chore of summer was done, the regiment would fill up in a twinkling.[53]

The County Fair

The fair was only a few days off and the excitement for it was building. The Jefferson newspaper invited everyone to come in and take advantage not only of the fair but of the opportunity to meet their fellow citizens who had just volunteered to represent Old Ashtabula in the field.[54] The news of Buckley's formal appointment to the command of the regiment just hit the local paper, and the opinion was expressed that there was no doubt that he would carry the mantle of honor he had earned for his service in the Nineteenth Ohio along with him into the Giddings Regiment. By the time the fairground gates opened to the public, Camp Giddings was, in one soldier's view, "in full blast." He described a merry scene: camp kettles singing, fine rations to enjoy, the solemn splendor of the guard walking his beat around the "tented field," and drum taps to salute the ears at the start and close of each day.[55]

The village was still buzzing about the stir Capt. Edward Hayes and his company had made when they marched into town the day before. Hayes's Boys were as fine-looking a set of fellows as any who had ever mustered.[56] Hayes came marching into Jefferson behind the famous Andover Brass Band, which paused in the village on its way out to camp to play martial tunes for the entertainment of the residents clogging the boardwalks.[57] Hayes's entrance was proof that patriotism beat every bit as strong in the hearts of these modern soldiers as it had in the breasts of their ancestors. Edward's grandfather had marched into Jefferson at the head of his regiment fifty years earlier almost to the day, during the height of the big scare of 1812. It was pointed out that compared to the luxury being enjoyed by the Twenty-Ninth's men out at Camp Giddings, Colonel Hayes's men had come into town a half century earlier lugging their own knapsacks, blankets, arms, and food.

With the addition of Hayes's men, there were now three partially filled companies in camp, and Buckley was reported on his way from Akron with another. Additional companies were expected by the time the fair opened. One was on its way from the Harpersfield-Austinburg neighborhood, another from Conneaut, and one each from Lake and Geauga Counties.[58] Even more companies were rumored to be on their way. Well-known artist Capt. Alonzo Pease was laying aside his paints and brushes and recruiting a company for the Giddings Regiment, and it was taken as fact in Jefferson that a company being raised by another supporter in Portage County would soon rendezvous at Camp Giddings.[59] That there had been no sign of any of them did not trouble anyone. At this rate, Ashtabula County might fill two regiments before the leaves turned. The county fair of 1861 seemed perfectly timed to celebrate the county's success in raising the Twenty-Ninth Ohio Volunteers.

The Jefferson editors encouraged everyone to come by asking the enticing question, "For where can there be as much seen, and so much pleasure had, at so small a cost, as at the County Fair?"[60] The fairgoers put on their best clothes and gathered at the fairgrounds in numbers that were counted immense. The dreadful state of national affairs was of course on everyone's mind, but it did not spoil the pleasures of the get-together. After four days, the fair had come and gone and the newspaper reported in language as flat as a barn floor, "The Fair is over." The crowds and the general excitement had left the residents of Jefferson exhausted, but satisfied. It had been a grand success, and the camp of the Twenty-Ninth Ohio had been its central and most enjoyable attraction.[61]

The visitors had been fascinated by the novel sight of an honest-to-goodness military camp set right down in the middle of the racing oval with horses whirling around the city of white tents. Soldiers with little brothers and sisters tagging along behind mixed freely in the crowd. To Clark, the staging of the fair simultaneous to his efforts to square away the three companies already in residence, while at the same time perfecting arrangements for those that would be coming in soon, was a mixed blessing. Once the fairgoers began to stream through the gates it was clear that admitting new soldiers to camp would have to stop for a few days. Clark could not maintain his standard of military decorum, and the grounds were too crowded to accommodate any more recruits. Besides, every cooking kettle and tent the state had sent was in use by the soldiers already there.[62]

But there was a brighter side to this grand interruption, and Clark had thought of it before the fair began. He wrote to Columbus requesting that a mustering officer be sent out so the three companies already in camp could take their oaths in front of the fair crowd.[63] To add to the drama, he suggested that the recruits make the change from civilian clothing to dress uniform with the fair spectators looking on. The sight of soldiers emerging from their tents dressed in fresh Union blue was bound to persuade at least a few of the fair visitors to enlist. The problem was, there were not enough dress uniforms on hand for everyone.

With one hundred regiments all needing equipment and uniforms, there was only so much the state could do. J. D. Ensign of the project's central committee went to Columbus to see if his influence could free up the logjam, and he succeeded. He returned to Jefferson at the reins of a supply wagon filled with brand-new dress uniforms, blankets, and sundry camp equipage and drove out through the camp gates and onto the racetrack.[64] There were enough uniforms in the wagon to fit up every man already in camp and, if it would help stir the recruiting pot, there were enough left over so that every new man arriving in camp would be rewarded with a uniform immediately upon taking his oath.

The sergeants pried open the crates and handed one to each man. Clark decided there was no time like the present and he ordered everyone to suit up for the three-company regiment's first dress parade. The Boys ducked into their tents and reappeared a few minutes later wholly transformed. Weapons still hadn't arrived, but that did not detract from the impression the Boys made in their spanking-new uniforms.

The Twenty-Ninth's display of the soldiers' quaint camp life, and the blue-wool pomp of the dress parade, must have convinced at least some visiting farm boys to enlist. Two weeks later, the Twenty-Ninth would send a well-drilled company in full-dress uniforms over to the Orwell fairgrounds, where they would pitch their tents and entertain the crowd during that village's fair.[65]

The Homer Boys

Some boys came into Jefferson by the dozen, marching down Chestnut Street with the brass band of their home village out front, crowds along the boardwalk cheering them on, and packs of children and dogs tagging along behind. Most wore the humble costume of the farmer. In their drab-colored ranks were veterans of the ninety-day Nineteenth Ohio, dressed in the gaudy homemade uniforms they had worn when they had trudged up the side of Rich Mountain, just a few weeks past. They came in smaller bands too, made up of boys who had all grown up in the same small neighborhood. A few men came alone without any affiliation at all, carrying their possessions in a cloth-covered valise dug out of a closet where it had sat since the last big trip to town. They came on foot, on horseback, and some crowded into the back of a farm wagon with brothers and sisters and a picnic lunch, the whole clan come along to see their boy safely off on his first step into the war. They were not coming in as fast as some had hoped, but they were coming.

To the officials who would command him, a soldier belonged to the regiment designated by the brass number and letter he wore on his hat. In time, he would be just one soldier among tens of thousands in the camp or battle line of a vast army sprawled along some Southern river with a foreign-sounding name, farther away from home than any one in his family had ever been. He would never be without a sustaining identity, though, because first and foremost he was and always would be, one of the Boys, whether of the Rock Creek Boys, or of Montville, or Pierpont. And in whatever might come, he would never be swallowed completely because his roots ran all the way back to northeastern Ohio, down deep into a village, or the neighborhood of farms set along a particular creek. He would be sharing everything that was to come with boys he had grown up with. Long into the future, when all of what would come in the war had been passed through and the new century was at hand, an old man named John Rupp remembered his first days of soldiering, in the fall of the year 1861. His group knew themselves from the start as the Homer Boys.

The one and only village in the township of Homer, in Medina County, was Homerville. There stood a few stores, a Methodist church, and the shop of a casket maker offering made-to-measure coffins cut, planed, and shaped from the neighborhood's black walnut. The hearts of John Rupp and a dozen other boys of the neighborhood were filled with loyalty. They packed their things and set off together toward the village mercantile, where they were directed to the farm of Russel B. Smith, recently retired from the Nineteenth Ohio.[66] They were country boys, clumsy and tentative, but two young men, Cains C. Lord, and an especially bright and deep-thinking twenty-five-year-old named John G. Marsh, had some soldiering experience from their just-concluded service in the Nineteenth Ohio. With Lord and Marsh as their drillmasters, Rupp and the others practiced their basic soldier steps on a rise of ground in the meadow of Smith's farm.[67] Smith oversaw their instruction and let them camp out on his ground. Other boys, too young to enlist just now, snuck away from their chores and hung along the edges of the pasture, watching and envying. Rupp's little brother, fifteen-year-old Henry, was there watching from the fence. In two years he would be old enough to leave the farm his widowed father tended and follow his brother into the Giddings Regiment.[68]

Passenger pigeons gathering for their southward migration rose in dark curtains and wheeled through the yellow haze. The grain lay cut and bundled in the fields. Stepping and wheeling back and forth across the pasture for hours on end was hard work, and the Boys worked up a thirst. There were several barrels of apple cider in the yard near the house, and frequent breaks in drill practice in which to take advantage of them. Periodically, they threw down the rake handles that served as make-believe muskets and lay down in the stubble to sip their drinks and speculate on the sights they would see and the marks they would make in the grand adventure to come.

A platform had been erected in their meadow camp from which their drillmasters hollered out the instructions as if calling a reel, and the Boys' families and friends came to stand atop it and watch their progress. In the evening, with the autumn moon as their light, the Boys turned the platform into a stage on which they capered about and entertained themselves with song and dance. They called each other "General," poked each other, and wrestled in the tall grass. Elias Roshon was a young man of their group from nearby Montville Township, blue eyed and of dark complexion. Elias was smaller than the rest, but boys much larger than he had a hard time getting the budge on him when they tried to throw him. After a while, the joshing ran down and they became quiet. Then, one of them proposed they take a solemn oath: that whatever happened in the days ahead, each would look out for the others.

Many men coming into camp shared a bond even deeper than that of a common neighborhood. For many men, service in the Twenty-Ninth Ohio would be a family affair. These men would take their chances together with kith and kin just as they had in all things. There would be dozens of pairs of brothers scattered through all the regiment's companies. Roswell and Willard Trall of Rock Creek, the Luce boys of Conneaut, the Hill brothers of Mogadore, the Sherbondy and Shanafelt brothers of Akron, the Atkins boys, the three St. John brothers from Rock Creek, the Masons, and the Yokes. Cousins like the Hoyts, Thad and Wallace, enlisted together, and sometimes a pair made of a nephew and uncle, like Jerome and Tobias Phinney, also of Rock Creek, signed up. In some families, every eligible male enlisted in the Giddings Regiment.

The musical Brainerd clan of Gustavus, in Trumbull County, came into Jefferson in a group large enough to form a nice-size squad all by themselves. James Treen had come to Akron from Birmingham, England, and gotten work on the canal steering the low, fat boats. He was to be elected first lieutenant of Akron's Company G, and serving beneath him in the same company were his sons, John, George, and James Jr., the last known affectionately as Gemmie.

Thomas Dowling of Painesville had married Annie Corgan at St. Conleath's Church, in the village of Newbridge, County Kildare, Ireland, and shortly after he had packed up his young family and set out for America, landing on a poor farm outside Painesville.[69] In autumn 1861 little Thomas decided he would go to war, although he was already in his forties. He went into town to enlist and took his sons, fifteen-year-old Peter and Michael, aged eighteen years, along for company. They all scratched an *X* on the enlistment paper. The Dowling men said their goodbyes, promised to send home their pay, and trooped off down the road into town, leaving their wife and mother standing in the dooryard and wondering how she would manage on this hard-luck farm without her men. She would spend every day of the coming years worrying over her gone-away man and boys, and her worry would be justified.

There were young men coming in who had never known a real family. Young men like Joe Winby, John Shaw, and at least eight others who came into the Giddings Regiment had been left to scratch for themselves on the dangerous streets of New York City. The kindhearted men and women of the Children's Aid Society put them on orphan trains and took them out to the open heart of Ohio, where folks in need of offspring took them in.[70]

Other boys had been more luckless than the orphans rounded up by the Children's Aid Society. The parents of the Morey brothers, Frank and his little brother, Gillespie, had both died when Frank was only five. The two little fellows stuffed their few possessions into the pockets of their knee britches and aimed themselves west, which was the general direction an older brother had taken when he ran away. The Morey boys worked their way cross-country, "boarding out" with farmers along the way. By the time the war came, they had made it as far as Ashtabula County, where they were working for a farmer named Baldwin near Rock Creek and living in his barn. They had served in the Morgan Riflemen in the Nineteenth Ohio, and they came to the conclusion that three years of army life could hardly be less settled than what they were used to, and it might be a far sight better. They signed up along with the other Rock Creek Boys. Frank's given name was Francis, but he thought that name too girlish for a soldier, and when the recruiter asked for his name, he changed it on the spot to Franklin.[71] Although young, and small in stature, their wanderings had made them tough as cobbles. Between them, they would be seriously wounded or made prisoner a half dozen times.

The Average Soldier

The average Giddings Regiment soldier was twenty-five years old, the same average age as all who served in the Federal army during the Civil War.[72] The Twenty-Ninth Ohio soldier could be a boy as young as eleven or a white-headed old man of sixty.[73] The largest group of the same age was the eighteen-year-olds, which was precisely true of the Union army. In the Giddings Regiment there were more than three hundred boys eighteen years of age. A recruit was supposed to be at least seventeen years old whether he had written permission from home or not, but the regiment had at least a dozen soldiers in it who were younger, as would be revealed decades later when they filed for disability pensions. But in the age before birth certificates and other forms of uniform identification, getting around the age requirement took only a little ingenuity.

The average Giddings soldier stood five feet six inches tall, which made him about two inches shorter than the average Union soldier, but he might have been as tall as six two. If he were one of the drummers, many of whom were actual boys, he might have been not much taller than a chair back. The majority had dark hair, blue eyes, and medium complexions. But some were fair skinned and had hair red as rust.

He was usually born in any of twenty different American states. Later in the war, some would enlist who had made their homes in states that lay south of the Mason-Dixon Line. He could have been born in a foreign country—most likely Germany, Ireland or England—but he might have been born in France, Switzerland, or Canada. Over half the Twenty-Ninth Ohio's soldiers had been born right in Ohio, which made the Twenty-Ninth Regiment, by their majority, an outfit of native sons. If he had not been born in Ohio, he most likely started life in New York or Pennsylvania.

His first name was typically plain and durable, like the boy himself. More often than not, he was named Robert, Thomas, or John, or the most common first name in the regiment, William. Many boys had been given first names that were unique and musical sounding when called at the morning roll: Ransom, Bevins, Montezuma, Valentine, and Noble. There were boys who had been named after heroes of the Old Testament: Levi and Isaiah, Abraham and Job, Moses and Solomon. Some boys had first names taken from the classics: Augustus and Julius, Cassius and Rex, Euclid, Romeo, and Horatio. There were those named after the big men in American history: Pulaski, Lafayette, Franklin, Columbus, Washington, and after the British military heroes Wellington and Nelson.

Regardless of their place of birth, most had had the benefit of the Reserve's forward-looking common-school education, which meant they had gone through the modern equivalent of the sixth or seventh grade, but some men, the Dowlings for example, were completely illiterate and could not write even their name. A handful like Nathan Parmater, Wilbur Stevens, Everson Hurlburt, Horatio Luce, and a few others had gone beyond the common-school bench, although none of these had attended a proper college. Amos Fifield, who was to be their surgeon, was the only man in the regiment who likely had the equivalent of a full college education. There were several lawyers in the regiment; Captain Fitch was one, but practicing the law did not require a college degree.

The majority were the grandsons of the pioneers who had come out from New England. Although midwesterners in their geography, they still retained some of New England's distinctive clipped speech. Those with limited vocabulary and spelling skills give clues of their speech in the letters they sent home. They sounded out their written words using the phonetics they had been taught, so that the writing of a word revealed how the boys spoke it. *Deer* was pronounced "deeyah," *speaking* became "speakin," and *pretty* became "poty." In comparison to the flat intonation of these men, the Irish among them spoke in a lilting singsong. The German voices heard in the company streets were thick, difficult to understand, and were ridiculed on that account.

A local newspaper claimed that the regiment was an ideal democratic society, being composed equally of farmers and mechanics. In the parlance of that day anyone who worked with his hands, but did not farm, was classed a mechanic, and the newspaper's proportioning of the regiment's vocational mix was accurate.

Just over half gave their line of work as farmer, which made sense because the Reserve was primarily agricultural.[74] The rest worked at trades practiced most anywhere, city or country. Very few men in the regiment had put on a boiled white shirt and dress coat to work. The average Twenty-Ninth Ohio soldier was a man with calluses on his hands: the outfit included tanners, boot makers, broom makers, makers of chairs, buggies, and boat oars; blacksmiths, machinists, millers, bakers and butchers, carpenters and bricklayers. Two dentists came along, and one man who gave his trade as druggist. There was a barber to cut a man's hair, a hatter to fit the hat a man set on his head, and a watchmaker to fix his timepiece if it broke. There were boys fresh from the school bench, students of law and medicine, and at least a dozen teachers. There were professional artists and musicians, and one whimsical young man who listed his vocation as gentleman. Most all these young men were used to long days of backbreaking work in the meanest of weather. This was good, because the war would require as much durability as it did bravery.

4

Recruiting Wars

FALL 1861

Competitors and Complainers

The days of the Ashtabula County fair of 1861 represented high times in Jefferson. At last the folk of the village had something to crow about. The Giddings Regiment was off to a rousing start. When the Jefferson company and those of many of its neighbors were excluded from the ninety-day war, the residents had felt besieged. Now they could stand straight up and answer, "Please announce, Mr. *Leader* [a rival newspaper], that Jefferson, in the county of Ashtabula with less than three hundred voters, has now in the tented field seventy-three men, being one-fourth part of its voting population."[1]

Not all these men had made their way into the Twenty-Ninth Ohio, although a fair number had. But there was a worm turning in the apple of the people's hope that their regiment would be filled quickly. The first three companies already at the fairgrounds had come in only partially filled, and none of the many promised companies had appeared yet. That recruiting might prove difficult was not yet generally admitted, but Maj. Thomas Clark had sensed the approach of the problem even during the euphoria of the fair. He reported to the state adjutant general that the Giddings Regiment was not filling as rapidly as he had anticipated.[2] Some of the problems standing in the way of completing the regiment were beyond the Jefferson group's control, and some could be laid at their doorstep.

Just as the Twenty-Ninth Ohio's recruiting campaign was getting underway, an observer in Ashtabula city surveyed the level of interest in enlistment and remarked, "The war spirit here is gradually dying out, and although there are plenty of chances to enlist, still the rolls are empty. A patriotic few endeavored to instill into the somewhat dormant minds of our citizens a little patriotic fire, but the reports of many of the three months men cooled it, in a much less time than it took to get it up to the sticking point."[3] A man named Gifford had recruiting orders to raise forty men for Captain Kinney's battery in the town of Ashtabula, but after days of trying to persuade men to join, he had yet to enlist so much as one man.[4] John F. Morse was trying to get up a company for the Giddings Regiment in Painesville. He didn't get far into his recruiting speech when former soldiers of the Seventh and Nineteenth Regiments stood up as a group and began loudly denouncing the government for failing to pay them.[5] Morse had been embarrassed by the outburst and his meeting nearly ruined. There were many more veterans lounging on the streets outside the hall complaining of unfair treatment.

Morse estimated that there were several hundred ninety-day soldiers hanging around Painesville, and if they were allowed to continue spreading their discontent at this crucial time, recruiting in these parts would drag to a full stop. Mustering and pay officers were already in Painesville doing their best to get things moving, but it would take a while. Morse would succeed in filling up his company, despite the griping of the ninety-day men, and would take it into Camp Giddings as Company F, but his road would be rockier on their account. Even after the veterans were paid off, they did not stampede into the Twenty-Ninth Ohio.

The regiment's founders had thought every Reserve veteran of the Nineteenth Ohio would be inspired by the chance to right the wrongs done them and rushed to enlist in their outfit. They did not. Ultimately, only one hundred veterans of the Nineteenth Ohio enlisted in the Giddings Regiment, every one of them a valuable commodity and appreciated, but hardly in numbers the promoters had expected.[6] For those who did join the Giddings project, it was a quick turnaround from their old outfit into the new, just enough time for them to visit home and say hello and goodbye to the folks before hurrying off to the rendezvous at Jefferson.

With the fair in full swing, the Nineteenth Ohio's soldiers were paid at last, and in bright new gold pieces.[7] The mayor of Ashtabula had anticipated that ready cash and soldiers might not mix, and he ordered the saloons and groggeries closed until the soldiers left town. Many veterans had gathered in Ashtabula for their pay, and the fat target presented by the assembly of over two hundred potential recruits in one place brought another problem into the light. A correspondent for the Conneaut newspaper in Ashtabula reported, "The town has been thronged with recruiting officers for the numberless different regiments being raised all over the country, and on Friday the number was considerably increased."[8] At the heart of the Giddings Regiment's recruiting problem lay the same problem hobbling the recruiting efforts of every outfit: there were too many men floating line and bobber in this same small recruiting pond and Giddings was powerless to drive them off. Preeminent among their competitors was Giddings's enemy Senator Ben Wade.[9]

Wade and another popular politician, John Hutchins, had decided to raise a regiment of their own. They started a few days after the Giddings group and in short order were well on the way to winning the race to put a Reserve-recruited, three-year outfit in the field.[10] By end of August, when only three partially filled companies were in residence at Camp Giddings, the Wade and Hutchins cavalry was reported nearly full.[11] The last company of Wade's Second Ohio Cavalry was mustered into the Federal service in their camp near Cleveland on October 10, 1861, weeks before the Twenty-Ninth Ohio would see its ranks filled to the prescribed level.[12] Wade's project had gone so well that he had far more men than could fit in one regiment, and he made plans to organize another, at Warren, Ohio.[13] As if to tweak Giddings's nose, the men who had enlisted in what was being called the Ashtabula company of Wade's cavalry decided to meet in Jefferson to elect their officers.[14] Just as the Twenty-Ninth's organizers were opening Camp Giddings, the village seemed to be overrun by Wade's men.[15]

W. J. Keen of Andover had served five years in the much-admired British cavalry, a credential that was apt to win over many men.[16] He set up his headquarters at the American House hotel in Jefferson, just a few blocks down the street from the fairgrounds.[17] Other Wade associates were in Jefferson taking advantage of the fair to buy cavalry mounts.[18] The only thing the editors of Giddings's hometown paper could do about the whole thing was to suggest that Wade's men were taking advantage of the locals by paying only eighty dollars for a horse that would have fetched one hundred dollars elsewhere.[19] Moreover, some residents complained that Wade's demand for horses had led to a carnival of horse thieving such as had never been seen in Ashtabula County.[20]

Not far into the future, some in the Giddings Regiment, like Josiah "Jack" Wright of Akron, would point fingers at those who had road-blocked the Twenty-Ninth Ohio's efforts to fill up. He would allege that Giddings's enemies were settling past political scores by thwarting the development of his regiment. Wright was most likely referring to Ben Wade, but Wade was not the only obstacle. Other men, many of them as it turned out, had high hopes for forming their own regiments.

Less than a thousand souls lived in the village of Conneaut, but in this small place local mayor Thomas J. Carlin was completing enlistment for the Conneaut artillery with the intent of taking them into the Second Ohio Independent Battery at the same time that the Twenty-Ninth Regiment was trying to recruit there. Ultimately, over twenty-five Conneaut men would enlist in the Twenty-Ninth, which sounded like a good haul considering the size of the village, but three times that many joined Carlin's battery.[21] Geneva, a little way up the lakeshore, was forming a battery of its own under command of a local favorite, Captain Kenney.[22]

There were opportunities for enlistment in Seventh and Twenty-Third Ohio Infantries, as well in the old Nineteenth Infantry, which was refitting itself for the three-year service, and had opened a recruiting office right in Jefferson. A man thinking of soldiering might also pick from one of several regular army regiments that were advertising for men. If a man preferred to see the war from horseback rather than on foot there were chances for service in the First, Second, or Sixth Ohio Cavalries. And there was nothing to prevent a Reserve man from joining a regiment being assembled in some other state. By late fall, tiny Windsor, in Ashtabula County, had men in homegrown outfits like the Seventh, Twenty-Third, and Twenty-Ninth Regiments, and in the Second and Sixth Cavalries, but it also had boys serving in outfits gotten up in Wisconsin, Pennsylvania, and Missouri.[23] It was rumored that a full company of Ashtabula County men had gone off to join a regiment in Buffalo, New York, causing one Twenty-Ninth Regiment officer to comment sarcastically that Giddings had decided to form his regiment simply to stop the outflow of the county's men into the "inglorious" service of other states.[24]

A Captain Graham from across the border in Pennsylvania was signing up men for his company in the Erie regiment in Conneaut, and at points even deeper within Ohio's Reserve. This was hardly considered poaching, at least not at this point. The Ohio-Pennsylvania line in these parts was merely a line on a map anyway, and the capitals of each state were far away. The Twenty-Ninth Ohio's recruiters capitalized on this transborder kinship. Capt. Edward Hayes of the Twenty-Ninth drew many men for his company from the Pennsylvania border communities of Espyville, Beaver Center, and Linesville, just across the great Pymatuning Swamp.

Just a few days after Giddings announced his plan to raise a regiment, Mr. Perry Devore, Esq., announced that he was busy raising a company of men in his home village of Springfield, Pennsylvania, just across the border from Conneaut. He was said to be wrestling with the decision whether to take his company into a regiment headquartered in Erie, Pennsylvania, or into the Giddings Regiment.[25] He decided in favor of his native state. The Giddings Regiment did not have a monopoly on the affections of men, even within the great man's near neighborhood.

Right in the village of Jefferson, population little more than 650, at least four outfits were actively recruiting, including a company being raised for service in the Seventh Kansas Cavalry by John Brown Jr. Just after Camp Giddings opened, Brown announced his intention to organize a company of mounted sharpshooters and take them back to the scene of his martyred father's exploits in Kansas.[26] Several weeks later, Brown paraded into Jefferson with his company following behind him in wagons. He stopped by the office of the *Sentinel* to receive a speech from William C. Howells and the cheers of the residents. To make sure there were no hard feelings between him and the promoters of the Giddings Regiment, he explained that his recruits had come from western Pennsylvania mostly, and before rolling away he and his men sent up three cheers for the boys out at Camp Giddings.[27] Over two dozen Ashtabula County men were riding to war with him, men who might just as easily have signed on for service in the Giddings Regiment, and every one of them possessed the same antislavery spirit the Giddings organizers were seeking in men for their outfit.[28]

Seven thousand county men had voted in the most recent national election, which was a rough measure of the men available for military service. However, not every one of them was a candidate for enlistment. The elderly and those recently immigrated from foreign lands were immune from having to place their names on the militia rolls. There were those who had no interest in military service and no amount of arm-twisting by recruiters would persuade them otherwise, and there were also the physically unfit. The recruiting pool was much smaller than it seemed on paper.

Thomas Clark had been a storekeeper and a trader of vast cargoes and he knew how to count quantities on hand. In early September he made an inventory of Ashtabula's supply of eligible men. By his tally, the cream off the top—at least a thousand men—were already in camps for the various branches of service, leaving him and any other concerned patriot to wonder how the county could possibly replace its losses in the field if the war ran much longer than a year.[29]

Too Tight a Hold

The Giddings group were themselves partially to blame for the frustration beginning to surface. They were holding the reins of the regiment-building enterprise tightly, maybe too tightly. They were using Giddings's special authority from Washington to decide who could join their regiment and who could not. When the regiment took its first steps, the normal process in place for raising troops was that a man interested in getting up an outfit, whether a company or a regiment, make application to the governor or the adjutant general, in Columbus. If approved, he was granted "recruiting orders." That letter, along with a blank enlistment roll, put him in the troop-raising business. By Giddings's special arrangement with the War Department, Giddings and his group had the exclusive right to decide who could recruit for them. In theory, they were hunting for men who shared their antislavery zeal, and their special status gave them the final say in deciding whether a man's views were sufficiently sympathetic to their own.

Soon after coming to Jefferson, Thomas Clark began issuing letters of authority to men who had passed muster as recruiters. Some men had gone ahead without that authority. He sent recruiting orders out to Edward Hayes at Burgh Hill, to the team of Messrs. Bingham and Phillips of Orwell, to J. F. Morse of Painesville, and to N. J. Smith of Conneaut, who was granted leave from this assignment and his recruiting authority transferred to Horatio Luce of nearby Kingsville.[30]

The Giddings group's recruiting policy ran headlong into the already confusing system that most patriots were practicing in the fall of 1861. Several men wishing to enlist recruits for the Twenty-Ninth Ohio were apparently ignorant of the need for special authorization from the Giddings group and continued to write directly to the state adjutant general's or governor's offices for their papers. The adjutant general's office was overwhelmed with correspondence from men who were seeking official authority to recruit. All of them could not possibly be answered, nor could effective track be kept of their activities.

Some men who had received their appointment to recruit from Columbus were out working tirelessly with the intention of bringing the fruits of their labor to the Twenty-Ninth Regiment, and in some cases, the Twenty-Ninth's organizers did not even know these men were working on the regiment's behalf.[31] When their efforts were made known to Thomas Clark, they were dismissed out of hand for not having gotten their papers from the Giddings group. Without direction from Columbus or Jefferson, they took their men to other regiments or threw their hands up in frustration and quit.

In early August, Governor Dennison again forgot the particulars of Giddings's arrangement with the War Department in Washington and handed out a recruiting officer's appointment in the Twenty-Ninth Ohio to A. D. Strong of Ashtabula city. Strong might have served in the Twenty-Ninth Ohio and brought many men along with him, but he had to send his appointment back to Columbus when Giddings informed him that only he could grant recruiting authorizations.[32] Strong would take his valuable services and those of his men into Jefferson, but his destination was the recruiting office of Wade's cavalry.[33]

County resident James Crane was all set to enlist former members of his company of Nineteenth Ohio men into a company for the Twenty-Ninth Ohio and get them into Jefferson on the double-quick. He wrote to the governor requesting a letter proving he had the right to enlist volunteers for the Giddings Regiment.[34] Unfortunately, he had made his application at the wrong office. He took his men elsewhere.[35]

It was thought that Giddings's famous antislavery politics would serve as a magnet for enlistment in the Twenty-Ninth Regiment. But in some corners of the Reserve his reputation worked against him. Mr. E. A. Ford, in neighboring Geauga County, had permission from the adjutant general to raise a company. He wrote to him in mid-August and began by saying, "While enlisting for our Company, the question is frequently asked, 'What Regiment will you connect yourselves with?'" He explained that many of his boys were against joining the Giddings Regiment because of an unspecified "principle dear to us all." Whatever the nature of their objection to Giddings, it was sufficient for Ford to steer his company away from Giddings and into the ranks of the Forty-First Regiment.[36]

Among the men to whom Clark had rationed out recruiting authority were Amander Bingham and J. B. Phillips of Orwell, a tiny place south of Jefferson on the Warren road.³⁷ Bingham successfully raised a company, but he did not bring them into the Twenty-Ninth's camp. Instead, he took his men into yet another cavalry regiment forming up in the area, the Sixth Ohio, which left the question hanging, had he used the recruiting authority given him by Clark to enlist his men with the intention of joining another regiment all along, or had he been carrying authorizations to enlist men for both regiments?³⁸ Some men were not playing fair, and for lack of ground rules, the play would become rougher.

Impostors

A few days after Fitch's company got into Camp Giddings, a man named Milton P. Pierce of Berea arrived in Jefferson and announced he was raising a company of riflemen for the Twenty-Ninth Regiment.³⁹ Pierce had appeared at the office of the *Sentinel* in early July, before Bull Run, and showed off the beautiful gray uniform and kepi to be worn by the four hundred men he had already raised. Howells gave him a warm endorsement in the local paper, referring to him in a friendly manner as "Mr. P."⁴⁰ He reappeared in Jefferson now and established his headquarters in a room at the American House. Pierce said his company of sharpshooters would rendezvous in Jefferson as soon as transportation could be arranged.

He was calling himself Captain Pierce, and there was no harm in that because a man was entitled to use an honorary officer's title while he was recruiting, although the rank was usually that of lieutenant. He was doing all the things a bona fide company raiser would do, such as holding war meetings and making official-sounding announcements, which were duly published in the Jefferson newspaper. The *Sentinel* quoted Pierce at full strength as saying he had just received written assurance from the state that they would arm his men with the best rifles. This alone might have galled Clark since Columbus had told him a few days earlier that they had no weapons to provide, whether rifles or slingshots. Of far graver concern to Clark was Pierce's claim that he had just received orders direct from the adjutant general assigning his company the honor position of Company A in the Giddings Regiment.⁴¹

The problem was that there was already one Company A in Camp Giddings, that being Captain Fitch and his men. Editor Howells failed to anticipate that the *Sentinel*'s boosting of Pierce might cause the fur to fly out at camp. This was a trouble that couldn't have come at a worse time. Thomas Clark fired off a letter to the adjutant general complaining that men were at work organizing companies for the Twenty-Ninth Ohio with "authority obtained elsewhere."⁴² Clark had been sending out the letters of authority and the man now in the village who "stiles himself Capt. M. P. Pierce" had not been one of the recipients. Clark suggested that Pierce was using his claim that he and his men had been guaranteed the distinction of being assigned as the regiment's first company, Company A, as a selling point to enlist recruits, which in Clark's mind was a dishonorable thing.

To keep the whole project from suddenly unraveling, and maybe to call Pierce's bluff, Clark assured the adjutant general that Captain Pierce could come into camp on September 9, as he had stated he would, and he and his recruits could have the post of honor as Company A. Clark set one all-important qualification: that the men Pierce brought with him were identical to those whose names appeared on his enlistment roll. Clark warned that if Pierce came in with a different set of men, or tried to make up a roll after arriving, "after the style of a Kansas Lecompton Roll Book," a grave injury would be done to men like Fitch who had played by the rules.⁴³ Pierce was starting to look more and more suspicious.

Three weeks had passed since he had first arrived in Jefferson and announced that his company was all set to go, but not a single one of his men had yet been seen. Men who claimed to know Pierce had confided to Clark that they doubted he had either a company or the authority to recruit one.⁴⁴

If Pierce was playing at a game, his play was skillful. Around Jefferson, he was saying his authority to recruit came from the adjutant general, while telling the adjutant general at the same time that his authority had come from Giddings.⁴⁵ Pierce complained to the adjutant general that he had been unjustly kept out of the ninety-day service and that, by all appearances, he was being railroaded again.⁴⁶ All that was holding him back from bringing his company to Jefferson was a want of money, and if he could only be provided the train fare for a hundred men, he would bring them.[47] A recruiter was entitled to reimbursement by the state for out-of-pocket expenses incurred during the course of signing men up, and Pierce claimed he was already out the cost of enlisting over two hundred men.[48] If his motive was to defraud the government, he was going to an awful lot of work for a few hundred dollars.

Clark took Pierce out of the contest by making a small detour around the rules. Pierce claimed to have sent in a completed enlistment roll of some kind to the adjutant general, which was the correct procedure even in the Twenty-Ninth's special case, and he had beaten Fitch on a technicality. According to the rules, it was not the company that showed up first in camp that won the post of honor but the first to place its completed roll on file with the state adjutant general.[49]

Fitch had prepared his enlistment rolls bearing the names of his eighty-three recruits while still quartered in the village, but there had been a foul-up. Fitch handed the rolls to J. R. Giddings. Giddings did not know he was supposed to send them straightaway to the state, and they sat.[50] Clark sent Fitch's roll in forthwith, along with his apology for Giddings's ignorance. That satisfied the adjutant general, and Fitch and his men held on to their position.[51]

Pierce hung around Jefferson through the period of the fair, waiting for transportation for his phantom company of men, and shortly after that, without offering any explanation whatsoever, the *Sentinel* stopped publishing reports on his recruiting activities as abruptly as it had started. Pierce disappeared from view.[52]

The *Sentinel*'s endorsement of Pierce by blithely publishing his pronouncements was not the only time the Jefferson newspaper was appearing to act at cross-purposes with the hopes of the hometown regiment. Later in the fall, when the issue of filling the Twenty-Ninth Ohio became painfully acute, a Lieutenant Prentice settled himself in Jefferson to recruit a company of middle-aged men who would fight on principle alone, which meant they were the kind of high-minded men the Twenty-Ninth was looking to recruit. As it turned out, Prentice was not enlisting men for the Twenty-Ninth Regiment but for the Nineteenth Ohio Volunteer Infantry being organized for the three years' service, another competing enterprise to which the Jefferson newspaper gave a hearty endorsement.[53]

Giddings suffered two fits of the heart in late August, around the time the Pierce affair was being played out, reportedly triggered by a dispute over the disposition of offices in his regiment.[54] With considerable work remaining to complete his regiment, Giddings was hors de combat. There had been a small unpleasantness within the regiment. Comfort Chaffee, a local boy, had been elected first lieutenant of Fitch's Company A, but after holding that office only a few days, he was forced to resign in favor of Leverett Grover of Hartsgrove.[55] Grover was the thirty-seven-year-old farmer who had tried unsuccessfully to get his company of "Red Coats" into the ninety-day war. He came into camp and joined Company A with enough Hartsgrove men to force a new officer election. Chaffee did the politic thing and stepped out of his way, but not down. Chaffee would soon be appointed the Twenty-Ninth Regiment's first adjutant.

The casting for recruits in tight quarters was making men cranky and hypersensitive. Accusations were beginning to fly that one recruiter's turf was being invaded by men who had no official authority whatever to raise troops, or that a man's rightful efforts were being confounded by mysterious "others" who had the right papers but had set themselves crossways in the road of the organizer's interests.

On the last day of August, the adjutant general tried to end the squabbling going on from one end of Ohio to the other by publishing a general order. The order stated in plain language that the drumming up of recruits by men without special orders dispensed from his office was henceforth forbidden.[56] In the adjutant's opinion, the existing system had caused a "disastrous competition," which if allowed to continue would lead to an entire and permanent demoralization.[57] That was the first step. A complete overhaul of the recruiting process was in the wings.

To meet the endless demands for more and more men that might be placed on it by the federal government, something more refined, and fair, would be needed. The state of Ohio moved to put a new system in place. Completely comprehensive, it became a regular grassroots-driven troop-raising machine, capable of turning over every rock for soldiers in the most remote countryside or in the most populous city neighborhoods. The new policy established a grand pyramid with the governor and adjutant general at the apex and its sturdy base resting on all of Ohio.[58]

Henceforth, the governor would appoint representatives to sit on the military committee for each congressional district. They in turn appointed men to sit on the committees of every county within their purview. The county committeemen were instructed to appoint subcommittees in each of their townships. The township committee might spread its load further if the township population were large, like the metropolis of Cincinnati, by appointing men to run subcommittees set up within school districts. Every township committee was to send regular reports citing the hard numbers proving its success or confirming its shortcomings to the county committee in place above it, with the congressional military committee governing the whole district sending a grand tally every business day to the adjutant general in Columbus. Columbus would know with a glance at the bottom line how the state was progressing toward filling whatever quota the federal government had levied upon it.

To put an end to the divisiveness the old system had generated, any man wanting to raise troops would now have to apply first to his county or district committee, which would vouch for his moral character and give him their blessing. Only then would the adjutant general issue the necessary papers.

The general mission of the county committee was to stimulate enlisting. They did this by staging meetings featuring speakers capable of impressing upon the people the necessity of filling the ranks. They also supervised the work of the officers appointed to recruit for the various regiments within their domains. Using the old militia rolls as a starting point, the township committees were to canvass every household in every school district in their neighborhood and knock on every door to encourage the men who lived there to enlist. In their travels back and forth across the township, committeemen were to ascertain how many men had volunteered, and into what company and regiment they had enlisted.[59]

The raising of volunteers would now be conducted on a businesslike footing. No more would it be left to ephemeral blossoming of patriotism or to the civic pride of a few citizens in a particular village or county. If a draft became necessary, the machinery was in place make sure it went off smoothly. Not far into the future, the federal government would mandate changes that would demand an even deeper search for eligible men. For now, the state of Ohio was far out ahead of the thinkers in Washington.

The policy change affected prospective soldiers and civilians alike. District military committees, such as the one having jurisdiction over Summit County, ordered every county committee under their control to organize aid societies on the same plan. Henceforth, the accounting for soldiers and for all things that were donated for their support would operate under one banner.

By November 1861 the ladies of Summit County were ordered to procure socks, drawers, and blankets for soldiers already in the field. They were directed to report their progress to the society representative attached to the county committee, who in turn was obligated to report to their delegate sitting on the district committee, who then filed comprehensive reports to the Aid Society of Cleveland.[60] From this point forward the production of canned pickles, currant juice, mittens, the ominous-sounding belly bandages, and a host of other homemade goods needed for the health and comfort of Union soldiers lying in hospitals would be reported as tirelessly in the local newspapers as a township's production of recruits.

The newspapers would not always be forthcoming in their reporting of Union dead and wounded in a particular campaign or battle. But the newspaper appeals to women following every large battle to step up their scraping of rags for the lint used to pack hemorrhaging wounds told the truth of the scale of the bloodletting when the newspapers or the army would not. For the duration, everyone must pull his or her weight. Teenage girls would be staging "dime parties," strawberry festivals, masquerades, dances, concerts, and a thousand other money-raising events for the soldiers' relief. Even small children could contribute, and they were encouraged to plant gardens so their sick or wounded older brothers, and fathers, could be provided with vegetables.

Despite the state's overhaul of the troop-raising process, enlistment continued to stagnate. Letters to the editor complained that some young men seemed to be spending more time playing the Reserve's favorite game, baseball, than they did concentrating on their patriotic duties. Men indulging this pursuit were invited to take their clubs to Virginia, where they might "play ball to some purpose."[61]

The abuses and predations continued despite the reforms. Men who had been given recruiting authority with the understanding they would report with their men to Camp Giddings were persuaded midstream by fast talkers for other regiments to take their considerable number of enlistees elsewhere. In this period, the Giddings Regiment was deprived of dozens of men who had been enlisted for it specifically but at the last minute had been suckered away with airy promises of better opportunities in other outfits. George W. McNeil, member of Summit County's military committee, reported to the adjutant general that a recruiter for Senator John Sherman's regiment had created so much dissatisfaction in the mind of an Akron man who had been authorized to raise troops for the Giddings Regiment that McNeil thought it best for all concerned if the man were released from his commitment to the Twenty-Ninth and allowed to turn his catch over to Sherman.[62]

On the assurance he would take his recruits to Camp Giddings, William Hall of Medina had been given the necessary papers and enlisted a fair quantity of men. Around Halloween, he decided unilaterally to take them into the Seventy-Second Volunteer Infantry Regiment.[63] A Captain Hamilton had been authorized to enlist troops for the Twenty-Ninth Regiment in neighboring Geauga County. He went to work with a passion and in the twinkling of an eye had enlisted nearly a hundred soldiers. On their way to Camp Giddings, he and his men were waylaid by a recruiting officer for the Forty-First Regiment. He persuaded Hamilton to abandon whatever obligation he felt to the Twenty-Ninth Regiment and take his boys to Camp Wood, which he did. Colonel Clark hurried a letter off to the adjutant general demanding that Hamilton's men be returned to the Giddings Regiment. He cared nothing about recovering Hamilton because in his view one so "wavery" could not be trusted. Clark got neither Hamilton nor his men.[64]

Some recruiting officers for other regiments, Wade's cavalry in particular, were so bold that they walked into Camp Giddings and lured away soldiers right from under the officers' noses.[65] Recruiters for Wade's cavalry registered complaints at high levels that the Twenty-Ninth Regiment was guilty of the same discreditable practice.[66]

The adjutant general announced that men would no longer need to report in large groups. Hereafter, they could come into the camp singly if they wished, where they would be assigned to companies not yet full.[67] This last accommodation spoke to the reality of the diminishing numbers of men willing or available to volunteer.

Breaking the Sacred Bond

There had been recruiting problems right from the start. The disgruntled Nineteenth Ohio veterans had thrown a wet blanket over the Giddings enterprise. The Giddings name had not been the irresistible magnet the founders had supposed it would be. Unexpected competition had come at them from Ben Wade and countless others. The flawed recruiting system itself had slowed them. The organizers had been fooled by men who they believed were working on the regiment's behalf, but were not. And the organizers themselves were partly to blame for insisting they alone should decide who could recruit for them. Those looking for a solution identified what they believed was one of the root causes: mothers here on the Reserve, and likely every other place, were holding their sons back.

A boy wishing to join the regiment had to be at least eighteen years of age, and if he were under the age of twenty, he had to get written permission from his parents. By the end of the war, several hundred young men served in the regiment who had needed a parent's permission to enlist. During their organization at Camp Giddings, only four parents came to the camp, got their sons by the ear, and took them home.[68] Each of these soldiers "claimed as a minor" and taken home, was at least eighteen years old—old enough to legally sign the rolls, but not old enough to do it without his parents' permission.

The common belief was that it was the mother rather than the father who required persuasion. The mother was the repository of morality, chief nurturer, caretaker of home, which was the most pleasant of all places, and the embodiment of woman as civilizer. It was well accepted that away from female influence, men became degenerates, a danger to which soldiers, especially young ones, were known to be vulnerable. If the rebellion was to be crushed, that bond had to be broken, and a campaign began to remove this tender obstruction. An image began to appear about this time, whether in paper and ink, or a word picture conveyed in a poem, or in the lyrics of a song, or an essay. It might change slightly in its details, but it would persist in about the same form through the war years.

Decades after, the exact scene would be memorialized in an expensive stained-glass window in the Buckley Chapel in Akron. The scene was that of a young soldier saying goodbye to his mother. He stands on one side of the front gate in his uniform, with his equipment strapped in place, cap in his hand, and his head bowed. On the other side of the gate stands his mother, either wringing her hands in her apron or reaching over the gate to touch his face. When it came time for Ashtabula to make her contribution of young men in the war's first days, the newspaper editors encouraged every mother to be like the Roman matron who, when asked for her jewels, presented her sons. Stock platitudes encouraging mothers to place their sons on the "altar of liberty" ran in the local newssheets throughout the war. A long story called "The Young Volunteer" printed in the Jefferson newspaper had a young man of the village named Frank as its protagonist.[69] He was keen to enlist in the Twenty-Ninth Ohio. Two village men are discussing the news that Frank has enlisted. Says one, "Well, this must be a pretty hard sacrifice for Mrs. White to let him go, as he is her only son, and her darling too—for I know she dotes on him."

No boy ever loved a mother more than he, and Frank had not enlisted earlier out of regard for her feelings. Soon after the soldiers had begun to gather at Camp Giddings, Frank approached his mother and said, "Mother, I wish I could enlist. Wouldn't you like to have me?" The mother replied, "Oh no, I can't spare you Frank," and she thought the topic ended for once and for all. But a while later Frank said, "Mother, on the first of November I shall be 18 years old," and then he turned and walked away. She knew what her son meant. Wrestling with the dilemma made her sick. She worried that if Frank returned, he would no longer be the innocent boy she had sent to war.

He came to her one evening and they talked of everything except what was on both their minds. The boy took his mother's hand, looked into her face, and started, "Mother . . . ," then could say no more. He dropped his head into her lap and cried like a child. Mother's resistance broke. She gave her permission, and Frank went to be a Giddings Regiment soldier. She had done the right thing after all and for just the right reasons, as her townsman reflected: "Mrs. White will bear this as well as any mother I know of—she has the real Spartan pluck, and the spirit of '76, and is full of patriotism. Then she is so bent on having slavery destroyed, that I really believe she would lay her only son, whom she loveth, on the Altar, to accomplish it—if she thought God and her country called for the sacrifice."

The Economics of Soldiering

Men were coming into the Twenty-Ninth Ohio Volunteer Infantry for many reasons. There were men like Pulaski Hard and Wilbur Stevens who had missed the chance to lead troops to glory in the ninety-day war, and also the soldiers of the disbanded companies from Jefferson and other Reserve places, which had gotten all fitted up for the summer's war but had not been allowed a part in it. The ancestors of men like Edward Hayes had made names for themselves in America's earlier wars, and the time had come for their descendants to prove they were cut from the same cloth. There were the veterans of the ninety-day Nineteenth Ohio, who had taken a hand in the revolt at Buckhannon and were looking to restore the county's reputation.

Some young men enlisted because every other young man in the village was going off to see the big show and no one wanted to be left behind. In some men, patriotism lay dormant and they hadn't really given much thought to the matter of enlisting until they got inside the village hall on the night of a war meeting, where the general hoopla swept them up to the front to the enlistment rolls. Some men, like Myron T. Wright, presently recruiting up an Akron company for the Twenty-Ninth, were genuine patriots. And many boys enlisted to escape the endless tedium of village life or the isolation of farming.

There were young men who had been reared on the popular romantic literature of the day, which glorified combat: books by Sir Walter Scott and James Fenimore Cooper, and poems such as Tennyson's "The Charge of the Light Brigade." Some of these simple farm boys nurtured secret visions of themselves as knights gallant, so devoted to a cause that one's personal welfare became a trifling matter.

The Nineteenth Ohio veterans had threatened to withhold their services until they were paid, which might make them appear mercenary. A man fought for many reasons all mixed together in the same pot, one motivation difficult to separate from the other. One of the reasons men volunteered was that being a soldier paid a regular wage. For many men, service in the Giddings Regiment or in any other was their best hope for escaping perpetual hard times.

Howells recalled that most of Ashtabula County's residents were poor. Most lived on half-improved homesteads in houses as flimsy as tents. They came into Jefferson but twice a year: to visit the county fair and to stop by the *Sentinel* office to pay their annual subscription. They paid with apples, cheese, and wool, because, according to Howells, no one had any cash.

By 1861 a generation was coming to the age when a young man looked to strike out on his own. But the opportunities their grandfathers, and fathers had enjoyed when they came to this part of Ohio were drying up. The frontier had passed hundreds of miles to the west, and the Western Reserve was now a settled land. The best ground had been cleared and put under cultivation years before. By the arithmetic of some, a young man's chances of material success if he stayed in the county were less than one in ten.[70]

We think of life in that age as simple and charming, just as William Dean Howells portrayed it. The reality was quite different. A good many of the soldiers in the Twenty-Ninth Ohio knew lives that were relentlessly hard if they were lucky, precarious and often brutal if they were not.

When a family lost a boy in the war, his survivors, parents in most cases, were entitled to apply for a pension of about eight dollars per month. To perfect their claim they had to show to the government's satisfaction that they had depended on their dead son's soldier pay to make ends meet. Discount by half the pension applicants' natural tendency to exaggerate their poverty, and you are still left with a grim picture of the lives most of the enlistees led as civilians. Most children had been "working out" since they were twelve years old or younger, the parents having sent them to work on the farmsteads of neighbors able to pay cash for their labor. The boys lived for months at a time in the neighbor's hayloft, worked in the fields, and tended the sheep and cows, while their sisters scrubbed floors and did the wash. Hundreds of the regiment's boys came from small profitless farms, most encumbered by mortgage or back rent. For many, the family's entire fortune consisted of one or two spindly cows grazed in already worn out pastures, thick with stumps left over by the original pioneers; large families were forced to depend on the produce of a single garden plot. Many of the boys came from families in which one or both parents had been broken by the land before they had fully broken it. The end of the growing season did not mean vacation. Families moved their industry inside, where they dyed rags for the makings of rugs to sell on trips to the village, repaired the neighborhood's clocks or boots on the family kitchen table, worked in a grain mills for the discount that was given on a sack of flour, and took in the wash of neighbors who could afford that extravagance. At the end of the year, a family was lucky if they had fifty dollars to show for it all.[71]

The news of Fort Sumter had set Ohio afire and nothing was needed to convince young men to enlist. After Bull Run, it was a different story. To secure a recruit now it was necessary to make persuasive arguments, and the organizers of war meetings and the editors of the newspapers each took an oar. Appeals to a young man's patriotism met him at every turn, but that was no longer enough. The newspapers began to point out on a regular basis the considerable financial benefit that a man would derive from his army service. Compelling, commonsense editorials argued the financial advantages of soldiering. A private soldier earned thirteen dollars per month, which, it was pointed out, was the highest wage paid the soldiers of any army in the world, and, as the *Sentinel* argued, "Young men out of employment will find this as a good opening as is it is more than the wages of hands in most business particularly in these dull times."[72]

Some parents feared that a soldier's pay, coupled with unsupervised adolescence, was a surefire recipe for evil. One newspaper editor anticipated that objection and advised parents to stop worrying, because "his [the soldier's] situation is such . . . that he cannot squander his means . . . and can send home major portions of the same to his family."[73] To put an even brighter face on it, pounders of the enlistment drum argued that a soldier's enlistment was good not only for him and his family but for the whole local economy: "The soldier confers a favor upon those he leaves behind. . . . He not only earns money . . . but his absence from the community tends to create a demand for labor. . . . 500 men in a county can better be supplied with work and be better paid than 1,000."[74] The total value of the benefits to the soldier, in addition to his monthly wages, was published regularly in all the Reserve newspapers.[75]

Among the many rewards given the soldier were: board and clothing found, travel costs, a federal bounty of $100, and eligibility for certain pensions, which in America's previous conflicts had been paid in land, 160 acres of it.[76] Adding all these together, the soldier might receive remuneration of nearly $500 in his first year alone.[77] This at a time when a modest house and lot could be purchased for about that, and a whole working farm—land, implements, and buildings included—for what could be earned in two or three years in uniform. These arguments ended with a warning: the war might not last a year, and a man would be foolish if he did not act quickly to reap the multiple, lucrative benefits of army service.[78]

None of these inducements could have been lost on young men from straitened circumstances, like Franklin Potter, or on all the other impoverished boys old enough to join up. By enlisting, they would be helping their families as much as the Union.[79] If the young man did the arithmetic, the decision to enlist became easier.

There were a few young men in the ranks who came from comparatively secure backgrounds, but the money one might earn as a soldier proved a powerful inducement even to them. Eighteen-year-old Pvt. Wallace Hoyt's father, John Hoyt, owned property and speculated in others, had held paying local offices, and owned the home in which Wallace had grown up—a rarity in the case of most Twenty-Ninth Ohio soldiers.[80] The father was considering seeking an officer's appointment in his son's regiment. Wallace advised him to go ahead, but the advantages he ticked off had nothing to do with restoring the Union or uprooting slavery: "The money is just what you want to pay your debts with and it can be easily obtained from the government as any business you can do." As Wallace explained, any hardships that might fall on the family because of his absence would be more than offset by his army pay. "Mother can spare you for a year or two for the sake of having money enough to make her comfortable for years after you return."[81] John Hoyt would mull this advice over for several months before acting on it.

Buckley Takes Command

A week after the fair closed, Col. Lewis P. Buckley rode into Camp Giddings escorted by Capt. Pulaski Hard's company of Summit County men.[82] Hard's failure in trying to get into the ninety-day Nineteenth Ohio, and the humiliation that followed, were behind him now. Hard had been ably assisted in recruiting up the first Akron company in the Twenty-Ninth by Myron T. Wright, the energetic miller's son from Johnsons Corners, and by a Vermont-born six-foot-two sailor named James Grinnell.[83] Wright was rewarded for his tireless recruiting by winning office as the company's first lieutenant, and Grinnell took the second lieutenancy.

In the first days of September, Wright departed Akron with forty more recruits. En route to Jefferson he planned to stop in several Summit County villages to round up more men who had signed his enlistment roll.[84] With Hard's arrival, the makings of four companies were now in camp.

A second Summit County company, Company G, would arrive in late September. It would be the result of the recruiting work of three men. James Treen, English-born canal boat skipper; Akron auctioneer and part-time town constable Josiah J. Wright; and thirty-five-year-old Canadian-born John S. Clemmer of Mogadore had failed to recruit enough men to fill their own companies, and they had combined their catch into one company.[85] Josiah Wright, who preferred to be called by his middle name, Jack, had gotten his recruiting orders directly from the adjutant general's office, in Columbus, and had gone to work at once scouring Akron, buttonholing prospective recruits wherever he found them and using his considerable gift of blarney to sign them up. Akron's leading newspaper, run by Wright's close friend Sam Lane, gave him a boost by saying that Jack was energetic, indomitable, and plucky. Lane added, "Let everybody desirous of joining a company, 'fall in' before the tickets are all taken."[86]

Upon arrival in Jefferson, Clemmer was elected captain. Nearly six feet tall, with blue eyes set off by prematurely gray hair, he was to be one of the regiment's most popular company commanders, remembered by his men as genial and hearty in his manner and fond of leading the men in singing, both in camp and on the march.[87] As a civilian he spent his days managing the production of a local pottery and devoted his evenings to leading the Mogadore glee club.[88] Not long after arriving in camp, Clemmer was presented with a dress uniform by his townsmen so splendid that it was the envy of every other officer.[89]

Clemmer's enthusiasm was extinguished temporarily when a letter came to him at Camp Giddings from the office of the state adjutant general revoking his commission forthwith. He had failed to submit his company's morning reports. The regiment could not afford to lose someone as popular as Clemmer, and Thomas Clark intervened on Clemmer's behalf to get the matter straightened out and Clemmer's commission restored.[90]

Ultimately, three companies, Company D, Company G, and Company H, all recruited in Summit County, would take their place in the regiment. The question gets asked, and was asked then: why did these Summit County men not join a regiment in their own neighborhood? Summit County's population was about the same as that of Ashtabula County. Akron, seat of Summit County, had ten times the population of tiny Jefferson. The answer lay partly in the founders' decision to secure the services of Lewis P. Buckley—it had proved to be the recruiting magnet for Summit County men the Jefferson group had hoped for. An Akronite himself, Capt. Jack Wright answered, perhaps with tongue slightly in cheek, that no other regiment had extended an invitation to them.[91]

Up in Conneaut, Horatio Luce, a twenty-two-year-old schoolteacher, was putting together his company for the Twenty-Ninth, which would be designated its Company E.[92] He had begun his military career a few months before as a fifer in Captain Hoyt's company of Ashtabula County men in the ninety-day war. For his valor at Rich Mountain he had been promoted from the ranks to first lieutenant.[93] Coming into Luce's company was his younger brother, Charles. Charles gave his age as eighteen, but he was really only sixteen.[94] He exchanged the hoe he was using to weed plants on his father's strawberry plantation on the east side of Ashtabula city, picked up his older brother's fife, and enlisted in the Twenty-Ninth's band.[95] Luce was being assisted in his recruiting of men for his company by the most cheerful storekeeper in the Reserve, Theron S. Winship. Winship was admittedly a young man more used to the light rigors of running his mercantile than the hardships of war. But the Conneaut newspaper said that if he applied as much energy to his military service as he had to promoting his store he was certain to make a mark in the war.[96] Always out in front of the competition, Winship had begun organizing several weeks before the war even began. So many young men wanting to be soldiers had taken up residence in and around his house that the neighbors had taken to calling it Fort Winship.

In late September a group of nine young men came into camp to enlist in Captain Luce's Company E. In this squad was Nathan Parmater. He had grown up along the banks of the Saint Lawrence River in New York, the youngest of seven children. When he turned twenty-one, he left home and headed west, as each of his brothers and sisters had done before him. Parmater was keen on bettering himself and he enrolled at the best Ashtabula County had to offer by way of higher education, which was the Kingsville Academy, north of Jefferson. Parmater thrived on the student life there with its warm associations, taking classes when he could afford it and supporting himself by teaching country school. He had great affection for his fellow students, especially those who were female, and for his teachers, with whom he formed lifelong bonds.

He was close to finishing his schooling when the war came and he and his best friend, fellow student Alonzo Sterrett, decided to leave their studies and become soldiers. Enlisting in Luce's company was automatic. He had been a student with them at Kingsville Academy. Moreover, although he was only twenty-two, Luce was already a seasoned officer.

Young men were leaving Conneaut in droves for service in various outfits. The principal medical doctor of the village, Amos Fifield, had gone to be an army surgeon, and the printers at the newspaper had gone off to war en masse. Anyone could see times were changing. Winship assuaged his customers' fears that the war would tip village life on its head, by placing a windy ad in the local paper suggesting a lingering innocence that service in the Twenty-Ninth Regiment would not demand much more than was required on weekend drills in the Old Militia. He assured his loyal customers that although he was on a war footing for now, and working hard for the interests of the Twenty-Ninth, he did not intend to give up interest in his store or his customers. "Trusting that the fortunes of war will allow me to again resume the pleasurable task of weighing sugar and tea, and measuring calico and tape, I take my leave at present. Remember and call at the 'old stand' where, if you do not find the undersigned, you will find those who will attend to all your wants."[97]

Winship was a man who knew something about how to dress a store window to attract buyers, and he borrowed the grandest flag in the village from its owners at the *Reporter* newspaper office and took it down to the recruiting booth he had set up at Camp Giddings. Unfortunately, a soldier had made off with the flag, saying he would return it to the newspaper office for him, but to Winship's distress, the flag did not show up.[98] The staff at the *Reporter* were not excessively upset with Winship's losing the village's best flag, and continued in their commitment to rally around the village's brave troops. They pledged to continue to help the Twenty-Ninth Ohio by stepping away from their typesetting chores whenever a potential recruit wandered into the shop, and signing him up.[99] The *Reporter* was Ben Wade's mouthpiece, just as the *Sentinel* had been Giddings's, and allowing the printing shop help to enlist recruits for the Twenty-Ninth Regiment was as close as Wade ever came to assisting the Giddings project.

Camp Giddings

SEASON OF COMPLAINT, LATE FALL 1861

The Village and the Camp

The goodwill the fair had engendered spread through the whole of September and on into October. Jefferson opened its arms to the soldiers, so that the camp seemed an extension of the warm society of the village. Citizens brought out baskets filled with enough supper to feed several hundred soldiers, and the soldiers repaid their kindness by putting on a dress parade. Everyone had a grand time, although one soldier fresh to camp observed that the clumsy soldiers did better justice to the victuals than they did to their drill.[1]

The people of Jefferson devoted themselves to making the soldiers' stay at camp as comfortable as possible. To improve their sleeping accommodations a drive was begun to collect quilts and coverlets, and strips of old carpet.[2] To enliven their rations, farmers brought apples and tomatoes. One soldier was seen carrying the gift of a "whaling big cheese" down the village streets, and the village folk were encouraged to follow the donor's good example.[3]

Friends and family who lived close enough to allow easy travel to camp continued to devote themselves to their pet companies. A caravan from the neighborhood of Pierpont rolled in one afternoon with banners flying. They set up a feast for their Boys in Company B and passed a pleasant afternoon with their soldiers.[4] It was hoped that the memories of such visits would cheer the Boys in the future, when they sat around the gloomy campfires of distant places that the war would surely contain.

In October the weather grew too fickle for picnics on the field, the society between the camp and the village moved inside. Sawdy Tyrrell, proprietor of the Jefferson House hotel, arranged a military ball to celebrate Halloween and invited all the Twenty-Ninth's officers and men to join the village's young folks for an evening of dancing. The hall was decorated with patriotic bunting, pumpkins, and corn shocks.[5] One shy soldier recounted, in the style of the country's most popular humorist, Artemus Ward, how he had straightened himself and asked a young woman if she would like to dance. "I asked Senator so-and-so's daughter if she wouldn't glide in the mazy dance. She said she would and so we glode."[6] Young boys still not in the army service roamed the village streets after dark, frightening the residents with their awful yowling and throwing cabbage heads at peacefully disposed citizens.[7]

Gradually, the regiment was becoming less dependent on the village. Theron S. Winship was appointed regimental quartermaster, in charge of managing their commissary and supplies. He had recruited many of the soldiers of Company E, and he had been their unanimous choice to serve as first lieutenant. With Winship gone to his new post, the company's efficiency fell to the point that Buckley and Thomas took notice. For the good of the men, Winship resigned his higher post as quartermaster and returned to his company. An Akron man, Oscar Gibbs, was appointed in his place.[8]

They were soldiers now, but unlike future wars, in which recruits would assemble at huge depots far from home, the Twenty-Ninth Ohio's preparation was taking place in the Boys' backyards, and close proximity to home had its benefits. If a bored or homesick boy could not get a furlough, he skirted the rules and took a French leave, or simply a French, as the Boys were fond of putting it. A soldier could run back home most anytime he wanted and say hello to the folks.[9] After only a month in camp, a considerable number of soldiers were absent on these informal furloughs.[10] Except for the occasional knockdown, typical among young men thrown together for the first time with those from competing villages, and from different lots, life in camp was as peaceful as in the home village.[11]

Into this convivial atmosphere marched the regiment's sixth company. Capt. John F. Morse had finally overcome the obstacles thrown in his path by the unpaid ninety-day veterans and found enough men in Lake and Geauga Counties for the makings of Company F. Morse had come in earlier than he had planned. He had enlisted sixty men, but recruiters for Wade's cavalry had stolen a significant number of them. To put an end to this body snatching, Morse gathered up the men he still had and escorted them to what he hoped was the sanctuary of Camp Giddings.[12] Squads of new recruits were arriving almost daily and being assigned to companies already there that were still short of men.[13] Interlopers representing other regiments snuck into camp and spirited some of them away. One of the regiment's most promising officers left after a single day at Camp Giddings to pursue better opportunities.[14]

Alvin Coe Voris was a hard charger in Summit County Republican politics and a successful lawyer. His antislavery credentials were sterling. Years earlier, he had stolen a slave right off the James River, Virginia, plantation of ex-president of the United States John Tyler.[15] He had already made a sizable contribution to the Giddings Regiment by enlisting many of the soldiers of Company H. He left to take a command slot in the Sixty-Seventh Ohio Infantry and would ultimately lead it to glory. Such a charismatic leader would be missed. Jonas Schoonover, a thirty-five-year-old New York–born farmer was appointed recruiting lieutenant in his place. Schoonover would remain in Summit County for the time being and continue his fishing for men in what would become Summit County's third company to go into the Twenty-Ninth.[16]

The soldiers were improving so rapidly in their drill that they gave promise of being one of the best regiments in the service, so the county newspapers bragged. The men of Pulaski Hard's company were in advance of the others in their proficiency. The soldiers of other companies stopped in their own drill practice to admire Hard's men perform the complex Zouave skirmish drill.[17] The Boys were coming on strong as soldiers, but there were not enough of them. By the time the leaves began to drop from the trees, only six of the ten companies could show presentable numbers when they lined up for morning roll call, and most of the companies were still short of men.

"Hurrah for the Soldier's Life"

New arrivals in camp were made welcome with a hot meal and hearty congratulations all around for having joined the best regiment in the Reserve. The very next morning the newcomer was introduced to the fixed routine of army life. The soldiers were awakened by reveille at half past five, played not by a bugler but by fife major Richard Noonan. They swept their tents, aired the straw-filled sacks that served as their beds, washed up, and hurried out for roll call, and after that to breakfast. At seven in the morning came surgeon's call. The rest formed up on the track for squad drill, or if assigned to it, the ritual of guard mounting. A soldier was free to pursue his own endeavors from around eleven in the morning through dinner. At half past one, drill was practiced by company, followed by battalion drill, in which the regiment practiced complicated battlefield movements like right oblique. After that, soldiers cleaned up themselves and their gear for the daily dress parade, which came off at five. Unless on guard duty, or working off a punishment, a soldier was at leisure until nine in the evening, when tattoo was sounded and he was expected to go to his tent, and stay there, and come out only if nature called. Taps sounded a half hour later, demanding candles and lanterns be put out, and after a full day of activity, and all became quiet.[18]

Each company was assigned its own beeline-straight street, and at the head of each company street stood the tent of its captain, with Old Glory flying from the peak, and just behind that, the two tents in which Buckley and Clark lived. There were two water pumps in camp and a short line of tents for men posted to guard duty, and just beyond the track stood the wood-frame buildings being used for cooking and tending the sick. Pickets stood sentry duty around the camp and at the main gate on the side nearest the village, but from the sound of it, no one, soldier or civilian, had any difficulty coming or going as he pleased.

Getting the hang of the military vocabulary, as vexing to some as mastering a foreign language, made for grand humor. One novice sergeant of the guard, identified as Lew Low to protect him from embarrassment, addressed the man that came out to relieve him, "Who comes there?" To be properly military, Lew should have said, "Halt relief—advance Sgt., and give the countersign." Instead, he became flummoxed, and the best he could come up with was, "Stop Relief. Come up here, Sergeant, and give an account of yourself." Everyone within hearing bent over in laugher. Even Buckley chuckled, and commented, "Lew, you haven't waked up yet."[19] The recruits advanced in their education by fits and starts. Overall, as Jack "Stand Back" Wright observed, "Each day draws the reins a little more military fashion, and when a fellow gets so he thinks he knows it all, he finds he has just commenced learning."[20]

Soon, the sameness of every day began to wear. The soldiers found ways to counter the enforced monotony of camp life and took their fun where they could find it. According to one, they did "everything allowable and many things not laid down in regulations." Of an evening, a stroller down a company street would find the occupants of one tent studying the Bible, while in the next a noisy game of euchre was being played. A soldier stood in the company street preaching a sermon, while another boy down the line recited Hamlet, and always, there was singing, fiddling, and dancing.[21] A particular Irish ballad with its tenor flourishes and opportunities for fireside harmonizing, and the melancholy lyric "I'll take you home again, Kathleen," was especially popular in the camp.

Huddled together up the company street were a group telling funny stories and planning practical "joax," while another knot of recruits formed a "traveling menagerie" going from one end of camp to the other, entertaining the men by posing as "wax-worx," in the phraseology of Artemus Ward, whom many boys were fond of imitating. One entertainment that drew crowds for several evenings until it became stale was put on by two big fellows who threw a blanket over themselves and lumbered up and down the street in imitation of an elephant.[22] So, as one soldier put it, "by all these and many unmentionable devices we manage to squander our days, weeks, and months to the tune of $13 per month and rations."[23]

The village provided entertainments of its own. Pvt. Nathan Parmater went into Jefferson one evening for a "mite society," which consisted of getting acquainted with the local girls, and he did not return to camp until after midnight, which was a curfew violation for an enlisted man. But Parmater had been invited on this foray by some of the elected officers, and they could come and go as they desired. Several men had been drummed out of Horatio Luce's company for some infraction, but discipline seems not to have been a problem, which might have had more to do with the easygoing relationship between officers and the hometown boys who had just elected them than the strict application of military law. With the easy granting of furloughs to men who had barely been in the army a month, the running back and forth from camp to home without them, and the frequent intrusions into camp by friends and family, a soldier might get the idea that army life was as democratic as at home. Parmater reported only one other breach of the rules, and it proved that a plain private was as entitled to his rights as much as any officer: "There was some excitement in camp today caused by putting one of Co. 'A's men in jail for not falling in for breakfast and saucing the Lieutenant but the Lieutenant was blamed and the man soon released."[24]

Some of the enlisted men were beginning to show a penchant for rowdiness. A group of them went into town to see the magic show of a traveling entertainer.[25] "Herr Kline" had just started his performance when the Boys saw he was rather "worse for the use of the ardent," which is to say he was drunk. The Boys pushed him aside and took over the stage and, being clumsy, broke most of his props.[26] No punishment was meted out. Herr Kline had been drunk after all and had received his just deserts. Drunkenness on the part of a practitioner of the show business was expected; they were known to be a low class of men.

As a bulwark against a soldier's moral decay, Buckley made attendance at Sabbath service mandatory. Lacking a chaplain of their own, the soldiers walked the few blocks up Jefferson Street on Sunday mornings and observed services at one of its churches. In the afternoon, local preachers drove their buggies out to camp and conducted a second service.[27] Russell H. Hurlburt, a thirty-five-year-old Iowa farmer, had returned to Ohio and set to work recruiting for the Twenty-Ninth Ohio. He had an interest in theology and volunteered to officiate at Sunday service. The soldiers liked him. His preaching style held their attention. He was just as much a hit with the officers. Thirty-two of the regiment's officers endorsed his official appointment, and Hurlburt became the chaplain.[28]

Jonas Schoonover made final preparations over near Akron to bring Company H to Camp Giddings. When the war broke out, he had been quick to organize war meetings in his village, serving as speaker, secretary, or whatever job required filling. He had been delegated by his village to organize a company of dragoons, but there had been no room in the ninety-day service for them. He was rumored either to have served in the Mexican-American War or to have recruited men who had. Schoonover got an appointment as a recruiting lieutenant for the Twenty-Ninth Ohio, and he applied himself to the work, ultimately enlisting nearly every man in the company.[29] He and his recruits, escorted by thirty mounted troopers from a local militia outfit and behind them a caravan of well-wishers in carriages, set out from Akron. They pulled up in front of the Empire House hotel in Akron to receive speeches from local dignitaries. They took the morning train for Ashtabula on November 5 with final connections to Jefferson via wagon.[30]

Forty-year-old Josiah J. Wright, Jack to his friends, and soon to be second lieutenant of Akron's Company G, had been, among many other things, "one of the most efficient rogue catchers, and criminal detectives" on the Akron scene, having served that town as marshall and then constable.[31] Here in camp, he wrote frequently to Akron's *Summit Beacon,* posting as many as four letters a day. Despite his complaints that the regiment was being intentionally deprived of decent equipment, and that Giddings's enemies were working behind the scenes to derail the project, Wright found that soldiering fit him right down to the ground. Young men already in wonderful physical condition when they enlisted were becoming as tough as hoe handles. Complaints about the quality and lack of variety in their army-issued rations notwithstanding, every man seemed to be putting on weight. Wright himself reported contentedly that he had never slept so sound or eaten so heartily. In brief, he exclaimed, "Hurrah for the soldier's life."[32]

The fatigue uniform for everyday soldiering—blouse, shirt, pants, and kepi forage cap—arrived the week before Halloween.[33] Long-delayed loads of camp equipment, hospital stores, and rations now came into camp on a semiregular basis. The first two companies, A and B, were now fully equipped from head to toe with most every necessary of war, including uniforms, canteens, knapsacks, and haversacks. Three more companies had enough uniform pieces to outfit each man for both field and dress parade. But, with the exception of the lucky first two companies, the men were still without weapons. Until the rest were delivered, most of the men would have to continue to simulate the real thing by practicing their drill with one arm cocked.

"Present Arms!"

In early October, a persistent rain began to fall, turning everything to mud and making life in camp disagreeable. The first frost covered the fields in late October, which was considered late for this region of harsh climate.[34] The track infield, churned to mud by marching soldiers, froze into rock-hard furrows at night, making movement of any kind a chore. Despite everyone's best efforts, the regiment would not fill up. The first big push to fill the regiment, begun in August, had reached its zenith and was now waning. Companies A through E were nearing the magic number of one hundred, but Company F, which had come into camp weeks before, was still struggling for recruits.[35] Companies I and K were woefully undermanned, and two Summit County companies, G and H, which both had solid cores, needed more men. There were now as many as seven hundred men in camp, but that was far short of the one thousand needed to take to the field. Jack Wright returned to Akron in late October to hunt for recruits and returned to camp with an additional dozen men in tow for Clemmer's Company G.[36] He had hoped for more, and falling short of his goal gave him the blues.

Some blamed the change in weather for the slowdown in the regiment's recruiting success.[37] The long season of cold would soon arrive, when everyone burrowed down for the winter, and winter was a notoriously poor season for recruiting. Even if the regiment had enough men, it could not go to war without weapons, and when they might arrive was anyone's guess. When Grotius Giddings's company had been slow to receive its rifles, his father had publicly vowed that he would buy every man a musket from his own pocket.[38] The weapon he promised to buy them was the Enfield rifled musket; it and the Springfield were judged to be the two finest infantry muskets in the world. Giddings had reminded the state of his namesake regiment's need for arms months ago, but his request had gone unfilled, and Giddings was not using his influence to secure Enfields or any other weapons for his Boys in Jefferson.

In early October, another messenger was sent to Columbus to hurry their weapons along, and he had slightly better success.[39] Camp had been open nearly two months when the first shipment of two hundred muskets arrived, but these were only enough to arm two companies.[40] These were state-of-the-art .577 caliber Enfields, giving the men of the other companies the hope they too would soon be polishing the barrels of these British-made wonders.[41] To keep things on a democratic footing, and prevent envy of one company by another, the Enfields were saved for special drill and guard duty.[42] Most of the soldiers had been in camp for several months now and they still had no muskets, leading them to wonder if they would have to fight the rebels with their bare hands. There was no shortage of pistols. Nearly every man seems to have brought at least one along in his valise. Advertisements ran regularly in every newspaper explaining the dire need for the soldier to equip himself with a sidearm. An advertisement ran every week through the war's first year in the Conneaut newspaper:

> To Soldiers and Volunteers. No man should enter the U.S. service without the protection of a small pocket revolver to defend him in sudden and unexpected assaults. The government furnish no such arms, and the volunteer should purchase one before going from home. The best revolvers in our opinion is Smith and Wesson's 7 hole or Sharp's 4 hole Repeater. These can be had in Conneaut at N.Y. prices and are invaluable to the soldier.

D. K. Carter's mercantile in Conneaut sold a dozen different models.[43] The dangers of recruits handling pistols were widely reported from the outset. One sage suggested that volunteers and pistols be treated in the same way as the sexes at a model boarding school: lock them both up separate and safe, and then throw away the key.[44] At Camp Giddings, the Boys amused themselves with their personal sidearms until a recruit in Captain Fitch's company shot off his trigger finger.[45] Buckley ordered every revolver in camp unloaded and forbade the soldiers to load them again.[46]

In early December wagons carrying coffin-size crates pulled into camp, and when the covers were pried off, the soldiers were not happy with what they saw stacked inside.[47] The .69 caliber muskets they lifted from the crates were hardly as sleek and shiny as the Enfield but appeared to be an artifact of some earlier war. Because of its immense bore, blacked barrel, and massive hammer, the men immediately took to calling it "shoulder cannon."[48] The Pondir musket was named after the Philadelphia businessman who had contracted with the government to furnish ten thousand of these Belgian-made rifles.[49] Some of them were already rifled when shipped from Europe, while others, like those provided the Twenty-Ninth Ohio, were smoothbore when they arrived in the United States and had to be "modernized" locally.[50] At the Cincinnati foundry of Miles Greenwood and Company, workers paid the outlandish sum of $1.25 per weapon to have imparted the twists that would allow firing of the deadly minié ball.[51] The Pondir was heavy to carry, and of variable quality, but in the hands of a soldier who learned to load the weapon properly and brace against the heavy recoil, it was considered the equal of the Enfield in accuracy.[52] Its heavier bullet could punch its way through heavy brush that would turn the lighter bullet fired by the Enfield. General Rosecrans preferred them over the Enfield. He had seen a soldier armed with a rifled smoothbore drop a rebel at a distance of nine hundred yards, and the weapon was capable of repeated execution at four to six hundred yards.[53] Based on its appearance alone, the soldiers did not have anything generous to say about their new arms. "Pvt. W" complained: "Friday our guns came, so we have now got what is generally denominated Arms, but if it was allowable for me to express my private opinion, I should say they were long tubular pieces of iron, with wood fastened to one end, one of the boys says [the barrel] was made by running iron around a woodchuck hole, others claim that they were used by our 4 fathers in the war of the Revolution."[54]

Unknown to the complaining boys in camp, many Ohio troops had done no better in the arms they were provided. Enfield rifles were in such scarce supply that the federal government could provide less than fifteen hundred of them for use by Ohio troops through all of 1861. In the same period, Uncle Sam delivered five thousand of the .69 caliber Pondirs to Columbus.[55] The majority of Ohio regiments were being armed with converted U.S. arsenal-manufactured smoothbores, or with less desirable European muskets.[56] Some Ohio regiments were even less lucky. The Ninth Ohio carried old-fashioned smoothbore muskets until well into 1863.[57]

Whether the Pondir would even fire, and if so, whether it could be made to hit anything, was a question the soldiers would not be allowed to answer while at Camp Giddings. Target practice was not a feature of the soldiers' training and even if it were, they had no ammunition. They would have to wait until they got nearer the seat of war before getting any.[58] The regiment made a distinctive appearance drawn up for review armed with the giant Pondirs, weapons that drew good-natured teasing from soldiers in regiments that had been supplied with more desirable weapons. Despite complaints about them, one old soldier would recall years later that the Pondir had been a "successful shoulder hitter."[59]

Season of Complaint

Some of the soldiers in camp were becoming convinced that their regiment had been singled out for mistreatment, just as their predecessors in the Nineteenth Ohio Infantry had been. In their view, the Giddings Regiment had become a dumping ground for inferior matériel while other regiments were being furnished the best of everything. The Pondir musket was one example, but there were others. The tents were stamped B.C. in an antiquated style of lettering that proved to the camp wags they were anything but modern. Back in the sunny days of the county fair, the soldiers had been tickled to death with their new uniforms, and the bystanders impressed. By December the soldiers looked like ragamuffins. Blouses and trousers had disintegrated into tatters, seats of the soldier's britches now resembled swiss cheese, and soles had peeled completely from shoe bottoms after drilling in wet weather.[60] Besides affecting the soldier's vanity, these shoddy goods were causing his pocketbook to suffer.

The government provided his food, such as it was, and his clothing, to a point. Each soldier was allowed $3.50 per month for his uniform. It benefited him to make his pants, coat, drawers, and shoes last as long as he could, because when he mustered out at war's end, if any of his clothing allowance was left unspent, it was turned over to him in cash. If he wore out more than $3.50 worth of army-supplied clothing in a month, and had to draw new, the U.S. government would lighten his final pay to settle the account.[61]

Sounding like a small-town haberdasher, the government proclaimed that the clothing it provided was not only of the most durable kind but would be offered to the soldiers at the lowest wholesale prices. The clothing provided Ohio troops at Camp Goddard, near Zanesville, in the early days did not measure up. The pants provided them were made of a trashy satinet, more appropriate for the dance floor than the drill field.[62] Rascally contractors had palmed these shoddy goods off onto the state, and Governor Dennison was attacked from all quarters for the miserable quality of clothing. An investigation into clothing fraud was threatened and reforms were promised.[63] After ruminating on the matter, Pvt. W's messmate concluded facetiously, "A man who cannot fight naked, is not worthy of a position in the ranks of this great army."[64] His lieutenant made a gift of a fine flag to the company. He presented it to the captain in a private ceremony rather than at assembly, because he feared that the men would use its sacred folds to patch their pants.

When it grew colder, the government sent a shipment of long-tailed sack overcoats out to Camp Giddings and charged them to each soldier's clothing account. The coats kept out neither wind nor cold. One soldier estimated that they could not have cost Uncle Sam more than $1.17 apiece, including freight, but the government charged $7.50 for them, more than two months' worth of his clothing allowance.[65] The coats had somehow escaped the factory minus their pockets, a deficiency being remedied in Company G by Captain Clemmer's wife. She had come out from Mogadore and set up a seamstress shop in camp to fix them.[66] If uniforms wore out this quickly, a man was forced to consider the prospect of coming home at war's end penniless, having turned over all his hard-earned wages to the government just to settle his clothing account.[67]

Earlier, camp had been the happy scene of boys fussing over their first-ever attempts at cooking, and the large black kettles sang with the good things they contained. By late fall, their appetite for army rations had worn as thin as the seats of their pants. As Pvt. W pointed out, the civilian's idea of how a soldier lived, and especially how he was fed, fell short of the truth. Pvt. W found a sign nailed over the door of his company mess that summed up the men's attitude toward their rations: "Soldiers are tough cusses, but they can't eat hay."[68] By December the bill of fare, or bill of unfair, as the soldiers called it, had been reduced to just two items.

John G. Marsh of the Homerville Boys described the menu for his sister: "For breakfast, bread and beef, and coffee. For dinner: beef, bread, and cold water. For supper: coffee, bread, and beef; quite a variety, don't you think?"[69] This was an adequate variety if one were forced to eat it for a while, but to face it three times a day for months on end was getting hard. The soldiers were growing less shy about expressing their dissatisfaction, sometimes taking it to the absurd, as one soldier reported, "for now every pleasant morning, when our rations are being delivered, the boys will get themselves into line, flap their wings and caw, caw, caw, like a thousand crows at the sight of a feast."[70]

Griping was the natural province of the private soldier, and some of it was perfectly natural to his condition, no matter how good or bad, and the Giddings soldiers indulged their rights. The sharp-tongued officer hiding behind the pseudonym S. B. took more direct aim at men he believed were responsible not only for the regiment's seeming banishment in Jefferson, but for all its other problems too, and his attacks were duly published in Akron's leading newspaper. What bit at him was the fact that their persecutors were not outsiders, but their own neighbors.

> Oh for a forty horse power doctor to cure that disease called "'blab.'" Blab about J. R. Giddings—blab about a place eleven miles from nowhere—blab about the mud; blab about snow—blab about the abolition regiment; blab, blab, blab. . . . Use your influence to have other Regiments get clothed soonest and with the best clothing, and equipped with the best arms, only after all this is done, let us go, don't keep us here any longer.[71]

S. B. was shorthand for Stand Back, which in the parlance meant "clear the decks and get out of the way." A few months hence, the veil covering S. B.'s identity would be removed and he was revealed as the outspoken forty-year-old 2nd Lt. Josiah "Jack" Wright.[72] Wright blamed all of Giddings's political opponents including one man of Giddings's own party, whom Jack identified by his appearance as a "tow-headed rat."[73] In Wright's mind, some men preferred to join regiments that had far less to prove, outfits that were treated to "cheap puffs" in their local newspapers. He was fed up with the bad-mouthing from which the Twenty-Ninth had suffered, but from his frustration had grown determination: "God helping us, we will endeavor to wipe out the blab-stains that have been heaped upon us. Send your goodies to other regiments and forget that any of your boys are here. Your boys are good and brave and want nothing so much as a fair field with the enemy in sight."[74]

This was not an isolated case of paranoia on the part of Lieutenant Wright. Soldiers in other regiments had learned of the Twenty-Ninth Ohio's plight and were sympathetic to it. One soldier confirmed, in a letter to his hometown newspaper, that the Giddings Regiment was being maligned.[75] The sense of besiegement was not confined to the soldiers languishing at Camp Giddings. Wounds that had been opened by challenges to the region's patriotism were still unhealed by late November. The Akron newspaper editor set their critics straight on Summit County's enlistment record.[76] He prefaced the county's accomplishments by stating, "The denizens of other portions of Ohio have been wont to sneer at this portion of the State, and though acknowledging our power and potency in the matter of voting, have been led to question our patriotism on the score of furnishing volunteers for the war." He then pointed out that the county had put 870 men into service already, 130 more men than their quota required. Such a stirring achievement gave him the right to admonish the cynical: "We advise those who have hitherto been in the habit of sneering at, and blowing about 'Cheesedom' to sweep before their own doors before attempting to lecture us about the untidiness of ours." As they wrapped themselves in blankets against the icy winds blowing in off Lake Erie, the Giddings soldiers began to feel more and more that they had been intentionally forgotten in this dreary village.

Some men were in fact saying some ugly things about the Giddings Regiment. Activists in the anti-slavery movement disliked being called abolitionists, a term that carried a ton of depreciatory baggage. To be called the Abolition Regiment was a heavy enough burden, but now their most malicious detractors had branded the outfit the "nigger regiment."[77] Little doubt lingered in the minds of the soldiers: they were a marked regiment, and would have to fight.[78]

Slipping Away

The weakening sun cut a lower arc through the sky with each succeeding day. Winter was in the air, and in these parts it was not to be taken lightly. Camp Giddings was never intended as an all-season camp, and the Boys had only thin canvas for protection. Any time now, the fierce snowstorms for which this country was famous would roll in, followed nearly always by days of cold so intense that an ax bit struck against a tree shattered as if made of glass. The people in Jefferson began to feel a genuine concern for the soldiers out at camp. Cold and wet were known agents of sicknesses of all sorts.

In the British army during the Crimean War, three men had died of sickness for every man who had been killed in battle or died of wounds.[79] The experience of the American army in its most recent war down in Mexico had not been much better. It would be years into the future before the causes of common killing diseases were discovered, and until then the soldiers would suffer mightily. Common sense suggested some preventatives.

Advocates of public health suggested that the officials in charge of the army arrange the camps so that they were well ventilated, dry, and insofar as possible, sanitary. So important a thing as the health of the soldier, it was cautioned, must not be left solely to the men in charge of the army. Veterans of previous wars counseled that the soldier must take responsibility for his own health. In his cookery he must avoid fatty or obviously tainted food, which would prove nigh impossible in this army if a man wanted to eat. He should take pains to keep dry, keep his skin clean, and carry spare socks. The soldier was reminded that if he became ill while in the field he would not be able to run down to the local drugstore for a cure. The soldier had best prepare himself for the inevitable by turning his knapsack into a traveling apothecary.

On hand in every mercantile, or by mail order, were a plethora of remedies a soldier might chose from, for example, Perry's Pain Killer for cuts, bruises, and injuries of all sorts. There was Dr. Richardson's Bitters for toning of the soldier's system and regulation of his bowels if they should become disordered, Atwood's Quinine Tonic Bitters for the ague and the dozen different fevers known to drift in the vapors above Southern swamps, and scores of other patent medicines in brightly colored bottles with claims all their own, including those guaranteed to heal gunshot wounds and saber cuts.[80] In mid-December death visited camp for the first time.

Pvt. W reported simply, "Last night the first death in the regiment occurred. The deceased was a private like the rest of us."[81] Charles Clopp (or Clapp), an eighteen-year-old laborer from Hudson, Ohio, had died.[82] His parents came out to camp to collect his body and take it back home escorted by an honor guard.[83] That an otherwise healthy young man had died did not attract much notice. Nine children of the same Summit County family had been snatched off recently by diphtheria all within a few days, and right up the street from camp three children of the village, none much younger than the regiment's soldiers, had been carried off by the same lethal caller.[84] With so much sickness even in peaceful times, and generally so little to be done about it by the average country sawbones, the soldiers of the regiment were lucky to have a doctor tending them who had had formal medical training. Caring for the sick at the camp hospital in the fairgrounds exhibition hall, and wearing the green sash of the regimental surgeon, was Amos Fifield, twenty-eight-year-old physician of the village of Conneaut.

Tall and thin as a rail, he was known for his sunny disposition and was the pet of his widowed mother and older sisters.[85] He had big shoes to fill. His father, Dr. Greenfield Fifield, was a local legend.[86] The elder Fifield was the archetype of the selfless frontier doctor and beloved by everyone in the village, and Amos decided to follow in his footsteps. He had benefited from as good a medical education as mid-nineteenth-century America could offer. Most doctors of his day, if they had any formal education at all, attended lectures for a year or two at the nearest medical college and then served an apprenticeship of variable duration in the office of an older practitioner. Fifield had studied for two years at the Cleveland Medical College and then went to New York to study at the prestigious College of Physicians and Surgeons.[87] In 1860 he married his first cousin Maria Kellogg, daughter of his mother's brother, Abner Kellogg.[88] He got an appointment as the Twenty-Ninth Ohio's surgeon, and went straight to Camp Giddings and began setting up his hospital.[89] His first duty was to examine new recruits to see if they could stand the physical rigors of soldiering. It would be found later that some of the men he approved were so broken down that they could not shoulder a pack from one side of Jefferson Street to the other.

By late fall Fifield was as busy as any man in the regiment. It was well known and even expected that most soldiers came down with some illness shortly after arriving in camp. Nathan Parmater had fallen ill two days after his arrival and moved from his tent into the camp hospital. No sickness was to be taken lightly. A simple sore throat could lead to something far worse. Clopp had been the first to die in camp, but not the first in the regiment. William L. Wildey was in his mid-forties when he departed his Rock Creek farmstead, leaving behind his wife, Hannah, and four daughters.[90] Wildey was known to be of excellent health. He came down with a severe cold. It was thought that a soldier stood a better chance of recovery if he were allowed to return to his home with its familiar surroundings and a loving family to attend him, so Colonel Buckley gave Wildey a pass and ordered him to report back to Camp Giddings when he was better. The local doctor diagnosed his case as "bilious pneumonia" and in a few days he was dead.[91]

When the regiment finally left Jefferson, the camp hospital was broken up and the patients distributed among the families of the village.[92] Despite the best efforts of the village to nurse them back to health, two of the left-behind soldiers died. Albert Rogers (or Rodgers), a nineteen-year-old private of Company B from Harpersfield, died in Jefferson a few days after the regiment left, and Pvt. James S. Pike of Company E died there a week later in his thirty-seventh year.[93] All told, for so large a group of men, the absence of mortal sickness at Camp Giddings had been quite extraordinary. It was a record for healthfulness that would not stand long.

As winter approached and soldiering became more of a chore and less of a lark, the soldiers' enthusiasm for army life cooled in proportion to the weather. An officer could resign when he felt like it and leave the army without disgrace or punishment. The private soldier was in for three years or the duration, whichever came first, and there was no release from this obligation short of discharge for disability, debilitating wounds, or death. If a man had made up his mind that he just wasn't cut out for soldiering, he walked off and was declared a deserter. Several soldiers decided it was better to slip away while close to home rather than in some distant Southern place. Robert Hill, a nineteen-year-old miller from Chatham Center, walked away from camp in November, and a few days later forty-four-year-old Russell Goodrich went absent without proper leave.[94] Goodrich's absence was not considered worth reporting because of his age and intemperance.[95] Privates John Hall, Urias Reifschneider, and Reuben Wagoner ran off within a few days of each other and were never heard from again.[96] John Blodgett of Company K was left sick in a private home in Jefferson when the Twenty-Ninth departed, and he failed to rejoin the regiment.[97]

New recruits were still coming into camp as November 1861 ended, and although those lost to disease, or the impulse to run away, were thought replaceable, the grinding down of the regiment had begun.

"The Emblem of Universal Freedom"

LATE FALL 1861

Rumors

One morning in late November, the villagers looked out from their warm houses and saw snow falling, and falling hard. A sleigh was seen cutting a path down the village streets of Conneaut, and the newspaper declared that the "merry season" was at hand.[1] Some of the soldiers in camp enjoyed themselves by throwing snowballs, but for most men there was little in this first snow for merriment. Later in the day, with the snow bowing tents and muffling noise, news came in that Wade's cavalry would be leaving its camp in Cleveland for the war.[2]

While the Giddings Boys stood in the snow, their chief rivals were giving and receiving champagne toasts beneath the gaslit chandeliers of Cleveland's finest hotel.[3] Then, good news of their own. A rumor circulated through camp that they were to be sent to the front even though the regiment was still undermanned.[4] Seven of the ten companies were ready to go, but Company F, which had been in camp for weeks, was still not up to the hundred-man goal, and Companies K and I were likewise short.[5] The rumor proved false before the Boys had fairly begun to pack. The same rumor roared through camp a few days later. Pvt. W reported, "Last Thursday was the day we were to leave this land of mud, lawyers and pretty girls, so the early part of this week was all bustle and confusion . . . none of us knowing what to do, consequently we done almost everything that ought not to be done and left the balance to our officers."[6] Things were speedily put in order, but just as they were ready to march, an order came for them to eat the rations they had stowed in their packs. They threw themselves down around the embers of that morning's fires, yanked at chunks of tough, cold beef and puzzled over what to do about this latest disappointment.

This lifting up of their hopes and dashing them again was more than some men could stand. Pvt. W was accounted to be an impudent fellow, so his company delegated him to go to Colonel Buckley and find out from the old man why their departure had been canceled. After rehearsing his speech outside Buckley's tent, he gathered his courage, entered, and then came right out and asked the colonel "why we wasn't allowed to march." The colonel looked up from his papers and replied that he thought the private and his mates might be competent enough *to* march, but they were not competent to decide *when*. The private's tongue froze, and all he could do was touch the visor of his cap and flee.[7]

Their exit had been triggered by an order from Columbus. Buckley had received orders from Columbus at the end of November that the regiment be ready to move on December 4, and he ordered Clark to arrange transportation.[8] The day came and went without confirmation from Columbus and the regiment continued to sit. They would suffer through a dozen of these rumors, making men suspicious of the wisdom of army officials and stretching their emotions as tight as piano strings.

The absurdity of saying one's good-byes over and over, and packing up to move only to reverse course and sit some more, was hard on the nerves, but it was also embarrassing. Adjutant Comfort Chaffee wrote a touching farewell speech to the village that was published in the *Sentinel* back in the first few days of December. "A few days more and the 29th which contains many husbands, fathers, and sons of your readers, will have left Camp Giddings, and Ashtabula County, (some of them probably not to return), for the field of action."[9] The regiment did not move, and like the others, Chaffee returned to sitting on his hands. The empty rumors of marching were having a telling effect not only on the soldiers but on their friends and family, as one private explained: "We have bid our friends goodbye at least a dozen times. We have been home and kissed our mothers, sisters, and sweethearts for the last time, three or four times over; barrels and barrels of tears have been shed, and in fact the thing is getting ridiculous. . . . Give us action . . . we want the excitement of active service."[10]

By late November even the stoic Colonel Buckley had had enough, and he ordered Thomas Clark to write to the to Columbus and remind the officials of the regiment's existence, and most important, to encourage the adjutant general to remove them to some warmer clime. At the very least, as Clark pointed out, the general should move them to some location where they might find weapons, and overcoats. At this late date, some of the soldiers had only the thin blouses issued them in the summer long past. He reminded Buckingham that their requisition for basic matériel had been superseded not once but several times by the requests of regiments that were clearly favorites of the administration. He also reminded Buckingham that the soldiers had not been paid yet and their families were beginning to suffer. He then dipped his pen into the ink of sarcasm. If these things were not remedied, Clark promised that the regiment would begin daily prayer for the defeat of the governor in the next election. However, the Twenty-Ninth Regiment would forgive these oversights if the adjutant would get them to a warmer place (Kentucky had been a rumored destination) before Camp Giddings froze solid, and the soldiers along with it.[11]

Buckingham was a military man with a West Point education, and he was unused to being addressed like a common storekeeper.[12] Moreover, Clark's remarks sounded like insubordination. Buckingham censured Clark in writing, but the words failed to put Clark in his place. He wrote again, admitting that his remarks had been "peppery" but that he would gladly take two such chastisements per week if it got the Twenty-Ninth Regiment equipped faster and on the road. Within ten days, the regiment had its muskets and winter clothing.[13]

Some of the soldiers had been sworn in during the high times of the fair, but now the regiment could not get a mustering officer to come out and officially muster those who had come since.[14] Buckley was in command, but after four months of serving in that position, even he had not been sworn into the U.S. service. Thomas Clark continued as second in command, until now in an unofficial capacity. An election was held in late November, and Clark was elected lieutenant colonel by a unanimous vote. The post of major on the field officer staff, third in the hierarchy of authority, remained vacant. The private soldiers could not come to agreement as to who should have that post.[15]

Unbeknownst to the enlisted men, Thomas Clark had realized back in mid-November that the regiment might be spending the winter at Camp Giddings. Winter overcoats had not yet been received, although the weather by then was "rather uncomfortable," which was an understatement. For lack of winter clothing or orders to move to a milder climate, Clark asked Adjutant General Buckingham for permission to erect winter barracks at Camp Giddings, putting up some new buildings, and utilizing the existing buildings on the fairgrounds.[16] Those soldiers who lived close by could winter with their families. Clearly, Clark was beginning to grow desperate: sending any of the regiment's precious enlistees away meant a dismemberment that might not easily be repaired. The days of early fall, in which the Giddings group, including Clark, had felt so full of confidence that they could be picky about who recruited soldiers for the regiment, were far behind them. For the first time, Clark, writing at Buckley's request, asked for the adjutant general's help, and it was needed "now." The area around the regiment had been thoroughly canvassed for recruits, and the counties from which they had recruited had already met their quotas. The Twenty-Ninth was still short at least one hundred men. Clark asked if the adjutant had any parts of companies not yet organized that he might send them. Given his past, testy relationship with Adjutant General Buckingham, Clark's words were given as if on a bended knee. While he had Buckingham's attention, he pointed out that the adjutant general was complicit in depriving the regiment of a full company of men promised to it. Clark reminded Buckingham that the adjutant general had given him verbal and written assurances that they should have the company. But the more explanations the adjutant general offered, "the meaner the whole transaction looked." The company in question had been "decoyed" from the Twenty-Ninth into the Forty-First Ohio Infantry. Having injured the Twenty-Ninth by this injustice, the adjutant would only be making "reparation" by sending any spare men he had to the regiment. As it turned out, Buckingham did not send them so much as a drummer boy.

As snowdrifts grew toward the tops of the tents, threatening to entomb the occupants, hope sank down near the region of despair. Speaking for the rest, S. M. informed their followers in Akron, "We have given up all hope of getting away this winter."[17]

Flag Day

> Too much importance cannot be attached to furnishing regiments with colors. Their flag is the rallying point, when broken and thrown into disorder by the enemy's fire; around it they will make their last and most desperate stand, and beneath its folds will meet a soldier's death with a soldier's heroism. It is the idol they worship, and to save it from desecration, they will willingly part with life itself.[18]

Thus one man explained the grave importance of an infantry regiment's flags. Except for the small flags that marked the tent of each company's captain, the Giddings Regiment went through most of its stay at camp without any regimental colors. By November 1861, Ohio had seventy to eighty regiments in the field or about to take to it, and only a tenth of these had been supplied with their colors.[19] It was not guaranteed that they should have any. The government did not provide this luxury. If the men of the regiment wanted a stand, comprised of two flags, one state, the other national, someone would have make them, or get up the money to have them made.

At $140, the cost of making up the two flags was not insignificant. The duty to raise such a sum was given automatically to the women of the neighborhood. As to why this work devolved to the women, a writer offered: "The Ladies are the ones that should be interested in a movement of this kind, for the soldier's eye would burn with a brighter luster, and his arms be nerved with a stronger purpose, mid the thunder and smoke of battle, could he but know that his flag was a donation from the willing hands and loving hearts of the wives, mothers, and sisters of Ohio."[20]

If a woman were not patriotically minded, there were commonsense reasons why she should apply herself actively to this project, and to the work of the soldiers' aid societies. It was reported that in John Brown's hometown of Hudson, Ohio, every eligible man in the village had gone off to war. The young ladies of Hudson and every place else would have time on their hands. "Consequently, the young unmarried ladies in this, and for like causes in every other community, must very sensibly feel the effects of the war; as their chances for matrimony are reduced in a very remarkable degree, and the prospect of a long, tedious and monotonous winter lies spread out before them."[21]

War work would also serve as a tonic for the melancholy that women felt over the loss of their sons, husbands, and suitors. The flags would remind the soldiers that the women would always be mindful of his behavior on the battlefield and in the morally dangerous army camps.

The Twenty-Ninth Ohio might lack a good many things that other regiments received, but they would have their colors. Miss Stanhope of Williamsfield took charge of the project in Ashtabula County and began asking for donations of ten and twenty cents.[22] By early November it looked as though fund-raising in Ashtabula County had come up shy of the mark. Colonel Buckley published an appeal reminding the citizens of Summit County that they had three companies of their boys in the Twenty-Ninth Ohio, and he suggested that the ladies might want to show that they remembered them by taking hold of the fund raising.[23] To fire their civic competitiveness, which was never a very difficult thing to do, he pointed out that the ladies of Warren and Trumbull Counties had gotten up enough money to furnish the Wade-Hutchins cavalry with not one but two very nice stands of colors.[24]

The project was a success. Contrary to the legend of the Twenty-Ninth Regiment, their flags were not handmade by the ladies.[25] In late fall a county resident was passing the show windows of Hawk's store in Cleveland and pulled up short when he saw what was on display. Behind the glass were the Twenty-Ninth's new flags, Old Glory, and next to it the dazzling blue State. Both were judged to be unusually rich in their embroidery and gilding.[26] G. W. Crowell and Company of Cleveland, doing business as makers of flags and banners for "Military Companies, Civic Societies and Sunday Schools," had made both flags.[27] On Wednesday, November 27, 1861, Joshua Reed Giddings rode through the coagulating mud and snow out to camp. This was to be his only documented visit to the regiment that bore his name.

Two weeks after suffering "fits of the heart," he had left the regiment-building project as it was just beginning and returned to his consulate post in Montreal. He was not well, but he was full of his usual energy. He wrote to his son Addison in Jefferson, speculating as to how the Giddings family might profit from the rising interest rates spawned by the war and from the government demand for beef to feed its soldiers.[28] He also used his influence to have Addison appointed his vice-consul in Montreal, securing for his youngest son a comfortable haven far removed from the dangers of combat. Giddings had returned to Ohio late in September, but he did not stop by Jefferson to see how his regiment was progressing. He went instead to visit his son Grot's company, now in service with the Twenty-Third Ohio. In contrast to the Twenty-Ninth's condition, Giddings found his son's regiment stunning and well equipped.[29]

He came out to camp to present the Twenty-Ninth Ohio Volunteer Infantry with their flags, and his speech to them would be part benediction and part history lesson. He held his arms out in front of him and began. He reminded the soldiers that the people of the Reserve had been injured by the treatment of its soldiers in the Nineteenth Ohio. There had been the slave-catching incident, and the disgrace of Lieutenant Stratton and his men, which had thrown the people's hopes in the mud. He explained that this regiment had been born of those disappointments. He said that every soldier and officer standing before him had been examined, and found to be the sort of man who would sooner die than give comfort to rebels and despots by returning slaves. If any of the men standing in front of him believed that the aim of the war was to restore the Union, he reminded them, "This is emphatically a war of principle, a war against the enslavers of mankind by whatever name they may be called. It is a war which is honorable, and patriotic men may gracefully lay down their lives in behalf of our common community."[30]

There was at least one man standing out in front here who could not pass Giddings's litmus test. Lewis P. Buckley would never sanction disobedience of a military order, whether a slave depended on him for rescue or not. He had been a lifelong Democrat, a party not generally sympathetic to antislavery. But two years would pass before any clue surfaced suggesting Buckley's political affiliations. In commending Buckley's service to the country, the editor of an Akron newspaper reported that Buckley had *not* been "a very strong abolitionist," which was the faintest of endorsements, considering he was then in command of the Abolition Regiment.[31]

He had been called as a witness in the court martial of Lieutenant Stratton, and the others accused of having stolen property from a rebel sympathizer. He wrote to state adjutant general Buckingham on August 21 and stated that although it was his great desire to see Stratton and his men honorably acquitted, his health was imperfect and he begged to be excused from attending. Rosecrans and McClellan had been vilified in the Reserve's newspapers, a pummeling Buckley did not feel was warranted: "I do not by any means feel disposed to censure Genl's McClellan or Rosecrans for they could not have done otherwise and done their duty." Moreover, Buckley concluded that Stratton's punishment had produced a salutary effect on the troops.[32]

Nearing the dramatic climax, Giddings turned toward Colonel Buckley: "To you Sir, as commander, I present these beautiful standards for the use and benefit of the Regiment.... Wherever you go, let them be borne aloft, and respected as the emblem of universal freedom to all who seek your protection. Preserve them unstained, except for the blood of your enemies."[33] With that, he untied the plain cloth hiding the two flags. The wind caught at the gold fringed edges and the flags flashed into view, heavy silk shimmering sluggishly. From the base of its ball bat–thick wooden staff to its cast-iron eagle finial, each flag was twice as tall as the average solider. The grave honor of lifting it into battle would test the courage and physical strength of the soldiers who carried it. The effect of so much sudden color against the monochromatic background of camp was startling. There was not a heart in the regiment that did not beat with emotion that the emblems of such a mighty cause had been given to them for care. On behalf of his men, Buckley pledged, "And now, fellow soldiers, in the presence of this assembly, and before high heaven, we swear upon the altar of our country to defend this flag so long as there shall be one true heart to lift it to the breeze."[34] Every man then vowed the flags should remain untarnished as long as a single one of them lived.[35] These flags would do some hard traveling, and some of it to places the soldiers would not want them to go. Weather and battle, and defacement by rebels, would turn these particular flags to smoky ribbons in a short while.

Sleight of Hand

In the middle of a December night the men were aroused from their chilly slumbers by the shout "Fire!" One of the tents along the street of Company E was burning. The next morning a group of soldiers stood near the smoking pile talking. One of the boys concluded that they could not march away from Jefferson now, because the regiment "*has burnt its tail.*"[36] There were many reasons why the regiment had not moved. Without their knowing, Buckley had been partly to blame. In late September the rumor circulated through the camp that every regiment in Ohio was to be shipped to the front in a few days regardless of their level of preparedness. Buckley immediately wrote to the adjutant general reminding him that Giddings had gotten assurance from the War Department in Washington that the Twenty-Ninth could remain in its camp until it was completely filled, and that assurance had induced its officers to enlist in the regiment.[37]

Buckley had predicted back in September that two weeks more would about fill the regiment up, but he requested that the adjutant general honor the War Department's pledge to Giddings if it should take as long as six weeks. It would take much longer than that. His letter to the adjutant may have taken the Twenty-Ninth Ohio out of an earlier rotation into the war, which in turn was causing all the carping and finger pointing. Buckley had his reasons for wanting more time to organize.

He was worried that if the regiment were sent far away from its recruiting grounds it might never fill up. He could look down the war road and see what was coming, and it would in no way resemble the Nineteenth Ohio's outing in western Virginia. The war that lay ahead would demand far harder service, and an undersized regiment would quickly be whittled down, and maybe out of existence. Better to risk the demoralization that came from lingering too long in camp than to see the Giddings Regiment disbanded early in its career because it had rushed into the war with too few men.

The regiment had been steadily gaining manpower. Around the time of Halloween, there were seven hundred soldiers and officers in Camp Giddings, and a month later, as Thanksgiving approached, the regiment could count 850 soldiers and officers present and ready to go.[38] The fear had already set in that they might have to spend the entire winter here on the edge of this remote Ohio village, or worse. One soldier wrote, "I will close by saying that all our fears are that we will never see actual service."[39]

With his men beginning to resign themselves to having to spend the entire war in Jefferson, Buckley took action. A total of 956 officers and enlisted men had been listed on the rolls, but once that high point was reached, their strength began to erode.[40] By the time they left Camp Giddings, that number had fallen to 900.[41] The Twenty-Ninth Ohio Volunteer Infantry would never be as strong as it was at this moment. It was time to leave.

Colonel Buckley did some administrative sleight of hand to get them away. With the New Year just two weeks away, men from the filled companies were shifted to the two companies that were short of men, I and K. He ordered his company captains to "detail" a prescribed number of men from each company into the two weakest companies. In the army style, captains were to ask their men if anyone wished to volunteer.[42] A man joined up to fight with the neighborhood company in which he had enlisted, and leaving it to take up company life with a set of strangers was no small thing. But there were certain benefits in transferring allegiance to another company.

Pvt. W had lobbied comrades in his old company by telling them that if they transferred with him, and elected him to office, he would look after their interests. When the votes were counted in their new company that evening, Pvt. W was still a private. His friends had their own dreams of a lieutenant's shoulder boards, and each had voted for himself. As to the qualifications of the men who were elected officers, he remarked, "The biggest fool in the lot was made captain, the next first Lt., and so on down."[43] Enough men transferred into the last companies to allow the Twenty-Ninth Ohio to report that its organization was complete.[44] Russel B. Smith, forty-two, the Nineteenth Ohio veteran who had supervised the drilling of the Homer Boys on his farm, would lead Company I to war.[45] Company K would have as its captain Alden P. Steele, a short twenty-seven-year-old Connecticut native.[46] They had everything by way of manpower and equipment that they required. Their new flags were cased and ready, and they would also have their own songs.

In the darkest days of December, a member of Captain Clemmer's company wrote two songs just for the regiment.[47] Soldiers borrowed the printing press at the *Sentinel* and ran off copies so every man in camp could learn the words, and Clemmer was leading the boys in learning to sing them. "Dixie for the Twenty-Ninth," to be sung to the tune of the wildly popular "Dixie," was the better of the two: part recruiting advertisement, and part tribute to the counties that had sent their sons into the regiment. The rhyming was awkward, but the sentiment shone bright as gold.

> Old Ashtabula's boys shall raise
> Our banner to the Southern breeze,
> And braves to make the rebels tremble,
> Will from Summit's plain assemble . . .
>
> And if you want to drive away the sorrow,
> Come and join the Twenty-Ninth tomorrow,
> The Northward breeze shall hear our story,
> To home and friends from fields of glory . . .
>
> Away! Away! The Twenty-Ninth in Dixie
> Away! Away! Away down South in Dixie!

The "Full Rigged Volunteer"

"Camp life to Volunteers is at first a novelty, next a monotony, and lastly a consummate bore." Thus Pvt. W expressed his view of army life.[48] One day in mid-December, Buckley ordered everyone to harness themselves into the complicated network of belts and straps from which their knapsacks, haversacks, canteens, cartridge and cap boxes, belts and bayonet sheaths, blankets and guns depended. They were to prepare for a march out into the countryside. Pvt. W described his own struggles to get himself arranged: "After divers ineffectual attempts, I succeeded in getting mine on somehow, nearly everything was wrong side up, but no matter, I had complied with the order—'put them all on,' and that you must learn is the height of soldier's ambition—obey. You have seen caricatures of Santa Clause have you not? Yes. Well, that approaches the ridiculous, but a full rigged volunteer caps the climax of the ludicrous."[49]

The regiment went out into the countryside only a few miles, but that was enough to take them into a neighborhood so isolated that one soldier claimed the inhabitants had not yet heard the news that a regiment had been camped in Jefferson for the last months. They found the residents so deeply bedded in the teachings of John Brown that it was doubtful they knew much of anything else, including the fact that there was a war on.[50]

As soon as they got back to camp, one soldier slid out of his outfit and frisked about like a madman. When asked by his captain why he had behaved so, he replied, "I am altogether too young a colt to carry a knapsack."[51] The Boys were always first to laugh at their own ineptitudes, so there was comedy to be taken in this first clumsy field maneuvering. Despite the horseplay, the more reflective soldiers could sense they were making their final preparations for the deadly serious work ahead. There were other signs. The company cookhouses were ordered closed down, and the companies divided into messes of several men each, which was the cooking arrangement used by fighting regiments.

Christmas was near, but even at this late date new recruits continued to come into camp a man at a time.[52] However, with the season of bad weather at hand, this trickle was expected to dry up. A mustering officer had finally visited, and the soldiers had been officially sworn and mustered in.[53] All the officers had been elected but were not sworn, pending a few last-minute adjustments. Three men offered themselves as candidates for the major's post vacated by Thomas Clark's election to lieutenant colonel. Of the three men who wanted the job, only Capt. John S. Clemmer could round up a clear majority, and he won the election.[54] Neither the governor nor anyone could say now that the regiment was not ready. All that was needed now was an opening into the war and the orders that would send them there.

Away at Last

A few days before Christmas, a stretch of Conneaut Creek above the mill froze solid, and the villagers strapped on skates and passed these shortest days of the year flying up and down the ice. Evenings, everything was mostly still, except for the sound of sleigh bells and laughter. The young folks, Young America, as this generation was called, bundled up beneath piles of blankets and buffalo robes and rode sleighs through the dark countryside to parties in neighboring villages, some returning not until morning. Their arrival at this ungodly hour was duly noted by the morally vigilant.[55] Gift giving was popular then, and although there was a war on, and some complaining that they were in the midst of hard times, the advertisements in the newspapers this season showed that the possibilities for presents were nearly endless.

Over in Tallmadge, near Akron, the ladies were decorating tables for the two hundred guests they hoped would attend their Savory Supper on Christmas night. The money they hoped to take in would go to buy material they would turn into pillow covers and socks and drawers bound for the soldiers' hospitals just now beginning to appear as a feature of the war's landscape. The banquet would feature oysters, meats, biscuits, cakes, pies of all kinds, and hot coffee, and for a few pennies, one could take a chance on drawing a prize at the game of post office. After dinner, they would adjourn to the schoolroom to hear the Honorable Sydney Edgerton speak on the seriousness of the times.[56] Mostly, life appeared to come off as usual in this happy season, much as it always had.

For Reserve soldiers already at the front, the war was still little more than a pleasant excursion to a novel place. A soldier of Carlin's battery had sent home to Conneaut some stalactites he had collected in a cave near Rolla, Missouri, and the villagers regarded the glittering globs with as much curiosity as if they had been snatched from the surface of the moon. Out at Camp Giddings, spirits had been on the descent for weeks, but of a sudden, glad news burst through camp, and it proved to be the best Christmas gift any soldier could hope for.

Orders had arrived at Buckley's tent several days before Christmas and unlike the others that had preceded it, these appeared to be the real thing. The regiment was to break camp and report themselves to the troop collection point at Camp Chase, in Columbus.[57] From there, they would step off directly into the war. Where they would be going was a mystery, but the soldiers hoped it would be to the land of magnolias and warm breezes.

The announcement of their going produced universal sadness in the village. The officers had been perfect gentlemen, and the common soldiers had been industrious and intelligent. Many had been regular attendees at the village churches and at its social gatherings and welcomed guests at family firesides. There had been none of the brawling, drunkenness, or depredations against civilians that were almost expected of young men in military camps.

There had been small breaches of decorum, as when the soldiers took over the stage from Herr Kline, but that had all been in good fun, and in no way resembled the carryings-on in less fortunate places like nearby Canton, where a soldier was shot dead right in the town's commercial hall for disobeying an order.[58] The soldiers at Camp Giddings had been well behaved, and more important, soldiers and villagers had become friends.[59] After the regiment left, the board members of the county agricultural society would inspect the fairgrounds and find that the soldiers had demolished many of the buildings so thoroughly that not a stick remained, and they had done similarly to much of the grandstand, and to the fence that enclosed the grounds. None of this had been done out of maliciousness but only from the soldier's need to stay warm. The gentlemen of the agricultural society would grouse about the damage and the cost of repairing it, but the matter was soon forgotten.[60]

Though they had done their level best to keep their soldiers entertained and comfortable, the citizens realized that monotony and frustration had piled up out at camp so high that the soldiers could no longer see over it into their future.[61] "God-speed to the 29th Regiment," in whatever role they might be placed, was the common sentiment.[62] As a memento, the Jefferson newspaper printed the name of every man in the regiment and his place of residence.[63]

The soldiers publicly expressed their gratitude for the many kindnesses done them by the residents of Jefferson in a notice published in the village newspaper.[64] The soldiers' feelings about the village had soured over the months, along with everything else, until some of them had come to believe Jefferson the worst place in the world. Several weeks after they were gone from Jefferson, one soldier of the village's very own Company A wrote to the *Sentinel* to express his belief that local feeling toward the regiment had been "ungenerous."[65] In a very short time, most all of them would regret ever having left.[66]

Christmas morning 1861 the sun came up red and swollen and hung on the bottom of a blue sky. It was severely cold but otherwise pleasant. The soldiers were up before first light and began packing their gear. Some men had not been to bed at all. The night before, which was to be their last Christmas Eve at home for how long no one could say, the officers blacked their boots, put on their best uniforms, sashes, and swords. They spent the night at homes and halls decorated with evergreen boughs and holly sprigs laced with patriotic bunting, with Christmas trees in the corners blazing with candles. To the accompaniment of piano and fiddle, they had waltzed young women in fancy gowns across polished plank floors. The war was very far away that night.

Reveille was sounded at six in the morning, a hasty breakfast prepared and eaten, and the kettles and tin plates packed away in piano-size travel chests.[67] Hundreds from the village and the surrounding countryside had come to say their final goodbyes. Fires had been built in front of every soldier's tent along all the company streets, and around each fire stood groupings of the soldier's loved ones with the soldier at the center. There were embraces, jokes to soften the discomfort of the moment, and there were tears. The imposing military spectacle of guard mounting was carried out at Camp Giddings, Jefferson, Ohio, for the last time.

On Command, the canvas city upon which the residents had become so used to looking went down all at once, exposing private scenes of leave taking. Wagon teams now appeared simultaneously on every part of the fairgrounds and the men pitched in to load mess chests, tents, tent pins and poles, kettles, and personal baggage aboard. Soldiers had crammed every corner of knapsacks, haversacks, and pouches full of every sort of item, each and every one regarded as indispensable, and it took one or two teams and wagons to carry the impedimenta of a single company, and several more to hold the regiment's general gear.

Decades later, Thomas Clark would look back on this day, when every man carried too much, of too many things, and reflect, "A soldier learns in time that the real necessities of life are few. Yet the artificial and fanciful are many."⁶⁸ They had come to this place as farmers, mechanics, students, and teachers and were leaving this day as soldiers, drilled, armed, and uniformed, but only partially informed as to what being a soldier in this war might mean.

Wagons full to the gunwales creaked out and lined up along Beech Street, pointed north. Then the drums of each company beat to arms and the sergeants hollered, "Fall in, men, fall in." Soldiers slung their knapsacks and stepped up to form their line.⁶⁹ This was it; there would be no going back. Even stalwart men unused to crying turned away and swiped at their eyes, hiding runaway emotions behind a cough. Mothers, wives, sisters, and sweethearts reached out to capture a soldier's hand, saw that it was senseless to persist so and turned loose. This might be the last time they would see their son, husband, or brother. Part of that was the romanticism of the time; war all mixed up with notions of glory and grand sacrifice, and part of it was perfectly justified.

The soldier standing by the fire in front of his tent, anxious for the good-byes to end so he could get away from this too-quiet place, could not see what lay in store, for him or for the boy next to him. His eyes were fixed on the snow-covered ridge north of town, which blocked his view of the Plank Road, which led up to the railhead in Ashtabula, and beyond that somewhere lay the war, and he was starved for a look at it. When they marched out of Jefferson, they were, by one head count taken this day, 923 men strong, including their officers.⁷⁰ Many of these first boys would falter or fall, and others would step forward to take their places, so when the War was done, 1,542 men could rightfully claim they had done service in the Twenty-Ninth Ohio Volunteer Infantry.

The drummers of the regimental band took up the long roll, and each company, with its own flags flying out in front, started in motion. The officers mounted their horses. Out front and center were their new flags, splendid beyond measure, and behind them, the regimental band throwing a lively tune into the cold air. The music was cut off in midstream by command, and after a dramatic pause Buckley's clear voice: "Shoulder arms, right face, mark time," and then band music again, and once more Buckley: "Forward, march!"⁷¹

They swung through the camp gate in perfect arrangement, south to Jefferson Street and east to the public ground surrounding the courthouse, where they stacked arms and listened to farewell speeches. When that was done, they shouldered muskets again and made another turn around the square to give the locals one last look.⁷² They turned up Walnut Street and pointed themselves north. The hurrahs died away and the crowd watching from the courthouse became still. Many a silent prayer was intoned, and tears wiped away, as the regiment moved out of sight. The last soldier in the last rank paused on the ridge above the village, waved his hat, and then disappeared.

"At the Threshold of an Untried Life"

CAMP CHASE, COLUMBUS, DECEMBER 1861–JANUARY 1862

Three Trains in the Night

The road up to the town of Ashtabula was piled deep with sticky snow that almost pulled the soldier's shoes from his feet. This march was hard work compared to what the Boys of the Twenty-Ninth had been used to at Camp Giddings. Although some of them had been to war, all of them were green as grass, if the surplus of stuff every man carried was any measure. Years down the road, Col. Thomas Clark would reflect, "We stood at the threshold of an untried life."[1]

They were cheered at every farmhouse along the way, and when the long column of soldiers, followed by their train of forty wagons, arrived in Ashtabula, eight miles distant, there was a huge crowd waiting for them, larger even than the one that had gathered to catch a glimpse of Lincoln when he came through on his inaugural train, a year earlier.[2] The curious had come out to get a look at the spectacle of so large a group of armed men in this hitherto peaceful place.[3] The regiment drew up and uncoiled itself in the town square. The locals thought the regiment looked fierce and concluded it would unlikely have any superiors in the volunteer army.

They paused in Ashtabula an hour, while a special train was coupled together. It was an extraordinary twenty-one passenger cars long plus an additional half dozen freight cars packed with their baggage.[4] There was a stove in each of the cars. The atmosphere inside was redolent of wet wool and tobacco smoke. The windows were soon covered with a layer of frost so thick that they could not see out. For many of these backward boys, it was the first time they had ever taken a ride on a railroad train, and they were enjoying it immensely. The locomotive whistled up brakes and sagged forward.

At Painesville a thousand people had collected at the station.[5] When the Twenty-Ninth's train pulled in, a cheer went up that rent the multitudes. The residents surprised the regiment with box lunches for every company, and one for each of the field officers.[6] They stopped in Cleveland long enough for their special train to be broken down into three trains for better speed and then hustled on through darkened towns, headed south and east over the hills just west of Homerville and Medina, and down into the flattening terrain around Columbus. Soldiers tired from the day's march and general hullabaloo dozed in their seats and watched the yellow lights of houses and villages fly past. They arrived in Columbus at seven in the morning, just as the city was awaking.[7]

Paris on the Scioto

The regiment stayed aboard the cars just long enough to finish off box lunches. Then they shouldered their gear and set off on a four-mile march through the city toward Camp Chase, out on the city's west side. One Twenty-Ninth Ohio officer marching along the street overheard a spectator remark that the Giddings Regiment was the best by all odds of the numerous regiments that had already passed through the city.[8] In comparison to the frozen, more northern place they had just departed, Columbus was warm as spring.[9] The Boys put their feet on the National Road, crossed the bridge over the Scioto River, and filed into their new home.[10] How long they would be lodging here at Camp Chase, no one knew.

The federal government had set up two camps for the reception of Ohio boys into the arms of Uncle Sam: Camp Dennison, over near Cincinnati, and this place. Like their camp in Jefferson, Camp Chase sat on the site of a racetrack. The neighbors considered it an eyesore, and the soldiers who lived there a public nuisance. Soldiers were inclined to sneak out of camp after dark to raid gardens and chicken coops and steal anything that wasn't tied down.[11] Pvt. Nathan Parmater judged the camp nicely situated on its four-hundred-acre field. It had been designed to accommodate four thousand soldiers in its row upon row of completely identical wood-frame barracks, each measuring fourteen by twenty feet, and was at present nearly full. With a hospital, laundry, cookhouses, and other conveniences, the camp was a city unto itself.

The barracks were drafty and overrun by rats, but wooden walls were preferable to thin canvas in this climate, and each cabin-size barrack was equipped with a good stove and plenty of wood.[12] The place was muddier even than Camp Giddings, but the soldiers liked it better the more they saw of it.[13] They piled into their shanties, stowed their traps, and went outside to take a look around.[14] Pvt. Wallace B. Hoyt lost no time in letting his parents back home in Rock Creek know, "The boys all feel fine and full of fun and I never enjoyed myself better."[15]

Of immediate interest to the newcomers was the prison just inside the edge of camp. Within the sixteen-foot-tall plank palisade were 350 real live rebels.[16] To add to the novelty, Negro slaves attended several of the captured Confederate officers.[17] Ohio's capital city held eighteen thousand souls, and to untraveled boys from Richmond Center and Cherry Valley it was the first city of any rank they had been privileged to explore. They could not have found Paris more fascinating. Willis Sisley, a farm boy private in Capt. Wilbur Stevens's company, sent a letter to his brother Reason, who had unwisely chosen to stay home: "10 of us Boys best acquainted got a pass yesterday and went up to the city and a beautiful place it is. We was through the State House and the state prison. You have no idea what is going on in the world. I have seen more inside of the last two weeks than I ever seen in my whole life."[18]

Columbus was famous for its miserable streets, and the hogs that roamed them, but it had a cosmopolitan air. Over two dozen passenger trains called daily at the grand depot. Hacks stood in lines in front of it, ready to haul visitors up to one of the city's fine hotels. At all hours of the day and night passenger trains squealed and groaned into the depot and when the passengers stepped down it was seen that they were mostly blue-uniformed soldiers, faces burnished by the prairie winds of the flatland states lying back toward the Mississippi. These western boys alighted briefly to stretch their legs and then were quickly back on, bound east to join the big troop buildup going on around Washington, or down below the Ohio River. The city had a spanking-new state capitol building, institutions for the insane, deaf, and blind, its own medical college, a finishing school for young females, and several newspapers, including a foreign-language sheet for the city's prosperous population of Germans.[19]

If a soldier had money, there were any number of entertainments for his diversion. The grand State Theatre was hosting a production of *The Hunchback of Notre Dame*. Music halls, like the Varieties or the Apollo, featured the antics of the cork-darkened comics in Matt Peel's Ethiopian Minstrelsy, and the chaste but highly amusing performance of a troupe of traveling female Zouaves. A soldier might apply himself to the Scientific Game, beneath the fancy gaslights of the swanky Winant's Billiard Room. For those soldiers from the countryside seeking a first experience in that vein, there was the novelty of houses of ill repute out on the edge of town.[20]

Shop windows in the downtown were filled with every product of the Western world, and many things from places more exotic. On display behind plate glass were fancy Swiss clocks, mink victorines, and sprawling horsehair settees with gleaming walnut arms carved into the likenesses of angel heads. There were shops that did a thriving business outfitting soldiers on their way through to the war.

Displayed for sale were swords, hats, ingenious tin mess kits, and knapsacks guaranteed to be waterproof or the buyer's money cheerfully returned. From the sutlers set up out near the camp, a soldier could satisfy his wants in gloves, handkerchiefs, knives, pipes, combs, pocket mirrors, and 360 different styles of patriotically decorated stationery.[21]

Columbus had always gotten its strength from the rich agricultural lands that surrounded it. Now, with a war on, factories were sprouting up in every neighborhood. Hundreds of young women had left farm life behind, which was a revolutionary migration, for the cash wages they could earn in the factories. Gentle hands, more used to applying a damp rag to a child's fevered forehead, spent long days sewing soldiers' knapsacks and uniforms, assembling the extra-large minié-ball cartridges needed for the refitted muskets of the type the Twenty-Ninth Ohio carried. The ladies turned out upward of forty thousand of these "cure-all pills for Secesters" in a single day.[22] The more trusted convicts from the state penitentiary applied themselves to the contract manufacture of war matériel, from cannon balls to camp kettles and everything in between.[23]

The regiment celebrated New Year's Day 1862 by holding their first dress parade since arriving at Camp Chase. The day began in the usual fashion, with reveille at six, but after lunch, a new element was injected into the daily routine. The men were ordered to collect all their soldier paraphernalia, attach it to their "pusson," and form up for an inspection more formal than anything that had been tried at Camp Giddings.[24] Though most of them had been soldiers now for several months or more, Pvt. W reported that an inspection of this sort was wholly new to the men. He thought he made a fine appearance and was sure he would be singled out for praise. At the order "Inspection, Arms!" he drew the rammer and dropped it into the Pondir's gaping muzzle, but it would not go down. "There I stood, in sight of the whole battalion, spectators and Colonel with the barrel of my gun half-full of something, I did not know what."[25] He discovered that some of the boys in his mess had been using the barrel of his musket as a "receptable" for their used tobacco quids. He was chewed out in turn by Colonel Buckley and then by his own captain and then excused.

With little required by way of military duty except to stand guard one day in four, the boys had plenty of spare time in which to enjoy the capital city's entertainments.[26] But most of these took money, and the soldiers currently had none.[27]

Clothed in Patriotism

> What astonishing notoriety some characters can get . . . there is Mr. Payday; a few months since, he was barely known; yet it is astonishing now to see how eagerly his acquaintance is sought. The Mssrs. Pay-Rolls are much thought of, in fact are very popular with the masses; yet strange to say, by some hocus pocus they are condemned by the firm of Red Tape and Circumlocution faster than antiquated crackers are on the Potomac.[28]

Thus, Capt. "Stand Back" Wright wrote for the edification of their friends in Summit County. Despite the promises that they would be paid "next week," many next weeks had come and gone, and not one of them contained a payday. The official explanation was that there was some minor defect in the payrolls that had been prepared by the company clerks.

The government had swung the inducement of a regular payday in their faces to get them to enlist. The boys had fulfilled their end of the bargain, but the government had not, and it was affecting morale. They were all, according to S. B., "wretchedly disappointed."[29] Most of the soldiers, both men and officers, had left families behind who were depending on their husband's or son's army pay to purchase the necessaries of life. Cash was always scarce and hard won, but with their husbands and sons gone, the flow had dried up altogether. These were a people used to pitching in and helping a neighbor out, and concerned folks banded together to ease the sting of hardship on the home front.

Near Columbus, the young boys of the Sawbuck Rangers cut and hauled firewood to the families who had men in service so at least they would be warm. In Summit County officials had arranged for the payment of a small weekly stipend to the distressed families of unpaid soldiers.[30] The payments were admittedly hardly enough to keep starvation from the door. To take up the slack, the Akron newspaper editor encouraged local merchants and farmers to lend a hand to make sure that the soldier's family would not starve.[31] For those who did not realize the seriousness of their neighbor's plight, the editor finished, "Reader! Don't let this call go in one ear and out the other, but start right off, and do something towards carrying out its suggestions." The blanket of civic largess could only stretch so far. Until the soldiers were paid, needy families must be content to feed and clothe themselves in patriotism—that was the general, bitter sentiment of the soldiers.[32]

This issue was pressing in on the soldiers at the worst possible time. Before long they would be someplace far too distant from home to keep track of their family's well-being or to lend direct comfort if things came to the breaking point. It would be better if they could get their pay here in Columbus, so that they could go off to war with clear minds. Pvt. W wrestled down to the nubbins of the problem and found it might affect his willingness to fight: "It is all very well to talk about patriotism but let me tell you and all others concerned, that soldiers with families at home suffering for the bare necessaries of life, will make poor work fighting any but the powers that are to blame for such shabby treatment."[33]

A Condition in No Way Remarkable

Everyone knew that the army was filled with its inevitable demoralizations and calamitous evils.[34] It was a place of temptations, filled with tainted men doing their level best to steer innocent boys toward damnation. Young boys from village and farm would be thrown in with hard cases from big cities, who would be teaching them to use profane language, to gamble, and most hideous of all, to drink whiskey. The sale of intoxicants to soldiers in military camps was officially illegal. However, sutlers were known to be a devious bunch when it came to selling liquor. The camp merchant need only drop a couple peaches into a jar of whiskey and label it pickled peaches to stay within the law. To aid the soldier in hiding his own cache of the contraband, sutlers sold inventions like the Bosom Companion, which was a tin flask shaped and painted to resemble a hymnbook.[35] There was plenty of other proof to confirm the fears of the homefolks.

An officer of a regiment that had passed through Camp Chase a few weeks earlier had with his own eyes seen volunteer officers drunk as any common trash, sleeping "the critter" off in the middle of the city's sidewalks in broad daylight.[36] To battle this disgraceful behavior, the officer had founded a camp temperance society, but from the sounds of it, not many men took the pledge.

The First Ohio Regiment had hurried off to save the city of Washington in the first days after Fort Sumter. They returned to Columbus for discharge not long after, and a half dozen of its private soldiers, drunk, as it was reported, nearly tore the town apart. Enraged citizens came to the rescue, and a riot of fists and rocks got under way. The police wagon rolled up to haul the drunken veterans to the station house, but not before one of them had been beaten to a pulp by the outraged locals.[37]

It was not so much the bullet the family feared for their boy but the ruination that came from lifting the Fatal Bowl.[38] Even the most self-disciplined of young men was in dread danger of being turned into a drunken beast, or falling victim to one of army life's other well-known vices such as gambling and taking up with loose women. There was plenty of preaching from the pulpit and the newspapers to help him guard against these things. The soldier was asked to make a public promise that he would let no foul word pass from his lips and that he would condemn any man who indulged in this or any other of the "besetting sins of soldiering." He promised he would let whiskey alone, except if prescribed by a physician, and defend his self-respect on all occasions and under all circumstances.[39] His goal always: to return home as unpolluted as when he left.

The entertainments of the men at Camp Giddings while under the eyes of their nearby families had been innocent enough. The Reserve itself, in which most of these soldiers were raised, was famous as an abstemious place, at least by the people who lived there. Nearly every town and village had a branch of the Ladies' Temperance Society or of one or more of its affiliates, like the one in which Colonel Clark was a member. In reality, Reserve towns flowed with the contents of the Poisoned Cup as much as any other place in the state, and intoxicating beverages could be found even in the moral stronghold of Ashtabula County, if one was motivated to go looking. Some of the county's men who wanted to enlist in John Brown Jr.'s company of sharpshooters were rejected when it was discovered they were intemperate.[40] Akron had over forty "grog shop doggeries" that plied their villainous trade. The newspapers campaigned against them periodically and incited the citizens to rise up and close them down. Even the circumspect village of Jefferson, where the temperance movement had been especially vigorous, had at least one groggery of its own tucked away among its stately churches and homes, disguised as a grocery.

Three men of Capt. Horatio Luce's company had been ceremonially drummed out of Camp Giddings. The event created a sensation that was orchestrated to have a salutary influence on those who witnessed it.[41] The stated reason for their banishment was "irregular bearing," code words for indulging an appetite for strong drink. One evening shortly after Luce's men were sent away, an officer-led squad of Twenty-Ninth Ohio soldiers, armed with muskets and hatchets, descended on the establishment of a man suspected of selling liquor. The squad stove in whiskey barrels with their musket butts, while others held the owner and his patrons at bay with bayonets.[42] Their officer mistook barrels containing vinegar and coal oil for "death-at-forty-rods," and ordered them destroyed along with the rest. The soldiers were applauded for their temperance crusading. They had proved to the villagers that the Twenty-Ninth was one regiment that had not been wet-nursed on the bottle.

Now, only a few hours from home, some of the soldiers and their officers forgot the powerful prejudices of their people against the use of alcohol and embarked on a spree. Colonel Buckley, known always to be an acerbic gentleman and a stern disciplinarian, may have turned a blind eye toward it. This was after all their last chance to blow off steam before they shoved off into the hazards of war. Buckley had call on occasion to point out to the men that they were "too full of the toddy," a condition that, Pvt. W pointed out, was "in no ways remarkable among us patriotic volunteers, both officers and privates."[43] An enlisted man was almost expected to kick up his heels once away from home, but an officer was supposed to be made of higher moral stuff, and thus a vacation from hometown morality was not warranted. According to Pvt. W, the regiment's officers were the worst offenders. He observed, with tongue partially in cheek, that the Twenty-Ninth Ohio could not move to the front until the officers sobered up long enough for them to do so.[44] The newspaper editors back home in the Reserve published these soldier accounts verbatim, suggesting that despite their communities' prohibitions against strong drink, such things were forgivable in the current crisis.

Alcoholic beverages were always in demand around army camps, and priced accordingly. The soldiers at Camp Chase pled poverty. But the impoverished soldier could still have a fine night on the town for himself and his friends if he knew how to work it, and it wouldn't cost him a penny. Columbus had any number of German groceries and beer gardens, all of which dispensed lager beer. Jack Wright heard one German beer seller lament that soldiers from Camp Chase marched into his establishment in military cadence calling out, "'left, left, left.' . . . Den dey trink up all my peer mitout any pay, an say 'left, left, left'—again, and ven I looks up tey pes all left—an tey left no money to pay mit my peer all trink up."[45] Technically, this sort of rowdyism amounted to petty thievery, but the complainant was after all only a thick-tongued German.

Pvt. W made the round of Columbus's scenic attractions and the first stop on his tour was the state penitentiary. He found the nine hundred inmates uniformed in striped pants and jackets and trained to move in perfect unison whenever a bell was rung. They reminded him of a herd of zebras, or better yet, of a company of soldiers. In fact, he observed that if the convicts had muskets they could be mistaken for soldiers.[46]

The regiment was in a Federal army camp now, and fully governed by all its sundry regulations. A boy could no longer run home whenever he felt like it, as soldiers had at Camp Giddings, but, as Pvt. W reported it, they could leave Camp Chase whenever they pleased, whether they had a proper pass or not. The two other regiments in camp just now were filled with soldiers who were mostly German, and these "Dutchmen" regarded the native Yankee sons of the Giddings Regiment as model soldiers. If any Twenty-Ninth boy wanted to pass the "Dutch Guard" on his way to the city, he simply said he was a "regular" and the German guard let him pass with no tougher challenge than "I spose that so."[47] If the guard was not a naive German, the soldier approached the gate and worked a deal: if the guard would pass him out, he would return the favor the next time it came his turn to stand guard. So well-traveled was this underground route that when Pvt. W's company was called out for a dress parade one afternoon, he claimed he was the only one who showed up. Everyone else had gone into town.[48]

With their poor handle on the English language, these "Dutchmen" of Colonel Bausenwein's Fifty-Eighth Regiment were gullible, and natural targets for ridicule. Not very polished just now, they would soon prove they could fight and die as well as any native-born Ohioan at places like Fort Donelson, Shiloh, and Vicksburg.

False Start: Reprise

On January 11, at one in the morning, an unusual time for anyone to be up except for those on guard duty, Colonel Buckley made the rounds of the company captains and gave them orders. Their men were to fix two days' rations and be ready to march by nine.[49] Wallace Hoyt was doing duty this week as cook for his mess. He hurried to fix rations for the road and found time to fire off a last-minute letter to his mother telling her that the whole camp was astir and that they were on their way at last.[50] The orders had catapulted the Boys into high spirits.[51] Now they were getting somewhere. The stir had started that Friday evening in Governor Dennison's office when an urgent dispatch came in from General McClellan in Virginia. He needed every Ohio soldier that could be sent, and he needed them on the double-quick.[52] After threatening the village of Romney, in western Virginia, earlier in the month, rebel general Thomas Jackson was pressing in again, this time in full earnest. If Jackson took Romney, he would effectively block any coordinated movement between the severed halves of the Union army and continue his destructive raids on the Baltimore and Ohio Railroad track that ran alongside the Potomac, connecting Washington and the West.

Governor Dennison assured McClellan that he would start fourteen regiments of infantry on the road immediately.[53] The soldiers were packed and ready at the appointed hour, but Mr. Red Tape had failed to order up enough teams to cart all of them and all their baggage to the depot, and most of the day had run off the clock before the mistake could be set right.[54] The Giddings Regiment marched out the gates of Camp Chase in fine style, with the skillful musicians of one of the "Dutch" regiments leading the way. The soldiers of less lucky regiments lined up around the gate and passed the Twenty-Ninth Regiment through with cheer after cheer.[55] They had gone but a mile when a messenger rode up and told them the order had been countermanded.[56]

The Boys filed right and countermarched back to Camp Chase.[57] The Twenty-Ninth Regiment was praised for its efficiency in following the order, but to the men in the ranks the praise fell flat. This had been nothing more than another in a long line of false starts.[58] After a hot cup of coffee, spirits lifted, and the soldiers spent that evening in their normal fashion, gathered around the hot stove, cracking jokes, singing, and predicting what they would do to the rebels when they got the chance.[59] John G. Marsh promised his little sister that when they did get to the war, he would send her a lock of hair from the head of Jeff Davis.[60] To the more observant among them, the cat was out of the bag as to where they *might* eventually be headed. The Boys conjectured that they might be bound for any number of places in the war. The old Nineteenth Ohio was currently doing active service near Louisville, Kentucky. Carlin's battery of Conneaut men was down in Missouri, and other Ohio infantry regiments were doing service at a dozen more points. The Twenty-Ninth might be off to join any of them.

It had even been rumored that the Twenty-Ninth Ohio was headed for an unexciting post in Indian country, out in the dusty precincts of Ft. Leavenworth, Kansas. Had they proceeded this time, their destination would have been Romney, Virginia.[61] As it turned out, Romney was past saving by the time Mac's telegram came into Dennison's office the night before. Stonewall Jackson and his men had taken Romney earlier in the day and easily dispossessed the sick and dispirited Union force assigned to hold the place.⁶² Kelly's brigade, under the direction of its newly appointed commander, Gen. Frederick West Lander, loaded their baggage, burned what they could not carry, and beat it back down to safety on the Potomac below Cumberland, Maryland. There they went into a camp that they named Camp Kelly in honor of their former commander, Brig. Gen. Benjamin F. Kelly.⁶³

Paper-Collar Soldiers

The Boys were in a sour frame of mind when they were called out again. They had been summoned to parade in a grand review to mark the inauguration of Governor David Tod. They formed up brigade-style on State Street and with three other regiments marched onto the grounds of the lunatic asylum, which seemed a fitting location for what followed. They stood until nearly frozen, waiting for outgoing governor Dennison and governor-elect Tod to take their places on the reviewing stand. They marched by the front of the platform, not once but several times. The boys of Company G were lucky to be wearing mittens knitted for them by the loving hands of the ladies of Akron's Soldiers' Aid Society.⁶⁴ Most men had to stand in the ranks and suffer, warming bare hands beneath the flaps of their coats and stamping their feet to stave off frostbite, while officers of all ranks in each of the regiments were called forward one at a time and introduced to the new governor.⁶⁵ Buckley thought the Boys had showed themselves poorly.

The other regiments had done even worse. Even the *Ohio State Journal* had been forced to admit that the more recently organized outfits were deficient in their evolutions.⁶⁶ S. B., always on the lookout for someone to harpoon, targeted the ineptitude of the German adjutant who had been appointed to run the show.⁶⁷ He appeared to have been mounted aboard a drunken horse. The inept adjutant "managed to turn sixty two summer-saults—stood on his head for an hour—led his horse around the ring by the tail, and actually shouldered the horse and pulled off his boots (not the horse's) to salute the Governor."

Nathan Parmater summed up the men's feelings about being bothered to entertain dignitaries: "The boys think that when they wish to see them again, they had better come to us."⁶⁸ The soldiers covered the four cold miles to camp, crossed the grounds that by now had been churned by marching feet into a "vast sea of mud that had neither bottom nor shore," and went to their barracks to thaw and await developments.⁶⁹ There was generalized bellyaching that they had not enlisted to playact as white-glove soldiers for government men in stovepipe hats. In two short weeks, Columbus had lost its charm.

The Well-Seasoned Recruit

When the Twenty-Ninth arrived in Columbus it had been as balmy as spring. The day after they arrived, a damp wind pushed a steady mix of rain alternating with snow, chilling men to the bone and bringing on "hard" colds in half the men in the outfit.⁷⁰ Sixteen boys in Wallace Hoyt's company were sent to the post hospital.⁷¹ Ten days later the number reporting for sick call had risen to eighty.⁷² So many men were laid low that there were not enough men to hold roll call. After just two weeks in Camp Chase, the health of the regiment was under full assault and giving ground every day. Some of the men were suffering from camp fever, the catchall term for the host of diseases to which troops were exposed in large camps. Many of the soldiers had acquired racking coughs that would nag them throughout the war, and for some men the cough would never leave.⁷³ Those men not down with colds were breaking out in a disease with a track record of causing death in green troops: measles.⁷⁴

Miniepidemics of childhood diseases were common when soldiers first assembled with men from other regions and even with men from different areas of the same state. These first bouts with disease were expected, and troops were not considered well seasoned and ready for active service until they had passed through this first scourge of soldiering.⁷⁵ Of the two thousand regiments that would serve in the Federal army, not a single one escaped an outbreak of measles.⁷⁶ Lethal complications could and did develop. Ultimately, measles sent five thousand boys to their graves.⁷⁷ To assuage any alarm this might cause, the army issued a bulletin claiming that disease mortality in the army was less than that of any American city, whose population included the aged, children, and even babies. One Ohio editor scoffed at the report and tweaked the army for its sluggishness in moving against the enemy by saying that if low mortality was the government's objective, it had made a distinguished success.[78]

Amos Fifield's skills were soon recognized and he was appointed post surgeon, in charge of the entire camp. Before he took over, conditions in the post hospital had been less than ideal, but under his hand, medical affairs were straightened up to a degree that the men of other regiments who had lay languishing there came to regard him as a godsend.[79]

Before he was a private in Company I, twenty-year-old Elias Roshon had been a farm boy, like his friends in the Homerville squad, and like them he had always been healthy as a horse. However, four days after arriving here, Roshon, began to feel poorly.[80] Several boys in his shack had already broken out in measles. Over the next few days, Roshon got sicker and sicker with the symptoms that preceded the scabby proof of the malady, and after refusing to take the medicine the doctor prescribed, he was put into the post hospital. After six days of cough and fever, the measles started to come out on Elias, and come out fast. The crisis in the pathology of the disease had been reached, but Roshon confessed, "I feel awful mean today." While those soldiers who had escaped the disease spent their days drilling and lounging, Roshon lay in his bed, looking out at the cold rain and thinking more about his home than any time since he had been a soldier. Two weeks after he had begun to come down with the disease, Roshon was discharged from the hospital, although he was still not feeling up to par.

Luck was with the Twenty-Ninth at Camp Chase. Not a single soldier of the regiment died while they were encamped there. Columbus was as far as Jesse J. Rockwell, an eighteen-year-old private in Company B, would travel in this war, however. He took sick while the regiment was making final preparations to depart. In another few weeks, he would be dead.[81] The rest of the sick vowed to avoid the hospital at all hazard, and wheezed, coughed, and scratched at half-healed measles. In their first scrape with disease, the Giddings Regiment had dodged the bullet.

Two dozen enlisted men were left behind in the hospital, which would be a problem for them and for the regiment. The complex riddle of how a private with little or no cash was to go about transporting himself several hundred miles to the front was left to him to cipher. Several soldiers who had been made patients in the post hospital would never return to the regiment and would end up being listed as deserters.[82]

Farewell, Ohio, Farewell

A last-minute fine-tuning of the officer staff was made as the regiment readied itself to move into the war. James Treen had been elected first lieutenant by his men while at Camp Giddings and was a shoo-in to take Clemmer's place as its captain. Buckley preferred 2nd Lt. Jack Wright for the post.[83] Treen was competent at the helm of a canal boat, but in Buckley's opinion he could not steer soldiers. He wanted Wright leap-frogged over Treen to the rank of captain, and Treen kept in his post as first lieutenant. William Palmer Williamson, Palm as he was known to his many friends back home in Akron, was promoted from sergeant major of the regiment to second lieutenant of Company G, and regimental orderly Cary Russell moved up to fill Palm's post.[84]

On January 17 company and staff officers presented themselves at Buckley's tent for a quiet ceremony. Judge Chaffee of Jefferson, father-in-law of Lt. Everson J. Hurlburt, had come down from Jefferson to administer the oath of office to Lewis Buckley. Buckley then called forward each of the officers. One man after the other placed his left hand on the Bible, raised the other, and repeated, "I do solemnly swear or affirm that I will faithfully support the Constitution of the United States and the Constitution of the State of Ohio . . ."[85]

A week after the fruitless march to the depot, orders came down for the regiment to move out, and this time the order would not be countermanded. On January 17, 1862, the *Ohio State Journal* broke the news that the Giddings Regiment, along with the Sixty-Second and Sixty-Sixth Ohio Regiments, had received their marching orders. They were to leave for the seat of war the following day, with the Sixty-Seventh Ohio scheduled to start after them. Their destination was reported again as Romney, in western Virginia.[86]

They had numbered over nine hundred men and officers when they left Jefferson two weeks earlier to come to this place. Sickness had already reduced that number by fifty-five.[87]

The moment they had been awaiting for months was finally at hand. But as Nathan Parmater explained, "Orders to prepare to leave were obeyed reluctantly, for many of the boys do not wish to go until they are paid."[88] The flaw in the regiment's accounting discovered by the army paymaster meant that the company clerks had to sharpen their pencils and redo the arithmetic. Worse, it meant that the Twenty-Ninth would have to wait until the next pay period ended before they could resubmit the books. An anonymous correspondent using the name Mr. Lobby had come down to cover the regiment's departure. In a phrase, he found the soldiers penniless and ragged. He reported that the officers were so impoverished that they hadn't the cash to buy either saddles or bridles for their horses, leaving the reader with the comic picture of the officers riding to the Columbus depot bareback, like any simple farm boy. When back issues of the newspapers in which Lobby's observations were published finally caught up with them, he was attacked for being a naive amateur and alarmist who had no business broadcasting the state of the soldiers' pocketbooks to the public.[89]

The soldiers countered that they were in as good a condition as any other regiment at Camp Chase—a true enough statement since the Giddings Regiment was not the only one that had not been paid. On the same news page, a soldier pointed out to the civilians at home that he and his comrades were so poor they could not afford a penny to buy a postage stamp. Clearly, men like Jack Wright believed that it was all right for the soldier to express in print his worry that his children were crying for bread, but he did not want any outsiders taking potshots at his poverty.[90]

Capt. Edward Hayes had come down with the fever while at Camp Chase, and when the regiment moved out, he was left behind.[91] He lay in his quarters completely unattended for twenty-four hours. A hungry wharf rat the size of a terrier wandered in and bit this descendant of famous patriots through the nose while he lay in his delirium. Several Reserve newspapers picked up the story, with one editor running its lurid details under the headline "Volunteers Exposed to Rats."[92] Akron booster extraordinaire Gen. Lucius V. Bierce had come to the helpless Hayes's rescue and taken him to his favorite Columbus hotel, where he was properly looked after until he recovered. Hayes admitted he had brought only seventy dollars to Camp Chase, thinking that would last him until he was paid the six hundred dollars the government owed him. But his money had soon run out, and he found himself sick, broke, and alone. The *Telegraph* reporter added his own comment to the exposé: Hayes had been made so poor by government bungling that he didn't even have the money to hire someone to keep the rats from devouring him alive as he lay on his cot.[93]

One evening a few weeks hence, the men sat around the evening campfire talking of this and that. Soldiers from other regiments had gathered round to add their two bits, and these visiting sages counseled them that they should have staged a mutiny at Columbus. As Jack Wright remembered it, "We are told by some knowing croakers that we ought to have claimed our rights at Columbus, that we ought to have refused to move until we were paid; until we had dress coats for privates, until we had good tents . . . that we should have had some influential politician lobbying for us."[94] Bristling and defensive, Jack answered that he, for one, had sworn to serve his country and obey orders, and that was good enough for him, while in the next breath he walloped the same old nail once again: "Does it require the wire-pulling, sneaking, conniving, meddling of a dirty politician to induce the Government to pay her soldiers?"[95] The situation had become so grievous and potentially volatile that Buckley wrote to the adjutant general expressing his fear that "trouble" might erupt were the men not paid before they exited Ohio.[96]

Despite their misgivings about leaving, the Boys shouldered their gear and marched out of Camp Chase. The thermometer was dropping, and the sky was throwing a mix of rain and snow that reduced itself after a while to buckshot-size sleet that popped against kepi visors and coat sleeves.[97] There was no music to pipe the way this time around. The regiment's band had stowed its instruments and slogged along with the rest. With heads pulled back turtlelike into coat collars against the weather, the soldiers picked their way through sooty snow piles and arrived at the depot in Columbus at midday.

A few months back they had been individuals, farmers and mechanics mostly. Now they were a compact blue army. They could perform complicated drills while touching shoulders with a thousand other soldiers, mount a guard, cook and care for themselves, and follow orders, generally. That they had not been paid rankled everyone from colonel to private, but surely the government would come through and care for them as it had promised.

The bad taste in their mouths over the slights done some of them back in the long-ago day's of McClellan's campaign in western Virginia with the old Nineteenth Ohio faded, and the accusations that they were men of too lofty ideals and too little fight in them stung slightly less now that they were on their way. The recruiting skirmishes, enmity toward the Giddings Regiment's detractors who had tried to derail their organization, and frustration over their protracted stay in Jefferson had all begun to dissolve with time and distance. They were armed and equipped, not to their complete satisfaction, but in truth they had made out better than many Ohio regiments. In each company, and high up in the regiment, officers were in place that the privates had chosen to lead them, and the few petty rivalries over office seemed long behind them. They had everything required to fight, and fight well, and, courtesy of J. R. Giddings, they had a special purpose and identity. All they had asked all along was a good field and a fair chance at victory, and they now had that in their sights.

They stood around in the mud for two hours, attracting little notice. They were just another regiment on its way out of town. Finally, their train pulled in and the Boys piled aboard. Trailed out behind this locomotive of the Ohio Central was a string of first-class carriages, with red-velvet upholstered seats and a woodstove in each well-lit and cheery car.[98] Most of the Boys still hadn't a clue as to their exact destination, only that they were all going down to Dixie's Land.[99]

PART II

With the Eastern Armies

8

A Good "Breaking-In"

WINTER ON THE UPPER POTOMAC, 1862

Set Down in the Mud

The regiment rode in first-class cars on the Central Ohio Railroad eastbound out of Columbus.[1] A half day out of Columbus it was clear they were headed east, in the direction of the war's big things. At the end of this road lay the land of newspaper headlines and mighty armies. Their competitors in Wade's Second Ohio Cavalry had drawn a far less lucky card and were putting in their time performing dusty, tedious scouts down in Kansas, far from the war's exciting center.[2]

They dismounted the cars at Bellaire, on the Ohio River, unloaded themselves and their baggage, loaded it onto wagons, and unloaded and loaded again onto to a ferry that took them across the river and to the western Virginia side. The quality of the transport furnished them by the Baltimore and Ohio Railroad for the next leg of their journey did not please them. They were crammed onto dilapidated freight cars better suited to hauling cattle to market than men to war.[3] Rough planks had been installed down each side for seating, and one ran the center. If a man wished to recline, it was on a floor covered in wet straw.[4] When the soldiers of the Sixty-Seventh Ohio, coming up behind them, saw the condition of the cars, they balked and would not get on. These cattle cars were the last straw, but the real issue was they had not been paid. They would sit the war out right here at this rail siding if need be, and the government could go to hell.[5] Lt. Col. Alvin Voris gave the stump speech of his life, and a mutiny was averted.

As the Twenty-Ninth's train ascended the west slopes of the Allegheny Mountains, the weather turned cold and rainy. The cars leaked, both through the roof and the sidewalls from which some of the boards had been knocked off, but riding in them was preferable to squatting in the open on a flat car, which some of the Boys were forced to endure for want of enough boxcars.[6] Capt. Josiah Wright believed shady government contractors were responsible.[7]

The Boys were flatlanders and few of them had ever been in such a country. They had entered a region of deep-cut valleys and mountains so high their flanks disappeared into the clouds before a soldier's eye could measure their full height. The track hunted the course of creek bottoms when it could, with the thick brush crowding in so close a man could snatch a handful of it through the open door. The steam engine struggled to climb passes and flew down the reverse pitch like a runaway bobsled, with brakes screeching and the soldiers hooting. The train twisted along a road the Boys thought the most crooked they had ever seen, steel or dirt.[8]

Each of these miles-wide valleys had side spurs, anyone of which could conceal an entire army. The valleys grew successively wider as the train picked up and followed the Potomac River. In the easternmost of these ran the fabled Shenandoah. But they were not going that far south and east. They were entering a neighborhood more forbidding than the Shenandoah. Here, the valleys were steeper and narrower, the weather more tempestuous. Most of them were farmers, and on this first journey, and on all the others that would follow, they surveyed the land with the interest of prospective buyers. Capt. Josiah Wright rendered his opinion: "I can say it consisted of log cabins, dilapidated frame houses, dirty women and children, and big hills dipped in rain and mud and hung up to dry where they couldn't dry. . . . If a man owned a thousand acres of such land, and should show himself in Summit County, he would be sure to be put in the poorhouse."[9] Why the rebels would want to fight to keep such a worthless country they could not fathom. Their adversary in this campaign and in those that would occupy them in the coming months valued every square inch of this countryside very highly.

Gen. Thomas "Stonewall" Jackson had concluded the season's campaign in this area bordering the upper Potomac River with most of his goals achieved. His men had torn up track and burned buildings, rolling stock, and bridges. Presently, the entire stretch of the Baltimore and Ohio from below Cumberland on the upper Potomac clear down to Harpers Ferry, which guarded one of the vital approaches to Washington, had been cut. The line was the main conduit of commerce running from the Chesapeake back into the Ohio heartland. There were detours around the broken stretch, but they were costly and consumptive of time. What the Federals might do about it, and when, had been debated at army headquarters and in the White House for months. In the meantime, a mountain of goods bound for the East were accumulating in Cumberland, depriving the Union of their use, and providing a fat target for the rebels.

Jackson held Romney, twenty miles below Cumberland, Maryland. From it, he could prey on the railroad and block Federal incursions from the west aimed at the Shenandoah valley. Jackson was becoming a man to be feared. His mere appearance on the skyline above Romney the week before the Twenty-Ninth Ohio arrived in this theater was enough to convince the Federals to abandon it to him. Jackson left a portion of his command in Romney and returned with the bulk of his men to Winchester, where he was setting up winter camp.

Brig. Gen. Frederick W. Lander had the misfortune of being in command of the troops that handed over Romney. Giving up without a fight had not been his idea. Officials in Washington had him ordered to leave.[10] After departing Romney, Lander high-tailed it back toward Cumberland. The week before the Twenty-Ninth Ohio arrived, he had staked out a camp at Patterson's Creek, six miles below Cumberland, which his many friends in the eastern newspaper establishment emphasized, was on the Virginia side of the Potomac. If the overly cautious plodders in Washington would give him the resources, he would march straightaway to Winchester and destroy Jackson forthwith. In the eyes of many, Lander was just the sort of general the army needed.

Lander's name had always been a harbinger of success in battle, but he was now clinging to his toehold on Virginia soil with too few men. A news correspondent traveling with him reported, "If we [Lander's division] are conquered, Ohio must ask why we are left here without reinforcements, and Gen. Lander in command, who swears all the rebels in Virginia, shall not make him cross the Potomac."[11]

Lander's force was too small, by his accounting, to both guard the railroad and drive the rebels away from the tracks, and he demanded more men. Maj. Gen. Nathaniel P. Banks had a large army sitting on the safe side of the Potomac, near Harpers Ferry, but he was not going to loan him any. The obvious source of reinforcements was Ohio. There were whole regiments at Camp Chase waiting for a summons, and the railroad remained open in that direction. Lander leaned on McClellan, McClellan leaned on General Buckingham, back in Columbus, and before long, the Twenty-Ninth Ohio was on a train bound for Patterson's Creek.[12]

George McClellan, their tentative and grandiloquent commander at Rich Mountain, had ridden the newspaper headlines generated from his small western Virginia victories directly into Washington, where he had been placed in command of the entire Army of the Potomac. Lincoln had charged McClellan with the responsibility of turning the legions of dispirited amateurs who had run from Bull Run into an army capable of taking Richmond and putting a quick end to the Confederacy. Lincoln also wanted the B&O Railroad repaired and set to running again, but McClellan was dubious about investing the money and men to fix it and keep it open. After all, a small raiding party with a bucket of coal oil, a lucifer match, and some pry bars could wreck a bridge whenever they desired.

Their train dropped down onto the north branch of the Potomac River, on the Maryland border, passed through Cumberland, and several miles below there, it stopped. The Boys had reached the end of the line. The railroad jumped the Potomac to the Virginia side at a point where Patterson's Creek came down out of the Virginia mountains, crossed over it, and ran the rest of the way to Baltimore. Jackson had wrecked both bridges here and torn up the track from this point east. Before debarking the train, they were issued ammunition for the very first time, a clear sign that they were now in the land of their enemy.[13] Soldiers rubbed the cinders from eyes fogged by three nights without sleep and stepped down.

The enlisted men hadn't a clue as to their destination on this march until they slogged into Camp Kelly, down on the flats on the Maryland side of the river.[14] The area assigned to them for camp was like everything else around here, many inches deep in mud. The *New York Times* ran a news flash written by a field correspondent for the *Cleveland Herald* on the scene at Patterson's Creek. "To-day, our force was joined by the Twenty-ninth and Sixty-second Ohio Regiments, and two heartier looking regiments I think never entered the state of Virginia."[15] The Giddings Regiment had made the pages of a big eastern newspaper without firing a shot.

A General Who Fights

They were now members of Lander's division, responsible for holding the far-right flank of the Army of the Potomac. Frederick West Lander was one of the best-known men in America: explorer of the Far West, Indian fighter, road builder, and top draw on the lyceum circuit, where he lectured on his many adventures. All that accomplished and he was not yet forty years old. McClellan and Lander had been close friends, and when McClellan came east, he brought him along. The Boys of the Twenty-Ninth who had been in the Nineteenth Ohio had last seen Lander scouting the way up Rich Mountain for them, and once seen, it would be impossible to forget him. He stood six feet tall, wore his hair long in the style of the frontiersman, and preferred a tight uniform that showed his muscular physique to good advantage. He was expert with both bowie knife and fists and could out-cuss and out-drink the roughest muleskinner in the army. One of his orderlies remembered him as the wickedest man he had ever met.[16] He also had a tender side. He was an intimate of leading artists and poets of that day and was himself a composer of melancholic poetry. He had captured the heart of the darling of the American stage, Jean Davenport, and had recently married her.[17]

At the battle of Philippi, in western Virginia, he caught the public's eye by riding down on the rebels like a Plains Indian and getting off pistol shots while ducked low behind his horse's neck. He had gotten newspaper coverage a second time for the part he'd taken in containing the Federal disaster at Ball's Bluff.[18] Lander had been shot in the leg in the aftermath of that fight, and the bullet had carried a piece of his bootstrap into the wound. The wound looked healed, but Lander had not yet returned to normal. He had been a loose cannon as McClellan saw it, and now, with the plentiful soldiers and matériel being sent to him at Patterson's Creek, he was a loaded loose cannon.

In later years, the soldiers of the Twenty-Ninth Ohio would remember that they had spent their first winter in the war guarding the railroad, which in a narrow sense was true. The reality was they had taken part in a grander strategy; at least that is how the general who commanded them here saw it. Lander was confident that if McClellan would turn him loose, he would get everything done in a single week that army planners thought required many. He could reopen the railroad, retake Romney, and march cross-country and knock out Jackson at Winchester. The plan finally agreed to, and the one in which the Giddings Boys were to have a part, called for a more conservative approach. Lander was authorized to rebuild the railroad to his east and to continue planning to knock out Jackson, but he would have to move cautiously.[19]

Back in the peaceful days, when the trains still ran, Patterson's Creek was a day's trip from Washington, a hundred miles to the east the way the crow flew, but it might just as well have been ten thousand miles, given the faraway look of this place. Camp Kelly was jammed tight into the river flats and up on the narrow shelves hanging above. There were several thousand men here already, Ohioans mostly. Just across the Potomac, near the wreckage of the bridge crossing the creek, was the camp of the Seventh Ohio Volunteer Infantry.

The Seventh Ohio had been recruited back in the Reserve as a ninety-day outfit, but not far into their career, their commander had persuaded them to convert to the three years' service. They had been actively campaigning in the mountains directly to the west since June, and in comparison to most of the Boys of the Twenty-Ninth, the Seventh Ohio's men were already battle-hardened veterans. In command of their brigade was the Seventh Ohio's organizer and leader, forty-year-old former Ravenna, Ohio, fur trader, Erastus B. Tyler.[20] The Sixty-Sixth Ohio Infantry would join them in a while. These three regiments would fight side by side for the next three years. Soon after they arrived, it was rumored that Buckley would lead the Third Brigade, but Tyler got the job. Buckley approached him and pledged, "I consider the fortunes of the Twenty-Ninth, either for weal or for woe with the Third Brigade."[21]

The scene visible to the soldiers in the Twenty-Ninth Ohio as they settled in was both dismal and impressive. Miles of white tents stood sharp against the black mud and the pine-covered hills. The rain fell without letup, drenching everyone and everything. Cloud bottoms covered the surrounding hills and the river itself in a shroud. Soldiers by the hundreds were digging channels in the mud into which they hoped water would run, instead of across the dirt floors of their tents. Muskets and cannon were being fired continually to keep the barrels dry, in readiness for the combat it was believed might begin at any moment. The place was miserable, but the scene was one any romantic might enjoy. "Seelye," an anonymous newspaper correspondent of Company A to the Jefferson newspaper, wrote, "If we could only forget the mud it would be a situation that could not fail to catch the eye of the poet and painter. The swollen river, the canal and its locks, and the railroad winding among the hills covered with green mountain pines, that bristling green stand like upright spears, altogether is a picture that enchants as long as the eye gazes."[22]

He referred to the Chesapeake and Ohio Canal, an engineering feat for its day that ran across the rear of their camp. The shore of the Potomac lay several hundred yards to their front. The fresh, white-timbered superstructure of the newly rebuilt bridge stood out in the half light with rope-and-plank scaffolding dangling off the sides.[23] If the Boys wanted to cross over to the other side to visit friends in the Seventh Ohio, or explore, they had to wait for a train headed that way, or walk on the planks laid end to end between the rails.[24] Their diminutive but brave adjutant, Comfort Chaffee, volunteered to carry a message posthaste across the river, and for a moment thousands of troops on both sides paused in their work and looked up to see him racing his horse along the narrow planks, the swirling dark waters of the Potomac far below. When he safely reached the end of the span, the soldiers on the flats and hillsides gave him three cheers. Despite its discomforts, Lander believed this location perfect for his plan. With reinforcements now on hand, and more arriving everyday, he looked things over and concluded that he could hold this soggy place against twenty thousand of the enemy.[25]

The Giddings Boys, following the lead of soldiers arrived just before them, uncrated axes and went to work on the surrounding slopes cutting bundles of pine boughs. These "Maryland feathers" were preferable to trying to sleep on a blanket unrolled into the mud of a floorless tent. But even with a scaffold of pine boughs, the Boys awoke most mornings to find several inches of water running beneath them.

Passing Time

Within a few days of their arrival, the first letter from the front by a soldier of the Twenty-Ninth Ohio appeared in the Jefferson newspaper. It reported their long journey had ended safely, the details of what they were doing, and, as near as could be figured, where they were located. Seelye began his letter by admitting that the citizens of Jefferson might not want to hear anything more about the outfit that had once been their darling. He felt free to observe now, that the village itself had been divided in its support of Wade's cavalry versus the Giddings Regiment.[26] In the weeks that followed their departure from Ohio, the Giddings Regiment was front-page news in Akron and in Jefferson too, despite any lingering bad feelings against them in the village. Some single editions featured up to a half dozen long, chatty letters from the officers and enlisted men.

Several soldiers considered themselves de facto correspondents for their favorite newspaper back in the Reserve and wrote directly to the editors. The friends and families of others felt at liberty to personally walk letters addressed to them down to the newspaper office, where they were fitted in with reports of military affairs elsewhere. None of the correspondents in the regiment seemed to know anything of Lander's wider fame, and if they did, they were not humbled by it. They knew only that "we are in Lander's Brigade, and it is said he is a fighting man."[27] Rumors of a chance to prove whether that was true were being churned out by the camp gossip mill before they'd finished unpacking.[28]

An attack on Romney was in the offing. The Giddings Boys were put under marching orders the day they arrived. Three days' rations were cooked and stowed in every haversack, and rifles kept close so that a soldier could lay his hands on it in a hurry. They might be starting out this very night.[29] But the mix of snow and rain continued falling, and movement was impossible.

While everyone waited for the weather to clear, the soldiers continued their adaptation to life in a large army camp. They could not practice their drill, and lacking any other military duty other than guard mounting, soldiers were faced with long hours and nothing in particular to fill them. Capt. Josiah "Jack" Wright was carving a pipe from the root of the mountain laurel; he planned to send it to the editors of the *Summit Beacon*, to prove that his knife was at least as sharp as his tongue.[30] Chaplain Hurlburt moved into Wright's tent, leaving him to wonder whether the reverend had taken this action because he was a good man, or a bad man in need of spiritual supervision.

Soldiers collected in knots to argue rumors up and down. The few newspapers coming into camp were passed around until the print had been rubbed off by handling and by the rain. During any interlude in precipitation, there was sightseeing in the surrounding hills, and the enlisted men continued their experiments in cooking. Most soldiers, though, filled their days with letter writing or sleep. For those who smoked, oak leaves would have to suffice. Universal poverty had placed a plug of the genuine article from the sutler's establishment beyond reach.[31] Colonel Clark endeared himself to the common soldiers by sharing what he had left from his personal supply. The drinking spree in which some of them had indulged back in Columbus was suspended for the time being. The enlisted men were too strapped to buy a small square of shortcake, let alone a strong drink.

Every regiment had a band and a corps of fifers and drummers, and all seemed to want to practice simultaneously and at all hours.[32] No soldier who experienced it, however hardened he became, grew tired of the touching ritual of day's end. From far up the river the sound of taps slid down and was taken up in turn by musicians in every regiment. A drummer boy stepped into the company street to play the "tearing roll," followed by a measured tap—tap—tap, announcing it was time for every soldier to put out his light and go to bed.[33]

After living for several days in a depressing half light, the men had concluded that the sun did not shine in this "God-forsaken part of the globe."[34] They settled into camp life with some amount of complaining, but overall their spirits were high. Captain Wright assured the folks back home in Summit County, "We are well and hearty, and don't care a snap for anybody, nor any other man. We, almost all of us, are most extremely ready for all necessary brushes, except shoe brushes, those we have no further need of."[35]

Conditions had not dampened their appetite for battle. Pvt. Elias Roshon promised his father, "We will give them shot and shell, and land them on the other side of Jordan."[36] If they did not march today, it would be soon from the looks of things. They were waiting only for the streams in the mountains above to recede enough to allow crossing, and then they would march.[37] By Roshon's overoptimistic count, there were thirty thousand troops gathered here already, and he had heard that another fourteen thousand were on their way from Ohio.[38] Within a few weeks, Lander's division would grow to over fifteen thousand, on paper at least, far more than the ten thousand men normally allotted an infantry division.[39] Any soldier would be duly impressed by the congregation of armed men at this place, and trains were arriving with fresh reinforcements from the West with soldiers standing atop the boxcars hollering greetings to those on the ground. The Twenty-Ninth Illinois pulled in, loaded with young fellows so powerful looking that they put Seelye in mind of the old Rail Splitter himself.[40]

Unlike back home in the Reserve, where the white-tailed deer was rarely seen, these hills still held a "right smart chance" of game.[41] A group of six soldiers went hunting, to have something to do and to supplement their rations. Buckley had given them permission, with the warning that they would all be thrown in the guardhouse if they returned empty-handed. They crossed the bridge and ventured into the hills. Night was coming on when soldier Perry Decker raised his Enfield and downed a fine buck, which the Boys took turns dragging back to camp.[42] Other hunting parties returned to camp with the occasional turkey, and in some cases, "a deer with the wool on," which was soldier code for a farmer's sheep.[43]

They had yet to fire a shot at the rebels, but their muskets were already causing wounds. Four men would be lost to the regiment during their stay here, all by accidental discharge of their rifles. In each case, the resulting injuries were identical: loss of the trigger finger of the right hand. Each of these men had been alone, either hunting or performing picket duty.[44] One soldier claimed that he had been using his musket as a walking stick, fingers wrapped around the business end of the barrel to get up a steep hillside when the trigger caught on a laurel bush.[45] However these incidents occurred, Chaplain Hurlburt was keeping count and reported the most recent in late February by saying, "This makes finger shot-off No. 4 in the 29th."[46] One soldier thus wounded failed to return from his medical leave and was never heard from again, causing some to speculate whether the loss of his finger had really been an accident.[47]

The Giddings Regiment, and the other fresh outfits gathered at Camp Kelly, were by all standards green as grass, and Lander heartily disliked untested troops. He was even unhappy with the weapons they had brought. He considered the Belgian-made muskets, the Twenty-Ninth's Pondir musket included, to be the scourge of the army.[48] It had been discovered through hard field usage that they misfired, or would not fire at all. The proficiency of the gunners being sent to him also fell below his standard. In his opinion, his artillery could not hit a thing.[49]

After years out west associating with trappers and traders, Lander was hardly a dilettante, but he looked over the troops rapidly accumulating around him and concluded that his command was more of an armed mob than an army.[50] Indiana troops, known for their freebooting ways in western Virginia, were coming in, and Pennsylvanians of the 110th Pennsylvania were also added to Tyler's brigade. The Pennsylvanians had been in the war just a few weeks, but they had lost no time in establishing a reputation as roughnecks. They had been sent to the town of Hancock to defend it from Jackson's depredations, but they destroyed it as thoroughly as Jackson could.[51]

Despite their inferior equipment, inexperience, and lack of discipline, Lander was confident these men would do what was asked of them.

Riding the Locomotive

A week into their stay, they were assigned legitimate soldier work. Against the cold and damp, the enlisted men wore the wool coats issued in Jefferson, and some who could afford them, officers mostly, pulled on waterproof coats and leggings. They got over the river and joined the Seventh Ohio. This was to be a reconnaissance-in-force to feel out the enemy presence between Patterson's Creek and the South Branch bridge, where the south fork of the Potomac joined the main river at a place called Green Springs.[52] They were the first to travel on this portion of the line since Jackson had wrecked it the preceding summer. No one knew what might lie in their path. A train arrived within ten minutes and they all piled aboard.

Colonel Tyler invited Captain Fitch of Company A to stand on the catwalk hanging from the nose of the locomotive with him and serve as lookout, although they could see little, blinded as they were by the worst rain and sleet storm any of them had ever seen. The camps of the many regiments were passed, then the picket line of Lander's division, and after that they were in a country belonging to the rebels.[53] They steamed forward at a slow trot, stopping periodically to let off squads of men to beat the side valleys for rebels. Other soldiers, fully rigged, and with canteens and sundry gear banging at their sides, ran out ahead of the train to check the condition of the track, signaling back that it was safe to proceed.

Eight miles up the line they came into a tiny hamlet, deserted except for a solitary resident who told them the rebel cavalry had passed through a few days before. At South Branch Bridge, not so much as a stray dog was visible. Tyler threw out a skirmish line that awoke a few rebels, but they vanished into the hills. As luck would have it, the rebels had left behind sizeable quantities of oats and corn, enough to fill four boxcars, and the soldiers set to work loading it aboard. Burning buildings was strictly against orders, as was the seizing or molestation of any rebel property without authorization from the very top. By the time the Twenty-Ninth Ohio got down from the cars, it was nearly dark, but the place was well lit. The store houses were already burning. According to Sgt. John Marsh, this had been the work of the Seventh Ohio.[54] Next, a secesh house went up in flames; accidentally, it was reported facetiously, by a careless soldier's lantern. The scene they had created was taken by most as grand: soldiers running hither and thither in the rain, flames roaring, the shadows of burning buildings and soldiers tangled up in the steam and smoke.[55] Having completed their work, the train started back to Camp Kelly tail end first.

They paused where men of Captain Fitch's company had been ordered out on scout, and Fitch cupped his hands and yelled against the rain and darkness for them to come in. Eleven men did not return, but it would not be wise to linger here, and there was nothing for it but to push on for camp. Two days came and went and the men Fitch had left behind had not returned. He organized a search party and set out on foot to bring them back. When found, the boys did not seem any the worse for wear. They had drawn what rations they needed from secesh in the neighborhood.

On returning from their first foray into enemy country, the Boys looked for a dry place to sit down and share their first adventure in real soldiering with the folks at home. John Marsh gave all of the details to his family and got back a rebuke from his sister. To her, the outing sounded like plain mischief. He tried to explain that the warehouses to which the torch had been applied were mostly empty anyway. As for the rest of the destruction: "I am very sorry Hester don't approve of burning & destroying the rebel property; perhaps if she would inform the Secretary of War, or Gen. McClellan of her scruples, they would take some action to have it stopped."[56] As far as Marsh was concerned, the Virginians were just beginning to receive their due.

Frozen Mountains

A week later, with the rain and snow finally let up, a general movement was again ordered, and Camp Kelly began to boil with activity. They were on their way to oust the rebels from Romney. The soldiers were rousted from their tents at five in the morning. Baggage, including their tents and cooking utensils, was to follow them on another train. The locomotive that was to take them down the line pulled a string of "hog cars," and the Boys rode them down to Green Springs. The rest of the way to Romney would be covered on foot. Lander would lead the remainder of his command to Romney via the main road.[57] Tyler's brigade would take the back roads there.

The climb out of the valley had carried them into a country as elevated and frigid as the Alps. Capt. Josiah Wright found the air up at these heights so thick with frost that he could bite it, and it could bite him back.[58] In campaigns through here a few weeks before, soldiers of both sides had had to stay awake at night and make endless circles around a tree just to keep the blood flowing. Some men had frozen stiff as statues, still clutching their muskets. The damp chill weather they had complained of at Camp Kelly had been merely a temporary thaw, and the coldest winter in western Virginia's history had returned.[59]

There were frequent stops in which the road had to be cleared of soldiers to allow the cavalry and artillery to pass to the front. To escape being run down by artillery and cavalry passing to the front, soldiers jumped down into the water-filled ditches. Before long, although it was against standing orders, they tore down fence rails and built giant bonfires.[60] With soldiers stopping too regularly to make fires, they made only five miles and halted at midday in a high meadow.[61] Here, they would spend their first night in the field as soldiers.

They set to work pulling down haystacks, wrapped themselves in hay, and lay down around fires to sleep. They had just tucked themselves in when Buckley called them shortly after midnight: "Fall in, Twenty-Ninth." They shouldered weapons and started off in the direction of Romney at a trot.

Lander had come up to Romney and found the rebels had recently fled. He wanted Tyler to get his command up to the intersection of the Romney road and the Winchester pike. Jackson's men would soon be passing on their flight back to Winchester, and Tyler was to bag the lot of them. It sounded simple enough on paper, but countless streams snaked through this valley of the Little Cacapon River, crossing the road a score of times. Most of these watercourses were not bridged and were too fast flowing to freeze. Men already chilled deep into their bones stumbled along in the dark and waded streams as high as their belt buckles. Some men tripped and fell headlong into the water and had to be reeled in by their comrades. With no time to stop and build fires, wet wool froze to the hardness of boiler plate, and the soldiers trudged along like tin men, growing a thicker layer of ice at every stream.

The sun rose through an ice fog, sun dogs slanting down on each side of it, predictive of still colder weather. They had reached the Winchester pike, a few miles east of Romney.[62] A scouting party was sent ahead and the regiment stamped its feet and waited. Intelligence came back that the rebels had gotten to this crossroads before them and escaped; the bird had flown. John Marsh reported their frustration: "They gave us the slip, their forces numbering over eight thousand strong, vamoosed over the rough and rugged rocks and rippling hills, the ragged rascals ran, being so wild that we could not get within gunshot of them."[63]

They marched back to the meadow they had left in the dead of night, arriving there as the light was failing and the thermometer sinking. Men had fallen out on the march back and gone instantly to sleep. Just as quickly, they had frozen fast to the ground. Friends had to pry them free.[64] This camping place would be known by many names: Camp Steele, Camp Haystack, Heights of Hampshire, Pine Levels, Camp Misery, Breezy Heights, and Camp Starvation. To most men, "the Levels" seemed adequately descriptive; it appeared to be the only horizontal real estate in this tilted country.[65]

When the Twenty-Ninth Ohio marched out of Camp Kelly, Seelye had been ordered to stay behind and count stores.[66] He admitted he had not been present in ancient times to witness the exodus of the chosen people out of Egypt, but the departure of Lander's army from Camp Kelly, which he did witness, could not have exceeded it in grandeur or scale.[67] When he saw the soldiers pile their tents and blankets next to the track and steam away, he felt a throb in his gut that this had been a mistake. Several days passed and he saw their baggage still sitting where they had deposited it. His friends were out there somewhere in the frigid mountains nearly as bare as the day they were born. He hitched a ride on a train going as far as French's Store, and got off to walk the rest of the way to Tyler's camp. The way there was well marked by heaps of smoldering fence rails.

Seelye made his way up to the high bench where the Boys were camped. He cautioned the folks back home to take the stories conveyed to them in letters from sons and husbands with a grain of salt. Soldiers were inclined to exaggerate. Some soldiers delighted in sending home stories that would cause their mothers to cry "La, me! Did you ever?"[68] But there was enough in his account of hard conditions the Boys had suffered on their all-night march to trap Jackson, and in their camp at the Levels to alarm even skeptical mothers. There was enough misery in it to wreck men's constitutions by the dozens, and many of them would soon be applying for medical discharges, claiming they had contracted rheumatism in these mountains. A soldier's claim that he suffered from rheumatism was difficult to prove or disprove. Medical science believed exposure to cold and wet could cause it. Cynics believed it to be the malady of goldbricks.

Seelye had not gone far when he began to see familiar faces. Lt. E. B. Howard and several of his men had taken over a blacksmith shop and were shoeing the regiment's horses. The owner no longer needed it; he was locked up back in the stockade at Camp Kelly under suspicion of aiding the rebels. Further on, Seelye came to a log cabin in which Clark, Dr. Fifield, and Adjutant Chaffee were quartered. Colonel Clark was standing outside personally handing out the daily ration of salt pork, crackers, and coffee. Seelye had lugged a bag of mail up the mountainside, and when that was discovered, the regiment crowded round him. Those who did not receive a letter walked away with head down and hands in pockets, displaying a sadness that pulled at Seelye's emotions.

Several companies shared quarters in a small white-clapboard Methodist church; others set up camp inside two barns and a house. The last three companies to organize at Camp Gidding had drawn the short straw. Their boys built shanties using fence corners for two walls, and rails covered with pine branches for a roof.[69] Notwithstanding circumstances, they judged themselves to be comfortably situated.[70] Some soldiers reported that rations were scarce, just enough of a supply of salt pork and waterproof crackers to stave off actual starvation, but some soldiers reported the supply as plentiful.

The farms surrounding them were well stocked with herds of cattle and sheep. Despite the prohibition against molesting civilian property, Seelye noted that the ground was covered with shucked-off feathers and the hides and bones of cattle and sheep. Beehives chock-full of honey made their way mysteriously into camp. The companies taking up lodging in one of the barns first prepared it by slaughtering the sixty or so chickens that lived there.[71] All told, although the weather was atrocious, Private Roshon noted, "we made them feed us good while we stayed with them we had a good time milching the cows."[72] Generally, regardless of how the veterans might look back at it years later, they were faring quite well.[73] The weather was another matter. Temperatures fell to zero at night and recovered little heat during the day. Drill was out of the question. Soldiers were too busy avoiding death by freezing. Most boys occupied their time here cutting down trees and breaking limbs and branches into firewood. As rations grew short and the weather colder, bonds were welded from shared privation, at least in some companies.

There had been a quasi-mutiny in Capt. Edward Hayes's company. Hayes had been laid low by sickness as the regiment had been packing to leave Columbus and could not join them on their trip to the Potomac. With time on their hands, his men sat around their fires at Camp Kelly and began to suppose that Hayes had taken the easy way out. He was resting on clean sheets while they slept in the mud. They had been duped into enlisting his company, and were it not for him, they might be enjoying quarters in the arms of some other regiment posted anywhere but here. He returned to them emaciated and pale, which was proof to some of his men that he had not been playing possum.[74] Some of the men would not relent in their suspicions. They had gotten up a petition, signed by many of the enlisted men demanding that he resign. He persuaded the hardheaded among them to hold their petition in abeyance until they had seen his leadership in one battle. After that, he would submit to their will.[75]

Hardship stripped a man down to his essentials, so that his idiosyncrasies could be easily seen, and comical but affectionate nicknames were being assigned appropriate to them. One unkempt soldier who had somehow gotten himself dirtier than the rest was called Mud Hen.[76] Eighteen-year-old Pvt. Wm. D. Haynes was saddled with the nickname Joshua R. Giddings, for what reason can only be guessed.[77] The genius of the company was "Beauregard." Down the road a ways, Beauregard's superiority would get him into serious difficulty, and no one would find anything comic in his punishment. In this icy place, they were learning to lift themselves above difficulty, and the outward sign of that was their friendly joshing. One soldier seen trying to break hardtack with his teeth was stopped by another: "That is nice bread you are eating," to which he replied, "Yes, mother baked it this morning."[78] Reduced now to crackers and pork, they acted out a satire on their condition, the details of which Capt. Josiah Wright reported back to Akron:

> Bill, step over to Hanscom's and get me a couple of pounds of that nice cheese . . . only eight cents a pound, and that sutler of the 7th charges sixteen for a poorer article.—Jeb, go down cellar and fetch up some cider and apples, and you Tom go up stairs and get some them hickory nuts . . . keep out of my room there Sir, I left my watch on the piano.[79]

They were picking up some pointers here about how to get by on very little. Recipes were perfected for making the most of what they had on hand. It did not take an iron kettle large enough to boil laundry in order to get a hot meal. Soldiers discovered here in their camp at the Levels that a canteen left outside burst into two equal halves by the ice expanding within it, and the result was a pair of excellent lightweight skillets.[80] A breakfast could be made by tamping down a ration of salt pork into a tin cup, bringing it to a boil two or three times, skimming off the water, and then seasoning it to taste with imaginary pepper. As an alternative to that, hardtack pounded into crumbles could be stirred into one's coffee, turning it into "oysters." Men learned how to make shelters by forcing the crotches of sticks into the ground, and making walls and roofs from whatever covering nature provided. Such structures were primitive, but they were capable of keeping soldiers alive on the coldest nights, if the inhabitants huddled together.

Back home in the Western Reserve, notices of deaths of soldiers carried off by disease began to appear with increasing frequency. These announcements took up just a line or two, giving the place and date of his demise and a few words telling what a good and patriotic soldier he had been and how much he would be missed. These were still individual tragedies. The long lists of soldiers wounded or killed in a single battle that would fill many columns in future newspaper editions had yet to appear. An anonymous letter writer who called himself Company G offered a wry prayer to the Akron newspaper: "God grant that Mr. Conservatism at Washington will come to the conclusion ere long, that 'somebody has got to be hurt' before this war is ended."[81] Few back home had yet to arrive at that reality, and with all quiet on the Potomac and most every place else in the war, the social gatherings that had filled winter life on Ohio's Western Reserve for decades continued. They now took on a purely benevolent purpose, but were no less enjoyable on that account.

While their soldiers sat at Camp Starvation, a masquerade ball was held in Mogadore at the Union Hall, every penny of the proceeds to go to the sick soldiers. It was noted that John Clemmer was not available to manage the music for this particular production since he was serving now as third in command of the Twenty-Ninth Ohio. The ubiquitous and popular Akron Liedertafel, composed of Akron's "very best" German citizens, provided the music for attendees, who danced the schottische, shuffles, figures, and pirouettes. A half hour into the party, masks came off and the invitees laughed for having failed to recognize near neighbors.[82] For the benefit of their Soldiers' Aid Society, the young women of Copley tried something that had never been attempted in the village. They staged an exhibition of tableaux, in which groups of actors stood stock-still atop a large table as if figures in a three-dimensional painting, separated from the audience for set and costume changes by a curtain hung from the ceiling, and lit by oil lamps placed on the floor. They depicted charming and historical scenes like "Pocahontas Saving John Smith," "Irish Courtship," and "The United States vs. the Southern Confederacy," with musical interludes furnished by the Copley Cornet Band, which played favorites like the "June Bug Quickstep."

There was a compact notice that Alvin Nims, Company D, Twenty-Ninth Regiment had died of erysipelas at the hospital in Cumberland, and just below that an invitation to attend a "Dime Party" being put on by the Akron High School Girl's Soldiers Aid Society, to which "all are cordially invited to attend, and have a good time generally."[83] And below that, for those who needed pictures to better understand the complex operations of the various armies, an announcement that the famous Willard's Panorama had come to town, and had on display twenty-five very finely painted scenes of the great American Rebellion, with accompanying lectures by Professor Willard, both words and illustrations judged not only educational, but artistic. Sheet music for piano or voice was for sale in the stores. The chaplain of a regiment posted near Fortress Monroe had heard the slaves singing a song of peculiar sweetness with just enough wildness to bring out the full meaning of the words. He took down the words and melody, and now "The Song of the Contrabands: O Let My People Go" was available in Akron for twenty-five cents. Also available was another song for which the critic predicted great popularity, "Battle Hymn of the Republic." Obituaries of "old pioneers" ran in nearly every newspaper. The grandfathers of the soldiers, the men and women who had come out from New England and settled the Reserve, were slipping away and taking their way of life with them.

Taken Sick

Most of the enlisted men had been strong enough to carry an anvil in each hand, or throw hundred-pound bundles of wool onto a boxcar hour after hour without complaint. Several days of war in these frozen mountains had made it clear that it was impossible to judge by a man's outward appearance whether his constitution could absorb the enormous physical strain of soldiering in rough country day after day, on inadequate rest and nourishment. The large rough-and-tumble man, it was seen, could fall and not get up again, while a man half his size kept going. A lesson was being taught to the men, only three weeks into their war, about their variable capacity to be soldiers. Patriotism counted, but there was a measuring instrument buried within every soldier, preset at the limit of what he could take, and once that was reached, he could take no more, and some men were already reaching the end. Many boys had been too sick to make this chilly march and had been left behind down on the river.

When the Boys arrived at Camp Kelly, they sat down in the mud and became sick. Nearly everyone complained of some malady: sore throat, chills, headache, and worse. Chaplain Hurlburt visited the Federal hospital in Cumberland within a day of the regiment's arrival and found it jammed with more than fifteen hundred sick soldiers.[84] Private Roshon, still not up to snuff from his bout with the measles at Camp Chase, came down with the contagion affecting most of the men, and he documented its onset in his diary.

> Sat. Jan. 25: to-day I was here in camp this four noon I cooked some rice soup for the Boys it was a good dish in the afternoon i was taken with the chill fever the chill was on me about 2 hours in the night. I had a fit.
>
> Sun. Jan. 26: this morning I feel some better only I am sore all over as if I had been pounded to deth I have an awful sore throat.[85]

Roshon had been lucky. For the less fortunate who could not recover on their own resources, it was a ride back into Cumberland, where more advanced medical treatment awaited. The soldiers had good reason to fear being sent to the hospitals in Cumberland.

Dr. Charles Tripler, commanding the army's medical department, believed that his work in organizing and provisioning hospitals for the Army of the Potomac was at a successful conclusion. He was stunned to learn of the condition of Lander's division near Cumberland. He had not even known that McClellan's army had a division posted in that far-flung place.[86] He immediately dispatched an inspector and got back a report confirming his worst fears:

> The regiments composing the command were scattered in all directions for some 40 miles over the hills. The sick, numbering 1,200, had been abandoned in the city of Cumberland, and were in a wretched condition. They were quartered in close, compact, ill-ventilated rooms, where the police is bad, food badly cooked and improperly served out, men of different regiments reeling and staggering through the streets with fevers, seeking shelter and medical attendance.[87]

Lander, a dynamo in any matter that he found stimulating, apparently had not visited Cumberland; if he had, he was indifferent toward conditions suffered by his sick men. He had demanded the best of soldiers be sent to him, but he had not made any preparations for caring for their inevitable sickness. Apparently, his medical establishment in Cumberland was without even the basic necessities. It had been the general of a neighboring command who alerted Tripler on the dire situation. Tripler took immediate steps to set things right. Buildings were rented, and huts built housing fifty patients each to serve as hospitals, local women were hired to sew bed sacks, and arrangements made for the Sisters of Charity, a Catholic order of nuns, to serve as nurses. Tripler ordered ambulances, carloads of bedding, and hundreds of boxes of basic medical stores sent at once. He assigned a physician of known competence to Lander's command with the instruction that he exert himself. Surgeon George Suckley took to the streets of Cumberland and rounded up the wandering sick; in his first week he collected fourteen hundred of them.[88] The Giddings Regiment's adjutant, Theron S. Winship, the enthusiastic storekeeper from Pierpont and currently second in command in Luce's company, was assigned duty as a hospital inspector under Dr. Suckley.[89]

The medical department was filled with men who were masters of organization, capable of pulling rabbits from hats and moving mountains. In time, with sufficient resources given them, the department would become the model of treatment for the world's more advanced armies.

Pvt. Charles Dudley, a farmer's son from Austinburg, was well liked by his comrades and officers. He had come down with pneumonia at Camp Chase and spent time in the post hospital, but was well enough to depart with his regiment.[90] He fell sick again at Camp Kelly and was sent into Cumberland when conditions there were at their worst. Seelye visited him and found him low and failing.[91] They talked quietly about his religious condition, and Dudley whispered that he was penitent, and trusting in his Redeemer. He died two days later, a sacrifice in the cause of Union, it was noted, as surely as if he had been killed in battle. Poor Dudley; his having gone to Cumberland, or that he was sick at all, escaped the notice of the officer who took the morning roll call, and under the heading "Register of Deserters," his name was written in his company's book as having deserted his company.[92] Afterward, someone corrected the mistake in the company books, but that did not right the wrong. Back at the adjutant general's office in Ohio, his name was placed on the state's roll of dishonor and can still be found there.[93]

Eight men perished of disease in the Cumberland hospital in January and February, and seven more in March. Four more soldiers lingered on there after the regiment had moved up the road, all of them dying before May Day.[94] Even at this early date the common soldier had learned to eschew the advice of the army surgeons, Dr. Fifield included, and stayed clear of the hospital as long as he could still stand. Even Capt. Josiah Wright, who had access to hospitals far better than those to which the enlisted men were sent, concluded, "I had sooner die on the road as go to the hospital."[95]

A strong wind came up suddenly one night and blew down Surgeon Fifield's tent, and the Boys howled to see the notorious blue pills, bottles of quinine, and packets of Dover's powders "going it" in every direction.[96] Packets of one popular purgative, cayenne pepper, broke open, and everyone within range were victims of sneezing and watering eyes.[97] One of the remaining medicines was prescribed for Pvt. Newton P. Hummiston. He described his recent bout of sickness for his mother back in Ohio: "I have had a hard cold but I went to the doctor and got something for it and threw it in the fire and I got better soon."[98]

The enlisted men had begun to go down with astonishing regularity. But though the benefits of being an officer translated into vastly improved odds of surviving sickness, even they began to drop away.

Lt. William Hall of Company I resigned the very week the regiment arrived on the Potomac.[99] Lt. Leveret Grover of Company A had been loaded for bear when he came into Camp Giddings and got immediately down to wrestling for an officer's rank in the company he had helped recruit. But he found the rough and tumble of life at Camp Kelly too severe and resigned after a brief stay on the sick list in Cumberland.[100] The soldiers worried over Colonel Buckley's health, but regardless of his age and previous problems, he was enjoying the robust health of men half his age. Their hope was that he would come through the future unscathed.[101]

Without doubt, most of these men were genuinely ill, some gravely, as proved by their ultimate deaths. Josiah Wright, cynical in all matters, judged at least some to be suffering from nothing more than "the white feather disorder." A battle would come at some point, and some men did not have the stomach for it.[102]

Their suffering had already been considerable. Chaplain Hurlburt informed the residents back home that although the soldiers of the Twenty-Ninth Ohio had not yet been given an opportunity to fight, they had seen service:

> Had you followed us in our marches and countermarches—up and down the mountains—through deep gorges—fording the streams—sleeping in the woods—living on short rations—men sick, and dying in miserably managed hospitals—others dragging out a miserable existence in camp rather than go to the hospital—disabled men waiting for a discharge till hope is gone, and they lie down to rot and die. . . . Reader, these are facts. . . . Who will say that the Twenty-Ninth as not "*seen service.*"[103]

Spirits were again headed downward. Some of the early enlisted men had now been gone over half a year and neither they nor anyone had yet to see a dollar from the U.S. government. Someone had left the regimental muster rolls behind in Wheeling when they passed through the town. Rumors continued that they would be paid any day now, but as Chaplain Hurlburt reported, "every other camp rumor is believed save this one. Not a boy in the regiment will believe it."[104]

The oceanic mud had narrowed the artery of military supplies coming down from Cumberland. Their ration of "hard bread," referred to in most of the army as hardtack, was the most relied on stomach filler on the soldier's menu. It was now reduced to three crackers per day, and increased to five on the days a march was scheduled.[105] The sutler sold chunks of soft bread, but no one had a nickel to buy it.

Wallace Hoyt asked for a loan from his parents and got back a single dollar. His letter acknowledging receipt of it revealed the regiment's universal poverty. "I did not spend that dollar that Father sent me until 2 or 3 days ago because I could not find money enough to change it. But my boots giving out I bought a new pair of government shoes second hand at a quarter of a dollar and managed to get it changed."[106] No one, officers included, had so much as four quarters, and their loved ones back home were doing no better.

Hardships for their families back home were mounting. Summit County would continue to pay the soldiers' families a weekly allowance, but it was barely enough to keep starvation from the door.[107] Some soldier's families had given up the struggle and gone to the poor farm, which to the soldiers was an abomination.

Captain Wright was reading the Akron newspaper out loud to the soldiers collected around him up at Camp Starvation. He had finished one article and begun reading the next, and before he could check himself, it was too late to back out. The newspaper appeal told the truth of how desperate some of their families had become.

> Who can estimate the courage that will have been infused into their hearts, and the strength that will come into their good right arms from the knowledge that their loved ones at home are kindly remembered and cared for by their thoughtful neighbors during their patriotic and perilous absence? . . . Reader! don't let this call go in at one ear and out at the other, but start right off, and do something towards carrying out its suggestions.[108]

Tears ran down cheeks raw and reddened by exposure. It was an outpouring of frustration and humiliation that caused even their stoic captain to weep. They regarded themselves as patriots, but as the anonymous "Richard" pointed out, "money makes the mare go."[109] Colonel Buckley wrote to the governor pleading their case for pay. Common soldiers came teary eyed into Buckley's tent, to show him letters from family back home giving stark examples of their destitution. Governor Tod had passed the letter along to the War Department in Washington hoping it would shock the authorities into action.[110] It occurred to the soldiers that Giddings should be doing something to help them. Richard could not choke down his bile as he and others wrapped themselves in bundles of straw: "This is Old Gid's regiment, who promised so much for it, and always has an eye on it. Old Joshua, that good man. I wish his eye could find some Sibley tents for us, and show us the paymaster."[111]

Giddings's interest in military matters was confined to pleasant recollections of his soldiering in the War of 1812, and he published an inquiry in the local newspaper wondering if veterans still living would enjoy meeting him for a reunion before their Last Muster was called.[112]

While stalled in Ohio, the soldiers had feared that the war might end before they had seen the big show. Now their apprehension was renewed. Elsewhere in the Union army, the soldiers were enjoying victories. Despite the complaints of hard-line newspapers pushing for a more vigorous prosecution of the war, and Lincoln's impatience, it seemed to the Boys that the Union army was in ascendancy everywhere. Maj. Gen. Ambrose Burnside had sailed a fleet down to North Carolina and successfully landed his army without serious opposition. There were successes at places like Cedar Keys, Florida, and Mill Springs, Kentucky; and there was fighting going on far out west at Val Verde, New Mexico Territory. In the first half of February, a hitherto unknown western general named U. S. Grant had taken two strategic Confederate forts in quick succession, and as a direct result, Federal forces walked into and occupied Nashville. Just down the Potomac the vast army of McClellan was colossal, and growing mightier every day. Surely, Richmond could not stand against such a machine once it was started in motion. The news of these was read by the regiment's soldiers stuck along the upper Potomac and the conclusion to be drawn was clear: this war would be over by June, and everyone would be home in time to put in a late crop.[113]

What they saw of the Confederacy in their small theater made such a thing not only possible but likely. The residents were ignorant and lived in log shacks, the likes of which had not housed anyone in the Reserve for over a generation. The soldiers believed that the distinctive local dialect was a reflection of low intellect and no education. "You are a right nice brought up set of fellas," and, "You are right smart looking men," were the phrases one friendly farmer had greeted them with when they appeared on his property. The Giddings Boys mimicked his words around camp for days.[114] The captured or deserted rebels that passed through their camp were ragged and equipped no better than a Rock Creek farmer rigged up to go squirrel hunting in the woods out back. By comparison, from the volume of rail traffic that came steaming into Camp Kelly, the Union could prevail if supplied from the western states alone.

Their grimmest prospect was that the Twenty-Ninth Ohio might spend their war doing nothing more than guarding the railroad in this backwater, as cut off from the real action as they had been back at Camp Giddings.[115] Their chaplain imagined them having been sent just as easily to Grant's army, where they would now be sharing victories. Instead, as he said, the fates had turned them into these mountains.[116]

"A Surcease of Tramping"

Lander remembered that he had an entire brigade at Camp Starvation, and Tyler's men were ordered to stow what little they had brought with them and move out. They would not be returning to Camp Kelly. Their destination was Paw Paw, western Virginia, the next stop of consequence to their east on the B&O Railroad. Lander was already gathering his force there for the next strike. The Third Brigade climbed down from their perch at the Levels and picked up the line of the railroad. To stay clear of the mud, some men hopped from one railroad tie to the next the entire dozen miles into Paw Paw.[117] Many soldiers could not keep up. Lander believed that the use of the "ardent" fortified a man's spirits as well as his body, and although they were short on hard bread and salt pork, there was whiskey enough in the supply train to give each soldier a regular ration.[118] For some men, such stimulation was not enough. Montezuma St. John was already sick when he started to Paw Paw with the others, and he played out. Wallace Hoyt carried Monte's pack, but even that did not help, and St. John lay down in the snow while his regiment marched away.[119]

They marched through the village of Paw Paw and out again, up a high hill and into their campsite. Dark was coming on, and their assigned ground looked unlivable. But they now knew what to do. Groups of soldiers subdivided into work details. Some went off to collect brush to build wikiup-style huts, others gathered the pine boughs that would cover the frozen ground. Other boys collected armfuls of kindling and got a fire going, while their friends got in line to draw rations, lugged them back, and cooked for the squad. After supper they nested into the pine duff and went to sleep. The most memorable attribute of this camp was the wind, which made taut rope tremble and whine and caused men to lean forward as if breasting a river. The locals knew that these gales were a precursor of a warmer season. There would be more winter, and plenty of it, but spring was coming.

While most of his soldiers slept, Lander and a force of infantry and cavalry pushed on ahead toward Bloomery Gap, the last opening in the mountains between them and Winchester. A dispirited irregular rebel outfit held the pass. Lander leapfrogged ahead of everyone and galloped down on the rebels, waving a pistol in one hand and holding his reins in the other.[120] It had all been confusion and crossed wires, but Lander and his bodyguard shot or captured every single rebel in sight.[121] The Twenty-Ninth Ohio had taken no part, but Lander's clean-out of the rebel nest gave them their first look at men killed in battle.

Down in the town of Paw Paw, a crowd of soldiers had gathered around a building hoping for a peek at the rebel prisoners locked up inside. A covered wagon was parked next to that building, and it held something of even greater interest. Someone brought a lantern over and raised it into the opening at the wagon's rear. Inside were two dead Union soldiers, both still in their gore-spattered uniforms. One was of middle age, the other a soldier so young that from the smoothness of his cheeks it appeared to Chaplain Hurlburt that he had yet to take his first shave. Hurlburt gazed on them and his thoughts turned to the sacrifice they had made.[122] Decades later, one old veteran would recall having lifted the wagon flap and looking inside at the dead. To him and the others, such things were still novel. He also reflected that a day came when the sight of dead men was commonplace, and therefore of little interest to the soldier.[123]

On February 17, 1862, the baggage left behind at Camp Kelly finally caught up with them, including their tents. Disgusted with them when they had been uncrated at Camp Giddings, the soldiers at Paw Paw were now delighted.

> Yesterday our tents and baggage came along, although they were the same old worn out, good-for-nothing tents brought from Camp Giddings, they seemed like old friends, in this hour of extremity, for we had been living for two weeks in the bushes. You need not be alarmed if we should be compelled to bring them back into Jefferson, as things equally unexpected have already befallen the Twenty-ninth. We have had the promise of new tents and many other things which we have never received. Please excuse this little fault-finding, as I am nervous to-day from the effects of a cold and want of rest.[124]

It still took fifteen wagons to carry all of the regiment's paraphernalia. Each wagon required a four-horse team to pull it, and a soldier sitting jockeylike on the wheelhorse to steer it along.[125] The stock provided was a rough mix of horses and mules, sometimes harnessed together, which was something that would have been ridiculed back home. Some of the beasts were hardly capable of pulling a wagon when it was empty, and many were hardly broken. One mule refused to have his bridle removed and sent the half dozen soldiers who picked up the challenge flying. They concluded wisely that it was better to step back from some contests, and the mule wore his headdress to bed. Regardless of the difficulties of managing such heavy transport, the soldiers were happy to see their wagons again. In them were the tangible reminders of home and its attendant comforts. They were still soldiers after all and not common vagabonds.

Soldiers writing letters back to Ohio wrote of many things, but in this period all the soldiers wrote about two incidents: their hard camp at the Levels and the celebration of Washington's birthday here at Paw Paw. The Father of the Country had passed back and forth through this place in his own youth, surveying this area when it and the mountains to the west were still wild. The men of the Seventh Ohio made an arch of boughs high enough to walk under, and across it they twisted pine sprigs into the letters spelling out Washington's name and those of some of their officers. Flags had been fixed to the tops of their fine, conical Sibley tents.[126]

At sunrise on February 22, the big guns fired a salute, sending a boom rolling up the slopes. The wind had died down, the day milder than most they had seen here. Soldiers sorted through their packs for their cleanest shirts, polished guns, belts, and buckles and marched down the mountainside to the lower campground, where they joined a celebration that all came to regard as the grandest thing they'd ever witnessed. Lander's ten thousand assembled by brigades, each of the regiments dressed in their best uniforms, flags distinctive to each planted in their front. Lander galloped onto the reviewing ground, his white charger throwing globs of Virginia mud cartwheeling, followed by his personal bodyguards, each as fancily decked out as he. He wheeled his horse up and down the line, and when he paused in front of a particular regiment, their band took up a martial tune in salute. The music quieted at the wave of Lander's hand, and he delivered a speech appropriate to this day of patriots.[127]

When he came to the Twenty-Ninth Regiment, they fired a thirteen-volley salute, one for each of the colonies. The regiment then broke down into columns and returned his compliments by filing past him in review. Then, Tyler's brigade formed in hollow squares, and Lander made a speech just for them: "Upon my 3rd Brigade, I depend and expect much, do your duty as soldiers worthy of the great cause in which you are engaged; do your duty as American Soldiers, and I will lead you to victory. I will give you the front position in the next forward movement, a chance to open the ball."[128]

The men let go with a cheer that shook the hills.[129] When it was over, soldiers climbed back up to their camp and set about cooking a holiday dinner of beans and hard bread. As Nathan Parmater recorded, "Thus it goes nothing to do for weeks only show ourselves once and a while to our officers, and scour our guns, to the tune of $13 per month."[130]

The soldiers found Paw Paw aptly named, because getting any kind of work done required them to paw and paw in the mud, so they joked. The cold and wind kept men locked in their tents and brush huts. When the weather allowed, men searched the hills for specimens of laurel root from which to whittle rings, then folded them within the pages of a letter and mailed them to sweethearts left behind. For a time, every man in the regiment made them.

An enlisted man was responsible for his own laundry, not having the luxury enjoyed by their officers, who could hire it out. Soldiers carried loads of washing not done since leaving Columbus to the nearest creek. Work like this on a winter day took the bark off a man's fingers, and after trying his own hand at doing laundry, Nathan Parmater concluded that henceforth, "I should never blame the women for being 'cross' on washing day for it was more of a task than I was aware of."[131]

The Boys were drawn to the peaks that surrounded them, and they climbed them. Parmater thought he'd reached the peak of the one he was climbing, but once up to it, discovered that the real summit had been hidden from view and was still far above.[132] High up, he and his friends came across piles of stones set at regular intervals, which they interpreted as the resting place of some extinct race of Indians. They climbed higher, jumping upward from crag to crag, and got to the top, and for what could be seen from there, the effort had been worth it.

> To the East was seen the Blue Ridge with heavy clouds resting upon its summit and even on its side hiding the summit from sight. And to the North as far as the eye could extend could be seen peaks and ridges towering toward Heaven, this side of which lies the Potomac and the lower camp Tylor consisting of 15,000 men whose tents looked like mere specks in the distance. And the Canal could be seen winding its way along the side of the river until it disappeared at the foot of a high ridge where it entered a tunnel of some length. And also the B & O R.R. could be seen with its smoking engine halling its long train of cars, which looked more like a little boys hand wagon than a train of cars.[133]

In Parmater's philosophy, the works of man were puny in comparison to those of the Maker of All Things. Seelye made the trip to the top and described it for the less traveled back home: "Occupying an elevated position in the world—saying nothing of society—where we overlook a country that has more land to the acre than a Buckeye ever dreamed of."[134]

News came into the Twenty-Ninth's camp of Segal's victory over the rebel Price in Missouri, which set off a round of cheering and hat tossing.[135] Nathan Parmater was cheered by the news of Union victories beyond their small theater of war. "We hear good news from our army in Kentucky and hope we shall continue to hear such until all the rebels are made to bite the dust or throw down their weapons of rebellion and come back into the *glorious* Union."[136]

Dissatisfied with the progress of his armies, Lincoln ordered every Federal force everywhere to advance against the insurgents. February 22 was set as the jumping-off day.[137] The day came and went at Paw Paw, but the soldiers remained immobile. The army planners for this theater were still applying the finishing touches to a campaign that would put them in motion, and maybe into the history books. A week after Washington's birthday, the soldiers were summoned from their blankets at three in the morning. Orders were to cook three days' rations; in three days of marching they could reach just about any point in the state of Virginia, so it was imagined. And in the time it would take to eat the ten days' extra rations stowed aboard their wagons, they might reach any point in the Confederacy. Every soldier was issued one hundred rounds of ammunition.[138] This looked serious.

A few days before, orders from Washington had arrived at Lander's headquarters. He was to proceed east with his army and take it to the foot of the Shenandoah, below Winchester. There, Lander was to join his army with Banks's and they would proceed together and overwhelm Jackson. Lander's feeling was that if Jackson would not stand and fight, he could at least burn Winchester to the ground.[139] His army could not start out from Paw Paw until the tricky business of crossing Banks's army onto the Virginia side of the Potomac could be worked out. In the meantime, the Giddings Boys devoted themselves to keeping warm and attached to the ground so they would not be blown away by the late winter winds.

Turned Back

On March 1, Tyler's brigade took the advance of Lander's whole division, just as Lander had promised. They had orders to march to Bloomery Gap. They did not get started until after four in the afternoon. The road was in good condition, and better yet, it seemed to be leading in the direction of Winchester. But having a decent road on which to march did not seem to be in the regiment's cards. Tyler's men were shunted off onto a much poorer road that went up and down like a series of ramps. After crossing a bridge made of artillery wagons over the Big Cacapon River, they stopped an hour before midnight. The Boys were too played out to build fires for warmth, or to make coffee. They rolled into their blankets and fell instantly asleep in the snow.

Next day, they sat around their fires awaiting further instructions. An order came through late in the afternoon that everyone was to reverse course and leg it back to Paw Paw, no explanation given. The march in the direction of Winchester had suggested battle, and the Boys were disappointed in the extreme.[140] They lifted their packs and started out their retrograde. Snow began to fall, a few flakes at first and then a general opening of the skies, covering men in white faster than they could brush it off and making the footing over rocks and tree roots tricky, especially in the pitch dark.

Snow filled the valleys surrounding Paw Paw from wall to wall, muffling the noises made by thousands of soldiers. Then came the explanation as to why they had been turned around: their general had died.

The affair at Bloomery Gap and the Washington's birthday review had been Lander's last hurrah. An infection had rekindled itself in his old leg wound, so it was reported afterward, and Lander fell ill. While the Twenty-Ninth Ohio was on the road to Bloomery Gap, the telegraph wire connecting Paw Paw to headquarters in Washington buzzed with hourly updates on Lander's condition. His staff reported that Lander was too ill to lead his army and that he might be sick for many days to come.[141] However, he had risen from prostration to lead his men before this, and his staff was hopeful he would do so this time. The updates on Lander's condition became more ominous.

Lander had been asleep for twenty hours under the influence of morphine; administered by his physicians, it was supposed to subdue the pain of his Edwards Ferry wounds.[142] At supper hour, he died.[143] There had been no word from officials in Washington as to what his command staff should do in this sad crisis, and lacking that, Lander's assistant ordered Tyler to turn around and come back to Paw Paw. His men could better endure this late-winter storm in Paw Paw than on the high pass at Bloomery.[144] Gen. Robert C. Schenck immediately applied for Lander's job, but it went to brigadier general of volunteers James Shields.[145]

Lander's death would go down in the Twenty-Ninth's history as the reason their march to Bloomery Gap had been halted.[146] The real reason they had made the march at all was that there had been miscommunication at high levels. It had all been a mistake. Banks was crossing the Potomac to the Virginia side with utmost caution, which was taking extra time, as anything involving Banks was apt to. If Lander's division got to the valley too far ahead of Banks, Jackson could come out from Winchester and destroy him, and then turn his attention next on Banks. McClellan discovered this timing error the day Tyler's brigade started out on the shortcut to the valley, and he fired off a telegram to recall them, but they were already on their way.[147]

The following day the division was called out to see Lander's remains off to Washington. He had been the first Union officer of his rank to die in the war, and his popularity alone demanded a funeral of high pomp and formality. After it left here, Lander's flag-draped coffin jolted through the mud of Washington's streets aboard a caisson. McClellan walked alongside, hat in hand, as one of the pallbearers.[148] He looked upon the coffin and remarked to a subordinate that he wouldn't mind trading places with Lander.[149]

The public wept. Lander's success at Bloomery Gap, however modest, had been the only Union victory for many months along the Potomac. His devil-take-the-hindmost charge at Bloomery Gap had electrified the nation.[150] His was the type of go-ahead generalship that was sorely lacking just now, and he would be missed. He had cleared all the rebels from his department just as he had promised, and he could have done much more had he not been hindered in executing his program by the timid in Washington.[151] The editor of the Akron newspaper held Lander so high that he did not clip a eulogy from a larger newspaper, as was practice, but wrote his own. "Gen. Lander was at once the terror of the rebels and the pride of his own army, and his loss will be most deeply deplored by the forces under his command."[152] Men in the Giddings Regiment did not share the opinion.

Chaplain Hurlburt, close to the common soldiers, and their spokesman, said that in the Twenty-Ninth Ohio anyway, not a single tear had been shed. Lander lacked "soul," which in the parlance of the time meant he had no sympathy for the welfare of his soldiers. Lewis P. Buckley believed that Lander had exposed his soldiers to unnecessary hardship. Further, Buckley knew Lander to be a thoroughly dissipated man, and he had not died of honorable wounds but in a drunken fit. In Buckley's judgment, the sooner the army was rid of such leaders, the better.[153]

"Show Us the Paymaster"

Chaplain Hurlburt was writing a long letter while seated on a tree stump when he cut the letter short.[154] The best kind of news had just come in. The regiment's pay had at long last arrived. Soldiers were called into line by companies to collect their money. Privates received $43.50, in scrip mostly, but still spendable at the sutler's, which is the direction many of them immediately headed.[155] Bread in any form, other than waterproofed and hard as rock, was highly prized, and the sutler had soft bread in stock. Even with pay filling a soldier's purse, ten cents was too high for a small chunk of what back home would be considered rough-quality wheat bread, and they went without. Butter, which the Boys called sauce, cost even more, but it was one luxury they could not do without. After these small spending sprees at the sutler's booth, most every soldier sat down to write a letter home, and enclosed with it a little of the "needful." How much of his pay a soldier sent to his family back home depended on their need, and his sympathy toward it. Newton Hummiston, a twenty-one-year-old house painter from Akron, wrote home to his mother and gave her an accounting of his spending.

Bought pair of boots	5.00
A Rubber blanket	2.00
Repairing boots	1.25
Stationary	.75
Sundries	10.00

After paying his other "just and necessary debts," five dollars remained, all of which he folded into his letter with the proviso, "By next Pay Day I hope to send you more but you must be thankful for small favors and larger ones in Proportion."[156] Sgt. John Marsh requested that his father use some of the ten dollars he had sent home with the chaplain to buy a new dress for each of his sisters. He wanted them to look as pretty as the other girls of Homer Township when they attended singing school. He earmarked ten cents to buy candy for his nieces and nephews, and told them it had come from their Uncle John.[157]

Most soldiers sent home at least half their pay, holding some back for the purchase of treats at the sutler's, or improvements in their personal gear. At the top of the list was a good pair of boots. The government provided brogans, but these wore themselves into shapeless forms with flapping soles and all the stitching rotted out after just a few weeks of service. Boots, made to order by the shoemaker back home, were the ideal, but a pair could cost a full month's pay or more, so for most soldiers the army shoes they had been issued would be patched, sewed, and stuffed with rags to keep them going a few more miles until money could be saved to buy something better.

An officer's pay was substantial, far more than a professional man could make back home.[158] The lowliest second lieutenant earned over a hundred dollars per month, and Colonel Buckley $212.00, which was enough to pay nearly twenty private soldiers. A few weeks later Lt. Eleazer Burridge of Company F made a "flying" visit to Akron, knocked on Mrs. Buckley's door out on the west side of town, and presented her with a "gift" of one hundred dollars.[159] The money had been collected among the regiment's officers as token of their love and admiration for her husband. But more than regular pay, custom-made boots, or any other thing, the soldier yearned for news from home.

The deeper he traveled into the war, the more he craved news from home, whether reported in letters from his family or in the hometown newspapers. Sergeant Marsh asked his sister in Homerville to write often, and of anything: "Who works the place this summer and who are the gossips going to have married next and how many chickens have you, what young ladies have beaux or is that business at a standstill since the war broke out and so many have gone soldiering. Write everything good, bad and indifferent. I have plenty of time to read it all and more than that, time that I don't know what to do with."[160]

Small changes had taken place in the regiment during this winter's test of their durability. William P. Williamson, Palm to his comrades, was every inch a soldier, so much so that he had caught the eye of General Tyler. Tyler chose him as his aide-de-camp, and James B. Storer, the ironmonger's son from Akron, took his place. While some men moved up, one company commander moved out, and back home to Ohio.

Capt. Pulaski Hard had struggled mightily to get into the war. No one could fault his dedication to the cause of flag and country. He got as far as Paw Paw but could go no further. He had suffered some from a bowel complaint while at Camp Giddings, and while riding into Cumberland on business of some kind, he was taken by it again. Captain Hard checked into a local hotel to recover, but rest and better food than was available back at camp did not turn the trick. He had been able to carry on through the application of stimulants and anodynes, but by the time they reached Paw Paw, he was too bent over with pain to mount his horse. Fifield advised him to resign, and he did.[161] After he got home, he kept to his rooms in Johnsons Corners.[162] Myron T. Wright took over command of the company, using the honorary rank of captain until the official paperwork came through confirming his new rank.

Their march out of these cold mountains had been canceled, but that proved to be a lucky stroke. It had given the army planners enough time to arrange to transport the entire force by rail, thus saving the soldiers a long difficult march. To the common soldier, like Homerville boy Pvt. John C. Rupp of Company I, Lander's passing meant one important thing: "It looked as though we might now have a surcease of tramping around and accomplishing nothing."[163] Their first two months in the war had been uncomfortable to say the least, and for those who had gone off to take their chances in the hospitals, it had been dangerous too. But as Private Rupp recalled years later, when the grand futility of it had been softened, it had been a necessary and valuable "breaking-in." Now, for the first time since arriving at the seat of war, everyone, officers and privates alike, knew where they were going. They were about to move east and destroy Jackson at his stronghold in Winchester.

9

The Ball Opens

THE BATTLE OF KERNSTOWN, MARCH 23, 1862

Into a Better Country

On March 8, Tyler's brigade marched down to the railroad, where they were to take the cars to Martinsburg, Virginia, twenty miles north of Winchester. Sixty-nine of the regiment's soldiers were culled out near the railhead and sent off to Cumberland. They were too sick to keep up with the regiment. They would slow the forward progress, and their presence would be a depressing influence on those who were still healthy. Chaplain Hurlburt thought that many more should have fallen out, but from fear of the medical establishment, or loyalty to their comrades, they kept their place in line.[1]

Thousands of soldiers had gotten to the railroad ahead of them, and it was not until dark that their turn came to board. The cars were so crowded that soldiers had to lie one atop the other.[2] They paused briefly at dawn at a place named Sleepy Creek and then steamed on into the rising sun.

Lincoln had reorganized the army while they slept. General Order no. 2 discarded management of the army by department and reorganized it on the corps system. Overnight, the Twenty-Ninth Ohio had become part of an army of forty thousand. The primary concern to the ordinary soldier coming from this change was that his mail routing had changed, and soldiers wrote home to make sure their families knew how to find them. Future letters should be addressed: Army of the Potomac, 2nd (Shields) Division, Banks's 5th Corps.

A few miles more and they were at Back Creek, in the last valley separating them from the Shenandoah. The railroad line lay broken from here on, and their division could not cross, even on foot, because the rebels had burned the bridge. Boys of a dozen regiments stood atop the cars and watched the engineers rebuild it. During their stop here the Giddings Boys were issued "gum blankets," rubberized sheets made to protect a sleeping soldier from damp ground.[3] They had a look at the new commander of their division. Gen. James Shields sat on his horse and watched them pass by. Shields took particular interest in Company I of the Twenty-Ninth Ohio as it filed past. Sgt. Rollin Jones heard him express his astonishment that it seemed to be made up entirely of boys.[4]

Shields was close to Buckley's age, short in stature, with blazing blue eyes, mustachioed, and dark headed. He had landed on the East Coast from Ireland while still in his teens, sized up the opportunities available to him in his new country, and moved out to the Illinois prairie. Like Lander, he had made a mark for himself in the Mexican-American War, fifteen years earlier.[5] He had gotten into politics in Illinois, which brought him into a collision with Lincoln. He challenged Lincoln to a duel, but a peace was worked out by their seconds before the two went at each other with broadswords on a sand spit in the Mississippi River.[6] Shields suffered from wanderlust, like many men of his time, which pulled him further and further into the West. He served not only as a senator from Illinois and Missouri but as the first senator from Minnesota He was mining in the jungles of Mexico when the war started. He had been waiting around Washington for appointment to some command, and then Lander died.

A bumpy eleven-mile tramp along what remained of the railroad bed brought them to Martinsburg. The soldiers were entering the realm of Jackson. The destruction he had applied to the railroad the past summer went on for miles along here, and no soldier who walked this way failed to comment on it. Hundreds of railroad cars had been backed onto bridges and burned. They lay now in forty-foot-high heaps.[7] The torch had been applied to over forty locomotives, which sat now disfigured and rusted, and to all the railroad shop buildings. The air in this neighborhood reeked of destruction.

They struck the Martinsburg Pike and stepped out onto it, headed south. When clouds parted to the south, the Boys got their first view of the Blue Ridge rising up to the east and south.[8] Beyond the Blue Ridge, ninety miles distant, lay Manassas and, just beyond that, Washington. The soldiers looked toward the horizon as they strode along and they were elated. There was flat land up ahead.

They now began to sing as they marched, adding a snap to the downbeat. They were singing the most popular marching song in the army, which began with the line, "John Brown's body lies a-mouldering in the grave," and they would be singing it in all the marches that followed.[9] A popular magazine had published a new set of lyrics for the same tune the previous winter. Julia Ward Howe's "Battle Hymn of the Republic" was a hit with civilians, but the soldiers would always prefer their version.

They stopped for the night in a pleasant orchard belonging to some unfortunate farmer. Most of these boys were farmers and they knew how much backbreaking work went into building up a nice place, and in the privacy of letters home some sympathized with the owners of places appropriated by soldiers for their camp. Pvt. Alvinson Kinney took pity on such a farmer and wrote to his father, "How wold you like to have 5 or 6 hors teams drive up through your wheat field and take the rails to burn and turn out 15 horses to feed if we shold march through."[10]

All along, disease continued to whittle them down. They had left one of their own behind at Martinsburg. Pvt. Conant Brainard was a thirty-three-year-old farmer from Harpersfield. He seemed to have stood the banging the regiment had endured in the mountains, but he doubled over with a bellyache on the way to Martinsburg and fell out. In early April, a letter arrived at the Brainard farm back in Ohio. Lorinda Brainard was the mother of his four sons, the youngest of whom was a newborn. She unfolded the letter and read.[11]

> Martinsburg, Berkley County, Va.
> March 31, 1862
> Mrs. Conant Brainard
>
> Dear Madame
>
> With profound regret I have to inform you of the death of your husband, he being under my special care for some days previous to his death. His death was caused by inflammation of the liver and finally resulted in congestive chills. Your personal well-fare and that of your children was his special regret at leaving the world, with that single exception his death was peaceful, calm, and Christian—which fact is truly a source of gratitude toward God, and filled with a happy hope of reunion beyond this vail of flesh and tears. His death occurred last night at 12 o'clock in [the] Post Hospital at Martinsburg, Berkley County, Virginia. He was buried in the Martinsburg Cemetery . . .
>
> The place of his interment is a beautiful spot, beautifully decorated with everything one could wish. While in the hospital he was visited twice a day by the ladies of Martinsburg, and done all for him that was in their power for his comfort. His personal effects were as follows and delivered to Sgt. B. A. Smith of Co. B, 29th Reg't Ohio

Volunteers and will be delivered to you by him: one blouse, one pair boots, one pair pants, one vest, one money purse, one pocket book, two shirts, one knapsack, one knife, fifteen dollars in paper money, and seventy cents in silver.

Very Respectfully,

    G. F. Koop, Surgeon
84" Regt. Penna Vol
Surgeon Post Hospital

If his friends in his company had been around Martinsburg when he died, a collection would have been taken up to send his body home to Ohio. But they were not, and Lorinda was left without the comfort of having her husband close to her in the local cemetery.

In announcing the death of Charles Dudley, several weeks earlier, Seelye had cautioned those at home not to fret too much about the health of their loved ones in uniform. Dudley, he explained, might just as easily have fallen ill at home. But the increase in announcements of soldier deaths in the local papers no longer supported his theory. Notices of soldiers who had died of disease from Harpers Ferry to St. Louis had begun to spot the newspaper pages more densely, single editions giving the news of not one, but a half dozen deaths, headed by captions such as "Another Soldier Gone" or "Another Empty Chair." Union soldiers were being swept off by the thousands, and the war's first full-scale bloodletting had yet to happen.

In their overnight stay in the orchard on the way to Winchester, Lt. Ebenezer Howard of Company E rode out into the countryside and returned to camp leading a string of a dozen horses taken from a secesh farm, along with the family's two slaves.[12] Confiscation of a man's property, including his slaves, was illegal. Howard seemed to be performing the mission that Giddings had set for them, but his would be the first and last instance of any Twenty-Ninth Ohio soldier going out of his way to free a slave. What became of one of the slaves Howard liberated was disclosed in a small piece in the Conneaut newspaper a while later. When Mrs. Ebenezer Howard stepped down onto the train platform in Conneaut, after visiting her husband at the front, it was seen that she had brought back "a good looking Contraband" with the stated intention of putting him, or her, to work on the family farm.[13]

What became of the second contraband that Howard freed is suggested by Nathan Parmater, who was applying himself to cooking for his mess and generally doing his company's housekeeping. He made a notation in his diary that he had been asked by an officer in his company, of whom there were few about at the time except Lieutenant Howard, to provide board for the officer's "waiter," which he agreed to do for a little extra money. There was no white person in Virginia who would have gone to work serving a Union officer. Officers of the Giddings Regiment had begun to acquire "servants" of their own, and as far as is known all of them were contraband.

On March 12 the soldiers got orders to march. This time they were to leave their knapsacks and carry with them only full canteens and muskets.[14] They had not gone far when important news came: Jackson had vacated Winchester. They continued along the pike and set up camp four miles north of the town.[15] They remained here for the next five days, while Jackson's whereabouts could be discovered, his plans fathomed, and their response formulated. Waiting wasn't nearly as hard as it had been just two weeks earlier. The weather had shifted from rain and snow to full sunshine. This country had a prosperous look to it, and because of that, the soldiers felt happy. They were in general agreement that this was some of the prettiest farm country they'd ever seen, Ohio included.

Still, it did not look completely like home. The houses were set too far back from the road and had pastures or crops right in the front yard. In the Yankee settlements back in Ohio, the farmhouses stood up close to the road, with the working land out back.[16] Most of the residents here were passionately Confederate, but they were not against selling a home-cooked meal to a hungry Union soldier. Parmater was able to get a meal of "victuals" at a "secesh" house not far from camp for twenty-two cents and felt well satisfied with the bargain.[17]

The ground on which they were camped had recently been a battleground. The Boys idled away the hours examining unexploded artillery shells and picking up deformed minié balls.[18] Soldiers sat around the campfire at night and discussed the regiment's prospects for battle, and they badgered each other good-naturedly about who would skedaddle and who would face the fire like a veteran. The south wind blew rain in their faces and sometimes the sounds of rifle fire, which at times seemed quite heavy.[19] Some thought it sounded like a skirmish, but most had never been in a skirmish, so no consensus could be reached.

From their camp, the Boys could look around and see "a right smart of soldiers."[20] Sixty thousand soldiers were spread out in the fields close by, a full third more souls than occupied all of Cleveland, which the boys regarded as the most populous place on the planet. "The 29th is finally swallowed up in the Grand Army of the Potomac; but she is not lost; no more than the north star is lost in the heavens above. The 29th is *the* acknowledged Regiment in the Brigade, while all know the 3rd Brigade as the *fighting* Brigade of the Division," wrote Adjutant Chaffee to the Jefferson newspaper; never mind that most of the Giddings Boys had not yet fought.[21]

Chaffee saddled his horse and rode into Winchester to do some sightseeing and pick up a few things for the officer's mess. The Union naval blockade was having the intended effect. Salt was selling for fifteen dollars a barrel, sugar for as much as four shillings a pound, and a sheet of letter paper a staggering ten cents. Coffee could not be had at any price. He acquired some Confederate scrip to send home as a souvenir.[22] Winchester was a thriving market town of five thousand people with well-kept houses, some of them very fine, public gardens, finishing schools, and academies.[23] After too many weeks in the sterile mountains, a town this size was a natural magnet for the soldiers. Moreover, it was the first real Southern town any of them had ever visited. Seelye hitched a ride into town for a look-see. He was impressed by the ancient and aristocratic feel of it. He also noted that the black inhabitants were far meeker than those of the same race in the North.[24]

On their last day in camp, just north of Winchester, the officers and sergeants practiced their men in shifting from marching columns into battle lines, a maneuver that seemed to them a sign of things to come.[25]

The Sound of Distant Fire

On March 18 the drummers sounded the long roll, and thousands of soldiers emerged in full battle gear from woods and fields and found their places in their companies. Companies formed into regiments, making a several-mile-long column, and the men got on the road to Winchester.

Jackson was retiring toward Strasburg, and they gave chase. They passed through Winchester and on to Kernstown, where a pretty creek called Obequon cut the pike. They halted at noon, having covered a dozen miles. They boiled coffee and ate raw cabbages "borrowed" from a farmer's garden.[26] Jackson's cannon boomed from up ahead, which caused the Boys to quicken their steps. Shields's artillery replied and a small but brisk artillery duel arose sufficient to suggest to the soldiers that their first battle would immediately follow. They had come within three miles of Strasburg but could go no further. Jackson had burned the bridge over Cedar Creek, and his men were standing in line of battle on the other side, daring the Federals to come closer.

With his superior numbers, Shields might have crossed and pitched into the rebels and overwhelmed them. But the shots were being called by General Banks, and although he had shown himself a forceful U.S. congressman and governor, he was more timid as a general. No one in command thought to improvise a bridge. The light was going out of the day, and Nathan Parmater and his best friend, "Chum" (Alonzo Sterrett), spread their gum blankets on the ground and slept.[27]

Footsore soldiers awoke to an on-again, off-again rain. The bogeymen who had menaced them from the opposite bank had vanished. Shields's soldiers waded across Cedar Creek, something that had seemed impossible in the twilight of yesterday. The Federal artillery came up and fired a few desultory shots at Jackson's rearguard, but he would not cooperate by standing and giving battle. The division turned around and began its march back to Winchester. It rained part of the way, and the rain turned to heavy snow as they made their way back to camp on the Martinsburg Pike.

Firing could be heard wherever they happened to be now, but always at a distance too great for them to participate. Seelye expressed their common frustration: "As I write, I hear the distant roar of arms occasionally, and cursing my luck that keeps me from the dance."[28] They had marched nearly twenty-five miles in a single day, with only one cracker per man to eat, and they had done it in seven hours.[29] One bit of good news came to them on this march: the grand Sibley tents they had been promised would be waiting for them.[30]

The Federals now had Winchester in hand, and secure in that knowledge, Banks moved back toward the east, leaving Shields to hold the town. Scouts of Jackson's cavalry commander, the daring Turner Ashby, had observed Tyler's brigade pulling back through the town on the way back to their old camping spot and concluded that these Federals were leaving. When this intelligence reached Jackson, he put his army of thirty-five hundred back on the pike toward Winchester.

The Giddings Boys spent the day enjoying their new tents, writing letters, and resting from their march to and from Strasburg.[31] All was quiet in their camp until four in the afternoon the following day. Artillery and musket fire was heard pounding and popping back in the direction of Winchester, but who was firing, and to what purpose, could not be discerned.[32] At five, while soldiers were lighting fires and getting their rations ready to cook supper, they were ordered into line and started on the road to Winchester as fast as marching men could move.

Darkness reached Winchester ahead of them, and since they were without tents and the night cold, they returned to their camp, near Stephenson's Depot. The commotion that had deprived them of supper had been raised by Federals skirmishing with Ashby's cavalry near Kernstown. The next day, March 23, 1862, Ashby continued to press Shields's outposts. Stonewall Jackson heard the same noise that was presently rolling down to the Giddings Boys, mounted his horse, and rode that way to survey the situation.

The Ball Opens

A heavy wet snow had come down the day before and was melting to slush this Sunday morning. Sabbath was being observed quietly, as it was in any army camp. Halfway into it, cannonading was heard again from the direction of Winchester, but this time it was accompanied by a heavier volume of rifle fire, rising and falling in distinctive, more or less continuous waves. The drummers hurried along the company streets beating the long roll. The Giddings Boys formed into columns four men wide and started up the pike at a half trot with Colonel Buckley leading the way on horseback. Seven hundred sixteen soldiers and officers of the Twenty-Ninth Ohio were here to see this day. Over two hundred men, the contents of at least two full companies back in Jefferson, had fallen away by the agent of sickness. The Twenty-Ninth's case was not exceptional. This process of subtraction had worked on the other regiments just as efficiently.

On arriving in Winchester, they paused to load their rifles. Soldiers planted rifle butts onto the pike's hard surface and tore the strings securing the contents of the finger-size paper cartridges with their teeth. Powder was poured down the barrel, the deadly minié ball set atop the muzzle, and all of it clanged home with ramrod. For safety's sake, hammers were brought back to half cock, a copper primer placed on the nipple, and their rifles were ready for business. Because most men were from rural backgrounds, the army assumed gun handling was second nature, and it was taken for granted that every man possessed some degree of marksmanship. The soldiers had practiced loading, which was part of the standard infantry drill. They had already fired a volley of blank charges in honor of General Lander on Washington's birthday this past winter. There were the seventy veterans of the old Nineteenth Ohio Volunteers among them who had fired the volley that set the rebels running at Rich Mountain, but that had only required the discharge of a single round in the general direction of the enemy. Most of the Giddings Boys marching through Winchester this blustery March day had little or no experience in firing a heavy-caliber rifled musket, let alone accurately, nor had most of them tried the complex reloading process with enemy bullets swarming around them. Even if a soldier had fired at a living thing like a deer, or a farmer's sheep, what was coming would be the first time the large majority of them had ever pulled the trigger of a weapon aimed at a human being.

On order, rifles came up to the shoulder and they marched toward Kernstown, several miles up ahead. Puffs of smoke bloomed on the horizon, followed in a second by the receipt of a succession of booms. What had caused the ruckus into which they were presently headed would become clear within the next hour, but its larger implications would remain hidden to some of these soldiers for the remainder of their lives.

When Jackson's boss, Gen. Joseph E. Johnston, responsible for defending Richmond, learned of Jackson's withdrawal beyond Strasburg, he suggested to Jackson that he keep the Federals tied up in the valley and thus unavailable to reinforce any threat on Richmond.[33] Jackson got to Kernstown just after midday, and the intelligence that greeted him was persuasive: only a handful of regiments had been left behind to dispute his reentry into Winchester.[34] It was a Sunday, and Jackson was not normally inclined to allow his soldiers to perform any duty except attend religious services and read their Bibles. But the enemy was here, and he would fight them. No more Federals could be allowed to leave the Shenandoah valley.

As the Twenty-Ninth Ohio neared Kernstown they came upon a Federal battery, guns planted with muzzles pointed to the south, attended by crews who were all practiced motion and concentration. A few hundred yards more and wounded Union soldiers making their way back toward Winchester began to file past them.[35] By indisputable signs, the ball had opened. They crested a low rise and paused near the toll gate where a west-running road named the Cedar Creek Turnpike intersected the Valley Pike. From here, the soldiers were spectators to the opening scenes of a battle in which they would soon play an important role.[36] Through openings in the trees, they could see a Union battery at work east of the pike and another to the west. The rebels had a battery of their own posted on an elevation on the west side of the road, two miles ahead. Its rumble could be heard, and felt through the shoe bottoms, but the guns themselves were invisible to them.

Ashby's cavalry was in plain view, troopers riding at a gallop toward the east end of the Union line. Jackson's infantry could be seen, flags flying, bayonets flashing. If the enemy reached the Union right, where rebels appeared to be trending, the Union army would be flanked. These soldiers were not expert in military tactics, but from their vantage point the situation looked precarious. To a common soldier like Nathan Parmater, generalship would seem to call for a preemptive stroke: choke off the rebel advance and storm *their* battery.[37]

Just after they arrived at the toll gate, Tyler's brigade was ordered forward to support a Federal battery.[38] The rebels moved up a battery of heavier guns and began lobbing well-placed shots into the guns and the troops supporting them, killing and wounding men. It was clear that silencing the rebel guns was paramount.[39] At four o'clock Tyler moved his brigade out along the Cedar Creek road with orders to take the rebel battery and turn Jackson's flank.[40] Before getting everyone moving he made them a speech:

> Men, you are to fight,—to take that battery. The 7th Ohio and the 7th Indiana will make the charge. I want you to reserve your fire until your order comes, then bring your man. I want you to keep your mouths shut, and I will make noise enough if I have a chance. If you are cool, you will win. Let every man keep his place and obey orders.—Forward, march![41]

Tyler led his men down a shallow ravine that coursed along the rear of a wood.[42] *Hardee's Tactics* prescribed that columns march by rows of four men abreast, which would make easy work of shifting into a battle line two men deep when the proper moment came. Tyler's men now entered a neighborhood of rough, wooded terrain, the eight-man-wide blue mass moved steadily through a half-mile-wide woods. Shells from unseen guns began to hunt for them in these woods, throwing up giant clods of earth, bringing down branches, and wounding soldiers. When the woods thinned enough to allow it, Tyler ordered the whole brigade to make a half wheel to their left, which they did with amazing efficiency, given they had practiced it only a few times, and that was on a parade ground. They were about to come down directly onto the enemy's left flank, and they had not been detected.[43]

The enemy had thrown a skirmish line out into the trees ahead, but it was driven with ease, giving the impression that the rebel force was too thin to block their advance.[44] Tyler's men stepped out of the woods in a thick line of regiments, with the Seventh Ohio on the right, the Twenty-Ninth Ohio on the left near a mud road known to the locals as Middle Road, and the rest of the brigade between them.[45] They got a look at the terrain in front of them. Ahead three hundred yards the land rose from west to east along a sandy ridge, and along its low crest ran a waist-high stone wall—a stone fence, as most of these men with New England roots called it. In between was cleared pasture mostly, with a long gentle downward roll to it most of the way, then up again toward the wall. For the Twenty-Ninth, the only cover would be on the near side of a long, shallow hogback.[46] At the top of the field sat the enemy battery. They would rush across the field and take it before the rebels knew what had hit them.

A Fence Made of Stone

The Twenty-Ninth Ohio trotted through the last of the woods. Reaching open ground, their officers turned them loose, and they charged forward yelling like tigers. The Seventh Ohio had stopped to take down a rail fence, and just as they stepped over, they were struck by gunfire. Men shrieked and fell. The Seventh Ohio closed its ranks and pushed forward.[47] Just clear of the woods, the Giddings soldiers began taking fire from rebels concealed behind rocks and brush piles. Pvt. Alvinson Kinney remembered their surprise: "The enemy was in a holla and we did not know That They were quite so clost until we were close upon Them and They run alittle wase and got behind a stone fence where They give it to us for awhile."[48] Kinney had been one of those far enough forward for a view of something striking. Several hundred men in rebel gray and tan rose as one from behind the wall up ahead and were presently leveling several hundred muskets at them, and before the thought could fully register, the entire length of the wall burst into flame.

The line of the woods they had exited angled upward toward the right, which put the Seventh Ohio a hundred yards closer to the rebel line than the others, and they took the brunt of the rebels' first organized fire.[49] By instinct, most of the Giddings Boys threw themselves to the ground, and most of the enemy's first fire flew over their heads.[50] They got back on their feet and leaned into the fire coming from the wall.

The Giddings Boys held their fire until they came within fifteen yards of the wall, where they stopped and delivered a volley accompanied by an unearthly yell.[51] The wall exploded a second time, and the blue wave advancing on it staggered.[52] Individual soldiers hunkered down and continued to fire, but the place had become too hot to stand, and the Federals were forced to fall back.[53] The Seventh Ohio was pressed sideways and backward by the weight of the fire, as if blown off course by a great wind. To hurry them along, two rebel guns near the wall began firing canister, cans of egg-size iron balls that turned a cannon into a giant shotgun.[54] Some of the Seventh Ohio's soldiers hung on near the wall, but between them and the Twenty-Ninth Ohio, on the left and rear, regiments unraveled. Parmater recorded the early action in his diary: "But they [his comrades] were soon up and firing at them but they poured so hot a fire into us that the 7th Ohio took to the trees and the 7th Ind. And the 1st Va. broke and did likewise while the 110th Pa. broke and fell back into the 29th Ohio and went through our ranks and broke us up. But we soon rallied and came up in good shape."[55]

Men got separated from their companies and ran, they knew not where. The entire line slipped backward, individuals pausing to turn and fire at the wall, and some soldiers shooting wildly in every direction. The men recovered and re-formed into fighting units. This had been merely a confused reaction to coming under fire for the first time, not a stampede. The regiment stood its ground, loaded, and fired three aimed volleys on command. They started forward with Companies A through D in the lead and the others right behind.[56] Some of the Twenty-Ninth's soldiers fell back to the leading edge of the wooded grove they had just left, and they stayed there. Kinney was too young and too unworldly to take the pose of the warrior. He admitted to his parents that he and some of the others had taken to the trees because they were afraid.[57]

Kimball's brigade, made up principally of Ohio troops, had been standing ready to support Tyler's men. Shields's right-hand man on the field, aide-de-camp R. C. Shriber, could see that more rebels were coming down and taking up places behind the wall. There were rebels barricaded there three rows deep, all of them crowding to the front for a chance to shoot a Yankee. It was clear that the battle would be decided at this point, and Shriber ordered Kimball up to begin work on Tyler's left. The soldiers of the Fifth Ohio, Kimball's brigade, went at the wall as if the fate of the nation depended on the outcome. Four color bearers went down in as many minutes. Their Captain Whitcom carried their flag forward until he, too, fell—shot dead.[58] With this act of derring-do, the battle became general.

There were four thousand Federals condensed in a line several hundred yards long, all firing. Tyler's men began fighting without orders. For the next two hours it was a fight of enlisted men, in small groups or singly, banging away at the rebels bobbing up and down behind the wall, some Federals getting up to carry out a three-man charge, falling back, continuing to load and fire. Fighting contained a multitude of novel sounds, one being the distinctive flat slap of a rifle bullet colliding with flesh and bone. Some boys fell without a sound, as if the air had been let out of them. Others screamed and began tearing at their clothing to see where they had been hit. Rifled muskets had a killing range of a thousand yards, and the rebel fire was coming at them from a fraction of that. Bullets cut furrows in the sod and blasted chunks from stones and men. A tree in the rear of Company K was chewed to pulp so thoroughly that a private standing near looked up in wonderment and commented that he "would give fifty dollars for seven feet from the body of that tree to carry with him to Conneaut."[59] For a time, it seemed every cubic foot of air had at least one missile speeding through it. As Seelye expressed it, "Many pressing invitations were given for eternity, yet the passing over Jordan was too sudden for the nerves, and comparatively few invitations were accepted."[60]

Parmater's company had been placed in the ravine on the leeside of the hogback and were unable to see enough to fire more than a few unaimed shots. Companies to their right had a better angle at the rebels and kept up a busy, persistent fire. Sheltered behind whatever protection the terrain provided, the regiment's soldiers went at their work with a vengeance, the men frequently standing up to fire, neither side giving an inch. The opposing sides were close enough to exchange jibes and challenges, the rebels yelling, "Remember Bull Run," to remind the Federals of the beating they had taken there, while the Union boys hollered, "Remember Cross Lanes," which had been a notable rebel defeat in western Virginia the previous summer.[61]

Confederates who raised themselves above the wall too high were struck by one or several balls, jerking them upright as if lifting them by their belts, spinning them around and backward. Some of the Giddings Boys laughed and jeered at these contortions, hooted, and by turns, swore. John Marsh confided to his father later, "I would aim at them when only forty or fifty yards from me as coolly as I ever did aim at a squirrel."[62] Pulaski Hard's resignation had left twenty-two-year-old 1st Lt. Myron T. Wright in command of Company D. Two companies were actually under his command, which for this battle constituted a division within the regiment.[63] Wright had been wounded in the first charge out of the woods when a canister ball struck his lower left leg. His trousers were soaked red from the knee down and his boot was filling with blood. When the second charge was ordered, Wright pointed out his injury to his superior, who took little sympathy on him and yelled, "For God's sake . . . lead this charge!" Company D was short on leadership just now, so Wright hobbled out ahead of his men and got to within a few rods of the wall. He could go no farther and was now in a fix. The two companies under his care would be left leaderless if he departed the field.

Wright signaled his dilemma to Colonel Buckley, who made his way over and authorized William P. Williamson to take his place. Lieutenant Williamson came up and Wright saluted him. A brief conversation followed that sounds more like the dialogue of two British officers at Waterloo than two sons of a midwestern state. Wright addressed Palm, "To you I entrust my command." Rather than asking, "Why?" Williamson responded in his own grand way, "What is the occasion, Sir?" Wright pointed to the blood running down his leg and Williamson pledged, "Captain, it shall be retrieved."[64]

A few minutes later Palm went down, the sword he had been waving above his head still in his hand. A bullet had pierced his right eye and passed through his head, killing him instantly. Just before leaving Cleveland with the old Nineteenth Regiment in the war's first May, he had married a seventeen-year-old girl named Fannie Frost. That November, a son was born and they named him Willie P. Williamson.[65] Palm was the first man in the Twenty-Ninth Ohio to die in battle.

Before everyone on this end of the field began firing, the rebel position at the wall was as clearly delineated as any the regiment would face in the war. But a dozen or more discharges of several hundred muskets and the rapid firing of the rebel artillery produced a blanket of smoke so thick that all a soldier could see were the legs of the man standing next to him. Alvinson Kinney got control of his initial fear and settled down to loading and firing, telling his parents afterward that for the rest of the battle he had not trembled a particle. The noise and confusion made the success of his aim difficult to confirm, "I don't know whether I kiled one o not but I tride poty hard."[66]

Colonel Buckley's demeanor on the battlefield was no different than that which he displayed in camp. "Calm and placid as a summer's day," was how one soldier described it.[67] Captain Fitch was out in the thick of it, exhorting his men to "keep cool and aim well." Maj. John S. Casement of the Seventh Ohio was standing next to Fitch, holding his own horse. A swarm of bullets perforated Casement's coat, but Fitch was untouched.[68] Harvey Beckwith, a teenage private in Company E, had not been so lucky. A ball passed entirely through his chest and seriously wounded the soldier behind him.[69] Beckwith was dead on the field.

The incontrovertible logic of superior numbers began to tell. At most, there had been seventeen hundred rebels behind the wall, and Federals in twice that strength had been hammering at them for two hours. By small gradations, the battle was turning in the Federals' favor. Col. A. C. Voris of Akron, formerly of the Twenty-Ninth Ohio, but now leading his own regiment, the Sixty-Seventh Ohio Infantry, came up on the left of the Giddings Regiment and got his companies positioned to fire several volleys down the length of the wall. Rebels began to fall back from the wall, and it took only a moment for the domino effect of departing rebels to reach the neighborhood of Tyler's brigade.[70] As the sun began to go down, Tyler ordered a charge.[71]

Soldiers took bayonets from their belts and seated them in their sockets. Everyone started forward at once, regimental organization taking a backseat as they swept toward the wall. They ran with flags tipped forward and men cheering so loud their noise drowned out the cacophony of battle. Enough rebels remained to deliver a killing fire, but the men now seemed immune to it. They drove the rebels who tried to hold their ground at the point of their bayonets.[72]

The rebels still fighting from behind the wall now ran for the timber, "like the old hare and we after them," as Kinney described it.[73] Jackson's soldiers stopped and rallied around their battery, but the advancing Federals poured fire on them, and they gave up and fled. Some of Tyler's men continued the chase, shooting at gray-clad figures moving off in half light through the trees, until they were ordered back. For the first time in hours quiet came over the pastures and woodlots. The Twenty-Ninth Ohio's first battle was over.

The rebels had left three pieces of artillery and their dead and many of their wounded. It was now dark as pitch. Most of the Giddings Boys collapsed on the ground in the vicinity of the wall and slept as if under the influence of ether, with one hand gripping their rifles lest Jackson should return.

Nights of Eternal Length

In some men, the electric current that had carried them through that afternoon was not completely discharged, and they could not sleep—Sgt. John Marsh, for one.

> The excitement through which I had passed made sleep impossible, so I took a stroll over the Battlefield to see the effects of our fire. It was terrible. The small bushes were cut all to pieces and every tree was filled with balls. The Dead lay thickly in these woods and behind the Stone Wall, some torn all to pieces with shell, some badly mangled with Grape Shot, but by far the largest portion was killed with Rifle Balls. It was curious to note the different expressions on the faces of the Dead. Some seemed to have died in the greatest agony, others wore a smile even in death, and still others seemed possessed of the very spirit of cruelty and revenge. I can think of nothing to express their look except "infernal."[74]

Surgeon Amos Fifield had been on the field during the battle, removing bullets and bandaging wounds. He treated all the wounded in the Twenty-Ninth Ohio and those of many other regiments. He bound Myron Wright's wound for him and made sure he was placed in an ambulance beside Valentine Viers, an eighteen-year-old barrel maker and currently a private in Wright's company. Viers had been shot in the lower leg, the ball angling downward several inches and coming to rest in a purple bulge under the shinbone. Their ambulance broke down somewhere in the woods on the four-mile ride into Winchester. The Medical Department had sent enough ambulances along to carry the wounded, but when they were hitched up to bring the wounded in, it was discovered conveyances had been worn out by officers who had used them for buggy riding. Some cavalry happened along and found Myron Wright lying in the open. They wrapped him in a blanket, propped him against a tree, and rode off after Jackson.

Fifield was in Winchester working on the wounded, and he was keeping an eye out for Wright and Viers. The evening advanced toward midnight and the two still hadn't come in. Fifield got into his buggy and backtracked to the battlefield. He found the two sitting against a tree and brought them back to Winchester.[75]

Shortly after the firing ceased, squads of men assigned to hospital duty appeared on the field. They built bonfires to illuminate their work and as rallying points to collect the wounded. Wounded men were laid near the fire.[76] The squads searched the field all that night, holding lanterns close to faces to see if life remained and loading the wounded into wagons. The wounded lay strewn about everywhere. Marsh drifted through the scene of carnage and did what he could to help: "I wandered beyond the battle ground and in a thicket of pines found three wounded men. Their groans were heartrending. The cold night air had stiffened them so that they were in the deepest agony. I built a fire, brought them some water from a mud hole nearby and then went back to show the ambulance where to find them."[77] By sunrise, over four hundred wounded Federals, and many more than that of wounded rebels, had been gathered in Winchester, each of them awaiting his turn with the surgeon. Burying the dead, both Union and Confederate, could wait until morning.

Eighty-six rebel dead were dragged from behind and near the wall and laid in a mass grave the next day.[78] A rebel officer was found stumbling among the dead at the wall, both eyes and his nose gone.[79] Union boys calmed him and made sure he got medical treatment along with the rest. The normal debris lying around after any battle, inanimate and still living, were a museum to these first-timers: a boot with the owner's foot and lower leg still in it drew attention and remark. A rebel private was found lying among the gravely wounded, shot twice through the chest. He asked the Federal officer who found him whether he was acquainted with General Banks. The officer nodded his head that he was. "Tell him that I want to take the oath of allegiance, for I have three brothers in the Federal service, and I want them to know that I die true to the Union."[80]

The regimental surgeons and their assistants were as inexperienced in warfare as the soldiers now lying in front of them on floors and tables. Even the well-trained doctor, with years of practice under his belt, was unprepared for the deluge of torn, bleeding men in every stage of extremis. They were amazed at just how shot to pieces a man could be and still live. In Winchester, the number of surgeons present was found inadequate to do the work at hand. Some surgeons neglected to report for duty in Winchester and instead rode off the next day with their regiments, as if their duties were limited to attending them only. When surgeons began setting up shop in various buildings in town and instructed orderlies to bring basic medical supplies, it was discovered that there was none of almost anything necessary to comfort or save a soldier.

Lander's division had come down out of the mountains gravely deficient in medical supplies, and even normal medical stores due them since coming into the Shenandoah valley had not been forthcoming, because quartermasters and commissary officers were uninterested in performing their duties.[81] Medical supplies bound for Shields had been waylaid in faraway Baltimore, and until they arrived, men would suffer. The army had not yet recognized that battles, whether won or lost, would produce an army of the stricken requiring a whole range of supplies. The medical director of Banks's corps suggested that in future enough medical supplies be forwarded so they could satisfy the needs of twenty thousand sick and wounded soldiers, over a period of three months. In his judgment, "A supply of medicines and stores on hand, according to my experience, is as necessary to an army in the field as it is to have a supply of subsistence."[82] Procedures for collecting the wounded, and nursing and feeding them, were imperfect; help for the wounded must come from other places, some of them unexpected.

The women of Winchester were infamous for their loyalty to the Confederate cause, and for the venomous asides they made to any passing Union soldier. But with the bloody produce of a battle filling their town, they pitched in to comfort the wounded of both sides. For several days, the ladies brought cooked meals in pails and baskets and served them to the soldiers. A wounded soldier in the Sixty-Seventh Ohio who benefited from their charity remembered, "They didn't hesitate either to tell us that they were our enemies, as we were theirs; that we had come as invaders of their country; but all the same we were in distress, and they were disposed to return good for evil."[83] There was much about Winchester worthy of note, but singular in the memories of the Union soldiers was the unfriendly attitude of the female residents toward them.

Colonel Buckley was a man who would not gladly suffer disrespect from any quarter. A story ran in an eastern newspaper that Buckley and a group of officers were walking on a Winchester street when they encountered a fashionably dressed young woman. Being a gentleman, Buckley made her a slight bow, and she responded by spitting in his face. He took her across his knee and spanked her with the flat of his sword in front of a crowd of spectators. The Akron newspaper denied the story on Buckley's behalf, but if it had been Buckley, the editors were proud that his name was tied to so fitting a punishment of Southern insolence.[84]

Boys wounded in this battle were getting an introduction to life in an army hospital following combat. Myron Wright had to suffer the agony of the daily probing of his wound, which was the practice of the day, done to keep the wound open and draining, and to remove fragments of uniform, bits of leather, and even fragments of brass buttons that had been driven into the wound by the slow-moving minié ball. His surgeon eschewed a surgical instrument and used his two bare fingers, pushing one into the exit hole and the other into the entry until both fingers joined in the middle.[85]

Wright shared his room in Winchester with two wounded from the Seventh Ohio. One had died not long after being brought in, and the second man could not possibly last until morning. "Thus you see it is not the most desirable spot on earth for a wounded man to pass the nights of eternal length, amidst the groans and shrieks of dying men and those suffering amputation; but it is only a phase in war, and we are all willing to acknowledge that war cannot be carried on without some loss of life and comfort."[86]

Among the Twenty-Ninth Ohio's casualties was its surgeon, Amos Fifield. He was amputating a leg that had become gangrenous in a hotel that he had taken over as a hospital, when he nicked his right hand with the point of his scalpel.[87] Within a few hours, his hand had swollen to twice its normal size, and within thirty-six hours his entire arm, from fingers to shoulder, was red and inflamed. He now became a patient in his own hospital. Surgeons who attended him there were able to draw out enough of the poisoned blood to allow him to keep the arm, and after a few days he was able to return to Conneaut to complete his recuperation. He had been there only a day when the poisoning returned, and for days Fifield hovered between life and death. He would pull through, and return to the regiment, but his right arm, so essential to his work, would cause him suffering for the rest of his days.

The soldiers took time to write home, to report that they had been in their first fight and that they, anyway, had come through. News came along into the brigade's camp of Union victories at Island Number Ten and Corinth. The victory at Island Number Ten in particular received as much newspaper space as Lincoln's election victory. The Conneaut newspaper headlined it "Battle of the World." John Marsh described for his family how the news was greeted in their camp: "I will bet my ears if you could have heard the shouts and cheers that went up from the regiment after regiment and the bands playing the Star Spangled Banner. I guess we surprised the natives in our demonstrations of joy, for the rapid strides Freedom was and is every day making."[88] Marsh supposed that the news of these larger battles, seemingly more decisive and bloodier than the one they had just fought at Kernstown, had pushed any coverage of the regiment's first battle off the news pages.

State of Suspense

The *Ashtabula Sentinel,* in Jefferson, published a few lines about the battle three days later: "The 29th have doubtless had a taste of battle. The news from the East reports a battle near Winchester, Va., in which Gen. Shields took part and was wounded. Our boys must have been in this fight and doubtless did well."[89] Friends and families wanting specific news of how many in the regiment had been killed or wounded, and their identity, would have to suffer through a period of excruciating suspense.[90] Much of the first news of the battle was nothing more than recitations of Shields's own overblown accounts: Jackson's men were whipped and demoralized. He had beaten a crafty antagonist and proven that Stonewall Jackson was not invincible.

Published accounts emphasized the rebel army's well-known "accustomed fleetness of foot and determination to get out of the way."[91] It was reported that during the retreat the rebels had thrown their wounded out of wagons so they could get away all the quicker, and Jackson had had to pour barrels of whiskey into his soldiers to make them go into the battle.[92] Nearly all the rebel dead and wounded had been shot in the head or chest, which was simple proof that the Union troops, particularly from Ohio, were better marksmen. Every report of the battle managed to shoehorn in one singular story. As the Union boys had marched through Winchester on their way to the fight, the local women had heckled them with the boast that Jackson would be back by suppertime to enjoy the meal they were preparing for him. Well, Jackson did not appear in Winchester for his supper, nor would he ever, if the Boys had something to say about it.[93]

The Akron editors had learned that Palm Williamson was the only man of the neighborhood who had been killed, but as to the fate of the several hundred other Summit County men in the Twenty-Ninth Regiment, all concerned would have to keep to their anxious waiting.[94] Captains William Fitch and Myron T. Wright got out letters as fast as they could whenever a soldier under their command died of disease or wounds, in the hopes that their families would be spared the shock of reading the news in the newspapers.[95] But even they did not always know what had become of a soldier after he was sent away to a distant army hospital.

A Seventh Ohio soldier had been wounded attacking the wall at Kernstown, and after a while his parents got notice that he was well enough to return home. They drove to the train depot in Warren, Trumbull County, to meet him, but he was not among those stepping down. The next day a hearse pulled up at their front door and in it was their son's body.[96]

After three weeks, one of the Twenty-Ninth's soldiers sent a letter to the newspaper giving firsthand details of the late battle. Seelye identified the wounded, at least those he had seen wounded. Myron T. Wright wrote a long letter to the Akron paper while propped up on the pillows of his bed in a female boardinghouse, which had been turned to use as a hospital in Winchester.[97] Although both men gave colorful and detailed accounts of the battle, and named men who had been thought killed or wounded, neither was taken as official.

In Wright's account, all had behaved splendidly. There had been injury and loss of life of course, but other Ohio regiments had suffered more. Theron S. Winship sent a letter to the Conneaut newspaper written in the style of an earlier age. Picking up the action where Tyler turned the brigade from the road and into the woods, "But hark, the firing has ceased—what can it mean? They are attempting to flank us on the right. Three quarters of a mile of woodland, fences, underbrush and limestone rocks must be traversed within ten minutes or the day is lost. Query: can it be done? Yes was the response of three thousand brave hearts."[98] By most accounts, the loss of life on both sides had not exceeded two hundred. Lt. E. B. Howard, who had little basis for comparison, exclaimed to his newspaper, "We are on the largest battle ground on record."[99] He provided the village folk with his foremost impressions of the battle. On charging the wall he heard the Giddings Boys set up the most the most unearthly yell he ever heard. The Boys took cool aim whenever the soft felt hat worn by the rebels showed itself. He described the satisfying spectacle of four to six thousand rebels, all wearing gray homespun, moving at a "smart gallop" for the rear.

Chaplain Hurlburt had gone home before the battle to deliver the soldier's pay to their families. While there he was given a valise full of small presents—tokens of affection from wives and mothers, such as photographs of children, baked treats, personal letters, and embroidered handkerchiefs for a soldier to fold into his knapsack and take out in lonely times to remind him of the love that awaited his return. But when Hurlburt got back to the regiment he found that several of the soldiers for whom they were intended were dead and buried.[100]

Not only had several soldiers been taken by disease in his absence, several officers had resigned in the short time he had been away. Having missed the fight at Kernstown, he talked to the men and recorded their impressions of it and sent them along to the newspaper. Ever sensitive to how the Twenty-Ninth Ohio was treated in the press, he pointed out that the exploits of the Seventh Ohio had received plenty of blowing in the newspapers, while the actions of the Twenty-Ninth Ohio were left out entirely, implying that they had not fought. Based on their unhappy experience at Camp Giddings, the Boys were vulnerable to irritation, and now some verbal snipers suggested they had taken a backseat to other outfits at Kernstown. This hypersensitivity to perceived assaults on their performance was not unique to the Twenty-Ninth Ohio. A feud broke out in the Ohio newspapers almost immediately between soldiers and supporters of the Fifth and Seventh Ohio Regiments, each side claiming their regiment had been the first to take the stone wall.

It was a dispute that would not be settled anytime soon, if ever. Veterans who had been there would be arguing over it over a half century later. Capt. Josiah Wright of the Twenty-Ninth Regiment got his oar in the water and claimed that the Giddings Boys had been first over the wall at Kernstown, claiming for his regiment the prize without offering a single fact in support.[101] The extent to which a regiment's bragging could be believed, aside from the record of its deeds found in official reports, seemed dependent on its casualties.

The bullet holes in the Seventh Ohio's flag were counted and found to number twenty-eight. Its soldiers invited any regiment to produce a flag as riddled. The death toll in the Seventh Ohio amounted to twenty-three officers and enlisted men, and that of the Sixth Ohio only five less. Rebel bullets had made three perfect holes in the Twenty-Ninth's flag, a fact that General Tyler, their brigade commander, found worthy of noting in his official report of the battle. The Giddings Regiment's killed in action equaled precisely the number of holes in their flag: three, which was the smallest number of fatalities suffered in any of the regiments in Shields's division.[102] At least one more soldier not listed among the killed in action received his death wounds at Kernstown and died not long after.[103]

Years later, the Seventh Ohio's historian, and onetime private, stated his opinion on who had taken the stone wall at Kernstown. Lawrence Wilson had been pinned down within a few yards of it, which gave him the best seat in the house. In his opinion, those who gave the Seventh Ohio exclusive credit for taking the wall were in error—nearly every regiment in Tyler's brigade was represented, very little attention being given at the moment to organization.[104]

Firsthand reports of the Twenty-Ninth's fight at Kernstown were still finding their way into the Ohio newspapers when the news hit of the war's greatest battle to date. Grant's previous victories had been announced with congratulatory headlines such as "Bully for Grant," followed with multiple exclamation points, and celebrations at home, and in the army camps in the Shenandoah valley. The battle, which would come to be known as Shiloh, after the church around much of the fighting had whirled, had been a victory for the Union, but the incomprehensible numbers of soldiers who had perished there, both Federal and Confederate, extinguished the urge to celebrate. Grant's losses were reported to be twenty thousand and those of the rebels, double.[105] At thirteen hundred killed, wounded, and missing, the casualties of Kernstown had been puny by comparison.

The newspaper in Jefferson tried to soften the shock of Shiloh by comparing it to history's more sanguinary battles. Napoleon's soldiers had suffered as much at Borodino, Austerlitz, and Waterloo, and for far less noble a purpose.[106] The people believed that this war was God's rod upon them for the nation's sinful ways, and their preachers continued to remind them of that. For those who may have been keeping count, it was becoming clear that a corner had been turned at Shiloh, and the road they were now traveling was leading somewhere darker than any had imagined.

A few days before Kernstown, Mr. Hiram Ewell of Mogadore traveled east to bring his sick son back to Ohio. Cpl. John Ewell, Company G, Twenty-Ninth Ohio, was sick in the hospital at Cumberland. Mr. Ewell stayed with him, hoping for him to get well enough to make the trip home, but he died of congestion of the lungs. Mr. Ewell brought his son home. A funeral service was held at the Brimfield Center cemetery with many of John's friends in attendance. He had been a popular boy at home and in his regiment. The preacher quoted Jeremiah, third chapter, and noted that found in John's personal effects was the Bible that he had been given along with the other soldiers in his company when they left Akron. Inside the front flap he had written, "Father, if I do not live to see you again, take this in remembrance of your son, who went from home to do his duty."[107]

Everyone in the fight at Kernstown had done what was asked of him. The soldiers had been obedient and brave, and their officers universally gallant. Lt. James Treen, the canal boat pilot from Akron, wrote an odd, defensive-sounding letter to the newspaper. He stated that he had acted as honorably on the field as any officer, and if anyone did not believe it, he would gladly give up his office and take a place in the ranks.[108] This suggested that someone had found his leadership wanting, although if that were the case, Treen would have been better off keeping it to himself, because it was never mentioned publicly by anyone, save him.

Shields singled out Tyler's brigade for special praise: "This brigade . . . achieved the decisive movement of the day. They drove the forces of the enemy before them on the left flank, and by hurling this flank back upon the reserve consummated this glorious victory."[109] Of the victory Shields concluded, "The blow has struck terror into this country."[110] If Shields had counted Jackson as one of those discomfited by the result of the battle, he had miscalculated. More than two decades later the soldiers of the Twenty-Ninth Regiment, like most Union soldiers in the fray, still did not understand what they had faced, or what the fight ultimately accomplished. In the regiment's published history, J. Hamp SeCheverell wrote, "Stonewall Jackson, the pride of the South and by many considered the bravest general in the rebel army, was whipped, and that, too, by a force much inferior in numbers, many of whom had never faced death before."[111] The truth was Tyler's brigade alone had nearly the manpower of Jackson's entire force.[112] As further events would reveal, Jackson was hardly whipped. His besting had not really been a defeat at all. He had accomplished his goal of keeping the Federal army in the valley.

The Giddings Boys had passed their first test. The question of whether they would fight had been answered. They had been bloodied, but in general, fortune had blessed them and their loss had been light. They had taken part in a great thing, and most were anxious for the next opportunity in which they might do even more. Not every man was happy at the prospect of further battle. For Adj. Comfort T. Chaffee, the fight at Kernstown had been enough to satisfy his longing for battle. He wrote home, "Suffice it to say that it was a very hard fought battle, and that none of us are anxious that it should become necessary for us to be in such close quarters again."[113]

Not all of their hurt boys had been wounded in body. The transformation of boys into monsters that John Marsh had seen troubled him. "The fact is, in battle man becomes a demon, and delights in the work of death. If his best friend falls at his side he heeds it not, but presses on eager to engage in the wholesale murder. When I was a boy, I was a great admirer of military heroes, now; their honors seem tarnished with blood, and the tears of widows and orphans."[114] Marsh wrestled with this moral dilemma. After a while, he came to the conclusion that killing would be necessary if the Union was to be restored, and he put it aside.

The soldiers awoke the morning after the battle in a state resembling a hangover. They had gone to bed without making anything to eat, or fire to cook it over. Most dropped to the ground where they stood and went immediately to sleep. This morning, they untwisted themselves from the ground, rose to a sitting position, and regarded the battlefield upon which they had fallen asleep. The ground was as thoroughly turned over as if plows had been pulled across it. Slushy snow lay in patches, some of them tinted pink to show where some unlucky boy had been hit or lay afterward. A breeze came up, drifting thousands of bits of cartridge paper into windrows. The field around them was covered with broken rifles, knapsacks, coats, and hats. The pockets of the rebel dead had been turned inside out by souvenir hunters. It looked like the armies had been picked up by their feet and shaken. Before they could wash the grimy residue of battle from their faces, orders came for them to harness up their gear and get ready to march. Jackson was in retreat, and where he went, they must follow.

10

Chasing Jackson

MARCH–JUNE 1862

Slow Motion

There was a fine home in Luray, Virginia, up in the Shenandoah valley. Its owner had left it weeks before without locking the door. That would have been useless with thousands of Union soldiers passing back and forth through the village in their movements up and down through the valley in the past weeks. The house remained just as it had been when its owner said his good-byes to it and rode off, just before the Yankees arrived. In the front room were an imported carpet, a splendid rosewood piano, and the owner's personal library of leather-bound books. Presently, Lt. Gurley G. Crane of the Twenty-Ninth Ohio Volunteer Infantry sat at the fine mahogany table in the center of the room. He got out his pen and a sheaf of blank paper and began to recount for his parents, back in Cuyahoga Falls, Ohio, what the regiment had seen and done in the two months since their grand victory at Kernstown.[1]

Not long ago, it seemed, they had left Ohio nearly a thousand strong in officers and soldiers, every one of them full of resolve and ready for a scrap. They had helped beat Stonewall Jackson in their first battle, at Kernstown. Nine weeks had passed since that grand day, and the events that had transpired since then had pushed the Twenty-Ninth Ohio Infantry to the breaking point. Over a hundred and fifty of them were locked up in rebel prison, dozens more wounded and dead, and some of them had become so dispirited that they deserted. To cap their misfortune, one of their beloved flags was presently tacked to a wall where it was defiled by the rebels who had taken it from them. How to pick and arrange the words to make what had happened to them in just two months understandable to someone who had not been there to see it? Gurley Crane fixed his pen in his fingers and began the attempt.

The morning after their fight at Kernstown, the soldiers started in pursuit of Jackson, south, in the direction of the Shenandoah's source. The wounded rebels encountered in every house along their route confirmed how badly they had injured Jackson's army. Despite the public boasting by their high officers as to Jackson's sorry condition, they regarded him as dangerous and followed him up the valley with caution. Their grand commander, Nathaniel Banks, was now with them in person supervising this pursuit, and he had brought with him the thousands of soldiers in Brig. Gen. Alpheus S. Williams's division. Shields was there too, recovered enough from his Kernstown wounds to take up personal command of his division again, although he was doing it from the seat of a buggy rather than on horseback.[2]

The soldiers were glad to see him and hurrahed him into camp. He had led them to victory, and he could do so again. The army got on the Valley Pike and headed toward Strasburg, the next town south. They paused on the crests of hills to look down upon themselves: dark columns spanning entire valleys, disappearing out of sight up and around hills and then appearing again, wagon trains many miles long bringing up the rear, artillery batteries and cavalry troopers hustling back and forth.

Chill, wet weather had dogged them since Kernstown and persisted through most of April. The weather was not entirely to blame for their inability to chase Jackson down and destroy him. Jackson would not stand and fight. He was moving in retreat more slowly than he ever had moved forward, but the Union commanders seemed unwilling to put the capable machine at their disposal into full throttle.[3] Instead, each day's activities were a duplicate of the preceding day's. A few pieces of artillery in Jackson's rearguard would pause at a point of their choosing and throw a few shells into the Union advance. Ashby's cavalry would ride down to challenge the Federal skirmish line, which brought Banks's army to a full stop. Soldiers stood idle until a battery could be rushed forward to throw a few shells of their own, at which point the rebel gunners would limber up and depart. The next day this routine would be repeated.

On their first day out from Kernstown, the Twenty-Ninth Ohio was thrown out ahead in a broad skirmish line. About noon, it looked like Jackson would cooperate and fight. Ashby's cavalry came out of the woods, whooping and firing as they rode, and the regiment formed itself into hollow squares, which was the prescribed tactic for infantry versus cavalry. After a single volley, the enemy troopers turned and rode back out of sight.[4] The next day the Federal advance reached Strasburg, and it appeared to the Boys that their pursuit of Jackson had already petered out. They were ordered to make camp and organize what gear they had. From such preparations, the common soldier drew the conclusion, as did Nathan Parmater, "Things look as if we were going to stay here for some time; the boys think that we will act the same part that the troops have acted nearly all winter near Washington, that is to watch one an other across the creek."[5]

In their blankets at night, the soldiers could hear skirmishers popping at the rebels, and the thud of an occasional shell exploding, but for the most part life for the soldier in these days was peaceful. Their baggage caught up with them two weeks after Kernstown, and in a few hours their camp began to look like home again.[6] They were in a fertile region. The valley floor was miles wide and filled with farms, some taking up many thousands of acres. The soldiers called these giant farms plantations.

There were sermons from their chaplain on Sundays. The Sabbath was just right for doing wash down in the creek. Colonel Buckley objected. To his thinking, soldiers should wash themselves by all means, but washing their laundry would have to wait. He sent them to their tents, where they engaged in group Bible reading and quiet study of the Scriptures.[7] Wallace Hoyt found it important to let his parents back home know that he and his comrades from Rock Creek, Ashtabula County, had not strayed far from the path in which they had been raised: "The Creek Boys are right side up with Jesus."[8]

This valley seemed one vast wheat field, and every few miles along the Shenandoah River sat an abandoned flouring mill. There were more than a few millers in the Twenty-Ninth Ohio, and they set to work making flour. Each company put some of its boys to building ovens, large enough to bake a dozen loaves at a time.[9] When they got to mixing dough, one of the more knowledgeable among them noticed they were missing the critical ingredient. Bread making would have to wait until they got yeast.[10]

The weather was now more agreeable than anytime since they had left Camp Giddings, and they were now well fed. They were called out to have telegrams read to them, congratulating them on their victory at Kernstown, and Shields continued to pat their backs, as Pvt. Nelson Gillett reported: "We was praised up so by the General in the fight at Winchester that he thinks he will try it again. Our regiment had the name of doing the best of any regiment there and had the least men killed."[11]

Sgt. Rollin L. Jones was not with them. He was doing duty as a printer for the army post office back in Winchester. Jones walked out to the cemetery where the regiment's dead were buried to pay his respects.[12] He noticed a gravestone from which relic hunters had taken many chips. Here lay Maj. Gen. Daniel Morgan, a hero of the Revolution, and the inscription so impressed him that he copied it down and kept it with him for the rest of his life. It said something about the man and soldier Rollin hoped to make of himself: "Patriotism and valor were the chief attributes of his character."[13] Rollin would rejoin the regiment in a few weeks.

Their spirits were high. As Cpl. Wallace Hoyt expressed it, "Soldiering agrees with me first rate. I don't think I could work at anything that would suit me better. The excitement is just what I like."[14] Many of the regiment's soldiers were hardly out of boyhood, and they enjoyed playing pranks. Pickets took over a barn for an outpost and amused themselves at the owner's expense by pretending one of them had smallpox.[15]

In mid-April, Jackson was reported to be making a stand at Mount Jackson, the next town up the Valley Pike. Colonel Buckley's voice was heard an hour past midnight: "Get up and eat your breakfast." On rolling out of their blankets, the soldiers discovered that Buckley had done them the kindness of going up and down the company streets and stoking their campfires back to life.[16] They marched out toward Mount Jackson by the light of the moon. There was musket fire up ahead, and the rumble of artillery. When it grew light enough, the soldiers could see a column of smoke rising into the sky beyond the town. They had seen enough of this same drill in the past few weeks: Jackson had crossed the river and fired the bridge, but Union cavalry drove off the enemy and put out the fire.[17]

Shields spread his entire force into battle line a half mile from the river, as if he intended to cross over and give chase. There was plenty of daylight left for that, but the men stood in their ranks and waited, and waited some more. The only thing disputing their crossing was a piece of rebel artillery, and the Twenty-Ninth Ohio was ordered up to drive it away.[18] They advanced to within musket range of the gun and began to cross an open field when the gunners opened on them. At the sound of the report, and the howl of the shell, most soldiers threw themselves down. Parmater thought that foolish. In his limited experience, the shell sounded closer than it really was. When the next boom shook the ground Parmater noted that the shell had landed much closer than he had estimated, throwing up a geyser of dirt twenty feet high. Ever after, he snugged tight to the ground whenever he heard a shell.[19] The rebel battery limbered up and drove off. They pursued Jackson for a few miles, but by then it had grown too dark to proceed safely. Next day they "captured" Mount Jackson and then marched a few miles more into New Market.[20]

"In the Name of the United States and Uncle Abe Lincoln"

For the Union soldiers who marched into Mount Jackson, conquering Richmond could not have produced more satisfaction. Mount Jackson had been taken "in the name of the United States and Uncle Abe Lincoln," reported Lt. E. B. Woodbury to the folks in Jefferson.[21]

Capt. Horatio Luce, the strawberry grower's son, had been appointed provost marshal of Mount Jackson, and he took his Company E with him to act as military police, while the rest of the regiment went into camp with Shields's division at New Market. There was a bridge to guard here, and order to maintain. The mountains hereabouts were beautiful, the valley astonishingly so, but as for the town itself, "Mount Jackson, like all Virginia towns that we have passed through, looks old and deserted, smoky and dirty, but little pride taken in beautifying their houses."[22] The town was quiet, except for the passage of freight wagons passing through on their way to the front, seven miles to the south. Soldiers who had deserted Stonewall's army began to filter home, and although they had taken an oath that they would not take up arms against the Union, they needed watching.[23] That Jackson's men were leaving him was another sign that his army was on the ropes.

The boys of Company E had taken up lodging in an abandoned home, and they found life in it far preferable to sleeping out of doors. All kinds of good things to eat were available in the town, and at reasonable prices. Cash was always a concern, but a soldier could earn a little extra here on his off-duty time by working as a ward attendant at one of the hospitals.[24] Life here was pleasant but exceedingly dull. They hunted for ways to pass the hours.

Parmater carved a pipe, prospected for showy quartz specimens, and wrote ten-page letters to his girlfriend, Ipsa, but he still could not fill the day. He found an old fishing net and he and his friends went off one day to try their luck. Fishing did not pan out. On their return, they came across the house of a Mr. Weems, located in the middle of his six-thousand-acre plantation. Weems was serving in the rebel army and his property was now their property, so Parmater figured. He took three books and a small picture as souvenirs of his visit.[25] At home, stealing was a sin, and Parmater was a pious young man. But here in the enemy's country, these strictures did not apply, nor did they apply to cadging free meals from civilians, or stealing "rabbit with the split hoof," soldier code for pigs or sheep.

The ceaseless spring rains made everything dreary, and the gloom they cast penetrated the soldiers of Company E in Mount Jackson. The regiment's sick were sent to the hospital here and put in the same beds recently occupied by Stonewall Jackson's sick.[26] Boys who died during the night were carried out to the front porches of the hospitals. To the boys of Company E fell the somber duty of standing guard over them until morning. Alma Dalrymple, a twenty-four-year-old private in Company A, got sick in late March but had been able to walk to the hospital. Five days later he fell into a delirium and died.[27] His father complained that the Twenty-Ninth Regiment had been forced to sleep on the cold, hard ground without tents and with only one blanket for warmth for nearly two months. His son had died of typhoid fever, but surely, in the father's view, the physical hardships heaped on his son had been the root cause.[28] Parmater's squad escorted Dalrymple's remains to the burying yard, where the raw-pine-plank box was covered with the flag and put in the ground, with three volleys to send him on his way.[29]

The Homerville Boys were known as an especially hardy group, proud of their physical strength and resilience. Nevertheless, by early April 1862 only two of the group who had practiced drill in their captain's pasture the preceding autumn, John Marsh and Phil Hawk, were still on their feet. John Rupp, Jeb Bair, and all the others had fallen out of the war already and were in army hospitals or back home in Ohio trying to get well.[30] Everyone in the regiment was sick with something, from sore throats that caused most men to speak in a hoarse whisper, to coughs that would not go away, to bowel problems.

A snow fell in late April, which seemed to be a last wringing-out of the wet weather that had hung over them for weeks. Parmater opened the door of the house he and his mates had lived in for going on two months, and he felt the novel sensation of warm sun on his face. He noted that spring came all at once. Overnight, the fields turned green, the peach trees put out their flowers, and the whole valley looked like one vast meadow.[31] All of nature seemed to be tendering the soldiers a joyful welcome.[32]

Parmater walked out one evening just as the sun was going down behind the mountains to the west. "The golden light ringed the fields giving them a most lovely appearance. It looks more as though peace and plenty reigned than that black war was in the land."[33] One night a wildfire was seen moving along the crest of the Blue Ridge, a marvel that drew the attention of the soldiers who were still up to see it, looking as it did like the gunfire that had pulsed along the wall at Kernstown. The war seemed very far away up here in these pristine valleys. Distanced from the war's larger scenes, and unmolested by Jackson, it was easy to fall into the belief that a similar stasis had taken hold of the armies everywhere, and if this were so, the war might go on forever. Their hope that the war would be over come summer, in plenty of time for them to be home to celebrate the Fourth of July, began to melt away.[34]

The main body of the regiment, camped near New Market, had seen no more action than the provost guard left at Mount Jackson. New Market had been a busy trading center of twelve hundred, but the Union soldiers who first entered it found it mostly boarded up and deserted, as if in anticipation of a hurricane. Merchants had come out from Richmond, taken over vacant shops, and were selling their wares to the soldier market at prices not even the officers could afford.[35] Most every enlisted man needed shoes, some were going barefooted, and those who had shoes did not have socks. The Valley Pike was a miracle of modern paving and at first glance was thought superior to anything they had marched on. However, its compacted surface made every soldier footsore. To make matters worse, the lucky few who got new government shoes found them to be worthless. After a few miles of tramping, thin leather wore off the edges of the soles, revealing them to be made of wood, like some Dutch boy's shoes.[36] Willis Sisley, a private in Company C, although a farmer by trade and not a cobbler, invented the perfect footwear to defeat these paved roads and sent an order home for his father to fill:

> These paved roads is awful hard on leather. I have seen boots with a plate of iron all oer the heel and half of the sole. You know about the size of my flat foot. It is about like yours. Don't get them too short. Get a midlen thick sole and have the heels chuck full of good nails. Have the sole stick out midlen well. Have the feet lined and have them midlen high. Get Dick Mullens to make them if you can get as solid a pair as he can make and have them midlen nice for there will be thousands looking at them. The best fellow has the best pair here.[37]

The men admired Shields for his victorious ways, but in his oversight of the quartermaster department, he was a failure. In fairness to him, the supply line along which shoes and other necessaries flowed ran far into their rear and was vulnerable to interruption.

They awoke one morning in late April in their camp near New Market, and as they were boiling coffee, it occurred to them that every man had slept the whole night through without disturbance. Jackson's army had moved off and taken most of his rear guard with him. This time, Shields did not go after him. It had taken him the whole month of April, but in Shields's view, Jackson had finally realized that the Federals could not be scared off.

The Boys began to wonder if Shields subscribed to their belief that blood would have to be spilled if the rebellion were to be put down. The artillery skirmishing of the past six weeks had harmed hardly a soul. An officer in one of Shields's batteries recalled that the only casualty in all of it had been a kitchen stove smashed to pieces by an errant cannon shot.[38] Shields had cavalry with him, but sending them out to maintain contact with Jackson, or at the least to trace his whereabouts, did not figure in. From appearances, Jackson had moved outside the boundaries of this department, and what he did in future could trouble the sleep of others. In the last week of March, and the entire month of April, the Federals had progressed only thirty miles from where they had started, around Winchester. However, Banks and Shields believed that their movements against Jackson since Kernstown had been a success. The enemy had not only been prevented from retaking Winchester but had been pushed out of sight entirely. Eastern newspapers, which officers seemed to rely on for intelligence as much as any other source, were reporting that Jackson had left the valley and was on his way to the defense of Richmond. The valley was safe.

McClellan's huge army had finally departed Washington in armadas carrying men and mountains of supplies and was taking up positions above Richmond. It was becoming clear to even the pudd'nheads here at New Market that whatever McClellan did far away near Richmond would have an effect on them.

After weeks of quiet, a succession of rumors sprinted down the company streets, taken as gospel one day and discarded the next. It was reported that the rebels had pushed McClellan into the Chesapeake and were sending an overwhelming force to Jackson in the valley.[39] The Federals in the valley might be falling back. Parmater noted that the thought of giving up without a fight made the Boys shut their teeth tight.[40] A group of thirty Negroes passed through on their way north, believing that now was the time to get free, before their masters returned, along with Jackson's army.[41] The most recent rumor guessed that they were to move back down the valley to Strasburg, and it proved to be the only one that was accurate. This was not a fallback or anything like it. Strasburg was the first waypoint on the way out of the valley. Then it was confirmed: the Boys were leaving the valley and joining McClellan for the conquest of Richmond.

By driving Jackson from the valley, the fears of the authorities in Washington had been calmed enough for them to authorize Banks to leave the valley and join Gen. Irwin McDowell's army at Fredericksburg. They would then march overland toward Richmond, block the escape of rebels not crushed by McClellan's mighty army, and the rebellion would be over. A Union prisoner recently escaped from Jackson reported to General Banks that Stonewall was seen departing over the Blue Ridge. Another report absolutely confirmed that he had left the valley and was bound for Richmond. In Banks's opinion, these were facts, and he reported them as such to Secretary of War Stanton on April 30: "There is nothing to be done in this valley this side of the fortifications this side of Strasburg."[42] And, in case Stanton did not receive the telegram or failed to understand it completely, Banks wrote again, stating that not only was Jackson gone but he would not likely return to the valley, ever. Jackson's army was demoralized, reduced in numbers, and on half rations. He would have to go to Richmond just to avoid starving to death.

General Banks got a little ahead of himself and proposed that if authorized he would march his corps out of the valley toward Washington, and chances were good that he could win victories along the way that would lift his army from its doldrums and electrify the nation.[43] Banks must have reacted with some surprise when he received a telegram from Stanton notifying him that Shields's division, which represented two-thirds of Banks's army, could leave the valley, but Banks was to stay put, just in case. Shields's men were now officially assigned to Gen. Irwin McDowell's command, presently readying for the march to help McClellan. McDowell lost no time in wiring Shields that he was delighted that the president had honored him by placing Shields's gallant division under his supervision.[44] Shields replied a few days later that he would be ready to march with his eleven thousand men as soon as he could round up his outlying detachments.[45]

The big news of their division's move east, where headlines and probably history waited on them, took a few days to trickle down to the ranks. Soldiers consulted their road maps and saw that their destination was over 120 miles distant, but even if they had to cover it on foot, it would be worth it to be in on the last days of the Confederacy.

The quiet days Parmater and Company E had spent in Mount Jackson ended on May 10, when they were ordered to form up with all their gear. They marched all night and reached their regiment outside New Market. The happy news that they would be joining the big show was dampened a little when orders arrived in camp for everyone to turn in their tents. A few could be retained for hospital and office work, but most, along with every other piece of baggage, was to be left behind.[46] Every man in the command, the officers most of all, sent up an immediate complaint.

Their gracefully conical and thoroughly modern Sibley tents had been promised them for months, and once delivered the Boys had been allowed to enjoy them for less than a month. McDowell, whom the soldiers already regarded as cruel without having met him, had his reasons for taking away the tents and they were good ones. He had seen that an army encumbered by too much trumpery traveled slowly, and he issued the order demanding a reduction of baggage.[47] In the past months the officers had lodged themselves in private homes near the regiment's camp, and if not that, then in the comfortable Sibleys. Some officers balked when ordered to turn them in, and some threatened to resign. Wallace Hoyt thought the hoopla noteworthy enough to report in a letter home:

> May 10, 1862
> Camp Buckley near Haymarket, Va.
>
> Dear Mother
>
> As there is a chance to send out mail I thought I would send you a line. We made an advance to Harrisonburg but the next day we retreated back to here. Yesterday we turned our tents over to the quartermaster so we are left out of doors. But they served the whole of Shields' Division alike. A good many of the officers are resigning on account of the tents being taken. . . .[48]

There was likely more smoke than flame in the regiment over the tent issue. Several of the Twenty-Ninth Regiment's officers had resigned, but Hoyt was mistaken in supposing that they had found the test of going without tents too severe a strain on their patriotism. Lieutenant Crowell of Company A and Captains Alden Steel and John Morse of Companies K and F, respectively, left the regiment within two weeks of their first battle.[49] Parmater did not know the reason behind their resignations, but had heard some soldiers guess that these officers thought they would be safer back in Ohio.[50] After Kernstown their little adjutant, Comfort T. Chaffee, had expressed the hope that he would never again see the likes of what he had seen at Kernstown. Now he, too, resigned, and a few days into April he was on his way back home.[51] Two other officers, Lt. Seth Wilson of Company I and 2nd Lt. Henry Mack of Company H, turned in their resignations. Back at Camp Kelly, resignations by Pulaski Hard and Leveret Grover were accompanied by explanations. Both had fallen victim to disease. For those who resigned after Kernstown, no explanation was offered, leaving the privates an interesting topic for campfire bull sessions.

When Buckley forwarded the batch of officer resignations on to Ohio, he sent a note expressing his view on what sort of man should be considered to take the places of those gone. Instead of those who were not present for duty half the time, and those who always asked to be excused when danger presented itself, only men of real merit should be rewarded by promotion. Buckley pledged that as the opportunities presented themselves, he would "endeavor to sift such men out of the 29th Regiment

Ohio Volunteer Infantry."[52] Buckley blocked one officer from promotion who was entitled to it by his seniority, and he made no bones as to why he had done it. The man drank too much—to the point he had to be hospitalized.[53]

McDowell took away their tents but gave back something of considerable value to the enlisted men. There would now be enough room in the wagons to carry knapsacks and blankets, and in the long march that lay ahead to lighten a soldier's load by even a pound would count for quite a lot.[54]

Buckley was making a name for himself. In the absence of General Tyler, he would command the Third Brigade on its march out of the valley. On the evening of their departure, he circulated a bulletin through the camps warning the soldiers that they would be passing through country still held by the enemy and that anyone who fell behind was sure to be captured. In addition, the names of stragglers were to be taken down, their pay stopped, and their company officers held responsible.[55]

No one was joyful at the prospect of walking from one side of Virginia clear to the other, but they packed their things and wrote letters home. Wallace Hoyt was finishing a letter to his parents when a soldier came hurrying down the company street calling for the last mail the men would be able to send home for the foreseeable future: "We are preparing to make a long march all that are not fit for duty are sent back to the hospital and their guns turned over to the quartermaster. The Boys from the Creek are all well myself included and will march but the mail is ready and I must adjourn. I will write after the march is over."[56] Shields's division got itself sorted out and on the road.

Marched to Death

They were started on what the soldiers regarded as one of the greatest marches of the present war. No sooner had they left camp than the poor whites and the "darkies" from the surrounding countryside moved in to pick through the blankets, clothing, and sundry things the soldiers had discarded.[57] The head of Shields's column soon came upon the white tents and blowing banners of General Banks's headquarters. He had arrived at this place ahead of them, but he was headed back into the valley, not out of it. Shields and his staff rode over to Banks to say goodbye. Banks and his officers wore the look of doom on their faces. Shields's officers could barely contain their enthusiasm, shook hands all around, and rode back to the head of the division as if they were leading a grand parade.[58]

The climb out of the valley was by easy up-and-down grades in the direction of Luray. The first two days out were the warmest they'd seen since leaving Ohio. Thousands of marching feet ground the road into reddish flour, which caked sweating men and animals and made breathing hard. There were pretty views to be had along here normally, but fires were burning in the forests, and the soldiers could not see beyond the smoke and dust encasing their columns.[59] They made camp and the first thing the soldiers did was rush down to a brook to souse the road dust from face and hair.

Next day they made another hot and dusty twenty miles and passed through Luray. The regiment's band got out front and played "Yankee Doodle" as they swung through, bringing smiles to the faces of the black people, and turning the expressions of the white residents sour as green apples.[60] Just a couple of days of marching had filled the ambulances to overflowing with men too sick or sore footed or plain worn out.[61] Another day's hard marching and they would be free of the valley. It rained the next day, which settled the dust well enough but turned everything back to mud. Just as they got settled in for sleep, near Front Royal, on the east flank of the Blue Ridge, the sharp toot of a steam locomotive was heard, and the men were glad to hear it. Being close to a railroad always lifted their spirits, and the entire regiment raised itself and cheered. At last, they were out of the wilderness to which they'd been consigned since arriving at Patterson's Creek.[62]

The weather remained "lowry," the soldier's word for a sky that was gray and drizzly, but they trudged along. The road up to Manassas Gap was broken and the country rough, but they climbed through it happy to have mastered the last mountain standing between them and Richmond.[63] A mysterious man on a horse had shadowed them from the ridgelines above. Eight miles out, near Gaines' Cross Roads, the scouts ran into some rebel cavalry, and where there was cavalry there might be infantry. The new adjutant, Theron Winship, galloped all the way back to Shields to warn of the danger, and when artillery and cavalry rushed forward, the rebel scouts were driven off.[64]

The road they were marching tracked the course of the famous Rappahannock River. In the legend they'd all grown up with, the boy George Washington was said to have thrown a coin across it, further down at Fredericksburg, and that was where they were headed. Beyond Chester Gap, the river continued south, but Shields's division was eastbound, which meant they had to get across. It almost went without saying by this time: the bridge had been wrecked by the rebels. They marched down the river three miles before they found a place where thousands of men, many unable to swim, could ford its swift current. Most of the men took turns floating across in an abandoned skiff that had come bobbing along. Some men swam across. They stripped down to their underwear, or less, which caused their comrades to hoot and jeer. It was all in good fun.[65]

One evening the men camped in a church large enough to accommodate most of the regiment. Chaplain Hurlburt always liked to be close to his boys, and he unrolled his blanket in the amen corner, near the pulpit, while the soldiers filled every other part, including the choir loft. An old Negro who had been pressed into service to drive one of their wagons settled himself in the loft and remarked, "Wal, dis child hab been in dis yer gallery a heap ob times before, but not in sich a shape as dis."[66] Chaplain Hurlburt made note of the man's remark, and sent it along to the newspaper.

Another day's march and they arrived in Warrenton, less than twenty miles below the Bull Run battlefield. Warrenton contained fine homes, churches, and stores and was set in a countryside of carefully tended farms, groves, and pretty streams. Shields's boys were among the first Union troops to enter the place since Virginia had seceded. In future days, Warrenton would be visited by a succession of armies. The soldiers who saw it now would note that with each subsequent visit it deteriorated more, until when they last saw Warrenton it was as dirty and beaten up as every other Southern place. Soldiers of Parmater's company stood guard while the brigade passed through. Parmater was inquisitive and outgoing by nature, and he found a lady of high cultivation who was willing to talk to him at length. She told him that she felt it wrong for the Union soldiers to invade her country and also that the South could never be subdued.[67]

The next day they rested. The soldiers cleaned their guns and mended their raggedy gear. Accidents with their weapons continued to pester them. Forty-four-year-old Pvt. Elijah Curtis of Conneaut was struck in the shoulder blade by the discharge from a gun handled by a soldier in Company K. The surgeon removed the ball and dug out what remained of the shattered bone, but the word was that Curtis would not survive.[68] In their history to this point, more of the regiment's soldiers had been wounded by accident than had been shot intentionally by the rebels at Kernstown. By May 19 they reached Catlett's Station, on the Orange and Alexandria Railroad, and were now in the outer rings of McDowell's army. Here they came into contact with eastern troops for the first time.

Six regiments of McDowell's men, dressed in neat new uniforms, white shirts, and spotless gaiters, were facing each other across a meadow getting ready for a mock battle. The Giddings Boys could not resist throwing a few remarks in the direction of the untested soldiers of Gen. Abram Duryea's brigade, and the easterners could not help but offer comments back regarding the dilapidated condition of Shields's soldiers. Soldiers from both outfits stepped out of the ranks and banged away at each other with fists until one or the other said uncle.[69]

They tramped along making good mileage, although the road now was clogged with soldiers and wagons from at least twenty regiments. It appeared as though they were marching through one vast army camp, the entire neighborhood alive with military purpose. Wherever they stopped, the Boys fell to the ground and slept. Those who had energy left played baseball.[70] The country hereabouts had not been visited much by the armies as yet, and the fields and woods stood green, and the farms and villages neat and orderly. Their line of march was taking them to Fredericksburg. They had come a hundred miles since New Market, and the long daily marches were taking a toll. Parmater had been bothered by a pain in his side since they'd started, and he could no longer draw a full breath. He rode the last of the way in an ambulance, which was hardly better than walking, so hot and jarring was the ride.[71] There was no dishonor in riding, and a soldier who knew when he had reached his limits was wise to take an ambulance. Continuing on foot could lead to the grave.

Four otherwise healthy men had died within a day of each other in early April and the stated cause was "hard marching."[72] A long march produced stragglers, but most caught up with the regiment later that day. Many had fallen out on this march, but some of them did not show up in camp later in the day. It would take some time to determine what had become of them.

In the history of the Twenty-Ninth Ohio Volunteer Infantry there was but one period in which soldiers deserted in numbers enough to signify a failure in morale. By war's end, the total number of men who walked away never to be heard from again did not exceed the average for the Union army, or even Ohio forces taken separately.[73] A few men had deserted the regiment before, and a few more would after, but the tide of desertion in the Giddings Regiment began to rise on this march to join McDowell and would crest in a few weeks, largely as a result of events this march generated. How or why a soldier deserted was hardly ever explained, unless he was captured and returned to the regiment by force. Once found gone, a notation was entered in the regiment's descriptive books, as in the case of Pvt. Isaac Wells of Company G: "May 22, 1862, Fredericksburg, Va., While on the march he slipped away."[74]

The Boys came into Falmouth, just above Fredericksburg, barefoot and in uniforms that were tattered and patched. They were the most impoverished-looking soldiers ever seen in the Union army. All the blue had been bleached from their uniforms by sun, rain, and snow, and they looked as gray as any rebel's. To fix their sorry appearance, Shields had requisitioned new uniforms and shoes and arranged that they be sent ahead to meet them at Catlett's Station, on the road to Falmouth. But the new things had not arrived. The smartly uniformed eastern soldiers called them Shields's Foot Cavalry or Shields's Bushwhackers, and when such remarks were made loud enough to be heard, companies pulled themselves over to the side of the road to watch the fists fly and cheer on their champions.[75]

It was reported that Lincoln was here at Falmouth to review McDowell's army before it started out to help McClellan. The soldiers set to work brushing life back into their uniforms, chipping off appliqués of mud, polishing buckles and gun barrels, and, for those who still had them, blacking their shoes. Parmater was too sick to go far from the hospital tent, but he carried with him a spyglass through which he watched Lincoln review the troops.[76] Dozens of regiments paraded past Lincoln, his long thin figure in plain dark suit and tall hat standing out clearly among so much soldier blue.[77] Lincoln did not cut a military figure in the least; he was a civilian, and a plain one at that, and the soldiers found in his homely appearance something they could love. One boy who saw him close up would say later that he looked just like "anybody," which meant he looked like them. Lincoln was interested particularly in seeing the heroes of Kernstown, and he was touched by their worn-out appearance.

After the review, everyone marched back to camp and made final preparations for their next move. McDowell had delayed his plans to embark for the Peninsula for two days to allow Shields's men a chance to rest, and after that they would load up and march to the support of McClellan. Shields's division was to have the post of honor and lead McDowell's army out of Fredericksburg, which was a salute to their experience and hardiness. The Boys had been back in camp less than an hour after meeting Lincoln when news of a debacle back in the valley roared through the camps, and that news would turn the grand plan to aid McClellan on its head.

Jackson had not left the valley at all. He had been in camp far up the valley, near a place called Port Republic, strengthening his army and laying plans to retake the real estate he had relinquished a few weeks earlier. After Shields left, Jackson had come down the valley much stronger than he had been last seen going up it, and he attacked Banks's outposts at Front Royal. He got Banks on the run out of Strasburg, and the run would not stop until Banks had reached the Potomac at Harpers Ferry, which is where Banks had started out the winter before.

There was a keen urgency to what must now be done. Jackson was in four places at once, and if not checked, he might well be battering at the walls of Washington by the day after tomorrow. Lincoln and Stanton moved nervous fingers around on the map of the valley, interpreted lines and shadings, measured distances from one point to another, and the prudent response came into focus. McDowell's movement to support McClellan would have to be scratched, and his army, including Shields's division must start for the valley at once. His men had already beaten Jackson once, and they could do so again.

In Jackson's bold move lay an opportunity. He was on the banks of the Potomac, above Martinsburg, and if McDowell drove into the valley from the east, and Gen. John C. Frémont and his western Virginia army pushed in from the west, they could cut him off and finish him. McDowell protested that trying to link up with Frémont in broken country with few roads was a tricky proposition at best, and McClellan tried to point out that Jackson's raid was only a diversion to weaken his hand. However, panic drove the decision making in the White House just now, and the end result was that the Twenty-Ninth Ohio and all of Shields's command was to be turned around to repeat a march that they had just finished.

The order for them to return was met in Shields's division with shock, and then anger. Few of the officers saw any sense in it.[78] There was cussing a-plenty and slapping of gauntleted gloves against knees, but orders were orders. The enlisted men remained uncomplaining. Such things were beginning to seem normal. They pulled their cap visors down low and began the march back. Coming here had been tough enough, but this time they would have to march faster, without rest or letup.

They moved via Manassas Junction, the scene of the battle of Bull Run, which the Boys found desolate. The armies had tramped the ground down so thoroughly that not a weed could poke through, and trees had been cut down for miles around, leaving fields of stumps. They drew close enough that the rebel fortifications could be seen, and resting atop them were artillery pieces pointed in the direction of Washington. On closer inspection, these guns were found to be nothing more than carved and painted tree trunks.[79] The sense of alarm intensified the nearer they approached the capital. At Manassas, they ran into soldiers still shaky from their flight from Thoroughfare Gap, the pass through the last tall ridge this side of Washington. The refugees told them they had escaped destruction by Jackson's tens of thousands by the skin of their teeth, and only then by the good sense and lightning-quick reactions of their commander.

These were the soldiers of Brig. Gen. John White Geary's command. In civilian life, Geary had most recently been a farmer, but before that he had led a Lander-like life out in the Far West. He had raised an oversize regiment of fifteen hundred Pennsylvania volunteers. They would be split into the Twenty-Eighth and 147th Pennsylvania Infantry Regiments, and the artillery battery they had brought with them would come to be known to all as Knap's battery. A month before, Geary had been promoted to brigadier general of volunteers and had hopes he would go much higher before the fighting ceased. Currently, he was in charge of protecting a fifty-mile stretch of the Manassas Gap Railroad, running toward the valley.

Winding up the grade into Thoroughfare Gap, Shields's division met a few more of Geary's soldiers coming down. He had neglected to call in his pickets when he executed his strategic retreat.[80] Shields's men were coming up the road in uniforms now hanging from most of them in stitched-together patches, devoid of shoes, carrying with them only the weapons they needed to defend themselves. What they found at Geary's former camp angered everyone who saw it. To keep the rebels from getting it, Geary had burned a bounty of supplies, including perfectly good uniforms and all his soldiers' tents, and had made bonfires of rifles and carbines superior to anything these men were shouldering. His officers had departed in such haste that they left even their swords and photographs of loved ones. "The all-firedest scare I ever heard of," was how Col. Nathan Kimball described it.[81]

Geary had relied on intelligence given him by a jittery runaway slave who came into his camp telling of Jackson's hordes rolling down the valley and poised to overrun Geary at their convenience. He passed this information along, undigested, to Washington, with the warning that large bodies of rebels had been seen all along his front. He was later chastised for his overreaction, and his actions at Thoroughfare Gap were seen by some as disgraceful, although Geary had friends in the newspaper business who praised him for saving his command and giving early warning to Washington. Shields could not find a rebel within twenty miles of the gap, but just now Geary's report of marching rebels fed the panic in Washington.

Worry began to gnaw at the Boys on their way back to the valley. They had left their sick behind at the hospitals in Mount Jackson, Strasburg, and Winchester when they left the valley, some of them brothers or cousins, and comrades at the very least, and these places had been right in the path of Jackson's rampage. The steps of the weary marchers were quickened by the hope that they might get there in time to save them.

Swept Up

They did not know it just now, but they were too late to save the Boys they'd left behind. Banks's medical staff had done the best they could to get these unfortunates to safety before Jackson overran them. But some men were too sick to move, and for others there had not been enough time. Patients opened their eyes to see rebels in tall cavalry boots standing at the foot of their cots. Jackson's men judged some of them too sick to travel. They were allowed to keep to their hospital beds upon giving their word that they would give up their fight against the rebellion. Others were rousted from the hospitals and herded onto wagons, to begin the long bumpy ride up the valley and out of it again to Lynchburg, where the rebels had established a prison camp.

Pvt. Daniel Platt had been left at the hospital in Strasburg with a lamed ankle, along with the others unfit to march to Fredericksburg.[82] As Jackson approached, the staff loaded the infirm aboard wagons and ambulances and horses, with those who could walk trying their best to keep up. Banks's exodus jammed the pike, slowing everyone's escape, and between Strasburg and Winchester, Ashby's cavalry stampeded down on the head of the train and took sixty Twenty-Ninth Ohio soldiers prisoner. Platt was in the middle of the column and had a few seconds to consider his course. He jumped down from the wagon and ran for the brush, thus saving his hide, except for a buckshot wound to his already sore ankle. Later, he claimed to have seen Ashby's troopers murder some of the captured for an offense no greater than not walking fast enough to keep up. Platt said he saw one soldier of Company H, Wellington Gillett, shot down in this manner.[83] His recognition of the corpse might have been faulty. Gillett was reported as having died in the hospital at Mount Jackson five days earlier.[84]

George Treen also claimed to have seen the rebels murder two Twenty-Ninth Ohio soldiers, although no record shows any Giddings Regiment soldier to have been killed during Jackson's juggernaut down the valley. Treen and eighteen other soldiers well enough to walk had gotten out ahead of the main body of refugees and were hobbling toward Winchester when they were set upon by rebel cavalry. While others in his group were shot down or taken prisoner, Treen "skedaddled" and found his way into the Union lines.[85] A small piece in the *Ashtabula Weekly Telegraph* stated that the "painful suspense" had been cleared up concerning the disappearance at Strasburg of Steadman J. Rockwell, an eighteen-year-old corporal in Company E.[86] He and Lt. Andrew Wilson of Company B had flown ahead of Jackson, but the rebels got on their trail. The two men were forced to hide out on a secesh property.[87] Their hiding place was discovered and they were taken prisoner, but their captors were in a hurry, and they did not take Rockwell or Wilson with them. A month later both men would be back home in Ashtabula County with a grand tale to tell. Who had been taken was not known for some time.

Most all of the dozens of soldiers belonging to the Giddings Regiment swept up by Jackson spent no more than a few hours in rebel hands, some no more than a few minutes. Jackson's men were moving too fast to make bringing prisoners along convenient. Besides, many of them were sick and in need of special attention. The hundreds of wagons the rebels had captured were filled with things of more value to them than prisoners. Tons of rations, ammunition, and every kind of sundry military supplies were being loaded aboard for the return trip south. Prisoners signed their parole pledges and Jackson passed on. Pvt. John Watson of Company G was in the hospital in Winchester suffering from a lung disorder when Jackson took the town. Too unwell to be moved from his bed, he was paroled where he lay.[88] Under this oath of honor, a soldier swore that he would not take up arms again until he was officially exchanged for a Confederate prisoner of equal rank.[89] There was nothing to prevent a man from picking up a rifle and continuing the fight as soon as the enemy went out of sight. But a soldier's promise that he would not do so seemed to count for much, which explains why so many of the soldiers captured by Jackson ended up back in Ohio rather than rejoining the regiment directly.

Four lucky boys were discharged from the hospital at Strasburg a day before it was captured on May 25, and they had arrived home in Summit County before the news of its capture hit the local newspapers.[90] Jehiel Lane Jr. had been sick at Strasburg, gotten better after the regiment marched away, and was acting as a cook in the hospital.[91] His father, who had been sick with lung fever in the very same hospital, made it out earlier on the day Jackson came calling, but he had not been heard from since and was presumed to be among the captured in the wagon train.[92] Pvt. Euclid Supplee had come down with the measles and been sent to the hospital in Strasburg. After one week of convalescence, he felt well enough to rejoin the regiment. He and several others had gone no more than a few miles before they were made prisoner by elements of Ashby's cavalry.

Some of the captured were too weak from recent illness to walk to prison. The rebel guards took pity on them and allowed them to ride U.S. army mules that had been cut loose from captured wagons. A soldier could not sit comfortably for days after riding one of these razor-backed beasts, but it was only through the kindness of their captors that these men survived the trip. Supplee's group was herded back into the town of Winchester with a rebel brass band at the head. When the band struck up tunes favored in the rebel army, the prisoners sang "Yankee Doodle" so loudly that the band gave up.[93]

Euclid was one of the hundreds of sick Federals thought healthy enough to stand the march to prison. When Jackson's retrograde began, Euclid and the others were ordered out of the depot building in which they had been confined. A mounted rebel officer rode up and down their line ordering those unable to march to step out. Thinking it would be better to ride to prison than walk there, Euclid stepped forward. He was returned to the building in which he had been locked up while others, like Newton P. Hummiston, the youthful private who had written to his mother back in Paw Paw and enclosed part of his pay with the suggestion she be grateful for small favors, filed south out of Winchester toward an uncertain fate. Frémont's cavalry made a dash into Winchester and freed Supplee. His experience had taught him there was advantage in riding through the war rather than walking it, and once recovered enough from his ordeal, Supplee joined the Sixth Ohio Cavalry.[94]

More Federal soldiers—the sick and those who had received severe wounds at Kernstown—lay in the hospitals in Winchester. At word of Jackson's approach, hundreds were carried on their cots to waiting boxcars that took them on a jury-rigged line to Martinsburg, thence to Harpers Ferry, and then on to hospitals in Frederick, Maryland. Some soldiers, including over two dozen of the Twenty-Ninth's men, could not be gotten out of the way in time and were scooped up in Winchester and taken along by the rebels, regardless of their state of health. One Twenty-Ninth Ohio soldier was left where he lay. He had been paralyzed by a bullet at Kernstown and could not be moved. The *New York Times* listed the names of a dozen of these, some of whom had been sick at the hospital set up in the town's Union Hotel by Surgeon Amos Fifield, in which three of them had been serving as nurses.[95] Capt. Josiah Wright wrote later that several soldiers had been left behind in the valley to guard a flouring mill when the Twenty-Ninth Regiment left for Falmouth, and they had been swept up by Jackson along with the rest.[96]

Many of the Giddings Boys left behind had been put in the hospitals or assigned light duty in them, on account of the most common affliction in Shields's division—sore feet.[97] When Shields's division marched to Falmouth, nearly a thousand soldiers could not make the march because they were lame, and they were lame because they had been going barefoot or had been trudging the pike's hard surface in leather scraps that had once been shoes. Lack of footwear was far more serious an issue than the soldier's personal comfort. Poor shoes, or no shoes at all, had cost Shields nearly five times his loss at Kernstown.

II

"Up the River and Back of the Mountains"

THE BATTLE OF PORT REPUBLIC, JUNE 9, 1862

Return to the Shenandoah

Nathan Parmater was too weak to walk back to the valley. He and the other sick rode on boxcars to Manassas, where the line quit.[1] The lame and halt would have to ride in ambulances. There were only half enough ambulances to haul them further, and Parmater gave up his spot and started out on foot. He struggled up to Thoroughfare Gap and caught up to Shields's supply train, hitched a ride on a wagon, and overtook his regiment near White Plains. The soldiers were as worn out as the invalids who had followed along behind them.[2]

The Boys had prayed for a day of rest, and it appeared they would be allowed half of one anyway. At midday they were directed off the road and ordered to set up camp. Their rest was interrupted just before dark. The enemy was closer than Shields thought, and he believed a nighttime march would close the distance. As Parmater described it, "We filed into the road just after dark, but of all the marching I ever did this went ahead of all."[3]

If Shields had sent scouts ahead, they had misinformed him about the condition of the road. Alternating rain and sun had cut ruts into it as tall as a wheel hub, and in some places the rain had washed the whole road away and left the earth's bouldered crust exposed, so men had to climb as much as march. Shields had not considered how to pass thousands of men—and all his wagons, artillery, and cavalry—over a narrow road enclosed tightly on either side by steep banks. Soldiers walked only a few yards before having to stop and stand in place while tangles were straightened out up ahead. They walked a few feet, which was a tonic to aching backs and legs, and stopped again. The best they could make was three miles in four hours, and by the time morning came, the Boys felt more used up than if they'd marched thirty miles.[4]

Men fell down and could not be coaxed back onto their feet. The regiment stopped for sleep an hour before sunrise, but two hours later, they were called out onto the road for more.[5] Five days after starting, they limped into Front Royal, having made the march back in half the time it had taken to get from this same point to Falmouth on the way out. The cavalry drove off the small rebel force holding Front Royal, but instead of pressing ahead to join hands with Frémont, who was coming toward Luray from the west, Shields paused.

McDowell arrived the following day, got a fire going under Shields, and ordered him to move toward Strasburg, at once. Jackson had sniffed out the plan to trap him and was falling back at full speed from the Potomac. If Shields moved with celerity, they could intercept his strung-out army and chop it to pieces. Most of that day passed away before Shields got his command ready to march, and when they did, it was on the wrong road. It was night by now, with cold rain coming down by the bucket before he got his division off the road to Winchester and onto the right road to Strasburg. Nothing more could be done in the dark, and the soldiers marched back to their starting place and slept on the ground.[6] During the night it was learned that the last of Jackson's rearguard had already passed south of Strasburg, and any further movement in that direction was useless. Jackson had won this leg of the race.

The Deluge

The rain falling on them topped everything anyone had ever seen or heard of. In Pennsylvania the same storm had washed away farms and entire villages. Here, the roads were impassable and creeks that a few days before could be stepped over were now full-fledged rivers. The Shenandoah had become a monster. Shields was slow to formulate a plan of attack. A few men would have been enough to scout the condition of the bridges in the area. Instead, he sent the entire Twenty-Ninth Regiment on a series of profitless marches that occupied the last days of May and the first few of June. After one of these, the normally unquestioning Nathan Parmater wrote in his diary, "Just before dark we were ordered to march and soon fell in and marched back to the bridge and encamped on our old ground making some 13 miles march for What?"[7] After a week of wandering, they were ordered back to the place they had started out from.[8]

From what Shields could gather, Frémont was closing in on Jackson from the opposite side of the river and expected to overtake him near the hamlet of Port Republic, a day's march up ahead. Shields pushed an advance up the riverbank in mud so deep wagons sank to their axles, bringing everything to a stop until wagons and horses could be levered and pushed clear of the mud. At a place called Conrad's Store, the last bridge between this place and Port Republic, fifteen miles further up, was found burned.[9] The soldiers waited in the pouring rain for three days while their commander pondered his options. Then it came to him: the river was as unfordable to Jackson as it was to him, and without a bridge, neither he nor Jackson could get an army across. Shields decided on the course he might have considered the day he arrived at Front Royal.

He could capture the bridge at Port Republic, and if Jackson was on Frémont's side, he would burn it. Jackson would be stranded on the wrong side for a direct escape from the valley, and Frémont could hammer him to bits.[10] If Jackson tried to cross, Shields would attack his front, and Frémont his rear, like the cow in Lincoln's story stuck half-over a fence, assailed by dogs from both sides, unable to kick or gore. How he would accomplish this when the army in front of his eyes could make only a handful of miles in twenty-four hours—with soldiers who were hungry, at least a third of them shoeless, and some without even pants—was known only to Shields.[11] McDowell knew the condition of the river. Three of his staff officers had been swept off their horses trying to cross a minor tributary and nearly drowned. Before washing his hands of Shields's plan, McDowell wired Secretary of War Stanton:

> General Shields asks, as a condition of being able to stampede the enemy to Richmond, some cavalry of a kind I am unable to give him. The [First] Rhode Island [Cavalry] is as good as I have; and as to his preventing the enemy's escape "somehow," I fear it will be like his intention of crossing the river somehow. His command is not in a condition to go to the places he names.[12]

Their purpose now seemed to be their own survival as much as cornering Jackson.[13] In this weather, there was no chance of supplies reaching them. Some of the Boys had appropriated a bushel basket of counterfeit Confederate scrip and found that in these rural precincts it could be easily passed.[14] Trouble was, there was little for sale. They bought a quantity of flour but discovered that flour and water stirred together in a cup did not produce a fit meal for a soldier. Supper consisted of one cracker and a cup of coffee, and on some nights, soldiers went to sleep with no supper at all. Parmater had a dream. He was in a large dining hall. Just as he sat down to feast, his lieutenant yelled at the men to wake up. "Oh how better if the Lt. had only let me gotten my breakfast before he awoke me."[15]

The Boys now had some protection from the elements. The shelter tent, or shelter half, as it was also called, had been issued to the Twenty-Ninth Regiment at Falmouth, and each soldier now carried his house with him—half of it anyway. A complete A-frame structure without floor or flaps could be formed by buttoning the two halves together. Those soldiers taller than the average had their choice of sleeping with either head or feet exposed to nature. Parmater took to calling these leaky shelters tuggies, probably for the amount of tugging it took two men to pull the fabric tight and to attach it firmly to the ground with whatever stake was handy. Soon they would call every soldier shelter by that name. The Boys did not think much of the shelter half at present, but over time it would be found serviceable for an endless variety of uses, and in later years the pup tent would be the subject of poems, songs, essays, and after-dinner speeches.

Before McDowell left to go back east, he warned Shields against breaking his division down into pieces: doing that, in these conditions especially, would make mutual support impossible if a separated part got into a tight spot. Shields immediately discarded this sage advice. He had learned, on good intelligence, that the rebel general James Longstreet was coming up the road with his thousands, and Shields now had two rebel armies to fret over.[16]

Shields dispatched the Fourth Brigade, Col. Samuel Carroll commanding, ahead to Port Republic. Later, Shields would stick to his story that he had sent Carroll there for one purpose, which was to burn the bridge. Carroll's brigade had been picked for this work for the simplest of reasons—its men had shoes. The Twenty-Ninth Ohio and the other regiments of Tyler's brigade would follow the next day. Shields held his two remaining brigades near Luray, to fight off Longstreet if he came this way.

Shields was convinced that he was closing in on an enemy in its death throes. Jackson's men were reported half-starved, out of ammunition, dispirited, and deserting in droves.[17] He thought Jackson's famous cavalry nothing more than a band of half-trained freebooters. Tyler called his men together on Saturday evening, June 7, 1862, and gave them a talk. He admitted that they had already done far more than could be expected of any men.[18] He told them Shields had ordered them to march to Port Republic and asked if they were up to such a challenge, and they responded with a cheer.

With Carroll's brigade already strung out on their way to Port Republic, and Tyler under orders to start when daylight came, Shields went to bed, but he was unable to sleep. The thought had overtaken him that his plans might go off the rails and into the ditch.[19] He got up and wrote a dispatch to Colonel Carroll:

> Such is my anxiety that I rise from my bed to write to you. . . . The enemy has flung away everything; knapsacks and their stragglers fill the mountains. They only need a movement on the flank to panic-strike them, and break them into fragments. No man has had such a chance since the war commenced. Few men ever had such a chance. You are within 30 miles of a broken, retreating enemy, who still hangs together. Ten thousand Germans [Frémont's command] are on his rear, who hang on like bull-dogs . . . and yet there is a strange want of enthusiasm in the command. . . . I am pestered about shoes and stockings and clothing by officers like Colonel Gavin. . . . Take 5,000 of the enemy prisoners; then there will be time to clothe you.[20]

The Two Luckiest Boys in the Army

Tyler's brigade got on the road the next morning and marched five miles before stopping to eat the single cracker that would constitute that day's menu. The valley closed in on them as they slogged along, farms more scattered. Hills crowded in on their left. On their right was the river, with large trees, parts of buildings, and dead cattle tumbling over and over in the current. If a man slid down the greasy, eroding bank here, he would end up in the Potomac faster than an express train could take him. The rain had moved off for now, but clouds hung in the treetops. Sounds had a way of ricocheting off the walls of this narrowing corridor. The soldiers could hear the boom of artillery coming from the other side of river, but it was hard to say where exactly it originated, or what it signified.[21] Frémont's army was over that way, dogging Jackson's steps.

The going was tough. Jackson's men had had trouble making more than a few miles a day on this same stretch, and that had been before this deluge. A rider galloped up to the head of their column with troubling news. An advance group of Carroll's brigade had reached the Port Republic bridge, but before they could burn it, the rebels had swarmed out of the town and driven them back.

Tyler's soldiers jogged the remaining miles toward the village. Buckley was leading them, and Maj. John Clemmer was riding up and down the column, making sure the company captains were keeping the men closed up. The Giddings Regiment had in it this day four hundred men and officers. They had been in the field now six months, and they were losing nearly a hundred men a month. At this rate, the regiment would be extinct by autumn, whether they fought another battle or not. As the Twenty-Ninth Regiment dogtrotted toward Port Republic, a messenger rode up with a pouch full of dispatches, and in it were approvals of thirty-day furloughs for two Akron men. Sgt. C. H. Edgerly and Pvt. William Dennison shook hands and climbed on a baggage wagon headed back to Luray.[22]

Seven miles out, the sound of steady cannonading rolled down to them. Frémont and Jackson were fighting it out on the other side of the river near a hamlet named after the local tavern, Cross Keys. From the intensity of the racket, Jackson was not giving ground. A long stream of Carroll's wounded making their way to the rear began to pass Tyler's column, and offered an unsolicited warning: a bloodbath was waiting for them just up ahead.[23] Tyler advanced his brigade to within one mile of the bridge, spread them out in battle line, and prepared to receive the enemy. Jackson did not wish to accommodate them just then. Tyler drew the boys back to where the road ascended a rise and camped in a fringe of trees at the base of the hills. There were rebels on the other side of the river, in clear view, and a lot of them, if the forest of gun barrels and bayonets glistening in the dimming light were any indication.[24]

Having boasted to Secretary of War Stanton and others that this time Jackson was "bagged," about to be "thundered down" upon, and "hammered to pieces," Shields had locked himself onto a path from which there could be no turning back. To recall the troops he had sent forward to Port Republic might trigger a rout of the entire army.[25] There was braggadocio in Shields's orders over deeds yet accomplished, which betrayed to his listeners that he himself had doubts, and that doubt was picked up by his officers and passed down through the ranks.

Tall Odds

Tyler's brigade had arrived near Port Republic on June 8, in time to cushion the fallback of Carroll's brigade. The rebels across the river could be clearly seen with the unaided eye and counted individually with a spyglass. From appearances, the enemy outnumbered them at least six to one.[26] "Must we stand here and be murdered?" was the query that came to the mind of their new adjutant, Theron S. Winship.[27] Whether Shields would bring up the rest of the division, which was still a full day's march or more away, no one knew, but given the looks of things, they could not look to him for salvation.

The men stirred themselves several hours before the sun came up and were getting about the business of boiling coffee when shells began to drop in their camp. They were being bombarded by a rebel artillery battery, and to their dismay, the fire was traced to their side of the river.

By seven o'clock, they were formed into the standard two-man-deep line of battle and marched onto a level farm field.[28] The ground had been planted in wheat, from the rise on which they'd camped all the way up to the near side of the village. The fog lifted just enough to disclose the lay of the land in front. To their left was the steep-sided base of the Blue Ridge, and standing out from it was a flattened spur known to the locals as the Lewiston Coaling. In peaceful days, the locals had gone there to make charcoal. Gurley Crane looked up and saw Union gun crews manhandling artillery onto it. He had one of those out-of-place-and-time revelations in which a man's thoughts turned to home. It looked a great deal like Chuckery Hill, back home in Akron.[29]

The valley floor here was no more than a half mile wide.[30] Ahead of them on its surface were darkish boulders, which through binoculars were seen to be the corpses of the Seventh Indiana soldiers, killed the day before. The sun had not yet cleared the Blue Ridge and the narrow flat in front of them was still in half dark. They were in a place that was "up the river and back of the mountains," as Capt. Josiah Wright would describe it.[31] Frémont was on the other side of the river, but with Jackson in control of the only link between them, Frémont and his army might just as well have been in China.

At a council of war held with his officers the night before, General Tyler revealed a stubborn streak. He would not back away in the face of Jackson, although it seemed to many of the officers, Lewis P. Buckley included, that the best course of action was to backtrack down the river and wait for the remainder of Shields's division.[32] Before going in, Buckley had confided to Lt. Col. Thomas Clark that their defeat seemed imminent.[33] Capt. Edward Hayes saw the thick columns of rebels coming toward them and in a low voice told Sgt. Rollin L. Jones that they were about to be "whipped awfully."[34] His doubts about the battle's outcome did not diminish his fighting spirit one iota. He declared they would make the rebels pay dearly for every foot of ground. From appearances, they were about to be sacrificed.

Tyler put most of his guns on the Coaling and threw his infantry out along an east-west lane that ran down to the bank of the south fork of the river where an old mill stood. Soldiers piled their knapsacks by company, checked their cartridge and primer boxes, and lined up.[35] The Twenty-Ninth Regiment was directed to the extreme right of the whole line, tight up against the river.[36] The battle opened with an artillery fight, and the soldiers stood in line and watched shells popping open above the ground in front and crashing through the treetops.[37] The flags of three rebel regiments came into view advancing along their right near the river, and Tyler's brigade marched forward to stop them.[38]

A stout board fence stood in their way and brought the right end of Tyler's line to a stop.[39] While soldiers were still climbing over and through, they were staggered by a volley.[40] By good fortune, no one in the Twenty-Ninth Ohio was hit. Once everyone got over, they formed back into battle line, made sure elbows were touching, as was required, and stepped out onto the wheat field. The Twenty-Ninth Ohio was ordered to support Huntington's battery, and the soldiers had an up-close look at the destruction artillery caused to humans. Cannonballs ripped holes in the rebel lines, sending knapsacks, muskets, men, and parts of men tumbling through the air.

The rebels closed to within a hundred yards and broke out in their distinctive holler, half yell and half screech, and charged. Buckley's voice was heard above the riot of sound, "Aim low men, and at every shot let a traitor fall!"[41] The Giddings Boys held their fire until the buttons on a rebel's coat could be counted, then fired with a yell of their own, and the gray men recoiled. Tyler's line moved forward with a will, driving the survivors back toward a post-and-rail fence. But when they got within easy range, the rebels hammered a broadside of bullets into them.

Men were knocked out of the line here and there, screaming in pain, or noiseless and dead. They absorbed the shock and fired back. Unlike at Kernstown, where at times it had been every man for himself, the Twenty-Ninth's officers called for firing by volley, and for three hours there was a give and take as opposing lines lit up with the orange of a thousand muskets being discharged simultaneously. The Giddings Boys fought their way forward through the battle fog and up to the position where the rebels had made their stand.[42] The rebel dead and wounded lay in lines in the wheat as neatly as if they had been laid out for counting. The Twenty-Ninth Regiment had advanced from their starting point over a third of a mile, overrun the rebel line, and taken prisoners.[43] In one lunge, Company F by itself had captured twenty-five rebel prisoners.[44] When asked where the remainder of his comrades had gone, one captured Confederate answered, "I can show you where the remainder of our regiment is . . . it is up there, along that fence."[45]

By one account, Cpl. John Kummer made a lone dash into the enemy lines and came away with an enemy flag.[46] In later years, that act of bravery would be properly credited to Sgt. Allen Mason of Company C. It was he who had stormed into the rebel line and picked up the battle flag of the 7th Louisiana Tigers.[47] Following their first successful charge, the Twenty-Ninth began to sag under the weight of the rebels' renewed musket fire, and Buckley ordered a second charge.[48] They drove the rebels again, and for a time, the Boys seemed capable of driving them wherever they chose.[49] Even the doubters were becoming believers. Lt. Jack Wright recalled, "The Twenty-Ninth went right into the face and eyes of the enemy, with tremendous odds against them, and actually drove the enemy back some hundred rods with an awful slaughter—really piling up the dead Secesh."[50] Then, it all began to fall apart.

Black smoke was seen boiling into the sky from the bridge up ahead, and everyone knew what it meant.[51] Jackson's reinforcements had crossed to their side, burned the bridge, and stranded Frémont on the opposite bank. There would presently be hell to pay. Rebels under Gen. Richard S. Ewell were coming up the road, and Tyler's brigade had nothing in reserve. Still, they stood their ground. Captain Hayes was reported to have picked up a musket, taken careful aim at a rebel color bearer, and "lowered his sheet without further ceremony."[52] His company then fought their way further forward, but this was as far as Hayes and his boys would get.

Cpl. Charles Robinson defied the rebels by taking up a position forward of the regiment's line. After an especially well aimed shot he laughed, turned back to his friends, and yelled, "I emptied a saddle that time," which were the last words attributed to him; no sooner had the words left his mouth than a shell took off the back of his head.[53] Other soldiers were seen to be evidencing the same sort of odd behavior shown by bystanders at a train wreck. Pvt. George Stohl fought steadily, laughing the whole time as though "the scrape were gotten up for fun."[54]

Rollin Jones was standing close enough to Lewis Buckley to hear the sickening thud of a bullet striking flesh. Buckley's horse had been shot through the nose and thrown him hard to the ground. Jones and Captain Hayes rushed over and got Buckley on his feet and into the saddle of another horse.[55] Two more horses went out from under Buckley. His sword was broken at the hilt by a musket ball.[56] Bullets were flying so thick and fast that soldiers wondered how any of them could still be standing. Buckley's face did not seem to show a trouble in the world, and the soldiers who saw him there that morning took heart from his example and stood their ground.[57]

A soldier standing next to Rollin Jones was struck and bled to death in a moment. The smell made Jones instantly sick, and he began to doubt whether he would ever again want to go into the realm of battles.[58] Adj. Theron Winship had three horses shot from under him and his sword belt clipped off by a bullet.[59] In later years, Nathan Parmater would report that he had been struck in the chest by a bullet, but the small Bible he had stowed in his breast pocket stopped it.[60]

Lt. Carey H. Russell fired all six shots from his navy revolver and then stood fully upright to reload, indifferent to the entreaties of his men to get down.[61] Hands and faces were smeared with the greasy gunpowder of the cartridges they were furiously loading, and the soldiers began to resemble raccoons. After a while, barrels became too fouled to load. Rammers had to be driven home by upending the musket and pounding the muzzle against the ground. Lieutenant Russell moved up and down the line helping men clear the jams. Pvt. George Braginton's gun would not fire at all, and he sat down in the battle line and disassembled it into its several components, fixed the problem, and resumed combat.[62] Two "Irish Boys" from Akron, Pvts. John Burns and John Campbell, stripped themselves down to shirts and pants, rolled up their sleeves, and went at the rebels workmanlike.[63]

Pvt. Samuel Hart had been wounded in the early going when a bullet blasted his musket from his hand. He wrapped a rag around his hand, picked up a musket he found on the ground, and kept at his work. He would have two more rifles broken by bullets before he quit.[64] These battles were the events of a lifetime, but soldiers remembered them for the small, odd things they had seen or felt. One boy came up to Rollin Jones and offered him a glob of johnnycake that he had found while rummaging through a dead rebel's knapsack, but Jones's stomach was hardly settled enough for such a mess.[65]

Officers began to fall as steadily as the soldiers. Lt. Everson Hurlburt was one of the first men to go down. A ball had torn through his lower arm. He fought on one-handed. Major Clemmer was struck in the leg just below the knee, the ball shattering the tibia. Surgeon Fifield was there with them and got the ball out, but Clemmer was out of action.[66]

If it had been a fight just between these two bodies of men on the right, Tyler might have gained the day, but an even more desperate combat was unfolding on their left. There, atop the Coaling, a struggle for possession of the Union battery was taking place, and it was the key to the battle. There had been charge and countercharge through the shady tangle of trees, brush, and roots, with scores of men killing or being killed in an area no larger than a barn floor. The big guns continued to shred everything forward of the muzzle with grapeshot, even with rebels now getting right in among the guns. Men were beaten to a pulp with muskets swung clublike, stabbed, and shot, not once but many times. No one, rebel or Yank, had seen anything like this.

The men fighting it out on the flat had enough going on in their vicinity to occupy them and did not likely hear nor note what was happening up there. The fury being unleashed atop the Coaling acted like a magnet, pulling men from all parts of the field toward it. The Giddings Regiment was being pulled in that direction, too, although still tightly engaged with the enemy in their front. They had not drifted far in that direction when blue-uniformed men began staggering away from around the Coaling and onto the road leading back to Conrad's Store.[67]

Some said that the Twenty-Ninth Ohio had advanced too far to hear the order to retreat and began their backward movement only when someone noticed they were alone on the field with the whole of Jackson's army bearing down on them.[68] They had been hotly engaged and were bracing for attack by a rebel regiment that had moved to within musket range under the cover of brush at the river's edge. That threat was superseded by one more immediate.[69] Rebel cavalry came from out of nowhere, it seemed, and were charging down on them. They formed themselves into hollow squares—the prescribed defense against mounted enemy—as neatly as if they had been on dress parade, and braced for the collision.[70] Now, the rebel artillery was turned on them, and men were jolted out of line by grapeshot and went down now by twos and threes. The Giddings Regiment closed up the holes and continued to load and fire, as they backed away.[71] Back on the rise where the Twenty-Ninth Ohio had begun this day, musician Gurley Crane was assisting Dr. Fifield with the wounded. He saw the entire, awful panorama, and when the tide of retreat washed over him, he was carried backward with it.[72]

Buckley knew that if the officers could not keep their men in hand, an ugly stampede would result. He got out front of his regiment and, in a voice famous for its ability to be heard at great distances, soothed the panicky, "Don't hurry men, I am an old man. I can't run, and I won't run."[73] With lead and iron sizzling past their heads, they formed in companies as if doing so was the most ordinary thing in the world.[74] Firing as they went, the soldiers worked back toward the road, with rebels shooting at them now from ahead and from both sides.[75]

They reached the road but had gone scarcely a hundred yards on it when the rebel cavalry stormed in again, riding hard right over the tops of the Boys they could reach, swinging sabers, firing revolvers, and demanding surrender. The rebels now turned captured guns on them as they fled, throwing canister and solid shot onto the road ahead and into the trees, and what remained of the regiment's order after it had been broken by the cavalry, was hammered into molecules by artillery. Colonel Clark's horse was shot dead and pitched over on top of him, wrenching his leg.

The rebel cavalry followed the Boys into the woods, keeping the scare at a boil and stringing what remained of the Twenty-Ninth Ohio out into a ragged line two miles long.[76] Some of the rebel riders had worked themselves up to the top of the ridge, blocking the escape route over the crest. Rollin Jones heard men in that direction hollering "Halt!" and thought they were Federals trying to form a last defense. When he got too close, it turned out they were rebels, and with so many of the enemy around him, further resistance seemed unwise, and he surrendered to their demand to drop his rifle or be shot dead.[77] One man recalled that some men in the regiment had been lured out into the open by rebels flying a flag of truce.[78] Lt. George Washington Dice had been leading Company D since Kernstown. He was a sober young man, not given to exaggeration. What remained of his company was encircled by rebel riders and upon their order, "Halt you damned Yankees, surrender!" he and his men lowered their rifles. The rebel cavalry drew a circle around Dice's captured squad and started to shoot them down.

The survivors ran for the woods.[79] Such a thing might have happened. The cavalry's blood was hot for revenge. Their adored leader Turner Ashby had been killed by Federal infantry a few days earlier.

Capt. William Fitch found himself near Buckley and suggested he best take to the brush with the rest of them.[80] Fitch rallied the thirteen men who remained near him and formed the rear guard of Tyler's brigade. Pvt. Henry Turner, and Sergeants Roberts and Wilder, knelt and fired, unhorsing two cavalrymen and slowing the onslaught just long enough for their comrades to get deep enough into the forest that cavalry could not follow.[81] But the rebel cavalry charged in and broke them, too. The rebel colors the Boys had taken during the fight were now retaken by the rebels, and then the inconceivable: the Twenty-Ninth's flag was being paraded around the field by a mounted rebel, the long silk tail being pulled through the mud.[82]

Jones and the other captured men were rounded up and marched in a group back onto the field. The dead of both sides lay around them, and the rebel infantry were already turning out the pockets of the Union dead, looking for trophies.[83] The battle was over, but the sense of confusion persisted. A big, proud fellow in the Fifth Ohio named Scotty had mounted a horse and was seen pulling a piece of rebel artillery behind him, oblivious to the fact that his side had lost and he was a prisoner of war.[84]

General Frémont came up onto a ridge overlooking Shields's side of the river a few hours after the battle there had ended. He saw parties of rebels out on the field below him, gathering in their dead and wounded, and Union prisoners lining up for the march off to prison. Rollin Jones and over a hundred other soldiers and officers of the Twenty-Ninth stood in that long line of captured with the prospect of life in a rebel prison now a certainty. Lt. Col. Clark was taken prisoner. His sword, the one inscribed with his name and presented to him by friends in his temperance organization when he went to war, was taken from him. It would next be seen in public many years in the future, resting atop the Stars and Stripes that covered his coffin. The sister of the rebel who had forced it from him hunted for Clark by ads she placed in the Ohio newspapers, and it was returned.[85]

In futility, and foolishness, Frémont ordered a few shells lobbed down onto the field, which did not change things, except to anger Jackson.[86] Many of Tyler's dead and wounded were left on the field.

Capt. Horatio Luce had labored hard to enlist men in his company, and he was much loved by them. Some of his townsmen recalled that it had been he, William T. Fitch, and Theron Winship who had been the driving force behind the entire Twenty-Ninth Regiment.[87] He had gone down late in the fighting, his chest pierced by a musket ball. Sgt. A. J. Andrews was near Luce when he was hit, but he had to press forward with the others. He returned to Luce's body with two others and they had carried him a mile when the rebels rode in and smashed things up, and they had to leave him.[88] There had only been enough time for him to open his captain's coat and remove his watch and a few personal items before taking to the hills. To increase their father's grieving, his younger brother, sixteen-year-old Charles, was reported captured, his exact fate unknown.

Emory Luce arranged to have a family friend go to Virginia with the hopes of recovering his oldest son's body and perhaps finding out what had become of his youngest.[89] By the time he arrived at the seat of war, Charlie Luce had returned safely and was under Winship's wing.[90] Back home, Horatio Luce would be eulogized in the newspaper by a fellow officer, and his last utterance would be quoted. Winship reported that the dear old Stars and Stripes had been waving over his best friend's head when he fell and that with his last breath he looked up to it and said, "Boys, defend it!"[91] Winship could not conclude his letter of condolence to Luce's father without saying, "A terrible responsibility rests upon someone for this disaster. I do not feel like turning this letter into a criticism upon recent movements of this Division, but perhaps I can have a heart for such work at another time—should I attempt it; *it would be severe.*"[92]

Jackson was not heartless, but he had important business above Richmond, and with Frémont's artillery hurrying him along, there would be no time to bury the Union dead. It was later reported that the corpses of Union boys had been eaten by hogs.[93] After the battle, four days passed before a Union detachment of twenty-eight ambulances arrived at the field under a flag of truce to collect the dead and wounded.[94] The Federal rescue party was turned away after ministering to just a few of the dead and dying.[95] As they were moving the corpse of one soldier, it let out a groan.

There was life in this man yet, despite his appearance. George Eastlick was a plain private in Company C, formerly a farmer near Turnersville, Pennsylvania, where Captain Hayes had done some of his recruiting. Eastlick was taller by a head than most of the soldiers in his regiment, but since most soldiers tended to shoot high, his height was a liability in battle. A rebel musket ball knocked a chunk out of his skull the size of a potato, with enough velocity to send it into the soldier standing behind him, injuring him. Captain Hayes was standing nearby and saw Eastlick topple. All could see his wound was irrevocably fatal and he was one of those left on the field.[96]

Once found, Eastlick was able to walk the seven miles back to Shields on his own.[97] He survived the jolting ride back to a hospital near Washington, where a talented surgeon with new ideas and a willingness to try them out was assigned Eastlick's case. Where other men were dying of something as small as an infected cut, Eastlick survived. Eventually, he would find small fame in this grisly wound. Decades later, he could open the pages of the *Medical and Surgical History of the War* for visitors to his farm and show them the write-up of what had happened to him.

Most who fell at Port Republic had done nothing in their service to attract attention other than be killed in this place. Pvt. Jonathan Everhart of Company I had been cut in two by a solid shot, leaving behind a widow and three children in Medina.[98] Frederick Johnson had been one of the several dozen of the Twenty-Ninth's Boys who had "boarded out" before the war, living in the flouring mill where he worked, sending three-quarters of his wages home to his widowed mother.[99] He was now dead on the field at Port Republic, the second son of his family to die in a war that was little more than a year old. His brother Charles had been a victim of a careless gun handling in the Seventh Ohio Infantry several months earlier.

Those who had made it out onto the road ahead of the rebel cavalry were hurried along by the sound of firing directly in their rear, and by one soldier's account, they ran all the way back to Conrad's Store, where Shields was sitting.[100] The Confederate general Charles S. Winder, who had been in command of the rebel line pummeled by Tyler's men an hour earlier, pursued the main body of Federals for four miles, broke up a rearguard stand, and pushed them another four miles before Jackson ordered him to break off the pursuit.[101] The last lucky soldiers of the Twenty-Ninth Ohio to get onto the road ahead of Winder stopped to take a last look backward in the direction of their disaster. Buckley could be seen for a moment in the snarl of rearing horses and flashing sabers down there at the edge of the hills, and then they all seemed to vanish.

Cut to Pieces

The night of the battle Winship made his rounds through their camp and observed, "The dear old 29th presents tonight a very sorry aspect indeed."[102] Gurley Crane counted up the men who had made it out and there were only ninety-four, including him.[103] Those who remained were dumbstruck with fatigue and sick at heart. Camp was now a place of mourning, soldiers cheering throughout the night whenever a man thought lost appeared at the edge of the campfire.[104] Winship waited into the next day, walking about with the list of the missing in hand, removing a name from it each time a soldier thought lost showed up.

Two days later, they were amazed to see Colonel Buckley, uniform torn by briars, face and hands blotched with blood spatter, being helped into camp. He was in good spirits, telling the Boys better days would come, but he had been changed. He was already an old man, drawn and pale on his best days. Now, all these characteristics seemed exaggerated. That he had just had a long, anxious walk and was suffering the effects of having been thrown hard to the ground when his horse was shot were the hopeful explanations of his appearance. He was known to have generous recuperative powers.

Buckley had escaped the rebel cavalry and taken charge of eighty men of the four fragmented regiments of Tyler's brigade. With him were thirty-four of the Twenty-Ninth's soldiers and officers, including

Captain Fitch and Lieutenants Dice, Benjamin N. Smith, and Frank P. Stewart. They had traveled under cover of the forest canopy, using the road when it seemed safe enough. They bivouacked the first night in an abandoned building.[105] They had fed themselves on wild plants.[106]

Lt. Andrew J. Fulkerson, Company H, assembled his own group of thirty refugees in the woods.[107] They spent the first night near the battlefield and, in a bold move the next morning, attacked a nearby house occupied by rebels. They took five prisoners and their provisions. One of the captured, a cavalryman, agreed to guide them back to Luray, if they would turn him loose when they got there. Along the way, a black woman gave them a loaf of fresh-baked bread, and a male contraband helped move them along the river in his canoe. This was the first instance of contrabands helping Twenty-Ninth Boys out of a tight spot, but it would not be the last. Capt. Jonas Schoonover was one of those thought to have been captured or killed. He had lain for two days in the woods hiding from the rebel outriders before judging it safe enough to walk back to Luray.

Like Fulkerson's group, Christopher Beck and George Ellis decided the best course of action was to stay close to the lingering rebels rather than try to outrun them. The pair spent the night of the battle hiding under a rebel battery.[108] They brushed up against rebel cavalry patrols and had to hide in fencerows until they passed, but both made it back to Union lines. In total, eighty soldiers whose comrades thought them dead or captured made it back to the regiment.[109] Still, when Winship was done with his accounting, there was no disputing what the soldiers had seen on the field.

The casualty list that ran in the Jefferson newspaper was several inches wide, tightly packed with small print giving a man's name and his fate.[110] The Twenty-Ninth Regiment had been cut to pieces, as most of the survivors expressed it, and it was no exaggeration. They had gone into battle with as many as 450 soldiers and officers. Now, even after all the survivors had finally appeared, they were but 225 men of all ranks.[111] They had suffered as badly as any regiment in this engagement, Union or rebel, with the exception of the Sixty-Sixth Ohio. That regiment was under the command of Col. Charles Candy, a convivial old veteran of the regular army who had worked his way up from the ranks. His outfit had suffered more in aggregate. They had been in the hand-to-hand fighting up on the Coaling, but they had the benefit of having gotten out in time to avoid the wrath of the rebel cavalry.

Never again would Capt. Josiah Wright feel compelled to defend the honor of the Giddings Regiment. This time the injury done to the regiment had been bloody enough to satisfy any of their critics. The newspapers back home expressed dismay at the Twenty-Ninth's fate at Port Republic but stopped short of pity for them. That they had suffered mightily on the battlefield and held up their end of the fight was not in doubt. So few of them remained that the question now was whether they would continue to exist as a regiment at all.

The fates played strange, deadly tricks in war, causing men to ponder the what-ifs for the remainder of their days. Soldiers in this war were intrigued by the slight wrinkles of fate, which spared one man and hustled away the man standing at his side. Most applicable to their recent debacle: what if Lincoln's order to quit the plan to trap Jackson and bring everyone back to Falmouth had gotten to Shields in time for him to recall Tyler from Port Republic? That order had in fact been sent from Washington to McDowell, and he had dispatched a special courier at a gallop out from Front Royal to carry it to Shields.[112]

Around the campfires of this war, and in all the decades afterward, soldiers were fond of speculating and estimating things for which there were no proofs. How much lead could a man dodge before he was at last hit? One man would argue that a soldier's body weight in lead was about right, and if one ounce more than that was fired in his direction he would be done for.[113] Another soldier made a careful study and concluded that at least six hundred pounds of lead and iron would have to be fired at him before his number was called.[114] Such arguments of course persuaded a man how improbable it was that *he* would be shot, thereby allowing him to suppress the instinctive urge to turn tail and run. Or, if the six hundred thousand men now in the Union army lined up shoulder to shoulder, how long of a line would they form? Twenty-three miles was one considered guess, which led to further conjecture as to how long it would take a general on foot to inspect them all, and what if that general were on horseback or riding a locomotive?

Two weeks earlier, the civilian war managers in Washington had believed Jackson's destruction the most important goal in the whole of war, and they had gotten the ball rolling that led to the undoing of the Twenty-Ninth Ohio Volunteers at Port Republic. Now, Lincoln and Stanton concluded no good could be accomplished by keeping Shields in the valley. However its timing, the late order stood: "That it being the intention of the President that the troops of the Rappahannock be employed else-where, General Shields will cease all further pursuit, and bring back all his division to Luray and get it ready for the march to Fredericksburg."[115]

"Who Is to Blame?"

News of what had happened was slow in making it out of the valley and back to the Reserve via the East Coast newspapers. Nine days after the battle of Port Republic, the Jefferson newspaper quoted a report from Washington stating that Jackson had attacked the Federal advance on Monday morning and driven it back onto Shields's main body. Buckley was reported badly wounded. His men charged three times, just to get to him, but did not succeed.[116] "The 29th has again been in a hard fight where they have doubtless suffered much more than they did at Winchester," commented the editors.[117] It had been rumored that Capt. Horatio Luce had been killed on the field, but that could not be confirmed, pending publication of the official reports. "We have nothing but the most vague rumors respecting them," and until something solid came in, the people would have to endure another anxious wait.[118]

The newspaper in Conneaut was the first to publish the particulars of the battle. So startling was the news that the *Reporter* got out an extra, and at the center of it was a firsthand account from the regiment's adjutant and their townsman, T. S. Winship: "The bloody scenes of the 9th are past, and some few of us are comparatively safe; and although I have no heart to do so, nor am I in a fit condition, mentally or physically to write, yet I feel that the anxious friends of us all at home, must be apprised of our fate."[119]

They had marched hundreds of miles in thirty days, in heat and dust, rain and mud, been out of this valley and nearly to Washington, and then back again, and all of it had culminated in this battle. "My blood runs cold when I think of the carnage on that field—it now only surprises me that any escaped," wrote Winship.[120] The townsfolk were overjoyed when they got out of bed and walked to the village center to see their very own "bronzed warrior" among them again, home for only a day on a "flying" visit.[121]

Captain Fitch wrote to the newspaper after the battle with his own long compilation of the regiment's killed, wounded, and missing. He spared the civilians at home the bloody details, except to say the Twenty-Ninth had done "nobly," but the enemy had been too many for them, and they'd been compelled to retreat.[122] The brigades of Tyler and Carroll had held a little over three thousand soldiers, and a full third had been made casualties. It would be weeks before anything resembling the real scope of the regiment's loss could be measured, but the loss had been terrific: 14 to 17 dead on the field and another half dozen to die shortly of wounds, 40 to 50 or more wounded, and 114 soldiers and officers taken prisoner.[123] For the captured at Port Republic there would not be any on-the-spot paroles granted; capture in battle meant prison.

Pvt. Henry P. Turner of Hartsgrove had been one of the soldiers Captain Fitch had rallied to make a last stand at Port Republic and had been shot down by a rebel trooper after he had laid down his musket and surrendered.[124] He had been an exemplary soldier, and in his off-duty time he had assisted the chaplain in conducting divine service and had handed out the mail when it came through.[125] Turner's funeral was preached in Hartsgrove on a Sunday and his empty coffin was lowered into the ground. It was a pleasant shock to his family and friends to see his name listed among the captured enlisted men being held at a place called Belle Isle in Richmond.[126]

A few soldiers wrote long accounts of the battle. Most, however, kept their impressions of what had happened to themselves, giving the folks at home a sentence or two about it and a promise they would tell the whole story when they got home. Few soldiers were competent enough writers to attempt description of such things. Franklin Potter's diary entry on the evening of the battle was typical of the average soldier's brevity: "This morning got breakfast and then formed in line of battle the enemy opened on us we 29th went to support a battery we drove the enemy back the enemy flanked us on the left and drove us back we had to make for the woods."¹²⁷ Wallace B. Hoyt wrote home to tell his parents that they had been whipped, and to let them know how some of the other Rock Creek Boys had come out, so that news of their fates could be given their family and friends:

> Monty Branty is wounded in the head sevearly, frank mory in the foot the ball went through it length ways. Bill Munson in the arm, Lieut. Hurlburt in the arm, and Lieut. Morice in the leg, and Sargt. Hoyt is missing, taken prisoner probly. Frank Mory was also left on the field with others we could not carry off. I came out all right with the exception of sore feet for we have been marching so far that my shoes, as well as others['] was all worn out and we could draw none, so I went barefoot and one of my nuckles skinned with a piece of shell. But they are calling us to fall in to discharge our guns and I must adjurn.¹²⁸

The *Sentinel* ran a piece they titled "Incidents Occurring in the 29th at the Battle of Port Republic," in which the exploits of local men were ticked off, with each man having his own short paragraph.¹²⁹ Captain Hayes had perhaps been the bravest man on the field. He had seized a musket from a fallen soldier when the contest burned hottest, firing right alongside his men. Lt. E. B. Woodbury had been taken prisoner but was unharmed. James March, Company A, had been shot both above and below the knee, and while being removed from the field the ambulance overturned and he was captured. Eli Young of the same company fired all of the forty rounds he had been given, ran to the rear for more, and returned to take up the fight again, but he was captured anyway.

They had lost some of the backbone men of the enlisted ranks. Cpl. William A. Hart was fighting his county's battles in the Mexican-American War while most of the soldiers in his company were still in their frocks. A minié ball shattered his ankle, but he propped himself up and continued to fight. He made it out and eventually into a Washington hospital. A friend from his company visited him there and saw that Hart had lost his leg, but none of his spirit. In a letter to the Akron newspaper announcing Hart's fate, his friend wrote, "He was much esteemed by his comrades in arms—may he not be forgotten by his friends in Summit County."¹³⁰ For a reversal this stark, and for the loss of so many good men, someone must be held accountable.

"Who Is to Blame?" was the typical headline of stories about Port Republic that now filled the newspapers from Jefferson to Cincinnati. Everyone had an opinion as to who had been responsible for the failure to destroy the bridge at Port Republic, as if that alone had been the cause of the Federal disaster.¹³¹ No one was quite ready to acknowledge Jackson's resourcefulness. Colonel Carroll's friends were absolutely positive that he had been ordered to hold the bridge and not to destroy it. But Shields had quickly gotten on record that the defeat had been caused exclusively by Carroll's failure to obey his order to burn it. It was a dispute that would never be resolved. No one on either side in the debate seemed willing to pull back and take in explanations that went beyond the battlefield.

No criticism was laid at the doorstep of the White House, where Lincoln and Stanton had been swept along in the Jackson panic and sent armies, which had been promised McClellan back into the valley. Shields had generously shared the praise for his victory at Kernstown with his commanders. Now, with a defeat to explain, and fingers being pointed in his direction for failing to keep his brigades together, he worked feverishly to shift the weight onto others—mostly onto poor Carroll. He had failed to burn the bridge the day before the battle, and when Tyler came up, he too had let the bridge stand.¹³² Shields also criticized Tyler for deciding to stand in the face of an overwhelming opponent when it would have been more prudent to back away.¹³³

"This division had not been defeated," Shields stated proudly.¹³⁴ He had prepared a position at Conrad's Store so strong that Jackson not only feared to attack but ran away. Had he not received orders from Washington to desist, he would have run Jackson down the next day and slain him. Ultimately, McDowell, who had been bounced like a billiard ball from one purpose to another in the preceding weeks, would take the blame. He already had one strike against him with the earlier Federal debacle at

Bull Run laid at his door. The raking over the coals he would soon be subjected to by the defense lawyers in the court martial of Gen. Fitz John Porter, a fellow officer he had gone to court to help bury, included accusations that McDowell had been indifferent to the welfare of Shields's soldiers.[135] During the march from Falmouth, McDowell was alleged to have ordered them to retrace ten miles of their weary steps to rebuild a fence that they had taken down in their passing.[136]

Orders to march and remarch these men to death had come directly from the White House, as did the policy that no property be molested, secesh or otherwise. McDowell did not even agree with giving the Confederates such "rosewater" treatment, as he called it. Shields's promotion to major general had been pending in the Senate. After the disaster at Port Republic, it was rejected. Shields would remain in the war a few months longer before resigning and returning to California and getting into the railroad business.

Men in high office, with axes to grind known only to them, would interpret this campaign and lay the blame for its failures where they would. It was too complicated a game for the common soldier. His eyes were on the condition of the road at his feet, his prospects for a decent meal, and his odds of staying clear of the hospital. On the topic of imperfect generalship, the private soldier had nothing to say. Wallace Hoyt began a letter to his parents after the battle, "There has been a great change in the regiment,"[137] which was really a taking stock of their entire hard experience of the past six months.

At Luray the Giddings Regiment gathered its broken pieces and got ready to march back to the environs of Washington. Each man would have to lug his own traps. The knapsacks of the missing were slung into a soggy pile and burned.[138] Marching light and unencumbered, as Jackson's men did, made no allowance for sentiment.[139] The Twenty-Ninth Ohio Regiment needed many things just now: soldiers and officers to take the place of those who were gone, new uniforms and shoes, and more to eat. What they needed most of all was expressed by Buckley: "We have got to rest by God . . . we have run enough and must rest now, rest—we are all worn out."[140]

12

"Rest Now, Rest"

ALEXANDRIA, VIRGINIA, JUNE–JULY 1862

"Too Much Music"

Shields's division had been wrecked. Some if was not entirely his fault: the long marches ordered by others, the gear that was already half worn out when he took command back in Martinsburg, the mix-ups in supply that kept the soldiers nearly starved. The rest lay at his doorstep. The mountain of supplies he now needed before he could consider marching east showed that they were no longer much of an army: 9,200 caps, 12,000 pairs of shoes, 12,000 pants, 12,000 pairs of shirts and drawers, 5,000 haversacks, and 6,100 canteens.[1]

Two months earlier, his men had numbered eleven thousand and more. Now, what was left of Shields's division amounted to less than three thousand, and a large percentage of those men were now too tired or discouraged, or naked, to go on. After Kernstown, Shields's men would have followed him anywhere, even through the gates of hell, as they were fond of expressing it. Now, it would be hard to find a single private who still had confidence in him.

Luray, where his division was recovering, was filled with "so-called sick," both enlisted men and their officers, who would never again be of use to the army. Even the horses were beyond restoration.[2] Discipline had gone out the window and confusion and disorder had taken hold. Shields's division, the pride of the Potomac two months before, was by every measure now in a "bad state," officers resigning right and left, and men beginning to desert in numbers.[3] Wallace Hoyt observed that the officers in the Twenty-Ninth were nearly all threatening to resign. The reason seemed clear enough to him: "They are afraid we shall get a little too much music of the kind we got at Port Republic and as they are no musicians it has no charm for their ears."[4] Lewis P. Buckley was one of those threatening to pack up and go home.

Buckley wrote a three-page letter to the adjutant general back in Ohio in which he summarized the events that had overtaken the Twenty-Ninth Infantry since they'd left Camp Chase, six months ago.[5] Buckley admitted that it was not seemly for him to speak disrespectfully of his superior officers, but Shields's want of military capacity had ruined his men, and Buckley felt obligated to "speak plainly." Through his poor generalship, Shields had finished the process begun by Lander: the destruction of one of the finest divisions in the army. Fortunately for the Twenty-Ninth, he did not follow through on his resignation. Had he done so at this low point, the entire organization below him might have unraveled.

The pain in Nathan Parmater's chest and side had never gone away, and the surgeon gave him a thirty-day furlough to return to Ohio and restore himself. He went home on the trains, making the big loop through Washington, where he saw the Long Bridge and the unfinished capitol. He put up at the Soldiers' Retreat, a giant, government-run boardinghouse in which soldiers in transit stayed. Then, on through Pittsburgh, with its burgeoning, smoky industries, and all of a sudden he was back home, near Kingsville. He was delighted to find that the residents were still interested in the Giddings Regiment: "Everyone is very anxious to have me call on them and it is almost impossible to get through the streets without having to stop and talk to someone about the 29th."[6] He was home to rest, but his schedule was jam packed with church sings, corn hoeings, and shopping expeditions in which he bought a new pair of shoes and an improved spyglass. He wore his uniform for a visit to Kingsville Academy, where he called on his old teachers and soaked in the attention paid him by the students. Sitting in the pew at his church, he was struck by the quiet and order of the place. He would have done anything to get away from the regiment, but after a few weeks at home he grew lonesome for it.

A week after Port Republic the Boys finally got new uniforms.[7] Their appearance was being restored, but their manpower was not. Their losses in the recent battle aside, the evaporation of the Giddings Regiment into thin air continued by various mechanisms. Pvt. John W. Hurry of Company A injured himself in the week after the battle, making him the sixth soldier in the regiment to accidentally shoot off his trigger finger.[8] And for the first and last time in the regiment's history soldiers began to desert in significant numbers.

Soldiers had deserted the regiment before, always one soldier at a time, for reasons that were likely personal and had nothing in particular to do with the regiment. Now, having reached Front Royal, with its outlets to the populated world, nine soldiers left in one forty-eight-hour period, suggesting that there had been whispered discussions beforehand in which plans were made to walk away.[9] Beyond that, sickness continued to take men from them.

In May alone, at least sixteen men had died of disease, and several times that number were in hospitals or back home trying to recover from illness. In June, five more soldiers would die.[10] The summer months were notorious for the camp diseases of dysentery and typhoid fever, which took down men by the dozens in other regiments; but the Twenty-Ninth Regiment's health seemed to stabilize in this period. The Boys continued to get sick, and many would die, but not at the rate that had troubled them through winter and spring. Officers came down with the same sicknesses as the enlisted men, with the symptoms of racking cough, fever, and bilious complaints of the bowels, but not one had succumbed as yet. Many dozens of the Boys who had gotten sick had been sent back to their homes to finish recovery. Once separated from it for any reason, they found getting back to the regiment daunting.

Pvt. Elias Roshon was captured at the hospital in Mount Jackson and immediately paroled. He got a furlough and went home. He found that returning to the regiment was not as easy as it had been to leave it.[11] His father took him as far as Medina, where he got on a stagecoach, which took him to Cleveland; then he continued by train to Columbus, and then out to Camp Chase, where he was brought to a halt by a mountain of red tape. He got over that obstacle, although that did not mean that his next step would be transportation back to the regiment, in Alexandria. First, he had to report to Camp Dennison over a hundred miles away. When he arrived in Cincinnati, he found three thousand soldiers in line ahead of him, all needing to be examined by a surgeon before they could return to their outfits. Finally, with five or six other boys from the Twenty-Ninth for company, it was back to Columbus, where they caught the train for Bellaire, on the Ohio River, and then on to Alexandria.

The anguish of their debacle at Port Republic had seemed too much to bear, but within a few weeks, the wound of it began to heal over. Theron S. Winship would continue for a while longer trying to recover the body of his friend Horatio Luce from the battlefield. The result of his efforts was announced in the Conneaut newspaper six weeks after the battle: Luce's body had not been recovered and in all likelihood would never be.[12] The pain of Winship's disappointment was assuaged by the gift of a fine horse from fellow officer Lt. E. B. Howard. In a public thank-you to Howard, he wrote, "Experience has taught me, while horse flesh is very uncertain on the battle field, it is also *invaluable on the retreat,* for this and other reasons I prize your present highly."[13] Winship's spirits were mending.

The battle at Port Republic had been a thing of horrors, but after the passage of only six weeks the Boys could already tell funny stories on themselves. Pvt. Norman Cochran was struck by a spent ball during the fight. A comrade saw him limping and asked what was the matter. Norman replied, "Oh! There is a furlough growing on my leg."[14]

City Lights

On June 21 the regiment left the valley by a road that had become so familiar they could march it in their sleep. They paused for a few days near Bristoe Station, Virginia. They had marched four hundred miles in the past four weeks to get to this place, which for some men was as much as they could take. Eight soldiers were found gone the next morning.[15] They had deserted, which was bad timing, because the final leg of their trip did not require marching.

The division got on the Orange and Alexandria Railroad cars and rode up to the western bank of the Potomac River. After two hours of travel the church spires of Alexandria came into view. Alexandria sat across the Potomac from Washington. Alexandria was a city famous for the patriots who had lived in its blocks of elegant row houses, and for its slave pens. A photograph of Alexandria's waterfront at the war's start shows a few pleasure skiffs pulled up onto the riverbank and a Russian frigate sitting at anchor out in the wide reach of the Potomac with its sails lowered. By the time the Giddings Regiment arrived, all that had changed. Rows of piers poked out into the water and dozens of ships were tied to them, with more sitting in the slack water offshore, waiting their turn to unload the materials of war. Smaller steamers churned from one side to the other carrying messages of critical importance, and sightseeing soldiers. Give it a few weeks more, and this once sleepy place on the Potomac would exceed New York harbor in its energy.

Their train came to a stop and they got down. They were to have no respite from the rigors of marching and battle. They were ordered to march down to the bank of the Potomac.[16] Three steamers, recently returned from taking men and supplies down to McClellan, were tied up at the dock. They sat high in the water, showing they were empty and ready for new cargo, and smoke from their stacks showed that the boilers had been fired and the ships were getting up steam. Shields's worn-out division was bound for above Richmond and these ships would take them there. Few men among them felt glad at the prospect, and some felt the time for mutiny had arrived. They had been promised a rest, but from appearances there was not going to be one.

Buckley's feelings about it made it all the way down to the lowliest private. Pvt. Alvinson Kinney told his parents that Buckley had threatened to resign in protest. He let it be known that if he were in their place, he would be looking for someone's head over which to break a rifle stock.[17] Wallace Hoyt was a youth through and through, and for him any place he had not been was a place worth seeing. He told his parents, "As far as me I had as live [leave] go to Richmond as anywhere."[18] Pvt. Burton Pickett of Company expressed a similar sentiment: "For my part I don't care where we go if we can clear the rebells out."[19]

The Giddings Regiment did not have a chance to test their colonel's suggestion. Loading went slow. By dark, all the Ohio regiments had moved baggage, men, and horses aboard the steamers, except for the Twenty-Ninth Ohio. Their turn would have to wait for the sun to return. During the night Lincoln and Stanton were getting no sleep at all. Telegraphic reports were coming from McClellan's staff, and the news was not good. The addition of Shields's division, despite their reputation for hard fighting, could not tip the scales of battle around Richmond in the Union's favor. The orders to sail down to the Peninsula were canceled. They would have their rest after all.

Buckley's preference was that they all be given a thirty-day furlough home, which would give the regiment time to recuperate and do a little recruiting to make up for the attrition of the last six months. If not that, he was willing to have the Twenty-Ninth installed in one of the forts that were going up around Washington. After the trip down to join McClellan was cancelled, they did not get any orders that pointed them toward field action, and it began to appear they might be occupying this pleasant hillside camp for some time to come. On that belief, many of the officers obtained furloughs and went home, including Buckley.

Capt. Myron T. Wright went back to Akron and opened a recruiting office on the west side of Howard Street in offices recently vacated by Messrs. Beebe and Elkins, the owners of the *Summit Beacon*, and by mid-July he was ready for business.[20] Men thinking of joining the Twenty-Ninth Ohio could come in and have Wright or his assistants, Sgts. Adam Hart and Washington Shanafelt, answer in private all the myriad questions that had to be answered before a man signed the enlistment papers. Was the Federal bounty two dollars or three for joining an old regiment? Could he have a friend or family member who was going west file on a piece of land for him under the Homestead Act of 1862 so that he would not be left out on the best chance for getting ahead in life that had ever come down the pike? And the biggest question of all: why should he join the Twenty-Ninth Ohio when so many other outfits were competing for his services? Capt. Ebenezer Howard and two assistants had been dispatched to Ashtabula County on the same business.

The regiment was now missing its three top officers. Buckley was home in Ohio, Thomas Clark was locked up in a rebel prison in Salisbury, North Carolina, and Major Clemmer was out of action with a shattered leg. Captain Fitch of Company A was next in line to take charge of the regiment, but he was on sick leave. Next in line after Fitch, Capt. Wilbur Stevens of Company B took acting command by merit of seniority. In their camp, with plenty of good things to eat, light duty to perform, and the excitement of the nation's capital just over the river, this leadership vacuum did not seem to matter much to the men of the Twenty-Ninth.

Wallace Hoyt had written to his parents after Port Republic, "Since I wrote to you last there had been a great change in the regiment."[21] Their discomfiture at Port Republic had been the latest and most dramatic of these changes, but change had been the constant since the day they got into their camp at Patterson's Creek. To the plain soldier these evolutions meant little. Being shifted from one purpose to the next, serving under one general, with his own loud and lofty goals, in one season, then seeing him gone and replaced by another when the next season came round, seemed to be the ordinary course of a soldier's life within a big army. The officers were disheartened, but not the boys in the ranks.

Wallace Hoyt's greatest concern at the moment was fulfilling his mother's request that he visit a picture saloon and have his profile made for her. Alvinson Kinney wrote to his widowed father on stationary purchased from the sutler decorated with a color drawing of Union soldiers charging into a cloud of smoke with flags flying and captioned "The War for the Union."

> We are in camp now wresting. . . . I have written four letters and have not received any answer. We herd that our letters got wet and wrotted in Washington. Perhapaps that is the reason why we don't get eny. How are you getting along and how the rest of the folks there getting along? I am injoing myself the best. we are in sight of alexandra and Washington. . . . we get soft bread and plenty of it.[22]

By this time, Kinney had gotten himself a rubber stamp to fix on his letters in place of his scrawled signature: "*A. A. Kinny. CO. B 29 O.V.I.*"

The Boys were satisfied with their station here, on a breezy hill with a pleasing view of Washington across the river. They made boat excursions down the river to see the home of the Father of the Nation, at Mount Vernon, and took strolls through the city of Washington with its spectacle of monuments and imposing public buildings. For those hungry for a taste of life in a city frenetic with the business of managing the nation's war, there was the day and night hullabaloo along Pennsylvania Avenue: saloons offering cold beer in giant glass schooners, plates of oysters and clams, cheeses and crackers. Cpl. Burton Pickett summed it all up in a letter that must have astonished his unworldly family.

> We are in the prettyest camp we ever was. It is on the banks of the potomac 8 miles from Washington. I was up at washington yesterday we had a gay old time we went from Alexandria on a steamboat it is a nice place but the capitol beats any thing ever I saw. It is made of marble and covers over four acres of ground it isn't shaped like a house or a barn anything else it looks more like a mountain than any thing else.[23]

The Boys were getting their first taste of summer in a Southern place, a mix of heat and humidity that produced an ocean of sweat with even the slightest exertion. For the soldiers of this war it was wool for all seasons, right down to their wool flannel drawers and socks; the only lighter fabric allowed or procurable was the cotton in their shirts. Elias Roshon, recently returned from his furlough home, went out to stand for a general inspection along with the rest one afternoon in July. The inspection, followed by three hours of drill, made him dizzy and so overheated he thought he might "croak." "I tell you I took a good drink when I got back to camp."[24] Still, they were in a civilized place, with many small luxuries, and if he desired it, a soldier could refresh himself with a glass of iced lemonade purchased cheaply from one of the vendors that hung around the Union camps. It was here at Alexandria that the regimental band, of which they were uncommonly proud, packed up and went back to Ohio.[25]

Congress had concluded that the War Department was spending $4 million per year just to support regimental bands, and a bill was passed into law ordering all regimental musicians mustered out. From now on, the entire brigade would share a band, made up of musicians from each of its regiments. The law had gone into effect while they were in Alexandria. The musicians were encouraged to trade their cornets for muskets and stay on as soldiers. A few were invited into the brigade band, but most musicians in the Twenty-Ninth Ohio decided to go home.

Flush Times Ahead

Lincoln reorganized their army once again. The various departments had been operating at odds with one another, and from distances that made cooperation difficult. With the stroke of a pen, outfits that had histories and personalities their own, won by time spent in the mountains of western Virginia and the Shenandoah valley, went out of business. Now, they would march under one banner: the Army of Virginia. Soldiers who had enjoyed easy duty were pulled out of the forts around Washington and placed on a new footing.

Tyler's brigade would remain in Banks's corps, which was now called the Second Corps, and would continue to be led by him. Banks had been the unfortunate victim of Washington's micromanagement of the war in the valley, and of Stonewall Jackson. Those unhappy days were water under the bridge, and with enough men behind him now, Banks was ready for redemption. Whether he or anyone else could work efficiently with the new army's top general was a question that would shortly be answered.

The Army of Virginia was to be headed by Lincoln's personal choice for the job, Gen. John Pope. Pope, like Lander and Shields, had served in the Mexican-American War and after that lived the life of an explorer in the Far West. He came to the East with a share of the credit for Union victories won at New Madrid, Island Number Ten, and far down south in Corinth, Mississippi. Pope cut an imposing figure, perfectly coiffed and uniformed, with a blockish head and a face that hinted at the bully in him. Pope was already on the scene in Alexandria, visiting the camps and making unspecified "inquiries" about the army's past failures in command. He overlooked asking one question that would have revealed much to him. Most of the Boys had come down recently from the valley, where all of them had been either whipped by Stonewall Jackson or worn out by marching toward or away from him. Had Pope asked, they would have warned him about Jackson's astonishing capacity to read his opponent's mind and jump on any opportunity that presented itself.

The new army would take the pressure off McClellan, and if McClellan went back on the offensive, they could support him. Unfortunately for McClellan, the time for satisfying his increasingly anxious requests for more men had gone. The combat phase of McClellan's grand plan above Richmond began the day before the Twenty-Ninth Regiment got on the cars for Alexandria. The new rebel commander, Robert E. Lee, would not sit in his defenses while McClellan maneuvered, nor would he wait for Washington to supply the additional men McClellan thought would guarantee him the upper hand. Although outnumbered, Lee got the rebel army out of its defenses and onto McClellan's flank and rear, and by the time Tyler's brigade was boarding ships to come to his aid, it was clear that McClellan had been bested. While the Giddings Regiment slept on the wharf waiting to board, McClellan was already removing his army with its thousands of wagons and herds of beef toward the river that had brought them.

There had been a great change in the Twenty-Ninth Ohio Volunteer, just as Wallace Hoyt had observed. So too with life back home on the Reserve, where evolutions were being felt; nothing like a revolution just yet, but clear signs that one was coming.

In northeast Ohio, the winter past had been nearly as severe as the one their boys experienced in the mountains of western Virginia, with deep snow and air so cold that cast-iron pump handles snapped in two as if made of wood. Spring came late and settled itself uncertainly. When the weather finally warmed enough to put in crops, persistent rains turned farm fields into ponds. The early summer visited some villages with tornadoes, remarkable for their rarity in this region. A string of sunny days in June, with rains falling conveniently at night, soon filled every farm field with wheat, oats, and hay, giving the whole Reserve a look of universal abundance.

Then the weather turned against them. By the end of July, a drought had taken hold in Ashtabula County, while forty miles to the south, rain fell as if on demand.[26] The earth split open and the grain lay slumped in the fields. Thunderclouds churned up every afternoon on the western horizon and promised relief, but only a few drops made it to the earth, and the peculiar phenomena of the dust devil became a common occurrence, frightening cattle and carrying wash hung out to dry and chickens into the next county.[27] In early August 1862, the rains returned. The fields revived and turned as golden and bright as a new psalmbook, as one observer described it.[28]

The pastures of the Reserve were thick with sheep, and sheep were immune to the vagaries of weather. Those who raised them were presently in high feather. The federal government was desperate for the wool to make uniforms for hundreds of thousands of new soldiers. Handsome returns were filling the local sheep growers' pockets, some men feeling so prosperous that they were storing the early summer clip, on speculation that the market would take prices even higher. The thought that their own soldiers were going nearly naked for want of cloth to make uniforms did not seem to cross anyone's mind.[29] The only problem with bumper crops in wheat and wool was the scarcity of farmhands.

Cash-paying jobs had begun to appear, which to most in this cash-poor country came as a boon, and the jobs could be had without signing the enlistment rolls for any of the many regiments now recruiting in response to the president's latest call for troops. By the end of summer, the wages for unskilled work shot past what a soldier could earn, and the opportunities were many.

A man who knew his way around livestock could sign on as a teamster for any number of enterprises that had contracted with the army. These jobs paid twice what a private made, and a man did not have to endure the discipline or danger of a soldier's life.

The Atlantic and Great Western Railroad was all set to expand.[30] Ads were placed in the newspapers asking for one hundred fifty thousand railroad ties, cash to be paid to the Reserve lumbermen who would bring them in quantity. Plans were being made this summer of 1862 to give Akron more direct railroad connections to the region's important places. It would be a few months yet before the new trains started running, but the savvy were positioning themselves for greater output and increased sales.

Shops around Akron became busier than their owners had ever imagined they would be, turning out steam engines, stoves, lightning conductors, and stamped-metal roofing. Foundries went into high gear, hammering out plows and wagon axles. Men would need these things, not just for work in this neighborhood, but in the West, and some men were making plans to head that way and start a new life, even though there was a war on. Contingents of pioneers out of this part of Ohio had already taken their New England ways far down into southern Iowa and out into Minnesota, sending notes home to the local papers telling of rich soil and cheap land that nature had already cleared of rocks and trees.

Between the battles of Kernstown and Port Republic, the Homestead Act had passed Congress, fulfilling the Republican Party's promise to liberalize the process by which a common man could get his hands on government-owned land. Now, western land, out beyond the Mississippi mostly, could belong to anyone willing to live on it for five years and make modest improvements. Nearer to home, men were wanted to peddle the Little Giant sewing machine, which featured an automated hemmer, the salesman to be given a liberal salary, expenses, and a commission on each machine he sold.

Women and children made up the workforce at what would be known as the Barber Match Company in Akron. Small hands were just right for the tedious work of cutting pine planks into smaller and smaller pieces, down to the size of a toothpick, coating the business end with phosphorus, and keeping the finished matches carefully separated so the whole building wouldn't take fire and burn to the ground.[31]

A stout-built immigrant in Akron missed the oatmeal he'd eaten for breakfast back in Germany. Ferdinand Schumacher experimented with roasting his own, put the surplus in jars for sale in his grocery, and they disappeared off the shelf.[32] Schumacher's product was thought just the right fare for sick and wounded Union soldiers, and he got a contract with the army's quartermaster department and started filling orders. Not yet through the first year of the war, Schumacher had gone from being a small grocer to emperor of several multistory red-brick mills filled with dozens of men working every day of the week, nights and Sundays included, which until then had been a rarity.

Coal beds lay around Akron, in some places sticking out of the ground in shiny black ledges, but before the war no one paid that much attention to them.[33] With the war, much of which ran on steam, Summit County's plentiful supply of coal was all of a sudden another boon. Half a dozen men took up the business, hurrying wagon trains of coal from this point to that, employing men at the mines, separators, and offices. Everything was expanding and moving at a faster clip. A business that might have taken decades to develop in a time of peace could by the occurrence of this dreadful scourge of war, be up and successfully running in a matter of months.

By the end of the first year of war, Akron was taking on a new look. The change was troubling to the old pioneers but exciting and full of opportunity to the men in shirts boiled white who now stood on every corner scribbling out contracts for this and that and talking offhandedly in thousands of dollars where the year before business folk had argued over pennies.

New buildings were going up in Akron, large brick commercial affairs with space for stores, offices, and banks, on lots where the ruins of earlier structures had blighted the avenues for years. Shopkeepers could not make change in silver or gold coins, those metals being scarce as hen's teeth, and instead made change in postage stamps. Items less important in past years began to move nearer the top of lists of goods advertised for sale in any given shop. Large supplies of mourning clothes, in bombazine, silk, or a more conservative wool, or linen for summer, were kept in stock, and a new patented metal coffin, guaranteed to prevent the decay of the contents during long railroad journeys, could now be had from the local purveyors of furniture and musical instruments.

The Fourth of July in Conneaut had been a grand but circumspect affair, with the firing of cannon, just as in past years, the singing of "Hail Columbia" by the village chorus, music by the Italian band, and tables spread so heavily with food that if anyone went away hungry it was not the fault of the food committee. There had been nonstop oratory by local clergy, politicians, and old pioneers recounting the nation's history to that point, pledging renewed dedication to the cause of liberty in the name of the Founding Fathers, as well as a full reading of the Declaration of Independence. The minister of a small congregation of the village, Lyman Daniel Ames, gave a toast to "J. C. Frémont, the Pathfinder—The man who comprehends the genius of Republican institutions, and sees the most direct way to end rebellion."[34]

None of this was called a boom as yet; circumspect people would not admit to flush times at home with so many boys off at war risking their lives and limbs for the liberties the civilians enjoyed. Nevertheless, compared to the dim outlook for business that had persisted into the first months of the war, this was the start of something very much resembling a bonanza. While entrepreneurs looked to the future, some Reserve residents looked to memorializing their recent past.

The very same residents of Jefferson who had taken charge of the building of the Twenty-Ninth Regiment got out ahead of their neighbors in other counties with a proposal to be the first county in the Reserve, and maybe all of Ohio, to have a monument erected to the memory of those who had given their lives in the current war.[35] Men were appointed to look into funding, and to arrange for architects to submit plans. This go-ahead plan blazed hot for a week or two until some realist put the brakes on it. The war, as it was appearing now, might go on through all of this summer, maybe for unknown seasons to come, and the tablet the committee had in mind might prove too small for all the names that might be chiseled into it.

Guardians of the morals of towns and villages complained that morality was in decline. The city of Ashtabula had always been somewhat rougher around the edges than calmer places like Jefferson. It was on Lake Erie, after all, and catered to sailors who put in there from all points. One town father observed that in the past year over a dozen sinkholes of inequity had taken root, where drunkards, thieves, and gamblers were manufactured wholesale.[36] Most mercantiles here and elsewhere had refrained from selling liquor, since doing so in this famously abstemious region of Ohio could invite public sanction and ruin a business. Now stores openly advertised "natural" or "pure" wines for sale, and harder stuff also, although these stronger spirits were still hidden behind the storekeeper's claim that they were being sold for "strictly medicinal purposes."

Ashtabula had at least some young men who were as protective of the city's standards as the old folks. A man named Eugene Charlemagne, regarded as the town's "degenerate jour," had lived in the town for some time without resorting to honest means. Worse, he had been discovered living with the widow of a Union soldier.[37] The young vigilantes searched the house and found Eugene tucked into a ball behind the chimney. They dragged him outside, trussed him up, set him on a rail, and paraded him through town ahead of a crowd of jeering and whistling boys and men. He was carted to the depot, where upon his promise to catch the next train out and not come back, he was released. Charlemagne didn't get on the train, though, and when found on the streets the next day he was given a "rather severe drubbing."[38]

The cataloging of Southern atrocities continued in the Reserve's newspapers unabated. The latest reports in this line were of Winchester's women attacking retreating Union soldiers with butcher knives and clubs and throwing boiling water onto soldiers from windows above the street. Soldiers lying sick or wounded in the valley hospitals were bayoneted in their beds by rebel bullies.[39] One editor concluded, "If we go to war with Indians, we should expect to be scalped."[40]

Women working on behalf of the Soldiers' Aid Society held a money-raising activity nearly every day, even in the remote corners of the Reserve. They set aside examples of every article that was home manufactured and took them down to churches and town halls, where they were boxed and shipped to the army hospitals. The Reserve's newspapers published long lists of each lady's contributions, right down to the number of chickens she had put up and the number of apples dried, with her name published along side it, like the old New England congregations, which had published a list of every member's contributions, shaming those who had given little to give more. The women of Conneaut wrote to Governor Tod and offered their own homes to any Ohio soldier in need of convalescence—a kind offer that the governor declined since he had no power over the sick and wounded after they were discharged from the hospital.[41]

New regiments were poised at Camp Chase for their turn into the war, complaining of the waiting that preceded it, as had the Twenty-Ninth Regiment.[42] Into this second real year of fighting, Ohio's contributions in regiments would pass the one hundred mark, with the 105th Ohio Volunteer Infantry taking shape in Ashtabula and neighboring counties. Times were changing, that much was clear, and as a reminder of how far the Reserve had come, three Indians stepped out of the past it seemed and into the village of Conneaut.

The woman of the group was dressed in the old way, in garments the locals regarded as fantastic, and although the two men were dressed slightly more modern, they still bore the characteristics of the original inhabitants of these forests. The residents reflected that it had not seemed all that long ago the Indians had been a regular feature on the landscape. The report of their appearance held a certain sadness, that all of what had been was gone, replaced by farms and towns. The visitors did not linger in the village but moved on eastward, their destination and purpose a mystery.[43]

Poor Fellows

Major Clemmer's trip out of the valley had been no more comfortable than that of the wounded enlisted men. He rode his horse seventeen miles from the battlefield at Port Republic before he got to a place where his leg wound could be fully examined.[44] By then the leg was swollen and he was in extraordinary pain. It took two days for the four-horse ambulance to cover the miles into Luray, where he was loaded into a wagon and taken to Front Royal. There he was placed on a cot and put aboard the railroad for Washington. His treatment, as compared to that given the ordinary soldier, diverged at that point. He hired a cab to take him from the depot to the National Hotel, where he rented a room.

A friend found him there. It did not seem proper for an officer to cry, but Clemmer admitted that when his friend entered his room, both broke down and wept. A private surgeon was called for, and after a week of lying in his blood-crusted, powder-blackened uniform he was given clean clothes. Women from back home in Mogadore who happened to be in Washington came to his aide, bringing bandages to wrap his leg. One brought a bouquet of flowers to cheer him, and they put him in mind of home, with its familiar faces, green lawns, pleasant walks, and fragrant flowers. Soon he began to feel well enough to travel, and no less a personage than Ohio congressman Sydney Edgerton arranged for his transportation home.

Nine days after he had been hurt, Major Clemmer was delivered to his home in Mogadore, still on the same cot he had been laid down on in Front Royal. His wife and three daughters fussed over him, and for this he was glad. When the cannon were fired at their Fourth of July observance, he asked the town's residents to think of their boys who had been killed or maimed. He hoped to be able to return to the Twenty-Ninth Regiment, but his was one of those wounds that never healed. It remained open and leaking pieces of bone for the remainder of his life. His days as a warrior were over.[45] The Twenty-Ninth's soldiers, who did not have the pocketbook of their officers, took their chances in one of the army hospitals popping up around Washington like mushrooms in a wet season.

By the end of July 1862, hundreds of shattered boys were being carried off every ship coming back from the Peninsula and laid in the open on Washington's docks. With their own boys suffering similarly, the editor of the newspaper in Ashtabula city admitted, "The talk and novelty of civil war is over and its stern realities are upon us."[46] To make that hard fact even plainer, an Ohio woman living in Washington began a series of letters to her friends in Austinburg, Ashtabula County, on the medical treatment given the county's common soldiers. The letters were thought important enough to publish in the Jefferson newspaper.

For a Victorian woman, her description of the interior of an army hospital after a major battle was neither romantic nor demure, but it was something she felt the people back home needed to hear. "I spend my leisure hours in the Judiciary Square Hospital. Oh, such sad, sad scenes as I meet every day!"[47] She went on to report that the week before over eight hundred of McClellan's soldiers, mutilated and hacked to pieces, had arrived in a pouring rain, fresh from the battlefields above Richmond.

She overheard stories telling how men were dying on the battlefields. They did not say things like, "Tell Mother I died for my Country." The cruel reality was that stricken soldiers shrieked and begged, and she let the readers back home in Ashtabula County know that. The terrible machine of war was churning out mutilated young men far faster than hospitals could be arranged to house them, and the time for sparing comfortable civilians the awful details had passed.

> You may read the most graphic descriptions of battlefields and scenes and their attendant horrors but you can never realize any of it unless you step into the wards of some hospital, filled with wounded soldiers—flesh wounds of every description; eyes out, noses gone, jaws shot off, scalps torn up, arms gone, hands blown off, legs shattered and splintered, thighs shot through, feet cut open with pieces of shell—and these are the slightly wounded, they will tell you. Among the severely, or dangerously wounded, you find them shot through the body, some seeming perfectly riddled with bullets, and living, and "likely to get well," the doctors say. One poor fellow shot in the lungs, and another in the liver, living and "may recover."[48]

Men suffering from typhoid were collected in one long ward, skin the color of candle wax, eyes dead, some delirious, gasping their last hours away, and calling out for loved ones. The dead were carted out, the bedding changed, a new sufferer installed, and the cycle begun again. There was no mention in her letter of brave boys giving their lives for a noble cause or of sacrifices placed on the altar of freedom—just the hard, inescapable reality of war. Boys condemned to death by sickness or wounds held daguerreotypes of loved faces so tightly in their hands that they could not be pried away. Boys who knew they must die took her hand and would not turn loose of it; they sobbed and pleaded with her to get them out of this place and take them back home to Ohio.

She walked out two miles north of the city to visit Cliffburne Hospital, set up in a former barracks, where three hundred of the wounded of Shields's division lay knocked to pieces.[49] Going from ward to ward, up and down the long plank floors, she found boys from Ashtabula, Austinburg, Hartsgrove, Jefferson, and Morgan. They had arrived in a group at ten o'clock on a Saturday night after a long trip out of the valley. The hospital had been notified of their arrival, but there had been neither provisions nor staff on hand to meet them. The hospital, it seemed, was locked for the night. The neighbors took pity on so many wounded men lying out in the elements and they opened their homes, churches, and public halls to shelter them and rounded up food and refreshments.

The Religious Order of the Sisters of Mercy had charge of the nursing, and the Austinburg lady thought they favored the rebel boys being treated in the same hospital. In this later opinion, she was likely mistaken. The Sisters of Mercy had proven their selflessness in alleviating suffering decades before they took on this assignment, and none in the order had ever been south of Washington. Anti-Catholicism was prevalent in the Reserve, as elsewhere; parishes in the countryside of Ashtabula County, nonexistent. Few in the county had ever seen a woman dressed in a nun's habit, and the sisters of this order wore one that was particularly severe and foreign looking, and, to top it off, they were mostly Irish born.

Despite her prejudice against Catholic nuns, the Austinburg lady's heart was in the right place as she operated a one-woman relief society. At the start, she visited the soldiers during her leisure hours. Two months later she wrote, "I have ceased to make an effort toward anything not connected with the soldiers, now that I feel I have it in my power to alleviate, even in a slight degree, their sufferings."[50] She had adopted boys lying in several hospitals, walking to each with her heavy baskets. She bought loaves of bread with her own money, toasted slices and buttered them, and took them in a pail out to the hospital, along with lemons and sugar.[51] She bought stationary, oranges, newspapers, and dozens of pairs of slippers. She pressed for donations from friends back in Ashtabula County and got them, including barrels carefully packed with pillow cases, clothing, and wheels of the Reserve's famous cheese.

The soldiers were overjoyed to find a woman in the wards, and when they found out she was an Ohioan like them, those that could walk followed her as she made her rounds. A kind man back in Norton Township had sent a fine maple sugar cake to her for the soldiers. So many of them gathered round her that she was embarrassed to tell them there was not enough of the cake to go around, to which they replied, "Just let us look at it; it will do so much good, if made in Ohio."[52] She wrote last good-byes home for dying men and came to realize, after all her work, that there was nothing of interest to her any longer other than easing the suffering of the soldiers.

What she saw in the hospitals troubled her: men with broken limbs swollen and distorted, the bones going unset for lack of doctors; soldiers who had been patients in these places for months and had yet to see a single vegetable or piece of fruit, although vendors on the streets of Washington always seemed well supplied. A mere four surgeons were assigned to care for over a thousand soldiers at Fairfax Seminary Hospital. But it was not within the province of a woman in that age to agitate publicly for changes in anything.

The lady from Austinburg was onto something here, and she would not let it rest. Helen Cowles Wheeler[53] came from one of the Reserve's first families, one in which the parents had taken an approach to child rearing still novel for its time. The family felt that daughters were every bit as deserving of education as sons, and that a woman not only was capable of standing on her own two feet but had an obligation to. Her aunt, Betsy Mix Cowles, had been one of the first graduates of Oberlin College, male or female, and she had never shrunk from the opportunity to assail slavery and had been one of the county's antislavery organizers.[54] Some thought it unseemly for a woman to speak publicly, but Betsy never hesitated, and neither did her niece.

Within two weeks of the arrival of the wounded from Port Republic, Ohio residents living in the Washington vicinity met in a home at 512 Twelfth Street and formed the Ohio Soldiers' Association.

It was the members' job to visit every hospital in which Ohio boys were housed, obtain his name and condition, and then to report that information to Governor Tod.[55] More important, the members asked that the address of the association be published, so that families and friends anxious for a boy's fate could begin their search by writing to them. The *Sentinel* gave Helen Wheeler front-page space to bring her observations of the sorry conditions in hospitals to the attention of the county's residents.[56] Congress should be looking into these irregularities, and with Mrs. Wheeler's urging, Ohio congressmen John Hutchins and Albert Gallatin Riddle did.

Mrs. Wheeler had done for the people of Ashtabula County what Matthew Brady would do in a few months for the people of New York City. Those walking along busy Broadway saw his hand-lettered sign on the door, "The Dead of Antietam," and the interested climbed the flight of steps to his studio and went inside to look into the eyes of the men in photographs. These men, mouths opened in unnatural ovals, eyes staring, and limbs arranged in impossible ways were the cost of this war. The same could be said of Mrs. Wheeler's exhibition of letters as a reviewer said of Brady's exhibition: the lists of sick, dead and wounded of the war were read in the morning newspaper and then forgotten along with the coffee.[57] After her letters, they could no longer be so easily dismissed.

Decades later, when a history of Ashtabula County was written, the jolt Mrs. Wheeler's letters had given the people was still remembered.

Prelude to Misfortune

With each passing day, the weather in Alexandria grew hotter. The period of lounging in their camp had come to an end. Orders had come in that they were to head south. Tyler's brigade boarded the cars at Alexandria on July 25, bound for a point above Culpeper Court House, Virginia. The Boys nearly suffocated in the cattle cars, but this was better than going it on foot. They had ceased complaining about such things. They got down to Warrenton and set up camp. Changes continued to overhaul them. General Tyler had been ordered to Washington, D.C., and Gen. John White Geary took his place as commander of this brigade of mostly Ohio soldiers.

To fortify its reduced numbers, Geary brought his Pennsylvania regiment, which had nearly as many soldiers in it as all the Ohio regiments combined, and along with them Knap's battery, in which his adored son Eddie was serving. The brigade was called out to say good-bye to Tyler and listen to his moving farewell address.[58] He had led them nearly forever it seemed, and he had been rock steady in all weather. All was hurry up just now, and introductions to Geary would have to wait.

They got their first good sight of Geary on the march down toward Culpeper Court House as he and his staff rode up and down the division's column. He was a giant of a man by the yardstick of any age. It took a draft-size horse to seat his six-foot-six, 250-pound muscular bulk, and mounted upon it he appeared invincible. Geary was a man of high native intelligence. He had begun college at fourteen, interrupted it to go to work to pay off his deceased father's debts, returned, and graduated after studying engineering and law. After that, he worked as a surveyor, land speculator, and railroad construction engineer. Then came the Mexican-American War and Geary's life was transformed. He had always had an interest in things military and had enlisted in the local militia as a youngster. He rose to become lieutenant colonel of the Second Pennsylvania Infantry, although he was only twenty-seven, and led it in a glorious charge at Chapultepec, during which he was struck five times by musket balls. He came home a self-proclaimed hero, although some would dispute the facts he put forward to prove it.[59]

He parlayed his Mexican-American War record into an appointment as postmaster of San Francisco before California was a state, and he served as the city's first mayor. In 1856 he accepted a presidential appointment as governor of Kansas Territory, tried to steer a neutral course between proslavery and antislavery forces warring there, failed, and got out of the territory by the skin of his teeth and only then by making his exit during the dead of night and armed with two pistols.

If his great bulk was not enough to intimidate, there were his dark eyes, which he fixed on those who addressed him. He was a strict Methodist in temperament if not in doctrine, disinclined to tell or enjoy a funny story. He quoted easily from the English poets, and was well versed in Greek and French. He loved each of his children dearly and maintained a deeply romantic relationship with his wife. To the men who served under him he was regarded as something of a martinet, imperious and sometimes severe. He was not averse to applying the flat of his sword to the backside of soldiers who did not jump to obey him.

Geary had been farming in Crawford County, Pennsylvania, in the several years preceding the war, his political career looking stalled out with him still in the prime of manhood. When the Giddings Boys met him, Geary's military career was on the advance, and if he had anything to say about it, it was just getting started. He had already commanded troops in minor victories along the Potomac, and he had been honorably wounded. He had also displayed a knack for magnifying his own achievements, and he was supported in this by partisans in the news business.

The Boys were glad to be back in Banks's care and out from under McDowell. Their new high general, John Pope, promised to give the rebel citizenry the exact kind of war the editors back in the Reserve had been arguing for. Henceforth in Virginia, civilians living within a five-mile radius of any guerrilla depredation would be called out en masse to repair the damage, women and children being no exception.[60] If his soldiers were fired on from a house, they were ordered to burn it, arrest anyone around, and send them off to prison.[61] All disloyal male citizens were to be arrested immediately, except those willing to take the oath of allegiance to the United States. Those who refused would be taken outside Union lines and warned that if they ever returned they would be treated as spies—swung from a rope.[62]

Not a word of this escaped Robert E. Lee, who loved his native state and its people as much as any man could love anything. In Lee's view, Pope needed to be "suppressed."[63] Having cowed the civilian population, Pope turned his attention on his own men. He published a proclamation, unwise in some minds, since he'd not won anything in this theater yet, which went ahead of even McClellan's bombastic pronouncements back in western Virginia in the summer of '61. He ordered every company in the Giddings Regiment, and in every other outfit, called out to have the circular he'd written read to them:

> Let us understand each other. I have come to you from the West, where we have always seen the backs of our enemies; from an army whose business it has been to seek the adversary. . . . I have been called here to pursue the same system. . . . Meantime, I desire you to dismiss from your minds certain phrases, which I am sorry to find so much in vogue amongst you. I hear constantly of "taking strong positions and holding them," of "line of retreat," and "bases of supplies." Let us discard such ideas.[64]

He promised his soldiers they would soon have the names of new and victorious battles to stitch upon their battle flags. Immediately, there was talk of Pope being a braggart, an outsider, and a backbiter. Back home in Ashtabula County the citizens were impressed by Pope's talk. Pope had "snap."[65] For the soldier in the ranks of the Twenty-Ninth Ohio, all this big talk meant little at the moment, except that they would now be required to carry an extraordinary one hundred rounds of ammunition at all times, and that the thinning baggage trains would be reduced further, increasing the weight of the soldier's load.[66] "We expect to start to march for Gordonsville this morning where we shall have undoubtedly some fighting to do—which will be done without flinching on our part if they will fight us with even numbers."[67] So wrote Wallace Hoyt to his parents in the first days of August.

The camp rumor as to where they were headed this time proved faultless. While Pope finished assembling all the far-flung parts of his new command, Banks's corps was to get out ahead of Pope's army and strike for Gordonsville, thirty miles below Culpeper Court House.

Lee's army depended on supplies that came to it on the railroad via Gordonsville. Take Gordonsville, and Lee would be forced to holler uncle and give up the game. That Lee would not allow such a thing without a huge brawl would have occurred to the simplest soldier, especially since he had kicked McClellan off the Peninsula and was now free to consider other moves.

There had been little to occupy the soldiers in the five days they spent at Little Washington (so called to avoid confusion with the nation's capital), waiting to continue their march to Gordonsville.[68]

Finding shade of any kind was the order of their days here. One of the boys in the Twenty-Ninth Regiment had procured a pair of boxing gloves and the soldiers traded turns knocking each other down.[69] Chaplain Hurlburt concluded his Sunday evening service by announcing that failing health had compelled him to resign and that he would be leaving them. Hurlburt had been the soldiers' friend, and more than that, their outspoken champion, and he would be missed. Parmater's company, like the others, was desperately short of officers, a condition that was worsened here by the resignation of their second lieutenant, Albert Durkee.

Camping in Little Washington was not altogether healthful. Increasing numbers of Banks's men were presenting themselves at morning sick call with complaints of chills and dysentery, which were the unmistakable clinical signs of malaria, and typhoid. Their campground looked pleasant enough from a distance, situated on a cleared rise of ground, with pure, cool water available from the nearby river. Closer examination by an inspector with the Medical Department seemed to show a correlation between the ways the soldiers had set up their camps in this place and the "crowd poison" that spawned killing diseases.[70] Conditions seemed worst in the camps of the Second Division, where the inspector saw that the "sinks," or latrines, of one regiment ran up to within thirty feet of the tents of its neighbors. The company streets were no more than four feet wide, and the shelter tents pitched so that they nearly touched. Offal and the carcasses of slaughtered cattle lay decomposing in the grass behind every regiment. The inspector recommended some commonsense changes in housekeeping, and Banks issued orders that they be carried out.[71]

At an early hour on August 6, they got on the road to Sperryville, marching right up the edge of the Blue Ridge and getting into camp far after dark.[72] The Twenty-Ninth Ohio had acted as guards of Banks's ten-mile-long supply train on this march and had spent the day gagging on the red dust of the entire column.[73] At sunrise the next day they turned southeast, away from the blue mountains and into a dry country. A few hours after moving away from water, their beef cattle and horses lay convulsing at the roadside, lathered and foaming at the mouth from too much heat and too little water, and for the men it had not been much different.

Five miles out from Sperryville, word came down the column that they would stop early this day; the water found up ahead was too scarce for men and animals to pass without stopping.[74] A stream curved in nearly to the roadside.[75] Boys slipped out of their uniforms and ran into the water for a general frolic. The next day, news came down the column: there were rebels up ahead.[76] An officer came down to their swimming hole and ordered the boys to cease their sporting and form up. They marched through the hottest part of the day, men falling out without authority wherever a tree threw a shadow, and then on again.[77]

The Giddings Regiment was about to step into its third battle with only 173 men, including officers.[78] Of staff officers, they had none at all, and some companies were so short of officers that the sergeants were giving the orders. They were without their flags, or at least one of them, and their rock, Lewis P. Buckley, was not with them. Even their brass band was gone.

Despite these impediments, the regiment's desire to fight remained intact. Webster B. Storer left his Akron iron business and went Warrenton to visit his son Sgt. James B. Storer and to take the pulse of the regiment. He made no comment on their anemic size, saying only that the soldiers were in good spirits and ready for a scrap.[79] As Wallace Hoyt had said, they would do what was asked of them without flinching. Of their prospects for what lay ahead, Nathan Parmater wrote in his diary, "I expect that our little 200 will have a chance to show their spunk."

Twenty-one-year-old Burton Pickett was devoted to his aging father, whom he'd left to tend the family farm alone in the face of declining health. Burton had siblings, but they were small girls, children really, and not yet capable of contributing to the work of hardscrabble farming. When Burton went off to war, his father had lost his best and only hand. There had been an interruption in the flow of letters to and from Ohio this summer, which left soldiers like Burton anxious for news. He wrote to encourage his father to lighten his daily load of work by spending the army pay Burton had sent home to hire a helper.

Dear Father,

I take this pen to write you a few lines to let you know that I am well but I am afraid you can not say that. I heard your knee was lame agan is it very bad? I hope it aint. I wish you would write and tell me you dont know how hard I want to hear from you and to hear how you get along with your work. Father, I am writing this in a hurry I am Seargt of the guard today down and town and I shall have to go in five minutes . . .

I will help you all as long as I live and have my health . . . I wish you would write and let me know how you get along. Ma what shall I say to you? I have not time to say mutch but I hope you are well and dont have the headache as mutch as you did.[80]

A few more lines and he stowed pen and tablet in his pack and along with the others filed into the road for the last leg of their march to Culpeper Court House, Virginia, with the hope that when next they wrote home, there would be victories to report.

13

"South of Anywhere"

THE BATTLE OF CEDAR MOUNTAIN, VIRGINIA, AUGUST 9, 1862

Sunstruck

At the dawn of this day, an orange sun came up in a sheet-iron sky unshaded by a single cloud, and it was immediately so hot that is was impossible to draw a full breath. Each soldier carried a knapsack, a full canteen, and a musket that alone weighed fifteen pounds. The twenty pounds of ammunition each carried was stuffed into cartridge boxes, the excess into pockets. Four miles out from Culpeper Court House dust was seen billowing up into the still air to the south, signal that a large enemy force was coming their way.[1] Leaving the valley, they had hoped it was the last they would see of Gen. Thomas Jackson. Whether they lived or died, were captured or remained free, kept their limbs or lost them, was still up to him as much as their own generals, and he was coming up to test them again.

The Twenty-Ninth Ohio Volunteer Infantry marched through the town of Culpeper Court House. Passage through any rebel town was an event worthy of touristlike comments, but in their preoccupation, how Culpeper Court House and its people appeared to them went unreported. The whole of the Twenty-Ninth Ohio took up little room in the column. The Ohio regiments of their brigade, the Fifth, Seventh, Twenty-Ninth, and Sixty-Sixth, combined would have barely filled a single regiment back at the mustering camps a year earlier.[2]

Geary's own regiment, the Twenty-Eighth Pennsylvania, was by itself nearly as large as the rest of the entire brigade. By the accounts of the newspaper reporters who covered its exploits, the Twenty-Eighth Pennsylvania had already made high marks in the war. The truth was that their campaigning to this point had been practically bloodless.[3] With the signs of a serious fight up ahead, the Twenty-Eighth Pennsylvania was detached to guard a hill strung with telegraph wires, and the strength of Geary's brigade had been cut in half.[4]

The sun was already far past its zenith by the time they'd made a half dozen miles south out of Culpeper Court House. Capt. Wilbur F. Stevens rode at the head of the Twenty-Ninth, the sun and the weight of unsolicited responsibility bearing down on him. With all the field staff officers gone and the next in line, Capt. William Fitch of Company A, absent, command of the regiment devolved to him. Nothing really is known of Stevens's behavior in their battles to this point. Nothing critical had been said of him, by his men or his superiors. At Kernstown he had been briefly flummoxed by the nerves that every man felt before his first combat. He had recovered his composure and gone in at the head of his company, and there is nothing in the record to suggest he did not stay with them. Fifty years later some of the men who had known him in the army would claim to remember a few things about his temperament: when asked for a decision his face became red, and he would hesitate uncomfortably and cough into his hand. Stevens was bothered continually by back pain, fatigue, and jumpy nerves. Most damning in the eyes of those in the regiment who did not like him, Stevens was developing a reputation for falling off the water wagon and going on sprees, which rubbed the abstemious of his fellow officers, like James B. Storer, the wrong way. The indulgence in alcohol by some of the Twenty-Ninth's officers was not a rarity, nor did it mean necessarily that Stevens would not be a dynamo in combat. He was not the active physical type. He was of average height, but heavy; phlegmatic in makeup, according to his doctor; and not cut out for hard, physical work. If any man was susceptible to the heat of this day, it was Stevens.

Their division, under command of Gen. Christopher C. Augur, was out ahead of Banks's corps, and the Seventh Ohio in the lead of everyone. They had been marching since daylight, and with every mile covered they had seen an increasing numbers of men lying in the ditches, eyes rolling, with foaming mouths, oblivious as to whether they were back home hoeing among the corn rows or on a ship to Cathay. This heat was killing men as surely as if they had been shot through the vitals.[5] A few miles south of Culpeper Court House, Elias Roshon saw five men fall out of the brigade's column, victims of the melting heat, three of whom he claimed died.[6]

Aside from the terrible percentage of men who would be ingested by the machinery of war on this field, everyone who was here, from private to high general, remembered the heat for the rest of their lives. Scientists near Washington stepped outside to read their weather instruments at midday and penciled down their observations: 95 degrees and pushing higher, the air saturated with water, and not so much as a breeze to push it away.

The colonel of the Sixty-Sixth Ohio Volunteers, marching ahead of the Giddings Regiment, was Charles Candy. The army had been his home since he enlisted at age eighteen. He had sympathy for the private soldier, having been one himself. Candy had ridden and walked with the First U.S. Dragoons over the dry plains of Texas and New Mexico, where water was so scarce men drank from muddy hoof prints and were glad to have it.[7] He had served as assistant adjutant general to General Lander and saw service at Ball's Bluff before resigning and taking on the command of the Sixty-Sixth Ohio Volunteer Infantry.[8] Although many of the details of the coming battle would be lost to his memory, Charles Candy would always remember the heat: "It was the hottest day I ever experienced in the field, and during the remainder of my service [I] never knew troops to suffer more for water, and what little we could get had to be strained through our handkerchiefs into our mouths so as to wet our parched lips, anything so it was wet."[9] Geary's brigade continued south out of Culpeper Court House down the main-traveled highway known as the Culpeper Road. They came up to the outskirts of the developing fight. Skulkers warned them there were secesh just ahead, and hordes more coming. Geary's men dragged themselves forward by fits and starts.

The Wait

Two hours past midday, Geary's brigade finally got to Cedar Run creek. A few of the boys waded in to drink and sport. They climbed to within a hundred yards of long ridge atop which ran Mitchell's Station Road.[10] It had taken six hours to go seven miles from Culpeper Court House out to this ridge, where Mitchell's Station Road fed into highway.[11] At the top of the ridge, Federal batteries were unlimbering their guns. Banks had given Augur specific instructions as to how his division should be placed, and the soldiers got off the Orange Road and filed to the left into two lines, with their right on the road, and their left tailing off in the direction of Cedar Mountain.[12] Their line ran roughly parallel to Crittenden Lane, a long farm driveway that intersected the Culpeper Road a mile to the south. To their generals observing enemy movement from the ridge, the driveway could be located by the line of trees behind it. Just now, increasing numbers of rebel infantry were appearing in the fringe of those trees, their lines parting to admit artillery batteries, then closing tight again.

The right of the frontmost line was taken by the Seventh Ohio, with the Sixty-Sixth Ohio to its left. The Giddings Boys took their place on the rear of the slope, fifty paces back of the Seventh Ohio. To their left, the Fifth Ohio Volunteers lined up. The right side of the Twenty-Ninth was anchored on the highway, which would be their guideline in any forward movement. Their assigned duty at this point was to protect the artillery and await developments.

The man in command of the division that day was as unknown to them as Geary. Christopher Augur was a veteran of the Mexican-American War and an Indian fighter in the regular army. When the war broke out, he had been commandant of cadets at West Point. If pointed out as the division's leader, he may have impressed his soldiers as having the most extravagant mustache in the army. By reputation, Augur was a capable leader of men in battle, but he would have only a limited opportunity to demonstrate that today.

Augur had no need of field glasses to size up the terrain. The field on which the infantry would fight the battle was less than a mile square, and most of its important phases would be conducted in an area half that. Between the ridge behind which Geary's brigade waited and the Crittenden Lane lay a rolling field planted in Indian corn with scattered clumps of brush. Further off to the right of the Orange Road was a large patch of woods that ran all the way to the Crittenden Gate.

How they had come to be in this place would be something for generals and politicians to argue over in the coming months. Pope would blame Banks for precipitating the fight. He had attacked when he should have waited for Maj. Gen. Franz Sigel's corps to come up.[13] Banks would defend himself by waving Pope's order. He did not have a copy of it actually, since Pope's instructions to him were relayed to him verbally, but he had been through enough to have one of his aides write it out:

> General Banks to move to the front immediately, assume command of all forces in the front, deploy his skirmishers if the enemy advances, and attack him immediately as he approaches, and be reinforced from here.[14]

It would come down to the kind of argument that had gotten going in the wake of Port Republic over whether Shields had ordered the famous bridge held, or burned. For the common soldier none of this had any bearing on what was to happen here in the lee of Cedar Mountain, Virginia, August 9, 1862. Fine points could be argued up and down, but that was best left to others; once the armies were moved into killing range, events would proceed to an outcome that had little to do with the debates of generals.

Geary's brigade hugged the ground back of the ridge for an hour in comparative quiet. Then, rebel infantry rode out and drove in the Federal pickets on the left, and the batteries directly above them on the ridge began firing a challenge. Soon after, the rebel gunners got their range and shells began dropping into the brigade. The soldiers sidled over to get behind the steeper part of the slope to avoid annihilation by rebel artillery. As yet, not a single musket had been discharged.[15] Late afternoon passed into the supper hour while the soldiers endured artillery fire that seemed to be coming from two places at once. They had lain on the reverse slope of this ridge for days it seemed, protecting two batteries while the overshots of rebel gunners landed among them, tearing up the ground and the occasional soldier. Some men who had been here would claim later that they had been made permanently deaf.

It came as a shock after hours of this painful assault on the ears when the guns above them went silent.[16] Williams's division, across the road on their right, had begun its assault. In their own sector, Generals Geary and Henry Prince had spied Gen. Jubal Early's rebels gathering to attack their left. Then lines of rebel infantry came stepping out of the woods along the Crittenden Lane with flags unfurled and muskets lowered, advancing right toward Geary. He ordered his first line onto the field to dispute the rebel approach, and Prince's line stepped out on their left. It was six o'clock in the evening now, too late in the day to begin a fight of this scale, but the armies were arranged and they would fight it out regardless of the hour. The Seventh Ohio had officers in it as good as any in the Union army, and its soldiers, to a man, were resolute under fire. This was to be the third time in as many battles they would be used as the shock troop of their brigade. The Seventh Ohio, with the Sixty-Sixth Ohio on its left, went up and over the ridge in double line of battle and down into the cornfield below.

Into a Cloud

It was a curious thing to look upon, the Seventh Ohio Volunteer Infantry disappearing into a cloud. That is what the Giddings Boys too curious to lie in place saw when they crawled to the top of the long ridge to get a peek at the show that was unfolding on the other side. The sun was lowering and in their eyes, and the dust the combatants raised as they marched toward collision made it difficult to see. The batteries that had been trading shots for the past two hours had packed the field with smoke. The infantry of each side got within range of each other and fired a volley, and then the Seventh advanced into the smoke their firing had made. One minute they were seen there, raising rifles to shoulders among the corn rows, and the next, gone. From then on, the Seventh Ohio appeared to be at work within a thunderhead that pulsed with orange light. There were terrible sounds coming from within it: shouts, screams, gunfire, swearing, and even snatches of song.

Parmater's best friend, Alonzo Sterrett, had remained in the town counting Banks's supply wagons.[17] Finishing that, he recalled, "I went up to the scene of Battle alone feeling that I could render some good service."[18] He arrived in time to see the batteries exchanging fire, and an hour later, he saw the Federal infantry start their advance. Shortly, the world contained in the fields below him exploded, "The roar and din of battle was terrible, far exceeding anything I ever heard before because it was on a much grander scale." In a few moments more, he found useful employment in taking charge of the hundreds of maimed and bleeding boys who began to stream back from the battlefield.

The soldiers of the Giddings Regiment were safe by comparison. Soldiers would do anything to break the unbearable strain of waiting like this, clowning included. Every outfit had at least one man, it seemed, who knew everything there was to know, and was always happy to share his wisdom with others whether he had been invited to or not. The "genius" of the Giddings Regiment was a private of Company K they called the Commodore. The Boys did not like a know-it-all, but the Commodore had a sense of humor and for that, they tolerated him. He talked in a drawl and his words whined out through his nose. The Giddings Boys had developed a saying to be addressed to one whose company was not wanted, "Well, you can good day now; good day, sir." Here, on the backside of Mitchell's Station Road, the Commodore would not stay down. He had raised himself just when a shell passed over with the sound of a locomotive and nearly took his head off. He dropped to the ground quicker than he had ever been seen to do anything, and commented to the shell, "Waal, yew kin good day' naow."[19]

The Seventh Ohio had enjoyed the dubious honor of opening the infantry battle. They barely got to the base of the ridge behind which they had sheltered, and down into the corn, when a sheet of flame broke from a long line of concealed infantry ahead on their right.[20] They halted and were producing orderly fire when swarms of grapeshot coming from the Crittenden Lane struck them square in the front, tearing ragged holes in the line. There were now rebel guns taking aim at them, and rebel infantry stacking up behind.[21] The Seventh Ohio closed ranks and worked its muskets as one gray regiment after another stepped out to meet them and add their fire.[22] In the hour they had been fighting, the Seventh Ohio transited the whole of the cornfield and had closed to within a few hundred yards of the lane, leaving a thick trail of wounded tangled in the cornstalks.

Gen. Samuel Crawford's Union men to the right of the road had not suffered the crossfire of artillery and musket, and their charge across a wheatfield and through the woods gained an irresistible momentum as it went and smashed the rebels back. They made it all the way up to one of the batteries that had been tormenting them from the Crittenden Gate, and drove the survivors off in a panic. With their left turned, the whole rebel line was on the verge of coming unglued. It would only take one more push, maybe from Geary. His assault line was stalled but might drive further if it were reinforced, and he ordered the Fifth and Twenty-Ninth Ohio Regiments to their support.

The Giddings Regiment rose with a shout and got to the top of the ridge, where they were immediately swept by a hurricane of lead.[23] They took the line of the Orange Road as their compass arrow and set off in the direction of the Crittenden Gate. It was difficult to make out any target clearly with the smoke and the sun in their eyes. Some of the Seventh's men had made it through the corn and were all the way into the meadow in front of the Crittenden Lane, where they were presently mixed in with rebel soldiers.[24] According to one account, the Giddings Regiment stood and fired a volley down into the field, the effect of which killed and wounded not only rebels but soldiers in the Seventh Ohio.[25]

They Twenty-Ninth Ohio marched down the slope and into the edge of the cornfield, blinded by smoke and sweat, stumbling over bodies, knapsacks, and broken rifles left in the wake of the Seventh Ohio's advance. Furious sounds assailed them from their right, across the Orange Road, where Crawford's men fought.

The rebel guns turned their attention on the Twenty-Ninth Ohio, and a moan escaped the regiment as canister struck them head-on. The cornstalks provided at least the illusion of turning a bullet, and with that as their only cover, the Twenty-Ninth moved up. They came to a hollow in the rear of the Seventh Ohio in which that unit had laid their dead and dying.[26] They worked forward and into contact with the left end of the Seventh Ohio.[27] When the soldiers of the Seventh saw they were not alone any longer, they gave a glad cheer for the old Twenty-Ninth.[28] The Giddings Regiment laid down volleys of cover fire, under which the Seventh Ohio was able to collect its parts and fall back toward the ridge. No sooner had the Twenty-Ninth Ohio fought its way up to the Seventh's position than the situation near the Crittenden Gate changed dramatically.[29] What happened to the Giddings Regiment next was described by John Marsh as "perfect pandemonium."[30]

Stonewall Jackson had come up into the woods near the gate, and for the only time in his career, he took his sword from its scabbard, waved it over his head, and demanded his men stand and do their duty. The rebel line tottered but held. A brigade of A. P. Hill's division had finally come up, and General Winder's soldiers began throwing Crawford's Federals back through the wheat and woods. The Twenty-Ninth was now a small island of resistance, without connection to the troops on its right or left. Just then, the rebel line ahead of them renewed its push. Fire began to come at them from three directions at once, the most murderous of it from a body of rebel infantry on a rise in front of them, just beyond the cornfield.

Their objective now became the rise from which they were being tormented. The Giddings Boys steadied themselves, picked out targets, and fired. They fought through the rest of the cornfield, into the edge of the meadow, and drove the rebels off the knoll.[31] They had reached the high-water mark of their advance, and by the account of one Twenty-Ninth Ohio soldier, they had made it further forward than the Seventh Ohio.[32] But no force on earth could push them further, and most men lay down, continued to load and fire, and wondered how they would get out of this place.

Who commanded the Twenty-Ninth Ohio at the battle of Cedar Mountain was an issue that would become the center of a poisonous dispute decades from this day. Wilbur F. Stevens signed his name to the official, after-action report required of every regimental commander, and he also signed his name to the official casualty list. The facts contained in SeCheverell's *Journal History* were checked by a committee of Twenty-Ninth Ohio veterans before it went into print. SeCheverell stated unequivocally that Stevens had led the regiment that afternoon, and the newspaper reports published at the time of the battle did not contradict him. Not long afterward, a soldier visited Stevens in Washington, where he was recovering from exhaustion. Stevens told him he had collapsed near the end of the fighting and had to be carried off the field. One of Stevens's men had been wounded during the battle and was taken to a field hospital in the rear. He saw Stevens lying there and overheard the army surgeons discussing his case. He heard them say that Stevens was suffering from prostration, a term synonymous with overexposure to heat. Stevens's account stood unchallenged until his widow filed for a pension around the turn of the century. Then, James B. Storer and others launched a campaign to block her.

On battle day, Storer was filling some of the duties of adjutant and was also serving as the regiment's color bearer. With his own eyes he had seen Stevens throw himself into a ditch as the regiment approached the battlefield, and he was sure Stevens had stayed in it until the fighting was over. When asked to speculate why Stevens got into the ditch, Storer answered in a single word: cowardice. Stevens had shown the "white feather."³³ Storer claimed it was he who led the regiment back out to safety, although he was only a sergeant. The conflicting recollections dragged up in the Widow Stevens pension case substantiate one thing, certainly: it had all been very confusing.

On Their Own Hook

The Sixty-Sixth Ohio had gone in on orders from Geary no more specific than "advance." After that, nothing more was heard from Geary or his staff. Candy remembered they had "gone in on their own hook," and got out the same way.³⁴ Their dead and wounded stood as testament to the Sixty-Sixth's sticking power, driving the enemy in front of them, closing up their thinning ranks, and going forward again. All the official reports had the Sixty-Sixth advancing in a parallel line with the Seventh Ohio on its right, welded together as if they had linked arms. But keeping contact with them, or anyone, that afternoon was beyond possibility. Once they got into the cornfield, Candy lost sight of the Seventh so completely that it was impossible for him to see what troops were fighting on his right. On its way to the relief of the Sixty-Sixth Ohio, the Fifth Ohio found soldiers of the Twelfth U.S. Regulars cowering in the corn, and calling them cowards did not get them moving. They stepped over the fainthearts and made it through the cornfield and into the open, where they were torn by grapeshot, but they continued to advance, driving the rebels back. The Fifth Ohio's colonel, John H. Patrick, believed their success might have been widened had they been reinforced, but, "for some unexplained reason we were left to the kind mercy of the enemy." Without cover fire from the rear, or leadership, the half of the regiment that were still on their feet had to fight for their lives as they retreated back toward Mitchell's Station Road.³⁵ Their division and their brigade were headless.

With night falling, and the Sixty-Sixth dangerously forward in the salient they had hammered open, Candy decided to save the survivors and retrace their steps. It was not until around nine o'clock that night, and after he had led his men back out to safety, that he learned that Geary had been wounded and that he, Charles Candy, had been in command of the brigade through most of the fighting. He said that if he had been sought, he would have been found easily enough. He was in the front line with his men, which was where a commanding officer worth his salt would be. Why no one had come from the rear to inform him of Geary's departure he never learned.

Both Augur and Geary had left the fields with wounds. From General Augur's timekeeping, Geary received a bullet wound to his elbow near the time that the Twenty-Ninth started out from the ridge. General Augur stated in his official report of the battle that he had seen the Seventh and Sixty-Sixth's line weaken, and it had been he who ordered the second assault wave forward. Just then, he took the wound that rendered him hors de combat. It was seven o'clock.³⁶ Geary stated in his own report that his last act in the battle had been to order the Fifth and Twenty-Ninth Ohio Regiments to the attack, and before the words had entirely left his mouth he was hit.³⁷

Upon receipt of his wound, Augur dispatched his adjutant to find General Prince on the right and turn over command to him.³⁸ However, Prince did not get the message. He had been captured while riding across the field seeking aid for his own men. Somehow, Union general George S. Greene learned that command of the division had fallen to him, but by then it was too late to alter the outcome. In his official report, Geary did not name the officer to whom he turned over command, if to anyone. In Charles Candy's opinion, no one was in command. Regardless of who gave the order or at what time, the Twenty-Ninth went into its worst combat to date as leaderless from behind as it was in the ranks. How long they occupied that impossible position with fire coming at them from the front and right, assailed at close range by both cannon and hundreds of muskets, is impossible to say; something less than an hour, but more than twenty minutes.

For whoever commanded the Twenty-Ninth Ohio Infantry, it was clear from the backward passage of the Federals on their right, if not the distinctive rebel yelling in that direction, that the whole Union right was giving way. With the sun low behind them, the rebel line came forward from the lane in a corona. To stay in this place meant death, or capture, and Stevens ordered the soldiers to fall back.³⁹

Firing as they went, with the rebels close on their heels, they made it back to the reverse slope of the ridge, where they had been supporting the Union guns. Some did not make it out of the corn and were captured. Wallace Hoyt, the inveterate letter writer was captured, and his cousin Thad.

All of it had been a blur in which the normal movement of time ceased to apply. The only order they had been given was to advance, and after that, nothing. They had come into this battle with eight officers at most in the whole of the regiment, and nearly every one of those had been hit, along with most all their sergeants. While the Twenty-Ninth's soldiers lay and continued firing from the ridge, the rebels pressed Crawford back through the woods on their right, but having accomplished that, the battle refused to end. Now, the Tenth Maine was fed into the meat grinder on their right, and after them, the soldiers of Gordon's brigade. The battle had drowned the senses and absorbed the soldiers so completely that when it quieted enough to look up, the Boys were surprised to discover it was now night. Things of such complexity were difficult to summarize, but Parmater tried:

> We lie close behind the battery a little behind a hill for two hours with shells striking and bursting all around us, and at six we were ordered to charge over the hill where there was two our Regts on the left and Williams on the right had engaged the enemy some 20 minutes previous, it was in a perfect shower of balls that we passed over the hill, but we could not stand very long as we received no reinforcements while the enemy had, so we had to fall back, which was done firing and then came cheer after cheer from the Rebels, and thus the shades of evening came upon us.[40]

Storer said he had gathered the command, or at least those Boys who were within the sound of his voice, and got them off the field. Parmater got out by his lonesome. He was swept along in the ebb tide and made a stand with other Union boys forming a defensive line in expectation the battle would continue. He went to hunting for his regiment after things quieted down, past midnight, and although he looked through the entire night, he found only six of them.[41]

When SeCheverell compiled the regiment's history, thirty years later, he gave an account of the battle that had little to do with the reality of it. He had not been there and relied it was said on the memories and diaries of men who had. His account had the entire brigade charging forward in one grand rush. They were driving the rebels back by bayonet point until all of them were stopped by rebel reinforcements. He got the particulars wrong, but the feel of that late afternoon in the cornfield, just right:

> Comrades gave up their lives so gently that it was scarce possible to tell the living from the dead. The fatal missile struck the victim, leaving the lifeless clay in the same attitude which the living body occupied. During the fatal period death assumed a real character while life, seemed but a dream.[42]

Badly Shot

As the light began to dim, things were seen and heard that seemed to be the conjurings of dislodged spirits. When matters on the right appeared quite hopeless, a regiment of Pennsylvania cavalry appeared, its men perfectly shined and uniformed, and charged at full gallop into the woods jammed with rebels. An infantry regiment about to be sacrificed on the right stepped onto the ridgetop with a brass band at their head and, with the sound of bass drums and martial music, went down into the region where the long tears of musket fire and screaming men were the dominant sounds.[43]

The rebel infantry continued to push Geary's brigade from behind the ridge, and back across Cedar Creek, before they too ran out of steam. Geary's brigade fell back behind Gen. James B. Ricketts's division and camped on the banks along Cedar Run. Those that remained of the Twenty-Ninth Ohio made it off the field singly or in small knots. Elias Roshon could locate only two of his comrades before it became too dark and dangerous to continue searching: "If ever there was a lonesome set of boys, us Boys was them."[44] To the soldiers who stumbled from camp to camp hunting their own, it appeared that the Twenty-Ninth Regiment, Volunteer Infantry, as an organization, no longer existed.[45]

From the sounds coming at them in the dark, and the artillery lightning on the near horizon, Banks's men had every reason to believe the battle would be renewed the next morning if not sooner. The low sun had blinded men as they fought, and they cursed it. It had actually killed men this day and driven others mad. But it had gone down at last, and the Federals moved back into the darkness beyond Cedar Run. A light breeze had pushed the smoke away, and a full moon came up in a clear sky.[46] Men collapsed wherever they last stopped marching and were sound asleep before their bodies crumpled into the grass. Before sleeping, Nathan Parmater entered one final comment in his diary: "The day has been one that I never wish to witness again."[47] Like a snapping turtle with its head cut off, the battle continued to fix its jaws reflexively on anything at hand.

Teamsters had foolishly lit fires to boil their coffee near where Alonzo Sterrett had lain down to rest among strangers. Rebel gunners saw the light and dropped shells into the camp, which was enough to stampede them. Federal guns came up quickly and extinguished the rebel artillery fire. Entire meadows were covered with stricken men, and a surgeon's tent was set up in the middle to minister to them. While the generals had been perfecting their battle plans, the army surgeons had been picking out places to set up field hospitals. Initially, a house was selected, but as the battle spread, it was thought too near the fighting, and another, safer site was found for the surgeons' work, in a grove on the lee of a ridge.[48] Some wounded were struck a second and third time as they were being carried from the battlefield and were killed.[49] Around one of the houses in which the surgeons had set up shop, four hundred wounded men were laid in the grass. Rebel shells dropped into these places, injuring men further or killing them outright.[50] The wounded of Augur's division were carried to the field tents in the rear, where their wounds were bound and a few urgent operations performed on the spot. They were then forwarded into Culpeper Court House while the battle rushed toward climax.[51]

Hardly a soldier or officer in the Twenty-Ninth Ohio had not been hit in some fashion.[52] There had been only one officer with Sgt. John Marsh's company when they went in, and he had been struck down in the early going. Marsh took charge. At the zenith of their advance he was struck on the side of the neck by a piece of shell. The force of the impact spun him round three full times before he fell to the ground unconscious. His comrades thought he must certainly be dead, and they pulled his corpse out of the worst of the fire and laid him down. To their surprise, he came to his senses and was able to walk off the field, although in a daze.[53] When Captain Stevens made out his casualty list, five days after the battle, Marsh was still missing. The shot had severed the leather strap of his haversack and cut nearly through the sword strap slung round his neck, but by the good fortune of stout-made U.S. army leather, he had been spared. The other Homerville Boys had come through more or less intact. Phil Hawk had been run over by a cavalry horse but was none the worse for wear. Their worst casualty was Jeb Bair, and he had been flattened not by a bullet but by sunstroke.[54]

In Culpeper Court House, surgeons would labor for two days without letup before the work of removing bullets and amputating fingers, hands, arms, and legs was finished.[55] The town of Culpeper was now a hospital. Wounded men were carried into the three largest churches; and into the Piedmont, Virginia, and Depot Hotels, where tobacco and slave traders had stayed in another time; and into the Masonic Hall, and a cigar factory. Still, enough room could not be found for all of them, and the surplus spilled out onto the open lots surrounding the railroad depot.[56] A surgeon new to his posting with the Seventh Ohio Infantry told of the nature of some wounds: "Those wounded by balls were mostly hit in the breast, abdomen and legs; and what is indeed surprising, is that a ball could traverse through the lungs, or from one shoulder to the hip of the other side, or through the face, or even the head, and the soldier lives and gets well. It is astonishing how badly a man can be shot and yet live."[57]

The army's medical department had improved since the oversights and crossed wires of Cumberland and Kernstown. Trains of twenty cars and more began pulling into Culpeper Court House forty-eight hours after the battle ended, and up to five hundred stretcher cases at a time were loaded aboard, laid on beds of hay, and sent off up the line with attendants to nurse them, and dispense water and bread.

Most of the wounded in Geary's brigade were sent out of Culpeper Court House as soon as it was determined they could survive the trip and were put into the freight cars for the seventy-mile ride to Alexandria, where they were crowded into either the Mansion House or Marshall House general hospitals.[58]

"I May See You Again . . ."

Alonzo Sterrett was driven by an impulse to help in any way he could, so he went out on the battlefield by himself the morning after to collect the wounded, and to bury the dead. The two armies occupied the several days after the battle putting the fallen into the ground, a severe and unpleasant job given the unrelenting heat. The dead of both sides were found intermingled, showing that much of the killing had been done at close range.[59] Every soldier deserved a grave of his own, and a marker, even if it were nothing more than a piece of crate with his name and regiment penciled on it, but here that was not possible. The slaughter had been too great; moreover, the heat had blackened and bloated the faces of the dead so thoroughly that a soldier's mother could not have recognized him. The soldiers of Geary's brigade who had fallen in the field near the Crittenden Lane had been ransacked of everything that might have helped identify them.[60] Shallow trenches were dug, the dead were laid in them side by side and covered with red dirt, and that was the best that could be done.

A week after the battle Nathan Parmater and Alonzo Sterrett visited the battlefield. Parmater noted for his diary the quality of burial to which the dead had been treated: "The dead were all taken care of, some of them but poorly for I saw some of their feet sticking out of the ground."[61] Like a man coming out of his cellar to survey storm damage, Parmater marveled over large trees that had been chopped off mid-trunk by Federal artillery.

Pickets from the Twenty-Ninth were assigned duty on the edge of the army, which had collected itself at Culpeper, and the domain of the recent battle six miles south of town was their lonesome beat. The ground was covered with dead horses, broken caissons, and dismounted cannon. Red mounds showed the places where a soldier lay buried, the larger of these showing where many had been laid en masse. It was claimed in SeCheverell's *Journal History* of the regiment that a pair of dead boys were found on the field, one in blue, and the other gray, arms interlocked in their death struggle, and it may have been true.

The combat had been horrific. Casualty ratios had exceeded those of much larger, future battles, including those infamous for the scale of bloodletting.[62] In round numbers, nearly half of Geary's brigade had been killed, wounded, or captured.[63] In the Seventh Ohio, thirty died on the field, including three officers. The sad accounting afterward showed nearly two-thirds of its men had been casualties. Losses in the Fifth and Sixty-Sixth Ohio infantries had been nearly as heavy. The Giddings Regiment's losses had been least in the brigade, but they had been fewest in number of the several regiments in it.

The Twenty-Ninth Ohio had gone into the battle with about 180 men of all ranks, and when roll was called the morning after the battle, only eighty-three men were present to answer.[64] It would take years for the dust to settle, final records to be gone through, and some attempt made at establishing the regiment's actual loss at Cedar Mountain. Depending on who did the accounting, from fifty to sixty-five men had been killed, wounded, or gone missing.[65] It would be confirmed within a few days by rebel authorities that ten of the missing had been captured. From six to as many as eleven boys had been killed in action or would die soon enough to have their deaths attributed to the battle.

The boys had been shot in every conceivable place: foot, hand, head, face, chest, and groin. Two men limped back to the regiment on broken ankles. Not a single man had been shot in the back, showing they'd kept their faces to the enemy even as they retreated. Nearly every one of the officers had been wounded, none killed.

Lt. William Neil of Conneaut was as full of élan after the battle as he had been before it. He would fight on if the regiment had only a dozen men left in it, stating that he was "anxious to play another game of draw poker with Mr. Secesch, and he declares if he ever does, that he'll 'chip one,' and try for ten better."[66] Behind the bravado lay the sad truth: the Giddings Regiment had been reduced to the size of a company, and another such battle might send them out of existence.

Some of their best soldiers were now gone.[67] Capt. Josiah Wright's friends at the *Summit Beacon,* in Akron, found his name on the casualty lists published in the *New York Herald*.[68] The nature and extent of his injuries were not stated. Wright had been struck in the shoulder by a bullet, and, in his words, it had been "an ugly old slap."[69] The bullet had lodged in a place too tricky to attempt digging it out, and he would carry it with him always as a souvenir. Like George Dice and a half dozen other of the wounded, 2nd Lt. E. J. Hurlburt had been shot in the foot, but after a period of recuperation he would resume his duties, minus the second toe of one foot, which had been amputated by army surgeons.[70] Cpl. Burton Pickett had tried his best to describe for his family the grandeur of the Capitol in Washington, which to his unworldly eyes looked more like a mountain than anything else. He had closed out his last letter home with a few words for his younger sisters: "Margy and Hannah . . . think of your brother here in the enemy's country I may see you again sometime but it is doubtful. this war is going to last a long time. I must stop writing my love and best wished to all."[71] Burton had been hit in the leg at Cedar Mountain and died in one of Culpeper Court House's makeshift hospitals five days later.[72]

Pvt. Alvinson Kinney had written home last to say he had enjoyed Washington the best of any place. His only distress was that the stream of letters from home had dried up and left him wondering how the folks at home were doing, and whether his letters were getting out to them. He had been seventeen years old when he enlisted, and it had taken his widowed father's permission for him to do it. He did not come off the field with the others after the battle, and Kinney was listed as missing in action.[73] A few days later he had still not appeared. He could not be found in the hospitals, and he was not among those whose capture could be confirmed. At some point afterward, his fate was changed to "killed, August 9, 1862, Cedar Mt., Virginia."[74] What became of him was a mystery that was never solved.

14

"In the Hands of Devils"

PRISON STORIES, 1862

Beyond Hope

When Wallace Hoyt and the boys captured at Cedar Mountain were herded into the rebel prison camp set up on an island in the James River in Richmond, they were greeted by old friends. The 120 boys captured at Port Republic were already there. Belle Isle, however, had not been their first stop in the rebel prison system.

While what remained of the Twenty-Ninth Ohio headed north through the mud toward the safety of Shields, the captured took up the march south, in the direction of the rebel prison. Within an hour of Tyler's retreat, relative quiet returned to the battlefield. Those who had not made their way out were driven from their hiding places behind bushes and fallen trees and herded onto the road. They passed by the Lewiston Coaling, with its blasted treetops and dead men lying in tangled piles, some dead horses wedged between trees still leaning into their traces as if waiting for the command to pull the abandoned guns away.[1]

A rebel colonel rode up and said that if it were up to him he'd hang them all, on the spot.[2] Stonewall Jackson rode up to the group, quiet and handsome on his sorrel horse. He spoke sympathetically to some of the boys and instructed the guards, "Give those boys the best of attention. Let them suffer no abuse, for they are our equals."[3] Soldiers who were there and heard and saw Jackson, like Pvt. W. E. Baldwin of the Twenty-Ninth Ohio, sensed greatness in him.

The afternoon of the battle the prisoners were marched up into the mountains through Brown's Gap and past long lines of wagons stamped "U.S." on the canvas sides. They heard cannonading behind them, and the sound gave them hope that they would be rescued. It had been nothing more than Frémont firing a few salvos toward the rebels as they disappeared into the mountains. They slept their first night in captivity on the ground, with the rain coming down and nothing to eat except for the crumbs in their pockets. They crossed down out of the Blue Ridge the next day, and the last of the hope that they would be saved receded behind them.

The second night, the guards crowded them into a barn. The Twenty-Ninth's boys climbed into the hayloft and fell asleep. They had not been asleep long when a rebel called from below, "If you Yanks want anything to eat you had better come down and get it."[4] The guards had lit cooking fires and passed out rations. The prisoners dangled the bacon over the flames and made cakes of flour and water baked on flat stones set close to the fire. Some soldiers thought this the finest meal they ever ate in the army, whether guests of the Confederacy or soldiers of Uncle Sam.

On the third day they were marched into Charlottesville. Tables had been set up, and atop them sat platters of roasted turkeys, chickens, bread, butter, pastries, and cups of wine. They were even more surprised when the local ladies invited them to step forward and load plates.[5] Some boys thought it might be a trick, but they overcame their shyness and were fed. After dinner they were marched through the town to the courthouse, where they were made to stand while the residents gaped at them as if they were circus animals.[6] On the fifth day they got on boxcars that took them to their place of residence for the near term, Lynchburg, Virginia. No man would find the experience of capture and confinement pleasant, but just how harsh this chapter of a soldier's life had been depended on who told the story, and when it was told, whether a few weeks or decades afterward.

In peaceful times, Lynchburg had been a pleasant, prosperous town of seven thousand residents. The long trains passing through every day carried bundles of tobacco mostly, but since the war, the boxcars carried rebel armies.[7] The trains dumped cargoes of wounded and sick rebels on the depot platform and steamed out, leaving the burden of how to care for all these soldiers on the shoulders of the civilians.[8] The arrival of Jackson's sick and wounded coming down out of the valley this summer had threatened to sink the city entirely. Prices of every necessary went sky high, and blankets, flour, or soap could not be bought at any price. Gangs of rebel deserters controlled the streets of this hitherto law-abiding place after dark, making the citizens afraid to go out of their homes. Adding to their difficulties, three thousand and more Federal prisoners of war began arriving.

Some Twenty-Ninth Ohio soldiers had gotten here ahead of the group from Port Republic. The sick swept up by Turner's cavalry in the big panic at Strasburg were already there, penned up in a rail enclosure on a bank above the river adjacent the local fairgrounds. The Giddings Boys taken at Port Republic were escorted through the gates and onto the grounds fitted up to incarcerate these "Northern tourists with military proclivities."[9]

The Boys complained about the small size of the rations dispensed to them, and their quality: stale potatoes, salt beef, crackers, and buggy bread. According to Rollin Jones, the prisoners were without tents, blankets, or even fires by which they might cook or keep warm. But they were well used to such hardship and these things could be tolerated. What Jones could not stomach was the harsh treatment dispensed by the guards.

Soldiers of the Twenty-First Virginia Regiment had been detached to guard them, and in Rollin's opinion, "if devils ever formed themselves into a regiment they could not equal these men in coarse brutality." Jones had seen guards entertaining themselves by thrusting their bayonets at prisoners just to see them jump. One Union prisoner was shot dead, so it was reported, for no more offense than walking too near a guard. Men escaped from here, and those caught were made to drag the ball and chain around the grounds. For Jones, these things were to be remembered always, and revenged.[10]

Brutality was really not in the Twenty-First Virginia's line. They were a crack outfit, well disciplined, and better educated than most. They had come into the war with the accoutrements of gentlemen soldiers: linen gaiters, white shirts, and even neckties, with white gloves and spare white blouses packed in their French-made calfskin knapsacks.[11] The soldiers of the Twenty-First Virginia disliked guard duty as much as Jones disliked being guarded by them. One rebel soldier in the outfit wrote years later, "It was the unanimous desire of the regiment never to have charge of prisoners again."[12]

News of the outside world seemed to filter in to the rebel prisons wherever the soldiers were held, and when the news came to them that the Twenty-First Virginia had suffered terribly at Cedar Mountain, Jones was glad.[13] To his own men, the Twenty-First's commander, Col. Richard Cunningham Jr., was a hero and "a brave and Christian soldier."[14] Rollin Jones thought him the most disagreeable and tyrannical of them all. At Cedar Mountain, Cunningham had been so ill he could barely stand or speak, but he was still out front leading his regiment close by the Crittenden Gate when he was killed by a bullet near the spot where General Winder received his fatal wound.[15]

The Forty-Second North Carolina took over guard duty at Lynchburg, and the prisoners were herded into the fairgrounds proper, where they took up housekeeping in old tents, while other prisoners were placed in stalls in a livestock barn. A line was drawn down the floor dividing the barn into halves, with the Union prisoners on one side, and the rebel guards on the other.[16] The Carolinians' colonel

George Gibbs was scarcely hardhearted, and although unable to do better for the prisoners, he at least registered complaints with authorities above him.[17] Under Gibbs's management, daily rations were improved, and hospital tents were erected in the camp. Twenty-five hundred Union soldiers were confined here for two months at most, and of these less than a hundred had died, which was a fair record of healthfulness. But in Rollin Jones's mind, these men had not died in the normal course of camp living but had been murdered by the inhuman conditions forced on them.

The Union dead from the hospital were placed in plank coffins, respectful treatment it would seem, and carried to the graveyard. One suspicious prisoner made a chalk mark on one outgoing coffin and claimed he had seen the very same coffin return from the graveyard and then go out again three times. If they had firewood, the incessant rain prevented fire building. The soldiers who had been placed in tents complained they were so old and rotten that they had to squat together inside in stormy weather, each man holding the rent ends of canvas nearest him to prevent the whole affair from blowing away. Other prisoners had neither tent nor stall, only the canopy of the sky over their heads.[18] During most of their long campaigns, even in the dead of winter, Jackson's men had not been allowed the luxury of tents of any condition.

John Rupp of Company I was locked up in Lynchburg along with Rollin Jones and the others, and fifty years later, in admittedly more conciliatory times, he wrote of his experience. He did not remember their imprisonment there as a nightmare, nor did he remember the rebels guards as monsters. There was one well on the grounds but no pump with which to bring the water to the surface, but in Rupp's memory that deficit had been a source of merriment and not privation. The prisoners sold their watches and jackknives to the guards and with the money bought tin cups. "We affixed strings to our cups, and it was comical to see the boys at the old well dangling their numerous cups. There was plenty of wrangling too, when cup-strings would get twisted or water be spilt."[19] Jones claimed the prisoners were prohibited from building fires and were given nothing to warm themselves through the cold rainy nights. In the Lynchburg prison camp of Rupp's memory, the captives were allowed out of the stockade under escort to collect firewood, and fire building was routine. Jones claimed the prisoners were made to sit in their own filth. But Rupp recalled that the prisoners were allowed to go down to the local creek to bathe and do laundry.

Orders came that the prisoners were going away at last, directly back into the Union lines, it was supposed, and excitement overtook them. Instead, a train of boxcars with tobacco litter took them east and deposited them even deeper into the Confederacy. They were marched across a bridge in Richmond and onto an eighty-acre island in the river called Belle Isle—beautiful island. The island was more like a wildlife refuge in the middle of the town, and had once been the locale of an ironworks; if the war would end, promoters had dreams of building a first-class racetrack.[20] Three Twenty-Ninth Ohio boys were not along to make this trip. They had died at Lynchburg and had been taken out to the prisoner graveyard, which was close enough to the prison stockade that the inmates could witness its grim expansion. Among the dead was Pvt. Newton P. Humiston, the young man who had sent some of his first pay home to his mother in Akron with the advice that she be grateful for all gifts, big and little.[21]

Beautiful Island

If prison was their fate, fortune had at least been kind to Shields's soldiers in the timing of their confinement here. Belle Isle would have two separate incarnations during this war. Conditions here were worse than at Lynchburg, but Belle Isle was presently nothing like the hellhole it would become. A hundred-foot-high bluff took up most of the island, and the prison had been set up on the sandy flat below it. In its physical situation the prison camp was regarded as a pleasant enough place—it was airy, there was plentiful fresh water, and even bathing in the calmer channel of the river when the rebels permitted it. The five thousand prisoners held there were allowed to exercise as much as they liked as long as they kept to the flat below the bluff. The locals disliked having a prison camp in their midst as much as the prisoners disliked being their uninvited guests. Odors emanating from the camp's privies and the smells generated by too many males living in close contact drifted out over the city and offended sensitive noses. Like in Lynchburg, the prisons in Richmond strained the city's pinched resources.[22] Prices of every staple were so high in the city that Rollin Jones wondered how the city's poorer class lived.

In August 1862 the rebel officer in charge of Richmond's prisons was sent to Lynchburg to deal with the Union prisoners still there. Taking over for him was a one-armed Swiss émigré, physician Henry Wirtz.[23] Some of the Boys would meet him again down in Georgia at a place called Andersonville. The exchange system worked so smoothly that two weeks after the last of the Twenty-Ninth's prisoners left, Belle Isle was closed, and the use of it returned to quieter occupations.[24] In 1863, as the battles enlarged in scale and frequency, so too did the numbers of men who fell into rebel hands, and Belle Isle would be reopened to accommodate them. Conditions would deteriorate severely: men forced to the edge of starvation sickened and died, or lived in holes burrowed in the ground. Roving gangs of prisoners took down their own weak like packs of wolves, the camp commandant powerless to stop them.

The Twenty-Ninth Ohio's captured officers included their lieutenant colonel, Thomas Clark, taken at Port Republic. He and the other captured officers had been separated out from the enlisted men at Charlottesville and sent off to imprisonment at Salisbury, North Carolina, where their treatment had been far superior to that of the enlisted men. Mail came and went at Salisbury at least as efficiently as it had when mailed direct from a Union army camp. Lt. Carey H. Russell wrote to his sister in Mogadore from the "Buckeye Men's Mess" at Salisbury,

> Dear Sister Mollie:—I avail myself of this, my first opportunity, of writing you and letting you know my whereabouts and "how-a-bouts." Of course you have heard of our fight at Port Republic and its results. I escaped without any serious injury. I was struck in the left leg by a spent grape shot, which bruised and made it sore for about a week, but it is all right now. We have been very well used ever since our capture, those having us in charge doing all in their power to make us as comfortable as possible. We are very nicely fixed here, 11 of us having a fine big room; the location is very healthy, and if it were not for being prisoners, we would be very well contented; but we are all hoping for an exchange soon.[25]

The exchange process had already brought some of these officers back to Richmond en route home. On John Rupp's first night in Belle Isle, some of the regiment's captured officers had been allowed onto the island to see how their men were holding up, and a brief, sad reunion was held. Next morning the officers were marched off, and the privates were left behind to wonder if they would ever see them again.[26]

Sustenance here was slim pickings: a half loaf of bread per day, a cup of black-eyed bean soup, a small piece of bacon or beef, and on some days, nothing at all.[27] There were sutlers even here, and a prisoner could purchase items from him to supplement the prison fare, but most soldiers did not have money.

If a man grew sick here, he was on his own. Unlike Lynchburg, medical attention was lacking entirely. Jones estimated that by the time he left, five to ten prisoners a day were dying of disease on Belle Isle. Medicines could be purchased from the guards, but medicines were scarce and expensive. Two Twenty-Ninth Regiment soldiers captured around the hospitals at Strasburg had died of disease here before Jones and Rupp arrived, and one more died while he was there.[28]

Here at Belle Isle, the suffering and dying went on in the open. Twenty or more soldiers could be seen at any one time lying on the ground, dead or headed that way, talking deliriously of home and food.[29] Some of the captured were housed in captured Sibley tents, the same kind of tents they had enjoyed until they were taken away by official edict a few months earlier. The rest took their chances out in the elements, and although cold and wet, they were lucky it was summer. Few fires were allowed, and access to them was limited to the prisoners assigned to cooking duty.[30] The soldiers milled around the lower island all night to keep the cold at bay, and during the day they wriggled into the sun-warmed sand.[31]

There was a bridge across to the shore, but it was heavily guarded, and the narrow channel separating it from Richmond was a regular cataract in times of heavy rain. Attempting to swim to freedom would be foolhardy. Even if a man made it across, he was in the heart of the rebel capital, chock-full of rebel troops. One of the south's few foundries capable of producing quality armaments in any real quantity, the Tredegar Iron Works lay directly across the river, the work going on there easily observed from the island. For entertainment, Rollin Jones watched the employees wheel out new artillery pieces for test-firing. The workers lobbed shells up the river, throwing up tall geysers of water and occasionally bursting a gun, at which the prisoners cheered mightily. The Virginia statehouse and the grand statue of George Washington could be seen, but for most of those locked up here in the James River that was as much of Richmond as they would see until they marched through the city three years later, and by that time most of it would be burned and flattened.

The captives had the privilege of writing and receiving letters, and newspapers found their way into camp. Specific news of what their own regiment had done in their absence could be gotten firsthand, from the Boys who arrived from Cedar Mountain. This group, which included Wallace Hoyt, was marched onto the island in mid-August.[32]

Captives in Their Own Country

On September 11, 1862, civilians in plug hats and starched collars appeared on the island. Jones and five hundred lucky men were called out and told their time had come to leave the island. They were to be "exchanged," but what that entailed exactly no one knew.[33] Jones was in high spirits and was certain he could march fifty miles that day if need be. The column had gone but a dozen miles when the effects of months without exercise and spotty diet caught him. The guards were on horseback, and Jones and the others struggled to keep up. They crossed over Richmond's rings of entrenchments, which were said to run from this river all the way to the York River, over twenty miles distant.

The rebel officer in command apparently took pity on their sorry condition. He went into a warehouse along the way and threw loaves of bread to them from a window.[34] As night came on Old Glory was seen fluttering in the twilight. The U.S. flag-of-truce steamer *Cossack* was tied up to the wharf at Aiken's Landing. Jones and his comrades had reached the point agreed upon for transfer of prisoners from one side to the other.

The *Cossack* had just disembarked five hundred Gray Backs who were well clothed and appeared to have been well fed while in Yankee hands, something the Twenty-Ninth's boys noted and resented.[35] An officer appeared in Federal blue to take charge of them, and crates of hard crackers were pried open and passed around. Every Union soldier complained about hardtack, but on this occasion Rollin Jones commented that he had never tasted anything better. Although hardtack was impervious to moisture, in theory, it was not impervious to bugs. Many stories, lighthearted most of them, passed around the camps and circulated through the Ohio newspapers telling of the relentless assault of insects on the soldiers' rations. Representative of these was a piece appearing in the Conneaut newspaper that suggested that the insects were intentionally put in the crackers to save the army the cost of hiring mules to haul them. When the crackers were needed, the quartermaster simply whistled, and they came by themselves. There was also the story that four crackers were seen one evening performing battalion drill with as much precision as any soldier.[36] Jones and the others boarded the side-wheeler for the trip north, and at last Jones felt himself free of the rebels.

His saltwater voyage had elements of a pleasure excursion. He was looking at history passing by the ship's rail and he shared his good fortune with his brother and sister in a long letter. He saw the masts of the frigate *Cumberland* sticking up out of the water, sunk recently by the *Merrimac;* and then he saw the *Monitor,* looking scrappy and ready for another fight. Some soldiers got seasick, but the giant swells did not bother Jones in the least. The *Cossack* passed through the blockading Union fleet, which was idling under steam and ready for action. Porpoises rode ahead on the bow wake, the sun shone on the surface of the ocean as if in a painting, and the sea breeze was a tonic to men who had been in prison for months.

The *Cossack* got all the way up to Washington, but the freed soldiers were told they could not get off. They were stunned, and then angry. An officer tried to explain to them that even though they were back in Union hands, their captivity would continue until they could be exchanged for a like number of rebels.[37] They were headed for Fort Delaware, a Federal fortress at the top of the Chesapeake.

Samuel Hart, who was a private then, and destined to remain a private, told a story in later years that, while they were stopped at Washington, President Lincoln rode up to congratulate them on their release from prison and expressed his hope that the war would soon be over. The Boys cheered so loudly that Lincoln's horse reared and spun, and although not a graceful rider, Lincoln kept his seat. "Shout away Boys, I would rather be thrown from a horse than to have you stop shouting for it shows there is plenty of life and fight in you yet."[38] After taking on coal and rations, the steamer set off back down the Chesapeake. They glided past Mount Vernon. It was mostly hidden by giant trees, but Jones could see enough of it to identify it by the illustrations he'd seen in books as a child. Abruptly the voyage stopped. The steamship *Cossack* had run aground on an oyster bed, and the soldiers broiled in the sun. Ships stopped and tried to pull them off, but they sat for four days until a steam tug strong enough to do the job came along.

After a trip of eighty miles, they were at last on the ocean, and the ship set course for the north. Ten days after starting from Aiken's Landing, the *Cossack* turned into the broad mouth of the Delaware River and tied up at the receiving pier of an island on which stood the nation's mightiest fortress, Fort Delaware. Rollin Jones and the first group of Twenty-Ninth Ohio soldiers released from Belle Isle stepped down the gangway and onto Northern soil. Fort Delaware had been built to block foreign vessels from sailing up the river to Philadelphia. Pentagon-shaped, it had been designed on a scale so colossal that it became a destination for tourists who picnicked on the grounds and strolled beneath its massive stone walls. Its first residents, aside from the soldiers posted there, were rebels captured by Shields at Kernstown.

After landing, an officer came up and mistook Jones and his mates for rebels on account of their ragged and filthy condition. They were being marched toward the rebel prison barracks when the misapprehension was checked. They were stripped of everything they wore, issued new coats, pants, shirts, and shoes, and after that were allowed to move freely around the island. They had plenty to eat and no duty to perform. They would have preferred to have been sent back home to serve out their parole, just as some of their friends taken by Ashby's cavalry had been allowed to do.[39] Conditions were better here than at Lynchburg, or at Belle Isle, but they still felt themselves imprisoned.

The Radicalization of Rollin Jones

As to what role the black man should play in the war, the newspapers back in the Reserve, the *Sentinel* in particular, were always a step ahead of what Lincoln judged the country might tolerate. The editors argued that the black men in the North could be better employed than doing the pick-and-shovel work for the army. Instead, they should be suited up, armed, and allowed to fight on the battlefield. The antislavery set in Ashtabula County had urged the president to emancipate the slaves in the Confederacy. "We believe that the President can break the back of the rebellion almost instantly in this way, and that it can never be done any other way."[40] Lincoln had the same thing in mind, but he chose to wait until he had a decisive Union victory.

Had such a proclamation been issued before Rollin Jones's capture at Port Republic, he would have opposed it. The lore of the regiment reported that every man in the regiment had been questioned about the strength of his antislavery beliefs, and if he was not a diehard on the issue, he was rejected. Like Lewis P. Buckley, Jones had been a lifelong Democrat, and their service in the Twenty-Ninth Ohio had not changed their political allegiance—at least not at first. In his march out of the valley to Lynchburg prison, Jones had seen with his own eyes the South as it had lived for generations, and it changed his opinion about the plight of the black man: "My respect for slavery all vanished on the route from the battlefield of Port Republic to our prison in Lynchburg, while on either side could be seen the slave driving the baggage wagon, and doing the drudgery of his rebel masters; the black man and woman working in the field, while a traitorous master was fighting against the welfare of his country."[41]

As a prisoner of war, he had lost his freedom, and he felt sympathy toward a whole race of men who had never known any. He claimed to have put a very large question to the common rebel soldiers who were his captors in Lynchburg: Why do you fight? They told him they fought to preserve slavery.

History would show that very few rebel soldiers held that belief, but Jones took it at full strength. His heart had been hardened against the rebels by the coarse brutality they had shown him and the other captives, and when Jones considered it, all the killing and dying on the battlefields had been but a larger expression of the Southerner's cruel nature; a nature that made ownership of other humans acceptable. The rebels had started this and they must henceforth feel the iron hand, including the forfeiture of their slaves. Jones saw a group of rebel prisoners being off-loaded at Fort Delaware one day, and his comments on their appearance showed that he had turned a corner: "I could but feel grateful that I owed allegiance to such a Government as the United States, when a crowd of ragged, dirty and half-starved rebels landed at the wharf. A better idea of the infernal regions cannot be formed, than to look upon a collection of rebels clad in their garb covered with dirt." Citizens of Baltimore who visited Fort Delaware took pity on the plight of the nearly naked rebels and sent clothing out to them. Jones learned of this act of charity and saw the donors as no better than secesh sympathizers.

Despite the founders' claim that the regiment's membership was pure antislavery, in the end, the opinion of its soldiers was bound by extremes, as was likely the case in any Union regiment. On the one end there were soldiers like Sgt. John Marsh, who declared proudly that he had always been a "full-blooded Abolitionist."[42] At the other extreme stood men like the regiment's quartermaster, Oscar Gibbs, who would express his opinion of Lincoln's rumored emancipation of the slaves by saying, "We are not positive as to wheather the President has come out with his promised Proclamation since the 1st of the year declaring the Slaves free in the Rebel war States or not, and can as little as we know being perfectly satisfied that the Government is on the virge of ruinin all for the Nigger."[43]

John Brown Jr. was pursuing the true purpose of the war, as Giddings defined it, down in Missouri. By Brown's count, he had already freed seventeen hundred slaves.[44] Not long after that, he was forced to quit the war because of the unfortunate onset of rheumatism.[45] He would soon be buying a plot of ground on a picturesque island in Put-in-Bay, on Lake Erie, and making plans to move his family onto it.[46]

Two officers with roots in the Reserve carried on the tradition of the mutinous boys of the old Nineteenth Ohio at Buckhannon who had threatened bloodshed against their officers if a slave they had liberated was returned to his owner. Both men were serving in the Seventh Kansas Cavalry when the provost guard came into camp and arrested them for refusing to return fugitive slaves. The investigation did not go far before the charges were dropped and they were restored to command.[47]

No one in the Twenty-Ninth had freed a slave, except for Lt. E. B. Howard, nor had anyone uttered a word on the topic. The people back home could at least take pride in the fact that they had not *refused* safety to any contraband that came into their camp either, if that had happened, which had not been the case with other Ohio regiments, including one that was camped next door to them near Martinsburg the past spring.

The Twenty-Ninth Ohio's brigade mates in the Sixty-Sixth Ohio Infantry came from counties nearer Columbus than Akron. A contraband belonging to a Mr. Cunningham ran away and attached himself to the Sixty-Sixth Ohio as a "voluntary aid."[48] When the owner presented himself in the Sixty-Sixth's camp and asked for the return of his property, their colonel was reported to have said, "If the nigger is yours, take him, but I want you to know that this regiment ain't catching runaway niggers, especially when they are making tracks further South."[49] He had the black man produced and given back to his owner. A newspaper correspondent who had visited Tyler's camp around the time of Kernstown found the soldiers' attitude toward the contraband ungenerous, to say the least: "One thing we noticed among our soldiers—the utter contempt they manifest for the nigger. I don't believe anything could induce our boys to take one of them home with him."[50]

Men like Jack Wright, Theron Winship, Myron Wright, and their Chaplain Hurlburt had been faithful correspondents to the Reserve newspapers. However, not once in their dozens of letters did any one of them ever suggest that they were fighting this war to free the slaves. It was a rare letter that did not include a renewed promise to smite the traitors and crush the unlawful and evil rebellion, but nothing in any of them ever set the eradication of slavery as the regiment's purpose. John Marsh was a careful observer of men at war, and he concluded a soldier fought for many reasons, each entirely his own.

Nearly all have some motive besides patriotism; some men are seeking the bauble reputation even at the cannons mouth, some fight for glory, more for money, some are reckless, and fight because they are seeking death. You may think it strange Ida, but it is none the less true.[51]

The Amateur Sutler

Wallace Hoyt and his cousin Thad had been among the Rock Creek Boys captured at Cedar Mountain and were currently cooling their heels at Fort Delaware. His family had written to him asking a great many questions regarding the battle. He declined to give the details, saying only that except for a bullet hole in his blouse, he'd come through without a scratch.[52] How long they would be staying at Fort Delaware no one knew. He closed a letter to his little sister, Hattie, with his new official status, "Released Prisoner of War," but that did not mean he would be released from the island any time soon.[53] The fall progressed into November, and having lived long enough on army rations, Hoyt wrote home requesting his mother's cooperation in filling his grocery list. By the quantities he requested, it seems Wallace was thinking of going informally into the sutler's business.

> What I want is 8 pounds of butter, 30 pounds of cheese and a little honey if you can spare it. My sweet tooth aches awfully for some honey and a pair of boots I believe you now have already for me. And such other fixings as you are a mind to send to me. I wish on the reception of this you send me $10.00 by mail the truth is we get nothing but bread and beans. The beans are put in a kettle that holds 200 gallons without leaking over when boiled up without force of the [illegible] so you can see that beans have the soup rather strong for the stomach. So you can see I have concluded to board myself and eat things which will not make me sick so when I am called into the field again I can stand another campaign.[54]

Wallace Hoyt was not a spiteful boy by nature, but the sequestered life at Fort Delaware had worn thin, and nerves began to fray. Letters from home were always important, but here in this place with little to keep him busy, letters became vital. A month went by without any word from home.

> I have not received any news from you since the 19th of October which makes it just 4 weeks to the day in which time this makes the third letter I have written to you in succession with no show for an answer whatever! I might as well now inform you that it is no amusement for me to write! And that nothing except the hope of receiving an answer would entice me to at all and hereafter for every letter you receive from me you will at least have to write me one if not two in return. . . . We are exchanged, but our prospect of staying here is just as good as it ever was and I wish you would not delay one moment the sending of the money and things I sent for in my letter previous to this. I presume Thad's folks has got his things ready now and all you will have to do is just get together and put them in one box. . . . I have no news to write in fact I ought not to write any! That is if I should serve you right. Give to all inquiring friends.[55]

In mid-December, the longed-for box of delicacies arrived. The boots he had requested were inside, but Hoyt had grown some since he'd placed the order, and they would not fit. He recouped part of his investment by selling them on a promissory note to a friend. He sent off a thank-you to his parents:

> I received my box yesterday with much pleasure although the box was knocked open when we received it and all the things were pretty well messed up. The berry jam was all over everything and the can that the jam was in was gone. Still, we are highly pleased with our things.[56]

The Rock Creek Boys and the others had resigned themselves to spending the entire winter locked up on the island. The reason they had spent two months here already was a mystery to the Boys, and in their mind a waste. Two days before the first anniversary of their leaving Jefferson, the Boys were released from bondage.

Woodchoppers

A sharp wind blew across the river, kicking up spray onto the dike that surrounded the island. The wind curved around the high corners of the fortress, creating what Hoyt thought a doleful sound. The sky was clear, but it was bitterly cold. He and six hundred others were ordered to pack their duds and report at the landing. They got onto a boat along with a guard of thirty soldiers, a captain, and a surgeon who was full of fun and whiskey too. The ship passed across the Delaware and into a canal leading to the Chesapeake.

The guards warned they would shoot any man who stepped off; consequently twenty did get off at the very first lock and disappeared. After that, the rest of the Boys got off whenever they wished to stretch their legs, catching up with their ship, and getting back aboard. Whiskey was plentiful, and on this rare occasion, free. The boat got stuck in the ice.[57] The crew fought to free it and they fought with each other, too, and such a salty brand of swearing Hoyt had never heard.[58]

The hoped-for next stop would be the Twenty-Ninth's camp, wherever it might be, and then a happy reunion. After a short march from the wharf in Annapolis, they found themselves at Camp Parole along with several thousand other Union soldiers.[59] They had gotten off Fort Delaware's island, but they were still stuck tight in the exchange-and-parole system.

Hoyt fell behind on his own letter writing for the next several weeks. He would be busily occupied, although not militarily. He caught up with his parents at the end of January 1863, after he had finally rejoined the regiment. He gave his return address in his high-spirited way as "Head Quarters of the Rock Creek Squad." He began, "I will assume the historian and give you a history of my travels commencing at the time we left Fort Delaware." He gave good descriptions of the ancient town of Annapolis and of the activities that he and the others partook freely while at Camp Parole. On a typical day he walked about the town, attended Catholic mass for its entertainment value, ate dinners as good as anyone could hope for at the local hotels, and generally enjoyed himself.

The Rock Creek Squad's purses were empty, and one of them came upon a fine scheme for making money. A civilian was looking for a crew to chop firewood, and if these boys knew anything at all, it was how to split wood. Hoyt and his friend agreed to serve as cooks. The money all of them earned was to be shared equally, as was democratic. Wallace and the others took it upon themselves to vacate their lodgings at Camp Parole without permission from any officer and moved into a shack they had built in the woods to be nearer their work.

Some of the captured had been away from the regiment now for nearly half a year, and in their absence there had been significant changes of all kinds, not least of which was an effort to stop the leakage of soldiers from the regiment. Locating the many dozens of men whose whereabouts were unknown would require some detective work. Adj. Theron S. Winship was assigned the duty of locating Hoyt and his friends and bringing them back to the regiment. Hoyt and his comrades were at their chopping one day, when a horseman in a Union officer's uniform rode up. Adjutant Winship had ridden around the countryside a good deal, but he had succeeded. The Boys had worked just long enough to blister their hands, which had earned them only enough to pay for their axes, and little more. When they settled up with their employer and divided the profits, each boy was thirty-one cents richer.[60] It would be a while yet, but most of those who had been captured in the valley and at Cedar Mountain would be back with the regiment, where they would once again "cook grub in the enemy's country."[61]

15
Narrow Escapes
THE SECOND BULL RUN CAMPAIGN, AUGUST 1862

His Excellency the Ambassador

A few days after the battle of Cedar Mountain it was discovered that Jackson had slipped away, and that was happily interpreted by the Federals to mean Jackson had been beaten into retreat. While the soldiers who had fought at Port Republic were still reporting the details of that fight to the Ohio newspapers, reports came of this larger and bloodier battle. In the first newspaper accounts, Jackson had wielded an army of fifty thousand, several times larger than his opponent's, but the Federals had fought so nobly that the outcome had been a toss-up, with each side suffering two thousand casualties.[1] The battle was decidedly the bloodiest of the war, so went the reports, proven by the grim fact that it had taken two full days to clear the dead from the field. Since Gen. Nathaniel Banks occupied the battlefield after Jackson withdrew, Banks was regarded as the winner.[2] The newspapers confidently predicted that Stonewall would not stop running until he reached the fortifications of Richmond.[3]

A week passed, and the long lists of Union killed and wounded conveyed the truth of what had happened at Cedar Mountain better than the misinformed reporting. Banks had been bested, and after months of denigrating Stonewall Jackson, the newspaper editors in northeastern Ohio were forced to concede, "Jackson outwitted our generals . . . it must be admitted that he has shown thus far much skill as a general."[4] That Tyler's old brigade had been in the hottest parts of the late battle was reported in every newspaper far and near, and for the folks at home on the Reserve with such a heavy investment in it of their sons and husbands, their fate was feared. The friends of the Giddings Regiment were confident the battle would go down as another glorious chapter in the history of the regiment.[5] The people could still feel pride even in defeat: "The Western Reserve sacrificed more of her sons on the altar of her country than did any other section of the Union."[6] The Seventh and Twenty-Ninth Ohio Regiments, in particular, had stood as a wall to the storm and held Jackson in check.[7]

It was known to everyone that their ranks had been paper thin going into the battle, and the contest between Banks and Jackson could only have depleted them further.[8] When the final accounting of their losses was made known, the Conneaut newspaper took to calling them a "remnant band."[9] Lt. James Treen wrote to Capt. Josiah Wright to express his anxiety for their fate: "I don't know, Captain, what they will do with the poor 29th."[10]

While his namesake regiment hovered on the edge of its existence, Joshua Reed Giddings wrote to his son from the summer retreat of a wealthy friend outside Montreal, "Molly and I are sitting in a spacious parlor attached to my bedroom . . . where we enjoy every luxury of the City, and all the quietude of the country, with such hearty welcome as to render it very agreeable."[11] Back in June 1861, he had seen the war as the wonder of the coming age. But it was becoming apparent that he had been referring to more than the sweeping away of slavery. The war had also brought economic opportunities, and from the start Giddings had worked to position his son Joseph Addison Giddings so the family could gain the most from them.[12]

In the war's opening days, Giddings had written to his old friend Nathaniel P. Banks requesting he appoint his son Joseph Addison to some important post in either his quartermaster department or the more lucrative commissary department. The younger Giddings succeeded in getting neither. Addison seemed better suited to making money than gaining a reputation on the battlefield. He remained in Ashtabula County, where, with his father's coaching, he tried for a big strike in the business of providing beef on the hoof to the army, but too many men had gotten into that line ahead of the Giddings men. A few months later, with the Twenty-Ninth Regiment in its camp at Jefferson, Giddings brainstormed with Addison how the rising interest rates generated by the war might be used to their advantage.[13]

The war advanced through its first year and Giddings had yet to hit on the right opportunity for Addison, but in the Federal defeat at Cedar Mountain, and the failure there of a personal friend, there might be a silver lining. Nathaniel P. Banks had been pummeled by Jackson in the Shenandoah Valley, and at Cedar Mountain, and his career in this theater of war was coming to an end. By autumn he would be sent into the Deep South to take command of the Department of the Gulf. Giddings believed that Banks owed him for his elevation to high position as much as any man, and he began laying plans to call in the debt.[14] The cotton being confiscated in the Gulf region was becoming nearly as valuable as gold, and with the Mississippi River still not open to the north, mountains of it were piling up in Banks's neighborhood. In a short time, Addison would be going south, with his father's instructions that he boldly approach Banks and tell him frankly what it was he desired, which was authority to deal in confiscated cotton.[15] Some men would blithely say that men like Addison were merely savvy Yankee entrepreneurs. Others would identify them as a new class of men entirely, with a label that was coming into use in the American lexicon: war profiteers.

In the hundreds of letters he had written in all the months the soldiers of the regiment he had founded had been in active service, Giddings mentioned them not at all. The news of their discomfiture at Cedar Mountain, with the report that there were now less than a hundred of them, reached him in Canada, and his reaction was, "Our 29th is pretty much annihilated. It should be disbanded or filled up."[16] That is the last word Giddings ever wrote about them. What Giddings thought of them, or whether he thought of them at all, did not matter to the soldiers. If the soldiers who remained had anything to say about it, they would never be disbanded.

Loved and Lamented

While the Union army continued to falter and stumble, the fortunes of one small piece within it began to improve. Two weeks after the battle of Cedar Mountain, Capt. Josiah Wright wrote to Colonel Buckley in Akron, "I have the honor and exquisite pleasure of announcing to you that the 29th has got her much 'loved and lamented' flag again."[17] After a long, peculiar odyssey, worse for wear and perfectly riddled with bullets from Port Republic, their flag was back where it belonged. When last seen at Port Republic it was being paraded by a rebel cavalryman. It was next seen on the streets of Lynchburg, Virginia. According to Wright, "The Secesh at Lynchburg had a jolly time over that flag—paraded it through the streets with pomp and splendor, music, cheering and speeches, drinking, etc."[18] The flag had been stolen back from the rebels who had taken it. Who recaptured it, and how it was returned to them just after the battle of Cedar Mountain, was a story of variable facts.

John Rupp had been captured at Port Republic. His recollection was that on the second night of their march toward prison, the men of the Twenty-Ninth had been herded into a barn. While the dismounted cavalrymen guarding them dozed, Cpl. Nelson Bailey snuck the flag from their captors, hid it in his coat, and burned the staff. The guards cussed when they awoke and found their prize was gone, but the major in charge took no further action.[19]

The story that came to Myron Wright was that not one, but several "brave boys" had taken the flag from its staff on the way to Lynchburg and one of them had concealed it on his person throughout weeks of confinement.[20] It may not even have been a Giddings Regiment soldier who had risked his life to steal back their flag.

The *Sentinel* in Jefferson ran a story clipped from the pages of the *Wheeling Intelligencer* that contradicted Rupp and Wright. It was based on a letter by Sgt. J. M. Goudy of the First Virginia Infantry. He reported that a soldier in his outfit had escaped from Lynchburg prison, and sewn within the lining of his coat was the three-by-nine-foot flag of the Twenty-Ninth Ohio.[21] He had stolen it from the prison guard's room. Even when carefully folded, the flag was bulky enough to fill a steamer trunk. How anyone could conceal something so gigantic in the lining of an infantryman's coat was not questioned. Now it was back with them, and the Boys were looking forward to stitching the names of the regiment's battles on it: Winchester, Port Republic, and Slaughter Mountain, or Cedar Mountain, as the battle would become known.

In the 1920s a very old man appeared in the Citizens' Library in Jefferson.[22] He had a donation of sorts he wished to make, preceded by a story. A library was in the business of preserving the history held in its books, and to him this possession told as much about history as any book. He had once been a private in the Twenty-Ninth Ohio Infantry and, by his longevity, was now custodian of a relic sacred to them all. He had his regiment's flag. He realized that he would not live much longer, and the question of who would care for it after he was gone worried him. Chauncey Coon told the librarian one more thing before he went home and died: of the several flags that the Twenty-Ninth Ohio had carried and worn out through the war, this one had been ripped from the wall of a rebel prison and returned to the regiment. A few days later, a large wood case was delivered to the library and in it was the flag.[23] That flag has survived to this day and is hanging in a new display case on the library wall in Jefferson, and it happens to be the Stars and Stripes. With its return to the regiment, the painful disgrace of having lost it was in part repaired.

An Advance in Reverse

At home, faith in Gen. John Pope remained high: "We expect and hope that the next important news we have from Pope will electrify the hearts of the people with the glad tidings of the overwhelming defeat of Jackson."[24] Despite the upset at Cedar Mountain, Pope had met the expectations placed on him. The rebels had shown their backs to *him* just as he had predicted, and not a single Confederate could be found all the way down to Gordonsville.[25]

The Giddings Regiment spent three days near the battlefield, made disagreeable by the sights and smells and the ferocious heat. They worked at burying the dead and standing picket duty. The regiment's pickets went out one morning to take up their posts, and the brush booths in which their rebel counterparts had sheltered from the sun were empty. Three days went by after the battle before Banks got his army on the road out of Culpeper Court House in Jackson's direction. Nathan Parmater recorded the result: "Our force advanced this morning but loe and behold the enemy had skedaddled."[26] Banks ordered everybody back to Culpeper.

The Giddings Boys moved into Culpeper Court House, where they set up tents and got down to the normal duties of camp life. A wishful rumor floated that they might be staying here a good long while, but the soldiers knew in their hearts that nothing but more hard service waited.[27] The soldiers visited wounded friends in the town and wrote letters home to let friends and families know how they had fared in the last battle. Chum Sterrett began his letter:

> Aug. 13, 1862
>
> Dear Innis,
>
> I hasten to write to you this my first opportunity since the Battle that you may know that I am still unharmed and well as usual; though at times when the terrible and bloody battle raged I did not much think I would escape with my life.[28]

A general review was ordered on August 15 and the soldiers had been in the field long enough to know that an inspection of this scale was the precursor of a difficult march at the end of which might lie another battle. With so few of them left to fight it, they worried over the result. Other regiments that had been worn down to their present size had been folded into the ranks of another outfit by the stroke of some higher authority's pen. One more fight like Cedar Mountain and there would not be enough of them left to send into another regiment. The Ohio soldiers in Geary's brigade knew that friends back home were trying to get them all out of the field so they could recruit and rebuild. Their old friend General Tyler, stationed now in Washington, was doing his best to make that happen, but the order releasing them had not come down, and they would not be spared what lay ahead.[29]

Parmater had been out on a foraging expedition and returned to Culpeper Court House to discover the regiment packing its things. They had been ordered to prepare for a march. Pope had promised they would advance, always, and never show their backs to the enemy. But for reasons beyond the understanding of a common soldier like Parmater, they were not headed south, the direction Jackson had gone, but north.[30]

The normal frustration of getting an army uncoiled from its camps and onto the road occupied the Giddings Boys for most of a day, first ordered into marching line, then out, then back again. The whole army got in motion, everything and everyone headed back toward the Rappahannock, which a week earlier had been the rear. Soldiers idled about waiting for the logjams to clear and groused. They crossed the river at Rappahannock Station and slept on their rifles.[31]

Jackson had not retreated. The news filtered in that he had sidestepped them and was moving toward the Rappahannock River, putting Washington in danger again, touching off a wave of panic that exceeded that produced by his rampage through the valley earlier in the summer.

Lee had concluded that McClellan was not merely consolidating his forces after the Seven Days' battles, but was actually withdrawing his army, and rather than going on foot, he was taking every man and every scrap of equipment that could be loaded on ships. That would take time, and Lee saw an opportunity to strike and destroy Pope before any linkup with McClellan could take place.

Pope's army lay in a triangle formed by the Rapidan River below him and the Rappahannock above. He had pushed his army as far as the Rapidan south of Culpeper Court House, but on receipt of the news of Jackson's movement across that river, Pope ordered his army back to the north bank of the Rappahannock and spread them out in a ten-mile line to oppose the rebel crossing. To a soldier like Elias Roshon, every day of the next few seemed like battle, with troops ordered to move quickly from one point to the next, artillery banging away, and recurrent rumors of rebel riders already across the river and ready to strike. The meeting of the main bodies of the two great armies would not take place for a few days yet. Banks's men were gathered between Rappahannock Station and Beverly's Ford and were under orders to sleep with their rifles close to hand. Every sunrise was greeted with the booming of artillery that continued into the night, accompanied at all hours by the popping of the skirmishers, which at times broke out into full-scale fights as Lee's army probed for vulnerabilities in the Federal line.

The Rappahannock River, hardly over a man's shoulder in most places, was all that separated the tens of thousands of soldiers on opposite banks, and the war's largest confrontation might spring into life at any point, at any time. On August 21 a brigade of Stuart's cavalry tried a crossing near the Twenty-Ninth's post, and after a fierce little fight his horsemen were driven back.[32] A Federal force tried the same thing the next day, hoping to unravel the flanks of the moving rebels, and failed. A mile-long line of rebel soldiers would appear on the opposite bank in plain view, and the Twenty-Ninth would be called into battle line to take them on. After an hour's wait, the rebels had moved off to test the Union line at another point.

Their redoubtable Adj. Theron Winship returned from a quick trip back to Ohio and found the Twenty-Ninth near Beverly's Ford. The soldiers were in battle line, nerves on edge, and no one seeming to know what to expect. One minute they were called up to fight, the next hustled off to another point on the river.[33] The Boys were tired and very hungry. With the abrupt and unexplained halt in the flow of rations, soldiers snuck away to scour the neighborhood for food.

The countryside hereabouts was farmland, but it no longer much resembled it. The camp building, marching, and fighting of armies had made this entire region barren, from the Rappahannock up to the old battlefield at Manassas. Not a fence rail remained, houses had been abandoned, and passing soldiers had demolished them for the lumber in them. The crops had been trampled into the dirt and the cattle carried off. Green corn was at the bottom of the list of staples a soldier might "requisition," but it was the only thing now left in the fields. With every soldier in Pope's army looking for the same article, a soldier had to walk miles in his hunt for a few ears. Most of the soldiers were suffering from dysentery, a condition that was not helped by eating raw corn. This campaign would be remembered by the soldiers as much for their diet of green corn as for anything else.[34]

Lee now sent half his army on a wide sweep that would put it in Pope's rear and astride the Federal line of supply and communication with Washington. Geary's brigade marched up the river to Sulfur Springs, directly below Warrenton, and camped, with Robert E. Lee just across the river; and then a few days later moved up the Rappahannock to a place called Waterloo. Believing that Banks had sacrificed them at Cedar Mountain without good reason, the morale among the officers of his many regiments was said to be in the cellar, and the enlisted soldier's confidence in Pope was sinking lower with each passing day of hunger, poor rest, and crossed-wire marching.

Winship was normally glib and, like most of the officers, inclined to avoid criticizing any superior in public. Now he sarcastically characterized Pope's movement as a masterly "advance" on Washington, which had been equaled but once, and that was in McDowell's "advance" on Washington from Bull Run, a year earlier.[35] Sgt. John Marsh described these futile days as simply "the mess on the Rappahannock."[36]

Parmater dropped out of one of these marches up and down the Rappahannock and went to sleep by the roadside, and no one seemed much interested if he spent the rest of the war there. There were only three officers left in the entire regiment here to keep the Boys to their duties: Winship, Capt. Jonas Schoonover, and Lt. Andrew "Jack" Fulkerson.[37] Parmater confided his feelings about the unhappy state of morale in the retreating army to his diary: "We have no rations or anything else so the boys do about as they please."[38] He and a friend, Pvt. Daniel Morley, had left camp on a corn-gathering expedition, even though everyone had been ordered to stay put and be ready to go into battle at a moment's notice, and when they returned the regiment had packed up and left. The two soldiers walked up the road with shells exploding all around them and found their regiment in another new camp, only a few miles from the one they'd vacated that morning.

The situation was deteriorating quickly. Jackson had gotten his army across the river two days before and wasted no time in marching around the right of Pope's army. Around dark on August 26, he fell like a poleax on the railroad at Bristoe (Bristol) Station. The rebels captured the Federal pickets, derailed two railroad trains, cut the telegraph wires connecting the disparate parts of Pope's army, and raised a general ruckus. Jackson's presence set nerves in Washington on an even keener edge and mystified Pope. Mountains of supplies sat in warehouses and boxcars at the next stop up the line of the Orange and Alexandria Railroad in Manassas Junction. Before Pope could pull the supplies out of the way, Jackson swept in and captured it all, hauling away what his soldiers could carry, destroying a good deal of what they could not. The smoke billowing from Manassas Junction could be seen from the regiment's camp and from the president's house, in Washington.

Pope's plans for defending the line of the Rappahannock went out the window. However, he saw an opportunity taking shape by which he might insert a wedge between the two wings of Lee's army and defeat them one at a time. He ordered his army back from the river and toward Warrenton Junction, and from there up the line of the Orange and Alexandria to the vicinity of Manassas Junction. If everyone would just follow his orders, he was confident he could bag the whole of Lee's army.

Pope decided Banks would have a limited role in what was to follow. In the parrying along the line of the Rappahannock, Banks's corps had been placed in reserve, which explained why the Boys had been moved up and down the river to plug holes. With Jackson now in his rear, Pope ordered all of his army to come on at top speed to Manassas, all except for Banks. His men were given the unglamorous assignment of bringing up the rear of the whole operation and hurrying the army's supplies forward to Manassas Junction on the railroad. If he found himself confronted by an enemy too strong to resist, Banks was at liberty to burn both trains and supplies, but only after he had tried his best to fight the enemy off.[39]

Cut Off

By march and countermarch, Geary's soldiers moved north and east toward the Orange and Alexandria Railroad at Warrenton Junction, and then up the tracks a few miles to Catlett's Station, where they camped.[40] The field corn they had scavenged during the march they roasted over the coals just enough to soften it so it could be eaten without breaking teeth. At the same time they were sparking fires, Jackson's men were preparing feasts of good things looted from the warehouses at Manassas: lobster salads, fat cured hams, cakes and fresh fruit, finishing it all off with good cigars that had been meant for Union officers.

A wall of dirty smoke hung on the horizon to the north, in the vicinity of Manassas Junction, and the sounds of fighting drifted down to them from that direction. The rebel general Richard Ewell had been blocking the road just below Bristoe Station when Gen. Joseph Hooker's division came up. Ewell bloodied Hooker's nose and then smoothly retreated to rejoin Jackson, who was now safely installed behind the embankments of an unfinished railroad cut close by the old Bull Run battlefield. Banks's corps was again marching in the wake of its old nemesis, Stonewall Jackson.

The Giddings Regiment marched up the line of the railroad toward Bristoe Station, where the day before Jackson's men had stormed through, and rested a mile short of it. The Twenty-Ninth Ohio was assigned camping ground adjacent to a field hospital packed with soldiers wounded in the fighting along the railroad the day before. The wails of the stricken mixed in with the steady rumble of artillery fighting, and the noise of the two kept the men from sleep.[41]

The sky to the north flashed yellow with artillery fire, the report reaching them a few seconds later. The volume of this noise had been building for two days and was now more or less constant. It was clear that a large battle was on the verge of exploding just a few miles away, and what part they might have in it was unknown.[42] The battle of Second Bull Run was underway.[43] The news of it came to them by rumor, and on the wind. In his diary entry of August 29, Nathan Parmater observed, "We are in the rear and to the left of all the rest of our troops, there has been a severe fight kept up all day, west of Manassas near the old Bull Run field, reports say that Jackson is surrounded, the cannonading has been very constant, but we are too far off to hear the musketry." In Washington, the roar of artillery could be distinctly heard from the rooftops where nervous citizens had posted themselves.[44] The Giddings Boys were only a half dozen miles from the center of the hurricane where tens of thousands of muskets were being discharged simultaneously, but by some oddity of acoustics, rifle fire could not be heard. Messengers rode to them during the day with word that the largest battle of the war was being fought up the line. Jackson was surrounded, and his surrender imminent.[45] The signs that could be read by a common soldier by the next day told a different story. The sick and disabled with them were being sent away, which was taken by the soldiers as an indication that severe fighting lay directly ahead for them.[46] Whether Pope had prevailed or not, it was obvious that they were now holding the exposed end of the Union line. People in Ohio read the bulletins published in the newspapers and felt genuine dread for the safety of Banks's corps, in which so many Ohio boys were serving.[47]

The colonel commanding the brigade in Geary's absence galloped up to their camp, pulled his horse to a sliding stop, and ordered the men into line of battle on the double-quick.[48] Nothing came of it except to startle the soldiers and prompt a march of one mile forward up the railroad line and into the whistle-stop of Bristoe Station.

Nearly two days after the fighting had begun, the battle country to the north had grown mysteriously quiet. News confirmed that the enemy had bested Pope, and then the more startling realization: the enemy was in possession of Manassas, a few miles away, and the Twenty-Ninth Ohio and their comrades were now cut off from the main body of the army.[49] If Lee chose, his next move might be to turn his victorious army loose on them. At Bristoe, one hundred railroad cars and several locomotives stood on the tracks, and hundreds of wagons were parked nearby, all full of military supplies. Lest any of it fall into rebel hands, the Giddings Regiment was ordered to burn it all.[50]

A soaking rain had fallen that morning, but there were plentiful combustibles in and around the mile-long train, and at noon the Giddings Boys got down to work. Before they put it all to the torch, the Boys were given a rare treat. Parmater described the scene: "Before it was burned we were allowed to take what we could get hold of, some got clothes, of all descriptions and some eatables, and swords, etc. After the trains got fairly on fire there was one constant cracking from the ammunition on it."[51] Unfortunately, the officers had neglected to move the men to the east side of the tracks before the torches were applied, and to reach the road which led out of here and to safety, soldiers dodged and ducked through openings in the line of burning cars.[52] The colossal fireworks that started up when the flames bit into the ammunition cars were impressive, and dangerous. Bullets began to fly pell-mell from the burning cars and soldiers crouched for cover.

Banks put his army on a circuitous escape route that would take them around the rebels and up to the vicinity of Centreville, where Pope was regrouping the army. Sooty soldiers, some loaded down with plunder taken from the boxcars, set out cross-country, headed east and then north. By the end of this eventful day they arrived on the banks of Bull Run, the stream where the battle of First Bull Run, the event that the Twenty-Ninth's soldiers believed explained their existence, had been fought little over a year ago. They were marching through the margins of a battlefield upon which one hundred thousand soldiers had maneuvered and fought through the preceding three days. The wasted landscape smoldering in the near distance showed how gigantic and ferocious the fighting had been. Lee's men might pop up anywhere, jack-in-the-box fashion, and lay similar waste to them. They had steered clear of him so far, but they were by no means out of the woods.[53]

Chantilly Plantation

Lee might have attacked Pope as he limped toward Centreville, but in consideration of his men's exhaustion, he did not. Maj. Gen. Henry W. Halleck, head of the army, spurred Pope to take advantage of his superior strength and strike Lee before he got too far from the battlefield. Pope arranged for the attack, but Lee outfoxed him. He had sent Jackson on another sweep, which would put him between Pope and the safety of Washington. A report of rebel infantry marching in the rear of his army got Pope's attention, and he snapped out of the befuddlement that had bothered him since pulling back from the Rapidan and began issuing orders. The plan for attacking Lee was scrapped. Everyone was to get back to the fortifications of Washington as fast as they could.

Down on the banks of Bull Run, Banks's corps got to within a mile of Pope at Centreville, when new orders came—get to Washington.[54] The column wheeled right, in the direction of Fairfax Court House, and came up to a place called Chantilly Station, where a particular sort of hell was about to break loose. Jackson and the Federals had collided, and a sharp three-hour fight took off in the middle of a thunderstorm as fierce as the combat. Brig. Gen. Philip Kearny's division, which had been marching parallel to them, passed forward into the thick of this nasty fight, while Banks's soldiers stood in reserve.[55]

The fight went on until night fell and Jackson called it off. The Twenty-Ninth's soldiers were well aware that Jackson had tried again to cut them off at this place, and Kearny's men had saved the day but suffered mightily to do it. General Kearny had ridden by mistake into the rebel lines and had been shot down. Everyone, North and South, mourned the loss of so brave a man.

Chantilly marked the end of the Second Bull Run campaign, and already another was taking form in Robert E. Lee's mind. For the soldiers in the Giddings Regiment, it was hard to tell where one campaign ended and another began. Since they'd entered the war, everything seemed cut from the same bolt of cloth. Except for the few pleasant weeks at Alexandria, it had all been marching, hardships, fighting, and narrow escapes. Having given much of themselves, the Confederacy was no nearer defeat than when they stepped down from cars above Patterson's Creek.

Capt. Jonas Schoonover was keeping a war diary. It did not survive passage into the modern age, but it was still around when SeCheverell wrote the regiment's history, in the 1880s. SeCheverell was no longer with the regiment and had nothing of his own on which to rely, and he admitted that he had relied extensively on Schoonover's diary. What the men of the Twenty-Ninth were about to see made a lifelong impression, whether on Schoonover or anyone else.

The Boys had been marching through the rain after watching the fight at Chantilly and came up to the railroad platform at Fairfax Station. It was one of those scenes from the war that seemed to have been staged, lit garishly by dozens of lamps and lightning flashes, and for its music the drumming of rain on a tin shed roof, the shouts of teamsters cussing the mud and worn-out teams. The army surgeons had pushed tables together on the train platform so that many of them could work at once. Upon this makeshift operating table wounded men were laid and shifted about, waiting for the surgeons' attention: "Wounded boys were subjected to ofttimes bungling butchery of ignorant alleged surgeons, a number of whom were busily engaged in depriving poor fellows under their charge of wounded legs and arms, and in many cases hastening their death thereby. This worse than murder by men, the majority of whom, when at home, had never even witnessed a capital operation, cannot be too highly condemned."[56] Whoever described this scene for SeCheverell's history admitted that some of these surgeons were "first-class carvers" by the war's end, but the cost of their education had been untold suffering and death. Just as the generals passed blame for their misfortunes on to others, Schoonover fixed the cause of much of their own suffering on surgeons. That it had been the relentless clamoring for war from uncompromising places like Jefferson, Ohio, and Charleston, South Carolina, that had caused these miseries was not of interest to the soldier, now or ever. The Boys passed beyond the place of horrors and lay down on the ground in a cold rain.[57] Next morning they got ready for the short march into Alexandria, but before they could go, one last duty was fulfilled. There were valuable army stores at Fairfax Station, and what could not be carted back to Washington would have to be destroyed. Adj. Theron S. Winship was assigned command of the detail, and the Boys of the Twenty-Ninth Ohio got torches going. In less than an hour all that was left of ship-size stacks of army supplies were smoking heaps. With ash snowing down, they started out for the safety of Washington.[58]

A march of twenty miles brought them through Alexandria, where one of the war's most heartrending scenes was displayed. A special correspondent to the *Ohio State Journal* began his description of it by saying there was nothing to be gained by concealing the cruel truth of what he had seen:

> Alexandria is a vast hospital. The streets are crowded with ambulances and barouches fitted with the dead and dying, and the wounded. Boat load after boat load is moving off the wharves for Washington—train after train is leaving the Orange and Alexandria railroad with their bloody freight. All day and all night the procession moves. Soldiers who cannot be carried in ambulances, walk and limp by the side of the roads or lie down until some friendly hand comes to their relief.[59]

The regiment pushed through the jam and up the Potomac a few miles more, where they rested for the night in the lee of Fort Albany, an earthwork bastion built the year before to guard the approaches to the Long Bridge into Washington.[60] They marched up the river the next day, passing one earthwork fort after another, and then close by the foot of the knoll upon which stood the grand white home of Gen. Robert E. Lee. Then it was over the Aqueduct Bridge and into Georgetown, District of Columbia.[61]

The folks came out and gave the Giddings Boys water and things to eat, friendly treatment that to Nathan Parmater seemed odd after being in the enemy's country so long.[62] The regiment had successfully walked a tightrope from Culpeper Court House to Georgetown. Whether the run of luck that had followed them here would continue, only providence knew. The war's single bloodiest day waited for their brigade not far from here, on the banks of a sluggish Maryland creek with the pleasant-sounding name of Antietam.

At the Bridge

Adjutant Winship hoped their arrival in the fortifications in Washington meant rest, and recruitment.[63] But they passed through Georgetown without stopping, and pushed up to Rockville, Maryland, fifteen miles from the capital. Lee had crossed into Maryland, which was Union soil, and was making for Frederick city, a day's march to the north. Nathaniel Banks had been left behind in Washington. It was explained to the soldiers that his health had failed. Gen. Alpheus S. Williams was appointed in his place. Pope's career in this theater was finished too. He was dispatched out West to subdue Sioux Indians who had broken out of their Minnesota reservations and were cutting a bloody swath across the prairie. The big question now was who Lincoln would pick to lead the army to stop Lee's invasion of the North. Winship had a strong opinion of who that man should be: "McClellan is the man for the country and the army—he's the 'pet' and pride of the great American army, and if permitted to—by the powers that be—will surely lead them to glorious victories. To those at home who are disposed to deprecate his qualities as a General I would say—show us a better man or hold your peace. We are satisfied with him."[64]

Senator Ben Wade of Jefferson did not share Winship's opinion. He was said to be telling a humorous story around Washington: "Place him [McClellan] before an enemy and he will burrow like a woodchuck. His first effort is to get into the ground."[65] The editor in Jefferson had held a grudge toward McClellan going back to the days of the Rich Mountain campaign, and his recent squandering of an army of one hundred thousand down on the Peninsula had not raised him in the editor's eyes. McClellan's generalship was a complete folly, and moreover, he was likely insane. In future, McClellan should never be allowed to command so much as a corporal's guard.[66] Lincoln however, agreed with Winship, and McClellan was put back in command as the army worked its way north to head off Lee.

The great Federal army marched north in three columns, each many miles long, a day behind the rebels. Geary's soldiers marched in the center column within an army that was going out of business. A general order came down reorganizing the army yet again. The short, dubious history of the Army of Virginia was at an end.[67] The Giddings Regiment was once more in the Army of the Potomac, and Banks's old command was now the Twelfth Corps. Brigadier General Geary had been given command of their division.

While passing through Georgetown, the "brave old man" of the regiment, Lewis P. Buckley, rode through the throngs of bystanders crowding the army's route and rejoined his boys after a long absence in Ohio. He was immediately given charge of the brigade. After a few days of marching, he fell ill again and was sent back to the hospital in Rockville.[68] Captain Fitch had returned, but both he and Schoonover had been detached for work at brigade headquarters. With them gone, the regiment was down to just two officers: Theron S. Winship, and Lt. Jack Fulkerson.[69]

They passed through countryside with an easy roll to it. The Boys found it to be as pretty as could be found anywhere. Substantial houses of red brick or whitewashed plaster were seen along the road here, surrounded by orchards, wonderfully cultivated fields of yellow grain, and pastures filled with fat cattle. They crossed the knee-deep Monocacy River on a warm and golden day and camped in a field where the rebel army had camped the night before. An Indiana soldier of their corps was lolling in the grass when he spotted an envelope. He was happy to find that it contained three small cigars. The cigars had been wrapped in a letter that when read by him and his comrades appeared to be Lee's plans for the campaign. McClellan now knew where Lee was headed and he got the army moving at top speed.

The Twelfth Corps marched into the city of Frederick, Maryland, on Sunday, September 14, 1862. Geary's division was first to enter. Five minutes after their arrival, a dozen columns converged in the city.[70] The bells of the city's churches were calling their faithful to service when the sound of cannon fire up on South Mountain, twenty miles to the east, came down, tremors registering through the cobblestones and rattling window glass. McClellan's army had caught up with Lee, and battles were being fought for control of the gaps through which the Federals must pass to get to him.

The army was up before daylight the next day and strapping on gear for the march toward Sharpsburg. Winship was supervising the pack-up and getting the Twenty-Ninth ready to move when an orderly rode up with instructions. He was to take them back the way they had come, and back down to the Monocacy River.[71] The Giddings Boys stood and watched their brigade line its way out of town until it passed out of sight into the hills to the west and then marched back down to the Monocacy River, which they had forded two days before.

The order of battle for the Army of the Potomac for the coming battle included the Twenty-Ninth Ohio. In his history of the regiment, SeCheverell did not suggest that the regiment had fought in it, but he was vague as to their actions in that period and offered nothing to answer the question of why it was they had not marched up to Antietam with the rest of the brigade. The truth was they had been spared the dangers of Antietam for a simple reason: there may have been enough enlisted men in the regiment to fight a battle, but they had too few officers present to lead them into it. With only two officers present, Winship and Fulkerson, they marched back to the Monocacy and honorably fulfilled the work given them.

The tracks of the Baltimore and Ohio Railroad crossed the river here over an iron bridge. Lee crossed his army and blew it up. McClellan's soldiers could get across, but the supplies on which they would depend could not. Trains of cars loaded with Union supplies continued to steam forward until they reached the bridge. Guards were needed to protect the tons of accumulating matériel until the bridge was repaired, and the Twenty-Ninth had been given the duty.

On September 17 they awoke to an unnerving sound. The trestling on the bridge had been repaired and trains began to roll over the river that morning, but they were not the source of the deep rumbling noise that came to them presently. The Boys looked to the west, expecting to see a colossal thunderstorm moving their way, but the sky was clear. So many cannon were being touched off somewhere to the west, with such frequency, that it came to them as one uninterrupted thudding. Their friends in the Ohio regiments of their brigade were up there under that ungodly pounding. On this, the war's bloodiest day, the Seventh Ohio Volunteer Infantry was enduring yet another cutting in half, and a doubling of its reputation for bravery, around landmarks on the Antietam battlefield with the homely names of Dunker Church and the East Wood.

It seemed noteworthy to SeCheverell to memorialize an interesting incident that occurred here at the bridge. A rebel prisoner passed them. He had fought them at Port Republic, as he explained, and further stated that he personally had fired seven shots at Colonel Buckley.[72] The Seventh Louisiana soldier was amazed when told that Buckley was still alive. He asked to see him to verify the fact, and Buckley was summoned. The rebel complimented him for his bravery and that of his men. He said that all but fifty of his comrades had been killed, wounded, or captured in the Twenty-Ninth's second charge that morning. Buckley responded, "I commend your bravery, but condemn your cause."[73]

After completing their duty, the regiment marched back to Frederick. Frederick was by then a very different place than the one they had marched through just three days before. The great battle of Antietam had flooded the place with thousands of wounded. Although SeCheverell left the next two months of their history blank, they were to be the most important in the regiment's life.

FREDERICK, MARYLAND, FALL 1862

The Appearance of Angels

Normally, September in Frederick, Maryland, was bone dry. But people living in the vicinity of the places where the armies collided began to observe that battles seemed to produce their own weather. At Antietam a hundred thousand soldiers had each fired forty rounds and more, which made for countless rifle discharges in a single day, each shot making enough smoke to fill a parlor. Added to that was the smoke from artillery, and from burning buildings. All of it combined and pushed high into the regions where weather was made. In the aftermath of Antietam it rained, and kept raining.

Nathan Parmater began to feel sick again on the march to Frederick and fell out. He walked along as fast he could and caught up with his regiment when it stopped. Then the fever came and he could not walk at all. For him, it was a ride in a conveyance he wished to avoid: "I had to get into the dreaded Ambulance, dreaded by one so sick that he cannot sit up but has to lie flat on his back and have his sore and feverish frame shook nearly to death."[1] What he could see of the countryside looked beautiful compared to desolate Virginia, and when he made it into Frederick, or Frederick City, as the Boys knew it, he found it likewise picturesque. At Frederick he was laid in a tent, and for the only time in the war, he began to feel sorry for himself.

> Sept. 14—I remained with the teams today in a hospital tent which was put up for the sick while the Regt. went some three miles S. to guard a bridge. I could eat nothing and my fever was gaining. The Dr. that was left to take care of us was sick so that we got nothing to help us.
>
> Sept. 15—Remained in the tent on my pile of straw without much care or any medicine.
>
> Sept. 16—Today as yesterday only getting still worse, all the time. I began to think by this time that I would rather go to that much dreaded 'hospital' than lay here without care or anything to help me.

At last, an ambulance came by and took them to the Steiner Building, on the corner of Church and Market Streets, and he was put in a room that before the armies came to town was a billiard hall. There were thirty-two boys with him, most of them wounded from Antietam. Although he would know other army hospitals, this was the only period he did not make a daily record.[2] He could scarcely raise himself from his bed to drink the brandy and quinine that finally broke the fever.

Angels appeared to him in his delirium, bringing him little delicacies. One of these was a local woman named Mrs. Cooper Smith, whom he called Mother, and a pretty young lady, from Ohio as it turned out, whom he called Sister, after the custom of his religion. When he was recovered enough to write in his diary, he did not write about the things of sickness or the sufferings of the wounded, or their stories of how they had come to be laid next to him. He wrote about what he could see from the front window. Life, normal human activity, was going on there in the street, farmers come to town to sell ducks and chickens and produce, and the sight and sound of it refreshed him. Those in the beds around him who survived the first days were after a while all on the mend and at times were quite merry.

By the end of October, he was able to take short walks around the city. Mother Cooper continued to bring him meals: chicken stew, sweet potatoes, and good tea. The warm days of autumn had disappeared while he was sick, replaced now with days of chill rain. Then a snow fell, which took the last of the colors from the trees and covered the mess made by tens of thousands of soldiers like a clean bed sheet.[3]

On days when it was too blustery to venture out, Parmater and the others pulled up around the stove, read to each other, and played checkers. He wrote long letters to his beloved Ipsa. There had been talk of marrying when the war was over. When the weather was agreeable, he took tramps out into the countryside and came back with his pockets full of hickory nuts and fallen apples. He knew the Giddings Regiment was in the city, and one late October day he set out to visit them in their camp on a rise not far from town. He was greeted with, "How do you do Sergeant?" They had learned of his promotion before he had. They were happier than they had been; just about the happiest ever. Like Parmater, the regiment was on the gain. They had not fought at Antietam, but no one among them regretted it. The days of yearning for another battle in which to prove themselves had passed the way of their innocent overfilling of knapsacks back when they had left Camp Giddings.

Captain Fitch and seventy-eight of his men were detached to lay out a field hospital and raise two hundred tents to accommodate the army of wounded. They had scarcely finished when they were ordered to erect another hospital of the same size. The wounded now had protection from the weather, but no arrangements had been made for cooks or nurses. Fitch took the bull by the horns and detailed his men to fill those duties. The remainder of the Twenty-Ninth settled into work as guards, some assigned duty at any of the dozens of hospitals that now filled the town.[4] Most every building in the city, including brick barracks built by the British in an earlier war, had been converted to hospital use.

They would remember Frederick as fondly as home. It was a place with whole blocks of splendid houses and shops and clean streets.[5] Despite their somber duty, Frederick suited the Boys of the Twenty-Ninth right down to their shoes. Capt. Josiah Wright would recover from his nasty gunshot wound from Cedar Mountain and rejoin the regiment here. Of life in Frederick he wrote, "To us it seems an extremely comfortable location; we fear, (as General Shields would say) 'rather out of the regular course,' for we are provided with good comfortable tents and stoves, plenty of good rations, and clothing the best we have ever had."[6] The soldiers took pride once again in their camp, busied themselves sweeping its packed dirt streets, and arranging furniture inside their tents, and by the time the Boys were done with their fixings, Captain Wright thought their camp bore a striking resemblance to the Crystal Palace.[7]

Two officers of Company I, Smith and Woodbury, and the company's top sergeant, John G. Marsh, set up a snug retreat for themselves in three eight-by-ten-foot tents. One was furnished with a bench, table, chair, and camp stool and served as their sitting room. They used the second tent as their bedroom, and their cook slept and fixed meals in the third.[8] Intermittent snows fell, making deep drifts, but inside, by the heat of a sheet-iron stove, the officers enjoyed meals of bread and butter, beefsteak and potatoes, sauces, cheese, pickles, and codfish cakes. Many of these delicacies had been sent by the kind folks at home. Soldiers regained the pounds marched off them in their recent campaigning, and most everyone enjoyed good health. The size of the camp required to accommodate them more closely resembled that of a large hunting party than a regiment. Best of all pleasant things in their time here, news came from home that new recruits were on the way.[9]

Stragglers

By summer 1862 the War Department caught the scent of a significant problem: the armies had far more soldiers on paper than were actually present for duty. In the Twenty-Ninth Ohio, five hundred men should have been present to answer their names at roll call, but only a fraction of that did. An order went down from the top to find out where half the army had gone. In early July, Buckley went home to Akron to gather in his phantom soldiers. The newspapers published the order he had returned to carry out:

> By authority of the Brigade Commander, it is hereby ordered that all absentees, members of this command, whose leaves of absence have expired, and those who are absent without leave, do report to their Commander at the earliest possible moment, or render themselves subject to the severest penalty which the law provides for the punishment of deserters.
>
> By command of,
> Lewis P. Buckley, Col.
> 29th Ohio Infantry[10]

After less than seven months' active service, the regiment could not *officially* account for over three hundred of its soldiers.[11] The newspapers reported that Buckley had come home to collect the brigade's "stragglers," which was an unpleasant label, not much better than being called a deserter.[12] To take the sting out of a number this large, Winship explained in a note accompanying the list he sent to brigade headquarters, "You will notice that a large number of men, who are here reported absent are 'supposed' to be at the places named, but official notice to that effect has not been received."[13] It was not that the Twenty-Ninth Ohio's officers did not have a good idea as to what had become of their men, but that the actual "paper" from whomever had issued the soldier's furlough home from the hospital had not made its way to the regiment. Winship was obliged to put all the missing soldiers on the list, and the list was published in the newspapers, for their friends and neighbors to read. Few men on the list had run away.

Disease had bitten deeply into the regiment the past winter and spring, and hundreds had been sent off to army hospitals. The custom practiced by the Medical Department in the first half of 1862 was to send a soldier home after he had been discharged from the hospital. The surgeon in charge was required to send the regiment a notice stating the soldier's date of release and the place to which he had been furloughed. Once home, the soldier was required to report his status to the adjutant general of Ohio, and he would in turn send notice to the soldier's regiment, but these notices, from the hospital, or from Columbus, failed to catch up with the regiment. This leak was being repaired at higher levels, and the fix would take the soldier's post-hospital furlough home out of the picture.

Henceforth, when a soldier was discharged from the hospital, but still in need of recuperation, he would spend it under the watchful eyes of army authorities rather than at home in Ohio.

Nathan Parmater had been sent home after his first siege of illness, and he was on the list as having overstayed his sick leave, but desertion had hardly been his intent. The transportation pass by which he could travel free on the railroad from his home down to Columbus had not come through and he was delayed through no fault of his own.

The day after the list of absentees was published, Parmater presented himself at Camp Chase after a brief stop at the governor's office, where he made his case for appointment as a recruiting officer for his regiment. He found such a crowd of soldiers waiting to be examined by army doctors, preparatory to returning to their outfits, that there was little he could do except make himself a bed out of his overcoat and go to sleep in one of the old barracks. The appearance of some of the other names on Buckley's list of loafers was absurd, and some would have laughed were it not such a humiliating matter.

George Eastlick's wounding had been memorable in its grotesqueness; it was certainly disabling, and a hospital course of unusual length was expected. His name appeared on the list, although he was at that moment in a hospital bed in Washington after having a quarter of his skull blown away at Port Republic. Newton P. Hummiston's name was on the list, too. He could not have cleared his name from the list if he'd wanted to since he had died at the prison camp in Lynchburg. Some men acted immediately to have their good names restored. Sgt. M. E. Owen of Company I, presented himself at the newspaper office in Jefferson, and the next edition confirmed that he had the proper papers.[14]

The number of men Buckley was hunting turned out to be very small. Over two hundred of the soldiers on the list had already been discharged by reason of medical disability, or were about to be, and would never to return to the regiment.[15] Deciding whether each of them was truly disabled was out of Buckley's hands. While he was back in the Reserve scouring the countryside for the lost, over two dozen more soldiers would be culled from the regiment by army doctors at Camp Chase and dozens more at hospitals across the north.[16]

Many of these men had fallen victim to legitimate illness or injury. A significant number had no business being in the army in the first place, and after a few weeks or months, their disabilities became obvious and they were discharged. Buckley had said that when raising an army, or a regiment, it was necessary to take the good with the bad, which applied not only to a man's morals, but to his physical condition, too, and those who had been "swept in" had been swept out nearly as fast. Soldiers were supposed to strip for their enlistment examination, but Captain Fitch recalled years later that not a single man, in his company at least, had been ordered to disrobe.[17] As a result, men were passed into the regiment with grossly disqualifying handicaps.

One soldier had limped along in the regiment for nearly a year. On examination by doctors at Camp Chase, it was seen that he had been missing a sizable chunk of leg bone since birth. Having a too-short leg did not disqualify him for other work, however. Four days after being discharged, he took a job driving a six-mule team for an army contractor for triple the wages he had earned as a soldier. A year later, he passed the physical for enlistment in the Second Ohio Heavy Artillery and did two years' service in it.[18] Joining him in the artillery branch was another Twenty-Ninth Ohio soldier whom Fifield had given the stamp of approval even though he'd suffered for years from a large, protruding hernia.[19] The same soldier's brother had enlisted in the same company but had to be discharged when it was discovered that he had one leg several inches shorter than the other.[20]

Getting a discharge stating that a man was unfit for service did not imply that the condition was permanent, nor did it disqualify him from enlisting in another outfit. Montezuma St. Johns, last seen lying in the snow helpless while his regiment marched away to Paw Paw, was certified as a physical wreck and discharged. He and another Twenty-Ninth Ohio soldier who had been discharged were both restored enough within a few months to sign up for service in yet another regiment being raised in the neighborhood, the 125th Ohio Volunteer Infantry.[21] No one in the Twenty-Ninth thought the less of a man for changing allegiances. The little drummer boy of the Twenty-Ninth Ohio, J. Hampton SeCheverell, spent only half as much time in service with the Twenty-Ninth as he spent in the Second Ohio Heavy Artillery, in which he'd enlisted after the regiment's band was dismissed. The exodus of men from the Giddings Regiment via medical discharge would reach its zenith in the next few months and would decline sharply thereafter.

"Rally for the Dear Old 29th"

Most every Union regiment was short of men after one year in the field. The Ohio regiments in Geary's brigade were poorer than most. Towns that had enlisted their sons in them formed special committees, and they visited Washington to make their case at the War Department: these regiments must be allowed to go home and recruit back up to strength or risk going out of existence.[22]

General Tyler, who had led them at Port Republic, had done his best to help the Boys of his old command, but he had not succeeded. A delegation of civilians from Cincinnati representing the interests of the Fifth Ohio visited the chief of the army to plead the facts, and even the governor went to Washington to lend his voice.[23] General Halleck rejected them all out of hand: "No Sir Governor, it can't be done—if there is but one man in the Third Brigade [formerly Geary's], and his is a lame drummer boy—it [he] must remain with the balance of the force."[24] If the Twenty-Ninth was to be restored, the men themselves must see to it, and the approach of the war's first draft coincided perfectly with the Twenty-Ninth's efforts.

No one doubted that men would enlist to avoid the personal humiliation of being forced into service, and citizens wishing to avoid embarrassment to their town or county would push them in the direction of the nearest recruiting officer. Recruiting officer was a post of distinction, one worth competing for. Parmater had applied but failed to win the appointment.[25] Instead, two of the Giddings Regiment's most eloquent and energetic officers won that office and were detached back to the Reserve with the mission to enlist as many men as they could, and quickly.

Myron T. Wright would work the Akron area, and Ebenezer B. Howard would turn over rocks for recruits in Ashtabula County. Both men had enlisted soldiers for the Giddings Regiment at the start, and their experience was needed. Competition for recruits was even keener now than it had been during the peak of the recruiting wars. Howard began his campaign by running off a stack of broadsides and sticking them in store windows from Jefferson clear over the state line into Pennsylvania:

RECRUITS WANTED

ON TO THE RESCUE!!

RALLY

FOR "THE DEAR OLD 29TH !"

The ranks of the 29th Ohio Regiment

having become thinned by the rigors of a tedious winter campaign and the severe battles of Winchester and Luray, it has become necessary that new enlistments be immediately made to fill them, and again are the gallant sons of "Old Ashtabula" called upon to aid their brothers now in the field. The call is imperative. Our brave boys fought so heroically in the unequal contest at Luray, need assistance; they expect that their comrades at home will lend them a helping hand, and come up to their rescue, and the vindication of the cause of our glorious Union. Will you aid your brothers? I believe you will.

I have returned for the purpose of re-

cruiting, and wish to obtain all the good men I can. My headquarters for the present will be in Ashtabula.

The pay in this regiment is as good as is offered in the service anywhere.

Lt. E. B. Howard
Recruiting Officer"[26]

July 19, 1862

He had mislabeled the battle at Port Republic as Luray, and in truth the wages paid the Twenty-Ninth were the very same paid soldiers in any other outfit, but in expressing the spirit of the regiment—that they had been tried but not broken—he was right on the mark. Any who joined them now would have a share of the reputation already won.

The North seemed no nearer crushing the rebellion than it had been, and in some ways that goal was more distant. In the fall elections, Lincoln's party had lost seats, and John Marsh concluded from the result that the North's zeal was flagging. Even in his tiny hometown of Homerville, deep in the loyal Reserve, there were mutterings of discontent from a group of his very own neighbors whom Marsh referred to as the mysterious "bloody Bones Democracy."[27]

There had been reverses, huge bloodlettings, stalled-out offensives, and the losses to the army through the agents of disease had been much higher than anticipated. The people had put their shoulder to the wheel, and the president had been supplied with all the men he'd asked for. Thus far, all of it had come to naught. The chances for a short decisive war had been squandered through bad generalship, like that of McClellan and Pope, and by the unexpected brilliance of rebel generals. This war would not be ending anytime soon, and for it to be prosecuted with the kind of vigor Lincoln's supporters now demanded, not only would the army's losses have to be made good, but hundreds of thousands more men fighting under the flags of new regiments would have to be thrown into the fight.

In July, Congress passed the Militia Act, which would allow the president to call up three hundred thousand men for nine months, but that was not done because the leaders anticipated the war would be over that quickly. The act's real purpose was to force the states to identify every eligible man between eighteen and forty-five and list him on the militia rolls. It would be from this pool that men would be drafted, if it came to that.[28]

In early August, Secretary of War Stanton called for three hundred thousand nine-month troops and a few days later sent out instructions as to how the men should be enrolled and a draft conducted.[29] This call was on top of Lincoln's earlier call for three hundred thousand men. The deadline to supply the levy in each state was set for September 3; after that, the deficit would be filled by the coercion of "militia drafting."

Every township's honor was now at stake. The war meeting burst back onto the scene with a vigor that made the meetings of a year earlier seem as sedate as the gathering of the local library board. Anything that could be done, must be, and there was much to do.

A few months earlier the Reserve had been assigned the responsibility of providing their share toward the filling of the 105th Regiment. William S. Crowell had been first lieutenant of Company A in the Giddings Regiment, and when the 105th Regiment began organizing, he resigned his office and went to work recruiting for it. He had little difficulty in raising men, seventy of them having been recruited in Ashtabula County.[30]

In August the counties in Giddings's old congressional district were assigned the duty of immediately filling yet another new regiment, the 125th Ohio Volunteer Infantry.[31] Fortunately for the Twenty-Ninth Regiment and the other old regiments, Governor Tod emphasized that the people should first devote themselves to filling up the depleted ranks of the old regiments, rather than the new.[32] At the very least, for every recruit raised for a new regiment, one man was to be enlisted for a regiment already at war.[33] There was one other important inducement to enlisting in an old regiment: if a recruit signed up to serve in a new regiment like the 125th Ohio Volunteer Infantry, he was in for a full three years. If he joined an old regiment, like the Twenty-Ninth, the clock of his period of enlistment was set back to the date of the Twenty-Ninth's mustering-in, which meant that he would have nearly a full year knocked off his service. Whether the government would hold to this promise would not be answered until some who enlisted under it were packing up to return home.

Friends of the Union

Capt. Myron Wright had a reputation as a speaker who could draw crowds and hold them, and when word came to the small town of Montrose, Summit County, that he would address them that evening, the news spread like electricity.[34] Lt. Edward Curtis had come along to help stir the passions of a crowd so large that it overflowed the schoolhouse. Wright held the crowd in silence for over an hour with a talk he called "The Thousand Excuses Given for Not Enlisting," in which he laid out all the reasons men came up with to keep from enlisting, and he then "scientifically" took the starch out of every one of them. He got the folks chuckling and murmuring, "just so, just so." He then got deadly serious. He spoke of what the Giddings Regiment had already done and what it could do and would do if its ranks were filled again. His finish brought the crowd to its feet: "Come go with me and help to maintain our Liberty." Three men stepped up and enlisted in the regiment then and there.

Between speaking engagements and home visits to persuade men to enlist, Wright was helping Buckley corral the regiment's wayward men. He tracked down and arrested Joseph Earnsparger, who was found hiding in Brimfield.[35] Later, he treed John Wilson at Canal Fulton and had him put in shackles and hauled off by the town marshal.[36]

A sundown war meeting in Jefferson in early August filled the room so quickly that the event was moved out of doors into the courtyard. Among the speakers were two of the same men who had launched the Twenty-Ninth Regiment, Abner Kellogg and Darius Cadwell. Senator Ben Wade, home on the congressional summer recess, came out to whip the crowd. Best of all, it was rumored that old Giddings himself had come down all the way from Montreal to give a talk.[37] By mid-August the boosters could state confidently that Ashtabula County would in all probability escape the draft.

Captain Crowell's company of 120 recruits had marched out of Jefferson for the training camp of the 105th Ohio Volunteer Infantry, in Cleveland, and the happy expectation was that the county's quota for recruits—to be provided by the "old regiments," including the Twenty-Ninth Ohio—would be filled just as easily.[38]

Over in Summit County a war meeting was held in the Presbyterian church in Bath Center, and a resident came forward and offered five dollars from his own pocket to the first man who would enlist.[39] One did, and ten dollars was offered to the next man, and up and up with the biddings until three men had signed the enlistment roll. The cheering and stamping of feet brought a seventeen-foot length of stovepipe down onto the heads of the ladies, blackening their faces and covering their clothing in soot, which dampened the frivolity not at all. An underage orphan boy named Billy Long came forward and said he would go to be a soldier, which touched the hearts of those in attendance and motivated them to dig to the bottoms of their pockets.

Some would require the inducement of cash money before they signed the enlistment rolls. If a township could not produce enlistments, it could at least collect money to pay bounties, and tiny Orrville in neighboring Wayne County excelled in both. In the race to round up recruits, the village, with a population of less than four hundred, claimed to have enlisted eighty soldiers, and in addition had collected $1,250 to be paid in bounty premiums.[40] Lists of individuals who had enough generosity or wealth to cough up fifty-dollar bounties from their own pockets were published, to show, or shame, the others into seeing that deep digging was now required.[41] Orrville's residents boasted it was certainly beating its neighboring townships, and as far as they were concerned, their recruiting success put them "out ahead of the world." The newspapers pointed out over and over that if a man signed up now he would be paid a cash bounty, while those men who waited and were drafted would get nothing except their army wages.

The nonmonetary contributions of individual families were also roundly saluted. Three families in Greensburg, Summit County, had given a combined thirteen boys to the service, some of them only seventeen years old, showing that the parents, and their sons, loved their country above all else.[42]

Unlike at the war's start, women were now attending the war meetings right alongside their men. Their more direct involvement might serve as an additional stimulus to enlistment, and the means by which they might affect it was suggested in a story that was being passed through the Reserve newspapers. At a war meeting in New York State, the speaker urged the women to take their men by the hand and lead them up to the enlistment rolls. When one man hesitated, his woman said to him in voice loud enough to be heard throughout the hall, "Ira, you know what you said before you came here tonight—that you would enlist. If you don't do it, go straight home and take off those breeches, and let me have them and I will go myself."[43]

When the draft was first announced, it was predicted that every real friend of the Union would rejoice over its advent, because it would steer men at risk of being drafted into enlisting voluntarily.[44] By reputation, the Reserve was a stronghold of patriots and antislavery zealots, every last man champing at the bit for a chance to exterminate the traitors and crush slavery. The war's demand for more and more soldiers began to reveal what men were really made of, and in the Reserve they appear to have been made of the same stuff as men elsewhere. But Ashtabula and Summit Counties were not the political monoliths that their leading newspapers portrayed them to be, a fact that the impending draft brought into sharper relief in a variety of ways. Some men would not go regardless of how much money was dangled carrotlike in front of them.

John Marsh's sister had tipped him to the existence in Homerville of a group that had threatened bloody resistance of some sort if the draft were carried out. It came to nothing, but that was not universally true. At East Liberty, a few miles south of Akron, a meeting was held to stimulate volunteering for the 107th German Regiment. As the speaker was making his points, a mob began to throw rocks at him, hurrahed for Jeff Davis, and broke up the meeting entirely.[45] While attempting to leave the place, he discovered someone had cut the leather on his harness trace nearly through, and if he had set out without discovering it, he might have been killed. Later investigation revealed some members of the mob had signed a document pledging violent resistance to the draft. A dozen of the cowardly rascals were arrested and locked up in the Akron jail, and a warning was given to any others considering sedition that they would be severely punished under the new federal laws.[46] In Cleveland, something very much like a riot took place on the day names were to be drawn for the draft.[47] A mob attacked the draft commissioner, smashed things up, and forced the commissioner to postpone the event. Their complaint had been that the draft fell too hard on the working man and that the rich would escape. When next it was held, three companies of soldiers from a nearby mustering camp were stationed near the hall to enforce order. Thereafter, men eligible for the draft sought less violent ways to stay out of the war.

The "Square-Toed Measles" and Other Excuses

If a man could demonstrate to the satisfaction of the enrollment commissioner that he was physically unfit for service, his name would be removed from the militia rolls, and he was henceforth exempt from the draft. So many Summit and Ashtabula County men were coming forward claiming lifelong disabilities that the residents were amazed to learn that their population contained so many defective men. The examining committee came to Jefferson, and the place looked nothing like the village of vigorous, hard-working folks it had the day before. The newspaper in nearby Conneaut observed, "We are being informed that an army of disabled men have besieged the capital of this county—Jefferson was thronged last week with the poor and needy, weak and wounded, sick and sore. We suppose the streets looked as though some or our great hospitals had cast their inmates out into the open air of neglect and destitution."[48]

By early September, it was publicly admitted that a staggering one thousand otherwise eligible men had applied for exemption from military service in Summit County alone.[49] When the statistics were compiled, it turned out to be in excess of even that. The army of men presenting themselves for disqualification was larger by three hundred than the body of soldiers Summit County had placed on the field of honor to this point.[50] Akron expressed a fey shock that so much of its male population was disabled.[51] One brawny man complained of an agonizing and long-established liver ailment, and when asked to point out the location of the pain he pointed toward his shoulder. Other men with legs as muscular as an elephant's came crawling in and in feeble voices complained that childhood illnesses had left them weak and unable to do a day's work. The thick calluses on their hands, and the statements of their neighbors to the contrary, undercut their acting performances. One man claimed he had been permanently disabled by measles, and when the surgeon asked him if it had been the "square-toed measles," the man nodded his head sadly and said, yes, it had been that exact variety that ruined him.[52]

In an age in which birth records were imperfectly kept, men showed up for examination claiming they were well past enrollment age and already retired, although by appearance they were plenty youthful enough. Some Ohio men were taking a more painful way to avoid service. It was known for a fact that a man in Alliance, Mahoning County, had chopped off the forefinger of his right hand with an axe, attributing the fresh injury to accident, while the newspaper pointed out logically that this "soft impeachment," in a right-handed man, was impossible.[53] It was well known that a man could not be a soldier if he were unable to use his teeth to tear a cartridge, and prospective enrollees for the draft showed up toothless, and some fitted out with new dentures, and both classes stamped unfit.[54]

Such things might be expected of men in counties where antiwar sentiment was simmering, but hardly in the Reserve. In its final remark on the issue, the Jefferson newspaper stated, "It would be a happy state of things if our community *was* more healthy, but we shall leave it to the Doctor to decide who ought to be exempted."[55]

Following the same path to freedom runaway slaves had recently used for a noble purpose, draft dodgers took the steam ferry from Conneaut and Ashtabula across Lake Erie to Canada. The Reserve newspapers admitted that some of these men were not merely transients passing through, but their own neighbors. The Conneaut newspaper wrote, or ran a piece clipped from another newspaper, decrying the scandalous practice: "Some brave 'sojers' living in the Lake region smelling the draft from afar, packed up a few traps and commenced their line of march upon the skedaddle principle for the coward's asylum, in British America. The majority of the men in town enlisted. . . . Not daring to return to their deserted homes, they are now wandering like vagabonds among strangers in a strange land. . . . Let a monument of straw be erected to their memory where their coward souls have quaked out from their timid, sickly, imbecile, granny-dear bodies."[56] As for the towns that harbored the dodgers, "We wish them luck with the sneaks. A man that is sufficiently mean to desert his country will steal, and it would serve the residents right if their whole town was stolen, dogs, cats, chickens, geese, and—their wives."[57]

News that men were running away to Canada found its way into the Twenty-Ninth Regiment's camp, and Elias Roshon gave his opinion of them: "I heard the drafted men was running away to Canaday for fear they would be drafted I wish they would ketch them and hang them darn cowards they are as bad as Secesh."[58]

It was not that Ashtabula County had reached the bottom of the manpower barrel but that young men were no longer coming forward to enlist of their own will. Some defended this potential embarrassment by explaining that every eligible man was *already* in the U.S. service, a claim the editor of the Conneaut newspaper found preposterous after surveying the crowd at a visiting circus: "To our astonishment, we could count the sturdy, good looking young manhood by the hundreds. Surely, thought we, the country somewhere must be full of soldier timber."[59] Ashtabula County's neighbor to the south, Trumbull County, claimed that it had already contributed more volunteers than any other Ohio county and thus would not have to stare the draft in the face.[60] But even in that patriotic stronghold there were still plenty of eligible soldiers hanging back, and that irritated two young ladies of Warren, Ohio.

If shaming the town's young men into enlisting might do the trick, the girls were ready to pitch in. Identifying themselves in letters published in their town newspaper in a rather revolutionary form of address as "Beck" Patch, and "Lib" Fleming, the two girls made a startling proposal. They and the thirty-three other young women they had organized would happily take the place of a like number of young men who were working as clerks in the town's dry goods stores if they would only take off their aprons and enlist. As further inducement, Lib and Beck promised the jobs would be returned to them when the war was over.[61] Some, but not all, of Ashtabula County's townships had met their quotas, but even if a single man had to be drafted, the whole county would have to endure the assault on its pride.

Spinning the Wheel of Destiny

Part of the purpose of this first draft had been to pressure men into voluntary enlistment, and it succeeded. Between July 2 and August 22, Ashtabula County produced another six hundred recruits, bringing the total number of sons and husbands it had sent into the war to over two thousand.[62] The county had already dug deep to fill the quotas of soldiers laid upon it, but they had gone only halfway into the barrel. Over two thousand men had not gone into the service yet, and with the particulars of each man now listed out on the new militia rolls, the county knew who he was and where to find him. If the war's appetite for new troops continued, the time might come when every nonexempted man in the county might be called upon to do his part. For the time being Ashtabula was out ahead of Summit County in this latest enlistment competition by a neck.[63]

Old Ashtabula could rightfully claim it had done more than most counties in Ohio. It had contributed over 4 percent of its population to the war by summer 1862, while the average of the whole state had been 3 percent, and some counties, such as Crawford and Franklin, had given only 2 percent.[64] In their recruit production to date, Ashtabula had done more than its fair share, but the residents of other Ohio counties, including many that had little enthusiasm for antislavery or South bashing, had done more. Athens County, home to William T. Sherman, had sent 6 percent of its population to war.[65]

Allen County, with its large population of German and Irish immigrants, was ahead of everyone. It had already fielded fifteen hundred volunteers, which, given its smaller population of about twenty thousand, meant it had more than doubled Ashtabula's contributions of manpower for the war effort.[66] The decades of warlike threatening by the antislavery population of the Reserve had not converted directly into soldiers, and now those who opposed the war were making inroads.

A year earlier, a man who expressed any sentiment opposing the war was in danger of being run out of town, or worse. The Democratic Party had been crushed by the Lincoln tidal wave in 1860, but with a full year of disappointment on the battlefield, its members began to crawl out from under the wreckage. When the 1862 fall election ballots were counted, it was seen that the Democratic Party was back in business, even on the Reserve, and some of its membership now suggested publicly that the war might be ended through negotiation. The Twenty-Ninth's soldiers were universally opposed to the idea. Such a thing would strip their sacrifices of meaning.

Just in case the reader had been asleep for the past eight weeks, the newspapers hoisted last-minute warnings: "Drafting! Look Out!"[67] Every man should realize that his town, and his county, would be humiliated if so much as a single man were forced into service.[68] Ashtabula County's draft would be small, if one were needed at all. The draft was set for September 3. Just before it was to come off, with procedures as carefully detailed as for a hanging, it was postponed until September 16; the explanation being that the federal government had failed to arrange for arms and equipment for the drafted soldiers.

Although Lt. E. B. Howard had been at work enlisting for the Twenty-Ninth Ohio for two months, it was reported that all his new men had been raised within the last few days preceding the draft, suggesting that his batch of men had waited until the last dog was nearly hung to take Howard up on his offer.[69] Myron Wright's catch of recruits had left Akron for Camp Chase a week earlier, to be mustered into the Federal service there, and then on to join the regiment at Frederick.

It was not until early October that the wheel of destiny began to turn. In most places, the apparatus was not a wheel but a simple box. The name of each man was copied from the militia rolls and written at the center of a one-by-three-inch paper, the paper folded and placed in a box, and the box given a good shake. The provost marshal pulled names until the township quota was met.[70]

Statewide, the names of four hundred twenty-five thousand men had been placed on the militia rolls, but of these only twelve thousand were drafted.[71] Few of the drafted ever served a day in the army.[72] In Ashtabula County, less than a handful of men were overtaken by the draft, and some of them were allowed to enlist even though their names had been pulled. Most of this crop was sent into the Sixth Ohio Cavalry, and none to the Twenty-Ninth Volunteer Infantry.[73]

It would take several months for the town of Conneaut to recover from its disgust and reflect with at least some humor on the number of unpatriotic men found living within in its limits. The village was still bothered by rutting hogs tearing up the streets, and in a report of the most recent campaign to subdue them, the editor poked fun at the fakers who tried to dodge military service. "A pound for the imprisonment of hogs has been erected in town, on the corner of Sandusky and Monroe. The institution has already had a salutary effect upon the grunters in our streets, by rendering them polite and obliging. In many instances, it has had the same effect upon them that the draft had upon bipeds last fall—causing a wonderful skeddadling to parts unknown."[74]

New Faces

One September afternoon the soldiers idling in the regiment's camp near Frederick, Maryland, heard the bright sounds of a brass band, and it was coming their way. Capt. Myron T. Wright was coming up the road, and right behind him was a cornet band blaring away for all it was worth, and behind that, a hefty column of brand-new soldiers.[75] This single infusion of over 160 men doubled the size of the Twenty-Ninth. Not only had Wright and Lieutenant Howard succeeded in enlisting new soldiers, they had persuaded a dozen skilled musicians to join up.[76] The regimental bands had been broken up the previous summer, and these men were officially members of the brigade band, but they were enlisted in the Twenty-Ninth Ohio, and the Giddings Boys would have music again around their campfires. There were no rifles for the recruits as yet.

The Twenty-Ninth Ohio's recruits were put to work erecting tents and nursing the wounded, the latter a sobering but safe way to learn military routines.[77] Soldiers who had been away sick in army hospitals so long it was thought they might never come back began to return. There were the men working their way through the last steps of the prisoner exchange program, and sometime soon they would be sauntering back into camp. Companies began to get their officers back.

On his way back to the regiment the past August, Adjutant Winship laid over in Baltimore and attended a happy reunion arranged for officers just released from prisons in Richmond and Salisbury, North Carolina. They all took rooms at the National Hotel and had themselves a fine meal, which for men used to a prison diet of sour bread and wormy pork turned the day into a festival. Among the released officers were Colonel Clark, Captain Hayes, and Lieutenants Gregory, Neil, Nash, Wilson, Smith, Russell, and Woodbury. They were thin from prison rations but in good spirits and ready as ever to "whip their weight in bacon, or secesh."[78] These officers were entitled to a furlough home, and they took it and did not rejoin the regiment until later that fall of 1862 in Frederick.[79]

Captain Burridge and Lieutenants Dice and Hurlburt were doing well with their wounds from Cedar Mountain and would be released soon from the hospital at No. 25, 4 and ½ Street, in Alexandria.[80] Capt. Wilbur Stevens would recover from whatever malady felled him at Cedar Mountain and return to his place. With those above him in rank or seniority now back with the regiment, the odds of command ever falling on him again were slim. Best of all, Colonel Buckley had been restored to health, and with the energetic Adjutant Winship assisting him, everything in the Giddings Regiment was running smooth as oil again.[81]

The most outspoken man in the regiment was gone for good. Captain Josiah J. "Jack" Wright, Akron's one-time sheriff and Summit County's most popular auctioneer, had been a capable officer. His contributions to the Giddings Regiment had been substantial. He had raised Company G, defended the regiment's reputation against all comers, and advocated for the soldiers' timely pay and fair treatment. His belief in the regiment had never faltered. Wright had minimized his wounding at Cedar Mountain "as an ugly old slap," which was his style. In truth, the wound had been a dangerous one. The bullet had ripped through his upper chest and lodged under his shoulder blade in a location the surgeons thought too risky to try removing, and Jack was forced to resign.[82] There would be no more of his cynical and comic commentaries on life in the regiment. Major John S. Clemmer would not be returning either. Throughout the summer and fall he had kept up hope that the miserable leg wound he'd suffered at Port Republic might heal, but as winter approached it was evident that was not to be, and he had to resign.[83]

Slighted

The regiment was still woefully short of officers, as were most other Ohio outfits that had gone through the trials of the past year, and the governor took it upon himself to solve the problem by appointing replacements. There was immediate resistance to this policy in the Twenty-Ninth's camp. The soldiers were decidedly down on the governor's policy of appointing outsiders to places of command, and the noncommissioned officers felt downright slighted that their constancy and dangerous service had not been rewarded with promotion. Adj. Winship expressed the soldiers' grievance: "What incentive I ask is there for the faithful, brave and competent sergeants who have stood the hardships, and acquired the experience of a campaign when the Governor will take it upon himself to fill vacancies as fast as they occur from the ranks of citizens, instead of from the ranks of the army. There is a great disposition among the men to ignore the new-fledged '*shoulder strap.*'"[84] General Halleck sided with the soldiers and sent a circular out to the loyal governors discouraging the policy of appointing outsiders to old regiments. Before it could be considered, the issue came to a head in the Twenty-Ninth's camp.

Back in Camp Giddings, Wallace Hoyt had written to his father encouraging him to secure an appointment as an officer in the Twenty-Ninth. John Hoyt had finally taken his son's advice and got himself an appointment as second lieutenant. The boys of Company B would not take orders from him, and after a few days, he was forced to pack up and return to Morgan, Ohio. He told Wallace that his health had failed, but the truth of it was that he had been forced to resign because the boys would not accept him.[85]

"Be It Ever So Humble"

Late in the night, when everything at his guard post was quiet, Sgt. John G. Marsh let his imagination free. The Boys' stained, weather-beaten, and snow-steeped tents became silver-humped objects of beauty under the pale winter moon.[86] In the shapes of rocks and shrubs up on the flank of South Mountain, Marsh saw the ghosts of the dead from Antietam, come down to sit above the town and watch.[87]

Marsh had proven himself in combat. He would stick while others might run. He was a good leader and had advanced to the rank of first sergeant in his company. Buckley complimented him personally for getting more discipline into Company I than it had ever had. Here in Frederick, with the regiment's fortunes fast improving and old friends now back in the regimental family, loneliness began to gnaw at him.

Alone in his tent one night with the wind shaking the canvas walls and the rain slashing down, he took a piece of foolscap and moved a tallow candle close by so he could write. The cornet band was practicing in a nearby tent, playing a song the boys knew as "Home Sweet Home," and when they came to the line "Be it ever so humble, there's no place like home," a vibration began in his heart, and he had to admit to his little sister Ida, who was his confidant, that he was homesick.[88] There were times, he told her, that he wished he were a boy again.[89] In these quiet hours, he pictured what his family might be doing just then. "I imagined you all Sitting around the Stove, Ida & Eva eating apples, cracking hickory nuts, and laughing. Father sitting by the table reading the paper and mother in her corner by the cupboard, and the everlasting knitting in her hands and I flatter myself with the thought you all think Sometimes of the absent and wish he would come into the House that minute."[90]

There was time here to catch up on letter writing and sending and receiving packages home. Sergeant Marsh had picked up a revolver on the battlefield at Cedar Mountain, and he sent it back home by Adams Express for safekeeping until he returned.[91] Soldiers enjoyed the local markets, but buying anything was out of the question. The regiment's clerks still could not seem to get the payrolls right enough to suit Mr. Red Tape, and five months had passed since they were last paid. Soldiers and officers were strapped and dependent on boxes from home to supplement army rations.

Nathan Parmater attended a church service, which, he noted, was the first occasion in months that he'd paid attention to religious matters. Sergeant Marsh visited a Catholic church, still an oddity back home in the Reserve, and wrote a long letter to Ida poking fun at their mysterious rituals of kneeling, dipping fingers in water, and making the sign of the cross on the forehead.[92] There was an order of Catholic nuns in Frederick, but before the war not one had ever been seen outside the high wall surrounding their convent. Now, with so many wounded to care for, and half of their convent in use as a hospital, they could be seen on the town's streets almost every day. They walked in groups in perfect lockstep, and Marsh thought them better drilled than half the Union army.[93]

The times were pleasantly quiet but not wholly uneventful. A messenger rode into town at a full gallop in early October with the announcement that Lincoln was on his way. He had been to Antietam to visit the army and to prod McClellan to pursue the rebels. Frederick broke loose when the president arrived in a simple army ambulance. Soldiers fired their muskets and yelled until their throats were raw. Cannon were fired, church bells rang, and the ladies showered his uncovered head and plain dark clothing with flower petals. A thunderstorm came to town on Lincoln's heels, of such suddenness and power that it seemed to some soldiers like some Old Testament scene and Lincoln the calming hand of Moses in the tempest.[94] He went immediately into the hospitals, pausing at bedsides to take a wounded soldier's hand, thank him for his devotion to the country, and inquire how he was getting on. Lincoln's eyes glistened with tears, and the soldiers knew in their hearts his concern for them was genuine.[95] Of all public men, the soldiers loved Lincoln best. John Marsh had seen him with his own eyes in Frederick, and he sent his opinion of him to sister Ida:

> Do you think that any of these men remembered that he was a Republican President, while they were Democrats? Or that he had issued a proclamation of which they perhaps did not approve? I assure you they did not, but they all used the language of that old Abolitionist Horace Greeley, "God bless Abraham Lincoln" and I say Amen to the prayer; for I think him the wisest, the greatest, the most honest, the Best of All American Statesmen. And so will history speak of him in the future.[96]

On a midnight in late October, everyone was drummed from sleep. It was reported Stuart's cavalry was about to descend on the town. The new recruits among them were anxious to see a fight close-up. A soldier correspondent in the regiment who identified himself as "C" observed their excitement: "It would have done you good to have been here and heard the extravagant expressions of the new recruits. It is the first time they have been called out on an expedition of this kind. Each one—In his own estimation was to come back the hero of the day, with at least one secesh scalp hanging to his girdle."[97]

But their fervor was cooled when it began to rain and kept on raining until morning finally came and they were ordered back to camp without anyone having seen so much as a sign of the enemy. The newcomers were beginning to learn something already known to the veterans. Soldiering consisted to a very great extent of getting up in the middle of the night, stumbling down the road in pursuit of an enemy who would not materialize at their convenience, and then standing around in all manner of disagreeable weather until someone in the high ranks above decided the whole movement had been a mistake.

Into the start of the season of winter, an event occurred in the Twenty-Ninth's camp that drew spectators onto the roofs of nearby buildings and to the edges of the parade ground, where they could get a better look at it. With the regiment now on the increase, Buckley was not about to lose a single man. Desertion had become a plague to the whole army, and although in the Twenty-Ninth it had never been anything resembling that, there had been desertions. Sterner actions were now required to discourage it.

John B. Nowling, a twenty-nine-year-old private in Company F, had deserted with several others when the regiment passed through Bristoe Station the past June. He had been arrested while loitering around Washington and brought back to the regiment in early December. Nowling was known to his comrades as Beauregard. They regarded him as a know-it-all and a shirker. He was tried by a court martial for his crime and found guilty. Every soldier in the outfit was ordered to fall in on the parade ground and in a moment Nowling was brought up in irons under an armed escort and made to stand in front, facing Buckley. Colonel Buckley read the official sentence and then extemporized: "Private John B. Nowling, alias "Beauregard," Justice though tardy, has overtaken you. You came into the regiment a bad man, you are about to go out of it branded a bad soldier. . . . I do sincerely hope your future conduct may be better than your past, and that this may be a salutary warning to you throughout life."[98]

Jack Mowery of Company A spent the next hour pricking the letter *D* for deserter onto Nowling's hand and hip. When done, he daubed his work with india ink to ensure its permanence. Nowling was marched out of the camp led by three fifers playing "The Rogue's March." The men stood in total silence throughout. As to the rightness of Nowling's disfigurement, the editors in Ohio thought such punishments too light. They favored shooting one or two dozen deserters as an example. About the same time as Nowling's drumming-out, William E. Gray, a thirty-eight-year-old sergeant of Company K was shot dead by soldiers of the provost guard in Frederick. What he had done to earn this end was never explained in the regiment's record books.[99]

Changed Faces

The editor in Conneaut had reached the end of his tether with the never-ending war meetings and he led off an editorial with the singsong complaint "War, War, War":

> We shall be glad, and we believe our readers will be also, when the 600,000 men embraced in the last two calls of the President are filled up. Our eyes are tired of opening exchanges which invariably rest upon such heading as, "War Meeting," "Men Wanted," "Will There Be Drafting," "Tremendous War Meeting," etc. It is so all over the country, it is so in our paper, and it cannot be otherwise. . . . All other news has ceased to have a place in the papers, therefore they are newsless, dull and uninteresting.[100]

Actually, the newspapers were filled with things of interest, which showed openings into a new age and the closing of the old.

Soldiers from the county had died by now in Southern places more distant than most any resident had ever traveled, including one boy who died while fighting Sioux Indians in Minnesota. Civilian boys died at home as well, in ways that show that the inventions of industry were not only marvelous but dangerous. A local nineteen-year-old was lying on a large belt at a rolling mill when the machinery started up without warning and he was carried feet foremost into the jaws of a mechanical shear, which crushed him into a shapeless mass.

The Reserve's stores offered sheet music for a new song which went, "Say, Darkies, hab you seen de massa, / Wid de muff-stash on his face, / Go long de road some time dis mornin', / Like he gwine to leab de place?" And other newsworthy things: the father of Horatio Luce, dead on the field at Kernstown, brought oddly shaped sweet potatoes he had grown into the newspaper office to show how closely they resembled serpents and fur seals; a preacher predicted with scientific certainty that the end of the world would come in 1867, or 1868 at the latest; the state of Ohio had begun a campaign to raise $100,000 to buy artificial limbs for maimed soldiers; and an officer in the 105th Regiment about to ship out to the front published a thank-you to the citizens of Ashtabula County for their infinite kindness. Lincoln's face, it was observed, had become care worn, and some feared for his health; the Prince of Wales was to be married, but the bride was unannounced; and Gen. Tom Thumb was to be married to Miss Lavina Warren, who was another subject in P. T. Barnum's Lilliput's Kingdom. There was news of wagon trains crossing the Missouri River bound for the Far West, and of a telegraphic wire now connecting New York with "our golden sister," California, followed by speculation that the day was not far off when thoughts might be sent on the backs of lightning bolts.

Of war news: McClellan had resisted Lincoln's urging to follow Lee's army after Antietam and crush it, and for that, and other things, he was out and Burnside was in. A girl from Oberlin seeking to avenge her father and brother, who had both been killed in battle, donned men's clothing and enlisted in the Tenth Ohio Cavalry, where her sex went undetected for days.

Of news nearer to hand: a mud-throwing war broke out between Howells at the *Sentinel* and the editor of the *Conneaut Reporter* over something neither man could clearly remember. Gangs of roving dogs chased horses down the main streets of settled places, crippling them and their riders. And in Jefferson, the county fair committee had decided after long consideration that the fair would go on as it always had despite the deepening crisis. Gen. James Garfield, who was now running for Congress, would address the fairgoers on the last day. Smallpox had been confirmed in Akron, but by the time of its announcement, vigilant doctors had already nipped it in the bud.

In politics: it was now a fixed fact that the Democrats had pushed many Lincoln supporters from office in the October and November elections. During their election celebrations, Ashtabula city Democrats fired a cannon, which shattered the windows in nearly every store on the street. And a man in Kingsville was led away from his home in irons on the charge of having said or done something to "discourage" enlistments.

There was an announcement in the paper that the postprison furlough of the Twenty-Ninth's Lt. E. B. Woodbury was ended, and he would gladly carry any letters from family and friends of the Boys back to the regiment, in Frederick; and in that same edition, an open letter by a Union soldier wondering if he was alone in noticing the peculiar sensation caused by the passage of a minié ball close-by the face, which he described as a momentary feeling of deathly sickness accompanied by the smell of a newly opened funeral vault, or of a certain kind of fungus found in the woods and never intentionally disturbed by man or beast, and he asked any soldier who had noticed the same to kindly write to him confirming that these were real things and not fancies peculiar to his mind. For those civilians interested in the sounds of a full-scale battle as it came to a soldier's ears, a correspondent for a big newspaper tried his best to give them some earthly basis of comparison: "You hear a drop, drop, drop, as a few of the skirmishers fire followed by a rattle and roll, which sound like the falling of a building, just as some of you have heard the brick walls tumble at a great fire."[101]

All this and more, as the saying went, as 1862 wound down and away into history. Everyone and every thing seemed to be in motion in this new America, except for the army. The citizens had put their hearts into producing yet another harvest of their own sons and sent them along to war, and they had buried the many who had already perished. They had earned the right to excoriate generals like George McClellan, who had squandered an army of one hundred thousand; a feat without parallel in American history, so it was reported, and they had earned the right to criticize the high politicians who had allowed wicked men like McClellan to keep his job. Harder measures were called for: "The North has been laughed at for its imbecility. . . . With a million men in the field, the rebellion can be terminated in six months. But the blows will have to fall thick and hard. There must be no more sieges—no more surprises—no more retreats. 'Whip or be whipped' should be the watchword; and the best man wins."[102] The Boys also believed they had earned the right to speak, and be heard, and in the case of the appointment of John Hoyt, they were.

Battles stand high for what young men could discover about themselves, and they were important, but they were not entirely what made boys into soldiers. The Twenty-Ninth's war seemed to break itself into geologic epochs in which the participants were one way at the beginning, and something different at the end. The first of these reached its end here at Frederick. Less than a year ago they had come into the war through a back door on the upper Potomac. They had marched over a thousand miles from the sideshows of the war into its big shows, much of it purposeless and lethal. They had started out nearly a thousand strong, been taken down to a tenth of that, and here at Frederick, regenerated themselves. The Boys had seen war close-up in all its guises, sublime and horrible, and much of their hardship had been the result of the imperfect management by a string of generals. Lander, Shields, Banks, and Pope had each in their day promised much, and delivered little, except hardship and bloody, futile fighting. All of them were gone now, their stars sunk out of sight as quickly as they had risen. Gone too were the lives of twenty-five Giddings Boys given on Virginia battlefields, a dozen more who had died of their wounds afterward, and many dozens more who had perished in army hospitals.

A student in the Lutheran seminary at the Pennsylvania crossroads town of Gettysburg had a brother and many friends in the Twenty-Ninth Ohio. He had not seen them since they went off to war, and finding they were posted only thirty miles away at Frederick, he made them a visit. He remarked on the soldiers' reverence for Buckley, which he expressed as like that of children toward their father.[103] Most remarkable to him was the change in the boys he had grown up with. It was something in their faces, hard to put a finger on, but visible to him nonetheless. They no longer resembled the boys they had been.

Christmas Dinner Postponed

The Boys would have liked to spend the winter in Frederick, with its kindly residents and city conveniences. Their duties here had been military work, but hardly as taxing, or as dangerous, as what they were used to. Once all the paroled prisoners returned, they would muster over four hundred soldiers, which was as many as had come down out of the mountains and into the valley this past spring. They were rested, refitted with good equipment and clothing, and well led by tested and proven officers whom they knew and liked. They were ready for whatever lay ahead. They were lacking a chaplain, which most boys regarded as nonessential anyway, but the minister of a diminishing congregation back in Conneaut was making application for the job. It seemed likely they would be here in Frederick at least through the holidays, and the soldiers were pleased with that prospect.

A year before, the officers had enjoyed a Christmas ball put on for them by the people of Jefferson, but for most boys the warm rituals of the holiday had slipped by in a flurry of packing up. This year would be different. Captain Fitch asked the home folks for donations of things he might use to treat his men to a real Christmas dinner.[104] Boxes were filled with the traditional fixings and ready for freighting to Frederick when news came in mid-December that the Twenty-Ninth Regiment had left for the front and chances were they had already taken part in the battle of Fredericksburg. Pending news of their movements, the crate holding their homemade Christmas dinner feast sat in a corner of the newspaper office in Jefferson.[105]

17

Our Valley Forge

DUMFRIES, VIRGINIA, WINTER 1863

"From the Fighting Part, by God!"

In early December 1862, the Twenty-Ninth Ohio left the Frederick camp they had occupied for nearly three months and marched down to the depot to rejoin the Army of the Potomac.[1] They had not gotten far when news came of the ugly defeat of the Union army at Fredericksburg.[2] Newspaper correspondents atop the ridges on the opposite bank of the Rappahannock had seen every detail of it from start to finish, and for once accurate accounts of the outcome were published almost immediately. The bloodletting had been awful and the result obvious. The Federal army, under Ambrose Burnside, had sustained almost thirteen thousand casualties, many of the wounded frozen to death that night on the battlefield under a rare display this far south of the northern lights. The people in the Reserve, as elsewhere in the North, found the losses appalling and pointless. Afterward, the Army of the Potomac had withdrawn to the north side of the Rappahannock and gone into winter camp.[3] As to Burnside's prospects for future success, Col. Thomas Clark's opinion mirrored that of the nation: "We hardly think Burnside will reach Richmond via Fredericksburg, unless he goes as some of us did—as prisoners."[4]

The regiment crossed the Potomac on a pontoon bridge, and then over the Shenandoah at Leesburg, where they were once again on rebel soil. On their first day out from Harpers Ferry, guerrillas pounced on the tail of the column and made off just as quick with a sutler's wagon. Three companies of the Twenty-Ninth Ohio chased them without success.[5] They trudged on to Fairfax Court House and then down to the Bull Run battlefields. A brawl broke out between the Giddings Regiment's soldiers and those of a Pennsylvania regiment over who should have the right to a pile of rails, firewood being in short supply.[6] The Twenty-Ninth's boys enjoyed fires that night, implying that the Pennsylvanians had been defeated in the battle of the fence rails.

The defeat at Fredericksburg had taken the hurry-up out of their march, and the regiment paused for nearly a week near Fairfax Station, pending instructions from headquarters as to where among the various parts of the Army of the Potomac they should spend their winter.[7] As a Christmas gift to the enlisted man, Geary gave everyone the day off.[8] The Twenty-Ninth's officers shared a pauper's repast of three government pies, a slice of pork, a few beans, and a cup of coffee. "It was a fine dish for a soldier, and plenty good enough for a prince," reported Lt. E. B. Woodbury.[9] A more traditional Christmas was enjoyed at the headquarters of their general, John White Geary, whose staff serenaded him with carols, decorated cut evergreens, and placed them in front of his tent. They repaired later in the day to a supper Geary hosted featuring a fresh turkey with celery stuffing.

The Giddings Regiment was on the road again two days after Christmas, when it ran into a spot of trouble. A rebel fort on the south side of Broad Run thought at first to be deserted was poked a little and found to be manned. A hot little fight flared up and the rebels were driven away. It had been another nameless skirmish resulting in a few more deaths and injuries. But no one in the Twenty-Ninth had been harmed.[10] They were nearing their winter camp, but getting into it might involve a fight larger than the affair on Broad Run.

Scouts rode up to Geary's headquarters, near Fairfax Station, and reported that Jeb Stuart's cavalry had attacked a Federal outpost manned by troops of the Fifth, Seventh, and Sixty-Sixth Ohio Regiments at a place called Dumfries, killed many, and taken the rest prisoner.[11] The Twenty-Ninth's boys doubted the truth of the intelligence, knowing what a hard lot the Ohio regiments would be for anyone to take, Jeb Stuart included.[12] They set off to "rescue" the Ohio regiments. They pulled up to the ford at Occoquan Creek at midnight, and Geary ordered Buckley to put his men into an abandoned fortification with the instruction to hold it at all costs.

The next morning, near Occoquan Creek, the Twenty-Ninth got into battle line, muskets capped and loaded, and with Companies A and F under command of Captain Fitch thrown out into the tangle of stunted oak and pine as skirmishers. The sound of cannon fire came banging from the woods dead ahead. The veterans paid it little mind since it did not involve them directly, but the fresh recruits looked around nervously and considered the possibility they were about to be eaten alive. One new man relaxed a bit after a full brigade came up and deployed behind them, saying, "Thunder, the rebs can never muster men enough to whip all that crowd," which caused the veterans to chuckle.[13]

The new general of the Twelfth Corps came up in person to see what lay ahead, and the Giddings Boys got their first look at Henry W. Slocum. At age thirty-six, their leader was one of the youngest major generals in the Union army. West Point trained, he came into the war as colonel of a New York regiment and had been severely wounded at First Bull Run. He advanced in command and led men in the Seven Days' battles, Second Bull Run, and Antietam. Slender in physique, with prematurely grayed hair, and generally nondescript looking, he was bookish by nature and sometimes overcautious, but neither was he inclined toward braggadocio.

Slocum and his staff rode forward into the woods to see what the bother was. Shortly after, they came out of the woods much faster than they had gone in. Next, Fitch's skirmishers came running, and right behind them were the hard-riding rebel troopers of Stuart's cavalry. A few aimed shots from Geary's artillery stopped the rebel charge, and cut one trooper completely in two. Captain Fitch rallied his skirmishers, and they fired a single volley that unhorsed two more of Stuart's riders and started the rest on the run.[14] After it was over, Slocum rode over to Colonel Buckley and asked him in what part of Ohio his regiment had been raised, and Buckley replied, "From the fighting part, by God!"[15] The troops that came up to the scene remarked that the Twenty-Ninth Ohio's men were like "rein-deer," which the Boys took as a compliment for the quick, easy way they had moved through the brush.[16] They marched into the village of Dumfries, Virginia, without further molestation and rejoined the men they had come to rescue.

Their old friends in the Fifth, Seventh, and Sixty-Sixth Ohio Regiments were recovering from a more serious encounter they'd had with Stuart's cavalry two days earlier. When the Twelfth Corps had come into this neighborhood a week earlier, the Ohio regiments of Candy's brigade had been detached to guard this important rear link in the Federal supply line leading back to Washington. They had been hard at work building fortifications, setting up camp, and seeing to their dinner when cannon shells began to fall, followed by the charge of eighteen hundred rebel troopers. The fighting went on for hours, until the rebels were finally persuaded to back away.

The Seventh Ohio's autumn had been less pleasant than the Twenty-Ninth Ohio's, at Frederick. After Antietam they were posted near Harpers Ferry, where they were put to work shoveling dirt to make forts. After Gen. Joseph K. Mansfield's death at Antietam, Gen. John White Geary was given command of the division. Around Thanksgiving the Federals had crossed the Potomac from Sharpsburg and raided Shepherdstown. They succeeded in killing Redmond Burke, the Guerrilla King. The *New York Herald* gave Geary the credit, and Geary clipped the news pieces flattering to him and sent them home to his wife. An officer who had actually been at Shepherdstown complained that Geary had had nothing to do with the success of the operation whatsoever.[17] In early December the Seventh Ohio accompanied Geary on a reconnaissance to Winchester. Geary wrote to his wife that he had taken Winchester, killing rebels along the way and capturing 130 more.[18] The Seventh Ohio's historian had been with Geary at Winchester, and he recalled that the infantry had not even set foot in the town.[19] On their approach, Geary had sent forward a white flag of truce demanding the town surrender. The town officials replied that they would be glad to but thought it wise to let Geary know that smallpox was loose in the town, and Geary turned around and headed back to the Potomac.

Fallen Castles

Dumfries lay mostly in ruins, but not because of the war. It had once been a beehive of a place with several thousand residents, most all of whom were involved in some way with the lucrative tobacco trade. But tobacco had ruined the soil, which then silted up Quantico Creek, which connected Dumfries to the Potomac. By 1812 the town had been strangled.[20] Presently, poor log cabins housed squatters who were as hungry and dispirited as any soldier had ever been. The rest of what had been Dumfries was a collection of tumbledown walls overgrown with vines and grand stone staircases that led nowhere. General Geary saw in the worn-out land and its ruins a memorial to the greedy Southern aristocracy, which had made fortunes on the backs of slaves, spoiled the land, and then moved on to lay waste another place.[21] The common soldier was fascinated with the antiquity of this place, which to them seemed a land of fallen castles.

The one hundred twenty thousand soldiers of the Army of the Potomac lay in their vast camps, filling every ridge and valley between Fredericksburg and Falmouth, twenty-five miles south of Dumfries. The center of action nearest Dumfries was at Aquia Landing, ten miles below them on the Potomac. With the army's gigantic appetite for supplies, Aquia Landing was becoming a very busy port. New wharves poked far out into the Potomac, and a railroad spur ran right up to the ships. Warehouses were going up, and the tens of thousands of wooden crates that could not be fitted into them were stacked into two-story-high rectangles with alleys in between through which quartermaster and commissary personnel walked with hands full of thick sheaves of bills of lading. Many Giddings soldiers visited, either on work details or to take in the marvelous activity of the place.

Camping on the outer ring of the Army of the Potomac at Dumfries had its advantages. Where the main army camped below them, every house was pulled down for its lumber, and by this winter's end hardly a tree was left. The long, low ridges that ran from Dumfries down to the Potomac were still covered with timber, a handy source of material for camp building and heating. The Potomac River, with its entertaining spectacle of passing ships and the possibility of catching eel and other fish to fortify army rations, was a four-mile hike.[22]

The Twenty-Ninth Regiment was assigned a campground on a wooded hillside north of town, with a commanding view of the surrounding country.[23] Compared to last winter's camp, way up in the mountains, the Boys hoped the weather here in this more southern location would be downright temperate. At first the soldiers wrote home to report they were enjoying days of sunny warmth, far different than what the folks back home would suffer through in a typical January. But then the wind carried in a cold rain, which turned to snow, followed by freezing cold, and this cycle turned out to be the status quo of their Dumfries winter.

Our Valley Forge

Burnside had put the army out on the roads back toward Fredericksburg in an effort to redeem himself, but the weather had not cooperated, and the whole army got stuck in the mud. After that, he was out and Joe Hooker was in. The Boys liked Fighting Joe, both for his reputation of fairness toward the soldiers and for his record on the battlefield. He cut a fine, confident figure on his horse. In battle he could be found in the front line, and the soldiers liked that. Unknown to them, Hooker was inclined to make much of things he had not yet accomplished. Lincoln knew of this and other deficits, but hired him despite them. Hooker was now full of ideas as to how to get the tens of thousands of dispirited boys back into fighting trim.

For starters, he had a strategy for improving the health of the men, which began with improvements in their rations. Fresh bread was now issued several times a week, along with fresh meat. But SeCheverell wrote in his history that their winter in Dumfries was worthy of comparison to the suffering of Washington's army at Valley Forge, what with the bad weather, the long distance between their camp and their assigned outposts, and the scarcity of almost everything.[24] The soldiers in the Twenty-Ninth who wrote of their experiences this winter of 1863 had a completely different take on it.

There was plenty of "sweet" to satisfy the most acute hunger for it. The army thought it beneficial to the soldiers to issue each mess five pounds of sugar in the form of molasses.[25] Boys like Pvt. Cass Nims and his friends sat around the fireplace in their huts, dipped into the jars in which it was packaged, and took turns licking the spoon.[26] And a newfangled food was added to their army ration. Desiccated potatoes and a dried assortment of other garden items formed into the shape of a brick were thought by medical authorities to have disease-fighting qualities.[27] The soldiers found the gray, tasteless mess contained as much gravel as vegetable, but it was thrown into the cook pot along with anything else.

The local people were suffering through times every bit as hard as the lot of the soldiers, but the soldiers took little pity on them. Cass Nims, an eighteen-year-old farm boy, told his widowed mother that the pickets enjoyed themselves by forcing the people to feed them.[28] His heart softened over their plight and he wrote a month later, "The women and children are on the point of starvation and all that they get to eat the soldiers give them and that ain't much for we ain't much to give."[29]

Like Cass Nims, one soldier would write home to say that they were going hungry, and the soldier sharing the same bunk would write that they had plenty of provisions, leaving neighboring parents at home to compare the two accounts and scratch their heads over which gave the reality.[30] The Seventh Ohio Volunteers were camped nearby, but their historian remembered the winter of 1863 in Dumfries as nothing resembling a Valley Forge. The Twenty-Ninth's gloomy memories of the Dumfries winter were perhaps colored by the unhappiest event of their stay here.

"Wherever Fortune May Place Me"

In mid-January 1863, Col. Lewis P. Buckley sent a letter to the Akron newspaper, "I have had in contemplation for some time, in behalf of the 29th, through you, to thank the people of Akron, as well as the counties of Summit and Medina for their instrumentality in assisting to put into the field one of best regiments Ohio can boast of."[31] He went on to emphasize the bravery its men had shown and their devotion to duty despite difficult circumstance. It sounded very much like a farewell, and it was. A few days later he sent in his letter of resignation.[32] He had tendered his resignation back in July, but men of his skill were in short supply, and the War Department gave him a thirty-day furlough instead. He resigned again, and his furlough was extended. This time his resignation was accompanied by a letter from Dr. Amos Fifield. He had examined Buckley and found him to be suffering from tuberculosis of both lungs.[33] If Buckley stayed on, it would be at the risk of his life. The only hope for him now was to return to the quiet of civil life.[34]

The signs of consumption were well known to everyone, but his officers had made a gentlemen's agreement: they would never mention the exact nature of Buckley's problem, not now, not decades into the future. The stated hope of his men and officers was that he would recover, but they knew few ever did, and the elderly never. Buckley had promised to give everything he had to the Twenty-Ninth, and he had. He had shown them that there could be dignity, and even heroism, in defeat, as at Port Republic, but the escape on foot through the woods from there back to Shields had used him up, and after that he was never the same. His absences had grown progressively longer and closer set, and he had been injured again this past November in a fall from his horse.[35] Buckley was known as a superb horseman, and his tumble showed as much as anything that he was faltering. He had rallied to lead the march down to Dumfries and was still full of pluck, but that alone could no longer carry him.

If there was a public ceremony at Dumfries to mark Buckley's passage out of the regiment, no one wrote about it. He slipped out quietly without letting anyone except a few of the officers know, perhaps in order to spare his Boys the trying emotions of a good-bye. He was already gone from the regiment by the time the news was announced to the soldiers.

Officers and sergeants formed a committee, collected contributions, and made him two gifts. One was a fine military saddle. The second was the costliest sword they could find, chased along its length with elegant designs, with a gilded hilt set with pearl. The scabbard was gold plated from end to end, inlaid with pearl, and decorated with Masonic inscriptions.[36] And there were words to accompany these tokens of affection: "We feel that the reputation of the Twenty-Ninth Ohio as a fighting Regiment is mainly due to your example and teachings."[37]

From his room in Washington, where he had gone to recover his strength for the long trip home, Buckley wrote a good-bye, which was read to all the soldiers. "Permit me to say, that wherever fortune may place me, you will find me one whose memory must be dead, were I to forget the 29th; whose heart must be cold in death when it beats not for their individual happiness."[38] Buckley had been a Democrat. Sam Lane, editor of Akron's most ardent pro-Republican newspaper, commented, but he also allowed that Buckley was indeed a brave man and even expressed the hope that if Buckley was able to return to the war, it would be with a general's star on his shoulders.[39]

Another officer of great value to the Twenty-Ninth escorted Buckley home, and he would not be returning. When Theron S. Winship had announced his intentions to give up his store, back in autumn 1861, and go into the Giddings Regiment, his townsmen expressed doubt that someone as mercurial as he could adapt to army life. But he had proven the doubters wrong by making a reputation for high courage and a remarkable devotion to duty. He had lost pieces of his health everywhere the regiment had stopped—diarrhea, fevers, and finally ulcerations of both eyes—and by the time he reached Dumfries little of his constitution remained. Stooped over by the weight of an unmade decision, he visited his friend Capt. Edward Hayes in his tent one evening at Dumfries. He asked for Hayes's counsel: should he resign or stay? To Hayes the answer seemed clear. Winship could do no further good for himself or the regiment by staying on, and Winship took the advice and went home.[40]

Youth was no inoculant against physical collapse. Alfred Bishop was twenty-three when he enlisted in Captain Stevens's Company B in its early days and was elected its first lieutenant. There is a picture of him in the uniform he bought to celebrate his election to that office: white-leather gauntlets, fancy dress coat with many buttons, and on his head a kepi with an extraordinarily tall, slouchy crown to which he had pinned the brass hunting horn of the infantry, and above it the shining number 29. Like Winship, he left without a published testimonial, speeches, or presentation swords. His friend Oscar Gibbs sent the news home ahead of his leaving, "He had done duty for weeks at a time when he was unfit for it, but he cannot do justice to himself by remaining any longer and will resign. We all regret the necessity of his leaving but think it best."[41]

In a few weeks, Capt. E. B. Howard of Company E would be leaving, too. Howard had worked hard for the regiment, most recently during the recruiting expedition back in Ohio. He had been the only man in the regiment to emancipate slaves in the field, sending the one he'd liberated near Martinsburg back to Ohio to work on his farm. Not everyone liked Howard. Sergeant Parmater would run into Howard on the street a few months forward, and the meeting, at least for Parmater, was uncomfortable. In his opinion Howard had left them with little honor to himself, and with few friends in the company he once commanded. Parmater did not record his reasons for thinking thus.[42] Their first captain, Horatio Luce, dead on the field at Port Republic, had left tall boots for Howard to fill.

Col. Thomas Clark was still hobbling on the leg that had been crushed beneath his fallen horse at Port Republic, but he was well enough to take command after Buckley left. Taking the place of Adjutant Winship was James B. Storer of Akron. Capt. Myron T. Wright was acting major on the field staff, filling the vacancy left by John Clemmer, but appointments to fill Clark's vacated spot as second in command would have to wait pending the clearing of logjams for appointments back in Columbus. Captain of Company A, William T. Fitch, was next in line to ascend to Clark's post, but he was sick as much as healthy. Buckley, Reverend Hurlburt, Josiah Wright, and Winship had all made their imprint on the Twenty-Ninth Ohio and had spoken and written the words that defined it, and all were now gone. However, the life of the regiment was as much a work in progress as the Capitol dome in Washington, and as the familiar voices that had chronicled its stages receded, new voices came forward to reflect on and record what it was becoming.

A New Voice

The regiment had been without a chaplain since Russell Hurlburt had resigned and gone home, months ago. A new man of God appeared in their camp at Dumfries in the middle of March. He made his entrance so quietly that some time passed before all the Boys knew he was even among them. Reverend Hurlburt had been their noisy advocate on the touchy issue of their delayed pay. Conducting regular religious services was not at the top of his agenda. He had been more concerned with the material welfare of the soldiers, an interest that endeared him to them. Hurlburt liked rubbing elbows with them, pitched his tent on the company street, and traded bits of gossip as eagerly as any private.

The new man was of a different sort, not better or worse, but different, and his observations of the soldiers with whose spiritual care he was now officially entrusted were therefore different. When the war began, Lyman Daniel Ames had been presiding over the dwindling congregation of a Conneaut church.[43] He had been born in Vermont, where he was ordained into the faith of the Christian Church, also known as the Disciples of Christ.[44] He preached at churches in Vermont and New Hampshire before coming out to Conneaut sometime before 1854, and in his years in the village, he had not done anything to get his name in the paper. The sermons of some preachers were quoted regularly in the local newspapers; Ames's were not. He had a wife named Clara, a nine-year-old boy named Georgie, who was his father's delight, and an older son, Edward, who was a soldier in the Second Ohio Independent Battery. Ames was a fastidious man. Each time he wrote a letter, whether for business or to his wife and children, he made note of it in his diary and gave each a number.

At age fifty, with diminishing prospects at home, plying his profession in the army seemed an attractive option. He had never been a soldier, but he had come to believe that the soldiers of this war cried out for spiritual guidance, and he saw himself as the man who could provide that to them. He was careful of his finances and kept track of every penny in his diary. An army chaplain was paid one hundred American dollars per month, the equivalent of a captain's pay and several times more than he had earned in Conneaut. The army provided forage for his horse, gave him a tent, as much stationery as he could use, and an allowance with which to buy the officer's uniform he wore. He was subject to little or no supervision. A man might put little into the job or invest himself entirely in it. He applied to the governor for the job and got it.[45]

On arriving at Dumfries, he took lodging in the house of a Mrs. Long and shared mess arrangements with Colonel Clark. He arrived just in time to conduct funeral services for J. C. Hammond of Company H, who had died in the camp hospital the day before.[46] A few days later he visited the enlisted men for the first time. He offered religious counsel to every soldier he visited but found only one man interested in improving his spiritual condition. Several weeks passed, and Nathan Parmater wrote in his diary, "We have a new Chaplain but he has never spoken to us yet."[47]

After a month in camp, Ames conducted his first Sabbath service. He preached, and handed out temperance tracts that had been donated by a lady back home. It was in his nature to worry a great deal over what the soldiers might think of him, but when it was over, he was able to state that his new flock had at least listened politely and there had been no signs of impatience or boredom.[48] The soldiers in camp had not jumped at the chance of working one-on-one with Ames. He found a more receptive audience in the camp and brigade hospitals, where the population of sick and discouraged soldiers was increasing daily.

Tuggies

Nathan Parmater was left behind sick at Frederick. After Christmas, his hospital closed and he was sent to a camp for convalescents a half mile from town. There with him were the maimed and blinded of Antietam, and some men were there who were only acting lame to get a discharge.[49] He shared a tent with German-speaking soldiers, which was convenient because Parmater had decided to teach himself the language and could practice what he had learned from his book. Near the end of February, the camp was closed down and Parmater's days in Frederick were at an end. He would take with him pleasant memories. "I have been very kindly treated here, the ladies are noted for their hospitality towards the soldiers, but it is not for a soldier to choose his place of residence while under Uncle Sam."[50]

He was shipped off to Camp Ohio, two miles outside of Georgetown on a rise near Fort Gaines, and put in a tent with six others. The skyline of Washington could be seen in the distance and he took the streetcars one day to see it close-up. The U.S. Patent Office was high on his list of places to tour, because he was, as he admitted, "always quite a hand to see Yankee inventions."[51] He sat in the gallery of the Senate, "where so much fighting is done with the tongue," and inspected the grand murals decorating the walls of the rotunda, the roof of which was incomplete and draped with scaffolding. Aside from this one-day outing, there was little to occupy him, and he fell victim to what he called "the blues."

As they were being marched to yet another camp, an officer asked if there were soldiers present who wanted to return to their regiments. Parmater stepped forward and, after a brief stay at Camp Distribution, was on a ship that took him down to Aquia Creek. He hiked the rest of the way into Dumfries, where he found the Boys living on a sidehill in small huts made of logs and covered with old tents.[52]

The shelter tents they had been issued months ago had turned out to make handy little houses, but spending the winter in a low, open-ended tent in this climate was out of the question. The Boys set themselves to house building as soon as they arrived. The soldiers of the Twenty-Ninth used the word *tuggy* to describe their quarters, whether a simple tent or something more elaborate. Quartermaster Oscar Gibbs described the construction of his own hut here at Dumfries: "I have built up with small logs a square two feet high the size of my tent and barked it up and have my tent set on it. I have had built also a brick fireplace and chimney which makes my feet not only warm but pleasant and I would like very much to be permitted to remain in [it] through the winter for fear of worse accommodations."[53] The building material for most of these cabinlike structures could be had in the surrounding forests, and the universally accepted roof was made of shelter halves and old tents that the soldiers had scrounged. The enlisted men built their huts on a scale to accommodate the number of friends who planned to live in them, from two to six boys in most cases. Boards and nails could be purchased to knock together bunks of one to two stories along either wall, and pegs or nails were driven into the walls to hang gear when a soldier came in from picket duty. For chimney building there was a plentiful supply of mortar at hand with the pernicious mud everywhere, and even a good supply of bricks, authentic relics some of them. Parmater's tuggy boasted a chimney made of bricks from far-off Scotland in a time so distant the Boys thought them marvelous. In late winter, to stem the epidemic of typhoid and other camp fevers thought caused by camping too long on the same ground, these tuggies were ordered abandoned and the Boys moved a few hundred yards to a new spot. By then, tuggy building had been distilled to an art form, and Parmater and his friends set to work at once:

> Six of us have built one out of split logs, and have put up bunks three stories high, and built a chimney out of bricks which were taken from the Old Court House which is said to be the second one built in the U.S. and were brought from Scotland, and on two or three were found the prints of dogs feet very plainly and were made while the bricks were green which makes them "imported" dog tracks over a hundred years old.[54]

Some officers who were lucky enough to find them rented rooms in the few remaining buildings in town and slept on what passed for real beds. The enlisted men and their noncommissioned officers lived in their tuggies and made the best of it, and although they looked comfortable enough compared to living in a tent, and even quaint from a distance, life in was far less than cheery, and for some men, perilous.

The typical hut was windowless and cramped. The fireplace dumped as much smoke into the interior as it sent up the chimney, and it seems most of the Boys had by now taken up a vice that added to the murk. As Asst. Surgeon Elwood Haines observed, "the Volunteer smokes!" Haines found spending the day in the cook's tent preferable to asphyxiation in the quarters he shared with a man who indulged. No amount of weatherproofing could keep a tuggy dry. In rain, the worn-out canvas roofs leaked like sieves, and they collapsed when it snowed. To get a higher ceiling, some soldiers dug down into the soil a few feet before laying the first row of logs on the edges of the excavation, and in doing so tapped into the soggy, malignant soil.

Outside, the soldiers lived in a narrow gray-white band of ground fog and smoke. The floor of this world was made of the infinite mud. Mud was a routine inconvenience at home, and every boy, city or farm, was accustomed to it. But this Virginia mud was a different article altogether. Every step in camp cemented another five pounds of it to the shoes, and moving a wagon a few feet required the swearing and struggling of a dozen men, and even with that, whole mule teams would disappear in it up to the tops of their ears. Mud: a simple mix of water and Virginia soil, discomfited the soldier at the bottom of the army's organization, and had unseated its highest general, Ambrose Burnside.

Upon arrival in Dumfries, the men of Candy's brigade were beset by lice, something very few men would admit to, and no soldier in the Twenty-Ninth Ohio ever mentioned it in letters home to mother. Boiling their clothing in the company kettle was the best, although imperfect, method for getting rid of them. On any pleasant day, soldiers could be seen outside their huts picking through their clothes and removing the tiny bugs one at time. A soldier thus employed in the neighboring camp of the 147th Pennsylvania was said to be "doing his knitting" and was the object of good-natured kidding. One man trying to free himself from this nuisance was chided by his friend, "Hello, Freddie, you better get up and shake that shirt, then write home to your parents that you stood where hundreds fell."[55] A much more dangerous, invisible pest took hold of the soldiers at Dumfries, owing in part to the manner in which the army toileted.

Typically, a Twenty-Ninth Ohio soldier was quick to report home on the details of every feature of life in the winter camp of the Army of the Potomac, but Victorian propriety prohibited descriptions of his toilet arrangements. The foul condition and dangerous location of latrines had been a scandal in the Army of the Potomac from its beginning. Typhoid fever was observed to flare up where soldiers paid inadequate attention to sanitary matters. Hooker ordered the mess cleaned up, and the number of cases of soldiers coming down with typhoid was cut in half, but Boys still died from it nonetheless.

The best and most comfortable "sink" consisted of an elevated board for seating placed over a deep trench. Under Hooker's direction, the trench was to be dug away from the huts and separated from all water supplies. The worst were too shallow, so that they overflowed every time it rained, or were dug too close to where the soldiers slept and cooked their food. Maintaining even the most carefully placed and constructed latrine depended on the soldier's aim while "straddling the ditch" and on his willingness to use it. A detail was supposed to cover the day's deposits with a fresh layer of soil. But with everything melting to mud, maintaining the outlines of a trench was impossible. The weather this winter was more stormy than clear, and soldiers needing to do their business in the night might not challenge the elements by a long walk to the company latrine, using instead the backside of the hut.

Soldiers went for weeks, and some went throughout this entire winter, without a complete change of clothing or a bath. Even for a man educated in matters of hygiene, like Asst. Surgeon Haines, the opportunity to take a proper bath and put on a clean uniform was so rare that it won special mention in his diary.[56] By March it seems the soldiers had given up hope of ever getting clean. The general inspector came around to look them over. He remarked that the regiment was too filthy to stand inspection and he rode off.[57]

"A Case Demanding Sympathy"

Twenty-nine-year-old Elwood P. Haines had completed most of his formal medical training by the time he enlisted, and once that became known, he was assigned duty as the regiment's hospital steward. With Dr. Amos Fifield assigned charge of the brigade hospital, and Asst. Surgeon Sylvester Burrows resigned and gone home, Haines was now in charge of the regiment's hospital. Until now, his clinical experience had been limited to dispensing pills, bandaging injuries, and keeping records. As soon as he took over, the hospital was overwhelmed with sick soldiers.

Typhoid fever was the principal culprit. In Haines's opinion, the cause was "damp quarters."[58] In the next-door camp of the 147th Pennsylvania, Lt. Col. Ario Pardee Jr. commanding, every company was ordered to report to the surgeon's tent when the drums sounded sick call, where every soldier was compelled to swallow a "hot dose," which was a cocktail of quinine, red pepper, and whiskey. Even the boys who had a taste for the whiskey component found this preventative hard to swallow, but as one 147th soldier said, "it was die dog or eat the hatchet."[59]

Most every soldier in the Giddings Regiment suffered from at least one of typhoid's early symptoms: poor appetite, headache, cough, generalized aches and pains, fatigue, and diarrhea, so it was hard for a soldier to judge when he should give up and go to the hospital or tough it out on his own. When the inextinguishable fever set in, along with the other unmistakable signs—severe belly pain and breath that came so hard it felt like an elephant was sitting on his chest—he was in for the battle of his life. Captain Fitch had been sick with typhoid on and off for months. In mid-March, the bottom fell out of the bucket. He got himself into a room in town and for the next few weeks fought off death's repeated assaults.[60] A few of the other officers fell sick, but none of them died. The enlisted men admitted into the camp hospital fared less well.

Pvt. George Root of the Rock Creek neighborhood was one of the new men in the regiment. He was one of dozens whom Haines was treating simultaneously, almost all of them suffering with typhoid. He stayed up with Root all night, but despite cupping, cold baths, and dosing with arcane chemicals, Root continued to fail, and he was not going quietly. Wallace Hoyt reported home on the condition of the Rock Creek Boys and Root's plight: "The boys are all well except George Root, it is not thought that he can live long last night he was out of his head and would yell so that you could hear him all over camp."[61]

Although they were only forty miles from Washington with its ever-improving hospitals, conditions for the sick in Dumfries were primitive, if conditions in the hospital of their neighboring regiment was a measure. The Pennsylvanians' hospital consisted of a twelve-by-sixteen-foot canvas tent. The sick were laid on the ground on a bed of pine branches and covered with a gum blanket. The interior of the hospital was lit by candles, and heat came from a small sheet-iron stove, which covered the sufferers and the attendants in smoke, there being no chimney.[62] Conditions likely improved by the time George Root took sick, in March, but the surgeon's treatment regimen for the victims of typhoid had not. Believing that water fueled the fever, well-intentioned doctors would not allow a stricken man a drop of it, despite how loudly he might scream for it. Wallace Hoyt was right in his prediction that Root would not live. He hung on a few more days and then died.

From the day he arrived at Dumfries, Reverend Ames spent an increasing part of his days, and nights, at the camp hospital, comforting the sick, reading to them, and praying with or over them. Ames learned quickly that a sick man's fate seemed written on his face—whether he would recover, or was on his way down. Elias Waltz was one of the new musicians that had been enlisted this past fall and played their way into Frederick. Chaplain Ames followed the course of Waltz's battle with typhoid:

> April 1: Cold and windy this morning. Called on the sick—found all doing well except Mr. Waltz. He is evidently declining and feels discouraged and homesick. His is a case demanding sympathy and kindness.
>
> April 6: The sick improving except one—Waltz fails. Says but little.
>
> April 9: Waltz expressed a firm conviction in God, said it looked light ahead.
>
> April 10: Silas [Elias] Waltz died last night at 10 and ½ o'clock. Son of David Waltz of Johnson's Corners, Summit Co. O. He was a good man, he died in faith.

The pestilence continued into April and then receded, but it never disappeared.

National Pastimes

Some soldiers positively thrived during their Dumfries winter. With death notices of soldiers appearing regularly back home, Cass Nims wrote home to assure his mother that he was healthy as ever. He always knew he had been tough as a bear. He did not know what it meant to be sick.[63] While the sick fought their individual struggles, the majority of the soldiers carried on their military duties. The Twenty-Ninth's stretch of picket line was over three miles long, and its nearest end over a mile from camp. Once on it, the soldiers standing picket duty had to hunker down in the brush and hide or risk being potshot by bushwhackers.[64] Their anxiety was warranted. An entire patrol of Illinois cavalry disappeared one night on the road outside Dumfries.[65] The footprints of the twenty partisans who had waited in ambush and three Union cavalry sabers in a nearby field were all that was ever found of them.[66] Off-duty, soldiers kept their rifles leaned up by the door of their huts for quick use. Jeb Stuart's cavalry had not returned, but with his reputation for surprise, he might fall on them at any moment and drown them all in the Potomac.[67] With time on their hands, the soldiers amused themselves when an opportunity presented.

Surgeon Haines and Nathan Parmater followed the impulse toward self-improvement and the avoidance of idleness cherished by their New England ancestors. Haines finished reading Dickens's *Little Dorrit* and sailed into *A Tale of Two Cities,* mixing in perusals of *Harper's Magazine* and dime novels with serious study of treatises on the most up-to-date surgical methods. Lt. Curtis invited Haines to his quarters in town, where they spent an evening smoking cigars and discussing the authenticity of the Bible.[68] Other officers gathered together clublike and enjoyed suppers of Potomac oysters and any other delicacies that could be scared up. Parmater continued his pursuit of mastery of the German language. Soldiers hiked or hitched rides down to the Potomac to fish and watch the world float by.

The stream of letters from Ohio had dried up yet again. It was rumored that bags of letters had been thrown overboard by disloyal ship captains, or that mountains of soldier-written letters and letters intended for them were rotting on army wharves at Washington. By this time, most soldiers continued to write simply because it took a bite out of the endless hours of tedium, regardless of whether their letters were reciprocated. After each snow the soldiers came out of their huts and snowballed until everyone was soaked and hoarse with laughter.[69] On every dry day they searched out a mud-free plot of ground and played "ball," and as spring developed the game became almost a mania.

There were walking explorations by the enlisted men, and from the amount of writing that was devoted to it, the local cemetery was a popular attraction. It was said to hold over two thousand graves, most all of them ancient. As proof of their antiquity, trees that had been thin saplings when the deceased was laid in the ground had absorbed all but a corner of the gravestone.[70] For the officers who had the benefit of horses, there were pleasant rides out into the countryside. Reverend Ames went out one day with Colonel Clark to inspect their long picket line. He was impressed by an army's vigilance in the enemy's country, and in it saw a moral: "How important that the sentinels be true and faithful. . . . Were we as watchful against sin how much happier and wiser we should be."[71]

As to the nature of the sins he was seeing committed in his soldier flock, Ames did not enumerate. No boy writing home to honored parents admitted openly that he had indulged in liquor, but there were oblique taunts to parents that a boy might, if he wanted, now that he was a grown-up soldier out in the world. Sgt. John Marsh wrote to his sister in late winter that he was considering taking up drinking as an antidote to his deepening loneliness: "I am going to get drunk as a hog just to see how it seems some of these days. The boys seem to feel good when drunk."[72] The use of alcohol in the army, particularly by its officers, had become a genuine scourge. One officer from the Western Reserve cried out against the rampant use of "Rifle whiskey" in a piece published in the Akron newspaper: "The sale of whiskey is doing more to demoralize the army than any other thing that exists. The rebels can ask for nothing more of the Butternut Democrats than to engage in the sale of whiskey to our soldiers, which is the mainspring of insubordination, desertion, and unlooked for disasters."[73] After one battle, an officer was found dead as a doornail on the field. He was carried off and laid in a row along with the rest. When he was rolled over he gasped and sounded far more drunk than dead: "Ben, John, where is my whiskey flask?"[74] The newspapers regularly ran stories of intemperance in the army, with graphic and sometimes even humorous accounts of the how it affected two classes mainly: officers, and enlisted men who happened to be Irish.

The Twenty-Ninth's Fife Major Richard Noonan, alias Fifer Dick, was so proficient with his instrument that one admirer in the regiment said, "He can get all out of a fife that ever was in it, or all that ever could be; and he can put more in, and then blow that out."[75] He entertained the boys by using his fife to imitate every animal in creation, from a canary to a pig. He was claimed to have tricked one of the regiment's Irish soldiers into believing he could get music out of a stick. One of their soldiers wrote the story down, complete with comic dialect, and sent it back to Akron for the amusement of the newspaper readers. To complete the stereotype the writer pointed out that the victim of Noonan's charade had also been "full of the critter," meaning drunk.[76]

In February the men of Captain Fitch's company, who still identified themselves as the Jefferson National Guards, honored him with a surprise testimonial.[77] The Jefferson Boys formed on the parade ground, called Captain Fitch to step up front, and presented him with the gift of a fancy sword and belt. Cpl. Washington Dutcher made a speech in which he pointed out that Company A had yet to lose a man in battle and the thanks for that went to an all-seeing God, and to Captain Fitch for his superiority of command.[78] Fitch responded appropriately by telling them that he prayed fervently that they might never gather together to lament the loss of a slain comrade. The cook ended these solemn proceedings by banging the dinner gong and hollering, "Fall in for pork and coffee." The Boys moved off down the company street and gave three cheers for the captain and three more for the cook.

Home Fires

Back in Akron, Capt. Josiah Wright had gotten his old job back as town marshal and was waging a battle to clean up the town's trash-choked alleys. He finished his published warning to scofflaws, "I wish it to be distinctly understood that I will not have this matter fooled with any more."[79] He continued to perform duties for the men he had recently commanded. Soldier Warren Hall had survived the regiment's battle only to die of chronic diarrhea at Frederick. His remains were shipped home to Mogadore and laid out in his father's parlor. Hall was known for his odd sayings and funny speeches that had lifted the Boys' spirits when they were low, and such a man deserved a fine funeral, and former captain Josiah Wright took charge of its planning. Major Clemmer delivered a moving eulogy, and Maj. Myron Wright commanded the military squad that marched his coffin to the graveyard.[80]

Akron paused to note the passing of its soldiers, give them a proper testimonial, and then forward again full speed to the work of building, and improving itself.[81] Tenants were moving into a splendid new three-story business block at Market and Main, and another three-story brick building had gone up on Howard, opposite the post office, the upper story fitted up with much crystal and polished wood for the use of the Odd Fellows. A newly prosperous citizen had put up a house made entirely of stone, with other palacelike features previously unseen in Akron. Several new churches were going up, indicating that business in the ecclesiastical line was booming along with everything else.

The mood in the army after Fredericksburg was reported to be grim, but the atmosphere in Akron was bright and forward looking. The new retail store of Wesner and Co. featured a showroom laid out to the extraordinary dimensions of twenty-five by one hundred feet, its long rows of glass display cabinets lit by dozens of gaslights. The grand opening was attended by hundreds. The editors of the *Summit Beacon* looked around and concluded that despite the war, there was solid evidence of unusual activity and enterprise in their little city. "Now is the time, while business is good, and money plenty, for our citizens to embark in any substantial improvements which they have in contemplation," and the captains of an emerging order sensed the possibilities and plunged ahead.

A new machine shop, with a work floor as spacious as some farm fields, had gone up near the railroad depot and was throwing smoke and clang out into the street. Drowsy Middlebury, just outside town, had been known for years for its production of stoneware, but even that predictable, handwork industry was transformed. Horses that had walked in circles to move the clay-grinding turnstiles were retired in favor of mighty steam engines that provided power to drive a complex array of crushers and molders capable of producing hundreds of identical vessels per work shift.[82]

Over in Jefferson, men were prospering, too, from the produce of the farm fields, pastures, and woodlots, and the time had come for the village to have a place of its own in which to store its money and see it grow. A meeting was held of the town's wealthier men and plans made to capitalize its first bank with $100,000. The same men who had worked to build the Twenty-Ninth Regiment—Kellogg, Ensign, and Woodbury—were behind this venture and pledged $14,000 from their own purses to see it a reality.[83]

Men might profit directly from the service of the county's soldiers. The government had promised to pay a pension to men who had been sickened or maimed while in the Federal service, and for those who found the red tape too tedious or incomprehensible, men like Samuel L. Fenton, Pension Agent, of Conneaut had opened for business to represent them. He took out advertisements featuring a self-written testimonial stating, "The records of my office prove better and more rapid success therewith, than any other man in this part of the state."

Only one man in the community had devoted himself to a purely altruistic venture, one that seemed true to the county's passion for lifting up the victims of bondage. Reverend Olds had warned his congregation that war was coming so certainly that even the blind could see it. Now, with the slaves freed by the Emancipation Proclamation, he had left his pulpit in Jefferson and gone south to the environs of Corinth, Mississippi, where he was educating contrabands, returning to Jefferson only when donations were needed to fund his project.[84]

Cash-strapped soldiers in their muddy camp in Dumfries read the local newspapers that came to them and could see that those who had stayed home were getting ahead in the game of life. If and when a soldier returned, he might never catch up. Rollin Jones's best friend in the army, Sgt. Allen Mason, imagined that the boys of his village who had not gone soldiering might all be princes by the time he returned. But in the soldier's life, he was gaining things more valuable than money: "I shall be just as independent as they are rich. They can't run over me a bit for I think I am just as good a man as walks the streets of Andover. But we will wait until I get there and see how things run."[85]

Akron took interest in the predictions from the world's fashion capitals as to how a woman's hat should look this spring of 1863. The "sky-scrapers" popular in the previous season were replaced by the porkpie, resembling in shape a cheese, with feathers and clusters of imitation bugs pinned to the crown. In dresses, the edict was against flounces and for gimp braid. Prices for all things had risen and the prices for women's apparel along with them, as one editor observed: "Female gear of all kinds have gone up prodigiously. Hats that used to cost $15 now cost $30."[86]

Older women had no need of such shows of vanity. The soldiers' grandmothers, who were the Reserve's original generation or daughters of it, stuck to the old ways and continued to wear the same simple costume their grandmothers had worn back in Massachusetts: plain black dress, starched apron, and small lace bonnet cinched so tight over the brow that it pinched the face into a perpetually sour look. That severity of dress would pass when they did, and they were passing on these days at an alarming pace. They took the homely entertainments of an earlier time with them. One old man wrote to the newspaper to lament the disappearance of the custom of paring. Young people had once gathered to pass the days of winter by peeling and quartering apples, then crushing them for sauce and cider. That this would disappear along with so many other things seemed assured, with so many young men now gone off to the war and young women spending almost all of their time producing suppers, sings, and entertainments, all to raise money for the Soldiers' Aid Society.

The Reserve's people were encouraged at every turn to dig deep in their pockets for cash donations, to plant double the usual number of rows in their gardens and give the surplus for the good of soldiers in hospitals, and to give of themselves to every project that came along to ease the suffering of the soldiers. The people's hearts were open, and some took advantage. A lady in mourning clothes came into the Odd Fellows rooms in Akron and told a sad story. Her husband had died recently in the Federal service, and to compound her difficulties, her sister had taken deathly sick. While on her way to take care of her she had been robbed. Her husband had been an Odd Fellow, too, and knowing them to be a generous order, she requested "just a little" so she could continue on her way. The men gave her twenty-five dollars. After she left, the benefactors discovered they had been neatly conned. They sent a wire ahead to the authorities in Cleveland, and on getting down from the train, this "female Jeremy Diddler" was arrested.[87]

In early April, the nation's most famous humorist, Artemus Ward, kept a large audience at Empire Hall in Akron in stitches with his pithy stories in dialect poking fun at the foibles of the modern age. His long monologue "Sixty Minutes in Africa" was especially well received.[88] Circuses continued to parade in and out of town. Editors protecting the public morality cautioned Akronites to think twice before taking wives and children to the circus because the clowns had a tendency toward the profane and vulgar, and among the worst offenders was the chief jester and co-owner of the most popular show, Thayer and Noyes.[89]

The majority in Akron had hoped that one earlier town enterprise had fallen, never to rise again, but it resurrected itself and was back in business this winter of 1863. Akron's Democratic Party newspaper had been flattened by the Lincoln steamroller, but with antiwar sentiment being voiced openly now in the wake of the army's semisuccesses and outright failures, all attended by huge losses in men and wealth, it reopened proudly under its new banner, *The Akron Democrat*.[90] In reporting the Federal failure at Fredericksburg of a few weeks before, the editors of the *Democrat* had dared suggest the unmentionable: fifteen thousand Union boys had been needlessly and perhaps criminally led to their slaughter. Lane and Elkins, editors of the *Summit Beacon,* were always on the lookout for local traitors. They took the *Democrat*'s comments as a recommendation that the president be assassinated, and they went for their competitor's throat: "If anything were lacking before to demonstrate the disloyalty and utter devilishness of the conductor, or conductors of the *Akron Democrat,* the contents of last week's issue of that treasonable sheet had dispelled all doubts on the subject."[91]

The officers of the Ohio regiments at Dumfries were well posted on the developing antiwar politic at home, and they did not like it. They put their heads together and issued a joint communiqué expressive of their feelings and had it published in the Akron newspaper:

> The people have divided themselves into two parties, each claiming to have the same end in view—the one sustaining the Government in the determination to fight the contest out, the other opposing the administration and calling for compromise. The latter are traitors—enemies in the dark,—more to be feared than the armed rebels before us. . . . Pretending to be the friends of the soldier, you have declared the army demoralized, the soldiers tired of the war, opposed to the administration, and desirous of compromise upon any terms.[92]

A while later the enlisted men of Company E got into the act. By unanimous vote they composed and had published a similar declaration, demanding their friends at home put a stop to such copperhead organizations as the Knights of the Golden Circle and others who were suggesting that the war should be stopped and the Confederacy allowed to go its way. Speaking in one voice, the Boys of Company E threatened to return to Ohio and put down the copperheads themselves.[93] For his part, Cass Nims said that if it were left to the common soldiers of the opposing armies to settle the dispute, "They would get together and have a drink and let it go at that."[94]

As spring 1863 came on in Virginia, dogwood, crab apple, and a hundred other wild things were "blowing out" with flowers, as the soldiers described it, and the soldier's spirits were lifted. Hooker was planning something big–what, the soldiers did not know—and to get them ready he had ordered a top-down cleanup of the camps and the soldiers who lived in them.

The Boys were spending more time out of their huts than in, purging themselves of winter's accumulation of mud and blacking shoes now that a shine would last more than a few minutes. They polished the barrels of their rifles until they shone like silver, as any proud soldier would who now carried a brand-new Enfield, which all along had been the weapon of their dreams. Here at Dumfries the Twenty-Ninth had turned in their old Belgian muskets and drawn the modern British-manufactured

Tower Enfield. Hooker's army warmed itself in the April sun, cleared its throat of the winter's smoke and soot, and regarded itself.

They were more than 135,000 Union soldiers within a day's ride of Dumfries, and Hooker was going to make good use of them. As soon he took over, he had begun to return the army to a more disciplined routine with drills and inspections. The ongoing battle with the Virginia mud had limited the practice, but with spring on its way, the frequency increased. Soldiers had not seen such attention to military ways since the old days. Back home, the citizens in northeastern Ohio seemed as charmed by Hooker as his soldiers were. For those who had seen a likeness of him, every lineament of his winning face showed that he was absolutely confident of the future. Others, who had seen him close-up were troubled by his weak chin, which suggested a deficiency in fortitude.

Hooker was husbanding the strength of his army, and with the roads dried up, so too was the possibility of a furlough home. Many of the Boys had not been home for almost two years, but if the next big push succeeded, they might all be home by autumn. Cass Nims wrote to his widowed mother, "I think it won't be long before we shall all have everlasting furlough and that is the kind that I want."[95] Some soldiers would not take a furlough even if it was offered for reasons emotional, as Allen Mason explained to his mother, "I was in hopes that I could get a furlough after a while and come home but I guess it is just as well as it is for if I came home it might make me homesick after I come back. . . . The longer I am away the better I shall know how to appreciate home and friends."[96]

Soldiers were allowing themselves to be hopeful again for the army's success, if only just a little. Hooker's plan for the coming campaign would take full advantage of his superiority of numbers over Robert E. Lee. It was a plan that was elegant in its simplicity and audacious in its objectives. He would anchor the rebel army, in place at Fredericksburg, with a large force, while marching eighty-five thousand of his soldiers in a grand maneuver that would take them up the Rappahannock and down on Lee's flank in a haunted, brushy country known as the Wilderness. The logic of it was indisputable: Lee would have to fall back to Richmond, or give battle to two Federal forces, either of which was large enough to overpower him. Once the two parts of Hooker's army linked up, Lee's destruction and the fall of Richmond were guaranteed.

The Giddings Regiment was now 450 strong, four times the number that had marched away from Cedar Mountain.[97] The paroled prisoners, including Wallace Hoyt and Rollin Jones, had returned earlier in the winter, and sick men who had been away for months were now back with them. However, as soon as one leak in the army was plugged, another opened.

Dr. Jonathan Letterman, medical director of the Army of the Potomac, sent inspectors out from Washington and found that enlisted men were being given medical discharges for the most trivial of complaints. Examining boards made up of three surgeons from each brigade were established, in theory, to give each applicant a thorough physical and discharge him only if he were found completely unfit for service. But the tightening came too late to stop the flow of men out of the regiment. While they were at Dumfries, thirty-two enlisted men got discharges for disability, and twice that number applied. One of the original Homer Boys, William Cooper, wanted out—an effort that was not supported by his captain, Russel B. Smith, as John Marsh reported in a letter to his father: "Would you believe it. Cooper had the assurance to Send pension papers to Capt. Smith to be certified to, he said that his back was hurt at the Winchester fight, and he had been unable to do anything Since, *poor fellow.* He sent fifteen P.O. stamps to prepay the return, but Capt. Smith sent his papers back unsigned, and postage unpaid."[98] Cooper persisted through other channels and got his discharge. Other soldiers succeeded on even flimsier grounds. Pvt. Sidney Wilder was discharged in February for a condition of the scalp thought bothersome to his company.[99]

Easter Sunday came and went without any observation in the regiment's camp. Chaplain Ames had planned an outdoor service, but a surprise snowstorm canceled it.[100] Instead, he went down to the regimental and brigade hospitals to read scripture to the afflicted and pray with them. A soldier whose acquaintance he had not yet made died that day, and another anonymous boy was on his way down.

Ten days later an order came down from the very top: get into marching order and be ready to step off at sunrise. They'd received orders like this in other times and at other places, but this one varied significantly. This time the soldiers were to cook and have stowed in their packs rations enough to last them eight days—five packed in the knapsack and three in the haversack.[101] Added to his load were the sixty rounds of cartridges each soldier was ordered to carry on his person.[102] There were complaints about leaving a place in which they had invested so much to make comfortable. They had just completed their brand-new and best-ever huts and were loath to leave them.[103] The Boys wondered where they were headed and, more important, how they would get there. The roads were beginning to dry but were still without firm shore or bottom. Still, everyone got down to work, and by the next day they were packed and ready.[104]

It was five days more, and then not until most of that day's light had been burned, that they finally got on the road in a cold rain. At last, they were leaving this winter's camp and the Boys "felt finely," which in their idiom meant spirits were sky high, and they cheered themselves as they slogged along.[105] Their destination was unknown to them, but that mattered little. Wallace Hoyt got off a last-minute letter home to his mother and assured her, "We will undoubtedly turn up somewhere and then you will hear from me."[106]

18

Saving the Life of the Army

THE BATTLE OF CHANCELLORSVILLE, MAY 1–3, 1863

"Some Place Unknown to Us"

Sgt. Allen Mason wasn't a soldier who was inclined to worry too much about his welfare. Like most of the Boys, he was trusting in fate, and his experience to this point had shown him that he could survive most anything the soldier's life brought his way. He had been wounded at Kernstown and had earned a reputation for fearlessness at Port Republic, where he had made a one-man charge against a line of Louisiana Tigers and come away with their battle flag. On the last morning of the coming battle, his best friend in the regiment, Rollin Jones, was hunkered down close to him in the rifle pits, not far below the crossroads at a place called Chancellorsville. The rebel gunners were sending grapeshot, railroad spikes, lengths of chain howling inches over their heads.[1]

So Jones was surprised when Mason leaned in close and confided that he was absolutely sure he would not survive the day.[2] The odds of a soldier getting killed just had to be increasing with each additional minute spent here, and this fight had been ratcheting upward for the past two days and was likely to go far over the top of anything any of them had ever seen before. Doubts like these flitted through every soldier's mind at such times, but the first heat of combat usually cooked them off, and a soldier paid them no more mind. Now these doubts had gotten a grip on Mason, and they would not relent.

The rain made mud and slowed their march the first day out of Dumfries.[3] The next day was cool and pleasant, and they cheered themselves as they marched along, crossed Aquia Creek, and paused for the night near Stafford Church.[4] Armies had contended for ownership of this neighborhood for going on two years, and it looked the worse for wear. What remained showed that the Union soldiers who held it most recently were plain vandals, as well as scroungers. It was said that Stafford Church had hosted the wedding of George Washington, but it had been ransacked for anything of use or value, and someone had even climbed into its cupola and made off with its clock.[5]

They pulled over to the side of the road to let General Slocum and his escort gallop past. That night, as the soldiers buttoned together the halves of their shelter tents, they could hear the friendly sound of locomotive whistles and the boom of heavy rail cars coupling, two miles away, down at Aquia Landing. They expected to move out again the next morning, but foul weather made movement impossible and the men lay low in their little tents. They would remain in this camp for several days, waiting for the roads to dry and for army planners to perfect arrangements to fit tens of thousands of men onto the roads and in the right order. From a high hill, the Potomac was in view, and to the south, the hazy hills opposite Fredericksburg, where Lee's army had spent its winter. Pending orders, they played ball and read the newspapers.

Rumor back in Ohio claimed that Hooker had banned newspapers from the camps out of fear the blatant leaks of intelligence they contained might fall too easily into the hands of the enemy, with whom the soldiers freely traded. Pvt. Franklin Potter wrote home to assure his parents that newspapers were still available the camps, but the soldiers did not read them because they balked at paying the ten cents charged for them by peddlers.[6] Professor Thaddeus Lowe's balloon could be seen from their camp, and every soldier who saw it wrote home to tell he had seen this marvel of this modern age with his own eyes.[7]

Potter wrote to his parents from here to let them know that Captain Fitch was getting better and that they should expect to see him in the neighborhood before too long; and he thanked them for their gift: "I received the sugar you sent us the night before we left Dumfries and it was very thankfully received and you may know it tasted good too and you have my thanks and best wishes and I hope I may live to see you all once more and eat warm sugar with you."[8] From the might of the Federal army he could see assembling around him, there was a fair chance this campaign might succeed, and his fond wish be fulfilled.

They drew new uniform parts here while at Aquia Creek, and with their shining new rifles and new faces, the regiment looked as good as it ever had. And they had a new decoration to fasten upon their uniforms. Hooker had come up with a scheme by which the corps and division of every soldier in the Army of the Potomac could be seen at a glance. The men of Slocum's Twelfth Corps would be identified by a five-point star, each division within the corps distinguished from the others by its color. Geary's division would wear a white star. The Twenty-Ninth Boys drew their white cloth star and sewed it to the front piece of their kepis. Many things in the future would change, but this most recent mark of their affiliation with Geary's White Star Division would not.

Chaplain Ames missed another Sunday opportunity to preach. He was too busy with work delegated to him by the regiment's officers: issuing clothing, helping the men clean up for inspections, and keeping the regiment's records up to date.[9] They had hoped on leaving Dumfries that the season of sickness was over, but Ames was being called on to read words over the graves of the departed as much as ever. The regiment's sick had been loaded into wagons and were making this journey with them. Sgt. George Sherbondy of Akron died in the camp at Aquia Creek, and another boy was on his way down. Sherbondy left behind a younger brother. Pvt. Charles Sherbondy of Company D was an imaginative boy, but his greatest asset would be his durability. He would live far into the coming century and would be the regiment's last survivor.[10]

The whole army seemed to be in motion now, coming in and marching out. Every day for a week, one outfit after another had started out on the roads leading west. While they waited for their turn, the Boys caught up on their letter writing. As always, mail from home was slow to reach them and came by circuitous ways. Franklin Potter got a letter from home that by some mystery of the army mail system had been routed through New Bern, North Carolina. Wallace Hoyt got off a last letter to his parents before stepping off into what lay ahead. He'd already said his good-byes to them when he wrote to them from Dumfries, so this one was written as much to allay his anxieties as theirs.

> Sunday eve, April 26, 1863
> Aquia Creek, Va.
>
> Honored Parents,
>
> As we march tomorrow morn at sunrise I don't know as I shall have a better time to write you a line. . . . There is business ahead and the boys are ready . . . and undoubtedly we shall have some hard marching if not fighting before I have a chance to write to you again. As my bedfellow is teasing me to go to bed I will close. If you can read this you can read hyroughgliphics.[11]

They got on the road again at four in the morning on April 27, and this time their march would be direct and zephyrlike. Sergeant Marsh described the great, hopeful army on the move:

> We started at 7 o'clock a.m. for some place unknown to us. It was a pleasant morning, sun shining brightly, birds singing sweetly, and Regt. after Regt. moved off with colors flying,

keeping step to the inspiring music of fife and drum. It was a sight worth seeing, the long columns of marching humanity, the thousands of glistening bayonets, the gaily caparisoned horses and richly draped officers, the shining brass cannon, the flaunting banners.[12]

They turned south and east, toward Falmouth, before going into camp at a farm owned by a man named Blackburn at a place called Locust Hill.[13] They had put sixteen miles under their belts in the afternoon alone, even though each man now carried a load heavy enough to kill a mule.[14] No soldier had ever carried this much weight. The army had learned from its mistakes, one of which was that a moving army was soon jammed to a standstill by too many wagons. Hooker's planners scientifically calculated the maximum weight an average soldier could heft, and found it to be forty-four pounds.[15] On this march, wagons would be left behind except for those needed to transport medical supplies and ammunition. Wallace Hoyt commented wryly, "Last year we loaded our knapsacks into the wagon, this year we loaded the wagons into our knapsack."[16]

They had brought plenty of ammunition. Slocum's corps alone was hauling eight hundred thousand rifle cartridges.[17] Despite the load, stragglers on this march were remarkably few.[18] The Boys had just slipped out of their packs when they were ordered out on picket duty. Soldiers cussed their bad luck and took up their posts. At his outpost, Sergeant Marsh was too weary to stay awake. He made himself a bed of pine boughs and fell into a sleep as sweet as a poet's song, undisturbed by thoughts of rebels.[19] Two hours before sunrise, they were hurried back onto the road. They passed the turnoff to Fredericksburg and kept to the road taking them further up the Rappahannock to a crossing called Kelly's Ford.

General Hooker was here in person at Mount Holly Church, three miles from the ford, and the Boys were heartened to hear of it.[20] They had clicked off twenty miles that day and went into camp at sunset with the entire Twelfth Corps camped around them. Two soldiers of their brigade, both unknown to Chaplain Ames, had collapsed and died during the march. Such things were now a matter of course.[21] After hardtack and coffee, the soldiers wrapped themselves in their blankets, with the expectation that on the morrow Lee would dispute their crossing of the river just below and a great battle would be fought.[22]

They were rousted from their sleep at three hours past midnight and set to tramping down to the river before they'd even had a chance to make coffee.[23] They strode into their assigned position within Geary's division a few miles out, and within ten miles of starting, they joined the thousands of Slocum's corps. The soldiers worked out the kinks of a long winter and eased into the swinging stride of the rout step. Above the river crossings, they combined with the Eleventh Corps. The whole army sang "John Brown's Body" as they flowed south to the Rappahannock. Every soldier who wrote of this march was impressed with the perfect energy and organization of it.

Some soldiers felt like foundered horses under the heavy load, but on they went without decrease in speed.[24] About ten in the morning General Slocum rode up to the regiment and ordered them to deploy to the right of the road as skirmishers.[25] A few rebels resisted their advance but fell back without harm to either side. They made Hartwood Church by midmorning, and for the first time in many months the heavy boom of cannon was heard, coming to them from somewhere over the river.[26] They moved down to cross over the Rappahannock.[27]

The Eleventh Corps crossed on the pontoon bridge, while the Twelfth Corps covered them, and once safely over, the Eleventh Corps took up position to cover the Twelfth Corps's crossing.[28] From here down to their destination, the Twelfth Corps would lead the way, with Geary's division out in front of it and Candy's brigade out ahead clearing the road.

The rebel army was not there to block them, and once safely over the river the soldiers winked at one another, confident that they'd gotten the jump on the rebels. Two prisoners being marched to the rear warned the Boys that they would smell powder for certain if they tried to get over the next river.[29] Late in afternoon they wound down to the banks of the Rapidan River at a crossing called Germanna Ford, where their cavalry captured eighty rebels at work on a bridge. The prisoners admitted they had been told Hooker was coming, but they had not believed it.[30] Soldiers of the First Division had already begun wading across, and some were carried away in the current and drowned. Geary ordered his division to a stop until a footbridge was constructed of material the rebels had piled up. By dark the soldiers were bedding down on a rise on the opposite bank. The rest came down into the light thrown by torches stuck in the bank at the foot of the bridges and passed back into the dark on the other side.

The Giddings Boys got across the Rapidan and went immediately to sleep where they halted.[31] It had been a day for the history books. In a single day's march they had crossed not one but both the rivers that had been costly barriers to the soldiers of earlier campaigns. They awoke with the realization that they were deep into Lee's side yard.

They marched southeast and got onto a road leading east, toward Fredericksburg and Lee's army. The road was made of thick boards, giving the foot a bounce with every step. Geary's division had the advance and Candy's brigade was out front of the whole army using this road.[32] Mounted rebel skirmishers pestered their flanks, but they pushed them aside dismissively and moved forward through a country of tangled brush and close-set trees, anxious to be out of it. Midmorning, the Twenty-Eighth Pennsylvania, Candy's brigade, ran into the only real resistance thus far, and one of their favorites was shot dead by a rebel officer leading mounted rebel scouts.[33] His death was avenged on the spot when the rebel Captain Irwin was tumbled from his saddle by a well-aimed rifle shot and his horse and personal belongings taken by the Pennsylvanians as trophies.

Crossroads

To the men of the regiment now marching upon it, the name of this road would be enough to locate in memory the battle into which it led. The Orange Turnpike carried them through a marshy, brush-choked land of tea-colored creeks known locally as the Wilderness. Up the road a few miles, they came to a clearing, and in the clearing was a large brick tavern with many chimneys, columned porches, and a dozen rooms for wayfarers through this lonely country. It struck the soldiers as odd to see so grand a place in such a wild country. The owner had named the place and the small collection of buildings around it Chancellorsville, in honor of himself. The Twenty-Ninth Ohio's part in the coming battle would take place within five hundred yards of this building, and sometimes within a hat's toss of its porches. The common soldiers who fought in sight of it would not know it by its proper name until afterward. Chaplain Ames referred to it as the Brick Tavern, Eight Mile House, the Big Brick House, or the Inn. It stood nearly on top of the intersection of the Orange Plank Road, which continued on east into Fredericksburg, and the road coming up from the south out of the deepest parts of the Wilderness, and continued north up to United States Ford on the river. The soldiers who fought here would know this intersection as Chancellor's Crossroads.[34]

The head of the Twelfth Corps's columns arrived at this crossroads at two in the afternoon.[35] According to SeCheverell, Candy's Brigade was the first Union outfit to reach this vital waypoint.[36] John Marsh recalled the scene as they came out of the brush and into the clearing: "They [the rebels] were working on their fortifications here, and intended to stop our advance here, but the Yanks came down on them like an avalanche, killed eight of them, captured nearly a hundred and the balance ran away. General Joe Hooker seems to have surprised them completely as all the prisoners say they never expected us on this road."[37]

Thousands of soldiers of the Twelfth and Fifth Corps came up the road behind them and began stacking themselves into an area around the house no more than three-quarters of a mile square. The Eleventh Corps, with its heavy concentration of German-speaking soldiers, marched up and took position on the right of the south-facing line of Hooker's army, back west along the Orange Turnpike. Two more army corps had crossed the Rapidan above them and were presently paused no more than an hour's march north. By John Marsh's optimistic calculations, there were now one hundred thousand of them on this side of the river.[38]

George Gordon Meade, commanding the Fifth Army Corps, had arrived at the Chancellor Inn ahead of Slocum, and when the Twelfth Corps's commander rode up, the normally reserved Meade was delirious with excitement. They were squarely on Lee's flank, and if they continued to push east a few miles more, they would roll up whatever force Lee could field against them. Most important, one more hour of marching and they would be out of the Wilderness and into a more open country where the huge army could better maneuver. Meade's spirits fell when Slocum told him that he had just gotten an order from Hooker: all of them were to halt here and regroup.[39] The big push could wait until morning.

The army crammed itself onto the ground around the manor house this last evening of April 1863, and sensing they'd stolen a march on Lee, the soldiers were happy. Slocum deployed his soldiers into battle lines and moved the mile-long line of his corps off the Orange Turnpike and into the low timber below the road, its left end anchored below the Inn, and the rest parallel to road leading back the way they had come.[40] Candy's Brigade took up a line astride the Plank Road on the far left of Slocum's line.[41] They camped in the same order in which they had marched down here, which would make it easy to get everyone up and moving when they took up the movement toward Frederick again the next morning. The Boys settled down for the evening in a patch of timber with the Plank Road and the Inn at their backs.[42]

On this eventful day, Chaplain Ames had passed a milestone in his life's experience. He had watched a skirmish and seen men firing weapons with the intent to kill. He was anxious to see his first battle. So, too, were nearly a third of the soldiers in the Twenty-Ninth, for whom the sights and sounds of combat would be wholly new.

A last look around before the light went out of the day and the Boys could see the thousands of soldiers like them clustered within sight of the Chancellor Inn. A sense of "general hilarity" prevailed that night, as one soldier recalled. The army sang and joked as it went about camp chores, chopping firewood and preparing supper.[43] The lowering sun caught the bayonets of legions more taking their places in lines that reached all the way back to the river crossings. Artillery batteries pulled up and wheeled into their places, scouts with intelligence to report and officers seeking orders rode up to the Chancellor Inn, and then off again at a full gallop. A long hike with a heavy load seemed a small price to see such a spectacle.

The soldiers of the White Star Division were just bedding down when an order came down from General Geary.[44] Soldiers set to work felling trees and clearing the brush in front of them, opening up a field of fire. There would be much to remember about this battle, odd, small things some of them, but perfectly representative to the man who stored it away. The steady rumbling sound made by several hundred men of the Twenty-Eighth and 147th Pennsylvania Regiments using their bayonets as impromptu hatchets that night stuck with Rollin L. Jones for the rest of his life.[45] Others went to work out in front of their lines stacking and weaving a shoulder-high brush barrier called an abatis. Any attackers would lose momentum when they came to it, making easy targets.

Every soldier not assigned to cutting trees and brush in the Pioneer Corps, under command of the Twenty-Ninth's Lt. Edward Curtis, started excavating a trench along the entire division line.[46] Lacking shovels, the soldiers dug with swords, tin plates, boards, spoons, and even bare fingers.[47] Geary directed that the larger logs be piled into the road at the crossroads, effectively barricading it. Geary posted his artillery batteries on a hardly perceptible swell 250 yards southeast of the Chancellor Inn, from which they could sweep the roads to the south and east.[48] When the work was done, they considered themselves "pretty-well fortified."[49] No one expected they would fight here, and they were leaving in the morning anyhow, but Geary was a cautious man who did not like surprises, so they dug. They had got all the way down here without detection, and prospects were they would improve upon that come sunrise. Those men otherwise unemployed rolled into their blankets for a few hours' sleep with the knowledge that the whole of the rebel army was no more than five miles to the east.[50]

It was already showing patchy gray light in the east by the time most of the Boys finally finished chopping and digging. Hooker's plan for this day was to send his army east toward Fredericksburg in a three-pronged movement. Meade's corps would push east along a road that followed the river above, Sykes's division of Meade's corps would move out on the Orange Turnpike, and Slocum's corps on the Plank Road, which looped south and east of the crossroads through a matted, miasmic landscape before it rejoined the turnpike. A few miles out from here, on more open ground, Hooker's men would spread out into a several-mile-long battle line, at which point Hooker would arrive and oversee the denouement of Robert E. Lee.[51] Then, as Hooker said, the rebels should turn to God for pity, because he would have none for them.

Recalled

The Boys awoke, stretched, and rummaged through haversacks for a breakfast of cold salt pork, crackers, and creek water. They were anxious to get back on the road and take up the same fast clip that had brought them here. But the sense of hurry-up dissolved with the morning's fog, and soldiers lounged, mending gear and jaw-boning. Some began letters home, which was an activity usually taken up in idle times. Half the day's light had burned before they got the order to form up and continue the march that had been suspended the afternoon before. It was spring as yet, but the day had grown very warm, even for this Southern neighborhood.[52]

They headed out on the Plank Road, Candy's men taking their place in the column today as reserve to the rest of the White Star Division.[53] A short way out the brigade reached a woodlot, and they spread out in line of battle with the right resting on the road.[54] Minutes ticked off the clock. The soldiers stood and sweated while regiments were jockeyed into their assigned places. Then the whole line started noisily forward into the timber. Soldiers struggled in the thick, dim interior of the woods to keep the elbow-to-elbow alignment required for the advance of a battle line. Some thickets could not be penetrated at all and the scrub split the line into fragments. A soldier could see that if he stopped to get his breath, he might never catch up with the regiment, and if he were not very careful, a soldier could wander right into a concealed enemy before he even knew it. Worse yet, if fighting began in any of these boggy snarls and a man was hit, he might sink out of sight and never be found.

Candy's men marched only a few rods when the skirmish line out ahead drew the fire of a rebel battery blocking the road.[55] The Twenty-Ninth was ordered off the road and into the woods. The soldiers waited there in the spring woods expecting the enemy's main force to come up and give battle, but he did not come.[56] After an hour of waiting, they moved up to support Brig. Gen. Thomas Kane's brigade of Geary's division, which had been more hotly engaged with the rebel skirmishers. At the precise moment they reached Kane, a courier rode up with an order: everyone was to disengage and return to the lines at the crossroads they had departed little more than an hour earlier.[57] Lee had not risen to Hooker's bait and stayed put at Fredericksburg. He got the bulk of his army on the roads to Chancellorsville and was presently preparing to block Hooker's further approach. A mile above Geary's division, the noise of it unheard through the dense thickets, Sykes's division, Meade's corps, had marched less than three miles when it ran into full battle. Sykes was driven back, but he rallied his men, and continued to drive ahead, getting so far forward that he had to back up to align his advance with Geary's division below him. The leading elements of Geary and William's divisions had run into trouble of their own when two miles from their starting point they encountered a substantial portion of Lee's army spread out to receive them on the Orange Plank Road. When it sunk in that Lee had not fled, but had turned and confronted him, Hooker lost his nerve and ordered everyone back.[58]

Emboldened by the fizzled Federal advance, the rebel skirmishers harassed Geary's men all the way back to the crossroads. It had taken an hour and a half at most to move as far as Kane's brigade, but it took four hours to get back to their rifle pits, what with the stopping and starting again to load and fire at the rebels now sifting through the trees after them. Coming out, the skirmishing had been desultory, on their return the tempo of rifle fire quickened to a steady popping. To add to the Federals' discomfiture, rebel artillery began to assault them. Nathan Parmater had been under artillery fire at other places, so he had some expertise in the matter. He characterized the rebel cannon fire on the way back as "severe."[59] Only one Twenty-Ninth soldier had been hurt, when struck by a shell fragment, but the shelling succeeded in scattering the Federals from the road and required they form up all over again before continuing their backward march.[60] The Twenty-Ninth got back to the exact place they had started from at five o'clock, with the daylight beginning to weaken, and took up their place in the dug line.[61]

As dusk an event occurred that mystified and irritated the commander of their brigade, Col. Charles Candy. Without orders from him directly, nearly half his brigade got up and moved off in the direction of Capt. Joseph Knap's battery, posted near the trenches in the woods to the left of the Plank Road.[62] Who had done it and why would be clear momentarily. On their return to the crossroads, an hour earlier, sharpshooters had been sent out into the woods to feel the enemy and keep his skirmishers at bay. Now they came back toward the lines on a dead run. A full rebel regiment had chased their skirmish line back into their works and were coming at them on the Plank Road as coolly as if they were marching on a parade ground. Geary had sensed the enemy might make a rush to take his guns.

THE BATTLE OF CHANCELLORSVILLE, MAY 1–3, 1863

Several hundred muskets, borrowed from Candy, and Knap's guns, roared all at once and broke the rebels, sending them drifting back into the darkening woods and leaving a swath of dead and wounded men.[63] During the artillery firing, one of the guns discharged prematurely and exploded, killing and wounding several of the Seventh's soldiers. The accident was attributed by Col. William Creighton of the Seventh Ohio to carelessness of the gunners of the Fifth U.S. Artillery.[64] Further, the Seventh's historian blamed a section of Battery F of the regulars for depressing their guns so acutely that shells plowed into the Ohioans, causing great consternation among the soldiers and nearly a riot.[65] The Twenty-Ninth soldiers were up from their places and moving to take part in the defense of the battery two hundred yards to their left when the order was countermanded.[66] The attack had already been repulsed.

It was suppertime and the Boys would have liked their coffee despite circumstances, but with the enemy so close, fires were disallowed entirely.[67] They went to work deepening and widening the trench line.[68] Those who were not digging or dragging brush lay down behind their barricades with rifles ready and pointed into the darkness.[69] It was obvious that the rebels were employed in the same way as they, and not very far from their own lines.[70] They could hear clearly the rebels scraping at the dirt and cutting trees. The heaviest of the skirmish fire died out by ten o'clock, but gunfire flared throughout the entire night as rebel skirmishers probed Geary's line for weak spots.[71]

They had marched out that morning expecting there would be business to do when they met Lee's army. Instead, there had been a turnabout ordered from high up before they'd had a chance at him, and their day had amounted to little more than the debating of skirmishes, punctuated by the emphatic thud and flash of cannon shells. The Twenty-Ninth had filled a reserve role this day and that was all.[72] Chaplain Ames knew it would be his job to minister to those who would go down in what was headed their way. Before retiring to his blanket, he wrote in his diary, "All await a grand opening of one of a series of the greatest Battles ever fought."[73]

Bloody Day, Afternoon, May 2, 1863

The soldiers were still wiping sleep from their eyes when a brigade-size column of rebels strode rather nonchalantly out of the woods south and east of the crossroads, and by appearances they were headed toward the center of Geary's position.[74] Gunners of the Fourth U.S. Battery sent grapeshot wailing over the heads of the Boys in the trenches.[75] "No one [was] hurt but they made us hug the ground close you bet," was how John Marsh summarized this first action of the second day.[76] The rebels moved off, and the Boys lay in the lee of their trenches, intensely studying the tree line across the clearing. Most of the forenoon passed, but no more rebels were seen.

Just before midday the enemy made his appearance again. Col. Thomas Clark got the regiment up and out of the breastworks and into the woods to the left of the road, but elements of Geary's division had gotten to the scene ahead of them and driven the rebels off.[77] The Twenty-Ninth Ohio returned to the rifle pits without anyone having fired a shot.[78] Deprived of the road for the time being, a heavy column of rebel infantry was seen a short time later defiling into a clearing no more than a half mile away. This time, Lt. Edward D. Muhlenberg's battery took a turn, and their fire left dead and injured rebels scattered across the surface of the Plank Road.[79] At midafternoon an order came for the Twenty-Ninth and Seventh Ohio Regiments to pile knapsacks and prepare to move out along the left of the Plank Road.[80] Important observations had prompted this order.

To their right, along the Federal line, General Sickles had received intelligence that another, much larger column of rebels was passing through the forest far below the Plank Road. Through the thickening haze, several columns of enemy infantry and artillery were seen moving along a ridge to the south a mile and a half away. Sickles concluded that Lee was in retreat, and he ordered his Third Corps forward, between the Twelfth and Eleventh Corps, and out into the Wilderness to cut the enemy's train.[81] Slocum ordered Geary to form up his division and move out onto the Plank Road on a reconnaissance in force to discover what the rebels in front of him were up to. Like Sickles, Geary believed he was going forward to cut off an enemy *retreating* toward Gordonsville and away from Chancellorsville.[82] As far as the Boys knew, they were going out simply to clear the woods along the road of enemy skirmishers and sharpshooters.[83]

The Twenty-Eighth Pennsylvania led the way, with the Seventh Ohio right behind and the Twenty-Ninth Ohio behind the Seventh. The Pennsylvanians made contact with the enemy and were persuaded by the volume of fire slamming through the trees at them that the whole rebel army was blocking their way. Some of the Pennsylvanians lost their courage entirely and set out for the rear, which took them through the center of the Twenty-Ninth Ohio's line, breaking it temporarily.[84] As was their nature, the Seventh Ohio shouldered the less stouthearted aside and moved up, with the Twenty-Ninth right behind them.[85] The skirmishing grew hot here in the woods bordering the Plank Road, producing just as much noise and smoke as full-scale battles on other fields. The Seventh Ohio drove the rebels back, tree by tree.

It had taken no more a march than five hundred yards from the crossroads for them to determine that the rebels were not retreating. Geary's blood was up and he was willing to give the rebels as much battle as they might wish. Knap's battery came up on his order, unlimbered, and sent grapeshot howling down the road, taking off heads and arms and dropping rebels where they had stood. The rebel infantry recovered and directed their fire onto the guns, and Geary ordered Knap and his gunners to withdraw.

The rebel infantry in this place outnumbered the Seventh, and with the numbers beginning to tell, the Twenty-Ninth went in to give them a hand. As they came up, the boys of the Seventh cheered them and waved their hats. In concert, the two regiments drove the rebels back.[86] Geary would have fought the battle along this line if allowed to do it, but an order came down from Hooker himself that everyone disengage and get back to the crossroads, and quickly. The Twenty-Ninth and Seventh Ohio Regiments were too closely locked with the rebels to make an immediate withdrawal possible, even if they were inclined to obey the order. They stayed at their work until they were nearly out of ammunition.[87]

During the two or three hours of that long afternoon, Capt. Myron T. Wright had been ordered to take his Company D forward of the rest to pinpoint the enemy and draw his fire.[88] They slipped forward through the brush out ahead of the regiment but had gone only a short way when they came upon two full rebel regiments. Wright dispatched a runner to Geary with the report of what they had found, while he and his Boys stood still as stones behind trees, close enough to the rebels to hear them conversing.[89] The enemy moved off and Wright's company let out their breaths. They were only thirty-four in number, a full two hundred yards forward of support, in a woods that seemed to be the thoroughfare of an aggressive enemy. They were continuing forward when excited whispers came back from the Boys out front for everyone to stop and get down.

They had walked nearly up to the muzzles of camouflaged rebel cannon. Alongside the battery were a thick line of infantry, as much as a brigade of them standing atop trenches of their own. Wright's Boys had not approached this close without detection, and the rebels raised their muskets and began shredding the undergrowth with lead. Wright ordered his men to return fire and they did, with telling effect. Above the noise, Wright could hear Federals on the road hollering the order to withdraw. No sooner had they reached their regiment than the rebels rose and fired a volley, which the Twenty-Ninth and Seventh Ohio's answered. The most intense fight of the day engulfed them and caused the battle's first significant quantity of wounds in the Twenty-Ninth.[90]

As the afternoon ran down, Wright and his men made their way back to their lines with the fire of an advancing rebel line coming up behind them. Musket balls were raining down, but Wright's soldiers did not hurry. They stopped every few yards to fire back. On reaching the trenches, they stepped calmly into them and took their position, displaying a coolness that made Wright proud to know he was in the company of such men.[91]

Geary's reconnaissance had established several critical facts: the rebels were out front of them in sizable numbers, well dug in, and intent on staying there.[92] He would have to save his thanks to his men for what they had just done for some more peaceful occasion, because within minutes of settling into their places in the line the world around Chancellorsville exploded.

Fiery Heavens: Night, May 2, 1863

The smoke and dust had made a magnifying lens of the atmosphere, and the sun hung red and gigantic above the Orange Turnpike, to their west. A mile back in that direction, where the Eleventh Corps held the right of the Federal line, hell was breaking loose. At first, the noise of it could not be heard, but then it came on, like the sound made by the collision of locomotives. The foot traffic that had been seen passing across the Federal front earlier that day had been Jackson's wing of Lee's army. Jackson had marched his men through a country thought impassible for large bodies of troops and brought them down hard on the unprotected end of the whole Federal line, held by the Eleventh Corps. The Federal soldiers, Germans many of them, were not expecting thousands of rebels to come yelling like maniacs out of the trees just as they were getting their suppers, and when they did, the "affrighted Dutchmen lit out, many of them not even stopping to fire their guns."[93] No commands or imprecations by their officers could stop them once they started. On came the terrified mass of thousands, up the Orange Turnpike and alongside it, and their stampede now posed more of a threat to Geary's men than the rebels themselves. John Marsh described the effect of this tidal wave sweeping headlong into them: "Back they came past our position officers and men mixed up in a shameful rout: in vain we tried to halt them, the enemy in our front hearing the confusion poured in a volley, and that hastened them on; nearer and nearer came the tide of battle on our right, balls began to whistle near us, shells to explode around us, and the shouts of the enemy were in fearful proximity to us."[94]

Not every boy in the Twenty-Ninth maintained his calm in the face of the hysteria. Cass Nims confided in a letter home, "Father I felt like running when the 11th Corps broke . . . such butchery. The Rebbs would cut them down like grass when they run."[95] Cass overcame the instinct to flee along with the others, pulled his cap down low, and waited it out. Jackson's men were coming up fast behind the Eleventh Corps refugees, stopping only to fire volleys into their backs. The road west to the point of crisis was jammed, making any sensible response to Jackson's drive more difficult. Two or three regiments of Kane's brigade in the trenches nearer the breech were swept along in the flood, but the soldiers of Candy's brigade stayed put.[96] The Eleventh Corps soldiers who had kept their muskets fired them wildly, and horses still wearing their saddles but without riders plowed through Candy's line, injuring one soldier in the Twenty-Ninth.[97] Jackson was coming on hard, and Slocum's corps braced for the shock.

Colonel Candy ordered his officers to corral those who could be stopped and put them into his own lines. Most had thrown away their weapons and were useless.[98] Gen. Alpheus Williams was in command of Slocum's other division, and had been in line to the right of Geary. Williams's men had left their entrenchments and gone to the relief of Gen. David Birney, Sickles's corps, who was struggling to check the rebel juggernaut, and when Williams's boys returned to their old line, they found the right end of it in possession of the rebels.[99]

The flood tide of the wild throng passed. The fear of being stampeded out of the safety of their lines by their own men subsided. The Boys had hardly regained their composure when rebel bullets began streaking down the length of Geary's line.[100] The enemy lightning bolt would strike them next, and they prepared for the impact.

Jackson's onslaught ran out of steam and daylight by the time it came up against the soldiers of Sickles's corps, and for a time this evening large-scale infantry fighting waned. The sun went down and its afterglow lit the top of the battle fog, making the dark darker and the sense of gloom deeper.[101] The Giddings Boys lay behind their barricades, rifle hammers at half cock, waiting for the other shoe to drop.

Soon after it grew dark, the Twenty-Ninth got orders to move into entrenchments to their right, which took them nearer the fighting. Clark found room for seven of his companies in their new position, and the remainder marched back to their original line in the woods south of the Orange Turnpike.[102] Rollin Jones was in one of the companies that moved up to fill in a gap in the line. Even as a very old man he would remember clearly the eerie feeling of filing into the dark, deserted earthworks, the air electric with danger, the soldiers who had recently occupied them vanished as if by magic; whether overrun and captured or fled for their lives, no one knew.[103]

As darkness tried to descend, the rebels struck units of Sickles's corps, which had pushed far out from the Federal line on Slocum's right earlier. As John Marsh wrote of it a few days later in a letter home to his sister, "Then commenced one of the grandest scenes I ever imagined or dreamed of." Not a man who witnessed what was about to transpire ever forgot it, and all of it took place within a half mile of the Twenty-Ninth's position, giving every soldier who was there a ringside seat to the most terrible artillery fire ever seen on the continent. Sergeant Marsh wrote:

Our forces had massed their cannons on a range of hills in fair view of the place I stood, and as the Rebs came on fifty cannon opened on them all at once, while a long line of flame burst from the tens of thousands of rifles. You have heard the noise one cannon makes, Ida. Just imagine fifty pieces on our side, and an equal number on the enemies, fired at least three times a minute, and fifty thousand rifles joining in chorus. But the tumult increased, for our reserve of fifty cannon come up and joined the fray. The earth trembled with the roar of one hundred & fifty pieces of cannon, the whole heavens seemed all ablaze with the flashes.[104]

If such a thing were possible, the unsettling keening of the rebel yell was heard lifting above the general tumult. The Federal gunners off to their right, at previously tranquil places named Hazel Grove and Fairview, fed double loads of canister into their guns, taking down whole rows of rebels with every pull of the lanyard. Sickles's men were all mixed in out there with the rebels in a frantic, confused combat garishly lit by musket fire and artillery explosions. John Marsh stood and watched it all. No mortal could live beneath this kind of pounding, but the rebels apparently could, and on they came.

The Giddings Boys climbed atop the breastworks to get a better look. They were spectators to something terrible and yet grand, and their hearts stuck in their throats.[105] The movements of the battle line could be clearly seen by the long lines of light generated by musket fire as one side pushed the other only to be pushed back in its turn. The muzzle flash of the big guns illuminated ghastly tableaus of rebel infantry coming up to the mouths of the guns and disappearing. An hour before midnight the convulsions relented and the big guns went quiet. Soldiers off in the dark continued their private combats, but after a while even those ceased. Occasionally a gun boomed and the Boys studied the full arc of the shot with grave self-interest. The trajectory of each round was carved in the night sky by its burning fuse. It paused at its zenith bright as the evening star and then dropped down onto its target.

At midnight lines of walking specters came out of the trees and rushed Williams's line.[106] Capt. Clermont Best opened on them at close range with his thirty-four guns. It was delicate work, and imperfect, what with the opposing lines so close, but it succeeded, although at the cost of great suffering to Williams's boys. Oddly, this far into the night, a wind came up and pushed at the smoke where it lay stuck in the blasted trees. The moon broke through, lopsided in its phase, rags of smoke trolling across it. Several soldiers were startled by the fact of its appearance, amazed that the laws of nature still applied after such a battering. The whippoorwill called out in the dark woods and to the soldiers he seemed to say, "Why we, Hooker, why we Hooker."[107]

A new sound came up to the boys behind the breastworks. There were wounded men lying thickly on the ground out in the jungle of roots and vines to the west and south. The lines were too closely set now, and skirmishers too active, to risk leaving the protection of the trenches to help the thousands of crying men. In such a place, rest was elusive. The fighting on Geary's right where Williams's division was holding on continued until 3:00 a.m. But at last the battling burned down. Marsh, unconscious of the fact that it was now May 3, wrote, "Thus ended the 2nd of May. I wrapped a blanket around me and lay down in the Rifle pitts hoping to get some sleep as for three nights I had slept but little, but picket firing, false alarms, and other things kept me awake most of the time."[108]

The Giddings boys had been here for just over two days, under fire through most of it in some fashion, but the full weight of battle had yet to sweep them. Nathan Parmater looked back over this day before trying to rest: "Although there has been some hard fighting done today, yet it is merely called skirmishing in such a large army."[109]

An hour after midnight the Twenty-Ninth Ohio's turn came to serve picket duty. The soldiers picked for the detail crawled out forty yards into a no-man's-land of flattened brush and saplings with blown-out tops. "We were so near the Rebel pickets we could hear every movement. Here we lay flat on the ground watching the demonstrations of the enemy until the dawning of another day of blood and death."[110] Disoriented rebels stumbled out of the darkness and into the lines of the White Star Division and were escorted to Geary's headquarters for interrogation. After questioning them, Geary concluded that the character of the coming contest was disclosed.[111] Tomorrow there would be work to do.

THE BATTLE OF CHANCELLORSVILLE, MAY 1–3, 1863

Sunrise, May 3, 1863

Some soldiers seemed unaffected by their proximity to the maelstrom. John Marsh had been able to sleep for a full hour before the Twenty-Ninth Ohio was called into action, and he awoke feeling refreshed. Most had not slept a wink in three nights. With the sky in the east just beginning to lighten, rebels in wide-massed columns stepped out through the curtain of trees and acrid fog to their right, got within rifle range, and opened fire. Stonewall Jackson had been severely wounded the night before, and Gen. J. E. B. Stuart had taken command of Jackson's wing. This early morning he sent them smashing against the line of the Third Corps and the line of Williams's division of the Twelfth Corps, holding the line to the right of Geary.

The Federal line no longer looked much like it had the night before. Jackson had hammered it into a new shape. Viewed from above, it now resembled an upright basket, with Slocum's corps holding most of the bowed-out bottom, facing generally south, with Geary's division posted in the lower right corner, a third of a mile below the crossroads. Jackson's wing of Lee's army had reorganized during the night, and at first light they came at the Federals in regiments three deep. At the same time, Lee's wing was assembling in the brush beyond Slocum's line, with the intention this day of joining his wing with Stuart's, and together they would drive Hooker back into the Rappahannock. The way it was shaping up it would be the job of Slocum and Sickles to stop him, and they formed their soldiers into blocks two and three regiments thick to do it.

Most of the Twenty-Ninth's soldiers had spent the night out front of the trenches, behind the abatis.[112] The rest passed the night forward of even that exposed point. They had been sent out into the pitch-black woods to listen for rebel movement. Now, with massed rebels surging against the Federal line on their right, everyone out front of the trenches ran for it, hurdled the last barricades, and jumped down into the rifle pits.[113] No sooner had they gotten settled than the sergeants yelled, "Pile knapsacks." They stripped themselves of unnecessary gear and got ready to fight.[114] The next half hour was full of the ungodly racket of many thousands of firearms going off on their right. Then the battle swept up the road and enveloped them, too.[115]

Presently, the entire field above them and to their west, from the Chancellor Inn out to the tip of the salient Sickles had pushed forward the day before, rocked and smoked as the rebel legions moved in for the kill, and Hooker's men disputed the attempt.

The Giddings Regiment had come into this fight with only one field officer, Thomas Clark. The next man in the chain of command by merit of his seniority was William T. Fitch. But he had been too ill to march with them. Capt. Wilbur Stevens was next in rotation. Clark had fallen ill on the way here from Dumfries, and Stevens had managed their march. Clark had been too ill to lead yesterday, too, and it was Stevens who had led the regiment on the reconnaissance in force out on the Plank Road, during the nervous hours of the Eleventh Corps's rout and the terrible artillery fire of last night.[116] Clark was in command again this morning as the crisis loomed, and he ordered Stevens to move three companies into a gap in the trenches between the Sixty-Sixth Ohio and the 147th Pennsylvania.

Clark marched the remaining seven companies up the line to the right and nearer the contracting epicenter of the Federal line. They had been ordered to support the New Yorkers of Gen. George S. Greene's brigade of their division.[117] Williams's division, Slocum's corps, had melted away, leaving a dangerous gap to Geary's right. Greene spread his men out to hold what was now the open right end of the Union line. He ordered the Ohio boys who had come to his aid into a shallow trench, with the instructions to cover him.[118] They would remain here for two long hours, troubled more by the raking rebel artillery than rifle fire.[119] The Giddings Boys began taking casualties, but they were not alone in their duress.

Greene's soldiers fought hard, but the corps standing between them and the brunt of Stuart's drive were leaving their lines and moving off with their many wounded and away from the fighting. Another crisis was developing, this time on the left, and Greene ordered the Ohioans back to their division to attend to it.[120] Geary's own line was now under direct threat, this time from the south, where Lee's wing of the rebel army was seen massing in the clearings a half mile away, closing the gap between his army and Stuart's.

At the Guns

Col. Thomas Clark later stated that one of the regiment's two wings had been ordered back to support Knap's battery. Knap's battery was normally assigned to Geary's division, and thus it is understandable that any guns posted in Geary's sector were regarded as belonging to Knap. Clark's companies had been sent to protect guns, but they were not likely the guns of Knap's battery. At three that morning, Knap had been ordered to move his guns to the west of Slocum's line, where Stuart's wing of Lee's army was getting ready to advance, and he stayed there for the remainder of the fighting.[121] For two days and nights Geary's boys had enjoyed the protection of a thick knot of guns dug in around the crossroads, which included all of Knap's dozen guns. Now, most of these had been sent away to avert the crisis a half mile to the west, and in a while all that would remain to dissuade the rebels now massing astride the roads aimed toward Geary were four guns of Muhlenberg's Fourth U.S. Artillery, four pieces of Capt. John T. Bruen's battery, and two of Best's.[122]

Clark may have been confused about the affiliation of the guns he had been sent to defend, but he was crystal clear in describing their location. They had been "placed to rake the Plank Road leading *from* the Chancellor House [Inn]."[123] That was about the same position held by Knap's battery in the preceding two days. The gun crews rounded up what little ammunition remained and began firing both south and west, everyone setting themselves for what was clearly becoming the final phase of the battle of Chancellorsville. Clark spread his men around the guns with orders to hold this ground despite the cost.[124] Rebel artillery fire plunged in and around them, and fighting the instinct to bury their faces in the dirt, the soldiers loaded and fired their rifles.

Each shell seemed to make its own distinctive noise. Some flew with a basso howl that could be felt deep in the gut, some chugged and lurched like a steam engine, and some made a piping sound like a fife. Each of them was a severe test of the nerves. One Ohio soldier in Candy's brigade who was there that morning near the same guns the Twenty-Ninth was protecting considered the possible defenses against an artillery shell and concluded, "Folks say a fellow can dodge shells if he keeps a sharp look out & and so he can maybe, if it don't come very near him, but I made up my mind that I didn't want to trust the safety of my head to any skill in dodging. The best thing one can do is to lie low and take up as little space as possible. I don't believe many of us stuck up very far above the ground."[125] Sgt. E. F. Smith of the Twenty-Ninth Ohio found that getting low to the earth was no guarantee of safety. Myron Wright was lying next to him when he became unnaturally still. Smith had been struck square in the forehead by a shell fragment; he died an hour later.[126] They had been under heavy artillery fire before; most recently down below Culpeper Court House last August, but in John Marsh's estimation, what they were being subjected to now "beat Cedar Mountain blind."[127]

During his few private moments back at Dumfries, Asst. Surgeon Elwood P. Haines liked to think of his life back in Ohio, with its Sundays spent in church, and evenings at home singing with his wife. This day there would be no vacant moments for wistful reflection. He had been on leave home, and rejoined the regiment on the afternoon they arrived near the Chancellor Inn. He had been along on their march out toward Fredericksburg, the hardest part of which for him had been wading through bogs. Only one Twenty-Ninth Ohio soldier required his skills that day. The next day, May 2, a few more needed his help, although none of them was dangerously hit. This morning, the wounded began to stack up as soon as the sun cleared the low trees, and Haines became very busy. He would struggle far into the night to keep up with the inventory of dangerously hurt boys.[128]

Back at the crossroads, Geary's division held their line in the woods just south of the Orange Turnpike. It appeared to Geary that they were hemmed in by fire from three sides and in imminent danger of being cut off completely. The Federal army that they had seen fighting off to their right since the time the sun came up seemed to have gone away. The right end of his line ran a hundred yards in the direction of Fairview, and after that the Federal trenches were disturbingly empty, except for the corpses of soldiers and the wounded who had not been carried off. Rebels now held this part of the line, and they stood up, loaded, and fired endlong into Geary's line. If this continued, the right of his line would be turned and Candy's brigade destroyed.

Just then, Geary received orders to reform his line at right angles to the south-facing line they'd held, with one end anchored at or close to the Inn. They would at least have a chance to face their tormentors. Geary had just finished adjusting his line when Hooker himself stepped down from the porch at the Inn and ordered him to return his soldiers to their trenches in the woods south of the road.[129] This would be one of the last orders Hooker gave to any of his commanders that morning.

As the Boys started out to reoccupy their original line of entrenchments, knots of mounted officers with pennants flying that identified them as the headquarters staffs of the Third and Twelfth Corps rode into the clearing west of the Inn, followed by infantry, all of the procession moving off the field.[130] Low on ammunition and completely out of it in some cases, it was senseless for them to fight on, and Hooker had given them permission to withdraw. Their departure left everything to Geary's right in the hands of the enemy. By the accounts of the generals in charge of it, the retreat had been orderly. This was not an impression shared by the common soldiers. Sgt. John Kummer of Company G had gotten glimpses of Hooker's army moving off behind them along the Orange Turnpike, and in the clearings bordering it, and the word he chose to describe the huge retrograde was "unmanageable." Lawrence Wilson, the Seventh Ohio's historian, who was there to see it, characterized the general atmosphere: "Pandemonium and wild panic reigned supreme."[131]

Capt. Clermont Livingston Best was serving as Slocum's chief of artillery. He had dug in his guns last night at Fairview, just below the Plank Road to the west of the Inn, putting the gunners and those infantrymen he could round up to work throwing up waist-high, horseshoe-shaped walls around each gun, placing them side by side facing west. He'd held on this morning as long as he could and was still firing even after the Third and most of the Twelfth Corps had departed the field. The rebels had gotten in close, sighted their own guns on Best's position, and began dropping horses, gunners, and their officers. Best concluded there was nothing left for it but to give the order to limber up what remained and withdraw.[132] The rebels rolled their own guns up and turned them, and those Best had left behind, in Geary's direction. Solid shot and canister began ripping along the length of Geary's line.

Hooker was "leaning" against a porch column at the Chancellor Inn, which was an oddly relaxed posture, given that there was no longer anything between him and Lee's army except for the divisions of Geary and Maj. Gen. Winfield Scott Hancock. Hancock's men were putting up a fight around the Inn. Geary's right had been clearly turned by this time and was being bent back upon itself by continuous hammer blows.[133] A cannon shot smashed into the pillar against which Hooker was leaning and knocked him senseless.[134] After regaining consciousness, he, too, left the field.

Maj. Gen. Darius Couch rode forward to the left of Geary's line and found Geary there, striding up and down through his trenches, swinging his sword above his head, indifferent to the bullet storm. Geary hollered above the roaring, "My division can't hold its place; what shall I do?" Couch had seen with his own eyes that the enemy had the right of Geary's line, and having just come from Hooker, he knew there would be no help coming. There was nothing Couch could offer except to say, "I don't know, but do as we are doing; fight it out."[135] Around midmorning, an undersized, patched-together brigade of Couch's corps, Hancock's division, under command of Col. Edward Cross, took up a position out on the Plank Road south and east of Geary. Cross must have found the going too hot. He and his remnant brigade were there so briefly that his presence went unnoticed by Geary or anyone in Candy's brigade.

Geary had started the day with three brigades. When the order had come for Geary to get his division out of the forward trenches and reformed into a line that faced in a more westerly direction, with his right end to be anchored at the Chancellor Inn, the brigades of Kane and Greene moved back to the Inn, but they did not stop there. These two brigades simply kept on going, taking themselves off the battlefield and out of the fight. By the time Geary discovered their errant movement, they had strayed too far to recall.[136] Geary had lost two-thirds of his division. All that remained to him now was Candy's brigade, two regiments of Greene's brigade, and six pieces of artillery.

A year earlier, Geary was defending Thoroughfare Gap when, by his thinking, he had been on the verge of being overrun by a rebel force many times greater than this own. He had burned all his supplies and hurried away toward safety before all his men could even be called in. The rebel threat had proved to be the construction of his imagination, and critical colleagues had ridiculed him, calling the affair Geary's Last Stand. Now, with almost every other Federal force departing the field as fast as they could, he was about to face another, and few would ever dispute its authenticity.

Last Stand

At eventide the day before, there had been five army corps on the field up and down the Orange Turnpike. All that remained of that mighty army were a few cut-up brigades. In these last hours of the battle of Chancellorsville, they stood alone against Lee's army.

Hancock was leading an undersize division of the Second Corps in defense of a line north of the Orange Turnpike, struggling to hold off the enemy advancing toward the Chancellor Inn from the west and beginning to overlap the right of his line. While Geary was getting his division into a new line faced to the west as ordered, Hooker came up to him and ordered him to do nearly the opposite: get back to the trenches below the Plank Road. It was at this point that Greene and Kane's brigades marched off the field and into the woods north of the Inn.[137] Below the turnpike, the single brigade remaining in Geary's division hurried back into the trees toward their breastworks—ostensibly to slow the advance of the rebels coming up the road from the south. Candy's brigade double-quicked it back to the rifle pits and prepared to take on Lee's army. They did not stop at the rifle pits but leapt over the outer lip and kept on going into the fire zone between the trench line and the abatis, clearing it of rebels who had gotten through, pushing those back who were coming up to it. Only after winning this breathing space did they return to the trench line.

The soldiers knew they were in for it. Their position was far forward, and with most of the Federal army leaving or already gone, there would be no support coming their way. However, there was at least one happy discovery when they filed in behind the familiar breastworks. There were Union boys already there, and the Sixtieth and 102nd New York Regiments waved their hats and hurrahed a welcome. The New Yorkers either had not gotten the order to leave when the rest of Greene's brigade had moved back toward the Inn or were too full of fight to obey. When the Twenty-Ninth Ohio arrived, the New York volunteers were firing as fast as they could load, and the targets were innumerable with the rebels coming on now in waves right up to the trench line, and in some places already occupying it. This remnant of Greene's brigade had actually taken several dozen men of the Twelfth Georgia Infantry prisoner, along with their battle flag.[138]

Three rebel batteries totaling nearly twenty guns were posted less than a mile away. They now concentrated their fire on what remained of the Federal artillery at the crossroads and on the soldiers in the trenches below them. The guns slammed shot and canister through the brush, tearing Candy's line from end to end. Like an iron bar hammered over the edge of an anvil, Candy's line was bent back upon itself. It took on the shape of a V, with the point aimed south, in the direction of the newest threat. At some points in the line, soldiers were now firing their muskets with their backs nearly touching. The rebels reasonably supposed that too few men remained to oppose them, and confident of that, they advanced to annihilate the last of the Federal resistance.

Despite the bludgeoning the armies were giving and receiving, humanity remained. Union litter bearers crept out in the no-man's-land between the lines and carried wounded comrades and rebels alike out of the fire, and back toward the Chancellor Inn, where they were collected for transportation to the field hospitals. Inside the Inn, army surgeons were busy amputating limbs and throwing them out the sitting room windows into piles in the side yards. Dead men lay under canvas tarps in long rows outside the house.

Cass Nims had been detailed to carry the wounded. He was not a large young man, and the work of it nearly killed him.[139] David Y. Cook of Company G would not leave his comrades despite a dangerous gash in his shoulder and their insistence that he take himself to the rear.[140] Some soldiers were grabbed by the rebels during the close-in fighting. Others seemed simply to have vanished into the smoke. Albert Hall had been working along with the rest of Company G when a piece of shrapnel banged against the thick leather flap of his cartridge box. He patted it in gratitude and said, "You have saved my life." A second later, while his friend was still smiling at his remark, Hall disappeared.[141]

The oldest private in Company G, German-born John F. Weidle, age thirty-eight, was struck in the leg, and his friends concluded that he needed immediate medical attention. Sgts. Wilbur F. Chamberlain and John Kummer volunteered to carry Weidle to a hospital set up in the woods behind the Inn.[142] They made it safely through the shell fire blanketing the fields and into the woods. When they arrived at the hospital, rebel shells began falling through the trees, punching holes in the building's roof and walls, and setting it on fire. There were still sixty boys inside too hurt to walk. Kummer and Chamberlain got as many of them out as they could, but the fire got too hot for them and there was nothing more that could be done. There was no time to stand and fret, with the rebels now no more than thirty rods from the Chancellor Inn. Kummer picked up one of the dozens of wounded soldiers lying outside on the ground and departed. Chamberlain, who had been standing next to him a moment before, was nowhere to be seen—captured, it was supposed, given the nearness of the rebels. The other possibility was that he had gone into the house again and not made it out.

The fighting now became furious along the shrinking line of Candy's brigade, and soldiers who had run out of ammunition slashed at their attackers with bayonets. Rebel battle lines advanced right to the brow of the pits, some so close they threw down their guns and surrendered when finding Candy's soldiers still there with rifles pointed in their faces. The rebels had seen what looked like the entire Federal army retreating back toward the Inn and were surprised that anything this far forward was still manned. Smoke had settled in so thick that soldiers from neither side could see each other until they had closed to within a few yards of each other. Disoriented men used the direction of bullets squalling past them as a weathervane by which to aim—that and the rolls of orange inside the smoke canopy that identified yet another rebel line.

The battalion-size regiment Geary had brought into the war, the Twenty-Eighth Pennsylvania, had drawn the lucky straw going down to Cedar Mountain and guarded a telegraph installation in the rear while the rest of the brigade suffered. They had made a reputation for themselves on the bloody day of Antietam, back in September, where the Pennsylvanians lowered their heads and went forward in a bayonet charge that checked Jackson's advance near the Dunker church. Over forty of them had died to secure their regiment's good name, and five times that number had been wounded.[143] After that, five of its companies were transferred to a new outfit, the 147th Pennsylvania. Both regiments were fighting here this morning. The Twenty-Eighth Pennsylvania was faced to take the brunt of the rebel attacks and was suffering in proportion. Geary was standing next to the Twenty-Eighth's commander when Maj. L. F. Chapman was spun around by a bullet and died at his feet.[144]

Geary's line was taking fire from three directions, and some bullets were whining into them from what seemed like behind. To meet the most pressing threat, on their flank, the line was extended at a right angle to their original works, and the soldiers took up firing in three directions at once.[145] Whole rows of rebels were going down, so close to them that it was difficult to miss. "We came close enough to the Rebbs so that they could be reached easy enough with our bayonets and they stood their ground," was how Cass Nims explained the face-to-face nature of the fighting to his father, with a slight tip of his hat to the courage of the enemy.[146]

So much now depended on the steadiness of their officers, and none of the Twenty-Ninth's faltered, including Capt. Wilbur F. Stevens, and Colonel Clark thanked him afterward in his official report. Capt. Edward Hayes moved up and down the line, giving encouragement and calming the anxious.[147] Back at Camp Chase, Buckley would not endorse James Treen's election as captain of his company because he did not feel him competent to handle it. But here, Captain Treen demonstrated the sort of coolness under fire that Buckley himself was known for. Treen had two of his sons in this fight with him, and the bullet holes that perforated his coat and pants were adequate evidence to his soldiers of how willing he had been to risk everything for the good of his men. Although twenty-two-year-old George Hayward was only a sergeant, he had command of Company E this day. No one thought to document his acts of bravery, but on a day when acts of courage were routine, his bravery was singularly conspicuous, and for it he was given a battlefield promotion.[148]

Candy's brigade had shown uncommon pluck this morning, but such things could hold them to this place only so long in the face of the storm. In his official report, Geary stated that General Slocum ordered him to retreat. He went on to say that Candy's brigade retired by the left flank as neatly as if on the parade ground.[149] With the memory of these final minutes still fresh, Col. Thomas Clark wrote his official report of the battle. In it, he recalled that *no* orders to retreat from Geary or from anyone else were passed to them.[150] The officers in the front line made that decision on their own.

Colonel Creighton of the Seventh Ohio, Lt. Col. Ariel Pardee of the 147th Pennsylvania, and Col. Thomas Clark huddled together in the line of their tiny redoubt and considered their predicament. Many of the soldiers were disabled and could no longer fight, and the enemy was pouring in, with hundreds more coming up behind. This council of officers concluded, "It seemed worse than useless to maintain our positions longer."[151] Creighton stated that they had only considered withdrawing after taking stock of their situation: they were completely unsupported.[152]

"Fix Bayonets! Charge!"

Getting out of this hot place could be far more hazardous than staying put, if they were not careful about it. To safeguard their withdrawal, the officers ordered an improbable maneuver. The officers yelled up and down the line, "Fix Bayonets!" and then a few seconds later, "Charge!" Yelling like madmen, everyone rose up, climbed over the breastworks, and rushed toward the enemy. The rebels may not have been materially harmed by this charge, but they were dumbfounded. The minute it took them to recover was just what Candy's men needed.[153] The Boys withdrew from the woods, firing as they went, and into the narrow cleared field south of the Orange Turnpike. They paused, got back into battle line facing the rebels, and steadied themselves. Then an order came down the line for another bayonet charge, and they lunged forward. By some accounts, they charged not once but twice more from this position before pulling back onto the turnpike.[154] There might have been more charges than that; it all happened so quickly and the confusion had been so great, it was hard to say. Nathan Parmater tried to put a number to it in his diary entry of that evening, the excitement of the day still running high in him as he tried to make sense of it:

> Candies Brigade was on the left center and had to fall back as the enemy was getting in our rear, so after an hour of shelling we fell back from our rifle pits, but when the enemy came charging upon us at the left of our works Candies Brig. charged them back, and they rallied and charged us back, this was repeated several times but as they were gaining ground on the right, we had to fall back and form a new line, it was by quick time and under a heavy shower of iron hail that our Brig. escaped being taken prisoners.[155]

Charles Candy was not a man to spend too many words describing any event, however grand. He said only that upon their return to the breastworks the enemy set upon them immediately in overpowering force. His men were going down fast under a raking fire but giving as much as they were taking. When the time came, they made an orderly retreat, pushing the rebels back with their own counterattacks, buying time until what remained of the guns at the crossroads could get off safely. Once on the turnpike, they lay down to the left of where their artillery had been hoping to hold the rebels off a few moments longer. Shells exploded on the planks, sending wood shrapnel flying and convincing the survivors that to stay here meant capture or death.[156] Those who got out first took the shortest route directly past the Chancellor Inn and into the woods above it, where they rejoined the brigades of Geary's division that had preceded them. Others, including the boys of the Twenty-Ninth and Seventh Ohio Regiments, were blown north and east by the storm and into the cleared field east of the road that ran back up to the river and opposite the Inn. At the moment of their fallback, the rebels had surged up to the Inn and were firing into their flank. There were fewer than a hundred Union soldiers of what had once been Hooker's invincible army within sight of the place.[157] Once across the open field, they got into the woods paralleling the road leading up to U.S. Ford, and there they hoped to find shelter.[158]

The final moments of the Federal defense of Chancellorsville were compacted into a world of fire and confusion that ran from the fields surrounding the burning Inn to the section of trench line held by Candy's boys, below the crossroads. The gray men came up now in lines and files decorated with the flags of several rebel regiments, all angled forward, and surged into the clearings within sight of the Inn, as the fire of dozens of rebel guns cleared the terrain ahead of them. The question of which Union outfit had been last to leave the field would be debated in coming years, but hardly with the kind of public passion that had attended the argument over which regiment had taken the stone wall at Kernstown. Kernstown had been a Union victory after all, while Chancellorsville would go down as a reverse, and there was little to crow about in defeat.

Major General Hancock watched the fighting that rolled up and down Geary's line with understandable interest. Geary was protecting his flank. Hancock saw his mission clearly: face his division both east and west from the Inn and keep a corridor open above Geary's single brigade, by which it and any other Federals who had not yet departed could make a fighting retreat and get off the field. In Hancock's words, Geary's resistance had been "stern, but unsuccessful," and Geary had been forced to retire.[159] As to the time of Geary's withdrawal, Hancock said only that it had been "subsequent" to his receipt at ten o'clock of an order to begin withdrawing his own troops from around the Inn, and an hour later Hancock's withdrawal had been completed and his division had taken up a defensive line a half mile north of the Chancellor Inn. The time of his withdrawal was completed by Hancock's watch—11:00 a.m.[160] By Hancock's reckoning, his soldiers had been the last to hold the field against the rebels. Certainly, Hancock had no intention of staking a claim for this distinction for his own men, while diminishing the valor of others. He may have simply been mistaken.

Two of Geary's brigades had left the field by ten o'clock as a result of confused or errant orders, or without any at all. Candy's brigade had not, and by the accounts of soldiers who were there with him, they did not retire from the battlefield until *after* almost all of Hancock's soldiers had departed. SeCheverell took the consensus of memories of officers who had been at Chancellorsville that morning. He reported in his history that when the Twenty-Ninth Ohio passed near the Inn on their way off the field, it was already in possession of the rebels, and that there were not one hundred other Federal soldiers of any command in sight of it.[161]

Col. Thomas Clark wrote two reports concerning the Twenty-Ninth Ohio's actions in the battle of Chancellorsville, and both were published, which suggests the compilers of the *Official Record* considered them noteworthy. He stated in both reports that every outfit except Candy's had left the field when, finding themselves nearly surrounded, they grudgingly fell back, firing as they went.[162] John Marsh wrote to his sister Ida while the memories were still fresh, and he stated, "The 29th changed front to the right and charged down on the Rebs making them skedaddle back at double quick, followed them a short distance, and then fell back to our old position, found *every Regt except ours had gone,* so Col. Clark ordered a retreat."[163] Marsh may or may not have been correct that the Twenty-Ninth Ohio Infantry had stood all alone against the rebels, but in those desperate moments it may have seemed that way.

Colonel Creighton, commander of the Seventh Ohio, was a hard, relentless fighter and a fastidious reporter of the plain facts of battles in which his regiment fought. He stated in his official report that it was eleven in the morning when the Seventh Ohio *and* Candy's brigade withdrew across the cleared fields east of the Inn and into the woods north of the road, where it began to lose yet more men.[164] As to the time of the Twenty-Ninth's withdrawal, Nathan Parmater wrote in his diary that evening that it had occurred at noon, which was the same time given by Colonel Clark. Neither Clark nor Parmater were suggesting that it had been literally noon. It is unlikely that either man had had time to pull out his pocket watch and note the exact time, but the commonsense understanding of the term *noon* places the time closer to twelve o'clock than the midmorning time of prior to ten o'clock reported by Hancock.

"Oh, 'Twas Sammy"

On gaining the woods across from the Inn, the survivors of Candy's brigade paused for a moment, but there would be no rest here. With the remnants of Federal resistance cleared from around the Inn, the rebel gunners concentrated their fire on the woods into which the last vestige of Hooker's army was getting away. Shells began crashing through the trees, bringing down limbs and setting the brush on fire.

The Giddings Boys had sustained a dozen casualties in the battle of Chancellorsville prior to this moment, most of them in the movements to and from the breastworks. It would take them no more than half an hour to pass through these woods, but the majority of their seventy Boys hurt or killed at Chancellorsville went down here in the trees, where terror reigned.[165] Capt. Myron Wright and his soldiers were moving along as quickly as they could when a shell exploded close by. Wright turned his head to see if the shell had caused injury. "The sad expression upon the faces of his comrades, each exclaiming, 'Oh, 'twas Sammy!' told the esteem they bore him. He uttered no sound or moved a muscle; an instant before he was a living, rational man, but now the pure spirit of the brave man."[166]

Samuel Shanafelt, age twenty-eight, was from Stark County, Ohio, and had been with the regiment since the preceding autumn, but he had made a name for himself as a man whom friends could confide in and rely on for good counsel. This was his first and last battle. With death falling all around, and the rebels on their heels, Sammy's body could not be carried along, and he was left where he had fallen. Later, Wright applied for a flag of truce so he could go back and recover the remains, but he could not get permission.

Cohesion had been maintained while they fought their last action in the entrenchments, and in their dropback to the Orange Turnpike. Once into the woods however, individuals and small groups were chipped off the regiment by the confusing terrain and the cascade of falling shells. Sgt. Charles F. Waldron of Company F and another Twenty-Ninth Ohio soldier had become separated from the others. They came across a stream, and knowing it would likely run into the Rappahannock, they followed it. At around two o'clock they came into a clearing in the forest. A house stood within it, and near the house stood a man in military uniform. By the time they got close enough to see he was a rebel, it was too late. He told them to halt and surrender. Waldron looked around, hoping to see some avenue of escape, but there were other troopers of the Fourth Virginia Cavalry there too, with horses tied up nearby ready to run Waldron and his friend down. The rebel hollered a second time, "Throw down your arms," and this time Waldron and his friend stuck the muzzles of their Enfields into the dirt to show they would not resist. A few more Union soldiers wandered in and were captured. The whole group was started on their way to the rear, where a stay in a Richmond prison awaited. The rebel who captured Waldron was a sergeant too, and appeared to be about Waldron's age, twenty-two. As he marched his captive along, the rebel looked as sad over Waldron's capture as Waldron was himself, and said finally "Well Sergeant, this is hard." Waldron comforted his captor, "It is one of the fates of war."[167]

Chaplain Ames had observed combat for the first time during the skirmishing on the way here. What he had seen in the days following was an altogether different animal—terrible, of course, but also sublime.[168] He was on his horse on the night of May 1, riding from one part of the field to another. He found a campfire burning in an open field at three in the morning and lay down to sleep. He was up early the next day and went down to the regiment. In spots, the fighting sizzled like water drops flicked onto a hot griddle, and men began to go down under minié balls and cannon fire. Then he rode away from the fighting to a Twelfth Corps field hospital north of the turnpike not far above the Inn, where the surgeons and attendants were doing a brisk business, and there he found real work to do.

Around sunset, artillery shells began to rock the hospital house from its foundation, and although it was getting dark, the staff broke down the hospital and moved everyone off to the north, beyond the reach of the rebel guns. On the morning of May 3, all the chaplains of the Twelfth Corps met to plan their own campaign, and Ames was assigned duty at the new hospital. The wounded began pouring in as soon as the fighting welled up. He stayed at his work until the rebel guns found this hospital, too. Ames wrote in his diary, "At daybreak rebel shells came flying thick and fast for a few moments through the Hospital Camp, causing a panic. Well and sick hastened to get away. One was killed. The effort to get out of range was too much for many."[169] Ames and the others returned when the shelling subsided and got back to their work. Then this house, too, began to quake with explosions. They packed up again and crossed to the far bank of the Rappahannock. Ames was not a military man, but from the medical department's leapfrogging back toward, and finally across, the river, it was clear the Army of the Potomac was once again getting the worst of it. As to the effect of seeing helpless men subjected to this compounded misery, Ames said, "I felt it seriously," which for a self-contained man was an expression of heartbreak. The soldiers of his regiment had seen enough of misery here to last a lifetime.

Any Twenty-Ninth Ohio soldier who paused for a second at the crossroads before entering the woods was within sight of the Inn; some had passed close enough perhaps to feel its tremendous heat. The once fine building was coming down. Fire started by rebel shells had eaten the floors, and without their support, the roof and then the upper walls tumbled in. The last stragglers who had hidden in the cellar to escape the perils of combat had fled, but there were dozens of wounded trapped inside. The Inn had descended into the inner ring of hell and was taking its occupants down with it. Close by, dismembered horses screamed and injured soldiers were seen trying to drag themselves out of the burning woods. Those who did not make it were caught by the brush fires, their location marked by screams and the popping explosions of unfired cartridges on their belts. The rebel cavalry had already moved in to round up the Union refugees.

Thousands of rebels collected near the burning Inn. Robert E. Lee came up into the clearing and his soldiers cheered and threw hats into the air. Hands reached forward to touch the flanks of his famous horse, Traveler.

The soldiers of Candy's brigade followed the course through the woods taken by the other brigades of Geary's division when they left the field. The route was not difficult to trace, populated as it was by retreating soldiers who had been slowed by the difficulty of carrying wounded friends and by men too badly stricken to be carried who had been left behind. A minié ball had shattered the knee of Cpl. Warren Wilbur of Company I, and he could not get away on his own. John Marsh was determined that Wilbur not fall into the hands of the rebels: "By coaxing and threatening I got help enough to carry him to a ravine which I thought would shelter him from the shells, which filled the air in all directions, but it was not deep enough to do any good. I made up my mind that it would be impossible to get him away, he weighed over two hundred, and could not help himself in the least."[170] The remainder of Marsh's letter was lost as it was passed down the family line after the war, so the rest of Marsh's journey off the field is a mystery, except that he survived it and got Corporal Wilbur out. Wilbur survived the trip into Washington, where he was put in an army hospital, but he died two weeks later.

The separated parts of the Twenty-Ninth Regiment collected somewhere in the woods and began to march. An hour later, they came upon the balance of their division. They halted and waited two hours to allow those who had gotten separated to come in. Lee's army might be coming up at any moment to finish them, but Lee's men were as exhausted as they, and Lee did not follow. Soldiers slept standing up in the ranks, or squatted when possible, until an hour before midnight. The White Star Division shook itself out into columns and marched north to within a mile and a half of the Rappahannock and into the line of defenses Hooker had ordered prepared. May 3, 1863, came to an end.

Cold, Hard Rain

Hooker's army was still on Lee's side of the river in a belly-shaped line with its back to the Rappahannock. Among them were thirty thousand soldiers still fresh as a daisy, having seen little fighting as yet.[171] No one knew for sure whether another fight, perhaps the real battle, would take place here, and whether all that had gone before had been only a preamble. But Hooker had had enough.[172] There would be no more battle for now. Lee had planned to push his advantage, but word came of the severe fighting to the west of Fredericksburg, where Maj. Gen. John Sedgwick was attempting an impossible linkup with Hooker, and Lee turned his attention in that direction. By the unhappy luck of the draw, the Twelfth Corps was assigned a place in this fallback line closer to the river crossings, which meant that they would have to stay and cover the retreat of everyone else before they, too, crossed over.

The Boys rested until four the next afternoon, when they were ordered, along with the Fifth Ohio, to reinforce Kane's brigade, already installed in prepared trenches. The rebels were in plain view on the other side of a field, working on lines of their own. They could hear the occasional dull snapping of picket fire, but compared to what they'd just been through, Nathan Parmater was impressed by the stillness.[173] Some of the soldiers began to notice that they could no longer hear properly, nor would they ever. The shelling had been too much for their ears. Geary ordered them to get to work strengthening their trenches, which, based on recent experience, meant the higher-ups anticipated an attack.[174]

A cold rain had began to fall, grew violent, and continued without letup for hours. The trenches filled, immersing exhausted boys in an ice-water bath and wetting the charges in loaded muskets. The Boys dried their weapons and loaded fresh cartridges. Cold followed the rainstorm, and the soldiers shivered in wet wool suits with neither sun nor fire to drive away the chill. The rebels were just out front on the other side of the clearing, but neither side was anxious to take up the fight again.[175] Favor smiled on them as midnight approached on May 5, and Parmater reported this blessing, and the discovery that followed, in his diary.

> May 6—We lie down last night very wet and most of the boys have no blankets or tents. At eleven we were ordered to keep still and after standing and nearly chilling to death for an hour we were allowed to build fires and warm and when we came to look round we found that nearly all of our forces had left and then we were informed that we were to cover the retreat across the river which we did soon after daylight.[176]

The army had packed up and gone during the night. The Twenty-Ninth got on the road leading north and slogged up to the river crossing. As Candy's brigade lined up to cross on the pontoons, another brigade tried to cut in front. Thomas Clark, always bristly over proper observance of military protocol and fair play in general, reported that the offending brigade's attempt to budge into line was only partially successful, suggesting that tempers had flamed up and their rightful place restored only after threats of a fight.[177] They got over in good order and faced the last obstacle of the Chancellorsville campaign.

When they had come down to this river a few days earlier, the roads were mainly dry and the route down to the water and across to the other side filled with singing soldiers, the miles melting under the veterans' long, easy stride. Their march down into the Wilderness had seemed no more than a dreamy glide. Here at the ford, the opposite bank was nearly perpendicular, the mud as slick as churned butter. It took the last reserve of energy a soldier had to make his way up, sliding backward a step for every step and a half gained. At last they gained the top, and for the first time in seven days they were beyond the torment of enemy artillery.[178]

They no longer looked much like the finest army on the planet, which is how Hooker had bragged about them to Lincoln. Many were without coats, knapsacks, blankets, and food—they had not even a chew of hardtack.[179] The wagon train that pulled into line behind them no longer carried crates of ammunition but the hundreds of their wounded. The Giddings Regiment had suffered, but just how severely would take days to tally. They had passed through a battle the scale and bloodiness of which could compare to nothing that had been seen before, or even imagined. Port Republic had been uniquely cruel and terrifying, and Cedar Mountain full of its own peculiar horrors. However, in the vernacular of a German-born corporal in Company G, they had seen the real "spe-i-der" at Chancellorsville.[180]

The man commanding their corps, Maj. Gen. Henry Slocum, was proud of them. They had been first to cross the Rapidan on the way in and the last to cross the Rappahannock on the way out. Severely pressed at the end, they had not given up a single battle flag. Rollin Jones was standing nearby when Slocum rode up to Charles Candy after the battle and told him, "Your steadiness saved the Army."[181] Without the time bought by the soldiers of Hancock, and Candy's brigade, the rebels might have rolled the beaten Federals back onto their reserves and drowned the whole lot in the river.

At the start, Hooker had held all the cards, but he had not played them all, as Lincoln had cautioned, nor did he play those he laid on the table with the daring he said he would. Decades later Hooker's failure still produced a bitter taste in the mouth of Homerville boy John Rupp. He looked back at the army as it had appeared when it climbed the muddy pitch above the last river on its way out and observed, "If we were not licked we thought we were, or our commander did, for we got across the river by a shorter route than the one by which we had come."[182]

19

Aquia Creek Interlude
MAY–JUNE 1863

"We Congratulate the Army"

The regiment came back to the same campground at Aquia Creek they had occupied for a week on their way down to Chancellorsville. They had left this same place a few days earlier the best equipped army on the earth and came back to it looking as if they had been tossed about inside a cyclone. Soldiers had come out of the battle hatless, coatless, and in some cases without their shoes. Chaplain Ames helped the quartermaster issue uniform parts and a variety of gear to soldiers who had lost or worn out what they had carried to battle. One-half of Slocum's soldiers had lost shelter tents, rubber blankets, and even their knapsacks. Franklin Manderbach had lost his knapsack. It was returned to him, but not in time for use in this war.

Pvt. Isham Blake, Fifth Florida Infantry, Perry's brigade, McLaw's division, CSA, had picked up a souvenir in Candy's trench line at Chancellorsville.[1] In 1888 a parcel was delivered to the governor's office in Columbus, Ohio, accompanied by a letter from Isham Blake's sister. Her brother had picked up the object packed inside at Chancellorsville, and she requested that it be returned to the owner, if he had survived the war and was still living. Inside was a Union army knapsack, which had stenciled on its flap "29th O.V.I." Its owner was identified by a paper her brother had found folded inside. The document was a certificate of promotion belonging to Cpl. Benjamin F. Manderbach of Company G. The governor saw the healing properties of such a gesture, located Manderbach in Akron, and forwarded the knapsack to him.[2]

They had gone in with nearly a million rounds of rifle ammunition and many came back with nothing but a few loose grains of gunpowder in the bottoms of their cartridge boxes.[3] The loss of equipment in the Twelfth Corps expressed the general wreckage of its men. Almost three thousand soldiers, nearly one-quarter of the Twelfth Corps's men, had been killed, wounded, or taken prisoner.[4] Slocum's corps had been so roughly handled in the late battle that some of the Twenty-Ninth's soldiers debated whether the Twelfth Corps would continue to exist.[5]

When Lincoln learned of Hooker's defeat, and the magnitude of it, he asked, "What will the country say, what will the country say?" In the part of the country defined by the boundaries of Ohio's Western Reserve the country said little. First stories of the battle were culled from the New York and Philadelphia papers and ran in the Reserve's newspapers under headlines set in type no larger than that announcing the everyday train wreck: "Terrible Battle! Great Loss on Both Sides," and in the same edition, "Hooker's Victory Complete."[6]

Jackson had thrown himself "impetuously" on the Union right, and the "German corps" (Eleventh Corps) had fled in disgraceful panic, that much was admitted. But Jackson's advance had been handsomely checked by Hooker personally when he rushed to the point of crisis on his magnificent charger and rallied the boys with quotable orders such as "Receive the enemy on your bayonets!" The casualties had been high, but the payoff magnificent. First reports said Lee's army was being driven back and slaughtered all along the line from Fredericksburg to Chancellorsville, and the Federals were tearing up rebel railroad, capturing supplies, and overwhelming whole batteries and regiments of the enemy. A wire had been intercepted from Lee to his government, in Richmond, crying out for aid: he could hold out only two days longer if not immediately reinforced.[7] As proof positive of the Federal triumph, a thousand rebel prisoners fresh from the battlefield were seen marching down Pennsylvania Avenue to the old capitol prison, looking not only beaten but starved.[8]

Later dispatches from the battlefield reported that Hooker had withdrawn back across the river, but this had not been a retreat. Indeed, as reported by the Conneaut newspaper, the retrograde movement had been a calculated ruse. Hooker had crossed his army back to the safe side of the river to hold Lee in place. In the meantime, Union Generals John J. Peck and Erasmus D. Keyes had taken Richmond, which had been Hooker's grand design all along.[9] For the few days it would take to disprove it, the readers of the Ashtabula County newspapers were electrified.

In Jefferson, any news at all of the battle had to be dug out of the back pages of the *Sentinel*. More prominent space was given to the latest installment of a serialized Gothic novel, *The Left Hand*. The news of the battle that did find its way into the paper was as optimistic as that reported in the Akron newspaper: "Our advice up to noon today [May 5] are [sic] that the victory of Gen. Hooker's army is more complete than at first supposed. All that the most sanguine could hope for has been realized. We congratulate the army and the country upon this most important success."[10]

Only in Ashtabula city did the editors risk censure by neighboring newspapers and publish something slightly closer to the truth. Hooker had withdrawn back over the Rappahannock after taking large losses. It was admitted that a golden moment had been lost, and that was lamentable; but it had not been Hooker's fault. His brilliant plans and the movements to carry them out had been confounded by high water in the Rappahannock.[11] In light of that, he was praised for saving his army.

Just a year earlier, the editors had tried to dull the shock of the carnage at Shiloh by comparing it to history's bloodier battles. It took a while, but when Chancellorsville's numbers were finally reported, there were no attempts made to scale down the amount of bloodshed. In truth, the losses had been awful. Over seventeen thousand of Hooker's soldiers had been killed, wounded, or taken prisoner. The bleeding at Chancellorsville had gone far beyond that of Shiloh, and outdistanced all the big battles since then, including Antietam, Second Bull Run, and Fredericksburg.

There was no public complaint against yet another reverse for the Army of the Potomac, nor did anyone protest the implementation of the first federal income tax, which occurred on the heels of the recent battle.

Bonds were being sold to raise money to fund the unimaginable cost of this war, but that would not be enough to make the mare go. Citizens would have to pay their share, and to make sure they did, the new law had bite to it. If a man did not willingly pay his 3 percent, he could be fined and jailed, and his property could be seized. As far as it was reported in the Reserve newspapers, not a single objection was raised, and if any letters were sent to the editors complaining of it, they were not published. How could a citizen with an ounce of patriotism in his bones resist helping finance the government in these days of peril, when so many others had given their lives or those of sons and husbands? The Akron newspaper gave tips on how to figure what a man owed, so he could be prepared and have cash in hand to pay the tax collector when he knocked on the door.[12]

The unrelenting campaign urging the public to do more and more for the sick and suffering in army hospitals rolled along with increasing purpose. The push for homemade and homegrown contributions had already gone up the age ladder, with exhortations for the old folks to put aside their mustard plasters and canes and do what they could. Now it moved down, and a campaign was initiated to encourage boys still in knee britches and little girls yet in braids to pitch in.

Will your kind hearts and willing hands work for the good of the soldiers? You may ask, "What can we do?" You can work in your gardens and fields, plant and cultivate potatoes, tomatoes, cabbages, onions & etc. You can gather strawberries, raspberries, currants, and blackberries, and your mothers will can them. Your apples, pears, peaches and plums can be cut, dried, and put in small bags—Then, these rich treasures . . . of your patriotic industry, sent to the Soldiers' Aid Society, and thence to the Sanitary Commission, will reach the soldier, help him to get well, and cheer his heart. Begin to plan and to work at once. Keep at it, and thousands of our brave soldiers will rise up and call you blessed.[13]

While some of its hometown soldiers were making their way back to Aquia Creek, an entertainment was being held over in West Andover, near the Pennsylvania border in Ashtabula County, in the neighborhood where John Brown's supporters had worked feverishly, and criminally, on his behalf. The locals had organized an exhibition of "brilliant" tableaux to be presented at the Methodist church, where at a cost of fifteen cents, the audience would be awed by human, still-life compositions such as: "Soldiers Farewell," "On Picket," "The Soldiers Return," "The Death of Minnehaha," and "Uncle Tom and Little Eva."[14]

Down South, their misguided countrymen in Vicksburg were living in holes in the ground to avoid the Federal shells and eating rats to keep from starving, and increasingly throughout the South not a needle could be found, nor a scrap of manufactured cloth on which to apply it. Here on the Western Reserve and elsewhere in the North, residents could buy almost anything that was essential to life, and much that was not. The war industries were perfecting theories of production on a large scale based on the interchangeability of parts, and these same novel principles were being applied to the manufacture of labor-saving inventions for the home and farm. Door-to-door peddlers came knocking to extol the benefits of one of these marvels, the Singer sewing machine. Its cost was substantial, but cheap really, when a housewife considered the work it could save and, as the new phrase in the American idiom reminded everyone, in these hurry-up days, "time is money."

The civic leaders of Conneaut had succeeded in erecting a pound at the public expense for containing free-ranging hogs and were now crusading for the erection of Conneaut's first jail. Ships came into the port, took on loads of lumber, got up steam, and started east on Lake Erie. As with every other commodity, the war demanded lumber for ships, wagons, barrels, gun stocks, and a hundred other things. This part of the Reserve had no shortage of trees, and the lumber business boomed. Some worried that if the denuding of the ancient forests continued at this pace, they would all wake up to find themselves living on a treeless prairie. Business in Conneaut was climbing upward and, along with it, crime. There was war news in the newspapers to read and letters from boys at the front to give it a personal face. Most readers of their soldier boy's letters would be disappointed; most soldiers were too humble to attempt description of such complex cataclysms as Chancellorsville, which is not to say the residents did not have firsthand news of it.

The villagers of Conneaut were privileged to entertain one of their own sons fresh from the battlefield. Pvt. Edward Ryon was here to tell of the Twenty-Ninth Ohio's close escapes and stirring encounters at Chancellorsville, and as proof that he had been in the thick of it all, he was wearing the coat in which he had fought, with the shoulder mostly torn out by a rebel shell.[15] As for the boys in the Twenty-Ninth at Aquia Creek, he reported them in "good spirits and anxious to try the fight over again."[16]

The news of the Italian patriot Giuseppe Garibaldi's illness in Europe seemed of high importance, given its positioning on the front page of the local newspapers. To give that event in faraway Italy a home connection, the Jefferson newspaper was running a continuing travelogue on its front pages, *From Venice to Florence and Back Again,* which may well have been written by its former son William Dean Howells, who was spending these trying days hobnobbing with Europe's rich and powerful.[17] Into June 1863, J. R. Giddings was reported back at his home in Jefferson, sick but recovering, and working nonstop toward completion of his epic *History of the Rebellion.* Interspersed with the war news from Texas, Alabama,

Virginia, and even California, there were columns of one-slug jokes, such as: "Why would negroes be the best standard bearers? Because they would never lose their colors," and in the joke column titled *Funny and Otherwise* another riddle, "Why are cowardly soldiers like butter? When exposed to fire they run."[18] Not all the war news supported the view that every Union soldier was a loyal patriot. A Captain Sweet of the 105th Ohio, an outfit to which Ashtabula County had contributed men, had been dismissed for giving vital information to Union soldiers who had disguised themselves as rebels to trap him.[19]

Whether Chancellorsville had been a horrific defeat or the most glorious of victories, the country was to observe a day of national fasting, as recommended earlier by President Lincoln. On the appointed day everyone was to suspend business as usual, meditate on the gravity of the nation's crisis, and send up prayers for its deliverance. In Akron most spent the day in church, as they ought have, but some did not, and the editor of the *Summit Beacon* chastised them:

> The day was pretty generally observed in Akron by the closing of business establishments, and would have been wholly so, but for the large number of people from the country, who either ignorant or willfully unmindful of the recommendation of the President, came in with their produce for sale and for purchase of supplies. . . . The day should have been kept as rigidly, and even more so if possible, than the Sabbath, on account of its great moral bearing upon the enormous rebellion against which we are now struggling.[20]

As soon as he could step away from his duties at Aquia Creek, Col. Thomas Clark wrote a letter to the Akron newspaper apprising the citizens of the Twenty-Ninth's fate in the late battle. Chaplain Ames did the same for the families of boys in his neighborhood of Ashtabula County. As to the condition of his soldiers, Clark wrote, "The wounded are all at this date doing well; and considering the length and severity of the contest passed through, our friends at home have great reason to rejoice that the list, especially the killed, is no larger."[21]

"War in Its Worst Form"

Parents wrote to their sons, anxious to find out how they had come through the fight, injured or not, but also to learn what it had been like to be in so large a battle as Chancellorsville. Cass Nims's father had written to his son wishing to know how he had fared, and Cass seated himself and took up his pen to reply. He told of how their brigade had skirmished mostly for the first two days, and that it was on the third and last day that their part in the fighting began in earnest. He wrote that the rebels had been close enough to touch and told of their three bayonet charges, against which the rebels had stood their ground. Also, that on the last morning the Boys had fought in front of the Chancellor Inn, that it had caught fire, and that the wounded prisoners remaining inside had burned along with it. He had been detailed, he wrote, to carry away the wounded from their lines.

"I wish I could picture it for you it was rough play," was as good as he could get it. He lacked the words or inclination to speak of his excruciating trials that day: going forward into patches of burning woods looking for stricken men with rebels all around, bullets cutting down slim trees, and boys. Cass performed his duty: lugging the dead weight of the wounded, although he himself was plenty scared. "You are right when you think that that I have seen war in its worst form for that was as hard a fight as ever was fought."[22]

The work had been rough indeed. When Geary's division turned out for inspection here at Aquia Creek, they were a shadow of what they had been.[23] Over twelve hundred of them had become casualties.[24] In Candy's brigade alone, over five hundred soldiers and officers were gone.[25] The Fifth Ohio had lost six killed, and in the Seventh Ohio, which seemed always at the center of the killing zones, sixteen men were dead on the field. Gen. John Geary's old outfit, the Twenty-Eighth Pennsylvania, had left seventeen of its boys dead near the crossroads, including their intrepid commander, who was shot dead while standing in the forward trenches next to Geary, and sixty more of its men had been seriously wounded. For all the dangers to which they had been exposed—the charges and counterchages, the rain of shells, the thousands of musket balls that had sizzled past heads, the holding out at the very end against an army many times larger than they—the losses in the Twenty-Ninth Ohio might have been much worse. They had suffered less than any of the regiments in their brigade. All told, they had taken over seventy casualties. One of every five soldiers and officers in the Twenty-Ninth who fought at Chancellorsville had been killed, wounded, or taken prisoner. Blessedly, only two or as many as four men had been killed in action—depending on who did the counting. Sammy Shanafelt and twenty-year-old Sgt. Edward F. Smith had been killed by artillery fire.[26] Three of their wounded died within ten days following the battle, one of whom was a nineteen-year-old farmer's son serving as a private in Company E named Thomas Schultz.

Pvt. Edward Ryon told the home folks in Conneaut that he had been allowed to visit the field four days after the battle and he found Schultz lying where he had fallen. Poor Schultz was near death and unable to communicate the details of his solitary misery, but he was still breathing. He was being transported back to the hospital in Aquia Creek when he died near Stafford Court House on May 12. Tom's friends had to wait four days to bury him. It took that long to find him a coffin, such things, or the material from which to make one, being scarce in this part of Virginia. They buried him on a hillside near the town.[27]

Forty-two of the Twenty-Ninth's soldiers had been wounded, and for several, their wounds led to amputation and an end to their war. Twenty-eight soldiers were taken prisoner, including the popular young man of Akron Lt. A. J. Fulkerson. Three of the captured were paroled on the battlefield and sent on their way. The rest were marched through Richmond to City Point, where they were paroled.

Two soldiers who were counted among the missing did not show up on prisoner lists provided by the rebel authorities, nor did they turn up in Federal hospitals after the confusion automatic to the transport and care of thousands of wounded finally settled. It was concluded that John Hill of Mogadore was missing, with all signs pointing to his death on the field. His younger brother, Hiram, Company G, had come through unhurt. Oliver Osmond of Company K also went missing during the last day of battle. Published years later, the *State Roster* would report of his fate, "no further record found," as if his disappearance owed to a record-keeping error.[28]

The Chapel in the Pines

Chaplain Lyman Ames had been through his first battle, which he described dichotomously as both "sublime and awful."[29] His duties in its aftermath brought him into intimate contact with the aspects of the latter description, and the strain was beginning to tell. He had been healthy when he arrived a few months earlier, but now he began to complain to his diary more and more of a variety of physical ills: sore throat, upset bowels, headache, and a level of weariness no amount of sleep could cure. He believed the Almighty was testing him.[30]

While the army lay at Aquia Creek, Ames teamed up with the chaplains of other regiments in the brigade to stage divine services. Compared to Dumfries, where services had been held sporadically, the Boys could now attend prayer meetings every Sunday, and on Wednesdays too. There had been a noticeable increase in the number of soldiers who came into the clearings behind the particular regiment where the meeting was set up, and Ames was gratified. He had found himself too busy with duties that rightfully belonged to the officers and their clerks to conduct regular divine services back in Dumfries, and when he did, the soldiers' hearts had seemed only lukewarm to his attempts. After Chancellorsville, there were promising stirrings in camp of something resembling a religious revival.

Two weeks after they'd arrived back in Aquia Creek he and the chaplain of the Sixty-Sixth Ohio worked to fit out a suitable place for regular Sunday service based on the "Union Plan." Members of the Pioneer Corps and details of soldiers from the various companies were placed at the chaplains' disposal. They spread pine boughs on the ground for a floor and built a bower of transplanted evergreens over the pulpit.[31] Services commenced at six in the evening, following the dress parade. The soldiers followed along in the program of hymn singing, prayer, spiritual discussions, and a sermon, and the band played religious tunes. After a few weeks of regular service, Ames saw that the boys were improving in their singing and in following along with the prayers. When called to the front of their piney chapel to pledge their lives to Christ, many boys stepped up freely and made vows.[32] It seemed to Ames that the soldiers were beginning to see that religious practice would improve their chances for the afterlife and make for a better life in the present.[33]

Nathan Parmater attended services not only because it provided the chance for him to worship, but also because the singing of the old hymns reminded him of home. The song of the soldiers lacked the sweetness imparted to it by female voices, but it was sweet enough given they were in a place of impending violence and among men of rough ways.[34] The spirits of the soldiers were lifted by their greater attention to things spiritual, but Ames's spirits were not. Following one Sunday service he wrote, "O! For a new reviving by the spirit fitting for the work before me."[35] There were things working against his crusade to establish a stronger spiritual influence in the regiment.

The Twenty-Ninth's officers seemed little interested in divine matters, and few of them attended Sunday services. By their absence, Ames thought they were making a poor example for the enlisted men.[36] He had other bones to pick with them. Ames had observed that discipline and drill kept the soldiers busy and immunized them against the unseemly conduct that came of boredom. But the Twenty-Ninth's officers were not dedicated to keeping them busy: "It is a fact never to be lost sight of that an army cannot be too much drilled, neither men nor officers. There is a great tendency to relax efforts in this direction by volunteers in our service, especially by the officers. They seem to think that [it] is not the business of their lives and it will not pay to look far in that line of duty which is to be only temporary."[37] Ames continued to wonder and worry if there was any regard whatsoever in high places for the moral condition of the soldiers. That there was little, or none, seemed proved to him by what he could see and hear of the soldiers' behavior, and it appears the soldiers did little to conceal the most obvious of their wayward tendencies even when he was around. "Some of the most depraving vices are permitted to go unrebuked and unnoticed," and to him the increasing use of foul language was the most disturbing: "Profanity is a heaven-provoking and heaven-defying sin, practiced by 99 of every one hundred. No vice more hardens the heart against divine truth—[none] more contagious. It grows into the social fabric of Co., Regt., Brig., Div., etc."[38] Chaplain Ames stayed at his work, and in the days after Chancellorsville it was particularly heart wrenching.

"Many a Valiant Soldier"

Parents of sons who had been casualties in the late battle wrote to the regiment asking for news of their boy. Ames was given these letters to answer. He wrote to Jacob Schultz, father of the soldier found on the field days after the battle, giving what details he knew and offering consolation. Daniel Platt Sr. had been in the Twenty-Ninth Ohio himself for a time, found the army life too hard for a middle-aged man, and was discharged. He left a son behind in the regiment. Pvt. Daniel Platt had gone missing at Chancellorsville, and his father wrote to the regiment asking if there had been any word. Ames happily reported that Daniel had been one of those captured, and was now safe at Camp Parole, in Maryland.[39] Ames's sympathy for parents who had sons in harm's way was made deeper by his own situation.

His son Edwin was with Grant's western army, which was closing in on Vicksburg, the last rebel sticking point on the Mississippi River. Newspapers came into the camp and from what Ames could read, the situation at Vicksburg was both cheering and depressing. The Federals were drawing nearer their prize but had been repulsed twice in direct assaults with much loss of life and were settling down for a siege. He had not had a letter from Edwin for weeks, nor had his wife, back in Conneaut, and he steeled himself against bad tidings. "Success and cause of joy, but the sacrifice of life awful! Result to Edwin uncertain, painful the suspense and dreaded the news! Oh! Father in heaven prepare me for it in Mercy!"[40]

The recent battle had put thirty-two of the regiment's soldiers into the hospitals.[41] Ames visited them, and the sight of their suffering, some of them with ghastly wounds, sickened him.[42] However, he was a curious man and when he had an opportunity to observe the surgeons perform a capital operation, he availed himself of it. "Many cases of interest. Saw an amputation of leg above the knee. Man took chloroform, was insensible to the pain. Better to lose a leg than life."[43] He was learning that the successful performance of his job required a strong stomach as much as anything else. For two weeks and more after the battle, ambulances continued to arrive regularly at the division hospital adjacent their camp with their cargos of broken boys still being found on the battlefield. The quantity of stricken streaming into the grounds around the tents of the Twelfth Corps hospital at Aquia Creek seemed to Ames to be as large as the army itself.

Army surgeons were used to gore, but the wounds produced by the uniquely intense artillery pounding to which soldiers of both sides had been subjected at Chancellorsville horrified even them. Some boys were missing great regions of abdomen, as if they had been bitten by sharks. Ames conversed with these torn-apart boys, whether of his regiment or another did not matter to him. "Among the wounded men today found many a valiant soldier. Prostrate and mangled yet strong of heart, full of fortitude to bear up under this sad fortune."[44] Eli Oberholtz, a private in Company H, had been wounded in the leg so badly that it was doubtful he would ever recover. But despite the death sentence that hung over him, Ames found him calm and hopeful.[45]

The wounded of the Twenty-Ninth were doing well, generally. But seven of them had been badly hurt and their recovery was doubtful, especially those who been left on the field for days.[46] Those who could speak complained of the indifference of the army surgeons who had been left behind near the battlefield to care for them.[47]

Corporal Wilbur, who had been rescued on the battlefield by John Marsh, seemed stable enough after a time to survive the steamer trip from Aquia Creek to Washington. There, his individual misery was added to that of the thousands of other wounded who were off-loaded onto the wharves, where they waited in unsheltered rows for wagons to take them to a hospital. After earlier battles, great crowds of citizens had come down to the water to see the transports discharge their cargoes of wounded; some came to gawk and some came to ameliorate the suffering. Now the strings of steamers that came in day after day with the wounded attracted little notice.[48] A section of the city had now been taken over entirely by coffin makers and embalmers who advertised their services with transparencies hung from the sides of buildings of the type that had been used to promote the election of Lincoln back in Akron. Like most other businesses in Washington, the business of caring for the dead was brisk. Caravans of wagons and ambulances, with cargoes of wounded soldiers and stacked coffins, had become a normal feature of life in Washington.

Capt. Everson J. Hurlburt of Company A had been seriously hurt. This was the third battle in which he had been shot, but his prospects of recovery were good. He was visited in the hospital by his brother, the regiment's first chaplain, Russell Hurlburt, and Lyman Ames made his acquaintance.[49] Pvt. D. B. Franklin, a thirty-four-year-old farmer in Company E, had been one of the enlistees that came to them at Frederick. Chancellorsville had been his inauguration to battle, and he had been hit in four places. He was brought from the battlefield nearly two weeks after it ended, arriving at the hospital with his wounds yet undressed and having received no medical care of any kind in the miserable interim. He and other unfortunates had lain on the field without food or water, helping each other as best they could. He did not do well in the hospital, and it was reckoned he would not live, but he surprised the surgeons and did.[50] Not all the Twenty-Ninth Regiment's afflicted bore visible marks of injury. At least two soldiers had been driven into madness by their experiences at Chancellorsville.

The regiment's star fifer, sixteen-year-old Bennett H. Wadsworth, also known as Benny Bates, was known to be sensitive and sometimes eccentric, but after the battle he began to evidence behavior that went far beyond that. Surgeon Fifield knew Benny to be a bit of a "hanger around" hospitals, whether he had been detailed there or not, but he had shown up at the field hospital in the woods back of Chancellorsville in a violent delirium. From what little sense Dr. Fifield could make of Benny's ranting, the fifer seemed to be saying a shell had exploded near his head, and concussion or brain fever resulting from that might explain his behavior.[51] Others thought Benny had begun acting more strangely than was usual for him about the time he had received a letter from the girl he'd fallen in love with back at Camp Giddings.[52] She had fallen in love with another boy. Rest and quiet did not restore Benny to his senses. He seemed better for a while, but then his mania returned at full gallop. His odd behavior elicited jeers and ribbing from his bunk mates at first, but after a while they took pity on him and let him be. But his insanity seemed to upset the balance of the regiment and he was put back in the hospital, where he came to the attention of Chaplain Ames: "One sad case has developed today. Ben Wadsworth, the fifer, shows evident signs of being deranged; if not his conduct is unaccountable. O! What is a man bereft of reason? A wild and frantic animal! Benny is a subject of pity more than censure, though his freaks are often ludicrous and vexing."[53] Benny was eventually put under lock and key at the hospital at Aquia Creek, and so pronounced was his delirium that he frightened even his attendants. He would remain with the regiment, in the hospital more than out of it, for the next several months until he was discharged in early autumn.[54] There was little that could be done for soldiers suffering from "head troubles." A soldier's changed behavior after battle was at first treated as a disciplinary matter for the provost guard to handle.

Pvt. John C. Greenlee of Company E was working in the ambulance corps in Aquia Creek when he put down what he was doing and just walked off, as if under a spell.[55] He would not respond to commands to turn around and come back and instead kept at his wandering as if being called by some invisible voice. The provost guard brought him back, but it was immediately clear that Greenlee's mind had slipped a cog. They locked him up, which for him turned out to be the right medicine, and after enforced rest and some counseling with Chaplain Ames he regained his senses and went back to soldiering.

"Perfect Cut Throats"

The Boys were in fine spirits, engaging once again in the tussle and teasing incidental to life in the company streets, which could make starting and completing a letter at the same sitting a challenge. Nelson Gillett warned his mother as he began to write, "You must excuse my writing for the best writer in the world could not write here, the boys are tearing things up."[56] Army life at Aquia Creek was good. Uncle Sam fed the Boys fresh bread still warm from the bakery every day, and there was fresh butter to buy from the nearby sutlers, who, on account of the prices they charged, the Boys had taken to calling "smugglers."[57] There was enough to do, but not too much. Boys were seen hurrying along the company streets just come from the sutler's wagon with their arms full of brushes and tins of blacking compound, which they passed out to friends already hard at work blacking boots, cartridge boxes, and belts in preparation for the dress parade held every evening.[58] Some of the soldiers were detailed to work on a new fort, to be named after their General Slocum, while others dug trees and replanted them to form tall arches at the heads of the company streets. These green constructions were decorative but they also provided shade for the canvas-topped tuggies and blocked the clouds of dust whipped up by freight wagons using the road down to the landing. But even with these things, there was less to occupy the Boys than at any time since they'd been in the army.

It would look untoward for officers to resort to the recreations of the private soldiers, such as playing ball, and lacking those, their lives were immensely tedious. Assistant surgeon Elwood Potts Haines's duties locked him onto a worn path that ran in only one direction and back again: from his office-tent, where he filled out reams of government paperwork and treated sprained backs and sore throats, to the hospital, where he dressed wounds. After a month of it, he threw up his hands: "Alas! This everlasting sameness."[59]

The army paymaster was not a popular fellow, except when he showed up with satchels full of greenbacks, but he had not been seen now for months. Pvt. Nelson Gillett's attitude toward him and his broken promises was, "He would lie as quick as he would eat." The books were gotten into satisfactory order in mid-May and the Boys were paid off. Chaplain Ames got a windfall of $125. With money in their pockets, the Boys went through their usual process of writing a letter to let the folks know they had been paid and that they should be on the lookout for the part of it the soldier had promised them. No soldier was foolish enough to trust the mails for safe transport of currency. After every payday, an officer, and sometimes their chaplain, was sent on a flying trip back to Ohio with the pay of the entire regiment, and on arrival he visited the men who had been entrusted with holding the money until parents or wives came round for it. In Ashtabula County, a Mr. Bushnell was the most relied-on man for such a responsibility, and the soldiers universally advised parents that they should call on him to get their money. After fulfilling the obligation every boy felt to send the biggest part of his pay, he looked for ways to spend a little of it on himself.

The soldiers were drawn to Aquia Landing with its huge wharves, squadrons of steam locomotives, and small armies of soldiers acting as stevedores. Many boys wrote of it in their letters for those at home who would never have the chance to see such a marvel. Christopher Beck chewed at the stub of his pencil in a struggle to pull up the right words to describe such a colossus for his mother: "It is a landing where all the provisions is unloaded for the hull army of the potomac but we are 4 miles from the landing the bars [rails] run to the dock so they can allmost be loaded from the boats there is some of the nicest engines here that I ever saw the track is laid so they can run the engines unto the boats in case we should have to lieve here but that time wont come."[60] There were things down at the landing to draw parts of a soldier's pay as well as his curiosity. Wallace Hoyt went down and found an "eating saloon" that served ham and eggs, for which he was especially hungry, emphasizing in a letter to his little sister that the meal had cost him the staggering sum of one dollar, which was the equivalent of two days of a soldier's hard-earned wages.[61]

Because of his protracted sickness back at Frederick, and his separation from the regiment during it, Nathan Parmater had gone without pay longer than his friends. To him that had been just as well because when he visited the landing he found it the abode of "a perfect gang of cut throats." Sutlers and peddlers there were taking advantage of the soldier's need and charging twice or more than the going prices.[62] There were sharpers hanging out at the landing looking for choice marks, like Parmater's good friend Cpl. Alfred Doty. Doty's pocket was neatly picked of twenty dollars, which was a heartbreaking sum for a boy to lose, being over a month's pay and the going price on a fine colt back home.[63]

"May Success Yet Attend"

Hot, muggy days cooled the mania for ball playing that had dominated their off-duty hours when they were here in April. The Boys now took to less physical pursuits. Those who had been exposed to more esoteric pastimes back home amused themselves by playing chess. The card game of bluff had taken hold of the Boys in Parmater's company. Where the creek entered it, the Potomac flared into a miles-long bay, with steep-banked pools covered by canopies of giant trees rooted into the banks. Whenever they had a few spare moments, the Boys retreated to these shady places to bathe and swim. Afterward, they climbed to the top of the ridge above the Potomac and sat watching passing ships flying the flags of many nations while they dried themselves in the breeze coming up from the river.

They had failed to pass muster with the general inspector when he had come to examine them back in the valley. At Dumfries, he had refused to inspect them at all. Here at Aquia Creek they were working hard to erase these black marks.[64] By late May they no longer looked like a regiment that had been knocked to its knees earlier that same month, nor did the Boys feel that they had been beaten. Boys like Nathan Parmater could see the improvement. Three weeks after Chancellorsville, the regiment formed up for the evening parade and Parmater judged, "The old 29th looked as well as it ever did, the boys are feeling finely."[65]

When they climbed up from Chancellorsville, Chaplain Ames had worried over what the defeat might do to their spirit. Within a few days, he was surprised to observe, "Men feel well, are not disheartened as at first supposed. May success yet attend."[66] Whatever disappointment they may have felt was short lived. It was not for boys to brood over the failures of generals. The soldiers had enlisted to fight, and when they were called upon to do it, they might just as well do it without grumbling, as Pvt. Elias Roshon expressed it.[67]

No man in the regiment believed they had been beaten at Chancellorsville, outgeneraled maybe, but not defeated. In Pvt. Nelson Gillett's words, "They [the rebels] was whipped at Chancellorsville, but dident know it."⁶⁸ In their reporting of Stonewall Jackson's death after being wounded in the late battle, even the Western Reserve's newspapers now admitted that Jackson had shown capabilities in his thankfully brief career that exceeded those of any Union general. The private soldiers' regard for the capabilities of their opposite numbers in the Confederate Army was also changing. Once regarded as nothing more than armed ragamuffins who ran at the sight of a Union soldier, they were now grudgingly admired for their courage. The rebel soldier's tenacity was such that Nelson Gillett commented after Chancellorsville, "It does seem as though the rebs would never give up until they are all killed."⁶⁹

What had gone wrong at Chancellorsville was a popular topic for discussion among the officers. Chaplain Ames was privy to their debates and listened keenly to what they had to say, and what they had to say about Chancellorsville ran contrary to what was being trumpeted about it back home: "The more we think upon the late battle, the more doubtful [we are] of its advantages."⁷⁰

The folks back home followed the failures of the Army of the Potomac in the newspapers, and when it had sunk in that Chancellorsville had been yet another reverse, they assumed that their boys would be bothered by the same war weariness that more and more troubled even the most patriotic civilians. The soldiers were tired of it, most of them, but they were far from thinking of giving up. Christopher Beck had mentioned in an earlier letter to his mother that his heart had grown weary and that he longed for the peace of home. But in his mind, those feelings did not add up to a loss of faith: "Who hent [ain't] tired of even hearing the word war but I hent so tired of it yet so that I cant stay my time and I am very glad that I enlisted when I did for now them that stayed at home till they had to go will always be called recrutes."⁷¹

However pleasant their stay here was, it was not a furlough from the realities of war. The produce of the battle was within their hearing, interrupting their sleep with reminders of what they had been through and what most had escaped. A captain of the Fifth Ohio had died in a hospital near the regiment. In his last hours, the captain's cries had awakened Chaplain Ames, and he had risen from his cot to locate their source.

> Friday night I was aroused from sleep by his wild and unnatural cries. Doubtful at first what it was I arose and went out until satisfied that it was some poor suffering human being—but supposed it was someone of the many wounded men suffering excruciating pain from their wounds. This Capt. of the 5th O.V.I. was not in good health before the late battle, but his Patriotism and Zeal in the cause of his country were such that he could not be persuaded to [go] home on leave. Soon after his return to camp, he fell sick. An inflammation seated in the brain which at once deprived him of reason. It was sad to hear him screech and scream. The expressions [he] used indicated what had occupied his mind—namely war. Fighting. The strife of the battlefield. His wife came from Cincinnati to see him go down into the darkness of the grave. Her unceasing care and efforts could avail nothing. Death had fixed its mask upon him and there was no discharge in the war. What a trial for a wife! War makes widows and orphans the world over. It is the same now as when inaugurated by the prince of darkness.⁷²

A Commotion

Capt. James Treen resigned for health reasons in late May, and within a few days he was back in Akron. He had been a canal boat captain before the war, but that mode of transport had been driven into a quaint corner of history by the railroads, and what he would do now as a citizen in the peaceful walks of life was uncertain. He had brought three sons with him to the regiment. One had been discharged months ago and two remained. In all, as the newspaper said, "A pretty good show of patriotism for one small family."⁷³ About a week later, their commander, Col. Thomas Clark, resigned, and his leaving caused a divide among the regiment's officers that would take months to heal.

Colonel Clark's health had been precarious for some time. A month's rest after the battle had not restored him, and in late May he went down to the landing and caught a steamer up to Washington on what was to be a leave of absence, but he would not be returning.[74] He left the regiment he had shaped without speeches or sword presentations or published testimonials thanking him for his service to them. All three of their original field officers were now gone, and almost at once serious discord surfaced among the regiment's officers.

The dispute was being played out so openly that Chaplain Ames, who had few close connections with any of the officers, recorded in his diary, "Friction in official machinery—bad tendency, demoralizing in effect upon privates. Ambition, selfishness and pride often ruin a good cause."[75] The friction that developed in the wake of Clark's leaving came from the question of which of them was best suited to take command. Capt. William T. Fitch of Company A was next in line, but he was still out sick, and whether he would ever return was doubtful.

The captain of Company B, Wilbur F. Stevens, was next in line for command, by merit of seniority. In the most recent battle he had gained additional experience in handling the entire regiment, not only on the march, but during the fight. In one of his last official acts as the regiment's commander, Thomas Clark had written his official report of Chancellorsville, and he had singled out Stevens for his invaluable assistance. Clark's public thank-you might be taken as his endorsement of Stevens as his successor. However, Stevens was a man with enemies, Adj. James B. Storer chief among them. He was convinced that Stevens had shown himself a coward at Cedar Mountain, and that was not forgivable, regardless of what Stevens had done at Chancellorsville. Stevens also drank a bit, and to the abstemious Storer, that alone disqualified him for command.

The regiment did not air its laundry beyond the boundaries of its camp, so the details of the dispute, who was striving for higher office, and by whom they were supported, were not recorded. But the clash was not merely a flash in the pan. Three days after he first mentioned it, Ames wrote in his diary that the "commotion" was continuing.[76] The squabble was not resolved to everyone's satisfaction. When they left this camp, Capt. Wilbur F. Stevens would be in command.

Colonel Clark's leaving meant change for the regiment, but by now change was such a regular thing that his going meant little. Colonel Buckley's powerful presence made him seem unbreakable, and therefore permanent. He *was* the Twenty-Ninth Ohio, but he had gone from them and yet the regiment lived on. They had passed through a bleak winter made dangerous by disease, and after that they had not only survived the war's greatest battle but added to their reputation as boys who would stick and not run. Everything around them had evolved from one thing into another since they'd come into the army: company officers and leaders of the regiment came and went, along with the generals who commanded their armies, the names and order of which had changed, too. Change in all things seemed to be the one thing a soldier could count on.

Many of these Boys were not yet fully grown, and some of them had truly been boys when they left home going on two years ago. They had changed right along, in ways that could be partly seen and in ways that could not be known unless a soldier cared to reveal it, and most did not. There was comfort in letting Mother know that he was building on the good start she'd given him, and that could be evidenced by the fact that he no longer resembled entirely the boy she had watched march away from the courthouse in Jefferson.

"They all tell me I have grown awful fast since I come to the regiment and I have, some," wrote Cass Nims to his mother, but he assured her that she would still be able to recognize him when they were reunited.[77] Likewise, a soldier's younger siblings at home were changing too. Secondhand, a soldier would discover that his little sister had grown enough that she was attracting shy young men with courtship in mind to her front porch. Younger brothers and sisters would write to share the good news that they had grown responsible enough to raise poultry of their own, with the proceeds to be contributed to the family accounts, or had made and donated things for the good of sick and injured soldiers.

Many of the soldiers directed their letters to younger sisters rather than their brothers. They offered advice on proper behavior and other matters, and good-natured teasing too, of the same kind they would have extended had they been home. Wallace Hoyt composed a letter to his sister from Aquia

Creek, decorated the margins with schoolboyish doodles, and said to her, "I hope you will improve your mind and get an education! According to all accounts you are a young lady . . . instead of a girl with a short dress. . . . and I don't know but I should address you as Miss Hattie instead of Hat!"[78]

"Strike Tents!"

They had been under orders to be ready to march since the day they'd arrived back in Aquia Creek, but at the same time, they were being encouraged to continue to improve and prettify their camp, which suggested to the soldiers that they would be staying put here through the foreseeable future. Near the last day of May, Parmater recorded the rumor that had gone through camp, "The news is that the Rebs are anticipating a move north, if so we will probably have work to do soon."[79] The air went out of that rumor when they were ordered to abandon their present camp, move everything up the line a half mile to an orchard-shaded spot, and build brand-new tuggies. The new place would provide better sanitation and respite from the dust. Prospects were they would not be marching anytime soon.[80]

The sound of cannon fire came up on the hot, smoky wind from the direction of Falmouth.[81] Rumor was that the Federals were crossing the river below Fredericksburg and Lee's army was retiring.[82] They might be headed that way, to rewrite the outcome of Chancellorsville. Another week passed and they were still in the same place, carrying out the same routine of drill and dress parades, filling sandbags, and laying them in place down at the new fort. After brigade drill on June 11, General Geary called them into line and made a speech. He praised them very highly for their conduct at Chancellorsville, saying Candy's brigade, with the help of the two New York regiments, had held the entire rebel army in check on the last morning. He also told them that prospects were very good for meeting the same enemy again.[83]

The regiment's sleep was interrupted during the night of June 13. Geary's staff, known for their merrymaking on Christmas Eve when the division was on its way down to Dumfries the year past, had come serenading down the company streets and brought a band to accompany them.[84] The next day, as they were putting away their cook things from supper, lighting pipes, and settling in around their fires, the real order came: "Strike tents, and load-up as quick as possible." And in one hour everyone was on the road in their proper place.[85]

They ate up the pitch-black miles on a north-leading road and at sunrise came up to the scene of last winter's confrontation with Stuart's cavalry on the creek outside Dumfries.[86] They rested during the heat of the day and started north again in the middle of the night, more troops pouring into the road ahead, and behind, as they moved along. The whole army was in motion again from the looks of things. By noon scores of men had fallen out, victims of heatstroke or of lungs too clogged with dust to breathe.

There was no stopping or even slowing: those who fell out were left where they dropped. They came up to the Occoquan River. There was no time to wait for the bridge builders. They plunged in, came up dripping on the other side, and pushed north.[87] Where they were headed was not yet clear, nor did it especially matter, to the common soldier in the Twenty-Ninth Ohio Volunteer Infantry. All a soldier could do was march with the rest on a road that would intersect the enemy at some point. Cass Nims said all that needed to be said: "I hope for the best and hope that we may whip them."[88]

20

Saving the Life of the Nation

THE GETTYSBURG CAMPAIGN, JUNE–JULY 1863

"A Good Deal Like Murder"

Leaving their camp near Aquia Creek, they pushed north, in the direction of Washington, which struck soldiers like Nathan Parmater as yet another "falling-back."[1] Their purpose would not be revealed for a few more days. Lee's army had crossed the rivers below them and slipped off to the west and was moving north behind the screen of the Blue Ridge. They were traversing a dry, treeless countryside made desolate by the marching, camping, and fighting of armies. Chaplain Ames acquired a long linen duster to protect himself from the sun and dust. His new coat did not protect him from the sickening heat, or the accumulating fatigue from marches that began before sunrise and ended when the army ran out of daylight.

Their commanders feared Jeb Stuart's cavalry might fall on their columns anywhere, at anytime. They went into camp at night in line of battle, but Stuart and his invincible riders did not appear.[2] They passed to the east of the old Bull Run battlefields without stopping even to boil noonday coffee. With what energy remained to him, Parmater wrote in his diary, "The day has been very warm and many a poor soldier boy fell dead while doing his duty trying to keep up with his regt. We reached F. [Fairfax] late at night. I think it has been one of the hardest marches we ever had on account of the heat."[3] The straps of packs and accoutrements bit into the shoulders, so that the flesh resembled that of a horse with a bad case of collar gall.[4]

Two days after clearing Dumfries, they came into a more open country just below the Potomac, north and west of Washington. They continued on toward the river, with every soldier in the regiment dogging it to keep up, until they arrived near Leesburg, a few miles from the Potomac River crossings, where they stopped and set up camp in a meadow.

As soon as their motion ceased, sickness caught up with Chaplain Ames, and he found out how hard it was to be a sick man in an army camp. Greasy food was hardly conducive to restoring a broken system, and the powerful medicine prescribed to him proved as bad as the disease.[5] The march to this place had dented the health of even Wallace Hoyt.[6] He had boasted that he had never known a day's illness since enlisting. Now he was feverish and shaky. They regarded Leesburg as a paradise compared to the wasted land around Aquia Creek. However, this was an army after all, and an army brought blight with it.

Some might call this war cruel, while others believed it justifiably harsh, but all agreed that the sheer meanness of it had been rising steadily. A year ago, while coming out of the valley, they had been ordered to retrace their steps at the cost of many miles just to repair a fence the boys had damaged so as not to offend its owner. Now, any citizen foolish enough to say a word in support of the Confederacy did so to his sorrow. A farmer near their camp in Leesburg had both his home and mill burned to the ground for that offense, and the Federals let it be known that others in the neighborhood would fare the same if they did not keep shut.[7]

The story would circulate of an incident that occurred this summer of 1863 during a march the Twenty-Ninth Ohio led along the eastern base of the Blue Ridge.[8] At noontime they came upon a prosperous house at the side of the road, and General Geary and his staff entered to have their lunch. Soldiers searched the barn and discovered a cache of guns. The woman of the house came out and warned them they would pay dear for any depredations. The Boys took no heed and set the barn on fire. One soldier ran to the house with a firebrand to get it going, too, when Geary came out. The soldier said he knew the man who owned the place, having been captured by him and locked up in the springhouse on this very farm, where he had then been abused. Geary commented, "For God's sake let me eat my dinner first." They all marched off, and behind them the house went up in flames. The war had grown more unforgiving as it went along, and so too the army's treatment of its deserters.

On June 19 the provost guard carried out the punishment of three deserters. "Beauregard," the Twenty-Ninth Regiment's know-it-all, had been branded on the hip back in Frederick for going on a lark in Washington and not returning, and the punishment was thought so severe that it attracted a considerable crowd.

Back at Jefferson, soldiers who grew homesick and decided to visit home took French leave without bothering to get a proper pass—a practice that continued after they left. These exercises of a free American's independence were something to chuckle over. Some Giddings soldiers had returned to the regiment at Dumfries with unexplained absences of several months. They were admitted back into the regiment with no more than a wrist slap, which consisted of forfeiture of their pay for the time they were gone.

Desertion was depriving the Army of the Potomac of more soldiers with every passing day. The authorities decided after much deliberation that the punishment must be made to fit the crime. If a man could take off for home whenever he saw fit, soon every soldier would be going home on a whim. Desertion gone unchecked degraded the morale of those who chose to stick tight to their enlistment commitment, or, as John White Geary expressed it, "Justice to the living requires some punishment for such crime."[9] Also, a suitable punishment would serve as a deterrent to other soldiers who toyed with the idea of leaving.

Every soldier who kept a diary recorded the event they were about to witness, and every letter writer reported it. Cass Nims began such a letter, "I saw a sad spectkle yesterday."[10] At high noon the soldiers of Slocum's Corps were called out and ordered to form part of a huge hollow square, left open at one end. The Giddings Regiment happened to be positioned so that every man in the outfit had a close-up view of what was about to happen. A wagon was pulled into the open end of the square of soldiers with three rough coffins aboard, followed by an ambulance.[11] Inside the ambulance were the condemned soldiers wearing black skullcaps, one of whom was already bloody from an escape attempt the evening before.[12] When they stepped down, one of them was observed to be an actual boy of no more than fourteen years. All were soldiers in Williams's division.[13]

William McKee deserted from the Forty-Sixth Pennsylvania Volunteers. He had been found in a house near the regiment's camp, dressed in a linen duster and a fur hat, which, given the heat, must have struck the officer who interrogated him as rather odd. McKee tried to pass himself off as a sutler. The deliberations of the court-martial took only a few minutes, and they returned with the judgment that McKee would be shot to death by musketry. His only statement in his defense: "I intended to go home for a little while, and then come back again."[14] Pvt. William Gruver of the same company as McKee had been caught and tried along with him, and the verdict of the court was identical.[15] The third unfortunate was a German-born shoemaker in the Thirteenth New Jersey who had deserted while on picket duty. His enlistment papers were shown to him, and he was asked if the signature on them was his. He answered yes, and his fate was sealed.[16] The three had been marched along with the rest of the Twelfth Corps up to Leesburg. Nathan Parmater gave the details of the unhappy ceremony:

> They were placed on their coffins, blindfolded with bandaging, and hands tied behind them. A file of eight men with muskets were marched into line in front of the condemned. The General read the sentence of the Courts [sic] Martial, the Chaplain read a prayer and the order was given, "Ready, aim, fire!" The three men fell backwards across their coffins, each man pierced by several balls. Such a sight I hope I shall never be called to witness again.[17]

The reactions of the soldiers varied, but all were saddened; even the stern disciplinarian General Geary was downcast. Cass Nims's account held a note of sarcasm: "That is the new way that they have of having funerals. Take the men there and dig their graves, fetch their coffins, kill the men and bury them."[18] Chaplain Ames's sympathies were more with the families of the executed boys, who had been left an inheritance of ignomy.[19]

Come September, when they were camped again near their old battlefield at Cedar Mountain, the regiment would be called out again to witness another execution of deserters. A full dozen would be executed then, and it would not come off as humanely as the one at Leesburg. One of the two doomed men belonging to their division was tipped over by the volley, but the other still sat on his coffin. One ball passed through his shoulder and another laid open his bowels and passed on to perforate both hands, which had been tied behind him. Another firing squad came up, but it took two more volleys to finish him off. Wallace Hoyt was undecided as to the justification of such work: "It looked a good deal like murder. But perhaps it wasn't."[20]

Back in the Union

Newspapers, their best source of intelligence on what their own army was up to, did not reach them here at Leesburg, and the answer as to where the Twenty-Ninth might go from here could be founded only on the changeable strength of rumor and false alarm.[21] Even their general, John White Geary, was in the dark. Lee's army was marching somewhere out ahead, and for all Geary knew, Lee's men had already made it to the neighborhood of Geary's home. He sent a letter to his wife advising her on what she should do if the rebels called:

> I think I would stay at home and brazen it out. Do not do anything to offend them if they come. Tell the rebels who you are and they will not dare to injure you, they know the retaliation will be terrible. Eddie and I are well. With love I commit to the kind care of Our Heavenly Father. Ever your loving husband J. W. G.[22]

After a week in Leesburg, orders came. They marched at midnight, crossed over the Potomac at Edwards Ferry into Maryland, and camped near the Monocacy bridge.[23] Ames had gained a little in health during their rest and mounted a mule for the ride north. The mule balked and Ames, weak as a kitten, was nearly thrown. Pounding along in a saddle did his sore bowels no good whatsoever, and he decided to ride in an ambulance. His traveling companion was John Greenlee, the soldier who had lost his mind at Chancellorsville and was still unstable.

They marched by way of Point of Rocks, where Joe Hooker rode past them on his way back to Washington, with the news trailing behind him that he had been fired, and Gen. George Meade appointed in his place.[24] The next day, they reached the town of Frederick, Maryland, a place that held fond associations them. Parmater had dear friends in the town, but there would be no pausing here to renew old acquaintances.[25]

The Boys knew by now that Lee was moving north, out of sight behind the mountains to their west, and they were marching to find him and bring him to term.[26] A Twenty-Ninth soldier who was recovering from typhoid in a hospital in Frederick heard his friends were camped nearby. He deserted from the hospital to join them.[27] He collapsed not long after they marched from Frederick and rode the rest of the way to their destination in an ambulance. He took his place in the battle line next to his friends, and he was grievously wounded.

Once it was clear that Lee had begun his second invasion of the North, every soldier recovering in a Union hospital who could carry a musket was ordered to return to his regiment. One of the Homerville Boys, John Rupp, had cut his arm with an ax while fort building at Aquia Creek, and he had been sent to the hospital. Suddenly, he found himself on a train headed to Frederick, where he located his regiment and took his place in line.[28]

Slocum's Twelfth Corps, of which the Twenty-Ninth was part, marched through Frederick city, into Taneytown, and out again. Geary's division found the Third Corps pulled over to the side of the pike, hurried past it, and made Littlestown by nightfall.[29] The Twenty-Ninth was now in Pennsylvania, a prosperous land undisturbed by war. At every rural crossroads, and in every village and town, the residents came out to cheer for the boys who had come to save them. Grateful hands passed soldiers all kinds of good things to eat: wedges of yellow cheese, fruits of all kinds, cakes, slabs of ham, and thick slices of homemade bread to wrap around it.[30] Flags hung from every window and it felt good to be back in a country where the citizens were unafraid to put out the Stars and Stripes.[31] Some soldiers would recall that this march had the feel of a celebration about it.

For some of the soldiers of Candy's brigade, the coming fight was a personal matter. The Twenty-Eighth Pennsylvania had been raised here, and some of its soldiers made their homes in the town of Gettysburg, which was the next place of consequence in their line of march. For the Ohioans, their homeland lay just over the Pennsylvania border, and with Lee on the loose and moving fast, the rebels might be soon marching through the streets of Jefferson unless brought to ground. To read the newspapers that published the ominous dispatches coming out of the governor's office in Ohio, that was entirely within the range of possibilities. Sgt. Rollin Jones saw that some soldiers were marching barefoot and carrying their shoes. They did not want to risk wearing them out and not being able to fight for want of shoe leather.[32]

Past Littlestown, they filed into the woods to the right of the Baltimore Pike and rested for the night. An hour after sunrise they were back on the road to Gettysburg, ten miles distant. Halfway there, near Two Taverns, they were directed off the road. While boiling coffee, they heard artillery fire to the north, but from the sound of it the soldiers estimated it was still many miles away and of no immediate concern to them.[33] Curious, some of the Boys climbed to the top of a hill and came back to report that the estimators had been wrong. They were in fact close enough now to see artillery shells puffing open on the horizon. The Boys were stretched out in the shade when an officer galloped up and yelled, "Hurry-up." Bugles sounded, drums rolled out the long tap, and they started up the road at a jog.[34]

The First and Eleventh Corps had been fighting already and taken many casualties, if the stream of wounded they were encountering was a reliable measure. Further on, skulkers idling beside the road warned them that certain death lay directly ahead. There were now soldiers lying at the side of the road, some faces covered with blankets, some not. They had died while being transported to the rear and had been dropped at the edge of the Baltimore Pike to lighten the load.[35] They wound their way forward through the road's jumble: groups of prisoners being escorted to the rear, and then something new to them: refugees, on foot and horseback, and some driving wagons piled high with dining room chairs and mattresses.[36]

As they trotted out the last mile of this day's march up to Gettysburg, the smoke and noise rolled through the town and out to them. The Federals first up to the battle had fought desperately but, outnumbered and outflanked, were falling back onto a long ridge that rose south of the town and terminated in the two hills off to their left.[37] Around suppertime Candy's soldiers filed into a wheat field two hundred yards to the left of the pike and slipped out of their packs.[38]

Round-Topped Hills: Gettysburg, July 1, 1863

After this eventful day of fast marching, the men who kept diaries were too tired to take note of their surroundings. These few facts they knew: the Eleventh Corps had been driven back through the town and was holding the right of the line, the First Corps was in the center, spread out in battle line along the ridge, and Geary's division on the left, two miles south of the town.[39] They camped within an easy walk's distance of the lesser of two round-topped hills. Tomorrow's battle would define the grave importance of this place, and future generations would enshrine it as one of the most notable of all American places.

The heat of the day expired with the darkness, and a light rain began to fall through which the Army of the Potomac moved up on the pike and continued to move all through the night. The whole army was on its way, and there could be no doubt that a battle on the scale of Chancellorsville awaited. For now, they did not seem to be in any immediate danger. General Geary, however, was in a tremendous stir. He had ridden out ahead on their way here looking for Gen. Oliver O. Howard, commanding the Eleventh Corps, and instead met Gen. Winfield Scott Hancock. Geary had last seen Hancock when the two had gotten into a shouting match on the last morning at Chancellorsville over which of them was giving the orders, and Geary had backed down.

Hancock was in command of the Second Corps and was giving orders until General Meade came up. He told Geary that the right of Federal line could take care of itself. The "threatening emergency" was on the left, where the enemy was reportedly preparing to flank them, and he ordered Geary to place his division there. Geary moved his men into a line that ran along the two round-topped hills.[40] He did not yet know these hills by their local names, Little Round Top and Big Round Top, but he immediately recognized their strategic importance. If the rebels got guns on these hills, they could fire down the entire length of the Federal line, and the battle would be over before they'd had a fair chance to fight it. Candy's brigade held the end of the whole Federal left. Geary ordered the Fifth Ohio and 147th Pennsylvania to climb to the tops of the two hills and watch for signs of the enemy.[41]

If they were on the scene of a great emergency, the soldiers did not know it. Fresh beef had been issued, and the boys lit small fires among the rocks and roasted their suppers on sharpened sticks and bayonets.[42] Slocum's corps was the only one in the Army of the Potomac that had traveled here with a supply train, and soldiers who had worn out what they had marching to this place drew new clothing.[43]

They were aroused before sunrise, and by five o'clock they were marched back onto the pike. Some of Candy's soldiers had a considerable hike to rejoin their brigade. Lawrence Wilson, presently a soldier in the Seventh Ohio, recalled that Geary had thrown skirmishers down the western slope of the smaller round-top, through the weird jumble of huge rocks known locally as Devil's Den, and out onto the Emmitsburg Road. He then sent a line of sharpshooters three hundred yards beyond even it.[44] Once everyone had been collected, they started up the pike.

Culp's Hill, July 2, 1863

The sun came up over the trees lining the pike and immediately it was stifling hot. The road ran north to the right of a long, low ridge upon which thousands of soldiers moved and then continued into the town, which was currently in the hands of the enemy. After an hour's march, they left the pike and defiled to the right onto a farm lane and up into a shady, rocky terrain. Through the tops of the trees they could see the summit of a considerable prominence known by the name of the family that had owned it. To soldiers already atop Culp's Hill, views disclosed the town of Gettysburg below waking up to a change in ownership. More directly below and to the left lay the town's cemetery, with its fine brick gatehouse, where thousands of blue-coated men were tending their coffee and digging rifle pits among the gravestones.

As the Giddings Boys approached nearer the base of the big hill, they could see a second, smaller hill four hundred yards to their right. The two hills were connected by a saddle, which appeared fairly level to the eye. A sluggish river that went by the name of Rock Creek flashed intermittently down below in the green haze.

The Federal line was taking the shape of a shepherd's crook: the shaft running from north of the Round Tops, where they had camped last night, up to the cemetery, where it then hooked to the right, following the contours of Culp's Hill. Slocum's corps had been assigned the defense of this ground, on the right of the line of the Army of the Potomac. The Baltimore Pike ran on a diagonal two to three hundred yards behind them and in the rear of the Union army. If the rebels turned this end of the line and got onto the pike, the whole army would be taken in flank, and reverse. The sound of soldiers working with axes came to them from up ahead, and they drew closer to it.

The benefit of fighting behind entrenchments had been demonstrated to them at Chancellorsville, where at the very end few had held off many. The regiments of Brig. Gen. George S. Greene's brigade, Geary's division, had arrived at Culp's Hill ahead of Candy, and every soldier was busily at work improving the natural advantage of high ground. At Chancellorsville, Greene's soldiers, New Yorkers all of them, built lines so strong that the rebels who came upon them regarded them as veritable forts. Here, on Culp's Hill, with plenty of slabby rock, fence rail, and trees of just the right girth, they were building defenses that far exceeded their previous efforts. Hollow log cribs high as a man's chest were being laid up, the interior filled with rock, and a stout log laid at the top with enough gap to allow a soldier to poke his musket out and aim at whatever came up the slope at him. Others built their breastworks of logs entirely, with uprights made of cordwood driven into the earth to brace the freestanding walls.[45]

The Spangler farm lane on which they moved terminated on this headland overhanging the creek valley. The soldiers of Kane's brigade were presently staking out defenses forward of a stone wall that ran along the half of the saddle to Candy's right and up and over the lower hill. They spread out into battle line here, but a short while later an order came for Candy's regiments to move left, nearer Culp's Hill.[46] They picked up and moved uphill a hundred yards and crowded into a swale in rear of the 137th and 149th New York Regiments of Greene's brigade, who were manning the line on the sideslope of Culp's Hill, where the topography eased itself onto the saddle.[47]

They leaned their muskets into pyramids close to hand. The Giddings Boys drowsed under the influence of fatigue and heat without a single musket shot to disturb them. Late in the afternoon, the sound of battle came to them from the left, in the vicinity of the rocky hills they had left just that morning, and along the ridge that ran down to them. The sound was oddly muffled, as if the disputants were conducting their battle under a featherbed, but to the ears of veteran soldiers here at the base of Culp's Hill, the sound was clearly that of severe fighting.[48] Next, artillery shells began to howl through the treetops.[49] A rebel battery on the far side of Rock Creek was throwing shells end-on into the ranks of the First and Eleventh Corps, to their left at Cemetery Hill. General Geary ordered two sections of his artillery to extinguish their fire, and after a half hour of counterbattery work, the rebel battery desisted.[50] Relative quiet returned to their sector.

A March to Nowhere, Night, July 2, 1863

After the war, Pvt. Henry Knapp reflected on his part in the great battle of Gettysburg, "For a soldier in the ranks to pretend to tell or explain the movements of a great army going into battle is preposterous, as he many times, hardly knows what regiment is on his right or left."[51] Of the grand designs for these affairs, the private soldier was ignorant: such things were the province of generals. In the case of the movement they were about to undertake, their own general, John White Geary, seemed as confused as the plainest private.

The afternoon had worn itself out, but the fight on their left—volcanic in nature from the very first, based on what could be heard of it here at Culp's Hill—pushed even higher, with no sign of having yet reached its climax. Soldiers fighting over there were making small plots famous, like the Peach Orchard, the Wheatfield, Little Round Top, and the Devil's Den. The sun was going down, and the rays of it passing through the smoke filter sinking down along the Emmitsburg Road produced a weak yellow light back where the Twenty-Ninth Ohio crouched. They had waited through the afternoon and early evening for the combustion of the battle back toward Cemetery Ridge to eat its way to them, but it had not. At seven o'clock Geary received an order from General Slocum. He was needed immediately on Cemetery Ridge, where the Federal line was in danger of being breached. Greene's brigade was to stay behind, and the boys of Kane's and Candy's brigades started out for the center of the fighting, with Geary leading the way.

Geary explained later that he had started out without any specific instructions as to his objective. Given the dangers, and the darkness settling-in, having started without plotting a destination would strike some as genuinely odd.[52] Williams's division had started out a half hour before him, and the orders to Geary had been no more specific than to head out by the right flank and follow Williams. Williams had gone beyond sight and hearing, and Geary followed what he thought was Williams's rear-guard.[53] It turned out to be the trail that stragglers were using to get themselves to the rear. Geary had gotten off track.

Within a half hour or less of their setting out for the Union center, small lights began to flicker and wink behind them up and down the line of Greene's brigade, followed in a split second by the report of hundreds of muskets. Within a minute, Culp's Hill was outlined in an orange corona.[54] The men of Jackson's old corps, under command of Gen. Dick Ewell, had materialized out of the trees in masses below Culp's Hill and were presently storming their way up the sides and onto the saddle. Preservation of the Union right now became as precarious, and grave, as the fight at Little Round Top, on the far left, where Col. Joshua Chamberlain and the Twentieth Maine were fighting to hold on. Greene spaced out what soldiers he had to fill the breastworks Kane's brigade had occupied. Col. David Ireland and the 137th New York Volunteers passed down the slope and spread out into a thin line to fill the breastworks previously taken up by an entire brigade; they soon found themselves the only regiment on the hanging end of the Union right. Ireland's boys fought like tigers, but there were too few of them and too many rebels, and before long the enemy got into the breastworks directly below them.[55]

Sorely pressed from three sides at once, Ireland ordered his boys to fall back up the slope to the end of Greene's breastworks. The line here ran along a narrow and short traverse across the lower reach of Culp's Hill, near the top of the saddle. If the 147th New York gave way, there was a fair chance the rebels would shortly be loose on the Baltimore Pike. That did not happen, but it cost Ireland's boys dearly to make sure it did not. Thirty-eight of their officers and soldiers died at Gettysburg and another eighty-six were wounded, most of them lost in the severe fighting of this evening of July 2, 1863.[56]

With the sounds of the desperate combat of Ireland's troops and the other outfits right behind, Geary continued to move away. He had missed the turn that would have taken him to the backside of Cemetery Ridge and continued south on the Baltimore Pike, in the direction of Two Taverns. He would soon have himself and his men so far in the Federal rear that staff officers sent out to locate him and bring him back could not find him.

It was full dark by the time Geary's two brigades passed by an old sawmill on Rock Creek. He moved them even further from where they were wanted, over the bridge spanning Rock Creek, and onto its east side, where he threw the Boys out into a skirmish line.[57] He later claimed that he had received an order from someone's headquarters to hold the line here. At nine o'clock, Geary ordered Kane to return to Culp's Hill, to be followed by Candy's brigade. It was getting on toward midnight before Candy got the order to move, and the soldiers began retracing their steps.[58] Taking up the positions they had vacated on Culp's Hill would prove far more dangerous work than leaving them.

General Greene had sent a message back to Kane, warning him that rebels had taken his trenches. Before the warning reached him, Kane had approached to within two hundred yards of his former position, when it lit up with fire, and bullets came whining toward them out of the ink. Kane poked at the line a little, which was enough to determine that there were rebels in it. He backed away and took another road up to Greene.[59]

The racket of Kane's discovery came back to Charles Candy's soldiers, informing them that the place had become dangerous. Rebels were known to be in the breastworks, perhaps lurking behind stone walls too, or hiding in the dark groves waiting to spring up and rip them with fire. Any errors in direction finding now could lead to disaster, and Candy proceeded with caution. Gray light was showing in the east by the time the Ohioans got back into their assigned position.[60] The Twenty-Ninth Ohio lay down on the duff-covered granite floor of a swale behind the right end of Greene's New Yorkers.[61] They had been on the move all night, "wandering," it seemed to one Giddings Regiment soldier, among briars and boulders.[62] Like at Chancellorsville, the Twenty-Ninth Ohio had been on the field for two days and had yet to sustain a serious casualty.

Dedication Day

It was autumn 1887 and the countryside outside Gettysburg was splendid with russet, reds, and yellows. A new growth of timber was making its way up below Culp's Hill, but rising above it stark and white were the carcasses of the old giants whose limbs had shaded the soldiers who had fought on this slanted ground a quarter of a century ago. They were so full of holes that they looked as if they had been attacked by armies of woodpeckers. Souvenir hunters had been at work on them for the past two decades, whittling and drilling for the bullets hidden within. Some had sawed trees off at the ground, taking the whole away to be cut up into sections in a more convenient place and then varnished and tagged with a brass plate, certifying that this lead-filled chunk of Pennsylvania forest was a True and Authentic relic of the war's most famous battle.

The useable parts of the walls of logs, stone, and dirt behind which the Boys had fought their part of the battle of Gettysburg had long since been carted off. After the battle, the field became immediately famous, and the passage of twenty-four years had not diminished fascination with it in the least. Granite monuments to what they had done were going up all over the field. Each of the loyal states had been given a day for its sons to dedicate their monuments, wander the hills and fields, and remember. This day, September 14, was Ohio Day. Over a dozen Ohio infantry regiments had fought here, along with two cavalry regiments, and four artillery batteries. All who could make the trip were here to mark their outfit's contribution to the victory. The Boys of the Twenty-Ninth Ohio Volunteer Infantry gathered to dedicate the monument they had raised to themselves. Half a lifetime had passed since most had been back here, and although they were no longer boys in the biological sense, they still called themselves that. One of their own had done the design. Frank O. Weary may have been the youngest soldier to serve in the regiment. He had slung a drum around his neck and begun marching with them when only fourteen years old, and by this time he was a modestly successful architect in Akron.

They pitched tents on the ground around their monument. Their families had been put up at hotels in the town, to protect wives and offspring from rough veteran talk and to allow the Boys the chance to celebrate without reproach.

Edward Hayes gave their dedication speech. He had come up the short distance from Washington, D.C., where he held a modest government post—the earnings supplementing his monthly pension for disability owing to severe wounds received on another battlefield, later in time, and far removed from this. Wilbur F. Stevens had officially commanded the regiment at Gettysburg, but he was not invited to speak, nor was his one of the two names they had chosen to engrave on their memorial.

By 1887, Stevens was trying his luckless after-the-war-life in the now settled-up Far West, although it was unlikely he would have attended had he lived just up the road. James Storer could not be present for reasons all of them knew. He had spent the last many years confined to his wheeled chair, in constant pain. Hayes said it would be difficult to single out any man's bravery where individual bravery had been a matter of course. Everything had changed since that day, until what had been was barely recognizable. As Hayes said, "Nothing but the ground remains . . . so thoroughly burned into our memories that it seems as if we, to-day, know every foot of it."[63] He remembered for them, lest any had forgotten, that they had come to this place knowing that in this battle, more than any other, the life of the nation had been at stake, and they had played their part in saving it.

The Fight for Culp's Hill, Morning, July 3, 1863

Chaplain Ames made his solitary way toward the hill in the predawn dark, the woods full of troops moving silently toward final positions in a strengthening of the Federal right. He found the Giddings Boys in the shallow hollow, Capt. Wilbur F. Stevens, commanding, in battle line and ready.[64] During the action of the night before, Greene's brigade, with reinforcements hustled over from the corps to their left, had kept the rebels from taking Culp's Hill, and nearing the end of this short summer's night, they still held the positions they had occupied when the first rebel attack had come. The enemy dead lay below the entrenchments, in some places tumbled atop each other three deep, showing how deadly the combat had been. But the rebels had succeeded in taking the lower breastworks, running down in the direction of Spangler's Spring, and the crest of lower Culp's Hill, and thousands more were poised a few hundred yards below, along Rock Creek, close enough in some places that their whispered conversations could be heard.

The enemy was ready to capitalize on their gains of the evening before, and when it got light enough, they would push up the slope leading onto the saddle, sweep the blue men from the breastworks there, and roll up the Federal right. Geary's men stood in their way. When they finally got back from their midnight ramble in the rear of the Union army, two regiments of Candy's brigade, the Fifth Ohio and 147th Pennsylvania, were placed in line to the right of Kane, along the Spangler farm lane, which ran west to the Baltimore Pike, facing the lower summit and saddle. The Sixty-Sixth Ohio had been sent up to the top of the big hill to assist the Sixtieth New York in defending it.

The Twenty-Ninth Ohio was placed in a ravine, as Capt. Edward Hayes described it, although it was too shallow to bear much resemblance to one. Others referred to it as a swale. Unless one had a trained eye for otherwise imperceptible undulations in the terrain, it would be difficult to see that it could provide any safety at all. The swale was near the position they had rested the day before and ran north from Kane's position and behind the base of Culp's Hill. From here, they could be moved quickly to the support of either of Geary's two fronts: whether in the refused line facing south, toward the lower hill, or due east fifty yards, where Greene's soldiers steadied themselves for the inevitable renewal of combat that would come with sunup.

Most of the artillery was ranged out of their sight back behind the pike. However, one Twenty-Ninth Ohio veteran seemed to recall that a Federal battery had wheeled into place right behind their position and that they had been ordered to lie flat in front of it. They were close enough that fireballs leaping from the barrels nearly touched them, and the muzzle blast lifted men from the ground.[65] Everyone made themselves thin as flapjacks. The guns were throwing shells down on the breastworks that the rebels had succeeded in taking the night before. After fifteen minutes of intense shelling, the Federal guns went quiet, and the rebels of Johnson's division, Ewell's corps, came up out of the woods bordering Rock Creek and attacked. In a moment, nonstop firing was general along the entire line.

It became apparent from the number of massed rebels coming up the slope from the creek bottom, firing and yelling in their peculiar style, that the big push would be directly against Culp's Hill and the saddle. Colonel Ireland's 137th New York boys stood behind their angled breastwork, with battle flags propped straight up at the center of their line, and went to work.

By the accounts of some soldiers, life in the swale in the rear of Greene's brigade was at least as dangerous as in the breastworks, and transit between the two was especially perilous. Bullets fired from fifty to several hundred yards away ricocheted off boulders and trees above the swale, hitting soldiers who were waiting there. An hour into the battle, the bedlam rose to an even higher pitch as the 147th Pennsylvania charged a wall hiding a line of enemy infantry on the Twenty-Ninth's right, and after a hot, stand-up fight, the Pennsylvanians drove the rebels away and back toward the captured breastworks. Periodically, the Twelfth Corps artillery added its measure of noise, some of the shells landing and exploding no more than a hundred yards from where the Giddings Boys waited for the call to action.

An hour and a half after the battle began, Captain Stevens was huddled with a group of officers in the swale when he was struck in the neck by a spent ball, which by his account caused him severe pain, and giddiness.[66] The injury did not bleed, nor did it even leave a mark. As to the velocity of the bullet, Adjutant Storer remembered many years later that it had struck Stevens with no more force than a schoolboy might apply to a marble with his cocked thumb. Whether the injury was sufficient to force any other man from the field, or whether his courage had failed and he used it as an excuse to cover his retreat, would be the bone of a fierce argument that broke to the surface decades later. Stevens believed he was substantially hurt, while to James Storer, he was showing himself to be the same coward he had been at Cedar Mountain. For now, Stevens followed the correct protocol. He showed the injury to Colonel Candy, who gave him permission to leave. Wilbur Stevens turned over command to Capt. Edward Hayes just as the fight for Culp's Hill neared one of its several climaxes.

Fifteen minutes after Stevens's departure, at about five forty-five in the morning, a messenger (Ireland himself, in one veteran's memory) made his way into the swale and passed an order to Hayes. The 137th New York's situation was desperate. The Twenty-Ninth Ohio was to move forward and relieve the 137th New York in the breastworks. They had run low on ammunition, and their musket barrels were so choked with grime from constant firing that a ball could not be forced down the barrel. Hayes was a cautious man, and he disliked taking his men anywhere he had not first reconnoitered. He made his way forward to the breastworks and found Colonel Ireland, who pointed out to him the portion of the line for which the Twenty-Ninth Ohio would be responsible.

Of the several men who led the regiment during the war, Edward Hayes was the only one who ever stated his philosophy of command. This was his first experience in giving orders to the whole outfit, and it came to him like a flash right here in the swale: what the regiment needed at times like this was not a "great commander" in the commonly understood sense, but one who could put the regiment properly into line, set it square at the enemy, and then let it go.[67]

Hayes returned to the swale and called the Boys together. He stood to his full height, even though bullets were singing through the boughs hanging above his head. "Boys, we are going to advance. I don't want a shot fired until you are in the trenches. 29th forward, double quick."[68] He turned and, with his sword held high, yelled, "March." They went forward at a half run, "with a shout that would have frightened a hundred Ciceroes."[69] Private Knapp supposed that they yelled not so much to frighten the rebels but to keep their own courage up.[70]

The crest of the swale lay between them and the breastworks, and getting over it was a hazardous enterprise. The rebels were firing from below the Federal line, and the bullets that missed their targets flew on and upward toward the next elevation, which was the crest of the low ridge they were about to cross. The Giddings Boys made it over the ridgetop and rushed down toward the breastworks, stopping to fire a volley of covering fire to allow Ireland's boys to pass through them to the rear. Colonel Ireland had seen a good deal of battlefield bravery here and in other places. He later told Hayes that the Twenty-Ninth's charge into the breastworks had been the finest thing he had ever seen done under fire.[71] The Twenty-Ninth Ohio's soldiers planted their colors at the center of their line and began fighting.

Uphill and to their immediate left, the 149th New York was perched on a ledge, nearly unassailable from below. The length of line the Twenty-Ninth was defending lay on the traverse directly above the saddle, and it was dangerously lower ground. To the rebels pushing up from below, this point looked like it might be easier to take than the others, and, driven by the fire slashing down on them from the Federal rifle pits, they took the path of least resistance to the top, which brought them within easy range of the Twenty-Ninth Ohio's muskets.

Out front of the Giddings Boys, the slope up from the creek gentled into a barn-sized tub, with a slight ridge on the back side that partially concealed the enemy until he had closed to within seventy-five yards of the breastworks. Boys in the front rank fired and then sidestepped out of the way for the rank behind them to come up and shoot. In this methodical manner, they resisted one attack after another and shot down a great many rebel soldiers. They were in tight quarters here, four men to the yard, but the breastworks were stout and a man was relatively safe unless he raised himself above the head log.

George Hayward, one of their heroes at Chancellorsville, beloved by his men for his selflessness, was the first Twenty-Ninth soldier to go down in this battle. He stood up and was struck dead immediately, a ball through the neck.[72] The rebel who had shot him was hidden within the fold of a boulder no more than twenty paces from the breastworks. He made the mistake of trying to pick off one more boy in their line, and the puff of smoke from his shot gave away his position. No less than a hundred rifles aimed a volley at him, and he was punched backward; his scream upon being struck was the last that was heard from him.[73] Henceforth, if a Giddings soldier wanted to locate the enemy's fire, he raised his kepi on the tip of his ramrod, and in most cases the cap was ventilated with bullet holes, but the smoke advertised the position of the rebel marksman, and the Boys swung their fire on the source.[74]

Against a murderous fire, the rebels continued to advance up the slope. Some came so close to the breastworks that they could neither advance nor retreat. They surrendered and were helped over the breastworks into captivity. Fifty-two rebels came up in a group in front of the 147th New York and surrendered, and from them it was learned that they were fighting their old adversary, the Stonewall division.[75]

All along the line, the soldiers of one regiment moved forward to replace another in regular shifts, like factory workers. After exactly two hours and ten minutes of nonstop firing, the Twenty-Ninth Ohio was relieved by the Twenty-Eighth Pennsylvania, and the Boys withdrew to the swale.[76] For want of rags to clean fouled gun barrels, soldiers tore strips from their shirts. Canteens were passed around and what was left in them shared. Water had become scarce, and the day was miserably hot, but the Boys were too absorbed in their work to notice.

At nine thirty, Colonel Candy ordered the Twenty-Ninth Ohio to get into line and prepare to move to a meadow to their right where the rebels seemed to be making headway. But the troops fighting there succeeded in driving the rebels back by themselves, and the Twenty-Ninth's services were not needed. A few minutes later, the adjutant of Greene's brigade came into the swale and reported that the 137th New York was being hard pressed again and was nearly out of ammunition.[77] The Twenty-Ninth responded with the same élan that had marked their first rush to the breastworks. This time the trip was far more costly.

A body of rebels had come up near the breastworks and had actually taken the right end of it, according to SeCheverell.[78] The regiment made a half wheel and charged toward the breach with bayonets lowered. Just as they reached the ridge, a bullet storm hit them square in the face. Two-thirds of the regiment's soldiers killed and wounded at Gettysburg went down in these few seconds. Those who survived the passage over the top continued forward into the breastworks, driving the rebels away.[79]

At no point along the Federal line had the enemy made a serious break. To continue the attack seemed folly, but Ewell ordered more men forward, up the slope, and into the narrow killing zone. The rocky ground below Candy's men was by now thick in some places with dead and dying men. By this time in the war, the Boys had grudgingly admitted that the rebel soldiers were possessed of superhuman endurance and valor, but even they could stand only so much. One group of nearly one hundred rebels, of the Fourth Virginia it was said, had raised a flag of surrender in front of the Seventh Ohio's segment of the line. The rebel general Edward Johnson's chief of staff, Maj. Benjamin Watkins Leigh, rode out and ordered it down. Leigh had been with Stonewall Jackson on the nighttime scout in which Jackson had received his mortal wounds, and it had been Leigh who covered Jackson's body with his own, to protect him from further harm.[80]

The Seventh Ohio aimed a volley directly at him and he fell, "pierced like a riddle."[81] The soldiers whom Leigh had admonished for their lack of resolve came up to the breastworks and surrendered. Later in the morning a squad of seven rebels waved a white rag from below in the rocks directly in front of the Twenty-Ninth Ohio, and the line went quiet long enough for them to come up and surrender.[82]

The terrain, and the intensity of the fire, did not allow the enemy to come forward in organized battle lines. They attacked in squads, carrying out as many as a dozen charges, every one of them shot to pieces as it came up. Not every rebel who got up to the lip of the breastworks intended to surrender. One man came up to the wall held by the Seventh Ohio and got his hands on their colors. The color bearer pulled a revolver and shot the man, but the attacker did not give up his hold until an officer stepped forward and with a swing of his sword neatly severed the rebel's hand. Afterward, many soldiers came over to see the oddity of his hand still clenched around the staff.[83]

In the several hours they spent here on the upper reach of the saddle at Culp's Hill, the Twenty-Ninth's soldiers fired upward of 150 rounds per man.[84] Every soldier here this morning was confident he had killed at least one rebel; some men claimed they had shot down a great many more than that. To show their coolness under fire, Capt. Myron Wright later gave examples for the citizens back home in Summit County of the wit and good humor the Boys indulged while in the breastworks. Pvt. Tom Bare, Company D, was a boy whom others depended on for his drollery in trying times. His comrades pestered him this perilous morning with a comic, dialectical phrase he had popularized in the regiment: "Domb, Domb, ish de boat [boot] on?" And he replied, "If it tant on now it won't get on at all."[85] Also evident was the wit of another jokester of Wright's company, Pvt. Ezra Spidel, who while taking a rest from the ceaseless loading and firing, was bothered by several bullets sizzling past his head. His mock complaint: "Well, I guess I might fire *another* volley," after which he went back to the business.[86]

Ireland's boys relieved the Giddings Regiment at a little after ten in the morning and were relieved in turn by them a short while later.[87] By then the fire had begun to slacken along the line at Culp's Hill. Without their knowing it as yet, the last concerted rebel assault of the morning had been beaten back. General Ewell, it was learned from captured rebel officers, had sworn he would take Culp's Hill and get his army onto the Baltimore Pike if it took every man he had, and he had failed.[88] The Boys peered through the gap below the head log and observed that there were no more targets moving on the slope below, and they stopped firing.[89]

They had been in the front line for a substantial portion of the morning's nearly eight-hour battle. Capt. Wilbur Stevens returned around noon. He was still too unwell to take back command, and he left it in Hayes's hands until late in the afternoon.[90] The noon hour passed in comparative quiet as the last of Ewell's men, hurried along by rifle fire, got down off the slope and back into cover along the creek. The thud of two artillery rounds, followed by the firing of a multitude of guns, announced the opening of James Longstreet's bombardment of the Union center along Cemetery Ridge. The boys here at Culp's Hill got low to the ground, which was prudent given the errant rounds from the rebel guns that presently came screeching overhead, injuring some of Candy's soldiers.

After an hour or so, the volume of artillery fire backed off its peak and then nearly stopped. Fifteen minutes later, they heard the crash made by the simultaneous discharge of thousands of rifles. The racket ripped along until about three o'clock, when the sounds of battle from that quarter lessened. They learned later that day that the rebels had come out of the woods opposite Cemetery Ridge in perfect ranks by the thousands, crossed the Emmitsburg Road, and moved up toward the Federal line. The Union boys on Cemetery Ridge "had had it all their own way" too, and the apex of the great battle of Gettysburg had been reached.[91]

The Twenty-Ninth Ohio Volunteer Infantry stayed at the breastworks until ten o'clock that evening. Picket fire snapped up and down along the line, some of it threatening to break out into something more serious, but it did not. The Boys were tired and they had not had anything to eat since yesterday's noon meal. There was no rest to be had here, even if a soldier could find room to recline. The pleas for help from the stricken rebels lying just beyond the breastworks made that impossible. During the evening, a group of twenty-five rebels who had worked themselves too far forward to retreat decided on surrender, and came up to the Twenty-Ninth's works and climbed over.[92] From behind their wall, the Boys could see that the fire had been terrific. The bark had been peeled from every tree in sight. As to what other destruction the battle had produced, they would have to wait for tomorrow to discover.

"Such a Sight I Never Saw," July 4, 1863

The Twenty-Ninth Regiment was back in the breastworks before sunrise on July 4, but there was no firing. A reconnaissance by the Seventh Ohio down into the valley of Rock Creek revealed that Ewell had left their front. The soldiers climbed over the works with the mists low over the creek bottom, to investigate their killings. Geary's division had fired 277,000 bullets and hundreds of artillery rounds into an area that measured four hundred by two hundred fifty yards, and most of that into an area half that size.[93] The rebels had removed some of their wounded from directly in front of the Twenty-Ninth Ohio but had left most of their dead. The Giddings Boys were assigned the task of committing their own dead to the ground and, after that, collecting and burying the enemy dead. "Such a sight I never saw," was how

Nathan Parmater described what he saw: numberless tableaux of death and mutilation, every one of them terrible beyond description.

The rebel dead lay in a region of still green shadows noisy with the buzzing of flies. The soldiers seemed as impressed by the damage done to the trees as to the rebels. Every tree within three hundred yards of the breastworks had been torn and girdled by the immense musket fire; the leaves and branches that were still attached were turned under and drooping.

The ground here was carpeted with the refuse of battle: pieces of photographs, shoes, canteens, blankets, knapsacks, ramrods, caps, and letters. The brush was festooned with entrails, pieces of scalp, and scraps of uniforms. The dead lay singly or, where an artillery shell or a trained volley had found them, in huddled groups of upward of a dozen. The corpses were decaying quickly in this heat, turning black and bloated, some with arms thrown out as if in protest of some huge injustice, others peaceful and without a mark on them, but dead as stone nonetheless. Here they found bodies cut entirely in two by shells and others hammered into mush by the strikes of dozens of bullets.

Lt. Edward T. Curtiss of the regiment's Pioneer Corps directed the burial detail. They lugged the dead to central points and buried them in long trenches. Curtiss paused in the morning's work and came up to the breastworks to rest. Private Spidel, the boy credited with the droll remark about firing *another* volley, asked Curtiss how many rebels he had buried so far. Curtiss said his detail had buried eighty-five, and that was just in the area within a few steps of the breastworks. Spidel's comment: "Just the number I killed."[94]

Around twelve hundred rebel dead were found out front of Geary's line from the breastworks down to the creek bottom.[95] The day's work succeeded in burying nine hundred of them. As further proof of the scope of their victory, over five thousand rifles were collected and piled in front of Geary's sector; five hundred alone were picked up directly in front of the Twenty-Ninth's part of the line.[96] During this inspection of horrors, putting it under the ground, there was trophy hunting, too. Soldiers of the Seventh Ohio had already gotten to the body of the rebel adjutant Leigh and taken his sword, watch, and diary.[97] Nathan Parmater was a well-educated, churchgoing young man by all accounts, and compassionate, but he wanted a souvenir. By the time he arrived, only Colonel Leigh's shirt studs remained. Parmater clipped them and put them in his pocket.[98]

These black and bloated soldiers with the staring eyes had wounded and killed boys of the Twenty-Ninth at Kernstown and Port Republic, and at Cedar Mountain. Jackson's men had crushed the right of the line at Chancellorsville, which started the dominoes falling in the Twenty-Ninth Ohio's direction. The rebels had now been paid back with interest, so the boys remarked as they moved about the slope and regarded the dead. Only as older men, with children of their own, of the same age of the dead thrown down here, would they comprehend what each of these corpses represented. Years later, a Seventh Ohio soldier would look back on the killing they had done here and reflect, "It would be a sad sight to see at this late day; but we were young then, and did not realize that many a mother would shed tears over her brave and fallen boy that might have been a support and solace to her in her declining years."[99]

Upward of 165,000 soldiers of both sides had fought here at Gettysburg. Nearly 7,000 of them had been killed and many times that number injured. For the three days the fighting in Pennsylvania raged, an atmospheric anomaly had covered the neighborhood of Ashtabula County with a dark smoky mist through which the sun could hardly be seen.[100] The first news of the greatest battle of the war came to the village of Jefferson through a similar murk. It was learned that some in the Twenty-Ninth Ohio had been wounded, but not severely, and that only one man in the regiment, Lt. George Hayward, had been killed.[101] The hard fact was that nine of the Giddings Boys were dead, or would soon die, and thirty-five had been wounded.[102]

Myron Wright's company had been especially hard hit. Among the five men lost from it was Pvt. Mathias Soden. He was the youngest of thirteen children of an impoverished family. He had gone to work for wages to help his family when he was a boy of eleven. He earned one hundred dollars during one summer's work; he took twenty-five of it in cash and the balance in cows, which he herded home with the hopes of starting his family off in the dairy business, and out of poverty.[103] At Dumfries, he had gathered the seeds of a cedar tree and sent them home with the request that his family plant them to see if they would take in Ohio soil.[104] Mathias had been shot in the abdomen during the second rush over the ridge toward the breastworks and was taken to the field hospital. An injury like his carried a mandatory death sentence, as any soldier knew, and he did not survive. Also gone was Ben Pontius, the young man who had made the sketch of Camp Giddings and sent it to his mother to show he was part of something large and purposeful. He had taken a ball in the head and was dead. Other boys of Wright's company had been grievously wounded. Sydney Kennedy's eye had been drilled out by a musket ball, but he recovered.[105]

Wallace Hoyt normally used an ink pen to write his letters, emphasizing his fine hand with flourishes. He found a small scrap of paper and a pencil and composed a note to his parents. The note would be a self-created artifact, proving in future years that he had been there. The letters making the words were shaky and imprecise.

> Gettysburg July 4th
>
> Dear Parents
> As there is
> A chance to send out mail
> I will send you a few lines
> I am now setting in the
> Rifle Pits where we fought all day yesterday.
> I am not hurt all though A great
> many of our regt are. firing
> has commensed and I must
> close this is the forth day's
> fight we are pretty well tuckered
> out we are whipping them
> Good by.   W. B. Hoyt[106]

The heat and humidity had been building for days, and on the night of July 4 the weather let go with a regular gully washer, which cleansed the air temporarily of its stench and filled the floors of their breastworks with rainwater. A soldier of Company I, Pvt. William Waterman, had stretched out atop the works for a nap and accidentally rolled off into the noxious water with a ker-chug that made the Boys laugh. Even the taciturn adjutant James B. Storer laughed.[107] For their first time since they had been with the Army of the Potomac, a glorious victory had been achieved, but for now there would not be time to celebrate.

In the Wake of Battle

The student at the Lutheran Theological Seminary at Gettysburg who had visited the regiment in Frederick heard they had been in the fight on Culp's Hill and he walked up from the town to visit them. He found them near the rifle pits they had defended. The Twenty-Ninth Ohio's dead lay beneath fresh mounds on a shady elevation close by. The student prayed over them, while the survivors packed their gear. He had wanted to spend more time talking to the soldiers about what it had been like to fight the great battle, but the drums called them to the road before he had a chance. He walked with them a ways and then turned back.[108]

The Twenty-Ninth Ohio had finished its work on Culp's Hill, but for their chaplain, Lyman D. Ames, the work was just beginning. He pitched in at the field hospitals, focusing his labors at first on the needs of the wounded boys of his own regiment. As the Twenty-Ninth Ohio marched away, he rode his horse down the pike, through the traffic of the last of the Army of the Potomac, and reached a loop in the course of Rock Creek where the Twelfth Corps hospital had been set up, around the house of a farmer named Bushman.

Slocum's corps was the only corps in the Army of the Potomac to have come to the battlefield with its own train of medical supplies. The wounded were handled efficiently and treated quickly compared to earlier battles, and individual suffering had thus been reduced. The surgeon in charge of the Twelfth Corps hospital reported with extreme satisfaction that it had taken merely six hours to collect all the wounded, provide them food and shelter, and dress their wounds. Within twenty-four hours every necessary capital operation—amputations mainly—had been performed.[109] Initially the wounded were sheltered in a large barn or in one of the farm sheds on the Bushman place, but they soon overflowed these and were laid in canvas wall tents.

This was only his second battle, but Chaplain Ames had already established a routine. The regiment's wounded were scattered around, and finding all of them was his first task. He made a careful list of their names and the nature of their wounds and prepared a list of casualties to be sent to the newspaper back in Conneaut.[110] Ames felt poorly going into the work here, and intimate contact with maimed boys, many of whom could not possibly recover, wore at him. Knowing they were to die, some boys bargained with their Maker and promised Ames that if they were spared, they would discard their rough soldier ways and lead a better life.[111] Some of the wounded of Slocum's corps improved enough to be sent off to a general hospital, while others failed at a regular rate of a half dozen or more a day, and their burial required Ames to stand in the rain and say his few words over them. Ames gave the rebel dead the same Christian ceremony.

Ten days after the battle, enough boys had been sent away, or died, to free up space in the Bushman barn for the staging of divine services. Soldiers on crutches, some helped by attendants, shuffled in to hear Ames's prayers, and some even knelt down on the packed-dirt floor, which was gratifying to him.[112] Civilians had come into the town from various places, some from very far away, in search of friends and loved ones. They made their way into the Twelfth Corps hospital and went up and down the rows, searching. Clement Marsh made the train trip out from Homerville, Ohio, and was currently walking the rows looking for a familiar face.[113] His journey had been difficult. The year his son, Sgt. John Marsh, went away to the war, the father had come down with rheumatic fever, which had blinded him for a time and left him too weak to work at carpentry, the trade he had practiced before the war with his son as his helper. He had come to Gettysburg to take his son home.

The parents of Pvt. Edward J. Brown had come on a similar mission. Brown had been severely wounded, and his parents came to get him and take him home, where their loving care would speed him to recovery. He died at his home in Jefferson a few days after his arrival.[114] The Twelfth Corps field hospital was broken up in favor of a larger facility near the town, and Ames tied his blanket to his saddle and rode up to Gettysburg, stopping to survey the battlefield along the way.

The town was wrecked—glass, brick, doors, and shattered window frames littered every street. The fields around it where the armies had fought lay covered with dead men. Hundreds of dead horses lay steaming in the heat waiting to be dragged into piles, doused with kerosene, and burned. Every barn and house was filled with soldiers, too gravely wounded to survive the short move into the army hospitals. Into the town came trains bearing the good-intentioned with baskets and barrels of bread; Sisters of Charity under escort of their priest, looking for work to perform; and friends and family, who upon stepping down from the cars, went immediately to searching every hospital ward, patch of woods, and broken fence line for their lost boys. Their constant inquiries slowed the work of the gravediggers, who were wrapping the dead in their blankets, pinning their names, if known, to their chests, and laying them in the ground. The stench was overwhelming. "But who shall describe the horrible atmosphere that meets us almost continually?" wrote one lady who had come to the town to help.[115] Chloride of lime had been spread in the streets and hospitals, but it did little to knock down the smell. Visitors were recommended to come equipped with camphor or cologne, with which to dampen the cloth held to the face, and a pillow, to muffle the sounds of anguish during the hours of attempted sleep.[116]

It would be months before the wreckage was cleared away. In the coming November, Lincoln would come out to say what he thought to be his few poor words on the occasion of the dedication of the national cemetery. Attendees would ride in carriages out to see the sights at Culp's Hill and find the ground there still covered with what were now regarded as worthy mementos: tin cartridge boxes, letters, New Testaments, belt buckles, uniform parts, knapsacks, haversacks, bloody tourniquets, and flattened minié balls. They would load up as much as could conveniently be carried and drive off to explore other parts of the field.[117]

Ames headed to Camp Letterman, a mile and a half northeast of Gettysburg on the York Pike. The railroad passed close by and the general hospital erected here had its own depot by which supplies came in and the recovering wounded moved out on their way to convalescent stays at hospitals in Philadelphia, Baltimore, and Washington. For the many who did not recover, there was a dead house on the grounds in which to store them, and an embalming house to prepare their remains. Rows of wall tents, each large enough to accommodate forty cots, were laid out in neat lines and among them at all hours moved a small army of stretcher bearers, quartermasters, guards, doctors, attendants, chaplains, and visitors from home. Fresh pine boughs were hung at the inverted V of both ends of the tents to purify the air.

The produce of women's handiwork back in northeastern Ohio, and from every other place in the loyal Union of States, and items purchased from the proceeds of dances and dinners hosted by supporters of the Soldiers' Aid Society in Akron and Ashtabula were here in abundance; the pipeline of caring was now open and flowing. The wounded boys lay in clean bedding, on pillow cases edged in tatting, the special decoration put on by some unknown Union woman and meant to cheer a wounded boy who lay in his fresh dressing gown, with clean socks, shirts and drawers, and even slippers. Soldiers were served ice water in which wedges of lemon and pieces of tamarind bobbed. For those who required its medicinal benefit, there was milk with a little whiskey and sugar added, and for those who could eat solid food, there was fresh bread, butter, and jam. For the amputees, of whom there were at least a half dozen in the Twenty-Ninth Ohio, a porridge made of farina thickened with cornstarch with a spoonful of brandy stirred in was thought beneficial.[118]

On some days the heat was insufferable. But Ames noticed that the boys did not murmur complaints about the heat, or any other thing.[119] There were as many rebels here as Union boys, and although segregated and under guard, the prisoners came out of their tents and rested beneath the shade of the grove of giant elm and sycamore that spread above, and the residents came out to stand and gape at them.[120] Ames continued to minister to his boys, called sometimes to the bedside of rebels too, when it was seen one of them was headed down. He visited a soldier of the Third North Carolina, A. Keith, who was not long for this world, and he found him possessed of a faith in Christ as strong as any Union boy's. The dying continued. Some cases once thought hopeful turned downward suddenly, and when told by the surgeons they would not survive the day, boys wrestled with the cruel reality of it. "The struggle of mind is often great when compelled to give up hope of recovery," Chaplain Ames observed of boys in this strait.[121]

He spent one month in Gettysburg. By then, almost all of the wounded had been sent away and his work was done. He disliked leaving the few wounded of the regiment still here. The case of soldier Tullis McCain caused him particular worry. Arrangements for Ames's rail trip down to the Army of the Potomac had been made, and he must go. He left without having a chance to say good-bye to the wounded boys, stewards, doctors, and other chaplains who had all become his friends through their common trials.

Tullis McCain, a brown-haired, blue-eyed farmer, had been fifteen years old when he signed up for the war, and he had seen plenty of it. He had been captured at Port Republic, and at Chancellorsville, while trying to pull a wounded comrade to safety, he had been hit in the abdomen. He made the march to Gettysburg along with the rest.[122] During the rush to the rifle pits on Culp's Hill, he had been hit in the upper leg, and a leg ruined by gunshot fracture was subject to removal by surgeons employing the circular method. He survived the battle by five weeks, and died at Camp Letterman a week after Chaplain Ames departed, still a few weeks shy of his eighteenth birthday. He left a widowed mother back in Ohio, who corrected the army's record keepers years later by stating that her boy's real name was Tullis.[123] Sgt. John Kummer eulogized him, pointing out that his determined spirit had held strong throughout his ordeal in the hospital, although he must have known the odds were long against his recovery. Before he died he was heard to say, "I am going to that glorious home."[124]

Sgt. John Marsh was not with his regiment as it marched down to the Potomac after the battle. Up on Culp's Hill during a lull in the fighting on July 2, he had taken paper and pencil from his knapsack at noontime and wrote a letter home.

> I am writing this while the Regt. is in line of battle near Gettisburg, PA. . . . It is now 12 [a.]m. . . . the appearances indicate that a great battle will be fought, of the results I have not the least doubt, victory, I feel will light on our banners; yet many must fall, and I may be one of them. . . . I write this letter now, it may be the last opportunity, and I would assure all that I love of my remembrances in this hour of tumult and danger. Don't think I fear, I would not be away from my post if a hundred deaths stood in the way.[125]

He folded the letter and stowed in it his pack, intending to put it in the mail sack the next time the mail was collected. We know this letter made it back to Ohio because it was preserved along with many others he wrote. John Marsh had been shot in the thigh in the last sweep up over the ridge to the rifle pits and was carried to the rear. His leg was amputated below the hip by surgeon H. Ernest Goodman of the Twenty-Eighth Pennsylvania. Few men survived amputation this high up on the leg. Marsh died the same day he was wounded.[126] His father took him home and buried him in the family's tiny cemetery plot next to his mother, Hannah, who had rested there since he had been a small boy. For company he had two ancestors who had been born before the Revolution. Before the end of all this would be reached, two of his cousins who had been his playmates in this pleasant countryside of hickory groves and murmuring creeks would join him there—like he, victims of the war.[127]

Marsh's last year in the war had been one of torment. At first it came to him as homesickness so intense he thought he would die of it, but a furlough back home had only increased his suffering. Increasingly, he felt surrounded by "shadows." His spirit had begun its descent at the Battle of Kernstown, where he had first seen soft-spoken boys he had known his entire life hooting and jeering as they shot down boys not unlike themselves. Before Kernstown, his letters to his closest confidant, fourteen-year-old sister Ida, had been as cheery as any soldier's. After that, they became something alarmingly different. He came to believe that war drew men into it with the bait of blaring bugles, dipping flags, and the flash of a thousand bayonets, but once inside, they were turned into monsters. Over time, the unsolved conundrum turned his heart into something charred and desolate, and long before Gettysburg any visions he had of himself living a normal life after the war had dimmed out and died.[128]

21

Journeying Forth

SUMMER–FALL 1863

The Pursuit of Lee

With plenty of prodding from Lincoln to run Lee down before he got back over the Potomac, Gen. George Meade finally got the army on the roads down to the river. The Boys commenced to log daily marches that began before sunrise and did not end until long after dark. In a single day's rainy march the regiment covered twenty-seven miles. The Maryland countryside was rich in crops and cattle, and mostly unblemished by war, and to the soldiers shouldering heavy packs and wearing worn-out shoes, that counted for a great deal. Nathan Parmater observed, "The boys think that a Md. Mile is not as long a Virginia mile."[1]

The army had been pushed so quickly through Frederick on the way up to Gettysburg that there had not been time for Parmater to go into the town to look up old friends. The army was moving now with as much speed, but not as much purpose. As they returned through Frederick, Parmater saw a better opportunity to steal away for a visit, but there were risks involved. "It was at the peril of getting a booting as I saw General Geary boot a man close to me for starting out ahead, but as he did not see my white star he thought that I belonged to the red star division."[2] He went into town and looked up a young woman named Tillie Ogal, whose acquaintance he had made during his stay there last fall and early winter. He gave her a photograph of himself to add to those she had collected from other Union boys.[3]

The regiment marched close by a tree from which a man hung by the rope around his neck. He had been caught by a Federal cavalry patrol, with maps of army camps and fortifications stuffed in his pockets. His clothes had been torn off, and although horribly decomposed, some of the Boys recognized him.[4] One soldier was certain this same old man was the peddler of patriotic sheet music who had come and gone from their camps as free as a bird way back when they were chasing Jackson up in the Shenandoah valley.[5] By the accounts of other soldiers, this was the very same man, with his distinctive long white beard, they had seen hanging from a tree around the time of Port Republic, over a year earlier.

They moved over into the deep valley between South Mountain and the Blue Ridge. They were expecting a fight anytime now, and they cleaned their rifles and rammed fresh charges in anticipation of it. The next day brought them to Keedysville, a tiny place sitting near Antietam Creek, and then onto the old battlefield itself. They passed over the famous stone bridge, pocked and chipped by the hailstorm of battle.[6]

The steady booming of a cannonade came to them from the Potomac, where they expected Lee would give battle, trapped as he was on their side with the rising river behind him. At Fairplay, with the Twenty-Ninth Ohio in advance, the brigade moved into a wheatfield. Rebel skirmishers were in plain sight, but neither side fired a shot. They were rousted from their blankets two hours after midnight and ordered into battle line, but it was hours before they got on the road down to the river. News had come in that the flood stage in the river had passed, and Lee was starting his army across to the safety of Virginia. They brushed up against rebel cavalry and shots were exchanged, doing little harm to either side, while from ahead of them, down by the river, came the sounds of a sharper engagement, but they were not called to join it.

The rebels had built strong breastworks on the heights on the opposite bank, and Geary's division was put to work building breastworks of their own. Bundles of wheat mortared in place with dirt and a log placed on top made for a strong wall. Works like these were better suited to defense than to an offense of the type needed to catch Lee, as the soldiers by this time knew.[7]

The Gettysburg campaign was over. Lee had crossed the Potomac back into Virginia. "It is to be regretted that he should have escaped at all but we have the satisfaction of knowing that he has met with a severe loss and will not be likely to appear in Pa. very soon again," commented Parmater. General Meade shared the sentiment.[8] Lincoln was not satisfied with having driven Lee from Northern soil; he knew that the war would not end in this theater until Lee was destroyed, and the best opportunity of doing that had just been squandered.

The Giddings Boys filed out of their breastworks and marched through rolling, wooded hills. Their skirmishers ran into a patrol of Mosby's cavalry, and three Boys were shot but none killed.[9] They came round again to the Antietam battlefield and marched through Sharpsburg. The Twenty-Ninth had not fought here, but most of the veterans of their brigade had, and as they passed by its battle-scarred buildings, soldiers wounded in the fight pointed out houses and churches in which they had been tenderly cared for by kindly disposed citizens.[10] Ten days after leaving Gettysburg, they went into camp near Harpers Ferry, at the confluence of the Shenandoah and Potomac Rivers.

Their townsman John Brown had made Harpers Ferry famous, as every one of these Reserve Boys knew. There was damage still unrepaired in the place, made by Brown's hand. Brown had captured the old federal arsenal and used it as a bastion and rallying point for the slaves he had expected to join him. The parents and grandparents of the regiment's soldiers would have regarded the ruins as a holy shrine, but to a member of the younger generation, like Cpl. Nathan Parmater, it was just another wrecked building in a landscape ruined by war. He noted in his diary that he had seen it, but of its connection to John Brown, he said nothing at all.

From their high perch above the Potomac, they could see the Heights of Bolivar, and on the other side of the river the Heights of Loudon. On the horizon to the north and west stood the peaks of the mountains in which they'd wandered their first winter in the war under Lander. They crossed the Potomac back into Virginia, then the Shenandoah, and followed it south.

They pushed east and south through Ashby's Gap, and then Manassas Gap, on half rations of hardtack and a few sips of water.[11] On they went through Haymarket, then White Plains, where they had staged on the way to Cedar Mountain. They marched into camp near Warrenton Junction, on the Orange and Alexandria Railroad.[12] Next morning they were on the road early and made for Kelly's Ford, on the Rappahannock, where not all that long ago they had crossed down to Chancellorsville with high-as-a-kite hopes for a war-ending victory.[13] These places had become as familiar to them as delivery stops were to the driver of the Adams Express wagon back home.

Much had changed in the three months since Chancellorsville—almost a third of the regiment fallen to wounds, death, and capture in two great battles—but with all that some things had not changed at all. They had been up and down the Shenandoah from its top to its bottom, out of the blue mountains to the west, following the course of rivers that ran from there all the way to the Chesapeake, and then over and back again like a dog chasing its own tail, as it sometimes seemed to the Boys. They had moved up and down the line of the Orange and Alexandria Railroad again and again. All these movements had culminated in battles for which the commanding general of the moment promised war-ending victory but did not deliver.

They had beaten Lee at Gettysburg, but it was now apparent he had not been beaten badly enough, because he sat on the opposite bank of the river as defiantly as ever, and their general showed little desire to cross over and finish him. They had had "tall fighting" up at Gettysburg, and at last their efforts had produced a victory, but to obtain it the Boys had endured hard times, before and since. Patience for long daily marches on a ration precisely measured to four and one-half pieces of hard cracker was wearing thin. The Giddings soldiers supplemented this slim fare with chunks of pork and beef cut from the few nervous pigs and cows that remained in the neighborhood until, as Cass Nims complained, "the Generals put a stop to it."[14] Now they were right back in the neighborhood they had started from, and to the soldiers things appeared little changed from what they had been, despite all the marching, fighting, and suffering. Virginia was an increasingly loathsome place.

Chaplain Ames finished his weary work at the Gettysburg hospitals. He took the railroad as far as Manassas, got a horse, and rode the rest of the way down to his regiment. He found them camped not far from the Rappahannock along with the Army of the Potomac. He had made a few friends among the officers, and he anticipated the pleasure that seeing them again might bring. But his reunion with them had an unsettling quality to it, which he was at a loss to explain. He could simply observe and record what he felt: "Everything seems like being with strangers."[15]

Cowardly Traitors

News had come on the march away from Gettysburg that Gen. U. S. Grant had achieved a victory at Vicksburg on par with their own. Cass Nims was heartened by the news of Grant's victory: "Mother don't things look encouraging I think."[16]

Their victory at Gettysburg, coupled with Grant's, pushed their hopes upward. The general feeling among the soldiers was that the rebellion could not survive through autumn. They had enjoyed this fantasy in earlier days, but now, back home in Ohio, the editors of the Reserve's newspapers agreed with their sons at the front: the end of the rebellion was in sight. For the first time since the war began, they began debating how the seceded states should be brought back into the Union. Fireworks began when the *Cleveland Herald* suggested that their wayward brothers should be treated with biblical kindness, which caused the editor of the *Sentinel* in Jefferson to get his hackles up. "Does the *Cleveland Herald* intend to say that the Rebels, after we have fairly wrenched them from our throats, are to be treated to the fatted calf, and welcomed back as prodigal sons?"[17]

To the Boys, the road to victory seemed short and direct. The only thing blocking their path was a movement of citizens resistant to Lincoln's prosecution of the war, known as "copperheads," who were feeding on the war weariness that seeped at times into the hearts of even the most patriotic. The copperheads had grown substantial enough in numbers to worry Lincoln about the result of the coming fall elections. The situation in Ohio worried him in particular. Despite the ceaseless pounding of the war drum by the pro-Lincoln newspapers, the antiwar sentiment was gaining followers even in the Western Reserve. Clement Vallandigham, one-time Democratic congressman from Ohio, had been exiled to the South for his incendiary antiwar speeches and writings, but the rebels found his tongue too sharp and banished him. Now from the safe haven of Canada, just across the big lake, he was directing his campaign for the governorship of Ohio.

The Boys read the local newspapers that circulated through the camps and learned of copperhead rallies taking place in their very own hometowns. In the early days of the war, the casual utterance of words running counter to war fever earned the misguided a tar and feathering. Now men were gathering openly in rented halls and giving loud expression to their sentiment for an end to the war and reconciliation with the South. Universally, the Twenty-Ninth's Boys threatened to come home and deal with the copperheads, if their parents did not move to subdue them. Cass Nims's feelings stood for those of all the Boys when news came through the camps of the draft riots that were tearing Manhattan Island from one end to the other: "But if you could only See how disheartened the Soldiers was when they heard of the mob in New York and mother ain't it enough to know that we that are fighting for our Country and to know that Traitors are in our land and them that are even Fathers are that had Sons in the army.... I would like to come home and Meet Northern Traitors. I should be attempted to take his life."[18]

Lewis P. Buckley was at home in Akron, busy still with the war's work. He was heading up Summit County's military committee and raising money for a new stand of flags for his old regiment. Silk flags were glorious to behold when new, but they were not durable. The regiment was still carrying the stand that Giddings presented them back at Camp Giddings. The flags were mostly worn out before the season's campaigning of 1863, and after Chancellorsville and Gettysburg they were merely fluttering ribbons. Buckley's bonds with his old outfit were strong as ever, even with its enlisted men. One of his inquiring letters found Sgt. John A. Kummer convalescing in an army hospital in York, Pennsylvania, after being shot through the chest at Culp's Hill. As to conditions in the hospital, Kummer reported that he and the other twelve hundred wounded were being well cared for "from a medical point of view," but he found hospital life confining.[19] To prevent soldiers from wandering away, the hospital grounds were surrounded by a high board fence, the boys allowed outside it once every four days, and then for only three hours.

Despite these strictures, Kummer was as full of resolve as ever: "God willing I shall yet have a hand in the finishing blow to this most wicked Rebellion."[20] Kummer was just as anxious to strike the "cowardly traitors" at work around his own dear Ohio home, but his intended weapon was the ballot. It was unclear whether soldiers in hospitals would be allowed to cast a vote. He posed rhetorical questions for the news readers at home to answer: "How is it: will they give us hospital folks a chance to vote? There are quite a number here anxious to give that exile Vallandigham a kick and [Brough a] vote. Will they let us do it?"[21]

Except for the news of the progress of copperheads in their own backyard, and of the New York riots, the Boys were in satisfactory spirits. Everyone, though, craved a change of scene. Five days after Chaplain Ames rejoined them, they started out in the direction of new things.[22]

Flatlanders at Sea

Riots had broken out in New York City while the regiment was chasing Lee down to the Potomac. The city's poor whites, Irish mostly, had been sparked to violence by the implementation of the draft; so it was at first reported, and for three days, the city teetered on the edge of destruction. Police trying to subdue the rioters had been beaten, stabbed, shot, kicked to jelly, and burned along with the rest of the victims. The mobs, estimated to number upward of fifty thousand, conducted a reign of arson and homicide until it finally burned itself out and order was restored by the state militia.

In Jefferson, Ashtabula County, the newspaper devoted as much ink to the New York riots as it had to the details of Gettysburg, and the depictions of the former were far more lurid. The favorite dark anecdote published in several newspapers was about a black child who had been pulled from beneath the bed where she was hiding and beaten to death by a gang of men, women, and even children. The *Sentinel* editor thought he could see through the smoke of this infernal outrage and into its real causes: "The history of New York during last week will go down to the future as the blackest record of that very corrupt city.... Supposedly against the draft, but [the riots were] in fact against the policies of the government in conducting the war ... manifestly excited by the copperhead politicians and newspapers ... *it was in fact a battle of rebellion,* where the rebels could fight under cover of a riot."[23]

The result of the rampage was to postpone the draft until August 19. This time, Lincoln thought it best to have troops on the scene—not militia, but Federal troops, better organized and more used to large-scale violence. Meade was ordered to recommend the troops that should be sent to New York, the order was passed to General Slocum, and he selected what he described for the White House as his very best soldiers. Among those picked to go were the Ohio regiments of Candy's brigade. The Twenty-Ninth's historian reported that the regiment went to New York to "quell the memorable draft riots." In fact, they had been sent there to maintain order in anticipation of any future disturbance of the peace. They did not reach New York City until more than a month after the riots had subsided.[24]

The Twenty-Ninth Ohio's destination was unknown to its members. It might be New York, and then it might be Charleston; either would suit. One Twenty-Ninth Ohio soldier expressed the group's sentiment: "The boys feel pretty well generally, to think they are going to leave the lonely state of Virginia," and that's what seemed to matter most.[25] They marched back up to Rappahannock Station and took the cars to Alexandria.[26]

The soldiers had little to occupy them by way of military work while they waited for the ship that was to take them out on the ocean, except to avoid heat exhaustion. Wallace Hoyt had his likeness made at a photographic studio to show he was nearing the end of his adolescence. In a letter sent home to accompany his latest photograph, he apologized for the spots on his face, which the picture showed: "My face was broak out with the heat but I will get you a better one when I get a chance."[27]

Most of the Boys went to work indulging appetites for good things to eat and drink. Not since the general spree that everyone seemed to have gone on just after arriving at Camp Chase had the regiment rushed to partake of the ardent as they did on this layover in Alexandria. Chaplain Ames commented on the general free-for-all, but pulled up short of rendering judgment. He busied himself in shopping for a proper mess outfit for himself and hiring a black servant named Charles McCarter from among the thousands of contraband living around Alexandria in freedmen's camps. He agreed to pay his man the fair sum of twelve dollars per month, very nearly a soldier's wages.

After six days of waiting, the S.S. *Baltic* pushed up to the wharf and threw down its gangway, and the sixteen hundred boys of the brigade began to board. The *Baltic* was an old commercial ship, retrofitted with an oversize steam-driven side-wheel, making it capable of a steady eight to ten knots. She was wide of stern with a black smokestack towering above the deck and mounting two large sailing masts. The steamer was the veteran of many transatlantic crossings, hauling immigrants from Europe to America. The *Baltic* had been used to evacuate Maj. Robert Anderson from Fort Sumter far back in the spring of 1861. As the boys stood waiting for their turn to board, they gaped at the ship that would take them out onto the sea. All were impressed by the ship's size. Pity the stay-at-homes back in rural Ohio; the soldiers were about to be treated to an adventure. Traveling in this novel way, cooled all the while by sea breezes, with the romantic Atlantic slipping by, was sure to put riding in boxcars or wearing out expensive shoes in the shade. They would soon regard the *Baltic* as the vilest tub afloat.

The enlisted men climbed down to the lower decks where it was dank, crowded, and insufferably hot. The officers rented upper-deck cabins for the outrageous sum of twelve dollars per day, but at least they were high enough to catch a cooling breeze in the event one passed by. The first night on board, still tied up at the pier, it was too warm to sleep below deck or above, so the men stayed up all night carousing.[28]

The next morning the hawsers were cast off and the *Baltic* started down the Potomac headed for salt water. Four hours out the ship ran hard aground at a place called Kettle Bottoms, and for the remainder of this day and a good deal of the next they sat and broiled. Two tugs came up and, with the high tide in their favor, tried to push the *Baltic* free, but she would not budge. On their first evening out, Chaplain Ames observed the effect of moonbeams dancing on the water, but they seemed innocent compared to the moonbeams dancing in men's heads. The regiment had brought liquor aboard. Ames noted in his diary, "Time killers get weary inventing methods, card playing and drinking chiefly relied upon. Excesses of men are surprising."[29] This was their first sallying forth under their new leader, Col. William T. Fitch, and he did little to rein in the generalized partying.

Seven ships hooked onto the *Baltic* and pulled all together, but even that did not do the trick. Once the supplies of whiskey ran out, the Boys began to show signs of close confinement in the sweltering heat. In a word, their chaplain noted that they had become uneasy.[30] Not only had they been stranded for four days, but rumor began circulating that the captain was in league with the copperheads. "The whole of this crew were engaged in the New York ryot. They say that the Pylott run us [aground] on purpose he has been dismissed and we have a new Pylott," Wallace Hoyt reported home, suggesting the antiwar traitors were at work even among armed soldiers.[31] A new skipper was brought aboard. His first thought was to lighten the ship by temporarily off-loading several hundred soldiers and tons of coal onto barges, and with the next flood tide they were high enough in the water to get free.[32]

The *Baltic* got out onto the rough Atlantic Ocean and set a course north. Few men aboard had ever been at sea, and the ship's rails were lined with seasick flatlanders. Two days out the ship steered back toward land and through the narrows into New York harbor. Everyone crowded onto the deck to take in the views, which were grand and beautiful. To the right was Brooklyn, with its sea of rooftops and church steeples, and to the left Jersey City. New York City lay at their feet with its dense collection of tall buildings in red brick and stone. The harbor was jammed with tugs, steamers of every description, and ships still coasting the sea in the old way, by sail. The Boys were in high spirits over their good fortune in being sent to such a wonderful place. They anchored at Governor's Island, at the lower tip of Manhattan, where the East and Hudson Rivers joined salt water. They disembarked and spread out to camp on the island.

The services of the Ohio regiments were not required as it turned out, which left plenty of time for the officers to visit the city.[33] Chaplain Ames went into Manhattan, visited Barnum's American Museum, Trinity Church, Wall Street, and the Custom House. Overall, New York City fell short of his expectations. He found it to be old and dilapidated. He ranged further uptown and into Central Park. He was delighted with its scale and artful arrangements of lawn, trees, and shrubs. Lest he should forget, he listed facts of it in his diary, gave the acreage of its fields and ponds, the length of its paved carriage roads, and the number of its annual visitors.[34] The city and its fabled attractions were off-limits to the enlisted men. Wallace Hoyt had hoped for a pass so he could legally visit the city, but with none forthcoming, he arranged his own excursion.

> Was only over one evening and then I run the guard and paid a boatman one dollar to row me over to Brolkyn and back. A distance of about 40 rods. Took the ferry boat there and went to New York. I forgot to tell you that I was accompanied by Sgt. Rickard the Color Sgt. of our reg't. Well, we went up Broadway several miles eat oysters, drank lemmonaid and smoked cigars and had a good time generally. Got back a little before daylight. If you want a description of the City I can't give it. Because I could not see the City on account of the houses.[35]

After ten days of thumb twiddling, they boarded the *Baltic* and steamed out of New York harbor the way they had come. The big guns mounted on the fort at the harbor narrows boomed a salute at them as they sailed past, and they were soon back on the Atlantic Ocean.[36] It was not a given that they would be returning to the Army of the Potomac. Having broken free of its orbit, they might just as easily keep sailing, not stopping until they reached Texas, which by one rumor was their real destination.[37] Everyone's mood soured when it was learned they had been ordered back to the Rappahannock.[38]

While they were away in New York, Meade had maneuvered the army one rung lower on the ladder of strategic rivers in this theater. Candy's brigade marched back across the Rappahannock, down to Raccoon Ford, on the north side of the Rapidan River, and went into camp. The sight of Cedar Mountain a few miles distant rubbed their noses in the fact that despite all they had been through in this long year, they were back again very near where they had been.

The soldiers were hardened by now to all the discomforts and frustrations of soldiering, and they were not disposed to dwell on them. Thus they took the poor sanitary conditions in their camps, and the diseases that seemed by more than coincidence to flourish in them, as a matter of course. Conditions had improved generally, but by fits and starts. Their camp here on the Rapidan was drained by parallel ditches, and since the rainy season had begun, water ran in them. Regardless of their proximity to cooking and sleeping areas, and of latrines, the soldiers used the water ditches to relieve themselves. They did their laundry and cleaned pots and themselves in one ditch, which turned the water the color of milk, and got drinking water from the other, even though better water was not all that far away, in the river. During heavy rains the ditches overflowed and their contents mixed. Water from the "drinking" ditch tasted of toads and rotten wood, and the Boys were warned not to drink from it unless *very* thirsty, although it seemed satisfactory to them for making coffee. Wallace Hoyt spoke of his regard for the quality of the water with words that were a summing up of the soldiers' infinite ability to stand up to anything: "I have no reason to complain. I can drink mud if the rest can."[39]

While here they were called out to witness another group execution of deserters. They found it as repugnant as the stump water they drank. Their chaplain likewise thought the display was of dubious value and questionable morality. Aside from this sorry exhibition, there was little to occupy the soldiers as the army sat on its heels. On a mid-September day when the low, wet clouds were driven along the ground by a chill wind, Chaplain Ames saddled his horse and rode out to see the front lines: "Here I could see the Rebel pickets and other troops moving about at their pleasure. They could see our men with equal plainness. No apparent disposition on either side to cross the stream; probably each in doubt of the strength of the other . . . neither ready to make the attack."[40] Ames was not a general, but military affairs seemed to have become as quiet here on the Rapidan as they had been on the Potomac in the war's early days.

Rumors came to the camp of a great battle fought far away below the Tennessee River, where the rebel army under Gen. Braxton Bragg, and the Army of the Cumberland led by Gen. William Rosecrans, had tangled, but the rumor did not report which side had prevailed. The very next day, they heard a dull booming from across the river, but it was of bass drums and not cannon. The booming was followed by the striking up of rebel bands playing joyful tunes, and much cheering and singing up and down the rebel side of the river.[41] They wondered what the rebels had to celebrate, and they soon learned. Rosecrans had been beaten.

The next day they broke camp and marched north by an order that caught even General Geary by surprise. As they trudged along under a bright moon, the soldiers kibitzed on where they were headed, and to what purpose. Up to Bealeton Station the next day, where the tracks were busy with the coming and going of many engines, each pulling a long line of cars in the direction of Alexandria. The entire Twelfth Corps was here now, or on its way—regiments, and artillery outfits, horses and mules, all loading onto the cattle cars and chugging off. They were headed to a point unknown, and while they waited for their turn, debates in favor of one destination and against another displaced discussion of every other topic. Chaplain Ames had his sensitive fingers on the regiment's emotional pulse this day: "Men are becoming tired of the monotony of marching over and over again the state of Va. Something new is their motto."[42]

The Grandest Feat of the War

The big question as to where they were bound was answered as soon as they got close to Washington, where fresher newspapers were passed around and better-quality rumors circulated. It was confirmed that Rosecrans had been whipped at Chickamauga, in northwestern Georgia. Worse, reports were coming up that he and his men were trapped in Chattanooga, with the river at their backs and the Confederates glowering down on them from the heights. The rebel army commanded every convenient approach by which supplies might come to Rosecrans, and the rebel cavalry was raiding at will, tearing up track, burning supply trains, killing escorts and teamsters. Rosecrans's army was already hungry, and he was warning the officials in Washington that if not resupplied and reinforced immediately, he would abandon Chattanooga. Lincoln could not allow that to happen. Chattanooga, gateway to the South, was the hub of important railroad connections that ran down to Atlanta, and a decision had been made to send the Eleventh and Twelfth Corps to Rosecrans's relief.

A story would be told many years from now explaining that the triggering event that took them from one theater of war to the other had *not* been Rosecrans's reverse at Chickamauga, but the New York riots. An old Twenty-Ninth Ohio veteran met another old man who had been a rebel gunner posted with a battery on the Virginia shore of the Potomac. The rebel had been at his post one day in August 1863 when a ship loaded with Yankee soldiers came along and stranded itself on a sandbar right in front of them. The ship made a fat, stationary target and the gunners were itching to pull the lanyard and blow the S.S. *Baltic* into the next century, but they were ordered to hold their fire.[43] Lee was not inclined to interrupt the departure of any Federal troops from his front, and because of that, the Ohio boys on the *Baltic* caught a very large piece of luck. It may have been nothing more than another old veteran yarn, but it played neatly in support of the theory that the New York riots had launched this gigantic rail movement of two whole army corps.

Lee was not apt to miss any development in the Union army. When he learned that several thousand of Meade's best fighters were leaving his front and preparing to sail off to New York, he felt it safe to proceed with his plan to detach Longstreet's corps from his own army and send it south to assist Bragg in dealing with Rosecrans. Longstreet's three divisions got on the cars, and two weeks later they appeared on the battlefield at Chickamauga at a make-or-break moment and turned the tide against Rosecrans. That in turn had gotten the Army of the Cumberland into its current predicament, locked up in Chattanooga.[44] So these hundreds of railroad cars jammed with thousands of soldiers had all been started on their way by whoever got the mobs fired up in Manhattan on the occasion of the draft.

That the Eleventh Corps and their own Twelfth Corps had been the ones picked to cut ties with the Army of the Potomac made no especial matter to the Boys. No one was sad to leave. The commonsense reasons for the separation seemed to point toward parts of Slocum's corps having been made already mobile by the recent trip to New York, and, more important, among its several army corps, these two had the shortest history with the Army of the Potomac. Severing their bonds with it would cause the least injury. Getting the two cut-loose army corps from one region of the country to another was more complicated. Nothing like it had ever been attempted.

It would take nearly thirty trains of twenty cars each to move the whole works of two army corps to their destination. As soon as one train pulled away, another pulled up empty behind it, and the loading began all over. All of it came off like clockwork. When their turn came, the Giddings Boys boosted each other up onto the cars. The soldiers crowded onto the roofs of the cars to enjoy the spectacle of this mighty movement of horses, mules, and men packed into the long strings of cars, and wagons, ambulances, and artillery parked end to end on flatcars, with their wheels chocked against motion.

Their accommodations for the long ride were common freight cars, with a rough bench running down each side for seating. The plan had been to fit forty soldiers into each car, but with one end of the car filled with their packs, weapons, and ammunition, thirty soldiers packed a car to capacity and left no room for anyone to lie flat. The officers got a car to themselves, but that too was jammed. On their first ride from Ohio down into the war, the Boys had complained loudly over the injustice of being put into cars used to haul livestock, but they had learned since that riding under any conditions was better than walking, and no one complained.

Their train aimed west and up the Potomac. The officers pointed out the muddy bench at Patterson's Creek where they had camped when they first came out, through Cumberland, where so many of their friends had sickened and died their first winter in the war, and then into the mountains where they had nearly frozen that first winter. The railroad men were working day and night to keep the line running efficiently and safely, but the Twenty-Ninth's trip was not without accident. Short of Benwood, on the Ohio River, their train smashed into the rear of the one carrying the Seventh Ohio, wrecking cars, and injuring several soldiers in the Seventh.[45]

At Benwood they got down from the cars and marched across the bridge spanning the Ohio River. They were glad for the walk across, which gave them a chance to shake out the kinks after being penned up in the cars for over four hundred miles. This was the first time many of them had seen Ohio in nearly two years, and their native state soothed eyes used to Virginia's desolation. They steamed through the night, reached Zanesville at breakfast time, and boomed forward toward Xenia. All along the line people came out to give them a proper homecoming. Cheers and hurrahs were thrown up at them as the train hustled along, and when it slowed, citizens trotted up to the car doors and handed up good things to eat and drink. Crowds gathered at the station at Xenia to salute these lean soldiers, their faces tanned from living out of doors.

The stop at Columbus was short, too short for some soldiers. They fell out to explore a little, even though they had been ordered to stick close to the regiment, and some of them missed the train.[46] Hours more and they were crossing the prairies on their way to Indianapolis. They paused there and marched to a giant shed filled with hundreds of tables, each set with plates of bread, cheese, and ham, and pails of hot coffee to wash it down.[47] Fortified thus, the travelers steamed down to the banks of the wide Ohio River to Jeffersonville and crossed over into Kentucky at Louisville, and then through Bowling Green without stopping. They had been on the road now for seven full days and their destination lay still further south.

On through the Kentucky countryside of emerald pastures and huge stands of showy hardwoods, through regions unmolested by war. Nearing Nashville, the country began to show the unmistakable signs of conflict. Nashville, in the Confederate state of Tennessee, was a hard-looking place. Once well kept and thriving, it had been degraded by the influence of war, and everything in it converted to use as a Federal supply base for the armies operating below it. Its streets were jammed with marching soldiers and army freight wagons driven by teamsters who cussed each other for the right of way. Knots of rebel prisoners were being marched along bound for prisons in the North, some of them taking the oath of allegiance to the Union right there in the street and then sent on their way. From this point south, rebel raiders were active, and the Boys were advised to keep their eyes peeled anytime they got down from the cars. They were back in the realm of danger.[48]

The next day the train got them down to Murfreesboro, Tennessee, and stopped. The hard riders of Gen. Joseph Wheeler's cavalry had stormed through the neighborhood the day before, and where there ought to have been a bridge there was presently a smoldering jumble of lumber and iron. The rest of Candy's brigade had gotten over just before the rebels struck, but the Twenty-Ninth Ohio was stranded.[49]

They got down from the cars and marched to Stones River along the line of the railroad. They passed within sight of woodlots where every tree had been blasted off at mid-height and the trunks riddled with bullet holes as thoroughly as those at Culp's Hill. The ground was strewn with broken wagons and caissons, torn-down fences, and fresh dirt mounds. A four-day battle had been fought hereabouts this past New Year, already famous for its ferocity and horrifying casualties. The Twenty-Ninth's soldiers saw that combats between these western armies were as bloody as any they'd experienced in the Army of the Potomac.

They were now in the land of cotton, the cultivation of which in no small way was responsible for the war. The country hereabouts was judged amazingly fertile, wild grasses growing higher than a man's head. And with a bale of cotton selling for seven hundred dollars, the plant was still being cultivated just as it always had. Cass Nims was duly impressed:

> Dear Mother,
>
> I have got some cotton seeds in its raw state. The seeds are all in them. I got it in Alabama. There are more niggers there than a few and it is fun to see them pick cotton. Wenches and young ones and all they had no overseers when we went through—they were ashamed to be out driving niggers in front of the yanks. I will send you a little cotton. Save the seeds and then plant them in the Spring.[50]

Gen. John W. Geary was an educated man, not a half-schooled country boy like Cass, and he referred to the colored inhabitants of the neighborhood with a more enlightened term: blacks. Cass was from a region of Ohio where most of the residents, by reputation, would have been disgusted to hear these recently freed slaves called niggers. Had Joshua Giddings been there to see what Cass saw, he would have rushed into the fields to rescue these victims of Southern aristocracy from their unhappy lot.

The bridge got fixed adequately to get foot traffic over, and the Twenty-Ninth crossed over Stones River intent on catching up with Candy's brigade somewhere below them on the railroad line to Chattanooga. The next day they made Bell Buckle, then Wartrace, and came to Normandy, Tennessee, a whistle-stop on the Nashville and Chattanooga Railroad, halfway between the two towns for which the railroad was named.

The Twenty-Ninth Regiment was culled out from the flow of troops heading south and put to work guarding the railroad, which was the very same work they'd been given when they first arrived on the Potomac. Guarding water tanks and tracks was hardly glamorous, but it was necessary, given the rebel cavalry's ease in cutting the railroad. Indications were that they might be here in Normandy for some time, so the Boys set to work building shanties, cheery-looking constructions, complete with fireplaces and chimneys to warm them in the coming winter should they be required to spend it in this place.

The Road Down to Chattanooga

The principal temperance advocates of the regiment, Lewis Buckley and Thomas Clark, were gone. Geary was mostly abstemious, and frowned on whiskey-fueled foolishness, but he was rarely at this little place, and the officers felt free to kick up their heels without censure. Their celebrations in Normandy produced enough noise and boozy capering that it was hard not to know that there were "high times in certain quarters," as Ames reported in his diary.[51] They may have been enjoying an extended jollification over the results of the fall election.

October 13, 1863, was election day back in Ohio, and soldiers old enough to vote cast their ballots from here in the field. Election clerks and judges were appointed in the regiment's camp to make sure everything was on the up and up, just like at home. The pro-Union newspapers in the Reserve had been whipping up support for their candidate for governor, John Brough, and taking every opportunity to point up the inherent evil of the copperhead candidate, Clement Vallandigham. Brig. Gen. John Hunt Morgan's rebel raiding party had cut deep into Ohio and caused damage and injury, and had made national headlines before he was caught and locked up. Now, with the election coming up and the eyes of the nation on Ohio, the *Summit Beacon,* in Akron, spread the alarm of another invasion: it was rumored that armed men from Indiana and Illinois were preparing to march into Ohio to ensure Vallandigham's success.

Ames realized what was at stake in this vote, and the possibilities made him nervous. "The election today in Ohio will tell for good or ill. If it is for freedom and Union our cause is strengthened and preserved. If otherwise it may be retarded and baffled."[52] The election was a referendum on Lincoln's conduct of the war, and in the White House that night the president did not sleep. He stood by the telegraph operator and checked the numbers sent to him by Brough, and by morning it was clear that the copperheads had been repudiated and Brough fairly elected.[53] Lincoln sent a telegram to the governor-elect, "Glory to God in the highest. Ohio has saved the Union."[54] Every Reserve county had given Brough a majority, but the rebuke of Vallandigham had not been monolithic. In Ashtabula County, one of five had cast votes for Vallandigham, and in Summit and Trumbull counties, two of five had braved the enmity of the majority and voted for the copperheads.[55]

At the front, the Reserve's soldiers had gone foursquare for Brough. Of the nearly one thousand soldiers from Summit and Ashtabula Counties now in the field and eligible to vote, no more than a dozen voted for Vallandigham.[56] The Boys of Company D in the Twenty-Ninth had thrown every one of their votes for Brough.[57]

Even the soldiers who sat cut off in Chattanooga stayed up past midnight waiting for the results, and when news came that Brough won, they came out of their tents into a cold rain and cheered.[58] State-wide, the soldier vote tallied as forty-one thousand for Brough and only two thousand for Vallandigham.[59] Akron cut loose with a victory celebration that surpassed the spectacle of bands, bonfires, and endless speechifying that had saluted Lincoln's election, three years before. There would be no more talk in the Twenty-Ninth's company streets of going back to Ohio to exterminate neighbors who had fallen under the spell of the copperheads.

With the excitement of the election come and gone, the Boys went back to standing guard duty. The White Star Division was responsible for protecting a forty-mile stretch of railroad that ran from Murfreesboro down to Tullahoma, and while Geary was out on a four-day horseback inspection of it, he stopped for the night in Normandy.[60] Rooms for officers were scarce in a place as tiny as Normandy, Tennessee. Chaplain Ames had a comfortable room in Mrs. Wilson's boardinghouse, and he invited Geary to share it with him. The two retired to their room for the night, and Ames had a chance to question his general about his religious beliefs. As the rain hammered the roof, Geary laid out his views. He was favorable to a pure form of Christianity, opposed to bigotry, sectarianism, intolerance, and superstition.[61] Geary apparently took a liking to Chaplain Ames. Before leaving the next morning he gave him a pass and a railroad ticket to Nashville for later use—both highly prized. Ames was used to indifferent treatment by officers whenever he went to headquarters. When he next visited headquarters, a few days after he and Geary had shared accommodations, lo and behold, he was treated with a noticeable increase of civility.[62]

Most of Geary's division had already gone south to the vicinity of Bridgeport, Alabama, and the rumor was that the Twenty-Ninth was to follow. With the railroad seeming to be as often broken as intact, transport to that point would be by their own feet, it was at first announced, and the Boys were not happy at the prospect.[63] Ames heard the soldiers' complaint and counseled, "Rough roads and bad weather will make it unpleasant but resolute hearts and strong muscles will overcome all difficulties. The great work must be done."[64]

Eight days into their stay in Normandy, events were transpiring down the line that demanded their service, and they would take the railroad after all. Geary had received an order from their new Twelfth Corps commander, their old acquaintance Joe Hooker, to gather his division at Bridgeport, Alabama, on the wide Tennessee River, twenty-five miles west of Chattanooga. A major operation was about to start. Chattanooga was the gateway to the South, and Bridgeport was the gateway to Chattanooga. Geary had only three regiments close enough to Bridgeport to get there by the time the whole operation was scheduled to jump off, and the rest, including the Giddings Regiment, was to come on quickly and catch up.

While in Normandy, they read in the newspapers reporting that Rosecrans had been let go. Ulysses S. Grant had been placed in command of the armies in Chattanooga and those gathering around it. Opening the supply line was his number one priority, and to accomplish it he had planned a campaign with two prongs. The army would push out from Chattanooga, while the new troops from the Army of the Potomac would advance from Bridgeport. After clearing the line of rebel resistance, the two would link up and the rebel siege would be ended.

The Giddings Boys packed up and moved down to the tracks to wait for the train that would take them down to Bridgeport, but the train did not come. When darkness came, the soldiers gave up, lay down on the soggy earth, and slept.[65] Ames had been sick on and off again since before the trip to New York, and the diarrhea that had plagued him came back now with a vengeance. Because of his condition, sleeping for more than a few minutes at a time was hard enough, but when he was able to fall asleep at last, he was jarred back awake. The officers were spending this last night before going to the front by staying up and amusing themselves with "games," which was Chaplain Ames's circumspect way of saying that some of them had been as drunk and rowdy as any shanty Irish.[66]

They left Normandy the next morning. Soldiers trotted ahead to detect any breaks in the track made by rebels or guerrillas lest the whole shebang derail. They reached Bridgeport in the middle of the night, where they learned that General Geary had gone ahead without them. This was the end of the railroad line. If there was an actual town here, the Boys did not see it. All the action was down at the banks of the river, where the Eleventh Corps was making its headquarters and the balance of the Twelfth Corps staging to cross over and move on Chattanooga. Trains steamed in and out and supplies were accumulating down at the flat along the river, waiting for the time when the railroad bridge was rebuilt and the direct road opened to the army locked up in Chattanooga.

They unloaded themselves and their baggage and lay down on the ground to rest, but there was little of that. Drum taps called them from their blankets in the middle of the night. The Giddings Regiment formed a column along with the 147th Pennsylvania, and horses pulling the guns and caissons of a section of Knap's Pennsylvania battery swung in behind them. They crossed the Tennessee River by the light of torches on two pontoon bridges, both bellied out by the current that churned the water into oily boils. Their recent journeying, which had begun when they shipped off to New York City, then back to Virginia, and now to this new country, was at an end. The days and weeks ahead would show whether their travels had brought them the "something new" that had been their hearts' desire.

Jefferson, Ohio, birthplace of the Twenty-Ninth Ohio Volunteer Infantry. On its surface as quiet as any village, Jefferson was infamous as the western citadel of the antislavery movement and the stronghold of John Brown. *Kelly ambrotype, Ohio Historical Society Library/Archives, Columbus.*

Appearing half-finished in 1860, Akron would be so transformed by the war that returning veterans would not recognize it. *Summit Memory, Akron-Summit County Public Library.*

(above) One of the war's rarest photographs: recruiting in Akron's downtown during the war's first days in April 1861. An observer characterized the emotional atmosphere as "supernatural." *Summit Memory, Akron-Summit County Public Library.*

(left) Jefferson, Ohio, resident Joshua R. Giddings, founder of the 29th OVI, led northeast Ohio's decades-long antislavery battles in Congress, but was forced from office just as the war he had predicted drew near. *Library of Congress.*

(left) The 29th Ohio's first and best-loved commander, Col. Lewis P. Buckley, whose motto was "Come boys, follow me." *Summit Memory, Akron-Summit County Library.*

(below) Impressed with the order and purposefulness of Camp Giddings, Pvt. Ben Pontius made this detailed sketch for his mother. *Ohio Historical Society Library/Archives, Columbus.*

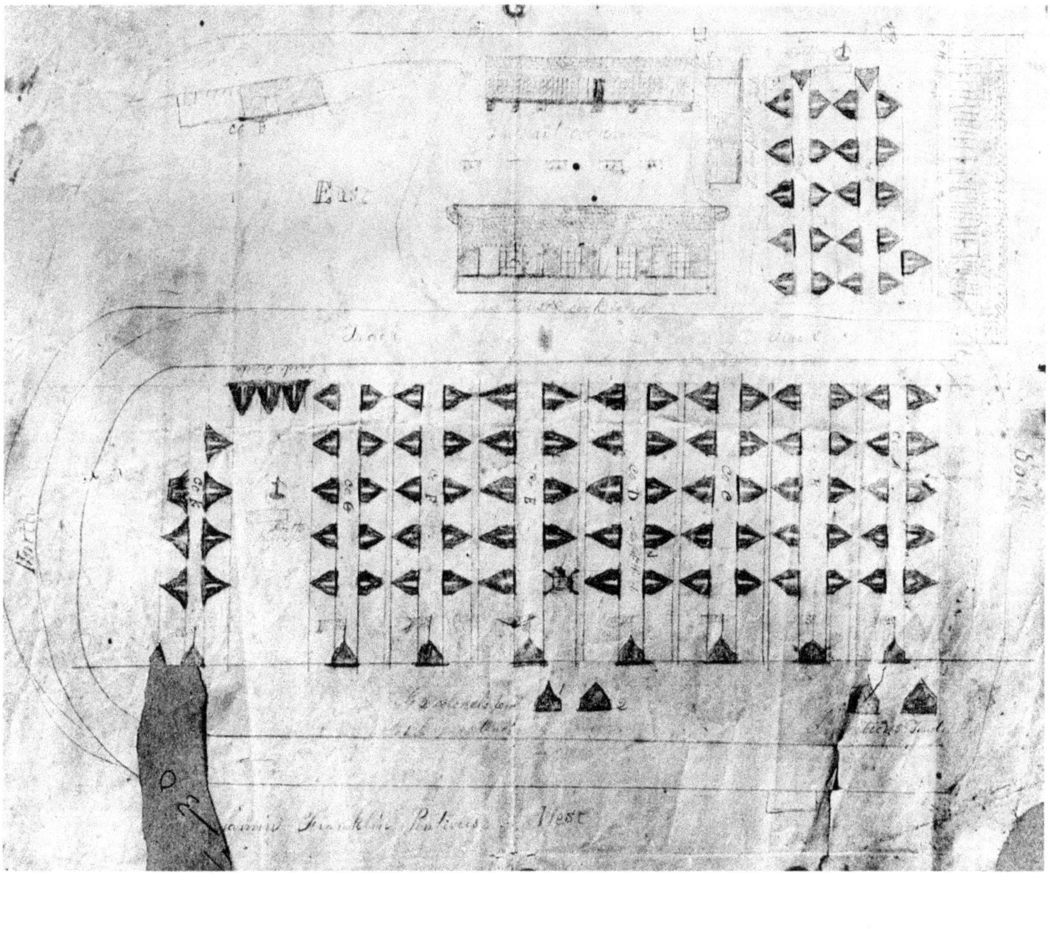

After several weeks of hard service, the veteran soldier bore little resemblance to recruit Pvt. Lorenzo Vallen, posed here in the full rigging of the untested volunteer. *John Gurnish Collection.*

Camp Chase, Columbus, a city unto itself. Farm boy Pvt. Willis Sisley, impressed with the camp and the city of Columbus, let his untraveled brother know, "You have no idea what is going on in the world. I have seen more inside of the last two weeks than I ever seen in my whole life." *Ohio Historical Society Library/Archives, Columbus.*

The final assault at Kernstown unraveled Jackson's flank and secured the Union victory. Sgt. John Marsh's long descent into despair began here on seeing combat turn boyhood friends into fiends. *Drawing by Alfred Waud,* Harper's Weekly, *April 12, 1862.*

Gen. James Shields led the boys to victory at Kernstown and to disaster at Port Republic. Colonel Buckley complained that incompetent generals, like Frederick Lander and Shields, had wrecked the 29th Ohio's division. *Library of Congress.*

RALLY
FOR "THE DEAR OLD 29th!"

The ranks of the 29th Ohio Regiment having become thinned by the rigors of a tedious winter campaign and the severe battles at Winchester and Luray, it has become necessary that new enlistments be immediately made to fill them, and again are the gallant sons of "Old Ashtabula" called upon to aid their brothers now in the field. The call is imperative. Our brave boys that fought so heroically in the unequal contest at Luray, need assistance; they expect that their comrades at home will lend them a helping hand, and come up to their rescue, and the vindication of the cause of our glorious Union. Will you aid your brothers? I believe you will.

I have returned for the purpose of recruiting, and wish to obtain all the good men I can. My headquarters for the present will be in Ashtabula.

The pay in this regiment is as good as is offered in the service anywhere.

Lieut. E. B. HOWARD.

July 19, 1862.   Recruiting Officer.

Sent home to make good the regiment's losses at Port Republic, Lt. E. B. Howard posted dozens of handbills advertising for recruits. He misnamed the battle as "Luray," but his confidence in what the regiment had done, and would do if reinforced, was genuine. *John Gurnish Collection.*

The hard reality of life within the walls of Fairfax Seminary Hospital and other Washington area hospitals was brought home to the residents of Ashtabula County in a series of published letters written by their neighbor Helen Cowles Wheeler. *"Fairfax Seminary converted to use as a hospital by the Army of the Potomac," by Edwin Forbes, Library of Congress.*

The regiment's boys were as much tourists as soldiers. The unfinished Capitol in Washington drew soldiers like Cpl. Burton Pickett. "I was up at washington yesterday we had a gay old time we went from Alexandria on a steamboat it is a nice place but the capitol beats any thing ever I saw. It is made of marble and covers over four acres of ground it isn't shaped like a house or a barn anything else it looks more like a mountain than any thing else." *Library of Congress.*

Ambitious Pennsylvania politician Brig. Gen. John White Geary commanded the 29th Ohio's division for better or worse from 1862 through the end of the war. *Library of Congress.*

In this panoramic sketch of the Battle of Cedar Mountain, the 29th OVI steps into the cornfield (exact center of drawing) to support the 7th OVI already engaged below the Crittenden Lane (marked by the loops of the Orange-Culpeper Road leading into the smoke forward of the woods in the upper right). A survivor wrote, "During the fatal period death assumed a real character while life, seemed but a dream." *Edwin Forbes, Library of Congress.*

Timothy Sullivan photograph, "Collecting and burying the Union dead on the battlefield at Cedar Mountain, Virginia, August 1862." The 29th Ohio's picket line stretched across the rows of mass graves seen in this photograph. Of the quality of these hasty burials Cpl. Nathan Parmater wrote, "The dead were all taken care of, some of them but poorly for I saw some of their feet sticking out of the ground." *Library of Congress.*

The regiment's first historian, J. H. SeCheverell, reported the severe winter of 1863–64 caused suffering in the regiment akin to that of earlier patriots at Valley Forge. Reporters for other regiments who spent the winter at Dumfries, Virginia, found conditions quite tolerable. *Alfred Waud drawing, "Winter Picket Duty," Library of Congress.*

"The Pontoon Bridges," by Edwin Forbes. The 29th Ohio's brigade led the 12th Corps's march to Chancellorsville, crossing both the Rapidan and Rappahannock Rivers in a single day, and landing them squarely on Lee's flank. Hopeful soldiers like Wallace Hoyt commented, "There is business ahead and the boys are ready." *Library of Congress.*

In the desperate final hours at Chancellorsville on May 3, 1863, the 29th Ohio's brigade (Candy's) stood nearly alone against Lee's army around the crossroads near the Chancellor Inn in the upper right of this drawing by Edwin Forbes. The battle was another Federal disaster, but to soldiers like Pvt. Nelson Gillett, "They [the rebels] was whipped at Chancellorsville, but dident know it." *Forbes, "Gen. Hooker's headquarters at the Chancellor house May 1, 1863," Library of Congress.*

The battle-worn veterans of Chancellorsville made frequent visits for recreation to the Federal shipping center at Aquia Landing, but always at their peril. Sergeant Parmater found it inhabited by "a perfect gang of cutthroats." *"Aquia Creek Landing," Library of Congress.*

Edwin Forbes's sketch of rebel skirmishers testing the Union defenses atop Culp's Hill, Gettysburg, on the morning of July 3, 1863. The 29th Ohio held the breastworks on the saddle below the crest at the extreme left. Commenting on the 1,200 dead and mutilated rebels found on this slope, the normally effusive Sergeant Parmater commented simply, "Such a sight I never saw." *Library of Congress.*

> Gettesburg July 4th
> Dear Parents
> as I there is
> A chance to send out mail
> I will send you a fiew lines
> I am now setting in the
> Rifle Pits where we fought
> all day yesterday. I am
> not hurt all though A great
> many of our regt are. fireing
> has commenced: and I must
> Close this is the forth days
> fight we are pretty well tuckered
> out we are whiping them
> Good by
> W B Hoyt

The most faithful letter writer of the regiment's Rock Creek Squad, Cpl. Wallace Hoyt found a moment in the rifle pits on Culp's Hill to pencil this note to his parents. *National Archives*.

Twenty years after the battle, trees cut in two by musket fire attracted the curious by the thousands, a grotesque testament to the intensity of the fighting on Culp's Hill. *Author's collection.*

Whitesides, Tennessee. The regiment spent the late fall of 1863 in the Raccoon Mountains west of Chattanooga keeping the Cracker Line open by endless mud digging on short rations, causing soldiers like Pvt. Cass Nims to complain about their new comrades in the Western army, "they are using us darned mean." *Library of Congress.*

(above) The assault on Dug Gap was the 29th Ohio's bloodiest day in their long war. To use the road on which Geary's troops are seen advancing toward the summit in this idealized drawing meant certain death. *Theodore R. Davis drawing,* Harper's Weekly, *June 4, 1864.*

(right) After consoling his father on the loss of his brother in the disaster at Dug Gap by saying, "It is what has happened," Cpl. Jerome Phinney was killed in the nightmarish fighting on the New Hope–Dallas line a few weeks later. *Brad Burroughs Collection, U.S. Army Military History Institute.*

(above) In the tangle of the New Hope–Dallas battle line, Georgia, May 1864. For the only time in the regiment's history, soldiers exhausted by days of nonstop fighting simply "played out" and walked to the field hospital. *"Photographic Views of Sherman's Campaign, . . . From negatives taken in the field by Geo N. Barnard, Official Photographer of the Military Div. of the Miss.," New York, 1866.*

(left) Lt. Rollin L. Jones was known as a lighthearted boy, but his psyche was ravaged by the experience of war. *Courtesy James C. Frasca Collection, U.S. Army Military History Institute*

Of Atlanta's destruction Sergeant Parmater observed, "The city itself is badly cut to pieces, with shot and shell, there are many nice buildings completely ruined, it is the nicest looking place I have seen in the south but it is rather desolate now as most of the inhabitants have left their nice homes and many of them are being torn down to make bunks for Yankees to sleep on." *Library of Congress.*

"Gen. Sherman's men destroying the railroad before the evacuation of Atlanta, Ga." The regiment's last duty before the march to Savannah was to destroy the railroad, work that became commonplace on the march across Georgia. *Photo by George Barnard, Library of Congress.*

The face of Maj. Gen. William T. Sherman was well known to the soldiers of the 29th Ohio, and several claimed to have talked to him. One soldier thought him as plain as a midwestern cattle dealer. *Photo by George Barnard, Library of Congress.*

Sergeant Parmater found the novel sight of contrabands marching at the rear of the 29th Ohio's column worthy of an illustration in *Frank Leslie's Illustrated*, and a few months later one appeared in that publication. *Library of Congress.*

The regiment's march to Washington took them through their old battlefield at Chancellorsville. The soldiers counted fifteen hundred skeletons lying within sight of the road through the Wilderness. By then, few soldiers were affected by such ghastly sights. *"Cold Harbor, Virginia (vicinity). Collecting remains of dead on the battlefield," photo by John Reekie, Library of Congress.*

The twentieth Corps of Sherman's army swings up Pennsylvania Avenue in the Grand Review, May 24, 1865. *Photo by Matthew Brady, Library of Congress.*

PART III

With the Western Armies

22

The Battles around Chattanooga

FALL 1863

Fighting by Moonlight

Geary's command was somewhere out ahead on this mountain road to Chattanooga. He had sent orders back for them to come up as fast they could. Chattanooga was twenty-five miles to the east, the way the crow might fly, but by the course the soldiers would march, far longer and much more difficult. The Tennessee River ran in coils from Bridgeport to near Chattanooga, where it relaxed into a giant loop. They marched along the river and into a steep-sided, winding valley, well into the night, coming to rest near a gorge at a place called Whiteside, above which stood the bulk of Raccoon Mountain.

Geary had pushed through here on the double-quick hours earlier and had marched his men over Raccoon Mountain and into the next valley, where Hooker ordered him to a stop. He had arrived at a place called Wauhatchie Station with the impressive, steep-sided majesty of Lookout Mountain dead ahead and Chattanooga out of sight the other side. Geary was ordered to stay here and hold the place while Hooker moved on toward Chattanooga. When Geary came down into Lookout Valley, he could plainly see rebels wiggle-waggling his arrival to each other from signal stations halfway up the mountain.[1] The rebel generals Longstreet and Bragg were up there, watching him descend into the valley. They were making plans to destroy him.

Until the rest of his division could join him, Geary had but fifteen hundred men, and parts of Knap's battery, in which his son Edward commanded a section. He worried that he had too few men to hold this isolated place if the rebels decided to come down off the mountain and strike him. Geary threw out pickets and ordered his men to sleep with muskets in their hands and cartridge boxes belted tight. During the evening, a citizen of the neighborhood came in and told Geary that he had seen Longstreet's men that very day, not up on the mountain but right down here where Geary was standing. Around ten thirty a few of his skirmishers tripped over their rebel counterparts and they exchanged shots. After that, the valley went quiet. Everyone seemed to sense that the other shoe was about to drop.

The moon illuminated a radius of one hundred yards around Geary's men, and shortly after midnight lines of rebel infantry stepped into the edge of it and began firing for all they were worth. Geary's pickets were shot down with the words of the challenge "Who goes there?" half out of their mouths, and the rebel line strode forward. The defenders formed a battle line in the shape of an L, corner out to the enemy, with their artillery tucked in behind, and began pouring fire out into the dark. Geary's men had a thirty-yard length of rail fence from behind which they loaded and fired, but aside from that it was a stand-up fight done out in the open, with soldiers aiming their muskets at the orange flashes that marked the enemy. One rebel rank would move up, be shot down or driven back, and another would come right in its place. Rebel prisoners informed Geary that he was up against the South Carolinians of Brig. Gen. John Bell Hood's division, Longstreet's corps, commanded in this rare nighttime assault by Brig. Gen. Micah Jenkins.

After three hours, Geary's men ran low on ammunition. Runners gathered what they could from the cartridge boxes of dead and dying men stacking up around them. The crews serving Knap's guns depressed the barrels, loaded short-fused spherical shot, and blasted holes in the enemy lines. The rebels were close enough that their yells "Pick off the artillery!" could be heard clearly above the roar. Knap's gunners began to go down two or three at a time, both men and horses tangled together in the guns. Although surprised, Geary had not been taken off guard, and except for the Negro teamsters who drove off at the first fire, Geary's line had not budged a single foot. The fighting went on by some accounts until the sky was going gray in the east. At last, the rebels backed away.

The rebels had suffered severely. Geary's gravediggers buried 153 rebel soldiers at the scene. To calculate how many of them had been wounded, Geary used what he said was the standard casualty calculation: for every man killed, five and one-half would likely have been injured, giving a total of one thousand rebels wounded. The rebels had inflicted three hundred casualties on Geary's men. Gen. George S. Greene had been shot in the mouth and cheek. Geary's darling son Lt. Edward Geary had been shot through the head while working his guns and died in his father's arms.

Up before light, with the last sounds of the battle up ahead still echoing through the mountains, the Twenty-Ninth marched cautiously from Whiteside, dropped into an opening in the valley, and Lookout Mountain came into their view for the first time. They got up to the scene of carnage at Wauhatchie and were immediately put to work. A drenching rain was falling, but their line needed strengthening just in case the rebels came down from the mountain again.[2] A few days later, Geary moved them up into the hills nearer the river. The Giddings Boys were assigned a camping spot on a hillside overlooking Kelly's Ferry Road.[3]

"Using Us Darned Mean"

Ames went to his work in the hospital on the river bank, comforting the dying and helping to load the wounded onto flatboats that were towed by steamer back to Bridgeport. He took over the chore of carrying soldier letters down to the ferry for posting and bringing back letters from home.

The road was full of men, pack mules, and wagons loaded with essential supplies on their way to Chattanooga. It appeared to Chaplain Ames that Lookout Mountain was a splendid natural fortification, clearly impregnable from this side of it.[4] Approaching a little closer, rebel guns could be seen peering down from the cliffs at the top. The enemy threw shells down from the top of Lookout Mountain occasionally, doing little harm, and shells from Federal guns on the other side could be seen arching up to the summit.[5]

They were now further into Dixieland than any of them had ever been, but they were still not in the land of the magnolia and the palm. The soldiers awoke in the morning to find the ground covered with heavy frost, and ice had to be jarred from the tops of water buckets. The supplies were beginning to flow from Bridgeport to Chattanooga, and trains of wagons stacked high with crates of food passed steadily by, but the soldiers who had opened the Cracker Line had barely a cracker of their own. They were living on half rations, and the horses were sickening and dying from lack of feed. This was not enough nutrition to fuel boys who spent their days at hard labor shoveling and draining the road, cutting timber, and laying the logs crossways on the roadbed to give it a bottom where it was swampy.[6] In these lean days, they resorted to their fallback food, field corn meant for cattle. Soldiers found that it could be made palatable by parching, and then softened by boiling. A cornfield lay not far from their camp, and the Giddings Boys competed with the rebels for the rights to it. The battle for the cornfield was conducted with fists and harsh words, and the boys of the Twenty-Ninth prided themselves on winning most of these disputes. Generally, pickets of both sides abided by an informal truce, coming out of the woods to trade Union coffee for rebel tobacco, and news.[7]

Sherman's army came up after a long march from Corinth, Mississippi. It took two days for all his rangy, lean-sided solders to march past them, adding thousands of soldiers to the already hungry congregation.[8] Cass Nims reported their current hardships, and his response to them, in a letter to his mother.

> I seat myself to write you a few lines to let you know I am well and enjoying good health. And hope these few lines will find you the same. We are on the same mountain yet but do not know how long we should stay. But I hope that we shall not stay long for they starve us here. They are using us darned mean after we drove the Rebs and they give all the rations to the Army of the Cumberland and if they catch fellows out foraging they make him work on the fortifications. They catched me but I ran away from them and came to the regiment before they had taken my name or regiment.[9]

There was an implied criticism in his letter of the generals who were running the show, pushing supplies toward the soldiers of the western armies and allowing newcomers from the Army of the Potomac to suffer. The new men from the East were known to these rough-and-tumble western boys as "paper-collar," white-gloved gentlemen, which struck the Giddings Boys as ironic but not amusing. Not all that long ago they had been provoked to fisticuffs when laughed at for their ragged, shoeless condition by the impeccably uniformed eastern soldiers they encountered when they came down out of the Blue Ridge, back in early summer 1862.

To General Geary, responsibility for his soldiers' current hard times owed to the inferior level of organization here in the West compared to that practiced in the Army of the Potomac. He confided to his wife his opinion of the western generals who were running things: "There seems to be considerable lack of brains among some of the officers about whom we read so much."[10] Cass Nims summed up the perceived feeling of the western troops toward the newcomers: "The Western Army don't like us much."[11] Its discipline had been the pride of the Army of the Potomac, holding the men together in the hardest of times. In this army, Geary found discipline to be nonexistent.[12] The soldiers in this western army wore whatever suited their fancy: some men dressing like riverboat gamblers or Rocky Mountain trappers, and wearing top hats, bowlers, fur hats, and even stovepipes tall as those favored by Lincoln. Geary issued a blizzard of orders to his soldiers throughout the coming months and afterward, each of which was read aloud to the assembled at roll call and then copied into the regimental books in the event the soldiers, or their officers, needed reminding of what Geary expected from them. First and foremost: the soldiers must wear the prescribed army hat and uniform, or face severe punishment.

Although everyone was hitching their belts a notch tighter for lack of rations, the real want of the Giddings Boys here in the mountains outside Chattanooga in late fall 1863 was for tobacco. Ames did not like habits of any kind, except for regular prayer, but he went to the ferry to get some for them, but found nothing.[13] Deserters came in every day, hungrier than they were, and broken in spirit to boot. They reported that thousands more just like them would give up and come into the Union lines if they could do it safely. The rebels in this part of the war looked to be about finished, and the Boys regarded the Confederacy now as more of myth than a reality.[14] There had been many rumors of impending action that would knock the last pins from under the rebellion, but affairs in the Wauhatchie valley remained quiet.

All the reinforcements were up that could be fitted into this end of the valley, and as soon as the roads dried to allow the movement of men and artillery, a campaign must begin. For now, the Boys were happy to be in camp, especially with the wildly variable weather. "It is warm enough to roast eggs here in the day and at night it will freeze a mule and they are the toughest things that there is in the Army," was how Cass Nims described the fluky late-fall weather in this Southern region.[15] The soldiers did their work every day, slashing timber and shoveling mud from the roadbeds, and returned to camp at night to enjoy the soldiers' simple pleasures of a well-tended fire and slowly improving rations.

Into the third week of November 1863, the fall rains finally subsided, and the roads once again had bottoms. In the lee of Lookout Mountain, everything took on the look of an army getting ready to fight. Hooker had collected roughly ten thousand soldiers in three divisions in and around this valley, and Sherman's army of three times that had marched by them and gone on toward Chattanooga. Grant intended to raise the curtain on this act of his program by taking the fight to Bragg up on the hills that looked down on Chattanooga. Hooker's role in Grant's original plan was to carry out a "demonstration" against the end of the rebel line atop Lookout, which meant he was to attack as if he intended to take it, but the real purpose would be to distract the enemy and hold him in place. Meanwhile, the big show would be at Missionary Ridge, on the other side of Chattanooga, where Generals William T. Sherman and George Henry Thomas would strike the main body of the rebel army.

Although others had judged it foolhardy even to try, Hooker believed he could take Lookout Mountain if Grant would give him a chance. His confidence was contagious, and Grant revised his orders. Hooker could go ahead with the attempt to conquer Lookout Mountain, but only if his demonstration proved it practicable, which left Hooker plenty of latitude as to how far his men might go. Religious services were being observed one evening in the camps of Candy's brigade when the prayers were cut short by the arrival of an order. The Twenty-Ninth and the rest of the brigade strapped on their gear, rammed dry charges into their rifles, and marched to the base of Lookout Mountain where its steep walls overhung the river.[16]

The Battle above the Clouds

Geary's division spread out in line of battle along Lookout Creek and waited for sunrise.[17] The boys dozed in place, or stayed up speculating on what might be required of them when the sun came up. By the account of one of his regimental commanders, Col. Eugene Powell of the Sixty-Sixth Ohio Infantry, Geary was unsure of his mission, at least the scope of it. During the night, Powell had been awakened by a courier from Geary's headquarters.[18] He rode over to Geary's tent and found not only officers of Geary's staff but men from the staffs of both Hooker and Grant, and from the solemn looks of things, Geary had just received news that was not to his liking. Geary broke the silence: "Colonel, I have sent for you: I have orders to make a demonstration upon Lookout Mountain. I wish to know where and how I am to cross that creek with my command." Geary then told Powell he intended to "show the world what his ideas of a demonstration meant." Powell was left with the distinct impression that Geary intended to exceed the scope of his orders and turn a demonstration into a full-out assault.

After some delays in getting his men over the creek, Geary led his men around the brush and boulders and up onto the mountain. The Twenty-Ninth Ohio's historian, Little Hamp SeCheverell, reported the assault on Lookout Mountain with the words, "Onward, upward, with loud cheers our columns rush to victory, carrying everything before them. A whole brigade is captured, and Lookout mountain, since famous in song and story, is ours."[19] His account was full of details of the sights and sounds of the battle that day, and of the geography of the mountain, and the grand scene at the top after the rebel resistance was pushed away. He omitted one important fact concerning the Twenty-Ninth's part in the battle: they had none. They had gone no further than Lookout Creek and had been only partial spectators. Cass Nims told the truth of it in a letter home: "We have been having hard times but we cannot grumble for the rest of our brigade has been fighting for three days steady and have taken Lookout Mountain." Of his regiment's duty while the battle was going on, out of sight on the mountain above them: "They took 2,000 prisoners and we had the devils to guard."[20] Col. William T. Fitch got the unvarnished version of the Twenty-Ninth Ohio's actions down in his official report to headquarters.[21]

Candy ordered him to cover the advance of the brigade over Lookout Creek and to bring the regiment up to the battle line after everyone had crossed. But before Colonel Fitch had advanced his boys one foot, Maj. Gen. Daniel Butterfield sent an order that Fitch was to stay where he was. While the rest of their brigade moved up Lookout Mountain and into the history books, the Giddings Boys set themselves to the inglorious, muddy work of hauling logs and setting them in place over the creek, and guarding the crossing. Up above, Hooker's men, led mostly by Geary's division, swept the rebels from Lookout Mountain. The morning after, the victors up on the summit raised the U.S. flag, and the sight of it as it came into focus through the clouds immediately became the stuff of legend.

The next day Hooker moved south and pitched into Bragg's left on Missionary Ridge at Rossville Gap, and, with Thomas's Federals swarming up above, the rebel army was forced into a full retreat.

Hooker brought his men up to the town of Ringgold, Georgia, with Bragg's artillery and trains in sight just on the other side, making their getaway through a gap with the same name as the town. The rebel general Patrick Cleburne was outnumbered, but he had no intention of letting Hooker pass without a fight, and when the Federal columns came up to the gap they were slammed by intense fire from atop Taylor's Ridge.

Geary ordered Candy's brigade, under command of the Seventh Ohio's Col. William R. Creighton, to storm the ridge. The Seventh was known as the Rooster Regiment because of its resemblance to that feisty bird in hard situations. Its boys were known to crow like roosters and flap their arms as they swung into battle, and many of their officers wore a rooster pin on their lapel. Creighton gave the boys a talk just before they started up: "We are ordered to take those heights, and I expect to see you roosters walk right over them!"[22] They got partway up, stalled, and then fixed bayonets to close the remaining distance to the ridgetop. Lt. Col. Orrin J. Crane was out front when he was mortally wounded. Creighton was not about to leave his friend's body to the enemy, and he led a charge to recover it and was fatally wounded. Cleburne withdrew only after winning enough time for Bragg to get the Army of the Tennessee safely to Dalton, Georgia. Further pursuit of Bragg was called off, and Geary moved his men all the way back to the neighborhood of Wauhatchie. The Seventh Ohio marched back with heavy hearts. Twelve out of thirteen of their officers had been killed or wounded, along with half their noncommissioned officers and soldiers.[23]

Crane and Creighton had many friends and admirers in the Twenty-Ninth, and when news of their deaths reached camp, it was as if a dark shadow had passed over. Ames had known both of them and commented that although the two had many failings, they were good soldiers, loyal and true, and he wished peace to their ashes.[24]

The Twenty-Ninth's regimental history was worded to suggest that not only had the Giddings Boys taken part in the grand triumph of Lookout Mountain but they had also been with Geary's division during the whole pursuit from Rossville down to the fire-swept ridge beyond Ringgold. J. Hampton SeCheverell wrote, "*We* moved on after the retreating army" and gave sufficient particulars to convince the reader that they had been there.[25] The truth was that they been left behind in the Wauhatchie valley.

Chaplain Ames got nearer the fighting than anyone in the regiment. He went sightseeing up to the top of Lookout and through his glass watched battle raging miles away, along Missionary Ridge.[26] As to the duty the Twenty-Ninth Ohio was performing while the rest of their brigade carried the fight to Bragg, and the duty they performed after it, Pvt. Christopher Beck, twenty-year-old farm boy of Company D, reported in a letter to his mother, "We have bin building brestworks and slashing timber and dug a road over raccoon mts to whitesides for our wagon would get shelled to go round the road but this work amounted to nothing to us."[27]

In the days immediately after the Seventh Ohio's undoing at Taylor's Ridge, the Twenty-Ninth Ohio's movements were frustrating beyond measure. They had been ordered to march to Ringgold a few days after the fight at Taylor's Ridge, but the regiment went only a mile before receiving orders to turn around and march back. Next, they were ordered to march to the top of Lookout Mountain and take up positions in the line of breastworks the rebels had recently vacated. They climbed to the top and were then ordered back down. Fitch reported to Geary asking what his regiment should do, and Geary sent him to Hooker. He rode over to Hooker's headquarters, and Hooker told him to report back to Geary. He turned his horse around and rode back to Geary's headquarters. Geary ended Fitch's hunt for something useful to do by ordering him to take his regiment back to their camp.[28] The Boys had been gone from their camp just long enough for soldiers from other outfits to tear down and carry off their shanties.[29]

"The Instrument of Almighty God"

During their midnight discussion at Mrs. Wilson's boardinghouse in Normandy, Geary had talked with Chaplain Ames dispassionately on religious matters, as if he were discussing an interesting aspect of philosophy. When Ames visited division headquarters after the battle of Wauhatchie, he found Geary in deep mourning over the loss of his adored son, which was understandable. Eddy had been the apple of his father's eye, an exceptionally handsome boy, whose poise in every situation and deportment in battle had earned him praise. Everyone who met Eddie immediately liked him. He had been his father's sounding board and his chief chum. Geary was normally taciturn, but after his son's death, Ames found him changed; more "approachable" was the word Ames chose.[30] Just how deeply his son's death had changed him, Geary confided only to his wife.

Geary was sunk in an impenetrable gloom after Wauhatchie, and in the days and weeks afterward it settled more heavily upon him. He saw his son's death as a divine punishment. "Oh, my God, I feel this chastisement for the pride I took in him."[31] Eddy's death had caused in him both a psychic and a spiritual transformation. He was no longer merely a patriot: "I am bereaved and transformed. Like the tiger robbed of his whelps, I have been like a destroying angel ever since . . . I have been the instrument of Almighty God, of carrying terror and terrible destruction wherever it pleased God to direct my footsteps. Under such impulses I stormed, what was considered the impassable and inaccessible heights of Lookout Mountain . . . this feat will be celebrated until time shall be no more."[32]

Geary had been there on Lookout Mountain, directing his men from the front, but credit for the taking of the summit belonged entirely to the soldiers. Just as Hooker said in his report, once the Boys got up steam they could not be stopped, and their rush to the top had not required any generalship. In fact, Hooker had ordered Geary to stop where he was, midway up, and consolidate his gains. Geary issued the order for the Boys to pull up and reorganize, but by then they had rushed too far up the mountain to get the order.

He might have left the town of Ringgold alone, but his soldiers had been shot at by rebel pickets concealed in a few buildings. Geary ordered them burned, along with a few other structures. However, for his wife, Geary reported that he had burned the *entire* town and then, with a dismissive sweep of his hand: "It contained about 5000 inhabitants and was a beautiful place."[33]

The season for campaigning had ended and the soldiers settled into their winter camps. Although the Twenty-Ninth Regiment had merely watched and not been allowed to fight, they had done enough by way of cutting timber and building defenses and marching, all of it on short rations, to feel that they were no longer newcomers on detached duty from the Army of the Potomac but worthy members of a new fraternity. Christopher Beck closed his letter home with the instruction to his mother, "Tell Alfred Drake I am in the army of the Cumberland."[34]

Parmater at Home

On the march back to the Rappahannock after Gettysburg, Nathan Parmater and six other men were ordered home to collect the regiment's share of drafted men and come right back with them. He would be gone the remainder of the summer and all of the autumn of 1863 and would not return to his regiment until nearly Thanksgiving, and after all that neither he nor the others returned with any new soldiers, drafted or otherwise.

The venture started out promisingly enough, but after a week at home, the squad's furlough expired. Having no clear direction on what they should next do, they reported to Camp Chase, in Columbus. They settled into an old barracks, while the officer went to the governor's office to see about getting authorization for them to go back to the Reserve and do a little recruiting.

There was little to occupy the time as they waited for recruiting papers. Some of the Boys went into Columbus and amused themselves by tearing down a Vallandigham banner during the height of the election furor. There were rats aplenty in their barracks room, and the Boys devised an elaborate trap that could be sprung by holding the end of a cord from a bunk. They'd spent only a few days here when the Boys began talk of taking French leaves back home, which meant absenting themselves from their posts without authorization. Two of them did just that. A few days later Parmater and the others got their recruiting papers and went home. They were officially in the recruiting business, but Parmater's heart was not in it: "I think I shall try to recruit my own health about as much as anything."[35] After three days of halfhearted hunting, he decided, "As recruits are rather scarce, I have concluded to go to hauling wheat for my brother."[36]

At first, he found his new routine at home to be "a very good way to soldier" compared to what he'd been used to at the front. He went berry picking, clumsily helped his best girl, Ipsa, doing laundry, and started a dozen other chores, but finished few. He boarded with a different friend or neighbor every evening, as if he was still on the march back in Virginia. He spent the majority of his days "bumming around." He visited the country school where Ipsa was the schoolmarm and impressed the drowsy scholars with his dress uniform and tales of a soldier's life.

One afternoon he took Ipsa and her sister down to the lake and let them fire a blank from his Enfield musket. The girls were awed not only by its bark and kick, but by the knowledge that it had been carried into combat and fired at real rebels.[37] He went to the county fair in Jefferson but found little there of interest to him except the fast trotting horses. He went to see the oddities of Van Amburg's Grand Menagerie, a circus featuring the fat girl, who weighed 675 pounds, and the Arabian Giant, who was nearly eight feet tall, and Parmater "had a good time generally," a phrase that in the course of the last several months had become the most popular expression in the Union army.

The only military duty required of him was to report to Capt. Everson Hurlburt in Jefferson once a week. Hurlburt and Sgt. Nelson Bailey were faring no better in the recruiting business, so they decided to run off some posters, and with three to four hundred dollars pledged by the good folk of the county to be paid as a bonus to every new soldier, he went away with his enthusiasm temporarily renewed.[38] Still, Parmater could not lift recruiting to the top of his chore list. He busied himself husking corn and chasing bees through the woods hoping to be led to their honey stash. He took his Enfield hunting but saw no game. Evenings, he attended church choir rehearsals and advanced himself to the rank of Sublime Master Mason at his local lodge. He and Ipsa exchanged promise rings and pledged "amour" to each other exclusively, for a period of one year. They had met around the time he had first come to Camp Giddings, and although they had had some ups and downs, the war and its long separations had not gotten between them. He missed the boys of his company, but having disconnected himself from the war, he seemed indifferent toward returning to it. On the other hand, he could not relax completely and enjoy his stolen vacation.

In November orders came for the recruiting squad to return to the regiment. Parmater said his good-byes and took the train to Columbus to wait for transportation south. Not all that long ago boys like him had thought Columbus the most cosmopolitan place on earth. Now he found the city rather dull and overall a "poor place to have much sport in."[39] At last the squad collected itself and got on a train headed south to rejoin the Giddings Regiment.

They were traveling with a contingent of Seventh Ohio boys who had been home on the same mission, when news reached them that the Seventh's beloved Colonels William R. Creighton and Orrin J. Crane had been killed in some action below Chattanooga and their regiment had been cut to pieces.[40] Parmater's detachment caught a freight train into Bridgeport, Alabama, which was the end of the line. Of a proper town, he could find no sign: it appeared to be one large military camp plunked down on the Tennessee River, in a steep-sided, oddly red-soiled valley. While waiting, Parmater watched a group of rebel prisoners being escorted over the river on a pontoon bridge when three or four of the pontoon boats suddenly sank. Seven rebels and two Federal soldiers could not be fished from the water, and drowned.[41]

They crossed the Tennessee and hitched a ride on an old steam engine pulling three flatcars, which took them part of the way. They stopped for the night at a place called Raccoon Mountain Coal Works. There was a hard, worn-out look to it, and it was walled in all around by close-sitting mountains. Union soldiers and columns of rebel prisoners passed them on their way back from the front, every one lean-looking from living on short rations. He found the regiment camped in a narrow valley between Lookout and Raccoon Mountains, four miles from Chattanooga.

"I found the boys looking very well, they have been living on about one third rations which is rather hard, the boys are at work building houses. It seems like old 'hard times' to get back to camp life," were

Parmater's impressions after being gone from the Boys for several months.[42] The supply line had been open for weeks by now, but the soldiers were still tightening their belts. The officers seemed to be eating as well as they ever did. Chaplain Ames was living in a wall tent with Lt. Col. Edward Hayes, second in command now to Colonel Fitch. Their accommodations featured a Sibley stove and plenty of hard crackers and bacon, while outside their horses continued to keel over for lack of fodder.[43]

Their work here consisted mainly of road building, but when off duty the soldiers explored the mountains and caves around them. Some made the long tramp around the toe of Lookout and into Chattanooga. They could see it had once been a flourishing town but was now knocked all to pieces. The Army of the Cumberland was filled with Ohio boys, and they had friends from back home in the town in the service of the 105th Ohio.

In their camp, the boys worked at increasing the size of their woodpiles in anticipation of winter. The custom of playing ball had been left behind with the Army of the Potomac. A new recreation popular in this rougher western army captured their interest. Chuck-a-luck was a game of chance consisting of a birdcage-size wire tumbler turned by a hand crank. The soldiers made cash bets that their chosen numbers would come up when the three dice came to a stop at the bottom of the cage. The game was surrounded by players at all hours, and to Chaplain Ames's distress, as much money was gambled away on the Lord's day as any other.[44]

For over two years, the boys in the Twenty-Ninth had been forecasting that the war would be over in a month, but events had made them eat their words. Their predictions this time were based on the observations of soldiers who had been privileged to see the condition of the South in *both* theaters, and the end now seemed inevitable. "The report is current here that Longstreet has surrendered, and if it is so this War is about played out for they are just whipped as hard as they can be," concluded Cass Nims, predicated on intelligence that unfortunately proved wrong.[45] Here at Wauhatchie, Bragg's disillusioned soldiers were throwing down their muskets and coming into the regiment's lines in numbers that seemed to prove the enemy's diminishing thirst for war. Cass had seen with his own eyes disheartened and worn-out rebels come out of the trees with hands in the air, eager to quit the fighting and go home.[46]

The same belief had taken hold of the citizens back home. Based on evidence from the battlefields it was clear: "The crisis has passed, and the worst is over," as the editor of Summit County's largest newspaper observed.[47] Surely if a nation could produce such startling abundance on the home front, while conducting a full-out war at the same time, the Confederacy could be toppled with one more push. The South had been choked into impoverishment by the Union naval blockade. The effect of it, combined with the enemy's inherent meanness, was now being evidenced by his treatment of Federal prisoners. A local officer locked up in Libby prison, in Richmond, sent the Akron newspaper editor a piece of the gray, gravelly bread they were fed by their captors.[48] He allowed that the rebels had permitted him and other Ohio officers to vote in the recent election but had mistreated them in every other way.

While the Giddings Boys were in their camp at Wauhatchie, the residents of Akron observed the national day of thanksgiving, and they had much to be grateful for besides the success of Union arms. The town was enjoying a level of prosperity without parallel in its history.

New businesses, churches, and lodge halls were going up around town, and those already in existence were making improvements. The progress of any civilized place could be measured by the improvements in its schools, and on the education-loving Reserve, these too moved forward, even though a bloody civil war raged. Although the pool of qualified teachers was diminishing in favor of the war's need for more and more soldiers, applicants were still required to stand for examinations and answer questions such as, "How many motions are made by the earth and what are they . . . state the diameter and circumference of the earth."[49] Accounts were published of the recent dedication of the cemetery at Gettysburg. Lincoln had attended and made a speech, but there was little attention paid to the few words he spoke.

Progress on the scale of Akron's had bypassed Jefferson, mostly because Jefferson lacked a railroad. That deficit would be corrected shortly, if the go-ahead boosters of the village's future had anything to say about it. Rumors were flying that surveyors had been spotted lugging chains through the woodlands and bogs just outside Jefferson. They were said to be marking out a course for a new railroad that would interconnect the Lakeshore Railroad with the Pittsburg and Erie.[50]

Every supper, picnic, lecture, dance, and performance of music or drama was organized with the purpose of raising money for the Soldiers' Aid Society. Homemade affairs all of them, but they showed that most folks had their hearts on the proper patriotic plane. The locals could escape the grimness of these war days and catch glimpses into a higher society that lay far beyond Jefferson through the eyes of people who had once been their neighbors. The marriage in Europe of William Dean Howells, son of the local newspaper editor, made a splash in the village. Mrs. J. R. Giddings, whose family was in Montreal, Canada, manning the American embassy, sent travel reports back to the Jefferson newspaper, describing her glittering nights at the theater, opera, and café. She was blessed, as she said, to live in a truly cosmopolitan place like Montreal.

New buildings and civic improvements were not changing Jefferson's skyline, as they were in Akron, but that is not to say the villagers were not making money on account of the war. Judge Norman L. Chaffee, who had taken a prominent role in putting the village on a war footing, was by practice a lawyer. With the war at hand, however, he had branched out and was making handsome profits in the wool market.[51] Other Ashtabula County men were making fortunes raising mules for the army.

Former captain in the Twenty-Ninth Regiment Josiah J. "Jack" Wright of Akron had never been one to bridle himself when it came to blunt talk. Now he publicly chided those who were making money as a consequence of the war. If they had any conscience, they should open their wallets and contribute to the various projects underway to raise bounty money that would encourage men to enlist voluntarily. The call to conscience by men like Wright was not entirely effective. There was not enough money in Jefferson's bounty fund to pay those who enlisted.[52] The village government would find it necessary to levy a tax to make up the deficit.

Women were regularly chastised by anonymous editorialists for spending too much on fripperies and flounces while soldiers suffered for want of things as basic as socks. In their defense, Miss Fanny Fern sent a letter to the newspaper reminding the reader that much of the weight of this war was being carried by women. They kept farms and businesses running without any male help whatsoever. The products of kitchens and sewing rooms had saved as many hospitalized Union boys from the grave as the rebels had sent there with bullets and shells. Fanny enumerated the private burdens that the women of this war were forced to shoulder: unwelcome thoughts of boys buried in heaps among which might be their own, or thoughts of a wounded husband or son left stranded on the battlefield, or languishing in a hospital or prison. A strong front had to be kept when her child moved a small finger down the lengthening columns of dead and wounded published in the newspapers in search of a father's name. At bedtime, she had to stand with brave face and listen to her children's pathetic entreaty that God please, please spare their father or big brother and allow him to come home to them. Fanny asked the question, "In this war did the soldier's wife suffer any less than he?" After taking the full tally of everything women were doing, Miss Fern concluded, "When I think of these solitary women scattered throughout the length and breadth of the land, my heart warms toward them; and I would hold them up for the world to admire."[53]

Such a woman was Mrs. Amos Fifield of Conneaut village, wife of Dr. Amos Fifield, the Twenty-Ninth Ohio's surgeon and current chief surgeon of Candy's brigade. She had turned the family home into a small hospital, continuing to care for the lame and afflicted of the village, and those of the war. Capt. N. J. Smith, former commander of the Second Ohio Battery, died of consumption in the Fifield home that fall.

The women, and everyone else who had an interest in the Brave Old Twenty-Ninth, began yet another period of excruciating anxiety. Sketchy news had come in of the bloody fighting around Chattanooga. Reports were that the Seventh Ohio had been roughly handled, and since it was well known that the Twenty-Ninth Volunteers always fought shoulder to shoulder with the Seventh, there was worry for the fate of the Giddings Boys.[54] But this constant worrying for news of their boys' health and welfare might soon be at an end, at least temporarily. If things worked out, their sons would be coming home to them on a special month-long furlough.

Veteran Volunteers

When Parmater got back to the regiment in early December, he found the Boys hungry, rain soaked, and locked in an obsession for playing chuck-a-luck. He also found every conversation dominated by the same topic: whether the regiment would reenlist or go out of existence when their three-year enlistment term of service expired, in the fall of 1864.[55] Col. William T. Fitch had sent a letter to the Akron newspaper in early November declaring his intention to reenlist the regiment for three more years.[56] It was not a cinch that enough soldiers would reenlist to make the quota. Adjutant James B. Storer was given charge of the project, and he began politicking along the company streets at Wauhatchie, extolling the benefits of reenlisting, overcoming the doubters, and signing men up.

The War Department in Washington recognized that the war could be better fought by veterans than by greenhorns and took steps to induce old regiments like the Twenty-Ninth Ohio to reenlist for three more years, or the end of the war, whichever came first. During the past summer, the War Department had begun offering enticements to soldiers who would reenlist, and by fall 1863 the campaign was pumped up and refined to include inducements a soldier could not easily dismiss. Aside from the pride a man might take in receiving the special title Veteran Volunteer, there was a bright chevron to wear on his coat sleeve, which announced that he had seen the spider and lived to tell of it. Now, there was talk of a guaranteed federal bounty of as much as four hundred dollars, which even in these high-wage, flush times was still a fortune, and more than a private could earn in more than two years of soldiering.[57] The townships back in Ohio were raising bounty money of their own, which could add as much as another $150 to the federal windfall. Added together, the federal and local bounties were enough to put a very sizable down payment against the purchase of a small farm that might give a boy's family a good start out of the financial hardship that had dogged families for generations. And there were other enticements besides cash.

With reenlistment came an immediate furlough home—whether for thirty or sixty days was not yet clear. Christmas was coming up and many had not been home for two years, and if they reenlisted now they would be assured of being at home at this brightest season of the year. Chaplain Ames hoped that a visit home would "moralize" those who had fallen from grace from their indulgence in vice; gambling was the worst of these sins at the moment.[58]

Most important, if three-quarters of them reenlisted, they could march to the war's finish behind their same flags, with the same officers, and in the same companies as they always had. Having been at war this long, no real patriot would want to be absent at the historic end.

Fitch's announcement to the Akron newspaper that the campaign to reenlist had been launched included his request that the residents help them: "And, Mr. Editor, I would most respectfully ask the assistance of our friends at home to help us in carrying out the object of getting home with the regiment to recruit, and re-enlist."[59] If keeping the townsfolk interested in the regiment would help, Lewis Buckley was willing to lead.

Buckley had taken charge of the campaign to raise money needed to buy the regiment a new pair of flags to replace the set Giddings had presented to them long ago at Camp Giddings. The "national colors"—the Stars and Stripes—was especially the worse for war, having been through all of the regiment's battles except for Cedar Mountain. Miss Maria Ackley of Akron and Miss Clemmer of Mogadore had between them raised the very substantial sum of eighty dollars.[60] Interested citizens in Ashtabula County had contributed another eighty dollars.[61] Buckley placed the entire sum in Maj. Myron Wright's hands, and he went to Cleveland in September and ordered them. Thanking all of those who had thought enough of the regiment to donate money, Wright assured them, "We will remember the friends who gave it, and be nerved with new energy, striking faster, deeper, and deadlier the new blows upon the enemies of our country."[62] As to what might be done with their old flags, objects made sacred by what had been sacrificed for them, and bona fide relics of the regiment's history, Wright said they were to be sent to Jefferson for safekeeping.

The new flags were shipped down to the Giddings Boys and presented to the entire regiment in a ceremony that featured the reading of an inspiring letter from the citizens of Jefferson.[63] Later that same day a rumor flew through camp that the requisite number of reenlistments had been obtained. The soldiers who believed it were to be disappointed.[64] The rumor proved false. Too many men were resisting the pressures to sign up, and the pressures were considerable.

No man wanted to deprive the others of a trip home. Choosing against reenlistment called into doubt one's patriotism. Men who decided against it feared they would be seen as sympathetic to the despised copperheads.[65] And, there was the pressure of staying true to the neighbor boys he'd accompanied into the war. The Rock Creek Boys got aboard the project, together in this as they had been in all things. Wallace Hoyt's cousin Thad; his boyhood friend Sgt. and Color Bearer Andrew Rickards, whom they all called Rickers; the Phinney boys; and his best friend in the world, Newton B. Adams, had all gotten on the reenlistment bandwagon. But Wallace had decided against reenlisting, and he would not be budged from his decision by Storer or by his own father. In a letter home, he explained:

> I should have been happy to comply with father's advice if I could only see it in the same light he does. Perhaps you would like to know my reasons if [it] so pleases you. I think I can do better. I don't know but you folks will think I am backing water because I don't stick myself for three years longer. If so just keep right on thinking. I know what I want about as well as any other man. I am not sorry in the least that I enlisted for three years! Nor, shall I be that I stay out the next three years.
>
> Your affectionate son
> Wallace B. Hoyt[66]

He had gone away from the environs of Rock Creek a boy, but his years as a soldier had earned him the rights of a man—foremost, the right to make his own decisions. He told his parents they should not expect him home with the others for Christmas. He would remain behind here on the Tennessee. There was no bitterness against those who did not reenlist. Some men simply "did not have the feeling," as Capt. Jonas Schoonover expressed it, and that was that.[67]

The reenlistment campaign caught the Seventh Ohio's soldiers with their spirits down. Creighton and Crane were gone, and there was a belief in the regiment that Geary had sacrificed them and all of the others without good reason at Taylor's Ridge. A generalized depression fell on them, and there was unhappiness with the officers who tried to replace the revered fallen leaders.[68] The feeling in the Seventh Ohio was understandably against reenlisting, and they decided to go home when their term expired, come spring 1864.

All the Twenty-Ninth's officers signed on for another three years, except for Capt. Wilbur F. Stevens. Given the enmity Storer felt for Stevens, it is doubtful that he even tried to persuade him to stay. Stevens had personal reasons for going home.

The enlisted men had not rushed to sign up, despite pep talks from the officers. After three weeks of agitation by Storer and others, enough difference of opinion still existed for Chaplain Ames to conclude that the prospects for them going home as a unit were not promising.[69] A few days later the corner had been turned. There were some difficulties yet to overcome, which necessitated visits by Fitch to headquarters for clarification of what exactly they would be paid, and when they might expect to ship home, but for now the thing looked more favorable.[70]

A few days later, the issue seemed in doubt again. Fitch and Hayes had gone to headquarters in Chattanooga again, hoping to get answers to their soldiers' questions. The Boys had been driven into their shanties by the rain and cold, where they waited impatiently to learn their fate. The officers poked their heads in and tried to soothe the agitation many now felt, while keeping their own expectations reined in. They wanted to protect their soldiers from more disappointment if it came to that.[71] The roads that they had broken their backs to build through the valley and up the slopes of the mountains were fast disappearing into the mud, and unless they started for home very soon, they would be stuck here all winter.

The muscle of every soldier in the division was now needed to keep the roads open. One day they returned to their camp after a long day of shoveling mud to be told there was nothing to eat whatsoever.[72] On December 18 there was good news: all doubt about reenlistment had been removed. Enough men had come forward to put them over the top.

But at retreat that very evening Fitch had to tell them that after a recount, it appeared that they were still eleven men shy of the mark.[73] Three more days of high anxiety passed before the entire regiment was marched down to headquarters, officially mustered out, and then in again as the Twenty-Ninth Ohio *Veteran* Volunteer Infantry, for three more years.[74] In the end, 335 men and officers reenlisted. About one in ten had chosen against it.[75] Nathan Parmater's heart was stirred by the dedication of those who had signed up again: "Who can think that our cause can fail when men who have been through what those here have, away from home and loved ones for over two years, and now living on almost nothing are willing to go on determined to see the end of the rebellion. May God bless all true Veterans."[76]

The trip back to Ohio was to start at once. Wallace Hoyt stood off to the side and watched them pack up, no longer part of the regiment in which he had grown from a boy into a young man. "The boys are all feeling fine because they are going where they can spend money again. Money will buy no luxuries here except cigars and those are 10 cents a piece which as you can buy at home for 2."[77] He was transferred over to the Seventh Ohio, where he was made welcome.[78] As things stood, he would spend the rest of his war with them. His time as a Rock Creek boy was over.

The very next day the regiment marched down to Kelly's Ford. However, the boat that was to take them to Bridgeport did not swing into view that day, or on the day after. The officers decided that if they wanted to get over to Bridgeport they had better set their feet in that direction, and after a single day's march of twenty-four miles up and down through the mountains, they got to Bridgeport in time to pile onto the day's last outbound train.[79] It was Christmas Eve and the soldiers celebrated by firing muskets out the doors of the cattle cars.[80]

The weather had turned cold, and the freight cars they rode in were not equipped with stoves. No one had thought to bring a blanket. They rolled up in their long coats and tried to get some rest on the rocking plank floor. They got into Nashville on Christmas night and marched to the five-story General Zollicoffer house. They began to doubt they would be home in time even for New Year's if they continued at this slow pace. Ahead at Louisville, several months' back pay awaited, and a hundred-dollar down payment against the promised reenlistment bounty. They would not get home in time for Christmas, but they would have money in their pockets when they did get there.

At Louisville the soldiers put up at the soldiers' home, in a hall big enough to accommodate the entire regiment. The paymaster arrived on schedule, which was a pleasant surprise, set up his table, and counted fat rolls of greenbacks into waiting hands. Their wallets now bulged with nearly two hundred dollars apiece.[81] To top it off, they were given the first square meal anyone had had in months. "All are feeling well—a few too well," commented Chaplain Ames after looking in on them."[82] The Boys were under guard, which irked them, but they were allowed to go into town if they went by squads. Some of them returned with whiskey, poor in quality, but sufficient in quantity to do the job. For those who wanted it, sleep was out of the question. Parmater observed the general frolic and wrote, "It has been a merry old time at the soldier's home today, some got drunk and some got drunker, but most of the boys behave very well."[83]

The steamed through Indianapolis and on toward Columbus, with the brownish Ohio countryside whirling by the windows. As they moved north into the Western Reserve, the ground was uniformly covered in white. They got into Cleveland around noon, and, believing the residents might like to see what a fighting regiment looked like, they brushed up their uniforms, chipped mud from shoe bottoms, and formed up. They took a few turns around the city in marching column with their drums and fifes out front. They marched with two sets of flags leading the way: the brilliant new stand they'd recently been presented, and the bullet-punched and smoke-stained pair they had rallied round at Chancellorsville and Gettysburg.[84] A reporter from the Ashtabula newspaper was on the scene to report their homecoming.

He recalled that not all that long ago they had marched through Ashtabula on their way to the war nearly a thousand strong, unproven then but anxious to show their courage. The column comprising the entire regiment now numbered less than three hundred, a wearing down for which the reporter pitied them.[85] For all they had done, and for their recent promise to go through to the end, the Boys expected a big, welcoming crowd, but they were in for a letdown. The people of Cleveland had witnessed the coming and going of too many regiments for them to be stirred by the passage of the Twenty-Ninth. Chaplain Ames thought the soldiers deserved better: "No preparation to receive us. No enthusiasm manifest. A multitude gazed and wondered. No effort to feed hungry men or make them welcome. A disappointment was felt by officers and men at this, for we expected a warm greeting from the people at home after a long absence and hard service."[86]

They marched out to the camp that had been arranged for them, on the outskirts of the city, and waited for the official papers that would allow them to return to the family hearth.

23

Home and Back Again

BRIDGEPORT, ALABAMA, WINTER 1864

A Month at Home

On New Year's Day 1864, the Boys awoke in their barracks outside Cleveland to find the bottom had gone out of the thermometer, and the way the north wind was shaking the barracks, the temperature was likely to plunge further. The regiment shivered and suffered through the first days of the area's coldest winter on record. Railroad brakemen were found frozen stiff as boards, fingers still wrapped around the brake wheel.[1] The officers allowed those who didn't mind spending the money to go into the city, take a hotel room, and thaw out.[2]

The officers had known when they left Tennessee that they would not get a furlough. They would be working out of the regiment's recruiting headquarters, which Colonel Fitch had set up at the American Hotel in downtown Cleveland. For the enlisted men, furlough papers had to be made out before they could leave for home, but many soldiers started for home without them. After the horse was already out of the barn, Fitch cut an order allowing everyone to go home at once. The proper papers would be sent to their homes.[3]

No one knew when the soldiers would be arriving, and families had not sent a wagon or cutter to collect their boys and bring them home. With the daytime temperature failing to make it above zero, travel was dangerous. The trains ran east along the shore of Lake Erie, but many of the boys did not live in any of the towns through which it ran. Getting home meant a cross-country hike of thirty miles or more. The soldiers turned in their rifles, buttoned up inadequate clothing, and set off through a stark white world.[4]

The towns and villages through which they tramped looked as deserted as doomsday, everyone inside pulled up close to the stove. But the weather became irrelevant once home was reached. To be icebound with one's loved ones suited the soldier just fine. Sunday was church day and the best opportunity for seeing old friends, but it was too frigid to safely venture out, and the boys stayed home, shared Bible readings around the fire, and caught up on the changes that had taken place in their neighborhoods in the two years they had been gone.

Chaplain Ames had been gone only ten months, long enough for the village of Conneaut to alter itself noticeably. Old Mrs. Fifield had passed on while he was away, and her homestead, which had been lived in by Fifields going back to the county's earliest days, was now occupied by folks who were complete strangers to him. The village had grown, not mightily, but enough for him to take note of new businesses. He saw new faces on the streets to replace those who had fallen in the struggle of living.[5] The frozen surface of Lake Erie as seen from Conneaut was stunning and weird. For the first time in memory, a sheet of ice covered it as far as the eye could see, leading observers to speculate that they would all be able to walk over to "the domain of the Kunucks [Canada]."[6]

Snowstorms arrived, some going on for days and depositing snow two feet deep, and even deeper in the places where the wind drifted it. For those who made it to the neighbor's house for a visit, pains were taken to make the soldier feel welcome and back in the bosom of home.

In Akron, sheltered from the alternating cycle of blizzard and subzero cold by its distance from the big lake, the townsfolk organized a grand fete to show their heroes how large a place they still occupied in the hearts of the citizens. Led by a brass band, the local militia outfit escorted the soldiers of the Twenty-Ninth Regiment and the Sixth Ohio battery to the ballroom in Cutter and Howe's Hall. Inside, tables heaped with platters of oysters and cold meats, cakes and pies, glowed under the gaslights. After they had filled themselves and the tables were cleared, and pipes and cigars lighted, the Akron Glee Club entertained with stirring patriotic songs that got everyone singing. With soldiers rising from their chairs to cheer and applaud him, the keynote speaker, Lewis P. Buckley, fixed himself on his theme:

> When I think that out of twelve hundred men who have been in the 29th Reg't only three hundred are left in its ranks, my bosom is filled with emotions mingled with sorrow and pride—with sorrow when I reflect that so many young men through sickness, wounds, and death have been compelled to leave the regiment; and with pride when I see those few who are left again go forth to the call of their country, by re-enlisting, resolving to help fight the battle out.[7]

As for how the rebel leaders should be treated when the war was over, Buckley took the hard line: "I would kill the vile wretches, and throw their worthless carcasses to the birds of prey."

Considerable heat was being generated by the recruiting campaign conducted by the Twenty-Ninth's officers. They combed the countryside for recruits, and in spite of the cold and snow, and the higher bounties being offered by townships in competing counties, they made a surprisingly respectable haul.

Approximately sixty-five new men were recruited in the month-long veterans' furlough; some had been enlisted as late as the day the regiment was scheduled to return to the front. Capt. Myron Wright had come home to Akron while the rest were still down near Chattanooga and worked through the months of November and December to get new men. Wright had persuaded thirty boys to enlist. In round numbers, these two catches produced one hundred new soldiers, triple the number needed to replace those who had not reenlisted.

Conneaut had stood foursquare for the regiment during its formation as much as any other place, and it outdid itself in this current round of fishing for men. The village's quota in the most recent Federal levy of troops was thirty-eight, and the village filled that without resort to the draft. Half the recruits were pledged to the Twenty-Ninth Regiment.[8] Chaplain Ames's presence in the village during the furlough, and his frequent talks to families about the soldier's life with his assurances that he would look after the soldier's moral condition once in the field, swayed some, although he was too humble to take credit.

Ames had business in Cleveland. The night before leaving, he had a premonition that his trip would end badly, but he went ahead and boarded the train in a snowstorm. Near Painesville his train collided with the rear of an express train that had gotten stuck in a snowdrift, smashing cars to splinters and throwing the dead and dying into a dreadful tangle. The cars caught fire and burned with passengers trapped inside. Recently retired surgeon of the Fourth Ohio Infantry, Harry W. McAbes, was brought into Ames's car. Ames was an experienced hand by now at giving aid in time of calamity, and he went to work. With the snow swirling against the windows he did what he could to comfort McAbes, but he was too badly mangled to live. Of him Ames said, "Escaping all perils of battle, he fell on his way home by one of those mysterious events that fall with crushing power when least expected."[9]

With the last ten days of their thirty-day furlough approaching, a warming southern wind began to blow, and overnight the roads and fields were turned to rivers and lakes, making a run up to the crossroads mercantile too difficult to undertake.[10] In the first days of February with their furlough nearly expired, the officers lobbied to have their time off extended, but the effort came to naught and everyone was ordered to be back in their camp at Cleveland by February 4.[11]

Parmater was weather bound during most of his furlough, which to him was not entirely a bad thing since it was in the home of Ipsa, his blue-eyed beauty. Although under the watchful eye of her parents, the couple managed to find moments in which they snuggled under a blanket together. Such intimacy meant a very serious advance in their romance, one that Parmater was prepared to make.[12] To amuse himself while confined inside, and to age his appearance, he'd had a friend dye his whiskers jet black.

It took a few days for everybody to get back to Cleveland and a few more to get transportation south arranged. When everything was packed and ready, they marched through Cleveland to the train depot. The wind coming in off the lake pushed a wet, heavy snow, coating uniforms, beards, and eyelashes.[13] This time, Clevelanders came out and cheered them, and the young ladies in the crowd threw the boys kisses as they passed by.[14]

They had been home to celebrate the first month of the new year 1864, and both soldiers and civilians could reflect back with satisfaction on the strides made in the year just passed. The rebellion was weaker in every respect, while the nation was vastly stronger. Surely the rebellion would be extinguished by the next holiday season if not sooner, and slavery blotted out and no longer a vexation to the people.[15] All the sacrifices that had been made on the home front seemed to be finally amounting to something. Buckley pointed out in the overheated banquet hall in Akron that the depleted ranks of the Twenty-Ninth Ohio Infantry showed what the soldiers had given.

What might be required of everyone to bring the war to its close was unknown. What was known was that none of the Twenty-Ninth Ohio's soldiers would be coming home again until it was over. The army was set up now to take care of the soldier in vast hospital complexes strategically placed around the nation. Now the army would care for him from the time he sneezed, or was wounded, until he was fully restored and ready to be shipped back to the front. To mark his own preparation for the return to war, Ames said a prayer in his diary. "The time has come. I must soon be off again. Things are all packed, ready. May we all soon return home in peace. Some must suffer, some must fall. May a great and merciful creator preserve and protect us all."[16]

Return to the Front

The railroad line into Cincinnati was crowded with trains carrying troops and war matériel down to the Ohio River. They got across the river on steam ferries and climbed onto another train, which roared across the winter countryside at the startling speed of twenty-five miles per hour.[17] Two days after departing Cleveland they arrived in Nashville. The boys were marched over to barracks no. 2, formerly the Nashville Female Seminary. Under orders to keep to their quarters at the seminary, Parmater and his best friend, Chum Sterrett, forged a pass and strolled into the city as blithely as any tourists. Parmater climbed to the top of the State Capitol dome and carved his and Ipsa's initials into the fancy woodwork.[18] That same day, misfortune struck the regiment and caused serious injuries to it, although they were still far from the fighting.

The seminary had been erected on low ground, and to keep the students from muddying their slippers, elevated passageways had been built connecting the buildings. The army officer in charge of the place recognized that these bridges were too flimsy to support much weight and had placed guards along them to limit the foot traffic. When the call sounded for breakfast, the soldiers crowded onto the porch outside the dinner hall door. The weight of one hundred boys jostling to get to the front of the line was too much for the porch, and it collapsed nine feet to the ground.[19] Thirteen of the boys pulled from the heap were found injured badly enough to require transport to U.S. Army Hospital no. 8, and two of them had been very seriously hurt. John Wiedle of Company G had been carried from the forward trench during the chaotic finale at Chancellorsville by friends, and he survived his wounds. Now his leg was so badly broken that army surgeons decided the only prudent course was to take it off below the knee. One other soldier, Pvt. Edward Spicer of Company D, sustained a head injury so severe it was thought he would not live. The rest suffered a variety of sprains, bruises, and broken bones and would not be joining the regiment for the rest of the trip south.

They headed south out of Nashville in a warm rain, part of a rail caravan five trains long. In the hill country below Nashville, the lead train lost traction while climbing a grade and stalled. Impatient with the wait, the Boys got down and looked for amusements. Nathan Parmater recorded one diversion the soldiers enjoyed: "The boys appeared to feel well and had a high time, some catching little Negros and putting them aboard the train, and anything for fun."[20] Whether the children were taken down from the train before it steamed away, he did not say.

The discipline applied to the enlisted men during the trip back to the front was reminiscent of the laxity they had enjoyed at Camp Chase back in 1861. Molesting civilian property was strictly against army rules, and back home the smallest transgression against this commandment would have been unthinkable for most. During one stop, the Boys carted off anything that was not nailed down. Parmater smiled at this small carnival of thievery: "The boys feel first rate, they do not steal anything that they cannot carry but they are very strong and appear to 'Lift' most anything that they see."[21] Army authorities took a more serious view. The pilfering and destruction of public and private property committed by Federal troops passing through Nashville prompted the War Department to stop the pay of commissioned officers in charge of them until restitution was made. Of the scores of regiments passing through the place, only seven outfits had given offense, and one of them was the Twenty-Ninth Ohio Veteran Volunteer Infantry.[22] The news was published in a large eastern newspaper for the whole country to read. The people of Jefferson, however, doubted their boys were capable of such a thing.

As they neared Bridgeport, Alabama, the unmistakable signs of war were illuminated in the cone of light thrown by the engine's headlamp. Abandoned buildings stood along the track, burned or dismantled, and at intervals, once-fine farm fields that had been tramped down to the consistency of pavement by hundreds of marching feet. The manifold refuse of the armies was scattered everywhere: trash, poverty, and despair.

The Boys got down from the train at Bridgeport at midnight and, without knowing it, had ended their last railroad journey of the war. Many of them had never ridden a train before they signed on for war. Now, they were experienced travelers. The regiment's war road stretched far out into the distance, and, except for those who were wounded or taken prisoner, they would be covering the remaining miles of it on foot.

From the siding, they were directed into a large wood-frame warehouse down by the edge of the Tennessee River.[23] An icy wind blew up from the river and through the slats in the walls. Fire building inside was not permitted, and the Boys wove themselves into their blankets and prepared to spend the coldest night anyone had seen in the army since they'd occupied Camp Starvation, in the western Virginia mountains. Although they were much fatigued from their journey, it was too intensely cold for any of them to sleep. Having grown weary of Virginia, they had longed for something new, but this evening it appeared that soldiering must always be more of the same, wherever it was done.

Winter Camp 1864: Bridgeport, Alabama

They hardly recognized Bridgeport, although they had passed through it only a few weeks ago. Large warehouses had grown up as if by magic down by the river, and more were under construction. A substantial shipyard was in operation, and there were steam-driven sawmills slicing trees into planks for boats and buildings. Bridgeport had become a major supply base in this theater, and it hummed with as much activity as Aquia Creek, back in Virginia. The first order of business for the Boys was to build shanties. Nathan Parmater recorded the details of the method that had become tried and true:

> March 2—The house is made of slabs by setting four posts so as to form an oblong square sides about ten feet and ends six and a half, Chimney and door take up nearly one end,

fireplace is built of stone and mortar made of common dirt, doors made of shakes gabled up with slabs and covered with four pieces of shelter tents, the walls are five feet high which accommodates its three inmates both for a sleeping place and a table, writing desk, a seat and a covering to our cupboard. Around the sides hang our rifles and equipments which are required to be clean and nicely.[24]

Measles took hold and sent soldiers to the field hospital, just as it had at Camp Chase in 1861, and like at Camp Chase, the disease affected the new recruits almost exclusively. Almost everyone came down with hard colds. Unlike former times, sick boys were sent to a hospital that was judged to be neat, quiet, and well conducted.[25] Compared to past winter camps, conditions here were nearly healthful. Only two of the Twenty-Ninth's soldiers succumbed to sickness through the entire winter. Ames said a few words over them, and three volleys were fired, followed by a procession to the gravesite. Chaplain Ames reflected on the occasion and remarked, "Thus men go by disease as well as battle."[26]

Their purpose here, other than to wait out the winter and prepare for the spring campaign, was to guard the railroad and the accumulating army stores. Their guard post was situated on a rise to the right of the railroad depot with an unobstructed view up and down the great river. They were to guard the river, too, and prevent civilians from crossing toward Chattanooga, where the bulk of the Federal army was spending its winter.[27]

The portion of line for which the Twenty-Ninth Regiment was responsible was within an easy walk of camp, unlike at Dumfries. Parmater was a noncom, a term that the sergeants had taken to calling themselves, and had charge of a squad of guards.[28] But once he had given his three corporals their instructions, he exercised the privilege of his noncommissioned rank and went back to his shanty and slept through his squad's guard shift, or trick, as he called their assigned hours.[29] The Boys were as happy in this camp as they had been any place in the army, but even though surrounded by friends he'd known his whole life, a soldier could still get lonely.

Come dark, the energy of Bridgeport was extinguished for the day. Except for the sound of a dog barking at shadows down past the bend in the river, or the rumble of a steam engine, the place seemed as peaceful as any place back home. Parmater studied the sheet of silver the moonlight made of the river, and watched the movement of the stars. These midnight meditations comforted a lonely young man like Parmater: the heaven he could see above him also covered his loved ones in Ohio.[30]

Rumors came and went that the rebel cavalry had gotten inside their lines and was preparing to gallop down on Bridgeport. On one occasion, the rebels were reported so close by that Geary ordered cannon run out and the defenses manned.[31] However, the raid did not materialize. General Geary had learned long ago that defensive works were a prudent investment of soldier labor, and within two weeks of their arrival, every rise of ground around Bridgeport was crowned with earthworks.[32] The Giddings Boys turned their energies to pick-and-shovel work, digging ditches and throwing up the dirt to form gun emplacements.[33] Duty of this type had to be performed per orders, but the soldiers' attitude toward it was not entirely military.

They had been issued a bounty of shovels and picks for this work, but when the work details were assembled at the start of one day's labor, it was discovered that there were too few implements to get anything done. Command ordered everyone to show up at headquarters with their spades, pickaxes, and wheelbarrows, so they could be counted. The soldiers reported as ordered but brought along only a few of the tools they really had. Despite the warning that the camp would be taken apart and searched, the Boys continued to hide the rest of the tools up their shanty chimneys and in other out-of-the-way places.[34]

Close proximity to a major supply depot had its benefits. For once in their service, the Boys had plenty to eat. What they did not have or could not buy from the sutler, they custom-ordered by way of letters home to the folks, such as the one written by Pvt. Elias Roshon on behalf of the Rock Creek Boys:

> Father, the boys concluded they would Send home for a box of things and they wanted me to write to you and have you tell the rest of the Boys folks I will tell you what kind of Stuff we want to have Some Cow butter about 25–30 pounds and have it well done up and some applebutter and we want some dried beet and some Cheese a big one about 40 pounds and dried apples and tell Marbrys folks and Kindigs folks and Archers folks will bring theirs to your home. . . . Oh Yes Edwin he wants his father to send him about 2 pounds fine cut tobacco and George Reed you to get him about 2 pounds of the same kind.[35]

The Phinney boys, Tobias and Jerome, of Rock Creek had put in their own order for good things from home not long after camp was arranged. Their parents speedily filled the request and shipped the box off on the first day of March. It was nearly two months in getting to them, and when opened, the Rock Creek Boys were disappointed to find that everything had spoiled.[36]

And before he forgot, Elias Roshon closed his February 26 letter with one last request: "Oh I want you to send me some Maple Sugar about four or five pounds if you have it." Elias was forthcoming in requesting so large a quantity of a delicacy that required so much labor to produce. He intended to divvy it up and pedal it to the soldiers. "I can sell it just as fast as I wast to."

Other Boys went into business for themselves, the soldiers in the camp making up their semicaptive clientele. On the way down from Ohio, Parmater purchased several pocket watches, and he had no difficulty unloading his small stock for five times what he had paid for them. Sgt. Ellis Green's tuggy mate sized up the prospects of making an extra dollar, invested ten dollars to buy cobbling tools and leather, and went into the shoe and boot repair business. Business was poor at first, but by the time they left here, he was making as much as thirty dollars in a single day, working at a table he set up in the company street.[37]

Their camp satisfied the Boys in nearly every way. Elias Roshon wrote, "Father we have got awfully nice weather here and a good place to stay and expect we will stay some time if we're not drove out by the rebels."[38] There was little chance that the rebels could make a dent in such a large establishment if they did attack, and the Boys hoped they might spend the rest of the war in this comfortable situation.

A Religious Revival on the Tennessee

Chaplain Ames found lodging in the rooms of the U.S. Christian Commission branch in Bridgeport. Their extensive installation consisted of rooms for meetings, storage for the reams of religious tracts that were handed out to the soldiers, and accommodations for visiting clergymen. At last he was in the presence of godly men who, like himself, enjoyed conversing for hours on end over moral conditions in the army. For the first time since he'd been with the regiment, Ames noticed that the soldiers were taking an interest in their souls.

At each service, Ames noticed an increase in the numbers of boys attending and in their interest in what he had to say to them. The chapel tent in Bridgeport filled to overflowing, with soldiers squeezed in on the benches and standing at the back shoulder to shoulder. One Sunday Parmater and his friend Chum Sterrett did not start early enough when the call to church sounded, and they found it so full they could not get inside. Col. William T. Fitch had had something to do with the surge in attendance. Previous commanders, Buckley for example, demanded the boys attend divine services, but it was not mandatory, nor would it ever be. Fitch applied a more forceful hand by personally chastising those boys who chose to ignore the call to church and instead observed the Sabbath by lounging about their shanties, smoking and gossiping.

The soldiers were now taking an active part in the service. As Ames described one Sabbath, "4 came forward by invitation seeking the mercy of God—one spoke. 8 arose at close for prayer, one other was prostrated."[39] These were evident signs that a movement toward grace had begun in this part of the army, and Ames's hope was that it would take hold and spread. One Sunday, Ames was preaching in the open air of the company street and he looked up from his work to see that even Capt. Wilbur F. Stevens, a man who in the minds of some was not a traveler on the higher path, was in attendance.[40] Ames noted with some surprise that Sabbaths here in the camps were beginning to resemble those back home.[41]

He was beginning to find his voice. Nathan Parmater heard one of Ames's sermons and said that it had been "good," which from Parmater was high praise. The chaplain's natural discontent did not allow him to take much satisfaction in his accomplishment. An early spring snowstorm knocked young leaves from the trees and set the soldiers to snowball fighting with the abandon of schoolboys. This downturn in the weather vanquished Ames's spirit, and he found himself once more feeling discouraged. His year in the war had brought him around to the discovery of an essential truth about himself: "It has never been my lot in life to be agreeably fixed in all respects and do not expect to be in the Army."[42]

A Hard Thing to See

While the soldiers at Bridgeport enjoyed comparative abundance, the civilians around them clung to the edge of existence. The soldiers had seen how the civilians in the neighborhood of last winter's camp at Dumfries had been further impoverished by war, but the condition of the people they encountered here on the Tennessee River made those back on the lower Potomac look like landed gentry. One of the commonest sights around Bridgeport was families displaced by the war, all their possessions tied up in an old sack, the smallest children piled aboard a worn-out horse and the rest walking alongside. Most were shoeless and coatless, though it was winter, and they slept on the ground without tents or blankets. They were bound for any place but this fought-over, stripped-off land. Until they could get where they were going, the refugees were dependent on handouts courtesy of the U.S. army. Parmater saw these dispossessed people and reflected, "It is a hard looking sight for Young Americans."[43] However, that was not to say Parmater was especially charitable toward them. They had made their own bed by supporting slavery and must now sleep in it. With that in mind, Parmater could observe them with the dispassion of an anthropologist:

> Was detailed for picket today, had charge of a post of three men, we were posted on a road leading into the country and close to a house or what was called a house, it was built of slabs and appeared to contain two families, two of whom I should call girls, they were about an average of the inhabitants of this country, they all appeared to chew tobacco and could spit as independently as any Young American just learning to use the weed. Their mode of washing clothes is to soak them and lay them on a small bench and pound them. They all appeared expert in carrying a large basket or jar (in fact most anything) on their heads, which causes them to be rather flat.[44]

Groups made up entirely of young women, except for one older man or woman who accompanied them, slumped along on broken-down horses or aboard shabby wagons. Some of the Boys were naive enough to think these groups were displaced families, even though the young ladies did not seem to share any familial resemblance. Their surgeon, Dr. Haynes, tended the neighborhood's malnourished babies and the parents. He ministered to a "Mrs." Carter. There was no Mr. Carter in sight. She had already buried one boy, all her remaining children were sick, and she had no one to help her. Worst of all, she had been diddled by soldiers.[45] To diddle in its most polite form meant to swindle, and in its least savory, it stood for sexual intercourse. Chaplain Ames had sworn before God to provide succor to humanity, and hereabouts was a bounty of opportunities. He rode along to help Haynes tend a refugee named Mrs. Thurman. Her children, mostly sick and all hungry, bore the colorful names Mexico, Texas, and Kansas. Ames found these refugees honest but profoundly destitute, and he pitied their plight.[46]

Other regiments had already been out on unprofitable scouts into the surrounding countryside, and in mid-March the Twenty-Ninth's turn came. They crossed the river and got on the road to Trenton, Georgia, near Lookout Valley. They saw only a dozen or so houses at most during their entire walk through lonesome valleys, all of them poor, and nothing of the enemy at all except for a few hapless rebels who were making their way home on furlough. They were back in Bridgeport the next day after a round-trip hike of thirty miles, and having not marched anything like this distance in months, everyone was footsore.[47]

There was only one matter about which the veterans complained: the winter had nearly passed and the bounty promised by the townships in which they had reenlisted had not been paid. Wallace Hoyt had not reenlisted, and with a note of I told you so, he reported the unhappiness of the Boys who had: "Most of the veterans are sick enough of there bargain. I am glad I did not go."[48]

The reason for the delay was traceable to a loophole in the arrangement by which a township was credited with recruits against which their levy was filled. Some townships had raised a surplus of recruits, but did not have the money left to pay their bounty. These men were assigned to a neighboring township that had not met its quota, with the understanding that in taking a credit for the soldier, it would pay his bounty. The soldiers would be paid, but it would take some time before the lists were straightened out and approved by the state of Ohio. Until then, the soldiers must endure the feeling they had been hoodwinked again, and grand plans for how to use the money had to be postponed, or scotched. Franklin Potter had promised his parents that he would devote his bounty to helping them pay down the note on the place they had just bought—and had bought only after he promised them he would help. However, after weeks of nonproductive hoping, he was frustrated: "After so much shifting around a trying to get a hundred dollars town bounty at some place, I am assigned to Burton, Geauga County. First I was assigned to Morgan, then to Burton."[49]

Ellis Green had promised his parents that he would use his bounty to help them accomplish a long-held family dream, which was to buy a small place of their own. With his assurance, they shopped and found a place. Ellis had looked it over during his veterans' furlough and gave it his approval. By end of March, the bounty money still had not been paid, and after putting off having to send bad news, he was at last forced to sit and write an apology for having gotten their hopes up: "I have been more than anxious for some time to get a letter hoping it would bring intelligence of the payment of that Bounty so that you could buy the place, but it seems they have not paid anything yet. I am fearful they do not intend to. I am sorry for your sakes."[50] He wrote again a few days later expressing hope that the bounty would be paid eventually, and if fate intervened and he were not around to hand it to them: "Would that I might do more if anything should happen to me, you get that Bounty, buy the lot of Martin at once and move on it."[51]

The townships in Ashtabula County took their obligation to the soldiers very seriously and sent a representative down to the camps in Bridgeport to untangle the knots by taking a headcount and documenting the township in which every soldier had enlisted.[52] This disappointment to the soldiers was temporary and had nothing in it of the venom they had spit over their late pay when they first came to Camp Chase, in 1861. By now, the veterans had grown used to government's inefficient and tardy ways.

A Death in His Family

The men who had not reenlisted were living in the camp of the Seventh Ohio with the expectation they would serve out their enlistments there. In late March, good news came to them. They were to move next door back home to the Twenty-Ninth Regiment.[53] They collected their traps quickly and returned that very day. Wallace Hoyt stayed behind one more night. He needed some time alone so he could think things through. A wind came up out of nowhere and howled for hours, making his tuggy tremble and squeak as though it had the ague.[54] The peach trees had blown out in gaudy blossoms, but a foot and a half of snow, freakish even in these parts, had stripped the flowers, and the cold snap that followed ruined the fruit buds. Hoyt's thoughts were heavy and confused.

His mother, Ester Hoyt, had died unexpectedly in late January. The Rock Creek Boys who had gone home on veterans' furlough set their entertainments aside and attended her funeral.[55] Wallace had not even known she'd been ill, and she was already buried when he learned of it. His mother had been his sounding board and intermediary in the disputes between him and his father. He was the oldest of her several children, next being his sister Hattie, age sixteen, and the youngest a four-year-old boy named Ellsworth. For a time, the family seemed on the verge of coming apart. His father was considering sending the children off to the care of others, which to Wallace was unthinkable.

In the wake of Ester's death, the father was again toying with the idea of enlisting. That his children were now motherless, and would be orphans if he left, did not seem to concern him, at least as Wallace saw it. Wallace asserted his position as eldest son and struggled to keep his family together. He wrote to Hattie,

> You may tell Father for me that if he goes into the service again I can never forgive him. There is no use of talking. I know as well as he that they cannot draft him. And even if they could it is his business to get clear of it if possible. . . . But if he is bound to go tell him to wait until I get home. There will be plenty of time then for him to see all that he will care about seeing. . . . It is not only my wish but I demand it.[56]

Unknown to him, his father had ignored his counsel and had been traveling to Cleveland and Columbus, hunting for recruits for a company he was raising. With the mother gone, the father expected his sister Hattie to take over the mother's weighty responsibilities, and Wallace cautioned his father against overworking her lest she get sick.[57] Her education would be put aside until the child next in line behind her grew old enough to step up, and Wallace sent her big brotherly advice on how she might keep up her learning while keeping house for her younger brothers and sisters:

> There is a great many things to be learned beside what is laid down in school books and it would be rather dull studying school books at home. But reading good interesting books is beneficial and interesting and iff you could appropriate an hour or two each day to reading you would find it pleasant and proffetable and you must tell Father that you want that any book you want that he thinks prudent for you to read to buy it and charge it to me. I am happy . . . to hear that Fran and Rosa are being educated but you wait patient and will not be long before your time will come.[58]

His enlistment would be up in August, and if his father chose war over his family, Wallace would be home to take charge. The worst of the situation was that his father was keeping him in the dark about his plans for the family. "I wish you would write some of your calculations for I want to know how you are agoing to get along."[59] And then a jab at his father regarding an acquaintance the father had taken in to help his sister: "I don't fancy Adalade's helping Hattie much for unless she has greatly changed she is no fit companion for Hattie. As you are her protector you should look to such things." In the margins of his letters addressing these serious matters, Wallace made schoolboy doodles of his name, and of the name of his home township, Morgan.

The Bridgeport Cotillion

Nathan Parmater spent his spare time in Bridgeport studying German with Chum Sterrett and planning brief sightseeing excursions. One of these took them down the river a short distance from their camp where mussel shells had been made into an oval mound, eight feet high, forty feet wide, and seventy feet long. The locals said it had been built by ancient Indians for some mysterious purpose, and was said to contain human bones. He and Chum discussed their futures, and hatched a plan to ensure their success in it. The U.S. army was looking for men to command colored regiments, and Parmater and Sterrett thought their chances as good as anyone else's and applied. Parmater had never expressed any interest in elevating the black man, but an officer's rank seemed easier to come by in one of these new regiments than it would be in his. In late March they received notice they had gotten over the first hurdle, and they made themselves ready to travel up to Nashville, where a board sat to examine candidates.[60] While waiting for authorization to attend, they put down their German lessons and applied themselves assiduously to reading manuals on military tactics.

In late winter the rumor was resurrected that the regiment would be returning to the Army of the Potomac.[61] Cumberland Gap, back in Maryland, was a guess. Pvt. Franklin Potter voiced the precampaign speculation that consumed the Boys in these springtime days of 1864 in a letter home:

> There is a rumor that we are going to move in a few days. Some think we are going to Nashville but it is hard to tell where we aare going to the front some think we are going to Nashville but it is hard to tell where we will move if we move at all. And I think that we wont go very soon though I may not guess right. It don't seem to me as though we was a going to the front.[62]

Duty called and Frank put his letter aside and came back to it a few days later, by which time guesses on where they might go had been sharpened to a finer accuracy:

> Monday evening and all is well. It has been nearly ninety and warm the dust is very bad. It is very disagreeable out or in the shantys and I have not heard from the box yet and I am afraid that I shall not get it before we have to move. It is thought that we would not stay here only three or four days and when we move I think we are going to Ringgold down below Chattanooga. It will be 4 or 5 days march if we have to march and I guess that we will.

Or they might stay right here in Bridgeport. John White Geary was a general and privy to information they were not, and the vegetable garden he had planted near his quarters was a plain statement that they would remain here.[63] Why would he go to the trouble of putting soldiers to work tilling, stretching string to make the rows straight, seeding, and watering if he knew he would not be around to enjoy the produce?

They had built camps like this in a half-dozen places, but their camp here along the Tennessee pleased them more than any other. They were in no real danger from either the rebels or disease, and there was enough of military pomp in the guard mounting, observance of reveille and tattoo, and light drill to give them a sense of purpose.

Far into April, some Boys applied their hand to interior decoration as if they would stay here forever. Parmater papered the walls of his shanty, covered the shelves with scalloped paper, and crowned the project with a bouquet of cut wildflowers.[64] The Twenty-Ninth Ohio was competing with their brigade mates in the Fifth Ohio to see who kept the neatest and most attractive camp.[65] Back in Dumfries, a year earlier, the general inspector found the Boys and their camp in so slovenly a condition that he refused to inspect them. Now, the Boys regularly swept the packed dirt of the company streets, parade grounds, and even the perimeter around the camp until they looked as clean as a dance floor. This time, when the general inspector came, he found their camp to be the cleanest and best kept he'd ever seen.[66]

One day would be as warm as summer back home, allowing boys to shed their coats and work in their shirtsleeves. Too stuffy and overheated inside their shanties, they moved cobbled-together tables and empty hardtack crates, which were their furnishings, outside to write letters home, play cards, read the newspapers, smoke, and talk. The very next day would come a freakish snowstorm, or cold so intense ice formed on water buckets as thick as window glass, accompanied by a wind that sailed along the river valley, carrying away anything that was not tied down. In their droll vernacular, this howling zephyr was a "right smart breeze," that at times closely resembled a "hurrycane."[67] Gradually, warm days won out, and it was spring. Apple trees and wild plants put out flowers in earnest, and what fields the soldiers had not tramped dead turned green.

Ball playing took over again, and it was played here in a more democratic way than back in Virginia. This spring of 1864, the officers now joined in their high-spirited frolics, taking turns knocking the hide off the ball. Other boys pitched quoits, a game in which the iron hoops of casks were lobbed toward a stake driven in the ground. A group of five or six unattached women lived in a hut near the Twenty-Ninth's camp, to what purpose no soldier was bold enough to admit. They joined the boys in their game of ball, and sang with them around the evening camp fires.[68] Rafts of migrating ducks filled the river from bank to bank, and large prehistoric-looking fish, long and flat of snout, could be seen rolling below the water's murky top. The boys tried for both, but had success with neither. Evenings the solders entertained themselves in a way that Parmater thought noteworthy to report: "The boys had quite a time this evening on the parade ground, they had a violin and formed three sets and had a regular cotillion, they appeared to enjoy it finely, probably bringing to mind some of their old times at home, but it must be a very great contrast especially at partners."[69] The frivolity was repeated on successive nights with one soldier in the center to call off the steps and another to fiddle the tune, while the boys paired up and sailed away in their giddy dance, making the dust fly.[70]

"There Is Something There to Be Done"

The manual of arms had become a rusty thing. Now, they polished it back to perfection. Officers were required to write down the names of the three best-appearing soldiers at each inspection, and the three worst.

The Boys had taken to wearing any style of hat they wanted, which was the custom of the western troops. Geary moved to stop this affront to military uniformity and ordered everyone to draw new forage caps, and to wear them from now on or be punished. Unfortunately, the lot from which they drew was all of one size—extra large, too big to fit even the melon headed among them, and the soldiers laughed at each other for their foolish appearance and the constant fidgeting with cap bills.[71] The Boys had also adopted the western armies' custom of wearing whatever blouse, jacket, and trousers that pleased them, but it did not please Geary, and he sent out an order prohibiting it. "The habit of wearing clothing other than the uniform of the Army on the part of many officers and enlisted men of this command has been so notorious that it must at once be stopped."[72] Some of the Boys had grown lax in showing proper respect to their officers. Discipline was being tightened, as it was leading up to the launch of any spring campaign, and Col. William T. Fitch thought it a good time to make them a cautionary speech. He warned, "Any enlisted man belonging to this regiment who shall in future be guilty of calling out at or making impertinent remarks to or concerning any officer in his vicinity when passing by will be arrested and tried by a court martial."[73]

An Indiana outfit came through, having marched the entire distance from Nashville, and crossed the river without resting—bound for Chattanooga and the front. By the first week of May, the volume of troops moving through in the direction of Chattanooga swelled to a flood. From such mighty movements the Boys concluded they would soon follow.[74]

They had lugged their long wool coats with them at the start of other spring campaigns and then thrown them away when the marching grew warm and difficult. The coats were expensive, and replacing one counted against a soldier's clothing allowance. Veterans, as they now officially were, planned ahead. Groups of boys from the same neighborhood back home packed their caped coats into a single box and expressed them back to Ohio. They did not think it necessary to label them with the owner's name. Mother could pick out the coat that belonged to her boy by the distinctive stitching she had employed in sewing pockets into the coat's interior.[75] Allen Mason sent his coat home to Andover, Ohio, in late April and lest his worrying mother interpret this as a sign that he was pessimistic about his fate he explained, "I should had to heave it away when we have to march."[76] Also, he felt his father could get some good use out of it. Mothers of the soldiers knew enough of war by this time to realize that the retreat of the spring rains and the lengthening days meant the season of peril was at hand. Mason's mother wrung her hands and wrote to him of her concerns. To comfort her he replied,

> Mother, you must not concern yourself about me. You have children at home to think of and care for without troubling yourself over me. I am old enough to take care of myself and if it shall please the Lord that I should return home by and by I shall try and return with as good a character as when I left home. If not, it is all the same, it makes but little odds where a man's bones are laid after he leaves this world.[77]

The signs of an impending movement were unmistakable, and to Chaplain Ames, ominous. The Boys dreaded taking the road out of here, knowing it would lead to battles and hard times, but they were determined to go forth and finish it.[78] They would never again know such a place as this camp.

The nature of the war into which they were about to pass would not allow such constructions, or the pleasures that attended them.

While the Boys danced around their campfires in Bridgeport, finishing touches were being applied to a grand plan for the dismemberment of the South. Grant had gone east to take command of the armies there, and his trusted lieutenant William Tecumseh Sherman was given charge of the western armies. While Grant ground Lee's army to dust in Virginia, Sherman would pilot this army south along the line of the railroad to Atlanta. Once Atlanta was taken, he would turn his army east toward the Atlantic, then wheel north through the Carolinas. When each was done, the Confederacy would be gutted.

In this theater, first things first: the rebel army, now under command of Joseph E. Johnston, had to be dislodged from its blocking position at Dalton, Georgia, thirty miles below Chattanooga, and astride the railroad line to Atlanta. Whether the rebels had any will or material capacity to resist was a question that could be answered only by pressing them, but from the sounds of it, they had little left of either.

Reports coming out of the rebel camps around Dalton, which were published in the Ohio newspapers and then mailed down to the Twenty-Ninth Ohio's camp for reading, showed the rebels to be in worse condition than the pitiful refugees the Boys saw everyday around Bridgeport. The strength of Bragg's army had been reduced by an epidemic of desertion to a mere thirty thousand; those that hung on were reported to be so starved that they were reduced to eating their mules.[79]

On May 3, 1864, the end of the Twenty-Ninth Ohio's time in Bridgeport was reached. Parmater recorded the news of it in his diary:

> The monotony of our camp life is at last broken, we received orders to march at 9 a.m. at which hour the camps of the first Division presented a lively seen, the shelter tents were taken away from the shanties and the knapsacks and haversacks being all packed and then came the usual scene of breaking camp, all the old rubbish such as old haversacks, knapsacks, old bottles and dried up bread all has to be scattered and it is generally used to throw at one another until its charge and recharge all through the camp.[80]

The soldiers shouldered their rifles, adjusted their rigging, and answered the insistent call of the drums. A week before they left, their destination was still a matter of wild conjecture. Cass Nims came closest with his guess, seemingly based on intelligence even his officers did not have, which gave the name of a town not far from the course line plotted out by the high generals for this campaign: "Report says that we are going to Rome, Georgia. There is something there to be done."[81] Their leaving was so abrupt that someone had forgotten to call in the soldiers doing guard duty on railroad. They returned to Bridgeport to find their camp deserted. The entire regiment had moved without leaving a note saying where they had gone.[82]

"They Called It a Demonstration"
THE FIGHT FOR DUG GAP, MAY 8, 1864

Across the Tennessee

The first day's march was uncomfortably warm, and heavy traffic on the road forced many stops and starts, which for boys standing in place saddled with heavy packs was a torture. Not a single soldier fell out this time, and they arrived at Shell Mound, Tennessee, with every boy in the Twenty-Ninth "feeling finely." After camp chores were finished, the Boys got up a game of ball down on the river flats, while others hiked up to Nickajack Cave for a look-see.[1] The last time Geary had been here, it had been with his now deceased son. He had watched Eddie and his chums launch a rowboat on a subterranean lake and disappear beneath the mountain. Eddie's smile had been so bright that it lit up the gloomy vault. The memory of that excursion with his lost boy was too much, and Geary hung back.[2] Sgt. Nathan Parmater and some of the others passed through the cave's gigantic lobby and squeezed through chutes that dropped far down into the earth.[3]

They picked up the pace the next day, marching over the road they'd built last fall, then down into the Wauhatchie valley, where Geary dismounted and lingered at the spot where Eddie had died.[4] They wound around the base of Lookout Mountain and kept going through the dusk until thousands of campfires in Chattanooga came into view.

The Eleventh and Twelfth Corps had been combined to form the Twentieth Corps, Army of the Cumberland. Col. Adolph Buschbeck's brigade of Pennsylvania, New York, and New Jersey soldiers had marched to this point to rendezvous with them, and for the first time in many months, the White Star Division was assembled in one place.[5] Charles Candy commanded the First Brigade, containing the regiments that had marched and fought side by side since Cedar Mountain: the Fifth, Seventh, Twenty-Ninth, and Sixty-Sixth Regiments of Ohioans, and the Twenty-Eighth and 147th Pennsylvania Infantries.

Col. David Ireland, who had saluted the Twenty-Ninth's charge to the breastworks at Culp's Hill, commanded the Third Brigade of Geary's division. To the boys of the Twenty-Ninth Ohio, this latest change in affiliation mattered little, except it required every boy who expected an uninterrupted supply of letters and packages to advise home of his new address: 20th AC, Army of the Cumberland, 2nd Div., 1st. Brig.

They were on the road to Ringgold long before sunrise, up and over Missionary Ridge, and across Chattanooga Creek. The sense of urgency was increasing with every mile, along with the volume of troops clogging the few roads that traversed these valleys. The countryside was mostly wild, except for occasional clearings in which sat small, rough farms and dooryard gardens showing early peas, corn spikes, and flowers. The whole of the Twentieth Corps was up now. The Giddings Boys were shunted off to the side of the road to allow their corps commander, Joe Hooker, and his escort to tear past.[6]

The trees were leafing out fast, softening the sharp edges of the giant rock slabs that tilted out from the mountainsides behind them.[7] They marched across the battlefield of Chickamauga, where ground creepers reached for the bones of the imperfectly buried. Every soldier took note of the way spring came on in this region: abrupt and irrepressible. White petals sifted down into drifts beneath every fruit tree and flowering shrub. General Geary saw the resurgence of life in the Georgia springtime, and paired a dark observation with his lyrical description, "All nature seems to be inclined to be peaceful, and to multiply and replenish the earth, each after its kind, and man alone is making preparations for the destruction of his race."[8] The prodigious preparations that had been made for this campaign were becoming more apparent as they hurried along to get to their small place in this immense enterprise. They were started on their third spring campaign since coming into this war, but this one was different. This one represented maybe not the exact end, but the beginning of the end.

Gen. William T. Sherman's one hundred thousand had been organized into three armies: the Army of the Ohio, the Army of the Tennessee; and the Twenty-Ninth's army, the Army of the Cumberland, commanded by Gen. George Thomas, nicknamed the Rock of Chickamauga for the immovable stance he had taken at that great battle. The soldiers of the several Ohio regiments of Candy's brigade would not have to look very far to see another Ohio state flag. Sherman's army now had in it seventy-eight Ohio infantry regiments, a dozen Ohio artillery batteries, and nearly as many cavalry outfits. Add them all up and there were twenty-five thousand Ohio sons waiting to get on the roads leading south out of Chattanooga this fine spring day.[9]

Geary's men made eighteen miles and got to within four miles of Ringgold. They were too tired to make anything but a rough camp, and "forage" a hog from a local farmer.[10] Next morning the marching was decidedly hotter, and dustier. Enemy patrols tiny as stick figures could be seen on the ridges to the east. Behind them, the rebel army was dug in around Dalton. Geary spread his soldiers out into line of battle, everyone moving cautiously now down into a pretty, compact valley, and camped at Pea Vine Church.[11]

The next day, the seven thousand soldiers of their division formed a double battle line and moved up the slope of Taylor's Ridge. Behind the marchers came the guns and caissons of Knap's Pennsylvania and Capt. William Wheeler's New York batteries, drivers popping whips and cursing to get the green-broke mules up the grade. The supply train carrying their ammunition came next, and last were the ambulances. They made the top, where the Seventh Ohio had met disaster late last year. They descended into the last valley, whereupon they got their first look at this neighborhood's most impressive geologic feature.

Just across this valley was a wall of rock sometimes called the Gibraltar of the South. Just behind it, Gen. Joseph Johnston's army sat in Dalton, waiting for them. The top was crowned with vertical rock palisades, from which it derived its map name Rocky Face Ridge. Driving the rebel army out from behind it was Sherman's first tactical puzzle of the campaign.

Ten miles long, rising six hundred feet from the valley floor, and as steep as a barn wall near the top, Rocky Face filled the horizon from one end to the other. There were only three ways through. The most direct way was by the railroad line that passed under a mountain called Tunnel Hill, past which the Twenty-Ninth's boys were currently marching, and then into Dalton via Mill Creek Gap. Inside the gap, steep cliffs reared up on either side, giving this narrow passageway the ominous name of Buzzard's Roost. Johnston was expecting them to come at him from this point and had planned for it. Sherman looked for a less costly way in.

Three and a half miles south of here, the locals had built a crude road up from the floor of Mill Creek valley that took advantage of a natural notch at the crest, which went by the name of Dug Gap. Dalton lay directly behind it. The third way through Rocky Face lay a dozen miles below Dug Gap. Snake Creek Gap passed through to the east and came out just west of a tiny stop on the railroad named Resaca, fourteen miles below Dalton. Just how anxious the rebels were to fight was something of a mystery.

The rebels had toughed out a winter behind Rocky Face far more difficult than that experienced by any Federal. They had been plagued by desertion, poor rations, and a plunge in morale, just as the Northern newspapers had happily reported. What the newspapers had not reported was that General Johnston had restored them, materially and in spirit. There were sixty thousand of them, twice what the newspaper intelligencers reported, and that number would grow even larger once they were reinforced by the army of the fighting Episcopal bishop Gen. Leonidas Polk.

The valley was filled with thousands of Federal troops. Not long after descending Taylor's Ridge, Geary's soldiers were ordered off the road, and none too soon. Cavalry general Judson Kilpatrick rushed by at the head of a vast procession of horsemen hurrying south, pausing to pick up Ireland's brigade of Geary's division, which was to accompany the cavalry on its business down at Snake Creek Gap. The Boys passed Gordon Springs, which loomed tall in the history of the Chickamauga battle. The land here looked better than what they had seen on their way to this point, the soil red but verdant, and the farms more prosperous looking. But there was no one at home in the neighborhood, and even the public house at Gordon's was deserted.[12] With the sun disappearing, they came up to the farm of a man named Hallowell and camped.[13] Many boys had played out on this march, Parmater among them, and it was dark by the time he caught up with the Twenty-Ninth at their camp, five miles east and south of Taylor's Ridge.[14]

A Year Ago at Chancellorsville

The veterans squatted around their fires boiling coffee this balmy night, remembering where they had been exactly a year before, which was working their way back to the Federal camps around Aquia Creek after their close shave at Chancellorsville.

The Boys were universally weary after so much up-and-down marching in the unexpected heat, and for the first time in several days, they were not roused from their slumbers in the middle of the night. The rising sun of May 8, 1864, threw yellow shafts through the smoke of unseen fires burning in the valley of Mill Creek. They drowsed about waiting for orders. Mid-morning came and went without much to do, and the soldiers grew hopeful that they might be given this Sunday to rest.[15]

Their old friend, Dr. Amos Fifield, took a moment off from his many responsibilities as chief surgeon of the brigade hospital and walked over to the Twenty-Ninth's camp to visit men he'd known since the early days back in Jefferson and many he had known since they were children. He met James B. Storer and, impressed by the adjutant's beaming good health, he clapped him on the back and told him he was as perfect a man physically as there was in the army.[16] All things seemed to be combining to assure Storer a happy future. He had risen far in the regiment, with the prospect of climbing further before the war was finished. Best of all, while in Akron during the veterans' furlough, he had married his childhood sweetheart.

The sound of firing had come to them as they crossed Taylor's Ridge yesterday from the vicinity of Tunnel Hill and below it. They could hear the dull pop of musket fire this morning, but it seemed far away. An hour before noon, the long roll of the drums demanded they get into their gear and form up immediately.

Orders from the Top

Geary had just received orders for the day's work from General Hooker, the text of which Geary quoted later in his official report: "March without delay to seize the gap in the Rocky Face Ridge called Babb's, and to establish yourself strongly at that point; take your two brigades and send word as soon as you are in position. Take no wagons and but few ambulances." In his report, Geary omitted the all-important qualifier in Hooker's orders: "Avoid a fight if you have to make it at a disadvantage."[17] Geary had been entrusted with an important mission in Sherman's plan for forcing Johnston out from behind Rocky Face. Sherman had pondered the options and decided that Thomas's mighty Army of the Cumberland would draw the rebels' attention at Mill Creek and Dug Gaps, while Maj. Gen. James B. McPherson slipped his army through Snake Creek Gap and cut the railroad below the rebels at Dalton.

The orders for this opening move of the Atlanta campaign passed down the chain of command from Thomas to Hooker, and from Hooker to the division commander he had chosen to carry out the afternoon's work at Dug Gap, Brig. Gen. John W. Geary.

Sherman intended these movements as feints merely. Battle was to be avoided unless the rebels came out from behind their works, something that was unlikely given the perfect defenses they occupied at the top.[18] As the Boys rested in the yard around the Hallowell place, important dispatches passed by telegraph wire, by signals waved through the heavy smoke, and by fast riders going back and forth between the generals. By the time the order had passed through multiple points on its way to Hooker, and thence to Geary, it had become as murky as the atmosphere hanging over the valley. As Hooker understood the orders, he was to get one of his divisions moving at once, on what was prescribed as a "reconnaissance," and once at Dug Gap, they were to "threaten" the rebels holding it. The order contained a proviso: the men going up to try the gap should avoid an engagement unless the rebels moved into the open.[19]

After a while, Thomas rode over to Hooker's headquarters to make sure the order had been carried out. After conferring with Hooker, he sent a message to Sherman assuring him that Geary had started out on what Thomas characterized as the reconnaissance, under orders to "feel" his way to the top, and if the rebels' defenses there were found weak, he was to stand pat and wait for reinforcements, of which there were plenty.[20] The entire Twentieth Corps was gathered nearby to exploit any opportunity.[21]

How much force should be applied at Dug Gap, whether a show of force or an attack, Geary felt empowered to decide. The action at Lookout Mountain had begun as an order for a mere "demonstration." His experience there had shown him that headlines waited on a bold commander who could turn limited opportunity into total victory. His boys had gone up the sides of that mountain like a tornado, sweeping aside what were thought to be impregnable rebel defenses, and had produced one of the war's most glorious scenes. They had done the impossible then, and they could do so again. Geary had neither a map, nor anyone on his staff familiar with the geography. He found a local farmer to serve as guide and got Candy's and Buschbeck's brigades formed up and ready to move.

Parmater was not with them. He had played out on the march down from Taylor's Ridge the day before. The doctors gave him a pass to ride along in an ambulance. The ambulances were ordered out of the column and parked near the ordnance train, and his friends marched off without him. He had a hard time of it that afternoon, alone and unattended, but as he admitted, not half as hard as his friends in the Twenty-Ninth Ohio.[22]

Test by Attack

The day had turned into a scorcher, and the road over which Geary's boys marched was narrow and hilly, but they made short work of the five-mile march across the valley to the base of Rocky Face.[23] Coming up to a small collection of buildings on Mill Creek known as the Babb's Settlement, Geary's skirmishers found a squad of rebel cavalry. The enemy took their time mounting up, splashed across the creek, and rode up the side of Rocky Face. No sooner had the two brigades filed into the opening than Geary ordered them to prepare immediately to attack. The Twenty-Ninth Ohio's soldiers moved to the left of the road and into a field, slipped off their knapsacks, and piled them by company for easy retrieval when they got back down.[24]

With the officers and noncoms moving men into battle formation, Geary brought binoculars to his face and studied the ridgetop above him. The slope of Rocky Face was covered with patchy brush and corrugated with ridgy spurs. Near the top of Dug Gap, the road passed between towering rock walls. The only passages through it, aside from the road, were by way of narrow clefts, just wide enough to admit men in single file, if at all. Geary saw rebels up top behind breastworks and rocks, and they were making no effort to conceal themselves. By anyone's appraisal, this was an ugly place to send troops. Still, after seeing what lay ahead, Geary remained convinced that the strength of these defenses could be tested only by attack.[25]

The Twenty-Ninth's officers had been given their orders: to make a strong demonstration and, if possible, carry the rebel positions.[26] They moved into double battle line, men standing elbow to elbow in lines a hundred men wide and four deep. The color bearers removed their new flags from canvas cases and moved front and center. The soldiers double-checked their cartridge and cap boxes and swung them around on their belts to the favored position. There was a pause while the Twenty-Eighth Pennsylvania took its place to their right. To the right of the Pennsylvanians, three regiments of Buschbeck's brigade got into line. In this storming of Dug Gap the Giddings Boys were to have the extreme left.

They were now facing Rocky Face dead-on and could see they had their work cut out for them. The slope was at least as steep as Lookout Mountain, the terrain covered in places with immense boulders, and the ground more rock than earth. The Dug Gap road zigzagged from their right to left, taking advantage of the contours, until it reached a perfectly vertical rock palisade at the top, where it joined a road that paralleled the ridgetop.[27] Tall outcroppings shouldered the uphill, Dalton side of the road. The naked eye could see gun barrels flashing up there in the late afternoon sun. There was a shorter route to the top, as they would discover, but that required a six-hundred-foot gain in elevation in nearly as many feet forward. Whether they could do better against the advantages of terrain and elevation than the rebels who'd tried it against them at Gettysburg would be determined by dangerous experiment.

Geary ordered three regiments of Candy's brigade to stay behind to guard the battery of highly accurate three-inch Rodman rifled guns set up in the yard.[28] For the first time since the Giddings Boys had been with them, the Seventh Ohio Volunteers would not be coming. The Seventh Ohio's historian thought that Geary remembered how roughly they had been handled on Taylor's Ridge last fall, and on that account, he ordered them to sit this fight out.[29]

Once they arranged themselves, the whole long line lurched forward and into the willows. They slowed as they came to the swampy thickets bordering Mill Creek and waded across its muddy bottom. Lines were dressed on the opposite bank, and the blue line shoved off in doubled battle lines, with the whole of the 119th New York Volunteers out front as skirmishers.[30] They had not gone far when the brass bands left behind at Babb's Settlement struck up the national anthem.[31] SeCheverell would state later that they blamed the musicians for alerting the rebels to their presence, which had not been the case. They had been watched from the moment they had come down over Taylor's Ridge yesterday.[32]

To the Top by Hard Ways

The Boys came under fire as soon as they started their climb, and bullets began to ping and whine down the slope. The 119th New York pushed the rebel skirmishers back up to the foot of the cliffs. The late afternoon sun broadcast directly onto the face of the ridge. Presently it was as hot as the interior of a steam boiler. Once onto the lower slope of Rocky Face, they realized that keeping their lines dressed and tight was impossible. They were in a mazelike region of mossy gullies and patches of scraggly timber. False ridges ran everywhere and, once explored, proved they did not lead to the top. The slanted ground was covered with a layer of flat, loose rock, making upward motion not unlike scaling the sides of a church steeple on which the shingles had not been nailed down. Progressing a single foot required grabbing at tree roots and vines, and clambering over boulder piles on slick-soled brogans. Setting up an aimed shot or finding cover in a hurry with the ground sliding out from under the soldier's feet would prove to be a torment.

Geary's plan was to stay to the right of the road, taking advantage of the scant protection of low timber and rocks.[33] Once near the top where the road passed through the cliff face, they would move left and storm the gap. The Twenty-Ninth Ohio anchored the left of the line, using the road visible through the stunted pines as a course line.[34] As soon as the climb began, the battle line was chopped into segments by the terrain, and not far onto the slope, the Federal line began to sag dangerously downward toward the road. The Twenty-Ninth Ohio, squeezed by the troops slipping downward from their right, found itself out on the exposed surface of the road, and the rebels opened on them.

Geary had ordered them to stay off the road but to follow its line, which was unfortunate, because the road at times was nearly perpendicular to the rebel line, making the Federals perfect candidates for being enfiladed. A bullet launched from the top had the entire length of the half-mile Union line to hunt for a victim. It was the worst possible moment for the regiment to the right of the Twenty-Ninth Ohio to lose its nerve, but the first crash of rebel gunfire broke the Twenty-Eighth Pennsylvania Volunteers, and her boys fled via the most direct route back to the bottom, wrecking the Twenty-Ninth Ohio's line.[35]

The second enemy volley went through the regiment like an ax, taking large chunks from the exposed right end of their line. They would be up here fighting for hours, but most everyone who went down this afternoon did so in the first forty minutes of the fight.

This was his first time leading the regiment in combat, and William T. Fitch was proving his mettle by leading his boys from the front. His tenure as the Twenty-Ninth's commander was cut short by a minié ball that tore into his shin just below the knee, shattering the bones. Second in command, Col. Edward Hayes was hit in the shoulder joint, the ball carving a deep cavity in bone and tissue. Adjutant Storer took a close-range blast of buck and ball, a musket load combining a .69 caliber ball and three buckshot. He collapsed to the ground, still conscious but unable to move his legs. Lt. Winthrop Grant, second in command of Company A, behind Everson Hurlburt, was shot dead, and Myron T. Wright's best friend, Lt. George W. Dice of Company D, went down with wounds in both face and chest. It was said later that most of those in the regiment who fell in these first moments were struck on the right side of the body, the explanation being that they were at that moment positioned at a left oblique relative to the rebels atop the palisade.[36]

They were now the only regiment on the rebel side of the road, within easy range of the rebel rifles and cut off from any supporting fire from Buschbeck's brigade. With three field officers down, and everyone too near the rebels to either attack or safely retreat, they were all of a sudden in the hottest kind of place a regiment could find itself.[37]

Three years of war and a natural talent to lead had prepared Maj. Myron T. Wright for this moment, and he took charge. With the right end hinged at the road, he passed an order down the line, and the entire regiment swung like a gate from below and upward, bringing all hands back into a line from which they could at least face the main threat squarely.[38] They were now within 120 yards of the summit, and their only protection was the fallen trees dragged off the road by its builders.[39] Getting to this point had cost them dearly, and as yet they still had not made an organized attack.

No sooner had the Giddings Boys righted themselves than the order came for the whole force to charge. Cheers went up along the Union line as the soldiers struggled to re-form a battle line, but were cut off in mid-breath by the shower of lead that slammed into them. The line reeled, recovered, and continued up. They reached the foot of the wall near the top, and with musket in one hand and the other searching for holds, soldiers began pulling themselves onto the cliff itself, or into the few fractured passageways that led to the crest. Some made it to the top, but too few to drive the attack home. Those who made it were shot down, and those who were not, jumped or were thrown off the cliff.

With the first assault repelled, the soldiers paused. It was hardly a safe place to re-form and catch breath. The rebels were directly on top of them, and it required little more than poking a rifle barrel over the edge and pulling the trigger to take down a Yankee. Hugging the cliff bottom seemed the best bet, although even there boys were hit by fire from their left and right. This first attack had been enough to fulfill Hooker's orders to Geary, which was to try the gap. Hooker's caveat to Geary that he should avoid a fight unless it could be made to his advantage seemed to have been adequately answered. Despite Hooker's instructions, Geary ordered a second attack.

To the soldiers struggling near the top, it could be seen that the rebels might have saved themselves the work of building breastworks. Nature had made them a superb defensive position.[40] Earlier that morning, there had been only two hundred and fifty troopers of the First and Second Arkansas Mounted Infantries up top, and their commander thought them more than enough men to hold it. By the time the Federals came up to Dug Gap, the number of defenders had increased threefold. The Ninth Kentucky Cavalry, eight hundred strong and resolute fighters all, took up positions along the top, leaving a quarter of their number to hold horses behind the crest. All told, there were nearly a thousand muskets now pouring fire down on the Federals.[41]

Gen. William J. Hardee, author of the published manual of drill and tactics that everyone had studied intently while learning the soldiers' arts back at Camp Giddings, galloped up to the crest of the palisades and was joined there by Gen. Patrick Cleburne. This was not the first time Cleburne had done battle here. Three months earlier he had retaken it from Indiana troops with little effort.[42] The generals encouraged the work and offered suggestions, although the rebels did not require guidance for this kind of turkey shoot.

The officers and noncoms rallied their boys, and they charged a second time, as Geary had ordered. The two regiments of Candy's brigade attacked the wall from both sides of the road, the Twenty-Ninth from the left, and the regrouped Twenty-Eighth Pennsylvania from the right. Carrying their flags into battle was always a dangerous enterprise, and on this cliff side more so. Color bearer Hammond W. Geer was first to go down, shot through both hips. Christian Remley lifted the banner from the ground and was immediately shot in the head and killed. Still, they climbed up, fighting and searching the wall for any breech that would lead to the top. The bottoms of these sloping rock crevices were a foot deep in shaley rock and leaf detritus, and too slim for more than a man at a time to climb through, and deathtraps all of them, with rebel muskets leaned over the top dumping fire onto the tops of the boys' heads. At this range, a twenty-pound rock dropped over the edge was enough to crush a man's skull, as the rebels soon realized. Sticks came into play, and muskets, where there was enough room to swing them.

The rebels had propped boulders and old cart wheels at the top and sent them bounding down the slope, knocking down trees and crushing an occasional Yankee. Done at first for fun, the rebels began to use them as weapons.[43] No one in the Twenty-Ninth Ohio was injured in this way, although it added to the terror every man felt. Avoiding one of these missiles meant having to give up shelter and scramble out of the way, which exposed a man to gunfire.

Against Hope

Some men made it to the top in this second attack, but all were beaten back with fists and clubs or shot. After the failure of the second assault, the soldiers slid down the slope 150 yards and regrouped. They fitted themselves in behind rocks or scraped at the ground with fingers to raise a furrow just high enough to maybe turn a bullet.[44] They clung to thin footholds, glancing backward down the slope in hopes of seeing support coming up to them.[45] Support never came, even though Geary had plentiful reserves down below.[46] Geary sent neither reinforcements nor ammunition up to the soldiers struggling at the top.[47] As at Cedar Mountain, the boys were fighting on their own hook.

Two organized attacks had failed, but man-to-man and small-group combats went on, each producing short, intense bursts of gunfire that overlapped and came to the listeners down below as a single continuous racket. They had been up in this place for going on four hours, fighting, scrabbling for cover, listening to the cries of the wounded who had fallen in places where their rescue meant nothing short of suicide. Two of the Giddings Boys were shot dead while trying to pull a friend to safety and several more wounded so badly in legs and arms that amputations were guaranteed if and when they could be gotten down.[48] Those who could be were carried by blanket or stretcher down to the base of the slope.

Stuck up here below the heights in this insufferable heat, unable to move up or safely down, water became a commodity as precious as ammunition. The wounded especially cried out for it. There was plenty of water down below in the creek, but no way to get to it and no effort being made to bring it to them. Soldiers made dangerous sorties to unsling canteens from those who no longer needed them. Late in the afternoon, they discovered that their cartridge boxes were empty. Checking up and down the line it was soon apparent that everyone was out. Boys crawled on their bellies to strip the dead and wounded of what they carried.[49] Then, even that ran out. As the light of day wore out, Geary had one more experiment to try.[50]

A half mile to the right of the gap, the rebel line appeared undermanned. He ordered the Thirty-Third New Jersey up to break through it. On signal, all the other regiments were to rush the heights as soon as the New Jersey boys got through. Once up, the New Jersey boys found the terrain as impossible as that at any other point along Rocky Face. A few did make it to the top, and as instructed, they let out mighty yell, which was the arranged signal for everyone to attack. With many men out of ammunition, and everyone long out of water, the Giddings Boys got up and tried it again. The result was no better: those in the lead were thrown backward as if struck by anvils, and sent rolling and sliding down the cliffside. With the sound of this last assault petering out, Colonel Ireland rode up to Geary and reported: McPherson's movement through Snake Creek Gap had succeeded.

Satisfied that he had accomplished his mission of "securing the enemy's attention," Geary deemed further effusion of blood unnecessary and called off the attack.[51] He had ordered three assaults to whip the rebels out of their stronghold; some who fought there remembered the number as five. If not for the news of McPherson's success, and the blessed arrival of night, Geary might well have ordered more.[52] At last, an order came up to the Twenty-Ninth that they should cease fighting. Myron Wright, who wrote the official report of the engagement, said that the Boys would have continued fighting with rocks and sticks if need be, had they not run out of ammunition, gone unsupported, and at last been ordered down.[53]

Getting the survivors back down, with the rebels still loaded for bear and shooting at any noise or movement, posed another problem. It was clear that such a thing could be tried only once full dark descended. To cover it, Geary brought up Capt. James D. McGill's battery and ordered it to direct fire at the ridgetop. The Fifth, Seventh, and Sixty-Sixth Ohio Regiments, positioned below, to the left of the road, were ordered to start firing up the slope, to cover the Twenty-Ninth's withdrawal, but the fire of hundreds of muskets was directed up the same corridor the Twenty-Ninth's soldiers were struggling to descend. The end of this day's business came to an ear-splitting crescendo, better suited to the opening of a battle than its conclusion.[54] Once aware that the Federals were backing down, the rebels began taking special aim at those trying to recover the killed and wounded.[55]

Men from each company in the Twenty-Ninth Ohio volunteered to stay near the top and keep up fire while the others got down. What remained of ammunition was collected and passed to them, while the rest began down-climbing. The survivors recrossed Mill Creek, stopping to drink and souse away the top coat of dust and gunpowder. They arrived on the ground around the Babb farm silent and spent. Still, they raised a cheer at the appearance of the Boys they'd left behind up there, now coming in one at a time.[56] They had not expected to see them again in this lifetime. John Davis, a middle-aged private of Company B, had traveled far in his life to get from Tipperary, Ireland, to this place. He fired the last shot of the battle and was the last Union soldier to come down off the gap.[57]

Body Counting

They stopped in their march away from the battle slope to pick up knapsacks they had piled five hours before. After every man present had pulled his from the pile, there were too many left. The cost of this engagement to the Twenty-Ninth Ohio Volunteer Infantry had been terrible. By first count, twenty soldiers had died up on the slope, and sixty-seven had been wounded, many of them severely. About a dozen more men would die of wounds inflicted on them at Dug Gap in the hours and weeks that followed, some in the hospital tent just up the road, others in hospitals at Ringgold, Chattanooga, Nashville, or at the end of the hospital line at Jeffersonville, Indiana.[58] At least one in three officers and enlisted men had been hit, resulting in injuries from the loss of eyes and limbs to gunshot fractures of the bones. Thad Hoyt had been shot through the leg, but his cousin Wallace had come through without a scratch.

Around ten at night the soldiers of Ireland's brigade of their division returned from their long march down to Snake Creek Gap and passed out the news to their friends in the Giddings Regiment that McPherson had gotten through.

It seemed obvious that the rebels up at the top would have as much difficulty moving troops down the narrow, gouged-out road as Geary's soldiers had going up, and that in the dark such a thing would be near impossible. Nonetheless, Geary ordered the division, the Twenty-Ninth Ohio included, to get out shovels and picks and commence building breastworks. When the sun came up, Geary could look around with satisfaction and see that the digging had nearly encircled his division.[59]

Geary's count of his casualties was wildly off base and came nowhere near the actual loss: Dug Gap had killed and wounded 350 of his men, and a third of those had been in the Twenty-Ninth Ohio. The rebels held the gap as securely as they had before the fight. Neither Geary nor anyone on his staff could ride up to the top and count the enemy dead. To set the stage properly, he stated with certainty that his boys had been opposed by a full brigade of Arkansas infantry and two regiments of Kentucky cavalry and that Cleburne had brought up his entire division.

Geary set about reporting the damage he had inflicted on the enemy. He gave the number of rebels killed at Dug Gap as sixty-nine, which he pointed out was better than a quid pro quo in bloodletting, since the quantity of rebel dead exceeded that in his own command. Based on the number of enemy dead, he used his casualty formula to determine that the number of enemy wounded was at least equal to his own.[60] The truth was quite different: the rebels had come away nearly unscathed.

Col. W. P. C. Breckinridge, who was directing the rebel defense and was in a better position than Geary to count his casualties, reported that the rebel loss in killed and wounded did not exceed twenty.[61] The day after the battle Geary wrote to this wife to inform her that he held the battlefield, which was patently false.[62] The rebels were still firmly seated at the Dug Gap. In his official report, Geary was careful to state that all his dead had been recovered. Maj. Myron Wright gave the truth of the matter in a letter sent to the Akron newspaper, "I very greatly regret that we were compelled to leave some of the dead on the field, as the enemy had fair range."[63]

The night of the battle Chaplain Ames took up his station at the field hospital, caring for the stricken until past midnight. The field hospital had done a land-office business since the first shots. The regiment's surgeon, Elwood P. Haines, went to work the afternoon of the battle and did not emerge from the hospital until the next morning. So many hours tending the dead and dying left him feeling used up, and Ames, who was not a young man, worse than that.[64]

The medical department of the army had jumped decades forward since the time of the regiment's first fight, at Kernstown. Back then there had been no formal arrangement for removal of the wounded, and inadequate supplies of food, medicines, caring attendants and qualified surgeons all worked to increase a wounded man's pain and lessen his chances of surviving. Here in the valley of Mill Creek the efficiency of the perfected system was demonstrated. Packhorses loaded with field dressings, tourniquets, splints, and folded stretchers now followed at the rear of every brigade, ready to respond quickly if the boys stumbled into something. Next up were the ambulances, fitted now with built-in lockers to carry essential supplies. The wagon boxes had been fitted with better springs to ease the misery of the passengers. Soldiers were now delegated specifically to hospital service and could not be ordered away by an officer and put to work elsewhere.

Wagons, reserved now especially for the use of the medical department, rolled up to a site near the Babb place and soldiers unloaded their cargoes: lamps, lamp reflectors, folding tables on which the surgeon performed his work, cots, blankets, bandages, sponges, stimulants such as tea and whiskey, and wood cases holding the surgeon's tools. Also set handy to the surgeon's hands were crates of thick green-glass bottles containing chloroform, which as an anesthetic was sovereign for capital operations.[65] Two hours after the first shots were heard up at the gap, a first-class hospital was open for business.

While Haynes tended the enlisted men, Amos Fifield tended the Twenty-Ninth's officers. The ball that had struck Lt. Col. Ed Hayes shattered his right shoulder joint and shoulder blade. Few men survived amputation of the arm this high up on the body. Hayes underwent a surgical "resection" in which Fifield sawed out the smashed lengths of bone. In Hayes's case, the ball of the shoulder joint was removed entirely.[66] He retained his arm and avoided becoming "another empty sleeve," a phrase being used more and more in the newspapers to note the alarming increase of amputees in every town, but with a large chunk of the bone gone, his arm would hang uselessly for the rest of his days.

Col. William Fitch had been shot with same kind of load that hit Storer, buck and ball. The ball had hit him in the right shin, several inches below the knee. Like Hayes, Fitch was put under and a resection performed.[67] He had gone down in the first moments of the attack, lost consciousness, and did not learn of the battle's outcome until he emerged from the haze of sedatives several days later and was told of it by a private soldier who had come to visit him. Fitch was hopeful that his leg would heal and that he could return to his regiment. But his leg would never support his weight, and hereafter he could move about only with the use of crutches.

The nature of Storer's injury lay deep in the uncharted realms of medical science. The ball that struck him in the lower back fractured vertebrae and injured his spinal cord.[68] The surgeons were able to dig the ball out, but his legs were as useless as if they had both been amputated and he could control neither bowel nor bladder. A week before the news of Dug Gap hit the newspapers, a telegraph message sent by a fellow officer notified his family of his wounds, which were believed mortal. They should come quickly. His bride, Helen, accompanied by his father, Webster, started out for the front.[69] The brother of soldier Curtis Lantz went with them to bring his remains back to Akron. Lt. E. T. Curtiss met them at the station in Nashville, and he had good news: Storer was still alive. Curtiss conducted them to Officer's Hospital no. 17, where they found Adjutant Storer comfortable and out of danger.

There would be no need for Lantz to go further south. He learned that his brother's body had been left to the rebels. Mrs. James Storer stayed behind to nurse her husband. It would be another three months before he could stand the trip back to Akron, and when his carriage pulled up in front of his home, he had to be lifted out and carried inside.[70] In the following months there would be hopeful signs. He was for a time able to stand on crutches. Over time, however, the paralysis became fixed and the excruciating pain constant. He would never walk again.

The quality of treatment dispensed by the army's medical department had improved steadily, but the soldiers' attitude toward army doctors remained the same. A Twenty-Ninth soldier wounded at Dug Gap wrote to the Jefferson newspaper from the USA General Hospital in Jeffersonville, Indiana: "Technically 'a [illegible] case,'—the surgeon-butcher's delight—fresh from the slaughter pens of Georgia, with nothing to do but 'keep up a devil of a thinking,' and afford the surgeon his daily recreation of probing, squeezing, pinching and cutting, (in which particular mode of scientific manipulation the 'gay and festive' Dr. S. has few if any equals and no superiors)."[71]

Within a few days of Dug Gap, the wounded thought stable enough to make the trip were taken by ambulance to Ringgold, placed onto rail cars—which by this point in the war were self-contained hospitals on wheels—and moved up to one of the several hospitals in Chattanooga. The dead of the Giddings Regiment had been laid out along the wall of the hospital tent to await their turn at burial.

In the Johnson Garden

On the day after their most severe test of the war, burial services were held near the hospital tent.[72] The dead were wrapped in a blanket or india-rubber sheet, removed a few paces from where they had lain on the ground, and were committed to the Georgia soil. The sounds of continuous cannonading rolled down from the vicinity of Buzzard's Roost, mixed with the rumble of an approaching thunderstorm. Lyman Ames and the chaplain of the Thirty-Third New Jersey, which had also suffered heavily, read scriptures. Many of the Boys had walked over to listen to Ames's remarks and say good-bye to friends they had known their entire lives and marched with since the beginning.

Among the dead was Ellis Green.[73] He had written to his parents from Bridgeport just before the march to Dug Gap began, to apologize for having gotten their hopes up for a place of their own. Franklin Potter was laid in next and, beside him, Cass Nims. Cass had enlisted in the Twenty-Ninth when he was just sixteen, had fought in all its battles, and had seen "war in its worst form," as he expressed it. From the start, he had expressed a belief that the end of war lay just around the next bend.

Allen Mason, the young man from West Andover whom Rollin Jones described as the best soldier he ever knew, had been shot through the lung at Dug Gap. He survived the moves in and out of a succession of hospitals, until, by the end of May, he was placed in the U.S. army hospital complex in Jeffersonville, Indiana. His friend Cpl. Charles Galpin visited him there and found him in low spirits. Mason asked Galpin to send his personal effects home to his parents. He tried to convince Mason that he would soon be well enough to carry them home himself. In his last letter from Bridgeport, Mason had reminded his mother that he was old enough to take care of himself and that whether he should return home safely was in God's hands. He died at Jeffersonville on May 29.[74]

Chaplain Ames was bone weary after forty-eight hours of work at the hospital. He had a sad obligation to fulfill before he rested. He rode over to the James Johnson house, which had served in the opening two hours of the battle as a triage station. He got down and prayed over the three fresh graves of boys who had died there on the afternoon of the fight. He duly recorded in his diary that Pvt. Amos Long and Sergeants Christian Remley and Mortimer Knowlton had been buried in the Johnson garden.[75] He said a few prayers, contemplated the meaning of their deaths, and rode off.

The early news looked bad, but the editor of the Jefferson newspaper, to whom the dispatches came, cautioned the readers against taking these preliminary reports at full strength. "Through private dispatches we hear there was hard fighting at Dalton, Georgia on the 12th in which the 29th suffered severely."[76] The date and exact location were wrong, but other details unfortunately true: their own sons Fitch and Hayes seriously wounded, Adjutant Storer of Akron mortally, as it was feared, and many other boys gone. "We regret with our friends of the 29th to hear this news, and sincerely hope the words 'severely wounded,' do not mean their worst in this case, and that our next report will be better, and that others of the regiment have escaped."[77]

The grim news was confirmed when the casualty lists were published almost two weeks after the battle. When the toll was counted, it was seen that twenty-six of their own had been killed in action at Dug Gap, and sixty-seven seriously wounded. Lt. George Dice of Company D had been wounded several times in earlier battles. He had been hit four times on May 8. He wrote to his mother from a hospital in Chattanooga.

> Dear Mother,
>
> It is with pleasure I seat myself to write you a few lines. My health is pretty good at present. The wound I received in the right breast is not healed yet but I expect to go to the Regt. today they are at Dallas, Ga. It was at Rocky Faced Ridge that I was wounded. I was struck four different times but there were but two balls that entered. They are in me yet. One below the left eye the other in the breast.
>
> Here mother I send you this note. I want you to keep it until I come home if I shall be so lucky. I shall close hoping to hear from you soon.
>
> Your son
> Geo M Dice
> Co. D 29th Ohio Vols
> Via Nashville, Tenn.[78]

"It Is What Has Happened"

As part of what had become his normal duties, Chaplain Ames immediately composed a letter for publication in the *Conneaut Reporter*. He tried his best, but there was no real way to sugarcoat what had happened at Dug Gap: "Sad indeed it is to relate, but it is true and must be told—many of our brave boys have fallen!"[79] Myron Wright assured those at home that the dead they had been able to recover had been given Christian burials. He gave their location, and said each grave had been plainly marked so they could be easily identified by the army's mortuary staff, or by loved ones from Ohio who might come down to bring them home.[80]

The news came hard to everyone, but harder still to some. Christian Remley's mother had already sacrificed her oldest boy to the Twenty-Ninth Ohio. Frederick Remley had been killed in action at Port Republic.[81] Now came news that her remaining boy, Christian, had been killed in action at Dug Gap.[82] Wright was near Remley when he fell and heard his dying words, "Tell my mother I died like a man, doing my duty in defense of my country."[83] The last words of their dead, here, and at other places were impossibly patriotic, but Wright's heart was in the right place. That even the bravest soldiers cried pitifully when grievously stricken would not have been proper to detail in this Victorian time, nor was it anything Wright, or anyone, wanted a boy's loved ones to have haunt them through the years. Better to give those at home a golden memory of their boy, and a purpose to his death. Wright reported that despite their losses, collective and private, morale in the Twenty-Ninth was still high, which was not the case with every soldier. Some were in anguish.

One of the Rock Creek Boys, a stocky young man named Jerome Phinney, had soldiered along from the beginning with his uncle, Richard Phinney. The two were close in age, and one was so rarely seen without the other that they were called the Phinney boys. Richard Phinney, Rickers as he was known to everyone, had been one of those killed at Dug Gap, and his was another of the bodies that could not be retrieved. Jerome wrote a letter home a week after the battle from a place he distinguished only as "Battle Field Georgia": "I could not get Rickers body to bury it. I got the last letter that you wrote to him and got the stamps that you sent to him. You must not take it to much to heart for it is what has happened. The both of us lost our Brother in the same day."[84]

John Kummer, seriously wounded at Gettysburg, and unable to return to combat, had joined the Invalid Corps, an army of honorably wounded men who wished to continue their service. They wore a distinctive robin's egg blue uniform and were often the object of derision. From his post in Indianapolis, Kummer had learned of the regiment's undoing at Dug Gap, and he wrote a tribute to the dead he had known best: Ellis Green, Christian Remley, and Pvt. George Braginton. Braginton, twenty-one years old, had died of wounds at a hospital in Nashville. Kummer thought the world of him. "He was a jovial tent mate, a cheerful companion on a long march, and a brave soldier on the battle-field." Then, the best thing that could be said of any soldier: "None of the fiery ordeals through which he passed ever discouraged him."[85]

The demonstration at Dug Gap shocked Akron, with so many of its sons gone down in a single afternoon. No loss of the war caused the town greater hurt. Throughout the winter the newspapers had persuaded the readers that the rebel armies, those in the western theater in particular, were incapable of fighting, and now the news of this tragedy.

The *Summit Beacon Journal* editor looked for someone to blame, and Geary, previously a darling of the Union-loving press here like everywhere, came under fire. Based on an unidentified source, the newspaper claimed that Geary had been imprudent on two counts. He was accused of failing to send out skirmishers, which was untrue. Second, and more suitable for debate, was the allegation that he had marched his line in a left oblique in the face of a murderous plunging fire, which any amateur knew was a suicidal maneuver to attempt when close up to the enemy.[86] The criticism of Geary taken up by the *Summit Beacon* in Akron had come through Webster Storer, and the source had most likely been an officer in the Twenty-Ninth whom he encountered in Nashville while visiting his son.

Geary's staff tent was reported by his critics to have resembled the press office of a large newspaper with officers and news correspondents scribbling away on pieces meant to enhance Geary's reputation. This time, the special correspondent to the *Philadelphia Press*, who was traveling with Geary, had little to say about Geary's conduct of the battle except, "Our advance up the mountain was personally superintended by the division commander, who was present with his staff, at all points, directing the movement of the lines and encouraging the men."[87] If Geary had been present on the mountainside, he must have been invisible; his presence there was never substantiated by anyone save the paper's correspondent.

Publicly, no one in the Twenty-Ninth Regiment ever said a word against Geary for his management of them at Dug Gap or at any other place. General Hooker, however, had started to distance himself from

Geary while the wounded were still being brought down off Dug Gap. By nine o'clock the night of the fight, Hooker wired Sherman's headquarters stating that he did not have all the details yet, but from what he could piece together Geary had been repulsed. "He went out with instructions to not make a fight unless to our advantage, from which I conclude that whatever the result he has realized an equivalent."[88] When the casualty lists came in, along with firsthand accounts, it was clear that Geary had not achieved an equivalent. Some question would always remain as to what exactly Geary had been ordered to do at Dug Gap. A few days after the battle, when it was still very fresh in his mind, General Thomas, commander of the Army of the Cumberland, confirmed the wording of the orders he had sent down the line through Hooker. Without equivocation, he stated that Geary had been sent to Dug Gap on a "reconnaissance."[89]

Word came to the Twenty-Ninth's camp in the days after the defeat on the heights that contradicted the good news they had heard earlier about McPherson's movement through Snake Creek Gap. The latest news, and what proved to be the truth, was that that having gotten through Snake Creek Gap with little loss, McPherson reached the railroad at a tiny place called Resaca and then backed away, leaving Joe Johnston's army unmolested. The Boys had done their part at Dug Gap, but McPherson had not done his, and an opportunity to destroy the rebels and end the war in this theater had been lost. If any Twenty-Ninth Ohio soldier among them believed their suffering had been in vain, he kept it to himself or spoke of it only in private.

No one questioned why Geary had not sent relief, ammunition, or water to the men stranded below the summit of Dug Gap, or why he had not called the attacking line back after its first repulse, which by itself had proven how difficult taking the gap would be. He was never made to answer why it was he chose to emphasize Hooker's words "seize the gap" and ignore the order's all-important proviso to avoid a fight unless it could be fought to his advantage.[90] For most of the Boys, going forward meant putting the past behind them. Jerome Phinney had summed it up in telling his father not to take such things too much to heart because they had happened and could not be undone. Other, weightier events soon put Dug Gap in the shade.

Lists of the Union wounded and dead who had fallen into the machinery of war at the Wilderness and at Spotsylvania Court House, Virginia, in these May days filled one full news sheet and ran onto a second in the big eastern papers. In anticipation of the spring campaign, the government had increased the capacity of the already gargantuan array of hospitals in and around Washington by twenty-five thousand beds, and soon after every hospital was bursting at the seams. In anticipation of the bloodshed, the U.S. Sanitary Commission had built up its cash reserves to buy supplies for the wounded soldier's comfort, but some of the necessaries—such as cotton lint to plug wounds, bandages, and especially belly bandages—could not be purchased at any price. These had to be homemade by the women in the North and the supplies of them, thought adequate for casualties produced by a normal spring campaign, were soon exhausted. Insistent calls on the generosity of the homefolk were regular fare in the Reserve's newspapers, but now they became desperate pleas.

> Will not each household in the city and country heed this call and furnish liberally of these? Bring packages of old cotton and linen to our rooms, and all will immediately be forwarded for relief of the sufferers. . . . The indications of a great battle now opening in the Southwest are a new draft upon our sympathies. We cannot do too much, and what is done, must be done quickly.[91]

True to the prediction of the Cleveland aid worker who composed this appeal, Sherman's army had already fought a bloody, full-scale battle of its own at Resaca, Georgia.[92] By the time the details of Dug Gap were reported back home, the Twenty-Ninth was already long marches away from Rocky Face Ridge and on the way to Atlanta. The Boys had witnessed and participated in great battles as yet unknown to their friends and families.

What had happened to the Giddings Boys did not add up to very much when placed against the backdrop of colossal suffering of the kind the Army of the Potomac was presently enduring.

This new phase of the war was taking down hundreds and sometimes thousands of soldiers day after day without letup. One Twenty-Ninth Ohio soldier who had been wounded at Dug Gap read the news of the appalling losses in Grant's army as it locked itself onto Lee. He put a macabre twist on a stock phrase that been used in the war's early days especially, to persuade mothers to give up their sons to the army: "All over this broad land, our country's altars are smoking with the sacrifices of her patriotic sons."[93]

Single editions of the Akron newspaper were now spotted with announcements of the deaths of up to ten of the neighborhood's young men. Most stated the simple cold facts: in what battle and in what part of the body the soldier had been shot, where he had died, the names of his parents, and where he had been buried. How the soldier's friends and family coped with such loss was not reported. Those were private things and not put on public display, except in rare cases, as with Charles Downey, eighteen-year-old private of Company D.[94]

A friend who had served with him in the regiment visited Downey's mother two months after Dug Gap to see how she was getting on. He signed his letter to the newspaper in which he reported his meeting with her with the letter F, which happened to be the last name of the man who had been responsible for Charles joining the Twenty-Ninth Regiment. Before the war, Charles had apprenticed himself to a tinsmith named William Faze. The older man enlisted in the Giddings Regiment, and Charles wanted to go with him. He was too young to enlist on his own, but he persuaded his mother to sign the permission and went off to war. While many boys spent their pay within a day of getting it, Charles was more saving with his money. By 1864 he had sent home over two hundred dollars with the instruction, "Mother take good care of my money but use whatever you need." While home on veterans' furlough, Charles's younger sister had died. He paid for her funeral and used what was left of his savings to buy his mother a small house set on an acre of land.

Charley had sent home a picture of a soldier, "this mother is my best friend, my messmate, and in all of our long marches my most intimate companion. And I send you therefore his likeness and ask you to love and respect it as the friend and companion of your boy." He had forgotten to give his friend's name. The mother handed "F" a cased ambrotype, and when he unsnapped the cover, he knew at once it was Curtis Lantz looking back at him. Both Charley and Curtis had fallen at about the same time and probably within feet of each other at Dug Gap, companions in this last thing as they had been in all things before it.

The whole blue-coated world seemed to be marching by the Twenty-Ninth's camp in the woods near the base of Dug Gap on the road leading south out of this valley. After several days of rest, the Boys were ordered to join the mighty procession, and in a few miles they were out of sight of the gouge through the top of the ridge where they had fought, and where some of their dead still lay. Myron Wright reported that their morale was high and the soldiers anxious to press on. From this point forward, no power on earth would turn them around.

25

Continuous Battle

THE APPROACH TO ATLANTA, MAY–AUGUST 1864

The Guns of Resaca

One week after the fight at Dug Gap, Chaplain Ames rode south to catch up with the regiment. The noise and motion he rode into west of Resaca told him a major battle was being fought just ahead. He could not penetrate the masses of wagons, artillery, and thousands of troops maneuvering for position and gave up trying. Next morning, he learned that the rebels had departed during the night and the Twenty-Ninth had gone after them. He rode across the battlefield, pausing to note the strength of the abandoned rebel forts, the signs of their hasty flight, and the many dead strewn about.

A few days earlier, Gen. Joe Johnston had vacated Dalton and moved his army down to Resaca, the next stop on the railroad to Atlanta. Sherman's plan was to pin Johnston against the river below Resaca and destroy him. He fitted his army into a line four miles long facing the impressive rebel entrenchments and a three-day battle was fought. Geary's division had fought nobly on the final day, but Candy's brigade, with the exception of some special work by the Fifth Ohio, had not been actively engaged, and the Twenty-Ninth Ohio not at all.

On the first day, Gen. John Bell Hood was sent to attack the Federal left and roll up Sherman's flank. Hooker got Brig. Gen. Alpheus Williams's division up in time to blunt Hood's attack and Geary's division filed onto the firing line to lend their weight. Candy's brigade came up last and did not get in on the glorious repulse.

Generals Sherman, Thomas, and Hooker galloped up at eleven on the morning of the third day and paused to perfect their plans. Some of the Giddings Boys were standing near enough to overhear their discussion. Hooker was asked by either Thomas or Sherman how many men it would take to capture an earthen fort that stood in a salient in the rebel line. There were guns in this fort enfilading the Union lines. Hooker staggered his superiors by saying, "Geary's division can, I think, carry that position if it can be done by anyone."[1]

Geary's boys trotted three-quarters of a mile through a narrow ravine and got into position for the attack. Ireland's brigade descended the ridge with flags flying, crossed a boggy creek, and stepped out to take the rebel guns. It was a grand scene and everyone, participants and observers, waved their hats and cheered at the tops of their lungs. The Giddings Boys were safely positioned behind breastworks and piles of railroad ties to the left and rear and had a ringside seat to the rare sight of a full brigade attacking in narrow massed columns by regiments.[2]

Ireland's boys and those of Brig. Gen. J. H. Hobart Ward's brigade, of Maj. Gen. Daniel Butterfield's division, got to the guns at about the same time, and Ireland's boys stabbed the butt of their flagstaff into the ground, staking their claim on it. There was little time to argue over bragging rights. The rebels still held their main line twenty yards to the rear of the fort and they began taking aim at the little fort, pinning the Federals to the ground. Geary ordered several regiments of Buschbeck's brigade to cross the half mile of open ground and join the men hunkered down near the rebel guns.

Geary's hundreds were in danger of being cut off and destroyed, if the rebels elected to step out from behind their breastworks. Geary's reaction was to send even more men out. The Fifth Ohio, of Candy's brigade, and several regiments from his other brigades moved forward to pull the rebel guns into their lines. By late in the afternoon, Geary had half his command out there beyond supporting distance.

The rebels launched a charge but were beaten back in a half hour's worth of some of the most concentrated musket and cannon fire of the war. Geary regarded the guns in the fort as valuable military assets, if not wonderful trophies, and he was not about to let the rebels get them back. Getting them into his lines would have to wait until dark. He sent orders forward for the beleaguered men to dig through the front of the fort and drag the guns back. The Twenty-Ninth Ohio had done little to this point, but with the stage set for creation of one of the division's memorable moments, the regiment's historian, "Little Hamp" SeCheverell, brought some of the Giddings Boys into the story.

He stated that a detachment from the Twenty-Ninth was sent forward, along with other Ohio outfits. The digging was done on hands and knees, and once through, lassos were snugged around the barrels of the cannon and they were pulled out, with much squeaking of wheels and sounds of men struggling with the mighty weight. All this was being done right under the noses of the rebels, and the guns had not been dragged far when they took notice of it. SeCheverell described the enemy's reaction:

> The rebels discovering this charged down upon us to recapture the guns. Expecting such an attack the First Brigade [Candy's] had moved forward into the ravine, and now waited the coming of the rebels. When close upon them a signal was given, which was followed by a sheet of flame along our entire line, dealing terrible destruction into the rebel ranks, immediately followed by a determined bayonet charge, which threw their lines into disorder, and they fled panic stricken over their fortifications, closely pursued by our command, whose loud huzzas sent Johnston's army in rapid retreat, abandoned all its cannon, hospital and commissary stores, and with their usual savagery leaving their own dead and wounded upon the field.[3]

It was true that some Ohio troops had been ordered to assist Col. George Cobham's Third Brigade in dragging the guns away, but that had been the Fifth Ohio, and not the Giddings Regiment or any part of it.[4] A Fifth Ohio soldier who was there wrote a detailed account of the episode, and he did not mention the Twenty-Ninth Ohio, nor did anyone else who reported the event. Myron T. Wright, in command of the regiment at Resaca and for everything that followed in the next ten weeks, wrote the official report of the regiment's part in the battle of Resaca. If anyone in his regiment had helped bring out the guns, Wright did not mention it, nor did he claim the regiment had taken part in shooting down the rebels who came storming out after them.[5]

At midnight the rebels had indeed been aroused by the sound of the guns squeaking and rattling away and they did not intend to let them go without a fight. They charged out of the breastworks and were repulsed without going far and sent back to their trenches. There had been no glorious counterstroke that turned the tide of battle and drove the rebels from the battlefield, as SeCheverell claimed. The rebels left a few hours later, but not because they had been hurled from the field. They had gotten away unnoticed while the Federals were asleep.

After the guns were hauled back into Geary's line, he immediately sent a dispatch to Hooker informing him of "this important achievement," and had them pulled down to headquarters. The rebel general Hood would state later that the guns were not worth the life of even one of his soldiers.

One or two of the Giddings Boys had been lightly wounded, but no one killed. The most serious injury to anyone in the Twenty-Ninth in the battle, or moving away from it, was sustained by Pvt. Samuel Hart. He had run afoul of a poisonous Georgia plant while climbing up a river bank after wading bare legged. The poison caused his leg to swell so badly he had to be sent to the hospital.[6]

The reputation of the soldiers of Geary's division had been lifted another notch by their act of daring in taking the guns, and compliments for their tenacity now came from unexpected quarters. Lt. Wilbur F. Chamberlain had been severely wounded at Dug Gap. While he was in the hospital, one of the Boys sent him a letter that Chamberlain thought was particularly noteworthy, and he sent it on to the Akron newspaper for publication. It had been found on the body of a rebel artillery officer at Resaca.[7]

> Resaca, Georgia,
> May 15, 1864
>
> My Dear Wife,
>
> John Thompson is going back to Cassville, wounded, and I thought I would drop you a line by him. The Yankees charged on my battery this P.M. and captured two sections of it, and many of the men in attendance were wounded. It was as daring an exploit as when my brother's battery was charged upon at Antietam by a New York regiment; they threw themselves into the Fort as unconscious of danger as so many ducks in a pond. Tell Joe and Will to stow away everything of value, fearing we should fall back from here, and if we do the Yankees will get everything within their reach. Hooker's command we had to fight them, or else the battery would never have been taken. I hear we are gaining on the Yankees in Va. And we would whip them here if it was not for Hooker's command. They all wear a white star.
>
> > Your husband until death,
> > W. W. Casper.

Of course, as the folks who read the Summit County newspaper knew, only Geary's soldiers wore the white star.

Geary was awakened on the morning after taking the guns and told that the enemy fortifications were empty. He sent out a reconnaissance to track the rebels, with his division right behind leading the Twentieth Corps. Two pontoon bridges had been pushed into place over the Conasauga River, but these were not enough to get everyone quickly across. The soldiers took off their shoes and socks, tied the shoelaces together, slung them around their necks, and waded to the opposite bank. They covered the next dozen miles at top speed, reaching the banks of the wider and deeper Coosawattee River, where Geary made a bridge spanning two old ferry boats and got everyone over.[8]

The White Star Division led the Twentieth Corps onto the road leading down to Calhoun, Georgia. The Twenty-Ninth's boys followed behind their supply trains and ate the dust of the whole division.[9] The enemy had gotten away, but if they hurried they might catch him. That night they camped on ground Johnston's army had vacated just hours before.[10] They were up early on the morning of May 18 with orders to march as fast as their feet could carry them, and they got onto the road aiming for Kingston. The valleys here were beautiful, and the fields were fine looking, but the houses, although large, were few and far between. They had penetrated the outer edge of the authentic, slavery-driven plantation system peculiar to the South.[11]

Two days later, after passing through a range of hills covered with the worst tangle of brush and close-set trees anyone had ever seen, they came into an opening. Just beyond lay the village of Kingston, on the railroad to Atlanta. There was heavy artillery firing ahead.

Butterfield's division had caught up with the rebel army and was shelling them vigorously. Hooker's corps spread out in a long battle line on both sides of the road and started a pursuit, which led back into the brush, thicker and more disorienting than what they had recently exited. A black man who had been a slave on the plantation of Col. H. F. Price, CSA, came up to them. He knew the country like the back of his hand and offered to pilot them.[12] He led them through the wilderness and up to the outskirts of Cassville. There was heavy rifle and cannon fire off to their left where the Fourth Corps was already engaging Johnston's army, which was spread out in an arc and waiting for the Federals. Geary's boys moved forward and got ready to fight.

The dark of night came down before anything further could be done. The Twenty-Ninth Ohio was assigned a place at the far right of the Twentieth Corps, on top of a ridge a half mile west of the town, with the rebel army visible in the near distance ready to receive them. When the sun came up it was obvious that the rebel army had decamped during the night, which was just as well because Sherman's army had outmarched its supplies. Hooker's corps paused at Cassville for several days while the army logicians moved the supply base down the line to Resaca. The Boys drew new clothing, cleaned rifles, and got ready for the next phase.

Death Finds Their Patron

While the regiment he had founded rested at Cassville, Joshua R. Giddings dropped dead as he was lining up a shot on a billiard table in Montreal.[13] His body was brought to Ashtabula County by special train, and a group of friends came to escort the hearse down to Jefferson. He lay in state for half a day so those who had known the Old Lion in life could get a last look. His flag-draped coffin was taken the short distance out to the village burying ground, and Giddings was lowered into the earth as the sun went down. The village girls cast flowers and garlands into the grave "in sweet token of the gentleness of his character and the presence of a spirit that could appreciate the beautiful in nature."[14] Polite eulogies saluted his decades-long struggle to overturn slavery, while acknowledging that he had not been popular with everyone. He had died like Moses of old, in sight of the Promised Land, but his eyes closed before he could see the glorious result of his life's work. There were no ringing of bells or closure of shops, schools, and offices, as there had been to mark the day John Brown was hung, nor was there any mention of his relationship to Brown.

The *Sentinel*, in his hometown of Jefferson, which had for decades been his trumpet, gave a lengthy account of his life, with the details of his rise from log cabin to the national political stage. Jefferson was also the hometown of the Twenty-Ninth Ohio, but of the connection between the two the newspaper mentioned nothing, not even that he had been its founder. His regiment routinely wrote eulogies for the fallen, even for lowly privates. When the news of Giddings's death reached them down in Georgia, no one composed a memoriam.

By the time he died, Giddings was said to be finally contented. He had completed his epic history of American slavery and the crusades against it, which is not to say he was entirely occupied with that or his consular duties. He had seen in the war opportunities to improve his family's fortunes. The war had spawned plentiful chances for making money, and by the ethical standard of that day, there was nothing wrong in trying to get ahead. Besides, other men in the hitherto sleepy and chronically cash-poor Jefferson were making money. Most all the Twenty-Ninth's founders had branched out into money-making ventures.

This summer of 1864, Judge Chaffee and Abner Kellogg seemed to be spending as much time increasing the size of their sheep flocks as they were in attending to their legal practices, which made sense to the pocketbook. Legal fees were as flat as ever, while the price of wool had gone through the roof and showed no signs of slowing. Several of the regiment's founders had started a bank in Jefferson in the midst of this terrible civil war, and it was reported doing very well. Most recently, two of Giddings's allies in Jefferson, Messrs. Wade and Ensign, both members of the regiment's founding group, had purchased a farm near Eagleville and were expecting to make their fortunes in raising mules to be sold to the U.S. army at top prices.[15] And to top it all off, the railroad would soon run through Jefferson, if the Lakeshore Line went ahead with its plans to build a shortcut from Ashtabula to the Pennsylvania coalfields.

Several of the founding group continued their contributions to the county's war effort by serving on various military committees, which was thankless, unpopular work that required the turning over of every rock for recruits, encouraging enlistments, trying to persuade the stingier townships to increase their bounty fund, and deciding who would go and who would not. One of their young men had not gone to war, even though he had been raised by one of the most vocal prowar advocates in Jefferson. William Dean Howells was sitting out the war hobnobbing with Europe's rich and royal in Venice, Italy. The taking of Lookout Mountain had quickly passed from fact into lore, and although thousands of miles away, Howells helped the myth along with his creation of lyrics for a new song, "Battle in the Clouds," the sheet music soon to be on sale in Jefferson and everywhere else.[16] This type of rousing patriotic song had been the mainstay of every public gathering since the war began, but they were being overtaken in popularity by songs far more somber.

"When This Cruel War Is Over" or, as it was better known, "Weeping, Sad and Lonely," expressed everyone's prayer for the end of the rebellion, when all would meet again. The sheet music for it could be bought at any local emporium and taken home to play and sing in the family parlor. The soldiers knew this song well and sung it in their camps this summer of 1864. Some officers forbid that it be sung because it depressed the spirits of the men. And there was another titled "The Vacant Chair," with the heart-tearing opening: "We shall meet, but we shall miss him." Another song popular with civilians and soldiers just now was "Tenting on the Old Campground," with its poignant lament, "Many are the hearts that are weary tonight, / Wishing for the war to cease." And then its haunting end, "Dying tonight, dying tonight, dying on the old campground."

The newspapers continued to run ads for the latest innovation in steel plows and countless other inventions, alongside bulletins from the war front, where progress was reported to be universal but the cost horrifying. Sandwiched in were innumerable anonymous poems, which more and more in this early summer of 1864 took as their theme the soldier boy who had died in some unknown leafy place with only the birds and spring flowers to salute his sacrifice. They bore stark titles like "Missing" or, even more stunning in its finality, "Dead." By this summer of 1864, hardly a household anywhere had gone untouched; there was legitimate grief to express, but the country was not immobilized by its sorrow.

Everyone seemed to be on the move this summer of 1864: building, inventing, selling, and laboring. Akron continued its building boom in factories, commercial buildings, and fine residences, even though the labor pool had been drained by competition for higher wages and by the government's relentless demands for more and more soldiers. Simple hod carriers in Cincinnati were demanding the huge sum of three dollars per day, and getting it. Closer by, in Cleveland, working men were joining together in meeting halls to discuss their grievances against employers.

The knack for invention had always been seen as a charming quirk in the Yankee makeup; now it was driving whole new industries and transforming old ones. Akron now had a steam-driven confectionary. The ingenious engine that drove it was a perfectly balanced blur of flywheels, pumps, pistons, and polished-brass eduction piping, all of it capable of producing hundreds of pounds of candy in a single day, each small piece absolutely identical in weight and size. At Willard's Drug Store in Ashtabula city a new-fangled soda fountain was installed, the druggist adding extracts of herbs and doses of patent medicines to the fizz water and dispensing it with a flourish from gleaming nickel spouts into a glass, which was drunk right there by the sufferer in hopes of curing some physical malady. Willard's owners proudly proclaimed this glowing apparatus to be the only thing of its kind outside New York City.[17]

Even in staid and thrifty Jefferson, new buildings were going up. The *Sentinel* had done business in the same building for years, the one in which a fugitive from the John Brown raid had been hidden, but it was moving into a new brick building closer to the center of the village.[18]

A few voices chided the wealthy of the North for indulgence in $200,000 houses and dressing their children in imported French fashions. Public displays of wealth at any time were still regarded as distasteful, but to broadcast one's success in the midst of the bloodiest war the nation had ever seen was, in the opinion of some, obscene. Further, such vanities resulting from this new, ceaseless striving for wealth threatened the simplicity of life that had always been the backbone of American life.[19] Before the war it had been impossible to judge by a person's appearance whether he or she were working folk or richer than Croesus. All of the older generation, regardless of their financial condition, wore the same somber black garments. They were nearly gone now, and a new class of instantly wealthy moved to the top of Akron's busy social scene and spent their surplus of cash in the town's dazzling emporiums.

But in this May of 1864, with the armies embraced in their death struggles, Akron's nouveaux riches sensed the animosity toward their conspicuous displays and took steps to rein themselves in. The Ladies' National Covenant had been formed with the ostensible purpose of curtailing spending on foreign-made goods. A group of Akron women convened under this banner in May 1864 and took a pledge that they would henceforth desist from buying imported luxuries like lace, india crepe, velvets, silks, hair ornaments, ormolu or marble ornaments, and furs, to name but a few. One of the women who attended said of their newfound commitment to do right, "We have hitherto lived pretty fast, and have been pleased with all sorts of foreign gew-gaws, and did all we could to keep up with the 'shining gold.'" They had seen the light, and from now on, "Home spun, home made, and home forever, be our motto."[20]

There seemed to be no end to the money, or the means by which it could be made. When the war began, Ashtabula County had been more forest than field, but three years into the war fields of stumps were replacing the shady groves. One alarmist decried the cutting down of the county's forests, which like everything in the Reserve, now seemed for sale. The trade in lumber was brisk, and the owners of every woodlot hurried to get into the business. Capt. E. B. Howard, recently resigned from the Twenty-Ninth Ohio, purchased a portable sawmill and got into the business.[21] If the denuding continued at this clip, the residents were warned that they might wake up one morning and find themselves in a landscape as desolate as the Sahara. Despite the warnings from a few romantics, the county's primeval hardwoods continued to go down, to be hauled off to the steam-driven sawmill and then fashioned into wagon boxes, oars, and ship planking. The managers of Conneaut's port boasted that in the year about to end, over three million board feet of lumber had been loaded aboard outbound lake boats—the equivalent of fifteen thousand six-story-tall oaks, hickories, and maples.[22] So much lumber had been cut, dressed, and shipped off that the residents of Ashtabula County found themselves in the midst of a firewood shortage, with the coldest season of the year already fastening down on them. For want of the preferred article, the editor of the Jefferson newspaper was forced to burn bituminous coal to keep from freezing.

Towns and cities in the Reserve that sat on Lake Erie were well positioned to take advantage of the surge in lake traffic, and all prospered, as did faraway places that shipped their output down to them. The unheard of town of Marquette, deep in the woods of Upper Michigan, had produced three hundred thousand tons of the richest iron ore ever mined in just six months, much of it coming to Ashtabula and Conneaut by big lake boats, to be off-loaded onto trains bound for the East. Much of it was needed in Cleveland, where it was fed directly into the giant foundries and mills that had sprung up there.

In this summer of 1864, Horace Greeley continued to promote the Union Pacific Railroad, with its plans for joining the Pacific and the Atlantic Oceans, and news came that the giant spool of cable allowing telegraphic communication between America and England had been nearly unwound into the depths of the Atlantic and would soon be ready for testing. Nearer to home, the railroads were putting up new depots, roundhouses, and shops in cities large and small throughout Ohio and other points. Bound for places more distant, in the preceding few months fifty thousand emigrants had passed through Fort Laramie, Wyoming Territory, on their way into the Golden West.

The only shortage of anything this summer was beef, all supplies of which were taken by the military. With most of the men gone by now, women and children were running the family farmstead. To those of the rural laboring class who had time to read the Summit County newspaper, they found an editorial that must have seemed a jest: "We urge Farmers to see that every one of their families who can be of any service to be got into the field. Many have boys over eight years of age that can do much in planting and cultivating." And if a child resisted the call to labor, the editor suggested, "put them on short rations awhile; that would be a more effectual discipline than scolding and whipping." Speaking directly to the children, he continued, "Boys, go it good and strong. The defense of the country has rendered laborers extremely scarce, and the Republic calls to you to put your little hands to the plow and hoe." Little girls were not exempt, though of smaller strength than boys, they too were exhorted to go out into the fields, if only to break clods and cover the seeds with dirt.[23] A citizen was driving along a main road through Tallmadge, in Summit County, and saw two women plowing, one holding the team, and the other the plow. This was hardly a rarity any longer, but still valuable for its lesson: "Let their noble example be imitated."[24]

There were plentiful stories in the newspapers, almost always under the heading A Singular Occurrence. They told of soldiers saved from death by a Bible stowed in the breast pocket and the Bible then sent home with the bullet still lodged in its pages, of razor-edged shrapnel deflected by a locket holding a miniature of a mother's face. Stories sharing a common theme, freshened by changing the place and time, appeared over and over. In one such common tale a soldier is sent to the hospital with a stomach complaint and the surgeons discover the only cure to be the delivery of her child. Other stock stories included the last-minute escape from living burial and the loyal dog. Of the latter type was the story of the wife of an Illinois officer who had gone to the Shiloh battlefield to locate her husband.[25] With three thousand fresh graves, it was difficult to find him. Then she saw the dog her husband had taken to war running toward her. He led her to the grave. She learned from his comrades that the dog had stayed outside the hospital and could not be enticed to give up his post, and after his master died, sat at attention by his grave for twelve days. The moral was that humans should show as much loyalty.

The public never tired of stories of prophetic dreams of the death or grievous injury to one's soldier-son. The little brother of an Akron soldier arose one morning and told his family that he'd had a bad dream about his older brother George, who had been in the fighting around Resaca. He would not give them the details because of the old saying that if a person relates his dream on the day following, the dream will come true. He waited until the day after that to be on the safe side. In his dream, he had seen George walking toward him. One of his arms was gone and he was being helped along by a friend, whom the little brother knew by name. A while later news came to the family that George *had* lost an arm at Resaca and that the friend who had helped him from the battlefield, and helped further by burying the arm, was the same soldier the little brother had seen in his dream.[26]

The Disappearance of Wallace Hoyt

Down in Cassville, Georgia, the soldiers were refitting after the mighty push that had gotten all of them from Bridgeport to here. The army's pause had given the Boys time to mend tears in pants and blouses made by the sharp Georgia brush, restitch shoes, and give their muskets a thorough cleaning. There had been no fighting to perform, but the Twenty-Ninth Regiment had been required to send men out on the skirmish line, and in brush this heavy, with rebel patrols probing the line, skirmishing was a dangerous occupation. When their skirmishers returned to camp, on May 21, Wallace Hoyt was not with them. Of the thirty or so soldiers who were out on the line, he was the only one who had not returned. Wallace had likenesses made of himself at least twice during the war, and he sent them home to his family in Rock Creek, Ashtabula County, to prove just how much he had changed. No photograph of him is known to exist. His appearance can only be guessed from the particulars given in the descriptive list of his company: brown hair, hazel eyes, eighteen years old when he enlisted, in 1861. He was somewhat shorter than the others, at five feet four inches when he enlisted, but he had grown since then, physically and in other ways. He had not seen home since he'd marched out with the regiment on Christmas Day 1861.

Wallace had reported life on the interior of the regiment as seen by a private soldier, from the time he first got to camp at Jefferson until several weeks before he went missing. He had fought in all the regiment's battles, stood picket duty and walked the skirmish line a hundred times in as many places, and had never been hurt. Likewise, he had been impervious to sickness, which was a rarity among soldiers, and he had been in a rebel prison. None of these had put a dent in his good health or his spirit. A neighbor of his before the war said he had been an especially rugged youngster, hardened by farmwork, and that might have had something to do with his long string of good fortune.[27] He had only three months left before his enlistment term was finished, after which he had planned to go home to Rock Creek and save what was left of his family. What had become of him would not be known for months.

The day after Wallace Hoyt went missing, Chaplain Ames conducted Sabbath service. He chose for his sermon John 17:1—"The Hour Is Come."[28] Although the soldiers had not been required to attend, nearly everyone not on duty came to listen and to ponder what would happen to their souls if they were suddenly swept from the earth. On the evening of May 22, orders came to prepare an astounding twenty days' rations and to send all sick and wounded to the rear. Only a few officers, and Chaplain Ames, had visited the town. Cassville had been a prosperous place, with seminaries, several churches, and a substantial school house. The competing armies had left the place utterly ruined.[29] After three days' rest in Cassville, they packed up and moved toward Atlanta.

The Battle of New Hope Church, May 25–28, 1864

Atlanta was only fifty miles distant, the way a crow might fly it, but getting there would not prove easy. The direct route ran through Allatoona Pass, where the railroad climbed through a range of hills. The rebels had built stout defensive works there, adding to those that nature afforded. With the difficulties of trying to take a fortified position in the mountainous terrain at Rocky Face still fresh in his mind, Sherman decided to bypass Allatoona and land his army on the railroad below Johnston, at Marietta. He got the army moving south and west, with the town of Dallas, Georgia, as their objective. Sherman had not gone far before Johnston ciphered out his sidestep and began moving his army to block it.

First day out from Cassville, Geary's boys crossed the Etowah River on a pontoon bridge, of which this army never seemed in short supply, and camped. Geary had orders to march at first light and, if found, to push the enemy before him. It was up-and-down marching with stops to repair the road and rebuild bridges so their artillery could pass; then the whole division advanced through thick woods in double column, coming out finally at the hamlet of Burnt Hickory, where they made rough camp.[30]

Geary's division moved out front and center of Hooker's three divisions, and Hooker with his staff and escort accompanied Geary on the next day's drive, which all hoped would get them to Dallas and well on the way to flanking the rebel army. At Pumpkin Vine Creek, the enemy had torn up the bridge planks and started the structure burning. Geary came up in time and put the fire out. He replanked the deck and got his division over in short order. Hooker rode forward to reconnoiter. He came galloping back with the sounds of gunfire on his heels and ordered Geary to get his men moving up the road. If they ran into trouble, they were to hold the rebels in place until Hooker brought the rest of the corps up. Ahead not more than a mile was a crossroads, and near it, in one of the neighborhood's rare clearings, sat a log church called New Hope.

The Seventh Ohio Infantry pushed forward in an extended skirmish line, and the Twenty-Ninth Ohio stepped out ten paces behind. The Seventh Ohio had not gone far when they ran into a strong line of rebel skirmishers, and musket fire began to snap in the tangle. Then a rebel infantry column materialized out of nowhere and let go a volley that cut through the Seventh Ohio, killing and wounding several dozen men all at once. The racket of first contact was still hanging in the air when thousands of rebels stepped out of the trees and came at them with flags tipped forward and yelling like wild Indians. Myron Wright got his men to change front on the fly, moving them into a half circle to defend against a flank attack. The fighting was immediately general up and down the line. This attempt to drive them back into the creek stalled out and the enemy slipped back into heavy cover.

They learned from rebel prisoners that they were facing the whole of John Bell Hood's corps. Their nearest support was five miles away, but Geary was not interested in merely holding the position. He reinforced the skirmish line, spread Candy's brigade out in a battle line with the other two brigades massed in support behind, and got everyone started forward on the attack. But Hood's men were not about to give an inch. Along with the other regiments, the Twenty-Ninth advanced, stopping on command to fire a volley, then the front rank opened to let the rear rank through for their turn at it. It took two full hours, and the numbers were against them, but they succeeded in driving the enemy a half mile. The enemy got behind what were obviously well-prepared defensive works, and coming up against it, Geary's attack ran out of steam. Geary wanted to deceive Hood as to his small numbers by keeping up the attack, but Hooker, who was supervising from over Geary's shoulder, ordered a halt. Geary's line had possession of a ridge, thick woods all around, but high ground nonetheless, and the Boys went to work, scraping up rudimentary breastworks, and prepared to hold on until help arrived.

Four hours disappeared in the bedlam of combat in narrow corridors of deer trails and wagon paths, sometimes over possession of a single tree. Support finally came up. Now, with the divisions of Williams and Butterfield on hand, Hooker ordered his thousands to attack. He got Williams's division out front, followed by Butterfield, with Geary's division right behind in reserve. The Federal battle plan sounded neat and organized as the generals later described it, but for the soldiers who did the fighting, it was neither. A half hour earlier, there had been too few boys to hold off the rebels; now there seemed to be too many in this tree-choked landscape. Regiments in the lead were forced to a stop by hard resistance, while outfits behind them continued to push up, which crowded the soldiers in the front right into the rebel guns.

The air had become fixed, making it tough to breathe with so much smoke hanging close to the ground. Around seven in the evening, the sun disappeared behind a black-and-purple wall of cloud. Williams's division had made headway, but in a half hour of hard fighting eight hundred of them had been killed or wounded, and they could go no further. Hooker ordered Geary up to relieve them.

It was nearly dark when Cobham's brigade and three regiments of Candy's brigade, including the Twenty-Ninth Ohio, moved out on the double-quick. A thunderstorm broke over their heads and boomed as loud as the fighting down below, slashing at the trees and pushing curtains of cold, stinging rain. Ravines became rivers and every low spot a swamp, but the soldiers rushing up to the line were oblivious to it all. Williams's ranks opened to let Candy's men through and sent up cheers and huzzahs to speed them forward. They closed on the enemy and delivered a terrific volley, rocking the rebels. They were advancing into the heaviest canister and shell fire they would see in this campaign, all the worse because they could not see where it was coming from.[31] There were small combats going on within the interiors of this flashing, smoky world, many conducted from distances no greater than ten feet, accompanied by much cursing and shouting. This last attack of the day was gaining ground. On they went until a rebel battery concealed in the brush opened on them and they were slammed to a stop.

The left end of the Twenty-Ninth Ohio hung in the air, and the regiment to their right had been driven back by the sheer volume of rebel cannon fire. Without support on their right or left, the Boys might have been obliterated were it not for a depression in the ground right under the barrels of the rebel battery. They flattened themselves in the mud bottom to avoid the muzzle blast and the iron balls that raced over them and off into the night, raising their heads to fire point-blank whenever their antagonists paused to reload the big guns.

They stayed at this close-quarters business until the rebel gunners were shot, or departed, and these particular guns quieted. No one in the Giddings Regiment learned of the precariousness of their situation until an officer from Geary's staff came up to them and ordered them to fall back. They withdrew to a position forty paces from the rebel line.[32]

Hooker's soldiers had driven Hood nearly three miles from Pumpkin Vine Creek and were now almost to the church at the crossroads. They were perilously close to Hood's main line. With lightning as their illumination, soldiers dug trenches with tin plates and bayonets, until some soldiers in the Second Brigade loaned them two picks and a spade. After that, they hunkered down in the water that soon filled their diggings. This close to the enemy, there was no peace for the soldiers manning the lines. The opposing lines were so near that boys from both sides were pulling logs for breastworks from the same pile.[33] Both sides kept up a desultory fire throughout a long night of cold and wet. The noise of the storm subsided, replaced by the sound of the hundreds of crying men who lay wounded between the lines.

Chaplain Ames had stayed with the supply train back near Pumpkin Vine Creek. He watched his regiment go up over a ridge and heard the storm of cannon and rifle fire that soon came from that direction. Wounded started to make their way back to the brigade hospital wagons at midday with reports that Candy's brigade was engaged in a terrible battle. After dark the sound of full battle boiled up in the near distance. At midnight, Ames rode up to the front line and found his regiment. What little he could learn at this late hour he committed to his diary: "A severe fight occurred this eve. A number of our men wounded."[34]

The sun came up over a bleak landscape. By the default of storm, darkness, and stiff resistance, they had landed on a ridge. Candy's brigade sat astride the road to New Hope Church with its left flank dangling in the air. A dense gloomy wood surrounded them. The ground had been pounded into grease and the treetops twisted and broken by the cyclone of artillery and high wind. Eighty yards away, the rebels sat in breastworks on their own ridge. Directly opposite Charles Candy's brigade, a rebel battery of seventeen guns was visible, and although it was barely dawn, they were already lobbing shells into Candy's line. The first order of business once it became light was to put the best marksmen in each regiment to work picking off the rebel gunners.

Much closer to Candy's line, rebel skirmishers held stout breastworks at the foot of this very ridge. Candy sent boys down to argue their possession. The enemy would not be budged, and the best Candy's boys could do was to scrape together breastworks of their own. Now the forward lines of both sides were no more than twenty yards apart. Their work this day, and for the next five days, would consist of attempts by small groups to push the line ahead a few feet. They worked under cover of darkness mostly, pick and ax employed on hands and knees in the mud and brush, with injury or death to the soldier whose mind wandered for a second and he raised himself high enough to make a target.

The day after the battle, Stanley's division of the Fourth Corps came up, and Candy's brigade was pulled out of the front line. Candy's brigade had been under constant fire for more than twenty-four hours. No one had eaten or had as much as a cup of coffee. The Giddings Boys turned over their position to the Thirty-Sixth Illinois Volunteers and descended into a gully behind the line where they enjoyed twelve hours of comparative peace. Half a day, or half a night, on the front line or in the skirmish pits, and half a day off became the program for the following days, with spirited artillery contests added for good measure. At some point in the first two days, General Sherman and his staff came up to watch the fighting.

Around the turn of the century, a Twenty-Ninth veteran claimed that not only had Sherman been there but that he and his mates had had actual contact with the famous man. Sherman came up to the rear of Company I and one of its soldiers, either unaware whom he was addressing or to prove himself as valuable a soldier as Sherman, asked the general to throw him a blanket, and without hesitation Sherman picked it up and tossed it to him.[35]

After two days, the physical and emotional fatigue produced by this continuous, close-range combat began to tell. For the first and last time in its history, boys from the Twenty-Ninth Ohio, and even their redoubtable Lieutenant Russell, who had seen more than his share of fighting, simply got up and walked away from the line and appeared at the brigade hospital. They did not show any signs of physical injury. They simply "gave out," was how Chaplain Ames diagnosed them.[36] Those who could not be counted on in a tight spot had been culled out long ago, and there were no accusations that these men had showed the white feather. For his part, Capt. W. F. Stevens had been leading his company in the hottest part of the fighting on the first day up from Pumpkin Vine Creek and been shot through the hand.

Geary had lost nearly four hundred men and officers killed, wounded, and missing in the first twenty-four hours of this battle, with more casualties to come before their stay here was over. Forty of the Twenty-Ninth's soldiers and officers were already down, all of them shot, it was said, within a few moments during the final assault on the first night.[37] Losses in the Fifth and Seventh Ohio Regiments had been more severe.

One Twenty-Ninth soldier had been killed outright on the first day, and another was conveyed to the field hospital gravely wounded. Ames saw Sgt. Joseph Marsh of Company K in the field hospital and pronounced that he must soon die of his wounds, and he did die shortly after Ames left him.[38] The fighting in this sector never rose to the furious level of the first day. Both sides were too well dug in to risk a full-scale attack. However, the fire was steady and more than capable of producing casualties. On May 29, four days after they had come up from Pumpkin Vine Creek, Company B was posted to the dangerous work in the skirmish pits. Three of their boys had been killed close up to the rebel defenses, and three of their comrades volunteered to bring them out.[39] One of these heroes had a special interest in recovering the fallen.

Spencer Atkins and his younger brother, Albert, enlisted in Company B back in 1861, on the same day. Albert was now one of those lying dead out there in the brush, and his brother went out to retrieve him. The rebels opened on the burial party with canister and musket fire, but the Boys persisted and got their dead back into the main line.[40] Among the dead was Jerome Phinney, the boy who had lamented in a letter to his father that he had not been able to perform this same service for his uncle, who had been killed and left behind at Dug Gap. One of the dead men the recovering party brought back into their lines was found to have life in him. Cornelius A. Davis was taken down to the hospital by the creek with a severe wound to the abdomen. He died within two hours, in time to be buried along with the others in a common grave on a ridge on the right side of the Dallas–Burnt Hickory road.[41]

Spurred by the gunfire drawn by the party sent out to rescue the Twenty-Ninth's dead, the rebels came down out of their works and charged down the slope. Geary's guns, loaded with double charges of canister and supported by the rifle fire from hundreds of muskets, broke the attack, leaving the ground covered in some places with rebel dead and wounded.[42] The regiment had been wounded again, but Ames found that the Boys in the front line were in good spirits and confident of eventual success.[43]

A week of fighting along this line had not produced Sherman's intended result. He had tried the center and then both ends of Johnston's line and met with bloody repulse everywhere. The fighting at Pickett's Mill, a mile north of Geary's line, had been an outright disaster. A Federal attack aimed at Johnston's right got jammed up in swampy terrain and impenetrable brush, and whole companies of soldiers were shot down where they stood, helpless to defend themselves against Cleburne's rebels, who enjoyed the advantage of high ground. Some rebel soldiers who had done this work regarded it as pure murder.

Maj. Gen. George Stoneman's Union cavalry got up to Allatoona Pass on June 1 and took it, and on the night of June 4, Johnston withdrew from the Dallas–New Hope line. After Gettysburg, Meade had given Lee a head start and then allowed him to get his army over the Potomac and back into Virginia. Sherman was not of that mind. He got his army moving immediately. On the first day of June, after seven days of continual fighting, the Boys got the order to move.

Chaplain Ames finished his work at the hospital and sat for a moment to tally their losses since leaving Bridgeport, less than a month before. One hundred thirty-two soldiers and officers had been killed, wounded, or were missing.[44] The field and company officer staffs had been decimated from the top down. At least another two dozen Boys, including Nathan Parmater, had fallen sick and were struggling to get well at hospitals back up the line. If the fighting continued at this pace for another month, the Twenty-Ninth Ohio would be as shorthanded as when they had marched into the corn at Cedar Mountain. Ames recorded the hard numbers and finished his diary entry, "Thus we melt away! A costly sacrifice on the altar of our country."[45]

Big Shanty

Hooker's soldiers left the ridge near New Hope Church, made a half dozen miles, and camped. The day after they left the ridge near New Hope Church, a steady rain began to pound at them. Evenings, except for those who were assigned picket duty, the Boys gathered round campfires to dry themselves and cook—luxuries they had not enjoyed for days. This close to the enemy, the dangers of camp were considerable. A soldier in the Seventh Ohio was asleep in his shelter tent when he was hit by a stray bullet. Chaplain Ames was out riding when a sharpshooter's bullet sizzled past his head, narrowly missing him.[46] Geary announced that Allatoona had fallen and that Sherman's engineers were already there, turning it into the army's next base of supply, which of course was good news; but the rain continued to fall, making the roads heavy and threatening to bring this immense operation to a full stop.

They packed up and moved up to Allatoona Pass, stopping at a point where the roads to Acworth and Big Shanty crossed. They were here to support the Twenty-Third Corps while it passed through toward Marietta. Chaplain Ames staged Sunday service in which he used the words "there is a time to all things" as the theme of his sermon, and he was surprised at the good attendance, especially given the recent bad behavior of the soldiers and their officers.[47]

Two days earlier the troops had been issued a ration of the beverage that their chaplain abhorred, and until it ran out, Ames worried that the regiment might be backsliding into its old ways. He observed, "Liquor—Spirituous fermented was issued to-day to men. Some took none, others doubled the dose. Officers used freely. Some men acted foolishly!"[48] Time and again he had seen with his own eyes that even a short stay in camp allowed vice to flourish.

The whiskey had been officially dispensed as a deterrent to the sickness that must come from living for days on end under this biblical rain. Sick men had begun to appear more frequently at surgeon's calls, but none of them as yet was "bad sick," as the soldier might say. The chaplain had been suffering from dysentery, the perpetual complaint of most of the men. On the rare occasions he could find it, he ate corn bread for relief. He attributed his own episodes to too much fatty pork, which, to compound its indigestibility, was currently fried in bacon grease. Bacon was not part of their daily fare, but the soldiers had gathered in big supplies of it as they marched up to Allatoona Pass.

Families along the route had hidden the produce of their smokehouses in the ground, shaping the surface and marking it so it looked like a grave. The soldiers sniffed out this subterfuge and despite the entreaties of the civilians that they would starve come winter, the soldiers carted away what they found—as much as half a ton of hams in one cache alone. Soon the soldiers took to digging up every fresh-looking grave they came upon. The officers put a stop to it when their digging produced the corpses of rebels that had been killed just a few hours earlier by Geary's skirmishers.[49]

Here at Big Shanty, hosts of troops passed by them on their way down to Marietta, flags out front and bands playing, despite the pouring-down rain.[50] It seemed to the soldiers watching this procession that the Federal losses of the past month had not really made a dent in the army—although it had. Candy's brigade had bled severely, and their strength was about to be reduced further. Two of its mainstay regiments, the Fifth and Seventh Ohio infantries, were about to go home.

The Seventh Ohio was already a battle-hardened outfit by the time the Giddings Boys joined them on the Upper Potomac in the first month of the year 1862. They had spearheaded many of the battles in which Candy's brigade fought. The clock on their term of enlistment had run down here, and they went home.[51] Most of the Fifth Ohio's boys went home too. The Fifth Ohio would carry on, but it would be filled mostly with boys from other regiments who still had time to serve but had not reenlisted as veterans. No one who had to stay was bitter because others got to leave. They were envious, of course, but happy for them, and they sent them off with cheers.

Chaplain Ames had a map and by it could measure the remaining steps to their prize: ten miles from this point in the mountains to Marietta, half a dozen miles from there to the Chattahoochee River, and a dozen miles beyond that lay Atlanta.[52] The Twenty-Ninth Ohio, and its corps, had received several orders in the past few days to join the mighty procession, but all of them had been countermanded.

The roads were too congested by the passage forward of other commands. The soldiers busied themselves with the futile work of drying clothes, and with the improvement in their defenses needed in case the army out ahead got turned around by the rebels and had to fall back to this place.[53] The air steamed when the sun came out during breaks in the storms, and at night there were awesome displays of lightning. The thunder was so loud in this Southern clime that it was both a novelty and a fright. Close by the Twenty-Ninth's camp several soldiers and horses went down like bowling pins when the tree under which they were standing was lightning struck.[54]

It was here, near Big Shanty, that Chaplain Ames met the poor woman who four years earlier had dreamed that flocks of blackbirds had descended around her so thickly that she feared she would be suffocated. Through her window Mrs. Adams could now see the dark-coated men of the Twenty-Ninth Ohio camped all around her house, everything within sight turned into a wasteland of tree stumps and excavations. The thousands of soldiers crowding the road and camped around her had stripped the landscape as thoroughly as the locusts of Egypt.[55] All this confirmed her belief that "all this trouble" had been foretold in her dream.[56]

The foul weather would not relent. The Twenty-Ninth had not had a more disagreeable time since they'd been out. The roads were nearly useless, and any movement of the whole army was reduced to turtle speed. Then a change for the better came their way. For the first time in almost a month, the sun broke through, a cool wind came up, and the roads began to dry as quickly as they had been turned to gumbo. The Boys shouldered their gear and got on the road, which took them south and out of the Allatoona Mountains and onto what they hoped would be flatter, more hospitable terrain.

They marched for only two hours and were ordered to stop right where they were and bivouac in battle line. When they started, the uninformed had believed they would march directly into Marietta. That would not be possible, as the Boys could now see. The outer ring of the rebel defenses was standing directly in front of them. The rebels were behind a long, interconnected line, ingeniously engineered to make the most of features of this twisted landscape. Dead ahead lay one of its most challenging segments: a low, denuded ridge that some locals knew as Pine Mountain, and most as Pine Knob.

The Makings of a Nightmare: The Battle of Pine Knob, June 15, 1864

Pine Knob stood three hundred feet above the surrounding terrain, which gave the rebels atop it a good view of the disposition of Sherman's army as it maneuvered down from the north. The enemy line described an arc: its left resting on Lost Mountain, not far from Dallas over to the west, then bowed out to take advantage of Pine Knob, continued several miles east to Brush Mountain, and beyond to the neighborhood's tallest eminence, Kennesaw Mountain. Sherman believed the rebels had spread themselves too thinly. He saw an opportunity to bring his superior numbers to bear.

The Boys could see that the sides of Pine Knob were veined with spurs and ravines. Getting to the top of it would not be an easy thing if the rebels chose to resist them. What the Boys could not see from below was that their enemy had honeycombed the sides of Pine Knob with earth-and-timber forts, lines of interconnected trenches, and artillery emplacements.[57]

On closer inspection, they were able to see rebels up on the top, both their camps and breastworks in clear view. The Federal gunners could see the same thing, and they wheeled up within easy range and began throwing shells up to the top.[58] The rebel high command, including Generals Johnston, Hardee, and Polk, had ridden to the top of the knob to survey the feasibility of holding it. Geary claimed that it was he who had seen this collection of rebel officers and ordered McGill's battery to fire on them. He learned later from prisoners that this was the spot where General Polk had been cut in two by a shell. A few days later, he wrote to his wife to tell her that one of *his* batteries had killed Polk. Others made far better documented claims for the credit, chiefly, Generals Howard and Sherman.[59]

When the Boys awoke their first morning in front of Pine Knob, they were pleasantly surprised to learn that the rebels seen plainly moving about on the summit of Pine Knob the day before had packed up and gone during the night. Whether the killing of their General Polk had persuaded all of them to abandon Pine Knob was a question for which Geary's soldiers would presently provide an answer. Sherman, Thomas, and Hooker rode over to Geary's division that morning, confirmed that the rebels had evacuated the summit of Pine Knob, and made plans for the attack.

At high noon, with artillery thudding from the right at Brush Mountain, and from the left in the direction of Kennesaw Mountain, Geary advanced his brigades, with Candy's brigade leading. They crossed two streams and arrived in the woods to the right of the knob.[60] Geary was sending his whole division in this time, nothing to be held back. Each brigade spread out in two lines. Candy's men got into position on the left, where the terrain on the skirt of the knob was most challenging. The ground ahead of them was a choppy arrangement of ridges and gullies. The skirmish line shoved off into the brush and with little difficulty drove the rebels from their first line of works. But there was no time to stand idly and admire the handiwork of their skirmishers.

A dispatch came up from Hooker ordering them to attack, immediately.[61] Hooker assured Geary that at the very moment his division started forward, the Fourth Corps, on his left, and Butterfield's division, on his right, would also attack.[62] In total, more than fifteen thousand boys would step off, and if they all went in at once, they might all be having breakfast tomorrow on the banks of the Chattahoochee with Atlanta in view.

Instantly, an all-out battle blew up from one end of Geary's line to the other. He stated in his report that the division got moving at precisely 2:15, but Charles Candy stated that the line did not begin moving until 5:00 p.m. That the hour had already grown late was also confirmed later by Myron Wright, who was in command of the Twenty-Ninth Ohio. He stated that he took the two hundred soldiers of the Twenty-Ninth onto the field at 5:30.[63] This discrepancy of three hours would not matter much in most affairs, but it would have a good deal to do with the nature of the fighting here, and its outcome.[64]

Candy put the Twenty-Ninth Ohio and Twenty-Eighth Pennsylvania in the first line, with the Giddings Boys on the right and the Fifth and Sixty-Sixth Ohio Regiments behind them.[65] The front line swung by the right flank to bring it square to the rebel line. Hooker, mounted on his magnificent gray stallion, rode along next to them.[66] The Boys swept over the first line of trenches and up to the second line, where they were stopped in their tracks by rifle and cannon fire.[67]

As they moved up to the fight, the Boys of Company D were surprised to see their captain, George W. Dice, coming across the field to join them, his frock coat buttoned over the bandages covering his chest wound, and a dark lump under his eye where a bullet from Dug Gap had lodged. The army surgeons had advised him against leaving the hospital with his wounds not yet healed, but he wanted to be with his men and he could not be talked out of it. He had gone only a few hundred feet when he was struck in the head and mortally wounded.[68]

The Giddings Boys fought their way down into the first ravine and locked in a struggle with the First and Twenty-Ninth Georgia Infantries. The fighting was at close quarters; at times the flagstaffs of Georgia and Ohio regiments crossed. The Georgians were forced back a step at a time. Their color bearer was shot and their flag went down. Someone in the Giddings Regiment almost had his hands on it when another rebel picked it up and got away with it. The Boys had succeeded thus far, so the veterans would later state, in killing, wounding, or capturing most all of the Georgians. The survivors ran up the slope, and the Giddings Boys charged after them.[69]

The line into which the rebels had fled was a masterwork of engineering. To make taking it even more difficult, they had built an abatis in front, dug a deep trench, and covered it with brush so it couldn't be seen by an attacker until he had already fallen into it.[70] The rebel artillery opened on the Giddings Regiment at point-blank range. Some of the Boys had seen the rebel gunners getting ready to fire and got down. Those who had not been thus forewarned were ripped by grapeshot. They had been fighting their way up the side of Pine Knob for two hours now. Darkness began to seep down into the smoky thickets. Neither side had any intention of giving ground. The Twenty-Ninth stayed put, close in to the rebel works, and concentrated on silencing the rebel artillery. Soldiers rose up for a second, fired, and ducked down again.

Then an order came for the Twenty-Ninth to fall back. They backed away from the rebel line and went to work building a line of their own. It was now quite dark, but such work was not any safer on that account. They were close enough to hear rebel officers ordering their men about, and any sound of their own digging and scraping drew the enemy's cannon and musket fire.[71]

A few days before, back at Big Shanty, Rollin Jones had been overcome by a premonition that he would not live through their next battle, just as his best friend, Allen Mason, had been convinced at Chancellorsville. At some point during this night at Pine Knob, with shapes materializing behind trees and then disappearing again, a rebel soldier rose up and shot him in the face, the bullet passing through and out the back of his neck. He was lucky. He would survive the physical effects of the wound, and in a few weeks he would be healed enough to rejoin his regiment. The many boys who knew Rollin well, however, said he was never the same after that.[72]

The battle went on until eleven at night, but the close-in fighting between individuals and squads continued through the night.[73] At daybreak, the Twenty-Ninth Ohio was relieved by the Sixty-Sixth Ohio, and they dropped back a hundred yards into the fallback line and rested on muskets.

With five hundred fifty men down, the battle had been a small disaster for Geary's division. Up the line to their right, near a church named Gilgal, Butterfield's assault had not been driven home with the tenacity of Geary's, nor timed to coincide with his. The rebels still sat in their main line. Geary's men had fought hard, and for a time a breakthrough in their sector appeared distinctly possible, but they had not been supported on either the right or left, as they had been promised.[74] The White Star Division had fought most of the battle with both ends of their line exposed. They had been in danger of destruction by flank attack and had been saved from that only by the quick thinking of the brigade commanders, Candy and Ireland, who had bent both ends of the line backward. Candy had good reason to be proud of his soldiers. The Twenty-Ninth Ohio and the Twenty-Eighth Pennsylvania had gotten to within thirty feet of the main rebel breastworks and, once there, had refused to budge.[75]

After their earlier battles in the war, soldiers had sent letters back to the Reserve newspapers to give the sights and sounds of mass conflict, with anecdotes showing which soldier had been particularly defiant or the best shot, or who had said something particularly amusing. That time had long since passed. Since Dug Gap, Myron Wright and Chaplain Ames had been the delegated carriers of bad news to the newspapers of their respective counties. Here at Pine Knob Wright had been wounded yet again, and even Chaplain Ames had been hit in the hand while giving first aid. To report the news of this battle, two new voices took their place: Pvt. George W. Halloway, and Capt. Everson J. Hurlburt. Their announcements provided the homefolks with only the stark essentials: "Co. A—Killed, Serg't A. L. Rickard, shot in head, Cyrus Roath, in breast. Wounded Corp'l G. B. Morey, in right ankle, severely, James O. Latimer, right thigh, severe." The list ran on for another several inches with the names of those killed, and those wounded in bowels, mouth, groin, arm or leg, with notation of those who had undergone amputation.[76]

Nine bodies of Twenty-Ninth Ohio soldiers were brought down from Pine Knob, laid out, and covered with blankets. Thirty more started on their way back to the division hospital after Surgeon Haynes did what he could for them at the field hospital.[77] For the dead, there was not enough time or safety to dig a grave for each man. They were laid side by side in a common trench and, after a short service, the dirt pushed in to cover them.[78]

The body of Pvt. Cyrus Roath of Company A, age twenty-one years, was found the next day and buried up on the slope by the soldier who discovered him. When they left Camp Giddings in 1861, every soldier's packs and pockets bulged with books, pistols, medicines, condiments, favorite blankets, personal clothing, and a hundred other things that were believed indispensable but were soon discarded. The soldier who found and buried Cyrus brought his personal effects down to Chaplain Ames for disposition. Ames made the inventory: two photographs, a few letters, four postage stamps, Roath's wallet, and a small case of needles with which he mended his clothes.[79]

Battlefield burials were meant to be temporary. Gravediggers followed in the rear of the army, giving the dead a better burial than the Boys had time for, or taking them away to one of the centralized cemeteries going up around the country. In the torn-up terrain on Pine Knob, covered with knocked-over trees and brush piles, exploring every remote place for the dead could not have been an easy thing. Cyrus Roath may lie up on that ridge yet, among the expensive homes built in the French chateau style.

As Ames led the others in prayers over the dead, his thoughts turned to his own son Edwin who was with the armies far down the Mississippi. He had not been heard from since April.

The rebel line running along the spurs of Pine Knob was found vacant the next morning, and Hooker's corps moved up a mile to keep contact. Like with the Army of the Potomac, now under Grant's command in the East, the war would no longer consist of battles interrupted by long periods of planning and recovery. The Federal armies had their hands on the enemy's throat, and the Union now had generals who would keep applying the pressure until he choked.

Candy's soldiers moved into the abandoned trenches and built more of their own. They were now on the next ring of the enemy's defenses out from Atlanta, which would be called the Mud Creek line. The rebel lines seemed to get stronger the further they advanced. Here they were made up of earth forts on unassailable ridges, stitched tightly together by complicated systems of mutually supporting trenches. A swampy creek ran between Hooker's command and the rebel lines and then curved to the northeast, following the natural defensive contours of high ground running toward the bulk of Kennesaw Mountain, and past that up to Brush Mountain. Geary's division was near the right end of the Federal army, with Cox's division below it, holding the bitter end of the rope. It was only four miles down this road to Marietta, and just beyond the town were the crossings over the Chattahoochee. Not a single Federal soldier could have predicted how much effort it would require to cover that short stretch of ground.

They would be stuck in these trenches for the next thirty days, putting up with sickening heat, mosquitoes that bred in every puddle, and flies that coated every surface so thickly they looked fur covered. Then there was the constant rain, with its byproduct of mud, and more mud. These were dismal places to be, even had it not been a time of war. The trenches filled hip deep with water, causing a soldier to endure leg cramps and chills, while at the same instant the Georgia summer sun broiled the parts of him above the water line.[80] Naturally, levels of sickness rose sharply, and many more beds in the division hospital were occupied by sick boys than by the wounded. When the fighting grew hot, however, the proportion reversed itself.

For the remainder of this summer 1864, the moments of complete quiet would be too few to count. The muggy atmosphere crackled around the clock with rifle fire and shook with the noise of terrible artillery disputes in which each side tried to hammer the other into backing away. The two armies sat glowering and deadlocked. Two weeks of fighting and mud struggle had passed since New Hope Church, and they were still no more than ten miles from it.

The army's march down from Resaca to New Hope had been metered by the names of towns through which it rolled full speed ahead. These days, Geary's White Stars, typical of the rest of Sherman's army, measured their progress by the names of neighboring farms, and even houses: the Dobbs house one day, forward the next day several hundred yards to the Barringer plantation, and a few hundred more on the day or days after to the Darby place.[81] At this rate they would be white-bearded old men by the time they got into Atlanta.

Through the rest of June and the first half of July, the standoff dragged on. The Twenty-Ninth's routine hardly varied: a day, or several days, in the forward lines; or out front of them in the skirmish line; a day or two of rest; and then back to the start of the cycle. They executed complex evolutions in support of this battery or that regiment, which advanced their lines less distance than a boy might throw a rock. The sameness of these days was broken by two big events, both brought on by the frustration of the generals who ordered them.

The Battle of Kolb's Farm, June 22, 1864

In the third week of June, Sherman ordered Hooker, with McPherson's corps supporting him on the right, to break free of the impossible terrain in their front and take Marietta from the southwest. Johnston knew something was up on the left of his line and sent Hood's corps out to stop it. For the first time in many days, the Giddings Boys got a chance to stretch their legs in a real march. They got on the road and covered the two miles down to the Powder Springs Road in a pelting rain. The Twenty-Ninth went to work immediately building breastworks. The vanguard of Hooker's corps had detected Hood's approach, stopped on a ridge astride the road, and thrown up stout barricades made of tree trunks and fence rails. This ridge overlooked the farm of the widow Kolb, which consisted of partially cleared fields cut by marshy streams and shallow ravines.

The Federals were stacked up three divisions deep behind their works, with two more divisions in place behind if they were needed. Hood got his men up and ordered an immediate attack against the center of the Federal line. Ten thousand rebels came up in perfect order and were immediately struck by volley fire and artillery. A ravine made a gap between the positions of Geary and Williams, and the rebels tried to force a wedge into it. The fire was too intense for anything to live for very long in it, and the rebels disappeared under a crossfire of bullets and close-range artillery, having gotten no closer to Geary than his skirmish line.[82]

It had been one of the war's grand things to see—this many rebel regiments coming across the fields all at once—but it took little more than an hour to break Hood's boys, and the aftereffect of such murderous work made for permanent, disturbing memories. The Twenty-Ninth's published history recalled the look of the field after the fighting ended that evening, to remind aging veterans who needed reminding of what they had witnessed: "At the close of this action a body of our skirmishers were deployed over the field, finding the enemy's dead and wounded scattered thickly about. In places they lay stretched across each other, literally heaped up, bloody, terrible—dead."[83]

No one in the regiment had sustained so much as a scratch, although they had fired their weapons at some point, making a small, long-distance contribution to the butchery.[84] Candy's brigade had been too far left of the center of the repulse to have a big part in it, but it had been the men of Geary's division nonetheless who had faced the brunt of the attack, which would entitle all his regiments to list this as one of their official battles. Fewer than three hundred Union boys had been hurt or killed along the entire line; Hood's losses were at least four times that. The rebel Stevenson made the sad admission that his division had by itself lost eight hundred men.[85] It had been a terrible waste of fine infantry. Hood got his men back into their fallback line and burrowed in. The road to Marietta was still not open.

SeCheverell rightfully did not claim any credit on behalf of his regiment for Hood's misfortune. Instead, his saga illuminated an event of the following day in which the regiment *had* played a glorious role. At about four in the afternoon of June 23, Federal artillery began a bombardment of the rebels atop Little Kennesaw Mountain, not far from the Twenty-Ninth's part of the line. One hundred guns went off all at once, and the rebel skirmishers got down to the business of picking off the gunners. A creek ran in front of the regiment, and across from it a blockhouse sat in the middle of the rebel line. According to the story, the gunfire originating from it annoyed Geary and he asked for twenty volunteers from the Twenty-Ninth to go out and capture it.

Lt. Rush Griswold of Company B and his boys breasted the storm of bullets and broke into the rebel trenches, driving the defenders away and capturing twenty-one of the enemy and killing and wounding several others. The squad moved up the trench line to the blockhouse and demanded its surrender. A rebel officer hollered out from inside, "You damned Yanks. Take us if you can!" Griswold's soldiers battered the door down. Everyone inside surrendered except for one enlisted man and the defiant officer, who fired on the Giddings Boys and was in turn killed. They held the blockhouse for two hours, but the rebels came up in strength and drove them off.[86]

One of their own had in fact been wounded that day, but not in the sortie out to the blockhouse. George Williams, an eighteen-year-old English-born farmer's son, had been shot through both thighs while helping move one of Geary's guns. He was brought to the hospital for treatment and for a time he seemed in a fair way to recover.[87] The hospital was not a peaceful place to convalesce. It had been shelled during his stay, shrapnel tearing through the tent, sending big trees crashing all around it, and requiring the attendants to disturb the patients and carry them outside.

Williams also suffered from dysentery in addition to his gunshot wounds, and he began to slip. Enlisted men must endure the trials of combat, and their officers had the duty of worrying over them, and their surgeon the responsibility to fix them when they were torn or sick. Chaplain Ames's job may have been the most difficult of all. He had to watch a boy like George Williams slide down and answer his big, last question:

> June 28—He ran down very fast during the day. I was with him in his last hour. Reason returned at the last; he said "Chaplain, do you think I am going to die?" Being told that he could not live but a short time he said, "Will you pray for me"? Prayer was offered, he appeared calm, clasped his arm around my neck like a child clinging to a father. Attempted to raise himself up, he had not strength & failed, not able to speak distinctly again, soon life ebbed out & the soldier boy's spirit had fled forever from Earth & all its scenes of war & strife & death.[88]

The Battle of Kennesaw Mountain, June 27, 1864

The Boys kept at the work of fortifying and manning the trenches and going out in front of them to trade shots with the rebels. Artillery shells, if not falling on them directly, detonated near enough that the burst could be seen, followed in a second by the thump. In late June, Sherman tried a second time to break the deadlock. He moved the army into position for what he hoped would be the campaign's decisive battle. This time, the army was to attack along the entire line. It got off to a good start, with the artillery firing in unison at 8:00 a.m. sharp on June 27, but the timing of the infantry assaults that followed was less perfect.

Geary's job was to take what ground he could and protect the flank of Maj. Gen. Oliver O. Howard's Fourth Corps making the main attack against spurs of Little Kennesaw, to his left. He got his men up and out of their trenches promptly at eight o'clock, spread his division out, with Candy's brigade on the left, and moved forward, driving the rebels in front of them. An ominous cloud of noise and smoke rolled down toward them. The sounds of men cheering escaped the cloud now and then, but after just an hour, the hopeful noise coming from Little Kennesaw faltered and then died. Howard's corps had charged in a line ten rows deep against a sharp angle in the rebel line, but they got into a place too narrow for such a thick formation and they had been shot all to pieces. Howard's troops began to recoil, leaving Geary's left flank exposed.[89] He refused Candy's line at a sharp angle just in case the rebels, emboldened by their pummeling of Howard, came out of their lines and attacked him. They did not.

Geary's White Stars had succeeded in advancing the Federal line several hundred yards, but on other parts of the field the morning's mass assaults had been a failure. During the fighting, the Twenty-Ninth Ohio had been ordered to the support of the Thirteenth New York Battery, posted on the top of an elevation overlooking the day's bloodiest fighting. Major Wright could not find suitable ground on which to place his men, and they returned to their brigade and dug in.[90] The Boys had been spectators to the battle of Kennesaw Mountain, and not participants.

No official report—submitted by Myron T. Wright, Charles Candy, or anyone else—mentioned any special, extra hazardous fighting done by the Twenty-Ninth Ohio that day. However, SeCheverell, who was not there, had been provided with recollections that they had done glorious and important work, and unlike the exploits of Rush Griswold's squad a few days earlier, this act of derring-do was corroborated by two Twenty-Ninth Ohio veterans who wrote separately of it many years later.

Sgt. Orlando Wilson of Company F recalled that General Sherman came up during the Kennesaw fight and saw for himself how the rebel sharpshooters were picking off Union boys. He asked for volunteers to go out and dislodge them. After a long pause, Wilson and Privates Henry Rood and Peter Dowling stepped out of the line of hesitant men and said they would try it. The regiment's history reported that at nine o'clock that morning, two men from each of the Twenty-Ninth's companies volunteered to go to the relief of an unidentified Pennsylvania regiment manning the same blockhouse that Griswold's squad had briefly taken in the earlier incident.[91]

This time the rebels gave up the blockhouse but stood firm in the lines behind it. The volunteers executed a flank movement under withering fire and got in the rear of the rebel works, capturing eleven prisoners, and held it until the Fifth Ohio Regiment came up and bolstered the position. One of the Twenty-Ninth's own, a Frenchman by birth, was hit and was carried back to the field hospital, where he died that evening. Wilson recalled that he and the others were each given the Medal of Honor for their bravery that day, and although years had passed, he and the others still cherished their medals.[92]

SeCheverell stated that it was at this moment that Howard's corps began their attack on the left. Two shells fell on the boys in this forward position, one round killing a dozen of them, and the second another half dozen; to what unit they belonged, SeCheverell did not say. The record shows that no regiment in their brigade or of any brigade in their division had been unlucky enough to have a shell fall on them and take out a dozen men. The Fifth Ohio had done exemplary work that day, driving the rebel skirmishers back into their lines under dangerous fire, but thankfully they had sustained only four casualties. The report filed by the Fifth's commander gave the details of their dangerous service that day, out ahead of the division and driving the rebels back into their lines, but he did not mention finding anyone from the Twenty-Ninth Ohio waiting for them when they came up to the rebel lines.[93] It may have happened as SeCheverell, John Rupp, and Orlando Wilson said it had; such displays of valor may have been too commonplace for their officers to single out in their official reports. SeCheverell, Rupp, and Wilson did not write of either rush to the blockhouse until twenty to fifty years later. By the passage of many years, events in the war had become compressed: they may have been recalling a single event, not two.

The evening of the battle of Kennesaw Mountain, the Twenty-Ninth Ohio was back out on the skirmish line, a dangerous duty that had been the hallmark of this campaign, and the Boys seemed to prefer it over life in the mainline trenches. As one of them who had walked the brush out forward of the lines recalled, "It was as home to us, for we felt that by this time we had learned the business."[94]

Atlanta Skyline

Sherman gave up any idea of pushing the rebels back by direct assault and returned to the safer stratagem of inchworm maneuvering. In the days after Kennesaw, he backed Maj. Gen. John Schofield's corps out of the line and got it sidestepping past Johnston's left. For the next two weeks of July, Geary's soldiers repeated what they had been doing every day since coming down from the Allatoona Mountains: skirmishing with the enemy's infantry, and sometimes cavalry, taking prisoners, losing a few men, and slowly but steadily driving the enemy back into yet another layer of his defensive line. In all this Geary made good use of his artillery, stopping his line to bring the guns up to batter the next rebel position and then starting the skirmish line ahead again to take possession of it. After one of these bombardments, the soldier found the bodies of a rebel colonel, seven of his privates, and seven horses.[95] McGill's battery had done the work.

Their hospital moved along with the Boys. Ames continued his regular visits to the front to check on them. Not infrequently, bullets hummed past him, not only on the line but while he was at brigade headquarters, in the rear.[96] On July 3 he learned that Marietta had been abandoned by the enemy, and, being a curious man, he saddled his horse and trotted up the road toward the town that had long eluded them. Everything within sight of the road had taken a beating from the Federal artillery. The buildings, if still standing, were scarred and chipped by shellfire; trees and fences around them were flattened.[97] When he visited the town itself, a few days later, he was surprised to find that Marietta had not been molested by either side.

Their third Fourth of July in the service came round, and to celebrate the occasion the Giddings Boys were issued a full ration of hardtack, bacon, and coffee, and everyone got a dram of liquor.[98] Even the soldiers in the hospital got a ration of ale. The brigade band came over to the hospital to entertain them, and small beer and music inspired the sick and wounded to sing along.[99] The soldiers of this war were always capable of creating cheering moments despite their hardships.

A soldier doing his duty along with the rest in Sherman's army wrote home to the newspaper in Conneaut to tell of such an event that took place the day before the Fourth of July. The soldiers were just beginning to stir their campfires back to life for breakfast when a brigade band began playing a hymn the boys had sung in their churches back home. Most everyone knew the words to "The Old One Hundred," and they began to sing. The bands on either side took it up, and the soldiers began singing all up and down the line. Before long thousands of voices were joined in this sanctifying hymn. The music died out after a while, but the normal gab and joking of young men preparing for yet another day of digging and fighting remained hushed.[100]

At last the Boys got into motion. They marched up a warren of twisting ridges and then down the reverse, busting brush all the way into the narrow valley of Nickajack Creek. Dead ahead, built into the sides and topping the ridges in front of them, sat the most intimidating line of defensive works any of them had ever seen. The Chattahoochee River lay just behind it.[101] Taking forts like this would be costly. For now, a rich reward waited for any boy who had the strength remaining to venture to the top of the nearest high ground, because the steeples and smokestacks of Atlanta shimmered from the other side of the river. "The sight of the city gave great encouragement to my men, who, seeing the prize which was to crown the campaign, looked cheerfully forward to its speedy possession," wrote their commander, John Geary.[102] Even Chaplain Ames, tired and sick, rode up to the top to take in the view.[103]

Sherman's last skillful maneuvering this side of the river would save them the horror of testing the rebel bastions lining the Chattahoochee. He succeeded in getting two bridgeheads established on the other shore, and Johnston began retreating across the river the next day.[104] Geary brought his command down to the banks of the Chattahoochee and set them to work beating the brush for the rebel stragglers. For the first time in a month, the regiment could sleep through the night without being disturbed by artillery, or callouts to support a skirmish line that had made contact with the enemy.

In their imaginations, the fabled Chattahoochee had grown to be as wide as the mighty Ohio, but once down to the banks it proved to be no wider in some places than Rock Creek, back in Ashtabula County. There were plenty of rebels on the other side, digging in, as was their custom, but they were not inclined to violence. The pickets on both sides of the river were close enough to holler friendly taunts and exchange gossip. In slack times, the boys at the bottom of the colossal military structure were always on speaking terms. They waded out to the middle of the Chattahoochee and traded coffee, of which they had plenty, for tobacco, of which they had none.[105] There was time here in the regiment's hillside camp above the river to contemplate the cost to them of having gotten this far. Within the ten days bracketing Sherman's big push on June 27, which came to be known as the battle of Kennesaw Mountain, a Giddings Regiment boy had been wounded every day. Gratefully, Pvt. George Williams had been the only one to die. However, the fights at Dug Gap, New Hope Church, and Pine Knob had cut deep gashes into them.

Since the start of this campaign more than forty men had died in battle; at least five more would die of their wounds in the weeks and months after the battles, and some wounded would not die of their injuries until forty years later.[106] One hundred thirty-two men had been wounded so badly they required hospital care; a handful had gone missing in skirmish and battle, including Wallace Hoyt; and dozens more had been sent away sick with intermittent fevers, dysentery, typhoid, and the other diseases incidental to soldiering.

They had been 350 strong when they crossed Mill Creek and started their climb up Rocky Face, back in early May. Now, on the banks of the Chattahoochee, they could muster only 150 men and officers.[107] Decades later they would claim they had been told by the mustering officer who came to give them their pay in this place that no regiment engaged in the campaign had lost as many men by this point in the Atlanta campaign.[108] Whether the mustering officer gave them reliable information or not, the Twenty-Ninth Ohio Infantry had paid mightily for the privilege of seeing the fabled city of Atlanta off in the distance.

They had nearly drowned in June's rain and mud. Back home in Ashtabula County the countryside was dying of thirst. An excursion party from the Conneaut newspaper rented a buggy in Ashtabula city and set sail down the Old Plank Road for Jefferson to see how their neighbors were faring.[109] They found little along the way of interest except for the dust, burned-out pastures, and struggling stands of corn and spindly wheat fields. Streams had left their beds and walked away. Wild fires burned through the fields, destroying valuable fencing, setting cattle free. Coming to Mill's Creek the day-trippers found a group of washerwomen on its banks. With cisterns at home empty and wells gone dry, women of the neighborhood had set up a day camp along one of the few streams that still flowed and were working and gossiping amid piles of laundry, boiling water in giant kettles, and pounding the wash clean in barrels.

Moving on to Jefferson, they passed by its notable sights: the old Giddings house, in which the recently passed old man had lived, the courthouse, and the town's finest hostelry, the American House. They could not leave without paying a visit to the man who had led the Twenty-Ninth Ohio, and also founded it, as he now claimed. They found Col. William T. Fitch flat on his back on a couch that he good naturedly called his "camp bed." He was as full of fire as ever from his top to his bottom. His injured leg, from which six inches of bone had been taken by Surgeon Fifield in the meadow below Dug Gap, was supported by a wooden birdcage apparatus secured to his leg with leather straps. He hoped to be up and moving shortly and back with his regiment.

For the first time in the Twenty-Ninth's career, there was genuine concern over how their losses would be made good without resort to the draft. The ability of Ashtabula County to supply volunteers to the Twenty-Ninth Ohio, and to the later regiments for which they'd been given responsibility, such as the 105th and 125th Ohio Infantries, was drying up. There were still eligible men left on the militia rolls, but no one knew how many of them would come willingly. The citizens were targets of unrelenting appeals to sign subscription lists by which they were obligated to contribute money to the local bounty fund, same as with a church tithing, and when they fell behind, the newspapers pestered them to pay up immediately.[110] In the war's opening days, Ashtabula County men had climbed over each other to get into the war. Many were now banding together in schemes to avoid it.

Men with cash could always buy their way off the hook by paying the three-hundred-dollar commutation fine or hiring a substitute. The less prosperous concluded that this was a rich man's war and a poor man's fight—but there were options. A group of one hundred sixty men in Geneva Township, in the northeast corner of Ashtabula County, men enough to restore the Twenty-Ninth Ohio from this one place alone, had organized a mutual protective association.[111] Each member put twenty-five dollars into a pool, and if his name was drawn in the coming draft, the fund paid the three-hundred-dollar commutation fee. The citizens back in northeast Ohio, anxious to save their neighborhood from the embarrassment of the next draft, recalled the ecstatic days of spring 1861, when men had been propelled into the army by nothing but patriotism. Now no amount of bounty money seemed adequate inducement. The town fathers of Akron were forced to concede that local backwardness in the matter of volunteering had become a downright humiliation.[112]

Back on the Chattahoochee their men, already in the war, rested. The Twenty-Ninth Ohio got their turn to cross to the other side of the last barrier between them and Atlanta on July 17. They took the pontoon bridge at Pace's Ferry at dusk, and once on the Atlanta side, got on the left branch of a two-headed road and marched east into the sultry Georgia night.[113]

26

Closing on the Prize

THE FALL AND OCCUPATION OF ATLANTA, JULY–NOVEMBER 1864

The Diarist Returns

Nathan Parmater had been left with the sick on the final approach to Dug Gap and was sent back up the line to Division Hospital no. 8, in Chattanooga, where he was put in a tent with four other boys. The same illness that had hit him on the march to Fredericksburg, back in 1862, was upon him again. The doctors dosed him with camphor, opium pills, whiskey, and quinine, but after taking the medicine he did not feel any better, and sometimes felt worse. Some days the most he could manage was a walk to the end of the tent to take a look at Lookout Mountain.[1] His regiment had marched far from the neighborhood where he'd last seen them, but he was still able to get some news of their travels. A soldier of Company C was in a nearby tent recovering from the amputation of his arm at Dug Gap, and from him Parmater got some particulars of the disaster he had missed by an eyelash. Over time, more wounded and sick from his regiment sifted back from the front into the Chattanooga hospitals, including his best friend, Chum Sterrett.

Life in a division hospital was dull but not unpleasant. The new recruits who had become patients complained about the food, but to veteran soldiers like Parmater, hospital rations were "First Best." There was plenty of soft bread, soups, fresh peas, and even lemonade once a day, and if they lacked anything, a lady from the U.S. Christian Commission visited every day with the promise that she would scour the local markets and bring it to them.

The Christian Commission conducted religious service every evening and twice on Sundays, which to the soldiers were as much entertainment as they were spiritual lessons. Saturday was the assigned day for changing clothes, which was easy enough to do, since the only item they had to change was their shirts. The hospital was short on socks and drawers and the boys went without. The long white shirts given to Parmater made a welcome connection with home. They were stamped "Northern Ohio," proving that the work of girls and women back home was reaching their soldiers.

It was hard to keep one's spirits aloft with from eight to fourteen boys dying every day in this hospital. Three of the five boys in Parmater's tent died. One soldier in his tent whom Parm liked especially, a boy called Sparks, had died so quietly during the night that Parmater was hardly disturbed by it. In early July, Parmater was judged well enough to tolerate the railroad trip to a larger hospital in Nashville. The cars that carried Parm and the others had built-in bunk beds, and each car had a water cooler and attendant. Although the ride was rough, and the stopping frequent due to breaks in the line, it was altogether superior to lying on a rough floor covered with straw and manure, which was the way the sick and wounded had ridden to the hospital centers not all that long ago.

Parmater was put in Cumberland Hospital in Nashville, which was a city unto itself with accommodations for three thousand sick and wounded. His ward consisted of two hospital tents stretched over wooden frames and joined at the ends. Each patient had an iron cot and ample white bedding. The walls were decorated with scalloped paper, and the pine plank floors were swept and scrubbed every day. Parmater found conditions here better than at Chattanooga, but the monotony identical. Anticipation of the next meal was all the soldiers had to look forward to.

Adjoining each ward was a framed cookhouse, and for those who could walk to it, there were tables set with white crockery plates and mugs. Boys capable of a longer walk visited the city's markets and brought back cucumbers, tomatoes, and peaches. The mainstay of their diet, here as in the field, was the same old boiled beef and army beans. It took as little as the gift of a genuine Illinois apple to brighten one of Parmater's days here. The soldier-patients got their pay even in the hospital, and the sutler's shop did a brisk business, especially in beer.

"Darkies," as Parmater called the contraband slaves who worked around the hospital, had a camp of their own on the grounds, where they did the hospital laundry and lived. Parmater thought the sight of them at work and at play worthy of a picture in *Frank Leslie's Illustrated*. There were Negro soldiers doing duty around the hospital, and relations between the races did not always come off smoothly. One of the colored soldiers, who had been pestered by a group of white soldiers, pulled his pistol and shot one of them in the leg.

Around the time that Sherman's army was getting across the Chattahoochee River, an examining board came round the hospital to see who was fit enough to return to the fighting. Although he did not feel recovered, Parmater passed the examination, and he blamed the doctor for his inhumanity; he was likely a copperhead. Boys were judged strong enough to fight who could still barely walk.

The "sick squad" was marched over to the Zollicoffer house under an armed guard and locked up in a large room until transportation south was arranged. The boys sat on the window sills and watched the busy life of Nashville traipse past. Parmater's trip back to the front was hardly as luxurious as the one away from it. To avoid the crowd inside the boxcars, he climbed onto the roof and made his bed. At Chattanooga his squad of three hundred was marched to a supply depot to draw muskets and then herded back onto the cars. Twenty miles out from Atlanta, he heard the sound of heavy cannon fire. On the Atlanta side of the river, the train unloaded its cargo, and the boys hoofed the last miles to their outfits.

Parmater found his regiment installed behind strong breastworks on the left of the railroad, three miles north of Atlanta, and living in their shelter tents close behind the lines. Constant rifle fire punctuated by the bang of artillery made an awful racket at all hours of the day and night, but as always the Boys were in good spirits. Parmater had been gone for three months and he noticed at once how few of them were left.[2] His own company could muster only thirteen men. Two weeks before Parmater's homecoming, the Twenty-Ninth had crossed the Chattahoochee and stumbled into a major battle with Hood's men.

The Battle of Peach Tree Creek, July 20, 1864

Sherman had spread his army out in an arc around the northern approaches to Atlanta and prepared to test the strength of its outer defensive ring. Upon getting across, Hooker's corps moved to the left along the river and then turned toward the city, where Peach Tree Creek joined the Chattahoochee. The land here was flatter than on the north side of the Chattahoochee, but just as choked with brush, and creased by marshy-bottomed ravines. Geary approached the twenty-foot wide Peach Tree Creek by stealth, softened the terrain ahead with artillery, and crossed.[3] During the night and the morning of the next day, Brig. Gen. Alpheus Williams's division and Brig. Gen. William T. Ward's brigade, Geary's division, crossed and took up positions to Geary's left and right. With everything in place, the Federals moved forward.

Geary's skirmish line ran into solid contact before going very far. Candy's brigade came up right behind, gained two ridges and then a third, upon which they paused and dug in.[4] The plan called for all of Hooker's divisions to move forward in unison, but because of the terrain and the speed of Candy's advance, the plan did not come off in synchrony. Candy had pushed out five hundred yards forward of supporting divisions on their flanks, and the skirmish lines of the divisions on either side of him had a time of it just keeping up with Geary's main line.[5] Geary spied a hill several hundred yards forward, and, deeming it an objective, he ordered the Thirty-Third New Jersey Infantry up to take it. Geary himself rode out to the hill to see what he could see.

While on his way, he met three rebel prisoners on their way to the rear. Geary had always placed great credence in what prisoners or locals told him. Back at Thoroughfare Gap, Virginia, in 1862, innocent to the possibility that locals in the enemy's country might want to deceive him, he had believed their faulty intelligence that his command was about to be annihilated, burned all of his supplies, and fled at top speed for a safer locale. Here in the meadow in front of his line at Peach Tree Creek, the three prisoners told him there was not a rebel force within two miles.[6] The Thirty-Third New Jersey was already more than a half mile forward of any help, but Geary ordered them to go forward even further. They had barely stepped off the hill when the battle of Peach Tree Creek flashed into existence, quick as a struck match.

Where a moment before there had been no enemy, there were now thousands stepping briskly out of the woods seventy-five yards away, yelling and firing as they came on. The boys of the Thirty-Third New Jersey ran for their lives and got back to the main line, but minus their flag. Geary came back at a gallop, leapt over the line, and yelled, "A general engagement! Hold your ground. I will bring up the main line!" and the boys cheered him for his élan.[7] The rebels quickly closed the ground and stormed Geary's line, which at this moment consisted entirely of Candy's brigade on a low ridge. In front of them was a cleared field several hundred yards wide, rare for this neighborhood. To the left of it lay the seemingly impenetrable thickets bordering Tanyard Branch, of Peach Tree Creek, and to their right, a ravine thought too deep for troops to traverse.[8] Candy formed a double line of battle and installed the thin line of the Twenty-Ninth Ohio behind, and the Twenty-Eighth Pennsylvania behind them as reserve. Candy's soldiers suddenly found themselves an island, with rebel waves pounding it from the front and overlapping its right and rear. If something was not done pretty quickly, they were going to be overrun.[9]

As soon as Myron Wright got his soldiers into position, he put them to work building a fallback defensive line just in the rear of Candy's main line. They were still working on it when the regiment on their right disintegrated. The Giddings Boys were now taking fire in their flank and rear. Myron Wright admitted they were forced to fall back in "some disorder."[10] Elsewhere along Hooker's line companies and regiments fell apart; soldiers scared out of their wits shucked their rifles and packs and hightailed it to the rear, their officers powerless to stop them. The Twenty-Ninth Ohio's retirement had not been a skedaddle. Wright re-formed them just back of the ridge while Candy held on, waiting for help.

Geary would not be rattled by any of it. He took stock of the situation, and while the ground and sky were torn by a level of fury that few of them had witnessed, he gave orders that averted disaster. If the rebels got control of his artillery, the day would be lost. He sent five regiments to defend it and stabilized his main line by changing front so that the ends were angled to deliver end-on fire into the rebels, and he brought up and fitted in his other two brigades. For Candy's soldiers, the arrival of the second and third brigades of their division could not have been timelier.[11] It had been only by desperate, sometimes hand-to-hand fighting that they had held on. With the whole of their division now up, everyone got down to the business of punishing the rebels for their audacity.

The enemy came on like a mob with flags, their officers galloping from point to point waving swords and urging the men forward.[12] It was one of the war's grandest scenes, perfectly sublime were it not for the musket and artillery fire that struck them, sending severed limbs and knapsacks tumbling. The bravery the rebels showed this day would long be remembered by the Union boys who shot them down.

From their place in the rear of the battle line, the Giddings Regiment was ordered to fall back to the line of works from which Geary had started the day. Their mission was to rally other troops that had been driven back. They stayed there until six o'clock, when they were moved up to support Candy, but by then the battle was sputtering out.[13] Charles Candy was a no-nonsense officer of the old school who called a spade a spade and did not apologize for the weakness of anyone. Therefore, when he stated that the Twenty-Ninth Ohio had been "compelled" to fall back under murderous fire that came at them both flank and rear, his word is to be trusted.[14] The Giddings Boys had been forced to give way, as everyone admitted, but not every one of them had fallen back. One veteran recalled that some of them stayed and fought through the hottest parts of one of the hottest battles ever fought.

A quarter century later, Sgt. Henry E. Clarke of Company B found a chair at the soldiers' home in Dayton, Ohio, and wrote a memoir of the battle of Peach Tree Creek.[15] He remembered this battle with special clarity because he had been captured. Some moments stood out in high relief: the peculiar stillness just before the rebel attack, the rebel kee-yip as they boiled out of the woods like wasps from a hive, and the smoke so heavy Clarke could not see the end of their line.

When the Twenty-Ninth Ohio fell back to the bottom of the ridge, he and some of the other Boys stayed behind to fight it out. The men tending the guns began to fall, and Clarke and his comrades stepped up to take their places. They turned a pair of guns toward the rebels threatening their flank and worked them for all they were worth. The rebels came on in droves, attacking the guns from the right, right rear, and front. Clarke and the others decided to stay and sell their lives as dearly as possible. Then, the inevitable: the rebels took the guns, and Clarke with them.

There had been other acts of heroism that afternoon south of Peach Tree Creek, things so small that only the soldier's family would know of them. All three of the Dowling men had enlisted in the Twenty-Ninth back in 1861, although the father, Thomas, was already in his midforties and well beyond the prime of life for that day, and his son Peter may have been as young as fourteen.[16] Michael had been one of the dozens who died of disease in the regiment's first months in the war. Peter was captured at Port Republic and again at Chancellorsville. Their father, Thomas, had been shot at Cedar Mountain, rendering his hand permanently useless. He stayed with the regiment, and was shot through the chest and shoulder at Gettysburg.[17] He was too shot up now to work a rifle. He talked his officers into letting him stay on as a litter bearer.

While carrying one of their wounded off the field at Peach Tree Creek, Thomas Dowling was shot through the lower chest, the ball passing through his lung and shoulder blade, and exiting near his spine. Although he was listed as wounded in the battle, he was in reality one of its dead. He made it home to Painesville, but died five years after the war ended, and no one disputed that the cause of death had been the wounds he sustained at Peach Tree Creek.[18] Dowling was one of a dozen in the Twenty-Ninth Regiment who were hit that day. Their color bearer had been shot, but their flag was safe. Two Boys had been killed. Henry Clarke had not been the only Twenty-Ninth Ohio soldier taken prisoner. John C. Shaw, one of the regiment's orphans from New York City, was also captured.

Shaw's parents died when he was nine, and after a brief stay with an uncle, he was placed in an orphanage. The Children's Aid Society took him in and sent him out to Ohio by train for adoption. He was a well-developed, yellow-haired boy of fifteen when he enlisted in Company C, and was sixteen years old when he was wounded in the leg, shoulder, and hand at Cedar Mountain. The story of how he was captured at Peach Tree Creek was passed to me by a retired Iowa farmer who happened to be Shaw's grandson.[19]

A rebel grabbed Shaw by the belt during the thickest part of the fight, stuck a pistol in his side, and greeted him, "How are you, Yank?" On the way to the rear, he was stopped by a rebel officer, grievously wounded in the legs, and leaned against a tree. He wanted to kill one more Yankee before he died and he demanded a pistol; the order was either refused, or the officer died before he could execute Shaw. Either way, Shaw was marched and freighted down to a prison camp some miles below Atlanta known as Andersonville. Shaw was to spend at least two months there. He was transferred to another rebel prison pen in Florence, South Carolina. Shaw came out of the rebel prison system a skeleton. Twenty-five years later, he still weighed but 120 pounds, although he was a tall man. His teeth had rotted out and his joints were perpetually swollen to twice their size from scurvy. His sons had to carry him up the flight of stairs to the doctor's office in the small Iowa town where he homesteaded after the war.

The evening of the battle of Peach Tree Creek, dusk had come, and the maelstrom that had threatened to pull every living thing around into it had relented. The evening relaxed into the now completely normal sounds of sporadic firing out on the skirmish line and the complex sighs and moans of the many hundreds of wounded men out between the lines. It had been touch and go for a while. The rebels had gotten to within a few yards of Geary's guns, close enough at times to touch the barrels before they were blown into molecules by grapeshot and canister or brained by swung muskets.[20] Geary's boys had repelled numerous charges in the three hours the battle had taken to fight, and they had stood their ground. They were too tired to make any sort of camp and fell on the ground in heaps and were instantly asleep not far from what is today the Bitsy Grant Tennis Center. One old veteran recalled coming into such a bivouac on the night of one of these battles: except for an occasional cough or dreamy mumble, the sleepers resembled dead men.

The morning after the battle of Peach Tree Creek, the soldiers walked out onto the field to inspect the damage and bury the dead. Not since Culp's Hill had they seen a landscape so thoroughly shredded.[21] Hardly a tree or bush had escaped destruction. The rebels had suffered severely. General Geary reported that he buried precisely 409 rebels in front of his line. Probably another two hundred of the Confederate dead had been carried away by their comrades.[22] All told, as many as twenty-five hundred rebels had been killed or wounded directly in front of his division.[23] The battle had been fought by two armies of twenty thousand each along a line that ran two miles. One of the spearheads of the rebel attack had been thrown against Geary, and he had deflected it.

Hood had replaced Johnston as head of the rebel army, and the battle of Peach Tree Creek had been his first test. His strategy of slowing Sherman by hitting a portion of his army with everything he had, failed. When it was over, Thomas's army had not been pushed back measurably anywhere.

A larger and more desperate battle would be fought two days later a few miles east and south of here. The battle of Atlanta would produce another ten thousand casualties on each side. Sherman's friend and protégé Gen. James McPherson would be killed. When it was over, both sides burrowed into the ground and began the siege of Atlanta. For this work, the soldiers of Hooker's Twentieth Corps would have a new general.

An incident had occurred that had not injured Joe Hooker physically but had hurt his pride, which to a man like Hooker was worse. By seniority, Hooker was next in line for the dead McPherson's job. Sherman thought better of giving it to him, and Hooker resigned in a huff. In his place, they would have the brave but cautious man who had commanded them in the Chancellorsville and Gettysburg campaigns, Maj. Gen. Henry W. Slocum.

Three weeks had passed since the battle of Peach Tree Creek when Parmater returned to his regiment. The Boys were already well seasoned in a type of military operation that had been new to them when they began it: laying siege to a city.

Siege

The Giddings Boys spent their duty hours in defensive works that had been dug deeper and were thrown up higher than any they'd held to this point. The rebels were entrenched behind works equally strong, and between the main lines, the skirmishers of both sides worked. Travel out to the skirmish pits was too dangerous in daylight and had to wait for night. Squads of soldiers crept out into the no-man's-land and dropped into holes big enough to accommodate four or five.[24] Dirt had been pushed up and banked in place with a few rails. The rebel pickets were only a few rods away, in pits of their own, and any man who showed his head above the dirt had a bullet immediately after him. Life in the main line was not much safer, with the constant zip of minié balls coming from sources unseen and the occasional explosion of big shells that came to them from places too far forward to locate. Parmater took his turn in the skirmish pits and in the line: "We retire regularly to rest in the main line but cannot tell whether we will awake in this world or another but trust ourselves to God who is able to keep us and try to do our duty as good soldiers."[25]

Just how dangerous life was, even behind the lines, was proven a few days after their arrival. Major Myron Wright was propped up in his hospital bed eating the wounded man's diet of applesauce, tea, Boston crackers, and cornstarch, listening to the steady thump of artillery, and writing a letter home to his old friend Lewis P. Buckley. He was wrestling with the question of what he would do with himself if his injury kept him from returning to his regiment when news came to him that several of the Boys had just been hit.[26]

The rebels had removed a six-inch Dahlgren gun from the gunboat *Chattahoochee* and mounted it in an earthen fort near Peachtree Street, a mile to the Twenty-Ninth's front.[27] The Boys had been standing in the rear drawing rations when a sixty-four-pound shell dropped on top of them. Sgt. Ransom Billings was killed instantly and Christopher Beck's leg taken off below the knee. Beck had been weary of the war a year into it, but had stayed with the regiment. After losing his leg, he made it up the line as far as Kingston, Georgia, before dying six weeks later.[28]

Nearly every soldier in the Twenty-Ninth Ohio had a story of a close call while in or behind these lines. Sgt. Cains C. Lord informed his father that a six-inch-diameter shell had come within a half foot of taking his head off while he was resting in his tent. The three other Homerville Boys he had tented with for years had all been lost fighting in this campaign.[29] Parmater was stunned at how perfectly reckless they had all become. They had learned that a bullet traveled faster than the brain, and if it were a man's fate to be hit, he would be hit. Sometimes the picket firing flared and threatened to rise to something general, but the boys slept through this kind of thing and did not rouse themselves until they judged it too close to ignore.[30]

There were rumors of a rebel army massing to assault them, and the boys put on their traps, but the "Johns" did not show, and they were disappointed.[31] Sherman's army was spread out in a battle line thirteen miles long, and although the rebels made daily attempts to break it at various points, they had not succeeded, nor had the Federals made much progress of their own. The two armies were locked together more tightly than they had been on the other side of the river.

Sherman was growing weary of the deadlock and decided to break it by sending a cavalry force of ten thousand in a pincer sweep aimed at cutting the railroad below Atlanta. If General Stoneman's part of the expedition could handle what opposition was thrown against it, he was to free the Federal officers from the rebel prison in Macon and then move on to liberate the enlisted men being held south of there at Andersonville. A few emaciated soldiers had escaped Andersonville and made their way back into Union lines with reports of conditions so dreadful that at first it was thought they must be exaggerating. Ames heard that Stoneman's great cavalry raid had failed, and a while later he saw the proof of it. What was left of McCook's cavalry passed near the hospital, both men and horses utterly worn out.

One morning before sunrise, every artillery piece in the Twentieth Corps went off up and down the line. They were answering a small barrage the rebel guns had sent over to wake them the morning before. The Giddings Boys rushed up to the works for a chance to enjoy the discomfiture of their enemies and laughed heartily at the sight of falling shells throwing up geysers of dirt, splintered lumber, and men.[32] Behind the line at the hospital, Ames heard the firing, terrible for its rapidity, and wondered what unfortunate part of the city had been on the receiving end of it.[33]

Regular battles had come off within their hearing at places down the line—Ezra Church, along the Lick Skillet road, and at Utoy Creek—but none of these had turned the trick. Sherman ordered the biggest guns in the Federal arsenal brought down from Chattanooga. Some of these were mounted in Geary's line, and they began throwing giant shells into the city at five-minute intervals. The Giddings Boys were no more than two miles away from the targets, more than close enough to hear the shell crashing through a roof, blasting down the walls, and setting the place on fire.[34] From inside the hospital, Ames could hear the church bells of Atlanta clanging the fire alarm.[35]

On the morning of August 22, the boys awoke to a novel quietude. They had received an order not to fire unless the rebels came at them in force. The pickets of both sides climbed out of their holes and met in the middle ground to swap rumors, and newspapers.[36] The fear of being wounded could be put aside at least for the moment. Other threats to one's health marched on. They tried their best to keep themselves clean by spit-bathing and discarding sweat- and dirt-encrusted clothes for new, but these were not adequate measures to fend off sickness, as in the case of disease caused by a diet deficient in fresh vegetables.

Made bold by his victory over the Federal cavalry, Maj. Gen. Joseph Wheeler took his rebel troopers north and onto the railroad at Marietta, then Cassville, and all the way up to Dalton, temporarily cutting Sherman's supply line. The soldiers in the trenches would suffer on account of Wheeler's raiding. With the line closed, the boys went without vegetables, and their incipient scurvy worsened. As soon as the railroad was reopened and supplies flowed again, including vegetables, the scurvy abated and the patient load in the division hospital dipped.[37] The form of scurvy that seemed to plague everyone in the siege line was mysterious to the army doctors who observed it, with its visible signs of yellow, listless eyes, sore joints, and loss of weight and energy.[38]

The soldiers labored on despite it, and kept free of the hospital—unless they fell to one of the diseases the scurvy had set them up for. Parmater was given pills for the illness that still pestered him, but he knew from experience that the cure could be worse than the disease: "Not feeling very well I reported myself to the Dr., he gave me some medicine and also reported me for duty, and as I did not feel able to stand both medicine and duty I threw away the medicine."[39] Cases of diarrhea, scurvy, congested lungs, and typhoid swelled the population of the division hospital to nearly three hundred. Some boys were clinging to life by a whisker and it took very little to push them over the edge. One boy under Ames's care died after a musket, leaned up against a tent pole by a visiting soldier, hit him on the head. The blow had not been hard, but it was enough, and the soldier died.[40] Fewer wounded came into the hospital, but their injuries were more perplexing. A large share of the wounded had suffered head injuries caused by artillery shells. The symptoms that Ames observed ranged from loss of reason to exposed brains, and there was little the surgeons could do to fix them. Ames continued to escort dead soldiers to the burial grounds. Few of the parents of enlisted men had the pocketbook to bring their son's remains home. For those who could afford it, clear advice was given on how the process should be approached.

In this age of Victorian funeral customs, parents might dress their stillborn infants in baptism gowns and pose the family around them for photographs, and ladies wove snatches of their deceased soldier's hair into decorative knots and placed them in lockets, rings, and necklaces. Thus, a correspondent for the sanitary commission did not think it ghoulish in the least to write home to Akron with a breakdown of costs for bringing a dead soldier home: metal coffin: $95; a nonmetallic model (but also fine): $50; embalming: around $25; and express shipment to Akron, about $35. It would behoove one, as the writer pointed out, to use the services of the Sanitary Commission because they were able to get a discount of five dollars per coffin. Interested parties should address their requests to W. R. Cornelius or Dr. Prunk, Market Street, Chattanooga, Tennessee, with the full name of the loved one, rank, and regiment, and they would take care of the particulars without further bother to friends or family.[41]

Heat and humidity required that an expired enlisted man for whom no embalming arrangements had been made be put in the ground immediately. By the end of August the hospital staff had built a neat burying ground and enclosed it with a stone wall. Fifteen boys from Geary's division were buried there, each grave clearly marked so that in future years visitors could find them.[42] Boys were buried by candlelight, with their rank, name, regiment, and name of their hometown written on a scrap of paper and placed in a corked bottle, put in with them at the foot of the grave, which was the method used by Chaplain Ames. A friend might supply a rude coffin, cobbled together from doors and siding scavenged from a building, but most went into the ground wrapped in an army blanket.

Ames was concerned that a soldier's grave be properly marked so it could be easily found, but there was no guarantee that the grave would be either found or respected once the army pulled out. It had become the job of the army's overwhelmed Quartermaster Department to come along after the armies and collect the dead in a central location, such as the cemetery in Marietta, where several dozen Giddings Boys would ultimately be reburied. The Sanitary Commission had begun a register, through which a loved one could verify a son or husband's death and discover the exact circumstances of it.[43] This service covered only those dead laid in the ground around the big Federal hospital complexes like at Chattanooga, and keeping track of who was buried in just that one place was an arduous task. Over six thousand were already buried there, and at the time of that grim census, the Atlanta campaign had not even begun.

Over all of the dead Ames prayed, "Peace be to their ashes. May their deeds of valor be remembered by a grateful people."[44] Ames never took for granted what the common boys were giving to end this rebellion. He admired them more than he did their officers. He would always find at least some of the officers suspect, either for their carousing or for allowing the boys of whom they had moral charge to imitate their bad behavior. A gunshot case was brought into the hospital and died soon after. He had gotten into a tussle with a soldier of the provost guard and been shot. Ames noted that both parties had been freely indulging.[45]

Parmater had been bothered, severely so since returning to the regiment, with what he described as "the disease common to camp life," by which he meant dysentery. Beans and boiled beef for every meal would not promote a cure, but it was eat that or die of starvation. Parmater stayed clear of the hospital by keeping to his tent when he could, resting, reading, writing letters, and working on his newest trinket project, which was fashioning a locket from two brass uniform buttons.

Ames suffered from the same scourge. He found the best relief came from working harder, and praying harder. He received a letter that his beloved son, Edwin, had finished his three years of service in the Second Ohio Light Artillery and had made it safely back to the family home, in Conneaut. Ames thanked God for the kindness shown him by allowing his son to pass safely through the war. But his peace of mind over improved conditions at home was short lived.[46] A short while later, he received a letter from his wife saying she was unhappy and discontented. Three years of worry and uncertainty was producing that effect in many people back home.

Progress

Camp gossip in the Giddings Regiment had predicted a general movement for days. The cease-fire Parmater had witnessed was Sherman's first step in it. With a big plan ready to be set into motion, he did not want a skirmish to spark into something larger. With one week in August remaining, he decided on a bold stroke. He pulled most of his army out of the line and sent them south and west to converge on the town of Jonesboro, twenty miles south of Atlanta. Slocum's corps was to fall back to the Chattahoochee River, where they would cover the river crossings. Parmater captured the complexities of the movement in a nutshell: "We are to guard the R.R. and wagon train while the right wing cuts itself loose and goes for the Johnnies."[47]

They started off at nine in the evening and by daylight were back at the Chattahoochee, two miles above the railroad bridge. The Boys set to work building trenches, clearing brush and trees to improve the field of fire, and with better material at hand, went to building shanties. Unknown to the boys on the banks of the river, the army had met the rebels at Jonesboro and broken them. Atlanta's last rail link to the rest of the Confederacy was in Union hands, and Hood made haste to evacuate Atlanta. No soldier who saw the spectacle of the city in its death throes ever forgot it.

It was after midnight on September 2 when the dark over Atlanta began to pulse red and orange. A few moments later, great explosions were heard, and ground tremors disturbed the boys asleep in their shanties, back on the Chattahoochee. They got up to take in the sight of flames throwing off tornadoes of sparks over the center of Atlanta, followed by more explosions. Some thought at first that the army was testing some new supercannon. When morning came, the intelligence arrived that the rebels had blown up dozens of boxcars loaded with ammunition, steam locomotives, and everything else that might be of use to Sherman. Geary's division moved forward at once into the city to see if the rebels had truly deserted it.

Two regiments of Ireland's Third Brigade were the first Union troops to get to the city hall. The boys of the Sixtieth New York and the 111th Pennsylvania climbed to the top and hoisted their flags, securing another first for the White Star Division.[48] The Giddings Boys were as anxious as the rest to get a look at the conquered city, but Candy's brigade was ordered to stay behind on the river. For the first time in many weeks, they could now come out in the open without fear. To celebrate this memorable occasion, Parmater waded into the Chattahoochee and had a good wash.[49]

That Sunday morning the brigade lined up and marched to Atlanta. By this time, Col. Charles Candy, the man who had commanded their brigade going back to the time of Antietam, had finished his enlistment term and departed.[50] Leading them on their triumphant march into Atlanta was their new brigade commander, Ario Pardee Jr. of the 147th Pennsylvania Infantry. He marched them so quickly that many boys had to drop out. Parmater concluded that their leader must have been anxious to "get to Town," which was enlisted-man parlance that the officers were in a hurry to get to the closest saloon.[51] They reached their old trench lines at noon, stopped for dinner, and then marched into the city proper. Parmater recorded the scene: "The city itself is badly cut to pieces, with shot and shell, there are many nice buildings completely ruined, it is the nicest looking place I have seen in the south but it is rather desolate now as most of the inhabitants have left their nice homes and many of them are being torn down to make bunks for Yankees to sleep on."[52]

They continued on through the town with their flags unfurled and the brigade band sending up a cheery tune. The passed along Whitehall Street, where commercial buildings stood shoulder to shoulder, some of them with large signs painted on the sides showing that the owner had been in the slave auction business. The black folk watching the parade cheered, while the white folk stood by looking downcast. The regiment continued through the devastated town and out into a rural area in the western outskirts, where they took possession of a recently abandoned section of rebel fortifications known as Whitehall Fort, after the ancient tavern that stood close by.

Pardee arranged his new command in the rebel works with his left near an old racetrack and his right on the Turner's Ferry road where it intersected the works and one of the city's major east-west roads, Green Street.[53] If a boy cared to walk over and inspect the colossal destruction Hood had ordered, his gunpowder magazine and the shops, sheds, cars, and locomotives of the Western and Atlantic Railroad were a mile away. Standing nearer at hand were the remains of the Atlanta arsenal.

What the artillery bombardment had started, the boys now finished. Enlisted men were not allowed to move into the houses that still stood, but they were not prohibited from taking them apart for the good shanty material they held. The eight-by-ten-foot shanty Parmater and his friends built featured French doors made from a pair of large shutters torn from a house near their camp. They spent a week here perfecting their huts, when orders came to tear off their shelter-tent roofs, pack, and move. They headed east and back through the city. The location of the place where they would spend the next ten weeks was never described exactly, except that it was two miles east and south of the place where they'd first camped and that it was distinctive for the two large siege guns that the rebels had left behind in a fort.[54] Parmater found the new location advantageous for tuggy building since there were more residences nearby than at their first city camp. Parmater strolled through the abandoned forts and the ruined neighborhoods, and he felt unaccountably lonely.

The Boys had long ago hardened themselves to so much destruction and death, caused to them or by them. Two and a half years earlier, when they had all been innocents, some of them had hiked down from their camp all the way into Paw Paw, Virginia, to stand and gape at the corpses of two dead Union soldiers in the back of an ambulance. Parmater took a walk one day and saw a soldier playing with a skull, tossing it around and throwing rocks at it, oblivious to the fact that it had once held someone's brains, and life.[55]

They had begun the Atlanta campaign four months ago, and that campaign was now over. What might come next was anyone's guess. Sgt. Parmater had not been with the regiment since the fight at Dug Gap, and came back after its last, which had been Peach Tree Creek. On the news of the surrender of Atlanta he said, "So now the Gate City is ours and that without much loss."[56] That was a true enough statement of the part he had seen. For his regiment, Candy's brigade, and the whole of Geary's division, the cost of it all had been very high.

The command of every regiment in the White Star Division, except three, had changed hands at least once. Of the seven thousand men of Geary's division who had come over Taylor's Ridge and into the valley over which Rocky Face towered, twenty-five hundred had been killed, wounded, or like Wallace Hoyt, vanished.[57] Another five hundred had fallen out along the way from the effects of disease. In their own brigade 143 had been killed, 750 wounded, and 30 captured or missing.[58] It was a wonder Candy's brigade had survived.

Garrison Life: Atlanta

Forty rebels too sick to march away with Hood had been left behind and were taken in by the division hospital, where Chaplain Ames now spent most of his time. They were dirty, ragged, and hungry boys, misguided in their loyalties, but boys nonetheless, and the surgeons and their helpers cared for them same as they did their own, even in death.

J. H. Chitty, Fifth Georgia Cavalry, had died before the city fell, his remains left behind for the Yankees to bury. W. E. Read, Company F, Fifty-Sixth Alabama Cavalry, came in very low and soon died.[59] Both men were buried with the same formality and prayers due any Union soldier, in a cemetery that Ames had helped the hospital director select. They were followed the next day by Pvt. Barney Brick of Chaplain Ames's own regiment. Brick had succumbed to disease. A few days later, Cpl. C. P. Douglass, Company C, Ninth Texas, was buried in a way that might have set him spinning in his grave. A black man by the name of Green Ward died at the same time as he. Ames was in attendance: "We buried them both this P.M. side by side in our chosen cemetery with our men. Service at the grave. Thus our common dust mingles to-gether in the embrace of Mother Earth."[60]

The city recovered itself, and a few days after its collapse the streets were again filled with an impressive level of activity, albeit most of it military. Thousands of rebel prisoners were marched in long columns past the hospital where Chaplain Ames worked, some of them falling out for a stay in it. Settled in one place again, the soldiers resorted to proven methods of entertainment. Ames observed that the "Provost business was brisk," his dry way of saying that the boys had located liquor and were raising Cain.[61]

The long campaign that had brought them all the way from Bridgeport was over, but Ames's services were in demand as much as they ever were, and he was used up by the work. Accommodations for him and the others working in the hospital would improve shortly. Sherman had ordered every resident having a relative in the rebel army to pack up and get out. A Mrs. Johnson owned a house on the grounds of the hospital, and when she moved out the Union officers moved in. For the first time in ages, Ames had a room to himself.[62]

A Dr. Cooper had come all the way from the medical director's office in Washington on a tour of the army's medical department in this theater.[63] Ames allowed that he may have been an excellent physician, but in manners and appearance he was coarse and slovenly. His worst attribute was that he had no sympathy for his fellow man, sick or healthy, which to Ames was an abomination. By contrast, Ames found the rebel surgeons who had stayed behind to care for their men, and who shared mess with Ames, to be gentlemen in every respect, and as dedicated to alleviating suffering as the Union doctors.[64] In their persons, their uniforms were simple but clean and neat.

The Boys did picket duty in this undisturbed place, lounged around the works, and when the sun burned too hot or it rained, got under the dirt roofs of the ingenious dugouts the rebels had left behind. They chewed over the many rumors that ran up and down the line: Sherman had chased down Hood and destroyed him, Jefferson Davis had thrown in the towel and asked for peace, and Phil Sheridan had cleared the Shenandoah Valley once and for all and destroyed every particle of material of potential use to the rebels. Only the last of these held up as being truthful.

One night after everyone had gone to bed, a rider galloped through their camp shouting the good news that Richmond had fallen. Everyone hustled out into the company streets to cheer and slap each other on the back, and every band in the division made joyful music. The whooping went on for three hours, until the boys blew themselves out and went back to bed.[65] The reaction of the soldiers in the Twenty-Ninth's brigade was subdued compared to the others because, as Parmater said, "They begin to think it does not pay to cheer until there is certainty of the dispatch being true."[66] Later news confirmed that Richmond had not fallen.

Rumors continued to speed in and out of camp, enjoyed for the round of debates each set off more than for the truth they might contain. From here, they might go to South Carolina, down to Texas or Mississippi, or up the line to Nashville. They might even return to the Army of the Potomac and help Grant crush Lee. A feeling persisted with some soldiers, like Sgt. Cains C. Lord, that the fighting here with Sherman was a sideshow and that the big show was in the East. "The fact of the matter is, the rebels have got their biggest and best army in Virginia, and their best generals. I wish we had such an army as the army of the Potomac down here. We would eat up Hood's army for breakfast."[67]

Wherever they might go, they were now more confident than ever of final victory. Sherman had sent a circular around congratulating the army on its successes, and the boys were in accord with his belief that "Nothing is impossible in an army like this."[68] One day in late September, Parmater marked the third anniversary of his life as a soldier and reflected in his diary on the war's only remaining mystery: "How little did we think that this war could last three years and yet the question is when will it end?"[69]

The Hired Men

Capt. Wilbur F. Stevens left without farewell speeches, published resolutions, or parting gifts. Some would say later that he had been driven out. In truth, he had gone home to get married and take care of his elderly parents, having honorably served his three-year term of enlistment. Dr. Amos Fifield went home too. The regiment's first surgeon had proved himself both "a good operator and executive officer," Ames thought.[70] The two dozen or so boys who had not reenlisted as veteran volunteers and had survived the campaign through mid-August went home without fanfare. Others arrived to replace them.

They had been in the forts west of town only a few days when a sixty-man squad of men in new uniforms marched into the camp, and not one of them had come voluntarily. The most recent draft had not succeeded in pushing men out ahead of it into voluntary enlistment despite the bounties offered. The citizens of the Reserve had always feared the embarrassment of having to resort to the draft, and by the summer of 1864, Ashtabula County had not come near reaching the bottom of the lists of eligible men. However, it had exhausted the supply of men who would enlist. Having accepted the ignominy of the draft, and the hiring of substitutes, the Conneaut newspaper encouraged the wealthy among them already exempt from service, including women, to show their patriotism by hiring a substitute to represent them on the battlefield.[71] Every man of this first allotment of new soldiers had not been drafted directly but hired as a substitute by a drafted man with a pocketbook fat enough to buy his way out.[72]

The hired men had come down to the regiment without an ounce of military training, as it appeared to the veterans. Parmater had been studying his tactics and drill books religiously for months, and perhaps on account of his leg up over the others in military knowledge he was given the duty of drilling them. He disliked acting as drillmaster for the "awkward squad" as much as he did filling out army paperwork.[73] Aside from the clumsiness expected of any new recruit, however, they seem to have been quietly fitted in, and the regiment went about its business. Parmater thought it pleasant to have so many men in his company again.[74]

Before they left Atlanta, the regiment would be restored to about the same manpower level it had enjoyed when it left Bridgeport, last May, and by some accounts as strong as it had been going way back to before their first battle, at Kernstown. In round numbers, nearly 280 new men came to them in Atlanta, 200 alone on the day before Halloween, none of them a volunteer.[75] Before this, the regiment had always been made up of men from a handful of counties in northeastern Ohio. With the arrival of the new soldiers, there were now men in their ranks from at least seventeen counties.[76] A few of the new soldiers came from much further away and may have once been sworn enemies of the Union.

Men motivated by the hefty commissions that might be made from it applied to the governor of Ohio for appointments to act as agents for their respective county in procuring enlistments in the Southern states. Mr. J. B. Phillips of Orwell, Ashtabula County, was one of these. Back when the regiment had been organizing at Jefferson, Phillips had been one of the lucky men to get authority to recruit for the Twenty-Ninth Ohio, but he did not bring a single soldier to the Giddings Regiment. He now turned his attention to a more profitable line. After getting his appointment, he went south and set up an office in Nashville, where he apparently enjoyed some success.[77] He focused on rebel prisoners who disliked the prospect of prison enough that they took the oath of allegiance to the Union and changed sides. Among the new men marched into the Twenty-Ninth Ohio's camp in Atlanta were five soldiers of distinctly Southern origins: two from Kentucky, one from Alabama, and two from Tennessee.[78]

As in any stationary camp, reviews were scheduled, and the Boys set to polishing themselves and their gear. The veterans had not practiced the foot-tripping evolutions of the drill since back in Bridgeport, and although they passed inspection when General Geary reviewed them, it was admitted that all—veterans and new men alike—had been awkward.[79] At one of these, General Sherman rode over. His was a familiar face to the boys of the regiment, but to Parmater he was an unknown. On seeing him for the first time Parmater remarked, "The General is a very plain looking man and makes one think of an old cattle buyer more than a noted General."[80]

The Erstwhile Cowboy and Other Adventures

Life in the regiment in this period was not without its adventures, some comic, some full of hair-breadth escapes, and as the fall progressed, some portending the serious work ahead. In late August, Capt. Jonas Schoonover had been assigned the duty of escorting 540 prisoners by railroad to Nashville.[81] The trip up to Nashville came off without a hitch. On the way back, just as the train was slowing on its way up a grade near Mill Creek, Alabama, they were ambushed by several hundred rebels. Schoonover and his detachment climbed onto the roofs of the cars, where they could take better aim, and a slow-moving gunfight began. The rebels shot thirty-four holes in the locomotive before backing off. The train continued down the line until rumor came of more rebels up ahead. The conductor stopped the train and refused to go further.

Friendly troops came up the next day, and they all got back on the cars and continued on to Chattanooga. Schoonover finished the account of his adventure by saying he would soon be back home with friends and family. His enlistment would expire in mid-October and he planned to muster out and go home.

Pvt. Samuel W. Hart of Company H had an adventure of his own. He had been in the hospital in Chattanooga for weeks, recovering from an adverse reaction to a poisonous plant he brushed against while fording the Oostanaula River after the battle of Resaca. He and some others were culled from the hospital and given the job of herding one thousand beef cattle down to Sherman's army.[82] It all began pleasantly enough with the cattle lowing and the soldier-cowboys singing sweet as wedding bells to the cattle. Then, Wheeler's cavalry rode down on them, yelling like Comanches and firing their guns, and Hart "got out of the cattle business in a hurry." He walked the rest of the way to Atlanta.

After a month of sitting, the Boys were eager for anything that would break the routine. The officers had been after them for some time to clean the company streets, which they resisted because by experience it seemed that as soon as they did, they were always ordered away, leaving the fruits of their housekeeping for others to enjoy. In late September they cleaned the streets, and an order came for them to move.

They were to take the cars all the way back up to Nashville, collect a drove of mules, and escort them back to Atlanta. Mule driving was not exactly in their line as soldiers, but a railroad ride to anywhere, for any purpose, was preferable to garrison life, and they set off in high spirits. They boarded the cars and got as far as the Chattahoochee River, where the train stopped and they were ordered off. They lounged near the track, waiting for the railroad line above to be cleared of rebels and repaired, but as soon as one break was fixed the rebels made another, and after two days the excursion was called off and they returned to their old shanties in Atlanta.[83] More interesting times were not far off, however.

Toward the end of October, the nights grew so cold that frost covered every surface when they came out of their tuggies in the morning. A warming sun took the chill off, and the days glowed with yellow warmth that put the Boys in mind of Indian summer back home in Ohio. This was the time of harvest, and better food for men and horses than the army provided was being cut and stacked by Georgia farmers just outside the city. The other brigades in Geary's division had already been out on "foraging expeditions," and in the week before Halloween the Giddings Boys got a chance at it. Geary's division marched out of the lines alongside a stupendous train of seven hundred army freight wagons.[84] They passed through Decatur, six miles outside Atlanta, and went eight miles more into a countryside where houses were as "rare as angel visits, few and far between," but the fields and pastures rich. Their brigade stayed behind while the others ranged out into the countryside, ostensibly to collect forage for the army's mules and horses. Although ordered to stay put, some of the Twenty-Ninth's boys went off foraging on their own.

> The boys get some molasses and frequently they bring in a crock of lard or anything they can get hold of, literally stripping some houses, killing the last cow, hog or sheep or whatever they can get hold of, without regarding the entreaties and tears of the women, telling them that the rebals must not tear up our R.R. then and cut our supplies off. It looks very hard but a soldier is in the habit of seeing all kinds of hardships.[85]

Three days after starting out, the column returned with their hundreds of wagons full to overflowing, with corn mostly, and a good deal of private property lifted from homes. Geary led several such expeditions out from the Atlanta works, collected twenty-four hundred wagonloads of corn in total, and three full wagons of sweet potatoes earmarked exclusively for use in his staff mess.[86] When the last of these foraging outings was done, the White Stars had denuded a swath thirty miles wide around the whole of Atlanta. It had been another regrettable necessity of a terrible war for which these civilians were entirely to blame, and seeing it thus, the boys were able to go about this work without remorse.

A week after the last wagon train had come back to Atlanta, and perhaps as a message that ravishment of the civilian population would not stand, the rebel general Alfred Iverson Jr., of Wheeler's cavalry, led an ineffectual attack against Geary's line. The rebels accomplished nothing more than driving Geary's pickets back into the main works. A few cannon shots and a musket volley or two was enough to unseat two dozen of the enemy, and they drifted away. One of the rebel dead was John Brower of the Third Georgia Cavalry.[87] Ames examined him before laying him in the ground and was startled by his youth. A soldier of forty years might be called a boy in this army, but this Georgia trooper truly was a boy. Ames looked at him and concluded that the Confederates must be desperate if they were dragging children into their armies.

Last Details: Election Day 1864

The presidential election of 1864 came round and Ohio continued the precedent of allowing its sons in the field and in the army hospitals to cast votes. Lincoln ran against the former commander of the Army of the Potomac George McClellan. Lincoln stood for pressing this conflict to its conclusion, while McClellan stood for a negotiated end to it.

Election Day was festive in the camps for its impromptu stump speeches and friendly teasing that a soldier was having the wool pulled over his eyes by his favorite party. The feeling in the regiment was powerful for Lincoln, but it was not universal. Elias Roshon, one of the original Homerville Boys, reported that among them it was all "Hurrah for Little Mac."[88] The Giddings Boys cast their votes in a tent on which some civic-minded and whimsical soldier had fixed a placard that read Town Hall. When the votes were counted only 40 or so of the 340 total were found marked in favor of McClellan. The sentiment of the regiment's Lincoln supporters was that they had sacrificed too much to be satisfied with anything short of total victory. Of ninety-six Ashtabula County soldiers, only two had voted for Mac.[89] Although Lincoln had feared he would be whipped, he easily won a second term.

Few soldiers would admit they had voted for McClellan. Those who had were the recently arrived substitutes, and little intelligent thinking was expected of them anyway, so the boys thought. One veteran soldier risked their censure and announced out loud that he had voted for McClellan. Parmater reported the consequence of such impetuosity: "There was one of our Veterans voted for Mack but he was always considered ignorant so not noticed much but the boys got a train in the evening and brought him out of his tent and exhibited him as one of the long eared gentry. I am confident that he will, yes and has, repented more than once already for what he has done."[90]

Back home, the citizens of Ashtabula County had cast more votes for Lincoln than any county in the state of Ohio.[91] Akron too had gone all out for Lincoln, and upon the news of his victory, the city broke out in jollifications marked by bonfires, parades, and torchlight processions. The black people of Akron staged a grand ball and supper of their own to celebrate the victory.[92]

Some of the boys had not been paid in months, but even without money, the Twenty-Ninth had its own Lincoln celebration. A quantity of "commissary" found its way into their camp. The soldiers indulged themselves and made a good deal of noise. There were a few fist fights caused by the ill-advised appearance of a few McClellan supporters, but as long as these misguided boys kept to the shade, affairs in camp were peaceful. To while away the hours some boys got drunk and stayed that way.[93]

"Where We Will Turn Up I Cannot Tell"

Two days after the election, fires were seen over near the center of the city. It was reported the army was burning its rubbish, but to the soldiers in camp it looked more than that. Over on the other side of the river, fires burned up the sides of Kennesaw Mountain casting its outline in orange against the night sky and warning of something important—of what the boys could not judge. On November 13, 1864, they were marched into the city to begin wrecking what remained of the city's railroad lines. The boys pried up the ties and made a giant bonfire, over which they laid lengths of the iron rails. When the iron was red hot, boys grabbed the ends and bent them into useless angles. It took only a company of soldiers to do this work. The rest found seats in the piles of ties and pondered their immediate future. Their Twentieth Corps had been alone in the city during most of the past two months. Now the Seventeenth Corps came marching in, with the Fourteenth and Fifteenth Corps right behind. Something big was afoot.

The streets of Atlanta were jammed with the traffic of a huge army gathering. The regiment's officers knew Sherman's plans no better than the privates, but by instinct they were already packing their things. Orders had come before the November election for everyone to draw enough clothing to last through a fifty-day campaign, and a short time later an order came requiring every soldier to draw an extra pair of shoes, even if the ones he had were still sound.[94]

Chaplain Ames, whose visits to division headquarters allowed him access to better-quality rumors, was in the dark as much as anyone. He saw one train after another come into the city with loads of ammunition and supplies. Civilians who had come down to deal with the U.S. army pushed and shoved for a seat.[95] Everyone not in uniform was trying to get out of the city as fast they could before the railroad north closed.

By November 14 the soldiers knew where they were going. They were marching east, toward the Atlantic Ocean. A move this deep into the enemy's homeland, depending on the countryside to feed sixty thousand hungry men and their livestock, ran square in the face of conventional military logic set down in the books Parmater had been reading. But he was confident they would come out all right: "This is a bold strike to cut off our own communications, while some two hundred miles distant in the enemies country, but we are strong enough to be bold."[96]

The whole army got up and in motion the next day. Two corps headed south on the Macon road, while the Fourteenth and their own corps, the Twentieth, marched east along the Augusta railroad in two columns so long that soldiers marching in them could see neither the head nor tail. By noon they were already out to Decatur. They paused for dinner there, got back on the road, and by night got up to the base of Stone Mountain, which some thought looked like a giant boulder. Behind them lay Atlanta, which could be located by an orange arc of flame beneath its smoke shroud.

Before leaving, Gen. John W. Geary had written to his wife to warn her that she should not expect to hear from him again for several weeks. Until then, "I commit you and the children to the care of Almighty God and humbly entreat His blessing upon you. . . . Where we will turn up I cannot tell."[97]

27 Tearing It Up

THE MARCH TO THE SEA, THE FALL OF SAVANNAH, AND THE CAROLINAS CAMPAIGN, NOVEMBER 1864–APRIL 1865

"The Blue Juniata"

So the story went, one evening deep in the Georgia interior, with his army arrayed around him, General Sherman sat at the fire in front of his tent. His ear caught the music of a song known to everyone in that day and he was mesmerized; so much so, that he let his famous cigar go out. When the music stopped, Sherman sent an orderly to locate the band and to tell them to play the tune again. Before long, the voices of half the army were sending the "The Blue Juniata" into the November night.

The lyrics were the lament of an Indian maiden for her lost warrior. She sang as she floated along a river called the Blue Juniata. The last verse seemed just right for this time and place: "Fleeting years have borne away / The voice of Alfarata; / Still sweeps the river on— / Blue Juniata!"[1] There was a longing expressed in the song for things that had passed beyond reach, so the soldiers' song might have been an expression of homesickness in this faraway place or of loneliness for friends who had been lost. They were out here destroying a distinctive way of life—evil in the minds of many, yes, but an undertaking uniquely and importantly American for better or for worse, and when they were done with their work, memories would be all that was left of it. The song might also have been a grieving for the loss of this whole grand experience of war. They had not gotten there yet, but some already had begun to sense that they would miss it. The war had been terrible, but every soldier would find something in it to keep him longing for its equivalent for the rest of his life: the friendships forged from dependence on each other when the chips were down, the shared experiences of misery and exultation, the being a part of something so gigantic and purposeful.

Folded in the back of the last volume of the Parmater diary is a four-page essay in his handwriting titled "Torn from the diary of a Veteran Volunteer of Co. E 29th Ohio . . . The March Through Georgia." Parmater wrote it down some time after the war. He borrowed some phrases, including those reporting the singing of this particular song on that particular occasion, from a book about Sherman by a popular writer of mass-produced biographies named Rev. Phineas Camp Headley.[2] This is not to say that Parmater had not sung "The Blue Juniata" that night along with the tens of thousands of others, nor does it mean that he had not witnessed the other scenes he described in his montage. The Reverend Headley's words simply did a better job of capturing the feeling of it. The rest of Parmater's essay is made of words that were his own.

There is a cinematographic quality to Parmater's word pictures, scenes that flash onto the screen of memory and fade out, with another image coming into focus, such as food from barns and gardens spitted on bayonets and carried off despite the pleading of women that they would starve without it. At the noonday halt for dinner: soldiers laying siege to houses and standing in the doorways grinning, with honey dripping into their beards; arms full of silver plate, bedding, and whatever else appealed to them. The day-to-day work of burning depots, tearing up track, and bending the rails over the fires. Lurid scenes most of them, and disturbing. Reflected firelight, and the nature of the work they were doing, turning boys' faces into those of leering savages, which was the transformation that had pained John Marsh's soul. Then, the army's evenings around its campfires: card playing, storytelling, and mass singing of songs of melancholy like "The Blue Juniata."

It took them about a month to cover the ground between Atlanta and Savannah. When they started none of the Boys knew Savannah was their destination. They pushed off around Thanksgiving and arrived at Savannah just before Christmas 1864. The going had been far easier than anyone expected, and faster. Sherman had divided his army of sixty thousand into two wings for this disembowelment of Georgia. By the time they were done, they had wrecked everything within a corridor 60 miles wide and 250 miles long. Outside Decatur, Sherman rode along with the left wing, commanded by General Slocum, of which Geary's White Star Division was part.

By Sherman's order, they were to feed themselves and their horses and mules from what they could find. Also by his order, they were not to trifle with civilians or their property, unless a headquarters officer deemed it of military value, and most of it was. There was a gap between the satisfactions of these two needs—to subsist and to destroy—which could be filled only by the application of individual conscience. Some men had little or no regard for orders, or the welfare of the civilians, and the people of Georgia suffered because of them.

Officers of other outfits turned a blind eye to the pilferage; Geary did not. He kept a tight rein on his men during their march across Georgia. Chaplain Ames was sympathetic to people of all kinds, including those in rebellion, and he deplored cruelty. He was present on every day of this march, but he did not mention a single act of meanness on the part of any soldier in the Giddings Regiment, nor, for that matter, in the division. The Boys were not angels. They had been instructed to take their food from the land, and doing that required some hardness of heart, but not cruelty.

The day after leaving Atlanta, the Twenty-Ninth Ohio Infantry took its place in the miles-long column and left their camp in the lee of Stone Mountain. The weather was perfect for marching: cool dry air and the sun just warm enough to take off the predawn chill. From one end to the other, the army sang "John Brown's Body." They marched through a wild country, provender limited this first day to sweet potatoes. The Boys had not gone far when they came across a rebel veteran who had lost both an arm and a leg at Stones River. The rebel's sorry condition stood for what was left of the enemy threat to them. Hood had taken his army far away to the north. Wheeler's cavalry was known to be about, but what he could do would be limited by his size. Sherman's army was sixty thousand strong, and by the experience of terrific battles and hazardous marches, they were irresistible.

They came into a country rich in all good things to eat: fresh pork, chickens, and molasses. They passed through a pretty town with the pleasant name of Social Circle that sat on the line of the Augusta and Atlanta Railroad, and then to Rutledge, where they had dinner. On the way out of town, they destroyed the track by prying it up and then flipping it over. They also burned the depot and all the cordwood that had been stacked up to feed the steam engines. They moved on and camped near the town of Madison, which Parmater said lay in nice country. Chaplain Ames rode into the town. Some of the houses were grand—"abodes of luxury," he called them—which meant the owners had made the fortunes by which they were built on the backs of slaves. Except for the jail, Madison had not been damaged by the fast-marching army—so far. Here, as everywhere they would pass, the black people were jubilant, the whites bitter. A group of black folk of all ages followed them out of town and stayed with them.[3]

They passed into a storybook country of huge manor houses, surrounded by gigantic crop fields, all of it worked by slave labor, and came to the plantation of ex-senator Joshua Hill. When the soldiers produced torches and prepared to burn him out, he claimed to be for the Union. They burned all his cotton and his cotton gin. The Boys took everything that could be eaten. They collared every horse and mule that might have benefited the Confederacy and harnessed them to their own wagons. Eatonton, Georgia, came into their path. The residents who had stayed behind here were frightened. Geary assured them that he and his men were here only to burn cotton and cotton yarn. The soldiers took from the people only what they needed to make a meal, and moved on.[4]

They marched up the line of the railroad, stopping to burn cotton, cotton gins, cotton mills, and cotton presses, and tear up the track, and got to a place called Buckhead Station in time for the midday meal, already ninety miles from Atlanta. Parmater noted that they had come so far south that roses were in full bloom even though it was late November. In the same breath he mentioned, almost as an afterthought, that before moving on they burned the station, water tanks, and anything else combustible that had to do with cotton or railroading.[5] They camped that night on a rich plantation on the Oconee River. The Boys had been told that this part of Georgia was not capable of producing much and had been picked over long ago for the use of the rebel army. Thus they were amazed at the abundance of most everything. Parmater commented, "The idea of starving the South out, is played out, they have plenty of everything to eat, a very pleasant and rich country."[6]

They turned south and followed the Oconee. By November 22 they approached Milledgeville, the capital of Georgia. They camped in a field on the Jordan plantation, which was a veritable food factory with a railroad spur of its own. Jordan was said to own one thousand slaves, and from appearances, he had lived like a feudal prince among serfs.[7] The Boys were not allowed to go into the town, but Chaplain Ames did. He found the state house "in a bad plight indeed," which was an understatement. Soldiers had ransacked the place from top to bottom, held uproarious mock legislative sessions in its chambers, and ruined everything that could not be carted off.

Even though the Giddings Boys were not privileged to go into town, they found enough to entertain themselves where they camped. Merchants had loaded up their merchandise and grocery stocks ahead of Sherman's army, taken it out to the edge of town, and buried it. But the Boys doing picket duty had little trouble locating it.[8] Both wings of the army reunited at this point. Sherman had sent them out from Atlanta in two wings to keep the rebels guessing about their real destination. From Milledgeville the army spread out into a line sixty miles wide and moved on.

The look of the country changed. Swamps began to slow their travel. They kept to the high, sandy ridges when possible and avoided the muck. Thick second-growth pine closed them in, but the columns of smoke that rose for miles all along their line assured them the army was all around them. They fell into a regularized daily routine: tearing up their assigned section of track, burning buildings, and foraging for dinner. They were now in full stride. As Parmater expressed it, "The expedition appears to be fed and oiled up . . . with sweet potatoes and sorghum and steam raised by burning cotton!!!"[9]

Five miles out from Hebron, the regiment found the bridge over Buffalo Creek burned. This was the first sign since starting out that the rebels intended to oppose them, but it did not produce any anxiety in the Boys. While they waited for the bridge to be rebuilt, they took turns at chuck-a-luck and encouraged the "Darkies" to entertain them with their "patting and dancing." There were enough black folk traveling with their regiment to make up a cotillion.[10] One night their pickets sounded the alarm and everyone was called out. They spent the rest of the night in line waiting for an attack. What the pickets had thought were rebels slipping up to them in the dark turned out to be cows, and the veterans enjoyed this joke on themselves.[11] They got onto the line of the Georgia Central Railroad, through Sandersville, destroying it as they went and, as Parmater characterized it, "playing smash, generally."[12]

The blanket of smoke covering the army became an annoyance. Earlier, the weather had been cold enough for ice to form. Now, the closer they got to the Atlantic, the warmer the weather. One boy in the Twenty-Ninth had become overheated and died, not from the heat directly, but from drinking too much water, as it was supposed.[13] Others had died in their division at the rate of one man per day. All of them had died of disease and none from wounds. Ames continued to keep a log of who had died, from what, and where his remains had been buried. At each gravesite, he lettered a board and installed it as a temporary grave marker. He made sure the grave was at least turfed over, then he rode on. The Giddings Regiment would lose three or four of their number to disease on this march, to malarial fevers mostly.

On the last day of November, they reached the low banks of the Ogeechee River, which ran off into a swampy country. The houses were few, but the size of the plantations even larger. One had a slave population of three hundred men, women, and children, not one of whom spoke any language recognizable to the Boys, by which they concluded these slaves had recently come from Africa.[14] At one plantation along the way, an indignant white woman stood her ground and protested their depredations. Chaplain Ames judged her to be a hard mistress by the poor quality of the shoes her slaves wore; most were not wearing any.[15] Whatever came to her, she had coming. Fifteen miles out from Millen, Georgia, the Twenty-Ninth was ordered into action. The rebels had burned a bridge over a creek and their skirmishers had staked a claim to the opposite bank. Maj. Myron Wright got the regiment into line and across the creek, and with a few shots they cleared the other side of rebels.[16]

They had now covered two-thirds of the mileage from Atlanta to the ocean. The first week of December 1864, their traveling carried them into a region where nature was more exotic than anything the regiment had seen in its long travels. The country hereabouts was more swamp than dry, with sluggish yellow rivers making double and triple loops. The swamps were so large that they bore names: Williams, Dismal, and Montieth. Trees grew here on giant roots that came right out of the water, and their limbs were draped with waving blankets of Spanish moss.[17] If ever there was a country that would be populated with the fabled alligator, this was it, and a local man produced a dead specimen for the boys to marvel over. On December 3 they crossed the river near Millen. There was a large rebel prison rumored to lie five miles north, and General Geary rode over to inspect it.[18]

Three thousand or more Union boys had been imprisoned within the eight-hundred-foot-square stockade. Inside, parallel to the walls, ran a rickety fence that was reported to be the dead line. Any soldier approaching it had been shot. On one side of the ground, the prisoners had built mud huts, and inside one of these lay three dead Union soldiers. Outside the wall, Geary found a long trench with a single board stuck at one end with the inscription "650 Buried Here." He was horrified by the foul, putrid atmosphere and realized that the stories of conditions at Andersonville prison were probably true. A Union soldier made his way into the Twenty-Ninth's line, and then into the division hospital where Ames worked.

J. H. Davidson of the 147th New York had escaped from the rebel prison pen at Andersonville. He reported that the prisoner's daily ration included one ounce of bacon, three spoonfuls of "syrup," which was a watered-down molasses, and half a pound of ground corncob. That was on the best of days. On the worst, nothing at all. On his arrival, the guards had taken his coat, blanket, boots, watch, and even his photograph of his dead sister, which he had carried through the war. The prisoners were suffering through the winter without shelter of any kind, except for the burrows they dug into the dank ground. He said there were 11,400 Union boys buried outside the palisade and more being added to that total every day.[19] Chaplain Ames interviewed the man, but he did not inquire whether Davidson had seen anyone in the prison from Geary's division, or perhaps someone from the Twenty-Ninth Ohio. He might have seen Wallace B. Hoyt there and solved the mystery of what had become of him after he went missing way back at Cassville, the past May.

As the prison hospital records would later show, Hoyt had been captured by a rebel cavalry patrol and sent to Andersonville. He had died in late October. An entry next to his name in the prison's dead book gave the cause of his death as scorbutus, which the soldiers knew better by the term *scurvy*.[20]

The railroad through these swamps ran atop a timber-braced levy. It was too narrow for the whole army to keep dry footed, and wading at times became the necessary route step. Wagons sunk to their axles and the mules pulling them went in up to their ears and sometimes drowned before they could be pulled free. The only efficient way across was for the soldiers to corduroy their path, which meant unpacking axes, cutting trees, and dragging them into place side by side in the mud and quicksand.

This weird and wild country bore few signs of human habitation. They marched now on a causeway made of white sand that had in it bits of seashell. From the composition of this road, the Boys concluded they must be getting close to the ocean. That speculation was confirmed when they learned the name of this route: the Old Savannah Road. They were in a hurry, marching now by night as well as day, which made for one of the most singular scenes Nathan Parmater had ever witnessed, or ever would witness, in his long life: "After dark passed through a dense swamp worthy of a picture in Frank Leslies Illustrated. A long line of soldiers, teams, and a goodly number of the 'Corps de Africa' of all sizes and sexes, wending their way through a dense swamp by the light of torches, the swamps are thick and the trees are covered with a thick gray moss hanging in fleecy rolls five or six feet long, from the limbs."[21]

Coming into the worst of the swamp country, where every river divided into a dozen channels and the plants looked distinctly tropical, they heard the distinctive boom of big guns. The locals informed him that these were enormous coastal guns being fired in Charleston harbor, one hundred miles away.[22] Chaplain Ames had just finished burying two Twenty-Ninth boys in a wood set back from the road when he heard the cannon booming. The sound revived his hope that their journey to the sea was nearing its end.[23]

The word in the Twenty-Ninth's camp was that there were Johnnies ahead.[24] There had been skirmishing along their course, but they had come this far without a scratch. They could move no closer to Savannah without fighting.[25] The Boys had drawn half rations during their march across Georgia, but except for the crackers and coffee, which were the soldiers' staple, their foraging had provided a bounty of things to eat. Of a sudden, foraging opportunities disappeared, and there was not so much as a single piece of hardtack to be found.[26] There were Federal ships lying up the river and offshore, ready to reestablish their supply line, but first Savannah had to go down.

Savannah Christmas

Geary's division got into battle line, with its left on the Savannah River.[27] The terrain was grown over with live oak, and vines as thick as cables covered the ground and looped up the sides of giant trees. South Carolina lay across the wide river, showing flat, cleared land and rice fields planted right up to the river's edge. South Carolina had started this war, as every boy looking at it across the river knew. They would attend to it in due course. Down the river, just four miles away, sat the object of their present interest: Savannah.

A rebel fort stood along the river blocking their progress. Headquarters had ordered Geary's division to charge across the waste and take it, and the Giddings Boys got ready to give it a try. The attack began an hour after midnight, but they had not gone far when their skirmishers sent back information that caused Geary to consider the cost of taking the fort. A water-filled canal would have to be crossed, close up under the rebel guns. Geary canceled the assault.[28] The soldiers took up the same work they had done on arrival at the outskirts of Atlanta, which was digging. From appearances, they were going to lay siege to the city.

One boy was struck by a piece of shrapnel, but the rebel artillery was otherwise ineffective, except in making the soldiers keep their heads down. Sharpshooters from both sides kept up a steady racket. One day the rebels floated a barge filled with explosives down the river to use against the Federal warships waiting off the coast. The Union batteries shelled it and drove it ashore. When the barge was examined, it was found to be a ghost ship, and loaded not with gunpowder, but flour. The Boys were hungry and would have loved to get their hands on its cargo, but that was not to be. Parmater captured the unwanted change in diet: "Fat living gone. Breakfasted on some beef, and that was all."[29]

During the day, the Boys cut trees and stacked the logs on the edge of the woods for use when dark came. At night, just as in Atlanta, working parties went out to advance their skirmish line and reinforce their rifle pits.[30] The rebels were alert as ever and sent bullets ripping toward them. No one in the regiment was hurt, but the work was dangerous.

Gunfire, the heaviest they'd heard since Atlanta, could be heard to their right, where the Union army was maneuvering for position. The key to mastering Savannah was Fort McAllister, the last major fortress between Sherman and the Atlantic. It stood on the marshy sand flats south of the city and was thought impregnable. While Sherman considered the best way to take it, the Giddings Boys set up their shelter tents and soon had things looking "camp style."[31]

The soldiers were hungry and stalemated, but their situation changed almost overnight. The news sped through the camp and was immediately confirmed that Fort McAllister had been taken. Gen. William Hardee's garrison of fifteen thousand rebels was still in Savannah, but with the army Sherman had at his disposal he could state with certainty, "I regard Savannah as already taken." The caravan of former slaves that had attached itself to the rear of his army as it marched across Georgia had not slowed their progress, but Sherman was always a stickler for keeping the army on the lightest footing possible. So, in preparing the operation to tip over Savannah, he stated, "My first thing will be to clear the army of surplus negroes, mules, and horses."[32]

From his cabin on the U.S. gunboat *Dandelion,* Sherman composed an official bulletin, which was published word for word in the Akron newspaper five days later. Of their sweep through Georgia he said, "The march was most agreeable." Lee could no longer look to this part of the country for succor. The Federal army had wrecked the country they had marched through without losing so much as a single wagon, and the soldiers were in better condition than when they'd started.

The destruction done by Geary's division alone had been stunning: nearly three thousand bales of cotton, fifty cotton mills, eleven flour mills, fourteen sawmills, bridges too numerous to tally, and twenty-six miles of railroad track and all the buildings that served it.[33] What they had taken for their own use had laid the countryside bare: nearly four hundred horses and mules, three hundred thousand pounds of corn and an equal amount of corn fodder, seven hundred beef cattle, and thousands of pounds of bacon, sugar, and potatoes, as well as barrels of molasses and salt. The Boys had even taken the burlap sacks in which the residents might have collected the scrapings that were left to them.

They had come upon a shoe manufactory during their march, accounted to be one of the largest in the South, with its own tannery and storehouse. Most of the stock of soldiers' shoes had been hauled away before they arrived, and those that remained were confiscated and turned over to Geary's quartermaster for issue to his own boys. From now on, the enemy would go as barefoot as the slaves. Geary did not mention burning it all to the ground, but his list of buildings destroyed during the march included three factories, and this was the only one he described in detail.[34]

Their stepping off into the Georgia interior had caused as much anxiety back home as if they'd passed to the dark side of the moon. The newspapers ran speculative pieces about their whereabouts and welfare, with titles like "Where's Sherman?" The Boys had gone without news of home for over a month. The army mail handlers had routed letters addressed to Atlanta over to the East Coast and sent them down to Savannah in steamships at the head of the fleet. A week short of Christmas Day 1864 the Twenty-Ninth's camp resembled a reading room at the public library.[35] Soldiers were downright greedy to hear of home, and when the letters came, everyone found a place to tear them open.

The supply line was now open to the North, but General Slocum found a way closer to hand to satisfy the hunger of his soldiers. There was a large rice mill not far from them, and Geary's division was assigned the job of running it for the benefit of the Twentieth Corps. Now they would have rice to go with their stringy beef, and their horses and mules would have rice straw. Rice was something new to most of the soldiers, and it took some experimenting to cook it just right, but everyone was happy to have it.

The Johnnies continued to toss shells into their line. Sometimes they came thick and fast, which made life uncomfortable.[36] Chaplain Ames drew the lucky assignment of escorting the body of a fallen officer to Hilton Head Island, and while there an order came for him to take the Twenty-Ninth's most recent pay back to Ohio for safekeeping. While waiting for ship's passage to New York, he learned that Maj. Myron Wright had been wounded.

The rebels sat snug in a series of earthen forts along the Savannah River, blocking the main road into Savannah. The Twenty-Ninth's brigade had been building a string of forts of their own from which to confront them.[37] The intensity of shellfire increased steadily the nearer the Boys came to completing their works. It was hardly safe to be out between the lines doing construction during daylight. Myron T. Wright was supervising the building of a connection between two new forts during the middle of the night on December 19 when a shell exploded near him. Shrapnel sliced into his left boot heel and fractured his foot.³⁸ He turned over command to Jonas Schoonover and was carried to the division hospital. The surgeons decided the best course was a resection of the tarsal bone.³⁹ Infection set in within a few days, and the surgeon amputated the foot to save Wright's life. One of Wright's friends in the Twenty-Ninth wrote home to Akron to report the sad news and to assure the residents that Maj. Myron T. Wright, one of the regiment's true heroes, would be among them again as soon as he was able to travel.⁴⁰

During the middle of the night on December 21, the rebel guns went quiet. Geary got a skirmish line out to confirm his suspicions that the rebels had gone. He roused the division and got everyone moving toward the city. A small lantern-lit caravan came out of the darkness to meet them. The mayor of Savannah and a delegation of aldermen were carrying a flag of truce. Geary accepted their surrender on behalf of General Sherman, and Savannah, one of the South's ancient centers of culture and commerce, was theirs.

The White Star Division was the first Federal outfit to march into the city, and leading them were the Giddings Boys.⁴¹ Geary rode directly to the city's most symbolic structure. He dispatched two of his soldiers to the top of the Cotton Exchange, and the Stars and Stripes and the White Star Division flag were run up the staff. Next, he moved on to the U.S. customs house, which he reclaimed for the Union, and the flag raising was duplicated.⁴²

On entering the city, the Boys found a mob of "low whites" and Negroes looting and burning. Geary was good at dealing with this kind of thing. He immediately ordered Barnum's brigade to restore order and by the time the sun was fully up, Savannah was quiet. As if prescribed by God, it had been precisely four years to the day that South Carolina had passed an act of secession. The black people roared their greeting and mobbed them as they marched. In their long career the Twenty-Ninth had entered many southern towns, but Savannah was the only one in which the white residents cheered and waved white handkerchiefs.⁴³

Geary ordered the Twenty-Ninth Ohio and the 28th Pennsylvania to march through the city and out to Fort Jackson, four miles beyond. Fort Jackson was one of the oldest in the country, a splendor of massive brick walls, every portal filled with the dark eye of a big gun. They found the rebels were gone from this place too. Before leaving, the enemy had set fire to the officer's quarters and barracks, blown up one of the magazines, and booby-trapped another so it could not be safely opened. Col. John Flynn, commanding the detachment, put out the fires, after which he raised the Stars and Stripes from the highest parapet and declared that the fort's dozens of guns and tons of supplies were again the property of Uncle Sam.⁴⁴

The hulks of rebel gunboats that had burned down to their waterlines lay smoking below in the river. Only one of them could still make war. The ironclad *Savannah* fired shells at them to prevent their occupying the fort, but it was hardly enough to dent their euphoria or slow their work.⁴⁵ To prevent it from falling into Union hands, the *Savannah*'s crew ran it aground and set it afire. The explosion made the ground under Fort Jackson tremble and produced a fireball that lit up the night sky for miles around.⁴⁶ In the afternoon a flotilla of U.S. warships came up the river. The Boys raised three hearty cheers for each that went by, which were answered in kind by the sailors on the decks.⁴⁷

The news of this milestone flew everywhere in the North via the telegraph wires. It would be a few days before the newspapers back home in Ohio caught up in their weekly rotation to report the details, which by then included Sherman's letter to Lincoln presenting the city to him as a Christmas gift.⁴⁸ Back home in Ohio, plans were underway to resurrect the kind of Christmas celebration the people had known before the war.

Lt. Gurley Crane was disabled by chronic dysentery and was out of the war and back home in Cuyahoga Falls, trying to get well. A Congregational minister of his town organized an old-fashioned Christmas. The children had suffered as much as anyone in the war, in particular during the holidays, which had been only quietly observed for the past several years, out of respect for the nation's crisis, and for those grieving around them. Now, with the good news coming in from Savannah, the minister felt it was time for festiveness.⁴⁹

He and his helpers put up three Christmas trees in a room at his church's Sabbath school and decorated them with red and silver garlands and tin stars. The children were treated to a fine supper made just for them and then led to the door of the Christmas room. The reverend had turned the lanterns inside down to half light to increase the drama, and when the door was thrown open, the children hurried forward. The trees sparkled with the tiny flames of dozens of tapers, and every branch had been hung with presents, each bearing the name of its recipient. After years of living in shadows, simple gladness was making its return.

All but two companies of the Twenty-Ninth went into camp in the southern part of the city. Companies C and G were to stay at Fort Jackson as a garrison force. The Giddings Boys set out to explore. Savannah was as nice looking a city as they had ever visited, with wide, straight-line boulevards, perfectly set block-size parks, fine houses, and commercial buildings. On Sundays, the Boys visited any one of the city's many churches, each with a fine organ and a choir. They strolled and took in the bigger-than-life marble monuments scattered throughout, like the one to the Polish hero of the Revolution, Count Casimir Pulaski. They found the streets a bit too sandy for their liking, but that was owing to the rebels having torn up the pavement and piled it in the river to obstruct the Union fleet.[50] Some of the Boys explored farther afield.

Two days before Christmas, Parmater and several friends commandeered a small boat and crossed the river to South Carolina. They found the country vacant except for a few Negroes and a chicken, which Parmater "captured" for use later. On Christmas Day wagons pulled up in front of their camp loaded with the lumber they were to use to build soldiers' shanties. There would be no taking apart of Savannah to build tuggies, as in Atlanta. Parmater roasted the captured chicken, which was a treat, but to him it did not seem much like Christmas. In the evening, someone put on a fireworks display. In the large camp of contrabands, near their own, the people held religious celebrations, singing and praying far into the night.[51]

On New Year's Eve there was a grand inspection of the Twentieth Corps. Sherman, Slocum, and Geary rode past them along Liberty Street in review, and the soldiers returned the compliment and marched past the generals in columns of companies. Some of the Boys stayed up all night New Year's Eve firing muskets into the sky, which was their way of "shooting the old year out and the new one in," as Parmater explained it. He found a moment of quiet before retiring to make an entry in his diary that was both a look back and a look ahead: "It is one year ago today that the old 29th reached Cleveland, Ohio on a Vet furlough, many have fallen since and yet we are far away from home but we trust God will allow us to reach home again ere another year passes by."[52]

"Ever a Fond Brother"

While recuperating from a leg wound in the hospital near Atlanta, Maj. Myron T. Wright had written a letter to Mrs. Susan Dice, mother of his fallen best friend, Capt. George Dice. Mrs. Dice would set great store in this letter, and the ones her son had sent to her from the war. Many years later, when she was a very old lady living with relatives out on the Kansas prairie, having these letters read to her was still her fondest enjoyment.[53] Wright told her that he had been with her son, George, the night he had been wounded at Pine Knob. He had helped load him on the stretcher and helped carry him from the field. He apologized for not having been able to be with her son when he died, two nights later. In case George had never described their friendship, Wright explained that he was writing to her as much more than her son's commanding officer:

> Since my entering the service in the spring of 1861 your son has been my constant comrade with the exception of such times as we were separated by wounds. And no one, not a near relative is more fitted to sympathize with you than I. He has ever been a fond brother and I feel that his loss is irreparable. He was only known to be loved and a large circle of friends in the army send you their heartfelt sympathy in this your bitter bereavement.[54]

The rest of his words might come down as a flowery relic left by a people who were too easily deceived, except that there were people living then, like Myron Wright, who believed them:

We do not however mourn as those without a hope but comfort ourselves with the just assurance that our loss is His infinite gain. And bowing in humble submission to the dispensations of God's holy will, we earnestly pray that He will comfort and abundantly bless you and sanctify this sad affliction to the good of all the friends of our beloved brother. May he grant speedy success to the cause of freedom in which your patriot son has so nobly perished and enable us to so improve our lives as to meet our darling friend in the blessed world where the blast of the bugle shall no more sound the dread war's alarms but all be peace and holiness.

A few days past Christmas he wrote a several-page official report of the Savannah campaign and ended in a matter-of-fact way, saying he had been wounded and turned over command to Jonas Schoonover.[55] Not long after he finished the report, he began to sink. George Halloway of Wright's own company visited him in the hospital late one evening. Wright grasped his friend's hand, and said to him, "George, I must die and I wish you to write to my mother and father, brothers and sisters and tell them that I tried to be a soldier, to do my duty in every respect, and that I hope to meet them in heaven."[56]

He died at one o'clock that morning, January 7, 1865. He was twenty-six years old. The officers paid to have his body embalmed and placed in a coffin. His parents were aged and too poor to pay for such a luxury. His friends escorted his body through the rainy night, past the slave auction blocks, through the gates of Factors' Row, and down to the wharf. A small boat took him out to one of the big ships anchored in the river, with its lights dancing in the mist. The officers composed a set of resolutions to mark Wright's passing and sent them to the *Summit Beacon* for publication. Addressing Wright's parents they said, "That in our sorrow at our loss, we think of the dear ones he left at home, whose bitter bereavement shares our sincere sympathy—the depth of whose sorrow we can judge by the depth of our own."[57]

The train carrying Wright's remains pulled into the station at Akron on a Saturday evening. In the preceding days, the mercury had stood at thirty degrees below freezing, and for days on end, the sun had been concealed by the ice fog that covered the city. This evening, though, the weather had turned springlike and rain had begun to fall. Myron's friends met him at the station, took his coffin down from the train, and escorted it the few miles south to his parents' home, in the village of Norton. At one in the afternoon the following Tuesday, a large congregation gathered at the cemetery in Johnsons Corners. Winter had returned and the temperature was well below zero. The mourners formed a circle around a dark rectangle cut in a field of white.

Rev. Carlos Smith preached, taking his theme from Proverbs 10:7: "The memory of the just is blessed."[58] When he was done with his words, the mourners shuffled forward to console the old folks, and toss a handful of soil into the grave before climbing into their wagons and leaving. In the spring, when the weather had finally softened, Myron's father had a fine white marble marker placed at the head of the grave. To anyone who was disposed to stop for a moment in their passing of this quiet place, the lettering cut into it told the story of Maj. Myron T. Wright's odyssey through the war and the manner of his death, and counted the span of his life, down to its months and days.

There is only one picture of Myron Wright. In it, his long blue officer's uniform is glossy and stiff with newness. His first attempt at a beard makes a shadow line along the edge of his jaw and the corners of his upper lip. His deep-set eyes peer out from under a shelf of his brow. By the time he was laid in the ground, many fine words had been written and spoken about him. The best of them were found penciled on the back of this small photograph: "Major Myron T. Wright Brave and *good* who was to be made Lieutenant Colonel if he recovered from his wound but he died from it."[59]

Jonas Schoonover, who had brought a Summit County company into Camp Giddings back in 1861, was now the regiment's colonel.[60] Six other men had held the post before him, and every one of them had been broken by the war in some way. Soldiers like Ulysses S. Hoxter and Almer B. Payne were now captains of companies in which they had once served as privates. Edwin B. Woodbury, son of one of the regiment's chief organizers, had begun military life in the regiment as a musician. He was now second in command.

Savannah Garrison

They passed the first month of the new year 1865 quietly. They did not know for sure where they would be headed after this. Troops could be seen boarding transports down at the river and steaming out, some going no further than the South Carolina side, where they unloaded. The troops crossed the stubbly fields and disappeared into a great swamp. It was rumored that Geary's division might spend what remained of the war right here in Savannah doing garrison duty.[61]

It rained hard through most of January, the runoff making puddles the size of small lakes. "Goin' fishin'" was the popular expression used by the soldiers to describe the cessation of all work duties due to the deluge. No one was going anywhere until the rain stopped, the river fell back into its banks, and the roads dried. The Boys devoted themselves to staying dry and warm. Getting up a supply of firewood had been the soldier's principal occupation wherever they had wintered. Here, in a developed city, getting it required a long hike to the outskirts of the city. Some of the Giddings Boys found a more convenient source. They waylaid Negroes returning from the same chore with their arms loaded with firewood and, in Parmater's phraseology, "confiscated" it.[62]

In this climate of cold and wet Parmater took sick for a few days, but after two years of experimentation the army doctors had finally settled on a diagnosis. He had been suffering all along from intermittent fever, in his case most likely malaria, and after a few doses of quinine, he was feeling fine again.[63]

As in all their settled stays in other places, drills were held, both by brigade and regiment. The brand-new flags presented to them by the grateful residents of Summit and Ashtabula Counties a year ago, back in Bridgeport, were worn from the fighting and marching. The state flag still had some service left in it, but the national flag—the good old Stars and Stripes—had been peppered to ribbons by shot and shell and was beyond use. An officer wrote to the Akron newspaper, appealing to its managers to take charge of the project, with the unneeded suggestion that the editor enlist the help of "the Ladies." To square things, the officer offered them a quid pro quo: provide them a new flag, and the Boys would turn over their used flag, with the graphic history of the regiment displayed in its folds, to the newspaper.[64] Their fond friend Lewis P. Buckley buttonholed everyone he knew on the city streets and asked for and received donations that ranged from fifty cents to a dollar, which earned the contributor the satisfaction of seeing his name printed in the newspaper.[65]

The Giddings Boys entertained themselves with strolls down to the foot of Bay Street, where they sat and watched schooners and steam vessels tied up along the wharf taking on cargoes of cotton bales, making steam, and moving down the river and out into the Atlantic. They played cards, and those dedicated to trying for their fortune at the chuck-a-luck tumbler continued to throw away their army pay. Parmater, normally conservative in the handling of his money, was drawn in and lost forty dollars before he regained his senses and backed off.[66] They had been about the deadly serious business of making war for three years, but many of them were still boys at heart, and they did those things that amused boys everywhere. For a few days, the regiment was overtaken with the high fun of wrapping twine around a tin can to serve as a fuse, stuffing it with gunpowder, and lighting it off.[67]

Within two weeks of its surrender, business activity in Savannah was again brisk, although the cotton filling its warehouses now belonged to Uncle Sam. The residents were mostly peaceable, although not all of them were agreeable to allowing the federal government to drain their life's blood of cotton away without compensation. In mid-January a group of citizens set fire to a stack of five hundred bales; better to see it go up in smoke than go to the Yankees. Speculators in large numbers appeared in the city bent on gaining control of some of the cotton for their own profit. The sutler authorized to sell to the Twenty-Ninth Ohio's soldiers charged prices that were considered outlandishly high, even for sutlers.

Good news made the rounds through camp in mid-January.[68] At Wilmington, North Carolina, the most powerful fleet in the history of naval warfare had fired twenty thousand shells into Fort Fisher and turned it to rubble. After small-scale but intense infantry fighting, Wilmington was conquered. By the looks of things, the Twenty-Ninth would be moving in that direction. What dangers the coming campaign would hold compared to others they'd faced was expressed in the convolutions of Pvt. Elias Roshon's letter home: "Give my best wishes to all the neighbors and tell them that we will be home before fall if we live so long but there is quite a risk to run. I think that we have run more risk than we will have to run again. I think the Confederacy is about played out! What do you think up there?"[69]

They were ordered to draw clothing and prepare rations for a march. Most any direction out from Savannah led into swamps, and some were oceanic, from what the soldiers could learn. Before passing out of sight again and back into the wilderness, the soldier attended to last details. Private Roshon sent home a package of silk cloth he had "captured" in a store somewhere on the march across Georgia.[70]

Orders to get under way came on January 19, and per tradition established long ago, soldiers got drunk and caroused through the night when they should have been sleeping. The order was countermanded, and they stayed put and nursed their hangovers. They heard that the Fourteenth Corps had crossed the river to the South Carolina side and had nearly drowned. The rebels had opened the floodgates in the rice fields and turned everything that was not already a swamp into one.[71]

"The Mother State of This Rebellion"

In late January the sun came out, and with it renewed orders to leave. The Giddings Boys marched through Savannah along Liberty Street and headed out along the river. Nathan Parmater marked the occasion with a sarcastic salute, "The rain is apparently over, it has cleared up cool tonight, so we will bid farewell to Ga. I suppose and give S.C. a call of Friendship!!!"[72] Geary's Boys were responsible for guarding the three-hundred-wagon caravan of the Twentieth Corps and making sure it kept up with the infantry column.[73] How they would get these several-ton conveyances, with their narrow iron wheels and heavy cargoes, through swamp country they did not know.

As in setting out on any serious enterprise, each soldier carried forty rounds of ammunition, with another half million rounds crated and ready in the division wagons, should they need it. Geary was prepared to build his own roads from Savannah clear up to the Potomac if need be. One freight wagon was packed with hundreds of axes, shovels, and picks and a special pioneer company of one hundred colored men who knew how to swing them had been enlisted in Savannah.

Before even crossing the Savannah River, they found themselves in continuous swamp.[74] The rains had raised the river far out of its banks and flooded everything. Thirty miles out from Savannah, Geary's division, Twentieth Corps, camped near the Fourteenth Corps, which was already positioned at the riverbank, and parts of the Fifteenth Corps had set up camp near them. Once again, the whole army was coming together.

The soldiers sought any spot of ground dry enough to pitch a tent. The Boys reverted immediately into life in the field, which meant plenty of joking and loud talk when the day's march was finished. They waited for a couple of days while the Pioneer Corps corduroyed five miles of road through the big swamp on the other side. They heard that the road builders had to sink and stack logs to a depth of five feet before they found a bottom. The rebels had slowed the work by laying "torpedoes," land mines that exploded when tread upon and injured Union boys.[75]

They sat in the dampish camp for several days. Affairs were growing rather dull, and the soldiers were anxious to cross the river and push on. Boats carrying sutlers and their inventories landed on the bank, and they sold out quickly, despite the outrageous prices. Some of the Boys got in line to buy "commissary." In Company H indulgence in cheap whiskey had set the Boys to quarreling, which produced the normal quantity of split lips and black eyes.[76]

They crossed the Savannah River at Sisters Ferry. On the South Carolina side, the division began slogging through a dense swamp on the worst road any of them had ever traveled. They came across a few scattered houses, each atop its own ridgy island, but by the time Geary's boys got up to them, it was obvious they had already been visited by other troops. Where there had been a house, there was now a smoking ash pile.[77] For the first time since they'd hurried up to Gettysburg, in 1863, they set a course for north.

Three years earlier to the day, they had begun their first march of the war. They had not reached their objective then, which was Romney, Virginia; they had stalled out in the icy mountains, and their adversary, Stonewall Jackson, had escaped. Fewer than one hundred of the soldiers who had marched that winter of 1862 were now present.[78]

The first actual village they came to north of the Savannah River was Robertsville, South Carolina. It had once been a nice little place, but soldiers had come through before the Twenty-Ninth and all that was left were blackened, leaning chimneys, which the soldiers called "monuments erected in the memory of Jefferson Davis."[79] They strode through and continued north, every house along the road a smoldering jumble.

On through swamp and forest, through places named Lawtonville, Beaufort Bridge, and then Blackville on the Augusta and Charleston Railroad. Every one of these places had been served in the same way as Robertsville. A few rebels blocked the route here and there, but they were brushed away as easily as a man swatting at a fly. As long as a soldier stayed close to his outfit, he was safe. Three Union soldiers had tarried at Robertsville, an indiscretion that cost them their lives. Geary had come upon a house outside the town owned by a Mr. Trowell. He would have ridden right past except several Negroes pointed out that there were three blue-coated soldiers lying dead in the bushes near the house. Trowell was responsible. He had signaled to some of Wheeler's cavalry when they came riding through that there were Yankees loitering nearby, and Wheeler's men shot them dead on the spot. Geary took Trowell into custody and intended to have him tried as an accessory to murder.[80]

They got up to the South Edisto River and stopped. Rebels had burned the bridges, and although the soldiers could wade across, their wagons could not. Work details from the Twenty-Ninth Ohio went out into the cold water and put their backs to the hard work of making a road of logs and sand. Log rafts had to be pushed down to the bottom by dozens of men and held there until thick wood pins could be sledge-hammered into place.[81] They had begun this sort of work soon after crossing into South Carolina, doing much of it by the light of torches, and it would occupy them every day for the next several weeks.

From the course they were taking, it seemed certain they were bound for the South Carolina capital, Columbia. They came up to the bank of the North Edisto River. Not only had the Johnnies burned the bridges here, but they were planted in the swampy cover on the other side and seemed interested in giving battle. Sharpshooters got to work on both sides, skirmish lines were thrown forward, and there were exchanges of artillery fire. Old hands like Parmater saw the affair as nothing more than a "little skirmish," although it would go down in the history books as a battle. A little more skirmishing the next day, and their opponents took flight. Some of the Giddings Boys were injured in this two-day affair, and one killed.

Capt. Wilbur F. Chamberlain wrote a letter to the dead boy's mother. John S. Rape had been one of the hired substitutes that had joined the regiment at Atlanta. Chamberlain had given him permission, which he now seemed to regret, to serve as a sharpshooter.[82] Rape borrowed money from his friends and bought a fancy shooting rig at the phenomenal cost of $104. He had also exchanged his blue uniform for a suit of gray, by which he could better avoid detection.[83] At the North Edisto River, he had gone forward and concealed himself behind a pile of fence rails—completely, so he thought. Preparing to pull the trigger, he was himself hit by a sharpshooter on the other side. The bullet struck him square in the forehead with enough velocity to pass through and wound another soldier. Chamberlain went through Rape's effects before burying him. They consisted of nothing save for an old pocketknife, a comb, and some tobacco. A friend of Mrs. Rape had written to Chamberlain asking him to write to the mother and describe for her the manner of her son's death and what his last words had been. From the tone of Chamberlain's reply, she also asked if her son had found religion before he died. Chamberlain wrote: "As to his hopes for the future I know but little, except that he led an inconsistent life for one who had hopes for a future world, yet he was a kind, good hearted boy. I deeply sympathize with you as I understand you have lost one Son previous to this one. No one can ever know what an immense amount you have suffered as a Mother. May you never endure a like loss again."[84]

Chamberlain explained to her how her son had bought his sniper's rifle and how he intended to use it. Soldiers of both sides despised sharpshooters as simple murderers who did their killing from hiding places, while a brave man fought out in the open, against an opponent who knew what he was trying to do and had the opportunity to do to him in kind.

Chamberlain had been with the regiment since the start. He had seen the war change and the change in the nature of the men who came to fight it; and in Rape's intent to commit legalized murder, the change was thrown in his face. In their first battle, Lt. William P. Williamson walked up to Myron Wright when the bullets were flying thick and most men were flattening themselves to the earth and addressed him in words that might have been spoken by a character in Sir Walter Scott, "What is the occasion, Sir?" To Chamberlain, such things must have occurred in a distant and very different war.

Foragers and Firemen

The left wing of Sherman's army, in which they marched, came within a few miles of the Saluda River, with Columbia, South Carolina's capital, on the other side. A squad of rebel cavalry was observed on the opposite side of Congaree Creek, where it passed near Two-Notch Crossroads. A skirmish group made up in part of Twenty-Ninth Ohio soldiers was sent across to deal with them. The firing was brisk for a moment, but the rebels departed before anyone was hurt.[85]

Their brigade was in advance of the whole corps, and for the time being they were unencumbered with the wagon trains. The wind came up and blew spring fires through the grasses. On the bank of the Saluda River they watched another army corps cross the river into Columbia. They did not go into the town, which they regretted. The next day they heard that the city had been burned to the ground. Rumor was that Union boys had been burning the state house when the wind carried sparks to other buildings.[86]

They were in a better country for foraging now. The Giddings Boys scoured the countryside around their rest stops and came away loaded with meat, meal, flour, and chickens, despite the teary protests of the farm women.[87] They did not suffer for want of victuals, but their uniforms hung from them in ribbons. Two weeks of constant immersion had swelled and burst the seams holding shoe to sole, and many were now going barefoot even though it was cold enough to change mud into sludgy ice.[88]

Geary hurried his men along so they could be first into the town of Winnsboro, on the railroad between Columbia and Richmond. Winnsboro was a pretty place of twenty-five hundred people in normal times. Currently, the population was swollen with refugees who had fled Charleston to escape the pounding the Federal fleet was administering. As they came up to it, a column of smoke was seen rising. They double-quicked the rest of the way and found a house burning. Parmater heard that its owner had started it going just to deprive the Yankees the pleasure of doing it. The Giddings Boys helped put the fire out and in doing so likely helped save the town from destruction.[89] As it turned out, they had not been the first Union soldiers to visit the town. Ario Pardee, commanding Candy's old brigade, believed the house had been torched by the foragers belonging to an army corps that preceded them. The plunderers had broken into every public and private building and terrorized the residents.[90]

The rebel cavalry chief, Gen. Wade Hampton III, sent a message into the town, requesting that a detail of Union soldiers be left behind as a safeguard until he could come up after the Federals marched on. In an arrangement that harked back to an earlier, more considerate style of warfare, Geary left two guards. When the rebel cavalry arrived, the guards were treated with the utmost respect, and before they were given safe escort back to Geary's lines, a crowd of grateful citizens gathered round them to thank them for their good hearts.[91]

A few days later, they passed through Rocky Mount, a tiny place of a few houses and a single store. It was one of the rare places they found unmolested since leaving Savannah, and Geary's boys left it in the same condition they found it. Geary would take pride in the restraint displayed by his men during all of this campaign. Not one of his boys had destroyed so much as a chicken house. As in the march through Georgia, they took what they needed to fill their stomachs and that was all. Boys like Pvt. Elias Roshon would write letters home claiming they had pillaged and burned wherever they went, but he described such things more to show the folks at home that they had given South Carolina its due than to put down an accurate record.

> I will give you a little of the history of South Carolina the Mother State of this rebellion we burned about every thing in the shape of a house except churches there was one county that we traipsed through that had only four houses left uninjured them was schools and

> churches the country where we passed was completely layed to ruin our army took every spece [speck] of about seventy miles wide and took everything as we went along.[92]

Whether he had done such things or not, Roshon felt sympathy for the people who lived in the path of this army.

> The folks up there [in Ohio] cant say they have hard times but supposing the rebels should tramp through our States and take every thing they have to eat in the world and nothing for your children . . . how many poor inacent child came up to me crying and asked me for some bread and I haven't enough such as it is.[93]

As they marched along the swamps became fewer, the country more elevated, and the farms neater and better cultivated. They reeled off at least ten miles a day on average, even though they'd had to build much of their own road. This was a different army than the one that had gotten mired to a stop during Ambrose Burnside's famous Mud March, in the winter of 1863—the soldiers so disgusted that officials in Washington wondered whether their morale could ever be restored. These boys on their way through South Carolina had complete confidence in their generals, and their generals in them. Here in the muck-bottomed swamps of South Carolina five hundred boys could build a passable road of a half mile's length in four hours, and drag and push stuck wagons free when mules could not, and they could do it day after day after day, most of them barefoot, and on short rations or none at all. The mornings were dark as nighttime with the rain, and fog enclosed their column like a cocoon. Heavy rain might halt them for a day or two only, and then it was back to work corduroying, pushing and pulling, and wading.

By late February, Geary's soldiers had crossed most of South Carolina. They had made two hundred miles since leaving Savannah. Considering the difficulties, they had made astounding progress.

At last they seemed to be climbing out of the swamp country into a hilly, forested land of faster-moving rivers. They now moved east as much as north, making for the coast, it seemed. The white people hereabouts lived on small no-account places, and the soldiers found them as ignorant as the slaves some of them owned. Near Hanging Rock, Parmater visited a family that cowered when he approached. They had been told for years that the Yankees would kill all their male children. They relaxed after Parmater assured them that was not his intention.[94]

In far northeastern South Carolina they descended down again into a land of quicksand and suspect roads which, when tread upon, were found to be only a crust with water running under them. The country was too poor here to fill the soldiers' bellies by what could be gathered by foragers working on foot. Geary mounted the men assigned to forage duty on good horses, so they could cover more ground and also serve as scouts. The foragers had ranged across the border and gone as far as Wadesboro in North Carolina before being chased back into South Carolina. After one such outing, they came galloping back to the column hollering, "Wheeler's Cavalry is after us."[95]

During the last week of March, Geary's division crossed the Pee Dee River and over into the last state between them and Virginia, and camped near the ghost town of Sneedsboro, North Carolina.[96] Parmater went out with a group of comrades to improve their menu, and he became separated from them in the cypress-gums and vine patches along the river. He came upon a band of "colored domestics" who had run away from their master. They cooked him a good meal, and afterward he "pressed" one of them into service to carry the food they gave him back to the Twenty-Ninth's camp.[97] Parmater had been lucky. One day Parmater and orderlies of the other regiments were called to headquarters to identify the body of a soldier of their brigade who had been bushwhacked.[98]

Elias Roshon felt himself one of the regiment's fortunate sons. For the first time in the war he was given a horse to ride and was sent out with a few other boys as a mounted forager. He got himself captured when ranging near Raleigh, North Carolina, and was sent to the rebel prison at Salisbury. No Union boy who was held there in the last months of the war would have anything kind to say of their treatment, and Roshon was no different: "We fared pretty hard for the time we was with them they took everything from our backs and the shoes from our feet and gave us one pint of meal for three days also ¼ lb of bacon that was our rations."[99]

By the time he and three hundred others finally got back into Sherman's lines, they were a hard-looking and hungry set of boys. Roshon had passed through another severe hardship, for which he thanked God. As to the story of his capture, and everything else in the war that he had seen and done, he told his parents they would have to wait until he got home. Then, "I can tell you the hole story from beginning to the end."

Near Rockingham, North Carolina, the travelers were again in a country of complete novelty. The pine forests dripped with pitch. In some places inside these vast pitch-pine plantations, the ditches were a foot deep with the powerful-smelling resin. There were factories nearby in the business of distilling the pitch into turpentine. Geary concluded that these buildings were of some military value, and he burned them, and along with them hundreds of barrels of turpentine, each sending a blue flame a hundred feet into the air.[100] They marched back into a world of muddy water and questionable roads, or no roads at all, over Rockfish Creek, Beaver Creek, Puppy Creek, and dozens more that had no names, and across big rivers like the Lumber and then the Cape Fear.

They were played out by the time they neared Fayetteville. The got into camp well past dark, and those wishing to eat had to stay up all night.[101] The chief ration just now was the famously tough army bean, which required hours of boiling before it was soft enough to prevent damage to a soldier's teeth. Thinking that they might remain here for a time, Parmater took his wash down to a small lake, but the bugles sounded assembly before he could finish, and he stuffed his wet laundry into his pack and started off in a hurry with the others and marched into Fayetteville on what mission they knew not. General Sherman wanted to review them.[102]

As the Giddings Regiment passed below him, General Geary pointed out their flags. Sherman thought them remarkable for the number of rents in them made by bullet and ball.[103] Federal gunboats had come up from Wilmington while they were there, which meant they were connected again to the civilized world. The Boys hurried to write letters and get them aboard to let their friends and family know they had survived passage through yet another wilderness.

Since the time they crossed into South Carolina, there had been small-scale fighting at places in the state that had little history before or after. At places like Whippy Swamp Creek, Barker's Mill, Duck Branch, the Big Salkehatchie River, Combahee Ferry, Cowpen's Ford, and Angley's Post Office, the few rebels who opposed them had been pushed aside without much trouble. The rebels were finding it more and more difficult to bring enough troops together in any one spot to offer much resistance. That changed when Joe Johnston, the chess master who had confounded them on the way to Atlanta, was put back in charge of the Confederate army in this region.

After Fayetteville, Sherman got the army moving toward Goldsboro, North Carolina, where he expected to unite with the thousands of soldiers coming toward them from the coast. Johnston decided to strike the left wing of Sherman's army before the linkup. A rebel force numbering twenty thousand came out onto a sandy pine flat near a place called Bentonville, and the first and last real battle of the Carolinas Campaign boiled up. The Union boys stood in ankle-deep water, taking shelter behind tree stumps as the rebels came at them in wave after yelling wave. There were bloody contests over regimental flags with fists, knives, and bayonets as the chosen weapons. Men who fought this battle said it had exceeded Chancellorsville or even Gettysburg in its ferocity.

Geary's division was miles away when the main body of the Twentieth Corps was hit. It was the dead of night when Geary heard that the main body of the Twentieth Corps was in battle, and he immediately got his soldiers out of bed and moving. He sent wagons of hardtack and coffee out ahead for the relief of the wounded, and from the sound of the battle that rolled back to them across the swamps and sand spurs, there would be many needing it. The next day Johnston moved his army away. The Twenty-Ninth Ohio's part of the battle of Bentonville had been limited to standing in reserve and listening to the last concerted exchange of artillery fire they would hear in the war. The battle produced four thousand casualties. No one in the Giddings Regiment had been injured. Lt. Palmer Williamson had been the first of the regiment to be killed in battle at Kernstown, and unknown to them at present, Pvt. John Rape had been the last.[104]

28
The Long Way Home
MAY–JULY 1865

"A Nation Born in a Day"

Chaplain Lyman B. Ames got the regiment's pay safely back to Ohio. He returned to Savannah in early February to find the Twenty-Ninth Ohio long gone. Getting back to them would not be easy. He boarded a ship heading north up the coast, hoping to catch up with them in their march through South Carolina. During a stopover on Hilton Head Island, the news came of the fall of Charleston, which Ames referred to as Babylon. There were expressions of joy everywhere in the flying of the Stars and Stripes and the sounds of salutatory cannon fire. Even the giant guns at Fort Pulaski, off Savannah, could be heard rumbling with celebration. He sensed that the sea island's black people would be affected most by the end of the Confederacy, and he took a particular interest in their reaction. He attended their impromptu "praise meetings" at a colored Sabbath school that had been established recently by a Northerner of good intentions. The students were restless at first in this new environment of desk sitting and book learning, but once settled they were as attentive as white children. Ames was given charge of three thirteen-year-old girls whom he found naturally bright. They showed evidence of having had religious instruction, although it had clearly been in the form of stories told to them, and not read. Perhaps here, on this sandy isle, was his life's mission. "Truly here is work for the Christian Philanthropist to raise up, educate, elevate & Christianize these '*freedmen.*'"[1]

The tide of activity seemed to be flowing in the direction of Charleston, and he made plans to get there. Once arrived, he spent his days touring the city's famous sights, recent and ancient. He took a boat ride in a drizzly fog out to Fort Sumter.[2] On another excursion, he sailed onto the bay to see Fort Moultrie, and then the famous floating battery from which some of the war's first shots had been fired by the rebels. It was half-submerged in the water and as rotten now as the Confederacy, which had placed guns atop it far back in the spring of 1861.[3] His real interest was talking to everyone he could find and recording the stories of which every man's life, both white and black were made. His pursued his inquiries with as much interest as a news correspondent covering life in a city the day after an earthquake.[4]

The white citizens interested in protecting their homes were taking the oath of allegiance and putting the Stars and Stripes at their doors to show they were "warm for the Union," and their property therefore off-limits to pillagers.[5] There were upward of ten thousand black people in the city, slaves one day, and the next as free as anyone else. He was seeing with his own eyes "a nation born in a day!"[6]

He witnessed processions of freedmen and -women carrying banners inscribed with hopeful mottos, marching through the streets behind the Twenty-Seventh U.S. Colored Infantry. Colored recruiting parties marched through the streets carrying the Stars and Stripes accompanied by brass bands, and everywhere they were surrounded by joyous colored men eager to enlist. He visited a public school, run now under the auspices of the U.S. Army, and found that two-thirds of the students were black, which Ames regarded as absolutely revolutionary. He also noted that the two races were kept separate.[7]

Both whites and Negroes took over abandoned houses, freely entering others to appropriate furnishings. In this casual freebooting, Ames found the behavior of the freedmen better than that of the poor whites. Some of the white residents he encountered were trying to rebuild lives and careers. One day he went to get his boots repaired and found not only the shoemaker but a lawyer and a jeweler all working in the same small space. Some people in Savannah were clinging to the old ways by intention or had been paralyzed by the instantaneous disappearance of a way of life they had assumed would go on forever. Ames was invited into the home of a Mr. Ryon. He had come down to Charleston from New York years before and made a fortune in railroad building. Before the fall of Charleston, he accounted his wealth to be one and a half million dollars. After the fall of the city, he doubted he was worth a penny. Some of Ryon's black servants had run off, but four stayed and would not leave his side.[8]

Ames climbed into the cupola of a tall building and took in the splendid panorama of Charleston, with its sandy-edged indigo harbor and two perfect rivers flowing into it. Forests, fields, and marshes surrounded this place of fine houses, grand public buildings, and parks set along neatly laid out streets. Down on the street level, he saw the harsher aspects of life in a city that had been turned upside down. He watched a group of Irish women begging for bread, or for a job by which they could earn the money to buy it, and he sympathized with their destitution. As he saw it, the rebellion was the cause of this suffering, and it was being unfairly visited now on these innocent women. Justice demanded that such punishment be reserved for the guilty men who had started the war.[9] He interviewed an Episcopal clergyman. Like Ames, he believed that Providence ruled the world and that everything would turn out good in the end. He also confided to Ames that he was fearful for the future safety of the blacks.[10] The Union army would not be here to protect them forever.

Ames spent nearly a month in Charleston. He was aboard the USS *Constitution* when news came that Lee had evacuated Petersburg, Virginia, where the two armies had been stalemated for many months. When he pulled into the harbor at Wilmington, North Carolina, he saw that every one of the dozens of ships in it was covered with banners and flags. He moved on toward the Twenty-Ninth Ohio and found them near Goldsboro on April 10. Great events were soon to transpire.

"Carry Me Back"

After the battle of Bentonville, the Boys continued on their way toward Goldsboro, North Carolina. They marched past a group of captured rebel officers, one of whom was pointed out to Parmater as Col. Alfred Rhetts, the Hotspur who had fired the first gun at Fort Sumter.[11] His capture proved that they had now pierced the vitals of the rebellion deep down into this cruel war's first minutes and rooted out the perpetrators. They crossed the path of several regiments of "sable soldiers," the name they gave colored regiments. Parmater had long ago given up his dream of going to officer school and leading such a unit. The friend who had shared this plan with him, Chum Sterrett, had succeeded and was presently serving as an officer with the Fortieth U.S. Colored Infantry, guarding the Louisville and Nashville Railroad in Tennessee.[12] Despite accomplishing his dream, Sterrett was troubled more and more by bouts of mental depression, which disabled him from performing his duties.

They reached Goldsboro on March 24. Their arrival there seemed to mark the end of the campaign. They were ordered to build shanties on an old cornfield that had been assigned as their campground. They were also ordered to draw new shoes and clothing. Geary reviewed his brigades and presented each with a fine triangular flag. Theirs was a blue silk field trimmed in yellow, and at its center the white star of the division. The main body of Johnston's army had been pushed back, but there were still rebels lurking, although in numbers too small to pose any serious threat. A detachment of foragers from the Twenty-Ninth went out into the country from here. A band of rebels drove one of their squads back to the detachment but gave up when they realized they were too few to try an attack against fifty armed

Yankees.[13] A few days before, two rebels had come right up to the Twenty-Ninth's picket line, drew revolvers, fired, and then ran off.[14] Such work showed the rebels were desperate and grasping at straws.

Mail from home caught up with them in Goldsboro. In Parmater's mail was a letter from Ipsa. Their romance, with its hopes of a future life, had sustained him through most of the war. Now, he held in his hands the last letter he would ever have from her. There had been some sort of falling out, and Parmater felt very, very sorry.[15]

On April 6 the officers assembled the regiment and read an official dispatch: Grant had taken Richmond. Having grown cynical of such reports, the Boys withheld celebrating. The next day, during an inspection, Geary himself confirmed the accuracy of the bulletin, which was authority enough even for the skeptics. It took two more days for the details of Grant's victory to sift down. As affairs stood in that sector, Lee was in flight and Grant right on his tail. With that news, the Boys let loose, each trying to outdo the other in a contest to see who could make the most noise with vocal cords and gunpowder.[16] Their rest in Goldsboro came to an end, and they set out on the road to Raleigh. It was only the first week of April, still too cold back home in northeastern Ohio for farmers to risk putting expensive seed in the ground, but here in North Carolina it was hot as blazes. Many men fell out, and by one account some even died from excessive heat. They rigged canvas shades to ward off the sun wherever they halted.

They got up on the morning of April 12 to the wild cheering of boys in regiments camped near them. One of their staff officers gathered them together and read the latest: Lee had surrendered the once invincible Army of Northern Virginia, which news was as good to them as if peace had been declared.[17] Their officers made short speeches to the Giddings Boys to mark the occasion, which lifted the soldiers into the highest of spirits. They slung knapsacks and headed out on the road to Raleigh.

Nearing Raleigh, they learned the rebels had evacuated it just ahead of them; battle would not be required to take it. They marched in and camped just west of the city's center. Raleigh was a pretty place, surrounded by beautiful country in which the trees showed their spring flowers, and cornstalks stood knee high and flashing green in the fields. Of immediate interest to the soldier-as-tourist was the state lunatic asylum. One man locked up in the place had become quite famous. He was about their age, spoke several languages, and sang for the visitors in a way that proved he was a man of refinement and education. He was not a lunatic as far as they could see. He told them his father had put him away in this place to prevent his going north to fight for the Union. The soldiers took an interest in his case and pledged it would be looked into.[18]

The Boys were ordered to collect their things and prepare to march, but before they got under way, the order was countermanded. Rumor came that Johnston had surrendered, and that the war in this theater, too, was over. The North Carolina air was full of rain and uncomfortable expectancy. Many of the soldiers had already turned in for the night when confirmation of Johnston's surrender came, and the whole camp erupted in a celebration that some soldiers continued past sunrise. The glad tidings of victory were snuffed out by a second bulletin: Lincoln had been assassinated in Washington while attending a play at Ford's Theatre.

The hearts of the soldiers, hitherto capable of withstanding any other sort of tragedy, were broken. They had lost their best friend.[19] In Akron the first reports of Lincoln's murder were disbelieved; the story must be some stupendous hoax.[20] Akron shuddered and braced itself. No one knew how the country would react to the death of the tall, ungainly man whose patience and wisdom had gotten them through. With Lincoln's death confirmed, there was a run on the local emporiums for black crepe, which soon draped every window and door. Flags that had been raised just a few days earlier in the wild jubilation that followed the news of Lee's surrender were now lowered. There had been plenty of bad news in the past four years, but none fell heavier than this. Stalwart men sobbed openly on the streets, regained composure, and then lost it again to fits of fury. The people were frantic in their desire to have the perpetrators identified and immediately punished, right alongside those who had started the rebellion. In a war that had held many dark ironies, the timing of Lincoln's murder was the blackest. For a few days, it seemed more than the people could bear. Akron shut down. Except for small gatherings of men and women who stood in the streets weeping and trying to make sense of something so profoundly senseless, people kept to their homes.

In the Giddings Regiment's camp, all was rumor: Lincoln was not dead, only wounded; Joe Johnston had not yet surrendered, and the war in this theater was still alive. The former proved false, the latter true. The surrender proceedings had contained troublesome wrinkles as to what portions of the remaining rebel forces still at large General Johnston could speak for, and questions had been raised over Sherman's authority to hammer out the details. The residents of Raleigh mourned right along with the Union boys and publicly deplored Lincoln's murder. Even the rebel boys who were being treated in the division hospital where Chaplain Ames worked condemned it.[21] The Federal soldiers were ordered to keep close to their camps, not only out of respect for Lincoln but for fear they would seek vengeance on the closest civilians. There were over a million Union soldiers in Southern places, all of them well armed and experienced in the art of destruction.

There were more rumors of peace and readings of official statements by their officers stating that Sherman and Johnston had reached terms. This was the most important historical moment of the age, and recognizing that, some soldiers copied the text of these announcements into their diaries. Peace was about to return to a region running from the Potomac all the way to the Rio Grande.[22] They would be on their way home as soon as Washington gave its approval. Geary gathered the division and paraded it past in review. He told them this was a rehearsal for a Grand Review they would be enjoying in Washington in just a few days, and immediately after that last piece of business was done, they would be back home enjoying the blessings of the freedom they had suffered to secure.[23]

The Boys had been tortured by rumors for going on four days. The dangers of battle were preferable to enduring the anxiety of so much uncertainty, made keener by the sudden absence of any real military purpose. General Grant was rumored to be in Raleigh, demanding the "Unconditional Surrender" for which he had long been famous.

But things had not worked out, so it appeared. Johnston's army still held to its weapons, and in consequence the whole army unfolded itself into columns and marched out of Raleigh. Rumor was they were going to run Johnston's army to ground and kill it, polite diplomatic maneuverings be damned. Geary's division got twelve miles out and camped, to awaken the next morning to the news that Johnston had surrendered. They rested for two days and then saddled up in their gear and headed back to Raleigh.[24] Reports as to why they were returning to Raleigh were too numerous to track and none of them to be believed.

Back in their cornfield camp in Raleigh, a newspaper made the rounds, and in it another official order was published, and this one seemed to be the genuine, conclusive article. If something was printed in a newspaper, the Boys held it to be fact.[25] Johnston's army had laid down its arms and quit. They could see the proof of it this time with their own eyes. Unarmed rebel soldiers strolled into their camp and mixed as easily with the Union boys as if they'd known them since boyhood. Soldiers of both sides approached each other, shook hands, and expressed their mutual happiness that the war was at last over. They had always treated each other thus, whenever they'd met, whenever there had been no officers around to enforce a hostility most boys did not feel. That night the sky above Raleigh was lit by a multicolored fan of fireworks the likes of which none of them had ever seen.[26] The very next day, solemn cannon boomed every half hour in respect for their good friend Abraham Lincoln. Flags were dropped to half-staff, all army business suspended for the day, and the soldiers told to subdue any loud talk.[27] The whole war had been just like this: joy smashed by gloom, and vice versa.

It would take a while for it to sink in completely, but they were now going home. Every step they took on leaving Raleigh would bring them closer to Ohio. That knowledge made the marching easy, although the distances covered every day were long. Over the Tar River to Oxford, and then to Williamsboro, ten miles from the Virginia line—the weather excellent, crops showing fair promise, the country now looking like a man could settle down here and make a good living.[28]

They crossed into Virginia on May 3 with their bands out front playing "Carry Me Back to Old Virginny."[29] Two years ago, they could not wait to leave this state. Now nothing could prevent them from getting back to it, because it was a waypoint on the course set for home. The "darkies" along the way were overwhelmed with joy to see Sherman's famous men come swinging along, and this time the deadliest weapons the Virginia women wielded were the lace handkerchiefs they waved as the boys marched by.

Full Circuit

They came up to near the Petersburg and Lynchburg Railroad and camped. Some of the Boys had ridden this line when they'd been captured at Port Republic, on their way to be locked up at the fairgrounds in Lynchburg. They found the Sixth Corps arrayed along the deserted trench lines and forts from which it had recently dislodged Lee. The Sixth Corps soldiers told them stories of affairs in the Army of the Potomac after the Giddings Boys left them. Battles at the Wilderness, Spotsylvania Court House, and Cold Harbor could rival anything the Boys had faced under Sherman.

Marching toward Richmond, rebels and their officers passed by, heading south, in the direction of their homes. The Boys were sick of marching by this time. There was no longer any crisis to hurry them, so why not stop and rest a day or two? And if they had to keep moving, they ought by rights be provided transportation.[30]

They were given a day's rest before marching through Richmond, but a cold rain spoiled the day and the Boys were quiet and felt lonesome.[31] Next day they set course for the city and the Boys entertained themselves with the chant "On to Richmond," which had been the theme that had dominated the generals' thinking until Grant took command. They paraded past the Army of the James, then crossed the river below Belle Isle and marched down Cary Street past Libby and Castle Thunder prisons, and out past the capitol building, with its grand square lined with the heroic statues of Washington, Jefferson, Franklin, George Mason, and Henry Clay. Chaplain Ames went into the state senate chamber, where important matters in the life of the Confederacy had been argued.[32] Everything pretty or useful had been burned; columns and chimneys of once fine buildings stood stark in this world of black and gray tones overhung with low clouds.[33] They camped that night near one of McClellan's old fields from the Seven Days' battles of 1862, close by the famous Chickahominy River, also made famous during McClellan's failed expedition to take Richmond. The Giddings Boys could see now that the fabled river was merely a stream bordered by marshy ground.

Over the North Anna River and then into a more open country that was familiar to all of them. In the western distance rose the Blue Ridge, and beyond it lay the Shenandoah River valley, which had loomed large in their history.[34] They lifted their feet over the ties of the Gordonsville railroad, which ran south in the direction they had marched that excruciating August day in 1862 on their way to fight Jackson at Cedar Mountain. They pushed west under orders to take nothing from the residents, not even a fence rail. Ames continued his fact finding and interviewed local farmers. They told him that farmland hereabouts, which before the war had sold for five dollars per acre, could not now be given away.[35]

Up before the light and on the road through Spotsylvania with the morning mist still hanging over the battle-ruined landscape. The Boys stopped to examine one oak tree, which they measured as twenty-two inches in diameter. It was of interest to them because it had been cut clean through by musket balls. Further proof of how hard the fighting had been here lay in the skeletons scattered about in the hundreds, some with scraps of uniform still clinging to the bones. Then, on up the road they had taken that hopeful early-May day in 1863, when tens of thousands of them had left the crossroads at Chancellorsville, confident they were about to destroy Robert E. Lee and end the war.

They passed through the battlefield itself, and soldiers fell out of the column to inspect points of interest close by the crossroads where they'd hung on against long odds. All of the regiment's twenty-seven soldiers who went missing at Chancellorsville were accounted for within two weeks after the fight, except for Pvt. John H. Hill, from Mogador. He or his remains were never found. Two months after John's disappearance, another thunderbolt struck the Hill family. John's younger brother Hiram had fallen to the same fate at Gettysburg. Whether any of his friends looked for some sign of John as they paused here in their victory march to Washington is not known. One man among them did go looking for a fallen friend.

Maj. Lansford Chapman of the Twenty-Eighth Pennsylvania Infantry had been killed on the last morning of the battle while rallying his men. Gen. John W. Geary had been compelled to leave Chapman's body to the enemy. Since then, although many of his friends and family had come here and looked for him, Chapman could not be found. Now, two years after the battle, in this same month of

May, Geary walked into the woods south of the Plank Road as if he were being drawn along by a beam of light. He immediately located the spot where he had seen his good friend go down.[36] A group, including a reporter from the *New York Tribune,* gathered around as shovelfuls of soil were carefully lifted aside and examined. Enough of Chapman was exhumed to identify him. The teeth, hair, and size of the corpse all fit Chapman. His pants had been stripped and the buttons cut from his coat, but enough of the coat remained for an officer in the group to recognize it. He had had the coat custom made for his major and presented it to him as a gift. Geary had the remains packed in a cracker crate and took them along to Washington, where they were shipped to Chapman's hometown for burial.

None of them would ever boast of what they had accomplished here; it had been a defeat after all. Across the road from the ruins of the Inn stood the woods where the rebel shells had fallen thick and fast, taking off limbs and killing men, including one of their favorites, young Samuel Shanafelt, and this was the place where, when he heard the news, Myron Wright had moaned out loud, "Oh, 'twas Sammy." Myron Wright, who had seemed immortal, had made it nearly to the end of the fighting but was gone too. Parmater observed that the place had returned to peacefulness: wounds to trees and earth were already on their way to healing over.[37]

They turned to a northerly heading and crossed the Rappahannock River at U.S. Ford, which was the way they had gone on their retreat from Chancellorsville. They passed toward Fredericksburg and took the same old road from Falmouth to Catlett's Station.[38] Marching deeper and deeper into their own history, the Boys noted that in this same month three years earlier, they had taken this road when Shields led them back and forth on their crossings to and from the Shenandoah valley. The marching then had seemed without purpose and so hard that some had fallen out and dropped dead at the side of the road, and others had just given up and deserted. Chaplain Ames now realized just how big a circuit they had made through the war, and he had shared with them only part of it.[39]

They passed near Bristoe Station on the Orange and Alexandria Railroad, where they had burned the Federal supply trains in the rear of Pope's army. They waded Bull Run Creek, its banks just as muddy as the last time they'd crossed it, in 1862. It was on that march, on the edges of the carnage of Second Bull Run, that they had seen the army surgeons sawing limbs by torchlight on the train platform at Fairfax. Hard, muddy marching got them to near Alexandria, where they rested quietly and mulled rumors—the one of primary concern to them was whether they would be mustered out immediately after this last review. As they could see now, their circuitous route toward Washington via their old marching routes and battlefields had not been arranged to give them a last look at painfully familiar places but to fit huge armies into spots around Washington convenient to the sequence they would appear in the Grand Review.

Just as he had done everywhere the regiment had traveled, Nathan Parmater climbed to a high point to take in the view and consider his future. He had not expected to hear from his beloved Ipsa again, but a letter from her had reached him, postmarked Baraboo, Wisconsin. What it contained he did not say, but he sent her a reply, and the fact that he did suggested that the breach that had opened between them could be mended. From an elevation near Fairfax Seminary, he could see the dome of the U.S. Capitol, in Washington, which he had first seen what seemed a lifetime ago when the war was new to him. Back then the dome was still a tangle of iron framing, and cows still grazed on the White House lawns. Now the dome was finished and shining. Nearer to view, the heights of Alexandria sprawled this side of the Potomac. That city had been the regiment's second home during much of their Virginia experience—the starting and ending point of many of their journeys and the outlet for those who had been through the prisoner of war system. Alexandria had been the place of healing for many dozens of Twenty-Ninth soldiers who had been patients in one of its countless hospitals and convalescent camps. They had started out from here on their sea voyage to New York, and their grand railroad voyage from the East to the West had begun here when they went to save Rosecrans, locked up in Chattanooga.

The Grand Review of the victorious armies would take a full two days, there were that many of them. The Army of the Potomac took its turn on the first day. The Twenty-Ninth Ohio's soldiers drew new clothing, blacked their shoes, polished brass, and got ready for their turn. The next day, May 24, 1865, they started across the Long Bridge over the Potomac. Nathan Parmater laid the details of this historic pageant in his diary.

The 15th and 17th A.C.'s passed ahead of us and the 14th A.C. followed us; passed up Maryland Avenew passing by the Capital and then around the North side of it then up Pa. Avenew; passing in review in front of the "White House" where the President, (A Johnson) and Lt. Gen. Grant and nearly all of the "Heavy" men of the nation were; The Streets were crowded with all classes and every balcony and window filled with spectators; many were the mottos all along the highway such as "Welcome Home," "Welcome Heroes of the West," "Ohio welcomes her brave boys Home;" and "We will all be gay and happy when Johnny comes marching Home" and the city was fixed up in fine style and nearly all of the ladies had boquets for the brave, some brought eatables out to us as we marched along, after we had passed in review; following the Corps came the long train of pack animals which created a great deal of mirth as they came packed in their usual style while on our southern marching, some with Raccoons others with goats, squirrels others with game cocks etc. riding on top of the packs. The cocks gave in their clear notes their usual amount of crowing as if on his native plantation; following along was two *very small* mouse colored Jacks each ridden by a small darkey.[40]

Afterward, the Boys marched through the city and arrived at a new camping place five miles out, near Bladensburg, Maryland, and set up tents in a regular, military order as if they might be here for some time. There was a surprise waiting at the conclusion of their settling in. It was their new national flag, the third to be provided them courtesy of the good people back home in Ashtabula and Summit Counties. On its red and white stripes were stenciled the thirteen battles in which they had fought.[41] It came with a letter from their old colonels, Buckley and Fitch, which Colonel Schoonover read to the regiment. The new flag stood as proof that although they had been gone a very long time, and other regiments had been raised after them in their home counties, each with its own claims on the affections of the people, the "Old Twenty-Ninth" had not been forgotten.

Chaplain Ames had been too busy at the division hospital to march with them in the Grand Review or watch it. Geary's boys had died at the regular rate of about one per day since they'd left Atlanta, and the end of the war did not mean soldiers were done dying. George Huntwork of Company F, age thirty-five, was one of the drafted men who came to the regiment in Atlanta. He had stood the march all the way from there to Washington, took sick with congestive chill two days before the Grand Review, and died the day after it. He was carried in a hearse to the new military cemetery at Arlington Heights, which had been laid out on the grounds below Robert E. Lee's former mansion.[42] Some of those who had died in the last twelve months were veterans, but the majority had been the new men. Some had died as close up as the ambulances that traveled at the rear of the division, and some as far away as hospitals in New York City.[43]

Enough of the soldiers and officers passed the time in Bladensburg by drinking liquor that their antics attracted the attention of Chaplain Ames.[44] He had preached and counseled against the use of intoxicants for over two and a half years, but it had not produced any change, and he could do nothing but stand back in futility and watch. Some soldiers' spirits were raised without the use of stimulants. The few men who had enlisted voluntarily in October of last year, and signed on for one year, were to be discharged at once.[45] The veterans who had been with the regiment from the start and reenlisted at Bridgeport sat anxious and waiting, hoping for a similar quick-out.

In the meantime, the company clerks were busier than they had ever been. The heavy, ledgerlike books of each company had been sent north by railroad for safekeeping when they left Atlanta. The books had found them now, and the clerks were working all hours to bring descriptive lists and clothing accounts up to date.[46] All the officers had gone into the city to celebrate the end of the war. Parmater got the scribbling in his company's books done and went in to Washington to see how it had changed in the two years since his last tour. No one knew when any of them might have a chance to come this way again, and all hoped it would never be in a time of war. He went first to the Capitol, where he stood under the rotunda in which Lincoln had recently lain in state while his fellow citizens had passed by him in their thousands to say a last good-bye. Parmater admired the grand oil paintings that were hung on its walls, especially the newest, a life-size likeness of General Grant in full uniform and holding a spyglass. He walked down to the Smithsonian Institution, which stood like a red-stone castle, and he marveled over the six Egyptian mummies on display, facial features still plain as day, although they had been dead three thousand years.[47]

Off-and-on-again rumors came that they would be going home: tomorrow, the day after, or the day after that. On June 9 the division hospital was broken up for the last time, the stakes pulled, and the canvas folded. Lyman Ames had tended hundreds of boys and buried dozens of them, going back to his first week with the regiment, at Dumfries, Virginia, during that long-ago winter of 1863. Sgt. Tunis Dykeman (Dikeman), Company I, 102nd New York, was the last. Ames wrote a letter to the soldier's widow in Hempstead, Long Island, to tell her that her husband had died of typhoid fever, that his remains had been properly buried by his company, and that he, Ames, had officiated. With the hospital closed and the sick that remained sent away to other places to try their luck at recovery, Ames was relieved of his hospital duties and ordered to return to the regiment.

Westbound Traffic

Orders came to the Twenty-Ninth Ohio at last, and they marched from Bladensburg to the station in Washington and boarded the cars of a westbound train at nine in the night, each company having its own boxcar this time. The Boys made their beds on the floor and slept. The train made slow time out to Relay House, Maryland, on the Potomac, on account of the line being jammed with troop trains. Their train passed near enough to Frederick as the sun came up for Parmater to catch a glimpse of its skyline. He thought of the friends who lived there. They had tended him in his illness and kept his spirits afloat. Further up the line he could pick out Observatory Heights, where he had climbed back in the winter of 1863 to carve his initials and those of Ipsa into the face of a rock.[48] They wound along the river and passed Harpers Ferry, where their neighbor John Brown had made the failed raid that had been the last straw on the nation's road to war. Then up to Paw Paw, higher yet on the Potomac, where Parmater saw another summit he'd climbed to scratch his and Ipsa's initials.[49] It was here in Paw Paw on a snowy night in 1862, in their mountainside camp, that the news of General Lander's death, down in the town below, had come to them.

They steamed into Cumberland, Maryland, a little after dark. Unlike their first days in the war, when so many of their sick had lain out in the streets of the town and died unattended, or nearly so, the residents now were fully prepared. They passed hot coffee and treats up into the cars while the soldiers' train paused at the depot. This section of the train ride ended at Parkersburg, West Virginia, where those of them who had served under Rosecrans and McClellan in the summertime war of 1861, in the Nineteenth Ohio Regiment, had first set their feet to war marching.

They boarded the steamer *Pickett*, moved down the Ohio River until it widened enough to accommodate a larger vessel, and climbed onto the *Ohio No. 3*. The sun went low, throwing purple and red on the water, the first stars came out, and the Boys stood on the deck and talked quietly as they glided along.[50] They had to go slow because the river was low, but that gave them better opportunity to admire the flags that were hung from every building along the northern bank, and to receive the hollered congratulations for a job well done by the people who came down to the river to see them. The boat reached Cincinnati, but instead of letting them off, so they could head in the direction of home, it steamed right past the turn off. They were not going home, not yet anyway. It appeared they were headed into the South, again. They got down to Louisville at suppertime, unloaded, and marched five miles out into the country and camped near Bardstown.

Getting Free

They were in Kentucky, and they would stay here until the mustering officer showed up, signed their discharges, and paid them off. The Boys waited, but the paymaster did not come. After a few days, the veterans concluded the government had decided to keep them here—for what purpose, no one knew. They had been warned about bothering civilians, but out of boredom more than genuine hunger the Boys took to raiding the local gardens. A rumor floated through that they were to be allowed a ten-day furlough, which angered the Boys more.[51] The furlough they wanted would be of the permanent variety. Soldiers being held similarly in other corps were heard to have deserted and gone home. If something was not done soon, the soldiers of the Twenty-Ninth Ohio would be taking French leaves of their own. Having been in the army for four years, they had all of a sudden forgotten how slow it ran.

They got their pay in late June, which enabled them to buy beer in quantity, and provided opportunities to haggle with the camp peddlers, but there was still no movement in the direction of home. Sergeant Parmater was officially part of the regiment's noncommissioned staff, and he was privy to information at the top. He actually saw the orders that plainly stated that the regiment was to be mustered out immediately, but they continued to sit. Parmater sewed new chevrons on the sleeve of his army coat and began writing a history of Company E; how far he got in it is lost. During a visit to the quartermaster, Parmater realized that the officer standing across the counter from him had the same last name as the good woman who had nursed him back to health in Frederick.[52] The man was the lady's brother. He learned from him that he had been just one of many sick soldiers she had taken care of before and after him. Caring so had worn Mrs. Coppersmith out, and she had died.

Chaplain Ames had gotten up on the morning of June 9 back in Washington and found the regiment had taken the train home ahead of him. He fell in with the Third Wisconsin Volunteers and began the long ride west. He landed in Louisville and made the dusty, hot hike out to the Twenty-Ninth Ohio's camp. At once, he fell into a mental state that paralleled that of the soldiers. His mind was unsettled and he was troubled with thoughts of his future.[53] Like the others, he felt the work was done, and he wanted to get home. His hope was to return home with the regiment. However, if they were not discharged soon, he would resign and go by himself.[54]

Ames found the soldiers demoralized and universally discontented, and the suspense as to when they might leave this place nearly unbearable. Colonel Schoonover had gotten a twenty-day leave and left them before the Fourth of July. Ames submitted his resignation. It was accepted, and he was once again a citizen. The change back to civilian life would be challenging, as he admitted, but he trusted it would also be full of agreeable things. He had given one talk to the Boys while here, which was his last to them for all time. He spoke to them with unusual candor, but on what topics he did not confide to his diary. He settled his financial affairs, sold his horse, and booked a passage on a steamer for Cincinnati.

He left the regiment with as little fanfare as was shown him when he had come to them in Dumfries, Virginia, in the winter of 1863.[55] Lyman Ames would find life in Conneaut comfortable, but that sensation would last only a few days, replaced by what he called an unsettledness of mind.[56] He set out for the oil boomtown of Pithole, Pennsylvania, hoping to make a big strike in a place that looked every bit as torn up and chaos filled as any battlefield.[57] It would take him a while to regain his bearings, but he would, and he eventually returned to the duties that had given him a measure of satisfaction before the war, when he had been a small-town pastor.

Back at Bardstown, July 4 came and it was reported that no one could go home until General Sherman came down and reviewed them one more time. They all liked General Sherman well enough, but the fourth was Independence Day, and independence is what they wanted now.[58] Only sixty of the boys fell in when they were called out. The rest ignored the order. Sherman did not arrive until later in the day, and those who were willing to march over a second time heard him praise their Twentieth Army Corps. He said they had never let him down. John White Geary, the general whose decisions had most directly controlled their fate for good or for bad since Cedar Mountain and in all that had followed, did not make them a good-bye speech, as far as is known.

Past the Fourth of July and deeper into the month, it was discovered that the regiment had not been discharged because of errors in their own record books. The clerks went over them in a fever, made the necessary corrections, and sent them on to headquarters for approval.[59] While the clerks worked, the Boys entertained themselves with cheap whiskey, which resulted in bruises and bloody noses, much as it always had. They also amused themselves by preying on the sutlers. "The boys are very anxious to help the Sutler sell out lately; today they sold him out in about 20 minutes (that is 'schooped' him)," by which Parmater meant they had charged his wagon en masse and taken what they wanted.[60]

On July 13, 1865, the mustering officer finally appeared and the Boys were mustered out of the service. The final papers required one more official stamp yet, but that would be waiting for them in Cleveland. The next day the "brevet citizens" turned in their shelter-half tents, which when issued to them years ago, were laughed at because of their small size. They had served their purpose, and the Boys had come to regard them with as much fondness as an innkeeper his lodging house.

The Tower Enfield muskets in which they'd set such stock were gathered and racked. A soldier could keep his musket for six dollars. Most of the Boys had seen enough of war and did not need this memento of it. While they waited for transportation home, an unexplainable loneliness descended over them all. With their tents returned to the quartermaster's department, they spent their last night in the field sleeping on the grass under a dome of stars.

They were awakened at three in the morning by the familiar tapping of the drums. This was the last time they would hear the sound that had insisted they leave their campfires at a hundred different places and get onto the road for a march to another place—and many times that road had led to skirmish and battle. They got onto the paddle wheeler *Melnotte* and pushed against the river current on their way back up to Cincinnati. They boarded the cars at Cincinnati and steamed through the night toward Cleveland. The Boys had traced the longest of courses through the war, just how long it had been, they would now have plenty of time to count by spreading maps and atlases on the kitchen table and with pencil and string put a number to all their miles. In round terms, it amounted to several thousand.

Last Parade

They stepped down from the cars in Cleveland and took a good wash at the depot. They squared their ranks, and fell in by company for the march to the public square. Many outfits had passed through Cleveland on their way home, and a reception committee had been formed, and public money earmarked, to give each one a proper welcome home. For the Giddings Boys, arrangements had been made for Leland's Brass Band to come up from Akron and lead them to the public square. They swung down the street in the easy, mile-eating lope that the citizens knew to be the distinctive step of veteran troops.[61] Colonel Schoonover was gone home on leave, so Maj. E. B. Woodbury was out front, accompanied by a delegation of citizens. When the Twenty-Ninth Ohio Volunteer Infantry had first passed through here, at Christmas 1861, they had numbered almost a thousand. There were but 235 on this last march through the city's busy streets, lined with citizens who had come out to see them pass and welcome them home.[62]

As they strode along, every soldier's mind turned to thoughts of those who had not completed the big circle back to this place. The exact number of Giddings Boys who perished during the war will never be known. The official numbers would not be published until twenty-five years after the war ended, and even then, they did not take into account the soldiers who would continue to die of wounds or recurrent, incurable diseases after the things of war were put away. Officially given as about 271 from all causes, the grim number of their loss might be two to three dozen higher.

The four men who died of wounds within a month following Dug Gap were not credited as killed in action, nor for any of their battles were those who hung on for a time and then died. The two men who had dropped dead of "hard marching" coming and going from the Shenandoah valley, in 1862, the soldier who drowned in the Savannah River, and the soldier shot dead by the provost guard under circumstances never explained did not fit into any neat category. The Twenty-Ninth Ohio Infantry had not been alone, of course. For almost every Ohio regiment, the experience of war had been deadly.

In the Twenty-Ninth Ohio, about six officers and 120 enlisted men had been killed outright in battle. One hundred fifty enlisted men had died of disease, but only one officer.[63] Their own accounting of their battle casualties published in the SeCheverell history stated 541 of them had been killed, wounded, captured, or were missing and never found.

Nearly every single one of them, soldier or officer, had spent time in hospitals trying to recover from sicknesses, most of which were capable of returning at any time, and with a vengeance. Lt. Gurley Crane resigned and came home in 1864, and died of chronic dysentery and "drowned lungs" within a week of Lee's surrender. Maj. Everson J. Hurlburt of Jefferson had been wounded as many times as any man in the regiment. His chest wounds from Chancellorsville and Gettysburg flared up in his first autumn home, and he died with the wife whom he'd married while they were at Camp Giddings at his side. Thomas Dowling died similarly, but he held on for a few years longer. Adj. James B. Storer struggled on for years, confined to his bed, blind and deaf in the last of them, dying eventually, as his doctor reported, of the gunshot wound he'd taken at Dug Gap in 1864, a half century earlier. Among the sixteen hundred Union infantry regiments organized for the war, the number of dead recorded on their muster-out rolls was adequate to earn the Twenty-Ninth Ohio Veteran Volunteer Infantry a place in the list of the three hundred regiments who had suffered most on the battlefield.[64]

The fallen were to be mourned but not fretted over. Lives, limbs, and health had been given in a great cause, and the boys marching this last mile pledged to live their own lives in such a way that they would prove the gift worthy of the cost. Not a single soldier would ever question the value of what they had done.

An important personage was at the square, waiting to make them a speech. Cleveland was not the regiment's hometown, but their career had been followed here, and the residents knew more than a little about them. Judge Daniel Tilden acknowledged what the soldiers already knew: that no one who had spent the war at home sleeping safely in their own bed could ever know what they had been through. While they had marched and suffered, every industry at home had prospered. The country they had set out to defend in 1861 had undergone great changes. The judge remarked that in Europe, America was no longer regarded as a conglomeration of individuals, each following his own course to material wealth, but as a nation with a conscience, and now as powerful as any on the globe.

The Twenty-Ninth Ohio was known in Cleveland as the Giddings Regiment or as the Abolition Regiment, as was pointed out in the newspaper article reporting the details of their homecoming, and the lore was republished that every one of the soldiers had been "abolitionized" during their training.[65] Everything they had done, as they themselves explained it, had been done to end the rebellion and restore the Union.

Judge Tilden assured them their name would always be spoken without hesitation in the same breath as that of the "Bloody Seventh," which the Boys must have taken as the highest compliment. The Seventh Ohio Infantry was Cleveland's pet. Judge Tilden knew the boys of the Twenty-Ninth were anxious to get home, so he kept his remarks short. He could not finish without trying to express the value the citizens placed in what the Boys had done: "Words cannot pay you. Gold cannot pay you. . . . Once more I bid you a hearty welcome. And now go home, and may the blessing of God attend you to the close of your life."[66]

On the conclusion of the address, the soldiers filed into the tents that had been set up and did justice to the fine breakfast the young ladies of the city served them. Done with that, the color bearers lifted the heavy staffs of their flags for the last time and led the way out to Camp Cleveland, where they were to be paid off.

They had carried three different national flags through the war. One of them, claimed to be their first, is displayed at the Henderson Memorial Public Library, in Jefferson.[67] What became of the other two is a mystery.

At Camp Cleveland, the Boys found other outfits in line ahead of them. The men of the Twenty-Eighth and Fifty-Fifth Ohio Infantries and Battery B of the First Ohio Light Artillery were waiting for the right papers and an officer to muster them out.[68] Many of the Giddings Boys did not wait and went home with the plan to come back later when the line had gone down. For those who stayed, it was the same old waiting. There were some skirmishes among the boys who imbibed too freely, but mostly they were quiet. Parmater thought that if this went on much longer he would die of the blues.[69] He went into the city and came back to find that the Paymaster had arrived and the Boys were being paid off.

Nathan Parmater had stayed true to the promise he'd made himself back at Camp Giddings on his first day as a soldier, which was to write in his diary every day. He turned back through the pages of his several notebooks and realized that he had made a book, and although it might never be published, it was a book nonetheless, and true to that form, it had a beginning and an end, and dramas, comedies, and tragedies filling its interior. He had been through all of it and done his best to record faithfully what he had done, seen, and felt. Now, before he set out for home, he made an entry in his diary to mark his last day as a volunteer soldier who had fought in the Great Rebellion:

> It is just 3 years and 10 months today since I first went into camp and became a soldier; what we have endured since that time this book tells above in part, but it all cannot be written in pen and ink. The Co. to which I belonged, (E) left Camp G[iddings] in 1861 with 97 men five of whom were discharged at the expiration of the first three years; not having reenlisted and 15 today; where are the rest? Many of them fill unknown graves in the far south, others are living cripples among friends at home; we mourn their loss but feel their lives were lost in a good cause; peace is ours at last and I hope a lasting one.[70]

The rest of the Boys started out of the war in the same way they had come into it: in small groups made up of friends who lived along the same road or creek. Those who still lay sick in army hospitals from New York to Indiana and at other places missed the homecoming given the others, and would make their solitary way home later this summer or fall. Stories would appear in the Ohio newspapers for the next year and sometimes longer of soldiers who had been thought lost in the war, and in some way had actually become lost, but showed up one day at their farmhouse doors long after every other boy had come home, so unrecognizable that the family dogs snarled at them as at any trespasser, and wives fainted dead away.

Leaving Cleveland, the Boys took the railroad to points nearest their villages and walked the rest of the way. Many who lived in the interior of Ashtabula County came back through Jefferson and passed by the fairgrounds, where in 1861 they had all stood on the threshold of an untried life, as Col. Thomas Clark remembered.

What Jefferson would do, now that the decades-long antislavery crusade was over, and the war won, remained to be answered. Here, as everywhere on the Western Reserve, hopes and plans for improved living through the miracle of commerce seemed to fill the vacancy. Before the war, an accounting of the entire village's cash resources did not exceed fifty dollars. Now, Jefferson residents counted nineteen pianos, nineteen melodeons, three organs, and over thirty automated sewing machines. Living in such an up-to-the-time place gave the *Sentinel* editor the right to issue a challenge of the type they'd put in print time and again during the recruiting competitions of the recently concluded war: "We feel a little like asking some village of our size to beat us, if they can."[71] Jefferson had been a village when the war began and would remain one always. But the impetus of war had transformed Akron. Its population had doubled to five thousand in the four years the Boys had been gone, and its boosters could rightly claim that it was no longer a town but a true city. Men with visionary ideas were already here and more would be coming, and the city would continue to build on the foundation of industry that had been laid during the war.

Even though the war had ended, there was still much related to it to occupy the people's minds. There would be the trial of the Lincoln assassination conspirators, congressional debates over how the vanquished South should be treated, and arguments in favor of and against giving the black man the right to vote. There were horror stories from the survivors of Andersonville prison and the frightful news of the sinking of the *Sultana*, which had gone down on the Mississippi River jammed with returning soldiers. Many of the seventeen hundred dead had survived the horrors of Andersonville and other dreadful rebel prisons, only to be scalded to death by exploded steam boilers or drowned. The war had been so overfilled with such terrible ironies, and the surplus seemed to spill over into the peace.

Formal observance of their homecoming would be celebrated in the coming days and weeks. In Conneaut the residents were planning a "Grand Social Hop" at Cleveland's Hall for the returned soldiers of the Twenty-Ninth, the 105th Ohio, and gunners of the Second Ohio Artillery.[72] The ballroom of the Jefferson House had been reserved for a special supper to salute the Boys, and a similar fete was planned in Akron, where the soldiers would gather one more time for a fine supper of oysters, cakes, and coffee, followed by the passing out of free cigars and emotional speeches.[73]

On their way home, what was left of the Rock Creek Squad paused in Jefferson to accept the blessing of the village that they might do as much honor to civilian life as they had the military life.[74] They continued down to Rock Creek, at the foot of the village, where as youngsters in the time before the war they had snuck away from chores to swim and slide down the rock ledges that passed under the bridge. Both the Phinney boys were gone, Wallace Hoyt too, and many of the others. The rain and sun had combined in just the right amounts this summer of 1865 to make for good crops in the fields they passed. They had come home too late for planting, but they would be here for the harvest.

They had seen war in its worst forms, and the last thing on the minds of the soldiers who walked the dirt roads to their homes this July day was revisiting any of it. That would change. In the future, most all of them would make at least one tour of memory, by railroad car and buggy ride. As white-bearded old men wearing the dark frock coats and wide-brimmed hats, which were the uniform of the favorite veteran organization, the Grand Army of the Republic, they would make long, painful hikes with a cane and an assistant to steady them. They would seek out the place of a camp, skirmish, or battle that held particular meaning. The year after Charles Lindbergh flew across the Atlantic Ocean, Samuel Hart, once upon a time a private in Company H, would travel out from the Golden West Hotel in San Diego to which he had retired, all the way back to Chattanooga. He would struggle up the hills and through the brush of the Wauhatchie valley until he found a rock shelf under which he and his mates had performed lookout duty. The ashes of the campfire they had built on a dreary afternoon back in late 1863 would still be lying there as if the soldiers had just stepped out for a moment.[75]

Just a few days after he got home, Nathan Parmater would be getting measured up for the two new suits of clothes he would need to begin the next chapter of his life. The very last entry in his war diary was dated August 10, 1865: "Returned to Geneva on the morning train and rode down to Mr. A. C. Cowles with E. R. C. where I spent part of the day in getting ready to go west which I expect to do soon."

Over to the east of Akron the Homerville Boys took transportation to Medina and then walked the rest of the way to their village, and out into the country, where most of them lived. Some were physical wrecks, bent over by fever and old injuries. Their packs were carried by comrades the last few miles in repayment of the same kindness done for them on some long-ago march. They passed by the farm meadow where in the golden autumn of 1861 a dozen country boys had gathered to practice military steps, and had drunk toasts of apple cider to celebrate their progress. Their drillmasters back then had been John G. Marsh and Cains C. Lord. Marsh had died at Gettysburg, but Lord was with them, although he had been permanently weakened by his stay at Belle Isle prison. Elias Roshon's capture had proved a mixed blessing. On his release from prison he had been sent directly to Camp Chase and discharged, thus avoiding the long frustrating detour made by the regiment to Kentucky. He was home now, and telling the whole story of his war, which he had been putting off telling until he got there.[76]

John Rupp had been one of those clumsy but enthusiastic country boys of Homerville village who had gone to be a soldier, leaving his little brother Henry to stand and admire from behind the pasture fence. Henry grew old enough to enlist without his father's permission, and he joined his brother's company. He had been with the Twenty-Ninth Ohio just a few months when he was killed at Dug Gap. The boys who had made it through that day, and all the perilous days before and after it, came up to a succession of farm gates. At each stop, a final good-bye was spoken, and a promise made to keep in contact over the shake of a hand. The dwindling band moved on down the road and repeated these shy ceremonies until there was only one soldier left to walk by himself the last steps of a journey that had contained millions.

Notes

Abbreviations

AGO	Correspondence to the Governor and Adjutant General of Ohio, 1861–66, series 147, Ohio Historical Society, Library and Archives, Columbus. (*Note:* The voluminous war correspondence of these offices has been partially catalogued. Full catalogue data for letters and documents cited in this work are provided when available.)
Giddings Papers	Joshua Reed Giddings Papers, MSS 53, Ohio Historical Society
Hudson Papers	James J. Hudson Papers, MC 1118, box 3, file 6, Special Collections, University of Arkansas Libraries, Fayetteville
MOLLUS	Military Order of the Loyal Legion of the United States, MOLLUS Museum and Library, Philadelphia
NA	National Archives and Records Administration, Washington, DC
OHS	Ohio Historical Society, Library and Archives, Columbus
OR	U.S. War Department, *The War of the Rebellion: A Compilation of the Official Records of the Union and Confederate Armies*, 128 vols. Washington, DC, 1880–1901
OVI	Ohio Volunteer Infantry
RG	Record Group
UAL	University of Arkansas Libraries

Newspapers

Beacon	*Summit County Beacon*, Akron, Ohio
Chronicle	*Western Reserve Chronicle*, Warren, Ohio
Journal	*Ohio State Journal*, Columbus, Ohio
Reporter	*Reporter*, Conneaut, Ohio
Sentinel	*Ashtabula Sentinel*, Jefferson, Ohio
Telegraph	*Ashtabula Weekly Telegraph*, Ashtabula, Ohio

Preface

1. Thomas Clark to Rollin L. Jones, n.d. (likely 1881, based on Clark's reference to a Twenty-Ninth Regiment reunion he had attended the preceding summer in Ohio). This letter was loaned to me through the courtesy of John Gurnish, Mogadore, Ohio.

Prologue

1. W. Williams, *Ashtabula County*, 49.
2. Howells, *Years of My Youth*, 81.
3. *Sentinel*, Dec. 21, 1850.
4. Weisenburger, *Passing of the Frontier*, 372.
5. Mathews, *Ohio and Her Western Reserve*, 175.
6. "What a Secessionist Says of Mr. Giddings," *Sentinel*, Apr. 17, 1861. This piece was reprinted from the *Avalanche* (Memphis).
7. Stewart, *Tactics of Radical Politics*, 142, 215.
8. Undated, unidentified newspaper clipping found in the Giddings Scrapbooks, Giddings Papers. For the probable period of this piece, see Roseboom, *Civil War Era*, 282–83.

9. Land, "John Brown's Ohio Environment."
10. Ibid., 43.
11. Ibid., 46.
12. Ibid., 25.
13. Ibid., 27.
14. Julian, *Giddings*, 370–71.
15. Land, "John Brown's Ohio Environment," 45.
16. Julian, *Giddings*, 370.
17. Retired from Congress against his will, Giddings continued to shape the conscience of the new Republican Party to insure it did not stray from its commitments to human liberty.
18. "Southern Chivalry," *Beacon*, June 20, 1861.
19. Roseboom, *Civil War Era*, 371.
20. "The Wide-Awake Republican Jubilee!" *Beacon*, Nov. 22, 1860.
21. Sandburg, *War Years*, 47.
22. "Mr. Lincoln's Journey," *Chronicle*, Feb. 20, 1861.
23. Ibid.
24. Sandburg, *War Years*, 51. The full text of Lincoln's speech in Cleveland was published in the *Conneaut Reporter*, Feb. 21, 1861, under the headline "Mr. Lincoln in Cleveland." The transcription appearing in that paper varied slightly from the version quoted in Sandburg: "It was not argued up, and cannot be argued down."
25. "Presidential Progress," *Telegraph*, Feb. 23, 1861.
26. "Mr. Lincoln at Conneaut," *Reporter*, Feb. 21, 1861.
27. Roseboom, *Civil War Era*, 373, 376.
28. "Speech of Mr. Giddings, Delivered at the Anti-Compromise Meeting Held in Jefferson, Dec. 24, 1860," *Sentinel*, Jan. 2, 1861.
29. "Compromise," *Beacon*, Dec. 27, 1861. The same anticompromise sentiment was expressed by a later piece in the *Beacon*, "Should There Be Any Further Compromise with Slavery!" Jan. 24, 1861.
30. *Beacon*, Mar. 20, 1861.
31. Ibid.
32. Salmon P. Chase to J. R. Giddings, Jan. 31, 1861, Giddings Papers; Stewart, *Tactics of Radical Politics*, 274. Giddings's salary of four thousand dollars per annum for serving as ambassador to Canada was detailed in the *Reporter*, along with the editor's guarded endorsement of his entitlement to the post, Mar. 28, 1861.
33. *Reporter*, Feb. 7, 1861.
34. "The Southern Flag" and "The Difference between the Gunners . . . ," *Sentinel*, Mar. 20, 1861.
35. "News of the Neighborhood," *Sentinel*, Jan. 16, 1861, taken from the *Warren Democrat*.
36. "The Times and the Men We Need: A Sermon Delivered by Rev. Olds at the Brick Church in Jefferson, Ohio, Sunday, Dec. 30, 1860," *Sentinel*, Jan. 23, 1861.
37. *Beacon*, July or Aug., 1855 or 1856.
38. Lyman Ames diary, June 10, 1864.
39. J. R. Giddings to Addison Giddings, June 10, 1861, Giddings Papers.

Chapter 1: "We Are All War"
"Let the Dogs of War Be Loosed"

1. Nathan Parmater diary, Sept. 23, 1861. A typescript and the handwritten volumes making up his war diary are found at the Ohio Historical Society, *Civil War Diary and Papers of Nathaniel L. Parmater*, 29th OVI, 5 cubic feet, call no. MSS246. Parmater's last name is spelled in some records as Parmeter, and his first name is given occasionally as Nathaniel. This book uses the form of the name by which he was known in the Michigan town where he lived for forty years after the war. The correct spelling of soldiers' names vexes the researcher. Some men in the regiment had their names spelled in a multitude of ways: Cains C. Lord, for example, appears as Gains Lord, Gaines Lord, Caius Lord, Gaius Lord, and even Lord Gains. The correct spelling of his name is found in legal documents prepared for his pension claim after the war. Cains C. Lord pension file, record group (abbreviated RG) 94, NA. Several members of the regiment who shared the last name Hurlburt were subjected to misspellings such as Hulbert, Halburt, Hurlbert, and Hurlbut, to name a few. Misspellings of soldiers' names abound in the Twenty-Ninth's records and in SeCheverell's multiple lists of membership in the regiment. For consistency in identifying a soldier in this work, I have relied on spellings

given in the *State Roster,* vol. 3, 351–93, unless a definitive spelling was found in pension files, military files, or correspondence to which a soldier signed his name.

2. Parmater diary, Dec. 24, 1861.

3. The Benjamin Pontius drawing of Camp Giddings is found at the Ohio Historical Society Archives/Library, SC 134.

4. Cox, "War Preparations," 1:84–98.

5. "Important If True," *Beacon,* May 2, 1861.

6. "Fugitives from Southern Oppression," *Beacon,* May 2, 1861. Although publication of unfounded stories of this sort lessened as the war progressed, rumors of the death of Jefferson Davis persisted through the entire war.

7. Ibid.

8. "Silence the Traitors," *Beacon,* Apr. 18, 1861.

9. *Reporter,* Aug. 16, 1862. A brief editorial, "War, War," expressed the Conneaut editor's loathing for the unvarying diet of continual announcements for war meetings and for war news in general.

10. "All Hail! Johnson's Corners," *Beacon,* Apr. 25, 1861.

11. *Beacon,* Apr. 25, 1861.

12. *Beacon,* Apr. 25, 1861.

13. *Beacon,* Apr. 25, 1861.

14. *Beacon,* Apr. 25, 1861.

15. Lane, *Fifty Years,* 353.

16. "Where the War Strength Lies—Population of the Three Classes of States," *Chronicle,* Apr. 24, 1861.

17. "The Feeling," *Telegraph,* Apr. 20, 1861.

18. "The Difference," *Beacon,* Apr. 25, 1861.

19. "War Begun—The Traitors Triumphant," *Beacon,* Apr. 18, 1861.

20. *Beacon,* May 23, 1861.

21. "Summit County Astir! Akron Fully Aroused!" *Beacon,* Apr. 25, 1861.

22. The full text of Giddings's Apr. 30, 1861, letter to Sen. Sumner is found in Julian, *Giddings,* 385.

23. Lane, *Fifty Years,* 352.

24. "The North as a Unit," *Beacon,* Apr. 25, 1861.

25. "Counsel to Volunteers—To Our Young Soldiers," *Beacon,* May 2, 1861.

26. "Fight, Fight, Fight!" The advertisement for Talcott's Hardware, typical of the war sloganeering used by Reserve merchants, ran in the *Sentinel* through May 1861.

27. "Presentations," *Beacon,* May 2, 1861.

28. Harper, *Ohio Handbook,* 7.

29. "From the Editor, Columbus, Apr. 26, 1861, to the Editor of the *Sentinel,*" *Sentinel,* Apr. 29, 1861.

30. *Sentinel,* Apr. 24, 1861.

Headquarters, Jefferson, Ohio

31. "'To Arms!!'" Headquarters, Jefferson, Apr. 21, 1861, *Sentinel,* Apr. 24, 1861.

32. "E. V. Smalley, lately one of the editors . . . ," *Beacon,* June 20, 1861.

33. Lane, *Fifty Years,* 357.

34. W. Williams, *Ashtabula County,* 50–51.

35. Ibid.

36. Ibid.

37. Ibid.

38. "Threads for Home-Spun Wear," *Reporter,* May 16, 1861.

39. "Flag Raising at Rome," *Telegraph,* June 22, 1861.

40. Ibid.

41. "The Court House for the last few days . . . ," *Sentinel,* Apr. 29, 1861.

42. "Rifle Companies," *Sentinel,* Apr. 29, 1861.

43. "Jefferson Light Artillery," *Sentinel,* June 6, 1861.

44. "Ashtabula Regiment," *Sentinel,* Apr. 29, 1861.

45. *Sentinel,* July 15, 1861.

46. "Capt. Crane," *Sentinel,* Apr. 29, 1861.

47. "The following is the roll of that known as the Ashtabula Companies . . . ," *Sentinel,* May 20, 1861.

48. Lane, *Fifty Years*, 355.

49. *Beacon,* Apr. 25, 1861.

50. Ibid.

51. Ibid.

52. "Gone into Camp," *Beacon,* May 2, 1861. Buckley's company departed Akron on Apr. 30, 1861. He and his fellow officers had personally pledged to pay Professor Marble and his musicians $650 for their services in the western Virginia campaign. Correspondence to the Governor and Adjutant General of Ohio, 1861–66, series 147, Ohio Historical Society, Archives and Library Division, Columbus. Catalog number cited when available. Correspondence from this collection cited hereafter as AGO.

53. "The Disbanding of Company 'C,'" *Beacon,* May 23, 1861. Hard continued to rankle from this affair years afterward and recounted the unhappy events in recollections of it he submitted to the Pension Department. Pulaski Hard pension file, NA.

54. Ibid.

55. "Morgan Riflemen," *Sentinel,* May 5, 1861.

The Origins of the Giddings Regiment

56. Dr. G. W. Dickinson, letter, July 16, 1861, in *Beacon,* July 25, 1861.

57. Brig. Gen. William S. Rosecrans report, *OR,* series 3, vol. 2, pt. 1, 216. Hereafter, citations to the *Official Records,* noted as *OR,* will take the following form: author of report or correspondence, volume number shortened to vol., part number abbreviated as pt., followed by the page number or numbers. With few exceptions, all cited documents are found in Series 1. For this reason, series number will be dispensed with and any exceptions noted.

58. "A. E. H.," letter, July 13, 1861, in *Beacon,* July 25, 1861.

59. Dickinson, letter, July 16, 1861; *Beacon,* July 25, 1861.

60. "The Late Gen. Garnett," undated piece from the *Wheeling Intelligencer,* published in the *Beacon,* July 25, 1861.

61. Rosecrans report, *OR,* vol. 2, pt. 1, 218.

62. *Reporter,* July 11, 1861.

63. "The Crops," *Beacon,* July 25, 1861.

64. Reserve soldiers in the Nineteenth began returning to their homes during the first week of Aug. 1861, upon expiration of their ninety-day enlistment term.

"Dark Peril"

65. "The Battle," *Reporter,* July 25, 1861. A field reporter for the Conneaut newspaper wrote a poignant account of the tortured emotional state of the residents of Ashtabula city on the night the Bull Run news came in.

66. *Beacon,* July 25, 1861.

67. Ibid.

68. "War News—The Defeat," *Sentinel,* July 25, 1861.

69. Ibid.

70. "Rebel Barbarities on the Battle Field," *Chronicle,* Aug. 14, 1861.

71. Ibid.

72. *Chronicle,* Aug. 14, 1861.

73. "A hospital filled with wounded men . . . ," *Journal,* Aug. 21, 1861.

74. *Reporter,* July 25, 1861.

75. SeCheverell, *Journal History,* 18.

Disappointment's Child

76. W. Williams, *Ashtabula County,* 52. Giddings's words and the circumstances under which they were spoken are recorded in the "Military History" section of this 1878 Ashtabula County history. This section was written by Twenty-Ninth Regiment veteran Rollin L. Jones.

77. "J. M. L.," letter, July 7, 1861, in "Disgraced Men of the 19th," *Sentinel,* July 18, 1861, taken from the *Cleveland Herald,* July 15, 1861.

78. "To the Public," from a letter written by two of the drummed-out soldiers of Stratton's company, dated July 16, 1861, taken from the *Trumbull Democrat* and reprinted in the *Sentinel* on July 22.

79. Ibid.

80. "Disgraced Men of the 19th," *Sentinel*, July 18, 1861. Extract from the letter of a Nineteenth Ohio soldier describing the affair, signed "J. M. L. (Leland)" and published in the *Cleveland Herald*. The soldier stated in part, "Our regiment came near being broken up today."

81. "The Disgraced Volunteers," *Sentinel*, July 22, 1861. The salient portions of General Order 29.

82. "The Flag Presentation," *Sentinel*, Dec. 4, 1861. The full text of Giddings's speech to the regiment in which he recounted the events of the Buckhannon affair and tied the regiment's founding directly to them was published in this account.

83. "Gen. Fitch Slave Catching," based on extracts of a letter by Pvt. E. T. Pritchard, Company K, Nineteenth Ohio, taken from the *Cleveland Leader*, reprinted in the *Sentinel*, July 15, 1861. Pritchard reported the event to his hometown newspaper in Cleveland, but oddly enough, no account of the incident written by an Ashtabula County soldier was ever published in a county newspaper.

84. Ibid.

85. Ibid.

86. "Blood Hounds?—No!" *Sentinel*, July 18, 1861.

87. *Sentinel*, Dec. 25, 1861.

88. "The Returned Warren Soldiers," extract of editorial from the Warren *Chronicle*, reprinted in the *Sentinel*, July 22, 1861. While the Nineteenth Ohio was still in its training camp in Ohio, the *Beacon* had raised a small furor over the poor quality of rations given its soldiers, while soldiers from other parts of Ohio were treated to the very best. The news of the victory at Rich Mountain was especially gratifying to Reserve residents because, as the *Beacon* editor noted, "There has been a disposition in certain quarters to depreciate the valor of volunteers from this part of the State, particularly from the Western Reserve, where most of the members of the 19th belong." *Beacon*, July 25, 1861.

89. "The Returned Warren Soldiers," *Sentinel*, July 22, 1861.

"What Does Ashtabula Do?"

90. "If Mr. Lincoln were equal to his duty . . . ," *Sentinel*, July 1, 1861.

91. Uncatalogued letter, Giddings to Dennison, AGO. From its content this undated letter can be placed in the period April–May 1861.

92. "The Nineteenth Regiment," *Sentinel*, July 25, 1861.

93. *Sentinel*, Apr. 21, 1861.

94. "Mr. Giddings returned home from Washington . . . ," *Sentinel*, July 15, 1861.

95. Harper, *Ohio Handbook*, 7. Lincoln's first call for troops, on Apr. 15, 1861, was for seventy-five thousand, of which Ohio's quota was thirteen thousand, or thirteen regiments. Ohio put a total of twenty-three three-month regiments in the field, initially intending to pay for the additional ten from its own pockets.

96. On July 13, 1861, Secretary of War Cameron issued a circular that stated, "No more troops will be received by this Department till authorized by Congress." *OR*, series 3, vol. 1, pt. 1, 327.

97. "Mr. Giddings returned home . . . ," *Sentinel*, July 15, 1861. This is the first documented notice of plans to form the Giddings Regiment.

98. "A Card—While recently at Washington . . . ," *Sentinel*, July 18, 1861. The *Sentinel* was published biweekly in this period—Monday and Thursday—which might explain the two-day delay in publishing the Giddings card.

99. Harper, *Ohio Handbook*, 10.

Chapter 2: Founders' Club
Acting in Concert

1. "The Flag Presentation," *Sentinel*, Dec. 4, 1861.

2. SeCheverell, *Journal History*, 18.

3. Stewart, *Tactics of Radical Politics*, 16–17.

4. Ibid., 276, 55.

5. E. B. Woodbury to Ohio Adjutant General G. P. Buckingham, Oct. 16, 1861, in which Kellogg is identified as Chairman Pro Tempore of the County Military Committee and J. D. Ensign as Secretary; 1 p. [series 147-14:157], AGO. Then, in a Dec. 17 letter to AG Buckingham, Woodbury signs as Chairman of the County Military Committee; 2 pp. [series 147-20:118], AGO.

6. W. Williams, *Ashtabula County*, 106.

7. Ibid., 105.

8. Ibid., 50.

9. "Arrival of the 29th," *Cleveland Daily Leader,* July 18, 1865. Upon their return to Ohio at the end of the war, the Twenty-Ninth was identified as the Giddings Regiment and as the Abolition Regiment. But in the official history of the U.S. army in the war, it was not the 29th Ohio that would win designation as the Giddings Regiment. Instead, the privilege of bearing the Giddings name would go to the Fourteenth U.S. Infantry, a regiment of regulars commanded for a time by Giddings's son Maj. Grotius R. Giddings.

10. "The New Regiment," *Sentinel,* July 29, 1861.

"Come Boys, Follow Me"

11. SeCheverell, *Journal History,* 18.

12. "Reception of the 19th," *Beacon,* Aug. 8, 1861.

13. Ibid.

14. J. R. Giddings to AG Buckingham, Aug. 8, 1861, 1 p. [series 147-4:119], AGO.

15. This sectional daguerreotype was made by pioneering photographer Samuel J. Miller and later made into an etching for publication titled "From the West, North Akron." Ohio Historical Society, 146–47, negative R55.

16. Grismer, *Akron and Summit County,* 171–75.

17. J. R. Giddings to AG Buckingham, Aug. 8, 1861, 1 p. [series 147-4:119], AGO.

18. Lewis Buckley to AG Buckingham, Aug. 26, 1861, 3 pp. [series 147-5:235], AGO; Buckley to AG Richmond, Jan. 19, 1863, AGO, uncatalogued.

19. Buckley to AG Buckingham, Aug. 26, 1861, 3 pp. [series 147-5:235], AGO.

20. *Akron Beacon and Republican,* May 30, 1896.

21. For an etching of Buckley, see Lane, *Fifty Years,* 359.

22. Cadet admission records for Lewis P. Buckley, U.S. Military Archives, U.S. Army Military Academy, West Point, New York, July 1, 1822.

23. Storke, *Cayuga County,* 348.

24. Ibid.

25. Auten, *Seneca County History* [Waterloo, NY] 1, no. 3 (Mar. 1985).

26. Ibid.

27. Geneva, NY, newspaper extracts, courtesy of Betty Auten, Waterloo, NY. Buckley married Mary Barton on Jan. 17, 1810.

28. Storke, *Cayuga County,* 348. Confirmed in *Abstracts of Early Wills,* Cayuga County, NY, which gives the date of Hugh's death as Nov. 9, 1812.

29. Geneva, NY, newspaper extracts. Mary Barton died on Feb. 17, 1813.

30. Avery, *Ingersoll Family,* 369.

31. Ibid. Justus Ingersoll was appointed to a variety of local government jobs in the villages around Batavia, NY, including state superintendent of stores, mentioned in an unidentified letter of recommendation, "Dear ____." In Buckley cadet admissions records, U.S. Army Military Academy, West Point.

32. Letters of recommendation in Buckley cadet admissions records, U.S. Military Academy.

33. *Akron Beacon and Republican,* Saturday, May 30, 1896; Lane, *Fifty Years,* 359.

34. Lewis P. Buckley student records, U.S. Army Military Academy.

35. Ibid.

36. Buckley pension file, RG 94, NA.

37. Lane, *Fifty Years,* 359.

38. Ibid.; Avery, *Ingersoll Family,* 369. Noah Ingersoll settled in Copley in 1836 and prospered, serving two consecutive terms as justice of the peace in Coventry. He was elected coroner of Summit County twice in the 1850s.

39. Lane, *Fifty Years,* 359.

40. Ibid.

41. Ibid.

42. Ibid.

43. Ibid., 1107.

44. GAR, *Our Memorial Chapel,* 4.

45. "New Companies for the 29th Regiment," *Beacon,* Aug. 22, 1861.

46. The first notice of Buckley's acceptance of the command of the Twenty-Ninth Ohio is found in Buckley to AG Buckingham, Aug. 26, 1861, 3 pp. [series 147-5:235], AGO. Buckley stated, "No doubt you see I have

accepted the Colonelcy of the 29th Regiment." The first published notice of Buckley's acceptance is found in the "The Twenty-Ninth Regiment," *Sentinel,* Aug. 19, 1861.

47. Buckley to AG Buckingham, Aug. 26, 1861.

48. J. R. Giddings, E. B. Woodbury, and Abner Kellogg to Gov. Dennison, Aug. 26, 1861, 2 pp. [series 147-5:136], AGO.

Cast in a Brilliant Light

49. All were reported in the *Sentinel* on July 4, 1861.

50. The passage of this comet and the sensation it caused were reported in the *Sentinel* and the *Beacon,* July 4, 1861; the *Chronicle,* July 12, 1861; and the *Journal,* July 24, 1861.

Chapter 3: Camp Giddings
First Steps

1. Clark's residence in Cleveland and his appointment as the regiment's major assigned the management of its organization were confirmed in "The 29th Regiment," *Cleveland Morning Leader,* Aug. 24, 1861.

2. On Aug. 1, 1861, Lewis P. Buckley wrote to Governor Dennison recommending that Clark be appointed to *any* active duty command vacancy. Buckley stated he knew Clark to be mature, vigorous, strictly abstinent, and a skilled master of the drill; 3 pp. [series 147-4:81], AGO.

3. SeCheverell, *Journal History,* 19.

4. Ellis, *Norwich University,* 2:369.

5. Ibid., 2:370.

6. Ibid., 2:369.

7. Further confirmation of Clark's service with the Nineteenth Regiment is found in a resume of his recent service in a letter sent to Governor Dennison, Aug. 4, 1861. Every captain of the Nineteenth endorsed his credentials by fixing their signatures to this letter; 3 pp. [series 147-4:23], AGO. Also in series 147-4:81.

8. Clark's service as drillmaster for the Nineteenth Ohio is reported in his obituary published in the *Cambridge (MA) Tribune,* Aug. 18, 1894. Search of the regiment's rosters and enlistment records does not reveal Clark's name. That he had an intimate connection to it is corroborated by SeCheverell. A biographical sketch of Clark published in the Roll of Honor for Norwich University states that Clark served as drillmaster at the front for the Nineteenth Ohio during the summer of 1861. Ellis, *Norwich University,* 458.

9. Thomas Clark to AG Buckingham, Aug. 20, 1861, 1 p. [series 147-5:57], AGO.

10. Ellis, *Norwich University,* 2:370.

11. Pvt. Oscar Brewster, letter, Camp Tyler, western VA, Feb. 26, 1862, in *Beacon,* Mar. 13, 1862.

12. Ibid.

13. SeCheverell, *Journal History,* 19.

14. "The New Regiment," *Sentinel,* July 29, 1861. The article announced that the fairgrounds of the Ashtabula County Agricultural Society would serve as the regiment's encampment.

15. *Reporter,* Oct. 10, 1861.

16. *Jefferson (OH) Star Beacon,* Dec. 23, 1996. Buildings present at the Ashtabula County fairgrounds when the regiment went into camp were identified in this modern article. The reporter ascribed the information to a report of the agricultural society's board prepared following the regiment's departure, in Dec. 1861.

17. Clark to Buckingham, Aug. 20, 1861.

18. Advertisement titled "Military Books," *Journal,* Aug. 23, 1861.

19. AG Buckingham's reply to Clark's request for weapons is found on the bottom of Clark to Buckingham, Aug. 20, 1861.

20. SeCheverell, *Journal History,* 19.

21. "The Twenty-Ninth," *Sentinel,* Aug. 22, 1861. The newspaper reported that Company A had gone into camp "last week," while the Pierpont Company had arrived on Monday, Aug. 19.

22. William T. Fitch pension file, RG 94, NA, gives his muster-in date as Aug. 14, 1861, three days before Clark arrived in Jefferson.

23. "Old Ashtabula First, This Time," *Journal,* July 24, 1861. Giddings had been in Columbus a few days before Bull Run on unknown business, perhaps to bolster flagging support for the Republican Party, which was being eclipsed by the new Union Party. *Journal,* July 18, 1861.

24. "Old Ashtabula First, This Time," *Journal,* July 24, 1861.

25. *Journal,* July 29, 1861.
26. "A Regiment in Ashtabula County," *Reporter,* Aug. 1, 1861.
27. "The New Regiment," *Sentinel,* July 29, 1861.
28. *Journal,* Aug. 8, 1861.
29. "Important to Recruits and Recruiting Officers," *Beacon,* Nov. 14, 1861.
30. "The New Regiment," *Sentinel,* July 29, 1861.
31. "The Twenty-Ninth," *Sentinel,* Aug. 29, 1861. "All question about the success of the filling up of the 29th is at an end."
32. "The New Regiment," *Telegraph,* July 27, 1861.
33. "The Twenty-Ninth," *Reporter,* Nov. 14, 1861. The newspaper reported that a six-gun battery was to be added "within days." The editor justified such an ambitious plan by reporting, optimistically, that all the regiment's companies were now full except one, and "that is filling fast."

Post of Honor

34. "The Jefferson Company," *Sentinel,* Aug. 15, 1861.
35. Fitch's age, place of birth, physical description, and residence before the war were found in his pension file, RG 94, NA.
36. Fitch obituary, *Sentinel,* Jan. 3, 10, 1895.
37. William T. Fitch pension file, RG 94, NA.
38. "Attention National Guards!" *Sentinel,* Aug. 19, 1861.
39. "The Jefferson Company," *Sentinel,* Aug. 15, 1861.
40. Everson J. Hurlburt pension file, RG 94, NA.
41. Wilbur F. Stevens pension file, RG 94, NA. Stevens's parents' place of birth and father's occupation are found in the censuses of 1850 and 1860 for Pierpont Township. Information provided through the courtesies of May Colling, Ashtabula, OH.
42. Muster rolls for Co. E, Regimental Books, 29th OVI, RG 94, NA.
43. Stevens pension file, "Deposition of Dr. Oliver S. Trunier," Pacific Grove, CA, Feb., 1897, taken in the widow's pension appeal case of Mrs. Wilbur F. Stevens.
44. Stevens pension file, RG 94, NA.
45. "Deposition of Bryon McArthur, late member of the 29th Ohio Infantry Regiment," Sept. 16, 1896, Tacoma, WA. Mrs. Wilbur F. Stevens widow's pension appeal case, NA.
46. "Pension Appeal Examiner's Summary of Facts," Stevens pension file, RG 94, NA.
47. Muster rolls for Co. B, Regimental Books, 29th OVI, RG 94, NA.
48. "Many times within the last few days . . . ," *Sentinel,* Aug. 29, 1861.
49. Maj. Thomas Clark to AG Buckingham, Aug. 29, 1861, 1 p. [series 147-6:58], AGO. Clark stated in part that he soon expected Hayes's Company C to have the "requisite" fifty men needed for it to muster as a company. That fifty men was the number necessary to come in as company as of Aug. 1861 is mentioned by E. A. Ford of Geauga County. E. A. Ford to AG Buckingham, Aug. 13, 1861, 3 pp. [series 147-4:135], AGO.
50. *Chronicle,* Aug. 21, 1861.
51. *Telegraph,* Sept. 14, 1861. Also published in "Soldier's Rations," *Sentinel,* Aug. 29, 1861.
52. "The Boys in Camp," *Sentinel,* Aug. 29, 1861.
53. "The New Regiment," *Sentinel,* July 29, 1861.

The County Fair

54. The Ashtabula County fair of 1861 was held from Tuesday, Sept. 2, to Friday, Sept. 6, 1861. *Sentinel,* Sept. 2, 1861. The dates of the fair and the schedule of events were also published in the *Telegraph,* Aug. 3, 1861.
55. "The Boys in Camp."
56. Capt. Hayes's Company C reported on Tuesday, Aug. 27, 1861, according to SeCheverell, *Journal History,* 19, or on Aug. 28, according to the *Sentinel,* Aug. 29, 1861.
57. "Capt. Hayes," *Sentinel,* Aug. 29, 1861.
58. "The Twenty-Ninth is filling up . . . ," *Sentinel,* Aug. 29, 1861.
59. "An Artist in the War," *Sentinel,* Aug. 22, 1861. Credited to the *Lorraine County News.*
60. "The time for holding the County Fair is close at hand . . . ," *Sentinel,* Aug. 19, 1861.
61. For an excellent account of the Ashtabula County fair of 1861, see "The Fair," *Sentinel,* Sept. 9, 1861.

62. Maj. Thomas Clark to AG Buckingham, Sept. 4, 1861, 1 p. [series 147-6:181], AGO.

63. Maj. Thomas Clark to AG Buckingham, Sept. 2, 1861, 1 p. [series 147-6:58], AGO. Clark to Buckingham, Sept. 4, stated that three companies would have their rolls complete enough to allow muster the following day.

64. "The Boys of the 29th," *Sentinel*, Sept. 9, 1861.

65. "To the Editor of the Sentinel," *Sentinel*, Sept. 19, 1861.

The Homer Boys

66. Rupp, "Fighting Regiment."

67. James Hudson, ed., "Civil War Letters from Frederick, Maryland: The War Correspondence of Sergeant John G. Marsh," *Old Northwest* 9 (Fall 1983): 237–53.

68. Henry Rupp pension file, RG 94, NA.

69. Thomas Dowling pension file, RG 94, NA.

70. That John C. Shaw had been an orphan in New York City and that he was placed in a Reserve home by the Children's Aid Society was confirmed by his grandson, Marion Shaw of Toledo, Iowa, during a visit with me, Feb. 1996.

71. Franklin Morey pension file, RG 94, NA.

The Average Soldier

72. Fox, *Regimental Losses*, 62. The mean age of Union recruits was twenty-five years.

73. Data for age at enlistment, physical description, place of birth, and vocation taken from the descriptive lists for each company found in the Regimental Books, NA. After the war, the wife of Col. William T. Fitch hand-copied the complete muster rolls and donated the copy to the Henderson Library, Jefferson, Ohio.

74. William Fox determined that 48 percent of the soldiers in the Union army had been farmers when they enlisted. *Regimental Losses*, 63.

Chapter 4: Recruiting Wars
Competitors and Complainers

1. "Please announce Mr. *Leader* . . . ," *Sentinel*, Aug. 29, 1861. The *Ohio State Journal* ran the *Sentinel*'s rebuke to the county's detractors in its Sept. 1, 1861, edition under the heading "The Ashtabula *Sentinel* says."

2. Maj. Thomas Clark to AG Buckingham, Sept. 4, 1861, 1 p. [series 147-6:181], AGO.

3. "From Ashtabula," *Reporter*, Aug. 29, 1861.

4. Ibid.

5. J. F. Morse to AG Buckingham, Aug. 9, 1861, 2 pp. [series 147-4:17], AGO.

6. A total of approximately seventy Nineteenth Ohio veterans enlisted in the Giddings Regiment. Company D of Akron held the most: twenty-eight of its one hundred men had seen service in the Nineteenth Ohio. The percentage of these men who served through all the Twenty-Ninth's service was higher than that of enlistees who had not served in the ninety-day Nineteenth Ohio Infantry. *State Roster*; W. Williams, *Ashtabula County*; Lane, *Fifty Years*.

7. "From Ashtabula," *Reporter*, Sept. 5, 1861.

8. Ibid.

9. In his MOLLUS membership profile Hayes complained that the "completion of the 29th Regiment was delayed by the authorization of a cavalry regiment on the same ground." There was only one other regiment of any sort, let alone a cavalry regiment, being recruited on this "ground"—the one being put together by Ben Wade. Military Order of the Loyal Legion of the United States (hereafter cited as MOLLUS), Insignia Record 7025, Lt. Col. Edward Hayes, MOLLUS Library, Philadelphia.

10. Secretary of War to Hon. B. F. Wade and Hon. John Hutchins, July 30, 1861, *OR*, series 3, vol. 1, pt. 1, 367. The *Sentinel* published a "card" from J. R. Giddings in its July 18, 1861, edition stating that J. R. had received assurances from the secretary of war that he would accept a regiment of infantry from "this" part of the state. A meeting of "interested gentlemen" was scheduled for July 25. The battle of First Bull Run intervened on Sunday, July 21.

11. "The Twenty-Ninth is filling up fast . . . ," *Sentinel*, Aug. 29, 1861.

12. Reid, *Ohio in the War*, 757.

13. "Another Cavalry Regiment," *Chronicle*, Sept. 18, 1861. Reported later in "Camp Warren," *Reporter*, Oct. 10, 1861.

14. "The Wade and Hutchins Cavalry," *Sentinel*, Aug. 29, 1861; *Reporter*, Sept. 5, 1861.

15. The *Reporter*, Sept. 5, 1861, gave the date of the Second Cavalry's officer election in Jefferson as Aug. 21, 1861. W. W. Williams gives the date of the regiment's organization as Aug. 20 and the place as Jefferson. W. Williams, *Ashtabula County*, 63. Whitelaw Reid gives the place of rendezvous as Cleveland and does not give the place of organization. Reid, *Ohio in the War*, 2:757.

16. "Cavalry Company," *Sentinel*, Aug. 19, 1861.

17. *Reporter*, Sept. 5, 1861.

18. "Horses for Cavalry," *Sentinel*, Aug. 29, 1861.

19. "The Horse Market," *Sentinel*, Sept. 5, 1861.

20. "Look well to your stable doors . . . ," *Sentinel*, Oct. 23, 1861.

21. "We Would Respectfully Suggest to the *Cleveland Herald* . . . ," *Reporter*, Oct. 24, 1861. A later piece in the *Reporter* listed the men enlisted in Carlin's Battery and in the Twenty-Ninth Ohio. *Reporter*, Nov. 7, 1861. Enlistment of Conneaut men in the Twenty-Ninth Ohio and in Carlin's battery was also listed in the *Sentinel*, Jan. 29, 1862.

22. *Reporter*, Sept. 5, 1861.

23. "Names of Volunteers, Now in the United States Army," *Sentinel*, Jan. 29, 1862. This edition published the name of every Ashtabula County man who had enlisted in the military service through the end of 1861, along with the name of the outfit in which he was serving.

24. "S. B." letter, Dec. 8, 1861, Camp Giddings, *Beacon*, Dec. 12, 1861. S. B. would be unmasked as Capt. Josiah "Jack" Wright of Akron.

25. "We learn that Perry Devore, Esq. . . . ," *Reporter*, Aug. 1, 1861.

26. "A Company of Sharpshooters," *Sentinel*, Aug. 19, 1861.

27. "John Brown's Company," *Sentinel*, Sept. 25, 1861.

28. W. Williams, *Ashtabula County*, 66. Nearly thirty Ashtabula County men enlisted in Brown's Company K, Seventh Kansas Cavalry.

29. Maj. Thomas Clark to AG Buckingham, Sept. 12, 1861, 3 pp. [series 147-8:27], AGO. Clark complained that little was being done to assist the Twenty-Ninth's recruiting efforts in Lake, Geauga, or Trumbull Counties, as had been expected, and at that point Summit County had provided the single company that marched into camp behind Colonel Buckley. In the overall confusion Clark was perhaps ignorant that in Summit County at least, recruiters were hard at work raising men for the Giddings project.

Too Tight a Hold

30. Maj. Thomas Clark to AG Buckingham, Aug. 31, 1861, 2 pp. [series 147-6:46], AGO.

31. So baffling were the ground rules of recruiting, and the role of the military committee in them, that J. F. Morse of Painesville wrote to Governor Dennison in October to inquire if the governor could provide him with the names of the men appointed as the Military Committee of Lake County, since he could not ascertain that important information even though he was on the scene; 3 pp. [series 147-10:170], AGO.

32. A. D. Strong to Gov. Dennison, Aug. 11, 1861, 1 p. [series 147-4:29,]AGO.

33. W. Williams, *Ashtabula County*, 63. Strong went on to serve as second lieutenant, Company F, Second Ohio Cavalry.

34. James Crane to AG Buckingham, Aug. 12, 1861, 1 p. [series 147-4:8], AGO.

35. The Twenty-Ninth Regiment lost the services of more than just A. D. Strong and James Crane and their men. E. D. Knapp of West Andover, Ashtabula County, had hopes of recruiting musicians for the Twenty-Ninth and wrote to the governor requesting direction. But like Morse, he was ignorant of the identity of the men appointed as his county's military committee. Knapp to Dennison, Oct. 14, 1861, 1 p. [series 147-13:107], AGO. Around the same time the military committee of Ashtabula County met and recommended to the governor that S. T. Prentice be given a recruiting appointment as second lieutenant in the Twenty-Ninth Regiment, and Lewis P. Buckley, colonel commanding, endorsed the recommendation. That is the one and only reference to Prentice. Ashtabula County Military Committee to Gov. Dennison, Oct. 16, 1861, 1 p. [series 147-14:157], AGO. As a last example of the confusion and imperfect coordination that caused difficulties for the Twenty-Ninth Regiment, William Hall of Medina had been given an appointment as a recruiting lieutenant for the Twenty-Ninth (whether by the Giddings group or the state is unclear) and had raised a substantial number of men. He changed his mind too, and took his men to the Seventy-Second Ohio Infantry after he had been assured by its organizers that he could have more time to perfect his company before going into their camp. Hall to H. C. Canfield, Oct.

31, 1861, 2 pp. [series 147-16:44], AGO. Knapp, Prentice, and Hall were never mentioned again in the annals of the Twenty-Ninth Regiment's career.

36. E. A. Ford to AG Buckingham, Aug. 13, 1861, AGO.
37. Maj. Thomas Clark to AG Buckingham, Aug. 31, 1861, AGO.
38. W. Williams, *Ashtabula County*, 63.

Impostors

39. "Capt. M. P. Pierce . . . ," *Sentinel*, Aug. 26, 1861. Three weeks earlier the Akron newspapers received a notice from Pierce meant for publication notifying the public that he was organizing a company to be known as the Ohio Sharp Shooters. *Beacon*, Aug. 8, 1861.
40. *Sentinel*, July 4, 1861.
41. "Captain M. P. Pierce . . . ," *Sentinel*, Aug. 29, 1861.
42. Maj. Thomas Clark to AG Buckingham, Aug. 31, 1861, AGO.
43. Ibid.
44. Ibid.
45. Ibid.
46. M. P. Pierce to AG Buckingham, Aug. 19, 1861. Pierce wrote two letters to Buckingham this day and references a third, which has not been preserved. Pierce's complaint that he had unfairly been kept out of the ninety-day service is contained in AGO, 1 p. [series 147-4:195].
47. Ibid.
48. Ibid.
49. M. P. Pierce to AG Buckingham, Aug. 19, 1861, 2 pp. [series 147-4:195], AGO. In his first letter to the adjutant general of this date Pierce enclosed the roll of men he had supposedly enlisted for the Giddings regiment. It was in this letter that Pierce claimed J. R. Giddings had promised that his company would be designated Company A.
50. Maj. Thomas Clark to AG Buckingham, Sept. 2, 1861, AGO.
51. Ibid.
52. Pierce did not get into the war. His name does not appear anywhere on the *State Roster*, as a member of either a ninety-day or a three-year outfit.
53. *Sentinel*, Oct. 23, 1861.
54. "Mr. Giddings on Saturday last . . . ," *Telegraph*, Aug. 24, 1861.
55. "The Twenty-Ninth Regiment," *Sentinel*, Aug. 19, 1861. The editor of the *Sentinel* was confused as to the regiment for which Prentice was seeking recruits. Two pieces appeared on the same newspaper page of this date, one tying him to the three-year Nineteenth Ohio, and the second to the Twenty-Ninth Ohio.
56. "Volunteering—The War Department . . . ," *Sentinel*, Sept. 5, 1861.
57. "General Order No. 51, Adjutant General's Office, Columbus, Aug. 31, 1861," *Journal*, Sept. 2, 1861.
58. "Head Quarters, Ohio Militia, Adjutant General's Office," *Reporter*, Oct. 10, 1861. The adjutant general's order, dated Sept. 27, 1861, announcing the adoption of the "Committee Plan," was published throughout Ohio.
59. "Meeting of the District Committee," *Beacon*, Nov. 7, 14, 1861. The practical operation of the district military committee was detailed in the minutes of the committee meeting in Ravenna on Oct. 29, 1861. The chief problem in the new system had nothing to do with its structure but rather with the fact that the townships were failing to send in their reports.
60. *Telegraph*, Nov. 7, 1861. A report of the district committee encompassing Summit County and Akron described the type and quantity of donated relief material counted up at Ravenna on Oct. 29. Goods collected by the district's women filled thirty boxes, each packed full with woolen socks, gloves, mittens, shirts, underdrawers, handkerchiefs, quilts, pillows, sheets, blankets, and towels.
61. "We see by the papers . . . ," *Reporter*, Oct. 3, 1861.
62. McNeil to AG Buckingham, 1 p. [series 147-14:32], AGO.
63. William J. Hall to H. C. Canfield, Oct. 31, 1861, 2 pp. [series 147-16:44], AGO.
64. Maj. Thomas Clark to AG Buckingham, Sept. 12, 1861, 3 pp. [series 147-8:27], AGO. In this letter Clark lays out the particulars of the Hamilton case. Interestingly, he proposed that the state set boundaries inside of which only one regiment could recruit. His proposal would eliminate the promiscuous practice of claim jumping but was not workable for a variety of reasons.

65. S. B., letter, Camp Giddings, Dec. 8, 1861, in "Army Correspondence," *Beacon,* Dec. 12, 1861. In the previously cited letter from Clark to AG Buckingham of Sept. 12, Clark complained that Camp Giddings had been "overrun" at times with recruiters from other branches of service, notably the cavalry and artillery, some being so bold as to walk right into the camp, single out a particular soldier, and draw him away from his duties for a sales pitch to jump ship.

66. John S. Matthews to C. P. Buckingham, Nov. 25, 1861 [series 147-18:10], AGO.

67. "Uniforms and Camp Equipage . . . ," *Telegraph,* Sept. 14, 1861. The Ashtabula city newspaper of this date ran the important announcement that men wishing to join the Twenty-Ninth Ohio at Camp Giddings no longer had to report in company-size groups.

Breaking the Sacred Bond

68. *State Roster.* The four soldiers claimed as minors and returned to their parents were Oscar Andrews, Albert Bentley, Miles Chadwick, and Cassius Giddings.

69. "The Young Volunteer," *Sentinel,* Feb. 5, 1862.

The Economics of Soldiering

70. "Westward Ho!" *Sentinel,* Feb. 7, 1856. Although it may have been a barely disguised promotion to encourage local abolitionists to pull up stakes and move west to bulwark the antislavery squatters in Kansas, the editorial appraised a young man's chances for getting ahead in the county, and the chances were slim. "There are in the County, hundreds of young men who have before them a life of restless ambition and struggle to improve their material interests, not one in ten of whom will ever succeed here."

71. The difficult financial circumstances of many soldiers' families before and after the war are poignantly described in affidavits found in the National Archives for the following soldiers: Thomas Bare, Levi Bean, Alexander French, Nelson Gillett, Ellis Green, George Hayward, Herman Holmes, Allen Mason, Tallis McCain, Benjamin Pontius, Franklin Potter, Cyrus Roach, Jesse Rockwell, and Matthias Soden, among many others. Pension files, RG 94, NA.

72. "Pay of Volunteers," *Sentinel,* Aug. 8, 1861.

73. "The Turning Point," *Reporter,* Oct. 24, 1861.

74. Ibid.

75. "The Pay of Our Army," *Reporter,* Aug. 22, 1861.

76. Ibid.

77. "Pay of Volunteers," *Sentinel,* Aug. 8, 1861.

78. Ibid.

79. Franklin Potter pension file, RG 94, NA.

80. Hoyt pension file, RG 94, NA.

81. Wallace Hoyt to "Dear Parents," Warrenton, VA, May 1862 (exact date illegible), Ohio Historical Society, Archives/Library, Manuscript Collection, Columbus. Material from the society cited hereafter as OHS.

Buckley Takes Command

82. "The Twenty-Ninth Regiment," *Sentinel,* Sept. 11, 1861. Buckley arrived on Monday, Sept. 9.

83. Descriptive list of Co. D, Regimental Books, 29th OVI, NA. Wright and Storer enlisted almost every man in their company.

84. "Gone to Camp," *Beacon,* Sept. 12, 1861.

85. Lt. James Treen to Assistant AG, Oct. 17, 1861, 1 p. [series 147-14], AGO.

86. "Jack Wright," *Beacon,* Sept. 19, 1861.

87. SeCheverell, *Journal History,* 14.

88. John S. Clemmer pension file, RG 94, NA.

89. S. B., letter, Camp Giddings, Nov. 11, 1861, in *Beacon,* Nov. 14, 1861.

90. Maj. Thomas Clark to Assistant AG Mason, Oct. 25, 1861, 1 p. [series 147-15:80], AGO.

91. S. B., letter, Camp Giddings, Dec. 8, 1861, in *Beacon,* Dec. 12, 1861.

92. Descriptive list for Co. E, Regimental Books, 29th OVI, NA.

93. For bravery at Rich Mountain, Horatio Luce was brevetted a lieutenant, an honorary rank he was entitled to hold while in the Nineteenth Regiment's service. Also reported in the "A Company for the 29th," *Reporter,* Sept. 12, 1861.

94. Charles Luce pension file, RG 94, NA.
95. *Telegraph*, July 18, 1861.
96. *Reporter*, Sept. 12, 1861.
97. *Reporter*, Sept. 26, 1861.
98. "Our Flag is There," *Reporter*, Oct. 10, 1861.
99. "A Company for the 29th," *Reporter*, Sept. 12, 1861.

Chapter 5: Camp Giddings
The Village and the Camp

1. Parmater diary, Sept. 25, 1861,
2. "A Suggestion," *Sentinel*, Sept. 19, 1861.
3. "A Good Example," *Sentinel*, Sept. 19, 1861.
4. "A Pleasant Meeting," *Sentinel*, Sept. 11, 1861.
5. "Military Ball," *Sentinel*, Oct. 23, 1861.
6. S. M., letter, Camp Giddings, Oct. 31, 1861, in *Beacon*, Nov. 7, 1861.
7. *Reporter*, Nov. 7, 1861.
8. Adj. T. S. Winship to AG Buckingham, Oct. 14, 1861, 2 pp. [series 147-13:199], AGO.
9. E. B. Howard, letter, Camp Chase (Columbus, OH), Dec. 26, 1861, in *Reporter*, Jan. 2, 1862.
10. Parmater diary, Oct. 7, 1861.
11. Parmater diary, Sept. 30, 1861.
12. J. F. Morse to Gov. Dennison, Oct. 2, 1861, 3 pp. [series 147-10:170], AGO.
13. Ibid.
14. *State Roster*, vol. 3, 382. All references to this work are taken from vol. 3, 21st–36th Regiments—Infantry. Hereafter only the page number will be cited.
15. Lane, *Fifty Years*, 583.
16. A. C. Voris to AG Buckingham, Oct. 14, 1861, 1 p. [series 147-13:63], AGO.
17. "G. G. C.—D. M.," letter, Oct. 19, 1861, *Beacon*, Oct. 24, 1861.

"Hurrah for the Soldier's Life"

18. S. M., letter, Camp Giddings, Oct. 16, 1861, in *Beacon*, Oct. 24, 1861. Fife Maj. Richard Noonan was a special favorite of Buckley, so much so he was referred to simply as Colonel Buckley's fifer.
19. S. M., letter, Camp Giddings, Oct. 11, 1861, in *Beacon*, Oct. 24, 1861.
20. "Stand Back" (Jack Wright), letter, Oct. 16, 1861, in *Beacon*, Oct. 24, 1861.
21. S. M., letter, Camp Giddings, Oct. 31, 1861, in *Beacon*, Nov. 7, 1861.
22. "Stand Back."
23. Pvt. W, letter, Camp Giddings, Dec. 8, 1861, in *Reporter*, Dec. 12, 1861.
24. Parmater diary, Oct. 9, 1861.
25. Parmater diary, Oct. 10, 1861. The announcement of Herr Kline's visit to Jefferson was made in "Magical Exhibition," *Sentinel*, Oct. 9, 1861.
26. Parmater diary, Oct. 10, 1861.
27. Parmater diary, Sept. 29, 1861.
28. Buckley to Gov. Dennison, Dec. 5, 1861 [series 147-19:146], AGO.
29. Descriptive list for Co. H, 29th OVI, NA. Schoonover signed up nearly every man in the company.
30. "Military Display," *Beacon*, Oct. 31, 1861.
31. Lane, *Fifty Years*, 580.
32. "Stand Back."
33. G. G. C.—D. M., letter, Oct. 19, 1861, *Beacon*, Oct. 24, 1861. The *Sentinel* reported that enough uniforms had arrived in camp the preceding week to outfit everyone present. The same piece reported that by this date, two companies had been armed. *Sentinel*, Oct. 23, 1861.

"Present Arms!"

34. "The First Frost . . . ," *Sentinel*, Oct. 23, 1861. Autumn's first frost was reported to have occurred on Oct. 20.
35. "Grafton," letter, Camp Giddings, Nov. 18, 1861, in *Beacon*, Nov. 28, 1861.
36. *Beacon*, Oct. 24, 1861.

37. "Camp Giddings," *Reporter,* Oct. 10, 1861.

38. *Beacon,* June 20, 1861.

39. *Beacon,* Oct. 9, 1861.

40. "Camp Giddings now presents . . . ," *Sentinel,* Oct. 23, 1861. Receipt at Camp Giddings of the regiment's first shipment of two hundred Enfield muskets was also noted by S. M., letter, Camp Giddings, Oct. 16, 1861, in *Beacon,* Oct. 24, 1861.

41. Research conducted by Dr. Richard Waters, Jefferson, Ohio, determined that two hundred Enfields were initially issued the regiment, followed by a second issue of 780 Pondir muskets. The balance of the regiment did not exchange their Pondir muskets for the more modern Enfields until after arriving at Dumfries, VA, Jan. 1863.

42. S. M., letter, Camp Giddings, Oct. 16, 1861, *Beacon,* Oct. 24, 1861.

43. *Reporter,* Aug. 20, 1862. Advertisements by the same merchant for pistols appeared in the Conneaut newspaper as early as Oct. 22, 1861.

44. "Threads for Home Spun Wear," *Reporter,* May 16, 1861.

45. "Casualty in Camp," *Sentinel,* Oct. 9, 1861.

46. Ibid.

47. Pvt. W, letter, Camp Giddings, Dec. 8, 1861, in *Reporter,* Dec. 12, 1861. The writer stated that the Twenty-Ninth Regiment's muskets were received the previous Friday, Dec. 6. Thomas Clark reported that this shipment of arms had been received in Camp Giddings that day. Clark to AG Buckingham, Dec. 5, 1861, 1 p. [series 147-19:6], AGO.

48. S. B., letter, Paw Paw, western VA, Feb. 17, 1861, in *Beacon,* Mar. 6, 1861.

49. Edwards, *Civil War Guns,* 28. On July 26, 1861, Pondir contracted with the government to supply what he described as the "beautiful Minie." This may not be the Twenty-Ninth Regiment's firearm since this batch of contracted rifles was the lighter .577 caliber French pattern.

50. Time-Life Books, *Arms and Equipment,* 35. Pondir imported upwards of thirteen thousand .69 caliber rifled muskets from Belgium during an unspecified time frame—most likely in 1861 and 1862. Some were originally smoothbore and had been rifled by the French. Todd, *American Military Equipage,* 1093. Records of the Ohio State Quartermaster's Department under "arms" received" noted the acceptance of .69 cal. percussion rifles. Following this entry is the parenthetical notation "rifled by John Pondir of Philadelphia." A few weeks before the war began, arms vendors began pushing the Pondir Belgian-made musket on Governor Tod. By way of recommendation, one dealer stated in a letter to the governor that Pondir had already sold sixty thousand of the "Austrian" .69 caliber muskets to the federal government. Now, he would gladly sell his remaining stock of twenty-five thousand to the State of Ohio at the bargain price of twelve dollars per musket, and to sweeten the deal, Pondir would throw in the accoutrements for free. A. Wellington Hart, who made this sales pitch to the governor, emphasized that there was only a "short time to act." A. Hart to Gov. Tod, Apr. 1, 1861, 3 pp. [series 147-30:89], AGO.

51. Todd, *American Military Equipage,* 1092.

52. Edwards, *Civil War Guns,* 92. So accurate was the .69 caliber Belgian that a Wisconsin soldier reported that one of his comrades using the weapon had brought a sack of squirrels into their camp and every one of the little critters had been shot through the head.

53. "Enfield Rifles for Ohio Troops," *Chronicle,* Nov. 20, 1861. The article is credited to the *Toledo Blade.* The piece reported that by this date thirty-four European-manufactured smoothbores had been rifled by Greenwood and Company and issued to Ohio troops.

54. Pvt. W, letter, Camp Giddings, Dec. 8, 1861, in *Reporter,* Dec. 12, 1861.

55. Todd, *American Military Equipage,* 1091–92.

56. Ibid.

57. Ibid.

58. S. B., letter, "Camp Kelley, five miles below Cumberland, Maryland," Jan. 21, 1862, in *Beacon,* Jan. 30, 1862.

59. Rupp, "Fighting Regiment." Rupp reported that the Twenty-Ninth Regiment's first large issue of muskets were "Belgian-made." These, according to Rupp, were exchanged for the Enfield sometime while in winter camp at Dumfries, Virginia, 1863. Diarist Elias Roshon noted in his entry of Jan. 19, 1863, that "some of the boys drawed guns and acquuipment." (The typescript of a diary written by Private Roshon covering the period Jan. through Nov. 1862 was given me by an Ohio friend. Included with the diary were typescripts of fourteen letters Roshon wrote to his family in Medina County during the war. Neither the identity of the transcriptionist, nor the custodian of the diary and letters, has been established.) Other companies may have been supplied with the superior Enfield musket before January 1862 when all of the Belgian muskets were replaced. Albert Durkee of

Co. E reported in his diary entry of July 7, 1862, "We got new Enfield rifles and turned over the old ones to the Government. Our company took 31 and it will not look like Camp Giddings when we had about 90 guns." Durkee diary, item 596, OHS.

Season of Complaint

60. Pvt. W, letter, Camp Giddings, Dec. 15, 1861, in *Reporter,* Dec. 19, 1861. The erstwhile soldier-reporter stated, "The dilapidated condition of our seatless pantaloons, and soleless shoes present to the mind of the observing outsider, unmistakable evidence that we are fast approaching the climax, and are real citizen soldiery."

61. "Soldiers' Pay, Rations and Bounty," *Journal,* Sept. 14, 1861. The clothing allowance for private soldiers was specified in the state adjutant general's General Order 51. The volunteer's pay and clothing allowance were explained frequently in the newspaper, as in "Pay of Volunteers," *Beacon,* Sept. 5, 1861.

62. "The 19th Regiment," *Beacon,* June 20, 1861.

63. Ibid. The Akron editors observed that Ohio, and to a lesser extent Pennsylvania and New York, had been the victims of shabby treatment at the hands of the federal government, while the troops of other states were receiving clothing and supplies of better quality.

64. Pvt. W, letter, Camp Giddings, Dec. 15, 1861, in *Reporter,* Dec. 19, 1861.

65. Ibid.

66. S. M., letter, Camp Giddings, Dec. 13, 1861, in *Beacon,* Dec. 19, 1861.

67. Pvt. W, letter, Camp Giddings, Dec. 15, 1861.

68. Ibid.

69. John G. Marsh to "My Dear Sister Almyra," Camp Giddings, Dec. 12, 1861, James J. Hudson Papers, MC 1118, box 3, file 6, Special Collections, University of Arkansas Libraries, Fayetteville. Hereafter cited as Hudson Papers.

70. Pvt. W, letter, Camp Giddings, Dec. 15, 1861.

71. S. B., letter, Camp Giddings, Dec. 8, 1861, in *Beacon,* Dec. 12, 1861.

72. In his letter of Jan. 22, 1861, S. M. identified himself as a soldier in Company G and pulled the veil from the pseudonymous S. B. by revealing him as an Akron detective and a current company captain. S. B. was none other than Josiah "Jack" Wright.

73. S. B., letter, Camp Giddings, Dec. 8, 1861.

74. Ibid.

75. S. M., letter, Camp Giddings, Dec. 13, 1861, in *Beacon,* Dec. 19, 1861. "Our Regiment has been much maligned. We have been called the 'nigger regiment,' &c. &c."

76. "Enlistments on the Reserve," *Beacon,* Nov. 28, 1861.

77. S. M., letter, Camp Giddings, Dec. 13, 1861.

78. S. B., letter, Camp Giddings, Dec. 8, 1861.

Slipping Away

79. "Health in Camp," *Journal,* Aug. 1, 1861.

80. "To Our Soldiers," *Journal,* Aug. 1, 1861.

81. Pvt. W, letter, Camp Giddings, Dec. 8, 1861, in *Reporter,* Dec. 12, 1861.

82. Descriptive list of Co. D, Regimental Books, 29th OVI, NA.

83. Pvt. W, letter, Camp Giddings, Dec. 8, 1861.

84. "Diphtheria has made its appearance . . . ," *Sentinel,* Oct. 9, 1861.

85. *Conneaut Herald,* Apr. 22, 1892.

86. W. Williams, "Biographical Sketch of Hon. Abner Kellogg," in *Ashtabula County,* 106.

87. *Conneaut Herald,* Apr. 22, 1892.

88. W. Williams, *Ashtabula County,* 121.

89. Amos K. Fifield to AG Buckingham, Aug. 25, 1861, AGO.

90. Widow's claim filed by Hannah Wildey, Wildey pension file, RG 94, NA. The descriptive list for his company gave Wildey's cause of death as typhoid.

91. Ibid.

92. "The soldiers of the 29th Regiment . . . ," *Sentinel,* Jan. 15, 1862.

93. "A soldier named Rogers . . . ," *Sentinel,* Jan. 8, 1861. Private Pike's death at Jefferson on Jan. 14, 1862, was recorded in the *State Roster,* 373.

94. With the exception of Goodrich, Hill, and Blodgett, the men described on this page as deserters may have simply signed the enlistment rolls but never reported to camp—a common enough practice but one that under military law constituted desertion. Their names may have been entered as deserters when the regiment's clerks were doing the final manpower accounting before leaving Jefferson. Roll of Deserters, series 108, State of Ohio, Adjutant General's Office, 1936, OHS.

95. Descriptive list for Co. E, "Deserters," Regimental Books, 29th OVI, RG 94, NA.

96. Descriptive list for Co. G, "Deserters," Regimental Books, 29th OVI, RG 94, NA.

97. Descriptive list for Co. K, "Deserters," Regimental Books, 29th OVI, RG 94, NA.

Chapter 6: "The Emblems of Universal Freedom"
Rumors

1. *Reporter*, Nov. 28, 1861. The first snow of the season had fallen the preceding Monday, Nov. 25.
2. Ibid.
3. "Grafton," letter, Camp Giddings, Nov. 18, 1861, in *Beacon*, Nov. 28, 1861. A separate notice describing the Second Ohio's send-off party in Cleveland is found in the same edition.
4. Ibid.
5. Ibid.
6. Pvt. W, letter, Camp Giddings, Dec. 8, 1861, in *Reporter*, Dec. 12, 1861.
7. Ibid.
8. Col. Thomas Clark to AG Buckingham, Nov. 29, 1861, 1 p. [series 147-18:54], AGO.
9. "Army Correspondence—Head Quarters, Camp Giddings, Dec. 2, 1861," Comfort Chaffee, letter, Camp Giddings, Dec. 2, 1861, in *Sentinel*, Dec. 4, 1861.
10. S. M., letter, Camp Giddings, Dec. 13, 1861, in *Beacon*, Dec. 19, 1861.
11. Thomas Clark for Lewis P. Buckley to AG Buckingham, Nov. 25, 1861, 2 pp. [series 147-17:221], AGO.
12. Coles, *Ohio Forms an Army*, 8.
13. Thomas Clark to AG Buckingham, Dec. 5, 1861, 1 p. [series 147-19:6], AGO.
14. Ibid.
15. Buckley to AG Buckingham, Dec. 5, 1861, 1 p. [series 147-19:146], AGO.
16. Major Thomas Clark to AG Buckingham, Nov. 15, 1861, 3pp. [series 147-18:36], AGO.
17. S. M., Dec. 13, 1861. Pvt. W concurred in the gloomy likelihood of spending the winter in Jefferson in his Dec. 15 letter from camp: "You may expect us to remain here this winter." *Reporter*, Dec. 19, 1861.

Flag Day

18. "Regimental Colors," *Beacon*, Nov. 14, 1861.
19. *Beacon*, Nov. 14, 1861.
20. Ibid.
21. "Hudson" to "Editors of the Beacon—," Nov. 22, 1861, in *Beacon*, Nov. 28, 1861.
22. "The 29th are to be honored . . . ," *Telegraph*, Nov. 16, 1861.
23. Lewis P. Buckley, letter, Camp Giddings, Nov. 8, 1861, in *Beacon*, Nov. 14, 1861.
24. Ibid.
25. In his speech accompanying the presentation of the flags to the regiment, Giddings stated that the flags had been "prepared" by the ladies of the county. Future, literal readings of the text of his speech led to the belief that the flags, the regimental flag in particular, had been sewn by the county's women.
26. *Reporter*, Nov. 28, 1861. Ads for G. W. Crowell and Co. appeared frequently in the Reserve newspapers throughout the war.
27. "Colors for the 29th Regiment" (under "Home Facts and Fancies"), *Reporter*, Nov. 28, 1861.
28. J. R. to Addison Giddings, Sept. 19, 30, 1861, Giddings Papers.
29. J. R. to Addison Giddings, Sept. 30, 1861, Giddings Papers.
30. *Sentinel*, Dec. 4, 1861. The full text of Giddings's speech was published herein.
31. *Beacon*, Jan. 29, 1863.
32. Lewis P. Buckley to AG Buckingham, Aug. 21, 1861, AGO. Stratton and the seven soldiers charged along with him took the train to Columbus, accompanied by the editor of the Warren newspaper. When the court-martial was convened in the case of Stratton and his men, not a single prosecution witness showed up. The charges were dismissed and all the accused were honorably discharged. *Chronicle*, Sept. 4, 1861.

33. "The Flag Presentation," *Sentinel*, Dec. 4, 1861.

34. SeCheverell, *Journal History*, 24. A substantial variant of Buckley's acceptance speech is found in W. Williams, *Ashtabula County*, 52.

35. S. M., letter, Camp Giddings, Dec. 13, 1861, in *Beacon*, Dec. 19, 1861.

Sleight of Hand

36. Pvt. W, letter, Camp Giddings, Dec. 15, 1861, in *Reporter*, Dec. 19, 1861.

37. Buckley to AG Buckingham, Sept. 30, 1861, 2 pp. [series 147-10:99], AGO. (The revised collection at OHS shows this letter as series 147-10:99).

38. In his Oct. 20, 1861 letter, a writer identifying himself as "Sojer Boy" reported there were seven hundred soldiers and officers at Camp Giddings. "Sojer Boy" letter, *Beacon*, Oct. 24, 1861. A month later, an anonymous soldier identifying himself as "HALT" reported in his letter of Nov. 18 that their numbers had reached 850. *Beacon*, Nov. 21, 1861.

39. HALT, letter, Camp Giddings, Nov. 18, 1861, in *Beacon*, Nov. 21, 1861.

40. The *State Roster* lists the total number of officers and men enlisted in the Twenty-Ninth through Dec. 1861 as approximately 960.

41. "Letter from Col. Buckley," Jan. 13, 1863, Dumfries, VA, in *Beacon*, Jan. 29, 1863. Buckley, who was in good position to know, stated, "When the Regt. was ordered to Camp Chase in Dec., it numbered nine hundred as brave and true men as ever marched forth to do battle." Comfort Chaffee, who as adjutant was responsible for the exact count, gave the strength of the regiment on the day it left Camp Giddings as 923. Comfort. T. Chaffee, letter, Dec. 22, 1861, in "Letter of the Adjutant," *Sentinel*, Dec. 25, 1861.

42. Pvt. W, letter, Dec. 15, 1861.

43. Ibid. Pvt. W could poke fun at the rush for office in Companies I and K, but there had been real trouble in one of them. The soldiers had elected Owen Martin, a young farmer from Ashtabula County, as their second lieutenant by a vote of fifty-six to nine. Clark and four other officers thought him intelligent, well educated, and adept at managing troops. But the vote for Martin was not open to inspection by the other nominees, and on that basis an unnamed party who had received only four votes attempted to have the election results thrown out. Clark took up Martin's cause directly with the governor of Ohio. The governor must have rejected Clark's recommendation, because William J. Hall was allowed to trade his private's stripes for a second lieutenant's shoulder bars, and Martin was returned to the ranks. This dispute is recorded in Clark to Gov. Dennison, Dec. 5, 1861 [series 147-19:146], AGO.

44. The names of soldiers transferring to these two companies and the dates on which they were transferred are listed in the *State Roster*, 3:351–93. Company I, with its compact core group from Medina County, just west of Akron, was inflated by the transfer to it on Dec. 13 of at least twenty-five volunteers from the regiment's other companies and it was mustered in the very next day. Company K had been recruited from various townships in Ashtabula County, but it too had been unable to fill out its roster. Two dozen men, mostly from Company A, were persuaded to transfer to its ranks. Company I would be the only one of the regiment's companies to be mustered into Federal service with its organization incomplete. SeCheverell, *Journal History*, 33.

45. Captain Smith's age, occupation, and place of birth are found in the descriptive list of Company I, Regimental Books, NA.

46. Alden P. Steele pension file, RG 94, NA.

47. *Beacon*, Dec. 12, 1861. The first of these songs, "Song of the 29th," was conveyed to the newspaper in S. B.'s letter of Dec. 2 and was also published in the *Sentinel*, Dec. 25, 1861. "Dixie for the Twenty-Ninth" appeared in the *Beacon* on Dec. 19 by letter from camp of Dec. 8.

"The Full Rigged Volunteer"

48. Pvt. W, letter, Camp Giddings, Dec. 8, 1861, in *Reporter*, Dec. 12, 1861.

49. Pvt. W, letter, Dec. 15, 1861.

50. Ibid.

51. Ibid.

52. "Adjutant" (Comfort T. Chaffee), letter, Camp Giddings, Dec. 22, 1861, in *Sentinel*, Dec. 25, 1861.

53. General Order 51, in *Journal*, Sept. 2, 1861. The adjutant general prescribed that companies elect officers prior to muster-in to the U.S. service.

54. "Adjutant" letter, Dec. 22, 1861.

Away at Last

55. "Christmas in Our Village . . . ," *Reporter,* Jan. 2, 1862.
56. "Christmas in Tallmadge," *Beacon,* Jan. 2, 1862.
57. "Adjutant" letter, Dec. 22, 1861. The exact date on which the regiment received its marching orders is unclear. The newspaper reported only that "it had been known for several days that the regiment would leave on Christmas Day."
58. "A Soldier Shot," *Journal,* Aug. 29, 1861.
59. "The Twenty-Ninth," *Sentinel,* Jan. 1, 1862.
60. The condition of the Ashtabula County fairgrounds after the Twenty-Ninth's departure was reported in an article by Carl E. Feather, *Jefferson (OH) Star Beacon,* Dec. 23, 1996, and was based on his review of the records of the county agricultural society.
61. *Reporter,* Jan. 2, 1862.
62. Ibid.
63. "The Twenty-Ninth," *Sentinel,* Dec. 25, 1861. "We give in this paper a full list . . ."
64. Ibid.
65. "Seelye," letter, Camp Kelly, Allegheny County, MD, n.d., in *Sentinel,* Jan. 29, 1862.
66. Lt. E. B. Howard, letter, Camp Chase, Dec. 26, 1862, in *Reporter,* Jan. 2, 1862.
67. "The Twenty-Ninth," *Sentinel,* Jan. 1, 1862. Details of the regiment's camp breaking at Jefferson were reported with unusual fullness in this piece.
68. Thomas Clark to Rollin Jones, n.d., John Gurnish Collection.
69. "The Twenty-Ninth," *Sentinel,* Jan. 1, 1862.
70. "To the Editor of the Sentinel, Head Quarters, Camp Giddings," *Sentinel,* Dec. 25, 1861. Adj. Comfort T. Chaffee's farewell letter to the village, Dec. 22, 1861.
71. "The Twenty-Ninth," *Sentinel,* Jan. 1, 1862.
72. Howard, letter, Camp Chase, Dec. 26, 1861.

Chapter 7: "At the Threshold of an Untried Life"

Three Trains in the Night

1. Thomas Clark to Rollin L. Jones, n.d.
2. "The 29th, Col. Buckley . . . ," *Telegraph,* Dec. 28, 1861.
3. E. B. Howard, letter, Camp Chase, Dec. 26, 1861, in *Reporter,* Jan. 2, 1862.
4. "Departure of the 29th," *Reporter,* Jan. 2, 1862.
5. "The Twenty-Ninth," *Sentinel,* Jan. 1, 1862, borrowed a piece from the *Painesville Telegraph* reporting the hearty welcome extended to the regiment on its stop at the town's railroad depot.
6. Parmater diary, Dec. 25, 1861.
7. The Twenty-Ninth's trip from Jefferson to Columbus is well described in Lieutenant Howard's letter from Camp Chase, as well as in the Parmater diary entry, both on Dec. 26, 1861.

Paris on the Scioto

8. Howard, letter, Dec. 26, 1861.
9. Wallace Hoyt to "Dear Mother," Camp Chase, Dec. 27, 1861, OHS.
10. SeCheverell, *Journal History,* 35.
11. Harper, *Ohio Handbook,* 13.
12. Howard, letter, Dec. 26, 1861.
13. Parmater diary. His entry was erroneously dated Dec. 25 but was more likely written on Dec. 26.
14. Ibid.
15. Wallace B. Hoyt to "Dear Father and Mother & Sister and Brothers," Camp Chase, Jan. 7, 1862, OHS. The war letters of soldier Wallace B. Hoyt, forty-three in all, are found in two places: Wallace B. Hoyt Papers, MSS 1282, OHS; Hoyt pension file, RG 94, NA. Citations to these letters hereafter distinguish the two sources.
16. Ibid.
17. *Journal,* Mar. 24, 1862.
18. Willis Sisley to his brother, Reason Sisley, Jan. 8, 1862, Sisley pension file, RG 94, NA.
19. Weisenburger, *Columbus,* 7.

20. Ibid., 14.

21. Typical of the assortment of military gear for sale in Columbus stores are the items found in the advertisements of the *Journal,* Dec. 31, 1861.

22. "Pills for the Seceshers," *Journal,* Aug. 23, 1861.

23. Weisenburger, *Columbus,* 17.

24. Pvt. W, letter, Camp Chase, Jan. 2, 1862, in *Reporter,* Jan. 9, 1862.

25. Ibid.

26. Ibid.

27. John G. Marsh to "Dear Father," Camp Chase, Jan. 15, 1862, Marsh pension file, RG 94, NA.

Clothed in Patriotism

28. S. B., letter, Camp Chase, Jan. 14, 1862, in *Beacon,* Jan. 23, 1862.

29. Ibid.

30. Ibid. The first mention of the establishment of a county government–sponsored support program for soldier's families is found in this S. B. letter.

31. "The Soldier's Family," *Beacon,* Feb. 6, 1862.

32. Ibid.

33. Pvt. W, letter, Jan. 13, 1862, in *Reporter,* Jan. 15, 1862.

A Condition in No Way Remarkable

34. "Temperance in the Army" was written by an officer at Camp Chase and reprinted from the *Journal* in *Beacon,* Dec. 4, 1861.

35. "Sutler's Expedients," *Beacon,* Nov. 14, 1861.

36. "Temperance in the Army."

37. "Disorderly Conduct of the Some of the Returned Volunteers," *Journal,* July 31, 1861.

38. "Temperance in the Army."

39. "Temptations of the Camp," *Beacon,* Nov. 28, 1861.

40. "Rejected," *Sentinel,* Sept. 11, 1861.

41. "The 29th Regiment Are to Be Honored," *Telegraph,* Nov. 16, 1861.

42. *Beacon,* Nov. 14, 1861. The soldiers' assault on the Jefferson liquor seller was reported by Stand Back in his letter of Nov. 11 from Camp Giddings. This incident was also reported in the *Telegraph,* Nov. 16, 1861.

43. Pvt. W, letter, Jan. 13, 1862.

44. Pvt. W, letter, Camp Chase, Jan. 17, 1862, in *Reporter,* Jan. 22, 1862.

45. S. B., letter, Camp Chase, Jan. 14, 1862, in *Beacon,* Jan. 23, 1862.

46. Pvt. W, letter, Camp Chase, Jan. 2, 1862, in *Reporter,* Jan. 9, 1862.

47. Ibid.

48. Ibid.

False Start

49. S. B., letter, Jan. 14, 1862.

50. Wallace Hoyt to "Dear Mother," Camp Chase, Jan. 11, 1862, OHS.

51. Parmater diary, Jan. 11, 1862.

52. *Reporter,* Jan. 15, 1862.

53. Ibid.

54. S. B., letter, Jan. 14, 1862.

55. John G. Marsh to "My Dear Sister Almyra," Camp Chase, Jan. 11, 1862, Hudson Papers.

56. Ibid.; Parmater diary, Jan. 11, 1862.

57. Parmater diary, Jan. 11, 1862.

58. S. B., letter, Jan. 14, 1862.

59. Marsh to "My Dear Sister Almyra," Jan. 11, 1862.

60. Ibid.

61. Mentioned in S. B., letter, Jan. 14; Parmater diary, Jan. 11; Hoyt, letter, Jan. 11, 1862.

62. Boatner, *Dictionary,* 492; Long, *Civil War,* 159.

63. "From Romney—Its Evacuation," *Wheeling Intelligencer,* Jan. 28, 1862, run in the *Beacon,* Feb. 6, 1862.

Paper-Collar Soldiers

64. S. B., letter, Jan. 14, 1862.
65. "The Review," *Journal*, Jan. 14, 1862.
66. Ibid.
67. S. B., letter, Jan. 14, 1862.
68. Parmater diary, Jan. 13, 1862.
69. Pvt. W, letter, Jan. 13, 1862.

The Well-Seasoned Recruit

70. Wallace Hoyt, letter, Camp Chase, Jan. 3, 1862, OHS.
71. Ibid. Hoyt reported this number as having been sent to the post hospital the same day.
72. Pvt. W, letter, Jan. 13, 1862.
73. Willis Sisley wrote, "Most of the boys have colds, and the rest have measles." Sisley, letter, Camp Chase, Jan. 8, 1862, Sisley pension file, RG 94, NA.
74. The outbreak of measles in the regiment while at Camp Chase is documented in Wallace Hoyt's letter of Jan. 3, 1862; in Pvt. W's letter of Jan. 13; in soldier depositions found in the pension file of Willis Sisley's survivors; and in the pension file of Pvt. Obed Phelps, RG 94, NA. Several Twenty-Ninth soldiers later claimed that they never fully recovered from the effects of this disease.
75. Steiner, *Disease*, 13.
76. Ibid., 14.
77. Ibid., 12.
78. "Health of the Army of the Potomac," *Chronicle*, Jan. 8, 1862, credited to the *Ohio Gazette*.
79. Pvt. W, letter, Jan. 13, 1862.
80. Roshon diary, Jan. 1, 1862.
81. Jesse J. Rockwell pension file, RG 94, NA.

Farewell, Ohio, Farewell

82. The regimental books of this or any other field regiment cannot be relied on for sufficient accuracy in consigning a soldier to the ignominy of desertion. Several soldiers of the Twenty-Ninth Regiment listed as deserters in the organization's own records (defects which were reproduced freely in SeCheverell's *Journal History*) turned out to be merely misplaced and were later honorably discharged. For the purpose of this work, a soldier has not been characterized as a deserter unless his name appears in both of the following postwar publications, neither of which depended solely on the regiment's own record keeping: the *State Roster* and Roll of Deserters, Adjutant General's Office, State of Ohio. Poor record keeping within the military system was widespread throughout the era of the Civil War, and it is entirely possible that the men listed as deserters in this book performed honorable service and were not in fact deserters. I apologize to the descendants of any soldier whose memory has been further tarnished by errors I have committed to print. With that qualification uppermost, deserters at Columbus, Ohio, Jan. 11–31, 1861, were: John Ardis, William Dady (Doty or Dody), William DeWitt, Gregory Youngs (Younst), Issac Roberts (Robert Issacs), and Joel (Joseph) Ritter.
83. Lewis. P. Buckley to AG Buckingham, Jan. 8, 1862, 2 pp. [series 147-22:180], AGO.
84. "The Twenty Ninth," *Sentinel*, Jan. 22, 1862.
85. Civil War Personnel Records, series 2106, box 52.697, file 29, 29th Ohio Officers' Certificates of Qualifications and Acceptances of Commissions 1861–1862, OHS.
86. "Orders to March," *Journal*, Jan. 17, 1862.
87. Chaplain Rufus Hurlburt, letter, Camp Kelly, Cumberland, MD, Jan. 23, 1862, in *Sentinel*, Feb. 5, 1862.
88. Parmater diary, Jan. 17, 1862.
89. "G," letter, Camp Kelly, Cumberland, MD, Feb. 3, 1862, in "From the 29th Regiment," *Beacon*, Feb. 13, 1862.
90. Ibid.
91. Hurlburt, letter, Jan. 23, 1862.
92. *Telegraph*, Feb. 22, 1862.
93. Ibid.
94. S. B., letter, Camp Cumberland, Allegheny Co., MD, Jan. 28, 1862, in *Beacon*, Feb. 6, 1862.
95. Ibid.

96. Buckley to Buckingham, Jan. 16, 1862, 1 p. [series 147-23:230], AGO.
97. S. B., letter, Camp Kelly, Jan. 21, 1862, in *Beacon,* Jan. 30, 1862.
98. Hurlburt, letter, Jan. 23, 1862.
99. Elias Roshon to "Dear Father," Camp City, MD, Jan. 20, 1862.

Chapter 8: A Good "Breaking-In"

Set Down in the Mud

1. Chaplain Hurlburt, letter, North Branch Bridge, Cumberland, MD, Camp Kelly, Jan. 23, 1862, in *Sentinel,* Feb. 5, 1862. A detailed account of the regiment's rail trip from Columbus to Cumberland is found in this letter.
2. The Wade-Hutchins cavalry left Ohio *after* the Twenty-Ninth Regiment, departing for its posting on the Missouri border on Jan. 27. Dyer, *Compendium,* vol. 1, 1473. The Second Ohio Cavalry's career would take it gradually eastward, landing it at war's end at Appomattox Courthouse, having covered as much ground as the Twenty-Ninth. Among its notable campaigns would be the Wilderness and Sheridan's Valley campaign, among numerous other history-making fights.
3. Hurlburt, letter, Jan. 23, 1862. There is considerable confusion as to what date the Twenty-Ninth Ohio departed Camp Chase, Columbus. SeCheverell and committee stated the date as Jan. 26, 1862. Dyer used data collected from the state adjutant general's office and reported in his *Compendium* that the date was Jan. 17. Pvt. Elias Roshon recorded their arrival date in his diary as Jan. 19, and confirmed this date in a letter to his father dated Jan. 20, in which he reported the regiment arrived the preceding day. Parmater also gives the date as Sunday, Jan. 19. A Twenty-Ninth soldier writing under the pseudonym Seelye reported that the regiment had departed Columbus on the preceding Friday and arrived at Camp Kelly (referred to in official army correspondence as Patterson's Creek) on Jan. 19, 1862. *Sentinel,* Jan. 29, 1862.
4. S. B., letter, Camp Kelly, MD, Jan. 21, 1862, in *Beacon,* Jan. 30, 1862.
5. Unsigned letter, 67th Regiment, New Creek, VA, n.d., in *Beacon,* Feb. 6, 1862.
6. Elias Roshon diary, Jan. 18, 1862. "This morning we came to Bellaire and then we crossed the Ohio River before daylight then we got on flatcars they leked like everything it rained day and night."
7. S. B., letter, Jan. 21, 1862.
8. An excellent account of the regiment's first of many rail journeys in the war is found in Roshon, letter to his father, "Camp City, Maryland," Jan. 20, 1862.
9. S. B., letter, Jan. 21, 1862.
10. "From Romney—Its Evacuation," *Beacon,* Feb. 6, 1862.
11. "Misc. Rebellion News: Gen. Lander's Command," *New York Times,* Feb. 4, 1862, credited to *Cincinnati Gazette,* Jan. 19, 1862.
12. Typical of the flurry of correspondence regarding the assignment of new Ohio troops to Lander's command is McClellan's adjutant's telegram to Ohio State Adjutant General Buckingham, Jan. 20, 1862: "General McClellan desires to know as soon as possible by telegraph what troops have left Ohio to reinforce Lander." *OR,* vol. 51, pt. 1, 519. The Twenty-Ninth Ohio had arrived at Patterson's Creek the preceding day.
13. S. B., letter, Jan. 21, 1862.
14. Roshon, letter, Jan. 20, 1862, to his father. "We didn't know where we were going til we stopped."
15. "Misc. Rebellion News: Gen. Lander's Command," *New York Times,* Feb. 4, 1862. Report of the arrival of the Twenty-Ninth Ohio at Camp Kelly appearing in the *Times* was credited to a letter in the *Cleveland Herald,* Jan. 20, 1862.

A General Who Fights

16. Beatie, *McClellan,* 480.
17. For sketches of both Lander and his wife, actress Jean Davenport, see A. Johnson et al., *Dictionary of American Biography,* 570.
18. Beatie, *McClellan,* 418.
19. Banks, whose division was blocking the upper approaches to Washington and gathering strength enough to cross the Potomac and move on Winchester, disagreed. Even after Lander had begun to execute his plan, at Patterson's Creek, Banks continued to quietly express his opposition that it would be impractical and wasteful to reconstruct the Baltimore and Ohio while any enemy force remained installed on the Virginia side—an opinion that proved true, at least in a tactical sense, because the rebels would continue to disrupt the line for several more

years to come. Thankfully, railroad crews became so used to repairing these bridges that they could have trains running over them within days, and then hours, of their being destroyed, with little interruption of commerce or military transportation.

20. Reid, *Ohio in the War,* 831–32.

21. Lewis Buckley to General McNeil (his "good friend" in Akron), Paw Paw, VA, Feb. 18, 1862, in *Beacon,* Feb. 27, 1862.

22. Seelye, "Army Correspondence, From the Twenty-Ninth," Camp Kelly, on the Potomac, Allegheny Co., MD, n.d., in *Sentinel,* Jan. 29, 1862.

23. In a letter to his father dated Jan. 20, 1862, Roshon reported that the main bridge spanning the Potomac had already been rebuilt by the time they arrived.

24. "Army Incident," *Sentinel,* Feb. 12, 1862.

25. Beatie, *McClellan,* 480.

Passing Time

26. Seelye, letter, Camp Kelly, n.d., in *Sentinel,* Jan. 29, 1862.

27. S. M., letter, Camp Kelly, five miles below Cumberland, MD, Jan. 22, 1862, in *Beacon,* Feb. 6, 1862.

28. Adj. Comfort Chaffee, letter, Jan. 24, 1862, in "Army Correspondence, From the Twenty-Ninth," *Sentinel,* Feb. 5, 1862.

29. Elias Roshon to "Dear Father," Jan. 20, 1862.

30. S. M., letter, Jan. 22, 1861, in *Beacon,* Feb. 6, 1862.

31. Ibid.

32. For a colorful description of the scene greeting the soldiers at Camp Kelly, see Hurlburt, letter, Jan. 23, 1862.

33. Ibid.

34. Hurlburt, letter, Jan. 23, 1862.

35. S. B., letter, Jan. 21, 1862.

36. Hurlburt, letter, Jan. 23, 1862.

37. Chaffee, letter, Jan. 24, 1862.

38. Ibid. An officer, whose education might be thought to make him a more accurate estimator, judged the numbers present at Patterson's Creek as inaccurately as had Elias Roshon. In his letter of Feb. 5, 1862, Seelye reported to the *Sentinel* that Lander's force numbered between twenty and twenty-five thousand. *Sentinel,* Feb. 12, 1862.

39. "Abstract from the Return of the Army of the Potomac for the Month of Feb. 1862," *OR,* vol. 5, pt. 1, 732. On paper, the aggregate of Lander's force at Paw Paw, western Virginia, was almost sixteen thousand officers and soldiers. But within a few weeks nearly five thousand were absent.

40. Ibid.

41. "From Our Regular Correspondent in the 29th," Seelye, letter, Camp Kelly, Feb. 5, 1862, in *Sentinel,* Feb. 12, 1862.

42. Ibid.

43. Roshon diary, Feb. 1, 1862.

44. Seelye, letter, Camp Kelly, Feb. 11, 1862, in "From the Twenty-Ninth," *Sentinel,* Feb. 26, 1862. Pvt. John S. Haddock (Hadlock) of Company E was found to have shot off his trigger finger while on picket duty.

45. Chaplain Hurlburt, letter, "Two Miles from Paw Paw, VA," Feb. 18, 1862, in *Sentinel,* Feb. 26, 1862. The soldier injured in this incident was Sgt. John Roff (Rolf), Company C, a twenty-eight-year-old farmer from Gustavus, Trumbull County.

46. Ibid.

47. Seelye, letter, Feb. 11, 1862. At least one incident similar to these took place several months later and received an informal investigation by the officers. They concluded that the wounding had been intentional, and a notation was made in the company records to that effect. Since no court-martial was convened, and no actual evidence presented supporting this conclusion, I have withheld the soldier's name. Regimental Books, 29th OVI, NA.

48. Beatie, *McClellan,* 470.

49. Lander to Maj. Gen. Marcy, Paw Paw, VA, Feb. 19, 1862, *OR,* vol. 51, pt. 1, supplements, 534.

50. Lander to McClellan, Patterson's Creek, Jan. 16, 1862, *OR,* vol. 5, pt. 1, 702.

51. Beatie, *McClellan*, 478. Williams had gone to Hancock to reinforce Lander and upon arrival found Lander's five regiments already there pillaging the town with impunity, as if that were the normal course. "They knew nothing of garrison, or other military duty, and were literally a mob—firing their guns right and left and generally playing the devil." The 110th Pennsylvania had been especially rapacious.

Riding the Locomotive

52. Excellent accounts of the Twenty-Ninth's first military operation are found in a letter of Adj. Comfort Chaffee, Jan. 29, 1862, and an extract of a letter from Captain Fitch, Feb. 2, 1862, both in *Sentinel,* Feb. 12, 1862.
53. John G. Marsh to "Well Almyra," Camp Kelly, Jan. 29, 1862, Hudson Papers.
54. Ibid.
55. Ibid.
56. John G. Marsh to "My Sister Almyra," Camp Tyler, VA, Feb. 25, 1862, Hudson Papers.

Frozen Mountains

57. Lander's movement to strike Jackson at Romney was apparently based on intelligence that Jackson was withdrawing most of his Romney garrison to Winchester. Lander telegraphed McClellan on Feb. 2: "I shall take Romney or be defeated within forty-eight hours" (*OR,* vol. 51, pt. 1, 523). This dispatch seems to have been the first notice to McClellan of Lander's decision to attack Romney. Only after receipt of news that Lander was already in motion toward Romney did McClellan begin to send a flurry of orders to Lander's neighboring commanders, Banks and Rosecrans, to assist Lander in whatever way they were able.
58. S. B., letter, Camp Paw Paw, VA, Feb. 17, 1862, in *Beacon,* Feb. 27, 1862.
59. Anecdotes depicting the unusually frigid weather in the mountains above the Shenandoah in winter 1862, and the suffering caused by it, are numerous. Notable among them is found in Tanner, *Stonewall in the Valley,* 73–74.
60. Ibid.
61. Of the several accounts of this march, none seems to agree perfectly on the time of day various points were reached. I have used the timeline reported in an unsigned officer's letter, Feb. 10, 1862, Camp Steele, VA, in *Sentinel,* Feb. 26, 1862.
62. Parmater's diary was apparently stowed with the regiment's baggage and did not catch up with them until a week later. Then, Parmater caught up with the events of the preceding several days in a single entry of Feb. 13, 1862.
63. Pvt. Alonzo Sterrett, letter (headed "Editors Gazette," likely the newspaper in Erie, PA), Feb. 22, 1862, by permission of Lewis Leigh, Fairfax, VA.
64. L. Wilson, *Itinerary,* 119.
65. *Sentinel,* Mar. 5, 1862. Of the dozen names given to this camp, only Seelye described the place accurately enough to identify its modern location. In his letter of Feb. 23, 1862, he referred to it as the Levels. This is the village of Levels, West Virginia, a village of 147 population in Hampshire County. An elementary school, several churches, and a country store and gas station compose the village core.
66. Seelye, letter, "In the Mountains of Virginia," Feb. 11, 1862, in *Sentinel,* Feb. 26, 1862.
67. Ibid.
68. Ibid.
69. Unsigned letter, Camp Steele, VA, Feb. 10, 1862, in *Sentinel,* Feb. 26, 1862.
70. Ibid.
71. Roshon diary, Feb. 7, 1862.
72. Ibid.
73. Unsigned letter, Feb. 10, 1862.
74. The official date of Hayes's return to duty was Feb. 3, 1862. Edward Hayes pension file, RG 94, NA, extract of absences taken from the returns of Co. C, 29th OVI. The date of his actual return to his company has not been established, but had likely occurred by Feb. 6, taking into account a three-day trip from Columbus to Cumberland.
75. H. Williams, *Trumbull and Mahoning Counties,* 275.
76. S. B., letter, Paw Paw, VA, Feb. 17, 1862, in *Beacon,* Mar. 6, 1862.
77. Capt. M. T. Wright, "Condition of Co. D, 29th Regt.," in *Beacon,* July 31, 1862.
78. S. B., letter, Feb. 17, 1862.
79. Ibid.

80. Recipes, instructions for building a survival shelter, and the how-to of making a portable skillet from an ice-ruptured canteen were all reported in S. B., letter, Feb. 17, 1862. S. B. wrote two letters to the Akron newspaper dated Feb. 17, 1862. The first was published in the Feb. 27 *Beacon*, while the second was printed in the Mar. 6 edition.

81. Unsigned letter, "Co. G.," Camp Kelly, below Cumberland, MD, Feb. 3, 1862, in "From the 29th Regiment," *Beacon*, Feb. 13, 1862.

82. *Beacon*, Feb. 6, 1862. Akron's busy social calendar announced in the newspaper is typical of the war period.

83. *Beacon*, Mar. 27, 1862.

Taken Sick

84. Hurlburt, letter, Jan. 23, 1862, in *Beacon*, Feb. 5, 1862.

85. Roshon diary, Jan. 25–26, 1862.

86. Medical affairs in Cumberland are extracted from a multipage report composed by Tripler summarizing the challenges and accomplishments of his command in this period. *OR*, vol. 5, pt. 1, 86.

87. Ibid.

88. Ibid. These final details were accomplished by Mar. 3, 1862.

89. MOLLUS, insignia record no. 8604, Capt. William Fitch. Fitch may also have been assigned as a Hospital Inspector. There is frequent reference in soldier letters of this period reporting his absence in Cumberland, where he was said to be "looking after" the sick.

90. Medical record card, Pvt. Charles E. Dudley, Co. C, USA Post Hospital, Camp Chase, RG 94, Records of the Adjutant General's Office, entry 534, Carded Medical Records, 29th Ohio Infantry Regiment, NA.

91. Seelye, letter, Camp Kelly, Feb. 5, 1862, in "From Our Regular Correspondent in the 29th," *Sentinel*, Feb. 12, 1862.

92. Regimental Books, Co. C, 29th OVI, NA.

93. Fortunately for his family and friends, the error was at least corrected in the *State Roster*, in which it was properly noted that Charles Dudley had died at Cumberland on Feb. 4, 1862.

94. Based on data published in the *State Roster*.

95. S. B., letter, Camp Tyler, VA, near Paw Paw, Feb. 23, 1862, in *Beacon*, Mar. 13, 1862.

96. Ibid.

97. *Sentinel*, Mar. 5, 1862. This incident was sufficiently entertaining to be reported by Chaplain Hurlburt, who described it for the homefolks in Ashtabula County in his letter of Feb. 27, 1862.

98. Pvt. Newton Hummiston to "Dear Mother," Camp Tyler, Mar. 1862, Hummiston pension file, RG 94, NA.

99. *State Roster*, 325, and confirmed in Adj. Comfort Chaffee's letter of Jan. 24, 1862, from Camp Kelly.

100. The *State Roster* indicates that Grover's resignation was not effective until Feb. 28, 1862. The reason for his resignation is given in Chaplain Hurlburt's letter of Jan. 23, 1862.

101. Pvt. Oscar Brewster, letter, Camp Tyler, Feb. 26, 1862, in *Beacon*, Mar. 13, 1862.

102. S. B., letter, Camp Tyler, Mar. 4, 1862, in *Beacon*, Mar. 13, 1862.

103. Chaplain Hurlburt, letter, Camp Tyler, Feb. 27, 1862, in *Sentinel*, Mar. 5, 1862.

104. Ibid.

105. Wallace Hoyt, letter, Camp Paw Paw, Feb. 4, 1862, OHS.

106. Ibid.

107. "The Soldier's Family," *Beacon*, Feb. 6, 1862.

108. Ibid.

109. "Richard," letter, Camp Tyler, Feb. 25 (26), 1862, in "From the 29th Regiment," *Beacon*, Mar. 13, 1862.

110. Buckley to Gen. McNeil, Feb. 18, 1862, in *Beacon*, Feb. 27, 1862.

111. Richard, letter, Feb. 25 (26), 1862.

112. "To the Surviving Officers . . . ," *Sentinel*, Feb. 26, 1862.

113. S. B., letter, Camp Paw Paw, Feb. 17, 1862, in *Beacon*, Feb. 27, 1862. Jack Wright wrote over two thousand words on the regiment's experience in the aborted campaign to trap Jackson on his departure from Romney.

114. Unsigned letter, Camp Steele, near Paw Paw, VA, Feb. 10, 1862, in *Sentinel*, Feb. 26, 1862.

115. *Sentinel*, Mar. 5, 1862. Chaplain Hurlburt stated his opinion of the regiment's dimming prospects for glory in his letter of Feb. 27, 1862: "From present appearances we judge that the 29th will *not* have the opportunity to distinguish itself on the battlefield."

116. Ibid.

"A Surcease of Tramping"

117. Hurlburt, letter, Feb. 18, 1862. Tyler's brigade, including the Twenty-Ninth Ohio, arrived in Paw Paw on Feb. 13, 1862. The duration of their stay at Camp Starvation had been one week.
118. Wallace B. Hoyt to "Dear Sister," Paw Paw, VA, Feb. 4, 1862, OHS.
119. Ibid. Montezuma St. John survived the cold march to Paw Paw. He was wounded several months later at the battle of Port Republic and discharged for disability from his wounds in Aug. 1862.
120. Beatie, *McClellan,* 488–95.
121. Hurlburt, letter, Feb. 18, 1862.
122. Ibid.
123. Leonard, "Balky Mule."
124. Hurlburt, letter, Feb. 18, 1862.
125. Hurlburt, letter, Feb. 27, 1862.
126. Sterrett, letter ("Editors Gazette"), Feb. 22, 1862.
127. Hurlburt, letter, Feb. 27, 1862.
128. Sterrett, "Editors Gazette."
129. Parmater diary, Feb. 22, 1862.
130. Ibid.
131. Parmater diary, Feb. 25, 1862.
132. Parmater diary, Feb. 23, 1862.
133. Ibid.
134. Seelye, letter, Feb. 23, 1862, in *Sentinel,* Mar. 5, 1862.
135. Parmater diary, Feb. 20, 1862.
136. Ibid.
137. Long, *Civil War,* 163–64.
138. S. F. Barstow to McClellan, *OR,* vol. 51, pt. 1, 545.
139. Lander to Marcy, *OR,* vol. 51, pt. 1, 534.

Turned Back

140. Parmater diary, Mar. 1, 2, 1862.
141. Barstow to McClellan, *OR,* vol. 51, pt. 1, 545.
142. Ibid., 544
143. Bartow to Chase, *OR,* vol. 51, pt. 1, 546.
144. Barstow to McClellan, *OR,* vol. 51, pt. 1, 546.
145. Schenck to Stanton, *OR,* vol. 51, pt. 1, 545.
146. SeCheverell, *Journal History,* 36–37.
147. McClellan to Banks, *OR,* vol. 51, pt. 1, 544.
148. Leech, *Reveille,* 130.
149. Ibid.
150. "Gen. Frederick W. Lander," *Telegraph,* Mar. 8, 1862.
151. Typical of the published eulogies extolling Lander was the one appearing in "Death of Gen. Lander," *Sentinel,* Mar. 12, 1862.
152. "Death of Gen. Lander," *Beacon,* Mar. 6, 1862.
153. Col. Lewis P. Buckley to AG Buckingham, June 26, 1862, 3 pp. [series 147-40:119], AGO.

"Show Us the Paymaster"

154. Chaplain Hurlburt, letter, Mar. 4, 1862, in *Sentinel,* Mar. 19, 1862.
155. Parmater diary, Mar. 5, 1862.
156. Hummiston (Hummison) pension file, RG 94, NA.
157. John G. Marsh to "Dear Father," Paw Paw Tunnel, VA, Mar. 6, 1862, Marsh pension file, RG 94, NA.
158. Boatner, *Dictionary,* 624.
159. "From the 29th—A Handsome Present," *Beacon,* May 1, 1862.
160. John G. Marsh to "Dear Ida," n.d. (likely on or around the regiment's first payday), Marsh pension file, RG 94, NA.

161. Pulaski Hard pension file, RG 94, NA. Hard was drafted into the 125th Ohio Infantry less than a year later. His service with that unit consisted in the main of recruiting, and he was formally discharged from further service with them in Nov. 1863, before they took to the field.

162. P. C. Hard, letter, Johnson Corners, Mar. 17, 1862, in *Beacon,* Mar. 27, 1862. Hard announced his return to Akron in this letter; Jack Wright had reported his failed health earlier.

163. Rupp, "Fighting Regiment."

Chapter 9: The Ball Opens
Into a Better Country

1. Chaplain Hurlburt, "Army Correspondence. From the Twenty-Ninth," letter, Camp Tyler near Paw Paw, VA, Mar. 4, 1862, in *Sentinel,* Mar. 19, 1862.
2. Parmater diary, Mar. 6, 1862.
3. Ibid.
4. Jones, "Bits of Gossip."
5. Boatner, *Dictionary,* 752.
6. Sandburg, *Prairie Years,* 1:283.
7. Summers, *Baltimore and Ohio,* 96.
8. Parmater diary, Mar. 11, 1862.
9. Wheeler, "Experiences of an Enlisted Man." Wheeler had been a sergeant in Alvin C. Voris's outfit, the Sixty-Seventh OVI, and was wounded at Kernstown.
10. Alvinson Kinney, letter, May 15, 1862, Kinney pension file, RG 94, NA.
11. Conant Brainerd pension file, RG 94, NA.
12. Parmater diary, Mar. 11, 1862.
13. "Mrs. Howard, Wife of Lieut. Howard of the 29th Regiment . . . ," *Reporter,* Apr. 9, 1862.
14. Parmater diary, Mar. 12, 1862.
15. The regiment was camped about one mile south of the modern village of Stephenson, VA. "Julius," correspondent to the Warren newspaper for the Seventh Ohio, reported that Camp Shields was three miles north of Winchester. "From the 7th Regiment," *Chronicle,* Apr. 2, 1862.
16. Parmater diary, Mar. 12, 1862.
17. Parmater diary, Mar. 13, 1862.
18. Roshon diary, Mar. 12, 1862.
19. Roshon diary, Mar. 14–15, 1862.
20. "From the 7th Regiment," *Chronicle,* Apr. 2, 1862.
21. Adj. Comfort Chaffee, letter, Mar. 14, 1862, in *Sentinel,* Apr. 2, 1862.
22. Ibid.
23. Delauter, *Winchester,* 1–3.
24. Seelye, letter, Winchester, VA, Mar. 18, 1862, in *Sentinel,* Apr. 2, 1862.
25. Roshon diary, Mar. 17, 1862.

The Sound of Distant Fire

26. Parmater diary, Mar. 18, 1862.
27. Ibid.
28. Seelye, letter, Mar. 18, 1862.
29. SeCheverell, *Journal History,* 38.
30. Parmater diary, Mar. 20, 1862.
31. Parmater diary, Mar. 22, 1862.
32. Ibid.

The Ball Opens

33. Tanner, *Stonewall in the Valley,* 119.
34. Ibid., 122.
35. Parmater diary, Mar. 23, 1862.
36. Ibid. Of the numerous accounts of the Kernstown fight written by Twenty-Ninth soldiers and officers, Parmater recorded his first impressions of the scene that presented itself to the Twenty-Ninth as they crossed

the field on the night before the battle. Although tactically imperfect, his observations seem a more genuine representation than those reports composed days, weeks, or years later.

37. Parmater diary, Mar. 23, 1862.
38. Julius, correspondent for the Warren newspaper, stated that the Third Brigade had been ordered to the support of Daum's battery. *Chronicle,* Apr. 2, 1862.
39. Report of R. C. Shriber, aide-de-camp, *OR,* vol. 12, pt. 1, 350–51.
40. Report of Nathan Kimball, Col., 14th Indiana, *OR,* vol. 12, pt. 1, 360–61.
41. Julius, letter, *Chronicle,* Apr. 2, 1862.
42. Ibid.
43. Ibid.
44. Alvinson Kinney to "Dear Father and Mother," Mar. 30, 1862, Kinney pension file, RG 94, NA.
45. Shriber, report.
46. Col. Erastus B. Tyler, *OR,* vol. 12, pt. 1, 360–61.

A Fence Made of Stone

47. Julius, letter, *Chronicle,* Apr. 2, 1862.
48. Kinney, letter, Mar. 30, 1862.
49. Shriber, report.
50. Parmater diary, Mar. 23, 1862.
51. Shriber, report.
52. Seelye, letter, Camp Kimball, Strasburg, VA, Mar. 30, 1862, in *Sentinel,* Apr. 9, 1862.
53. Shriber, report.
54. Ibid.
55. Parmater diary, Mar. 23, 1862.
56. Lt. Theron S. Winship, letter, Mar. 29, 1862, in *Reporter,* Apr. 9, 1862. Winship stated that the entire regiment fired three volleys, after which Companies A through D were ordered forward and the remaining companies placed in reserve behind them. Their objective was a long ridge that ran roughly parallel to the stone wall. Seelye, letter, Strasburg, VA, Mar. 30, 1862, in *Sentinel,* Apr. 9, 1862.
57. Kinney, letter, Mar. 30, 1862.
58. Shriber, report.
59. Chaplain Hurlburt, letter, "Camp Duvall, Thirty-Five Miles from Winchester," Apr. 15, 1862, in *Sentinel,* Apr. 30, 1862.
60. Seelye, letter, Mar. 30, 1862.
61. Hurlburt, letter, Apr. 15, 1862.
62. John G. Marsh to "Dear Father," Camp Tyler, Edinburg, VA, Apr. 10, 1862, Marsh pension file, RG 94, NA.
63. Myron T. Wright to "Dear Father," Mar. 25, 1862, in *Beacon,* Apr. 10, 1862, *Sentinel,* Apr. 16, 1862 ("In the *Beacon* we find a letter . . .").
64. Ibid.
65. Williamson pension file, RG 94, NA.
66. Kinney, letter, Mar. 30, 1862.
67. Seelye, letter, Mar. 30, 1862.
68. Ibid.
69. Kinney, letter, Mar. 30, 1862.
70. Voris, "Battle of the Boys," 4:95.
71. SeCheverell, *Journal History,* 40.
72. Ibid.
73. Kinney, letter, Mar. 30, 1862.

Nights of Eternal Length

74. Marsh to "Dear Father," Apr. 10, 1862.
75. M. Wright, letter, Mar. 25, 1862.
76. W. S. King, Surgeon and Medical Director, Fifth Army Corps, to Medical Director's Office, Mar. 31, 1862, *OR,* vol. 12, pt. 1, 344–45.
77. Ibid.

78. Hurlburt, letter, Apr. 15, 1862.
79. Ibid.
80. "Battle of Winchester: Winchester, Mar. 26," *Sentinel,* Apr. 2, 1862.
81. King report, Mar. 31, 1862.
82. Ibid.
83. Wheeler, "Experiences of an Enlisted Man."
84. "Good for the Colonel, but bad for the young lady . . . ," *Beacon,* Nov. 20, 1862.
85. "From the 29th Reg't," *Beacon,* Apr. 10, 1862; Wright, letter, Mar. 25, 1862.
86. M. Wright, letter, Mar. 25, 1862.
87. Amos K. Fifield pension file, RG 94, NA.
88. Marsh to "Dear Father," Apr. 10, 1862.

State of Suspense

89. "The Twenty-Ninth Have Doubtless Had a Taste of Battle," *Sentinel,* Mar. 26, 1862.
90. "The Battle of Winchester," *Sentinel,* Apr. 9, 1862.
91. Hurlburt, letter, Apr. 15, 1862.
92. Seelye, letter, Mar. 30, 1862.
93. Hurlburt, letter, Apr. 15, 1862.
94. "The Victory at Winchester," *Beacon,* Apr. 3, 1862.
95. Capt. William T. Fitch, letter, Luray, VA, June 11, 1862. In *Sentinel,* June 25, 1862. As to the fate of those succumbed to wounds at Kernstown, Fitch stated, "All those who have died in the hospital, I have in every case written to their friends, informing them of same."
96. "Deceased Soldiers," *Chronicle,* Apr. 6, 1862. The soldier in question was J. D. Hunt, son of Mr. and Mrs. Samuel Hunt of Champion, Ohio.
97. M. Wright, letter, Mar. 25, 1862. Wright's letter was thought so important it was reprinted in the Jefferson newspaper.
98. Winship, letter, Mar. 29, 1862.
99. Lt. E. B. Howard, letter, Camp Kimball, near Strasburg, VA, Apr. 1, 1862, in "Another Letter from the 29th," *Reporter,* Apr. 9, 1861.
100. Hurlburt, letter, Apr. 15, 1862.
101. S. B., letter, Apr. 16, 1862. Summarized, with editorial comment, in "The Twenty-Ninth," *Beacon,* May 8, 1862.
102. "Return of Casualties in the Union Forces, Shields Division," *OR,* vol. 12, pt. 1, 346.
103. Cpl. Levi Bean, Company B, died of wounds received at Kernstown on Apr. 2. *State Roster,* 360.
104. L. Wilson, "Kernstown. Who Charged."
105. "The Price of Battle," *Sentinel,* Apr. 23, 1862, 176B.
106. Ibid.
107. "From Mogadore," *Beacon,* Mar. 20, 1862. John Ewell died on Mar. 6, 1862, at Cumberland, MD. *State Roster.*
108. Jas. Treen, letter, Strasburg, VA, Mar. 1, 1862 (obviously misdated), in *Beacon,* Apr. 10, 1862.
109. Gen. James Shields, report, *OR,* vol. 12, pt. 1, 342.
110. Ibid., 338.
111. SeCheverell, *Journal History,* 40. In his initial report of Mar. 23, Shields gave Jackson's strength as fifteen thousand. In his follow-up report of Mar. 27, written after his staff had interviewed captured prisoners, he reduced his estimate to eleven thousand. *OR,* vol. 12, pt. 1, 335, 338.
112. By most accounts Jackson's force at Kernstown did not exceed 3,500. The strength of Tyler's brigade was officially reported as 3,255 present for duty and 4,397 aggregate.
113. Adj. Comfort T. Chaffee, letter, Strasburg, VA, Mar. 29, 1862, in *Sentinel,* Apr. 9, 1862.
114. Ibid.

Chapter 10: Chasing Jackson
Slow Motion

1. Gurley Crane to "Dear Parents," Luray, VA, June 12, 1862, in *Beacon,* June 26, 1862.
2. L. Wilson, *Itinerary,* 145.

3. Worsham, *Jackson's Foot Cavalry*, 74.
4. SeCheverell, *Journal History*, 42.
5. Parmater diary, Apr. 5, 1862.
6. Ibid.
7. Parmater diary, Apr. 6, 1862.
8. Wallace Hoyt to "Dear Father," "Edinburgh [Edinburg], Va. on Rock Creek," Apr. 6, 1862, OHS.
9. Parmater diary, Apr. 7, 1862.
10. Parmater diary, Apr. 11, 1862.
11. Pvt. Nelson Gillett, letter, Camp Buckley, near New Market, VA, May 10, 1862, Gillett pension file, RG 94, NA.
12. Jones, "Bits of Gossip."
13. Ibid.
14. Hoyt, letter, Apr. 6, 1862.
15. Parmater diary, Apr. 9, 1862.
16. Parmater diary, Apr. 17, 1862.
17. Ibid.
18. Ibid.
19. Ibid.
20. Parmater diary, Apr. 18, 1862.

"In the Name of the United States and Uncle Abe Lincoln"

21. Pvt. R. E. Woodbury, letter, New Market, VA, Apr. 30, 1862, in "Through the politeness of Lt. Crowell," *Sentinel*, May 14, 1862.
22. Gurley Crane, letter, New Market, VA, Apr. 19, 1862, in *Beacon*, May 8, 1862.
23. Parmater diary, May 1, 1862.
24. Gillett, letter, May 10, 1862.
25. Parmater diary, May 8, 1862.
26. Woodbury, letter, Apr. 30, 1862.
27. *Reporter*, June 4, 1862.
28. Ibid.
29. Parmater diary, May 2, 1862. Dalrymple died at Mount Jackson on May 2, 1862. Several of his kin soldiered on in Companies A and E.
30. John G. Marsh to "My Dear Sister Almira," Strasburg, VA, Apr. 2, 1862, Hudson Papers.
31. Parmater diary, Apr. 23, 1862.
32. Crane, letter, June 12, 1862.
33. Parmater diary, Apr. 26, 1862.
34. Parmater diary, May 1, 1862.
35. Huntington, "Operations in the Shenandoah."
36. L. Wilson, *Itinerary*, 155.
37. Willis Sisley to "Dear Father," New Market, VA, May 7, 1862, Sisley pension file, RG 94, NA.
38. Huntington, "Operations in the Shenandoah."
39. Parmater diary, May 5–6, 1862.
40. Parmater diary, May 5–7, 1862.
41. Parmater diary, May 7, 1862.
42. Banks to Stanton, Apr. 30, 1862 (two dispatches that day), *OR*, vol. 12, pt. 3, 118.
43. Ibid.
44. McDowell to Shields, May 2, 1862, *OR*, vol. 12, pt. 3, 125.
45. Shields to McDowell, May 5, 1862, *OR*, vol. 12, pt. 3, 134.
46. Ibid.
47. Shields, dispatch to Carroll, *OR*, vol. 12, pt. 3, 353. Regarding the order he had received from General McDowell commanding him to dispense with his wagons and baggage except for those wagons needed to haul rations and ammunition, Shields wrote to Colonel Carroll, "General McDowell writes me that Jackson marches 30 miles a day, and as he says, we can never catch a swift-footed enemy with such a train filled with trumpery. Mind this, and let your officers act upon it at once."

48. Wallace Hoyt, letter, Camp Buckley, near Haymarket, VA, May 10, 1862, OHS.

49. 1st Lt. William S. Crowell, Company A, resigned on April 13, 1862. *State Roster,* 355. Capt. John Morse, Company F, age 60, resigned on April 15, 1862. *State Roster,* 374. Capt. Alden Steele, Company K, resigned on April 11, 1862. *State Roster,* 390.

50. Parmater diary, Apr. 7, 1862.

51. Parmater diary, Apr. 10, 1862.

52. Lewis Buckley to Adj. Buckingham, Apr. 15, 1862, 2 pp. [series 147-32:175], AGO.

53. Lewis Buckley to Adj. Buckingham, Mar. 22, 1862, 2 pp. [series 147-32:178], AGO. The officer in question was 2nd Lt. James H. Grinnell (Grinnel) of Company D. Buckley, who could be rather unforgiving of human moral failings, characterized Grinnell's behavior as "licentious." Lieutenant Grinnell must have reformed his ways. He stayed with the regiment until he was discharged on June 14, 1864, having never risen above the rank of second lieutenant, the same rank he had been given when the regiment was organized in 1861. *State Roster,* 367.

54. Parmater diary, May 20, 1862.

55. Chaplain Hurlburt, letter, May 20, 1862, in "On the Wing," *Sentinel,* May 28, 1862.

56. Hoyt, letter, May 10, 1862.

Marched to Death

57. Hurlburt, letter, May 20, 1862.

58. Powell, "Shields in the Shenandoah."

59. Parmater diary, May 12–13, 1862.

60. Hurlburt, letter, May 20, 1862.

61. Ibid.

62. Parmater diary, May 14, 1862.

63. Parmater diary, May 15, 1862.

64. Hurlburt, letter, May 20, 1862. He reported that two of the captured Confederate scouts were placed in the custody of Captain Fitch.

65. Ibid.

66. Ibid.

67. Parmater diary, May 18, 1862.

68. Ibid. Curtis was discharged for disability in July 1862 and returned to Conneaut, Ohio. He lived until 1903. Curtis pension file, RG 94, NA.

69. The references to the fisticuffs that broke out when western troops first came into contact with eastern soldiers are too numerous to list. Lawrence Wilson spoke of it in *Itinerary of the Seventh Ohio* (p. 151), as did James Huntington in "Operations in the Shenandoah Valley" (p. 317).

70. Parmater diary, May 20, 1862.

71. Parmater diary, May 21–22, 1862.

72. *Register of Deaths,* Regimental Books, 29th OVI, NA. All of the deceased were privates in Company B. Herman Holmes and Jonas Newman died in Winchester, April 5–6, 1862. William Vanscoit died in Frederick, MD, on April 5, and Charles F. Bauer died in Winchester on April 19. Their deaths were noted in the *State Roster,* 360, 361, 362, and 360 respectively. The Pension Bureau documented Holmes's cause of death as typhoid fever. Holmes pension file, RG 94, NA. His comrades observed that Holmes had kept marching long after the time he should have given in and gone to the hospital. The men of their company attributed all of their deaths to "hard marching," and the company clerk recorded them thus in the company books.

73. Ohio raised nearly 320,000 soldiers for the Union army. Reid, *Ohio in the War,* 1:160. In her seminal examination of the elusive number of deserters, Ella Lonn concluded that 18,354 Ohio soldiers, or about one in eighteen, had deserted. Lonn, *Desertion,* 234. A huge ledger book bearing the title Roll of Deserters, series 108, Ohio Adjutant General's Office, 1936, can be examined at the Ohio Historical Society. The AGO initially listed 82 Twenty-Ninth Ohio Infantry soldiers in this ledger. Corrections were later made and names removed as the mountains of documents left in the wake of the conflict were collected and scrutinized, and individual cases reviewed. Final adjustments were made to the list in the 1930s, but it still contains errors. The names of 54 Giddings Regiment soldiers remain on this roll of dishonor. Over 1,500 men had served in the regiment during the rebellion. Using the Roll of Deserters as a benchmark, while keeping in mind its propensity for error, it appears that one in twenty-eight Twenty-Ninth soldiers turned their backs on war and walked away, far less than the average for an Ohio regiment. A study of whether each man on this ignominious list deserved his place on

it would occupy a lifetime for the regiment alone, and in all likelihood the endeavor would never produce a completely trustworthy number.

74. Register of Casualties, Books of the 29th OVI, NA.
75. Huntington, "Operations in the Shenandoah," 317.
76. Parmater diary, May 24, 1862.
77. Powell, "Shields in the Shenandoah."
78. Huntington, "Operations in the Shenandoah," 321.
79. Parmater diary, May 27, 1862.
80. Huntington, "Operations in the Shenandoah," 322.
81. Kimball's telegram containing his opinion of affairs at Thoroughfare Gap was wired to Secretary of War Stanton by McDowell, May 27, 1862. *OR*, vol. 12, pt. 3, 255.

Swept Up

82. "From the 29th," *Reporter*, June 18, 1862.
83. Ibid.
84. Pvt. Wellington Gillett, twenty-two, of Company C, died at the hospital in Mount Jackson, VA, May 20, 1862. *State Roster*, 365.
85. "Our Sick at Strasburg," *Beacon*, June 5, 1862.
86. "The Fate of Mr. Rockwell," *Telegraph*, June 21, 1862.
87. Ibid.
88. J. J. W., letter, Dec. 22, 1862, in "Another Soldier Gone," *Beacon*, Dec. 25, 1862. After many difficulties, Watson's friends got him back to Akron. He was found dead at his home before Christmas 1862 and buried with full military honors.
89. Boatner, *Dictionary*. The typical text of the *parole d'honneur* in use in this period is quoted in Boatner, 620.
90. "Soldiers from the 29th," *Beacon*, May 29, 1862.
91. "Soldiers Return," *Beacon*, June 12, 1862.
92. The elder Lane turned up eventually and was discharged in Oct. 1862, within a few days of his son. *State Roster*, 381.
93. Supplee, "Shenandoah Valley."
94. Ibid.
95. Reprinted in the *Sentinel* as "Northern Ohio Boys in Winchester When Taken by the Rebels," July 2, 1862, credited to the *New York Times*. The official record of the regiment's soldiers captured on or about May 25, 1862, does not distinguish where they were taken prisoner, giving the place generally as Strasburg. In a letter dated June 11, 1862, from Luray, VA, Capt. William Fitch listed an additional eight soldiers taken at Winchester. "Army Correspondence . . . ," *Sentinel*, June 25, 1862.
96. J. J. Wright, letter, Camp Wade, Alexandria, VA, July 16, 1862, in "From the 29th Regiment," *Beacon*, July 24, 1862. The mill guarded by Twenty-Ninth soldiers subsequently captured by Stonewall Jackson was located in Woodstock, VA, a village astride the Valley Pike between Mount Jackson and Strasburg.
97. Report of W. S. King, Medical Director, Dept. of the Shenandoah, May 29, 1862, *OR*, vol. 12, pt. 3, 286. Surgeon King estimated the numbers of sick left behind by Shields when he began his march to Fredericksburg as 84, while those left there as "disabled" numbered 870.

Chapter 11: "Up the River and Back of the Mountains"

Return to the Shenandoah

1. Parmater diary, May 27–28, 1862.
2. Parmater diary, May 28, 1862.
3. Parmater diary, May 29, 1862.
4. Ibid.
5. Parmater diary, May 30, 1862.
6. Huntington, "Operations in the Shenandoah," 325.

The Deluge

7. Parmater diary, June 6, 1862.
8. Parmater diary, May 31–June 6, 1862.

9. Conrad's Store was located on the south fork of the Shenandoah, near present-day Elkton, VA.

10. Shields to Col. Schriver, *OR,* vol. 12, pt. 1, 686.

11. Shields to Col. Schriver, *OR,* vol. 12, pt. 1, 359. On the readiness of this troops for battle, Shields stated, "We stand in need of salt meat, hard bread, coffee, and sugar. One-third of my command are without shoes, and sans culottes in a literal sense of the word; but we will soon have time to refit."

12. McDowell to Sec. of War Stanton, *OR,* vol. 12, pt. 3, 325–26.

13. Shields to Schriver, *OR,* vol. 12, pt. 1, 686. Shields wrote, "In this condition the first question was how to live, to obtain supplies, as none could reach us over such roads."

14. Parmater diary, May 31, 1862.

15. Parmater diary, June 6, 1862.

16. Huntington, "Operations in the Shenandoah," 303–37.

17. Shields to Schriver, June 8, 1862.

18. J. R., letter, June 19, 1862, in "Army Correspondence," *Chronicle,* July 2, 1862. This account of the battle of Port Republic was written by a Seventh Ohio soldier.

19. Shields to Brig. Col. Carroll, *OR,* vol. 12, pt. 3, 353.

20. Ibid.

The Two Luckiest Boys in the Army

21. Rollin L. Jones to "Dear Brother and Sister," Fort Delaware, MD, Oct. 4, 1862, *Sentinel,* Nov. 19, 26, 1862.

22. SeCheverell, *Journal History,* 45.

23. J. R., letter, June 19, 1862.

24. Parmater diary, June 8, 1862.

25. Shields to McDowell, June 4, 1862, *OR,* vol. 12, pt. 3, 335.

Tall Odds

26. Theron S. Winship, letter, near Luray, VA, June 12, 1862, in "Casualties in the 29th: Full Particulars of the Battle," *Reporter,* June 25, 1862. Published in the column bordering Winship's letter, under the title "Battle of Port Republic," was a long editorial on the import of Captain Luce's death as well as details of it extracted from a letter Sgt. A. J. Andrews had sent to his father. Most Federal participants overestimated Jackson's strength at Port Republic. Douglas Southall Freeman calculated the strength of all arms available to Jackson at Port Republic as 8,000. Freeman, *Lee's Lieutenants,* 217. Tyler's command and that of the portion of the Fourth Brigade present on the field is given generally as no more than 3,000. Col. Thomas Clark and Capt. William T. Fitch estimated Jackson's force as 25,000. Twenty years later SeCheverell stated that Jackson, by his own "official" reports, had 34,000 on hand for the battle. SeCheverell, *Journal History,* 48.

27. "From the Twenty-Ninth!! List of Killed, Wounded & Missing! Full Particulars: Letter from Adjt. Winship," *Sentinel,* June 25, 1862. Winship's letter was dated June 12, 1862, Luray, VA, and was copied by the *Sentinel* from a special edition of the *Conneaut Reporter.*

28. Capt. Wm. T. Fitch, letter, June 11, 1862, in "Army Correspondence. From the Twenty-ninth. Headquarters 29th Regt., Camp in the Field, Near Luray, Va.," *Sentinel,* June 25, 1862.

29. Gurley Crane to "Dear Parents," Luray, VA, June 12, 1862, in *Beacon,* June 26, 1862.

30. SeCheverell, *Journal History,* 46.

31. Lt. James Treen to Josiah J. Wright, Luray, VA, June 11, 1862, in "The Missing of the 29th . . . ," *Beacon,* June 19, 1862.

32. Jones, "Bits of Gossip." Capt. Edward Hayes took Rollin Jones into his confidence and told him that in a meeting of the officers on the eve of the battle, Lewis Buckley had voted for retreat.

33. Jones, letter, Oct. 4, 1862.

34. Ibid. Lt. George W. Dice, commanding Company D in the fight, wrote to his mother that he too had seen that their prospects were hopeless, but despite that the men fought like tigers. Dice to "Dear Mother," June 19, 1862, Dice pension file, RG 94, NA.

35. Rupp, "Fighting Regiment." Also in SeCheverell, *Journal History,* 46.

36. J. R., letter, in "Army Correspondence," *Chronicle,* July 2, 1862. There is some confusion about whether the Seventh or Twenty-Ninth Infantry held the extreme right flank of Tyler's line. A description of the battle and the placement of troops written by a Seventh Ohio soldier shortly after reported that the Twenty-Ninth took the right, and the Seventh Ohio formed the right center. The Twenty-Ninth's position at the extreme right of the

Federal line would explain in part their failure to hear the order to retreat and that they were last to leave the field. From the far right, their retreat back to the road was necessarily longer than that of the other regiments engaged.

37. Jones, letter, Oct. 4, 1862.
38. Parmater diary, June 9, 1862.
39. SeCheverell, *Journal History*, 46.
40. Jones, letter, Oct. 4, 1862.
41. SeCheverell, *Journal History*, 47.
42. Fitch, letter, June 11, 1862.
43. S. B., letter, Warrenton, VA, July 28, 1862, in "From the 29th," *Beacon*, Aug. 21, 1862.
44. SeCheverell, *Journal History*, 47.
45. S. B., letter, July 28, 1862.
46. Ibid.
47. Seymour and Baldwin, "Port Republic." Baldwin credited Allen Mason with capturing the battle flag of the Seventh Louisiana Infantry.
48. Ibid.
49. Crane, letter, June 12, 1862.
50. S. B., letter, July 28, 1862.
51. Jones, "Bits of Gossip." Jones stated in this letter, written while he was in captivity at Fort Delaware, that upon capturing the rebel flags, Captain Hayes told him for the second time that day that the regiment's prospects for success were slim.
52. "Army Correspondence."
53. S. B., letter, July 28, 1862.
54. Ibid.
55. Jones, "Bits of Gossip."
56. "Col. Buckley Safe," *Beacon*, June 19, 1862. Accounts of the battle of Port Republic given the newspaper by Lts. Treen and Grinnell are found in this edition under the titles "More from the 29th" and "Further from the 29th."
57. Jones, letter, Oct. 4, 1862.
58. Ibid.
59. Winship, letter, June 12, 1862.
60. Otsego County Centennial, *Heritage Years*, 17, 49.
61. S. B., letter, July 28, 1862.
62. Ibid.
63. Ibid.
64. Capt. Jonas Schoonover, letter, "Camp Bristow, near Manassas, VA," June 22, 1862, in "From the 29th Reg't," *Beacon*, July 10, 1862.
65. Jones, letter, Oct. 4, 1862.
66. John S. Clemmer pension file, RG 94, NA.
67. Parmater diary, June 9, 1862.
68. Unsigned letter (an Ohio soldier in Tyler's brigade), *Journal*, June 19, 1862. "The 29th did not get the order and was entirely surrounded."
69. Crane, letter, June 12, 1862.
70. Fitch, letter, June 11, 1862.
71. Crane, letter, June 12, 1862.
72. Ibid.
73. Jones, "Bits of Gossip."
74. Ibid.
75. Capt. Wm. T. Fitch to W. S. Crowell, n.d., in *Sentinel*, July 2, 1862.
76. SeCheverell estimated that the Twenty-Ninth Regiment fought the rebel cavalry in a running battle two miles long as they retreated from the field. SeCheverell, *Journal History*, 47.
77. Jones, letter, Oct. 4, 1862.
78. Pvt. Perry Decker pension file, RG 94, NA.
79. Dice to "Dear Mother," June 19, 1862.
80. Fitch to Crowell, n.d.

81. Ibid.

82. Jones, letter, Oct. 4, 1862. Jones states with clarity that at Port Republic both the national flag (Stars and Stripes) and the state flag—the two constituting the regiment's "stand"—were taken. In a letter several months later to his brother and sister he stated, "We captured a rebel battle flag, but this together with the National flag belonging to our Regiment were taken by the enemy. You have probably heard of the whereabouts of the Regimental flag. The Sergeant who had possession of it, made his escape from Lynchburg a few days before we left."

83. Ibid.

84. Ibid.

85. Thomas Clark obituary, *Cambridge (MA) Tribune,* Aug. 18, 1894.

86. Allan, "Valley Campaign," *Annals of the War,* 747.

87. "Battle of Port Republic," *Reporter,* June 25, 1862.

88. Ibid.

89. "Capt. H. Luce," *Telegraph,* June 21, 1862.

90. Winship's letter of condolence to Capt. Luce's father, Emory Luce, was published in the *Telegraph,* Saturday, June 28, 1862. Several pages of the same edition were mistakenly dated June 29. Another Winship letter, dated June 12, was published in the same edition under "Casualties in the 29th: Full Particulars of the Late Battle." A third collection of incidents of the battle of Port Republic was published in this edition of the *Telegraph* under "The 29th at the Battle of Port Republic."

91. Ibid.

92. Winship to Emory Luce, Luray, VA, June 11, 1862, in *Telegraph,* June 28, 1862.

93. Clouds, "Cross Keys."

94. Mumford to Jackson, *OR,* vol. 12, pt. 1, 732.

95. "Battle of Port Republic," *Reporter,* June 25, 1862. In his eulogy to Horatio Luce, found in the *Telegraph,* Theron Winship wrote, perhaps for the grieving father's benefit, that the officer accompanying the flag of truce onto the battlefield had promised Winship that he would try to locate Luce and give him a proper burial, but had failed. This pledge was not likely fulfilled because the truce arrangement apparently broke down, and the party was driven back from the field. *Telegraph,* June 28, 1862; Winship to Emory Luce ("Dear Sir"), June 11, 1862. Winship was one of several participants who lamented that Captain Luce was left on the field: "Poor Captain, I was obliged to leave him on the field, together with all our dead, and a portion of our wounded." Winship, letter, June 12, 1862, in "Casualties in the 29th: Full Particulars of the Late Battle," *Telegraph,* June 28, 1862. Winship's letter was also published in the *Reporter,* June 25, 1862.

96. Affidavit of Edward Hayes, Warren, Ohio, Oct. 28, 1867, George Eastlick pension file, RG 94, NA. Although bothered by a variety of complaints caused by his wound, Eastlick lived until 1930.

97. Jones, "Battery Horses." Jones met Eastlick at a Memorial Day observance in May 1889, having not seen him since the battle of Port Republic.

98. Everhart pension file, RG 94, NA.

99. Johnson pension file, RG 94, NA.

100. Decker pension file, RG 94, NA.

101. Brig. Gen. Chas. S. Winder, CSA, to Gen. T. J. Jackson, *OR,* vol. 12, pt. 1, 742.

Cut to Pieces

102. Winship, letter, June 12, 1862 ("From the Twenty-Ninth").

103. Crane, letter, June 12, 1862.

104. Winship, letter, June 12, 1862.

105. SeCheverell, *Journal History,* 48.

106. "Battle of Port Republic," *Reporter,* June 25, 1862.

107. "Further from the 29th," *Beacon,* June 19, 1862.

108. Capt. M. T. Wright, "Condition of Co. D, 29th Regt.," n.d., in *Beacon,* July 31, 1862.

109. Lt. James Treen to J. J. Wright, Luray, VA, June 11, 1862, in "The Missing of the 29th . . . ," *Beacon,* June 19, 1862.

110. Winship, letter, June 12, 1862.

111. Winship to Luce, *Telegraph,* June 28, 1862. Winship's calculation of the numbers present after the battle, including those who returned in the two days following it, are assumed reliable since it was his duty to make sure the company clerks were taking roll call and accurately recording the result. Another count of the

Twenty-Ninth's strength before and after Port Republic was reported as 460 and 230, respectively. J. R., letter, *Chronicle,* July 2, 1862.

112. McDowell to Schriver, June 8, 1862, *OR,* vol. 12, pt. 1, 356.

113. Frank Holsinger, Capt. Nineteenth U.S. Colored Infantry, Brvt. Major U.S. Volunteers. "How Does One Feel Under Fire?" MOLLUS—Kansas, *Kansas War Papers, War Talks in Kansas,* May 5, 1898, 1:301.

114. Wheeler, "Experiences of an Enlisted Man."

115. McDowell to Schriver, June 8, 1862, *OR.*

"Who Is to Blame?"

116. "Jackson Attacks Shields," *Sentinel,* June 18, 1862.

117. "The Twenty-Ninth," *Sentinel,* June 18, 1862.

118. Ibid.

119. Winship, letter, June 12, 1862.

120. Ibid.

121. "Battle of Port Republic," *Reporter.*

122. Fitch, letter, June 11, 1862.

123. The counting of the regiment's losses in the Port Republic engagement, as reported in three sources (all of which were imperfect), gives a range of men killed in action of from 14 to 17 (Fox, *Regimental Losses,* reports the higher number, with an additional 6 soldiers dead of wounds afterward), wounded 41 to 57 (SeCheverell reports the higher figure), and captured as 114. Fox, 319. SeCheverell reported the number of "missing" as 105. SeCheverell, 282.

124. Fitch to Crowell, n.d., in "Extract of a letter from Capt. Wm. T. Fitch to W. S. Crowell," *Sentinel,* July 2, 1862.

125. "R. D. N.," "To the Editor of the *Sentinel,*" condolence letter, *Sentinel,* July 2, 1862.

126. "Missing of the Twenty-Ninth," *Sentinel,* July 23, 1862. The circumstances of Turner's murder and plans for his funeral also appeared in R. D. N., letter, Hartsgrove, Ohio, June 22, 1862, in "To the Editor of the *Sentinel,*" *Sentinel,* July 2, 1862.

127. Potter diary, June 9, 1862.

128. Wallace Hoyt to "Dear Parents," Luray, VA, June 12, 1862. The quoted page will not be found in the balance of this letter at the Ohio Historical Society. It was kindly provided by the Friends of Andersonville, Andersonville National Historic Site Library, Andersonville, GA.

129. "Incidents Occurring in the 29th at the Battle of Port Republic," *Sentinel,* June 25, 1862.

130. M. Wright, "Condition of Co. D," 1862. Cpl. William Hart, forty-two, survived the amputation of his leg and was discharged in Dec. 1862 for wounds received at Port Republic. *State Roster,* 367.

131. "Who Is to Blame," *Journal,* June 23, 1862. In its June 26 edition, under the title "Port Republic Explanatory," the *Journal* reversed course and supported Carroll's argument that he had been ordered to hold the bridge rather than burn it. The editors thought that made simple military sense, and they believed him.

132. Shields to Schriver, June 13, 1862, *OR,* vol. 12, pt. 1, 684–85.

133. Ibid.

134. Ibid.

135. Fitz-Porter was arrested by Gen. John Pope for disobeying orders at Second Bull Run and convicted by a panel that some said was handpicked by McClellan's enemy, Secretary of War Stanton. Fitz-Porter was eventually exonerated and his rank restored.

136. McDowell, testimony at Fitz-Porter trial, *OR,* vol. 12, pt. 3, 289.

137. Hoyt to "Dear Parents," June 12, 1862, OHS.

138. Parmater diary, June 14, 1862.

139. Ibid.

140. Hoyt to "Dear Parents," June 12, 1862.

Chapter 12: "Rest Now, Rest"
"Too Much Music"

1. Shields to Schriver, June 10, 1862, *OR,* vol. 12, pt. 3, 367–68.

2. Schriver to McDowell, Front Royal, VA, June 10, 1862, *OR,* vol. 12, pt. 3, 368.

3. "General Shields' division is, I learn, in a bad state morally and materially—officers resigning and even men deserting." McDowell, at Fitz-Porter court-martial, quoting from his letter to Stanton, June 21, 1862, in *OR,* vol. 12, pt. 1, 288. Also quoted in *OR,* vol. 12, pt. 3, 417.

4. Wallace Hoyt to "Dear Father," Front Royal, VA, June 18, 1862, Hoyt pension file, RG 94, NA. Only one officer did resign that summer, and his exact reasons for resigning went unstated. Lt. Benjamin F. Perry, Co. C, resigned on June 20, 1862. United States, Adjutant General's Office, *Official Register of the Volunteer Force of the United States Army 1861–1865,* 1865–1867, Washington, Ohio Infantry, 95.

5. Buckley to Buckingham, June 26, 1862, 3 pp. [series 147-40:119], AGO.

6. Parmater diary, July 2, 1862.

7. Potter diary, June 16, 1862.

8. Potter diary, June 14, 1862. Hurry was discharged for disability on July 10, 1862. The loss of his finger likely was determined to have been accidental since he was granted a pension for disability caused by it. He died in the California Soldiers' Home in 1926.

9. Roll of Deserters, series 108, State of Ohio, Adjutant General's Office, 1936.

10. From the data contained in the *State Roster,* SeCheverell, and the Regimental Books, it appears that the following number of deaths from disease occurred from May through July 1862: May, 16; June, 5; July, 7. No deaths from disease were reported for Aug. 1862.

11. Roshon's odyssey was reported in his letter of July 10, 1862, to his parents, and in his diary entries of July 7–12, 1862.

12. *Reporter,* July 16, 1862.

13. *Reporter,* July 23, 1862.

14. Capt. M. T. Wright, letter, n.d., in "Condition of Co. D, 29th Regt.," *Beacon,* July 31, 1862.

City Lights

15. Roll of Deserters, series 108, State of Ohio, Adjutant General's Office, 1936.

16. Potter diary, June 28, 1862, "Went down to the river and staid until dark Staid all night 66, 5, 7th regiment[s] got on the boats and Staid all night." And in his entry of the next day, "Morning unloaded the boats and went through town and camped on the railroad." It is noteworthy that SeCheverell stated in print the obvious error, "after lying at this point for nearly a month we embarked on the transports," which was misremembered as to date, and, that they had actually boarded. SeCheverell, *Journal History,* 49.

17. Alvinson Kinney to "Dear Father," July 2, 1862, Kinney pension file, RG 94, NA. A portion of Kinney's letter is faded beyond reading, but enough of it is legible to understand Buckley's sentiment, "Part of the brigade got on the boats, they did not. . . . Cornel buckly had made up his mind to go home. He said he shold resign if they do not give us rest. He said if he was in the boys plases if they went to put us on the boat that he wold brek the gun stalks." Upon whom the gun stocks would be broken is illegible, but the obvious candidates would be those in places high enough to order the brigade's removal to the Peninsula.

18. Wallace Hoyt to "Dear Parents," Front Royal, VA, June 18, 1862, Hoyt pension file, RG 94, NA.

19. Burton Pickett, letter, June 19, 1862, Pickett pension file, RG 94, NA.

20. "Recruiting Rendezvous," *Beacon,* July 17, 1862.

21. Wallace Hoyt to "Dear Parents," Luray, VA, June 12, 1862, OHS.

22. Alvinson Kinney, letter, Camp Washington, VA, July 18, 1862, Kinney pension file, RG 94, NA.

23. Burton Pickett, letter, Camp Wade, VA, July 22, 1862, Pickett pension file, RG 94, NA.

24. Elias Roshon to "Dear Father and Mother," Camp Washington, VA, July 21, 1862.

25. Most musicians in the regiment's band were discharged on July 2, 1862, under General Order No. 65. *State Roster,* 354–55. The author of the regiment's published history, J. Hampton SeCheverell, had enlisted as a musician. The "Little Drummer Boy" may have been called that with friendly sarcasm—he was nearly six feet tall and twenty years of age. SeCheverell was taken prisoner at Strasburg, VA, in May 1862, where he was being treated for typhoid fever. SeCheverell pension file, RG 94, NA. In the history he wrote, he lists himself as having been discharged along with the rest of the band. SeCheverell, *Journal History,* 174. The *State Roster* gives a different version of his departure from the regiment. He is not listed as a member of the band, but is found listed with the privates of Company B along with the remark "Reduced from Musician—; discharged June 4, 1862 at Williamsport, Md., on Surgeon's certificate of disability." *State Roster,* 362. His own pension file sheds little light on the circumstances of his discharge. However, he did recover sufficiently to enlist in the Second Ohio Heavy Artillery, where he served much longer than he had in the Twenty-Ninth Regiment. After the war, he practiced dentistry in Jefferson and wrote feature stories for the local newspapers. He believed the latter was his true calling. He lived until 1910. He is buried in Jefferson.

Flush Times Ahead

26. "Harvest—The Crops," *Telegraph*, Aug. 9, 1862.
27. "Oh for Rain," *Reporter*, Aug. 6, 1862.
28. *Reporter*, Aug. 9, 1862.
29. "The Price of Wool," *Telegraph*, June 29, 1862.
30. Grismer, *Akron and Summit County*, 179–80.
31. Ibid., 190.
32. Ibid., 174–79. Schumacher eventually consolidated his mills with those of others in the Reserve, running all of them under the new name of Quaker Oats.
33. Grismer, *Akron and Summit County*, 182.
34. *Reporter*, Aug. 9, 1862.
35. "Monumental Proceedings," *Telegraph*, June 29, 1862. Ashtabula County's proposal for building a Civil War monument was also reported in the *Sentinel*, July 2, 1862. Messrs. Kellogg, Wade, and Cadwell served on the committee chaired by *Sentinel* editor W. C. Howells.
36. "Village Morality," *Telegraph*, July 5, 1862.
37. "Riding on a Rail," *Telegraph*, Mar. 15, 1862.
38. Ibid.
39. "The Women of Winchester," *Sentinel*, June 11, 1862.
40. "Rebel Atrocities," *Sentinel*, May 21, 1862.
41. *Reporter*, July 16, 1862. G. C. E. Weber, surgeon general of Ohio, thanked the women of Conneaut for their offer to take sick and wounded soldiers into their homes in a letter to Rev. Bartlett. Weber to Bartlett, July 11, 1862. In *Reporter*, July 16, 1862.
42. "From the 84th Regiment," *Beacon*, June 19, 1862.
43. "Lo the Poor Indian," *Reporter*, July 23, 1862.

Poor Fellows

44. "From Major Clemmer," *Beacon*, July 3, 1862.
45. Clemmer was forced to resign on Dec. 12, 1862. *State Roster*, 353.
46. "To the Young Men of Ashtabula!" *Telegraph*, July 26, 1862.
47. "Extracts from Letters by a Lady in Washington to Her Friends in Austinburg, Number II," *Sentinel*, June 25, 1862. During the summer of 1862, the *Sentinel* published a series of ten numbered letters written by Mrs. Wheeler. The first letter was published on June 18 and the last on Sept. 10. A last letter, addressed directly to the *Sentinel* editor during her visit home to Austinburg, was published in the newspaper on Sept. 24, 1862.
48. Ibid.
49. "Letters by a Lady," *Sentinel*, July 2, 1862.
50. "Relieve the Wounded! Women of Ashtabula County!" *Sentinel*, Aug. 6, 1862. This alarm to the women of the county was written by Mrs. "L. M." Giddings; most likely Lura Maria Giddings, Joshua Giddings's daughter. The main body of the piece consisted of material quoted from a letter sent to her from Washington by Mrs. Helen Cowles Wheeler.
51. Ibid.
52. "Letters by a Lady," no. 9, *Sentinel*, Aug. 20, 1862.
53. This series of letters were unsigned, but the *Sentinel* disclosed the writer's last name in the introduction to her last letter, which appeared Sept. 24, 1862: "From Mrs. Wheeler." She signed this last letter "H. C. M. Wheeler." W. W. Williams described Helen Wheeler's work in the hospitals of Washington during the Civil War and mentioned the series of letters written by her and published in the *Sentinel*. W. Williams, *Ashtabula County*, 102. Her letters, although disturbing to the genteel, had aroused interest in the suffering of the soldiers.
54. W. Williams, *Ashtabula County*, 100.
55. "Prompt Care of Sick and Wounded Ohio Soldiers," *Journal*, June 26, 1862.
56. Mrs. Wheeler's published letters were about ten in number. The four referenced in this work appeared in the *Sentinel* on June 25, July 2, Aug. 6, and Aug. 20, 1862.
57. *New York Times*, Oct. 20, 1862.

58. Roshon diary, Aug. 3, 1862.

59. Accounts challenging Geary's heroics in the Mexican War are noted in William Allan Blair's preface to Geary, *Politician*, x.

60. "Number 7, General Orders," *OR,* vol. 12, pt. 2, 51–52.

61. Ibid.

62. *OR,* vol. 12, pt. 2, 52.

63. *OR,* vol. 12, pt. 3, 917–19.

64. *OR,* vol. 12, pt. 3, 473–74.

65. Pope's address to his troops was published in the *Telegraph,* July 26, 1862, under the headline, "SNAP: Gen. Pope's Address to his Army."

66. *OR,* vol. 12, pt. 2, 52.

67. Hoyt to "Dear Parents," Aug. 3, 1862, OHS.

68. Most of Banks's corps, including the Twenty-Ninth Ohio, was camped at Little Washington, VA, from Aug. 1 to Aug. 6, 1862.

69. Parmater diary, Aug. 4, 1862.

70. Surgeon Thomas Antisell, "Services in the Medical Staff," 120.

71. Ibid.

72. Parmater diary, Aug. 6, 1862.

73. Roshon diary, Aug. 6, 1862. Roshon was among the Twenty-Ninth soldiers captured at the battle of Cedar Mountain; he did not rejoin the regiment until Nov. 8, 1862.

74. Parmater diary, Aug. 7, 1862.

75. Parmater and others give the location of their frolic of Aug. 7 as five miles south of Sperryville and eight miles north of Culpeper Court House, which places it near the present site of Woodville, VA, on State Highway 522.

76. Parmater diary, Aug. 8, 1862.

77. Ibid.

78. "The 29th Again Suffers," *Reporter,* Aug. 20, 1862. The *Sentinel* listed the regiment's casualties at Cedar Mountain and gave their effective strength going into the battle as precisely 173. "From the Twenty-Ninth," *Sentinel,* Aug. 20, 1862.

79. "A Visit to the 29th," *Beacon,* Aug. 8, 1862.

80. Pickett, letter, July 22, 1862. Pickett was wounded at Cedar Mountain on Aug. 9 and died in Culpeper Court House on Aug. 14, 1862.

Chapter 13: "South of Anywhere"
Sunstruck

1. "Julius," 7th Ohio Infantry, letter, Culpeper, VA, Aug. 13, 1862, in *Chronicle,* Aug. 27, 1862.

2. Gen. Christopher Augur, report, battle of Cedar Mountain, *OR,* vol. 12, pt. 2, 157. Augur stated the strength of Geary's Brigade as 1,121, including artillery personnel.

3. Geary, *Politician,* 53–54.

4. Geary, report, battle of Cedar Mountain, *OR,* vol. 12, pt. 2, 160–61.

5. Krick, *Stonewall Jackson,* 49. Among the dozens of documented examples of the killing effect of the heat that day, Krick cited one that was especially poignant. A young Union recruit died of the heat on the march and was buried along the route. He had come and gone so quickly from the Second Massachusetts that the regiment's chaplain could not recall his name.

6. The entries in Elias Roshon's diary were typically spare of detail; he used it to record distances marched in a given day, the dates of his pay, and the names of towns through which they passed. But even he found the effect of the heat of Aug. 9, 1862, noteworthy: "It was warm, the sunshine almost melted us down we only went 5 miles South of Culpepper Court House I saw five men that were sun struck three of them died the other two are unwell yet." Roshon diary, Aug. 9, 1862.

7. Charles Candy pension file, RG 94, NA.

8. Ibid.

9. Charles Candy to H. A. Tripp, Fort Leavenworth, KS, June 29, 1887, Gould Papers, Duke University Archives, Durham, NC. Candy stated that if it had not been for the kind attention of his adjutant that evening, he would have fallen victim to heatstroke himself, long after the sun had set.

The Wait

10. Geary, report, battle of Cedar Mountain. Geary apparently checked his pocket watch throughout the battle. He stated it was two in the afternoon when he got his brigade in line to support Best's battery.

11. L. Wilson, *Itinerary*, 179.

12. Augur, report, 157.

13. Pope, report, *OR*, vol. 12, pt. 2, 133.

14. Krick, *Stonewall Jackson*, 43.

15. Julius, letter, Aug. 13, 1862. Specific times at which regiments within Geary's brigade changed positions, and the Seventh marched forward, differ by at most an hour.

16. Augur, report.

Into a Cloud

17. Alonzo Sterrett to "Dear Innis," Aug. 13, 1862. The original of this letter is in the possession of Lewis Leigh Jr., Fairfax, VA. A copy of it is held by the U.S. Army Military History Institute, Carlisle Barracks, PA.

18. Ibid.

19. "S. B.," "Sketches of the Old 29th," undated essay, in *Beacon*, Feb. 12, 1863.

20. Julius, letter, Aug. 13, 1862.

21. L. Wilson, *Itinerary*, 184.

22. Julius, letter, Aug. 13, 1862.

23. Parmater diary, Aug. 9, 1862.

24. Wilson quoted his comrade M. M. Andrews, who stated that the following day, when the Seventh Ohio army was on the field burying their dead, bodies of soldiers belonging to the Seventh were found in the "meadow." L. Wilson, *Itinerary*, 194.

25. Julius, letter, Aug. 13, 1862. That the Twenty-Ninth Regiment had fired its first volley from this position is confirmed by John G. Marsh in a letter to his sister: "We had by this time reached the highest ground and we had fair sight of the Rebels. Giving them one volley, we pushed on." Marsh to "Dear Ida," Culpeper, VA, Aug. 14, 1862, Hudson Papers.

26. Ibid.

27. Capt. Wilbur F. Stevens, report, 29th Regt., Ohio Infantry, *OR*, vol. 12, pt. 2, 164–65.

28. Marsh to "Dear Ida," Aug. 14, 1862.

29. L. Wilson, *Itinerary*, 186–87. As to the status of Federal success on their right at the moment the Giddings Regiment relieved the Seventh Ohio, Wilson stated: "When the charge of Crawford's regiments broke up and put to flight Jackson's line of battle on the left, the 29th advanced and relieved the 7th which moved back to a place of safety across Cedar Run."

30. Marsh to "Dear Ida," Aug. 14, 1862.

31. Stevens, report. If Stevens had not participated in the battle, it is assumed he had been judicious enough to interview officers of the Twenty-Ninth Regiment who had. In his official report filed on Aug. 13 from Culpeper, he describes the regiment breaking out of the cornfield and onto the eminence in the meadow. L. Wilson, *Itinerary*, 193–94, states that the Seventh Ohio got as far as the meadow below the cornfield. The location of the hill that Stevens identified as the zenith of the regiment's advance can be established in part by the location of the stone marker bearing the inscription "29th O" placed on the field under the direction of J. Gordon Thomas with the guidance of Union veterans. According to the current farmer of the land upon which the Twenty-Ninth's portion of the famous cornfield is located, the marker had been moved because striking it damaged his field equipment. Care was taken, however, to move it aside, along a line perpendicular to the highway. The modern Dove Hill Road runs across this rise and intersects the modern highway from several hundred feet northeast of this extrapolated line. Modern topographical maps show only one prominence (elev. 434 ft.) in the terrain between the gate and the Mitchell Road ridge. This may well be the rise described by Stevens in his official report of battle.

32. Marsh to "Dear Ida," Aug. 14, 1862. Marsh stated, "Giving them one volley, we pushed on; got through the cornfield to where the 7th Ohio were . . . they gave way for our advancing column and on we went across a piece of bottom land to the hill beyond from which the Rebels had skedaddled as we came up."

33. James B. Storer, deposition, Aug. 27, 1897, Stevens pension file, RG 94, NA. The original of the Storer deposition was missing from Stevens's file. Dr. Robert Krick kindly provided me with a photocopy from his file.

On Their Own Hook

34. Candy to Tripp, June 29, 1887.
35. Col. John H. Patrick, 5th OVI, *OR,* vol. 12, pt. 2, 162–63.
36. Augur, report, 157.
37. Geary, report.
38. Augur, report.
39. Stevens, report.
40. Parmater diary, Aug. 9, 1862.
41. Ibid.
42. SeCheverell, *Journal History,* 52.

Badly Shot

43. Surgeon Denig, 7th Ohio Inf. Regt., to his brother, Aug. 12, 1862, in "From Culpeper," *Journal,* Aug. 19, 1862.
44. Roshon diary, Aug. 10, 1862.
45. Parmater diary, Aug. 9, 1862. Parmater reported in his diary that he could find no more than half a dozen soldiers of his regiment that night.
46. "The Late Battle at Culpeper Court House," *Sentinel,* Aug. 20, 1862.
47. Parmater diary, Aug. 9, 1862.
48. Antisell, "Services in the Medical Staff," 120.
49. Denig to brother, Aug. 12, 1862.
50. Ibid.
51. Antisell, "Services in the Medical Staff," 121.
52. "James" to "Dear Father and Mother," Culpeper, VA, Aug. 13, 1862, in "From the 29th—Since the Battle," *Beacon,* Aug. 21, 1862.
53. Marsh to "Dear Ida," Aug. 14, 1862.
54. Ibid. Pvt. Joel J. Bair was discharged for disability three months later. *State Roster,* 387. After recovering, he reenlisted in the regiment and served the remainder of his enlistment.
55. Ibid.
56. McParlin, "Operations of the Medical Department," xcii.
57. Denig to brother, Aug. 12, 1862.
58. Grier, "Report to the Surgeon General."

"I May See You Again . . ."

59. Pope, report, 134.
60. L. Wilson, *Itinerary,* 194.
61. Parmater diary, Aug. 17, 1862.
62. Thirty percent of the eight thousand Union troops who fought at Cedar Mountain were casualties. By comparison, Federal casualties at Gettysburg amounted to 24 percent, at Chickamauga 26 percent, Spotsylvania Court House 18 percent, and at Cold Harbor (regarded by Grant's critics as a senseless bloodbath) 12 percent.
63. Geary's casualties amounted to 465, which means 41 percent of the soldiers of his brigade were killed, wounded, or taken prisoner. "Return of Casualties in the Union Forces . . . at the battle of Cedar Mountain, Va., Aug. 9, 1862," *OR,* vol. 12, pt. 2, 137.
64. SeCheverell, *Journal History,* 53. James B. Storer took the count of what remained of the regiment on Aug. 11, 1862, at Culpeper.
65. The true number of the Twenty-Ninth Ohio's casualties at Cedar Mountain, as with all its other battles, remains elusive. Parmater took a count the day after the battle and reported that 80 men had been killed, wounded, or missing. Men continued to come in after that and their names were removed from the list of the missing. Capt. Wilbur F. Stevens, as commander of record of the regiment at Cedar Mountain, waited until Aug. 14 to submit his several-page official list, which was sent up the chain of command. Record group 94, Office of the Adjutant General, Volunteer Organizations of the Civil War, Regimental Casualties, Ohio, Infantry, units 7–61, NA. The names of every man on this list who had been killed or wounded, or was still missing five days after the battle, totaled 66. William Fox, the best-known scholar of the war's mortuary statistics, agreed with Stevens's accounting. Fox, *Regimental Losses,* 319. The regiment's historian, J. Hampton SeCheverell, put the total number

at 49, although both he and Fox had supposedly relied on returns filed with the state of Ohio. SeCheverell, *Journal History,* 282. Stevens listed the number of men killed, including those too grievously stricken to survive, as 7. Fox gave the number as 6, and SeCheverell nearly twice that many: 11. The *State Roster* named 9 men of the regiment who had been killed in action that afternoon and evening.

66. Theron S. Winship, letter, Alexandria, VA, Aug. 20, 1862, in *Reporter,* Aug. 27, 1862.
67. Roshon diary, Aug. 10, 1862.
68. "Capt. J. J. Wright Wounded," *Beacon,* Aug. 14, 1862.
69. J. Wright, letter, Aug. 16, 1862, in "From Capt. J. J. Wright," *Beacon,* Aug. 28, 1862.
70. Carded Medical Records, Lt. E. J. Hurlburt, 29th OVI.
71. Pickett, letter, July 22, 1862.
72. Carded Medical Files, Cpl. Burton Pickett, 29th OVI, NA.
73. RG 94, Office of the Adjutant General, Volunteer Organizations of the Civil War, Regimental Casualties, Ohio, Infantry, Units 7–61. Only three of the official casualty lists filed by the regiment's various commanders after each of its battles and campaigns have been preserved in this record group: Capt. Wilbur F. Stevens's report for the battle of Cedar Mountain, Lt. Col. Thomas Clark, Chancellorsville, and Capt. Jonas Schoonover for the Carolinas Campaign.
74. Kinney's father and his neighbors gave his first name as Alvinza, although he was carried on the rolls as Alvinson. Kinney pension file, RG 94, NA.

Chapter 14: "In the Hands of Devils"
Beyond Hope

1. Jones, "Battery Horses."
2. Hart, "When He Saw Stonewall Jackson."
3. Seymour and Baldwin, "Port Republic."
4. Hart, "Battlefield to Prison."
5. Ibid.
6. Rupp, "Fighting Regiment." That the Federal prisoners were made to stand on exhibit is also mentioned in Rollin Jones's letter of Oct. 4, 1862, to the *Sentinel.*
7. Morris and Foutz, *Lynchburg,* 6–9.
8. Ibid., 13.
9. Hart, "Battlefield to Prison."
10. Worsham, *Jackson's Foot Cavalry,* 96. Worsham stated that his regiment served guard duty at Lynchburg from June 11 until June 18, 1862.
11. Ibid., 27.
12. Ibid., 116.
13. The Twenty-First Virginia, Garnett's brigade, Jackson's division, sustained 39 killed and 78 wounded at Cedar Mountain, the highest number of casualties of any Confederate regiment. Krick, *Stonewall Jackson,* 370.
14. Worsham, *Jackson's Foot Cavalry,* 96.
15. Ibid., 112–13.
16. Rupp, "Fighting Regiment."
17. Morris and Foutz, *Lynchburg,* 20.
18. Hart, "Battlefield to Prison."
19. Rupp, "Fighting Regiment."
20. Parker, *Richmond's Prisons,* 14–15.
21. *State Roster,* 380. Hummiston (Humison) died at Lynchburg on July 28, 1862. Hummiston's death in prison was announced in the *Beacon,* Aug. 28, 1862, under "Death of Newton P. Humison." The spelling of Newton's last name was among the most variable in the regiment. Hummison, Humison, Humson, Hummaston, Humaston are all found in various records. In the *State Roster,* 380, his name is spelled Hueninston. In the pension documents, his mother, Clarissa, gave the spelling as Humiston. Humiston pension file, RG 94, NA. Newton had been a good son. As a young teen, he worked in a stove-making foundry, and once took a new stove and later a wagonload of coal home for his mother in lieu of part of his pay. When the war began, Newton was working in a livery stable harnessing teams. He turned pay from both jobs over to his mother, who made a scant living taking in laundry. For the loss of her son, the government paid her eight dollars per month. Also having passed away while prisoners at Lynchburg were William H. Jones of Summit County's Company D, captured at Port Republic and died July 21; and Hiram Sly of Company E, who had been captured at Strasburg and died at Lynchburg on July 6. *State Roster,* 368 and 369, respectively.

Beautiful Island

22. Parker, *Richmond's Prisons,* 15.
23. Ibid., 17.
24. Ibid., 19.
25. "From Lieut. Carey H. Russell, One of the 29th Prisoners," *Beacon,* July 24, 1862.
26. Rupp, "Fighting Regiment."
27. Hart, "Battlefield to Prison."
28. Two men captured at or near Strasburg, VA, were sent to rebel prisons in Richmond, where both died. Robert Sills, Company B, was "supposed" to have died there. *State Roster,* 362, and SeCheverell, *Journal History,* 175. James Whitney, Company F, died at Libby Prison on June 3, 1862. SeCheverell, 204. Whitney's name is not found at all in the *State Roster* listing the personnel of Company F.
29. Hart, "Battlefield to Prison."
30. Ibid.
31. Ibid.
32. Rupp, "Fighting Regiment."

Captives in Their Own Country

33. Rollin Jones, Fort Delaware, MD, to *Sentinel,* Oct. 4, 1862. Jones's letter is the longest wartime letter written by any Twenty-Ninth Ohio soldier or veteran in existence.
34. Hart, "Battlefield to Prison."
35. Ibid.
36. "Army Bread," *Reporter,* Jan. 21, 1863. This story was borrowed from the *Springfield Republican.*
37. Jones, letter, Oct. 4, 1862.
38. Hart, "Battlefield to Prison."
39. Jones, letter, Oct. 4, 1862.

The Radicalization of Rollin Jones

40. "The President's Policy," *Sentinel,* Aug. 13, 1862.
41. *Sentinel,* Nov. 26, 1862. In the publication of Sgt. Rollin Jones's Oct. 4, 1862, letter, which was his account of life in rebel hands as well as his political manifesto, the editors explained in a footnote that before the war Jones had been a Breckenridge Democrat, meaning he had been in favor of allowing the territories to decide whether slavery should be allowed after they had been admitted to the Union.
42. John Marsh to "Dear Ida," Apr. 13 (or Apr. 23), 1863, Hudson Papers.
43. Oscar Gibbs to "Dear Adelia," Jan. 7, 1863, Gibbs pension file, RG 94, NA.
44. "John Brown, Jr. closes a letter . . . ," *Reporter,* Apr. 9, 1862.
45. "Capt. John Brown," *Sentinel,* June 25, 1862. Brown's outfit was the Seventh Kansas Cavalry.
46. *Sentinel,* Oct. 29, 1862. This piece was credited to the *Sandusky Register.*
47. "Col. Anthony . . . ," *Sentinel,* July 30, 1862. The officers in question were a Colonel Anthony and a Captain Hoyt.
48. "A Contraband in Camp," *Journal,* Apr. 1, 1862.
49. "Our Boys Don't Like Cuffy," *Journal,* Apr. 1, 1862. The story reports the contraband's escape into the camp of the Sixty-Sixth Ohio.
50. Ibid.
51. Marsh to "Dear Ida," Mar. 16, 1863.

The Amateur Sutler

52. Wallace Hoyt to "Dear Parents," Fort Delaware, MD, Sept. 27, 1862, OHS.
53. Hoyt to "Dear Hattie," Fort Delaware, MD, Oct. 25, 1862, OHS.
54. Hoyt to "Dear Mother," Fort Delaware, MD, Nov. 1, 1862, OHS.
55. Hoyt to "Dear Mother," Fort Delaware, MD, Nov. 18, 1862, OHS.
56. Hoyt to "Dear Father," Fort Delaware, MD, Dec. 14, 1862, OHS.

Woodchoppers

57. Rupp, "Fighting Regiment."
58. Hoyt to "Dear Father," Dumfries, VA, Jan. 26, 1863, OHS.

59. Hoyt to "Dear Parents," Annapolis, MD, Dec. 23, 1862, Hoyt pension file, RG 94, NA. Wallace informed his parents that he had left Fort Delaware that day and was writing to them from his new situation at Camp Parole.

60. Hoyt to "Dear Father," Jan. 26, 1863.

61. Rupp, "Fighting Regiment."

Chapter 15: Narrow Escapes

His Excellency the Ambassador

1. "A Desperate Battle," *Sentinel,* Aug. 13, 1862.
2. "The Battle between Banks and Jackson," *Journal,* Aug. 14, 1862.
3. "The fight of Stonewall Jackson shows . . . ," *Telegraph,* Aug. 16, 1862.
4. "The Culpeper Battle," *Chronicle,* Aug. 20, 1862.
5. *Beacon,* Aug. 14, 1862.
6. "The Culpeper Battle," *Chronicle,* Aug. 20, 1862.
7. Ibid.
8. *Beacon,* Aug. 14, 1862.
9. "The 29th Again Suffers," *Reporter,* Aug. 20, 1862.
10. Lt. Treen, letter, camp near Luray, VA, June 11, 1862, in "The Missing of the 29th—Letter from Lt. Treen," *Beacon,* June 19, 1862.
11. J. R. Giddings to Joseph Addison Giddings, Aug. 22, 1862, Giddings Papers.
12. J. R. to Joseph Addison Giddings, May 30, 1861, "I should like to see Grosh [Grotius] in the field and you buy cattle," Giddings Papers.
13. J. R. to Joseph Addison Giddings, Sept. 19, 1862, Giddings Papers.
14. J. R. to Joseph Addison Giddings, Jan. 3, 1863, Giddings Papers.
15. Ibid. In letters of Apr. 16 and May 18, 1863, it is clear that Addison had started in their cotton scheme, at least to the extent of having purchased "cotton bonds." But with the prospect of the Mississippi River being opened soon by Union successes and an abundance of cotton flowing again, Joshua Giddings predicted the market in cotton speculation would tumble. Thus, he advised his son Addison to sell their bonds and get out of the business. To that end he advised Addison to go personally to New York City to dispose of them.
16. J. R. Giddings to Joseph Addison Giddings, Aug. 22, 1862. Giddings's son-in-law, George Julian, wrote a biography of Giddings that ran nearly five hundred pages. Julian knew Giddings intimately in this period, well enough to include mention of Giddings's favorite dog, a Newfoundland named Rover who had been trained to carry the newspaper and groceries. No mention whatsoever is made in Julian's biography of Giddings's founding of the Twenty-Ninth Ohio Infantry, suggesting that the regiment did not stand very high in the Giddings topography.

Loved and Lamented

17. J. J. Wright to Buckley, Washington, DC, Aug. 16, 1862, in "From Capt. J. J. Wright," *Beacon,* Aug. 28, 1862.
18. Ibid.
19. Rupp, "Fighting Regiment."
20. "The New Colors for the 29th," *Beacon,* Sept. 10, 1863, quoted a letter from M. T. Wright to Lewis Buckley, Sept. 5, 1863.
21. "The Flag of the Ohio 29th," *Sentinel,* Aug. 27, 1862.
22. "Exciting Past of Civil War Flag in Library Unearthed," *Jefferson Gazette,* Jan. 19, 1937. The story was related to the reporter by resident Mrs. A. L. Herold, wife of the brother of Twenty-Ninth Ohio veteran Chauncey Coon. Coon died on Nov. 21, 1921.
23. The regiment's national flag is on display at the Henderson Memorial Library, Jefferson, Ohio.

An Advance in Reverse

24. "The Culpeper Battle," *Chronicle,* Aug. 20, 1862.
25. "The fight of Stonewall Jackson shows . . . ," *Telegraph,* Aug. 16, 1862.
26. Parmater diary, Aug. 12, 1862.
27. Parmater diary, Aug. 15, 1862.
28. Soldier Alonzo Sterrett, letter, Aug. 13, 1862, provided courtesy of Lewis Leigh, Fairfax, VA.
29. Parmater diary, Aug. 15, 1862, "Gen. Tyler is trying to get us out of the field so that we may have a chance to recruit, but the boys do not look for much but hard service yet."

30. Parmater diary, Aug. 18, 1862.
31. Parmater diary, Aug. 19, 1862.
32. L. Wilson, *Itinerary,* 196–97.
33. "Ofcr. W," letter, Headquarters of the 29th Regiment, Monocacy Bridge, Sept. 16, 1862, in "Letter from the 29th," *Reporter,* Sept. 24, 1862.
34. Much ink was lavished on the scant diet of this campaign. It is mentioned by several Twenty-Ninth Boys contemporaneously, most notably in the Parmater diary, whose author spent a significant portion of the Second Bull Run campaign searching for green corn.
35. Ofcr. W, letter, Sept. 16, 1862.
36. John G. Marsh letters to "Dear Ida," Oct. 5 and Nov. 7, 1862, Hudson Papers.
37. Fitch returned to the regiment at Culpeper on Aug. 15. Parmater, Franklin Potter diaries, Aug. 15, 1862. Later, his neighborhood newspaper published correspondence from an officer writing under the nom de plume Ofcr. W (by deduction Adj. Theron S. Winship, who had written previous letters behind the pseudonym Pvt. W before his promotion) stating there were only two officers present to command the Twenty-Ninth during the Second Bull Run campaign and the march to Frederick, MD. Jonas Schoonover was named as one of the officers also present in this period. SeCheverell, *Journal History,* 54. Both Schoonover and Fitch were likely detached on duties away from the regiment, as they had been in earlier campaigns.
38. Parmater diary, Aug. 26, 1862.
39. Pope to his commanders, Aug. 27, 1862, *OR,* vol. 12, pt. 1, 210.

Cut Off

40. Parmater diary, Aug. 27, 1862.
41. Parmater diary, Aug. 28, 1862.
42. Ibid.; Potter diary, Aug. 28, 1862.
43. The battle of Second Bull Run was fought Aug. 28–30, 1862.
44. "Bloodiness of the Late Battles," *Journal,* Sept. 5, 1862.
45. Parmater diary, Aug. 29, 1862.
46. SeCheverell, *Journal History,* 55.
47. "Telegraphic News: Morning and Afternoon Report: Danger to Banks Corps Dreaded," *Journal,* Sept. 2, 1862.
48. Parmater diary, Aug. 30, 1862.
49. Parmater diary, Aug. 31, 1862.
50. SeCheverell, *Journal History,* 56. The date of the burning of the Federal supply trains at Bristol Station is confirmed in the Potter diary as Aug. 31.
51. Parmater diary, Aug. 31, 1862.
52. L. Wilson, *Itinerary,* 200.
53. Parmater diary, Aug. 31, 1862.

Chantilly Plantation

54. Parmater diary, Sept. 1, 1862.
55. L. Wilson, *Itinerary,* 201.
56. SeCheverell, *Journal History,* 56–57.
57. Parmater diary, Sept. 1, 1862.
58. Insignia record 8604, Theron S. Winship, MOLLUS Museum and Library, Philadelphia.
59. "Bloodiness of the Late Battles," *Journal,* Sept. 5, 1862.
60. Parmater diary, Sept. 3, 1862.
61. Parmater diary, Sept. 4, 1862.
62. Ibid.

At the Bridge

63. Ofcr. W, letter, Sept. 16, 1862.
64. Ibid.
65. "Wade's Idea of McClellan," *Sentinel,* July 30, 1862. Wade's joke was found sufficiently entertaining, and reflective of the Reserve's attitude toward McClellan, to be copied in the *Reporter,* Aug. 6, 1862.
66. "The Army of the Potomac . . . ," *Sentinel,* Aug. 20, 1862.

67. Long, *Civil War*, 265. General Order 129, Sept. 12, 1862, ordered the absorption of the Army of Virginia into the Army of the Potomac.
68. Ofcr. W, letter, Sept. 16, 1862.
69. Ibid.
70. "James," letter, Monocacy Station, MD, Sept. 16, 1862, in "From the 29th," *Beacon*, Sept. 25, 1862.
71. Ibid.
72. SeCheverell, *Journal History*, 58.
73. Seymour and Baldwin, "Port Republic."

Chapter 16: Restoration
The Appearance of Angels

1. Parmater diary, Sept. 11, 1862.
2. Parmater was unable to work on his diary from Sept. 18 to Oct. 23, 1862, when he was recovered enough to take it up again.
3. Potter diary, Nov. 7, 1862. The first measurable snow of this winter season fell on this day.
4. Capt. William T. Fitch, "To the Editor of the Sentinel," n.d., in "From the Twenty-Ninth," *Sentinel*, Dec. 3, 1862.
5. John G. Marsh to "Dear Ida," Dec. 5, 1862, Hudson Papers.
6. "T," letter, Camp of the 29th OVI, Frederick City, MD, Nov. 20, 1862, in "From the 29th—Trial and Sentence for 'Beauregard' for Desertion—Execution of the Sentence," *Beacon*, Dec. 4, 1862.
7. Ibid.
8. John G. Marsh to "Dear Ida," Nov. 7, 1862, Hudson Papers.
9. Ofcr. W, letter, Headquarters of the 29th Regiment, Monocacy Bridge, Sept. 16, 1862, in "Letter from the 29th," *Reporter*, Sept. 24, 1862.

Stragglers

10. "Attention—Soldiers," *Sentinel*, July 16, 1862. The official order signed by General Tyler authorizing Buckley to collect "stragglers" from all of the Ohio regiments in Tyler's command was also published in "To Whom It May Concern," *Beacon*, July 10, 1862.
11. "Attention—Soldiers," *Sentinel*, July 16, 1862. Appended to Buckley's order demanding those absent from the regiment report themselves immediately was a list, by company, of the several hundred men who were not properly accounted for.
12. *Beacon*, July 10, 1862.
13. "Attention—Soldiers, "*Sentinel*, July 16, 1862.
14. "Sgt. M. E. Owens of Company I . . . ," *Sentinel*, July 23, 1862.
15. By the end of 1862 approximately 213 soldiers in the Twenty-Ninth had been discharged specifically for disability. *State Roster*.
16. *State Roster*. Twenty-eight of the regiment's soldiers were discharged for disability at Camp Chase, in Columbus, in 1862.
17. Deposition of William T. Fitch, May 14, 1889, Abram Exceen pension file, RG 94, NA.
18. Beckwith pension file, RG 94, NA.
19. Decker pension file, RG 94, NA.
20. Ibid.
21. William Chalmers pension file, RG 94, NA.

"Rally for the Dear Old 29th"

22. "A special Washington dispatch . . . ," *Sentinel*, Aug. 27, 1862. The Fifth Ohio, with the help of the Cincinnati city council, applied to the War Department for permission to return to Ohio to recruit or, in lieu of that, be placed in one of the forts around D.C. and recruit there. It was reported in this piece that the Seventh, Twenty-Ninth, and Sixty-Sixth Ohio Regiments had made identical applications. Halleck refused to remove any of them from the field.
23. In a postscript to his Aug. 21, 1862, letter published in the *Reporter*, Aug. 27, 1862, Adj. Theron Winship mentioned that the governor of Ohio had recently visited Washington to lobby on behalf of a furlough for the Ohio regiments of the Twenty-Ninth's brigade.

24. Halleck's rejection of the request to remove these Ohio regiments from the field for a period of recruiting is quoted by T. S. Winship in his letter to the *Conneaut Reporter*, Aug. 27, 1862. A slight variation of Halleck's words is found in the *Beacon*, Sept. 4, 1862.

25. Parmater diary, July 17, 1862.

26. The text of the only surviving recruiting poster published by the Twenty-Ninth Ohio is taken from the original by courtesy of John Gurnish, Akron, Ohio.

27. Marsh wrote, "Tell me who is drafted & if any of the bloody scenes are enacted that were threatened by the bloody Bones Democracy in Homer, if they are drafted. Or do they come up to the ranks peaceably like—men I almost said." John G. Marsh to "Dear Ida," Oct. 12, 1862, Hudson Papers.

28. Murdock, *Bounty System*, 4–5.

29. "Another 300,000 Men to be Raised," *Beacon*, Aug. 7, 1862.

30. "Marched," *Sentinel*, Aug. 13, 1862.

31. "A New Regiment," *Sentinel*, Aug. 20, 1862.

32. "Fill Up the Old Regiments," Gov. Tod, Columbus, July 23, 1862, in *Beacon*, July 31, 1862. In late July 1862, Secretary of War Stanton raised the federal bounty paid men enlisting in "old" regiments to four dollars; twice what a recruit got for joining a new regiment. In a year of rapidly rising civilian wages, two dollars amounted to very little inducement. Sec. of War Stanton to New York Common Council on National Affairs, Washington, DC, July 26, 1862, in "Extra Bounty to Recruits for Old Regiments," *Beacon*, July 31, 1862.

33. "From Trumbull County Military Committee," *Chronicle*, Aug. 20, 1862.

Friends of the Union

34. B. V. Burroughs, letter, Aug. 11, 1862, in "Montrose," *Beacon*, Aug. 21, 1862.

35. "Skedaddlers and Deserters," *Beacon*, Aug. 28, 1862.

36. "Another Deserter in Limbo," *Beacon*, Aug. 28, 1862.

37. "War! War! War!" *Sentinel*, Aug. 6, 1862. More details of Jefferson's war meeting were published in "The War Meeting in Jefferson," *Sentinel*, Aug. 13, 1862.

38. "Marched," *Sentinel*, Aug. 13, 1862.

39. "War Meeting in Bath," *Beacon*, Aug. 7, 1862.

40. "Orrville Patriotism," *Beacon*, Aug. 7, 1862.

41. *Reporter*, Aug. 16, 1862.

42. "To Greensburg Belongs the Banner," *Beacon*, Sept. 4, 1862.

43. *Reporter*, Aug. 16, 1862.

44. "Another 300,000 Men to be Raised," *Beacon*, Aug. 7, 1862.

45. "Riot at a War Meeting—Discouraging Enlistment—Arrest of the Perpetrators," *Beacon*, Aug. 14, 1862.

46. "Secession in Ohio," *Reporter*, Aug. 16, 1862.

47. "Something akin to a riot . . . ," *Reporter*, Oct. 8, 1862.

The "Square-Toed Measles" and Other Excuses

48. *Reporter*, Sept. 3, 1862.

49. "Military Statistics of Summit County," *Beacon*, Sept. 11, 1862. Of the 1,325 claims that were filed for exemption, 650 were allowed.

50. "Military Statistics of Summit County," *Beacon*, Sept. 11, 1862. By July 2, 1862, 1,104 men had volunteered and were serving in the field. During July and Aug. 516 men had volunteered, bringing Summit County's total voluntary enlistment to about sixteen hundred.

51. *Beacon*, Sept. 11, 1862.

52. Ibid.

53. "One of the Shifts," *Reporter*, Aug. 20, 1862.

54. Ibid.

55. "Invalids," *Sentinel*, Sept. 3, 1862.

56. "Exiles. . . . ," *Reporter*, Aug. 27, 1862.

57. "An Asylum for the Cowards," *Beacon*, Aug. 28, 1862. This piece was borrowed from the *Detroit Advertiser*.

58. Elias Roshon, letter, Mar. 17, 1863, OHS.

59. "At the Circus—," *Reporter*, Aug. 6, 1862.

60. *Reporter*, Aug. 20, 1862. Taken from the *Warren Chronicle*.
61. Ibid.

Spinning the Wheel of Destiny

62. *Sentinel*, Sept. 3, 1862. The county assessor kept score of their recruiting efforts. As of July 2, 1862, when the recruiting drive began, Ashtabula County had enlisted 1,529 men. Between July 2 and Aug. 22, 1862, an additional 601 new troops were raised. Before exemptions, a total of 5,915 names appeared on the new militia rolls. The county's population was given in this year as 32,231.
63. "Military Statistics of Summit County," *Beacon*, Sept. 11, 1862. By this date, 5,037 men had been listed on the militia rolls. As of July 2, 1862, 1,104 men had volunteered and were serving in the field. Since July 2 an additional 516 men had volunteered, leaving a reserve available for future drafting of about 4,000 nonexempt men.
64. "Proportion of Volunteers," *Sentinel*, Aug. 27, 1862.
65. Ibid. These percentages were based on enlistments before May 2, 1861, as filed with the assessors in these counties. Like most places, Ashtabula County had enlisted far more soldiers in the war's first weeks than could be accepted by the state of Ohio.
66. "Proportion of Volunteers," *Sentinel*, Aug. 27, 1862. About 7.5 percent of Allen County's entire population was in uniform by the end of summer 1862.
67. "Drafting! Look Out!" *Sentinel*, Aug. 27, 1862.
68. Last Call! Drafting!" *Reporter*, Aug. 27, 1862.
69. "For the 29th," *Sentinel*, Sept. 3, 1862.
70. "Drafting," *Sentinel*, Sept. 3, 1862.
71. Murdock, *Bounty System*, 5.
72. Ibid. Of the total whose names were picked in this draft, only twenty-four hundred men actually went into the service. The rest claimed conscientious objector status, volunteered at the last minute to avoid the stigma of coercion, hired substitutes, were discharged for various reasons, or simply skedaddled.
73. "The drafted men from this county who had not volunteered, were on last Friday, mustered into the 6th Cavalry Regiment," *Sentinel*, Nov. 26, 1862.
74. "Pound," *Reporter*, May 20, 1863.

New Faces

75. Gurley G. Crane, letter, "Camp of the 29th, R.R. Bridge, Md.," Sept. 19, 1862, in "Later from the 29th," *Beacon*, Sept. 25, 1862. Crane reported on the fine sight of Myron Wright marching the new men into the regiment's camp. "James" stated that Wright marched 140 recruits into Frederick. James, letter, Sept. 16, 1862, in "From the 29th," *Beacon*, Sept. 25, 1862. The *State Roster* shows that a total of approximately 150 new soldiers came into the Twenty-Ninth during this period. The *Sentinel* reported that J. J. Hoyt, Lieutenant Howard, and Sgt. Henry M. Ryder left the county on Sept. 2 to join the regiment with 200 recruits, an apparent overappraisal of their recruiting success, which had been excellent in any event. "For the 29th," *Sentinel*, Sept. 3, 1862. Lewis P. Buckley, who was perhaps the best authority, stated that the Twenty-Ninth's recruiting campaign of summer and fall 1862 produced 163 recruits. *Beacon*, Jan. 29, 1863.
76. SeCheverell, *Journal History*, 58.
77. Ofcr. W, letter, Frederick City, MD, Oct. 2, 1862, in *Reporter*, Oct. 15, 1862.
78. T. S. Winship, letter, Washington, DC, Aug. 20, 1862, in "Letters from the 29th," *Reporter*, Aug. 27, 1862.
79. An early Nov. 1862 edition of the *Reporter* stated that Captains Burridge and Hurlburt, and Lieutenants Neil, Wilson, Gregory, and Woodbury rendezvoused at the railroad depot in Painesville at the conclusion of their furloughs and rode the cars together down to Frederick.
80. Winship, letter, Aug. 20, 1862.
81. Fitch, letter, n.d., in *Sentinel*, Dec. 3, 1862.
82. *State Roster*. Wright's resignation was effective Oct. 1, 1862.
83. Ibid. Clemmer's resignation was accepted on Dec. 12, 1862.

Slighted

84. W, letter, Sept. 16, 1862, in *Reporter*, Sept. 24, 1862.
85. John Hoyt's resignation was effective Nov. 1, 1862. *State Roster*. The Hoyt pension file contains a declaration in which Hoyt stated he served as second lieutenant of Company B from Sept. 8 until Oct. 27, 1862. Adjutant General's Office, report, Mar. 2, 1886.

"Be It Ever So Humble"

86. Marsh to "Dear Ida," Dec. 5, 1862.
87. Ibid.
88. John G. Marsh to "Dear Ida," Oct. 5, 1862, Hudson Papers.
89. Ibid.
90. John G. Marsh to "Dear Ida," Nov. 17, 1862, Marsh pension file, RG 94, NA.
91. Marsh to "Dear Ida," Oct. 12, 1862.
92. Ibid.
93. Marsh to "Dear Ida," Dec. 5, 1862.
94. Lincoln's visit to Frederick is described in the John Marsh letter of Oct. 5, 1862, to his sister Ida.
95. Ibid.
96. Ibid.
97. "C," letter, Frederick, MD, Oct. 13, 1862, in *Sentinel*, Oct. 22, 1862.
98. T, letter, Nov. 20, 1862.
99. Gray was shot by the provost guard on Dec. 10, 1862, the day the Twenty-Ninth Regiment left Frederick. *State Roster*, 390.

Changed Faces

100. "War, War," *Reporter*, Aug. 16, 1862.
101. "How They Fire in Battle," *Reporter*, Oct. 29, 1862.
102. "The Avalanche," *Telegraph*, Aug. 16, 1862.
103. "H. G. H.," letter, Gettysburg, PA, Nov. 20, 1862, in "A Visit to the 29th OVI," *Beacon*, Nov. 20, 1862. (The date of the letter was obviously misprinted in the *Beacon*.)

Christmas Dinner Postponed

104. Fitch, "To the Editor of the Sentinel," n.d.
105. "Latest from the 29th," *Sentinel*, Dec. 17, 1862. A telegram from a Twenty-Ninth soldier to the newspaper reported that the regiment had left Frederick for the front on the preceding Wednesday. It seemed probable that the regiment had been in the fight at Fredericksburg. Pending more accurate news, shipment of the Christmas box for Company A was postponed. "The Box for Co. A, 29th Reg't.," *Sentinel*, Dec. 17, 1862.

Chapter 17: Our Valley Forge
"From the Fighting Part, by God!"

1. E. B. Woodbury, letter, Dumfries, VA, Jan. 3, 1863, in *Sentinel*, Jan. 14, 1863. The regiment departed Frederick, MD, on Dec. 10, 1863.
2. The battle of Fredericksburg was fought Dec. 11–15, 1862.
3. "From Fredericksburg—The War," *Sentinel*, Dec. 24, 1862.
4. SeCheverell, *Journal History*, 59.
5. Woodbury, letter, Jan. 3, 1863. The theft of the sutler's wagon by rebel cavalry was also reported by "N" of Company G. N, letter, Fairfax Station, VA, Dec. 22, 1862, in *Beacon*, Jan. 1, 1863.
6. SeCheverell, *Journal History*, 59.
7. Ibid.
8. J. W. Geary to Mary Geary, near Fairfax Station, VA, Dec. 25, 1862; Geary, *Politician*, 75.
9. Woodbury, letter, Jan. 3, 1863.
10. SeCheverell, *Journal History*, 60.
11. "Co. A," letter, Dumfries, VA, Jan. 21, 1863, in "Army Correspondence—From the Twenty-Ninth," *Sentinel*, Feb. 4, 1863.
12. Ibid.
13. Ibid.
14. The repulse of Stuart's cavalry on Dec. 28, 1862, is described in the following accounts by Twenty-Ninth Regiment participants: Woodbury, letter, Jan. 3, 1863; C, letter, Jan. 21, 1863; Lewis P. Buckley to J. J. Wright, in *Beacon*, Jan. 15, 1863.
15. Cass M. Nims to "Dear Mother," camp near Dumfries, VA, Jan. 2, 1863, Nims pension file, RG 94, NA.

16. Ibid.
17. Geary, *Politician*, 69.
18. Geary to Mary Geary, Dec. 8, 1862; in Geary, *Politician*, 70.
19. L. Wilson, *Itinerary*, 219.

Fallen Castles

20. Woodbury, letter, Jan. 3, 1863. "Dumfries is all ruins. There are not more than twenty houses."
21. Geary to "My Dearest Mary [Geary]," Jan. 28, 1863, Dumfries, VA, in Geary, *Politician*, 86.
22. Woodbury, letter, Jan. 3, 1863.
23. Ibid. The location of the Twenty-Ninth's winter 1863 camp is given most precisely by Lieutenant Woodbury as lying on the slope of the area's tallest rise, overlooking the old town, and four miles inland from Dumfries Landing, VA.

Our Valley Forge

24. SeCheverell, *Journal History*, 62.
25. Cass Nims, letter, Dumfries, VA, Feb. 7, 1863, Nims pension file, RG 94, NA.
26. Nims to "Dear Mother," Jan. 2, 1863.
27. L. Wilson, *Itinerary*, 228.
28. Cass Nims to "Dear Mother," Dumfries, VA, Jan. 16, 1863, Nims pension file, RG 94, NA.
29. Cass Nims, letter, Feb. 7, 1863.
30. Elias Roshon told his parents, "We have got very good times here." Roshon to "Dear Father and Mother," Mar. 17, 1863. Twenty-Ninth Ohio soldier Thomas Fales reported, "We have very good provisions here." Fales, letter, Feb. 3, 1863, Fales pension file, RG 94, NA.

"Wherever Fortune May Place Me"

31. Buckley, letter, Headquarters 29th Regt., Camp at Dumfries, VA, Jan. 13, 1863, in "Letter from Col. Buckley," *Beacon*, Jan. 29, 1863. The same edition published the announcement of Buckley's resignation. The editor saluted Buckley's undaunted courage, while reminding the readers that he had been a lifelong Democrat and "not a very strong 'abolitionist.'" "Col. Lewis P. Buckley," *Beacon*, Jan. 29, 1863.
32. Lewis P. Buckley, letter of resignation, Dumfries, VA, Jan. 19, 1863, Buckley pension file, RG 94, NA.
33. Ibid. Statement of A. K. Fifield, Chief Med Officer, 1st Brigade, 2nd Division. Buckley pension file.
34. Ibid.
35. "Accident to Col. Buckley," *Beacon*, Nov. 13, 1862.
36. "Return of Col. Buckley," *Beacon*, Feb. 12, 1862.
37. Dumfries, VA, Feb. 2, 1863, published memorial to Colonel Buckley by the soldiers and officers of the regiment, in "Complimentary to Col. Buckley," *Beacon*, Feb. 19, 1863.
38. "Complimentary"; "Col. Buckley's Reply," *Beacon*, Feb. 19, 1863.
39. "Col. Lewis P. Buckley," *Beacon*, Feb. 12, 1863.
40. Statement of Edward Hayes, Winship pension file, RG 94, NA.
41. Oscar Gibbs, letter, Jan. 7, 1863. Bishop resigned effective Feb. 13, 1863. *State Roster*, 359.
42. Parmater diary, Aug. 19, 1863. Howard resigned Mar. 6, 1863. *State Roster*. By the start of the coming year, he would be engaged in Ashtabula County's thriving lumber business. He and a partner had each bought a portable sawmill. "Capt. E. B. Howard and Gilbert Sweet, Esq. . . ," *Reporter*, Jan. 20, 1864.

A New Voice

43. W. Williams, *Ashtabula County*, 162.
44. Biographical information on the life of Lyman Daniel Ames was developed by his descendant Edwin Lyman Ames, San Francisco, CA. Edwin Ames discovered that Rev. Ames had served in a church in Ashtabula. However, although the county history was careful to list the names of the pastor of every church from pioneer days through the 1880s, Rev. Ames was not listed as one of them. For that matter, W. W. Williams does not list Ames as a pastor at the Christian church of Conneaut. Instead, he is named as a pastor of Conneaut's Baptist church from 1863 to 1866; Ames was with the regiment during that period. W. Williams, *Ashtabula County*, 163. The two conclusions to be drawn: that Ames was replaced as pastor of the Christian church, or that he took a leave from the Baptist church to serve in the Twenty-Ninth. The former seems more accurate, based on the

research done by his descendant. Further, the timing of Ames's employment with the Twenty-Ninth follows the date, June 1862, that a new minister settled into work at the Christian church.

45. Ames's appointment has been dated to Feb. 19, 1863. SeCheverell, *Journal History,* 161.

46. Chaplain Lyman D. Ames, diary, Mar. 15, 1863. A typescript of the diary, apparently prepared by an Ames descendant, is found at the U.S. Army Military History Institute, Carlisle Barracks, PA, and at OHS: Civil War Diary of Lyman D. Ames, Chaplain 29th OVI, photocopied typescript, 158 pp., call no. VFM2972.

47. Parmater diary, Mar. 29, 1863. Parmater returned to the regiment at Dumfries from his long sickness on Mar. 10, 1863, five days before Rev. Ames arrived.

48. Ames diary, Apr. 12, 1863.

Tuggies

49. Parmater diary, Dec. 29, 1862.
50. Parmater diary, Feb. 23, 1863.
51. Parmater diary, Mar. 1, 1863.
52. Parmater diary, Mar. 10, 1863.
53. Gibbs, letter, Jan. 7, 1863, Dumfries, VA.
54. Parmater diary, Apr. 15, 1862.
55. Anonymous soldier, 147th Regiment, reminiscence of life in the Union camp, Dumfries, VA, winter 1863, *Snyder County Historical Society Bulletin* (Snyder County, Pennsylvania Historical Society) 1, no. 1 (1972): 343.
56. Asst. Surgeon Elwood P. Haines diary, Feb. 7, 1863.
57. Franklin Potter diary, Mar. 30, 1863.

"A Case Demanding Sympathy"

58. Haines diary, Feb. 1, 1863.
59. Soldier, 147th Regiment, reminiscence, 343.
60. Ames diary, Mar. 23, 28, 1863.
61. Wallace Hoyt to "Dear Parents," Dumfries, VA, Mar. 15, 1863, OHS.
62. Soldier, 147th Regiment, reminiscence, 341.

National Pastimes

63. Nims to "Dear Mother," Jan. 16, 1863.
64. Nims, letter, Feb. 7, 1863.
65. Pleasanton to Williams, Mar. 16, 1863, *OR,* vol. 25, pt. 1, 45.
66. Southworth to Stoneman, Mar. 16, 1863, *OR,* vol. 25, pt. 1, 46.
67. Roshon to "Dear Father and Mother," Mar. 17, 1863.
68. Haines diary, Apr. 11, 1863.
69. References to snowball fights and the playing of an early form of baseball were noted frequently by Nathan Parmater in his diary entries of winter and spring 1863.
70. Parmater diary, Mar. 12, 1863.
71. Ames diary, Mar. 30, 1863.
72. John Marsh to "Dear Ida," Dumfries, VA, Mar. 6, 1863, Marsh pension file, RG 94, NA.
73. "Capt. Lowrey Says," *Beacon,* Feb. 26, 1863.
74. "Not Dead Yet," *Beacon,* Aug. 7, 1862.
75. "Sketches of the Old 29th," *Beacon,* Mar. 12, 1863.
76. Ibid.
77. "Co. A," letter, Dumfries, VA, Feb. 4, 1863, in "Army Correspondence—From the Twenty-Ninth," *Sentinel,* Feb. 18, 1863.
78. Ibid.

Home Fires

79. "Clean Those Alleys!" *Beacon,* May 7, 1863.
80. "Another Brave Soldier Gone," *Beacon,* Jan. 29, 1863.
81. "Akron and Its Improvements," *Beacon,* Nov. 13, 1862.
82. "Manufacture of Stone Ware," *Beacon,* Dec. 4, 1862.

83. *Reporter,* Apr. 8, 1863. The remainder of the $100,000 needed to secure the Jefferson bank's charter was to be raised by selling stock at $100 per share.

84. *Reporter,* Nov. 1, 1863. Notice of Rev. Olds's appointment to this missionary post appeared in the *Reporter,* Apr. 8, 1863.

85. Allen Mason to "Dear Mother," Dumfries, VA, Apr. 2, 1863, Mason pension file, RG 94, NA.

86. "Spring Styles," *Reporter,* Apr. 8, 1863.

87. "A Female Jeremy Diddler," *Beacon,* Mar. 5, 1863.

88. "Artemus Ward," *Beacon,* Apr. 9, 1863.

89. "The Circus," *Beacon,* May 21, 1863.

90. "The *Akron Democrat,*" *Beacon,* Dec. 4, 1862.

91. "The Assassination of the President Recommended by the *Akron Democrat,*" *Beacon,* Jan. 1, 1863.

92. "The 12th army corps . . . ," *Reporter,* Mar. 17, 1863. This edition was erroneously dated Mar. 18 on the masthead.

93. "From the 29th O.V.I.—To Our Union Friends in Conneaut," *Reporter,* May 6, 1863.

94. Nims, letter, Feb. 7, 1863.

95. Cass Nims to "Dear Mother," Dumfries, VA, Apr. 2, 1863, Nims pension file, RG 94, NA.

96. Mason to "Dear Mother," Apr. 2, 1863.

97. "Letter from Col. Buckley," *Beacon,* Jan. 29, 1863. "Still it cannot now muster for duty over 450 men." The number in the regiment of all ranks present for duty at Dumfries around this time was cited by Lewis P. Buckley. Buckley, letter, Dumfries, VA, Jan. 13, 1863, in *Beacon,* Jan. 13, 1863.

98. John Marsh to "Dear Father," Frederick, MD, Nov. 17, 1862, Marsh pension file, RG 94, NA.

99. Sidney Wilder pension file, RG 94, NA.

100. Ames diary, Apr. 5, 1863. Easter Sunday 1863 was observed on Apr. 5.

101. Wallace Hoyt to "Dear Mother," Dumfries, VA, Apr. 16, 1863, OHS.

102. Ames diary, Apr. 16, 1863.

103. Parmater diary, Apr. 16, 1863.

104. Ames diary, Apr. 17, 1863.

105. Parmater diary, Apr. 21, 1863.

106. Wallace Hoyt to "Dear Mother," Apr. 16, 1863.

Chapter 18: Saving the Life of the Army
"Some Place Unknown to Us"

1. M. T. Wright, Capt. Co. D, 29th Ohio, letter, field near Aquia Creek, VA, May 9, 1863, in "The Killed, Wounded and Missing of the 29th—Incidents of the Great Battle," *Beacon,* May 21, 1863. Capt. Myron T. Wright wrote two letters describing the regiment's actions at the battle of Chancellorsville. Both were published in the *Beacon* of May 21, 1863. The letter referenced here covers the entire span of the battle. Wright's other letter on the battle, dated May 8, 1863, was printed under the title "Another Brave Patriot Fallen."

2. Jones, "Bits of Gossip."

3. Ames diary, Apr. 20, 1863.

4. Parmater diary, Apr. 21, 1863.

5. Ibid.

6. Franklin Potter to "Dear Parents," Aquia Creek, VA, Apr. 26, 1863, Potter pension file, RG 94, NA.

7. Parmater diary, Apr. 23, 1863.

8. Potter to "Dear Parents," Apr. 26, 1863.

9. Ames diary, Apr. 26, 1863.

10. Charles Sherbondy, obituary, *Akron Beacon Journal,* Jan. 6, 1939.

11. Wallace Hoyt to "Honored Parents," Aquia Creek, VA, Apr. 26, 1863, OHS.

12. John Marsh to "Dear Ida," May 1, 1863, Hudson Papers.

13. Ames diary, Apr. 27, 1863.

14. John Marsh to "Dear Ida," May 1, 1863.

15. W. R. Hopkins, Chief QM, Twelfth Army Corps, to Col. R. Ingalls, Chief QM, Army of the Potomac, May 23, 1863, *OR,* vol. 25, pt. 2, 559.

16. Hoyt to "Honored Parents," Apr. 26, 1863.

17. Hopkins to Ingalls, May 23, 1863.

18. Ibid.
19. Ibid.
20. Parmater diary, Apr. 28, 1863.
21. Ames diary, Apr. 28, 1863.
22. Parmater diary, Apr. 28, 1863.
23. Parmater diary, Apr. 29, 1863.
24. John Marsh to "Dear Ida," May 1, 1863.
25. SeCheverell, *Journal History*, 63.
26. Ames diary, Apr. 29, 1863.
27. Ibid.
28. Maj. Gen. Henry W. Slocum, report, *OR*, vol. 25, pt. 1, 669.
29. Marsh to "Dear Ida," May 1, 1863.
30. Parmater diary, Apr. 29, 1863.
31. Marsh to "Dear Ida," May 1, 1863.
32. Slocum, report, 669.
33. Brig. Gen. John W. Geary, report, May 10, 1863, *OR*, vol. 25, pt. 1, 728.

Crossroads

34. Sgt. John A. Kummer, letter, Aquia Creek, VA, May 9, 1863, in "Another Letter from the 29th—Full Particulars of the Fight . . . ," *Beacon,* May 21, 1863.
35. Ibid. Slocum confirmed in his official report of the battle that Geary's division had led the march from Germana Ford toward Chancellorsville. According to him, the first elements of his corps arrived by two o'clock. Slocum, report, 669. SeCheverell reported the regiment arrived "late in the afternoon of Apr. 30," giving the impression they had been one of the two regiments ordered to leave the road for the more arduous work of driving rebel horsemen out of the brush. SeCheverell, *Journal History,* 63.
36. SeCheverell, *Journal History,* 63.
37. Marsh to "Dear Ida," May 1, 1863.
38. Ibid. The number of Federals in the Fifth, Eleventh, and Twelfth Corps on the south side of the Rappahannock totaled approximately 54,000. Stackpole, *Chancellorsville,* 139.
39. Stackpole, *Chancellorsville,* 139.
40. Slocum, report, 669. Slocum placed the Twelfth Corps, generally in woods, on a line parallel to the Plank Road, with its left at the Chancellor Inn and the right at Hunters Run creek.
41. Charles Candy, report, Commanding First Brigade, *OR,* vol. 25, pt. 1, 734.
42. SeCheverell, *Journal History,* 63. The bivouac of Candy's brigade on the night of Apr. 30 is also located by Col. William R. Creighton, Seventh Ohio Infantry, in his official report. *OR,* vol. 25, pt. 1, 737.
43. Couch, "Chancellorsville Campaign."
44. Geary stated in his official report that it was he who gave the order for the men to build trench works during the late night and early morning of Apr. 30–May 1. Geary, report, 728.
45. Jones, "Bits of Gossip."
46. M. Wright, letter, May 9, 1863.
47. Candy, report, 734.
48. Geary, report, 728.
49. Kummer, letter, May 9, 1863.
50. Marsh, letter, May 1, 1863. That the common soldiers were aware of their proximity to Fredericksburg and Lee's army also was noted by Nathan Parmater: "We are now within a few miles of F. and there is an enemy in our front and we expect fighting soon." Parmater, diary, Apr. 30, 1863.
51. Stackpole, *Chancellorsville,* 139–40.

Recalled

52. Ames diary, May 1, 1863.
53. Candy, report, 734.
54. Creighton, report, 737.
55. SeCheverell, *Journal History,* 64. Rev. Ames, who accompanied them on this movement, estimated the high tide of their advance from Chancellorsville as one mile, an opinion shared by Nathan Parmater. Ames diary, May 1, 1863; Parmater diary, May 1, 1863.

56. Lt. Col. Thomas Clark filed two reports on the regiment's actions at the battle of Chancellorsville. The first was dated May 9, 1863, and the second May 30, 1863. They appear consecutively on pages 739–42, *OR*. Publication of two after-battle reports by a regimental commander is a rare occurrence in the *Official Record*.

57. Ibid. Slocum stated in his report of the battle that Hooker's order to return to their jumping-off point was received at one in the afternoon on May 1. Slocum, report, 670.

58. Couch, "Chancellorsville Campaign," 3:161. General Couch, commander of the Second Corps, had been stupefied and angered by Hooker's order to suspend the offensive, and he rode back to complain. By the time their discussion concluded, Couch was convinced that Hooker was a "whipped man."

59. Parmater diary, May 1, 1863.

60. Clark, report, 739.

61. Ibid.

62. Candy, report, 734.

63. Geary, report, 729.

64. Creighton, report, 737.

65. L. Wilson, *Itinerary*, 233.

66. Candy, report, 734.

67. Ames diary, May 1, 1863.

68. Geary, report, 729.

69. M. Wright, letter, May 9, 1863.

70. Geary, report, 729.

71. Kummer, letter, May 9, 1863.

72. M. Wright letter, May 9, 1863.

73. Ames diary, May 1, 1863.

Bloody Day

74. Parmater noted in his diary that the first assault on their line took place at seven on the morning of May 2. As it turned out, a rebel brigade going to relieve another lost its way and strayed into sight of the Federal guns posted near the crossroads. L. Wilson, *Itinerary*, 233.

75. M. Wright, letter, May 9, 1863.

76. Marsh wrote a nine-page letter detailing his experience at Chancellorsville. The cover page bearing the date of his writing it has not survived, thus an exact date cannot be given it. Hereafter this letter will be noted as: Marsh, letter, Chancellorsville, n.d.

77. M. Wright, letter, May 9, 1863.

78. Clark, report, 740.

79. Geary, report, 730.

80. Clark, report, 740–41. In his second report on the battle Col. Thomas Clark gave the time of their departure on this reconnaissance as two o'clock.

81. Slocum, report, 670.

82. Geary, report, 730.

83. Creighton, report, 737.

84. Marsh to "Dear Ida," May 1, 1863. Creighton, report, 737.

85. Creighton, report, 737.

86. Marsh, letter, Chancellorsville, n.d.

87. In his official report, Geary mentions the valor of these two regiments but names neither. Geary, report, 730. In his letter, Marsh reports with certainty that the Twenty-Ninth had gone forward to help the Seventh Ohio, *after* the right wing of Geary's division, Kane's brigade, had filled the road in the march back to Chancellorsville. Clark's report of the Twenty-Ninth's part in the battle is deficient in detail as to the Giddings Regiment's activity in the reconnaissance.

88. M. Wright, letter, May 9, 1863.

89. Ibid.

90. Clark, report, 741.

91. M. Wright, letter, May 9, 1863.

92. Couch, "Chancellorsville Campaign," 3:163. That the rebel force Geary encountered was fortified and prepared to stick is also found in Geary's official report on Chancellorsville. They had been found drawn up in line of battle, along strong entrenchments of their own, with cannon posted at intervals along their line.

Fiery Heavens

93. Marsh, letter, Chancellorsville, n.d.
94. Ibid.
95. Nims to "Dear Father," June 5, 1863.
96. John G. Marsh stated in his undated letter to his sister covering the events of May 2 that two or three regiments of Kane's brigade were dislodged by the refugees of the Eleventh Corps.
97. Kummer, letter, May 9, 1863.
98. Candy, report, 734.
99. Slocum, report, 670.
100. Maj. Henry E. Seymmes (Semmes), report, 5th Ohio Infantry, *OR*, vol. 25, pt. 1, 736.
101. Marsh, letter, Chancellorsville, n.d.
102. Clark, report, 731.
103. Jones, "Bits of Gossip."
104. Marsh, letter, Chancellorsville, n.d.
105. Ibid.
106. Slocum, report, 670. Between midnight May 3 and 3:00 a.m., rebels stepped out of the darkness in double battle lines in repeated attempts to drive the divisions of Williams and Berry from their defensive lines. A portion of Brig. Gen. Davis Birney's division, Sickles's corps, that had survived the deadly combat out in the salient returned to the main line and was sent immediately to extend Geary's line to prevent it from being flanked. Birney moved forward to drive the rebels in front of Williams's line away, found the enemy immovable, and retired. One of Birney's guns was captured, and the rebels turned it on Geary's line and began sending shot and shell down its length. Major General Slocum reported that this enfilading of Geary's line caused frightful destruction. The effect of this fire, in comparison to the hammering Williams's men were enduring, was not found noteworthy by anyone except Slocum.
107. William H. Tallman, memoir, excerpt, Dec. 1862–June 1863, vol. 106, Fredericksburg and Spotsylvania National Military Park, Fredericksburg, VA (original at U.S. Army Military History Institute, Carlisle Barracks, PA). Tallman was a clerk in the Sixty-Sixth OVI, Candy's brigade.
108. Marsh, letter, Chancellorsville, n.d.
109. Parmater diary, May 2, 1863.
110. SeCheverell, *Journal History*, 65.
111. Geary, report, 730.

Sunrise

112. Clark, report, 739.
113. SeCheverell, *Journal History*, 65. His is the only account having the Twenty-Ninth Regiment being driven back into the trenches by an attack coming directly from their front in the opening minutes of the fighting of May 3.
114. Marsh, letter, Chancellorsville, n.d.
115. Geary, report, 730. "Shortly after daylight on the morning of the 3d instant, the action commenced at a distance from our line on the right and rear of the army, and within half an hour it had reached my division and become general along the whole front."
116. Clark, report, 740 (his Chancellorsville report of May 9, 1863).
117. Ibid., 739.
118. Ibid.
119. Ibid.
120. Ibid., 741.

At the Guns

121. Capt. Joseph Knap, report, *OR*, vol. 25, pt. 1, 771. "At 3 a.m. Sunday, the 3rd, I was ordered to place Hampton's six guns near the headquarters of General Williams, on the right of the Twelfth Corps, and at 4:15 was ordered to report with my other six guns (Knap's) to General Reynolds, commanding First Corps, where they remained in position during the day."
122. Geary, report, 731.
123. Clark stated in his first of two official reports that after the regiment's support of Greene was deemed no longer necessary, he and the Boys were sent to protect "Knap's Battery," which was then posted so as to rake the Plank Road leading from the Chancellor Inn. Clark, report, 739.

124. Ibid.

125. Alexander T. Wilcox letter, 7th Ohio Inf., May 16, 1863, Camp Near Aquia Landing, VA, bound vol. 183, Fredericksburg and Spotsylvania National Military Park, Fredericksburg, VA (original in the Manuscript Collection of the United States Army Military History Institute, Carlisle Barracks, PA).

126. M. Wright, letter, May 9, 1863.

127. Marsh, letter, Chancellorsville, n.d.

128. Haines diary, May 1–3, 1863.

129. Geary, report, 731.

130. Couch, "Chancellorsville Campaign," 3:161. General Couch, who was there near the Chancellor Inn, and observed the withdrawal of these two corps, gave the time of their leaving the field as eight thirty.

131. Kummer, letter, May 9, 1863. "Pandemonium and wild panic reigned supreme" were the words used by Lawrence Wilson. L. Wilson, *Itinerary*, 239.

132. Capt. Clermont L. Best, Chief of Artillery, Twelfth Army Corps, report, May 10, 1863, *OR*, vol. 25, pt. 1, 675.

133. Couch, "Chancellorsville Campaign," 3:161.

134. Ibid. Couch gave the time of Hooker's wounding as between nine fifteen and nine thirty.

135. Ibid., 168.

136. Geary, report, 731. In Geary's defense, Hooker's contradictory order added to the confusion of an already chaotic situation.

Last Stand

137. Ibid.

138. Ibid.

139. Nims to "Dear Father," June 5, 1863.

140. M. Wright, letter, May 9, 1863.

141. Ibid. Hall survived and was discharged for disability in Sept., 1864.

142. Kummer, letter, May 9, 1863. Weidle, a native of Württemberg, survived the battle and was discharged for disability in Sept. 1864.

143. Fox, *Regimental Losses*, 264.

144. That Major Chapman was killed within Geary's sight is reported in various sources, the most interesting of which is Bates, *Martial Deeds*, 421–22. Geary stated in his official after-battle report that Chapman was struck "in my immediate presence." Geary report, 733.

145. Maj. Henry Symmes, report, Fifth Ohio Infantry, *OR*, vol. 25, pt. 1, 736. So confusing were the rapid changes in Candy's line to meet the rebel assaults that according to Major Symmes the Fifth Ohio got into the rifle pits by the rear rank and with its left and right ends reversed. This backward maneuver made little difference because by that time Candy's brigade was taking fire from all directions. Symmes is identified in this report as its likely author. The Fifth's commander, Lieutenant Colonel Kilpatrick, had been severely wounded in the battle.

146. Cass Nims letter dated June 5, 1863, Camp near Aquia Creek, Va. "Dear Father,"

147. Stevens, Hayes, and Treen were singled out for their valuable service during the battle by John Kummer. Kummer, letter, May 9, 1863, *Beacon*, May 21, 1863.

148. Clark, reports, May 9, May 30, 1863. The governor of Ohio promoted Hayward to the rank of second lieutenant within two weeks of the battle for gallantry.

149. Geary, report, 731. Geary stated, "When the order was given by me to retire by the left flank, the movement was executed in excellent order."

150. Clark stated in both official reports that he did not receive orders to retire the regiment from their island defense south of the Chancellor Inn and emphasized the point further by stating, for whoever cared to know, "I have since learned that an order was given for us to retreat, which order was not received, and it was only when a further defense was useless that we retired." Clark, report, 739.

151. Ibid., 741. Capt. Myron Wright confirmed the impromptu conference of the several regiment's officers in his letter of May 9, 1863.

152. Creighton, report, 738.

"Fix Bayonets! Charge!"

153. This bayonet charge was likely the last concerted Federal offensive movement on the battlefield. Its occurrence is noted in their official reports by Clark, 741, and Creighton, 738. Creighton stated that the Seventh

Ohio led this charge, which succeeded in driving the rebels back. Two to three more charges were executed a few moments later as Candy's brigade fought for breathing space to cover its withdrawal from the woods.

154. Reports of the number of charges made by Candy's brigade, Geary's division, into the woods south of the Plank Road below the Chancellor Inn vary. Major Symmes, Fifth Ohio, gave the number of charges in his official report as three in total. Symmes, report, 736. Candy mentioned one organized charge, but he may have been referring to the initial charge ordered by Hooker. In a June 5, 1863, letter to his father, Pvt. Cass Nims of the Twenty-Ninth wrote, "Our Regt. made three bayonet charges before we fell back." Nims pension file, RG 94, NA. In his diary entry of May 3, 1863, Nathan Parmater reported the number of charges as "several."

155. Parmater diary, May 3, 1863.

156. Creighton, report, 738.

157. SeCheverell, *Journal History*, 66.

158. As to the route of retreat from just east of the crossroads, Colonel Creighton stated, "About 11 a. m. the regiment and brigade withdrew across the cleared fields east of the brick house, retiring through the woods on the north side of the road, and losing a number of men from the enemy's guns shelling the woods as we retired. About 2 miles from the battle-field, on the road to the United States Ford, the regiment was halted, and rested until some time in the afternoon when it moved up the road a mile." Creighton, report, 738.

159. Maj. Gen. Winfield S. Hancock's Chancellorsville report, commanding First Division, Couch's II corps. *OR*, vol. 25, pt. 1, 314.

160. Ibid. Hancock, fighting on Geary's left and rear, stated that he and Geary were squeezed into what Hancock described as a "salient' close enough to each other that he could see Geary's battle flags. By Hancock's account, much work remained to him around the Chancellor Inn after Geary departed the field. Hancock recalled the half of his division fighting a half mile away facing the direction of Gordonsville, and made sure what guns he had left were hitched up and hauled to safety. He also stated that the inn, which was being used as a hospital, was set afire by rebel artillery *after* Geary's command left the field. The regiment's historian, J. Hampton SeCheverell, had not been with the regiment for over a year, but he doubtless interviewed men of the Twenty-Ninth who had been in the battle of Chancellorsville. Although uncorroborated by other participants, SeCheverell stated the rebels had full possession of the Chancellor Inn by the time the regiment passed into the woods opposite it on their way to safety. The consensus of officers in Candy's brigade places the time of the final withdrawal of their brigade between 11 a.m. and noon. Neither Hancock nor Geary ever asserted a claim of having been the last to stand alone against the combined wings of Lee's army.

161. SeCheverell, *Journal History*, 66.

162. Colonel Clark gave the time of their departure from the trenches as "near noon," an observation likely based more on the position of the sun than on his watch. Clark, report, 741. If the Giddings Boys had stayed in the trenches until twelve o'clock, all of them would have been dead or captured, which they were not. Likewise, Parmater, the faithful diarist who was fighting there, gave the time as "*about* noon," while the Twenty-Ninth's historian, J. Hamp SeCheverell, stated that they had made their final retreat in the "afternoon," which was a recollection made soft by the passage of two decades of storytelling and remembering. SeCheverell, *Journal History*, 66. Colonel Creighton gave the time of their retreat as 11:00 a.m. Creighton, report, 738.

163. Marsh, letter, Chancellorsville, n.d.

164. Creighton, report, 738.

"Oh, 'Twas Sammy"

165. M. Wright, letter, May 9, 1863.

166. M. T. Wright, letter, May 8, 1863, in "Another Brave Patriot of the 29th Fallen," *Beacon*, May 21, 1863. "I sorrow while the fate of war imposes upon me the duty of announcing the death of Samuel Shanafelt."

167. *Confederate Veteran* (Jan. 1896): 25.

168. Ames diary, May 1–3, 1863.

169. Ames diary, May 4, 1863.

170. Marsh, letter, Chancellorsville, n.d.

Cold, Hard Rain

171. Couch, "Chancellorsville Campaign."

172. Ibid., 3:171. Hooker assembled his generals at a midnight meeting on May 4 and after a discussion announced his decision to retreat to the other side of the river.

173. Parmater diary, May 4, 1863.
174. Parmater diary, May 5, 1863.
175. Haines diary, May 5, 1863.
176. Parmater diary, May 6, 1863.
177. Clark, report, 741.
178. Unless otherwise credited, the description of the Twenty-Ninth's activities from the time they collected in the woods after falling back from the crossroads at Chancellorsville until they successfully got over the Rappahannock is in M. Wright, letter, May 9, 1863.
179. Parmater diary, May 6, 1863.
180. Kummer, letter, May 9, 1863. Kummer attributed this bit of battlefield drollery to the highly popular, German-born Cpl. Christian Remley of Company G.
181. Jones, "Bits of Gossip."
182. Rupp, "Fighting Regiment."

Chapter 19: Aquia Creek Interlude
"We Congratulate the Army"

1. Compiled Service Records of Confederate Volunteers, 5th Florida Infantry, NA. Blake enlisted on May 15, 1861, for a period of three years. He was slightly wounded at Sharpsburg, and some time after Chancellorsville he was transferred to the First Florida Cavalry.
2. Benjamin F. Manderbach, "Personal War Sketch," Buckley Post, GAR, Akron, OHS.
3. W. R. Hopkins, Chief Quartermaster, 12th Army Corps, to Col. R. Ingalls, Chief Quartermaster, Army of the Potomac, *OR*, vol. 25, pt. 1, 558.
4. The effective strength of the Twelfth Corps before Chancellorsville was reported as 13,450 and its losses at Chancellorsville from all causes as 2,824. Major General Slocum estimated he lost 30 percent of his corps at Chancellorsville. Slocum, report, *OR*, vol. 25, pt. 1, 672.
5. Ames diary, May 16, 1863.
6. "Hooker's Victory Complete! All the Most Sanguine Could Ask!!" *Beacon*, May 7, 1863.
7. Ibid.
8. Ibid.
9. *Reporter*, May 6, 1863.
10. "Hooker's Victory Complete!" *Beacon*, May 7, 1863.
11. "Bad News," *Telegraph*, May 9, 1863.
12. "The Income Tax, "*Beacon*, May 7, 1863.
13. "To All the Boys and Girls in Ohio," *Sentinel*, May 20, 1863.
14. "The West Andover Soldier's Aid Society," *Sentinel*, June 17, 1863.
15. "Mr. Edward Ryon of this town . . . ," *Reporter*, May 20, 1863.
16. Ibid.
17. "From Venice to Florence and Back Again," *Sentinel*, June 3, 1863.
18. "Funny and Otherwise," *Sentinel*, July 8, 1863.
19. "Capt. H. C. Sweet . . . ," *Telegraph*, May 16, 1863. Credited to the *Cincinnati Gazette*.
20. "The National Fast Day," *Beacon*, May 7, 1863.
21. Thomas Clark, letter, near Aquia Creek, VA, May 20, 1863, in "Official Statement of the Killed, Wounded, and Missing of the 29th Regiment," *Beacon*, May 28, 1863.

"War in Its Worst Form"

22. Cass Nims to "Dear Father," camp near Aquia Creek, VA, June 5, 1863, Nims pension file, RG 94, NA.
23. Ames diary, June 9, 1863.
24. Geary, Chancellorsville report, *OR*, vol. 25, pt. 1, 733.
25. Sears, *Chancellorsville*, 490, table.
26. Fox reported the Twenty-Ninth Ohio's losses at Chancellorsville as 2 killed, 42 wounded, and 28 missing. Fox, *Regimental Losses*, 319. SeCheverell reported their number of killed in action as 4. SeCheverell, *Journal History*, 282.
27. *Reporter*, May 20, 1863. The Ryon story concerning the discovery and removal of Thomas Schultz from the battlefield was reported by Chaplain Lyman Ames in his letter of May 9 to the newspaper. He also reported

on Schulz's death in his diary entry of May 13, 1863. Ryon's account is found in the *Reporter*, May 20, 1863, "Mr. Edward Ryon of this town . . ."

28. *State Roster*, 392.

The Chapel in the Pines

29. Ames, letter, *Reporter*, May 20, 1863.
30. Ames diary, May 29, 1863.
31. Ames diary, May 20, 1863.
32. Ames diary, May 27, 1863.
33. Ibid.
34. Parmater diary, May 31, 1863.
35. Ames diary, May 17, 1863.
36. Ames diary, May 31, 1863.
37. Ames diary, May 27, 1863.
38. Ames diary, May 18, 1863.

"Many a Valiant Soldier"

39. Ames diary, June 3, 1863.
40. Ames diary, May 25, 1863.
41. Ames diary, May 10, 1863.
42. Ibid.
43. Ames diary, May 26, 1863.
44. Ames diary, May 16, 1863.
45. Ames diary, June 9, 1863. Private Oberholz survived and was discharged for disability. He died in 1914 in Wadsworth, Ohio, where he had been born and raised.
46. Ames diary, May 19, 1863.
47. Ibid.
48. Leech, *Reveille*, 232.
49. Ames diary, May 18, 1863.
50. Ames diary, May 16, 1863. Pvt. Franklin survived and was discharged for disability stemming from his wounds on Sept. 15, 1863. *State Roster*, 372.
51. Fifer Benny Bates pension file, RG 94, NA.
52. Dr. Amos Fifield, affidavit, Bates pension file.
53. Ames diary, June 6, 1863.
54. *State Roster*.
55. Ames diary, June 1, 4, 9, 1863. Greenlee was wounded at New Hope Church, GA, during the Atlanta campaign, survived, and was discharged at the expiration of his term of enlistment on Oct. 18, 1864. *State Roster*, 372.

"Perfect Cut Throats"

56. Pvt. Nelson Gillett wrote a letter addressed to his father dated June 1863 from Aquia Creek. The exact date is illegible. The letter closes with the words, "From your lonesome son Nelson to his Affectionate Father." Written as postscripts to this are letters to his mother, dated June 7, 1863, closed by "From a soldier to his mom," and three letters dated June 8, 1863, to his sister Flora, to his sister Amelia, and to his little brother Charly, whom he calls affectionately "rat." Gillett pension file, RG 94, NA. His apology for his poor handwriting attributed to the boys in his tent "tearing it up" is found in his postscript letter to his mother.
57. "J. W. C.," Co. D, 29th OVI, letter, camp near Aquia Creek, VA, May 26, 1863, in "From the 29th," *Beacon*, June 4, 1863.
58. Ibid.
59. Haines diary, May 26, 1863.
60. Christopher Beck to "Dear Mother," Aquia Creek, VA, June 9, 1863, Beck pension file, RG 94, NA.
61. Wallace Hoyt to "Dear Hattie," Aquia Creek, VA, May 31, 1863, OHS.
62. Parmater diary, May 14, 1863.
63. Parmater diary, May 15, 1863.

"May Success Yet Attend"

64. Nelson Gillett, letter, "Dear Mother," camp near Aquia Creek, VA, June 7, 1863, Gillett pension file. As to the impression the regiment had made on the general inspector he said, "We now have inspections every day. They have got a black mark against us and we have to make that up."

65. Parmater diary, May 25, 1863.
66. Ames diary, May 9, 1863.
67. Elias Roshon to "Dear Father and Mother," camp near Breck Station, VA, Apr. 26, 1863.
68. Nelson Gillett, letter to his father, June 1863. Gillett pension file, RG 94, NA.
69. Ibid.
70. Ames diary, May 18, 1863.
71. Beck to "Dear Mother," June 9, 1863.
72. Ames diary, May 24, 1863.

A Commotion

73. "Resignation of Capt. Treen," *Beacon,* June 4, 1863.
74. Ames diary, May 24, 1863.
75. Ames diary, June 8, 1862.
76. Ames diary, June 10, 1863.
77. Cass Nims to "Dear Mother," Dumfries Landing, VA, Apr. 2, 1863, Nims pension file, RG 94, NA.
78. Hoyt to "Dear Hattie," May 31, 1863.

"Strike Tents!"

79. Parmater diary, May 30, 1863.
80. By several accounts, the date of the Twenty-Ninth's change of camp was June 3, 1863.
81. Parmater diary, June 4–5, 1863.
82. Ames diary, June 5–6, 1863.
83. Parmater diary, June 11, 1863.
84. Parmater diary, June 13, 1863.
85. Ames diary, June 13, 1863.
86. Ames diary, June 14–15, 1863.
87. Ames diary, June 15, 1863.
88. Nims to "Dear Father," June 5, 1863.

Chapter 20: Saving the Life of the Nation
"A Good Deal Like Murder"

1. Parmater diary, June 14, 1863.
2. Ames diary, June 17, 1863.
3. Parmater diary, June 16, 1863.
4. Henry J. Knapp, "Gettysburg by a Soldier in the Ranks," *Jefferson Gazette,* Feb. 8, 1912. Knapp dated this incident generally as having taken place after the battle of Gettysburg, during the army's march in pursuit of Lee. At the time, he had been a nineteen-year-old private in Company H.
5. Ames diary, June 21, 1863.
6. Wallace Hoyt to "Dear Hattie," Leesburg, VA, June 24, 1863, OHS.
7. Parmater diary, June 25, 1863.
8. H. Knapp, "Gettysburg by a Soldier."
9. Geary to his wife, Leesburg, VA, June 20, 1863, in Geary, *Politician,* 93.
10. Cass Nims to "Dear Mother," Leesburg, VA, June 30, 1863, Nims pension file, RG 94, NA.
11. Parmater diary, June 19, 1863.
12. Ames diary, June 18, 1863.
13. Nims to "Dear Mother," June 30, 1863.
14. William McKee, Co. A, 46th Pa. Vols., case 18091938, LL445, RG 152, Records of the Office of the Judge Advocate General, NA.
15. William Gruver, Co. A, 46th Pa., case LL445, no case number, RG 152, Records of the Office of the Judge Advocate General, NA.

16. Christopher Krubert, Co. B, 13th New Jersey Infantry, RG 152, Records of the Office of the Judge Advocate General, NA, case18091938, LL445.

17. Parmater diary, June 19, 1863.

18. Nims to "Dear Mother," June 30, 1863.

19. Ames diary, June 19, 1863.

20. Wallace Hoyt to "Dear Sister," "Camp in the Fields, Near Culpeppers, Va.," Sept. 21, 1863, OHS.

Back in the Union

21. Parmater diary, June 25, 1863.

22. Geary to his wife, Leesburg, VA, June 19, 1863, in Geary, *Politician,* 92.

23. Franklin Potter diary, June 26, 1863.

24. Lynn, "At Gettysburg."

25. Parmater diary, June 29, 1863.

26. Ames diary, June 29, 1863.

27. Knapp, "Gettysburg by a Soldier." This copy of Knapp's recollections of Gettysburg provided by Dr. Richard Waters, Jefferson, Ohio. Knapp did not identify the soldier.

28. Rupp, "Fighting Regiment."

29. Ames diary, June 30, 1863.

30. Parmater diary, June 30, 1863.

31. Parmater diary, June 28, 1863.

32. Jones, "Bits of Gossip."

33. SeCheverell, *Journal History,* 69.

34. Hart, "At Gettysburg."

35. SeCheverell, *Journal History,* 69.

36. Rupp, "Fighting Regiment."

37. L. Wilson, "Candy's Brigade."

38. SeCheverell, *Journal History,* 69. SeCheverell erred in reporting that their position of that moment had been on or near Seminary Ridge.

Round-Topped Hills

39. Neither Parmater, Franklin Potter, Asst. Surgeon Elwood Potts Haines, nor Lyman Ames were specific about the location of their camp on the evening of July 1, 1863.

40. Brig. Gen. John W. Geary, commanding Second Division, report, July 29, 1863, *OR,* vol. 27, pt. 1, 825. Gen. John W. Geary's official report of his actions at Gettysburg caused a flap among his fellow high-ranking officers, who complained Geary had misstated facts to make it appear he alone had planned and managed the repulse of the rebels on the Union right. Gen. Alpheus Williams in particular, who commanded the Twelfth Corps for a time during the struggle for Culp's Hill and was therefore Geary's superior, felt justifiably slighted in Geary's official report of the battle and raised a considerable ruckus over the accuracy of claims Geary made for himself in it. Williams's extreme dislike of Geary far outlived the war. Ten years later he advised a student of the battle that Geary's reports were often "premeditated and wicked lies—They were written solely for his own exultation without the least regard for facts." Quoted in Pfanz, *Gettysburg,* 440. Geary was also criticized for expending too much ammunition during the fighting, for ordering the retaking of the trenches won by the rebels during his lost ramble in the Union rear, and for getting lost in the Gettysburg night on July 2. Most of Geary's failings at Gettysburg are described by Edwin B. Coddington in *Gettysburg Campaign,* 433–34. Unhappiness with Geary's actions even found its way into the battle memoir of Frank A. Haskell, who overheard General Meade voice his dissatisfaction with Geary's costly assaults to drive the rebels out of his trenches. Haskell, "Battle of Gettysburg," 190.

41. Col. Charles Candy, commanding First Brigade, report, *OR,* vol. 27, pt. 1, 836. Old veteran S. W. Hart of Co. H, 29th OVI, recalled more than a half century later that Candy's brigade, the Twenty-Ninth included, spent the night of July 1 at Little Round Top, which might not be taken literally but does shed light on the location of Candy's brigade within the line of Geary's division. Hart, "At Gettysburg."

42. H. Knapp, "Gettysburg by a Soldier."

43. Potter diary, July 1, 1863.

44. L. Wilson, "Candy's Brigade."

Culp's Hill

45. Jones, Capt., 60th New York Volunteers, "Breastworks," *Battles and Leaders,* 3:316.
46. Candy, report, 842.
47. Capt. Wilbur F. Stevens, commanding Twenty-Ninth Ohio Infantry, report, *OR,* vol. 27, pt. 1, 842. Stevens characterized the terrain in which they rested in reserve though most of July 2 as a "hollow." He gave the time of their arrival at this position as eight o'clock.
48. Parmater diary, July 2, 1863.
49. Col. William R. Creighton, Seventh Ohio Infantry, report, *OR,* vol. 27, pt. 1, 840.
50. Geary, report, 826.

A March to Nowhere

51. Knapp, "Gettysburg by a Soldier."
52. Geary stated, "When ordered thus to leave my entrenchments, I received no specific instructions as to the object of the move, the direction to be taken, or the point to be reached, beyond the order to move by the right flank and to follow the First Division." Geary, report, 826.
53. Ibid.
54. Parmater described the scene: "All quiet this morning, we were moved to the extreme right this morning, the enemy commenced on left in the afternoon and the fight was severe, they drove our men a little, some skirmishing along our line on the right, our Brigade was moved farther to the right, and soon after there was hard fighting where we left, we on the move nearly all night." Parmater diary, July 2, 1863.
55. Col. David Ireland, 137th New York Infantry, report, *OR,* vol. 27, pt. 1, 866.
56. Ibid. By comparison, Chamberlain's losses during the Twentieth Maine's defense of the left end of the Federal line amounted to 29 killed and 96 wounded. Fox, *Regimental Losses,* 233. Ireland's regiment was reinforced once they reached their last redoubt, assistance that the Twentieth Maine did not enjoy.
57. Candy, report, 836.
58. Ibid.
59. Brig. Gen. Thomas Kane, commanding 2nd Brigade, Geary's division, report, *OR,* vol. 27, pt. 1, 847.
60. Rupp, "Fighting Regiment."
61. Candy, report.
62. Parmater diary, July 2, 1863. General Greene stated in his official report that Candy's brigade returned to Culp's Hill at one thirty in the morning after their late night saunter in the rear of the fighting. Brig. Gen. George S. Greene, commanding Third Brigade, Second Division, report, *OR,* vol. 27, pt. 1, 857. It may have taken an additional two hours to sort out the line and move troops into their positions, which would correspond with the soldiers' claims that it had been more like three o'clock when they finally settled into their protective swale.

Dedication Day

63. Hayes, "Address."

The Fight for Culp's Hill

64. Ames diary, July 3, 1863.
65. Lynn, "At Gettysburg."
66. Stevens, report, 842.
67. Hayes, "Address."
68. M. T. Wright, Capt., Co. D, 29th Ohio Vols., letter, in "The Killed and Wounded of the 29th," *Beacon,* July 30, 1863.
69. Ibid.
70. Knapp, "Gettysburg by a Soldier."
71. General Greene was severely wounded at Missionary Ridge the coming fall, and Col. David Ireland took command of the famous Third Brigade. Ireland died of disease in Atlanta, GA, in Sept. 1864.
72. Hayes, report, 843.
73. SeCheverell, *Journal History,* 72.
74. Knapp, "Gettysburg by a Soldier."
75. Ireland, report, 867.

76. Hayes, report, 843. Hayes stated in his report that the Twenty-Ninth Ohio first went into the breastworks at 5:45 a.m. and were relieved two hours and twenty minutes later at 8:05 a.m.
77. Ibid.
78. SeCheverell, *Journal History*, 71.
79. Hayes, report, 843.
80. L. Wilson, *Itinerary*, 256n.
81. M. Wright, letter, *Beacon*, July 30, 1863.
82. Ibid.
83. Knapp, "Gettysburg by a Soldier." This incident, reported decades after the battle, should be taken with a grain of salt. However, it is figuratively correct in its representation of the determination of the rebel soldier fighting to take Culp's Hill. Rollin Jones also remembered this notable event, but he did not include the severed-hand portion. Jones, "Bits of Gossip."
84. M. Wright, letter, *Beacon*, July 30, 1863.
85. Ibid.
86. Ibid.
87. Ireland, report, 867.
88. Geary gave the time of the final rebel attack of the morning as ten thirty. Ewell's pledge to take the hill and the pike at any cost, as learned from his captured officers, is found in Geary's Gettysburg report, 830, as is Geary's statement of the time of the last rebel charge.
89. Hayes noted the time of the cessation of fire as eleven o'clock. *OR*, Hayes, report, 843.
90. Stevens, report, 842.
91. Parmater diary, July 3, 1863.
92. Ibid.

"Such a Sight I Never Saw"

93. Geary, report, 830.
94. M. Wright, letter, *Beacon*, July 30.
95. Geary, report, 831.
96. Ibid. Supported by Parmater in his diary entry for July 5, 1863.
97. Bertholf, "Twelfth Corps."
98. Parmater diary, July 4, 1863.
99. Bertholf, "Twelfth Corps."
100. "Dark Weather," *Sentinel*, July 15, 1863.
101. "Casualties of the Late Battle, *Sentinel*, July 15, 1863.
102. SeCheverell, *Journal History*, 74.
103. Matthias Soden pension file, RG 94, NA.
104. Matthias Soden, letter, Dumfries, VA, Feb. 6, 1863, Soden pension file, RG 94, NA.
105. The injuries to men in Company D were described in Myron Wright's letter to the *Beacon*, July 30, 1863.
106. Wallace Hoyt to "Dear Parents," July 4, 1863, "Rifle Pits, Gettysburg, Pa.," OHS.
107. Jones, "Bits of Gossip."

In the Wake of Battle

108. "H. C. H.," letter, Gettysburg, PA, Aug. 9, 1863, in "Another Visit to the 29th Regt. OVI—The People of Gettysburg," *Beacon*, Aug. 27, 1863.
109. Surg. Jonathan Letterman, U.S. Army Medical Director, Army of the Potomac, report, *OR*, vol. 27, pt. 1, 197. Letterman quoted directly from Surg. McNulty's report to him.
110. Ames diary, July 5, 1863.
111. Ames diary, July 18, 1863.
112. Ames diary, July 12, 1863.
113. Marsh's father arrived in Gettysburg to collect his son's body on July 16, 1863. Ames diary, July 16, 1863.
114. *State Roster*, 356. Pvt. Brown died on July 20, 1863.
115. Souder, *Leaves from the Battlefield*, 16.
116. Ibid., 22.
117. Ibid., 136.

118. Ibid., 38.
119. Ames diary, Aug. 2, 1863.
120. Ames reported that the morning report of that day showed 307 rebels and 308 Union soldiers at Camp Letterman. Ames diary, July 29, 1863.
121. Ames diary, July 28, 1863.
122. "J. A. K," Co. G, 29th Ohio, in "Death of Tallis McCain," *Beacon,* Sept. 10, 1863.
123. McCain pension file, RG 94, NA, and Carded Medical Records, in RG 94, 1780s–1917, entry 543, confirm McCain died Aug. 12, 1863, at Camp Letterman.
124. J. A. K., "Tallis McCain."
125. John G. Marsh's last letter, to "Dear Ida," was dated July 2, 1863, from Gettysburg. Hudson Papers.
126. Marsh pension file, RG 94, NA; and Carded Medical Records, 29th Reg., OVI, give the place of Marsh's death as the Twelfth Army Corps Hospital, Gettysburg, PA.
127. Marsh is buried in Ashland County, Ohio, in a small private cemetery known as the Marsh Farm Cemetery near State Route 58 and Sullivan Township Road 350, about four miles east of Homerville.
128. John G. Marsh to "Dear Ida," Feb. 17, 1863, Hudson Papers. In his letter of Mar. 16, 1863, to his little sister Ida, Marsh confided that he felt his future dark and joyless, and that there was little left to tie him to the earth.

Chapter 21: Journeying Forth
The Pursuit of Lee

1. Parmater diary, July 7, 1863.
2. Parmater diary, July 8, 1863.
3. Ibid.
4. Ibid. The hanged spy was reported in SeCheverell, *Journal History,* 75.
5. L. Wilson, "7th Ohio."
6. Parmater diary, July 10, 1863.
7. Parmater diary, July 13, 1863.
8. Parmater diary, July 14, 1863.
9. SeCheverell gives the date of their encounter with Mosby's men as July 18, 1863. SeCheverell, *Journal History,* 76.
10. Parmater diary, July 15, 1863.
11. Parmater diary, July 24, 1863.
12. SeCheverell, *Journal History,* 77.
13. The regiment reached Kelly's Ford, on the Rappahannock River, on July 26, 1863. Parmater diary, July 26, 1863.
14. Cass Nims to "Dear Mother," July 28, 1863, Nims pension file, RG 94, NA.
15. Ames diary, Aug. 12, 1863.

Cowardly Traitors

16. Nims to "Dear Mother," July 28, 1863.
17. "We'll Kill the Fatted Calf," *Sentinel,* Sept. 2, 1863.
18. Nims to "Dear Mother," July 28, 1863.
19. John A. Kummer to Lewis P. Buckley, General Hospital, York, PA, Aug. 11, 1863, in "From a Wounded Soldier," *Beacon,* Aug. 20, 1863.
20. Ibid.
21. Ibid.
22. O. J. P., letter, "From the Twenty-Ninth, Alexandria, Va.," Aug. 20, 1863, *Sentinel,* Sept. 2, 1863.

Flatlanders at Sea

23. "New York Riots," *Sentinel,* July 22, 1863.
24. SeCheverell, *Journal History,* 77.
25. O. J. P., letter, Aug. 20, 1863.
26. Ames diary, Aug. 16, 1863.
27. Wallace Hoyt to "Dear Parents," Aug. 24, 1863, OHS.
28. Ames diary, Aug. 22, 1863.

29. Ames diary, Aug. 24, 1863.
30. Ames diary, Aug. 25, 1863.
31. Hoyt to "Dear Parents," Aug. 24, 1863.
32. Ibid.
33. Ames diary, Aug. 31, 1863.
34. Ames diary, Sept. 2, 1863.
35. Hoyt to "Dear Parents," Aug. 24, 1863.
36. SeCheverell, *Journal History,* 78. Candy's Brigade departed Governor's Island, New York, on Sept. 8, 1863.
37. Wallace Hoyt, letter, Governor's Island, NY, Aug. 31, 1863, OHS.
38. Ames diary, Sept. 15, 1863.
39. Wallace Hoyt to "Dear Sister," Culpeper, VA, Sept. 21, 1863, OHS.
40. Ames diary, Sept. 19, 1863.
41. Ames diary, Sept. 22, 1863. The rebels were celebrating Bragg's victory at the battle of Chickamauga, which was fought Sept. 19–20, 1863. John Rupp of Company I recalled the rebel celebration on the banks of the Rapidan in "Fighting Regiment."
42. Ames diary, Sept. 27, 1863.

The Grandest Feat of the War

43. Hart, "Draft Riots."
44. Thayer, "Railroad Feat."
45. Ames diary, Sept. 30, 1863.
46. Ames diary, Oct. 2, 1863.
47. Ames diary, Oct. 3, 1863.
48. Ames diary, Oct. 5, 1863.
49. Wallace Hoyt to "Dear Mother and Sister," Murfreesboro, TN, Oct. 9, 1863, OHS.
50. Cass Nims to "Dear Mother," Nov. 19, 1863, Nims pension file, RG 94, NA.

The Road Down to Chattanooga

51. Ames diary, Oct. 25, 1863.
52. Ames diary, Oct. 13, 1863.
53. Sandburg, *War Years,* 2:451.
54. Roseboom, *Civil War Era,* 421.
55. "Home Vote of Ohio—Official," *Sentinel,* Nov. 18, 1863.
56. "The Full Vote of Ohio on Governor, Including the Soldier's Vote by Counties," *Sentinel,* Dec. 2, 1863.
57. Unsigned letter, Normandy, TN, Oct. 14, 1863, in "How the Old 29th Voted," *Beacon,* Oct. 29, 1863.
58. Roseboom, *Civil War Era,* 421.
59. Ibid.
60. Geary to Mary Geary, Oct. 18, 1863, in Geary, *Politician,* 126. Geary informed his wife he had that day returned from a four-day tour of the railroad. Ames gives the date of Geary's visit to Normandy as Oct. 15, 1863. Ames diary, Oct. 15, 1863.
61. Ames diary, Oct. 15, 1863.
62. Ames diary, Oct. 18, 1863.
63. Ames diary, Oct. 24, 1863. While the Twenty-Ninth waited for rail transport down to Bridgeport, word came that guerrillas had derailed a freight train below them, at Tullahoma.
64. Ames diary, Oct. 23, 1863.
65. Ames diary, Oct. 27, 1863.
66. Ibid.

Chapter 22: The Battles around Chattanooga
Fighting by Moonlight

1. Geary, report, Nov. 5, 1863, *OR,* vol. 31, pt. 1, 112–20. This portrayal of the battle of Wauhatchie, also known as Brown's Ferry, is based on Geary's official report.
2. Ibid., 118.
3. Ames diary, Nov. 1, 1863.

"Using Us Darned Mean"

4. Ames diary, Oct. 29, 1863.
5. Ames diary, Nov. 4, 1863.
6. Ames diary, Nov. 13, 1863.
7. SeCheverell, *Journal History,* 84. SeCheverell reported both the battle of the cornfield and incidents in which the Giddings Boys traded coffee for tobacco with the rebels.
8. Chaplain Ames noted the passage of Sherman's army through Lookout Valley in his diary entry of Nov. 20, 1863.
9. Cass Nims to "Dear Mother," Nov. 19, 1863, Nims pension file, RG 94, NA.
10. Geary to Mary Geary, Oct. 8, 1863, in Geary, *Politician,* 120.
11. Geary to Mary Geary, Oct. 19, 1863, in Geary, *Politician,* 127.
12. Geary to Mary Geary, Oct. 25, 1863, in Geary, *Politician,* 129.
13. Ames diary, Nov. 17, 1863.
14. Ames diary, Nov. 19, 1863.
15. Nims to "Dear Mother," Nov. 19, 1863.
16. Ames diary, Nov. 22, 1863.

The Battle above the Clouds

17. SeCheverell, *Journal History,* 84.
18. Powell, "Battle above the Clouds."
19. SeCheverell, *Journal History,* 85.
20. Cass Nims to "Dear Mother," Nov. 26, 1863, Nims pension file, RG 94, NA.
21. Col. William T. Fitch, 29th Ohio Infantry, report, *OR,* vol. 31, pt. 2, 419–20.
22. L. Wilson, *Itinerary,* 367.
23. Ibid., 286. The battle of Ringgold, also known as Ringgold Gap, was fought on Nov. 27, 1863, and marked the conclusion of the Chattanooga campaign.
24. Ames diary, Nov. 28, 1863.
25. SeCheverell, *Journal History,* 87.
26. Ames diary, Nov. 25, 1863.
27. Christopher Beck to "Dear Mother," Chattanooga, TN, Dec. 1, 1863, Beck pension file, RG 94, NA.
28. Fitch, report, 420.
29. Ames diary, Dec. 3, 1863.

"The Instrument of Almighty God"

30. Ames diary, Nov. 5, 1863.
31. Geary to Mary Geary, Nov. 2, 1863, in Geary, *Politician,* 131.
32. Geary to Mary Geary, Dec. 4, 1863, in Geary, *Politician,* 143.
33. Ibid., 144.
34. Beck to "Dear Mother," Dec. 1, 1863.

Parmater at Home

35. Parmater diary, Aug. 29, 1863.
36. Parmater diary, Sept. 3, 1863.
37. Parmater diary, Sept. 9, 1863.
38. Parmater diary, Sept. 28, 1863.
39. Parmater diary, Nov. 24, 1863.
40. Parmater diary, Dec. 1, 1863.
41. Parmater diary, Dec. 3, 1863.
42. Parmater diary, Dec. 5, 1863.
43. Ames diary, Dec. 8, 1863.
44. Parmater diary, Dec. 13, 1863.
45. Cass Nims to "Dear Mother," Bridgeport, AL, Dec. 16, 1863, Nims pension file, RG 94, NA.
46. Nims to "Dear Mother," Nov. 26, 1863.
47. "Thanksgiving Day," *Beacon,* Nov. 26, 1863.

48. "Vote in Libby Prison," *Beacon,* Dec. 10, 1863 ("We have in our possession . . .").
49. "Teacher Examinations of Oct. 31st 1863," *Beacon,* Nov. 26, 1863.
50. *Reporter,* Dec. 9, 1863.
51. "Sheep and Wool," *Sentinel,* Dec. 2, 1863.
52. "A tax of three thousand dollars . . . ," *Telegraph,* June 4, 1864. A tax in the significant sum of $3,000 was levied against property owners in Jefferson Township.
53. "Soldiers Wives," *Telegraph,* Jan. 9, 1864.
54. "The Brave Old 29th," *Beacon,* Dec. 10, 1863.

Veteran Volunteers

55. Parmater diary, Dec. 8, 1863.
56. Fitch, letter, Wauhatchie Valley, TN, Nov. 11, 1863, in "From the 29th—A Noble Resolve," *Beacon,* Nov. 19, 1863.
57. "Our Quota—Public and Private Bounties," *Beacon,* Dec. 17, 1863. In 1862 a Federal bounty of two or three dollars was thought adequate to pull in the hesitant recruit. As 1863 came to a close, the bounties amounted to the biggest pile of cash any plain boy had ever seen. The federal government promised to pay $300 to every new man who stepped up and enlisted and $400 to the veteran who chose to stay in the army after his three-year term expired. Townships raised bounties of their own to be paid on top of the federal bounty. The citizens of Akron raised a bounty fund adequate to pay every recruit that could be credited against their quota the tidy sum of $150. Even with these unheard of financial incentives, men were not coming forward.
58. Ames diary, Dec. 14, 15, 1863.
59. Fitch, letter, Nov. 11, 1863.
60. "Flags for the 29th," *Beacon,* Sept. 3, 1863.
61. Maj. M. T. Wright, letter, Cleveland, Sept. 5, 1863, in "The New Colors for the 29th," *Beacon,* Sept. 10, 1863. Wright stated that the national colors being replaced was the flag taken from them by the enemy at Port Republic.
62. Ibid. The replacement flags had cost $175. Contributions had totaled $176, which left one dollar in Buckley's hands. The editors of the *Beacon* apparently still regarded Buckley, with his known prewar association with the Democratic Party, as one not to be trusted completely with the surplus and published an insulting reminder: "We presume [he, Buckley] will see that it inures in some shape to the benefit of the soldiers." "Colors for the 29th," *Beacon,* Sept. 24, 1863.
63. Ames diary, Dec. 10, 1863.
64. Ibid.
65. Schoonover, letter, Lookout Valley, TN, Dec. 28, 1863, in "From Capt. Schoonover . . . ," *Beacon,* Jan. 14, 1863. To calm any anxiety that the soldiers who did not reenlist would be mistreated, Schoonover wrote, "Boys who did not have the feeling to reenlist have been well-accepted in the 7th Ohio, took their ranks with them, and not considered as copperheads (as was much feared they should be)."
66. Wallace Hoyt to "Dear Folks at Home," Wauhatchie, TN, Dec. 3, 1863, OHS.
67. Schoonover, letter, Dec. 28, 1863.
68. L. Wilson, *Itinerary,* 290.
69. Ames diary, Dec. 5, 1863.
70. Ames diary, Dec. 9, 1863.
71. Ames diary, Dec. 14, 16, 1863.
72. Parmater diary, Dec. 15, 17, 1863.
73. Parmater diary, Dec. 18, 1863.
74. Ames diary, Dec. 21, 1863.
75. Schoonover reported that the forty-five soldiers who had not reenlisted would be sent to the Seventh Ohio to serve out their original enlistment terms. Schoonover, letter, Dec. 28, 1863.
76. Parmater diary, Dec. 18, 1863.
77. Wallace Hoyt to "Dear Father," Lookout Valley, TN, Dec. 21, 1863.
78. Ibid.
79. Ames diary, Dec. 24, 1863.
80. Parmater diary, Dec. 24, 1863.
81. Parmater diary, Dec. 29, 1863.

82. Ames diary, Dec. 29, 1863.
83. Parmater diary, Dec. 28, 1863.
84. "For the *Telegraph*, Cleveland, Jan. 1, 1864." *Telegraph*, Jan. 16, 1864.
85. *Telegraph*, Jan. 16, 1864.
86. Ames diary, Dec. 31, 1863.

Chapter 23: Home and Back Again
A Month at Home

1. "The close of the old year . . . ," *Telegraph*, Jan. 9, 1864.
2. Ames diary, Jan. 1, 1864.
3. Ibid.
4. Parmater diary, Jan. 1, 1864.
5. Ames diary, Jan. 14, 1864.
6. "The close of the old year . . . ," *Telegraph*, Jan. 9, 1864.
7. "The Soldiers' Banquet," *Beacon*, Feb. 4, 1864.
8. "The following names have been mustered into the service as volunteers to apply on our quota for 38 men . . . ," *Reporter*, Jan. 20, 1864.
9. Ames diary, Jan. 20, 1864. The train wreck occurred the preceding day. The *Reporter* covered this commonplace but nonetheless tragic incident, adding details and portraying Ames as something of a hero for his care of the injured. Among the grievously hurt, the train conductor's scalp had been torn from his head. Ames applied first aid and likely saved the man from bleeding to death. The citizens of Painesville sent fifty sleighs out to the site and transported the injured back to the town. Two bodies were too badly burned to be identified. The newspaper pointed out that the army surgeon Ames had tried to help had successfully eluded death on the battlefield and was "illy reconciled to being smashed to death," in a train wreck. *Reporter*, Jan. 27, 1864.
10. Ames diary, Jan. 23, 1864.
11. Ames diary, Feb. 3–4, 1864.
12. Parmater diary, Feb. 3, 1864.
13. Chaplain Lyman D. Ames, letter, Feb. 15, 1864, Nashville, TN, in "From the 29th Reg't.," *Reporter*, Feb. 24, 1864.
14. Parmater diary, Feb. 8, 1864.
15. *Telegraph*, Jan. 16, 1864.
16. Ames diary, Feb. 4, 1864.

Return to the Front

17. Ames, letter, Feb. 15, 1864.
18. Parmater diary, Feb. 13, 1864.
19. Ames, letter, Feb. 15, 1864. The details of the porch collapse at Nashville were reported in the *Beacon*, with reference to a letter from M. T. Wright, which was not printed. *Beacon*, "Accident to the 29th," Feb. 18, 1864. The incident was also reported in the *Sentinel*. Below the list of injured was a letter from Col. Fitch in which he stated his formal opinion that the barracks commander, Capt. E. C. Ellis, was negligent. "Deplorable Accident," *Sentinel*, Feb. 24, 1864.
20. Parmater diary, Feb. 14, 1864.
21. Parmater diary, Feb. 10, 1864.
22. The "special dispatch" from Washington listing the offending regiments and demanding restitution was taken from the *Pittsburgh Commercial*, and printed under "Pay Stopped" in the *Sentinel*, May 4, 1864.
23. Ames diary, Feb. 16–17, 1864. The Twenty-Ninth Regiment arrived in Bridgeport at midnight on either Feb. 15 or 16. The intense cold of that night and the night following, and the attendant suffering of the men is also noted by Parmater in his diary, Feb. 15–16, 1864.

Winter Camp 1864

24. Parmater diary, Mar. 2, 1864.
25. Ames diary, Feb. 26, 1864.
26. Ames diary, Mar. 24–25, 1864.
27. Parmater diary, Mar. 2, 1864.

28. Parmater diary, Feb. 25, 1864.
29. Parmater diary, Mar. 14, 1864.
30. Parmater diary, Mar. 4, 1864.
31. Ames diary, Feb. 22, 1864.
32. Parmater diary, Mar. 4, 1864. On this day General Geary ordered the construction of a ring of earthen forts around Bridgeport.
33. Parmater diary, Mar. 30, 1864.
34. Parmater diary, Mar. 29, 1864.
35. Elias Roshon to "Dear Father and Mother," Bridgeport, AL, Feb. 26, 1864.
36. Cass Nims, letter, Bridgeport, AL, Apr. 30, 1864, Nims pension file, RG 94, NA.
37. Ellis Green to sister and parents, Bridgeport, AL, Mar. 27, 1864, Green pension file, RG 94, NA.
38. Roshon to "Dear Father and Mother," Feb. 26, 1864.

A Religious Revival on the Tennessee

39. Ames diary, Mar. 7, 1864.
40. Ames diary, Mar. 14, 1864. The original of the Ames diary has never been located. In the typed rendering of it, the transcriptionist, apparently in faithfulness to the original, typed the name of the mystery guest at his service as Ames had recorded it: "S_ _ _ _n," which the transcriptionist believed stood for "Sherman," as in Gen. W. T. Sherman. Sherman's presence there would have been significant enough for others to have noted it, which they did not. Given Captain Stevens's supposed disinclination toward matters religious, the reference obviously was to him and not to Sherman.
41. Ames diary, Mar. 27, 1864.
42. Ames diary, Mar. 22, 1864.

A Hard Thing to See

43. Parmater diary, Mar. 24, 1864. On Feb. 19, 1864, Parmater observed a group made up of females entirely, camped out in the open.
44. Parmater diary, Apr. 1, 1864.
45. Haynes diary, Mar. 16, 19, 20, 1864.
46. Ames diary, Mar. 31, 1864.
47. Parmater diary, Mar. 17–18, 1864.
48. Wallace Hoyt to "Dear Father," Bridgeport, AL, Feb. 29, 1864, Hoyt pension file, RG 94, NA.
49. Franklin Potter to "Kind Parents," Bridgeport, AL, Apr. 25, 1864, Potter pension file, RG 94, NA.
50. Ellis Green to "Dear Sister and Parents," Bridgeport, AL, Mar. 27, 1864, Green pension file, RG 94, NA.
51. Green to "Dear Sister and Parents," Bridgeport, AL, Apr. 5, 1864, Green pension file, RG 94, NA.
52. Parmater diary, Apr. 9, 1864. The emissary was a Mr. Warner of Kelloggsville, Ashtabula County, Ohio.

A Death in His Family

53. Wallace Hoyt to "Dear Father and Sister," Bridgeport, AL, Mar. 24, 1864, OHS.
54. Ibid.
55. Affidavit of H. E. Wooden, Co. A, 29th OVVI, affidavit, Hoyt pension file, RG 94, NA.
56. Wallace Hoyt to "Dear Sister," Bridgeport, AL, Mar. 28, 1864, OHS.
57. Hoyt to "Dear Father," Feb. 29, 1864.
58. Hoyt to "Dear Sister," Bridgeport, AL, Mar. 7, 1864, OHS.
59. Hoyt to "Dear Father and Sister," Mar. 24, 1864.

The Bridgeport Cotillion

60. Parmater diary, Mar. 31, 1864.
61. Rumors that they might return yet to the Army of the Potomac were reported by several soldiers, Nathan Parmater among them.
62. Potter to "Kind Parents," Apr. 25, 1864.
63. Green to "Dear Sister and Parents," Mar. 27, 1864.
64. Parmater diary, Apr. 19, 1864.
65. Parmater diary, Apr. 13, 1864.

66. Ibid.
67. Hoyt to "Dear Father and Sister," Mar. 24, 1864.
68. Parmater diary, Apr. 24, 1864.
69. Parmater diary, Apr. 15, 1864.
70. Parmater diary, Apr. 17, 1864.

"There Is Something There to Be Done"

71. Parmater diary, Apr. 8, 1864.
72. Commanding Brig. Gen. John Geary, Order Book, Regimental Books, 29th OVI, Apr. 5, 1864, NA.
73. Col. William T. Fitch, Order Book, Regimental Books, 29th OVI, Apr. 21, 1864, NA.
74. Parmater diary, May 2, 1864.
75. Cass Nims to his father, Louisville, KY, Feb. 10, 1864, Nims pension file, RG 94, NA. Cass did not properly estimate the severity of the Tennessee winter and sent his coat back home on the way down to Bridgeport.
76. Allen Mason to "Dear Mother," Bridgeport, AL, Apr. 26, 1864, Mason pension file, RG 94, NA.
77. Ibid.
78. Parmater diary, Apr. 29, 1864.
79. "The War—By News from Chattanooga . . . ," *Telegraph*, Jan. 30, 1864.
80. Parmater diary, May 3, 1864.
81. Cass Nims to "Dear Parents," Apr. 30, 1864, Nims pension file, RG 94, NA.
82. Rupp, "Fighting Regiment."

Chapter 24: "They Called It a Demonstration"
Across the Tennessee

1. Parmater diary, May 3, 1864. The town of Shell Mound (Shellmound), TN, as the boys of the regiment knew it, no longer exists. The town was alive and thriving through the 1930s. It was mostly inundated by the backwaters of Nickajack Dam built by the Tennessee Valley Authority in the 1960s. Nearby Nickajack Cave, considered by the soldiers to be a true natural wonder, was drowned by the same flood control project and is off limits except to divers.
2. Geary to "My Dearest Mary," Pea Vine, ten miles west of Dalton, GA, May 6, 1864, in Geary, *Politician*, 170.
3. Parmater diary, May 3, 1864.
4. Geary to "My Dearest Mary," May 6, 1864.
5. Geary, report, *OR*, vol. 38, pt. 2, 114.
6. Parmater diary, May 5, 1864.
7. Parmater diary, May 3, 1864.
8. Geary to "Dearest Mary," Mar. 4, 1864, Bridgeport, AL.
9. Downer, *Ohio Troops*, 26.
10. Parmater diary, May 5, 1864.
11. Ames diary, May 6, 1864.
12. Ames diary, May 7, 1864.
13. Ibid. In his official report of the campaign Geary gave the name of their last night's camp before the Dug Gap fight as "Thornton's farm." *OR*, vol. 38, pt. 2, 114.
14. Parmater diary, May 7, 1864.

A Year Ago at Chancellorsville

15. Ames diary, May 8, 1864.
16. Adj. James B. Storer to Commissioner of Pensions, Jan. 11, 1902, Storer pension file, RG 94, NA.

Orders from the Top

17. Perkins (Hooker's assistant adjutant general) to Geary, May 8, 1864, 10:30 a.m., *OR*, vol. 38, pt. 4, 76.
18. Sherman to Thomas, May 7, 1864, *OR*, vol. 38, pt. 4, 56.
19. Hooker to Whipple, Chief of Staff, May 8, 1864, 9:30 a.m., *OR*, vol. 38, pt. 4, 76.
20. Thomas to Sherman, May 8, 1864, 6 p.m., *OR*, vol. 38, pt. 4, 70.
21. After surveying the situation at Hooker's headquarters Thomas wrote to Sherman, "From what I saw today I think Geary will prevent enemy from getting in rear of McPherson. Such orders were given and for him

to feel up Hall's [Dug] Gap to see if the enemy occupied it in force, and if not to seize and hold until he could get re-enforcements." Thomas to Sherman, May 8, 1864. There was considerable confusion as to the name of the Gap through Rocky Face Ridge by which the road passed into Dalton. It is given variously in the Federal dispatches of that day as Rocky Face Ridge, Hall's Gap, Babb's Gap, John's Mountain, and Dug Gap. General Thomas referred to it as "Hall's Gap," the logic of which Geary explained in his official report: "The main road from Lafayette to Dalton crosses Mill Creek at Hall's Mill, thence winds up the steep ascent to an elevation of 800 feet from the valley, and there crosses over the ridge." Geary, report, 114.

22. Parmater diary, May 8, 1864.

Test by Attack

23. Geary, report, 114.

24. Rupp, "Fighting Regiment."

25. After giving a detailed description of the ominous topography of Dug Gap, Geary stated that he scanned the ridge *while* his soldiers were preparing the attack. In addition to the impenetrable natural defenses, he could now see the rebels moving about behind substantial breastworks, but despite these observations he did nothing to call off or modify the attack. Geary, report, 115.

26. SeCheverell, *Journal History,* 90.

27. Ibid.

28. Geary, report, 115.

29. L. Wilson, *Itinerary,* 296.

30. Geary, report, 115.

31. SeCheverell, *Journal History,* 90.

32. Breckinridge, "Atlanta Campaign." Breckenridge commanded the Ninth Kentucky Cavalry, which had arrived at Dug Gap the day before the fight. From his position up in the gap, Breckenridge observed the approach of Geary's division from across the valley. It had been Breckenridge's pickets who had ridden back into the gap after encountering Geary's skirmishers around the Babb farm on Mill Creek.

To the Top by Hard Ways

33. Geary, report, 115. Geary stated, "The general line of advance had inclined at an angle toward the Dalton road and my extreme left was now across it. The atmosphere was hot and stifling, and the ascent was one of the greatest difficulty. After a halt of fifteen minutes, the palisades were charged impetuously by portions of both brigades, Buschbeck's on the right and Candy's on both sides of the road."

34. In his official report, Myron T. Wright stated that the Twenty-Ninth had taken position on the *left* and not the right of the road, as Geary stated, when the Union line started up the ridge, and were thus separated at the very start from all other regiments making the assault. M. Wright, report, *OR,* vol. 38, pt. 2, 181.

35. Maj. Charles C. Cresson, 73rd Pa. Volunteers, report, *OR,* vol. 38, pt. 2, 256. Several participants reported the rout of the Twenty-Eighth Pennsylvania, but Cresson, who commanded the regiment to the immediate right, was the only one to name them in his after-battle report. SeCheverell did not identify the regiment, stating only that "a" regiment was, for some reason, moving by the left flank directly in front of them when the first rebel volley struck, sending its terrified soldiers back through the Twenty-Ninth Ohio. SeCheverell, *Journal History,* 90. The Twenty-Eighth Pa. rallied soon after and got back into the fight.

36. *Beacon,* May 26, 1864. Chaplain Ames commented on the nature of wounds sustained by the Giddings soldiers at Dug Gap. Appended to his letter were the names of the regiment's killed and wounded, making the longest casualty list of the war to appear in a Summit County or Ashtabula County newspaper. Ames, letter, May 14, 1864, under "We have just received the following from Chaplain Ames . . ." *Reporter, May 25, 1864.* Geary was criticized for imprudence in ordering his line up the mountain end-on, rather than parallel to the rebel works at the top, thus exposing the entire line to an enfilading fire; which sounded reasonable, but which the terrain would have made impossible. "Return of Messrs. Storer and Lantz," *Beacon,* May 26, 1864.

37. Myron T. Wright, letter, woods near Mill Creek, GA, May 10, 1864, in "The Killed and Wounded of the 29th," *Beacon,* May 26, 1864. Wright stated that Fitch, Hayes, and Storer fell in the early part of the engagement. In his official report of the fight at Dug Gap, Wright understates the importance of his order that the line of the regiment be swung like a gate. *OR,* vol. 38, pt. 2, 181. Without doubt, this unlikely maneuver, carried out under intense, close-range gunfire, saved many lives, since it stopped the enfilading of the regiment's entire line. Normally loquacious, Wright was a capable writer and a keen observer of detail. However, he covered the

regiment's ordeal at Dug Gap in just a dozen sentences. Wright wrote his report on the regiment's part in the Atlanta campaign from a hospital bed in Atlanta, where he was recovering from yet another wound and some undiagnosed camp disease. He was also trying to come to grips with the recent death of his best friend, Capt. George Dice, killed in action at Pine Knob, as well as the possible end of his own military career.

38. Ibid.
39. Ibid.
40. Breckinridge, "Atlanta Campaign," 278.
41. Ibid., 279.
42. Ibid., 278.
43. Ibid., 279.

Against Hope

44. Geary, report, 115. Vestiges of the saucers the Twenty-Ninth's soldiers scooped out to protect themselves, the lip on the uphill edge to divert rebel gunfire, can still be seen on the slope of Dug Gap.
45. That the Twenty-Ninth Ohio expected to be supported after reaching the rebel line is stated in SeCheverell, *Journal History,* 91; M. Wright, report, 181.
46. Geary, report, 115. The regiments of Candy's brigade assigned to guard McGill's battery were the Fifth and Sixty-Sixth Ohio and the 147th Pennsylvania.
47. Geary, report, 116. Geary reported that he sent the Fifth and Sixty-Sixth Ohio Regiments to the Twenty-Ninth's support left of the road near the gap. But by then it was nearly dark and the boys of both sides too exhausted to continue the struggle. The Fifth and Sixty-Sixth did perform valiant service by covering the Twenty-Ninth's retreat off the slope and carrying off the dead and wounded.
48. M. Wright, letter, May 10, 1864.
49. Ibid.
50. Geary, report, 115–16.
51. Ibid., 116.
52. Camp near Mill Creek Gap, Ga., May 10, 1864, in "The Campaign in Georgia: Geary's Division in the Battle at Rocky Face Ridge—A Desperate Fight of Five Hours—The Losses, &c.," *Philadelphia Press,* June 2, 1864.
53. M. Wright, report, 181.
54. Geary, report, 116.
55. M. Wright, report, 181.
56. SeCheverell, *Journal History,* 91.
57. Ibid. Pvt. John Davis, Company B, would be wounded in subsequent battles at New Hope Church and Pine Knob. He survived the war and mustered out with his company.

Body Counting

58. *State Roster.* Twenty soldiers were listed as killed in action and another twelve to sixteen died of wounds sustained at Dug Gap. Sixty of the wounded survived, many of them too severely disabled to return to the regiment. The *State Roster* and SeCheverell are frequently at odds, especially so over the distinction between "killed in battle" or "died of wounds."
59. Geary, report, 116.
60. Ibid.
61. Breckinridge, "Atlanta Campaign," 279.
62. Geary to Mary Geary, Babb's Gap, four miles west of Dalton, GA, May 9, 1864, in Geary, *Politician,* 172.
63. M. Wright, letter, May 10, 1864.
64. Asst. Surg. Elwood P. Haines, diary, May 9, 1864.
65. Surg. H. Ernest Goodman, report, *OR,* vol. 38, pt. 2, 148–49.
66. Edward Hayes pension file, RG 94, NA.
67. William T. Fitch pension file, RG 94, NA.
68. James B. Storer pension file, RG 94, NA; J. E. Herbst, Surgeon in Charge, USA General Hospital, Nashville, TN, statement, June 3, 1865, Storer pension file.
69. "Return of Messrs. Storer and Lantz," *Beacon,* May 26, 1864. The party left for Nashville on Friday, May 13, 1864.

70. "Adjutant Storer at Home," *Beacon,* Aug. 18, 1864.
71. Sgt. Newton B. Adams, letter, USA General Hospital, Jeffersonville, IN, May 24, 1864, in "From the Twenty-Ninth," *Sentinel,* June 1, 1864.

In the Johnson Garden

72. Ames diary, May 9, 1864.
73. Green's given name was Thomas E. Green. Everyone called him by his middle name, Ellis.
74. Charles Galpin, 29th OVI, affidavit, Mason pension file, RG 94, NA.
75. Ames diary, May 10, 1864.
76. "The Twenty-Ninth," *Sentinel,* May 18, 1864.
77. Ibid.
78. George Dice to "Dear Mother," June 6, 1864, Dice pension file, RG 94, NA.

"It Is What Has Happened"

79. Lyman Ames, letter, May 9, 1864, in *Reporter,* May 25, 1864.
80. M. Wright, letter, May 10, 1864.
81. *State Roster.* Frederick Remley, age twenty-four, German-born corporal in Company D, was killed in action at Port Republic. That Frederick and Christian were brothers was confirmed by Sgt. John A. Kummer, in "A Tribute to the Departed Heroes of the 29th by an Old Comrade," *Beacon,* June 16, 1864.
82. Kummer, "Tribute."
83. Ibid.
84. Jerome L. Phinney to "Dear Father," May 14, 1864, Phinney pension file, RG 94, NA.
85. Kummer, "Tribute."
86. "Return of Messrs. Storer and Lantz," *Beacon,* May 26, 1864. "Nearly all of those killed or wounded in that charge were hit upon the right side, the brigade having been very imprudently ordered by Gen. Geary to charge by left oblique, up a steep hill, as at Missionary Ridge, in the face of deadly plunging fire, without sending out skirmishers, as it is alleged he stated, on giving the order, had already been done."
87. "Campaign in Georgia," *Philadelphia Press,* June 2, 1864.
88. Hooker to Chief of Staff Brig. Gen. Whipple, May 8, 1864, 9 p.m., *OR,* vol. 38, pt. 4, 80.
89. At 6 p.m. on the evening of Geary's assaults on Dug Gap, when Maj. Gen. George H. Thomas sent a telegram to Maj. Gen. Sherman, Thomas did not yet know whether Geary's efforts had succeeded or failed—"Have not heard result of Geary's reconnaissance yet." He used the word "reconnaissance" twice in this dispatch to characterize the maneuver he had ordered of Generals Butterfield at Buzzard's Roost and Geary at Dug Gap. *OR,* vol. 38, pt. 4, 70.
90. The Twenty-Ninth Ohio's tragedy at Dug Gap might have been traceable to any number of forces working within John White Geary, or a combination of all of them: distraction with his son's death, coupled with the belief that God had made him an avenging angel; his belief that he was entitled to a higher rank and that one more grand victory like the one he claimed for himself at Lookout Mountain would make it impossible for his superiors *not* to promote him; or, he may simply have been an incompetent battle commander.
91. "Help for our Wounded—Old Cotton and Linen Wanted," in *Beacon,* May 26, 1864.
92. The battle of Resaca was fought May 13–16, 1864.
93. Sgt. Newton B. Adams, letter, "From the Twenty-Ninth, Jeffersonville [IN]," May 24, 1864, in "To the Editor of the Sentinel," *Sentinel,* June 1, 1864.
94. "F," letter, "Another Akron Boy Gone," *Beacon,* June 30, 1864. After his wounding at Dug Gap, Pvt. Charles Downey was taken up the line to Ringgold, Georgia, where he died in an army hospital on May 14, 1864. *State Roster.* Downey's best friend, Curtis Lantz, was killed at Dug Gap. His body was never recovered.

Chapter 25: Continuous Battle
The Guns of Resaca

1. SeCheverell, *Journal History,* 94.
2. Rupp, "Fighting Regiment"; Geary, report, *OR,* vol. 38, pt. 2, 118.
3. SeCheverell, *Journal History,* 95.
4. Kilpatrick, "Fifth Ohio." As to which regiment had secured the rebel guns and brought them into Geary's line, Kilpatrick stated, "From the time we relieved the One Hundred and Eleventh Pennsylvania at the top of the

hill until the guns were out and away, I never saw an officer or man of any regiment excepting our own and the fifty men under an officer of the Thirty-third New Jersey and the aide-decamp." Finally, Col. George Cobham, who was in overall command of the party, stated that it had been the Fifth Ohio, assisted by men of the Thirty-Third New Jersey, that pulled the captured artillery into the Federal line. *OR,* vol. 38, pt. 2, 278.

5. Capt. Myron T. Wright, 29th OVI, report, *OR,* vol. 38, pt. 2, 181–82.
6. Hart, "Cowboys."
7. "A Rebel View of the Situation," Beacon, June 23, 1864.
8. Brig. Gen. John W. Geary, commanding Second Division, report, *OR,* vol. 38, pt. 2, 121.
9. M. Wright, report, 182.
10. Ames diary, May 17, 1864.
11. Ames diary, May 18, 1864.
12. Ames diary, May 19, 1864.

Death Finds Their Patron

13. Julian, *Giddings,* 395. The date of Giddings's death is given by his son-in-law biographer as May 27, 1864, which may have been a typographic error. The *Sentinel* published news of his death and of his funeral, in Jefferson, on May 25, 1864, which means Giddings died some time before that.
14. "Death of Mr. Giddings," *Sentinel,* May 25, 1864.
15. Giddings to Joseph Addison Giddings, Dec. 12, 1863, Giddings Papers.
16. *Reporter,* Aug. 3, 1864.
17. "Soda Fountain," *Telegraph,* June 4, 1864.
18. "To be Moved," *Sentinel,* Nov. 25, 1863.
19. "Unseemly Extravagance," *Reporter,* May 25, 1864.
20. "The Ladies National Covenant," *Beacon,* May 19, 1864. The wealthy women of Akron who joined this organization were not representative of all women, most of whom continued to face hard economic circumstances caused by the absence of their men. A citizen riding through Tallmadge saw two women plowing—one driving a team of horses, the other holding the plow. Of such backbreaking, likely desperate work, the *Beacon* editor said, "Let their noble example be imitated." "Women as Field Laborers," *Beacon,* May 12, 1864.
21. "Capt. E. B. Howard . . . ," Reporter, Jan. 20, 1864.
22. "Port of Conneaut," *Reporter,* Dec. 30, 1863.
23. "All Hands to Work," *Beacon,* May 26, 1864.
24. "Women and Field Laborers," *Beacon,* May 12, 1864.
25. "A Faithful Dog on the Battlefield," *Beacon,* July 3, 1862.
26. "Another Empty Sleeve," *Beacon,* Aug. 18, 1864.

The Disappearance of Wallace Hoyt

27. Hoyt pension file, RG 94, NA.
28. Ames diary, May 22, 1864.
29. Ames diary, May 20, 1864.

The Battle of New Hope Church

30. A detailed route of their march to Burnt Hickory, Georgia, and the difficulties encountered are found in Geary, report, 122.
31. Ibid.
32. The day's final attack near New Hope Church by Candy's brigade was documented by General Geary in his official report, 124.
33. M. Wright, report, 182.
34. Ames diary, May 25–26, 1864.
35. Rupp, "Fighting Regiment."
36. Ames diary, May 27, 1864.
37. SeCheverell, *Journal History,* 100.
38. Ames diary, May 27, 1864.
39. SeCheverell, *Journal History,* 102.
40. Ibid.

41. Ames diary, May 29, 1864.

42. SeCheverell, *Journal History,* 102.

43. Ames diary, May 26, 1864. SeCheverell, *Journal History,* 282, reported that six men were killed at Dallas, Georgia, which corresponds to the number listed as killed in action in the *State Roster*. William Fox based his casualty lists on returns filed with the Adjutant General's Office; the same source was utilized by the compilers of the *State Roster,* but in his "Fighting 300 Regiments," he lists the number of Twenty-Ninth soldiers killed in the fighting around New Hope Church as two, which proved to be an error. Fox, *Regimental Losses,* 319.

44. Ames diary, June 1, 1864. Ames had good basis for detailing the Twenty-Ninth's casualties. He had access to the records of the regimental, brigade, and division hospitals where he spent most of his time. As part of his ex-officio duties, Chaplain Ames contributed some of his time to clerking on the regiment's books. He based his count of their casualties in the Atlanta campaign to this date on returns submitted by each company.

45. Ames diary, June 1, 1864.

Big Shanty

46. Ames diary, June 3, 1864.

47. Ames diary, June 5, 1864.

48. Ames diary, June 8, 1864.

49. Geary to Mary Geary, June 8, 1864, in Geary, *Politician,* 179.

50. Staging here below Allatoona Pass were the Fourth, Fourteenth, Twentieth, and Twenty-Third Army Corps. Geary, report, 125–27.

51. Ames diary, June 11, 1864.

52. Ames diary, June 9, 1864.

53. Charles Candy, report, *OR,* vol. 38, pt. 2, 156. Charles Candy stated that their duty here had been to support the Twenty-Third Corps.

54. Ames diary, June 10, 1864.

55. Geary to Mary Geary, June 8, 1864.

56. Ames diary, June 10, 1864. In his official report of the Atlanta campaign, Myron Wright gave the location of their camp near Acworth, GA, as being opposite the southeast corner of the Adams house, with its left on Big Shanty Road. M. Wright, report, 183.

The Makings of a Nightmare

57. SeCheverell stated that this was not their first look at Pine Knob. Two days earlier, the entire regiment had come down from Big Shanty to reconnoiter the rebel line and had found the rebels strongly entrenched. SeCheverell, *Journal History,* 104. In the official reports of their layover near Acworth, neither their brigade commander, Charles Candy, nor their own commander, Myron Wright, mentioned this reconnaissance. Geary stated that he had skirmishers from his command out front of the Federal line while at Acworth for the purpose of "feeling" the rebel defenses on the Brush Mountain–Pine Knob line, but he did not identify the units engaged in that work. Geary, report, 126.

58. Ames noted the time of this artillery fire aimed at the top of Pine Knob as 1:00 p.m., June 14, 1864.

59. The accepted account of the killing of General Polk was that Sherman had observed the collection of rebel officers atop Pine Knob and pointed out their presence to General Howard of the Fourth Corps. Howard ordered the Fifth Indiana Battery to fire.

60. Geary, report, 127.

61. Ibid.

62. Ibid.

63. M. Wright, report, 183.

64. Candy, report, 156.

65. Ibid.

66. SeCheverell, *Journal History,* 105.

67. M. Wright, report, 183.

68. The circumstances of George Dice's wounding and death were reported by Lt. George Halloway, letter, in "Casualties in the 29th Reg't OVI," *Beacon,* July 14, 1864.

69. SeCheverell, *Journal History,* 105.

70. Ibid.

71. Geary, report, 128.

72. Rollin L. Jones pension file, RG 94, NA.
73. M. Wright, report, 183.
74. Geary, report, 128.
75. Candy, report, 157.
76. "Casualties in the Twenty-Ninth," *Sentinel,* July 13, 1864. This list for the regiment's known losses at Pine Knob, GA, was supplied to the newspaper by Capt. E. J. Hurlburt.
77. The *State Roster* lists the names of nine of the Twenty-Ninth's soldiers as killed in action at Pine Knob, or Pine Mountain, as it was also called.
78. Ames diary, June 16, 1864.
79. Ibid.
80. Geary, report, 131.
81. Ames recorded the names of places camped at in this period in his diary.

The Battle of Kolb's Farm

82. Geary, report, 183.
83. SeCheverell, *Journal History,* 109.
84. M. Wright, report, 183. Maj. Myron Wright summed up their participation in the battle of Kolb's Farm with these few words: "At 10 a.m. 22nd moved to the front one mile; took position on a hill in open field near Kennesaw Mountain; threw up heavy works, Twenty-ninth fourth battalion of First Brigade; had some fighting, but no casualties in Twenty-ninth; remained here. Nothing of importance transpired until 7 p.m. [June] 27th." Brigade commander Charles Candy gave the events of June 22 in his front in an equally short form: "June 22, two regiments were thrown forward to take position on a range of hills in our immediate front, on which were posted the enemy's skirmishers; drove them off, and the rest of the brigade moved forward to occupy the hill and intrench, which was done." Candy, report, 157.
85. C. L. Stevenson, CSA, report, *OR,* vol. 38, pt. 3, 815.
86. SeCheverell, *Journal History,* 109–10. According to SeCheverell, Griswold's squad had charged across an open field, under fire the whole way, been in combat at close quarters while in the rebel breastworks, and then returned to their line under heavy fire. Amazingly, not one of them had been hurt; if any had been, SeCheverell did not report it. Chaplain Ames was at the hospital not far in the rear; he was startled by the fierceness of the artillery firing and noted its time. After the big guns went quiet, gunfire did not spark up anywhere within his hearing, including the part of the rebel line that Griswold stormed. There is nothing in the official record, including the reports of Candy and their own commander, Myron T. Wright, to corroborate this daring feat, which is not to say it did not happen just as SeCheverell claimed.
87. Ames diary, June 23, 1864.
88. Ames diary, June 28, 1864. George Williams, Company F, was buried on a hillside along the Sandtown Road, close by the tenant's house on the Dobbs place.

The Battle of Kennesaw Mountain

89. Geary, report, 134.
90. M. Wright, report, 183.
91. The taking of the rebel blockhouse was also reported by Pvt. John Rupp, Company I, 29th OVI, in "Fighting Regiment."
92. O. Wilson, "Medal of Honor." Wilson could not recall the name of the French-born member of Company F who died of wounds during the storming of the sharpshooter's nest during the battle of Kennesaw Mountain. None of the sources listing the regiment's casualties in this period confirm the wounding or death of this unidentified soldier. Any medal of honor Wilson and the others were given was likely devised by the army or corps. One hundred forty-three Ohio Civil War soldiers were awarded the Congressional Medal of Honor, but no soldier of the Twenty-Ninth Ohio appears on that elite list. Harper, *Ohio Handbook,* 15–22.
93. Capt. Rb't Kurkup, 5th OVI, *OR,* vol. 38, pt. 2, 173.
94. Rupp, "Fighting Regiment."

Atlanta Skyline

95. Geary, report, 135.
96. Ames diary, July 1, 2, 1864.

97. Ames diary, July 3, 1864.
98. SeCheverell, *Journal History*, 114.
99. Ames diary, July 4, 1864.
100. "Old Hundred in Camp," *Reporter*, July 27, 1864.
101. Scaife, *Campaign for Atlanta*. The reference is to Mr. Scaife's map, "Federal Approaches to the River Line," following page 82 in his book.
102. Geary, report, 136.
103. Ames diary, July 8, 1864.
104. Geary, report, 136. Geary stated that the rebels deserted the fortifications in his front and crossed the river during the evening of July 9, 1864.
105. That such meetings between pickets of the opposing sides occurred along the Chattahoochee is reported in SeCheverell in *Journal History*, 115, and by Chaplain Ames, who apparently saw it for himself on July 13, 1864. Ames diary, July 13, 1864.
106. James B. Storer's certificate of death gives the cause of his death as gunshot wound. Storer pension file, RG 94, NA.
107. SeCheverell, *Journal History*, 115. No precise number can be given to the Twenty-Ninth's total losses to this point in the Atlanta campaign except for those killed outright or who died of disease whose names appeared in the *State Roster*. SeCheverell prepared a table giving casualties in the regiment for the entire war. *Journal History*, 282. He obtained his data from the U.S. army, Adjutant General's Office, and from the adjutant general of Ohio (p. 10), in theory the same sources used by William Fox in his statistical summary of the war's important numbers. SeCheverell's table lists 42 killed in action, 132 wounded, and 4 missing for a total of 178 in the period from Dug Gap through Kennesaw Mountain.
108. SeCheverell, *Journal History*, 115.
109. "Superficial Glances," *Reporter*, July 6, 1864. "We went to Jefferson the other day . . ."
110. "The Bounty Fund," *Beacon*, Dec. 24, 1863.
111. "The *Warren Chronicle* says . . . ," *Reporter*, June 15, 1864. A drafted man was not eligible to collect any bounty, federal or local, but a scheme erected in Portage Township, Summit County, made a neat detour around that restriction. Not as boldly evasive of the draft as the Mutual Protective Association, but well thought out to maximize the financial benefit to a man in the unhappy event that he was conscripted. All a draft-eligible man need do was to subscribe his payment of thirty dollars to the township bounty fund. For that small hedge bet, the fund guaranteed that if he were drafted, they would pay him the same bounty paid a volunteer. "The Bounty Fund," *Beacon*, Dec. 17, 1863.
112. "Our Quota—Public and Private Bounties," *Beacon*, Dec. 17, 1863.
113. Geary, report, 136.

Chapter 26: Closing on the Prize

The Diarist Returns

1. Parmater diary, May 28, 1864.
2. Parmater returned to his regiment on Aug. 9, 1864.

The Battle of Peach Tree Creek

3. Geary, report, 136.
4. Ibid., 137.
5. Ibid.
6. Ibid., 138.
7. Clarke, "Peach Tree Creek."
8. Geary, report, 137.
9. Col. Charles Candy, report, *OR*, vol. 38, pt. 2, 158. Colonel Candy complained in his official report that his boys had been placed in this dangerous circumstance by the failure of Williams's division to protect his left.
10. Capt. M. T. Wright, 29th OVI, report, *OR*, vol. 38, pt. 2, 184.
11. Candy, report, 158.
12. Geary, report, 140.
13. W. F. Stevens, commanding 29th OVI, report, *OR*, vol. 38, pt. 2, 185.
14. Candy, report, 158.

15. Clarke, "Peach Tree Creek."
16. Peter Dowling pension file, RG 94, NA.
17. Thomas Dowling pension file, RG 94, NA.
18. Ibid.
19. Russell Shaw of Toledo, Iowa, and his wife spent a pleasant weekend at my home in Minneapolis in 1995.
20. Geary, report, 140.
21. Ibid.
22. Ibid., 141.
23. Geary was inclined to exaggerate the rebel casualties in front of his line. Livermore calculated that the rebels sustained about 2,500 casualties along the entire Federal line. Livermore, *Numbers and Losses,* 122. Hood left 600 dead on the field.

Siege

24. Parmater gives a detailed description of the skirmish pits in his diary entry of Aug. 11, 1864.
25. Parmater diary, Aug. 10, 1864.
26. Myron T. Wright to Col. Lewis Buckley, July 28, 1864, in "Further from the 29th," *Beacon,* Aug. 11, 1864. A second letter from Major Wright, dated July 26, 1864, was published in this edition of the *Beacon,* in which he thanked the ladies of Akron for their contributions to the sanitary commission, the benefits of which were clearly seen in Geary's division hospital, in which he was currently a patient. He assured the readers that their donations were dispensed on an equal footing to both officers and enlisted men, dispelling the rumor that the officers got all the best things from home, while the men in the ranks got only what the government provided. He also thanked Dr. Amos Fifield for having spared no effort in making hospital life more comfortable for officers and enlisted men.
27. Scaife, *Campaign for Atlanta.* The location of the rebels' Dahlgren gun is found in Scaife's map "Civil War Atlanta Summer of 1864," following page 130.
28. The *State Roster,* 368, gives Christopher Beck's date of death as Sept. 16, 1864.
29. Sgt. Cains C. Lord to "Dear Father," Aug. 1864, copy provided by courtesy of his descendant Greg Wickenburg, Brier, WA.
30. Parmater diary, Aug. 15, 1864.
31. Parmater diary, Aug. 16, 1864.
32. Parmater diary, Aug. 19, 1864.
33. Ames diary, Aug. 19, 1864.
34. Geary to his wife, Aug. 11, 1864, in Geary, *Politician,* 195–96.
35. Ames diary, Aug. 13, 1864.
36. Parmater diary, Aug. 22, 1864.
37. In his diary entries of this period, Ames noted the fluctuations in the number of sick men in the division hospital: higher when the supply line into Atlanta was closed, lower when it was open.
38. M. Wright to Buckley, July 28, 1864. Wright, among others, noted the appearance of a form of scurvy in their camps in this period, a malady that had been observed by their division surgeon at the start of the Atlanta campaign.
39. Parmater diary, Aug. 15, 1864.
40. Ames diary, Aug. 27, 1864.
41. "Interesting to those who have friends in the Army of the Cumberland," *Beacon,* Sept. 22, 1864.
42. Ames diary, Aug. 24, 1864.
43. "Sanitary Matters," *Beacon,* Apr. 7, 1864.
44. Ames diary, Aug. 24, 1864.
45. Ames diary, Aug. 28, 1864.
46. Ames diary, Sept. 1, 1864.

Progress

47. Parmater diary, Aug. 26, 1864.
48. Geary, report, 146.
49. Parmater diary, Sept. 3, 1864.
50. Col. Charles Candy resigned as commander of the First Brigade on Aug. 10, 1864. Ario Pardee Jr. assumed command a few days earlier, Aug. 4, 1864.

51. Parmater diary, Sept. 4, 1864.
52. Ibid.
53. Pardee was the only reporting officer who gave a precise description of the position held by the First Brigade during the occupation of Atlanta. Col. Ariel Pardee Jr., commanding First Brigade, report, *OR,* vol. 38, pt. 2, 160.
54. Unfortunately, the regiment's movement from the west side to the east side of Atlanta, to the place where they would spend the fall of 1864, is not given by the regimental commander, Capt. Wilbur F. Stevens, in his official report, likely owing to confusion as to whether he or Myron Wright, who was convalescing nearby, was responsible for reporting in this period. Ario Pardee Jr., commander of the First Brigade, did not mention the regiments of his command as holding any place other than the line west of the city. The Giddings Regiment's movements during this period of occupation were likely the same as those reported by the commander of the 147th Pennsylvania: "We took up the line of march at 9.30 a.m., reaching the city at 1 p.m. Here we were put into line of works built by the enemy on the west side of the city, where we remained until Nov. 15. We were, on account of the movement of the troops, obliged to change camp several times. We assisted in building the fortifications around the city." Lt. Col. John Craig, report, *OR,* vol. 38, pt. 2, 294.
55. Parmater diary, Sept. 6, 1864.
56. Parmater diary, Sept. 2, 1864.
57. Geary, report, 146.
58. Pardee, report, 160.

Garrison Life

59. Ames diary, Sept. 4–7, 1864.
60. Ames diary, Sept. 12, 1864.
61. Ames diary, Sept. 6, 1864.
62. Ames diary, Sept. 8, 1864.
63. Ames diary, Sept. 9, 1864.
64. Ames diary, Sept. 10, 1864.
65. Elias Roshon, letter, "Dear Mother and Father," Oct. 10, 1864.
66. Parmater diary, Oct. 10, 1864.
67. Lord to "Dear Father," Aug. 1864.
68. The full text of Sherman's message to the army was reprinted in SeCheverell, *Journal History,* 125–26.
69. Parmater diary, Sept. 23, 1864.

The Hired Men

70. Ames diary, Aug. 11, 1864.
71. "Representative Recruiting," *Reporter,* July 6, 1864.
72. Parmater diary, Sept. 14, 1864.
73. Parmater diary, Sept. 23, 1864.
74. Parmater diary, Oct. 30, 1864.
75. The *State Roster* lists 119 substitutes and 117 drafted men sent to the Twenty-Ninth Ohio in the fall of 1864. Parmater reported that a large contingent, containing 200 substitutes *and* drafted men, arrived at the regiment in Atlanta on Oct. 30, 1864.
76. Parmater diary, Oct. 12, 1864. Parmater acted as an election officer in the state elections of Oct. 11 held in their Atlanta camp. Part of his responsibility was to make a tally sheet for each county represented in the Twenty-Ninth Ohio. When it was organized back at Jefferson in 1861, soldiers came to the regiment from a half-dozen counties at most. Parmater was surprised to discover the regiment now had men in it from seventeen counties.
77. *Reporter,* Aug. 17, 1864.
78. Descriptive lists, 29th OVI, and pensioners on the rolls, NA. The circumstances under which these men found their way into the regiment is worthy of further research.
79. Parmater diary, Sept. 19, 1864.
80. Parmater diary, Sept. 25, 1864.

The Erstwhile Cowboy and Other Adventures

81. Col. Jonas Schoonover, letter, Battalion Camp Detachment, Chattanooga, TN, Sept. 14, 1864, in *Beacon,* Sept. 29, 1864.

82. Hart, "Cowboys."
83. Parmater diary, Oct. 2–4, 1864.
84. Parmater diary, Oct. 21, 1864.
85. Parmater diary, Oct. 22, 1864.
86. Geary to Mary Geary, Oct. 18, Nov. 1, 1864, in Geary, *Politician,* 208, 212.
87. Ames diary, Nov. 10, 1864. Geary gave the rebel losses in this nameless episode as 8 dead and 20 wounded. Geary to Mary Geary, Nov. 10, 1864, in Geary, *Politician,* 213.

Last Details

88. Roshon to "Dear Mother and Father," Oct. 10, 1864.
89. Parmater diary, Nov. 9, 1864. Parmater stated that a total of 384 votes had been cast by the regiment. Schoonover's diary, from which SeCheverell would quote for the remainder of his narrative, recorded an identical number. SeCheverell, *Journal History,* 127.
90. Parmater diary, Nov. 8, 1864. The boys formed a "train" to harass the unfortunate McClellan supporter. It is presumed this was something like a modern snake dance.
91. "Hurrah!" *Reporter,* Nov. 16, 1864.
92. "Grand Triumph Dance," *Beacon,* Nov. 24, 1864.
93. Parmater diary, Nov. 10, 1864.

"Where We Will Turn Up I Cannot Tell"

94. Parmater diary, Oct. 29, Nov. 2, 1864.
95. Ames diary, Nov. 7, 1864.
96. Parmater diary, Nov. 14, 1864.
97. Geary to Mary Geary, Nov. 4, 1864, in Geary, *Politician,* 213.

Chapter 27: Tearing It Up
"The Blue Juniata"

1. Lyrics by Marion Dix Sullivan.
2. Headley, *William Tecumseh Sherman,* 286. In describing the army's singing of "The Blue Juniata" at Sherman's request, Headley wrote, "The band and still another band, played a low accompaniment; camp after camp began singing; the music of 'The Blue Juniata' became for a few minutes, the oratorio of half an army." This exact phrase is found in Parmater's essay, except for his misspelling of Juniata.
3. Parmater diary, Nov. 19, 1864.
4. Ames diary, Nov. 21, 1864.
5. Parmater diary, Nov. 19, 1864.
6. Ibid.
7. Ames diary, Nov. 22, 1864.
8. Parmater diary, Nov. 23, 1864.
9. Parmater diary, Nov. 24, 1864.
10. Parmater diary, Nov. 25, 1864.
11. Parmater diary, Nov. 27, 1864.
12. Parmater diary, Nov. 26, 1864.
13. Parmater diary, Nov. 29, 1864.
14. Parmater diary, Nov. 30, 1864.
15. Ames diary, Nov. 24, 1864.
16. Myron T. Wright, report, Savannah Operations, *OR,* vol. 44, pt. 1, 288. Wright gave the date of this small action as Dec. 1. Parmater recorded it in his diary as Dec. 2, 1864.
17. Parmater diary, Dec. 3, 1864.
18. Brig. Gen. John W. Geary, report, *OR,* vol. 44, pt. 1, 274.
19. Ames diary, Nov. 28, 1864.
20. Hoyt died in the prison hospital at Andersonville, GA, on Oct. 24, 1864. Database report 21228, ref. 47 [3], 357 [418], information taken from the prison hospital records and provided by Bill Burnett, Friends of Andersonville, Andersonville National Historic Site, Andersonville, GA.
21. Parmater diary, Dec. 6, 1864.

22. Geary, report, 275.
23. Ames diary, Dec. 8, 1864.
24. Parmater diary, Dec. 11, 1864.
25. Ames diary, Dec. 11, 1864.
26. Parmater diary, Dec. 10, 1864.

Savannah Christmas

27. Parmater diary, Dec. 11, 1864.
28. Parmater diary, Dec. 12, 1864.
29. Parmater diary, Dec. 13, 1864.
30. Ibid.
31. Parmater diary, Dec. 15, 1864.
32. "Official Bulletin," *Beacon,* Dec. 22, 1864.
33. Geary, report, 282.
34. Geary, report, 271.
35. Parmater diary, Dec. 17, 1864.
36. Ames diary, Dec. 16, 1864.
37. Geary, report, 279.
38. M. T. Wright, report, 289. Wright's last official act as commander of the Twenty-Ninth Ohio was the completion of the report dated Dec. 28, 1864, on his regiment's part in the Savannah Campaign. He died ten days later.
39. Carded Medical Records, Myron T. Wright, 29th OVI, NA. Wright was wounded during the night of Dec. 19, 1864.
40. "W. E. C.," letter, post headquarters, Fort Jackson, GA, Jan. 4, 1865, in "From the 29th—Major Wright Wounded and Leg Amputated," *Beacon,* Jan. 19, 1865. The writer was likely Wilbur Chamberlain.
41. Parmater diary, Dec. 21, 1864.
42. Geary, report, 280.
43. Parmater diary, Dec. 21, 1864.
44. Col. John Flynn, Twenty-Eighth Pennsylvania Infantry, report, *OR,* vol. 44, pt. 1, 294.
45. Geary, report, 280.
46. Parmater diary, Dec. 22, 1864.
47. Ibid.
48. "Magnificent Christmas Present," *Beacon,* Dec. 29, 1864.
49. "Christmas at Cuyahoga Falls," *Beacon,* Jan. 5, 1865.
50. Parmater diary, Dec. 24, 1864.
51. Parmater diary, Dec. 25, 1864.
52. Parmater diary, Dec. 31, 1864.

"Ever a Fond Brother"

53. Dice pension file, RG 94, NA.
54. Ibid. Myron Wright's condolence letter to Dice's mother, Mrs. Susan Dice, Upper Strasburg, PA, was dated July 2, 1864, and is found in the Dice pension file, RG 94, NA.
55. Myron Wright, report, Dec. 28, 1864, *OR,* vol. 44, pt. 1, 289,
56. Halloway, letter, Jan. 8, 1865, "The Late Major Wright," *Beacon,* Feb. 23, 1865.
57. "Testimonial to Major Wright," *Beacon,* Jan. 26, 1865. A summary of Wright's war service and the details of the receipt of his remains in Akron are found under "Death of Major Wright," in the same edition.
58. "The Memory of Our Noble Dead: A Sermon Preached at the Funeral of Maj. Myron T. Wright . . . ," *Beacon,* Feb. 9, 1865.
59. John Gurnish Collection, Mogadore, Ohio.
60. "Promotions in the 29th," *Beacon,* Feb. 2, 1865.

Savannah Garrison

61. Parmater diary, Jan. 9, 1865.
62. Parmater diary, Jan. 20, 1865.
63. Parmater diary, Jan. 13, 1865.

64. Unsigned letter, Savannah, GA, Jan. 9, 1865, in "From the Glorious Old 29th—An Appeal for a New Flag," *Beacon,* Jan. 26, 1865.
65. "The New Flag for the 29th," *Beacon,* Mar. 16, 1865.
66. Parmater diary, Jan. 14, 1865.
67. Parmater diary, Jan. 20, 1865.
68. Parmater diary, Jan. 18, 1865.
69. Elias Roshon to "Dear Father and Mother," near Savannah, GA, Jan. 20, 1865.
70. Ibid.
71. Parmater diary, Jan. 21, 1865.

"The Mother State of This Rebellion"

72. Parmater diary, Jan. 25, 1865. Geary's division left Savannah on Jan. 27, 1865.
73. Brig. Gen. John W. Geary, report, *OR,* vol. 47, pt. 1, 682.
74. Parmater diary, Jan. 28, 1865.
75. Geary, report, 682.
76. Parmater diary, Jan. 30, 1865.
77. Parmater diary, Feb. 4, 1865.
78. Parmater diary, Feb. 5, 1865. He reported that in his company, Company E, only eleven were present for duty in early Feb. 1865. Nine others were still on the rolls, sick, or recovering from wounds in hospitals throughout the North.
79. Parmater diary, Feb. 5, 1865.
80. Geary, report, 683.
81. Ibid.
82. Capt. Wilbur Chamberlain's condolence letter to Mrs. Nancy Rape was dated Apr. 18, 1865, Raleigh, NC, Rape pension file, RG 94, NA.
83. The *Sentinel,* Apr. 19, 1865, published an itinerary of Sherman's campaign through the Carolinas written by an unidentified Twenty-Ninth Ohio officer. The entry for Feb. 12, 1865, reported, "Skirmishing at the South Edisto river, where John Rape of Co. G was killed, and James Miller, Co. I and several others were wounded. Rape and Miller were acting as sharp-shooters, and were dressed in gray uniforms."
84. Chamberlain to Nancy Rape, Apr. 18, 1865.

Foragers and Firemen

85. Parmater diary, Feb. 15, 1865. In his official report General Geary mentioned skirmishes with the enemy cavalry in two separate actions on Feb. 15. Geary, report, 685. Brigade commander General Pardee stated that "slight" skirmishing occurred this day at a point where Congaree Creek passed through a place called Two-Notch Crossroads. The firing had been brisk at times, but no one in his command was hurt. Pardee, report, *OR,* vol. 47, pt. 1, 706, Pardee).
86. Parmater diary, Feb. 18, 1865.
87. Parmater diary, Feb. 19, 1865.
88. Elias Roshon to "Dear Father and Mother," Goldsboro, NC, Mar. 30, 1865.
89. Parmater diary, Feb. 21, 1865.
90. Brevet Brig. Gen. Ariel Pardee Jr., commanding First Brigade, report, *OR,* vol. 47, pt. 1, 707.
91. Geary, report, 687.
92. Roshon to "Dear Father and Mother," .
93. Ibid.
94. Parmater diary, Feb. 27, 1865.
95. Parmater diary, Mar. 6, 1865.
96. Parmater diary, Mar. 4, 1865. Geary, among others, confirmed this date in his official report. Geary, report, 689.
97. Parmater diary, Mar. 5, 1865.
98. Parmater diary, Mar. 14, 1865.
99. Elias Roshon to "Dear Father and Mother," Alexandria, VA, May 7, 1865. Capt. Jonas Schoonover reported total casualties in the regiment during its march through the Carolinas as 13: 6 men wounded, 1 killed, and 6 missing—while foraging, it might reasonably be presumed. (Capt. Jonas Schoonover, "Report

of Casualties in the 29th Regt. O.V.I. from Jan. 27 to March 28, 1865," found in Regimental Casualties, Ohio Infantry Units 7–61, RG 94, NA.) Five of the six men listed as missing returned to the regiment, whether they had been captured or had merely gotten lost. Pvt. Thomas Bonner, Company A, was one of the substitutes who came to the regiment in Atlanta. The *State Roster,* 356, lists him as captured on Mar. 11, 1865, but then states "no further record." SeCheverell, *Journal History,* 171 and 281, shows him captured on Mar. 11, but provides no clue as to whether he was ever seen again.

100. Geary, report, 689.
101. Parmater diary, Mar. 12, 1865.
102. Geary, report, 691. Geary's division passed through Fayetteville, NC, on Mar. 12, 1865, and left it the next day.
103. "Sherman's Campaign: The Mar. of the 29th Regiment," *Sentinel,* Apr. 19, 1865. Portions of an unidentified Twenty-Ninth officer's diary were given two columns in this edition of the newspaper.
104. Pvt. John Rape was killed in the fighting along the Edisto River on Feb. 12, 1865. He was the last Twenty-Ninth Ohio soldier to die in action.

Chapter 28: The Long Way Home
"A Nation Born in a Day"

1. Ames diary, Feb. 19, 1865.
2. Ames diary, Mar. 9, 1865.
3. Ames diary, Mar. 18, 1865.
4. Ames had visited the offices of the *New York Herald* newspaper during a stop-over in New York City. His visit to Charleston might have been to gather observations for a news piece. Nothing of his was ever published, aside from the casualty lists he had sent to the newspaper in Conneaut.
5. Ames diary, Mar. 1, 1865.
6. Ames diary, Mar. 21, 1865.
7. Ames diary, Mar. 13, 1865.
8. Ames diary, Mar. 2, 1865.
9. Ames diary, Mar. 6, 1865.
10. Ames diary, Mar. 4, 1865.

"Carry Me Back"

11. Parmater diary, Mar. 20, 1865.
12. Alonzo Sterrett pension file, RG 94, NA.
13. Parmater diary, Mar. 26, 1865.
14. Parmater diary, Mar. 24, 1865.
15. Parmater diary, Mar. 27, 1865.
16. Parmater diary, Apr. 8, 1865.
17. Parmater diary, Apr. 12, 1865.
18. Parmater diary, Apr. 13, 1865.
19. Parmater diary, Apr. 17, 1865.
20. "The Terrible Calamity," *Beacon,* Apr. 20, 1865.
21. Ames diary, Apr. 20, 1865.
22. Parmater diary, Apr. 20, 1865.
23. Ibid.
24. Parmater diary, Apr. 25, 1865.
25. Parmater diary, Apr. 28, 1865.
26. Parmater diary, Apr. 29, 1865.
27. Ames diary, Apr. 29, 1865.
28. Parmater diary, May 1, 1865.
29. Ames diary, May 3, 1865.

Full Circuit

30. Parmater diary, May 9, 1865.
31. Parmater diary, May 10, 1865.

32. Ames diary, May 11, 1865.
33. Parmater diary, May 11, 1865.
34. Parmater diary, May 13, 1865.
35. Ames diary, May 13, 1865.
36. Bates, *Martial Deeds*, 421–22. Bates, who was not present, quoted an article written by the *New York Tribune* reporter).
37. Parmater diary, May 15, 1865.
38. Parmater diary, May 16, 1865.
39. Ames diary, May 15, 1865.
40. Parmater diary, May 24, 1865.
41. Ibid. Parmater did not make it clear in this diary entry whether the regiment received its last new flag before or after the Grand Review. John Rupp answered that question in a postwar recollection published in the *National Tribune*, Sept. 27, 1900, in which he stated that the Twenty-Ninth Ohio was presented with their last, national flag near the Capitol Building, and *then* marched forward for the Grand Review.
42. Ames diary, May 25, 1865.
43. The *State Roster* shows two Twenty-Ninth Ohio soldiers who died at Davids' Island, in Long Island Sound: nineteen-year-old Robert Stewart on Mar. 4, 1865, and forty-year-old Jacob Dunkel on Apr. 17, 1865.
44. Ames diary, May 26, 1865.
45. Parmater diary, May 27, 1865.
46. Ames diary, May 29, 1865.
47. Ames diary, June 9, 1865.

Westbound Traffic

48. Parmater diary, June 11, 1865.
49. Ibid.
50. Parmater diary, June 13, 1865.

Getting Free

51. Parmater diary, June 21, 1865.
52. Parmater diary, July 5, 1865.
53. Ames diary, June 19, 1865.
54. Ibid.
55. Ames diary, June 27, 1865.
56. Ames diary, July 6, 1865.
57. Lyman D. Ames left for the Pennsylvania oil fields on July 10, 1865. Ames diary, July 10, 1865.
58. Parmater diary, July 4, 1865.
59. Parmater diary, July 12, 1865.
60. Ibid.

Last Parade

61. "Arrival of the 29th OVI," *Cleveland Daily Leader*, July 18, 1865.
62. Parmater made out ration returns for everyone present for duty in the regiment at Bardstown, KY, on June 26, 1865, which by his count was 235.
63. My interpretation of the flesh and blood cost of the war for the Giddings Regiment is based on my examination of the numbers provided by the preeminent writers on the topic of Civil War mortality. In 1889, William Fox, *Regimental Losses,* was the first to publish an independent, scholarly analysis of the number of Union losses based on the often contradictory records scattered throughout various departments and offices of the army and federal and state governments. Thomas Livermore, with access to more complete data, followed Fox in 1900 with *Numbers and Losses,* his attempt to put a number to the war's dead. In his *Compendium,* published in 1908, Frederick Dyer assigned a number to each regiment's war dead. Dyer's numbers are often quoted, but he did not apply the same level of inquiry as Fox or Livermore. There appears to be some degree of cross-pollination from Fox into Livermore's work, and most certainly into Dyer's. To my knowledge, no definitive work on the topic has emerged since Livermore, other than PhD dissertations and treatises written for historical journals on very specific or localized Civil War mortality issues. Even with these sources as starting

points, any attempt to establish the precise number of dead for the Twenty-Ninth Ohio, or for any regiment, Union or Confederate, will fail. The attempt produces as many questions as answers. To begin, there is no agreement as to the exact number of men who served in the Giddings Regiment. SeCheverell, *Journal History*, 153, reported the total number of men who served in the regiment as 1,540. Fox, whose work appeared several years after SeCheverell's and who had access to the final, revised enlistment rolls on file with the State Adjutant General's Office, came up with a total enrollment in the Twenty-Ninth as 1,518, the number I rely on for my analysis. Fox, *Regimental Losses*, 319. Fox reported the number of dead in the Twenty-Ninth Ohio from all causes as 271 (ibid.). Dyer reported the exact same number for the regiment. *Compendium*, 1510. SeCheverell summarized the regiment's mortality from battles only, and made no attempt to put a final number to the men who had died of disease or accident. SeCheverell gave the number killed as 89, making no distinction between killed in action and died of wounds afterward. *Journal History*, 282. Fox combined those killed in action and those who died of wounds in some unspecified period of time after battle and arrived at the total of the regiment's battle dead as 120, which included 6 officers. *Regimental Losses*, 319. Only SeCheverell counted the regiment's casualties for each of its battles including killed, wounded, and missing and arrived at an aggregate of 541. *Journal History*, 282. To arrive at a percentage of men who became casualties in battle, it would be reasonable to deduct the approximate 300 drafted and substitute men who came to the regiment at Atlanta in 1864, by which time all of the regiment's costly battles had been fought. Deducting those 300 from the total enlistment of 1,518 provides a rough number of men who fought in at least one of the regiment's significant battles—1,218. Battle casualties based on SeCheverell's count show that 44 percent of the regiment's men and officers were either killed, wounded, or missing. How did the regiment's losses compare to those of other regiments in the Union army as a whole and to those of Ohio regiments in particular? Livermore determined that 2,898,304 men had served in the Union army, which included all units organized regardless of their length of service. *Numbers and Losses*, 1. Fox based his mortality study only on Federal units enlisted for three years; thus his number of total enlistments in the Union army was smaller than Livermore's. Fox calculated that the percentage of total deaths among three-year Ohio regiments such as the Twenty-Ninth was nearly 16 percent. *Regimental Losses*, 526. Livermore counted the total deaths in the Union army from all causes as 359,528. *Numbers and Losses*, 8–9. Livermore's number of dead against his number of total enlistments shows that 12.4 percent of those who served in the Federal army perished. In the Giddings Regiment, using the total enrollment number as 1,518 and the number of men in it dead from all causes as 271 reveals a mortality rate of very nearly 18 percent. Ohio historian Robert S. Harper reported that the state of Ohio furnished 319,189 men for service in the Union army. Harper, *Ohio Handbook*, 9. For the purpose of my analysis, I have deemed Harper's number of 319,189 sufficiently accurate. Of these, 35,475 died from all causes, which interestingly included those who drowned or were victims of homicide, suicide, execution, and sunstroke. Dyer, *Compendium*, 1:16. The number of Ohio's war dead reported by Dyer, supposedly taken from his own examination of the records, happens to be the exact number reported by William Fox two decades earlier. *Regimental Losses*, 526. Thus, the mortality rate for Ohio troops regardless of their length of service was slightly more than 11 percent. In summary, the butcher's bill for the Twenty-Ninth Ohio Infantry was slightly higher than that of other three-year regiments in the Union army, and significantly higher than the average deaths in the Union army overall and among Ohio regiments.

64. Fox, *Regimental Losses*, 319.
65. "Arrival of the 29th OVI," *Cleveland Daily Leader*.
66. Ibid.
67. In the 1990s, Dr. Richard Waters of Jefferson, Ohio, led the project to have the regiment's national flag, reputed to be its first, placed in a new case and returned to public display at the library. Fearing that handling this relic might destroy it, the flag was not unfolded. The names of the battles in which the regiment fought, stenciled or sewn along its stripes, would establish which of the regiment's national flags this is. Currently, its secrets remain hidden within its folds. The regiment carried two state (regimental) flags through the war. One of them has been restored and is housed at the Ohio Historical Society. What became of the other flag in not known.
68. Parmater diary, July 18, 1865.
69. Parmater diary, July 21, 1865.
70. Parmater diary, July 22, 1865.
71. "Musical Instruments," *Sentinel*, Aug. 9, 1865.
72. *Reporter*, Aug. 24, 1865.

73. Jefferson's celebration of their soldiers' return was held at the Jefferson House. Universal satisfaction was expressed for the music, supper, and excellent company. "A party given to the returned soldiers . . . ," *Sentinel*, Aug. 9, 1865.
74. "Veterans Returning," *Sentinel*, July 26, 1865.
75. Hart, "Civil War Scenes."
76. Elias Roshon pension file, RG 94, NA.

Bibliography

The goal of this work is to tell the story of the Twenty-Ninth Ohio Volunteer Infantry (OVI), as much as possible, in the words of the soldiers and officers who served in it. Initial fears that too little of what the men of the regiment said about themselves had survived were resolved early on. My research produced a surprising quantity of wartime letters, both published and unpublished, and several diaries. A review of extant Ohio newspapers of the period recovered more than 180 published letters written by the regiment's soldiers and officers. This does not include numerous letters written by soldier-correspondents of other regiments of their brigade in which the writers mentioned the Twenty-Ninth Ohio, nor does it include the many squibs written by the various newspaper editors to keep the homefolk posted on the regiment's whereabouts, health, personnel changes, and battles.

Most of the newspaper-published war letters were written by a compact group of soldiers, officers mostly, each of whom served as field correspondent for his favorite newspaper. Chaplains Russel Hurlburt and Lyman D. Ames, Colonels Thomas Clark and Lewis P. Buckley, and officers Comfort Chaffee, Wilbur Chamberlain, Gurley Crane, William T. Fitch, E. B. Howard, Jonas Schoonover, Theron S. Winship, E. B. Woodbury, Josiah Wright, and Myron T. Wright all composed at least a half dozen letters for public consumption. Other men published letters under a pseudonym; most prominent of these were "S. B.," who was revealed as Josiah Wright, and "Pvt. W" (later "Ofcr. W"), who most likely was Theron Winship. Soldiers using a nom de plume who cannot be identified, but who each wrote several letters, were "Seelye," "James," "J. R.," and one writer who signed his letters "Anonymous." The majority of these letters were published in the *Ashtabula Sentinel,* Jefferson, Ohio; the *Summit Beacon Journal,* Akron, Ohio; or the *Conneaut Reporter.*

A significant number of letters and diaries that were never published have survived. The largest body of letters by a Giddings Regiment soldier are those written by Sgt. Wallace B. Hoyt. Forty-six of his letters have been preserved. Most are found at the Ohio Historical Society. Several more Hoyt letters were discovered during research in his survivor's pension file at the National Archives, in Washington, D.C.

Thirty-three war letters of Lt. John G. Marsh have been identified. About twenty of them, written mostly to his little sister and favorite correspondent, Ida, were traced by historian James Hudson to Ida's descendant Mrs. Maryal Hantz Hunt. Copies of these letters are located at the University of Arkansas Library, Fayetteville. The others are found in the Marsh pension file at the National Archives. Professor Hudson published the group of Marsh letters written from Fredericksburg, Maryland, in the fall of 1862 with limited but valuable annotations. See "Civil War Letters from Frederick, Maryland: The War Correspondence of Sergeant John G. Marsh," *Old Northwest* 9 (Fall 1983): 237–53. From a bit of marginalia in his working notes it appears Hudson had considered publishing the entire body of Marsh letters under the title "If a Hundred Deaths Stood in the Way." His plan was not fulfilled, which is unfortunate because Mrs. Hunt apparently possessed rich details of Lieutenant Marsh's life and times, passed along through the family chain, which are not recorded elsewhere. A small group of Marsh letters was edited and published by C. Calvin Smith. See "The Duties of Home and War: The Civil War Letters of John G. Marsh, 29th Ohio Volunteers (A Selection)," *Upper Ohio Historical Review* 8 (1979): 7–20. The dozen letters surveyed in Smith's piece, and catalogued by Hudson, were those examined in the original form during research for this book in the Marsh pension file at the National Archives. A tantalizing lead toward the possible existence of Marsh letters other than those noted was suggested by the discovery of a stray notation for a forty-one-page piece prepared by Lyle W. Durham of Urbana, Illinois, in 1978. Unfortunately, Durham may not have published his work in any conventional way, and it cannot be located.

Pvt. Cass Nims's parents kept about a dozen of his letters and sent them to Washington, where they currently reside in the Nims pension file. Also found in the pension files were 110 letters written by various Twenty-Ninth Ohio soldiers, including Christopher Beck, George B. Dice, Thomas Fales, Oscar Gibbs, Nelson Gillett, Ellis Green, Newton P. Hummiston, Alvinson Kinney, Allen Mason, Jerome Phinney, Burton Pickett, Franklin Potter, Willis Sisley, and Matthias Soden. Care was taken in preparing the notes section of this book so that the reader might easily locate a letter I have cited, published or unpublished, and to that end the location of each is fully detailed. For simplicity's sake, the following bibliography does not encumber the reader with a catalog of several hundred soldier-written letters.

Located at the Ohio Historical Society are the typescripts of two remarkable diaries, those of Pvt. Nathan Parmater and Chaplain Lyman D. Ames. The society also possesses the original several volumes into which Parmater committed his impressions of the war as he saw and felt it. A transcription of the diary of Pvt. Elias Roshon and, by comparison, his far richer war letters were provided to me by an Ohio friend. Their provenance has not been established, as is the case also with the transcription of the sparsely written diary of Pvt. Franklin Potter. The Ohio Historical Society has custody of a similarly leanly written diary attributed to Lt. Albert Durkee. Like Potter and Roshon, Durkee used his diary as a daily accounting book of distances marched, places visited, pay and clothing drawn against his allowance, and for little else. Chaplain Ames and Nathan Parmater, and particularly Parmater, wrote in their diaries with an eye to future publication; that motivation, along with a genuine talent for observation and recording, make their diaries a marvel of insight into life inside the regiment. A transcription of the original diary of the assistant surgeon Elwood Potts Haines was supplied to me by its owner, John Gurnish of Akron. Haines's entries are as spare of detail as those of Potter, Roshon, and Durkee.

In total, more than three hundred soldier-written letters published in the newspapers of the period and, preserved in manuscript, are available to the student. Diaries and letters referenced in this work do not constitute the full catalog of the regiment's war writing. Since the beginning of this project over a dozen individual letters written by soldiers of the Twenty-Ninth Ohio Volunteers have appeared in the marketplace of Civil War relics. Every soldier who could write started a diary, and the letters that the boys sent home to Ohio once numbered in the many thousands. It is hoped that more of these letters, and even a comprehensive diary or two, will reemerge. Also, I rigorously examined state and national manuscript catalogs, but there is the possibility that something crucial to the Twenty-Ninth's story may have been overlooked.

The personal prewar and wartime correspondence of its founder, Hon. Joshua R. Giddings, provide insights into the great man's motivations in founding the regiment that took his name. His letters are found at the Ohio Historical Society. Also located there is the voluminous correspondence received by the offices of the adjutant general and the governor of Ohio. Found within that collection were several dozen letters useful in understanding the complex and sometimes difficult organization of the regiment. The letters from both collections have been cited fully in passing in the notes.

The commander of the division in which the Twenty-Ninth Ohio served, from the time of the Battle of Cedar Mountain, Virginia, in 1862, until the end of the war, wrote several hundred letters, most addressed to his wife and confidant, Mary Henderson Geary. Insofar as they have been preserved, no soldier or officer in his command wrote more letters than Brig. Gen. John White Geary. His wartime correspondence is housed at the Historical Society of Pennsylvania, in Philadelphia. During research, copies were made of the originals of the letters most directly bearing on the story of the regiment. Noted historian of the war Bell Irvin Wiley died before completing publication of a selection of Geary's war letters. *A Politician Goes to War* was completed by William Alan Blair, who wrote the preface and added valuable annotations. Of the Geary war letters collection in total, a large number were devoted to the mundane details of household management, personal finances, and local politics. Bell Wiley selected for publication those letters containing the most information covering Geary's war experience. Those letters served fully the purpose of this work. For ease of finding, and reading, reference is made to the Geary war letters as published in *A Politician Goes to War*.

Geary described for his wife nearly every campaign, march, and battle in which he participated. The letters of this complex and brilliant man are full of his pithy observations on the condition of people and places that the war brought within his view. Unfortunately, like the newspaper reports he shaped and the official reports to which he signed his name, his accounts to her of the battles that he directed are frequently exaggerated and detached from the chill reality. But even these portions of his letters are valuable because they reveal the defect of personality that blocked Geary from learning from his mistakes and therefore limited his abilities as a field commander—a failing that to the men he commanded sometimes proved fatal.

J. Hampton SeCheverell, the author of the regiment's *Journal History*, was with the Twenty-Ninth Ohio for only the first half year of its career. But although he had not been a witness to most of the events he wrote about, a committee of Twenty-Ninth Ohio veterans signed off on the authenticity of facts reported in his book before it was put into print in 1887. Others have already found fault with SeCheverell's effort. The modern reader of SeCheverell would be well advised to take nothing in it as gospel unless it can be substantiated elsewhere. As with all things historical, SeCheverell's work needs to be judged within the context of the time it was written. The committee was quite obviously in a hurry to get a history of the regiment published before the state elections of 1887 and the national elections of the following year. The outcome of these campaigns, the presidential campaign in particular, was of critical importance to them since a foremost issue under debate was whether veterans' pensions would be liberalized or reined in. The quality of their *Journal History*, which sadly was to be the only published history of the Giddings Regiment written by its own soldiers, suffers on that account, among others. Although much in it must be discounted and in some cases even dismissed, much remains of value to a student of the regiment.

Although veterans of other regiments in their brigade did, no soldier or officer of the Twenty-Ninth OVI ever published a memoir, which is not to say they did not write for publication about their experiences. For some of the Twenty-Ninth's veterans, a substantial part of the satisfaction with what they had done as the Boys of '61 came from seeing their reminiscences published in the pages of the Union veterans' favorite newspaper, the *National Tribune*. Some of these memoirs were written far past the turn of the century, by which time over fifty years had passed since the event took place. No particular discounting of the veracity of these postwar recollections, no matter how distant from the event under treatment, has been applied. As in the use of any account, written an hour afterward or half a century, reasonable corroboration of the events depicted was sought.

Manuscript Collections

Duke University Archives, Durham, NC

Gould Papers, Charles Candy to H. A. Tripp, Fort Leavenworth, KS, June 29, 1887.

Military Order of the Loyal Legion of the United States Library, Philadelphia, PA. (Hereafter referred to as MOLLUS.)

Insignia Record Number 7025, Record of Lt. Col. Edward Hayes.
Insignia Record Number 8604, William T. Fitch.

National Archives and Records Administration, Washington, DC.

Record Group 94, Office of the Adjutant General, Volunteer Organizations of the Civil War, Regimental Casualties, Ohio, Infantry, units 7–61.
Record Group 152, Records of the Office of the Judge Advocate General, Courts Martial Proceedings.
Record Group 94, Records of the Adjutant General's Office, Carded Medical Records of Volunteer Soldiers in the Mexican and Civil Wars, entry 534, 29th Ohio Infantry Regiment.

Civil War Union Volunteer Regimental Books, Record Group 94, Records of the Adjutant General's Office, entries 111–15, Ohio Infantry—29th–33rd , 29th Regt., Ohio Volunteer Infantry, 7 books.

Organizational Index to Pension Files of Veterans Who Served between 1861 and 1900, (microfilm) T289, 29th Regiment Ohio Volunteer Inf., rolls 400–401. (This is the finding aid to the soldier's or survivor's complete pension file in record group 94).

Compiled Service Records for Union Army Volunteers, 29th Regt., Ohio Volunteer Infantry.

Compiled Service Records of Confederate Volunteers, 5th Florida Infantry.

Ohio Historical Society, Library and Archives, Columbus

Lyman Daniel Ames diary, VFM 2972.
Buckley Post no. 12, GAR, post records.
Certificates of Qualifications and Acceptances of Commissions, 1861–62.
Civil War Personnel Records, series 2106, box 52.697, file 29, 29th Ohio Officers'.
Albert Durkee Civil War diary, Sept. 13, 1861–Aug. 8, 1862, vol. 596.
Joshua Reed Giddings Papers, 1821–66, MSS 53.
Governor and Adjutant General of Ohio, 1861–66, correspondence, series 147.
Grand Army of the Republic, Buckley Post no. 12 (Akron, Ohio), Personal war sketches, 1890, vol. 1028.
Wallace B. Hoyt Papers, MS1282.
Nathan Parmater Papers, MSS 246.
Ben Pontius Drawing, Camp Giddings, Jefferson, Ohio, SC134.
Rolls of Deserters, series 108, State of Ohio Adjutant General's Office, 1936.

Library of Congress

Consolidated Report of the Asst. Adjutant General, Feb. 9, 1935.

Pennsylvania Historical Society, Philadelphia

Maj. Gen. John White Geary correspondence, 1859–65. Geary Family Papers, collection no. 2062.

University of Arkansas Libraries, Fayetteville

James J. Hudson Papers.

U.S. Military Archives, U.S. Military Academy, West Point, NY

Lewis P. Buckley, Cadet Admission Records, 1822–23; student records.

Newspapers

Ashtabula Sentinel, Jefferson, Ohio, 1850–66.
Ashtabula Weekly Telegraph, Ashtabula, Ohio, 1860–66.
Cleveland Herald, 1861–62.
Conneaut Reporter, 1860–66.
New York Times, 1862–63.
Ohio State Journal, Columbus, 1860–65.
Otsego County Herald and Times, Gaylord, MI, Jan. 21, 1910.
Philadelphia Press, 1861–65.
Summit County Beacon, Akron, 1855–90.
Western Reserve Chronicle, Warren, Ohio, 1861–66.

Books and Articles

Abstracts of Early Wills, 1812, Cayuga County, NY.
Adams, George W. *Doctors in Blue: The Medical History of the Union Army in the Civil War.* Baton Rouge: Louisiana State University Press, 1996.
Allan, Col. William. "Stonewall Jackson's Valley Campaign." In *The Annals of the War Written by Leading Participants North and South,* edited by A. K. McClure, 725–49. Dayton: Morningside, 1988.
Antisell, Thomas. "Extracts from a Narrative of His Services in the Medical Staff during the Summer of 1862." In United States, *Medical and Surgical History,* app. to pt. 1.

Auten, Betty. *Seneca County History* [Waterloo, NY] 1, no. 3 (March 1985).

Avery, Lillian Drake, comp. *A Genealogy of the Ingersoll Family in America, 1629–1925.* New York: Grafton Press, 1926.

Bates, Samuel P. *Martial Deeds of Pennsylvania.* Philadelphia, PA: David and Co., 1876.

Beatie, Russel H. *The Army of the Potomac.* Vol. 2, *McClellan Takes Command, September 1861–February 1862.* Cambridge, MA: Da Capo, 2004.

Berthoff, G. D. "The Twelfth Corps . . . The Part They Took in the Big Battle of Gettysburg." *National Tribune,* May 11, 1893.

Bierce, Gen. L. V. *Historical Reminiscences of Summit County.* Akron: T. and H. G. Canfield, Publishers, 1854.

Boatner, Mark M., III. *The Civil War Dictionary.* Rev. ed. New York: Vintage Books, 1991.

Breckinridge, Col. W. P. C., CSA. "The Opening of the Atlanta Campaign." In Johnson and Buel, *Battles and Leaders,* 4:277–81.

Castel, Albert. *Decision in the West: The Atlanta Campaign of 1864.* Lawrence: University Press of Kansas, 1992.

Castle, Capt. Henry E., 137th Ill. Inf.. "The Shelter Tent." In *Glimpses of the Nation's Struggle,* MOLLUS—Minnesota War Papers, vol. 3.

Chamberlin, Maj. W. H., 81st OVI. "The Skirmish Line in the Atlanta Campaign." In MOLLUS—Ohio, *Sketches of War History, 1861–1865,* 3:182–96.

Clarke, Henry E. "Fighting Them Over: What Our Veterans Have to Say about Their Old Campaigns: The Fight for the Battery at Peach Tree Creek." *National Tribune,* May 31, 1883.

———. "Peach Tree Creek." *National Tribune,* Nov. 26, 1891.

Clouds, George K. "A Reminiscence of Cross Keys." *National Tribune,* June 4, 1883.

Coddington, Edwin B. *The Gettysburg Campaign: A Study in Command.* Dayton, OH: Morningside Bookshop, 1979.

Coles, Harry L. *Ohio Forms an Army.* Columbus: Ohio State University Press for the Ohio Historical Society, 1962.

Collins, Darrel L. *The Battles of Cross Keys and Port Republic.* Lynchburg, VA: H. E. Howard, 1993.

Couch, Darius N., Maj. Gen., USV. "The Chancellorsville Campaign." In Johnson and Buel, *Battles and Leaders* 3:155–71.

Coulter, E. Merton. *Travels in the Confederate States: A Bibliography.* Norman: University of Oklahoma Press, 1948.

Cox, Jacob D. "McClellan in West Virginia." In Johnson and Buel, *Battles and Leaders,* 1:126.

———. "War Preparations in the North." In Johnson and Buel, *Battles and Leaders,* 1:84.

Cozzens, Peter. *The Shipwreck of Their Hopes: The Battles for Chattanooga.* Chicago: University of Illinois Press, 1994.

Delauter, Roger U., Jr. *Winchester in the Civil War.* Lynchburg, VA: H. E. Howard, 1992.

Downer, Edward, T. *Ohio Troops in the Field.* Columbus: Ohio State University Press for the Ohio Historical Society, 1961.

Dyer, Frederick H. *A Compendium of the War of the Rebellion.* 2 vols. Dayton, OH: Morningside Bookshop, 1994.

Ebersole, Jacob, MD, 19th IN Inf.. "Incidents of Field Hospital Life with the Army of the Potomac." In MOLLUS—Ohio, *War History,* 4:327–33.

Edwards, William B. *Civil War Guns: The Complete Story of Federal and Confederate Small Arms.* Harrisburg, PA: Stackpole, 1962

Ellis, William A., comp. and ed. *Norwich University, 1819–1911: Her History, Her Graduates, Her Roll of Honor.* 3 vols. Montpelier, VT: Capitol City Press, 1911.

Fenton, E. B., 20th CT Vol. Inf.. MOLLUS—*Michigan War Papers,* 1:485–503.

Fox, William F. *Regimental Losses in the American Civil War, 1861–1865.* Albany, NY: Albany Publishing Company, 1889.

Freeman, Douglas Southall. *Lee's Lieutenants: A Study in Command.* 1 vol. abridged. New York: Simon and Schuster, 2001.

Geary, John White. *A Politician Goes to War: The Civil War Letters of John White Geary.* Edited by William Allen Blair. Selections and introduction by Bell Irvin Wiley. University Park: Pennsylvania State University Press, 1995.

Grand Army of the Republic. *Our Memorial Chapel, Dedicated Tuesday, May 30, 1876, with the Life and Services of Col. Lewis P. Buckley, and a History of Buckley Post no. 12, GAR.* Akron: Beacon Publishing Co., 1876.

Grier, William P., Assistant Surgeon, U.S. Army. "Extract from a Report to the Surgeon General." In United States, *Medical and Surgical History,* app. to pt. 1, xcix, 127.

Grismer, Karl H. *Akron and Summit County.* Akron: Summit County Historical Society, 1950.

Guardian Book. Vol. 1. Genesee County Surrogate Office, Batavia, NY.

Harper, Robert S. *Ohio Handbook of the Civil War.* Columbus: Ohio Historical Society for the Ohio Civil War Centennial Commission, 1961.

Hart, S. W. "At Gettysburg with the 12th Corps—Following Lee to Pennsylvania—At Scene of The Fighting on the First Day, July 1, 1863 at 5:00 p.m.—On the Hook of the Line—Pickett's Daring Exploit—Transferred to the Western Army—Kind Buckeyes and Hoosiers." *National Tribune,* June 23, 1927.

———. "At Ringgold." *National Tribune,* July 3, 1913.

———. "Fighting Stonewall Jackson." *National Tribune,* Oct. 13, 1927.

———. "From Battlefield to Prison: Recollections of the Battle of Port Republic and of Prison Life at Lynchburg and Belle Isle." *National Tribune,* Aug. 13, 1903.

———. "New York Draft Riots." *National Tribune,* Apr. 4, 1929.

———. "Their Cowboys Lost Some Cattle—An Extraordinary Time Down in Georgia." *National Tribune,* June 18, 1903.

———. "Thomas, the Ideal Soldier." *National Tribune,* Nov. 13, 1913.

———. "Visits Civil War Scenes." *National Tribune,* Nov. 29, 1928.

———. "When He Saw Stonewall Jackson." *National Tribune,* June 14, 1928.

Hayes, Col. Edward. "Address of Lieut. Col. Edward Hayes to the Twenty-Ninth Ohio Association at Gettysburg, Sept. 14, 1887." In *The Twenty-Ninth Ohio at Gettysburg 1863–1887,* edited by Memorial Committee of the Twenty-Ninth Veteran Volunteer Infantry. Columbus: Nitschke Bros., 1887.

Headley, Phineas Camp. *Life and Military Career of Major-General William Tecumseh Sherman.* New York: William H. Appleton, 1865.

Haskell, Frank A. "The Battle of Gettysburg." In *Gettysburg,* by Haskell and William Oates. New York: Bantam, 1992.

Historical Wyoming (Arcade, NY: Wyoming County Historian) 20, no. 3 (April 1967).

Holbrook, Stewart H. *The Yankee Exodus: An Account of Migration from New England.* New York: Macmillan, 1950.

Holsinger, Capt. Frank, 19th U.S. Colored Inf., Brvt. Maj. U.S. Vols.. "How Does One Feel under Fire?" MOLLUS—Kansas War Papers, *War Talks in Kansas,* May 5, 1898, 1:301.

Howells, William Dean. *Years of My Youth.* New York: Harper and Brothers, 1916.

Huntington, Capt. James F., Batt. H, 1st Regt. Lt. Artillery, Ohio Vols.. "Operations in the Shenandoah Valley, From Winchester to Port Republic, March 10—June 9, 1862." In *Campaigns in Virginia, 1861–1862,* edited by T. F. Dwight. Vol. 1 of *Papers of the Military Historical Society of Massachusetts.* Wilmington, NC: Broadfoot, 1989.

Isham, A. B., 1st Lt., 7th Mich. Cav.. "The Story of a Gunshot Wound." In MOLLUS—Ohio War Papers, *War History,* 4:429–43. Read to the commandery March 4, 1896.

Johnson, Allen, Dumas Malone, Harris E. Starr, and Edward T. James, eds. *Dictionary of American Biography.* New York: Charles Scribner's Sons, 1930–1937.

Johnson, Robert, and Clarence Buel, eds. *Battles and Leaders of the Civil War.* 4 vols. 1887–88. Reprint, Secaucus, NJ: Castle, n.d.

Jones, Rollin L. "The Battery Horses. They Were Not Ridden Away, But Were Killed . . ." *National Tribune,* June 27, 1889.

———. "Bits of Army Gossip: Interesting Reminiscences of an Ohio Captain." *National Tribune,* Apr. 3, 1890.

Jordan, Phillip D. *Ohio Comes of Age, 1873–1900.* Vol. 5 of *The History of the State of Ohio,* edited by Carl Wittke. Columbus: Ohio State Archaeological and Historical Society, 1943.

Julian, George W. *The Life of Joshua R. Giddings.* Chicago: A. C. McClurg and Co., 1892.

Kilpatrick, Robert Lang. "The Fifth Ohio Infantry at Resaca." In MOLLUS—Ohio, *War History,* 4:246–54.

Kinnear, J. W. "Twentieth Corp Remembered: The Surrender of Atlanta." *National Tribune,* May 31, 1883.

Knapp, Henry J. "Gettysburg by a Soldier in the Ranks." *Jefferson Gazette,* Feb. 8, 1912.

Krick, Robert W. *Stonewall Jackson at Cedar Mountain.* Chapel Hill: University of North Carolina Press, 1990.

Land, Mary. "John Brown's Ohio Environment." *Ohio Archaeological and Historical Quarterly* 57, no. 1 (Jan. 1948): 24–47.

Lane, Samuel A. *Fifty Years and Over of Akron and Summit County.* Akron: Beacon Job Department, 1892.

Leech, Margaret. *Reveille in Washington, 1860–1865.* New York: Harper and Brothers, 1941.

Leonard, Giles R. "A Balky Mule: A Prescription Which Started Him Running Down the Mountain." *National Tribune,* May 14, 1891.

Livermore, Thomas L. *Numbers and Losses in the Civil War in America, 1861–1865.* 2d ed. Boston: Houghton Mifflin, 1901.
Long, E. B. *The Civil War Day by Day: An Almanac, 1861–1865.* With Barbara Long. New York: Da Capo, 1971.
Lonn, Ella. *Desertion during the Civil War.* Lincoln: University of Nebraska Press, 1991.
Lynn, J. R. "At Gettysburg: What the 29th Ohio Did During the Three Days' Fighting." *National Tribune,* Oct. 7, 1897.
Marsh, John G. "Civil War Letters from Frederick, Maryland: The War Correspondence of Sergeant John G. Marsh." Edited by James Hudson. *Old Northwest* 9 (Fall 1983).
Mathews, Alfred. *Ohio and Her Western Reserve.* New York: D. Appleton and Co., 1902.
McConnell, Stuart. *Glorious Contentment: The Grand Army of the Republic, 1865–1900.* Chapel Hill: University of North Carolina Press, 1992.
McParlin, Thomas A., Surgeon, U.S.A. Medical Director. "Report of the Operations of the Medical Department of the Army of Virginia, May 2, 1863." In United States, *Medical and Surgical History,* app. to pt. 1, xcii.
Medina County Historical Society. *History of Medina County.* Fostoria, OH: Gray Printing Co., 1948.
MOLLUS (Military Order of the Loyal Legion of the United States). Ohio Commandery. *Sketches of War History, 1861–1865.* Papers read before the Ohio Commandery of MOLLUS. Vols. 1–4. Cincinnati: R. Clarke and Co., 1883–1903.
Morris, George, and Susan L. Foutz. *Lynchburg in the Civil War: The City, the People, the Battle.* 2nd ed. Lynchburg, VA: H. E. Howard, 1984.
Murdock, Eugene C. *Ohio's Bounty System in the Civil War.* Columbus: Ohio State University Press for the Ohio Historical Society, 1963.
Newton, George A., 129th Ill. Inf. "Battle of Peach Tree Creek." In *The Atlanta Papers,* no. 15, *GAR War Papers, Read before Fred C. Jones Post no. 401, Dept. of Ohio,* comp. Sydney Kerksis, 1:391–408. Dayton: Morningside Press, 1980.
Noyes, Edward. "The Ohio GAR and Politics from 1866 to 1890." *Ohio Archaeology and Historical Quarterly* 55, no. 2 (Apr.–June 1946): 79–105.
Ohio. Adjutant General's Department. "Twenty-Ninth Ohio Veteran Volunteer Infantry." In *Official Roster of the Soldiers of the State of Ohio in the War of the Rebellion, 1861–1866,* 3:353–93. Cincinnati: Wilstach, Baldwin and Co., 1886.
Ohio Gettysburg Memorial Commission. *Ohio Honors Her Brave Sons, Gettysburg, September 14, 1887.* Columbus: Nitschke Bros., 1887.
Otsego County Centennial. *Otsego County: The Heritage Years, 1875–1975.* Gaylord, MI: Otsego County Centennial, 1975.
Parker, Sandra V. *Richmond's Civil War Prisons.* Lynchburg, VA: H. E. Howard, 1990.
Pfanz, Harry W. *Gettysburg—Culp's Hill and Cemetery Hill.* Chapel Hill: University of North Carolina Press, 1993.
Powell, Eugene. "The Battle above the Clouds . . . Ordered to Make a Demonstration, Gen. Geary Bridges Lookout Creek and Assails the Heights." *National Tribune,* Aug. 8, 1901.
———. "Shields in the Shenandoah." *National Tribune,* June 12, 1902.
———. "The White Stars and Their Splendid Defense of Culp's Hill, Gettysburg." *National Tribune,* Sept. 20, 1888.
Reid, Whitelaw. *Ohio in the War: Her Statesmen, Her Generals, and Soldiers.* 2 vols. Cincinnati: Wilstach and Baldwin, 1868.
Robinson, William A. "The Song-Selling Spy." *National Tribune,* June 22, 1905.
Roseboom, Eugene H. *The Civil War Era, 1850–1873.* Vol. 4 of *The History of the State of Ohio,* edited by Carl Wittke. Columbus: Ohio State Archaeological and Historical Society, 1944.
Rupp, John. "With a Fighting Regiment. Story of the Four Years' Service of the Gallant 29th Ohio." *National Tribune,* Sept. 20, 27, 1900.
Sandburg, Carl. *Abraham Lincoln: The Prairie Years.* 2 vols. New York: Harcourt, Brace, 1926.
———. *Abraham Lincoln: The War Years.* 4 vols. New York: Harcourt, Brace, 1936–39.
Scaife, William R. *The Campaign for Atlanta.* Saline, MI: McNaughton and Gunn, 1993.
Sears, Stephen W. *Chancellorsville.* Boston: Houghton Mifflin, 1996.
SeCheverell, J. Hampton. *Journal History of the Twenty-Ninth Ohio Veteran Volunteers, 1861–1865: Its Victories and Its Reverses.* Cleveland, 1883.

Seymour, F. A., and Baldwin, W. E. "Port Republic." *National Tribune,* Sept. 25, 1884.
Souder, Mrs. Edmund A. *Leaves from the Battlefield of Gettysburg: A Series of Letters from a Field Hospital: And National Poems.* Philadelphia: Caxton Press of C. Sherman, Son and Co., 1864.
Stackpole, Edward J. *Chancellorsville: Lee's Greatest Battle.* Harrisburg, PA: Stackpole, 1958.
Steiner, Paul E. *Disease in the Civil War: Natural Biological Warfare in 1861–1865.* Springfield, IL: Charles C. Thomas, 1968.
Stewart, James Brewer. *Joshua R. Giddings and the Tactics of Radical Politics.* Cleveland: Press of Case Western Reserve University, 1970.
Storke, Elliot G. *History of Cayuga County, New York.* Syracuse: D. Mason, 1879.
Summers, Festus P. *The Baltimore and Ohio in the Civil War.* Gettysburg, PA: Clark Military Books, 1993.
Supplee, Euclid. "Shenandoah Valley . . . The Experiences of a 29th Soldier." *National Tribune,* May 16, 1889.
Tanner, Robert G. *Stonewall in the Valley: Thomas J. "Stonewall" Jackson's Shenandoah Valley Campaign, Spring 1862.* Mechanicsburg, PA: Stackpole, 1996.
Thayer, Capt. George A., 2nd Mass. Vol. Inf.. "Gettysburg as We Men on the Right Saw It." In MOLLUS—Ohio, *War History,* 2:24–42.
———. "A Railroad Feat of War." In MOLLUS—Ohio, *War History,* 4:214–234.
Time-Life Books. *Arms and Equipment of the Union.* Alexandria, VA: Time-Life, 1991.
Todd, Frederick P. *American Military Equipage, 1851–1872.* Vol. 2, *State Forces.* With Maria Todd/Damerel. New York: Chatham Square Press, 1983.
United States. Bureau of the Census. *Population Schedule of the Seventh Census, 1850, Ashtabula County, Ohio.* Washington, DC: the Bureau.
———. *Population Schedule of the Eighth Census, 1860, Ashtabula County, Ohio.* Washington, DC: the Bureau.
United States. Department of the Interior. National Parks Service, National Register of Historic Places Inventory—Nomination Form for Cedar Mt. Battlefield, p. 3. Union soldier Hawley's map of the location of the markers donated by J. Gordon Thomas is denoted map 6 in this file. Courtesy of Betty Shackelford, Rapidan, VA.
United States. Surgeon General's Office. *The Medical and Surgical History of the War of the Rebellion,* prepared by Surg. Gen. Joseph K. Barnes. App. to pt. 1, SCVII. Washington, DC: Government Printing Office, 1875–83.
United States. War Department. *The War of the Rebellion: A Compilation of the Official Records of the Union and Confederate Armies.* 128 vols. Washington, DC, 1880–1901.
Voris, Alvin C., Brvt. Maj. Gen., U.S. Vols.. "The Battle of the Boys." In MOLLUS—Ohio, *War History,* 4:95.
Waldron, Charles F. "Southern Battlefields: An Ohio Comrade Visits Places of Georgia and Tennessee." *National Tribune,* Mar. 14, 1901.
Weisenburger, Francis P. *Columbus during the Civil War.* Columbus: Ohio State University Press for the Ohio Historical Society, 1962.
———. *The Passing of the Frontier, 1825–1850.* Vol. 3 of *The History of the State of Ohio,* edited by Carl Wittke. Columbus: Ohio State Archaeological and Historical Society, 1941.
Wheeler, Xenophon, Sgt., 67th OVI, Capt. 129th OVI. "Experiences of an Enlisted Man in the Hospital in the Early Part of the War." In MOLLUS,—Ohio, *War History,* 6:276.
White, John D. "On the Move: The 29th Ohio Did Not Wait for Duty to Come to It." *National Tribune,* Nov. 29, 1900.
Williams, H. Z., and Bro. *History of Trumbull and Mahoning Counties, with Illustrations and Biographical Sketches.* 2 vols. Cleveland: H. Z. Williams, 1882.
Williams, W. W. *History of Ashtabula County, Ohio, with Illustrations and Biographical Sketches of Its Pioneers and Prominent Men.* Philadelphia: Williams Bros., 1878.
Wilson, John. "The Academy on the Knoll." *Wyoming County History,* Apr. 1986.
Wilson, Lawrence. "Candy's Brigade at Gettysburg." *National Tribune,* June 20, 1902.
———. "Cedar Mountain: Blue and Grey Unite to Mark Positions on This Famous Battlefield." *National Tribune,* Aug. 22, 1901.
———. *Itinerary of the Seventh Ohio Volunteer Infantry, 1861–1864.* New York: Neale Publishing Co., 1907; reprint, Whitefish, MT: Kessinger, 2008.
———. "Kernstown. Who Charged and Took the Stone Wall at the Battle." *National Tribune,* June 6, 1889.
———. "The 7th Ohio, Personal Reminiscences of a Promoted Private of Co. D Who Was There to the End," two installments, *National Tribune,* Jan. 14, 1904, Jan. 21, 1904.

Wilson, Orlando E. "Received a Medal of Honor." *National Tribune,* Nov. 27, 1907.

Worsham, John H. *One of Jackson's Foot Cavalry: His Experiences and What He Saw during the War, 1861–1865.* New York: Neale Publishing Co., 1912.

Writers' Program of the Works Projects Administration in the State of Georgia. *Georgia: A Guide to Its Towns and Countryside.* Athens: University of Georgia Press, 1946.

Writers' Program of the Works Projects Administration in the State of Ohio. *The Ohio Guide.* New York: Somerset Publishers, 1948.

Writers' Program of the Works Projects Administration in the State of Virginia. *Virginia: A Guide to the Old Dominion.* New York: Oxford University Press, 1946.

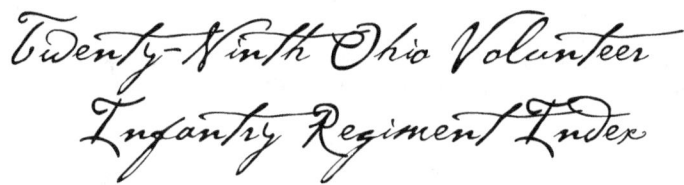
Twenty-Ninth Ohio Volunteer Infantry Regiment Index

(SEE ALSO GENERAL INDEX, FOLLOWING)

aka Giddings Regiment, ix
aka the Abolition Regiment, ix, 58, 59, 378; referred to as the "nigger regiment," 59
as Twenty-Ninth Ohio Veteran Volunteer Infantry, 290

amusements
  Akron supper during veterans' furlough, 293
  "ball" playing: during march to Falmouth, 124; at Dumfries, 210; on march to Chancellorsville, 216; at Aquia Creek, 243, 244; at Bridgeport, 301; on march to Dug Gap, GA, 304
  boxing, 154
  Christmas Eve 1863 celebrated by musket firing from boxcar doors, 290
  climbing Allegheny mountain peaks, 98
  in the company streets: at Bridgeport, 301; at Camp Giddings, 54
  dancing: at Camp Giddings, 52; refugee women join soldiers for evening cotillions at Bridgeport, 302
  drinking: admonitions against, 73; soldiers and officers on a spree at Camp Chase 1862, 74–75; Buckley blocks an intemperate officer's promotion, 123; Ohio officer identifies drinking as the scourge of the army, 210; alcohol-fueled carousing on the sea voyage to New York City, 269; officers observed intoxicated at Normandy, TN, 274–75; soldiers overindulge in whiskey at Louisville, 290; whiskey ration causes soldiers to act foolishly, 329; at Atlanta, 348, 352; at Sister's Ferry, GA, 363; at Bladensburg, MD, 375; at Bardstown, KY, 376
  fishing, 119, 210, 301
  gambling: Chuck-a-luck at Wauhatchie, 286; Chuck-a-luck during the march to Savannah, 355; card playing and Chuck-a-luck at Savannah, 362
  games: "Bluff" and chess, 244
  Halloween ball in Jefferson, 1861, 62
  hometown celebrations of veterans' return, 379–80
  humor, soldier: at Camp Giddings, 52, 54, 56, 65, 67; at Camp Chase, 72, 76; windstorm blows away surgeon's medicines, 94; at Cedar Mountain, 159, 210–11; march to Chancellorsville, 218; general hilarity in Hooker's army first night at Chancellorsville, 220; soldier comment on Hooker's retreat from Chancellorsville, 235; Gettysburg, 259, 260, 261; soldiers hide shovels to avoid manual labor, 296; oversized caps issued at Bridgeport, 302; soldiers favoring McClellan in 1864 election teased, 351; "playing smash" on the march to Savannah, 355
  letter writing, newspaper reading, and pipe carving at Camp Kelly, 87
  music, band: 36; regimental bands practice at Camp Kelly, 87; band plays "Yankee Doodle" on march to Falmouth, 123; regimental bands broken up and sent home, 146; new recruits at Frederick placed in brigade band, 195; bands lead the march into Virginia with "Carry Me Back to Old Virginny," 371
  music, singing: "John Brown's Body" on march to Winchester, 103; "John Brown's Body" on march to Chancellorsville, 218; around the campfires at Bridgeport, 301
  New Year's Day 1865 celebrated by firing muskets, 359
  practical jokes: Fife Major Noonan pranks Irish soldiers, 211; catching Negro children and putting them aboard trains, 295
  reading and studying, 210
  Sabbath service as entertainment, 241
  searching for laurel root from which to carve trinkets, 98
  snowballing, 210, 298
  swimming: in the Rappahannock, 124; on the march to Cedar Mountain, 154, 157
  tobacco: ground oak leaves serving for at Camp Kelly, 87; prevalence of smoking at Dumfries, 208; officers gather at Dumfries for cigar smoking and conversation, 210; shortage of at Wauhatchie, 281
  touching off tin cans filled with gunpowder, 362
  Washington's Birthday celebration at Paw Paw, 97
arms
  Enfield muskets issued, 56
  Buckley bans pistol loading in camp after recruit shoots off his finger, 56
  soldier disappointment with issue of Pondir musket, 56–57
  ammunition issued for first time at Camp Kelly, 85
  musket used for deer hunting, 88
  Gen. Lander's negative opinion of Belgian musket, 88
  100 rounds per man issued at start of Winchester march, 98
  inexperience in firing, 106
  Gen. Pope orders every soldier to carry 100 rounds, 153
  Tower Enfield muskets issued at Dumfries, 213
  ammunition carried by 12th Corps train to Chancellorsville, 218
  rain requires discharge and reloading of muskets, 235
  29th Ohio's division fires 277,000 musket rounds at Culp's Hill, 259

477

arms (cont.)
  enemy rifles collected in front of 29th Ohio's position on Culp's Hill, 260
  Parmater lets girlfriend fire his musket, 285
  muskets turned in at war's end, 377
  government allows soldiers to purchase, 377
battles and campaigns
  reconnaissance to and burning of Green Springs, VA, 88–89
  march to cut off Jackson at Romney, 89–90
  Kernstown, VA, 106–10; Sgt. Marsh describes the dead on the field, 110; soldiers' detailed accounts of sent to Ohio newspapers, 113; debate over which Ohio regiment drove the rebels from the wall, 114; Sgt. John Marsh disturbed by transformation of men in combat, 115
  Port Republic, VA, 132–37; regiment's officers predict defeat, 133; blame for argued, 140–41; order to join McClellan on the Peninsula cancelled, 144
  Cedar Mountain, 157–62; evening of battle, 162; dispute as to who commanded the 29th Ohio in the battle, 160
  Second Bull Run, 178–82
  Antietam campaign, 182–84; explanation for the 29th Ohio's nonparticipation in, 184; regiment's duties at Monocacy Bridge, MD, 184
  Chancellorsville, 219–35
  Gettysburg, 251–58; accusation of cowardice against Capt. W. Stevens, 256–57
  Lookout Mountain, and the battles around Chattanooga, 282–83
  Atlanta campaign: demonstration at Dug Gap, GA, 306–11; battle of Resaca, 318–20; battle of New Hope Church, 325–28; battle of Pine Knob, GA, 332; battle of Kolb's Farm, 333–34; battle of Kennesaw Mountain, 335–36; battle of Peach Tree Creek, 340–43
  Savannah campaign, 353–59
  Carolinas campaign, 363
  Bentonville, NC, 367
burials and treatment of the dead
  first battle dead seen, 96–97
  at Mt. Jackson, VA, 120
  several wounded and killed in action left on the field at Port Republic, 136, 143
  29th Ohio detailed to collect and bury the dead of Cedar Mountain, 164
  at Lynchburg prison, 168
  of executed deserters at Leesburg, 250
  enemy dead buried in front of 29th's division at Gettysburg, 259–60
  initial burial of regiment's killed in action at Culp's Hill, 261
  parents visit Gettysburg to collect sons' remains, 262
  Dug Gap: group burials at, 313–14; dead left on the field, 313, 314, 315
  New Hope Church: daring recovery of dead at, 328; location of group burial at, 328
  trench burial at Pine Knob, 332; personal effects of soldier killed at Pine Knob, 332
  burial of enemy dead at Peach Tree Creek, 343
  arrangements for shipping the dead back to Ohio, 345
  indifference to human remains, 347
  chaplain buries rebel and former slave side by side, 348
  unburied dead scattered on old Virginia battlefields, 372
camps, field
  4 miles north of Winchester, 105
  with Shields's division at New Market, 119
  Co. E posted as provost guards at Mt. Jackson, 119–20
  Camp Kelly, Patterson's Creek, VA, 85, 86
  Camp Misery (aka the Levels, Camp Haystack, Camp Starvation), western Virginia mountains, 89–92
  Little Washington, VA, 153–54
  Culpeper Court House, VA, 177
  Bristoe Station, VA, 180
  Leesburg, VA, en route to Gettysburg, 248–50
  near Raccoon Ford, VA, 270–71
  Normandy, TN, 274–75
  Wauhatchie Valley, TN, 279, 280; duties at, 280, 281, 283
  Mill Creek Valley, GA, 317
  Cassville, GA, 321, 324–25
  near Atlanta fortifications, 340, 343–44
  Goldsboro, NC, 369–70
  Raleigh, NC, 370–71
  Bladensburg, MD, 374
  Bardstown, KY, 375–77
camps, fixed and semifixed
  Camp Giddings: county fairgrounds buildings converted to military use, 30: soldiers' relationships with the village of Jefferson, 52; regiment ordered out on practice march, 66–67; departure from, Christmas Day 1861, 68–69; soldier's daily routine, 53
  Camp Chase, Columbus: layout described, 71; rebel prison on grounds, 71; duties at, 72; drill for the entertainment of governor-elect Tod, 76; staff and field officers sworn in, 77
  Alexandria, VA, June–July 1862, 144
  Frederick, MD, 185–86, 195–200; regiment's duties at, 186
  Dumfries, VA, 203–25; camp location, 203; duties at, 204, 210
  near Aquia Creek, VA, en route to Chancellorsville, 216–17
  Bridgeport, AL, 295–303; duties at, 296; general inspector praises regiment's camp, 301
  in Atlanta, 348–52
  Savannah, GA, 359–63
  Camp Cleveland, 377
casualties, accidental
  gunshot wounds at Camp Kelly, 88
  exceed battle wounds May 1862, 124
  sixth trigger finger shot off in supposed gun handling accident, 143
  in porch collapse at Nashville, 294–95
casualties, combat
  Kernstown: Lt. Williamson first man in regiment killed in action, 109; Capt. Myron Wright describes treatment of his Kernstown wound, 112; regiment's losses at, 114
  Port Republic, 138

Cedar Mountain, 163, 164; casualty rates exceed future, larger battles, 164; analysis of accounting methods of the regiment's casualties in this battle, 420n65

Chancellorsville, 232; in Slocum's 12th Corps, 236; in Geary's division and in Candy's brigade, 239; in 29th Ohio, 239–40; 29th Ohio soldiers in division hospital after Chancellorsville, 241

Gettysburg: casualties sustained in second charge to the rifle pits on Culp's Hill, 258; total casualties in regiment at, 261

Atlanta campaign: at Dug Gap, GA, 311, 314; at Resaca, 320; at New Hope Church, 327–28; Dug Gap through New Hope Church, 328; Pine Knob, GA, 332; Kolb's Farm, GA, 334; in Atlanta campaign through approach to the Chattahoochee, 337; decimated ranks of Sgt. Parmater's company noted, 340; caused by enemy artillery during Atlanta siege, 344; increase in head injuries at Atlanta from artillery fire, 345; cumulative casualties in 29th Ohio's brigade, 347–48

deafness caused by proximity to artillery firing, 158
official battle casualties, 377

casualties, nonphysical injuries (mental derangement)
attributed to shell fire at Chancellorsville, 242
deranged soldiers placed under Chaplain Ames's care, 242–43
deepening depression of Sgt. John Marsh, 264
soldiers with no apparent injury appear at New Hope field hospital, 327
residual mental injury to Sgt. Rollin Jones, 343
Alonzo Sterrett disabled by depression, 363

casualties, total
difficulty in establishing a firm number, 463–64n63
probable total mortality, 377–78
summation of published fatalities from all causes, 377
See also disease

copperheads
regiment's officers publish declaration characterizing Democrats as traitors, 213
soldiers of Co. E threaten to return to Ohio to put down copperheads, 213
soldiers' anger over traitors working against them back home, 267–68
soldiers who did not reenlist worry they will be regarded as sympathetic to, 289

desertions
"French leave" defined, 53
at Camp Giddings, 60
soldier unfairly listed as deserter, 94
on march to Falmouth, 125
on march from the Shenandoah valley after Port Republic, 143
Col. Buckley returns to Ohio to collect soldiers absent without authorization, 186–88
punishment of Pvt. Nowling at Frederick, 197–98
29th Ohio ordered to witness execution of deserters at Leesburg, 249–50
ordered to witness execution of deserters near Culpeper, 250, 270

comparison of desertion rate in the 29th Ohio to other Union regiments, 463–64n63
assessment of accuracy of army documents regarding cases in the 29th Ohio, 394n94, 400n82, 410n73

discipline
disrespect of officers at Camp Giddings, 54
soldiers disrupt a magician's performance, 54
soldiers banished from Camp Giddings for drinking, 74
soldiers at Camp Chase stiff German saloon keepers, 74
soldiers leave Camp Chase without passes by tricking German guards, 75
Cpl. Hoyt and comrades leave Camp Parole and move into a shack in the woods, 174
soldiers do as they please along the Rappahannock, 179
soldiers refuse to take orders from an outsider, 196
deserter punished at Frederick, 196–97
soldier shot dead by provost guard at Frederick, 198
general inspector at Dumfries finds regiment too dirty for inspection, 208
Chaplain Ames's opinion that lax discipline is the root of soldier vices, 241
foul language used by men and officers decried by Chaplain Ames, 241
Sgt. Parmater visits Frederick without authorization, 265
soldiers sight see in Brooklyn without a pass, 270
Gen. Geary orders soldiers to stop wearing nonregulation clothing, 281
soldiers forge pass and visit Nashville, 294
stealing near Nashville draws War Department's attention, 295
soldiers ordered to draw and wear standard issue hats, 302
Col. Fitch warns soldiers against making impertinent remarks to officers, 302
Gen. Geary maintains tight discipline on the march to Savannah, 354
soldiers at Bardstown, KY, raid civilians' gardens, 375–76
soldiers disobey order to attend Sherman's farewell speech to them, 376
See also desertions

disease
enlistees advised on precautions to be taken, 59
first deaths from at Camp Giddings, 59–60
measles attack at Camp Chase, 76
disability claims for rheumatism caused by exposure, 90
deaths at Cumberland, MD, 92, 115
soldier death at Martinsburg, 103–4
soldier deaths attributed to "hard marching" en route to Falmouth, 124
barefoot marching lands more soldiers in hospital than were wounded at Kernstown, 128
disease mortality in the Giddings Regiment through June 1862, 143
common types, 143
outbreak of typhoid, malaria, and dysentery at Little Washington tied to poor sanitary practices, 154
heatstroke at Cedar Mountain, 157
deaths caused by sickness at Belle Isle prison, 169

disease (*cont.*)
- prevalence of dysentery during 2nd Bull Run campaign, 179
- Gen. Hooker orders cleanup of latrines, 208
- typhoid outbreak in regiment's camp at Dumfries, 209
- prescriptive taken by 147th Pennsylvania to prevent typhoid, 209
- 29th Ohio surgeon's treatment regimen for typhoid, 209
- disease deaths on the march to Chancellorsville, 217
- army officials calculate maximum weight carried by each soldier, 218
- drinking water quality at Raccoon Ford, 270
- comparative good health enjoyed at Bridgeport, 296
- scurvy among troops at Atlanta, 345
- disease deaths during march to Savannah, 355–56
- Wallace Hoyt's death at Andersonville prison attributed to scurvy, 356
- postwar deaths from disease and wounds, 378

elections, political
- hospitalized soldiers request right to vote in 1863, 268
- soldiers reject Vallandigham in Ohio Governor's election of 1863, 274
- soldiers cast overwhelming 1864 vote for Lincoln in tent marked "Town Hall," 351

emancipation
- divergent views on, 172
- regiment's general indifference to, 172

enlistees, original, characteristics of, 37–38

entrepreneurs, soldiers as, 173, 174, 297

flags
- first pair presented at Camp Giddings, 63–65
- bullet holes at Kernstown, 114
- regiment's national flag captured at Port Republic, 136
- flag taken from them at Port Republic returned, 176–77
- Buckley raises funds for new flags, 288
- original flags sent to Jefferson for safekeeping, 289
- new pair of flags presented to the regiment at Wauhatchie, 289
- old and new flags carried through Cleveland late 1863, 291
- campaign to raise money for regiment's third set of flags, 362
- battle-damaged condition of remarked on by Sherman, 367
- third and last national flag presented at Bladensburg, MD, 374
- final disposition of, 378

Giddings, Joshua R.
- presents regiment's flags at Camp Giddings, 64
- sarcasm toward, 95
- absence of reaction to his death, 321

home, maintaining connections with
- sending pay to families, 100
- Sgt. Marsh requests local gossip from home, 101
- rumor that mail was left rotting on docks, 210
- maintaining connections to younger siblings, 246–47
- list of foods requested from home, 297
- solving family problems from a distance, 299–300
- long-delayed mail from home reaches regiment at Savannah, 358
- mail catches up with regiment near Goldsboro, NC, 370

humor, soldier. *See under* amusements

marches
- false start from Camp Chase, 75
- march to cut off Jackson's retreat from Romney, 89–90
- Camp Starvation to Paw Paw, 96
- snowy march toward Winchester aborted, 99
- into Paw Paw to see Gen. Lander's remains placed on train, 100
- from near Martinsburg to above Winchester, 103
- to first battle at Kernstown, 105–7
- pursuit of Jackson after Kernstown, 117–18
- Shenandoah valley to Falmouth, 123–25
- return to the valley, 129–30
- hungry, muddy march leading to Port Republic, 130–32
- out of the valley to Bristoe Station, VA, 144
- Culpeper Court House back to the Rappahannock River, 178
- Rappahannock to Bristoe Station, 180–81
- Bristoe Station to Georgetown, 181–82
- Georgetown to Frederick, MD, 182–83
- Potomac River to Dumfries, VA, 201–2
- Dumfries to Chancellorsville, 216–19
- to their old camp at Aquia Creek after Chancellorsville, 236
- Aquia Creek to Leesburg, VA, 247
- Leesburg to Gettysburg, 250–51
- pursuit of Lee from Gettysburg back to the Rappahannock, 265–67
- forced march from Bridgeport, AL, to reinforce Geary at Wauhatchie, 278–79
- Wauhatchie to Bridgeport, 290
- scout into Georgia from Bridgeport, 298–99
- Bridgeport to Dug Gap, GA, 304–7
- Resaca to Cassville, GA, 320
- to New Hope Church, 325
- New Hope Church to Big Shanty (Acworth), 329
- to Pine Knob, GA, 330
- back to the Chattahoochee, 346
- entering Atlanta, 347
- Atlanta to Savannah, 352–57
- 29th Ohio's division first to enter Savannah, 359
- Savannah to Raleigh, NC, 363–70
- North Carolina to Washington, DC, 371–73
- Grand Review, 373–74
- homecoming march through Cleveland, 377
- returning soldiers set out for their homes, 379–80

medicine: hospitals, army surgeons, and medical treatment
- battlefield triage at Kernstown, 111
- shortage of medical supplies and ambulances to treat Kernstown wounded, 111–12
- 29th Ohio soldiers left behind in Shenandoah valley hospitals captured by Jackson, 127
- wounded Maj. Clemmer's journey from the Port Republic battlefield to Ohio, 149–50
- graphic descriptions of conditions in Washington area hospitals, 150–51
- treatment of the Cedar Mountain wounded on the field, and in the town of Culpeper, 163

rail transport of wounded from Culpeper to
Washington hospitals, 163–64
Alexandria described as one vast hospital, 182
at Frederick, MD, 185, 186
Chaplain Ames finds hospitalized soldiers more
amenable to his preaching, 207
regimental hospital at Dumfries described, 209
medical discharges at Dumfries, 214
division hospital at Chancellorsville, 227
29th Ohio soldiers carry wounded to the rear at
Chancellorsville, 229–30
artillery fire destroys 12th Corps hospital at
Chancellorsville, 233
soldier found wounded on Chancellorsville days after
the battle dies, 240
29th Ohio wounded at Bushman Farm hospital and
Camp Letterman, Gettysburg, 262–63
care of wounded on the field at Dug Gap, GA, 312;
advanced rail transport to hospitals from, 313,
339–40
division hospital near Kennesaw Mountain
shelled, 334
a wounded soldier's last hour in the Kennesaw
Mountain field hospital, 335
field hospital patients given beer ration, 336
medicines given for intermittent fever, 339
medicine: soldiers' attitudes toward hospitals and army
surgeons
dread of hospitals and medicines, 94
incompetent army surgeons blamed for soldier
suffering, 181
riding in an army ambulance, 185
attitude toward surgeons of wounded left on the field
at Chancellorsville, 242
soldier's characterization of army surgeon as
butcher, 313
Sgt. Parmater throws away prescribed medicines,
345
morale
plummeting in late fall 1861, 57, 69
high spirits on arrival at Camp Kelly, 87
sinking at Camp Kelly, 94
jubilation after Kernstown battle, 118
officers threaten to resign when Gen. McDowell
prohibits tents and baggage, 122
officers protest order to return to the Shenandoah
valley, 126
mourning in the 29th's camp on the evening of Port
Republic, 137
officers resign to avoid another battle like Port
Republic, 142
visitor to the Regiment reports high morale before
Cedar Mountain fight, 154
buoyed by arrival at Frederick of 160 recruits, 195
Hooker's reforms restore morale, 213, 225
unaccountably high among enlisted men after
Chancellorsville, 244–45
distress at inability to recover the dead from Dug
Gap, 315
soldiers' resolve to persevere after Dug Gap, 317
at historic high in Atlanta, 349
demoralization at Bardstown, KY, 375–76

mythology of the Twenty-Ninth Ohio's war
each soldier tested for his abolition zeal before
enlistment, xii, 64, 378
timing of and motivations for the founding of the
29th Ohio, 20–22
participation of U.S. Senator Ben Wade in the
regiment's organization, 23
command at Cedar Mountain, 160
participation in the Antietam campaign, 184
hardships of winter 1863 at Dumfries, 204
role in suppression of the New York draft riot, 268
actions at Lookout Mountain and the battles for
Chattanooga, 282–83
capture of rebel gun at Resaca, 319
division's artillery kills rebel Gen. Polk, 330
capture of rebel blockhouse near Kennesaw
Mountain, 334, 335–36
soldier mans artillery in last stand at Peach Tree
Creek, 342
newspaper correspondents, soldiers as, 87
officer resignations, field
threatened over removal of tents, 122
threatened after Port Republic defeat, 142
officer resignations, staff
Col. Lewis Buckley resignation at Dumfries, 204–5
Col. Thomas Clark resignation after Chancellorsville
causes serious discord among 29th Ohio officers,
245–46
officers, general, attitude toward
Chap. Hurlburt and Col. Buckley criticize Gen.
Lander's indifference to his soldiers' welfare, 100
soldiers hurrah Gen. Shields after Kernstown, 117
Buckley accuses Gen. Shields of ruining his division, 142
Gen. Pope's fallback from the Rappahannock
criticized, 179
officer states McClellan will lead the army to
victory, 183
Burnsides's boast to take Richmond met with
sarcasm, 201
confidence in Gen. Sherman, 349
organization
timing of and motivations for regiment's founding,
20–22
the men behind the Giddings Regiment's birth, 23
Lewis P. Buckley accepts command, 27
predictions for early completion of organization, 31
characteristics of original enlistees, 37–38
enlistment spirit in decline post–Bull Run, 39
enlistment slowdown blamed on 19th Ohio
veterans, 39–40
recruiting competition, 40–42
reform of the recruiting process, 44–46
Capt. Josiah Wright assails unidentified men who
worked against the 29th's success, 58
Col. Clark attacks state adj. general for depriving the
29th of recruits, 63
Buckley requests the regiment be held back from the
war until up to full strength, 65
organization completed by shifting men to
undermanned companies, 66
Wade's cavalry blamed for 29th Ohio's slow
organization, 86

pay
- complaints of delay, 72–73
- poverty of soldiers and officers at Camp Chase, 78
- plight of impoverished families causes soldiers to cry, 95
- first pay day, 100
- soldiers account for how pay is spent, 100
- enlisted men's earnings compared to officers, 101
- chaplain takes regiment's pay to Ohio, 114
- by late fall 1862 regiment has not been paid for five months, 196
- pay and benefits of an army chaplain, 206
- soldier fears he might never catch up with stay-at-homes who are getting rich, 212
- army paymasters characterized as liars, 243
- soldiers paid at Aquia Creek, 243
- reenlisted veterans receive a windfall of cash at Louisville, 290
- disappointment at failure to receive veteran's bounties, 299

prisoner of war experiences
- most 29th Ohio soldiers captured by Jackson in Valley hospitals paroled and sent home to Ohio, 127–28
- circumstances of capture at Port Republic, 135–36
- survivors of Port Republic return to Regiment at Luray, 137–38
- Port Republic prisoners marched from Port Republic to the rebel prison at Lynchburg, VA, 166–67
- conditions at Lynchburg, 167–68
- enlisted men captured at Port Republic and Cedar Mountain moved to Belle Isle prison, Richmond, 168
- officers captured at Port Republic imprisoned at Salisbury, NC, 169
- soldiers captured at Port Republic and Cedar Mountain paroled and sent to Fort Delaware to await exchange, 169-70
- paroled prisoners rejoin the regiment at Frederick, 200
- circumstances of capture at Chancellorsville, 233
- soldiers captured at Chancellorsville paroled and released, 240
- captured at Peach Tree Creek, 342
- mass graves discovered at Millen prison pen, GA, 356
- rations at Andersonville prison reported by escapee, 356
- conditions at Salisbury prison 1865, 366–67

rations and ration preparation
- initial delight with, at Camp Giddings, 33–34
- acute dissatisfaction with at Camp Giddings, 58
- cooking ordered done henceforth by squad, 67
- frying pan made by splitting a canteen, 91
- cooking hardtack and salt pork in a tin cup, 91–92
- reduced to three crackers per day, 95
- Gen. Lander issues whiskey, 96
- celebration feast of beans and hard bread, 98
- soldiers build ovens and attempt bread baking, 118
- making a meal of flour mixed with water, 130
- supper consists of one cracker and a cup of coffee, 130
- plentiful soft bread at Alexandria, 145
- at Belle Isle prison, 169
- Union officer pries open crates of hardtack and feeds hungry released prisoners, 170
- published jokes about insect infested hardtack, 170
- subsisting on green corn during 2nd Bull Run campaign, 179
- officer rations at Frederick, MD, 186
- officer's bill of fare Christmas 1862, 201
- soldiers issued desiccated vegetables and molasses at Dumfries, 204
- fresh bread and butter at Aquia Creek, 243
- citizens present soldiers with a bounty of things to eat on the march to Gettysburg, 251
- issued fresh beef on first night at Gettysburg, 252
- hospital diet for wounded and amputees at Gettysburg, 263
- rations reduced to four and one half crackers per man per day after Gettysburg, 267
- Ohio residents feed soldiers en route to the relief of Chattanooga, 272
- reduced to hardtack and field corn at Wauhatchie, TN, 280
- soldier and officer rations at Wauhatchie compared, 286
- surplus of at Bridgeport, 296
- graves dug up to retrieve hams hidden by civilians, 329
- issued near Marietta, GA, 336
- for patients in Chattanooga hospitals, 339
- for patients in Nashville hospitals, 340
- foods gathered during foraging in Atlanta suburbs, 351
- foods foraged from Georgia civilians in march to Savannah, 354
- discovery of grocer's buried stock, 355
- rations dry up on arrival at Savannah, 357
- soldiers introduced to rice, 358
- limited to army beans in North Carolina, 367

rebel soldiers, attitude toward
- poor condition derided, 96
- accused of killing defenseless soldiers during Jackson's Valley sweep, 127
- accused of murdering surrendered soldiers at Port Republic, 135
- characterized as ragged and filthy, 172
- soldier thinks war could be ended by soldiers of both sides having a drink, 213
- tenacity at Chancellorsville praised by an enlisted soldier, 245
- old veteran expresses sympathy for parents of rebels shot down at Culp's Hill, 260
- Yankees trade coffee and news to rebels for tobacco, 280
- soldiers caught foraging are detailed to manual labor, 281
- dispirited condition of rebel deserters convince regiment's soldiers that the Confederacy is finished, 281, 286
- soldiers wade into the Chattahoochee River and trade rebels for tobacco, 337
- chaplain buries boyish rebel cavalryman and concludes the Confederacy is desperate, 351
- soldiers of both sides shake hands and exchange wishes for a happy peace, 373

recruiting (enlistment)
- mothers encouraged to give sons to the army, 46–47
- economic advantages of enlistment emphasized, 48–49
- 19th Ohio veterans in Giddings Regiment, 106

officers Myron Wright and E. B. Howard return to Ohio to recruit following Port Republic debacle, 145, 189–91, 194
friends at home work to have Ohio troops of Tyler's brigade taken out of the line and refitted, 178
recruiting campaign of 1862 hindered by raising of new regiments, 190, 191
soldier thinks draft dodgers should be hung, 193
success of captains Wright and Howard, 195
successful campaign to gather voluntary recruits late 1863, 293

religion
  Buckley makes Sabbath service attendance mandatory at Camp Giddings, 54
  Buckley orders men to desist from doing laundry on Sabbath, 118
  soldiers attend Catholic mass for entertainment, 174
  soldier pokes fun at Catholic nuns, and Catholic rituals, 196
  Chaplain Ames finds most soldiers indifferent to their spiritual condition, 206
  dramatic increase in Sabbath services after Chancellorsville, 240–41
  services conducted at 12th Corps Hospital at Gettysburg, 262
  attendance at service surges at Bridgeport, 297–98

skirmishes
  with Ashby's cavalry near Strasburg, 118
  with Jackson's artillery near Mt. Jackson, 119
  with Stuart's cavalry on the Rappahannock River during opening moves of the 2nd Bull Run campaign, 178
  29th Ohio called out to defend Frederick from rebel cavalry, 197
  guerrillas attack column and get away with a sutler's wagon, 201
  with a Pennsylvania regiment over rights to firewood, 201
  at Broad Run, VA, 202
  with Stuart's cavalry outside Dumfries, VA, 202
  with rebel cavalry on the march to Chancellorsville, 219
  with Mosby's guerrillas near Sharpsburg, MD, 266
  deployed at Kolb's Farm, 334
  as hallmark of the Atlanta campaign, 336
  with Wheeler's cavalry at Mill Creek, AL, 350
  with Iverson's cavalry during garrison duty in Atlanta, 351
  outside Millen, GA, 356
  in front of Savannah, 357–59
  North Edisto River, SC, 364

slaves (freedmen, contrabands), encounters with
  officers acquire "servants," 104
  Virginia black people seen as subdued in behavior compared to Ohio blacks, 105
  Chaplain Hurlburt's comic duplication of a former slave's dialect, 124
  Lt. Howard sends one of two liberated slaves to Ohio to work on his farm, 104
  Port Republic survivors aided by slaves, 138
  soldier converted to antislavery upon observing slaves working under their masters, 171–72
  Sgt. Parmater indifferent to John Brown raid sites at Harpers Ferry, 266
  Chaplain Ames hires black servant, 269
  soldier observes Tennessee "niggers" picking cotton, 273
  Negro teamsters flee at first fire battle of Wauhatchie, 280
  29th Ohio soldiers amuse themselves by putting Negro children aboard trains near Nashville, 295
  Gen. Geary attributes ruination of Dumfries, VA, to Southern slave owners, 203
  slave guides Geary's division to Cassville, 321
  contrabands employed in Nashville hospitals, 340
  conflict between colored soldier and white soldiers, 340
  colored residents cheer regiment's march into Atlanta, 347
  jubilant slaves join Geary's column in march to Savannah, 354
  slaves dance to entertain soldiers during march to Savannah, 355
  found looting in Savannah, 359
  soldiers waylay colored residents of Atlanta and steal their firewood, 362
  Sgt. Parmater is fed by runaway slaves, 366
  Chaplain Ames fears for the safety of freed slaves after the army goes home, 369

Southern civilians, relationships to
  at Camp Starvation, 91
  soldiers make fun of Southern dialect, 96
  pity owners of farms ruined by Union camps, 103
  purchasing home-cooked meals from, 104
  playing pranks on, 119
  stealing livestock and souvenirs at Mt. Jackson, 119
  Cpl. Parmater interviews a Warrenton, VA, lady, 124
  Shields's men ordered to retrace march and repair destroyed fence, 141
  sympathy for starving women and children at Dumfries, 204
  farmer's place burned for speaking against the Union, 249
  destitution of refugees at Bridgeport, 297
  slave-owning woman protests destruction, 356
  white residents of Savannah cheer the 29th's entry, 360
  sympathy for South Carolina civilians in the army's path, 366

sutlers
  disguising alcohol, 73
  goods too expensive for money-strapped soldiers at Camp Kelly, 87
  selling soft bread at Camp Kelly, 95
  paid soldiers visit sutler's booth, 100
  Cpl. Wallace Hoyt asks parents and neighbors for food, intending to sell it to his fellows, 173
  soldier purchases from at Aquia Creek, 243
  referred to as "smugglers," 243
  characterized as "cutthroats," 244
  high prices charged at Wauhatchie, 290
  at Nashville army hospitals, 340
  regiment's sutler at Savannah charges outlandish prices, 362
  supply beer at Bardstown, KY, 376
  soldiers at Bardstown overrun and destroy sutler's stand, 376–77

tents and shelters
- antiquated tents issued at Camp Giddings, 33
- straw sack beds, 53
- keeping clear of mud at Camp Kelley, 86
- fence rail and pine branch arbors at Camp Misery, 91
- wikiup construction, 96
- tents from Camp Giddings arrive at Paw Paw, 97
- "gum" rubber blankets issued, 102
- tents and baggage catch up with regiment at Strasburg, 118
- long-awaited Sibley tents issued, 122
- Gen. McDowell bans tents and baggage, 122
- shelter halves issued, 131
- officers and soldiers at Frederick in comfortable tents, 186
- officer accommodations at Dumfries, 206, 207
- Officer Gibbs's detailed building plan for his shanty at Dumfries, 207
- term "tuggy" as used by the 29th Ohio's soldiers, 207
- description of soldier huts at Dumfries, 207–8
- tuggies constructed during stay at Aquia Creek, company streets beautified, 243
- hut building at Wauhatchie, 285
- officers' accommodations at Wauhatchie, 286
- winter hut building at Bridgeport, 295–96
- decoration of huts at Bridgeport, 301
- soldiers dismantle Atlanta houses for hut-building material, 347
- shelter tent camp outside Savannah, 357
- army provides lumber for soldier huts at Savannah, 360
- shelter halves turned in at war's end, 377

tourists, soldiers as
- impressed by sights of Columbus, 71
- opinion of western Virginia countryside, 84, 87
- Shenandoah valley compared to Ohio, 104, 118
- Winchester, 105
- New Market boarded up and deserted, 120
- Washington, DC, 145
- area surrounding Manassas a wasteland, 179
- march through the 1st and 2nd Bull Run battlefields, 181
- favorable impressions of Frederick, MD, 186
- antiquities of Dumfries, VA, 203, 210
- Cpl. Parmater tours notable sights in Washington, 207
- federal shipping colossus at Aquia Landing draws curious soldiers, 244
- officers tour New York City, 270
- exploration of caves, mountains, and town of Chattanooga, 286
- exploring ancient shell mounds, 300
- exploring Nickajack Cave, 304
- Atlanta after its fall, 347
- novelty of Georgia swamp country, 356, 357
- Savannah, 360
- Charleston, SC, 368–69
- through ruined Richmond, 372
- Washington, DC, at war's end, 374–75

transportation
- rail: Ashtabula to Columbus, 70; Columbus to the Upper Potomac, 79–85; reconnaissance to and burning of Green Springs, VA, 88–89; Paw Paw to near Martinsburg, VA, 102; Bristoe Station, VA, to Alexandria, 144; Alexandria to Warrenton en route to Cedar Mountain battle, 152; Alexandria to Normandy, TN, 271–74; Normandy to Bridgeport, AL, 275; Bridgeport to Ohio, 290–91; return to Bridgeport, 294–95; Cincinnati to Cleveland, 377
- water: paroled prisoners sail to Ft. Delaware, MD, 170; on the Atlantic from Virginia to New York City and back, 268–70; riverboat to Bardstown, KY at war's end, 375; from Bardstown to Cincinnati, 377

troop strength
- peak strength reached at Camp Giddings, 65
- on leaving Columbus, 78
- sick left behind at Camp Chase, 77
- at the battle of Kernstown, 106
- before and after the battle of Port Republic, 138
- shortage of staff and field officers after Port Republic, 145
- before and after Cedar Mountain, 29th OVI reduced to less than size of a full company, 164
- shortage of officers in Antietam campaign, 184
- Gen. Halleck refuses to allow regiments of the 29th's brigade opportunity to recruit and refit, 188
- 160 new recruits join regiment at Frederick, 195
- on setting out for Chancellorsville, 214
- reduced by Atlanta campaign, 337
- fortified by arrival at Atlanta of "substitutes," 349

uniforms and equipage
- dress uniforms first issued at Camp Giddings, 35
- fatigue uniforms, kepis, knapsacks, canteens, and camp stores arrive, 55
- first uniform issue wears out within weeks, 57
- defective great coats, 57
- long overcoats issued, 57
- uniform draw against pay system, 57
- comic difficulties getting into full gear, 66–67
- enlisted men doing laundry, 98
- army-issued brogans soled with cardboard, 101
- soldiers dream of custom-made boots, 101
- Pvt. Willis Sisley orders made-to-order boots from home, 120
- Valley Pike wears out shoddy shoes; many soldiers going barefoot, 120
- Lincoln touched by pitiful condition of Shields's soldiers, 124
- new uniforms fail to meet them at Falmouth, 125
- knapsacks of Port Republic missing piled and burned, 141
- materiel loss in Shields's division in Shenandoah valley campaign, 142
- new uniforms issued after Port Republic, 143
- new uniforms drawn at Aquia Creek en route to Chancellorsville, 217
- on Hooker's order, soldiers draw white stars to identify corps and division, 217
- knapsacks piled prior to combat at Chancellorsville, 226

uniforms and equipment lost or damaged at Chancellorsville replaced, 236
knapsack captured at Chancellorsville returned to 29th Ohio soldier decades later, 238
knapsacks rub shoulders raw on march to Leesburg, 248
veterans ship winter coats home as campaign of 1864 nears, 302
uniforms drawn at Cassville, GA, 321
order to draw extra uniforms and shoes for march to Savannah, 353

Veteran Volunteer reenlistment
campaign at Wauhatchie, 288–90
number of soldiers and officers reenlisted as, 290
furlough home, 292–94

General Index

(SEE ALSO TWENTY-NINTH OHIO VOLUNTEER
INFANTRY REGIMENT INDEX, PRECEDING)

abolition (antislavery movement), ix, xii; Jefferson, OH, as epicenter of, 2; sentiment in the 29th Ohio toward, 172
Ackley, Miss Maria, 288
Adam's Express, 266
Adams, Cpl. Newton B., 289
Adams, Rev., 15
Aiken's Landing, VA, 170, 171
Akron, OH, xi, 13, 25, 50, 74, 172, 176, 210, 245, 255, 274, 315, 379; draft resistance in, 192; economic growth, 147–48, 211, 286, 321; Lincoln, support for, 4, 352; Lincoln's death mourned in, 370; military companies raised, April 1861, 16; National Day of Fasting observed, 239; 19th Ohio (90-day) soldiers celebrated, 18; veterans honored by, 293, 380; voluntary enlistment in, 338; women's fashions in, 212, 323
Akron Democrat, 213
Alexandria, VA, 143, 144, 181, 269, 271
Allatoona Pass, GA, 325, 329
Allegheny Mountains, 83
Allen County, OH, 194
Alliance, OH, 193
American Hotel (Cleveland), 292
Ames, Edwin, 241, 346
Ames, Rev. Lyman D., x; and Andersonville Prison escapee, 356; at Aquia Creek, 236, 240–42, 245; at Atlanta, 344, 345, 348; on the *Baltic*, 269; at Big Shanty, 330; at Bridgeport, 298, 302; in Cassville, GA, 325; at Chancellorsville, 217, 219, 220, 222, 233, 239, 244; in Charleston after its fall, 368–69; in Cleveland, 291; in Conneaut, 148, 292; counsels deranged soldiers, 243; and death of Pvt. Elias Waltz, 209; departs regiment at Savannah, 358; diary of, x, 206; at Dug Gap, 312, 313–14, 328; at Dumfries, VA, 206–7, 210, 214; and dying soldier, 335; on execution of deserters, 259; Gettysburg, en route to, 248, 250; at Gettysburg, 255, 261–63; hires freed slave as personal attendant, 269; life after war, 376; life before war, 206; at Lookout Mountain, 280, 283; in Madison, GA, 354; on March to the Sea, 355–56; in Milledgeville, GA, 355; at New Hope Church, 327, 328; in New York City, 270; at Normandy, TN, 274–75; on officers, 245, 269, 283–84, 286; ordered back to regiment, 375; at Painesville railroad disaster, 293; and rebel sharpshooter, 329; on rebel surgeons, 348; resigns and leaves regiment at Bardstown, 376; on soldiers, 267, 269, 271, 286, 288, 290, 294, 296–97, 302, 329, 335

Anderson, Maj. Robert, 269
Andersonville, GA, rebel prison at, 169, 341, 344, 356, 379
Andover, OH, 302
Andrews, Sgt. Addison, 136
Antietam, battle of, 184, 185, 186, 265
Antietam, MD, 182, 184, 265
antiwar sentiment, 13, 190, 267
Aqueduct Bridge, Washington, DC, 182
Aquia Creek, VA, 216, 217, 236, 238, 243, 248
Aquia Landing, VA, 203, 207, 216, 243
Army of the Cumberland, 340; besieged in Chattanooga, 271, 272, 284; service of Ohio soldiers in, 286
Army of the Potomac: at Chancellorsville, 226, 237; continuing defeats cause civilian war weariness, 245; 1864 rumor of regiment's return to, 300, 349; faces Lee across Rappahannock River, 267; at Gettysburg, 252, 261; pursues Lee toward Sharpsburg, MD, 183, 184; regarded by Western troops as "white glove" soldiers, 281; strength in spring 1863, 214; winter camp 1863, 201
Army of Virginia, 146, 183
artillery, Union: Best's, 12th Corps, 225, 228; Carlin's battery (Conneaut Battery), Geneva Artillery, 21, 22, 40, 67; 1st Ohio Light, 378; 2nd Ohio artillery, 389; 4th U.S., 222, 227; 5th U.S., 221; 13th NY, 335; 2nd Ohio Heavy, 188; Knap's Pennsylvania Battery, 126, 221, 223, 226, 227, 275, 280, 305; McGill's battery, 311, 330; Muhlenburg's Battery, Best's Artillery, 222, 227
Ashby, Col. Turner (CSA), 136
Ashby's Gap, VA, 266
Ashtabula, OH, 5, 6, 39, 150, 237, 322; economics of, 6, 149, 327; soldiers from, 20, 70; wounded soldiers at Cliffburne Hospital, 151
Ashtabula County, Ohio, xi, 147, 148, 274, 352; antislavery advocates, 171; and Bounty problems, 299, 338; Chancellorsville reports, 239; draft resistance 1862, 192–93; drafts in, 194, 349; Geneva Township protective association, 338; organization of the Giddings Regiment, 31; and Soldiers Aid Society, 238; and speculation, 147, 287, 327
Ashtabula County Agricultural Society, 68
Ashtabula County Fairgrounds, Jefferson, OH, 30
Ashtabula Sentinel, 15, 113, 198, 379; on blacks as soldiers, 171; on county's patriotism, 21; on Dug Gap disaster, 314; on financial benefits of enlistment, 48; and J. R. Giddings, 51;

Ashtabula Sentinel (cont.)
    on J. R. Giddings's funeral, 321; on mistreatment of county troops in the 19th OVI, 21; on New York draft riots, 268; on Port Republic battle, 140; on recapture of regiment's flag, 177; on treatment of the South after war, 267; war news placement, 237; Wheeler hospital reform campaign, 152

Ashtabula Weekly Telegraph, 78, 237, 291
Athens County, OH, 194
Atkins, Pvt. Albert, 328
Atkins, Pvt. Spencer, 328
Atlanta, GA, 271, 333, 344, 352; destruction of witnessed by regiment, 346; entered by Candy's (Pardee's) brigade, 347; siege of 343–46
Atlanta campaign, regiment's losses in, 337
atrocity stories, 4, 13, 19, 149
Augur, Gen. Christopher C., 157, 158, 161
"Augusta" railroad (Georgia Railroad), 352, 355
Austerlitz, battle of, 114
Austinburg, OH, 150
"Austinburg Lady, The," 150–52

Babb's Settlement, Mill Creek Valley, GA, 307
Back (Black) Creek, VA, 102
Bailey, Cpl. Nelson, 176, 285
Baldwin, Pvt. W. W., 166
Baltic, S.S., 269–70, 271
Baltimore, MD, 172, 195
Baltimore and Ohio Railroad, 75, 184
Baltimore Pike, Gettysburg, PA, 251, 252, 254, 256, 259
band, 123, 146, 194
Banks, Gen. Nathaniel P., 84, 111, 117, 121, 153, 158, 175, 176, 180, 183
Barber Match Co. (Akron, OH), 147–48
Bardstown, KY: 29th Ohio sent to at war's end, 375–77
Bare, Pvt. Thomas, 259
Barnum, P. T., 198
Bath Center, Summit County, OH, 191
Bealeton Station, VA, 271
"Beauregard," 91, 249
Beck, Pvt. Christopher, 138, 244, 245, 283, 284, 344
Beckwith, Sgt. Harvey, 110
Bellaire, OH, 143
Belle Isle Prison, Richmond, VA, 139, 166, 168–69, 380
Bentonville, NC, battle of, 367
Benwood, OH, railroad collision at, 272
Best, Capt. Clermont, 225, 228
Beverly's Ford, VA, 178
Bierce, Lucius V., 78
Big Cacapon River, VA, 99
Big Round Top, Gettysburg, PA, 252
Big Shanty (Acworth), GA, 7, 329–30, 332
Billings, Sgt. Ransom, 344
Bingham, Pvt. Amander, 43
Birney, Gen. David, 224
Bishop, Lt. Alfred, 205
"Black Strings," 3–4
Bladensburg, MD, 374–75
Blair, Pvt. Jeb, 120, 163
Blake, Pvt. Isham (CSA), 236
Blodgett, Pvt. John, 60

Bloomery Gap, VA, skirmish at, 96
Blue Ridge Mountains, VA, 103, 121, 154, 248, 249, 265, 372
Bluff (game), 244
Borodino, battle of, 114
bounties, 145, 191, 349; federal, 49, 288; local, 191, 287, 288, 293, 299, 322, 338; for Veteran Volunteers, 288, 290, 299
Bradley, Rev. Joshua, 26
Brady, Matthew, "The Dead of Antietam," 152
Bragg, Gen. Braxton (CSA), 271, 272, 279, 282
Braginton, Pvt. George, 134, 315
Brainard, Pvt. Conant, 103–4
Breckinridge, Col. W. P. C. (CSA), 312
Brick, Pvt. Barney, 348
Bridgeport, AL, 275, 279, 285, 290, 295–303
Brimfield, Summit County, OH, 13, 190, 191
Bristoe Station, VA, 144, 179, 180, 197
Broad Run, VA, skirmish at, 202
Brooklyn, NY, 270
Brough, Ohio Gov. John, 268, 274
Brower, John, 3rd Georgia Cavalry, 351
Brown, Pvt. Edward J., 262
Brown, John, 3–4, 238
Brown, John, Jr., 3, 41, 74, 172
"Buckeye Men's Mess," Salisbury Prison, 169
Buckhead Station, GA, 355
Buckingham, Ohio State Adj. General C. P., 30, 62, 63, 64, 84
Buckley, Hugh, 26
Buckley, Col. Lewis P., 61, 64, 66, 78, 101, 142, 184, 246, 293, 344; accepts command of the 29th OVI, 27; as Akron businessman, 27; Akron Union Light Infantry raised April 1861, 16; at Alexandria, VA, 144; in California Gold Rush of 1849, 27; at Camp Giddings and takes command of 29th OVI, 49; collecting brigade's absent soldiers, 187, 188; commands Tyler's Brigade on march to Falmouth, VA, 123; and Democratic Party, 64, 171; early life in New York, 26; at Frederick, MD, 183, 195, 197, 199; at Kernstown battle, 110; kindness to soldiers, 119; on Lander, 100, 142; at Occoquan Creek, 202; at Port Republic, 133, 134, 135, 137, 139, 141; and regiment's flags, 65, 267, 288, 362, 374; resignation forced by health, 204–5; Sabbath services, soldiers' attendance at, 118; on Shields, 142; on 29th OVI officers, 122, 123; at U.S. Military Academy, West Point, NY, 26; at Winchester, 112
Buckley Chapel, Akron, 47
Bull Run, battle of, 18, 179, 201, 248
Bull Run, second battle of, 177–81
Burke, Redmond, "The Guerrilla King," 202
Burns, Pvt. John, 134
Burnside, Gen. Ambrose, 95, 198, 201, 203, 208, 366
Burridge, Lt. Eleazer, 101, 195
Burrows, Asst. Surgeon Sylvester, 208–9
Burton Township, Geauga County, OH, 299
Butterfield, Gen. Daniel (Butterfield's division), 282, 320, 326, 331, 332
"Butternut Democrats," 210

Cadwell, Darius, 15, 24, 31, 191
Calhoun, GA, 320

Cameron, Sec. of War Simon, 22
Campbell, Pvt. John, 134
Camp Chase, Columbus, OH, 84, 143, 149, 187, 194, 269, 284, 295, 296, 299; alcohol use by regiment at, 74–75; layout described by Nathan Parmater, 71; outbreak of measles in, 76–77
Camp Cleveland, 378
Camp Dennison, OH, 71, 143
Camp Giddings, Jefferson, OH, 30, 54, 242, 268, 288, 379
Camp Goddard, 57
Camp Kelly, MD, 85, 87
Camp Ohio, DC, 207
Camp Parole, MD, 174, 241
Camp Taylor, Cleveland, 29
Canada, 267, 293
Canal Fulton, OH, 191
Candy, Col. Charles, 138, 157, 161, 224, 231, 257, 347
Canton, OH, 68
Capitol Building, Washington, DC, 207
Carlin, John (Conneaut Battery, Geneva Artillery), 21, 40
Carlin's Battery, 67
Carroll, Col. Samuel, 131
Carroll's 4th Brigade, Shields's division, 131
Casement, Maj. John S., 110
Cassville, GA, 321
Catholicism, 151, 174, 196
Catlett's Station, VA, 124, 180
Cedar Mountain, battle of, 156–64, 173, 174, 176, 177
Cedar Run, Culpeper, VA, 157, 162
Cemetery Hill, Gettysburg battlefield, 253
Cemetery Ridge, Gettysburg battlefield, 253, 259
Centreville, VA, 181
Chaffee, Adj. Comfort T., 32, 44, 62, 86, 105, 115, 122
Chaffee, Judge Norman, 77, 287
Chamberlain, Col. Joshua, 254
Chamberlain, Sgt. Wilbur, 229–30, 320, 364–65
Chancellor Inn, 219, 220, 225, 228, 231, 232, 233
Chancellor's Crossroads, 219
Chancellorsville, battle of, 216–35, 238, 245, 250, 252, 257, 260, 266, 291, 294, 372
Chantilly, battle of, 181
Chapman, Maj. Lansford F., 230, 372–73
Charleston, SC, 12, 182, 268
Charlottesville, VA, 166
Chase, Treasury Sec. Salmon P., 5
Chattahoochee River, GA, 329, 331, 333, 337, 338, 340, 346
Chattahoochee (rebel gunboat), 344
Chattanooga, TN, 271, 274, 275, 279, 293, 296, 302, 346
Chesapeake and Ohio Canal, 86
Chesapeake Bay, VA, 266
children as farmhands, 324
Children's Aid Society of New York, 36–37, 342
Chitty, J. H. (5th Georgia Cavalry), 348
Christian Church, 205
Christian Commission, U.S., 297, 334
Chuck-a-Luck, 286, 288, 355, 362
Cincinnati, OH, 140, 188, 245, 294, 322, 375, 377
Citizens Library, Jefferson, OH, 177
City Point, VA, 240
Clark, Col. Thomas, 206; appointment as state drill master April 1861, 29; on Gen. Burnside, 201; at Camp Giddings, 30; at Camp Kelly, 87; at Camp Misery, 90; capture at Port Republic, 136; censure by State Adj. Gen. Buckingham for insubordination, 62; at Chancellorsville, 222, 224, 226, 227, 230, 232, 235, 239; command of regiment after Buckley resignation, 205; at Dumfries, 210; on enlistment and recruiting, 41–42, 43; with 19th OVI in Rich Mountain campaign, 29; at Norwich Academy (University), 29; at Port Republic, 135–36; postwar letter to Rollin L. Jones, ix; release from Salisbury prison, 195; resignation at Aquia Creek, VA, 245–46; on Capt. Stevens at Chancellorsville, 246, 379; sword presented by Cleveland Sons of Temperance, 30
Clarke, Sgt. Henry E., 342–43
Cleburne, Gen. Patrick (CSA), 283, 310, 328
Clemmer, Maj. John S., 25, 49, 50, 58, 66, 92; resignation, 195, 206, 211; wounded at Port Republic, 134; wound treatment and return to Ohio, 149–50
Cleveland, OH, 70, 143, 191, 192, 291, 292, 293, 294, 322, 377
Cleveland Herald, 3, 266
Clopp (Clapp), Pvt. Charles, 59
Cobham, Col. George (Cobham's Brigade), 319
Cochran, Pvt. Norman, 143–44
colored regiments: 27th U.S., 368; 40th U.S., 369
Columbus, OH, 4, 15, 71, 72, 187, 272, 285, 290
"Commodore, the," 159
Conasauga River, GA, 320
Confederacy, in Western Reserve newspapers, 14
Confederate troops. *See* rebel troops
Congaree Creek, SC, skirmish at, 365
Conneaut, OH: Ames returns to, 376; Ames's son returns to, 346; changes in since 1862 noted by Chaplain Ames, 292; and draft resistance, 192, 193, 194; 4th of July 1862, 148; and Hooker, 237; Lincoln's inauguration train visits, 5; lumber industry, 238, 240, 323; recruiting for 29th OVI, 143, 293; veterans honored, 379; war meetings, 198, 200, 206, 211; women offer homes to convalescing soldiers, 149, 164
Conrad's Store, VA, 130, 135, 137, 140
Cook, Sgt. David Y., 229
Coon, Sgt. Chauncey H., 177
Cooper, James Fennimore, 48
Cooper, Pvt. William, 214
Coosawattee River, GA, 320
Copley, OH, 13
copperheads, 212, 267, 268, 274
Corinth, MS, 112, 281
Cossack (U.S. steamer), 170
Couch, Gen. Darius, 228
Cowles, Betsy Mix
Cracker Line, 280
Crane, Lt. Gurley G., 117, 132, 135, 137, 359, 378
Crane, James, 42
Crane, Lt. Col. Orrin J. (7th OVI), 283, 285, 289
Crawford, Gen. Samuel, 159, 160
Creighton, Col. William (7th OVI), 221, 231, 232, 283, 285, 289
Crimean War, 59

GENERAL INDEX 489

Crittenden Gate, 158, 159, 167
Crittenden Lane, 158, 159, 164
Cross Keys, VA, battle of, 132
Crowell, G. W. and Company, Cleveland, 64
Crowell, 2nd Lt. William S., 32, 122, 190, 191
Culpeper Court House, VA, 152, 156, 163
Culp's Hill, Gettysburg battlefield, 252, 253, 254, 255, 256, 263, 268, 273
Cumberland (U.S. sloop), 170
Cumberland, MD, 93, 163, 272
Cumberland Gap, MD, 300
Cunningham, Col. Richard, Jr. (CSA), 166
Curtiss, Lt. Edward, 190, 210, 220, 260, 313
Cutter and Howe's Hall, Akron, 293
Cuyahoga Falls, OH, 13, 359–60

Dallas, GA, 325
Dallas–New Hope Line, 328
Dalrymple, Pvt. Alma, 120
Dalton, GA, 283, 302, 345
Dandelion (U.S. gunboat), 358
Davenport, Jean, 85
Davidson, J. H. (147th NY), 356
Davis, Pvt. Cornelius, 328
Davis, Jefferson, 75, 192, 348
Davis, Pvt. John, 311
Decker, Pvt. Perry, 88
Declaration of Independence, 148
Delaware River, MD, 171, 174
Democratic Party, 14, 194, 198, 199, 205
Dennison, Ohio Gov. William, 20, 75
Dennison, Pvt. William, 132
Department of the Gulf, U.S. Army, 176
desertion, 60, 125, 197; punishment of, 197–98, 249–50
Devil's Den, Gettysburg battlefield, 252, 253
Devore, Perry, 41
Dice, Lt. George W., 17, 135, 137, 165, 195, 309, 314, 331
disease: at Camp Giddings, 59; dysentery during 2nd Bull Run campaign, 179; measles, 76–77, 296; in regiment, 1862, 120, 143; sick furloughs 1862, 143
Dixieland, 280
Doty, Cpl. Alfred, 244
Douglas, Cpl. C. P. (9th Texas Infantry), 348
Dowling, Pvt. Michael, 36
Dowling, Pvt. Peter, 36, 342, 335
Dowling, Pvt. Thomas, 36, 342
Downey, Pvt. Charles, 317
draft: in Ashtabula County, 192, 349, 350; commutation fee, 338; drafted and substitutes for Giddings Regiment at Atlanta, 349; exemption claims, 192; first, 190, 194; Geneva Township scheme for avoiding, 338; mechanics of, 194; resistance to in Ashtabula and Summit Counties, 192
drinking: at Bardstown, KY, 376; at Bladensburg, MD, 374; at Camp Cleveland, 378; on the Savannah River, 363; as scourge of the Union army, 210
Dudley, Pvt. Charles, 94
Dug Gap, GA, demonstration against, 304–17
Dumfries, VA, 202, 203, 209, 215, 216
Dunker Church, Antietam, 184
Durkee, 2nd Lt. Albert, 154

Duryea, Gen. Abraham, 124
Dykeman, Sgt. Tunis (102nd NY), last soldier buried by Chaplain Ames, 375

Early, Gen. Jubal (CSA), 158
Earnsparger, Pvt. Joseph, 191
East Liberty, Summit County, OH, 192
Eastlick, Pvt. George, 137, 187
East Wood, Antietam, 184
Eatonton, GA, 355
Edgerly, Sgt. C. H., 132
Edgerton, U.S. Congressman Sydney, 66, 150
Edwards Ferry, VA, 250
elections: Ashtabula County, 1864 landslide for Lincoln, 352; fall 1863, 274; hospitalized soldiers allowed to vote, 268; presidential election of 1864, voting in 29th's camp at Atlanta, 351–52
Ellis, Pvt. George, 138
Emancipation Proclamation, 211
Emmitsburg Road, Gettysburg, PA, 252, 253, 259
Enfield musket: issued to two companies at Camp Giddings, 56; issued to entire regiment at Dumfries, 213
Ensign, J. D., 15, 23–24, 34–35, 212, 321
Erie, PA, 41
Everhart, Pvt. Jonathan, 137
Ewell, Pvt. Hiram, 115
Ewell, Cpl. John, 115
Ewell, Gen. Richard S. (CSA), 134, 180, 254, 256–57, 259

Fairfax Court House, VA, 201
Fairfax Station, VA, 181, 182, 202
Fairview (Chancellorsville), 225
Falmouth, VA, 141, 203, 218, 247
Faze, Pvt. William, 317
federal income tax, 237
Federal Militia Act of 1862, 190
Fenton, Samuel L., 212
Fern, Miss Fanny, 287
Fifield, Surgeon Amos, 94, 204, 242; at Camp Chase, 77; chief surgeon, Candy's brigade, 287; Conneaut, prewar practice in, 60; at Dug Gap, 306, 312–13; at Dumfries, 208; at Kernstown, 111; physical examination of recruits, 188; at Port Republic, 134; resignation at Atlanta, 349; at Winchester, 112
Fifield, Mrs. Amos Kellogg, 287
Fitch, Capt. William T., 188, 200, 211, 269, 283, 288, 302; Antietam campaign, 183, 186; Aquia Creek, VA, too sick to take command at, 246; Cedar Mt., absent sick at, 156; Chancellorsville, absent at, 226; Co. A, organized and led into Camp Giddings by, 32; command of Co. A challenged by M. P. Pierce, 44; at Dumfries, 206, 209; Green Springs, VA, search for lost soldiers, 89; in Jefferson recuperating from wounds, 338; at Kernstown, 110; Lookout Mountain fight, 282; Occoquan Creek skirmish, 202; at Port Republic, 138–39; Sabbath services at Bridgeport, 297; and soldiers' furloughs, 292; typhoid fever, 217; at Wauhatchie, 286; wounded at Dug Gap, 308

flags: Geary presents each brigade with its own flag, 369; significance, 63; 29th Ohio (*see separate Twenty-Ninth Ohio Volunteer Infantry Regiment Index*)
Fleming, Lib, 193
Flynn, Col. John (28th Pennsylvania), 359
Ford, E. A., 42
Fort Albany, Alexandria, VA, 182
Fort Delaware, MD, 170, 171, 173
Fort Donelson, battle of, 75
Fort Gaines, DC, 207
Fort Jackson, Savannah, 359, 360
Fort Leavenworth, 75
Fort McAllister, Savannah, 357, 358
Fortress Monroe, 92
Fort Sumter, Charleston, 5, 12, 269, 368, 369
Frank Leslie's Illustrated, 340, 357
Franklin, Pvt. D. B., 242
Frederick, MD, 183, 184, 185, 197, 210, 244, 250, 251, 265; Union hospitals in, 128; new recruits of 1862 join regiment at, 195
Fredericksburg, battle of, 200, 201, 213
Fredericksburg, VA, 121, 124, 214, 217, 219, 234, 247
Frémont, Gen. John C., 126, 129, 136, 148
"French leave," 53, 249, 284, 376
Front Royal, VA, 123, 125, 129, 143
Frost, Fannie, 110
Fugitive Slave Law, 3, 4–5
Fulkerson, Lt. Andrew J., 138, 179, 183, 184, 240

Gaines Crossroads, VA, 123
Galpin, Cpl. Charles, 314
Garfield, Gen. James A., 198
Garibaldi, Giuseppe, 238
Garnett, Gen. Robert S. (CSA), 17, 18
Geary, Lt. Edward (Knap's Battery), 152, 280, 284, 304
Geary, Brig. Gen. John White, 126, 152–53, 201, 293, 250, 273, 281, 330, 337, 352, 365; appointed commander of Tyler's brigade, 152; Atlanta, first Union force to enter, 346; at Bridgeport, 296, 301; at Cedar Mountain, VA, 158, 161; at Chancellorsville, 220, 222, 225, 227, 230, 234, 247, 373; command of regiment's division, 202; Culp's Hill, 260; discipline, 248, 249, 265, 302; at Dug Gap, 306, 307–10, 312; at Gettysburg, 253–54; leaves division, 376; at Lookout Mountain, 282, 283; at New Hope Church battle, 325–26; at Normandy, 274; Peach Tree Creek fight, 340–43; Pine Knob assault planned with Sherman and Hooker, 330; at Resaca, 320; Ringgold, GA, 283; 7th OVI at Taylor's Ridge, 289; Savannah, surrender of, 359; second Bull Run campaign, absent during, 180; Shepherdstown, West VA, raid, 1862, 202, 203; son Edward's death, 280, 284, 304; Tennessee, order to move to, 271; at Thoroughfare Gap, 126; at Wauhatchie, 279–80; Winchester claims, 203
Geauga County, OH, 46
Geer, Sgt. Hammond W., 310
General Order No. 2, 102
General Tom Thumb, 198
General Zollicoffer House, Nashville, 290, 340

Geneva Township, Ashtabula County, 338, 380
Georgetown, DC, 182, 207
Germanna Ford, VA, 218
Gettysburg, battle of, 251–61, 264, 266–67, 291
Gettysburg, PA, 252, 262
Gibbs, Col. George (CSA), 167
Gibbs, QM Oscar, 52, 172, 205, 297
Giddings, Grotius, 3, 16, 56
Giddings, Joseph Addison, 176
Giddings, Joshua Reed, ix, 2, 3, 4, 21, 22, 56, 95, 176, 231, 273; appointment as U.S. consul at Montreal, 5, 7, 175; in Congress, 2; correspondence of, x; criticized by soldiers, 95; exploits war's economic opportunities, 176; and Harpers Ferry Raid, 3; *History of the Rebellion*, 238; and 29th OVI, 20, 23, 44, 176
Giddings, Mrs. J. R., 287
Gilgal Church, GA, battle of, 332
Gillett, Pvt. Nelson, 118, 127, 243, 244–45
Goldsboro, NC, 367, 369
Goodman, Surgeon H. Ernest (28th Pennsylvania Volunteers), 254
Goodrich, Pvt. Russell, 60
Gordonsville, VA, 153, 177, 222
Goudy, Sgt. J. M., 177
Governor's Island, NY, 270
Grand Army of the Republic, 380
Grand Review, 373–74
Grant, Lt. Gen. Ulysses S., 95, 267, 275, 281–82, 303, 371
Grant, Lt. Winthrop, 309
Gray, Sgt. William E., 198
"Gray Backs," 10
Greeley, Horace, 323
Green, Sgt. Ellis, 297, 299, 313
Greene, Gen. George S. (Greene's brigade, Geary's division), 161, 226, 228, 229, 280; at Gettysburg, 253, 254, 255, 256
Greenlee, Pvt. John C., 243, 250
Greensville, Summit County, OH, 191
Grinnell, Lt. James, 27, 49
Griswold, Sgt. Rush, 334
Grover, Capt. Leverett, 44, 94
Gruver, Pvt. William, 249

Hall, Sgt. Albert, 229
Hall, Pvt. Robert Warren, 60, 211
Hall, Pvt. William, 46
Hall, Lt. William, 94
Halleck, Maj. Gen. Henry W., 181, 188, 196
Halloway, Pvt. George W., 332, 361
Hammond, Sgt. J. C., 206
Hampton, Gen. Wade, III (CSA cavalry), 365
Hancock, VA, 88
Hancock, Gen. Winfield Scott; at Chancellorsville, 228, 229, 232, 235; at Gettysburg, 252
Hard, Capt. Pulaski, 17, 47, 49, 53, 101
Hardee, Gen. William J. (CSA), 310, 357
Hardee's Tactics, 107
Harpers Ferry, VA, 125, 201, 266
Harpers Ferry Raid, 3
Harpersfield, OH, 60
Harper's Magazine, 210

GENERAL INDEX   491

Hart, Pvt. Samuel, 134, 145, 171, 320, 350, 380
Hart, Pvt. William A., 140
Hartsgrove, OH, 44, 151
Hartwood Church, VA, 218
Hathaway, Capt. Henry, 32
Hawk, Pvt. Phil, 120, 163
Hayes, Capt. Edward, 33, 34, 205; Camp Chase, leaving sick behind at, 78; at Chancellorsville, 230; on Culp's Hill, 256, 257; 1887 speech to regiment's survivors at Gettysburg, 255; at Port Republic, 133, 134, 140; recruiting for Giddings Regiment, 33, 41, 42; release from rebel prison, 195; resignation demanded by soldiers, 91; and Veteran Volunteer reenlistment, 289; Wauhatchie accommodations, 286; wounded at Dug Gap, 309
Hayes, Col. Rutherford B., 16
Haymarket, VA, 26
Haynes, Asst. Surgeon Elwood, 208; at Bridgeport, 298; at Chancellorsville, 227, 231; and Dug Gap wounded, 312; at Dumfries, 208, 209, 210; and Pine Knob wounded, 334; tedium of army surgeon's life, 243
Haynes, Pvt. William D., 91
Hayward, Sgt. George, 230, 257, 260
Hazel Grove (Chancellorsville), 225
Headley, Rev. Phineas Camp, 353
heatstroke: at Cedar Mt., 154, 160; on march to Gettysburg, 247
Heights of Bolivar, VA, 266
Heights of Loudon, VA, 266
Hill, Gen. A. P. (CSA), 160
Hill, Pvt. Hiram, 240
Hill, Pvt. John, 240, 372
Hill, Pvt. Robert, 60
History of the Rebellion (Giddings), 238
Homer Boys (Homerville Boys), 35, 77, 120, 163, 214, 380
Homer Township, Medina County, OH, 35
Homerville, OH, 191, 235, 251, 262
Homestead Act of 1862, 145, 147
Hood, Gen. John Bell (CSA), 280, 281, 318, 326, 333, 346, 354
Hooker, Gen. Joseph, 203, 214, 220; Army of the Potomac, 203, 250; attack on Pine Knob, GA, 329; and camp sanitation, 208; at Chancellorsville, 219, 221, 228, 234, 235, 237; corps badges, 217; 1863 spring campaign plans, 214; and Geary, 284, 306–7, 316; Lookout Mountain, 282; at Missionary Ridge, 282; at New Hope Church, 325; resignation in front of Atlanta, 343; 2nd Bull Run campaign, 180; 12th Corps commander for operations around Chattanooga, 275
hospitals, field and camp: Antietam wounded in Frederick, 186; Army of the Potomac, Camp Letterman Hospital, Gettysburg, 263; Candy's brigade hospital at Dumfries, 208; Culpeper, VA, 163, 164; Geary's division hospital, Mill Creek Valley, GA, 312–13; Geary's division hospital, Pumpkin Vine Creek, GA, 327–28; Geary's division hospital outside Atlanta, 345; Officer's Hospital No. 25, Washington, DC, 195; Shield's division, Strasburg, 127; Steiner Building, Frederick, 185; 12th Corps hospital at Aquia Creek, 241–42, 245; 12th Corps hospital at Bush Farm, Gettysburg, 261; Tyler's brigade, Mount Jackson, VA, 119, 120; Winchester, VA, Female Seminary and hotels, 111–12; York U.S. Army Hospital, York, PA, 268
hospitals, fixed: Alexandria hospital (unidentified), 195; Alexandria hospitals after 2nd Bull Run, 182; Camp Chase, OH, 76–77; Cliffburne Hospital, Washington, DC, 151; conditions in, 150, 339–40; Cumberland, MD, Lander's division, 93, 163, 272; Cumberland Hospital, Nashville, 340; Division Hospital No. 8, Chattanooga, 339; Fairfax Seminary Hospital, Fairfax, 151 ; growth of Washington area hospitals 1862, 150; Jeffersonville, IN: U.S. Army General (Pavilion Plan) Hospital at, 313; Judiciary Square Hospital, Washington, DC, 150; Mansion House army hospital, Washington, DC, 164; Officers Hospital No. 17, Nashville, 313; transport to, 33–40; U.S. Hospital No. 8, Nashville, 294, 339. *See also* Ames, Rev. Lyman D.; Kummer, Cpl. John; Suckley, Surgeon George; Wheeler, Helen Cowles; Wright, Capt. Myron T.
"Hour Is Come, The" (scripture), 325
Howard, Capt. E. B., 172, 323; blacksmithing at Camp Misery, 90; Kernstown fight, 113; in Mt. Jackson, VA, 119; presents horse to Theron S. Winship, 143; recruiting, 145, 189, 194; resigns at Dumfries, VA, 205; slaves liberated near Martinsburg, VA, 104
Howard, Mrs. E. B., 104
Howard, Gen. Oliver O., 252, 330, 335
Howe, Julia Ward, 103
Howells, William Cooper, 15, 16, 43
Howells, William Dean, portrays prewar life in Jefferson, Ohio, 1; *Years of My Youth* (Howells), 1–2, 238, 287, 322
Hoxter, Ulysses S., 361
Hoyt, Ellsworth, 299
Hoyt, Ester, 299
Hoyt, Hattie, 299
Hoyt, John, 49, 196, 199
Hoyt, Pvt. Thaddeus, 36, 161, 311
Hoyt, Cpl. Wallace B., 36, 49, 96, 144, 347; aboard *Baltic*, 269; in Alexandria, VA, 269; at Aquia Landing, VA, 244; at Bridgeport, 299; in Brooklyn, 270; at Camp Chase, 71, 76; at Camp Kelly, 95; to Camp Parole, 174; captured at Cedar Mountain, 162; to Chancellorsville, 217–18; near Culpeper, 250; on Culp's Hill, 261; death of, at Andersonville Prison, 356, 380; death of mother, 299–300; decision not to reenlist, 289, 290, 299; disappearance at Cassville, GA, 324–25; at Dumfries, 209, 214, 215, 217; at Fort Delaware, 173–74; imprisoned at Belle Isle, 166, 170; love of soldiering, 118; march to Gettysburg, 248; march to Gordonsville, VA, 153; on officers' threats to resign, 122, 142; at Port Republic, 140, 141, 142; at Raccoon Ford, VA, 270; Rock Creek Boys, 118, 140, 209; on value of education, 246, 300
Hudson, OH, 4, 59
Hummiston, Pvt. Newton P., 94, 100, 168, 187
Huntwork, Pvt. George, 374

Hurlburt, Lt. Everson J., 32, 77, 134, 165, 195, 242, 285, 309, 332, 378
Hurlburt, Chaplain Russel H.: appointed chaplain, 29th OVI, 55; Aquia Creek, visit to brother at, 242; at Camp Kelly, 87, 88, 96, 100; on contraband wagon driver, 124; on Cumberland hospitals, 93; on first Union soldiers killed in battle, 96–97; at Kernstown, 114; lasting impression on regiment, 206; on regiment's service record, 94; resignation, 154
Hurry, Pvt. John W., 143

Illinois cavalry (unidentified), 210
Illinois regiments: 29th, 88; 36th, 327
Indianapolis, IN, 290
Indiana troops, 302; reputation for freebooting, 1862, 88; soldiers find Lee's plans for Antietam, 183
Ingersoll, Justus, 26
Invalid Corps, 315
"Ipsa," Sgt. Parmater's betrothed, 186, 285, 294, 370, 375
Ireland, Col. David (137th NY), 254, 256, 257, 258, 304, 310, 346
Irish: as target of drunkenness jokes, 210–11
Irwin, Capt. (28th PA VI), 219
Island No. 10, battle of, 112, 146
Iverson, Gen. Alfred, Jr. (Iverson's Cavalry division, CSA), 351

Jackemay, Sarah, 27
Jackson, Gen. Thomas (CSA), 75, 117, 121, 129, 130, 245, 258; attack on Banks, 125; at Cedar Mountain, 156, 160, 175; at Chancellorsville, 223, 226, 236; 1861 summer campaign, 84; at Mt. Jackson, VA, 119; at Port Republic, 146, 156, 166; 2nd Bull Run campaign, 179, 181
Jefferson, OH, 1, 73, 151, 183, 187, 200, 260, 267, 268, 295; as antislavery stronghold, 2; County Fair 1863, 285; and exemption from the draft, 193; military company organized in war's early days, 15–16; railroad arrives in, 286; prosperity in by war's end, 379; regiment's founders start bank in, 211; residents' opinion of soldiers at Camp Giddings, 68; soldiers return to, 379; war meeting before first draft, 191
Jefferson National Guards, 32, 211
Jenkins, Gen. Micah (CSA), 280
"Jeremy Diddler," 213
Jersey City, NJ, 270
Jones, Sgt. Rollin L., 102, 212, 235; Andover Guards, elected 2nd lt., April 1861, 15; as army postmaster in Winchester, 118; at Chancellorsville, 220; imprisonment, 166, 170, 171; marched from Belle Isle to Aikens Landing, VA, 170; march to Gettysburg, 251; and Sgt. Allen Mason, 212, 215; at Port Republic, 134, 135; rejoins regiment at Dumfries, 214; severely wounded at Pine Knob, 332
Johnson, Gen. Edward (CSA, "Stonewall Division," Ewell's Second Corps, Army of Northern Virginia), 256, 258
Johnson, Pvt. Frederick R., 137
Johnsons Corners, Summit County, OH, 13, 101, 361

Johnston, Gen. Joseph E. (CSA), 107, 303, 306, 318, 325, 328, 330, 333, 336, 367, 369, 370, 371
Journal History (SeCheverell), xii, 23, 160, 162, 164, 181–82. *See also* ScCheverell, J. Hampton

Kane, Brig. Gen. Thomas (Geary's division), 221
Kansas 7th Cavalry, 172
Keith, A. (3rd North Carolina Infantry), 263
Kellogg, Abner C., 23–24, 31, 191, 212
Kelly, Brig. Gen. Benjamin F., 76
Kelly's Ferry, TN, 280, 290
Kelly's Ford, VA, 218, 266
Kennedy, Pvt. Sydney, 261
Kennesaw Mountain, GA, 330, 331
Kennesaw Mountain, battle of, 335–36
Kernstown, VA, battle of, 106–10, 111, 114, 115, 117, 118, 163, 216, 260, 264
Kettle Bottoms, Chesapeake River, VA, 269
Key, Judge Thomas, 20
Keyes, Gen. Erasmus D., 237
Kilpatrick, Gen. Judson, 306
Kimball, Col. Nathan, 126
Kingston, GA, 320, 344
Kingsville, OH, 6, 143
Kingsville Academy, Kingsville, OH, 11, 50, 51, 143
Kinney, Pvt. Alvinson, 108, 110, 144, 145, 164
Knap, Capt. Joseph, 221
Knapp, Pvt. Henry, 253, 257
Knights of the Golden Circle, 213
Knowlton, Sgt. Mortimer, 314
Kolb's Farm, GA, battle of, 333–34
Koop, Dr. G. F., Post Surgeon, Martinsburg, VA, 104
Kummer, Cpl. John, 133, 228, 229–30, 264, 268, 315
"Kunucks," 293

Ladies National Covenant, Akron, 323
Lake County, OH, 53
Lake Erie, 172, 238, 292
Lander, Gen. Frederick West, 76, 84, 85, 87, 88,, 89, 93, 96, 97, 99; Lewis P. Buckley on, 100, 142; death of, at Paw Paw, VA, 99; eulogized by Western Reserve newspapers, 100
Lane, Pvt. Jehiel, 128
Lane, Samuel, 19, 50, 204
Lantz, Pvt. Curtis, 313, 317
Latimer, Pvt. James O., 332
Lee, Robert E.: Antietam campaign, 183; at Chancellorsville, 223, 226, 233; at Fredericksburg, winter 1863, 216; Gettysburg campaign, 250, 251, 265, 266; and Hooker, 214, 219; McClellan defeated by in Richmond, 1862, 146; and Meade, 267, 271–72; on Gen. John Pope, 153; in 2nd Bull Run campaign, 178, 179, 181, 182
Leesburg, VA, 201, 248, 249–50
Left Hand, The (novel), 237
Leigh, Maj. Benjamin Watkins (CSA), 258
Letterman, Medical Director Dr. Jonathan, 214
Levels, VA (aka Camp Steele, Camp Haystack, Camp Starvation, Pine Levels, Camp Misery, Breezy Heights), 90
Lewiston Coaling, Port Republic battlefield, VA, 132, 135, 164

Libby Prison, Richmond, VA, 286
Lincoln, Abraham, 183, 194, 197, 198, 267, 271; campaign of 1860 in Western Reserve, 4; election celebration in Akron, Ohio, 4; call for troops, 13, 22; Gettysburg Address, 286; at Gettysburg cemetery dedication, 262–63; and Hooker, 203, 236; inauguration train through Western Reserve, 4–5; and Meade, 266; New York draft riots, 268; regiment reviewed by at Falmouth, 125; regiment's impression of, 125; reorganization of army, 102, 146; and Gen. James Shields, 102; 29th's camp near Raleigh, news of assassination at, 370–71
Little Dorrit (Dickens), 210
Little Round Top, Gettysburg, PA, 252, 253
Littlestown, PA, 251
Little Washington, VA, 163
Long, Pvt. Amos, 314
Long, Billy, 191
Long Bridge, Washington, DC, 142, 183, 373
Longstreet, Gen. James (CSA), 272, 279, 280, 286
Lookout Creek, TN, 282
Lookout Mountain, battle of, 282–84
Lookout Mountain, TN, 279, 280, 281
Lookout Valley, TN, 279
Lord, Pvt. Cains C., 35, 344, 349, 380
Louisville, KY, 273, 290
Lowe, Prof. Thaddeus, 217
Luce, Pvt. Charles, 36, 50, 137
Luce, Emory, 136
Luce, Capt. Horatio, 36, 38, 42, 50, 119, 136, 137, 139, 295
Luray, VA, 117, 123, 128, 142, 189
Lutheran Theological Seminary, Gettysburg, PA, 199, 261
Lynchburg, VA, 167, 169, 171, 176

Mack, Lt. Henry, 122
Madison, GA, 354
Maine troops: 10th regiment, 161; 20th regiment, 254
Manassas Gap, VA, 123, 266
Manassas Gap Railroad, 126
Manassas Junction, VA, 126, 179, 189
Manderbach, Cpl. Frank, 236
Manley, G. W. (Akron photographer), 7
Mansfield, Gen. Joseph K., 202
Marietta, GA, 325, 328, 329, 333, 336, 345
Marsh, Clement, 262
Marsh, Hannah, 264
Marsh, Ida, 196, 197, 264
March, Pvt. James E., 140
Marsh, Sgt. John G., 90, 190, 191, 210; as abolitionist, 172; at Aquia Creek, 242; Army of the Potomac in motion described by, 217–18; at Camp Giddings, 58; at Cedar Mountain, 160, 163; at Chancellorsville, 219, 222, 224–25, 227, 232, 233; death of, at Gettysburg, 262, 264; on destruction of Green Springs, VA, 89; drill master for Homer Boys, 35; at Frederick, 186, 196, 197; Homer Boys in 1862, 120; at Kernstown, 109, 110–11; on medical discharge process, 214; in 19th OVI, 35; 2nd Bull Run campaign, 179 ; and siblings at home, 100, 101; on soldiers, 115, 172–73
Marsh, Sgt. Joseph, 328
Marshall House army hospital, Washington, DC, 164

Martinsburg, VA, 103
Maryland, state of, 182, 183, 265
"Maryland feathers," 86
Mason, Sgt. Allen, 133, 212, 214, 216, 302, 313, 314
Mason, U.S. Senator James, 3
Masons, 285
McAbes, Surgeon Harry, 4th OVI, 293
McCain, Pvt. Tallis, 263–64
McCarter, Charles (freed slave), 269
McClellan, Gen. George B., 121, 140; Antietam campaign, 184, 197, 198; candidate for president in 1864 election, 351; command of Army of the Potomac, 84; Peninsula campaign, 121, 178; regiment's favorable opinion of, 183; request for troops to Gov. Dennison, 75; Western Reserve newspapers' criticism of, 199; in Western Virginia campaign summer 1861, 17, 20
McDowell, Maj. Gen. Irwin, 121–22, 125, 141; Port Republic, 140; 2nd Bull Run, 179; and Shields, 121–22, 129, 130, 131, 138
McKee, Pvt. William, 249
McNeil, George W., 45
McPherson, Gen. James M. (McPherson's Corps), 311, 316, 333, 343
Meade, Gen. George Gordon, 219, 220, 250, 265, 266, 267, 270, 271–72
Medical and Surgical History, 137
Medical Department, U.S. Army, Cumberland, 111, 154, 187, 214, 312
medical discharges, 188, 214
medical treatment: amputations at Fairfax Station, VA, 182; soldiers' negative attitude toward, 94, 313
Medina County, OH, 46, 143
Melnotte (steam packet boat), 377
Merrimac, CSS (former USS *Virginia*), 170
Mexican War, 140, 146
Middlebury Academy, Middlebury, NY, 26
Middlebury Township, Summit County, OH, 211–12
Military Committee Plan, 45, 212
Milledgeville, GA, 355
Millen, GA, 356
Missionary Ridge (Chattanooga campaign), 282
Missouri, state of, 103, 172
Missouri River, 198
Mitchell's Station Road, Culpeper, VA, 157
Mogadore, OH, 49, 115, 150, 211, 240
Monitor, USS, 170
Monocacy Bridge, MD, 184, 250
Monocacy River, MD, 183
Montreal, Canada, 5, 16, 21, 64, 175, 287
Montrose, OH, 190
Morey, Pvt. Franklin, 36–37
Morey, Pvt. Gillespie, 36–37, 332
Morgan, Maj. Gen. Daniel (Revolutionary War), 118
Morgan, Gen. John Hunt (CSA), 274
Morgan Township, Ashtabula County, OH, 196, 299, 300, 171, 184, 189, 205, 215, 235, 260
Morley, Pvt. Daniel, 179
Morse, Capt. John F., 39, 42, 53, 122
Mount Holly Church, VA, 218
Mowery, George (Jack) Pvt., 197
"Mr. Lobby," 78

"Mr. Red Tape," 75
Mt. Jackson, VA, 119, 120, 127
Mt. Vernon, VA, 145, 171
"Mud Hen," 91
Muhlenberg, Lt. Edward D., 222, 227
Murfreesboro, TN, 273
Mutual Protective Association, 338. *See also* draft

Napoleonic Wars, 114
Nash, Lt. Thomas, 195
Nashville, TN, 96, 273, 294, 295, 302, 340
Nashville and Chattanooga Railroad, 273
Nashville Female Seminary, 294
National Day of Fast, 239
National Hotel, Baltimore, MD, 195
Neil, Lt. William, 164, 195
New Hope Church, battle of, 325–28, 333
New Jersey regiments: 13th, 249; 33rd, 310–11, 341
New Market, VA, 119, 120
New York, state of, 191, 198, 202, 247
New York City, NY, 152, 236, 270, 275
New York draft riots, 271–72
New York Herald, 165, 202
New York Times, 85, 128
New York regiments: 60th, 256, 346; 102nd, 375; 119th, 308; 137th, 253, 254, 257; 147th, 356; 149th, 253, 257
Nickajack Cave, Shell Mound, TN, 304
Nims, Pvt. Alvin, 92
Nims, Pvt. Cass, 203, 210, 213, 214, 246, 273, 303; burial at Mill Creek, GA, 313; at Chancellorsville, 224, 229, 230, 239; on civilian suffering, 203; on Copperheads, 267–68; at Dumfries, 210; on executions at Leesburg, 249–50; on Grant's Vicksburg victory, 267; on rebels, 213, 247, 286; on regiment's role at Lookout Mountain, 282; on Western troops' preferential treatment, 281
Noonan, Chief Fifer Maj. Richard, 210
Normandy, TN, 273, 274
North Carolina, march through, 366–71
North Edisto River, SC, skirmish at, 364
Norton Township, Summit County, OH, 151
Norwich Academy, 29

Obequon Creek, VA, 105
Oberholtz, Pvt. Eli, 242
Oberlin College, 151, 198
Occoquan Creek, VA, skirmish at, 202
Odd Fellows, 211, 212
Official Record, 232
Ogal, Tillie, 265
Ohio, state of, 180, 198, 217, 251, 299; first draft, results of, 194; Lincoln's dependence on, in election of 1863, 274; newspaper editors on deserters, 197; procedure for reporting absent soldiers, 187; quotas for, in president's calls for troops, 15, 22; regiments in service by summer 1862, 149; veterans' reenlistment furlough, 290
Ohio Central Railroad, 79, 83
Ohio Day, Gettysburg 1887, 255
Ohio No. 3 (steam packet boat), 375
Ohio River, 83, 272, 273, 294, 375
Ohio Soldiers' Association, 152

Ohio State Journal, 76, 77, 182
Ohio troops, cavalry regiments: 2nd (Wade-Hutchins), 23, 24, 30, 40, 42, 46, 53, 61, 64, 83; 6th, 128, 194; 10th, 198
Ohio troops, infantry regiments
1st, 73
5th: at Aquia Creek, 245; at Cedar Mountain, 161, 164; at Chancellorsville, 234, 239; at Dumfries, 301; at Gettysburg, 252, 256; at Kennesaw Mountain, 336, 380; at Kernstown, 109; at New Hope Church, 328; refused recruiting furlough, 188; at Resaca, 318–19
7th ("Rooster Regiment," "Bloody Seventh"), 86, 89, 113, 285, 289; at Antietam, 184; at Camp Kelly, 86; at Cedar Mountain, 157, 158, 159, 160, 163, 164, 175; at Chancellorsville, 221, 222, 223, 231, 232, 239, 283; at Culp's Hill, 258, 259, 260; Dug Gap assault, 308; at Dumfries, 204; at Gettysburg, 252; near Harpers Ferry, VA, fall 1862, 202; at Kernstown, 108; atop Lookout Mountain, 283; in railroad collision, 272; return home June 1864, 329, 378; at Taylor's Ridge, 283
19th (90-day service): companies contributed by Summit and Ashtabula Counties, 16; veterans joining Giddings Regiment, 106
28th, 378
29th (*see separate* Twenty-Ninth Ohio Volunteer Infantry Regiment Index)
41st, 42, 63
55th, 378
58th, 75
62nd, 77
66th: attitudes toward slaves, 172; at Camp Kelly, 77; at Cedar Mountain, 157, 158, 159, 161, 164; at Chancellorsville, 226; at Gettysburg, 256; at Pine Knob, 331
67th, 53, 77; mutiny over pay en route to Camp Kelly, 8
105th, 149, 190, 191, 149, 286, 380
107th, 192
125th, 188, 190
Olds, Rev., Jefferson, OH, 212
Orange and Alexandria Railroad, 124, 179, 180, 182, 266
Orange Plank Road, Chancellorsville, VA, 221, 222
Orange Road, Culpeper, VA, 157, 159
Orange Turnpike, Chancellorsville, VA, 219, 220
Orwell, J. B., 349–50
Orwell, OH, 35
Osmond, Pvt. Oliver, 240
Owen, Sgt. M. E., 187

Painesville, OH, 2, 39, 70, 293
"paper-collar soldiers," 76
Pardee, Col. Ariel, Jr., 209, 231, 347
Parmater, Cpl. Nathan L., x; at Aquia Landing, 244, 247; as Ashtabula County schoolteacher before war, 38; Atlanta siege, 343–44, 347, 348, 349, 352; at Bridgeport, 295–96, 297, 298, 300, 301–2, 303; at Camp Chase, 71, 78; at Camp Giddings, 11; at Cedar Mountain, 159, 162, 163, 164; at Chancellorsville, 221, 225, 232, 234–35; and contraband servant, 104; at Culp's Hill, 259–60;

Parmater, Cpl. Nathan L. (*cont.*)
    diary of, x, 11, 185–86, 379, 380; on divine services in camp, 241; Dug Gap assault, falls out sick before, 307; at Dumfries, construction of "tuggy," 207; early life, 50; on executions at Leesburg, 249–50; Falmouth, march to, 124–25; in Frederick, MD, hospital, 185–86, 187, 207, 376; Front Royal, marching around, 129; gambling, 362; German studies, 210; Gettysburg, march to, 248, 250; Grand Review, 373–74; on Harpers Ferry, 266; in hospital, Chattanooga and Nashville, 339–40; Capt. E. B. Howard, dislike for, 205; at Kernstown, 108; on leave to collect drafted men for regiment, 284–85; on Lee's escape, 266; at Louisville, 290; March to the Sea, 353–54, 355, 357; on Maryland countryside, 265; at Mt. Jackson, VA, 119, 120; officer appointment in colored regiment sought by, 300; on officer resignations, spring 1862, 122; at Paw Paw, VA, 98; at Port Republic, life saved by Bible, 134, 142–43; on rations, 130; recruiting officer post sought, 188; reenlistment decision, 288, 290; 2nd Bull Run campaign, 178, 179, 180, 181, 182; on Sherman, 350; on soldier theft of civilian property, 295; and South Carolina slaves, 366; sympathy for women, 98; Veteran's Furlough, 294; war losses in his Co. I, 379; at Warrenton, VA, 124; Washington, DC, last tour of, 374–75
Patch, Beck, 193
Patent Office, U.S., Washington, DC, 207
Patterson's Creek, VA, 84, 181, 272
Paw Paw, VA, 96–98
pay: complaints against government at Camp Chase, 72; officer's earnings compared to enlisted man's, 101
Payne, Capt. Almer B., 361
Peach Orchard, Gettysburg battlefield, 253
Peach Tree Creek (GA), battle of, 340–43
Pease, Alonzo, 34
Peck, Gen. John J. 237
Pennsylvania, state of, 189, 251
Pennsylvania regiments
    2nd (Mexican War), 152
    28th: Antietam, 229; at Cedar Mountain, 156; Chancellorsville, 219, 220, 222, 229, 239, 372; Dug Gap, 309, 310; Gettysburg campaign, 251, 258; officer death near Chancellorsville avenged, 219; organization, 126; Peach Tree Creek, 341; Pine Knob, 331
    46th, 249
    110th, reputation as hooligans, 88
    111th, 346
    147th: at Atlanta, 347; at Chancellorsville, 220, 226, 230; at Dumfries, 208, 209; at Gettysburg, 252, 256; organized, 126; over Tennessee River toward Chattanooga with the Giddings Regiment, 275
Petersburg & Lynchburg Railroad, 372
Philadelphia, PA, 171, 236
Philadelphia Press, 315
Philippi, VA, battle of, 22, 85
Phillips, J. B., 43
Phinney, Pvt. Jerome, 36, 289, 297, 315, 328
Phinney, Pvt. Tobias Richard "Rickers," 36, 289

Pickett (steam packet boat), 375
Pickett, Pvt. Burton, 144, 145, 154–55, 165
Pickett's Mill, battle of, 328
Pierce, Milton P., 43–44
Pierpont, OH, 52
Pike, Pvt. James S., 60
Pine Knob, GA, battle of, 330–33
Pioneer Corps, 220, 240
Pittsburgh, PA, 143
Platt, Pvt. Daniel, 127, 241
Platt, Daniel, Sr., 241
poems: "Dead," 322; "Missing," 322
Point of Rocks, MD, 250
Polk, Gen. Leonidas (CSA), 306, 330
Pondir musket, 56–57, 88
Pontius, Pvt. Benjamin F., 11, 261
Pope, Gen. John, 146, 153, 158, 177, 179, 181, 183
Porter, Gen. Fitz John, court martial proceedings, 141
Port Republic, battle of, 132–39, 140, 166
Port Republic, VA, 125
Potomac River, VA, 125, 182, 201, 203, 210, 244, 250, 266, 272; Upper, or North, Branch of, 84
Potter, Pvt. Franklin, 139–40, 217, 248, 260, 298, 300–301
Powell, Col. Eugene (66th OVI), 282
Price, Col. H. F. (CSA), 321
Prince, Brig. Gen. Henry, 158, 161
prisoner parole and exchange system, 127, 139, 143, 170, 171, 195, 240, 366–67
prisons, rebel: at Andersonville, GA, 169, 341, 344, 356, 379; Belle Isle Prison, Richmond, VA, 139, 166, 168–71, 195, 380; at Florence, SC, 342; Libby Prison, Richmond, VA, 286; Lynchburg prison camp, 127, 167–68, 171, 177, 187; at Macon, GA, 344; at Salisbury, NC, 145, 169, 195, 380
prisons, Union: at Camp Chase, 71; at Paw Paw, 96
Put-in-Bay, OH, 172
Pvt. "W.": at Camp Chase, 72, 74, 75; at Camp Giddings, 57, 59, 61, 66; visits State Penitentiary in Columbus, 74

Quantico Creek, VA, 203
Quartermaster Department, U.S. Army, responsibility for reburying dead, 345

Raccoon Ford, VA, 270, 271
Raccoon Mountain(s), TN, 279, 285
railroads: Lakeshore Railroad, 286; Pittsburgh and Erie Railroad, 286
Raleigh, NC, 370; residents mourn Lincoln's death, 371
Rape, Pvt. John S., 364
Rapidan River, VA, 178, 218, 219, 270
Rappahannock River, VA, 124, 178, 179, 210, 212, 217, 233, 234, 237, 266, 270
Rappahannock Station, VA, 178, 269
rations: at Camp Giddings, 33; reduced during movements June 1862, 130
Ravenna, OH, 4, 86
Read, W. E. (56th Alabama Cavalry), 348
rebel troops, cavalry
    Alabama: 56th, 348
    Ashby's cavalry, 106–7, 118, 127, 171

Georgia: 3rd, 351; 5th, 348
Iverson's cavalry division, 351
Kentucky: 9th, 309
Morgan's cavalry, 274
Mosby's cavalry (CSA, irregular), 266
Stuart's cavalry, 178, 201, 202, 210, 247
Virginia: 4th, 233
Hampton's cavalry (corps), 365
Wheeler's cavalry (corps), 273, 345, 350, 351, 354, 364, 366
rebel troops, divisions
    Johnson's "Stonewall Division," Ewell's Second Corps, Army of Northern Virginia, 256, 258
    McLaws's, 236
rebel troops, infantry regiments
    Arkansas (mounted infantry): 1st, 309; 2nd, 309
    Florida: 5th, 236
    Georgia: 1st, 331; 12th, 229; 29th, 331
    Louisiana: 7th, 133, 184
    "Louisiana Tigers," 216
    North Carolina: 3rd, 263; 42nd, 167
    South Carolina troops opposing Geary at Wauhatchie, 280
    Texas: 9th, 348
Register of Deserters, 94
Reifschneider, Pvt. Urias, 60
Remley, Sgt. Christian, 310, 314, 315
Reporter (Conneaut), 51, 138, 198, 314, 337, 349
Republicans, 14, 190, 147
Resaca, GA, battle of, 318–20, 333
Rhett, Col. Alfred (CSA), 369
"Richard," 95
Richfield, Summit County, OH, 13
Richmond, VA, 96, 168, 169, 170, 175, 237, 348; Hooker's plan for capture of, 214; march through the ruins of, 372; prisoners at Chancellorsville taken to, 240; regiment's celebration of surrender of, 370; regiment's officers released from prisons in, 195
Rich Mountain, western VA, battle of, 17–18, 56
Rickards, Sgt. Andrew, 289, 332
Ricketts, Gen. James B., 162
Riddle, U.S. Senator Albert Gallatin, 152
Ringgold, GA, 283
Roath, Pvt. Cyrus, 332–33
Roberts, Sgt. Marcus, 136
Robertsville, SC, 364
Robinson, Cpl. Charles, 134
Rock Creek, Gettysburg battlefield, 252, 253, 254, 256, 259
Rock Creek, OH, 17, 21
Rock Creek Boys, 37, 118, 173, 174, 209, 289, 296, 297, 299, 380
Rockville, MD, 182, 183
Rockwell, Pvt. Jesse, 77
Rockwell, Cpl. Steadman J., 127
Rocky Face Ridge, GA: Buzzard's Roost, 305; Dug Gap, GA, 305; as Gibralter of the South, 305; Mill Creek Gap, 305; Snake Creek Gap, GA, 305; topography, 305
Rodman, rifled artillery, 308
Rogers (Rodgers), Pvt. Albert, 60

Rolla, MO, 67
Rome, GA, 303
Romney, VA, 75, 84, 90
Rood, Pvt. Henry, 335
Root, Pvt. George, 209
Rosecrans, Gen. William S., 17, 20–21, 271, 272
Roshon, Pvt. Elias, 36, 244, 296–97, 380; in Alexandria, 146; at Bridgeport, 297; at Camp Chase, 77; at Camp Kelly, 87, 92; at Camp Misery, 91; captured and sent to Salisbury prison, 366; at Cedar Mountain, 162; on Confederacy, 363; Homer Boys, member of, 36; prisoner parole, difficulty rejoining regiment after, 143; at Rappahannock River crossings, 178; in South Carolina, 365–66
Rossville Gap, GA, 282, 283
Roster of Ohio Troops, 240
Rupp, Henry, 36; killed at Dug Gap, 380
Rupp, Pvt. John, 35, 101, 168–69, 176, 235, 251, 336, 380
Russell, Lt. Cary, 77, 134, 169, 195, 327
Ryon, Pvt. Edward, 238, 239

"S. B." 76, 145, 169, 195
Salisbury, NC, rebel prison at, 145, 169, 195, 366
Savannah (CSA ironclad), 359
Savannah, GA, 354, 359, 362–63
Savannah River, 357, 358, 363, 364, 377
Sawbuck Rangers, 72
Schenck, Gen. Robert, 99
Schofield, Gen. John, 336
Schoonover, Capt. Jonas, 25, 289, 350, 374; as Akron recruiting officer, 53, 55; in Antietam campaign, 183; departure from regiment at Bardstown, 376; at Port Republic, 138; at Savannah, 359; 2nd Bull Run campaign, 179; war diary of, 181, 182
Schultz, Jacob, 241
Schultz, Pvt. Thomas, 240
Scotland, 207
Scott, Sir Walter, 48
scurvy, 345
SeCheverell, J. Hampton (29th Ohio historian), xii; accounting of regiment's war casualties, 377; account of Cedar Mountain, 161, 164; account of Chancellorsville, 219, 232; account of Culp's Hill, 258; account of regiment's bold taking of a rebel fort, 335–36; account of regiment's daring at Resaca (uncorroborated), 318–19; account of regiment's origins, 23; account of regiment's participation in the taking of Chattanooga, 282–83; account of regiment's role in Antietam campaign, 184; account of regiment's soldiers taking a blockhouse (unsubstantiated), 334; account of 2nd Bull Run campaign, 181–82; claim that band playing at Dug Gap alerted rebels, 308; as drummer boy of 29th Ohio, xii, 188; enlistment in 2nd Ohio Heavy Artillery, 188; history of regiment (*Journal History . . .*), xii, 23, 160, 162, 164, 181–82, 184; on Jackson's troop strength at Kernstown battle, 115; on preparation for Lookout Mountain assault, 282; regiment's suffering at Dumfries compared to Valley Forge, 204
Sedgwick, Gen. John, 234
"Seelye," 86, 90, 94, 105, 106, 109

GENERAL INDEX   497

Seven Days battles, 202
Shanafelt, Pvt. Samuel, 233
Shanafelt, Washington, 145
Sharpsburg, MD, 183, 266
Shaw, Pvt. John, 36, 342
Shenandoah River, VA, 84, 130–31, 201, 266
Shenandoah valley, VA, 104, 348
Shepherdstown, West VA, 202
Sherbondy, Pvt. Charles, 217
Sherbondy, Sgt. George, 217
Sherman, U.S. Sen. John, 46
Sherman, Gen. William T.: Altoona Pass, 325; Athens, OH, native, 194; Atlanta, 333, 346, 348; Chattanooga, 281, 282; and Giddings Regiment at New Hope Church, 327; good-bye to regiment at Bardstown, 376; Grant's grand plan, Western armies' role in, 303; on March to the Sea, 353, 354, 358; Ohio regiments commanded by in spring 1864, 304; Polk's killing credited to, 330; supposed request for 29th Ohio volunteers at Kennesaw, 335; Rocky Face Ridge, GA, 306; Savannah, 359
Shields, Gen. James, 117, 121, 131, 132; accused by Buckley of wrecking his division, 142; appointed as Lander's replacement, 99; and Col. Samuel Carroll, 131, 140; Front Royal, 129–30; at Kernstown, 111, 115; life before war, 102–3; Port Republic, VA, disaster, 130, 140, 141; regiment passes by at Back Creek, VA, 102
"Shields's Foot Cavalry," aka "Shields's Bushwhackers," 125
Shiloh (Pittsburg Landing), battle of, 114–15, 237
Shriber, Adj. R. C., 108–9
Sickles, Gen. Daniel, 221, 222
Sigel, Gen. Franz, 98, 158
Simonds, Charles Stetson, 23
Singer sewing machine, 238
Sisley, Pvt. Willis, 71
Sisters of Charity, 93
Sisters of Mercy, 151
slaves: Chaplain Ames and, 368–69; at Camp Chase, 71; contrabands following Geary's division called "Corps de Africa," 357; freed by John Brown Jr. in Missouri, 172; freed by E. B. Howard, 104; freed Tennessee slaves observed picking cotton, 273; Geary employs black man as scout at Kingston, GA, 321; Geary's march into Savannah cheered by, 359; QM Gibbs's attitude toward, 172; Jefferson minister Olds's work in Corinth, MS, 212; jokes about blacks in Western Reserve newspaper, 239; Sgt. Rollin Jones's attitude toward, 171–72; on March to the Sea, 355, 356; Sgt. John Marsh's attitude toward, 172; in Mt. Jackson, VA, on their way north, 121; at New Market, VA, 123; regiment cheered by as it reenters Virginia, 371; regiment's refugees helped by at Port Republic, 138; regiment's soldiers' joke, 295; "sable soldiers" (colored infantry), 369; and Sherman's army, 358; 66th OVI attitude toward, 172; as soldiers and laborers at Nashville hospital, 340; soldiers steal firewood from, 362; as "waiters" for regiment's officers, 1862, 104; at Winchester, VA, 105
Sleepy Creek, VA, 102

Slocum, Gen. Henry W., 202; Candy's Brigade recommended to Lincoln by, 268; career pre-1863, 202; at Chancellorsville, 220, 235; Chancellorsville, march to, 216, 218; fort built at Aquia Creek named in honor of, 243; impressed with regiment at Occoquan Creek skirmish, 202; orders to Geary at Gettysburg, 253; 20th Corps at Atlanta, commander of, 343
Smith, Lt. Benjamin, 138
Smith, Mrs. Cooper, 185, 376
Smith, Sgt. E. E., 227
Smith, Capt. N. J. (2nd Ohio Artillery), 287
Smith, Capt. Russel B., 35, 66, 186, 214
Social Circle, GA, 354
Soden, Pvt. Mathias, 260–61
soldier pastimes: baseball played during Falmouth march, May 1862, 124; at Bridgeport, 301; dancing, at Bridgeport, 301; at Dumfries, VA, 210; hunting and fishing, at Bridgeport, 301
Soldiers Aid Society, 45, 92, 149, 237–38, 263, 287
Soldiers Retreat, Washington, DC, 142
songs: "Battle Hymn of the Republic," 103; "Battle in the Clouds," 322; "The Blue Juniata," 353; "Carry Me Back to Old Virginny," 371; "Dixie for the 29th," 66; "Hail Columbia," 148; "Home Sweet Home," 196; "John Brown's Body," 218, 354; "The Old One Hundred," 337; "Rogue's March," 198; "Star Spangled Banner," 112; "Tenting on the Old Campground," 322; "The Vacant Chair," 322; "Weeping Sad and Lonely," 322; "When This Cruel War Is Over," 322
song-selling spy, 265
South Branch Bridge, Green Springs, VA, 88, 89
South Carolina, 4, 357, 363–66
Southern civilians: depredations against at Camp Misery, 91; dialect ridiculed, 96; home-cooked meals sold to Union soldiers, 104
South Fork, Shenandoah River at Port Republic, 133
South Mountain, MD, 183, 265
Spangler Farm, Gettysburg battlefield, 253, 256
Spangler's Springs, Gettysburg battlefield, 256
Sperryville, VA, 154
Spicer, Pvt. Edward, 295
Spidel, Pvt. Ezra, 259, 260
Spotsylvania Court House, battle of, 316
Stafford Church, VA, 216
Stafford Courthouse, VA, 240
Stanton, Sec. of War Edwin M., 121, 138–39, 190
Stark County, OH, 233
Steele, Capt. Alden P., 66, 122
Stephenson's Depot, VA, 106
Sterrett, Cpl. Alonzo, 11, 38, 50, 159, 163, 177, 294, 300, 339, 369
Stevens, Capt. Wilbur F., 32, 38, 156–57; at Bridgeport Sabbath service, 297; at Cedar Mountain, 160; at Chancellorsville, 226, 230, 246; Co. B enlisted by in Pierpont, OH, 32; Co. B later commanded by, 33; command of regiment after Clark resignation, 246; command of regiment at Gettysburg, 255; command of regiment turned over to Capt. Edward Hayes at Culp's Hill, 257; at Kernstown battle, 156; New Hope Church, wounded at, 327; Pierpont,

OH, military company raised and drilled by, April 1861, 16; resignation at Atlanta, 349
Stewart, Lt. Frank P., 138
St. John, Pvt. Montezuma, 96, 188
Stohl, Pvt. George, 134
Stoneman, Gen. George (Stoneman's Cavalry), 328
Stoneman's Raid, 344
Stone Mountain, GA, 352
Stone's River, TN, 273
Storer, Mrs. Helen, 313
Storer, Sgt. James B., 17, 261, 378; at Cedar Mountain, 160–61; on march to Culpeper, 154; replaces Palmer Williamson as sgt. maj., 101; replaces Winship as adjutant, 205; and Capt. Wilbur Stevens, 160–61, 246, 256–57; Veteran Volunteer reenlistment campaign at Wauhatchie, 288, 289; wounded at Dug Gap, 306, 309
Storer, Webster, 154, 313
Strasburg, VA, 117, 118, 121
Stratton, Lt. Joel, 20
Strong, A. D., 42
Stuart, Gen. J. E. B. (CSA), 226
substitutes, 348, 349. *See also* draft
Suckley, Surgeon George, 93
Sultana (river steamboat) disaster, 379
Summit Beacon, 324; Akron Democratic newspaper attacked by, 213; Akron's building boom promoted by, 211; first Federal Income Tax supported by, 237; Ft. Sumter, response to news of, 13; Geary criticized by for disaster at Dug Gap, 315; on Hooker's victory at Chancellorsville, 237; on National Day of Fasting, 239; plea for care of soldiers' families, 72–73, 95; premature belief that the war is nearly over, 286; report of recruitment numbers through August 1862, 193; results of 1863 election, 274; rumor of invasion by out-of-state copperheads, 274; Sherman's announcement published verbatim in, 358; and Josiah J. Wright, 87, 165
Summit County, OH, xi. *See also* Jefferson, OH
Sumner, U.S. Senator Charles, 5
Supplee, Pvt. Euclid, 128
Sweet, Capt. Henry (105th OVI), 239

Tale of Two Cities, A (Dickens), 210
Tallmadge, OH, 67, 324
Taneytown, MD, 251
Taylor's Ridge, GA, 283, 289
Tennessee River, TN, 271, 275, 279, 285, 296, 298
Tennyson, Alfred Lord, 48
Thayer and Noyes Circus, 213
Thomas, Gen. George Henry, 282, 307, 316
Thoroughfare Gap, VA, 127
"Thousand Excuses Given for Not Enlisting, The," Myron T. Wright recruiting speech, 190
Tilden, Judge Daniel, 378
Tod, Ohio Gov. David, 76, 149, 152, 190
Trall, Pvt. Roswell, 36
Trall, Pvt. Willard, 36
Tredegar Iron Works, Richmond, VA, 170
Treen, Pvt. George, 36, 127
Treen, Capt. James, 36, 77, 115, 175, 230, 175, 230, 245
Treen, Pvt. James, Jr., 36
Treen, Pvt. John, 36
Trenton, GA, 298
Tripler, Surgeon Charles (Medical Dept., Army of the Potomac), 93
Trumbull County, OH, 193, 274
Tunnel Hill, GA, 304
Turner, Pvt. Henry, 136, 139
Twenty-Ninth Ohio Volunteer Infantry Regiment. *See separate* Twenty-Ninth Ohio Volunteer Infantry Regiment Index
Two Taverns, PA, 254
Tyler, Col. Erastus B., 178, 188; as commander of 7th OVI, 86; command of brigade at Camp Kelly, 86; departs command of brigade, 152; Green Springs, VA, 7th OVI and Giddings Regiment on reconnaissance to, 88; at Kernstown, 107, 110; Port Republic, 131, 132, 133
Tyrrell, Sawdy, 52

"Uncle Sam," 359
"Union Plan," for field chapel arrangement, 240
Union troops, brigades
   Buschbeck's brigade, 304, 309, 319
   Candy's brigade, Geary's division, 12th Corps (later 20th Corps), 270; at Aquia Creek, 247; Atlanta campaign, losses in, 348; Chancellorsville, 218, 220, 221, 227, 229, 232, 235, 239, 247; to Chattanooga, 273; at Culp's Hill, 253, 256; at Dumfries, VA, 202, 208; Gettysburg campaign, 251; Kolb's Farm, 334; New Hope Church, 325–28; New York draft riots, 268; Peach Tree Creek, 340–43; Pine Knob, 330–33; regiments contained in spring 1864, 304; Resaca, 318; reviewed by Sherman at Fayetteville, 367; at Round Tops, 255
   Carroll's brigade: Port Republic, 131–32
   Geary's brigade, Augur's division, Banks's corps, 188; Cedar Mountain, 157, 158, 162, 164; reorganized as division, 183
   Gordon's brigade, Williams's division, 162
   Greene's brigade, Geary's division: Cedar Mountain, 161; Chancellorsville, 226, 228, 229; Gettysburg, 253, 254, 255, 256
   Kane's brigade, Geary's division, 221; Chancellorsville, 224, 228, 229, 234; Gettysburg, 253, 254, 256
   Kimball's brigade, Shields's division, 108
   Tyler's brigade, Lander's (later Shields's) division, 86, 88, 115, 131, 152; at Camp Kelly, 86; Green Springs, VA, 88; tactical role in movement to retake Romney 1862, 89; Paw Paw, VA, 96, 97–99; reorganized as Tyler's brigade, Shields's 2nd Division, Banks's 5th Corps, Army of the Potomac, 102; at Kernstown, 108, 114
Union troops, cavalry
   Kilpatrick, 306
   Sheridan, 348
   Stoneman, 328, 344
Union troops, corps, Army of the Cumberland
   4th, 321
   20th: 11th and 12th Corps, Army of the Potomac, reorganized as, 304; falls back to Chattahoochee River, 346; Grand Review, 372

Union troops, corps, Army of the Potomac
- 1st: 251, 253
- 2nd: Chancellorsville, 229; Gettysburg, 252
- 3rd, 221, 224, 228, 251
- 5th (Banks's), 2nd (Shields's) Division, 102, 105, 157; pursuit of Jackson after Cedar Mountain fight, 177; 2nd Bull Run role, 179, 180, 181, 219
- 11th: Chancellorsville, 218, 219, 222, 223, 224; "the German corps," 236; Gettysburg, 251, 252, 253; to the relief of Rosecrans at Chattanooga, 271–72, 323, 324; reorganized as 20th Corps, Army of the Cumberland, 304
- 12th: Chancellorsville, 218, 219, 222, 224, 226, 228, 233, 236; at Culp's Hill, 252, 256; execution of deserters in, 249; to Gettysburg, 252; hospital at Aquia Creek, 242; hospital at Gettysburg, 282; led by Gen. Henry Slocum, 202; regiment assigned to, 183; to the relief of Rosecrans at Chattanooga, 271–72, 323, 324; reorganized as 20th Corps, Army of the Cumberland, 304

Union troops, divisions
- Augur's division, 163
- Butterfield's division, 12th Corps, Army of the Potomac, 218, 282, 320, 326, 331, 332
- Geary's White Star Division, 183, 217, 233, 247, 251, 266, 274, 275, 279, 290, 304–6, 311–12, 315; at Aquia Creek, 239; Atlanta campaign, 347–48, 350–51; Bentonville, 367; Carolinas Campaign, 363, 366; Chancellorsville, 218–19, 220–29, 231, 232, 234, 239; at Culp's Hill, 252–53, 259; at Kolb's Farm, 333; at Lookout Mountain, 282, 283; March to the Sea, 354–58; New Hope Church, 325–28; Resaca, 318, 320; at the Round Tops, Gettysburg, 252; Savannah, 359, 360
- Hancock's division, at Chancellorsville, 228, 229, 232, 235
- Shields's division, Banks's Army, 122, 125, 128, 142; assigned to McDowell's command, 121
- Stanley's division, Army of the Cumberland, 327, 347–48
- Williams's division, 12th Corps (later 20th Corps), 117; Cedar Mountain, 158; Cemetery Ridge, 254; Chancellorsville, 224, 225; execution of deserters at Leesburg, 249; Kolb's Farm, 334; New Hope Church, 326; Peach Tree Creek, 340; Resaca, 318

U.S. Ford, VA, 219, 231
U.S. Military Academy, West Point, NY, 25, 26–27
U.S. Sanitary Commission, 238, 316, 345

Vallandigham, U.S. Congressman Clement, 3, 267, 268, 274, 284
Valley Forge, 203
Valley Pike (Shenandoah valley, VA), 107, 120
Van Amburg's Grand Menagerie, 285
veterans' furlough, 288, 289–90
Vicksburg, MS, 238, 241, 267
Victorian, 150, 208, 315, 345
Viers, Pvt. Valentine, 111
Virginia, state of, 266, 269, 275, 303; western, 17, 18, 20, 21, 22, 24, 25, 27, 29, 75, 85. *See also individual towns*
Voris, Col. Alvin C., 19, 53, 83, 110

Wade, U.S. Senator Benjamin F., 15, 23, 40, 183, 191
Wade, Decius, 321
Wadsworth, Pvt. Bennet H., 242–43
Waldron, Sgt. Charles F., 233
Waltz, Pvt. Elias, 209
Ward, Artemus, 52, 213
Ward, Green (emancipated slave), 348
Ward, Brig. Gen. William T., 340
War Department, U.S., 186, 295
war meeting, 191, 197
Warren, Miss Levina, 198
Warren, OH, 6, 193
Warrenton, VA, 124, 152, 179
Warrenton Junction, VA, 266
Washington, DC, 248, 255; 1861 troop buildup, 71; 1862 army hospitals in, 150; heat in, 157; invasion by Jackson feared, 125; and Lee's army, August 1862, 178; 2nd Bull Run campaign, 180, 181; seen by regiment's soldiers summer 1862, 145; and wounded, 242
Washington, George, 124, 216
Washington's Birthday, 97
Waterman, Pvt. William, 261
Watson, Pvt. John, 127
Wauhatchie, battle of, 279–80
Wauhatchie Station, TN, 279
Wauhatchie Valley, TN, 283
Weary, Drummer Frank O., 255
Weems Plantation, VA, 119
Weidle (Wiedle), Pvt. John F., 229, 294
Wells, Pvt. Isaac, 125
West Andover, OH, 15, 238
Western and Atlantic Railroad, 147, 347
Western Reserve, ix, xi, 175, 236, 245, 267, 322–23; as abolition hotbed, , ix, 3; anxiety for the 7th OVI at Chattanooga, 288; Cedar Mountain battle sacrifices, 175; first Federal Income Tax, 237; merchandize available in, 238; railroad expansion 1864, 323, 379
Wheatfield, The, Gettysburg battlefield, 253
Wheeler, Helen Cowles, 150–52
Wheeler, Gen. Joseph (CSA). *See* rebel troops, cavalry: Wheeler's Cavalry Corps
Wheeler, Capt. William, 305
Wheeling Intelligencer, 177
Whitcom, Capt. (5th OVI), 109
White Plains, VA, 129, 266
Whiteside, TN, 279, 280
Wide Awakes, 4
Wilbur, Cpl. Warren, 234, 242
Wilder, Pvt. Sydney, 214
Wilderness, The, battle of, 316
Wilderness, The, VA, 214, 219, 232
Wildey, Pvt. William L., 60
Williams, Gen. Alpheus S. (Williams's division, 12th Corps), 117, 158, 224, 225, 249, 254, 318, 326, 334, 340
Williams, Pvt. George, 334–35, 337
Williamson, Lt. William Palmer, 77, 101, 109
Wilmington, NC, fall of celebrated in 29th's camp, 362, 369
Wilson, Lt. Andrew, 127

Wilson, Pvt. John, 191
Wilson, Lawrence (7th Ohio), 114, 228, 252
Wilson, Sgt. Orlando, 335
Wilson, Lt. Seth, 122, 195
Winby, Pvt. Joseph, 36
Winchester, VA, 84, 90, 99, 105, 112, 128, 138, 203
Winchester Pike, VA, 90, 104
Winder, Gen. Charles S. (CSA), 137, 160, 167
Winship, Lt. Theron S., 51, 136, 143, 172, 174, 178, 179, 182, 187, 195, 196; Antietam campaign, 183, 184; as Ashtabula County merchant, 7; assists Luce in recruiting for 29th OVI, 50; at Camp Giddings, 52; as hospital inspector in Cumberland, MD, 93; on Kernstown battle, 113; to Manassas Gap, 124; on McClellan, 183; at Port Republic, 132, 134, 137, 138, 139, 143; resignation of, 205
Wirtz, Col. Henry (CSA), 169
Wisconsin troops: 3rd regiment, 376
women, 191, 198, 212, 349
Woodbury, Edward B., 23–24, 25, 212
Woodbury, Lt. E. B., 119, 140, 186, 198, 201, 361, 377
wounded, care and treatment of, at Cedar Mountain, 163–64
wounds: accidental, at Camp Giddings, 56; at Camp Kelly, MD, 1862, 88; Pvt. E. Curtis injured, 124; Pvt. John W. Hurry, 143; inflicted to avoid draft, 193
Wright, Albert, 13
Wright, Capt. Josiah J., 40, 72, 74, 91, 128, 134, 176; Akron prewar civilian life, 55; on army hospitals, 94; as captain of Co. G, 77; on condition of rail cars, 83; on farmland quality along the Upper Potomac, 84; in Frederick, MD, 186; on Giddings Regiment recruiting, 58; on government's failure to pay its soldiers, 72, 78; at Kernstown, 114; resignation, 195; return to work as Akron town marshall, 211; on sickness at Camp Kelly as "white feather disorder," 94; on war profiteers, 287; wounded at Cedar Mountain, 165
Wright, Capt. Myron T., 205–6, 211; as acting major on field staff, 205–6; arrest of deserter, 191; in Atlanta hospital, 344; in Buckley's company, 19th OVI, 17; burial in Johnson's Corners, 361; as captain of Company D, 101; at Chancellorsville, 223, 227, 232–33; condolence letter to mother of George Dice, 360–61; at Culp's Hill fight, 258–59, 260; death of, 361; at Dug Gap, 309, 312, 317; gunshot wound treated, 112; at Kennesaw Mountain, 335; at Kernstown, 109, 113; at Peach Tree Creek, 341; recruiting for Giddings Regiment, 27, 49, 144–45, 189, 190–91, 194, 195, 293; and regiment's new flags, 288–89; at Resaca, 319; wounded at Pine Knob, 332; wounded at Savannah, 358–59, 361

York Pike, Gettysburg, PA, 263
"Young Americans," 298

Zanesville, OH, 57, 272
Zouave, 16, 19; skirmish drill, 53

www.ingramcontent.com/pod-product-compliance
Lightning Source LLC
Chambersburg PA
CBHW081352290426
44110CB00018B/2350